FIFTH EDITION

Learning Python

Mark Lutz

Beijing · Cambridge · Farnham · Köln · Sebastopol · Tokyo

Learning Python, Fifth Edition
by Mark Lutz

Copyright © 2013 Mark Lutz. All rights reserved.
Printed in the United States of America.

Published by O'Reilly Media, Inc., 1005 Gravenstein Highway North, Sebastopol, CA 95472.

Editor: Rachel Roumeliotis
Production Editor: Christopher Hearse
Copyeditor: Rachel Monaghan
Proofreader: Julie Van Keuren

Indexer: Lucie Haskins
Cover Designer: Randy Comer
Interior Designer: David Futato
Illustrator: Rebecca Demarest

June 2013:   Fifth Edition.

Revision History for the Fifth Edition:

2013-06-07	First release
2013-08-16	Second release
2013-11-08	Third release
2014-01-24	Fourth release
2014-05-02	Fifth release
2014-08-22	Sixth release
2014-10-29	Seventh release
2015-01-09	Eighth release

See *http://oreilly.com/catalog/errata.csp?isbn=9781449355739* for release details.

ISBN: 978-1-449-35573-9

[QG]

1420556271

To Vera.
You are my life.

Table of Contents

Part II. Types and Operations

Part III.   Statements and Syntax

Part IV. Functions and Generators

Part V. Modules and Packages

Part VI. Classes and OOP

Part VII. Exceptions and Tools

Preface

If you're standing in a bookstore looking for the short story on this book, try this:

- *Python* is a powerful multiparadigm computer programming language, optimized for programmer productivity, code readability, and software quality.
- *This book* provides a comprehensive and in-depth introduction to the Python language itself. Its goal is to help you master Python fundamentals before moving on to apply them in your work. Like all its prior editions, this book is designed to serve as a single, all-inclusive learning resource for all Python newcomers, whether they will be using Python 2.X, Python 3.X, or both.
- *This edition* has been brought up to date with Python releases 3.3 and 2.7, and has been expanded substantially to reflect current practice in the Python world.

This preface describes this book's goals, scope, and structure in more detail. It's optional reading, but is designed to provide some orientation before you get started with the book at large.

This Book's "Ecosystem"

Python is a popular open source programming language used for both standalone programs and scripting applications in a wide variety of domains. It is free, portable, powerful, and is both relatively easy and remarkably fun to use. Programmers from every corner of the software industry have found Python's focus on developer productivity and software quality to be a strategic advantage in projects both large and small.

Whether you are new to programming or are a professional developer, this book is designed to bring you up to speed on the Python language in ways that more limited approaches cannot. After reading this book, you should know enough about Python to apply it in whatever application domains you choose to explore.

By design, this book is a tutorial that emphasizes the *core Python language* itself, rather than specific applications of it. As such, this book is intended to serve as the first in a two-volume set:

- *Learning Python*, this book, teaches Python itself, focusing on language fundamentals that span domains.
- *Programming Python*, among others, moves on to show what you can do with Python after you've learned it.

This division of labor is deliberate. While application goals can vary per reader, the need for useful language fundamentals coverage does not. Applications-focused books such as *Programming Python* pick up where this book leaves off, using realistically scaled examples to explore Python's role in common domains such as the Web, GUIs, systems, databases, and text. In addition, the book *Python Pocket Reference* provides reference materials not included here, and it is designed to supplement this book.

Because of this book's focus on foundations, though, it is able to present Python language fundamentals with more depth than many programmers see when first learning the language. Its bottom-up approach and self-contained didactic examples are designed to teach readers the entire language one step at a time.

The core language skills you'll gain in the process will apply to every Python software system you'll encounter—be it today's popular tools such as Django, NumPy, and App Engine, or others that may be a part of both Python's future and your programming career.

Because it's based upon a three-day Python training class with quizzes and exercises throughout, this book also serves as a self-paced introduction to the language. Although its format lacks the live interaction of a class, it compensates in the extra depth and flexibility that only a book can provide. Though there are many ways to use this book, linear readers will find it roughly equivalent to a semester-long Python class.

About This Fifth Edition

The prior *fourth edition* of this book published in 2009 covered Python versions 2.6 and 3.0.[1] It addressed the many and sometimes incompatible changes introduced in the Python 3.X line in general. It also introduced a new OOP tutorial, and new chapters on advanced topics such as Unicode text, decorators, and metaclasses, derived from both the live classes I teach and evolution in Python "best practice."

This *fifth edition* completed in 2013 is a revision of the prior, updated to cover both *Python 3.3 and 2.7*, the current latest releases in the 3.X and 2.X lines. It incorporates

---

1. And 2007's short-lived third edition covered Python 2.5, and its simpler—and *shorter*—single-line Python world. See *http://www.rmi.net/~lutz* for more on this book's history. Over the years, this book has grown in size and complexity in direct proportion to Python's own growth. Per Appendix C, Python 3.0 alone introduced 27 additions and 57 changes in the language that found their way into this book, and Python 3.3 continues this trend. Today's Python programmer faces two incompatible lines, three major paradigms, a plethora of advanced tools, and a blizzard of feature redundancy—most of which do not divide neatly between the 2.X and 3.X lines. That's not as daunting as it may sound (many tools are variations on a theme), but all are fair game in an inclusive, comprehensive Python text.

all language changes introduced in each line since the prior edition was published, and has been polished throughout to update and sharpen its presentation. Specifically:

- *Python 2.X* coverage here has been updated to include features such as dictionary and set comprehensions that were formerly for 3.X only, but have been back-ported for use in 2.7.

- *Python 3.X* coverage has been augmented for new `yield` and `raise` syntax; the `__pycache__` bytecode model; 3.3 namespace packages; PyDoc's all-browser mode; Unicode literal and storage changes; and the new Windows launcher shipped with 3.3.

- *Assorted* new or expanded coverage for JSON, `timeit`, PyPy, `os.popen`, generators, recursion, weak references, `__mro__`, `__iter__`, super, `__slots__`, metaclasses, descriptors, `random`, Sphinx, and more has been added, along with a general increase in 2.X compatibility in both examples and narrative.

This edition also adds a new *conclusion* as Chapter 41 (on Python's evolution), two new *appendixes* (on recent Python changes and the new Windows launcher), and one new *chapter* (on benchmarking: an expanded version of the former code timing example). See Appendix C for a concise summary of *Python changes* between the prior edition and this one, as well as links to their coverage in the book. This appendix also summarizes initial differences between 2.X and 3.X in general that were first addressed in the prior edition, though some, such as new-style classes, span versions and simply become mandated in 3.X (more on what the X's mean in a moment).

Per the last bullet in the preceding list, this edition has also experienced some growth because it gives fuller coverage to more *advanced language features*—which many of us have tried very hard to ignore as optional for the last decade, but which have now grown more common in Python code. As we'll see, these tools make Python more powerful, but also raise the bar for newcomers, and may shift Python's scope and definition. Because you might encounter any of these, this book covers them head-on, instead of pretending they do not exist.

Despite the updates, this edition retains most of the structure and content of the prior edition, and is still designed to be a comprehensive learning resource for both the 2.X and 3.X Python lines. While it is primarily focused on users of Python 3.3 and 2.7— the latest in the 3.X line and the likely last in the 2.X line—its historical perspective also makes it relevant to *older* Pythons that still see regular use today.

Though it's impossible to predict the future, this book stresses fundamentals that have been valid for nearly two decades, and will likely apply to *future* Pythons too. As usual, I'll be posting Python updates that impact this book at the book's website described ahead. The "What's New" documents in Python's manuals set can also serve to fill in the gaps as Python surely evolves after this book is published.

The Python 2.X and 3.X Lines

Because it bears heavily on this book's content, I need to say a few more words about the Python 2.X/3.X story up front. When the *fourth edition* of this book was written in 2009, Python had just become available in two flavors:

- Version 3.0 was the first in the line of an emerging and incompatible mutation of the language known generically as *3.X*.
- Version 2.6 retained backward compatibility with the vast body of existing Python code, and was the latest in the line known collectively as *2.X*.

While 3.X was largely the same language, it ran almost no code written for prior releases. It:

- Imposed a Unicode model with broad consequences for strings, files, and libraries
- Elevated iterators and generators to a more pervasive role, as part of fuller functional paradigm
- Mandated new-style classes, which merge with types, but grow more powerful and complex
- Changed many fundamental tools and libraries, and replaced or removed others entirely

The mutation of `print` from statement to function alone, aesthetically sound as it may be, broke nearly every Python program ever written. And strategic potential aside, 3.X's mandatory Unicode and class models and ubiquitous generators made for a different programming experience.

Although many viewed Python 3.X as both an improvement and the future of Python, Python 2.X was still very widely used and was to be supported in parallel with Python 3.X for years to come. The majority of Python code in use was 2.X, and migration to 3.X seemed to be shaping up to be a slow process.

The 2.X/3.X Story Today

As this *fifth edition* is being written in 2013, Python has moved on to versions 3.3 and 2.7, but this 2.X/3.X story is still largely *unchanged*. In fact, Python is now a dual-version world, with many users running *both* 2.X and 3.X according to their software goals and dependencies. And for many newcomers, the choice between 2.X and 3.X remains one of existing software versus the language's cutting edge. Although many major Python packages have been ported to 3.X, many others are still 2.X-only today.

To some observers, Python 3.X is now seen as a *sandbox* for exploring new ideas, while 2.X is viewed as the *tried-and-true* Python, which doesn't have all of 3.X's features but is still more pervasive. Others still see Python 3.X as the future, a view that seems supported by current core developer plans: Python 2.7 will continue to be supported but is to be the last 2.X, while 3.3 is the latest in the 3.X line's continuing evolution.

On the other hand, initiatives such as *PyPy*—today a still 2.X-only implementation of Python that offers stunning performance improvements—represent a 2.X future, if not an outright faction.

All opinions aside, almost five years after its release, 3.X has yet to supersede 2.X, or even match its user base. As one metric, 2.X is still downloaded more often than 3.X for Windows at python.org today, despite the fact that this measure would be naturally skewed to *new* users and the *most recent* release. Such statistics are prone to change, of course, but after five years are indicative of 3.X uptake nonetheless. The existing 2.X software base still trumps 3.X's language extensions for many. Moreover, being last in the 2.X line makes 2.7 a sort of *de facto standard*, immune to the constant pace of change in the 3.X line—a positive to those who seek a stable base, and a negative to those who seek growth and ongoing relevance.

Personally, I think today's Python world is large enough to accommodate *both* 3.X and 2.X; they seem to satisfy different goals and appeal to different camps, and there is precedence for this in other language families (C and C++, for example, have a long-standing coexistence, though they may differ more than Python 2.X and 3.X). More-over, because they are so similar, the skills gained by learning either Python line transfer almost entirely to the other, especially if you're aided by dual-version resources like this book. In fact, as long as you understand how they diverge, it's often possible to write code that runs on both.

At the same time, this split presents a substantial *dilemma* for both programmers and book authors, which shows no signs of abating. While it would be easier for a book to pretend that Python 2.X never existed and cover 3.X only, this would not address the needs of the large Python user base that exists today. A vast amount of existing code was written for Python 2.X, and it won't be going away anytime soon. And while some newcomers to the language can and should focus on Python 3.X, anyone who must use code written in the past needs to keep one foot in the Python 2.X world today. Since it may still be years before many third-party libraries and extensions are ported to Python 3.X, this fork might not be entirely temporary.

Coverage for Both 3.X and 2.X

To address this dichotomy and to meet the needs of all potential readers, this book has been updated to cover *both* Python 3.3 and Python 2.7, and should apply to later releases in both the 3.X and 2.X lines. It's intended for programmers using Python 2.X, programmers using Python 3.X, and programmers stuck somewhere between the two.

That is, you can use this book to learn *either* Python line. Although 3.X is often emphasized, 2.X differences and tools are also noted along the way for programmers using older code. While the two versions are largely similar, they diverge in some important ways, and I'll point these out as they crop up.

For instance, I'll use 3.X `print` calls in most examples, but will also describe the 2.X `print` statement so you can make sense of earlier code, and will often use portable printing techniques that run on both lines. I'll also freely introduce new features, such as the `nonlocal` statement in 3.X and the string `format` method available as of 2.6 and 3.0, and will point out when such extensions are not present in older Pythons.

By proxy, this edition addresses other Python version 2.X and 3.X releases as well, though some older version 2.X code may not be able to run all the examples here. Although class decorators are available as of both Python 2.6 and 3.0, for example, you cannot use them in an older Python 2.X that did not yet have this feature. Again, see the change tables in Appendix C for summaries of recent 2.X and 3.X changes.

Which Python Should I Use?

Version choice may be mandated by your organization, but if you're new to Python and learning on your own, you may be wondering which version to install. The answer here depends on your goals. Here are a few suggestions on the choice.

When to choose 3.X: new features, evolution

If you are learning Python for the first time and don't need to use any existing 2.X code, I encourage you to begin with Python 3.X. It cleans up some longstanding warts in the language and trims some dated cruft, while retaining all the original core ideas and adding some nice new tools. For example, 3.X's seamless Unicode model and broader use of generators and functional techniques are seen by many users as assets. Many popular Python libraries and tools are already available for Python 3.X, or will be by the time you read these words, especially given the continual improvements in the 3.X line. All new language evolution occurs in 3.X only, which adds features and keeps Python relevant, but also makes language definition a constantly moving target—a tradeoff inherent on the leading edge.

When to choose 2.X: existing code, stability

If you'll be using a system based on Python 2.X, the 3.X line may not be an option for you today. However, you'll find that this book addresses your concerns, too, and will help if you migrate to 3.X in the future. You'll also find that you're in large company. Every group I taught in 2012 was using 2.X only, and I still regularly see useful Python software in 2.X-only form. Moreover, unlike 3.X, 2.X is no longer being changed—which is either an asset or liability, depending on whom you ask. There's nothing wrong with using and writing 2.X code, but you may wish to keep tabs on 3.X and its ongoing evolution as you do. Python's future remains to be written, and is largely up to its users, including you.

When to choose both: version-neutral code

Probably the best news here is that Python's fundamentals are the same in both its lines—2.X and 3.X differ in ways that many users will find minor, and this book is designed to help you learn both. In fact, as long as you understand their differences, it's often straightforward to write version-neutral code that runs on both

Pythons, as we regularly will in this book. See Appendix C for pointers on 2.X/3.X migration and tips on writing code for both Python lines and audiences.

Regardless of which version or versions you choose to focus on first, your skills will transfer directly to wherever your Python work leads you.

 About the Xs: Throughout this book, "3.X" and "2.X" are used to refer collectively to all releases in these two lines. For instance, *3.X* includes 3.0 through 3.3, and future 3.X releases; *2.X* means all from 2.0 through 2.7 (and presumably no others). More specific releases are mentioned when a topic applies to it only (e.g., 2.7's set literals and 3.3's launcher and namespace packages). This notation may occasionally be too broad —some features labeled 2.X here may not be present in early 2.X releases rarely used today—but it accommodates a 2.X line that has already spanned 13 years. The 3.X label is more easily and accurately applied to this younger five-year-old line.

This Book's Prerequisites and Effort

It's impossible to give absolute prerequisites for this book, because its utility and value can depend as much on reader motivation as on reader background. Both true beginners and crusty programming veterans have used this book successfully in the past. If you are motivated to learn Python, and willing to invest the time and focus it requires, this text will probably work for you.

Just how much time is required to learn Python? Although this will vary per learner, this book tends to work best when *read*. Some readers may use this book as an on-demand reference resource, but most people seeking Python mastery should expect to spend at least *weeks* and probably *months* going through the material here, depending on how closely they follow along with its examples. As mentioned, it's roughly equivalent to a full-semester course on the Python language itself.

That's the estimate for learning just Python itself and the software skills required to use it well. Though this book may suffice for basic scripting goals, readers hoping to pursue software development at large as a career should expect to devote additional time after this book to large-scale project experience, and possibly to follow-up texts such as *Programming Python*.[2]

---

2. The standard disclaimer: I wrote this and another book mentioned earlier, which work together as a set: *Learning Python* for language fundamentals, *Programming Python* for applications basics, and *Python Pocket Reference* as a companion to the other two. All three derive from 1995's original and broad *Programming Python*. I encourage you to explore the many Python books available today (I stopped counting at 200 at Amazon.com just now because there was no end in sight, and this didn't include related subjects like Django). My own publisher has recently produced Python-focused books on instrumentation, data mining, App Engine, numeric analysis, natural language processing, MongoDB, AWS, and more—specific domains you may wish to explore once you've mastered Python language fundamentals here. The Python story today is far too rich for any one book to address alone.

That may not be welcome news to people looking for instant proficiency, but programming is not a trivial skill (despite what you may have heard!). Today's Python, and software in general, are both challenging and rewarding enough to merit the effort implied by comprehensive books such as this. Here are a few pointers on using this book for readers on both sides of the experience spectrum:

To experienced programmers
> You have an initial advantage and can move quickly through some earlier chapters; but you shouldn't skip the core ideas, and may need to work at letting go of some baggage. In general terms, exposure to any programming or scripting before this book might be helpful because of the analogies it may provide. On the other hand, I've also found that prior programming experience can be a handicap due to expectations rooted in other languages (it's far too easy to spot the Java or C++ programmers in classes by the first Python code they write!). Using Python well requires adopting its mindset. By focusing on key core concepts, this book is designed to help you learn to code Python in Python.

To true beginners
> You can learn Python here too, as well as programming itself; but you may need to work a bit harder, and may wish to supplement this text with gentler introductions. If you don't consider yourself a programmer already, you will probably find this book useful too, but you'll want to be sure to proceed slowly and work through the examples and exercises along the way. Also keep in mind that this book will spend more time teaching Python itself than programming basics. If you find yourself lost here, I encourage you to explore an introduction to programming in general before tackling this book. Python's website has links to many helpful resources for beginners.

Formally, this book is designed to serve as *a first Python text for newcomers of all kinds*. It may not be an ideal resource for someone who has never touched a computer before (for instance, we're not going to spend any time exploring what a computer is), but I haven't made many assumptions about your programming background or education.

On the other hand, I won't insult readers by assuming they are "dummies," either, whatever that means—it's easy to do useful things in Python, and this book will show you how. The text occasionally contrasts Python with languages such as C, C++, Java, and others, but you can safely ignore these comparisons if you haven't used such languages in the past.

This Book's Structure

To help orient you, this section provides a quick rundown of the content and goals of the major parts of this book. If you're anxious to get to it, you should feel free to skip this section (or browse the table of contents instead). To some readers, though, a book this large probably merits a brief roadmap up front.

By design, each *part* covers a major functional area of the language, and each part is composed of *chapters* focusing on a specific topic or aspect of the part's area. In addition, each chapter ends with *quizzes* and their answers, and each part ends with larger *exercises*, whose solutions show up in Appendix D.

 Practice matters: I strongly recommend that readers work through the quizzes and exercises in this book, and work along with its examples in general if you can. In programming, there's no substitute for practicing what you've read. Whether you do it with this book or a project of your own, actual coding is crucial if you want the ideas presented here to stick.

Overall, this book's presentation is *bottom-up* because Python is too. The examples and topics grow more challenging as we move along. For instance, Python's classes are largely just packages of functions that process built-in types. Once you've mastered built-in types and functions, classes become a relatively minor intellectual leap. Because each part builds on those preceding it this way, most readers will find a *linear reading* makes the most sense. Here's a preview of the book's main parts you'll find along the way:

Part I
> We begin with a general overview of Python that answers commonly asked initial questions—why people use the language, what it's useful for, and so on. The first chapter introduces the major ideas underlying the technology to give you some background context. The rest of this part moves on to explore the ways that both Python and programmers run programs. The main goal here is to give you just enough information to be able to follow along with later examples and exercises.

Part II
> Next, we begin our tour of the Python language, studying Python's major built-in object types and what you can do with them in depth: numbers, lists, dictionaries, and so on. You can get a lot done with these tools alone, and they are at the heart of every Python script. This is the most substantial part of the book because we lay groundwork here for later chapters. We'll also explore dynamic typing and its references—keys to using Python well—in this part.

Part III
> The next part moves on to introduce Python's *statements*—the code you type to create and process objects in Python. It also presents Python's general syntax model. Although this part focuses on syntax, it also introduces some related tools (such as the PyDoc system), takes a first look at iteration concepts, and explores coding alternatives.

Part IV

This part begins our look at Python's higher-level program structure tools. *Functions* turn out to be a simple way to package code for reuse and avoid code redundancy. In this part, we will explore Python's scoping rules, argument-passing techniques, the sometimes-notorious lambda, and more. We'll also revisit iterators from a functional programming perspective, introduce user-defined generators, and learn how to time Python code to measure performance here.

Part V

Python *modules* let you organize statements and functions into larger components, and this part illustrates how to create, use, and reload modules. We'll also look at some more advanced topics here, such as module packages, module reloading, package-relative imports, 3.3's new namespace packages, and the __name__ variable.

Part VI

Here, we explore Python's object-oriented programming tool, the *class*—an optional but powerful way to structure code for customization and reuse, which almost naturally minimizes redundancy. As you'll see, classes mostly reuse ideas we will have covered by this point in the book, and OOP in Python is mostly about looking up names in linked objects with a special first argument in functions. As you'll also see, OOP is optional in Python, but most find Python's OOP to be much simpler than others, and it can shave development time substantially, especially for long-term strategic project development.

Part VII

We conclude the language fundamentals coverage in this text with a look at Python's exception handling model and statements, plus a brief overview of development tools that will become more useful when you start writing larger programs (debugging and testing tools, for instance). Although exceptions are a fairly lightweight tool, this part appears after the discussion of classes because user-defined exceptions should now all be classes. We also cover some more advanced topics, such as context managers, here.

Part VIII

In the final part, we explore some advanced topics: Unicode and byte strings, managed attribute tools like properties and descriptors, function and class decorators, and metaclasses. These chapters are all optional reading, because not all programmers need to understand the subjects they address. On the other hand, readers who must process internationalized text or binary data, or are responsible for developing APIs for other programmers to use, should find something of interest in this part. The examples here are also larger than most of those in this book, and can serve as self-study material.

Part IX

The book wraps up with a set of four appendixes that give platform-specific tips for installing and using Python on various computers; present the new Windows launcher that ships with Python 3.3; summarize changes in Python addressed by recent editions and give links to their coverage here; and provide solutions to the end-of-part exercises. Solutions to end-of-chapter quizzes appear in the chapters themselves.

See the table of contents for a finer-grained look at this book's components.

What This Book Is Not

Given its relatively large audience over the years, some have inevitably expected this book to serve a role outside its scope. So now that I've told you what this book is, I also want to be clear on what it isn't:

- This book is a tutorial, *not* a reference.
- This book covers the language itself, *not* applications, standard libraries, or third-party tools.
- This book is a comprehensive look at a substantial topic, *not* a watered-down overview.

Because these points are key to this book's content, I want to say a few more words about them up front.

It's Not a Reference or a Guide to Specific Applications

This book is a *language tutorial*, not a reference, and not an applications book. This is by design: *today's Python*—with its built-in types, generators, closures, comprehensions, Unicode, decorators, and blend of procedural, object-oriented, and functional programming paradigms—makes the core language a substantial topic all by itself, and a prerequisite to all your future Python work, in whatever domains you pursue. When you are ready for other resources, though, here are a few suggestions and reminders:

Reference resources
As implied by the preceding structural description, you can use the index and table of contents to hunt for details, but there are no reference appendixes in this book. If you are looking for Python reference resources (and most readers probably will be very soon in their Python careers), I suggest the previously mentioned book that I also wrote as a companion to this one—*Python Pocket Reference*—as well as other reference books you'll find with a quick search, and the standard Python reference manuals maintained at *http://www.python.org*. The latter of these are free, always up to date, and available both on the Web and on your computer after a Windows install.

Applications and libraries
As also discussed earlier, this book is not a guide to specific *applications* such as the Web, GUIs, or systems programming. By proxy, this includes the libraries and

tools used in applications work; although some *standard libraries* and tools are introduced here—including `timeit`, `shelve`, `pickle`, `struct`, `json`, `pdb`, `os`, `urllib`, `re`, `xml`, `random`, *PyDoc* and *IDLE*—they are not officially in this book's primary scope. If you're looking for more coverage on such topics and are already proficient with Python, I recommend the follow-up book *Programming Python*, among others. That book assumes this one as its prerequisite, though, so be sure you have a firm grasp of the core language first. Especially in an engineering domain like software, one must walk before one runs.

It's Not the Short Story for People in a Hurry

As you can tell from its size, this book also doesn't skimp on the details: it presents the *full Python language*, not a brief look at a simplified subset. Along the way it also covers *software principles* that are essential to writing good Python code. As mentioned, this is a multiple-week or -month book, designed to impart the skill level you'd acquire from a full-term class on Python.

This is also deliberate. Many of this book's readers don't need to acquire full-scale software development skills, of course, and some can absorb Python in a piecemeal fashion. At the same time, because *any* part of the language may be used in code you will encounter, no part is truly optional for most programmers. Moreover, even casual scripters and hobbyists need to know basic principles of software development in order to code well, and even to use precoded tools properly.

This book aims to address both of these needs—*language and principles*—in enough depth to be useful. In the end, though, you'll find that Python's more advanced tools, such as its object-oriented and functional programming support, are relatively easy to learn once you've mastered their prerequisites—and you will, if you work through this book one chapter at a time.

It's as Linear as Python Allows

Speaking of *reading order*, this edition also tries hard to minimize *forward references*, but Python 3.X's changes make this impossible in some cases (in fact, 3.X sometimes seems to assume you already know Python while you're learning it!). As a handful of representative examples:

- Printing, sorts, the string `format` method, and some `dict` calls rely on function *keyword* arguments.
- Dictionary key lists and tests, and the `list` calls used around many tools, imply *iteration* concepts.
- Using `exec` to run code now assumes knowledge of *file objects* and interfaces.
- Coding new *exceptions* requires *classes* and OOP fundamentals.

- And so on—even basic *inheritance* broaches advanced topics such as *metaclasses* and *descriptors*.

Python is still best learned as a progression from simple to advanced, and a *linear reading* here still makes the most sense. Still, some topics may require nonlinear jumps and random lookups. To minimize these, this book will point out forward dependencies when they occur, and will ease their impacts as much as possible.

 But if your time is tight: Though depth is crucial to mastering Python, some readers may have limited time. If you are interested in starting out with a *quick Python tour*, I suggest Chapter 1, Chapter 4, Chapter 10, and Chapter 28 (and perhaps 26)—a short survey that will hopefully pique your interest in the more complete story told in the rest of the book, and which most readers will need in today's Python software world. In general, this book is intentionally *layered* this way to make its material easier to absorb—with introductions followed by details, so you can start with overviews, and dig deeper over time. You don't need to read this book all at once, but its gradual approach is designed to help you tackle its material eventually.

This Book's Programs

In general, this book has always strived to be agnostic about both Python versions and platforms. It's designed to be useful to all Python users. Nevertheless, because Python changes over time and platforms tend to differ in pragmatic ways, I need to describe the specific systems you'll see in action in most examples here.

Python Versions

This fifth edition of this book, and all the program examples in it, are based on Python versions *3.3 and 2.7*. In addition, many of its examples run under prior 3.X and 2.X releases, and notes about the history of language changes in earlier versions are mixed in along the way for users of older Pythons.

Because this text focuses on the core language, however, you can be fairly sure that most of what it has to say won't change very much in *future* releases of Python, as noted earlier. Most of this book applies to *earlier* Python versions, too, except when it does not; naturally, if you try using extensions added after a release you're using, all bets are off. As a rule of thumb, the latest Python is the best Python if you are able to upgrade.

Because this book focuses on the core language, most of it also applies to both *Jython* and *IronPython*, the Java- and .NET-based Python language implementations, as well as other Python implementations such as *Stackless* and *PyPy* (described in Chapter 2). Such alternatives differ mostly in usage details, not language.

Platforms

The examples in this book were run on a *Windows 7 and 8* ultrabook,[3] though Python's portability makes this mostly a moot point, especially in this fundamentals-focused book. You'll notice a few Windows-isms—including command-line prompts, a handful of screenshots, install pointers, and an appendix on the new Windows launcher in 3.3—but this reflects the fact that most Python newcomers will probably get started on this platform, and these can be safely ignored by users of other operating systems.

I also give a few launching details for other platforms like Linux, such as "#!" line use, but as we'll see in Chapter 3 and Appendix B, the 3.3 Windows launcher makes even this a more portable technique.

Fetching This Book's Code

Source code for the book's examples, as well as exercise solutions, can be fetched as a zip file from the book's website at the following address:

> *http://oreil.ly/LearningPython-5E*

This site includes both all the code in this book as well as package usage instructions, so I'll defer to it for more details. Of course, the examples work best in the context of their appearance in this book, and you'll need some background knowledge on running Python programs in general to make use of them. We'll study startup details in Chapter 3, so please stay tuned for information on this front.

Using This Book's Code

The code in my Python books is designed to teach, and I'm glad when it assists readers in that capacity. O'Reilly itself has an official policy regarding reusing the book's examples in general, which I've pasted into the rest of this section for reference:

> This book is here to help you get your job done. In general, you may use the code in this book in your programs and documentation. You do not need to contact us for permission unless you're reproducing a significant portion of the code. For example, writing a program that uses several chunks of code from this book does not require permission. Selling or distributing a CD-ROM of examples from O'Reilly books *does* require permission. Answering a question by citing this book and quoting example code does not require permission. Incorporating a significant amount of example code from this book into your product's documentation *does* require permission.

---

3. Mostly under Windows 7, but it's irrelevant to this book. At this writing, Python installs on Windows 8 and runs in its desktop mode, which is essentially the same as Windows 7 without a Start button as I write this (you may need to create shortcuts for former Start button menu items). Support for WinRT/Metro "apps" is still pending. See Appendix A for more details. Frankly, the future of Windows 8 is unclear as I type these words, so this book will be as version-neutral as possible.

We appreciate, but do not require, attribution. An attribution usually includes the title, author, publisher, and ISBN. For example: "*Learning Python*, Fifth Edition, by Mark Lutz. Copyright 2013 Mark Lutz, 978-1-4493-5573-9."

If you feel your use of code examples falls outside fair use or the permission given above, feel free to contact us at *permissions@oreilly.com*.

Font Conventions

This book's mechanics will make more sense once you start reading it, of course, but as a reference, this book uses the following typographical conventions:

Italic
> Used for email addresses, URLs, filenames, pathnames, and emphasizing new terms when they are first introduced

`Constant width`
> Used for program code, the contents of files and the output from commands, and to designate modules, methods, statements, and system commands

`Constant width bold`
> Used in code sections to show commands or text that would be typed by the user, and, occasionally, to highlight portions of code

`Constant width italic`
> Used for replaceables and some comments in code sections

 Indicates a tip, suggestion, or general note relating to the nearby text.

 Indicates a warning or caution relating to the nearby text.

You'll also find occasional *sidebars* (delimited by boxes) and *footnotes* (at page end) throughout, which are often optional reading, but provide additional context on the topics being presented. The sidebars in "Why You Will Care: Slices" on page 204, for example, often give example use cases for the subjects being explored.

Book Updates and Resources

Improvements happen (and so do mis^H^H^H typos). Updates, supplements, and corrections (a.k.a. *errata*) for this book will be maintained on the Web, and may be suggested at either the publisher's website or by email. Here are the main coordinates:

Publisher's site: http://oreil.ly/LearningPython-5E

> This site will maintain this edition's official list of book *errata*, and chronicle specific patches applied to the text in reprints. It's also the official site for the book's *examples* as described earlier.

Author's site: http://www.rmi.net/~lutz/about-lp5e.html

> This site will be used to post more *general updates* related to this text or Python itself—a hedge against future changes, which should be considered a sort of virtual appendix to this book.

My publisher also has an email address for comments and technical questions about this book:

> *bookquestions@oreilly.com*

For more information about my publisher's books, conferences, Resource Centers, and the O'Reilly Network, see its general website:

> *http://www.oreilly.com*

For more on my books, see my own book support site:

> *http://www.rmi.net/~lutz*

Also be sure to search the Web if any of the preceding links become invalid over time; if I could become more clairvoyant, I would, but the Web changes faster than published books.

Acknowledgments

As I write this fifth edition of this book in 2013, it's difficult to not be somewhat retrospective. I have now been using and promoting Python for 21 years, writing books about it for 18, and teaching live classes on it for 16. Despite the passage of time, I'm still regularly amazed at how successful Python has been—in ways that most of us could not possibly have imagined in the early 1990s. So at the risk of sounding like a hopelessly self-absorbed author, I hope you'll pardon a few closing words of history and gratitude here.

The Backstory

My own Python history predates both Python 1.0 and the Web (and goes back to a time when an install meant fetching email messages, concatenating, decoding, and hoping it all somehow worked). When I first discovered Python as a frustrated C++ software developer in 1992, I had no idea what an impact it would have on the next two decades of my life. Two years after writing the first edition of *Programming Python* in 1995 for Python 1.3, I began traveling around the country and world teaching Python to beginners and experts. Since finishing the first edition of *Learning Python* in

1999, I've been an independent Python trainer and writer, thanks in part to Python's phenomenal growth in popularity.

Here's the damage so far. I've now written 13 Python books (5 of this, and 4 of two others), which have together sold some 400,000 units by my data. I've also been teaching Python for over a decade and a half; have taught some 260 Python training sessions in the U.S., Europe, Canada, and Mexico; and have met roughly 4,000 students along the way. Besides propelling me toward frequent flyer utopia, these classes helped me refine this text and my other Python books. Teaching honed the books, and vice versa, with the net result that my books closely parallel what happens in my classes, and can serve as a viable alternative to them.

As for Python itself, in recent years it has grown to become one of the top 5 to 10 most widely used programming languages in the world (depending on which source you cite and when you cite it). Because we'll be exploring Python's status in the first chapter of this book, I'll defer the rest of this story until then.

Python Thanks

Because teaching teaches teachers to teach, this book owes much to my live *classes*. I'd like to thank all the *students* who have participated in my courses during the last 16 years. Along with changes in Python itself, your feedback played a major role in shaping this text; there's nothing quite as instructive as watching 4,000 people repeat the same beginner mistakes live and in person! This book's recent editions owe their training-based changes primarily to recent classes, though every class held since 1997 has in some way helped refine this book. I'd like to thank clients who hosted classes in Dublin, Mexico City, Barcelona, London, Edmonton, and Puerto Rico; such experiences have been one of my career's most lasting rewards.

Because writing teaches writers to write, this book also owes much to its *audience*. I want to thank the countless *readers* who took time to offer suggestions over the last 18 years, both online and in person. Your feedback has also been vital to this book's evolution and a substantial factor in its success, a benefit that seems inherent in the open source world. Reader comments have run the gamut from "You should be banned from writing books" to "God bless you for writing this book"; if consensus is possible in such matters it probably lies somewhere between these two, though to borrow a line from Tolkien: the book is still too short.

I'd also like to express my gratitude to everyone who played a part in this book's *production*. To all those who have helped make this book a solid product over the years —including its editors, formatters, marketers, technical reviewers, and more. And to O'Reilly for giving me a chance to work on 13 book projects; it's been net fun (and only feels a little like the movie *Groundhog Day*).

Additional thanks is due to the entire *Python community*; like most open source systems, Python is the product of many unsung efforts. It's been my privilege to watch

Python grow from a new kid on the scripting languages block to a widely used tool, deployed in some fashion by almost every organization writing software. Technical disagreements aside, that's been an exciting endeavor to be a part of.

I also want to thank my original editor at O'Reilly, the late *Frank Willison*. This book was largely Frank's idea. He had a profound impact on both my career and the success of Python when it was new, a legacy that I remember each time I'm tempted to misuse the word "only."

Personal Thanks

Finally, a few more personal notes of thanks. To the late Carl Sagan, for inspiring an 18-year-old kid from Wisconsin. To my Mother, for courage. To my siblings, for the truths to be found in museum peanuts. To the book *The Shallows*, for a much-needed wakeup call.

To my son Michael and daughters Samantha and Roxanne, for who you are. I'm not quite sure when you grew up, but I'm proud of how you did, and look forward to seeing where life takes you next.

And to my wife Vera, for patience, proofing, Diet Cokes, and pretzels. I'm glad I finally found you. I don't know what the next 50 years hold, but I do know that I hope to spend all of them holding you.

—Mark Lutz, Amongst the Larch, Spring 2013

Getting Started

## CHAPTER 1

A Python Q&A Session

If you've bought this book, you may already know what Python is and why it's an important tool to learn. If you don't, you probably won't be sold on Python until you've learned the language by reading the rest of this book and have done a project or two. But before we jump into details, this first chapter of this book will briefly introduce some of the main reasons behind Python's popularity. To begin sculpting a definition of Python, this chapter takes the form of a question-and-answer session, which poses some of the most common questions asked by beginners.

Why Do People Use Python?

Because there are many programming languages available today, this is the usual first question of newcomers. Given that there are roughly 1 million Python users out there at the moment, there really is no way to answer this question with complete accuracy; the choice of development tools is sometimes based on unique constraints or personal preference.

But after teaching Python to roughly 260 groups and over 4,000 students during the last 16 years, I have seen some common themes emerge. The primary factors cited by Python users seem to be these:

Software quality
> For many, Python's focus on readability, coherence, and software quality in general sets it apart from other tools in the scripting world. Python code is designed to be *readable*, and hence reusable and maintainable—much more so than traditional scripting languages. The uniformity of Python code makes it easy to understand, even if you did not write it. In addition, Python has deep support for more advanced *software reuse* mechanisms, such as object-oriented (OO) and function programming.

Developer productivity
> Python boosts developer productivity many times beyond compiled or statically typed languages such as C, C++, and Java. Python code is typically *one-third to*

one-fifth the size of equivalent C++ or Java code. That means there is less to type, less to debug, and less to maintain after the fact. Python programs also run immediately, without the lengthy compile and link steps required by some other tools, further boosting programmer speed.

Program portability

Most Python programs run unchanged on *all major computer platforms*. Porting Python code between Linux and Windows, for example, is usually just a matter of copying a script's code between machines. Moreover, Python offers multiple options for coding portable graphical user interfaces, database access programs, web-based systems, and more. Even operating system interfaces, including program launches and directory processing, are as portable in Python as they can possibly be.

Support libraries

Python comes with a large collection of prebuilt and portable functionality, known as the *standard library*. This library supports an array of application-level programming tasks, from text pattern matching to network scripting. In addition, Python can be extended with both homegrown libraries and a vast collection of third-party application support software. Python's *third-party domain* offers tools for website construction, numeric programming, serial port access, game development, and much more (see ahead for a sampling). The NumPy extension, for instance, has been described as a free and more powerful equivalent to the Matlab numeric programming system.

Component integration

Python scripts can easily communicate with other parts of an application, using a variety of integration mechanisms. Such integrations allow Python to be used as a product *customization and extension* tool. Today, Python code can invoke C and C++ libraries, can be called from C and C++ programs, can integrate with Java and .NET components, can communicate over frameworks such as COM and Silverlight, can interface with devices over serial ports, and can interact over networks with interfaces like SOAP, XML-RPC, and CORBA. It is not a standalone tool.

Enjoyment

Because of Python's ease of use and built-in toolset, it can make the act of programming *more pleasure than chore*. Although this may be an intangible benefit, its effect on productivity is an important asset.

Of these factors, the first two (quality and productivity) are probably the most compelling benefits to most Python users, and merit a fuller description.

Software Quality

By design, Python implements a deliberately simple and readable syntax and a highly coherent programming model. As a slogan at a past Python conference attests, the net result is that Python seems to "fit your brain"—that is, features of the language interact in consistent and limited ways and follow naturally from a small set of core concepts. This makes the language easier to learn, understand, and remember. In practice, Python programmers do not need to constantly refer to manuals when reading or writing code; it's a consistently designed system that many find yields surprisingly uniform code.

By philosophy, Python adopts a somewhat minimalist approach. This means that although there are usually multiple ways to accomplish a coding task, there is usually just one obvious way, a few less obvious alternatives, and a small set of coherent interactions everywhere in the language. Moreover, Python doesn't make arbitrary decisions for you; when interactions are ambiguous, explicit intervention is preferred over "magic." In the Python way of thinking, explicit is better than implicit, and simple is better than complex.[1]

Beyond such design themes, Python includes tools such as modules and OOP that naturally promote code reusability. And because Python is focused on quality, so too, naturally, are Python programmers.

Developer Productivity

During the great Internet boom of the mid-to-late 1990s, it was difficult to find enough programmers to implement software projects; developers were asked to implement systems as fast as the Internet evolved. In later eras of layoffs and economic recession, the picture shifted. Programming staffs were often asked to accomplish the same tasks with even fewer people.

In both of these scenarios, Python has shined as a tool that allows programmers to get more done with less effort. It is deliberately optimized for *speed of development*—its simple syntax, dynamic typing, lack of compile steps, and built-in toolset allow programmers to develop programs in a fraction of the time needed when using some other tools. The net effect is that Python typically boosts developer productivity many times beyond the levels supported by traditional languages. That's good news in both boom and bust times, and everywhere the software industry goes in between.

Is Python a "Scripting Language"?

Python is a general-purpose programming language that is often applied in scripting roles. It is commonly defined as an *object-oriented scripting language*—a definition that blends support for OOP with an overall orientation toward scripting roles. If pressed for a one-liner, I'd say that Python is probably better known as a *general-purpose pro-*

---

1. For a more complete look at the Python philosophy, type the command `import this` at any Python interactive prompt (you'll see how in Chapter 3). This invokes an "Easter egg" hidden in Python—a collection of design principles underlying Python that permeate both the language and its user community. Among them, the acronym EIBTI is now fashionable jargon for the "explicit is better than implicit" rule. These principles are not religion, but are close enough to qualify as a Python motto and creed, which we'll be quoting from often in this book.

gramming language that blends procedural, functional, and object-oriented paradigms— a statement that captures the richness and scope of today's Python.

Still, the term "scripting" seems to have stuck to Python like glue, perhaps as a contrast with larger programming effort required by some other tools. For example, people often use the word "script" instead of "program" to describe a Python code file. In keeping with this tradition, this book uses the terms "script" and "program" interchangeably, with a slight preference for "script" to describe a simpler top-level file and "program" to refer to a more sophisticated multifile application.

Because the term "scripting language" has so many different meanings to different observers, though, some would prefer that it not be applied to Python at all. In fact, people tend to make three very different associations, some of which are more useful than others, when they hear Python labeled as such:

Shell tools

Sometimes when people hear Python described as a scripting language, they think it means that Python is a tool for coding operating-system-oriented scripts. Such programs are often launched from console command lines and perform tasks such as processing text files and launching other programs.

Python programs can and do serve such roles, but this is just one of dozens of common Python application domains. It is not just a better shell-script language.

Control language

To others, scripting refers to a "glue" layer used to control and direct (i.e., script) other application components. Python programs are indeed often deployed in the context of larger applications. For instance, to test hardware devices, Python programs may call out to components that give low-level access to a device. Similarly, programs may run bits of Python code at strategic points to support end-user product customization without the need to ship and recompile the entire system's source code.

Python's simplicity makes it a naturally flexible control tool. Technically, though, this is also just a common Python role; many (perhaps most) Python programmers code standalone scripts without ever using or knowing about any integrated components. It is not just a control language.

Ease of use

Probably the best way to think of the term "scripting language" is that it refers to a simple language used for quickly coding tasks. This is especially true when the term is applied to Python, which allows much faster program development than compiled languages like C++. Its rapid development cycle fosters an exploratory, incremental mode of programming that has to be experienced to be appreciated.

Don't be fooled, though—Python is not just for simple tasks. Rather, it makes tasks simple by its ease of use and flexibility. Python has a simple feature set, but it allows programs to scale up in sophistication as needed. Because of that, it is commonly used for quick tactical tasks and longer-term strategic development.

So, is Python a scripting language or not? It depends on whom you ask. In general, the term "scripting" is probably best used to describe the rapid and flexible mode of development that Python supports, rather than a particular application domain.

OK, but What's the Downside?

After using it for 21 years, writing about it for 18, and teaching it for 16, I've found that the only significant universal downside to Python is that, as currently implemented, its *execution speed* may not always be as fast as that of fully compiled and lower-level languages such as C and C++. Though relatively rare today, for some tasks you may still occasionally need to get "closer to the iron" by using lower-level languages such as these that are more directly mapped to the underlying hardware architecture.

We'll talk about implementation concepts in detail later in this book. In short, the standard implementations of Python today compile (i.e., translate) source code statements to an intermediate format known as *byte code* and then interpret the byte code. Byte code provides portability, as it is a platform-independent format. However, because Python is not normally compiled all the way down to binary machine code (e.g., instructions for an Intel chip), some programs will run more slowly in Python than in a fully compiled language like C. The *PyPy* system discussed in the next chapter can achieve a 10X to 100X speedup on some code by compiling further as your program runs, but it's a separate, alternative implementation.

Whether you will ever *care* about the execution speed difference depends on what kinds of programs you write. Python has been optimized numerous times, and Python code runs fast enough by itself in most application domains. Furthermore, whenever you do something "real" in a Python script, like processing a file or constructing a graphical user interface (GUI), your program will actually run at C speed, since such tasks are immediately dispatched to compiled C code inside the Python interpreter. More fundamentally, Python's speed-of-development gain is often far more important than any speed-of-execution loss, especially given modern computer speeds.

Even at today's CPU speeds, though, there still are some domains that do require optimal execution speeds. Numeric programming and animation, for example, often need at least their core number-crunching components to run at C speed (or better). If you work in such a domain, you can still use Python—simply split off the parts of the application that require optimal speed into *compiled extensions*, and link those into your system for use in Python scripts.

We won't talk about extensions much in this text, but this is really just an instance of the Python-as-control-language role we discussed earlier. A prime example of this dual language strategy is the *NumPy* numeric programming extension for Python; by combining compiled and optimized numeric extension libraries with the Python language, NumPy turns Python into a numeric programming tool that is simultaneously efficient and easy to use. When needed, such extensions provide a powerful optimization tool.

Other Python Tradeoffs: The Intangible Bits

I mentioned that execution speed is the only major downside to Python. That's indeed the case for most Python users, and especially for newcomers. Most people find Python to be easy to learn and fun to use, especially when compared with its contemporaries like Java, C#, and C++. In the interest of full disclosure, though, I should also note up front some more abstract tradeoffs I've observed in my two decades in the Python world —both as an educator and developer.

As an educator, I've sometimes found the *rate of change* in Python and its libraries to be a negative, and have on occasion lamented its *growth* over the years. This is partly because trainers and book authors live on the front lines of such things—it's been my job to teach the language despite its constant change, a task at times akin to chronicling the herding of cats! Still, it's a broadly shared concern. As we'll see in this book, Python's original "keep it simple" motif is today often subsumed by a trend toward more sophisticated solutions at the expense of the learning curve of newcomers. This book's size is indirect evidence of this trend.

On the other hand, by most measures Python is still much simpler than its alternatives, and perhaps only as complex as it needs to be given the many roles it serves today. Its overall coherence and open nature remain compelling features to most. Moreover, not everyone needs to stay up to date with the cutting edge—as Python 2.X's ongoing popularity clearly shows.

As a developer, I also at times question the tradeoffs inherent in Python's *"batteries included" approach* to development. Its emphasis on prebuilt tools can add dependencies (what if a battery you use is changed, broken, or deprecated?), and encourage special-case solutions over general principles that may serve users better in the long run (how can you evaluate or use a tool well if you don't understand its purpose?). We'll see examples of both of these concerns in this book.

For typical users, and especially for hobbyists and beginners, Python's toolset approach is a major asset. But you shouldn't be surprised when you outgrow precoded tools, and can benefit from the sorts of skills this book aims to impart. Or, to paraphrase a proverb: give people a tool, and they'll code for a day; teach them how to build tools, and they'll code for a lifetime. This book's job is more the latter than the former.

As mentioned elsewhere in this chapter, both Python and its toolbox model are also susceptible to downsides common to *open source* projects in general—the potential triumph of the *personal preference* of the few over common usage of the many, and the occasional appearance of *anarchy* and even *elitism*—though these tend to be most grievous on the leading edge of new releases.

We'll return to some of these tradeoffs at the end of the book, after you've learned Python well enough to draw your own conclusions. As an open source system, what Python "is" is up to its users to define. In the end, Python is more popular today than ever, and its growth shows no signs of abating. To some, that may be a more telling metric than individual opinions, both pro and con.

Who Uses Python Today?

At this writing, the best estimate anyone can seem to make of the size of the Python user base is that there are roughly 1 million Python users around the world today (plus or minus a few). This estimate is based on various statistics, like download rates, web statistics, and developer surveys. Because Python is open source, a more exact count is difficult—there are no license registrations to tally. Moreover, Python is automatically included with Linux distributions, Macintosh computers, and a wide range of products and hardware, further clouding the user-base picture.

In general, though, Python enjoys a large user base and a very active developer community. It is generally considered to be in *the top 5 or top 10* most widely used programming languages in the world today (its exact ranking varies per source and date). Because Python has been around for *over two decades* and has been widely used, it is also very stable and robust.

Besides being leveraged by individual users, Python is also being applied in real revenue-generating products by real companies. For instance, among the generally known Python user base:

- *Google* makes extensive use of Python in its web search systems.
- The popular *YouTube* video sharing service is largely written in Python.
- The *Dropbox* storage service codes both its server and desktop client software primarily in Python.
- The *Raspberry Pi* single-board computer promotes Python as its educational language.
- *EVE Online*, a massively multiplayer online game (MMOG) by CCP Games, uses Python broadly.
- The widespread *BitTorrent* peer-to-peer file sharing system began its life as a Python program.
- *Industrial Light & Magic*, *Pixar*, and others use Python in the production of animated movies.
- *ESRI* uses Python as an end-user customization tool for its popular GIS mapping products.
- Google's *App Engine* web development framework uses Python as an application language.
- The *IronPort* email server product uses more than 1 million lines of Python code to do its job.
- *Maya*, a powerful integrated 3D modeling and animation system, provides a Python scripting API.
- The *NSA* uses Python for cryptography and intelligence analysis.
- *iRobot* uses Python to develop commercial and military robotic devices.

- The *Civilization IV* game's customizable scripted events are written entirely in Python.
- The One Laptop Per Child (*OLPC*) project built its user interface and activity model in Python.
- *Netflix* and *Yelp* have both documented the role of Python in their software infrastructures.
- *Intel, Cisco, Hewlett-Packard, Seagate, Qualcomm,* and *IBM* use Python for hardware testing.
- *JPMorgan Chase, UBS, Getco,* and *Citadel* apply Python to financial market forecasting.
- *NASA, Los Alamos, Fermilab, JPL,* and others use Python for scientific programming tasks.

And so on—though this list is representative, a full accounting is beyond this book's scope, and is almost guaranteed to change over time. For an up-to-date sampling of additional Python users, applications, and software, try the following pages currently at Python's site and Wikipedia, as well as a search in your favorite web browser:

- Success stories: *http://www.python.org/about/success*
- Application domains: *http://www.python.org/about/apps*
- User quotes: *http://www.python.org/about/quotes*
- Wikipedia page: *http://en.wikipedia.org/wiki/List_of_Python_software*

Probably the only common thread among the companies using Python today is that Python is used all over the map, in terms of application domains. Its general-purpose nature makes it applicable to almost all fields, not just one. In fact, it's safe to say that virtually every substantial organization writing software is using Python, whether for short-term tactical tasks, such as testing and administration, or for long-term strategic product development. Python has proven to work well in both modes.

What Can I Do with Python?

In addition to being a well-designed programming language, Python is useful for accomplishing real-world tasks—the sorts of things developers do day in and day out. It's commonly used in a variety of domains, as a tool for scripting other components and implementing standalone programs. In fact, as a general-purpose language, Python's roles are virtually unlimited: you can use it for everything from website development and gaming to robotics and spacecraft control.

However, the most common Python roles currently seem to fall into a few broad categories. The next few sections describe some of Python's most common applications today, as well as tools used in each domain. We won't be able to explore the tools mentioned here in any depth—if you are interested in any of these topics, see the Python website or other resources for more details.

Systems Programming

Python's built-in interfaces to operating-system services make it ideal for writing portable, maintainable system-administration tools and utilities (sometimes called *shell tools*). Python programs can search files and directory trees, launch other programs, do parallel processing with processes and threads, and so on.

Python's standard library comes with POSIX bindings and support for all the usual OS tools: environment variables, files, sockets, pipes, processes, multiple threads, regular expression pattern matching, command-line arguments, standard stream interfaces, shell-command launchers, filename expansion, zip file utilities, XML and JSON parsers, CSV file handlers, and more. In addition, the bulk of Python's system interfaces are designed to be portable; for example, a script that copies directory trees typically runs unchanged on all major Python platforms. The *Stackless* Python implementation, described in Chapter 2 and used by *EVE Online*, also offers advanced solutions to multiprocessing requirements.

GUIs

Python's simplicity and rapid turnaround also make it a good match for graphical user interface programming on the desktop. Python comes with a standard object-oriented interface to the Tk GUI API called *tkinter* (*Tkinter* in 2.X) that allows Python programs to implement portable GUIs with a native look and feel. Python/tkinter GUIs run unchanged on Microsoft Windows, X Windows (on Unix and Linux), and the Mac OS (both Classic and OS X). A free extension package, *PMW*, adds advanced widgets to the tkinter toolkit. In addition, the *wxPython* GUI API, based on a C++ library, offers an alternative toolkit for constructing portable GUIs in Python.

Higher-level toolkits such as *Dabo* are built on top of base APIs such as wxPython and tkinter. With the proper library, you can also use GUI support in other toolkits in Python, such as *Qt* with PyQt, *GTK* with PyGTK, *MFC* with PyWin32, *.NET* with IronPython, and *Swing* with Jython (the Java version of Python, described in Chapter 2) or JPype. For applications that run in web browsers or have simple interface requirements, both Jython and Python web frameworks and server-side CGI scripts, described in the next section, provide additional user interface options.

Internet Scripting

Python comes with standard Internet modules that allow Python programs to perform a wide variety of networking tasks, in client and server modes. Scripts can communicate over sockets; extract form information sent to server-side CGI scripts; transfer files by FTP; parse and generate XML and JSON documents; send, receive, compose, and parse email; fetch web pages by URLs; parse the HTML of fetched web pages; communicate over XML-RPC, SOAP, and Telnet; and more. Python's libraries make these tasks remarkably simple.

In addition, a large collection of third-party tools are available on the Web for doing Internet programming in Python. For instance, the *HTMLGen* system generates HTML files from Python class-based descriptions, the *mod_python* package runs Python efficiently within the Apache web server and supports server-side templating with its Python Server Pages, and the Jython system provides for seamless Python/Java integration and supports coding of server-side applets that run on clients.

In addition, full-blown web development framework packages for Python, such as *Django*, *TurboGears*, *web2py*, *Pylons*, *Zope*, and *WebWare*, support quick construction of full-featured and production-quality websites with Python. Many of these include features such as object-relational mappers, a Model/View/Controller architecture, server-side scripting and templating, and AJAX support, to provide complete and enterprise-level web development solutions.

More recently, Python has expanded into rich Internet applications (RIAs), with tools such as *Silverlight* in *IronPython*, and *pyjs* (a.k.a. *pyjamas*) and its Python-to-JavaScript compiler, AJAX framework, and widget set. Python also has moved into cloud computing, with *App Engine*, and others described in the database section ahead. Where the Web leads, Python quickly follows.

Component Integration

We discussed the component integration role earlier when describing Python as a control language. Python's ability to be extended by and embedded in C and C++ systems makes it useful as a flexible glue language for scripting the behavior of other systems and components. For instance, integrating a C library into Python enables Python to test and launch the library's components, and embedding Python in a product enables onsite customizations to be coded without having to recompile the entire product (or ship its source code at all).

Tools such as the *SWIG* and *SIP* code generators can automate much of the work needed to link compiled components into Python for use in scripts, and the *Cython* system allows coders to mix Python and C-like code. Larger frameworks, such as Python's *COM* support on Windows, the Jython *Java*-based implementation, and the IronPython .NET-based implementation provide alternative ways to script components. On Windows, for example, Python scripts can use frameworks to script Word and Excel, access *Silverlight*, and much more.

Database Programming

For traditional database demands, there are Python interfaces to all commonly used relational database systems—Sybase, Oracle, Informix, ODBC, MySQL, PostgreSQL,

SQLite, and more. The Python world has also defined a *portable database API* for accessing SQL database systems from Python scripts, which looks the same on a variety of underlying database systems. For instance, because the vendor interfaces implement the portable API, a script written to work with the free MySQL system will work largely unchanged on other systems (such as Oracle); all you generally have to do is replace the underlying vendor interface. The in-process *SQLite* embedded SQL database engine is a standard part of Python itself since 2.5, supporting both prototyping and basic program storage needs.

In the non-SQL department, Python's standard `pickle` module provides a simple object persistence system—it allows programs to easily save and restore entire Python objects to files and file-like objects. On the Web, you'll also find third-party open source systems named *ZODB* and *Durus* that provide complete object-oriented database systems for Python scripts; others, such as *SQLObject* and *SQLAlchemy*, that implement object relational mappers (ORMs), which graft Python's class model onto relational tables; and *PyMongo*, an interface to *MongoDB*, a high-performance, non-SQL, open source *JSON*-style document database, which stores data in structures very similar to Python's own lists and dictionaries, and whose text may be parsed and created with Python's own standard library `json` module.

Still other systems offer more specialized ways to store data, including the datastore in Google's *App Engine*, which models data with Python classes and provides extensive scalability, as well as additional emerging cloud storage options such as *Azure*, *Pi-Cloud*, *OpenStack*, and *Stackato*.

Rapid Prototyping

To Python programs, components written in Python and C look the same. Because of this, it's possible to prototype systems in Python initially, and then move selected components to a compiled language such as C or C++ for delivery. Unlike some prototyping tools, Python doesn't require a complete rewrite once the prototype has solidified. Parts of the system that don't require the efficiency of a language such as C++ can remain coded in Python for ease of maintenance and use.

Numeric and Scientific Programming

Python is also heavily used in numeric programming—a domain that would not traditionally have been considered to be in the scope of scripting languages, but has grown to become one of Python's most compelling use cases. Prominent here, the *NumPy* high-performance numeric programming extension for Python mentioned earlier includes such advanced tools as an array object, interfaces to standard mathematical libraries, and much more. By integrating Python with numeric routines coded in a compiled language for speed, NumPy turns Python into a sophisticated yet easy-to-use numeric programming tool that can often replace existing code written in traditional compiled languages such as FORTRAN or C++.

Additional numeric tools for Python support animation, 3D visualization, parallel processing, and so on. The popular *SciPy* and *ScientificPython* extensions, for example, provide additional libraries of scientific programming tools and use NumPy as a core component. The *PyPy* implementation of Python (discussed in Chapter 2) has also gained traction in the numeric domain, in part because heavily algorithmic code of the sort that's common in this domain can run dramatically faster in PyPy—often 10X to 100X quicker.

And More: Gaming, Images, Data Mining, Robots, Excel...

Python is commonly applied in more domains than can be covered here. For example, you'll find tools that allow you to use Python to do:

- Game programming and multimedia with *pygame*, *cgkit*, *pyglet*, *PySoy*, *Panda3D*, and others
- Serial port communication on Windows, Linux, and more with the *PySerial* extension
- Image processing with *PIL* and its newer *Pillow* fork, *PyOpenGL*, *Blender*, *Maya*, and more
- Robot control programming with the *PyRo* toolkit
- Natural language analysis with the *NLTK* package
- Instrumentation on the *Raspberry Pi* and *Arduino* boards
- Mobile computing with ports of Python to the Google *Android* and Apple *iOS* platforms
- Excel spreadsheet function and macro programming with the *PyXLL* or *DataNitro* add-ins
- Media file content and metadata tag processing with *PyMedia*, *ID3*, *PIL/Pillow*, and more
- Artificial intelligence with the *PyBrain* neural net library and the *Milk* machine learning toolkit
- Expert system programming with *PyCLIPS*, *Pyke*, *Pyrolog*, and *pyDatalog*
- Network monitoring with *zenoss*, written in and customized with Python
- Python-scripted design and modeling with *PythonCAD*, *PythonOCC*, *FreeCAD*, and others
- Document processing and generation with *ReportLab*, *Sphinx*, *Cheetah*, *PyPDF*, and so on
- Data visualization with *Mayavi*, *matplotlib*, *VTK*, *VPython*, and more
- XML parsing with the `xml` library package, the `xmlrpclib` module, and third-party extensions
- JSON and CSV file processing with the `json` and `csv` modules

- Data mining with the *Orange* framework, the *Pattern* bundle, *Scrapy*, and custom code

You can even play solitaire with the *PySolFC* program. And of course, you can always code custom Python scripts in less buzzword-laden domains to perform day-to-day system administration, process your email, manage your document and media libraries, and so on. You'll find links to the support in many fields at the PyPI website, and via web searches (search Google or *http://www.python.org* for links).

Though of broad practical use, many of these specific domains are largely just instances of Python's component integration role in action again. Adding it as a frontend to libraries of components written in a compiled language such as C makes Python useful for scripting in a wide variety of domains. As a general-purpose language that supports integration, Python is widely applicable.

How Is Python Developed and Supported?

As a popular open source system, Python enjoys a large and active development community that responds to issues and develops enhancements with a speed that many commercial software developers might find remarkable. Python developers coordinate work online with a source-control system. Changes are developed per a formal protocol, which includes writing a *PEP* (Python Enhancement Proposal) or other document, and extensions to Python's regression testing system. In fact, modifying Python today is roughly as involved as changing commercial software—a far cry from Python's early days, when an email to its creator would suffice, but a good thing given its large user base today.

The *PSF* (Python Software Foundation), a formal nonprofit group, organizes conferences and deals with intellectual property issues. Numerous Python conferences are held around the world; O'Reilly's *OSCON* and the PSF's *PyCon* are the largest. The former of these addresses multiple open source projects, and the latter is a Python-only event that has experienced strong growth in recent years. PyCon 2012 and 2013 reached *2,500 attendees* each; in fact, PyCon 2013 had to cap its limit at this level after a surprise sell-out in 2012 (and managed to grab wide attention on both technical and nontechnical grounds that I won't chronicle here). Earlier years often saw attendance double —from 586 attendees in 2007 to over 1,000 in 2008, for example—indicative of Python's growth in general, and impressive to those who remember early conferences whose attendees could largely be served around a single restaurant table.

Open Source Tradeoffs

Having said that, it's important to note that while Python enjoys a vigorous development community, this comes with inherent tradeoffs. Open source software can also appear chaotic and even resemble *anarchy* at times, and may not always be as smoothly implemented as the prior paragraphs might imply. Some changes may still manage to defy official protocols, and as in all human endeavors, mistakes still happen despite the process controls (Python 3.2.0, for instance, came with a broken console `input` function on Windows).

Moreover, open source projects exchange commercial interests for the *personal preferences* of a current set of developers, which may or may not be the same as yours—you are not held hostage by a company, but you are at the mercy of those with spare time to change the system. The net effect is that open source software evolution is often driven by the few, but imposed on the many.

In practice, though, these tradeoffs impact those on the "bleeding" edge of new releases much more than those using established versions of the system, including prior releases in both Python 3.X and 2.X. If you kept using classic classes in Python 2.X, for example, you were largely immune to the *explosion* of class functionality and change in new-style classes that occurred in the early-to-mid 2000s. Though these become mandatory in 3.X (along with much more), many 2.X users today still happily skirt the issue.

What Are Python's Technical Strengths?

Naturally, this is a developer's question. If you don't already have a programming background, the language in the next few sections may be a bit baffling—don't worry, we'll explore all of these terms in more detail as we proceed through this book. For developers, though, here is a quick introduction to some of Python's top technical features.

It's Object-Oriented and Functional

Python is an object-oriented language, from the ground up. Its *class model* supports advanced notions such as polymorphism, operator overloading, and multiple inheritance; yet, in the context of Python's simple syntax and typing, OOP is remarkably easy to apply. In fact, if you don't understand these terms, you'll find they are much easier to learn with Python than with just about any other OOP language available.

Besides serving as a powerful code structuring and reuse device, Python's OOP nature makes it ideal as a *scripting tool* for other object-oriented systems languages. For example, with the appropriate glue code, Python programs can subclass (specialize) classes implemented in C++, Java, and C#.

Of equal significance, OOP is an *option* in Python; you can go far without having to become an object guru all at once. Much like C++, Python supports both procedural and object-oriented programming modes. Its object-oriented tools can be applied if and when constraints allow. This is especially useful in tactical development modes, which preclude design phases.

In addition to its original *procedural* (statement-based) and *object-oriented* (class-based) paradigms, Python in recent years has acquired built-in support for *functional programming*—a set that by most measures includes generators, comprehensions, closures, maps, decorators, anonymous function lambdas, and first-class function objects. These can serve as both complement and alternative to its OOP tools.

It's Free

Python is completely free to use and distribute. As with other open source software, such as Tcl, Perl, Linux, and Apache, you can fetch the entire Python system's source code for free on the Internet. There are no restrictions on copying it, embedding it in your systems, or shipping it with your products. In fact, you can even sell Python's source code, if you are so inclined.

But don't get the wrong idea: "free" doesn't mean "unsupported." On the contrary, the Python online community responds to user queries with a speed that most commercial software help desks would do well to try to emulate. Moreover, because Python comes with complete source code, it empowers developers, leading to the creation of a large team of implementation experts. Although studying or changing a programming language's implementation isn't everyone's idea of fun, it's comforting to know that you can do so if you need to. You're not dependent on the whims of a commercial vendor, because the ultimate documentation—*source code*—is at your disposal as a last resort.

As mentioned earlier, Python development is performed by a community that largely coordinates its efforts over the Internet. It consists of Python's original creator—*Guido van Rossum*, the officially anointed Benevolent Dictator for Life (*BDFL*) of Python—plus a supporting cast of thousands. Language changes must follow a formal enhancement procedure and be scrutinized by both other developers and the BDFL. This tends to make Python more conservative with changes than some other languages and systems. While the Python 3.X/2.X split broke with this tradition soundly and deliberately, it still holds generally true within each Python line.

It's Portable

The standard implementation of Python is written in portable ANSI C, and it compiles and runs on virtually every major platform currently in use. For example, Python programs run today on everything from PDAs to supercomputers. As a partial list, Python is available on:

- Linux and Unix systems
- Microsoft Windows (all modern flavors)
- Mac OS (both OS X and Classic)
- BeOS, OS/2, VMS, and QNX
- Real-time systems such as VxWorks
- Cray supercomputers and IBM mainframes

- PDAs running Palm OS, PocketPC, and Linux
- Cell phones running Symbian OS, and Windows Mobile
- Gaming consoles and iPods
- Tablets and smartphones running Google's Android and Apple's iOS
- And more

Like the language interpreter itself, the standard library modules that ship with Python are implemented to be as portable across platform boundaries as possible. Further, Python programs are automatically compiled to portable byte code, which runs the same on any platform with a compatible version of Python installed (more on this in the next chapter).

What that means is that Python programs using the core language and standard libraries run the same on Linux, Windows, and most other systems with a Python interpreter. Most Python ports also contain platform-specific extensions (e.g., COM support on Windows), but the core Python language and libraries work the same everywhere. As mentioned earlier, Python also includes an interface to the Tk GUI toolkit called tkinter (Tkinter in 2.X), which allows Python programs to implement full-featured graphical user interfaces that run on all major GUI desktop platforms without program changes.

It's Powerful

From a features perspective, Python is something of a hybrid. Its toolset places it between traditional scripting languages (such as Tcl, Scheme, and Perl) and systems development languages (such as C, C++, and Java). Python provides all the simplicity and ease of use of a scripting language, along with more advanced software-engineering tools typically found in compiled languages. Unlike some scripting languages, this combination makes Python useful for large-scale development projects. As a preview, here are some of the main things you'll find in Python's toolbox:

Dynamic typing
> Python keeps track of the kinds of objects your program uses when it runs; it doesn't require complicated type and size declarations in your code. In fact, as you'll see in Chapter 6, there is no such thing as a type or variable declaration anywhere in Python. Because Python code does not constrain data types, it is also usually automatically applicable to a whole range of objects.

Automatic memory management
> Python automatically allocates objects and reclaims ("garbage collects") them when they are no longer used, and most can grow and shrink on demand. As you'll learn, Python keeps track of low-level memory details so you don't have to.

Programming-in-the-large support
> For building larger systems, Python includes tools such as modules, classes, and exceptions. These tools allow you to organize systems into components, use OOP

to reuse and customize code, and handle events and errors gracefully. Python's functional programming tools, described earlier, provide additional ways to meet many of the same goals.

Built-in object types

Python provides commonly used data structures such as lists, dictionaries, and strings as intrinsic parts of the language; as you'll see, they're both flexible and easy to use. For instance, built-in objects can grow and shrink on demand, can be arbitrarily nested to represent complex information, and more.

Built-in tools

To process all those object types, Python comes with powerful and standard operations, including concatenation (joining collections), slicing (extracting sections), sorting, mapping, and more.

Library utilities

For more specific tasks, Python also comes with a large collection of precoded library tools that support everything from regular expression matching to networking. Once you learn the language itself, Python's library tools are where much of the application-level action occurs.

Third-party utilities

Because Python is open source, developers are encouraged to contribute precoded tools that support tasks beyond those supported by its built-ins; on the Web, you'll find free support for COM, imaging, numeric programming, XML, database access, and much more.

Despite the array of tools in Python, it retains a remarkably simple syntax and design. The result is a powerful programming tool with all the usability of a scripting language.

It's Mixable

Python programs can easily be "glued" to components written in other languages in a variety of ways. For example, Python's C API lets C programs call and be called by Python programs flexibly. That means you can add functionality to the Python system as needed, and use Python programs within other environments or systems.

Mixing Python with libraries coded in languages such as C or C++, for instance, makes it an easy-to-use frontend language and customization tool. As mentioned earlier, this also makes Python good at rapid prototyping—systems may be implemented in Python first, to leverage its speed of development, and later moved to C for delivery, one piece at a time, according to performance demands.

It's Relatively Easy to Use

Compared to alternatives like C++, Java, and C#, Python programming seems astonishingly simple to most observers. To run a Python program, you simply type it and run it. There are no intermediate compile and link steps, like there are for languages such as C or C++. Python executes programs immediately, which makes for an interactive programming experience and *rapid turnaround* after program changes—in many cases, you can witness the effect of a program change nearly as fast as you can type it.

Of course, development cycle turnaround is only one aspect of Python's ease of use. It also provides a deliberately simple syntax and powerful built-in tools. In fact, some have gone so far as to call Python *executable pseudocode*. Because it eliminates much of the complexity in other tools, Python programs are simpler, smaller, and more flexible than equivalent programs in other popular languages.

It's Relatively Easy to Learn

This brings us to the point of this book: especially when compared to other widely used programming languages, the core Python language is remarkably easy to learn. In fact, if you're an experienced programmer, you can expect to be coding small-scale Python programs in a matter of days, and may be able to pick up some limited portions of the language in just hours—though you shouldn't expect to become an expert quite that fast (despite what you may have heard from marketing departments!).

Naturally, mastering any topic as substantial as today's Python is not trivial, and we'll devote the rest of this book to this task. But the true investment required to master Python is worthwhile—in the end, you'll gain programming skills that apply to nearly every computer application domain. Moreover, most find Python's learning curve to be much gentler than that of other programming tools.

That's good news for professional developers seeking to learn the language to use on the job, as well as for end users of systems that expose a Python layer for customization or control. Today, many systems rely on the fact that end users can learn enough Python to tailor their Python customization code onsite, with little or no support. Moreover, Python has spawned a large group of users who program for fun instead of career, and may never need full-scale software development skills. Although Python does have advanced programming tools, its core language essentials will still seem relatively simple to beginners and gurus alike.

It's Named After Monty Python

OK, this isn't quite a technical strength, but it does seem to be a surprisingly well-kept secret in the Python world that I wish to expose up front. Despite all the reptiles on Python books and icons, the truth is that Python is named after the British comedy group *Monty Python*—makers of the 1970s BBC comedy series *Monty Python's Flying Circus* and a handful of later full-length films, including *Monty Python and the Holy Grail*, that are still widely popular today. Python's original creator was a fan of Monty Python, as are many software developers (indeed, there seems to be a sort of symmetry between the two fields...).

This legacy inevitably adds a humorous quality to Python code examples. For instance, the traditional "foo" and "bar" for generic variable names become "spam" and "eggs" in the Python world. The occasional "Brian," "ni," and "shrubbery" likewise owe their appearances to this namesake. It even impacts the Python community at large: some events at Python conferences are regularly billed as "The Spanish Inquisition."

All of this is, of course, very funny if you are familiar with the shows, but less so otherwise. You don't need to be familiar with Monty Python's work to make sense of examples that borrow references from it, including many you will see in this book, but at least you now know their root. (Hey—I've warned you.)

How Does Python Stack Up to Language X?

Finally, to place it in the context of what you may already know, people sometimes compare Python to languages such as Perl, Tcl, and Java. This section summarizes common consensus in this department.

I want to note up front that I'm not a fan of winning by disparaging the competition—it doesn't work in the long run, and that's not the goal here. Moreover, this is not a zero sum game—most programmers will use many languages over their careers. Nevertheless, programming tools present choices and tradeoffs that merit consideration. After all, if Python didn't offer something over its alternatives, it would never have been used in the first place.

We talked about performance tradeoffs earlier, so here we'll focus on functionality. While other languages are also useful tools to know and use, many people find that Python:

- Is more powerful than *Tcl*. Python's strong support for "programming in the large" makes it applicable to the development of larger systems, and its library of application tools is broader.

- Is more readable than *Perl*. Python has a clear syntax and a simple, coherent design. This in turn makes Python more reusable and maintainable, and helps reduce program bugs.

- Is simpler and easier to use than *Java* and *C#*. Python is a scripting language, but Java and C# both inherit much of the complexity and syntax of larger OOP systems languages like C++.

- Is simpler and easier to use than *C++*. Python code is simpler than the equivalent C++ and often one-third to one-fifth as large, though as a scripting language, Python sometimes serves different roles.

- Is simpler and higher-level than *C*. Python's detachment from underlying hardware architecture makes code less complex, better structured, and more approachable than C, C++'s progenitor.

- Is more powerful, general-purpose, and cross-platform than *Visual Basic*. Python is a richer language that is used more widely, and its open source nature means it is not controlled by a single company.

- Is more readable and general-purpose than *PHP*. Python is used to construct websites too, but it is also applied to nearly every other computer domain, from robotics to movie animation and gaming.

- Is more powerful and general-purpose than *JavaScript*. Python has a larger toolset, and is not as tightly bound to web development. It's also used for scientific modeling, instrumentation, and more.

- Is more readable and established than *Ruby*. Python syntax is less cluttered, especially in nontrivial code, and its OOP is fully optional for users and projects to which it may not apply.

- Is more mature and broadly focused than *Lua*. Python's larger feature set and more extensive library support give it a wider scope than Lua, an embedded "glue" language like Tcl.

- Is less esoteric than *Smalltalk*, *Lisp*, and *Prolog*. Python has the dynamic flavor of languages like these, but also has a traditional syntax accessible to both developers and end users of customizable systems.

Especially for programs that do more than scan text files, and that might have to be read in the future by others (or by you!), many people find that Python fits the bill better than any other scripting or programming language available today. Furthermore, unless your application requires peak performance, Python is often a viable alternative to systems development languages such as C, C++, and Java: Python code can often achieve the same goals, but will be much less difficult to write, debug, and maintain.

Of course, your author has been a card-carrying Python evangelist since 1992, so take these comments as you may (and other languages' advocates' mileage may vary arbitrarily). They do, however, reflect the common experience of many developers who have taken time to explore what Python has to offer.

Chapter Summary

And that concludes the "hype" portion of this book. In this chapter, we've explored some of the reasons that people pick Python for their programming tasks. We've also seen how it is applied and looked at a representative sample of who is using it today. My goal is to teach Python, though, not to sell it. The best way to judge a language is to see it in action, so the rest of this book focuses entirely on the language details we've glossed over here.

The next two chapters begin our technical introduction to the language. In them, we'll explore ways to run Python programs, peek at Python's byte code execution model, and introduce the basics of module files for saving code. The goal will be to give you just enough information to run the examples and exercises in the rest of the book. You won't really start programming per se until Chapter 4, but make sure you have a handle on the startup details before moving on.

Test Your Knowledge: Quiz

In this edition of the book, we will be closing each chapter with a quick open-book quiz about the material presented herein to help you review the key concepts. The answers for these quizzes appear immediately after the questions, and you are encouraged to read the answers once you've taken a crack at the questions yourself, as they sometimes give useful context.

In addition to these end-of-chapter quizzes, you'll find lab *exercises* at the end of each part of the book, designed to help you start coding Python on your own. For now, here's your first quiz. Good luck, and be sure to refer back to this chapter's material as needed.

1. What are the six main reasons that people choose to use Python?
2. Name four notable companies or organizations using Python today.
3. Why might you *not* want to use Python in an application?
4. What can you do with Python?
5. What's the significance of the Python `import this` statement?
6. Why does "spam" show up in so many Python examples in books and on the Web?
7. What is your favorite color?

Test Your Knowledge: Answers

How did you do? Here are the answers I came up with, though there may be multiple solutions to some quiz questions. Again, even if you're sure of your answer, I encourage you to look at mine for additional context. See the chapter's text for more details if any of these responses don't make sense to you.

1. Software quality, developer productivity, program portability, support libraries, component integration, and simple enjoyment. Of these, the quality and productivity themes seem to be the main reasons that people choose to use Python.
2. Google, Industrial Light & Magic, CCP Games, Jet Propulsion Labs, Maya, ESRI, and many more. Almost every organization doing software development uses Python in some fashion, whether for long-term strategic product development or for short-term tactical tasks such as testing and system administration.
3. Python's main downside is performance: it won't run as quickly as fully compiled languages like C and C++. On the other hand, it's quick enough for most applications, and typical Python code runs at close to C speed anyhow because it invokes

linked-in C code in the interpreter. If speed is critical, compiled extensions are available for number-crunching parts of an application.

4. You can use Python for nearly anything you can do with a computer, from website development and gaming to robotics and spacecraft control.

5. This was mentioned in a footnote: `import this` triggers an Easter egg inside Python that displays some of the design philosophies underlying the language. You'll learn how to run this statement in the next chapter.

6. "Spam" is a reference from a famous Monty Python skit in which people trying to order food in a cafeteria are drowned out by a chorus of Vikings singing about spam. Oh, and it's also a common variable name in Python scripts...

7. Blue. No, yellow! (See the prior answer.)

Python Is Engineering, Not Art

When Python first emerged on the software scene in the early 1990s, it spawned what is now something of a classic conflict between its proponents and those of another popular scripting language, Perl. Personally, I think the debate is tired and unwarranted today—developers are smart enough to draw their own conclusions. Still, this is one of the most common topics I'm asked about on the training road, and underscores one of the main reasons people choose to use Python; it seems fitting to say a few brief words about it here.

The short story is this: *you can do everything in Python that you can in Perl, but you can read your code after you do it.* That's it—their domains largely overlap, but Python is more focused on producing readable code. For many, the enhanced readability of Python translates to better code reusability and maintainability, making Python a better choice for programs that will not be written once and thrown away. Perl code is easy to write, but can be difficult to read. Given that most software has a lifespan much longer than its initial creation, many see Python as the more effective tool.

The somewhat longer story reflects the backgrounds of the designers of the two languages. *Python* originated with a mathematician by training, who seems to have naturally produced an orthogonal language with a high degree of uniformity and coherence. *Perl* was spawned by a linguist, who created a programming tool closer to natural language, with its context sensitivities and wide variability. As a well-known Perl motto states, *there's more than one way to do it.* Given this mindset, both the Perl language and its user community have historically encouraged untethered freedom of expression when writing code. One person's Perl code can be radically different from another's. In fact, writing unique, tricky code is often a source of pride among Perl users.

But as anyone who has done any substantial code maintenance should be able to attest, *freedom of expression is great for art, but lousy for engineering.* In engineering, we need a minimal feature set and predictability. In engineering, freedom of expression can lead to maintenance nightmares. As more than one Perl user has confided to me, the result of too much freedom is often code that is much easier to rewrite from scratch than to modify. This is clearly less than ideal.

Consider this: when people create a painting or a sculpture, they do so largely for themselves; the prospect of someone else changing their work later doesn't enter into it. This is a critical difference between art and engineering. When people write *software*, they are not writing it for themselves. In fact, they are not even writing primarily for the computer. Rather, good programmers know that code is written for the next human being who has to read it in order to maintain or reuse it. If that person cannot understand the code, it's all but useless in a realistic development scenario. In other words, programming is not about being clever and obscure—*it's about how clearly your program communicates its purpose.*

This readability focus is where many people find that Python most clearly differentiates itself from other scripting languages. Because Python's syntax model almost *forces* the creation of readable code, Python programs lend themselves more directly to the full software development cycle. And because Python emphasizes ideas such as limited interactions, code uniformity, and feature consistency, it more directly fosters code that can be used long after it is first written.

In the long run, Python's focus on *code quality* in itself boosts programmer productivity, as well as programmer satisfaction. Python programmers can be wildly creative, too, of course, and as we'll see, the language does offer multiple solutions for some tasks—sometimes even more than it should today, an issue we'll confront head-on in this book too. In fact, this sidebar can also be read as a *cautionary tale*: quality turns out to be a fragile state, one that depends as much on *people* as on technology. Python has historically encouraged good engineering in ways that other scripting languages often did not, but the rest of the quality story is up to you.

At least, that's some of the common consensus among many people who have adopted Python. You should judge such claims for yourself, of course, by learning what Python has to offer. To help you get started, let's move on to the next chapter.

## CHAPTER 2

How Python Runs Programs

This chapter and the next take a quick look at program execution—how you launch code, and how Python runs it. In this chapter, we'll study how the Python interpreter executes programs in general. Chapter 3 will then show you how to get your own programs up and running.

Startup details are inherently platform-specific, and some of the material in these two chapters may not apply to the platform you work on, so more advanced readers should feel free to skip parts not relevant to their intended use. Likewise, readers who have used similar tools in the past and prefer to get to the meat of the language quickly may want to file some of these chapters away as "for future reference." For the rest of us, let's take a brief look at the way that Python will run our code, before we learn how to write it.

Introducing the Python Interpreter

So far, I've mostly been talking about Python as a programming language. But, as currently implemented, it's also a software package called an *interpreter*. An interpreter is a kind of program that executes other programs. When you write a Python program, the Python interpreter reads your program and carries out the instructions it contains. In effect, the interpreter is a layer of software logic between your code and the computer hardware on your machine.

When the Python package is installed on your machine, it generates a number of components—minimally, an interpreter and a support library. Depending on how you use it, the Python interpreter may take the form of an executable program, or a set of libraries linked into another program. Depending on which flavor of Python you run, the interpreter itself may be implemented as a C program, a set of Java classes, or something else. Whatever form it takes, the Python code you write must always be run by this interpreter. And to enable that, you must install a Python interpreter on your computer.

Python installation details vary by platform and are covered in more depth in Appendix A. In short:

- Windows users fetch and run a self-installing executable file that puts Python on their machines. Simply double-click and say Yes or Next at all prompts.
- Linux and Mac OS X users probably already have a usable Python preinstalled on their computers—it's a standard component on these platforms today.
- Some Linux and Mac OS X users (and most Unix users) compile Python from its full source code distribution package.
- Linux users can also find RPM files, and Mac OS X users can find various Mac-specific installation packages.
- Other platforms have installation techniques relevant to those platforms. For instance, Python is available on cell phones, tablets, game consoles, and iPods, but installation details vary widely.

Python itself may be fetched from the downloads page on its main website, *http://www.python.org*. It may also be found through various other distribution channels. Keep in mind that you should always check to see whether Python is already present before installing it. If you're working on Windows 7 and earlier, you'll usually find Python in the Start menu, as captured in Figure 2-1; we'll discuss the menu options shown here in the next chapter. On Unix and Linux, Python probably lives in your */usr* directory tree.

Because installation details are so platform-specific, we'll postpone the rest of this story here. For more details on the installation process, consult Appendix A. For the purposes of this chapter and the next, I'll assume that you've got Python ready to go.

Program Execution

What it means to write and run a Python script depends on whether you look at these tasks as a programmer, or as a Python interpreter. Both views offer important perspectives on Python programming.

The Programmer's View

In its simplest form, a Python program is just a text file containing Python statements. For example, the following file, named *script0.py*, is one of the simplest Python scripts I could dream up, but it passes for a fully functional Python program:

```
print('hello world')
print(2 ** 100)
```

This file contains two Python `print` statements, which simply print a string (the text in quotes) and a numeric expression result (2 to the power 100) to the output stream. Don't worry about the syntax of this code yet—for this chapter, we're interested only

Figure 2-1. When installed on Windows 7 and earlier, this is how Python shows up in your Start button menu. This can vary across releases, but IDLE starts a development GUI, and Python starts a simple interactive session. Also here are the standard manuals and the PyDoc documentation engine (Module Docs). See Chapter 3 and Appendix A for pointers on Windows 8 and other platforms.

in getting it to run. I'll explain the `print` statement, and why you can raise 2 to the power 100 in Python without overflowing, in the next parts of this book.

You can create such a file of statements with any text editor you like. By convention, Python program files are given names that end in *.py*; technically, this naming scheme is required only for files that are "imported"—a term clarified in the next chapter—but most Python files have *.py* names for consistency.

After you've typed these statements into a text file, you must tell Python to *execute* the file—which simply means to run all the statements in the file from top to bottom, one after another. As you'll see in the next chapter, you can launch Python program files by shell command lines, by clicking their icons, from within IDEs, and with other standard techniques. If all goes well, when you execute the file, you'll see the results of the two `print` statements show up somewhere on your computer—by default, usually in the same window you were in when you ran the program:

```
hello world
12676506002282294014967032053376
```

For example, here's what happened when I ran this script from a Command Prompt window's command line on a Windows laptop, to make sure it didn't have any silly typos:

```
C:\code> python script0.py
hello world
12676506002282294014967032053376
```

See Chapter 3 for the full story on this process, especially if you're new to programming; we'll get into all the gory details of writing and launching programs there. For our purposes here, we've just run a Python script that prints a string and a number. We probably won't win any programming awards with this code, but it's enough to capture the basics of program execution.

Python's View

The brief description in the prior section is fairly standard for scripting languages, and it's usually all that most Python programmers need to know. You type code into text files, and you run those files through the interpreter. Under the hood, though, a bit more happens when you tell Python to "go." Although knowledge of Python internals is not strictly required for Python programming, a basic understanding of the runtime structure of Python can help you grasp the bigger picture of program execution.

When you instruct Python to run your script, there are a few steps that Python carries out before your code actually starts crunching away. Specifically, it's first compiled to something called "byte code" and then routed to something called a "virtual machine."

Byte code compilation

Internally, and almost completely hidden from you, when you execute a program Python first compiles your *source code* (the statements in your file) into a format known as *byte code*. Compilation is simply a translation step, and byte code is a lower-level, platform-independent representation of your source code. Roughly, Python translates each of your source statements into a group of byte code instructions by decomposing them into individual steps. This byte code translation is performed to speed execution —byte code can be run much more quickly than the original source code statements in your text file.

You'll notice that the prior paragraph said that this is *almost* completely hidden from you. If the Python process has write access on your machine, it will store the byte code of your programs in files that end with a *.pyc* extension (".pyc" means compiled ".py" source). Prior to Python 3.2, you will see these files show up on your computer after you've run a few programs alongside the corresponding source code files—that is, in the *same* directories. For instance, you'll notice a *script.pyc* after importing a *script.py*.

In 3.2 and later, Python instead saves its *.pyc* byte code files in a subdirectory named *__pycache__* located in the directory where your source files reside, and in files whose names identify the Python version that created them (e.g., *script.cpython-33.pyc*). The new *__pycache__* subdirectory helps to avoid clutter, and the new naming convention for byte code files prevents different Python versions installed on the same computer from overwriting each other's saved byte code. We'll study these byte code file models in more detail in Chapter 22, though they are automatic and irrelevant to most Python programs, and are free to vary among the alternative Python implementations described ahead.

In both models, Python saves byte code like this as a startup speed optimization. The next time you run your program, Python will load the *.pyc* files and skip the compilation step, as long as you haven't changed your source code since the byte code was last saved, and aren't running with a different Python than the one that created the byte code. It works like this:

- *Source changes*: Python automatically checks the last-modified timestamps of source and byte code files to know when it must recompile—if you edit and resave your source code, byte code is automatically re-created the next time your program is run.

- *Python versions*: Imports also check to see if the file must be recompiled because it was created by a different Python version, using either a "magic" version number in the byte code file itself in 3.2 and earlier, or the information present in byte code filenames in 3.2 and later.

The result is that both source code changes and differing Python version numbers will trigger a new byte code file. If Python cannot write the byte code files to your machine, your program still works—the byte code is generated in memory and simply discarded on program exit. However, because *.pyc* files speed startup time, you'll want to make sure they are written for larger programs. Byte code files are also one way to ship Python programs—Python is happy to run a program if all it can find are *.pyc* files, even if the original *.py* source files are absent. (See "Frozen Binaries" on page 39 for another shipping option.)

Finally, keep in mind that byte code is saved in files only for files that are *imported*, not for the top-level files of a program that are only run as scripts (strictly speaking, it's an import optimization). We'll explore import basics in Chapter 3, and take a deeper look at imports in Part V. Moreover, a given file is only imported (and possibly compiled) *once* per program run, and byte code is also never saved for code typed at the *interactive prompt*—a programming mode we'll learn about in Chapter 3.

The Python Virtual Machine (PVM)

Once your program has been compiled to byte code (or the byte code has been loaded from existing *.pyc* files), it is shipped off for execution to something generally known as the Python Virtual Machine (PVM, for the more acronym-inclined among you). The

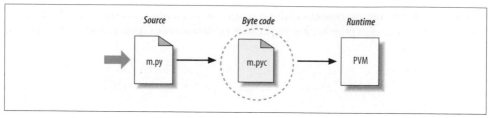

Figure 2-2. Python's traditional runtime execution model: source code you type is translated to byte code, which is then run by the Python Virtual Machine. Your code is automatically compiled, but then it is interpreted.

PVM sounds more impressive than it is; really, it's not a separate program, and it need not be installed by itself. In fact, the PVM is just a big code loop that iterates through your byte code instructions, one by one, to carry out their operations. The PVM is the runtime engine of Python; it's always present as part of the Python system, and it's the component that truly runs your scripts. Technically, it's just the last step of what is called the "Python interpreter."

Figure 2-2 illustrates the runtime structure described here. Keep in mind that all of this complexity is deliberately hidden from Python programmers. Byte code compilation is automatic, and the PVM is just part of the Python system that you have installed on your machine. Again, programmers simply code and run files of statements, and Python handles the logistics of running them.

Performance implications

Readers with a background in fully compiled languages such as C and C++ might notice a few differences in the Python model. For one thing, there is usually no build or "make" step in Python work: code runs immediately after it is written. For another, Python byte code is not binary machine code (e.g., instructions for an Intel or ARM chip). Byte code is a Python-specific representation.

This is why some Python code may not run as fast as C or C++ code, as described in Chapter 1—the PVM loop, not the CPU chip, still must interpret the byte code, and byte code instructions require more work than CPU instructions. On the other hand, unlike in classic interpreters, there is still an internal compile step—Python does not need to reanalyze and reparse each source statement's text repeatedly. The net effect is that pure Python code runs at speeds somewhere between those of a traditional compiled language and a traditional interpreted language. See Chapter 1 for more on Python performance tradeoffs.

Development implications

Another ramification of Python's execution model is that there is really no distinction between the development and execution environments. That is, the systems that compile and execute your source code are really one and the same. This similarity may have a bit more significance to readers with a background in traditional compiled languages, but in Python, the compiler is always present at runtime and is part of the system that runs programs.

This makes for a much more rapid development cycle. There is no need to precompile and link before execution may begin; simply type and run the code. This also adds a much more dynamic flavor to the language—it is possible, and often very convenient, for Python programs to construct and execute other Python programs at runtime. The eval and exec built-ins, for instance, accept and run strings containing Python program code. This structure is also why Python lends itself to product customization—because Python code can be changed on the fly, users can modify the Python parts of a system onsite without needing to have or compile the entire system's code.

At a more fundamental level, keep in mind that all we really have in Python is *runtime*—there is no initial compile-time phase at all, and everything happens as the program is running. This even includes operations such as the creation of functions and classes and the linkage of modules. Such events occur before execution in more static languages, but happen as programs execute in Python. As we'll see, this makes for a much more dynamic programming experience than that to which some readers may be accustomed.

Execution Model Variations

Now that we've studied the internal execution flow described in the prior section, I should note that it reflects the standard implementation of Python today but is not really a requirement of the Python language itself. Because of that, the execution model is prone to changing with time. In fact, there are already a few systems that modify the picture in Figure 2-2 somewhat. Before moving on, let's briefly explore the most prominent of these variations.

Python Implementation Alternatives

Strictly speaking, as this book edition is being written, there are at least five implementations of the Python language—*CPython*, *Jython*, *IronPython*, *Stackless*, and *PyPy*. Although there is much cross-fertilization of ideas and work between these Pythons, each is a separately installed software system, with its own developers and user base. Other potential candidates here include the *Cython* and *Shed Skin* systems, but they are discussed later as optimization tools because they do not implement the standard Python language (the former is a Python/C mix, and the latter is implicitly statically typed).

In brief, *CPython* is the standard implementation, and the system that most readers will wish to use (if you're not sure, this probably includes you). This is also the version used in this book, though the core Python language presented here is almost entirely the same in the alternatives. All the other Python implementations have specific purposes and roles, though they can often serve in most of CPython's capacities too. All implement the same Python language but execute programs in different ways.

For example, *PyPy* is a drop-in replacement for CPython, which can run most programs much quicker. Similarly, *Jython* and *IronPython* are completely independent implementations of Python that compile Python source for different runtime architectures, to provide direct access to Java and .NET components. It is also possible to access Java and .NET software from standard CPython programs—*JPype* and *Python for .NET* systems, for instance, allow standard CPython code to call out to Java and .NET components. Jython and IronPython offer more complete solutions, by providing full implementations of the Python language.

Here's a quick rundown on the most prominent Python implementations available today.

CPython: The standard

The original, and standard, implementation of Python is usually called CPython when you want to contrast it with the other options (and just plain "Python" otherwise). This name comes from the fact that it is coded in portable ANSI C language code. This is the Python that you fetch from *http://www.python.org*, get with the ActivePython and Enthought distributions, and have automatically on most Linux and Mac OS X machines. If you've found a preinstalled version of Python on your machine, it's probably CPython, unless your company or organization is using Python in more specialized ways.

Unless you want to script Java or .NET applications with Python or find the benefits of Stackless or PyPy compelling, you probably want to use the standard CPython system. Because it is the reference implementation of the language, it tends to run the fastest, be the most complete, and be more up-to-date and robust than the alternative systems. Figure 2-2 reflects CPython's runtime architecture.

Jython: Python for Java

The Jython system (originally known as JPython) is an alternative implementation of the Python language, targeted for integration with the Java programming language. Jython consists of Java classes that compile Python source code to Java byte code and then route the resulting byte code to the Java Virtual Machine (JVM). Programmers still code Python statements in *.py* text files as usual; the Jython system essentially just replaces the rightmost two bubbles in Figure 2-2 with Java-based equivalents.

Jython's goal is to allow Python code to script Java applications, much as CPython allows Python to script C and C++ components. Its integration with Java is remarkably seamless. Because Python code is translated to Java byte code, it looks and feels like a true Java program at runtime. Jython scripts can serve as web applets and servlets, build Java-based GUIs, and so on. Moreover, Jython includes integration support that allows Python code to import and use Java classes as though they were coded in Python, and

Java code to run Python code as an embedded language. Because Jython is slower and less robust than CPython, though, it is usually seen as a tool of interest primarily to Java developers looking for a scripting language to serve as a frontend to Java code. See Jython's website *http://jython.org* for more details.

IronPython: Python for .NET

A third implementation of Python, and newer than both CPython and Jython, IronPython is designed to allow Python programs to integrate with applications coded to work with Microsoft's .NET Framework for Windows, as well as the Mono open source equivalent for Linux. .NET and its C# programming language runtime system are designed to be a language-neutral object communication layer, in the spirit of Microsoft's earlier COM model. IronPython allows Python programs to act as both client and server components, gain accessibility both to and from other .NET languages, and leverage .NET technologies such as the *Silverlight* framework from their Python code.

By implementation, IronPython is very much like Jython (and, in fact, was developed by the same creator)—it replaces the last two bubbles in Figure 2-2 with equivalents for execution in the .NET environment. Also like Jython, IronPython has a special focus —it is primarily of interest to developers integrating Python with .NET components. Formerly developed by Microsoft and now an open source project, IronPython might also be able to take advantage of some important optimization tools for better performance. For more details, consult *http://ironpython.net* and other resources to be had with a web search.

Stackless: Python for concurrency

Still other schemes for running Python programs have more focused goals. For example, the *Stackless* Python system is an enhanced version and reimplementation of the standard CPython language oriented toward *concurrency*. Because it does not save state on the C language call stack, Stackless Python can make Python easier to port to small stack architectures, provides efficient multiprocessing options, and fosters novel programming structures such as coroutines.

Among other things, the *microthreads* that Stackless adds to Python are an efficient and lightweight alternative to Python's standard multitasking tools such as threads and processes, and promise better program structure, more readable code, and increased programmer productivity. CCP Games, the creator of *EVE Online*, is a well-known Stackless Python user, and a compelling Python user success story in general. Try *http://stackless.com* for more information.

PyPy: Python for speed

The *PyPy* system is another standard CPython reimplementation, focused on *performance*. It provides a fast Python implementation with a *JIT* (just-in-time) compiler, provides tools for a "sandbox" model that can run untrusted code in a secure environment, and by default includes support for the prior section's *Stackless* Python systems and its microthreads to support massive concurrency.

PyPy is the successor to the original *Psyco* JIT, described ahead, and subsumes it with a complete Python implementation built for speed. A JIT is really just an extension to the PVM—the rightmost bubble in Figure 2-2—that translates portions of your byte code all the way to binary machine code for faster execution. It does this as your program is *running*, not in a prerun compile step, and is able to create type-specific machine code for the dynamic Python language by keeping track of the *data types* of the objects your program processes. By replacing portions of your byte code this way, your program runs faster and faster as it is executing. In addition, some Python programs may also take up less memory under PyPy.

At this writing, PyPy supports Python 2.7 code (not yet 3.X) and runs on Intel x86 (IA-32) and x86_64 platforms (including Windows, Linux, and recent Macs), with ARM and PPC support under development. It runs most CPython code, though C extension modules must generally be recompiled, and PyPy has some minor but subtle language differences, including garbage collection semantics that obviate some common coding patterns. For instance, its non-reference-count scheme means that temporary files may not close and flush output buffers immediately, and may require manual close calls in some cases.

In return, your code may run much quicker. PyPy currently claims a *5.7X* speedup over CPython across a range of benchmark programs (per *http://speed.pypy.org/*). In some cases, its ability to take advantage of dynamic optimization opportunities can make Python code as quick as C code, and occasionally faster. This is especially true for heavily algorithmic or numeric programs, which might otherwise be recoded in C.

For instance, in one simple benchmark we'll see in Chapter 21, PyPy today clocks in at *10X* faster than CPython 2.7, and *100X* faster than CPython 3.X. Though other benchmarks will vary, such speedups may be a compelling advantage in many domains, perhaps even more so than leading-edge language features. Just as important, memory space is also optimized in PyPy—in the case of one posted benchmark, requiring 247 MB and completing in 10.3 seconds, compared to CPython's 684 MB and 89 seconds.

PyPy's tool chain is also general enough to support additional languages, including *Pyrolog*, a Prolog interpreter written in Python using the PyPy translator. Search for PyPy's website for more. PyPy currently lives at *http://pypy.org*, though the usual web search may also prove fruitful over time. For an overview of its current performance, also see *http://www.pypy.org/performance.html*.

Just after I wrote this, PyPy 2.0 was released in beta form, adding support for the ARM processor, and still a Python 2.X-only implementation. Per its 2.0 beta release notes:

"PyPy is a very compliant Python interpreter, almost a drop-in replacement for CPython 2.7.3. It's fast (*http://speed.pypy.org*) due to its integrated tracing JIT compiler. This release supports x86 machines running Linux 32/64, Mac OS X 64 or Windows 32. It also supports ARM machines running Linux."

The claims seem accurate. Using the timing tools we'll study in Chapter 21, PyPy is often an order of magnitude (factor of 10) faster than CPython 2.X and 3.X on tests I've run, and sometimes even better. This is despite the fact that PyPy is a 32-bit build on my Windows test machine, while CPython is a faster 64-bit compile.

Naturally the only benchmark that truly matters is your own code, and there are cases where CPython wins the race; PyPy's file iterators, for instance, may clock in slower today. Still, given PyPy's focus on performance over language mutation, and especially its support for the numeric domain, many today see PyPy as an important path for Python. If you write CPU-intensive code, PyPy deserves your attention.

Execution Optimization Tools

CPython and most of the alternatives of the prior section all implement the Python language in similar ways: by compiling source code to byte code and executing the byte code on an appropriate virtual machine. Some systems, such as the Cython hybrid, the Shed Skin C++ translator, and the just-in-time compilers in PyPy and Psyco instead attempt to optimize the basic execution model. These systems are not required knowledge at this point in your Python career, but a quick look at their place in the execution model might help demystify the model in general.

Cython: A Python/C hybrid

The *Cython* system (based on work done by the *Pyrex* project) is a hybrid language that combines Python code with the ability to call C functions and use C type declarations for variables, parameters, and class attributes. Cython code can be compiled to C code that uses the Python/C API, which may then be compiled completely. Though not completely compatible with standard Python, Cython can be useful both for wrapping external C libraries and for coding efficient C extensions for Python. See *http://cython .org* for current status and details.

Shed Skin: A Python-to-C++ translator

Shed Skin is an emerging system that takes a different approach to Python program execution—it attempts to translate Python source code to C++ code, which your computer's C++ compiler then compiles to machine code. As such, it represents a platform-neutral approach to running Python code.

Shed Skin is still being actively developed as I write these words. It currently supports Python 2.4 to 2.6 code, and it limits Python programs to an implicit statically typed constraint that is typical of most programs but is technically not normal Python, so we won't go into further detail here. Initial results, though, show that it has the potential to outperform both standard Python and Psyco-like extensions in terms of execution speed. Search the Web for details on the project's current status.

Psyco: The original just-in-time compiler

The Psyco system is not another Python implementation, but rather a component that extends the byte code execution model to make programs run faster. Today, Psyco is something of an *ex-project*: it is still available for separate download, but has fallen out of date with Python's evolution, and is no longer actively maintained. Instead, its ideas have been incorporated into the more complete *PyPy* system described earlier. Still, the ongoing importance of the ideas Psyco explored makes them worth a quick look.

In terms of Figure 2-2, Psyco is an enhancement to the PVM that collects and uses type information while the program runs to translate portions of the program's byte code all the way down to true binary machine code for faster execution. Psyco accomplishes this translation without requiring changes to the code or a separate compilation step during development.

Roughly, while your program runs, Psyco collects information about the kinds of objects being passed around; that information can be used to generate highly efficient machine code tailored for those object types. Once generated, the machine code then replaces the corresponding part of the original byte code to speed your program's overall execution. The result is that with Psyco, your program becomes quicker over time as it runs. In ideal cases, some Python code may become as fast as compiled C code under Psyco.

Because this translation from byte code happens at program runtime, Psyco is known as a *just-in-time* compiler. Psyco is different from the JIT compilers some readers may have seen for the Java language, though. Really, Psyco is a *specializing JIT compiler*—it generates machine code tailored to the data types that your program actually uses. For example, if a part of your program uses different data types at different times, Psyco may generate a different version of machine code to support each different type combination.

Psyco was shown to speed some Python code dramatically. According to its web page, Psyco provides "2X to 100X speed-ups, typically 4X, with an unmodified Python interpreter and unmodified source code, just a dynamically loadable C extension module." Of equal significance, the largest speedups are realized for algorithmic code written in pure Python—exactly the sort of code you might normally migrate to C to optimize. For more on Psyco, search the Web or see its successor—the PyPy project described previously.

Frozen Binaries

Sometimes when people ask for a "real" Python compiler, what they're really seeking is simply a way to generate standalone binary executables from their Python programs. This is more a packaging and shipping idea than an execution-flow concept, but it's somewhat related. With the help of third-party tools that you can fetch off the Web, it is possible to turn your Python programs into true executables, known as *frozen binaries* in the Python world. These programs can be run without requiring a Python installation.

Frozen binaries bundle together the byte code of your program files, along with the PVM (interpreter) and any Python support files your program needs, into a single package. There are some variations on this theme, but the end result can be a single binary executable program (e.g., an *.exe* file on Windows) that can easily be shipped to customers. In Figure 2-2, it is as though the two rightmost bubbles—byte code and PVM—are merged into a single component: a frozen binary file.

Today, a variety of systems are capable of generating frozen binaries, which vary in platforms and features: *py2exe* for Windows only, but with broad Windows support; *PyInstaller*, which is similar to py2exe but also works on Linux and Mac OS X and is capable of generating self-installing binaries; *py2app* for creating Mac OS X applications; *freeze*, the original; and *cx_freeze*, which offers both Python 3.X and cross-platform support. You may have to fetch these tools separately from Python itself, but they are freely available.

These tools are also constantly evolving, so consult *http://www.python.org* or your favorite web search engine for more details and status. To give you an idea of the scope of these systems, py2exe can freeze standalone programs that use the tkinter, PMW, wxPython, and PyGTK GUI libraries; programs that use the *pygame* game programming toolkit; win32com client programs; and more.

Frozen binaries are not the same as the output of a true compiler—they run byte code through a virtual machine. Hence, apart from a possible startup improvement, frozen binaries run at the same speed as the original source files. Frozen binaries are also not generally small (they contain a PVM), but by current standards they are not unusually large either. Because Python is embedded in the frozen binary, though, it does not have to be installed on the receiving end to run your program. Moreover, because your code is embedded in the frozen binary, it is more effectively hidden from recipients.

This single file-packaging scheme is especially appealing to developers of commercial software. For instance, a Python-coded user interface program based on the tkinter toolkit can be frozen into an executable file and shipped as a self-contained program on a CD or on the Web. End users do not need to install (or even have to know about) Python to run the shipped program.

Future Possibilities?

Finally, note that the runtime execution model sketched here is really an artifact of the current implementation of Python, not of the language itself. For instance, it's not impossible that a full, traditional compiler for translating Python source code to machine code may appear during the shelf life of this book (although the fact that one has not in over two decades makes this seem unlikely!).

New byte code formats and implementation variants may also be adopted in the future. For instance:

- The ongoing *Parrot* project aims to provide a common byte code format, virtual machine, and optimization techniques for a variety of programming languages, including Python. Python's own PVM runs Python code more efficiently than Parrot (as famously demonstrated by a pie challenge at a software conference—search the Web for details), but it's unclear how Parrot will evolve in relation to Python specifically. See *http://parrot.org* or the Web at large for details.

- The former *Unladen Swallow* project—an open source project developed by Google engineers—sought to make standard Python faster by a factor of at least 5, and fast enough to replace the C language in many contexts. This was an optimization branch of CPython (specifically Python 2.6), intended to be compatible yet faster by virtue of adding a JIT to standard Python. As I write this in 2012, this project seems to have drawn to a close (per its withdrawn Python PEP, it was "going the way of the Norwegian Blue"). Still, its lessons gained may be leveraged in other forms; search the Web for breaking developments.

Although future implementation schemes may alter the runtime structure of Python somewhat, it seems likely that the byte code compiler will still be the standard for some time to come. The portability and runtime flexibility of byte code are important features of many Python systems. Moreover, adding type constraint declarations to support static compilation would likely break much of the flexibility, conciseness, simplicity, and overall spirit of Python coding. Due to Python's highly dynamic nature, any future implementation will likely retain many artifacts of the current PVM.

Chapter Summary

This chapter introduced the execution model of Python—how Python runs your programs—and explored some common variations on that model: just-in-time compilers and the like. Although you don't really need to come to grips with Python internals to write Python scripts, a passing acquaintance with this chapter's topics will help you truly understand how your programs run once you start coding them. In the next chapter, you'll start actually running some code of your own. First, though, here's the usual chapter quiz.

Test Your Knowledge: Quiz

1. What is the Python interpreter?
2. What is source code?
3. What is byte code?
4. What is the PVM?
5. Name two or more variations on Python's standard execution model.
6. How are CPython, Jython, and IronPython different?
7. What are Stackless and PyPy?

Test Your Knowledge: Answers

1. The Python interpreter is a program that runs the Python programs you write.
2. Source code is the statements you write for your program—it consists of text in text files that normally end with a *.py* extension.
3. Byte code is the lower-level form of your program after Python compiles it. Python automatically stores byte code in files with a *.pyc* extension.
4. The PVM is the Python Virtual Machine—the runtime engine of Python that interprets your compiled byte code.
5. Psyco, Shed Skin, and frozen binaries are all variations on the execution model. In addition, the alternative implementations of Python named in the next two answers modify the model in some fashion as well—by replacing byte code and VMs, or by adding tools and JITs.
6. CPython is the standard implementation of the language. Jython and IronPython implement Python programs for use in Java and .NET environments, respectively; they are alternative compilers for Python.
7. Stackless is an enhanced version of Python aimed at concurrency, and PyPy is a reimplementation of Python targeted at speed. PyPy is also the successor to Psyco, and incorporates the JIT concepts that Psyco pioneered.

## CHAPTER 3

How You Run Programs

OK, it's time to start running some code. Now that you have a handle on the program execution model, you're finally ready to start some real Python programming. At this point, I'll assume that you have Python installed on your computer; if you don't, see the start of the prior chapter and Appendix A for installation and configuration hints on various platforms. Our goal here is to learn how to run Python program code.

There are multiple ways to tell Python to execute the code you type. This chapter discusses all the program launching techniques in common use today. Along the way, you'll learn how to both type code *interactively*, and how to save it in *files* to be run as often as you like in a variety of ways: with system command lines, icon clicks, module imports, **exec** calls, menu options in the IDLE GUI, and more.

As for the previous chapter, if you have prior programming experience and are anxious to start digging into Python itself, you may want to skim this chapter and move on to Chapter 4. But don't skip this chapter's early coverage of preliminaries and conventions, its overview of debugging techniques, or its first look at module imports—a topic essential to understanding Python's program architecture, which we won't revisit until a later part. I also encourage you to see the sections on IDLE and other IDEs, so you'll know what tools are available when you start developing more sophisticated Python programs.

The Interactive Prompt

This section gets us started with interactive coding basics. Because it's our first look at running code, we also cover some preliminaries here, such as setting up a working directory and the system path, so be sure to read this section first if you're relatively new to programming. This section also explains some conventions used throughout the book, so most readers should probably take at least a quick look here.

Starting an Interactive Session

Perhaps the simplest way to run Python programs is to type them at Python's interactive command line, sometimes called the *interactive prompt*. There are a variety of ways to start this command line: in an IDE, from a system console, and so on. Assuming the interpreter is installed as an executable program on your system, the most platform-neutral way to start an interactive interpreter session is usually just to type **python** at your operating system's prompt, without any arguments. For example:

```
% python
Python 3.3.0 (v3.3.0:bd8afb90ebf2, Sep 29 2012, 10:57:17) [MSC v.1600 64 bit ...
Type "help", "copyright", "credits" or "license" for more information.
>>> ^Z
```

Typing the word "python" at your system shell prompt like this begins an interactive Python session; the "%" character at the start of this listing stands for a generic system prompt in this book—it's not input that you type yourself. On Windows, a *Ctrl-Z* gets you out of this session; on Unix, try *Ctrl-D* instead.

The notion of a *system shell prompt* is generic, but exactly how you access it varies by platform:

- On *Windows*, you can type **python** in a DOS console window—a program named `cmd.exe` and usually known as *Command Prompt*. For more details on starting this program, see this chapter's sidebar "Where Is Command Prompt on Windows?" on page 45.

- On *Mac OS X*, you can start a Python interactive interpreter by double-clicking on Applications→Utilities→Terminal, and then typing **python** in the window that opens up.

- On *Linux* (and other Unixes), you might type this command in a shell or terminal window (for instance, in an *xterm* or console running a shell such as *ksh* or *csh*).

- Other systems may use similar or platform-specific devices. On handheld devices, for example, you might click the Python icon in the home or application window to launch an interactive session.

On most platforms, you can start the interactive prompt in additional ways that don't require typing a command, but they vary per platform even more widely:

- On *Windows 7* and earlier, besides typing **python** in a shell window, you can also begin similar interactive sessions by starting the IDLE GUI (discussed later), or by selecting the "Python (command line)" menu option from the Start button menu for Python, as shown in Figure 2-1 in Chapter 2. Both spawn a Python interactive prompt with the same functionality obtained with a "python" command.

- On *Windows 8*, you don't have a Start button (at least as I write this), but there are other ways to get to the tools described in the prior bullet, including tiles, Search, File Explorer, and the "All apps" interface on the Start screen. See Appendix A for more pointers on this platform.

- Other platforms have similar ways to start a Python interactive session without typing commands, but they're too specific to get into here; see your system's documentation for details.

Anytime you see the >>> prompt, you're in an interactive Python interpreter session—you can type any Python statement or expression here and run it immediately. We will in a moment, but first we need to get a few startup details sorted out to make sure all readers are set to go.

Where Is Command Prompt on Windows?

So how do you start the command-line interface on Windows? Some Windows readers already know, but Unix developers and beginners may not; it's not as prominent as terminal or console windows on Unix systems. Here are some pointers on finding your Command Prompt, which vary slightly per Windows version.

On *Windows 7 and earlier*, this is usually found in the Accessories section of the Start→All Programs menu, or you can run it by typing `cmd` in the Start→Run... dialog box or the Start menu's search entry field. You can drag out a desktop shortcut to get to it quicker if desired.

On *Windows 8*, you can access Command Prompt in the menu opened by right-clicking on the preview in the screen's lower-left corner; in the Windows System section of the "All apps" display reached by right-clicking your Start screen; or by typing `cmd` or `command prompt` in the input field of the Search charm pulled down from the screen's upper-right corner. There are probably additional routes, and touch screens offer similar access. And if you want to forget all that, pin it to your desktop taskbar for easy access next time around.

These procedures are prone to vary over time, and possibly even per computer and user. I'm trying to avoid making this a book on Windows, though, so I'll cut this topic short here. When in doubt, try the system Help interface (whose usage may differ as much as the tools it provides help for!).

A note to any Unix users reading this sidebar who may be starting to feel like a fish out of water: you may also be interested in the *Cygwin* system, which brings a full Unix command prompt to Windows. See Appendix A for more pointers.

The System Path

When we typed `python` in the last section to start an interactive session, we relied on the fact that the system located the Python program for us on its program search path. Depending on your Python version and platform, if you have not set your system's PATH environment variable to include Python's install directory, you may need to replace the word "python" with the full path to the Python executable on your machine. On Unix, Linux, and similar, something like **/usr/local/bin/python** or **/usr/bin/python3** will often suffice. On Windows, try typing **C:\Python33\python** (for version 3.3):

```
c:\code> c:\python33\python
Python 3.3.0 (v3.3.0:bd8afb90ebf2, Sep 29 2012, 10:57:17) [MSC v.1600 64 bit ...
Type "help", "copyright", "credits" or "license" for more information.
>>> ^Z
```

Alternatively, you can run a "cd" change-directory command to go to Python's install directory before typing **python**—try the **cd c:\python33** command on Windows, for example:

```
c:\code> cd c:\python33
c:\Python33> python
Python 3.3.0 (v3.3.0:bd8afb90ebf2, Sep 29 2012, 10:57:17) [MSC v.1600 64 bit ...
Type "help", "copyright", "credits" or "license" for more information.
>>> ^Z
```

But you'll probably want to set your PATH eventually, so a simple "python" suffices. If you don't know what PATH is or how to set it, see Appendix A—it covers environment variables like this whose usage varies per platform, as well as Python command-line arguments we won't be using much in this book. The short story for Windows users: see the Advanced settings in the System entry of your Control Panel. If you're using Python 3.3 and later, this is now automatic on Windows, as the next section explains.

New Windows Options in 3.3: PATH, Launcher

The foregoing section and much of this chapter at large describe the generic state of play for all 2.X and 3.X Pythons prior to version 3.3. Starting with Python 3.3, the Windows installer has an option to *automatically* add Python 3.3's directory to your system PATH, if enabled in the installer's windows. If you use this option, you won't need to type a directory path or issue a "cd" to run **python** commands as in the prior section. Be sure to select this option during the install if you want it, as it's currently disabled by default.

More dramatically, Python 3.3 for Windows ships with and automatically installs the new *Windows launcher*—a system that comes with new executable programs, py with a console and pyw without, that are placed in directories on your system path, and so may be run out of the box without any PATH configurations, change-directory commands, or directory path prefixes:

```
c:\code> py
Python 3.3.0 (v3.3.0:bd8afb90ebf2, Sep 29 2012, 10:57:17) [MSC v.1600 64 bit ...
Type "help", "copyright", "credits" or "license" for more information.
>>> ^Z

c:\code> py -2
Python 2.7.3 (default, Apr 10 2012, 23:24:47) [MSC v.1500 64 bit (AMD64)] ...
Type "help", "copyright", "credits" or "license" for more information.
>>> ^Z

c:\code> py -3.1
Python 3.1.4 (default, Jun 12 2011, 14:16:16) [MSC v.1500 64 bit (AMD64)] ...
```

```
Type "help", "copyright", "credits" or "license" for more information.
>>> ^Z
```

As shown in the last two commands here, these executables also accept Python version numbers on the command line (and in Unix-style #! lines at the top of scripts, as discussed later), and are associated to open Python files when clicked just like the original python executable—which is still available and works as before, but is somewhat superseded by the launcher's new programs.

The launcher is a standard part of Python 3.3, and is available standalone for use with other versions. We'll see more on this new launcher in this and later chapters, including a brief look at its #! line support here. However, because it is of interest only to Windows users, and even for this group is present only in 3.3 or where installed separately, I've collected almost all of the details about the launcher in Appendix B.

If you'll be working on Windows under Python 3.3 or later, I suggest taking a brief detour to that appendix now, as it provides an alternative, and in some ways better, way to run Python command lines and scripts. At a base level, launcher users can type **py** instead of **python** in most of the system commands shown in this book, and may avoid some configuration steps. Especially on computers with multiple Python versions, though, the new launcher gives you more explicit control over which Python runs your code.

Where to Run: Code Directories

Now that I've started showing you *how* to run code, I want to say a few words up front about *where* to run code. To keep things simple, in this chapter and book at large I'm going to be running code from a working directory (a.k.a. *folder*) I've created on my Windows computer called *C:\code*—a subdirectory at the top of my main drive. That's where I'll start most interactive sessions, and where I'll be both saving and running most script files. This also means the files that examples will create will mostly show up in this directory.

If you'll be working along, you should probably do something similar before we get started. Here are some pointers if you need help getting set up with a working directory on your computer:

- On *Windows*, you can make your working code directory in File Explorer or a Command Prompt window. In File Explorer, look for New Folder, see the File menu, or try a right-click. In Command Prompt, type and run a `mkdir` command, usually after you `cd` to your desired parent directory (e.g., `cd c:\` and `mkdir code`). Your working directory can be located wherever you like and called whatever you wish, and doesn't have to be *C:\code* (I chose this name because it's short in prompts). But running out of one directory will help you keep track of your work and simplify some tasks. For more Windows hints, see this chapter's sidebar on Command Prompt, as well as Appendix A.

- On *Unix*-based systems (including *Mac OS X* and *Linux*), your working directory might be in */usr/home* and be created by a `mkdir` command in a shell window or file explorer GUI specific to your platform, but the same concepts apply. The Cygwin Unix-like system for Windows is similar too, though your directory names may vary (*/home* and */cygdrive/c* are candidates).

You can store your code in Python's install directory too (e.g., *C:\Python33* on Windows) to simplify some command lines before setting `PATH`, but you probably shouldn't —this is for Python itself, and your files may not survive a move or uninstall.

Once you've made your working directory, always start there to work along with the examples in this book. The prompts in this book that show the directory that I'm running code in will reflect my Windows laptop's working directory; when you see `C:\code>` or `%`, think the location and name of your own directory.

What Not to Type: Prompts and Comments

Speaking of prompts, this book sometimes shows system prompts as a generic `%`, and sometimes in full `C:\code>` Windows form. The former is meant to be platform agnostic (and derives from earlier editions' use of Linux), and the latter is used in Windows-specific contexts. I also add a space after system prompts just for readability in this book. When used, the `%` character at the start of a system command line stands for the system's prompt, whatever that may be on your machine. For instance, on my machine `%` stands for `C:\code>` in Windows Command Prompt, and just `$` in my Cygwn install.

To beginners: don't type the `%` character (or the `C:\code` system prompt it sometimes stands for) you see in this book's interaction listings yourself—this is text the system prints. Type just the text *after* these system prompts. Similarly, do not type the `>>>` and `...` characters shown at the start of lines in interpreter interaction listings—these are prompts that Python displays automatically as visual guides for interactive code entry. Type just the text *after* these Python prompts. For instance, the `...` prompt is used for continuation lines in some shells, but doesn't appear in IDLE, and shows up in some but not all of this book's listings; don't type it yourself if it's absent in your interface.

To help you remember this, user inputs are shown in **bold** in this book, and prompts are not. In some systems these prompts may differ (for instance, the *PyPy* performance-focused implementation described in Chapter 2 uses four-character `>>>>` and `....`), but the same rules apply. Also keep in mind that commands typed after these system and Python prompts are meant to be run immediately, and are not generally to be saved in the source files we will be creating; we'll see why this distinction matters ahead.

In the same vein, you normally don't need to type text that starts with a `#` character in listings in this book—as you'll learn, these are *comments*, not executable code. Except when `#` is used to introduce a directive at the top of a script for Unix or the Python 3.3

Windows launcher, you can safely ignore the text that follows it (more on Unix and the launcher later in this chapter and in Appendix B).

> *If you're working along*, interactive listings will drop most "..." continuation prompts as of Chapter 17 to aid cut-and-paste of larger code such as functions and classes from ebooks or other; until then, paste or type one line at a time and omit the prompts. At least initially, it's important to type code manually, to get a feel for syntax details and errors. Some examples will be listed either by themselves or in named files available in the book's examples package (per the preface), and we'll switch between listing formats often; when in doubt, if you see ">>>", it means the code is being typed interactively.

Running Code Interactively

With those preliminaries out of the way, let's move on to typing some actual code. However it's started, the Python interactive session begins by printing two lines of informational text giving the Python version number and a few hints shown earlier (which I'll omit from most of this book's examples to save space), then prompts for input with >>> when it's waiting for you to type a new Python statement or expression.

When working interactively, the results of your code are displayed below the >>> input lines after you press the Enter key. For instance, here are the results of two Python print statements (print is really a function call in Python 3.X, but not in 2.X, so the parentheses here are required in 3.X only):

```
% python
>>> print('Hello world!')
Hello world!
>>> print(2 ** 8)
256
```

There it is—we've just run some Python code (were you expecting the *Spanish Inquisition?*). Don't worry about the details of the print statements shown here yet; we'll start digging into syntax in the next chapter. In short, they print a Python string and an integer, as shown by the output lines that appear after each >>> input line (2 ** 8 means 2 raised to the power 8 in Python).

When coding interactively like this, you can type as many Python commands as you like; each is run immediately after it's entered. Moreover, because the interactive session automatically prints the results of expressions you type, you don't usually need to say "print" explicitly at this prompt:

```
>>> lumberjack = 'okay'
>>> lumberjack
'okay'
>>> 2 ** 8
256
```

```
>>> ^Z                    # Use Ctrl-D (on Unix) or Ctrl-Z (on Windows) to exit
%
```

Here, the first line saves a value by assigning it to a *variable* (`lumberjack`), which is created by the assignment; and the last two lines typed are *expressions* (`lumberjack` and `2 ** 8`), whose results are displayed automatically. Again, to exit an interactive session like this and return to your system shell prompt, type Ctrl-D on Unix-like machines, and Ctrl-Z on Windows. In the IDLE GUI discussed later, either type Ctrl-D or simply close the window.

Notice the *italicized note* about this on the right side of this listing (staring with "#" here). I'll use these throughout to add remarks about what is being illustrated, but you don't need to type this text yourself. In fact, just like system and Python prompts, you shouldn't type this when it's on a system command line; the "#" part is taken as a comment by Python but may be an error at a system prompt.

Now, we didn't do much in this session's code—just typed some Python `print` and assignment statements, along with a few expressions, which we'll study in detail later. The main thing to notice is that the interpreter executes the code entered on each line immediately, when the Enter key is pressed.

For example, when we typed the first `print` statement at the `>>>` prompt, the output (a Python string) was echoed back right away. There was no need to create a source code file, and no need to run the code through a compiler and linker first, as you'd normally do when using a language such as C or C++. As you'll see in later chapters, you can also run multiline statements at the interactive prompt; such a statement runs immediately after you've entered all of its lines and pressed Enter twice to add a blank line.

Why the Interactive Prompt?

The interactive prompt runs code and echoes results as you go, but it doesn't save your code in a file. Although this means you won't do the bulk of your coding in interactive sessions, the interactive prompt turns out to be a great place to both *experiment* with the language and *test* program files on the fly.

Experimenting

Because code is executed immediately, the interactive prompt is a perfect place to experiment with the language and will be used often in this book to demonstrate smaller examples. In fact, this is the first rule of thumb to remember: if you're ever in doubt about how a piece of Python code works, fire up the interactive command line and try it out to see what happens.

For instance, suppose you're reading a Python program's code and you come across an expression like `'Spam!' * 8` whose meaning you don't understand. At this point, you can spend 10 minutes wading through manuals, books, and the Web to try to figure out what the code does, or you can simply run it interactively:

```
% python
>>> 'Spam!' * 8                                        # Learning by trying
'Spam!Spam!Spam!Spam!Spam!Spam!Spam!Spam!'
```

The immediate feedback you receive at the interactive prompt is often the quickest way to deduce what a piece of code does. Here, it's clear that it does string repetition: in Python * means multiply for numbers, but repeat for strings—it's like concatenating a string to itself repeatedly (more on strings in Chapter 4).

Chances are good that you won't break anything by experimenting this way—at least, not yet. To do real damage, like deleting files and running shell commands, you must really try, by importing modules explicitly (you also need to know more about Python's system interfaces in general before you will become that dangerous!). Straight Python code is almost always safe to run.

For instance, watch what happens when you *make a mistake* at the interactive prompt:

```
>>> X                                                  # Making mistakes
Traceback (most recent call last):
  File "<stdin>", line 1, in <module>
NameError: name 'X' is not defined
```

In Python, using a variable before it has been assigned a value is always an error—otherwise, if names were filled in with defaults, some errors might go undetected. This means you must initialize counters to zero before you can add to them, must initialize lists before extending them, and so on; you don't declare variables, but they must be assigned before you can fetch their values.

We'll learn more about that later; the important point here is that you don't crash Python or your computer when you make a mistake this way. Instead, you get a meaningful error message pointing out the mistake and the line of code that made it, and you can continue on in your session or script. In fact, once you get comfortable with Python, its error messages may often provide as much debugging support as you'll need (you'll learn more about debugging options in the sidebar "Debugging Python Code" on page 83).

Testing

Besides serving as a tool for experimenting while you're learning the language, the interactive interpreter is also an ideal place to test code you've written in files. You can import your module files interactively and run tests on the tools they define by typing calls at the interactive prompt on the fly.

For instance, the following tests a function in a precoded module that ships with Python in its standard library (it prints the name of the directory you're currently working in, with a doubled-up backslash that stands for just one), but you can do the same once you start writing module files of your own:

```
>>> import os
>>> os.getcwd()                                        # Testing on the fly
'c:\\code'
```

More generally, the interactive prompt is a place to test program components, regardless of their source—you can import and test functions and classes in your Python files, type calls to linked-in C functions, exercise Java classes under Jython, and more. Partly because of its interactive nature, Python supports an experimental and exploratory programming style you'll find convenient when getting started. Although Python programmers also test with in-file code (and we'll learn ways to make this simple later in the book), for many, the interactive prompt is still their first line of testing defense.

Usage Notes: The Interactive Prompt

Although the interactive prompt is simple to use, there are a few tips that beginners should keep in mind. I'm including lists of common mistakes like the following in this chapter for reference, but they might also spare you from a few headaches if you read them up front:

- **Type Python commands only**. First of all, remember that you can only type Python code at Python's >>> prompt, not system commands. There are ways to run system commands from within Python code (e.g., with `os.system`), but they are not as direct as simply typing the commands themselves.

- **print statements are required only in files**. Because the interactive interpreter automatically prints the results of expressions, you do not need to type complete `print` statements interactively. This is a nice feature, but it tends to confuse users when they move on to writing code in files: within a code file, you must use `print` statements to see your output because expression results are not automatically echoed. Remember, you must say `print` in files, but it's optional interactively.

- **Don't indent at the interactive prompt (yet)**. When typing Python programs, either interactively or into a text file, be sure to start all your unnested statements in column 1 (that is, all the way to the left). If you don't, Python may print a "SyntaxError" message, because blank space to the left of your code is taken to be indentation that groups nested statements. Until Chapter 10, all statements you write will be unnested, so this includes everything for now. Remember, a leading space generates an error message, so don't start with a space or tab at the interactive prompt unless it's nested code.

- **Watch out for prompt changes for compound statements**. We won't meet *compound* (multiline) statements until Chapter 4 and not in earnest until Chapter 10, but as a preview, you should know that when typing lines 2 and beyond of a compound statement interactively, the prompt may change. In the simple shell window interface, the interactive prompt changes to ... instead of >>> for lines 2 and beyond; in the IDLE GUI interface, lines after the first are instead automatically indented.

  You'll see why this matters in Chapter 10. For now, if you happen to come across a ... prompt or a blank line when entering your code, it probably means that you've somehow confused interactive Python into thinking you're typing a multiline statement. Try hitting the Enter key or a Ctrl-C combination to get back to the main prompt. The >>> and ... prompt strings can also be changed (they are available in the built-in module sys), but I'll assume they have not been in the book's example listings.

- **Terminate compound statements at the interactive prompt with a blank line**. At the interactive prompt, inserting a blank line (by hitting the Enter key at the start of a line) is necessary to tell interactive Python that you're done typing the multiline statement. That is, you must press Enter twice to make a compound statement run. By contrast, blank lines are not required in files and are simply ignored if present. If you don't press Enter twice at the end of a compound statement when working interactively, you'll appear to be stuck in a limbo state, because the interactive interpreter will do nothing at all—it's waiting for you to press Enter again!

- **The interactive prompt runs one statement at a time**. At the interactive prompt, you must run one statement to completion before typing another. This is natural for simple statements, because pressing the Enter key runs the statement entered. For compound statements, though, remember that you must submit a blank line to terminate the statement and make it run before you can type the next statement.

Entering multiline statements

At the risk of repeating myself, I've received multiple emails from readers who'd gotten burned by the last two points, so they probably merit emphasis. I'll introduce multiline (a.k.a. compound) statements in the next chapter, and we'll explore their syntax more formally later in this book. Because their behavior differs slightly in files and at the interactive prompt, though, two cautions are in order here.

First, be sure to terminate multiline compound statements like for loops and if tests at the interactive prompt with a blank line. In other words, *you must press the Enter key twice*, to terminate the whole multiline statement and then make it run. For example (pun not intended):

```
>>> for x in 'spam':
...     print(x)            # Press Enter twice here to make this loop run
...
```

You don't need the blank line after compound statements in a script file, though; this is required *only* at the interactive prompt. In a file, blank lines are not required and are simply ignored when present; at the interactive prompt, they terminate multiline statements. Reminder: the ... continuation line prompt in the preceding is printed by Python automatically as a visual guide; it may not appear in your interface (e.g., IDLE), and is sometimes omitted by this book, but do not type it yourself if it's absent.

Also bear in mind that the interactive prompt runs just *one statement at a time*: you must press Enter twice to run a loop or other multiline statement before you can type the next statement:

```
>>> for x in 'spam':
...     print(x)                    # Press Enter twice before a new statement
... print('done')
  File "<stdin>", line 3
    print('done')
        ^
SyntaxError: invalid syntax
```

This means you can't cut and paste multiple lines of code into the interactive prompt, unless the code includes blank lines after each compound statement. Such code is better run in a *file*—which brings us to the next section's topic.

System Command Lines and Files

Although the interactive prompt is great for experimenting and testing, it has one big disadvantage: programs you type there go away as soon as the Python interpreter executes them. Because the code you type interactively is never stored in a file, you can't run it again without retyping it from scratch. Cut-and-paste and command recall can help some here, but not much, especially when you start writing larger programs. To cut and paste code from an interactive session, you would have to edit out Python prompts, program outputs, and so on—not exactly a modern software development methodology!

To save programs permanently, you need to write your code in files, which are usually known as *modules*. Modules are simply text files containing Python statements. Once they are coded, you can ask the Python interpreter to execute the statements in such a file any number of times, and in a variety of ways—by system command lines, by file icon clicks, by options in the IDLE user interface, and more. Regardless of how it is run, Python executes all the code in a module file from top to bottom each time you run the file.

Terminology in this domain can vary somewhat. For instance, module files are often referred to as *programs* in Python—that is, a program is considered to be a series of precoded statements stored in a file for repeated execution. Module files that are run directly are also sometimes called *scripts*—an informal term usually meaning a top-level program file. Some reserve the term "module" for a file imported from another file, and "script" for the main file of a program; we generally will here, too (though you'll have to stay tuned for more on the meaning of "top-level," imports, and main files later in this chapter).

Whatever you call them, the next few sections explore ways to run code typed into module files. In this section, you'll learn how to run files in the most basic way: by listing their names in a `python` command line entered at your computer's system prompt. Though it might seem primitive to some—and can often be avoided altogether by using a GUI like IDLE, discussed later—for many programmers a system shell command-line window, together with a text editor window, constitutes as much of an integrated development environment as they will ever need, and provides more direct control over programs.

A First Script

Let's get started. Open your favorite text editor (e.g., *vi*, Notepad, or the IDLE editor), type the following statements into a new text file named *script1.py*, and save it in your working code directory that you set up earlier:

```
# A first Python script
import sys                    # Load a library module
print(sys.platform)
print(2 ** 100)              # Raise 2 to a power
x = 'Spam!'
print(x * 8)                  # String repetition
```

This file is our first official Python script (not counting the two-liner in Chapter 2). You shouldn't worry too much about this file's code, but as a brief description, this file:

- Imports a Python module (libraries of additional tools), to fetch the name of the platform
- Runs three `print` function calls, to display the script's results
- Uses a variable named `x`, created when it's assigned, to hold onto a string object
- Applies various object operations that we'll begin studying in the next chapter

The `sys.platform` here is just a string that identifies the kind of computer you're working on; it lives in a standard Python module called `sys`, which you must import to load (again, more on imports later).

For color, I've also added some formal Python *comments* here—the text after the `#` characters. I mentioned these earlier, but should be more formal now that they're showing up in scripts. Comments can show up on lines by themselves, or to the right of code on a line. The text after a `#` is simply ignored as a human-readable comment and is not considered part of the statement's syntax. If you're copying this code, you can ignore the comments; they are just informative. In this book, we usually use a different formatting style to make comments more visually distinctive, but they'll appear as normal text in your code.

Again, don't focus on the syntax of the code in this file for now; we'll learn about all of it later. The main point to notice is that you've typed this code into a file, rather than at the interactive prompt. In the process, you've coded a fully functional Python script.

Notice that the module file is called *script1.py*. As for all top-level files, it could also be called simply *script*, but files of code you want to *import* into a client have to end with a *.py* suffix. We'll study imports later in this chapter. Because you may want to import them in the future, it's a good idea to use *.py* suffixes for most Python files that you code. Also, some text editors detect Python files by their *.py* suffix; if the suffix is not present, you may not get features like syntax colorization and automatic indentation.

Running Files with Command Lines

Once you've saved this text file, you can ask Python to run it by listing its full filename as the first argument to a `python` command like the following typed at the *system shell prompt* (don't type this at Python's interactive prompt, and read on to the next paragraph if this doesn't work right away for you):

```
% python script1.py
win32
1267650600228229401496703205376
Spam!Spam!Spam!Spam!Spam!Spam!Spam!Spam!
```

Again, you can type such a system shell command in whatever your system provides for command-line entry—a Windows Command Prompt window, an xterm window, or similar. But be sure to run this in the same working directory where you've saved your script file ("cd" there first if needed), and be sure to run this at the system prompt, not Python's ">>>" prompt. Also remember to replace the command's word "python" with a full directory path as we did before if your PATH setting is not configured, though this isn't required for the "py" Windows launcher program, and may not be required in 3.3 and later.

Another note to beginners: do not type any of the preceding text in the *script1.py* source file you created in the prior section. This text is a system command and program output, not program code. The first line here is the shell command used to run the source file, and the lines following it are the results produced by the source file's `print` statements. And again, remember that the % stands for the system prompt—don't type it yourself (not to nag, but it's a remarkably common early mistake).

If all works as planned, this shell command makes Python run the code in this file line by line, and you will see the output of the script's three `print` statements—the name of the underlying platform as known Python, 2 raised to the power 100, and the result of the same string repetition expression we saw earlier (again, more on the meaning of the last two of these in Chapter 4).

If all *didn't* work as planned, you'll get an error message—make sure you've entered the code in your file exactly as shown, and try again. The next section has additional options and pointers on this process, and we'll talk about debugging options in the sidebar "Debugging Python Code" on page 83, but at this point in the book your best bet is probably rote imitation. And if all else fails, you might also try running under the IDLE GUI discussed ahead—a tool that sugarcoats some launching details, though sometimes at the expense of the more explicit control you have when using command lines.

You can also fetch the code examples off the Web if copying grows too tedious or error-prone, though typing some code initially will help you learn to avoid syntax errors. See the preface for details on how to obtain the book's example files.

Command-Line Usage Variations

Because this scheme uses shell command lines to start Python programs, all the usual shell syntax applies. For instance, you can route the printed output of a Python script to a file to save it for later use or inspection by using special shell syntax:

```
% python script1.py > saveit.txt
```

In this case, the three output lines shown in the prior run are stored in the file *saveit.txt* instead of being printed. This is generally known as *stream redirection*; it works for input and output text and is available on Windows and Unix-like systems. This is nice for testing, as you can write programs that watch for changes in other programs' outputs. It also has little to do with Python, though (Python simply supports it), so we will skip further details on shell redirection syntax here.

If you are working on a *Windows* platform, this example works the same, but the system prompt is normally different as described earlier:

```
C:\code> python script1.py
win32
1267650600228229401496703205376
Spam!Spam!Spam!Spam!Spam!Spam!Spam!Spam!
```

As usual, if you haven't set your PATH environment variable to include the full directory path to python, be sure to include this in your command, or run a change-directory command to go to the path first:

```
C:\code> C:\python33\python script1.py
win32
1267650600228229401496703205376
Spam!Spam!Spam!Spam!Spam!Spam!Spam!Spam!
```

Alternatively, if you're using the *Windows launcher* new in Python 3.3 (described earlier), a py command will have the same effect, but does not require a directory path or PATH settings, and allows you to specify Python version numbers on the command line too:

```
c:\code> py -3 script1.py
win32
1267650600228229401496703205376
Spam!Spam!Spam!Spam!Spam!Spam!Spam!Spam!
```

On all recent versions of *Windows*, you can also type just the name of your *script*, and omit the name of Python itself. Because newer Windows systems use the Windows Registry (a.k.a. filename associations) to find a program with which to run a file, you don't need to name "python" or "py" on the command line explicitly to run a *.py* file. The prior command, for example, could be simplified to the following on most Windows machines, and will automatically be run by python prior to 3.3, and by py in 3.3 and later—just as though you had clicked on the file's icon in Explorer (more on this option ahead):

```
C:\code> script1.py
```

Finally, remember to give the full path to your script file if it lives in a different directory from the one in which you are working. For example, the following system command line, run from *D:\other*, assumes Python is in your system path but runs a file located elsewhere:

```
C:\code> cd D:\other
D:\other> python c:\code\script1.py
```

If your PATH doesn't include Python's directory, you're not using the Windows launcher's py program, and neither Python nor your script file is in the directory you're working in, use full paths for *both*:

```
D:\other> C:\Python33\python c:\code\script1.py
```

Usage Notes: Command Lines and Files

Running program files from system command lines is a fairly straightforward launch option, especially if you are familiar with command lines in general from prior work. It's also perhaps the most portable way to run Python programs since nearly every computer has some notion of a command line and directory structure. For newcomers, though, here are a few pointers about common beginner traps that might help you avoid some frustration:

- **Beware of automatic extensions on Windows and IDLE.** If you use the Notepad program to code program files on Windows, be careful to pick the type All Files when it comes time to save your file, and give the file a *.py* suffix explicitly. Otherwise, Notepad will save your file with a *.txt* extension (e.g., as *script1.py.txt*), making it difficult to use in some schemes; it won't be importable, for example.

  Worse, Windows hides file extensions by default, so unless you have changed your view options you may not even notice that you've coded a text file and not a Python file. The file's icon may give this away—if it doesn't have a snake of some sort on it, you may have trouble. Uncolored code in IDLE and files that open to edit instead of run when clicked are other symptoms of this problem.

  Microsoft Word similarly adds a *.doc* extension by default; much worse, it adds formatting characters that are not legal Python syntax. As a rule of thumb, always pick All Files when saving under Windows, or use a more programmer-friendly text editor such as IDLE. IDLE does *not* even add a *.py* suffix automatically—a feature some programmers tend to like, but some users do not.

- **Use file extensions and directory paths at system prompts, but not for imports.** Don't forget to type the full name of your file in system command lines—that is, use python script1.py rather than python script1. By contrast, Python's import statements, which we'll meet later in this chapter, omit both the *.py* file suffix and the directory path (e.g., import script1). This may seem trivial, but confusing these two is a common mistake.

At the system prompt, you are in a system shell, not Python, so Python's module file search rules do not apply. Because of that, you must include both the *.py* extension and, if necessary, the full directory path leading to the file you wish to run. For instance, to run a file that resides in a different directory from the one in which you are working, you would typically list its full path (e.g., `python d:\tests \spam.py`). Within Python code, however, you can just say `import spam` and rely on the Python module search path to locate your file, as described later.

- **Use print statements in files**. Yes, we've already been over this, but it is such a common mistake that it's worth repeating at least once here. Unlike in interactive coding, you generally must use `print` statements to see output from program files. If you don't see any output, make sure you've said "print" in your file. `print` statements are *not* required in an interactive session, since Python automatically echoes expression results; `prints` don't hurt here, but are superfluous typing.

Unix-Style Executable Scripts: #!

Our next launching technique is really a specialized form of the prior, which, despite this section's title, can apply to program files run on both Unix and Windows today. Since it has its roots on Unix, let's begin this story there.

Unix Script Basics

If you are going to use Python on a Unix, Linux, or Unix-like system, you can also turn files of Python code into executable programs, much as you would for programs coded in a shell language such as *csh* or *ksh*. Such files are usually called *executable scripts*. In simple terms, Unix-style executable scripts are just normal text files containing Python statements, but with two special properties:

- **Their first line is special**. Scripts usually start with a line that begins with the characters #! (often called "hash bang" or "shebang"), followed by the path to the Python interpreter on your machine.
- **They usually have executable privileges**. Script files are usually marked as executable to tell the operating system that they may be run as top-level programs. On Unix systems, a command such as `chmod +x file.py` usually does the trick.

Let's look at an example for Unix-like systems. Use your text editor again to create a file of Python code called *brian*:

```
#!/usr/local/bin/python
print('The Bright Side ' + 'of Life...')      # + means concatenate for strings
```

The special line at the top of the file tells the system where the Python interpreter lives. Technically, the first line is a Python comment. As mentioned earlier, all comments in Python programs start with a # and span to the end of the line; they are a place to insert extra information for human readers of your code. But when a comment such as the first line in this file appears, it's special on Unix because the operating system shell uses it to find an interpreter for running the program code in the rest of the file.

Also, note that this file is called simply *brian*, without the *.py* suffix used for the module file earlier. Adding a *.py* to the name wouldn't hurt (and might help you remember that this is a Python program file), but because you don't plan on letting other modules import the code in this file, the name of the file is irrelevant. If you give the file executable privileges with a `chmod +x brian` shell command, you can run it from the operating system shell as though it were a binary program (for the following, either make sure `.`, the current directory, is in your system `PATH` setting, or run this with `./brian`):

```
% brian
The Bright Side of Life...
```

The Unix env Lookup Trick

On some Unix systems, you can avoid hardcoding the path to the Python interpreter in your script file by writing the special first-line comment like this:

```
#!/usr/bin/env python
...script goes here...
```

When coded this way, the `env` program locates the Python interpreter according to your system search path settings (in most Unix shells, by looking in all the directories listed in your `PATH` environment variable). This scheme can be more portable, as you don't need to hardcode a Python install path in the first line of all your scripts. That way, if your scripts ever move to a new machine, or your Python ever moves to a new location, you must update just `PATH`, not all your scripts.

Provided you have access to `env` everywhere, your scripts will run no matter where Python lives on your system. In fact, this `env` form is generally recommended today over even something as generic as */usr/bin/python*, because some platforms may install Python elsewhere. Of course, this assumes that `env` lives in the same place everywhere (on some machines, it may be in */sbin*, */bin*, or elsewhere); if not, all portability bets are off!

The Python 3.3 Windows Launcher: #! Comes to Windows

A note for Windows users running *Python 3.2 and earlier*: the method described here is a Unix trick, and it may not work on your platform. Not to worry; just use the basic command-line technique explored earlier. List the file's name on an explicit `python` command line:[1]

```
C:\code> python brian
The Bright Side of Life...
```

In this case, you don't need the special #! comment at the top (although Python just ignores it if it's present), and the file doesn't need to be given executable privileges. In fact, if you want to run files portably between Unix and Microsoft Windows, your life will probably be simpler if you always use the basic command-line approach, not Unix-style scripts, to launch programs.

If you're using *Python 3.3 or later*, though, or have its Windows launcher installed separately, it turns out that Unix-style #! lines *do* mean something on Windows too. Besides offering the py executable described earlier, the new Windows launcher mentioned earlier attempts to parse #! lines to determine which Python version to launch to run your script's code. Moreover, it allows you to give the version number in full or partial forms, and recognizes most common Unix patterns for this line, including the */usr/bin/env* form.

The launcher's #! parsing mechanism is applied when you run scripts from command lines with the py program, and when you click Python file icons (in which case py is run implicitly by filename associations). Unlike Unix, you do not need to mark files with executable privileges for this to work on Windows, because filename associations achieve similar results.

For example, the first of the following is run by Python 3.X and the second by 2.X (without an explicit number, the launcher defaults to 2.X unless you set a PY_PYTHON environment variable):

```
c:\code> type robin3.py
#!/usr/bin/python3
print('Run', 'away!...')            # 3.X function

c:\code> py robin3.py               # Run file per #! line version
Run away!...

c:\code> type robin2.py
#!python2
print 'Run', 'away more!...'        # 2.X statement

c:\code> py robin2.py               # Run file per #! line version
Run away more!...
```

This works in addition to passing versions on command lines—we saw this briefly earlier for starting the interactive prompt, but it works the same when launching a script file:

```
c:\code> py -3.1 robin3.py          # Run per command-line argument
Run away!...
```

The net effect is that the launcher allows Python versions to be specified on both a *per-file* and *per-command* basis, by using #! lines and command-line arguments, respec-

---

1. As we discussed when exploring command lines, all recent Windows versions also let you type just the name of a *.py* file at the system command line—they use the Registry to determine that the file should be opened with Python (e.g., typing **brian.py** is equivalent to typing **python brian.py**). This command-line mode is similar in spirit to the Unix #!, though it is system-wide on Windows, not per-file. It also requires an explicit *.py* extension: filename associations won't work without it. Some *programs* may actually interpret and use a first #! line on Windows much like on Unix (including Python 3.3's Windows launcher), but the system shell on Windows itself simply ignores it.

tively. At least that's the very short version of the launcher's story. If you're using Python 3.3 or later on Windows or may in the future, I recommend a side trip to the full launcher story in Appendix B if you haven't made one already.

Clicking File Icons

If you're not a fan of command lines, you can generally avoid them by launching Python scripts with file icon clicks, development GUIs, and other schemes that vary per platform. Let's take a quick look at the first of these alternatives here.

Icon-Click Basics

Icon clicks are supported on most platforms in one form or another. Here's a rundown of how these might be structured on your computer:

Windows icon clicks

On *Windows*, the Registry makes opening files with icon clicks easy. When installed, Python uses Windows filename *associations* to automatically register itself to be the program that opens Python program files when they are clicked. Because of that, it is possible to launch the Python programs you write by simply clicking (or double-clicking) on their file icons with your mouse cursor.

Specifically, a clicked file will be run by one of two Python programs, depending on its extension and the Python you're running. In Pythons 3.2 and earlier, *.py* files are run by `python.exe` with a console (Command Prompt) window, and *.pyw* files are run by `pythonw.exe` files without a console. Byte code files are also run by these programs if clicked. Per Appendix B, in Python 3.3 and later (and where it's installed separately), the new Window's launchers's `py.exe` and `pyw.exe` programs serve the same roles, opening *.py* and *.pyw* files, respectively.

Non-Windows icon clicks

On *non-Windows* systems, you will probably be able to perform a similar feat, but the icons, file explorer navigation schemes, and more may differ slightly. On *Mac OS X*, for instance, you might use PythonLauncher in the *MacPython* (or *Python N.M*) folder of your *Applications* folder to run by clicking in Finder.

On some *Linux* and other Unix systems, you may need to register the *.py* extension with your file explorer GUI, make your script executable using the #! line scheme of the preceding section, or associate the file MIME type with an application or command by editing files, installing programs, or using other tools. See your file explorer's documentation for more details.

In other words, icon clicks generally work as you'd expect for your platform, but be sure to see the platform usage documentation "Python Setup and Usage" in Python's standard manual set for more details as needed.

Clicking Icons on Windows

To illustrate, let's keep using the script we wrote earlier, *script1.py*, repeated here to minimize page flipping:

```
# A first Python script
import sys                    # Load a library module
print(sys.platform)
print(2 ** 100)               # Raise 2 to a power
x = 'Spam!'
print(x * 8)                  # String repetition
```

As we've seen, you can always run this file from a system command line:

```
C:\code> python script1.py
win32
1267650600228229401496703205376
Spam!Spam!Spam!Spam!Spam!Spam!Spam!Spam!
```

However, icon clicks allow you to run the file without any typing at all. To do so, you have to find this file's icon on your computer. On Windows 8, you might right-click the screen's lower-left corner to open a File Explorer. On earlier Windows, you can select Computer (or My Computer in XP) in your Start button's menu. There are additional ways to open a file explorer; once you do, work your way down on the C drive to your working directory.

At this point, you should have a file explorer window similar to that captured in Figure 3-1 (Windows 8 is being used here). Notice how the *icons* for Python files show up:

- Source files have white backgrounds on Windows.
- Byte code files show with black backgrounds.

Per the prior chapter, I created the byte code file in this figure by importing in Python 3.1; 3.2 and later instead store byte code files in the *__pycache__* subdirectory also shown here, which I created by importing in 3.3 too. You will normally want to click (or otherwise run) the white *source code* files in order to pick up your most recent changes, not the byte code files—Python won't check the source code file for changes if you launch byte code directly. To launch the file here, simply click on the icon for *script1.py*.

The input Trick on Windows

Unfortunately, on Windows, the result of clicking on a file icon may not be incredibly satisfying. In fact, as it is, this example script might generate a perplexing "flash" when clicked—not exactly the sort of feedback that budding Python programmers usually hope for! This is not a bug, but has to do with the way the Windows version of Python handles printed output.

By default, Python generates a pop-up black DOS console window (Command Prompt) to serve as a clicked file's input and output. If a script just prints and exits, well, it just

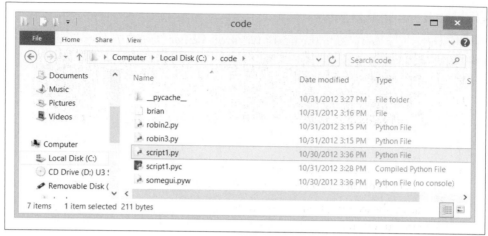

Figure 3-1. On Windows, Python program files show up as icons in file explorer windows and can automatically be run with a double-click of the mouse (though you might not see printed output or error messages this way).

prints and exits—the console window appears, and text is printed there, but the console window closes and disappears on program exit. Unless you are very fast, or your machine is very slow, you won't get to see your output at all. Although this is normal behavior, it's probably not what you had in mind.

Luckily, it's easy to work around this. If you need your script's output to stick around when you launch it with an icon click, simply put a call to the built-in `input` function at the very bottom of the script in 3.X (in 2.X use the name `raw_input` instead: see the note ahead). For example:

```
# A first Python script
import sys                    # Load a library module
print(sys.platform)
print(2 ** 100)               # Raise 2 to a power
x = 'Spam!'
print(x * 8)                  # String repetition
input()                       # <== ADDED
```

In general, `input` reads and returns the next line of standard input, waiting if there is none yet available. The net effect in this context will be to pause the script, thereby keeping the output window shown in Figure 3-2 open until you press the Enter key.

Now that I've shown you this trick, keep in mind that it is usually only required for Windows, and then only if your script prints text and exits and only if you will launch the script by clicking its file icon. You should add this call to the bottom of your top-level files if and only if all of these three conditions apply. There is no reason to add this call in any other contexts, such as scripts you'll run in command lines or the IDLE GUI (unless you're unreasonably fond of pressing your computer's Enter key!).[2] That may sound obvious, but it's been another common mistake in live classes.

win32
1267650600228229401496703205376
Spam!Spam!Spam!Spam!Spam!Spam!Spam!Spam!

Figure 3-2. When you click a program's icon on Windows, you will be able to see its printed output if you include an input call at the very end of the script. But you only need to do so in this one context!

Before we move ahead, note that the `input` call applied here is the input counterpart of using the `print` function (and 2.X statement) for outputs. It is the simplest way to read user input, and it is more general than this example implies. For instance, `input`:

- Optionally accepts a string that will be printed as a prompt (e.g., `input('Press Enter to exit')`)

- Returns to your script a line of text read as a string (e.g., `nextinput = input()`)

- Supports input stream redirections at the system shell level (e.g., `python spam.py < input.txt`), just as the `print` statement does for output

We'll use `input` in more advanced ways later in this text; for instance, Chapter 10 will apply it in an interactive loop. For now, it will help you see the output of simple scripts that you click to launch.

> *Version skew note*: If you are working in Python 2.X, use `raw_input()` instead of `input()` in this code. The former was renamed to the latter in Python 3.X. Technically, 2.X has an `input` function too, but it also *evaluates* strings as though they are program code typed into a script, and so will not work in this context (an empty string is an error). Python 3.X's `input` (and 2.X's `raw_input`) simply returns the entered text as a character string, unevaluated. To simulate 2.X's `input` in 3.X, use `eval(input())`.
>
> Be aware, though, that because this runs the entered text as though it were *program code*, this may have security implications that we'll largely

2. Conversely, it is also possible to completely suppress the pop-up console window (a.k.a. Command Prompt) for clicked files on Windows when you *don't* want to see printed text. Files whose names end in a *.pyw* extension will display only windows constructed by your script, not the default console window. *.pyw* files are simply *.py* source files that have this special operational behavior on Windows. They are mostly used for Python-coded user interfaces that build windows of their own, often in conjunction with various techniques for saving printed output and errors to files. As implied earlier, Python achieves this when it is installed by associating a special executable (*pythonw.exe* in 3.2 and earlier and *pyw.exe* as of 3.3) to open *.pyw* files when clicked.

ignore here, except to say that you should trust the source of the entered text; if you don't, stick to just plain `input` in 3.X and `raw_input` in 2.X.

Other Icon-Click Limitations

Even with the prior section's `input` trick, clicking file icons is not without its perils. You also may not get to see Python error messages. If your script generates an error, the error message text is written to the pop-up console window—which then immediately disappears! Worse, adding an `input` call to your file will not help this time because your script will likely abort long before it reaches this call. In other words, you won't be able to tell what went wrong.

When we discuss *exceptions* later in this book, you'll learn that it is possible to write code to intercept, process, and recover from errors so that they do not terminate your programs. Watch for the discussion of the `try` statement later in this book for an alternative way to keep the console window from closing on errors. We'll also learn how to redirect printed text to files for later inspection when we study `print` operations. Barring such support in your code, though, errors and prints disappear for clicked programs.

Because of these limitations, it is probably best to view icon clicks as a way to launch programs after they have been debugged, or have been instrumented to write their output to a file and catch and process any important errors. Especially when you're starting out, I recommend using other techniques—such as system command lines and IDLE (discussed further in the section "The IDLE User Interface" on page 73)—so that you can see generated error messages and view your normal output without resorting to extra coding.

Module Imports and Reloads

So far, I've been talking about "importing modules" without really explaining what this term means. We'll study modules and larger program architecture in depth in Part V, but because imports are also a way to launch programs, this section will introduce enough module basics to get you started.

Import and Reload Basics

In simple terms, every file of Python source code whose name ends in a *.py* extension is a module. No special code or syntax is required to make a file a module: any such file will do. Other files can access the items a module defines by *importing* that module —import operations essentially load another file and grant access to that file's contents. The contents of a module are made available to the outside world through its attributes (a term I'll define in the next section).

This module-based services model turns out to be the core idea behind *program architecture* in Python. Larger programs usually take the form of multiple module files, which import tools from other module files. One of the modules is designated as the main or *top-level* file, or "script"—the file launched to start the entire program, which runs line by line as usual. Below this level, it's all modules importing modules.

We'll delve into such architectural issues in more detail later in this book. This chapter is mostly interested in the fact that import operations *run* the code in a file that is being loaded as a final step. Because of this, importing a file is yet another way to launch it.

For instance, if you start an interactive session (from a system command line or otherwise), you can run the *script1.py* file you created earlier with a simple import (be sure to delete the `input` line you added in the prior section first, or you'll need to press Enter for no reason):

```
C:\code> C:\python33\python
>>> import script1
win32
1267650600228229401496703205376
Spam!Spam!Spam!Spam!Spam!Spam!Spam!Spam!
```

This works, but only once per session (really, *process*—a program run) by default. After the first import, later imports do nothing, even if you change and save the module's source file again in another window:

```
...Change script1.py in a text edit window to print 2 ** 16...

>>> import script1
>>> import script1
```

This is by design; imports are too expensive an operation to repeat more than once per file, per program run. As you'll learn in Chapter 22, imports must find files, compile them to byte code, and run the code.

If you really want to force Python to run the file again in the same session without stopping and restarting the session, you need to instead call the `reload` function available in the `imp` standard library module (this function is also a simple built-in in Python 2.X, but not in 3.X):

```
>>> from imp import reload          # Must load from module in 3.X (only)
>>> reload(script1)
win32
65536
Spam!Spam!Spam!Spam!Spam!Spam!Spam!Spam!
<module 'script1' from '.\\script1.py'>
>>>
```

The `from` statement here simply copies a name out of a module (more on this soon). The `reload` function itself loads and runs the current version of your file's code, picking up changes if you've modified and saved it in another window.

This allows you to edit and pick up new code on the fly within the current Python interactive session. In this session, for example, the second `print` statement in *script1.py* was changed in another window to print `2 ** 16` between the time of the first `import` and the `reload` call—hence the different result.

The `reload` function expects the name of an already loaded module object, so you have to have successfully imported a module once before you reload it (if the import reported an error, you can't yet reload and must import again). Notice that `reload` also expects parentheses around the module object name, whereas `import` does not. `reload` is a function that is *called*, and `import` is a statement.

That's why you must pass the module name to `reload` as an argument in parentheses, and that's why you get back an extra output line when reloading—the last output line is just the display representation of the `reload` call's return value, a Python module object. We'll learn more about using functions in general in Chapter 16; for now, when you hear "function," remember that parentheses are required to run a call.

> *Version skew note*: Python 3.X moved the `reload` built-in function to the `imp` standard library module. It still reloads files as before, but you must import it in order to use it. In 3.X, run an `import imp` and use `imp.reload(M)`, or run a `from imp import reload` and use `reload(M)`, as shown here. We'll discuss `import` and `from` statements in the next section, and more formally later in this book.
>
> If you are working in Python 2.X, `reload` is available as a built-in function, so no import is required. In Python 2.6 and 2.7, `reload` is available in *both* forms—built-in and module function—to aid the transition to 3.X. In other words, reloading is still available in 3.X, but an extra line of code is required to fetch the `reload` call.
>
> The move in 3.X was likely motivated in part by some well-known issues involving `reload` and `from` statements that we'll encounter in the next section. In short, names loaded with a `from` are not directly updated by a `reload`, but names accessed with an `import` statement are. If your names don't seem to change after a `reload`, try using `import` and *mod ule.attribute* name references instead.

The Grander Module Story: Attributes

Imports and reloads provide a natural program launch option because import operations execute files as a last step. In the broader scheme of things, though, modules serve the role of *libraries* of tools, as you'll learn in detail in Part V. The basic idea is straightforward, though: a module is mostly just a package of variable names, known as a *namespace*, and the names within that package are called *attributes*. An attribute is simply a variable name that is attached to a specific object (like a module).

In more concrete terms, importers gain access to all the names assigned at the top level of a module's file. These names are usually assigned to tools exported by the module

—functions, classes, variables, and so on—that are intended to be used in other files and other programs. Externally, a module file's names can be fetched with two Python statements, `import` and `from`, as well as the `reload` call.

To illustrate, use a text editor to create a one-line Python module file called *myfile.py* in your working directory, with the following contents:

```
title = "The Meaning of Life"
```

This may be one of the world's simplest Python modules (it contains a single assignment statement), but it's enough to illustrate the point. When this file is imported, its code is run to generate the module's attribute. That is, the assignment statement creates a variable and module attribute named `title`.

You can access this module's `title` attribute in other components in two different ways. First, you can load the module as a whole with an `import` statement, and then *qualify* the module name with the attribute name to fetch it (note that we're letting the interpreter print automatically here):

```
% python                   # Start Python
>>> import myfile          # Run file; load module as a whole
>>> myfile.title          # Use its attribute names: '.' to qualify
'The Meaning of Life'
```

In general, the dot expression syntax *object.attribute* lets you fetch any attribute attached to any object, and is one of the most common operations in Python code. Here, we've used it to access the string variable `title` inside the module `myfile`—in other words, `myfile.title`.

Alternatively, you can fetch (really, copy) names out of a module with `from` statements:

```
% python                          # Start Python
>>> from myfile import title     # Run file; copy its names
>>> title                         # Use name directly: no need to qualify
'The Meaning of Life'
```

As you'll see in more detail later, `from` is just like an `import`, with an extra assignment to names in the importing component. Technically, `from` copies a module's *attributes*, such that they become simple *variables* in the recipient—thus, you can simply refer to the imported string this time as `title` (a variable) instead of `myfile.title` (an attribute reference).[3]

Whether you use `import` or `from` to invoke an import operation, the statements in the module file *myfile.py* are executed, and the importing component (here, the interactive prompt) gains access to names assigned at the top level of the file. There's only one such name in this simple example—the variable `title`, assigned to a string—but the

---

3. Notice that `import` and `from` both list the name of the module file as simply *myfile* without its *.py* extension suffix. As you'll learn in Part V, when Python looks for the actual file, it knows to include the suffix in its search procedure. Again, you must include the `.py` suffix in system shell command lines, but not in `import` statements.

concept will be more useful when you start defining objects such as functions and classes in your modules: such objects become reusable *software components* that can be accessed by name from one or more client modules.

In practice, module files usually define more than one name to be used in and outside the files. Here's an example that defines three:

```
a = 'dead'                    # Define three attributes
b = 'parrot'                  # Exported to other files
c = 'sketch'
print(a, b, c)                # Also used in this file (in 2.X: print a, b, c)
```

This file, *threenames.py*, assigns three variables, and so generates three attributes for the outside world. It also uses its own three variables in a 3.X `print` statement, as we see when we run this as a top-level file (in Python 2.X `print` differs slightly, so omit its outer parenthesis to match the output here exactly; watch for a more complete explanation of this in Chapter 11):

```
% python threenames.py
dead parrot sketch
```

All of this file's code runs as usual the first time it is imported elsewhere, by either an `import` or `from`. Clients of this file that use `import` get a module with attributes, while clients that use `from` get copies of the file's names:

```
% python
>>> import threenames              # Grab the whole module: it runs here
dead parrot sketch
>>>
>>> threenames.b, threenames.c     # Access its attributes
('parrot', 'sketch')
>>>
>>> from threenames import a, b, c # Copy multiple names out
>>> b, c
('parrot', 'sketch')
```

The results here are printed in parentheses because they are really *tuples*—a kind of object created by the comma in the inputs (and covered in the next part of this book)—that you can safely ignore for now.

Once you start coding modules with multiple names like this, the built-in `dir` function starts to come in handy—you can use it to fetch a list of all the names available inside a module. The following returns a Python list of strings in square brackets (we'll start studying lists in the next chapter):

```
>>> dir(threenames)
['__builtins__', '__doc__', '__file__', '__name__', '__package__', 'a', 'b', 'c']
```

The contents of this list have been edited here because they vary per Python version. The point to notice here is that when the `dir` function is called with the name of an imported module in parentheses like this, it returns all the attributes inside that module. Some of the names it returns are names you get "for free": names with leading and trailing double underscores (__X__) are built-in names that are always predefined by

Python and have special meaning to the interpreter, but they aren't important at this point in this book. The variables our code defined by assignment—a, b, and c—show up last in the dir result.

Modules and namespaces

Module imports are a way to run files of code, but, as we'll expand on later in the book, modules are also the largest program structure in Python programs, and one of the first key concepts in the language.

As we've seen, Python programs are composed of multiple module files linked together by import statements, and each module file is a package of variables—that is, a *namespace*. Just as importantly, each module is a *self-contained* namespace: one module file cannot see the names defined in another file unless it explicitly imports that other file. Because of this, modules serve to minimize *name collisions* in your code—because each file is a self-contained namespace, the names in one file cannot clash with those in another, even if they are spelled the same way.

In fact, as you'll see, modules are one of a handful of ways that Python goes to great lengths to package your variables into compartments to avoid name clashes. We'll discuss modules and other namespace constructs—including local scopes defined by classes and functions—further later in the book. For now, modules will come in handy as a way to run your code many times without having to retype it, and will prevent your file's names from accidentally replacing each other.

 import versus from: I should point out that the from statement in a sense defeats the namespace partitioning purpose of modules—because the from copies variables from one file to another, it can cause same-named variables in the importing file to be overwritten, and won't warn you if it does. This essentially collapses namespaces together, at least in terms of the copied variables.

Because of this, some recommend always using import instead of from. I won't go that far, though; not only does from involve less typing (an asset at the interactive prompt), but its purported problem is relatively rare in practice. Besides, this is something *you* control by listing the variables you want in the from; as long as you understand that they'll be assigned to values in the target module, this is no more dangerous than coding assignment statements—another feature you'll probably want to use!

Usage Notes: import and reload

For some reason, once people find out about running files using import and reload, many tend to focus on this alone and forget about other launch options that always run the current version of the code (e.g., icon clicks, IDLE menu options, and system command lines). This approach can quickly lead to confusion, though—you need to remember when you've imported to know if you can reload, you need to remember to use parentheses when you call `reload` (only), and you need to remember to use `reload` in the first place to get the current version of your code to run. Moreover, reloads aren't transitive—reloading a module reloads that module only, not any modules it may import—so you sometimes have to reload multiple files.

Because of these complications (and others we'll explore later, including the `reload/from` issue mentioned briefly in a prior note in this chapter), it's generally a good idea to avoid the temptation to launch by imports and reloads for now. The IDLE Run→Run Module menu option described in the next section, for example, provides a simpler and less error-prone way to run your files, and always runs the current version of your code. System shell command lines offer similar benefits. You don't need to use `reload` if you use any of these other techniques.

In addition, you may run into trouble if you use modules in unusual ways at this point in the book. For instance, if you want to import a module file that is stored in a directory other than the one you're working in, you'll have to skip ahead to Chapter 22 and learn about the *module search path*. For now, if you must import, try to keep all your files in the directory you are working in to avoid complications.[4]

That said, imports and reloads have proven to be a popular testing technique in Python classes, and you may prefer using this approach too. As usual, though, if you find yourself running into a wall, stop running into a wall!

Using exec to Run Module Files

Strictly speaking, there are more ways to run code stored in module files than have yet been presented here. For instance, the `exec(open('module.py').read())` built-in function call is another way to launch files from the interactive prompt without having to import and later reload. Each such `exec` runs the *current* version of the code read from a file, without requiring later reloads (*script1.py* is as we left it after a reload in the prior section):

```
% python
>>> exec(open('script1.py').read())
win32
65536
Spam!Spam!Spam!Spam!Spam!Spam!Spam!Spam!

...Change script1.py in a text edit window to print 2 ** 32...

>>> exec(open('script1.py').read())
```

---

4. If you're too curious to wait, the short story is that Python searches for imported modules in every directory listed in `sys.path`—a Python list of directory name strings in the `sys` module, which is initialized from a PYTHONPATH environment variable, plus a set of standard directories. If you want to import from a directory other than the one you are working in, that directory must generally be listed in your PYTHONPATH setting. For more details, see Chapter 22 and Appendix A.

```
win32
4294967296
Spam!Spam!Spam!Spam!Spam!Spam!Spam!Spam!
```

The exec call has an effect similar to an import, but it doesn't actually import the module
—by default, each time you call exec this way it runs the file's code anew, as though
you had pasted it in at the place where exec is called. Because of that, exec does not
require module reloads after file changes—it skips the normal module import logic.

On the downside, because it works as if you've pasted code into the place where it is
called, exec, like the from statement mentioned earlier, has the potential to silently
overwrite variables you may currently be using. For example, our *script1.py* assigns to
a variable named x. If that name is also being used in the place where exec is called, the
name's value is replaced:

```
>>> x = 999
>>> exec(open('script1.py').read())     # Code run in this namespace by default
...same output...
>>> x                                    # Its assignments can overwrite names here
'Spam!'
```

By contrast, the basic import statement runs the file only once per process, and it makes
the file a separate module namespace so that its assignments will not change variables
in your scope. The price you pay for the namespace partitioning of modules is the need
to reload after changes.

> *Version skew note*: Python 2.X also includes an execfile('module.py')
> built-in function, in addition to allowing the form exec(open('mod
> ule.py')), which both automatically read the file's content. Both of
> these are equivalent to the exec(open('module.py').read()) form,
> which is more complex but runs in both 2.X and 3.X.
>
> Unfortunately, neither of these two simpler 2.X forms is available in 3.X,
> which means you must understand both files and their read methods to
> fully understand this technique today (this seems to be a case of aes-
> thetics trouncing practicality in 3.X). In fact, the exec form in 3.X in-
> volves so much typing that the best advice may simply be not to do it—
> it's usually easier to launch files by typing system shell command lines
> or by using the IDLE menu options described in the next section.
>
> For more on the file interfaces used by the 3.X exec form, see Chap-
> ter 9. For more on exec and its cohorts, eval and compile, see Chap-
> ter 10 and Chapter 25.

The IDLE User Interface

So far, we've seen how to run Python code with the interactive prompt, system command lines, Unix-style scripts, icon clicks, module imports, and exec calls. If you're
looking for something a bit more visual, *IDLE* provides a graphical user interface for

doing Python development, and it's a standard and free part of the Python system. IDLE is usually referred to as an *integrated development environment* (IDE), because it binds together various development tasks into a single view.[5]

In short, IDLE is a desktop GUI that lets you edit, run, browse, and debug Python programs, all from a single interface. It runs portably on most Python platforms, including Microsoft Windows, X Windows (for Linux, Unix, and Unix-like platforms), and the Mac OS (both Classic and OS X). For many, IDLE represents an easy-to-use alternative to typing command lines, a less problem-prone alternative to clicking on icons, and a great way for newcomers to get started editing and running code. You'll sacrifice some control in the bargain, but this typically becomes important later in your Python career.

IDLE Startup Details

Most readers should be able to use IDLE immediately, as it is a standard component on Mac OS X and most Linux installations today, and is installed automatically with standard Python on Windows. Because platforms specifics vary, though, I need to give a few pointers before we open the GUI.

Technically, IDLE is a Python program that uses the standard library's tkinter GUI toolkit (named Tkinter in Python 2.X) to build its windows. This makes IDLE portable —it works the same on all major desktop platforms—but it also means that you'll need to have tkinter support in your Python to use IDLE. This support is standard on Windows, Macs, and Linux, but it comes with a few caveats on some systems, and startup can vary per platform. Here are a few platform-specific tips:

- On *Windows* 7 and earlier, IDLE is easy to start—it's always present after a Python install, and has an entry in the Start button menu for Python in Windows 7 and earlier (see Figure 2-1, shown previously). You can also select it by right-clicking on a Python program icon, and launch it by clicking on the icon for the files *idle.pyw* or *idle.py* located in the *idlelib* subdirectory of Python's *Lib* directory. In this mode, IDLE is a clickable Python script that lives in *C:\Python33\Lib\idlelib*, *C:\Python27\Lib\idlelib*, or similar, which you can drag out to a shortcut for one-click access if desired.

- On *Windows* 8, look for IDLE in your Start tiles, by a search for "idle," by browsing your "All apps" Start screen display, or by using File Explorer to find the *idle.py* file mentioned earlier. You may want a shortcut here, as you have no Start button menu in desktop mode (at least today; see Appendix A for more pointers).

- On *Mac OS X* everything required for IDLE is present as standard components in your operating system. IDLE should be available to launch in *Applications* under the *MacPython* (or *Python N.M*) program folder. One note here: some OS X ver-

---

5. IDLE is officially a corruption of IDE, but it's really named in honor of Monty Python member Eric Idle. See Chapter 1 if you're not sure why.

---

sions may require installing updated tkinter support due to subtle version dependencies I'll spare readers from here; see python.org's Download page for details.

- On *Linux* IDLE is also usually present as a standard component today. It might
  take the form of an *idle* executable or script in your path; type this in a shell to
  check. On some machines, it may require an install (see Appendix A for pointers),
  and on others you may need to launch IDLE's top-level script from a command
  line or icon click: run the file *idle.py* located in the *idlelib* subdirectory of
  Python's */usr/lib* directory (run a `find` for the exact location).

Because IDLE is just a Python script on the module search path in the standard library,
you can also generally run it on any platform and from any directory by typing the
following in a system command shell window (e.g., in a Command Prompt on Windows), though you'll have to see Appendix A for more on Python's -m flag, and
Part V for more on the "." package syntax required here (blind trust will suffice at this
point in the book):

```
c:\code> python -m idlelib.idle          # Run idle.py in a package on module path
```

For more on install issues and usage notes for Windows and other platforms, be sure
to see both Appendix A as well as the notes for your platform in "Python Setup and
Usage" in Python's standard manuals.

IDLE Basic Usage

Let's jump into an example. Figure 3-3 shows the scene after you start IDLE on Windows. The Python shell window that opens initially is the main window, which runs
an interactive session (notice the >>> prompt). This works like all interactive sessions
—code you type here is run immediately after you type it—and serves as a testing and
experimenting tool.

IDLE uses familiar menus with keyboard shortcuts for most of its operations. *To make
a new script file* under IDLE, use File→New Window: that is, in the main shell window,
select the File pull-down menu, and pick New Window (New File as of 3.3.3 and 2.7.6)
to open a new text edit window where you can type, save, and run your file's code. Use
File→Open... instead to open a new text edit window displaying an existing file's code
to edit and run.

Although it may not show up fully in this book's graphics, IDLE uses syntax-directed
colorization for the code typed in both the main window and all text edit windows—
keywords are one color, literals are another, and so on. This helps give you a better
picture of the components in your code (and can even help you spot mistakes—run-
on strings are all one color, for example).

To run a file of code that you are editing in IDLE, use Run→Run Module in that file's
text edit window. That is, select the file's text edit window, open that window's *Run*
pull-down menu, and choose the *Run Module* option listed there (or use the equivalent
keyboard shortcut, given in the menu). Python will let you know that you need to save

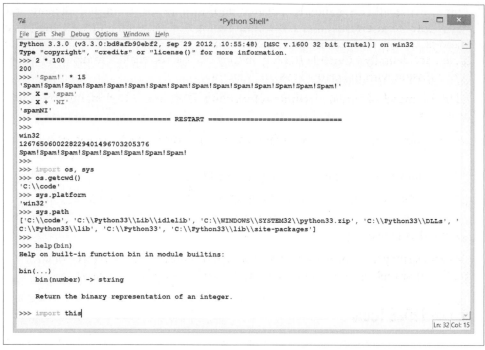

Figure 3-3. The main Python shell window of the IDLE development GUI, shown here running on Windows. Use the File menu to begin (New Window) or change (Open...) a source file; use the text edit window's Run menu to run the code in that window (Run Module).

your file first if you've changed it since it was opened or last saved and forgot to save your changes—a common mistake when you're knee-deep in coding.

When run this way, the output of your script and any error messages it may generate show up back in the main interactive window (the Python shell window). In Figure 3-3, for example, the three lines after the "RESTART" line near the middle of the window reflect an execution of our *script1.py* file opened in a separate edit window. The "RESTART" message tells us that the user-code process was restarted to run the edited script and serves to separate script output (it does not appear if IDLE is started without a user-code subprocess—more on this mode in a moment).

IDLE Usability Features

Like most GUIs, the best way to learn IDLE may be to test-drive it for yourself, but some key usage points seem to be less than obvious. For example, if you want to *repeat prior commands* in IDLE's main interactive window, you can use the *Alt-P* key combination to scroll backward through the command history, and *Alt-N* to scroll forward (on some Macs, try Ctrl-P and Ctrl-N instead). Your prior commands will be recalled and displayed, and may be edited and rerun.

You can also recall commands by positioning the *cursor* on them and clicking and pressing Enter to insert their text at the input prompt, or using standard cut-and-paste operations, though these techniques tend to involve more steps (and can sometimes be triggered accidentally). Outside IDLE, you may be able to recall commands in an interactive session with the arrow keys on Windows.

Besides command history and syntax *colorization*, IDLE has additional usability features such as:

- *Auto-indent* and unindent for Python code in the editor (Backspace goes back one level)
- Word *auto-completion* while typing, invoked by a Tab press
- Balloon help pop ups for a *function call* when you type its opening "("
- Pop-up selection lists of *object attributes* when you type a "." after an object's name and either pause or press Tab

Some of these may not work on every platform, and some can be configured or disabled if you find that their defaults get in the way of your personal coding style.

Advanced IDLE Tools

Besides the basic edit and run functions and the prior section's usability tools, IDLE provides more advanced features, including a point-and-click program *graphical debugger* and an *object browser*. The IDLE debugger is enabled via the Debug menu and the object browser via the File menu. The browser allows you to navigate through the module search path to files and objects in files; clicking on a file or object opens the corresponding source in a text edit window.

You initiate IDLE debugging by selecting the Debug→Debugger menu option in the main window and then starting your script by selecting the Run→Run Module option in the text edit window; once the debugger is enabled, you can set breakpoints in your code that stop its execution by right-clicking on lines in the text edit windows, show variable values, and so on. You can also watch program execution when debugging— the current line of code is noted as you step through your code.

For simpler debugging operations, you can also right-click with your mouse on the text of an error message to quickly jump to the line of code where the error occurred—a trick that makes it simple and fast to repair and run again. In addition, IDLE's text editor offers a large collection of programmer-friendly tools, including advanced text and file search operations we won't cover here. Because IDLE uses intuitive GUI interactions, you should experiment with the system live to get a feel for its other tools.

Usage Notes: IDLE

IDLE is free, easy to use, portable, and automatically available on most platforms. I generally recommend it to Python newcomers because it simplifies some startup details and does not assume prior experience with system command lines. However, it is somewhat limited compared to more advanced commercial IDEs, and may seem heavier than a command line to some. To help you avoid some common pitfalls, here is a list of issues that IDLE beginners should bear in mind:

- **You must add ".py" explicitly when saving your files**. I mentioned this when talking about files in general, but it's a common IDLE stumbling block, especially for Windows users. IDLE does not automatically add a *.py* extension to filenames when files are saved. Be careful to type the *.py* extension yourself when saving a file for the first time. If you don't, while you will be able to run your file from IDLE (and system command lines), you will not be able to import it either interactively or from other modules.

- **Run scripts by selecting Run→Run Module in text edit windows, not by interactive imports and reloads**. Earlier in this chapter, we saw that it's possible to run a file by importing it interactively. However, this scheme can grow complex because it requires you to manually reload files after changes. By contrast, using the Run→Run Module menu option in IDLE always runs the most current version of your file, just like running it using a system shell command line. IDLE also prompts you to save your file first, if needed (another common mistake outside IDLE).

- **You need to reload only modules being tested interactively**. Like system shell command lines, IDLE's Run→Run Module menu option always runs the current version of both the top-level file and any modules it imports. Because of this, Run→Run Module eliminates common confusions surrounding imports. You need to reload only modules that you are importing and testing interactively in IDLE. If you choose to use the import and reload technique instead of Run→Run Module, remember that you can use the Alt-P/Alt-N key combinations to recall prior commands.

- **You can customize IDLE**. To change the text fonts and colors in IDLE, select the Configure option in the Options menu of any IDLE window. You can also customize key combination actions, indentation settings, autocompletions, and more; see IDLE's Help pull-down menu for more hints.

- **There is currently no clear-screen option in IDLE**. This seems to be a frequent request (perhaps because it's an option available in similar IDEs), and it might be added eventually. Today, though, there is no way to clear the interactive window's text. If you want the window's text to go away, you can either press and hold the Enter key, or type a Python loop to print a series of blank lines (nobody really uses the latter technique, of course, but it sounds more high-tech than pressing the Enter key!).

- **tkinter GUI and threaded programs may not work well with IDLE**. Because IDLE is a Python/tkinter program, it can hang if you use it to run certain types of advanced Python/tkinter programs. This has become less of an issue in more recent versions of IDLE that run user code in one process and the IDLE GUI itself in another, but some programs (especially those that use multithreading) might still hang the GUI. Even just calling the tkinter `quit` function in your code, the normal way to exit a GUI program, may be enough to cause your program's GUI to hang if run in IDLE (`destroy` may be better here only). Your code may not exhibit such problems, but as a rule of thumb, it's always safe to use IDLE to edit GUI programs but launch them using other options, such as icon clicks or system command lines. When in doubt, if your code fails in IDLE, try it outside the GUI.

- **If connection errors arise, try starting IDLE in single-process mode**. This issue appears to have gone away in recent Pythons, but may still impact readers using older versions. Because IDLE requires communication between its separate user and GUI processes, it can sometimes have trouble starting up on certain platforms (notably, it fails to start occasionally on some Windows machines, due to firewall software that blocks connections). If you run into such connection errors, it's always possible to start IDLE with a system command line that forces it to run in single-process mode without a user-code subprocess and therefore avoids communication issues: its `-n` command-line flag forces this mode. On Windows, for example, start a Command Prompt window and run the system command line **`idle.py -n`** from within the directory *C:\Python33\Lib\idlelib* (`cd` there first if needed). A **`python -m idlelib.idle -n`** command works from anywhere (see Appendix A for *-m*).

- **Beware of some IDLE usability features**. IDLE does much to make life easier for beginners, but some of its tricks won't apply outside the IDLE GUI. For instance, IDLE runs your scripts in its own interactive namespace, so variables in your code show up automatically in the IDLE interactive session—you don't always need to run `import` commands to access names at the top level of files you've already run. This can be handy, but it can also be confusing, because outside the IDLE environment names must always be imported from files explicitly to be used.

  When you run a file of code, IDLE also automatically changes to that file's *directory* and adds it to the module import search path—a handy feature that allows you to use files and import modules there without search path settings, but also something that won't work the same when you run files outside IDLE. It's OK to use such features, but don't forget that they are IDLE behavior, not Python behavior.

Other IDEs

Because IDLE is free, portable, and a standard part of Python, it's a nice first development tool to become familiar with if you want to use an IDE at all. Again, I recommend that you use IDLE for this book's exercises if you're just starting out, unless you are already familiar with and prefer a command-line-based development mode. There are, however, a handful of alternative IDEs for Python developers, some of which are substantially more powerful and robust than IDLE. Apart from IDLE, here are some of Python's most commonly used IDEs:

Eclipse and PyDev

> Eclipse is an advanced open source IDE GUI. Originally developed as a Java IDE, Eclipse also supports Python development when you install the PyDev (or a similar) plug-in. Eclipse is a popular and powerful option for Python development, and it goes well beyond IDLE's feature set. It includes support for code completion, syntax highlighting, syntax analysis, refactoring, debugging, and more. Its downsides are that it is a large system to install and may require shareware extensions for some features (this may vary over time). Still, when you are ready to graduate from IDLE, the Eclipse/PyDev combination is worth your attention.

Komodo

> A full-featured development environment GUI for Python (and other languages), Komodo includes standard syntax coloring, text editing, debugging, and other features. In addition, Komodo offers many advanced features that IDLE does not, including project files, source-control integration, and regular-expression debugging. At this writing, Komodo is not free, but see the Web for its current status— it is available at *http://www.activestate.com* from ActiveState, which also offers the ActivePython distribution package mentioned in Appendix A.

NetBeans IDE for Python

> NetBeans is a powerful open source development environment GUI with support for many advanced features for Python developers: code completion, automatic indentation and code colorization, editor hints, code folding, refactoring, debugging, code coverage and testing, projects, and more. It may be used to develop both CPython and Jython code. Like Eclipse, NetBeans requires installation steps beyond those of the included IDLE GUI, but it is seen by many as more than worth the effort. Search the Web for the latest information and links.

PythonWin

> PythonWin is a free Windows-only IDE for Python that ships as part of ActiveState's ActivePython distribution (and may also be fetched separately from *http://www.python.org* resources). It is roughly like IDLE, with a handful of useful Windows-specific extensions added; for example, PythonWin has support for COM objects. Today, IDLE is probably more advanced than PythonWin (for instance, IDLE's dual-process architecture often prevents it from hanging). However, PythonWin still offers tools for Windows developers that IDLE does not. See *http://www.activestate.com* for more information.

Wing, Visual Studio, and others

> Other IDEs are popular among Python developers too, including the mostly commercial *Wing IDE*, Microsoft *Visual Studio* via a plug-in, and *PyCharm*, *PyScrip-*

ter, *Pyshield*, and *Spyder*—but I do not have space to do justice to them here, and more will undoubtedly appear over time. In fact, almost every programmer-friendly *text editor* has some sort of support for Python development these days, whether it be preinstalled or fetched separately. Emacs and Vim, for instance, have substantial Python support.

IDE choices are often subjective, so I encourage you to browse to find tools that fit your development style and goals. For more information, see the resources available at *http://www.python.org* or search the Web for "Python IDE" or similar. A search for "Python editors" today leads you to a wiki page that maintains information about dozens of IDE and text-editor options for Python programming.

Other Launch Options

At this point, we've seen how to run code typed interactively, and how to launch code saved in files in a variety of ways—system command lines, icon clicks, imports and execs, GUIs like IDLE, and more. That covers most of the techniques in common use, and enough to run the code you'll see in this book. There are additional ways to run Python code, though, most of which have special or narrow roles. For completeness and reference, the next few sections take a quick look at some of these.

Embedding Calls

In some specialized domains, Python code may be run automatically by an enclosing system. In such cases, we say that the Python programs are *embedded* in (i.e., run by) another program. The Python code itself may be entered into a text file, stored in a database, fetched from an HTML page, parsed from an XML document, and so on. But from an operational perspective, another system—not you—may tell Python to run the code you've created.

Such an embedded execution mode is commonly used to support end-user customization—a game program, for instance, might allow for play modifications by running user-accessible embedded Python code at strategic points in time. Users can modify this type of system by providing or changing Python code. Because Python code is interpreted, there is no need to recompile the entire system to incorporate the change (see Chapter 2 for more on how Python code is run).

In this mode, the enclosing system that runs your code might be written in C, C++, or even Java when the Jython system is used. As an example, it's possible to create and run strings of Python code from a C program by calling functions in the Python runtime API (a set of services exported by the libraries created when Python is compiled on your machine):

```
#include <Python.h>
...
```

```
Py_Initialize();                                      // This is C, not Python
PyRun_SimpleString("x = 'brave ' + 'sir robin'");     // But it runs Python code
```

In this C code snippet, a program coded in the C language embeds the Python interpreter by linking in its libraries, and passes it a Python assignment statement string to run. C programs may also gain access to Python modules and objects and process or execute them using other Python API tools.

This book isn't about Python/C integration, but you should be aware that, depending on how your organization plans to use Python, you may or may not be the one who actually starts the Python programs you create. Regardless, you can usually still use the interactive and file-based launching techniques described here to test code in isolation from those enclosing systems that may eventually use it.[6]

Frozen Binary Executables

Frozen binary executables, described in Chapter 2, are packages that combine your program's byte code and the Python interpreter into a single executable program. This approach enables Python programs to be launched in the same ways that you would launch any other executable program (icon clicks, command lines, etc.). While this option works well for delivery of products, it is not really intended for use during program development; you normally freeze just before shipping (after development is finished). See the prior chapter for more on this option.

Text Editor Launch Options

As mentioned previously, although they're not full-blown IDE GUIs, most programmer-friendly text editors have support for editing, and possibly running, Python programs. Such support may be built in or fetchable on the Web. For instance, if you are familiar with the Emacs text editor, you can do all your Python editing and launching from inside that text editor. See the text editor resources page at *http://www.python .org/editors* for more details, or search the Web for the phrase "Python editors."

Still Other Launch Options

Depending on your platform, there may be additional ways that you can start Python programs. For instance, on some Macintosh systems you may be able to drag Python program file icons onto the Python interpreter icon to make them execute, and on some Windows systems you can always start Python scripts with the Run... option in the Start menu. Additionally, the Python standard library has utilities that allow Python programs to be started by other Python programs in separate processes (e.g., os.popen,

---

6. See *Programming Python* (O'Reilly) for more details on embedding Python in C/C++. The embedding API can call Python functions directly, load modules, and more. Also, note that the Jython system allows Java programs to invoke Python code using a Java-based API (a Python interpreter class).

`os.system`), and Python scripts might also be spawned in larger contexts like the Web (for instance, a web page might invoke a script on a server); however, these are beyond the scope of the present chapter.

Future Possibilities?

This chapter reflects current practice, but much of the material is both platform- and time-specific. Indeed, many of the execution and launch details presented arose during the shelf life of this book's various editions. As with program execution options, it's not impossible that new program launch options may arise over time.

New operating systems, and new versions of existing systems, may also provide execution techniques beyond those outlined here. In general, because Python keeps pace with such changes, you should be able to launch Python programs in whatever way makes sense for the machines you use, both now and in the future—be that by swiping on tablet PCs and smartphones, grabbing icons in a virtual reality, or shouting a script's name over your coworkers' conversations.

Implementation changes may also impact launch schemes somewhat (e.g., a full compiler could produce normal executables that are launched much like frozen binaries today). If I knew what the future truly held, though, I would probably be talking to a stockbroker instead of writing these words!

Which Option Should I Use?

With all these options, true beginners might naturally ask: which one is best for me? In general, you should give the IDLE interface a try if you are just getting started with Python. It provides a user-friendly GUI environment and hides some of the underlying configuration details. It also comes with a platform-neutral text editor for coding your scripts, and it's a standard and free part of the Python system.

If, on the other hand, you are an experienced programmer, you might be more comfortable with simply the text editor of your choice in one window, and another window for launching the programs you edit via system command lines and icon clicks (in fact, this is how I develop Python programs, but I have a Unix-biased distant past). Because the choice of development environments is very subjective, I can't offer much more in the way of universal guidelines. In general, whatever environment you like to use will be the best for you to use.

Debugging Python Code

Naturally, none of my readers or students ever have bugs in their code (*insert smiley here*), but for less fortunate friends of yours who may, here's a quick review of the strategies commonly used by real-world Python programmers to debug code, for you to refer to as you start coding in earnest:

- **Do nothing**. By this, I don't mean that Python programmers don't debug their code—but when you make a mistake in a Python program, you get a very useful and readable error message (you'll get to see some soon, if you haven't already). If you already know Python, and especially for your own code, this is often enough —read the error message, and go fix the tagged line and file. For many, this *is* debugging in Python. It may not always be ideal for larger systems you didn't write, though.

- **Insert print statements**. Probably the main way that Python programmers debug their code (and the way that I debug Python code) is to insert `print` statements and run again. Because Python runs immediately after changes, this is usually the quickest way to get more information than error messages provide. The `print` statements don't have to be sophisticated—a simple "I am here" or display of variable values is usually enough to provide the context you need. Just remember to delete or comment out (i.e., add a # before) the debugging `print`s before you ship your code!

- **Use IDE GUI debuggers**. For larger systems you didn't write, and for beginners who want to trace code in more detail, most Python development GUIs have some sort of point-and-click debugging support. IDLE has a debugger too, but it doesn't appear to be used very often in practice—perhaps because it has no command line, or perhaps because adding `print` statements is usually quicker than setting up a GUI debugging session. To learn more, see IDLE's Help, or simply try it on your own; its basic interface is described in the section "Advanced IDLE Tools" on page 77. Other IDEs, such as Eclipse, NetBeans, Komodo, and Wing IDE, offer advanced point-and-click debuggers as well; see their documentation if you use them.

- **Use the pdb command-line debugger**. For ultimate control, Python comes with a source code debugger named *pdb*, available as a module in Python's standard library. In pdb, you type commands to step line by line, display variables, set and clear breakpoints, continue to a breakpoint or error, and so on. You can launch pdb interactively by importing it, or as a top-level script. Either way, because you can type commands to control the session, it provides a powerful debugging tool. pdb also includes a postmortem function (`pdb.pm()`) that you can run after an exception occurs, to get information from the time of the error. See the Python library manual and Chapter 36 for more details on pdb, and Appendix A for an example or running pdb as a script with Python's -m command argument.

- **Use Python's -i command-line argument**. Short of adding prints or running under pdb, you can still see what went wrong on errors. If you run your script from a command line and pass a `-i` argument between `python` and the name of your script (e.g., `python -i m.py`), Python will enter into its *interactive interpreter* mode (the `>>>` prompt) when your script exits, whether it ends successfully or runs into an error. At this point, you can print the final values of variables to get more details about what happened in your code because they are in the top-level namespace. You can also then import and run the pdb debugger for even more context; its postmortem mode will let you inspect the latest error if your script failed. Appendix A also shows `-i` in action.

- **Other options**. For more specific debugging requirements, you can find additional tools in the open source domain, including support for multithreaded programs, embedded code, and process attachment. The *Winpdb* system, for example, is a standalone debugger with advanced debugging support and cross-platform GUI and console interfaces.

These options will become more important as we start writing larger scripts. Probably the best news on the debugging front, though, is that errors are detected and reported in Python, rather than passing silently or crashing the system altogether. In fact, errors themselves are a well-defined mechanism known as *exceptions*, which you can catch and process (more on exceptions in Part VII). Making mistakes is never fun, of course, but take it from someone who recalls when debugging meant getting out a hex calculator and poring over piles of memory dump printouts: Python's debugging support makes errors much less painful than they might otherwise be.

Chapter Summary

In this chapter, we've looked at common ways to launch Python programs: by running code typed interactively, and by running code stored in files with system command lines, file icon clicks, module imports, **exec** calls, and IDE GUIs such as IDLE. We've covered a lot of pragmatic startup territory here. This chapter's goal was to equip you with enough information to enable you to start writing some code, which you'll do in the next part of the book. There, we will start exploring the Python language itself, beginning with its core *data types*—the objects that are the subjects of your programs.

First, though, take the usual chapter quiz to exercise what you've learned here. Because this is the last chapter in this part of the book, it's followed with a set of more complete exercises that test your mastery of this entire part's topics. For help with the latter set of problems, or just for a refresher, be sure to turn to Appendix D after you've given the exercises a try.

Test Your Knowledge: Quiz

1. How can you start an interactive interpreter session?
2. Where do you type a system command line to launch a script file?
3. Name four or more ways to run the code saved in a script file.
4. Name two pitfalls related to clicking file icons on Windows.
5. Why might you need to reload a module?
6. How do you run a script from within IDLE?
7. Name two pitfalls related to using IDLE.
8. What is a namespace, and how does it relate to module files?

Test Your Knowledge: Answers

1. You can start an interactive session on Windows 7 and earlier by clicking your Start button, picking the All Programs option, clicking the Python entry, and selecting the "Python (command line)" menu option. You can also achieve the same effect on Windows and other platforms by typing **python** as a system command line in your system's console window (a Command Prompt window on Windows). Another alternative is to launch IDLE, as its main Python shell window is an interactive session. Depending on your platform and Python, if you have not set your system's PATH variable to find Python, you may need to **cd** to where Python is installed, or type its full directory path instead of just **python** (e.g., **C:\Python33\python** on Windows, unless you're using the 3.3 launcher).

2. You type system command lines in whatever your platform provides as a system console: a Command Prompt window on Windows; an xterm or terminal window on Unix, Linux, and Mac OS X; and so on. You type this at the system's prompt, not at the Python interactive interpreter's ">>>" prompt—be careful not to confuse these prompts.

3. Code in a script (really, module) file can be run with system command lines, file icon clicks, imports and reloads, the **exec** built-in function, and IDE GUI selections such as IDLE's Run→Run Module menu option. On Unix, they can also be run as executables with the #! trick, and some platforms support more specialized launching techniques (e.g., drag and drop). In addition, some text editors have unique ways to run Python code, some Python programs are provided as standalone "frozen binary" executables, and some systems use Python code in embedded mode, where it is run automatically by an enclosing program written in a language like C, C++, or Java. The latter technique is usually done to provide a user customization layer.

4. Scripts that print and then exit cause the output file to disappear immediately, before you can view the output (which is why the input trick comes in handy); error messages generated by your script also appear in an output window that closes before you can examine its contents (which is one reason that system command lines and IDEs such as IDLE are better for most development).

5. Python imports (loads) a module only once per process, by default, so if you've changed its source code and want to run the new version without stopping and restarting Python, you'll have to reload it. You must import a module at least once before you can reload it. Running files of code from a system shell command line, via an icon click, or via an IDE such as IDLE generally makes this a nonissue, as those launch schemes usually run the current version of the source code file each time.

6. Within the text edit window of the file you wish to run, select the window's Run→Run Module menu option. This runs the window's source code as a top-level script file and displays its output back in the interactive Python shell window.

7. IDLE can still be hung by some types of programs—especially GUI programs that perform multithreading (an advanced technique beyond this book's scope). Also, IDLE has some usability features that can burn you once you leave the IDLE GUI: a script's variables are automatically imported to the interactive scope in IDLE and working directories are changed when you run a file, for instance, but Python itself does not take such steps in general.

8. A namespace is just a package of variables (i.e., names). It takes the form of an object with attributes in Python. Each module file is automatically a namespace— that is, a package of variables reflecting the assignments made at the top level of the file. Namespaces help avoid name collisions in Python programs: because each module file is a self-contained namespace, files must explicitly import other files in order to use their names.

Test Your Knowledge: Part I Exercises

It's time to start doing a little coding on your own. This first exercise session is fairly simple, but it's designed to make sure you're ready to work along with the rest of the book, and a few of its questions hint at topics to come in later chapters. Be sure to check "Part I, Getting Started" on page 1465 in Appendix D for the answers; the exercises and their solutions sometimes contain supplemental information not discussed in the main text, so you should take a peek at the solutions even if you manage to answer all the questions on your own.

1. *Interaction.* Using a system command line, IDLE, or any other method that works on your platform, start the Python interactive command line (>>> prompt), and type the expression **"Hello World!"** (including the quotes). The string should be echoed back to you. The purpose of this exercise is to get your environment configured to run Python. In some scenarios, you may need to first run a `cd` shell command, type the full path to the Python executable, or add its path to your PATH environment variable. If desired, you can set PATH in your *.cshrc* or *.kshrc* file to make Python permanently available on Unix systems; on Windows, the environment variable GUI is usually what you want for this. See Appendix A for help with environment variable settings.

2. *Programs.* With the text editor of your choice, write a simple module file containing the single statement `print('Hello module world!')` and store it as *module1.py*. Now, run this file by using any launch option you like: running it in IDLE, clicking on its file icon, passing it to the Python interpreter on the system shell's command line (e.g., `python module1.py`), built-in `exec` calls, imports and reloads, and so on. In fact, experiment by running your file with as many of the launch techniques discussed in this chapter as you can. Which technique seems easiest? (There is no right answer to this, of course.)

3. *Modules.* Start the Python interactive command line (>>> prompt) and import the module you wrote in exercise 2. Try moving the file to a different directory and

importing it again from its original directory (i.e., run Python in the original directory when you import). What happens? (Hint: is there still a *module1.pyc* byte code file in the original directory, or something similar in a __pycache__ subdirectory there?)

4. *Scripts.* If your platform supports it, add the #! line to the top of your *module1.py* module file, give the file executable privileges, and run it directly as an executable. What does the first line need to contain? #! usually only has meaning on Unix, Linux, and Unix-like platforms such as Mac OS X; if you're working on Windows, instead try running your file by listing just its name in a Command Prompt window without the word "python" before it (this works on recent versions of Windows), via the Start→Run... dialog box, or similar. If you are using Python 3.3 or the Windows launcher that installs with it, experiment with changing your script's #! line to launch different Python versions you may have installed on your computer (or equivalently, work through the tutorial in Appendix B).

5. *Errors and debugging.* Experiment with typing mathematical expressions and assignments at the Python interactive command line. Along the way, type the expressions 2 ** 500 and 1 / 0, and reference an undefined variable name as we did early on in this chapter. What happens?

You may not know it yet, but when you make a mistake, you're doing exception processing: a topic we'll explore in depth in Part VII. As you'll learn there, you are technically triggering what's known as the *default exception handler*—logic that prints a standard error message. If you do not catch an error, the default handler does and prints the standard error message in response.

Exceptions are also bound up with the notion of *debugging* in Python. When you're first starting out, Python's default error messages on exceptions will probably provide as much error-handling support as you need—they give the cause of the error, as well as showing the lines in your code that were active when the error occurred. For more about debugging, see the sidebar "Debugging Python Code" on page 83.

6. *Breaks and cycles.* At the Python command line, type:

```
L = [1, 2]          # Make a 2-item list
L.append(L)         # Append L as a single item to itself
L                   # Print L: a cyclic/circular object
```

What happens? In all recent versions of Python, you'll see a strange output that we'll describe in the solutions appendix, and which will make more sense when we study references in the next part of the book. If you're using a Python version older than 1.5.1, a Ctrl-C key combination will probably help on most platforms. Why do you think your version of Python responds the way it does for this code?

If you do have a Python older than Release 1.5.1 (a hopefully rare scenario today!), make sure your machine can stop a program with a Ctrl-C key combination of some sort before running this test, or you may be waiting a long time.

7. *Documentation.* Spend at least 15 minutes browsing the Python library and language manuals before moving on to get a feel for the available tools in the standard library and the structure of the documentation set. It takes at least this long to become familiar with the locations of major topics in the manual set; once you've done this, it's easy to find what you need. You can find this manual via the Python Start button entry on some Windows, in the Python Docs option on the Help pull-down menu in IDLE, or online at *http://www.python.org/doc*. I'll also have a few more words to say about the manuals and other documentation sources available (including PyDoc and the `help` function) in Chapter 15. If you still have time, go explore the Python website, as well as its PyPI third-party extension repository. Especially check out the Python.org (*http://www.python.org*) documentation and search pages; they can be crucial resources.

## PART II

Types and Operations

## CHAPTER 4

Introducing Python Object Types

This chapter begins our tour of the Python language. In an informal sense, in Python we *do things with stuff*.[1] "Things" take the form of operations like addition and concatenation, and "stuff" refers to the objects on which we perform those operations. In this part of the book, our focus is on that *stuff*, and the *things* our programs can do with it.

Somewhat more formally, in Python, data takes the form of *objects*—either built-in objects that Python provides, or objects we create using Python classes or external language tools such as C extension libraries. Although we'll firm up this definition later, objects are essentially just pieces of memory, with values and sets of associated operations. As we'll see, *everything* is an object in a Python script. Even simple numbers qualify, with values (e.g., 99), and supported operations (addition, subtraction, and so on).

Because objects are also the most fundamental notion in Python programming, we'll start this chapter with a survey of Python's built-in object types. Later chapters provide a second pass that fills in details we'll gloss over in this survey. Here, our goal is a brief tour to introduce the basics.

The Python Conceptual Hierarchy

Before we get to the code, let's first establish a clear picture of how this chapter fits into the overall Python picture. From a more concrete perspective, Python programs can be decomposed into modules, statements, expressions, and objects, as follows:

1. Programs are composed of modules.
2. Modules contain statements.
3. Statements contain expressions.
4. *Expressions create and process objects.*

---

1. Pardon my formality. I'm a computer scientist.

The discussion of modules in Chapter 3 introduced the highest level of this hierarchy. This part's chapters begin at the bottom—exploring both built-in objects and the expressions you can code to use them.

We'll move on to study statements in the next part of the book, though we will find that they largely exist to manage the objects we'll meet here. Moreover, by the time we reach classes in the OOP part of this book, we'll discover that they allow us to define new object types of our own, by both using and emulating the object types we will explore here. Because of all this, built-in objects are a mandatory point of embarkation for all Python journeys.

 Traditional introductions to programming often stress its three pillars of *sequence* ("Do this, then that"), *selection* ("Do this if that is true"), and *repetition* ("Do this many times"). Python has tools in all three categories, along with some for *definition*—of functions and classes. These themes may help you organize your thinking early on, but they are a bit artificial and simplistic. Expressions such as comprehensions, for example, are both repetition and selection; some of these terms have other meanings in Python; and many later concepts won't seem to fit this mold at all. In Python, the more strongly unifying principle is *objects*, and what we can do with them. To see why, read on.

Why Use Built-in Types?

If you've used lower-level languages such as C or C++, you know that much of your work centers on implementing *objects*—also known as *data structures*—to represent the components in your application's domain. You need to lay out memory structures, manage memory allocation, implement search and access routines, and so on. These chores are about as tedious (and error-prone) as they sound, and they usually distract from your program's real goals.

In typical Python programs, most of this grunt work goes away. Because Python provides powerful object types as an intrinsic part of the language, there's usually no need to code object implementations before you start solving problems. In fact, unless you have a need for special processing that built-in types don't provide, you're almost always better off using a built-in object instead of implementing your own. Here are some reasons why:

- **Built-in objects make programs easy to write**. For simple tasks, built-in types are often all you need to represent the structure of problem domains. Because you get powerful tools such as collections (lists) and search tables (dictionaries) for free, you can use them immediately. You can get a lot of work done with Python's built-in object types alone.

- **Built-in objects are components of extensions**. For more complex tasks, you may need to provide your own objects using Python classes or C language interfaces. But as you'll see in later parts of this book, objects implemented manually are often built on top of built-in types such as lists and dictionaries. For instance, a stack data structure may be implemented as a class that manages or customizes a built-in list.

- **Built-in objects are often more efficient than custom data structures**. Python's built-in types employ already optimized data structure algorithms that are implemented in C for speed. Although you can write similar object types on your own, you'll usually be hard-pressed to get the level of performance built-in object types provide.

- **Built-in objects are a standard part of the language**. In some ways, Python borrows both from languages that rely on built-in tools (e.g., LISP) and languages that rely on the programmer to provide tool implementations or frameworks of their own (e.g., C++). Although you can implement unique object types in Python, you don't need to do so just to get started. Moreover, because Python's built-ins are standard, they're always the same; proprietary frameworks, on the other hand, tend to differ from site to site.

In other words, not only do built-in object types make programming easier, but they're also more powerful and efficient than most of what can be created from scratch. Regardless of whether you implement new object types, built-in objects form the core of every Python program.

Python's Core Data Types

Table 4-1 previews Python's built-in object types and some of the syntax used to code their *literals*—that is, the expressions that generate these objects.[2] Some of these types will probably seem familiar if you've used other languages; for instance, numbers and strings represent numeric and textual values, respectively, and file objects provide an interface for processing real files stored on your computer.

To some readers, though, the object types in Table 4-1 may be more general and powerful than what you are accustomed to. For instance, you'll find that lists and dictionaries alone are powerful data representation tools that obviate most of the work you do to support collections and searching in lower-level languages. In short, lists provide ordered collections of other objects, while dictionaries store objects by key; both lists and dictionaries may be nested, can grow and shrink on demand, and may contain objects of any type.

---

2. In this book, the term *literal* simply means an expression whose syntax generates an object—sometimes also called a *constant*. Note that the term "constant" does not imply objects or variables that can never be changed (i.e., this term is unrelated to C++'s const or Python's "immutable"—a topic explored in the section "Immutability" on page 101).

Table 4-1. Built-in objects preview

Object type	Example literals/creation
Numbers	`1234, 3.1415, 3+4j, 0b111, Decimal(), Fraction()`
Strings	`'spam', "Bob's", b'a\x01c', u'sp\xc4m'`
Lists	`[1, [2, 'three'], 4.5], list(range(10))`
Dictionaries	`{'food': 'spam', 'taste': 'yum'}, dict(hours=10)`
Tuples	`(1, 'spam', 4, 'U'), tuple('spam'), namedtuple`
Files	`open('eggs.txt'), open(r'C:\ham.bin', 'wb')`
Sets	`set('abc'), {'a', 'b', 'c'}`
Other core types	Booleans, types, None
Program unit types	Functions, modules, classes (Part IV, Part V, Part VI)
Implementation-related types	Compiled code, stack tracebacks (Part IV, Part VII)

Also shown in Table 4-1, *program units* such as functions, modules, and classes—which we'll meet in later parts of this book—are objects in Python too; they are created with statements and expressions such as `def`, `class`, `import`, and `lambda` and may be passed around scripts freely, stored within other objects, and so on. Python also provides a set of *implementation-related* types such as compiled code objects, which are generally of interest to tool builders more than application developers; we'll explore these in later parts too, though in less depth due to their specialized roles.

Despite its title, Table 4-1 isn't really complete, because *everything* we process in Python programs is a kind of object. For instance, when we perform text pattern matching in Python, we create pattern objects, and when we perform network scripting, we use socket objects. These other kinds of objects are generally created by importing and using functions in library modules—for example, in the `re` and `socket` modules for patterns and sockets—and have behavior all their own.

We usually call the other object types in Table 4-1 *core* data types, though, because they are effectively built into the Python language—that is, there is specific expression syntax for generating most of them. For instance, when you run the following code with characters surrounded by quotes:

```
>>> 'spam'
```

you are, technically speaking, running a literal expression that generates and returns a new *string* object. There is specific Python language syntax to make this object. Similarly, an expression wrapped in square brackets makes a *list*, one in curly braces makes a *dictionary*, and so on. Even though, as we'll see, there are no type declarations in Python, the syntax of the expressions you run determines the types of objects you create and use. In fact, object-generation expressions like those in Table 4-1 are generally where types originate in the Python language.

Just as importantly, once you create an object, you bind its operation set for all time—you can perform only string operations on a string and list operations on a list. In formal terms, this means that Python is *dynamically typed*, a model that keeps track of types for you automatically instead of requiring declaration code, but it is also *strongly typed*, a constraint that means you can perform on an object only operations that are valid for its type.

We'll study each of the object types in Table 4-1 in detail in upcoming chapters. Before digging into the details, though, let's begin by taking a quick look at Python's core objects in action. The rest of this chapter provides a preview of the operations we'll explore in more depth in the chapters that follow. Don't expect to find the full story here—the goal of this chapter is just to whet your appetite and introduce some key ideas. Still, the best way to get started is to get started, so let's jump right into some real code.

Numbers

If you've done any programming or scripting in the past, some of the object types in Table 4-1 will probably seem familiar. Even if you haven't, numbers are fairly straightforward. Python's core objects set includes the usual suspects: *integers* that have no fractional part, *floating-point* numbers that do, and more exotic types—*complex* numbers with imaginary parts, *decimals* with fixed precision, *rationals* with numerator and denominator, and full-featured *sets*. Built-in numbers are enough to represent most numeric quantities—from your age to your bank balance—but more types are available as third-party add-ons.

Although it offers some fancier options, Python's basic number types are, well, basic. Numbers in Python support the normal mathematical operations. For instance, the plus sign (+) performs addition, a star (*) is used for multiplication, and two stars (**) are used for exponentiation:

```
>>> 123 + 222             # Integer addition
345
>>> 1.5 * 4               # Floating-point multiplication
6.0
>>> 2 ** 100              # 2 to the power 100, again
1267650600228229401496703205376
```

Notice the last result here: Python 3.X's integer type automatically provides extra precision for large numbers like this when needed (in 2.X, a separate long integer type handles numbers too large for the normal integer type in similar ways). You can, for instance, compute 2 to the power 1,000,000 as an integer in Python, but you probably shouldn't try to print the result—with more than 300,000 digits, you may be waiting awhile!

```
>>> len(str(2 ** 1000000))    # How many digits in a really BIG number?
301030
```

This nested-call form works from inside out—first converting the ** result's number to a string of digits with the built-in `str` function, and then getting the length of the resulting string with `len`. The end result is the number of digits. `str` and `len` work on many object types; more on both as we move along.

On Pythons prior to 2.7 and 3.1, once you start experimenting with *floating-point* numbers, you're likely to stumble across something that may look a bit odd at first glance:

```
>>> 3.1415 * 2            # repr: as code (Pythons < 2.7 and 3.1)
6.2830000000000004
>>> print(3.1415 * 2)     # str: user-friendly
6.283
```

The first result isn't a bug; it's a display issue. It turns out that there are two ways to print every object in Python—with full precision (as in the first result shown here), and in a user-friendly form (as in the second). Formally, the first form is known as an object's as-code `repr`, and the second is its user-friendly `str`. In older Pythons, the floating-point `repr` sometimes displays more precision than you might expect. The difference can also matter when we step up to using classes. For now, if something looks odd, try showing it with a `print` built-in function call statement.

Better yet, upgrade to Python 2.7 and the latest 3.X, where floating-point numbers display themselves more intelligently, usually with fewer extraneous digits—since this book is based on Pythons 2.7 and 3.3, this is the display form I'll be showing throughout this book for floating-point numbers:

```
>>> 3.1415 * 2            # repr: as code (Pythons >= 2.7 and 3.1)
6.283
```

Besides expressions, there are a handful of useful numeric modules that ship with Python—*modules* are just packages of additional tools that we import to use:

```
>>> import math
>>> math.pi
3.141592653589793
>>> math.sqrt(85)
9.219544457292887
```

The `math` module contains more advanced numeric tools as functions, while the `random` module performs random-number generation and random selections (here, from a Python *list* coded in square brackets—an ordered collection of other objects to be introduced later in this chapter):

```
>>> import random
>>> random.random()
0.7082048489415967
>>> random.choice([1, 2, 3, 4])
1
```

Python also includes more exotic numeric objects—such as complex, fixed-precision, and rational numbers, as well as sets and Booleans—and the third-party open source extension domain has even more (e.g., matrixes and vectors, and extended precision numbers). We'll defer discussion of these types until later in this chapter and book.

So far, we've been using Python much like a simple calculator; to do better justice to its built-in types, let's move on to explore strings.

Strings

Strings are used to record both textual information (your name, for instance) as well as arbitrary collections of bytes (such as an image file's contents). They are our first example of what in Python we call a *sequence*—a positionally ordered collection of other objects. Sequences maintain a left-to-right order among the items they contain: their items are stored and fetched by their relative positions. Strictly speaking, strings are sequences of one-character strings; other, more general sequence types include *lists* and *tuples*, covered later.

Sequence Operations

As sequences, strings support operations that assume a positional ordering among items. For example, if we have a four-character string coded inside quotes (usually of the single variety), we can verify its length with the built-in `len` function and fetch its components with *indexing* expressions:

```
>>> S = 'Spam'        # Make a 4-character string, and assign it to a name
>>> len(S)            # Length
4
>>> S[0]              # The first item in S, indexing by zero-based position
'S'
>>> S[1]              # The second item from the left
'p'
```

In Python, indexes are coded as offsets from the front, and so start from 0: the first item is at index 0, the second is at index 1, and so on.

Notice how we assign the string to a *variable* named S here. We'll go into detail on how this works later (especially in Chapter 6), but Python variables never need to be declared ahead of time. A variable is created when you assign it a value, may be assigned any type of object, and is replaced with its value when it shows up in an expression. It must also have been previously assigned by the time you use its value. For the purposes of this chapter, it's enough to know that we need to assign an object to a variable in order to save it for later use.

In Python, we can also index backward, from the end—positive indexes count from the left, and negative indexes count back from the right:

```
>>> S[-1]             # The last item from the end in S
'm'
>>> S[-2]             # The second-to-last item from the end
'a'
```

Formally, a negative index is simply added to the string's length, so the following two operations are equivalent (though the first is easier to code and less easy to get wrong):

```
>>> S[-1]                    # The last item in S
'm'
>>> S[len(S)-1]              # Negative indexing, the hard way
'm'
```

Notice that we can use an *arbitrary expression* in the square brackets, not just a hard-coded number literal—anywhere that Python expects a value, we can use a literal, a variable, or any expression we wish. Python's syntax is completely general this way.

In addition to simple positional indexing, sequences also support a more general form of indexing known as *slicing*, which is a way to extract an entire section (slice) in a single step. For example:

```
>>> S                        # A 4-character string
'Spam'
>>> S[1:3]                   # Slice of S from offsets 1 through 2 (not 3)
'pa'
```

Probably the easiest way to think of slices is that they are a way to extract an entire *column* from a string in a single step. Their general form, X[I:J], means "give me everything in X from offset I up to but not including offset J." The result is returned in a new object. The second of the preceding operations, for instance, gives us all the characters in string S from offsets 1 through 2 (that is, 1 through 3 – 1) as a new string. The effect is to slice or "parse out" the two characters in the middle.

In a slice, the left bound defaults to zero, and the right bound defaults to the length of the sequence being sliced. This leads to some common usage variations:

```
>>> S[1:]                    # Everything past the first (1:len(S))
'pam'
>>> S                        # S itself hasn't changed
'Spam'
>>> S[0:3]                   # Everything but the last
'Spa'
>>> S[:3]                    # Same as S[0:3]
'Spa'
>>> S[:-1]                   # Everything but the last again, but simpler (0:-1)
'Spa'
>>> S[:]                     # All of S as a top-level copy (0:len(S))
'Spam'
```

Note in the second-to-last command how negative offsets can be used to give bounds for slices, too, and how the last operation effectively copies the entire string. As you'll learn later, there is no reason to copy a string, but this form can be useful for sequences like lists.

Finally, as sequences, strings also support *concatenation* with the plus sign (joining two strings into a new string) and *repetition* (making a new string by repeating another):

```
>>> S
'Spam'
```

```
>>> S + 'xyz'                 # Concatenation
'Spamxyz'
>>> S                         # S is unchanged
'Spam'
>>> S * 8                     # Repetition
'SpamSpamSpamSpamSpamSpamSpamSpam'
```

Notice that the plus sign (+) means different things for different objects: addition for numbers, and concatenation for strings. This is a general property of Python that we'll call *polymorphism* later in the book—in sum, the meaning of an operation depends on the objects being operated on. As you'll see when we study dynamic typing, this polymorphism property accounts for much of the conciseness and flexibility of Python code. Because types aren't constrained, a Python-coded operation can normally work on many different types of objects automatically, as long as they support a compatible interface (like the + operation here). This turns out to be a huge idea in Python; you'll learn more about it later on our tour.

Immutability

Also notice in the prior examples that we were not changing the original string with any of the operations we ran on it. Every string operation is defined to produce a new string as its result, because strings are *immutable* in Python—they cannot be changed in place after they are created. In other words, you can never overwrite the values of immutable objects. For example, you can't change a string by assigning to one of its positions, but you can always build a new one and assign it to the same name. Because Python cleans up old objects as you go (as you'll see later), this isn't as inefficient as it may sound:

```
>>> S
'Spam'

>>> S[0] = 'z'                # Immutable objects cannot be changed
...error text omitted...
TypeError: 'str' object does not support item assignment

>>> S = 'z' + S[1:]           # But we can run expressions to make new objects
>>> S
'zpam'
```

Every object in Python is classified as either immutable (unchangeable) or not. In terms of the core types, *numbers*, *strings*, and *tuples* are immutable; *lists*, *dictionaries*, and *sets* are not—they can be changed in place freely, as can most new objects you'll code with classes. This distinction turns out to be crucial in Python work, in ways that we can't yet fully explore. Among other things, immutability can be used to guarantee that an object remains constant throughout your program; mutable objects' values can be changed at any time and place (and whether you expect it or not).

Strictly speaking, you can change text-based data *in place* if you either expand it into a *list* of individual characters and join it back together with nothing between, or use the newer `bytearray` type available in Pythons 2.6, 3.0, and later:

```
>>> S = 'shrubbery'
>>> L = list(S)                              # Expand to a list: [...]
>>> L
['s', 'h', 'r', 'u', 'b', 'b', 'e', 'r', 'y']
>>> L[1] = 'c'                               # Change it in place
>>> ''.join(L)                               # Join with empty delimiter
'scrubbery'

>>> B = bytearray(b'spam')                   # A bytes/list hybrid (ahead)
>>> B.extend(b'eggs')                        # 'b' needed in 3.X, not 2.X
>>> B                                        # B[i] = ord(x) works here too
bytearray(b'spameggs')
>>> B.decode()                               # Translate to normal string
'spameggs'
```

The `bytearray` supports in-place changes for text, but only for text whose characters are all at most 8-bits wide (e.g., ASCII). All other strings are still immutable—`bytearray` is a distinct hybrid of immutable *bytes* strings (whose b'...' syntax is required in 3.X and optional in 2.X) and mutable *lists* (coded and displayed in []), and we have to learn more about both these and Unicode text to fully grasp this code.

Type-Specific Methods

Every string operation we've studied so far is really a sequence operation—that is, these operations will work on other sequences in Python as well, including lists and tuples. In addition to generic sequence operations, though, strings also have operations all their own, available as *methods*—functions that are attached to and act upon a specific object, which are triggered with a call expression.

For example, the string `find` method is the basic substring search operation (it returns the offset of the passed-in substring, or -1 if it is not present), and the string `replace` method performs global searches and replacements; both act on the subject that they are attached to and called from:

```
>>> S = 'Spam'
>>> S.find('pa')             # Find the offset of a substring in S
1
>>> S
'Spam'
>>> S.replace('pa', 'XYZ')   # Replace occurrences of a string in S with another
'SXYZm'
>>> S
'Spam'
```

Again, despite the names of these string methods, we are not changing the original strings here, but creating new strings as the results—because strings are immutable, this is the only way this can work. String methods are the first line of text-processing tools in Python. Other methods split a string into substrings on a delimiter (handy as a simple form of parsing), perform case conversions, test the content of the string (digits, letters, and so on), and strip whitespace characters off the ends of the string:

```
>>> line = 'aaa,bbb,ccccc,dd'
>>> line.split(',')                    # Split on a delimiter into a list of substrings
['aaa', 'bbb', 'ccccc', 'dd']

>>> S = 'spam'
>>> S.upper()                          # Upper- and lowercase conversions
'SPAM'
>>> S.isalpha()                        # Content tests: isalpha, isdigit, etc.
True

>>> line = 'aaa,bbb,ccccc,dd\n'
>>> line.rstrip()                      # Remove whitespace characters on the right side
'aaa,bbb,ccccc,dd'
>>> line.rstrip().split(',')           # Combine two operations
['aaa', 'bbb', 'ccccc', 'dd']
```

Notice the last command here—it strips before it splits because Python runs from left to right, making a temporary result along the way. Strings also support an advanced substitution operation known as *formatting*, available as both an expression (the original) and a string method call (new as of 2.6 and 3.0); the second of these allows you to omit relative argument value numbers as of 2.7 and 3.1:

```
>>> '%s, eggs, and %s' % ('spam', 'SPAM!')          # Formatting expression (all)
'spam, eggs, and SPAM!'

>>> '{0}, eggs, and {1}'.format('spam', 'SPAM!')    # Formatting method (2.6+, 3.0+)
'spam, eggs, and SPAM!'

>>> '{}, eggs, and {}'.format('spam', 'SPAM!')      # Numbers optional (2.7+, 3.1+)
'spam, eggs, and SPAM!'
```

Formatting is rich with features, which we'll postpone discussing until later in this book, and which tend to matter most when you must generate numeric reports:

```
>>> '{:,.2f}'.format(296999.2567)          # Separators, decimal digits
'296,999.26'
>>> '%.2f | %+05d' % (3.14159, -42)        # Digits, padding, signs
'3.14 | -0042'
```

One note here: although sequence operations are generic, methods are not—although some types share some method names, string method operations generally work only on strings, and nothing else. As a rule of thumb, Python's toolset is layered: generic operations that span multiple types show up as built-in functions or expressions (e.g., len(X), X[0]), but type-specific operations are method calls (e.g., aString.upper()). Finding the tools you need among all these categories will become more natural as you use Python more, but the next section gives a few tips you can use right now.

Getting Help

The methods introduced in the prior section are a representative, but small, sample of what is available for string objects. In general, this book is not exhaustive in its look at object methods. For more details, you can always call the built-in `dir` function. This function lists variables assigned in the caller's scope when called with no argument; more usefully, it returns a list of all the attributes available for any object passed to it. Because methods are function attributes, they will show up in this list. Assuming S is still the string, here are its attributes on Python 3.3 (Python 2.X varies slightly):

```
>>> dir(S)
['__add__', '__class__', '__contains__', '__delattr__', '__dir__', '__doc__',
'__eq__', '__format__', '__ge__', '__getattribute__', '__getitem__',
'__getnewargs__', '__gt__', '__hash__', '__init__', '__iter__', '__le__',
'__len__', '__lt__', '__mod__', '__mul__', '__ne__', '__new__', '__reduce__',
'__reduce_ex__', '__repr__', '__rmod__', '__rmul__', '__setattr__', '__sizeof__',
'__str__', '__subclasshook__', 'capitalize', 'casefold', 'center', 'count',
'encode', 'endswith', 'expandtabs', 'find', 'format', 'format_map', 'index',
'isalnum', 'isalpha', 'isdecimal', 'isdigit', 'isidentifier', 'islower',
'isnumeric', 'isprintable', 'isspace', 'istitle', 'isupper', 'join', 'ljust',
'lower', 'lstrip', 'maketrans', 'partition', 'replace', 'rfind', 'rindex',
'rjust', 'rpartition', 'rsplit', 'rstrip', 'split', 'splitlines', 'startswith',
'strip', 'swapcase', 'title', 'translate', 'upper', 'zfill']
```

You probably won't care about the names with *double underscores* in this list until later in the book, when we study operator overloading in classes—they represent the implementation of the string object and are available to support customization. The `__add__` method of strings, for example, is what really performs concatenation; Python maps the first of the following to the second internally, though you shouldn't usually use the second form yourself (it's less intuitive, and might even run slower):

```
>>> S + 'NI!'
'spamNI!'
>>> S.__add__('NI!')
'spamNI!'
```

In general, leading and trailing double underscores is the naming pattern Python uses for implementation details. The names without the underscores in this list are the callable methods on string objects.

The `dir` function simply gives the methods' names. To ask what they do, you can pass them to the `help` function:

```
>>> help(S.replace)
Help on built-in function replace:

replace(...)
    S.replace(old, new[, count]) -> str

    Return a copy of S with all occurrences of substring
    old replaced by new.  If the optional argument count is
    given, only the first count occurrences are replaced.
```

`help` is one of a handful of interfaces to a system of code that ships with Python known as *PyDoc*—a tool for extracting documentation from objects. Later in the book, you'll see that PyDoc can also render its reports in HTML format for display on a web browser.

You can also ask for help on an *entire string* (e.g., `help(S)`), but you may get more or less help than you want to see—information about every string method in older Pythons, and probably no help at all in newer versions because strings are treated specially. It's generally better to ask about a specific *method*.

Both `dir` and `help` also accept as arguments either a real *object* (like our string `S`), or the name of a *data type* (like `str`, `list`, and `dict`). The latter form returns the same list for `dir` but shows full type details for `help`, and allows you to ask about a specific method via type name (e.g., help on `str.replace`).

For more details, you can also consult Python's standard library reference manual or commercially published reference books, but `dir` and `help` are the first level of documentation in Python.

Other Ways to Code Strings

So far, we've looked at the string object's sequence operations and type-specific methods. Python also provides a variety of ways for us to code strings, which we'll explore in greater depth later. For instance, special characters can be represented as backslash escape sequences, which Python displays in `\xNN` hexadecimal escape notation, unless they represent printable characters:

```
>>> S = 'A\nB\tC'           # \n is end-of-line, \t is tab
>>> len(S)                  # Each stands for just one character
5

>>> ord('\n')               # \n is a byte with the binary value 10 in ASCII
10

>>> S = 'A\0B\0C'           # \0, a binary zero byte, does not terminate string
>>> len(S)
5
>>> S                       # Non-printables are displayed as \xNN hex escapes
'A\x00B\x00C'
```

Python allows strings to be enclosed in *single* or *double* quote characters—they mean the same thing but allow the other type of quote to be embedded without an escape (most programmers prefer single quotes). It also allows multiline string literals enclosed in *triple* quotes (single or double)—when this form is used, all the lines are concatenated together, and end-of-line characters are added where line breaks appear. This is a minor syntactic convenience, but it's useful for embedding things like multiline HTML, XML, or JSON code in a Python script, and stubbing out lines of code temporarily—just add three quotes above and below:

```
>>> msg = """
aaaaaaaaaaaaa
```

```
bbb'''bbbbbbbbb""bbbbbb'bbbb
cccccccccccccc
"""
>>> msg
'\naaaaaaaaaaaaa\nbbb\'\'\'bbbbbbbbbb""bbbbbb\'bbbb\nccccccccccccccc\n'
```

Python also supports a *raw* string literal that turns off the backslash escape mechanism. Such literals start with the letter *r* and are useful for strings like directory paths on Windows (e.g., r'C:\text\new').

Unicode Strings

Python's strings also come with full *Unicode* support required for processing text in internationalized character sets. Characters in the Japanese and Russian alphabets, for example, are outside the ASCII set. Such non-ASCII text can show up in web pages, emails, GUIs, JSON, XML, or elsewhere. When it does, handling it well requires Unicode support. Python has such support built in, but the form of its Unicode support varies per Python line, and is one of their most prominent differences.

In Python 3.X, the normal str string handles Unicode text (including ASCII, which is just a simple kind of Unicode); a distinct bytes string type represents raw byte values (including media and encoded text); and 2.X Unicode literals are supported in 3.3 and later for 2.X compatibility (they are treated the same as normal 3.X str strings):

```
>>> 'sp\xc4m'            # 3.X: normal str strings are Unicode text
'spÄm'
>>> b'a\x01c'            # bytes strings are byte-based data
b'a\x01c'
>>> u'sp\u00c4m'         # The 2.X Unicode literal works in 3.3+: just str
'spÄm'
```

In Python 2.X, the normal str string handles both 8-bit character strings (including ASCII text) and raw byte values; a distinct unicode string type represents Unicode text; and 3.X bytes literals are supported in 2.6 and later for 3.X compatibility (they are treated the same as normal 2.X str strings):

```
>>> print u'sp\xc4m'     # 2.X: Unicode strings are a distinct type
spÄm
>>> 'a\x01c'             # Normal str strings contain byte-based text/data
'a\x01c'
>>> b'a\x01c'            # The 3.X bytes literal works in 2.6+: just str
'a\x01c'
```

Formally, in both 2.X and 3.X, non-Unicode strings are sequences of *8-bit bytes* that print with ASCII characters when possible, and Unicode strings are sequences of *Unicode code points*—identifying numbers for characters, which do not necessarily map to single bytes when encoded to files or stored in memory. In fact, the notion of bytes doesn't apply to Unicode: some encodings include character code points too large for a byte, and even simple 7-bit ASCII text is not stored one byte per character under some encodings and memory storage schemes:

```
>>> 'spam'                          # Characters may be 1, 2, or 4 bytes in memory
'spam'
>>> 'spam'.encode('utf8')           # Encoded to 4 bytes in UTF-8 in files
b'spam'
>>> 'spam'.encode('utf16')          # But encoded to 10 bytes in UTF-16
b'\xff\xfes\x00p\x00a\x00m\x00'
```

Both 3.X and 2.X also support the bytearray string type we met earlier, which is essentially a bytes string (a str in 2.X) that supports most of the list object's in-place mutable change operations.

Both 3.X and 2.X also support coding *non-ASCII* characters with \x hexadecimal and short \u and long \U Unicode escapes, as well as file-wide encodings declared in program source files. Here's our non-ASCII character coded three ways in 3.X (add a leading "u" and say "print" to see the same in 2.X):

```
>>> 'sp\xc4\u00c4\U000000c4m'
'spÄÄÄm'
```

What these values mean and how they are used differs between *text strings*, which are the normal string in 3.X and Unicode in 2.X, and *byte strings*, which are bytes in 3.X and the normal string in 2.X. All these escapes can be used to embed actual Unicode code-point ordinal-value integers in text strings. By contrast, byte strings use only \x hexadecimal escapes to embed the encoded form of text, not its decoded code point values—encoded bytes are the same as code points, only for some encodings and characters:

```
>>> '\u00A3', '\u00A3'.encode('latin1'), b'\xA3'.decode('latin1')
('£', b'\xa3', '£')
```

As a notable difference, Python 2.X allows its normal and Unicode strings to be mixed in expressions as long as the normal string is all ASCII; in contrast, Python 3.X has a tighter model that *never* allows its normal and byte strings to mix without explicit conversion:

```
u'x' + b'y'                         # Works in 2.X (where b is optional and ignored)
u'x' + 'y'                          # Works in 2.X: u'xy'

u'x' + b'y'                         # Fails in 3.3 (where u is optional and ignored)
u'x' + 'y'                          # Works in 3.3: 'xy'

'x' + b'y'.decode()                 # Works in 3.X if decode bytes to str: 'xy'
'x'.encode() + b'y'                 # Works in 3.X if encode str to bytes: b'xy'
```

Apart from these string types, Unicode processing mostly reduces to transferring text data to and from *files*—text is *encoded* to bytes when stored in a file, and *decoded* into characters (a.k.a. code points) when read back into memory. Once it is loaded, we usually process text as strings in decoded form only.

Because of this model, though, files are also content-specific in 3.X: *text files* implement named encodings and accept and return str strings, but *binary files* instead deal in `bytes` strings for raw binary data. In Python 2.X, normal files' content is `str` bytes, and a special `codecs` module handles Unicode and represents content with the `unicode` type.

We'll meet Unicode again in the files coverage later in this chapter, but save the rest of the Unicode story for later in this book. It crops up briefly in a Chapter 25 example in conjunction with currency symbols, but for the most part is postponed until this book's advanced topics part. Unicode is crucial in some domains, but many programmers can get by with just a passing acquaintance. If your data is all ASCII text, the string and file stories are largely the same in 2.X and 3.X. And if you're new to programming, you can safely defer most Unicode details until you've mastered string basics.

Pattern Matching

One point worth noting before we move on is that none of the string object's own methods support pattern-based text processing. Text pattern matching is an advanced tool outside this book's scope, but readers with backgrounds in other scripting languages may be interested to know that to do pattern matching in Python, we import a module called `re`. This module has analogous calls for searching, splitting, and replacement, but because we can use patterns to specify substrings, we can be much more general:

```
>>> import re
>>> match = re.match('Hello[ \t]*(.*)world', 'Hello    Python world')
>>> match.group(1)
'Python '
```

This example searches for a substring that begins with the word "Hello," followed by zero or more tabs or spaces, followed by arbitrary characters to be saved as a matched group, terminated by the word "world." If such a substring is found, portions of the substring matched by parts of the pattern enclosed in parentheses are available as groups. The following pattern, for example, picks out three groups separated by slashes or colons, and is similar to splitting by an alternatives pattern:

```
>>> match = re.match('[/:](.*)[/:](.*)[/:](.*)', '/usr/home:lumberjack')
>>> match.groups()
('usr', 'home', 'lumberjack')

>>> re.split('[/:]', '/usr/home/lumberjack')
['', 'usr', 'home', 'lumberjack']
```

Pattern matching is an advanced text-processing tool by itself, but there is also support in Python for even more advanced text and language processing, including XML and HTML parsing and natural language analysis. We'll see additional brief examples of patterns and XML parsing at the end of Chapter 37, but I've already said enough about strings for this tutorial, so let's move on to the next type.

Lists

The Python list object is the most general *sequence* provided by the language. Lists are positionally ordered collections of arbitrarily typed objects, and they have no fixed size. They are also *mutable*—unlike strings, lists can be modified in place by assignment to offsets as well as a variety of list method calls. Accordingly, they provide a very flexible tool for representing arbitrary collections—lists of files in a folder, employees in a company, emails in your inbox, and so on.

Sequence Operations

Because they are sequences, lists support all the sequence operations we discussed for strings; the only difference is that the results are usually lists instead of strings. For instance, given a three-item list:

```
>>> L = [123, 'spam', 1.23]          # A list of three different-type objects
>>> len(L)                           # Number of items in the list
3
```

we can index, slice, and so on, just as for strings:

```
>>> L[0]                             # Indexing by position
123
>>> L[:-1]                           # Slicing a list returns a new list
[123, 'spam']

>>> L + [4, 5, 6]                    # Concat/repeat make new lists too
[123, 'spam', 1.23, 4, 5, 6]
>>> L * 2
[123, 'spam', 1.23, 123, 'spam', 1.23]

>>> L                                # We're not changing the original list
[123, 'spam', 1.23]
```

Type-Specific Operations

Python's lists may be reminiscent of *arrays* in other languages, but they tend to be more powerful. For one thing, they have no fixed *type* constraint—the list we just looked at, for example, contains three objects of completely different types (an integer, a string, and a floating-point number). Further, lists have no fixed *size*. That is, they can grow and shrink on demand, in response to list-specific operations:

```
>>> L.append('NI')                   # Growing: add object at end of list
>>> L
[123, 'spam', 1.23, 'NI']

>>> L.pop(2)                         # Shrinking: delete an item in the middle
1.23
>>> L                                # "del L[2]" deletes from a list too
[123, 'spam', 'NI']
```

Here, the list **append** method expands the list's size and inserts an item at the end; the **pop** method (or an equivalent **del** statement) then removes an item at a given offset, causing the list to shrink. Other list methods insert an item at an arbitrary position (**insert**), remove a given item by value (**remove**), add multiple items at the end (**extend**), and so on. Because lists are mutable, most list methods also change the list object in place, instead of creating a new one:

```
>>> M = ['bb', 'aa', 'cc']
>>> M.sort()
>>> M
['aa', 'bb', 'cc']
>>> M.reverse()
>>> M
['cc', 'bb', 'aa']
```

The list **sort** method here, for example, orders the list in ascending fashion by default, and **reverse** reverses it—in both cases, the methods modify the list directly.

Bounds Checking

Although lists have no fixed size, Python still doesn't allow us to reference items that are not present. Indexing off the end of a list is always a mistake, but so is assigning off the end:

```
>>> L
[123, 'spam', 'NI']

>>> L[99]
...error text omitted...
IndexError: list index out of range

>>> L[99] = 1
...error text omitted...
IndexError: list assignment index out of range
```

This is intentional, as it's usually an error to try to assign off the end of a list (and a particularly nasty one in the C language, which doesn't do as much error checking as Python). Rather than silently growing the list in response, Python reports an error. To grow a list, we call list methods such as **append** instead.

Nesting

One nice feature of Python's core data types is that they support arbitrary *nesting*—we can nest them in any combination, and as deeply as we like. For example, we can have a list that contains a dictionary, which contains another list, and so on. One immediate application of this feature is to represent matrixes, or "multidimensional arrays" in Python. A list with nested lists will do the job for basic applications (you'll get "..." continuation-line prompts on lines 2 and 3 of the following in some interfaces, but not in IDLE):

```
>>> M = [[1, 2, 3],              # A 3 × 3 matrix, as nested lists
         [4, 5, 6],              # Code can span lines if bracketed
         [7, 8, 9]]
>>> M
[[1, 2, 3], [4, 5, 6], [7, 8, 9]]
```

Here, we've coded a list that contains three other lists. The effect is to represent a 3 × 3 matrix of numbers. Such a structure can be accessed in a variety of ways:

```
>>> M[1]                         # Get row 2
[4, 5, 6]

>>> M[1][2]                      # Get row 2, then get item 3 within the row
6
```

The first operation here fetches the entire second row, and the second grabs the third item within that row (it runs left to right, like the earlier string strip and split). Stringing together index operations takes us deeper and deeper into our nested-object structure.[3]

Comprehensions

In addition to sequence operations and list methods, Python includes a more advanced operation known as a *list comprehension expression*, which turns out to be a powerful way to process structures like our matrix. Suppose, for instance, that we need to extract the second column of our sample matrix. It's easy to grab rows by simple indexing because the matrix is stored by rows, but it's almost as easy to get a column with a list comprehension:

```
>>> col2 = [row[1] for row in M]     # Collect the items in column 2
>>> col2
[2, 5, 8]

>>> M                                # The matrix is unchanged
[[1, 2, 3], [4, 5, 6], [7, 8, 9]]
```

List comprehensions derive from set notation; they are a way to build a new list by running an expression on each item in a sequence, one at a time, from left to right. List comprehensions are coded in square brackets (to tip you off to the fact that they make a list) and are composed of an expression and a looping construct that share a variable name (row, here). The preceding list comprehension means basically what it says: "Give me row[1] for each row in matrix M, in a new list." The result is a new list containing column 2 of the matrix.

List comprehensions can be more complex in practice:

---

3. This matrix structure works for small-scale tasks, but for more serious number crunching you will probably want to use one of the numeric extensions to Python, such as the open source *NumPy* and *SciPy* systems. Such tools can store and process large matrixes much more efficiently than our nested list structure. NumPy has been said to turn Python into the equivalent of a free and more powerful version of the Matlab system, and organizations such as NASA, Los Alamos, JPL, and many others use this tool for scientific and financial tasks. Search the Web for more details.

```
>>> [row[1] + 1 for row in M]              # Add 1 to each item in column 2
[3, 6, 9]

>>> [row[1] for row in M if row[1] % 2 == 0]   # Filter out odd items
[2, 8]
```

The first operation here, for instance, adds 1 to each item as it is collected, and the second uses an `if` clause to filter odd numbers out of the result using the `%` modulus expression (remainder of division). List comprehensions make new lists of results, but they can be used to iterate over any *iterable* object—a term we'll flesh out later in this preview. Here, for instance, we use list comprehensions to step over a hardcoded list of coordinates and a string:

```
>>> diag = [M[i][i] for i in [0, 1, 2]]     # Collect a diagonal from matrix
>>> diag
[1, 5, 9]

>>> doubles = [c * 2 for c in 'spam']        # Repeat characters in a string
>>> doubles
['ss', 'pp', 'aa', 'mm']
```

These expressions can also be used to collect multiple values, as long as we wrap those values in a nested collection. The following illustrates using `range`—a built-in that generates successive integers, and requires a surrounding `list` to display all its values in 3.X only (2.X makes a physical list all at once):

```
>>> list(range(4))                          # 0..3 (list() required in 3.X)
[0, 1, 2, 3]
>>> list(range(-6, 7, 2))                    # -6 to +6 by 2 (need list() in 3.X)
[-6, -4, -2, 0, 2, 4, 6]

>>> [[x ** 2, x ** 3] for x in range(4)]     # Multiple values, "if" filters
[[0, 0], [1, 1], [4, 8], [9, 27]]
>>> [[x, x / 2, x * 2] for x in range(-6, 7, 2) if x > 0]
[[2, 1, 4], [4, 2, 8], [6, 3, 12]]
```

As you can probably tell, list comprehensions, and relatives like the `map` and `filter` built-in functions, are too involved to cover more formally in this preview chapter. The main point of this brief introduction is to illustrate that Python includes both simple and advanced tools in its arsenal. List comprehensions are an optional feature, but they tend to be very useful in practice and often provide a substantial processing speed advantage. They also work on any type that is a sequence in Python, as well as some types that are not. You'll hear much more about them later in this book.

As a preview, though, you'll find that in recent Pythons, comprehension syntax has been generalized for other roles: it's not just for making lists today. For example, enclosing a comprehension in *parentheses* can also be used to create *generators* that produce results on demand. To illustrate, the `sum` built-in sums items in a sequence—in this example, summing all items in our matrix's rows on request:

```
>>> G = (sum(row) for row in M)             # Create a generator of row sums
>>> next(G)                                  # iter(G) not required here
```

```
6
>>> next(G)                                    # Run the iteration protocol next()
15
>>> next(G)
24
```

The map built-in can do similar work, by generating the results of running items through a function, one at a time and on request. Like range, wrapping it in list forces it to return all its values in Python 3.X; this isn't needed in 2.X where map makes a list of results all at once instead, and is not needed in other contexts that iterate automatically, unless multiple scans or list-like behavior is also required:

```
>>> list(map(sum, M))                          # Map sum over items in M
[6, 15, 24]
```

In Python 2.7 and 3.X, comprehension syntax can also be used to create *sets* and *dictionaries*:

```
>>> {sum(row) for row in M}                    # Create a set of row sums
{24, 6, 15}

>>> {i : sum(M[i]) for i in range(3)}          # Creates key/value table of row sums
{0: 6, 1: 15, 2: 24}
```

In fact, lists, sets, dictionaries, and generators can all be built with comprehensions in 3.X and 2.7:

```
>>> [ord(x) for x in 'spaam']                  # List of character ordinals
[115, 112, 97, 97, 109]
>>> {ord(x) for x in 'spaam'}                  # Sets remove duplicates
{112, 97, 115, 109}
>>> {x: ord(x) for x in 'spaam'}               # Dictionary keys are unique
{'p': 112, 'a': 97, 's': 115, 'm': 109}
>>> (ord(x) for x in 'spaam')                  # Generator of values
<generator object <genexpr> at 0x000000000254DAB0>
```

To understand objects like generators, sets, and dictionaries, though, we must move ahead.

Dictionaries

Python dictionaries are something completely different (Monty Python reference intended)—they are not sequences at all, but are instead known as *mappings*. Mappings are also collections of other objects, but they store objects by *key* instead of by relative position. In fact, mappings don't maintain any reliable left-to-right order; they simply map keys to associated values. Dictionaries, the only mapping type in Python's core objects set, are also *mutable*: like lists, they may be changed in place and can grow and shrink on demand. Also like lists, they are a flexible tool for representing collections, but their more *mnemonic* keys are better suited when a collection's items are named or labeled—fields of a database record, for example.

Mapping Operations

When written as literals, dictionaries are coded in curly braces and consist of a series of "key: value" pairs. Dictionaries are useful anytime we need to associate a set of values with keys—to describe the properties of something, for instance. As an example, consider the following three-item dictionary (with keys "food," "quantity," and "color," perhaps the details of a hypothetical menu item?):

```
>>> D = {'food': 'Spam', 'quantity': 4, 'color': 'pink'}
```

We can index this dictionary by key to fetch and change the keys' associated values. The dictionary index operation uses the same syntax as that used for sequences, but the item in the square brackets is a key, not a relative position:

```
>>> D['food']              # Fetch value of key 'food'
'Spam'

>>> D['quantity'] += 1     # Add 1 to 'quantity' value
>>> D
{'color': 'pink', 'food': 'Spam', 'quantity': 5}
```

Although the curly-braces literal form does see use, it is perhaps more common to see dictionaries built up in different ways (it's rare to know all your program's data before your program runs). The following code, for example, starts with an empty dictionary and fills it out one key at a time. Unlike out-of-bounds assignments in lists, which are forbidden, assignments to new dictionary keys create those keys:

```
>>> D = {}
>>> D['name'] = 'Bob'      # Create keys by assignment
>>> D['job']  = 'dev'
>>> D['age']  = 40

>>> D
{'age': 40, 'job': 'dev', 'name': 'Bob'}

>>> print(D['name'])
Bob
```

Here, we're effectively using dictionary keys as field names in a record that describes someone. In other applications, dictionaries can also be used to replace searching operations—indexing a dictionary by key is often the fastest way to code a search in Python.

As we'll learn later, we can also make dictionaries by passing to the **dict** type name either *keyword arguments* (a special *name=value* syntax in function calls), or the result of *zipping* together sequences of keys and values obtained at runtime (e.g., from files). Both the following make the same dictionary as the prior example and its equivalent {} literal form, though the first tends to make for less typing:

```
>>> bob1 = dict(name='Bob', job='dev', age=40)            # Keywords
>>> bob1
{'age': 40, 'name': 'Bob', 'job': 'dev'}
```

```
>>> bob2 = dict(zip(['name', 'job', 'age'], ['Bob', 'dev', 40]))    # Zipping
>>> bob2
{'job': 'dev', 'name': 'Bob', 'age': 40}
```

Notice how the left-to-right order of dictionary keys is *scrambled*. Mappings are not positionally ordered, so unless you're lucky, they'll come back in a different order than you typed them. The exact order may vary per Python, but you shouldn't depend on it, and shouldn't expect yours to match that in this book.

Nesting Revisited

In the prior example, we used a dictionary to describe a hypothetical person, with three keys. Suppose, though, that the information is more complex. Perhaps we need to record a first name and a last name, along with multiple job titles. This leads to another application of Python's object nesting in action. The following dictionary, coded all at once as a literal, captures more structured information:

```
>>> rec = {'name': {'first': 'Bob', 'last': 'Smith'},
           'jobs': ['dev', 'mgr'],
           'age':  40.5}
```

Here, we again have a three-key dictionary at the top (keys "name," "jobs," and "age"), but the values have become more complex: a nested dictionary for the name to support multiple parts, and a nested list for the jobs to support multiple roles and future expansion. We can access the components of this structure much as we did for our list-based matrix earlier, but this time most indexes are dictionary keys, not list offsets:

```
>>> rec['name']                            # 'name' is a nested dictionary
{'last': 'Smith', 'first': 'Bob'}

>>> rec['name']['last']                    # Index the nested dictionary
'Smith'

>>> rec['jobs']                            # 'jobs' is a nested list
['dev', 'mgr']
>>> rec['jobs'][-1]                        # Index the nested list
'mgr'

>>> rec['jobs'].append('janitor')          # Expand Bob's job description in place
>>> rec
{'age': 40.5, 'jobs': ['dev', 'mgr', 'janitor'], 'name': {'last': 'Smith',
'first': 'Bob'}}
```

Notice how the last operation here expands the nested jobs list—because the jobs list is a separate piece of memory from the dictionary that contains it, it can grow and shrink freely (object memory layout will be discussed further later in this book).

The real reason for showing you this example is to demonstrate the *flexibility* of Python's core data types. As you can see, nesting allows us to build up complex information structures directly and easily. Building a similar structure in a low-level language like C would be tedious and require much more code: we would have to lay out and declare structures and arrays, fill out values, link everything together, and so on. In Python, this is all automatic—running the expression creates the entire nested object structure for us. In fact, this is one of the main benefits of scripting languages like Python.

Just as importantly, in a lower-level language we would have to be careful to clean up all of the object's space when we no longer need it. In Python, when we lose the last reference to the object—by assigning its variable to something else, for example—all of the memory space occupied by that object's structure is automatically cleaned up for us:

```
>>> rec = 0                          # Now the object's space is reclaimed
```

Technically speaking, Python has a feature known as *garbage collection* that cleans up unused memory as your program runs and frees you from having to manage such details in your code. In standard Python (a.k.a. CPython), the space is reclaimed immediately, as soon as the last reference to an object is removed. We'll study how this works later in Chapter 6; for now, it's enough to know that you can use objects freely, without worrying about creating their space or cleaning up as you go.

Also watch for a record structure similar to the one we just coded in Chapter 8, Chapter 9, and Chapter 27, where we'll use it to compare and contrast lists, dictionaries, tuples, named tuples, and classes—an array of data structure options with tradeoffs we'll cover in full later.[4]

Missing Keys: if Tests

As mappings, dictionaries support accessing items by key only, with the sorts of operations we've just seen. In addition, though, they also support type-specific operations with *method* calls that are useful in a variety of common use cases. For example, although we can assign to a new key to expand a dictionary, fetching a nonexistent key is still a mistake:

```
>>> D = {'a': 1, 'b': 2, 'c': 3}
>>> D
```

---

4. Two application notes here. First, as a preview, the `rec` record we just created really could be an actual database record, when we employ Python's *object persistence* system—an easy way to store native Python objects in simple files or access-by-key databases, which translates objects to and from serial byte streams automatically. We won't go into details here, but watch for coverage of Python's `pickle` and `shelve` persistence modules in Chapter 9, Chapter 28, Chapter 31, and Chapter 37, where we'll explore them in the context of files, an OOP use case, classes, and 3.X changes, respectively.

Second, if you are familiar with *JSON* (JavaScript Object Notation)—an emerging data-interchange format used for databases and network transfers—this example may also look curiously similar, though Python's support for variables, arbitrary expressions, and changes can make its data structures more general. Python's `json` library module supports creating and parsing JSON text, but the translation to Python objects is often trivial. Watch for a JSON example that uses this record in Chapter 9 when we study files. For a larger use case, see *MongoDB*, which stores data using a language-neutral binary-encoded serialization of JSON-like documents, and its *PyMongo* interface.

```
{'a': 1, 'c': 3, 'b': 2}

>>> D['e'] = 99                              # Assigning new keys grows dictionaries
>>> D
{'a': 1, 'c': 3, 'b': 2, 'e': 99}

>>> D['f']                                   # Referencing a nonexistent key is an error
...error text omitted...
KeyError: 'f'
```

This is what we want—it's usually a programming error to fetch something that isn't really there. But in some generic programs, we can't always know what keys will be present when we write our code. How do we handle such cases and avoid errors? One solution is to test ahead of time. The dictionary in membership expression allows us to query the existence of a key and branch on the result with a Python if statement. In the following, be sure to press Enter twice to run the if interactively after typing its code (as explained in Chapter 3, an empty line means "go" at the interactive prompt), and just as for the earlier multiline dictionaries and lists, the prompt changes to "..." on some interfaces for lines two and beyond:

```
>>> 'f' in D
False

>>> if not 'f' in D:                         # Python's sole selection statement
        print('missing')

missing
```

This book has more to say about the if statement in later chapters, but the form we're using here is straightforward: it consists of the word if, followed by an expression that is interpreted as a true or false result, followed by a block of code to run if the test is true. In its full form, the if statement can also have an else clause for a default case, and one or more elif ("else if") clauses for other tests. It's the main *selection* statement tool in Python; along with both its ternary if/else expression cousin (which we'll meet in a moment) and the if comprehension filter lookalike we saw earlier, it's the way we code the logic of choices and decisions in our scripts.

If you've used some other programming languages in the past, you might be wondering how Python knows when the if statement ends. I'll explain Python's syntax rules in depth in later chapters, but in short, if you have more than one action to run in a statement block, you simply indent all their statements the same way—this both promotes readable code and reduces the number of characters you have to type:

```
>>> if not 'f' in D:
        print('missing')
        print('no, really...')               # Statement blocks are indented

missing
no, really...
```

Besides the `in` test, there are a variety of ways to avoid accessing nonexistent keys in the dictionaries we create: the `get` method, a conditional index with a default; the Python 2.X has_key method, an `in` work-alike that is no longer available in 3.X; the `try` statement, a tool we'll first meet in Chapter 10 that catches and recovers from exceptions altogether; and the `if/else` ternary (three-part) expression, which is essentially an `if` statement squeezed onto a single line. Here are a few examples:

```
>>> value = D.get('x', 0)                # Index but with a default
>>> value
0
>>> value = D['x'] if 'x' in D else 0    # if/else expression form
>>> value
0
```

We'll save the details on such alternatives until a later chapter. For now, let's turn to another dictionary method's role in a common use case.

Sorting Keys: for Loops

As mentioned earlier, because dictionaries are not sequences, they don't maintain any dependable left-to-right order. If we make a dictionary and print it back, its keys may come back in a different order than that in which we typed them, and may vary per Python version and other variables:

```
>>> D = {'a': 1, 'b': 2, 'c': 3}
>>> D
{'a': 1, 'c': 3, 'b': 2}
```

What do we do, though, if we do need to impose an ordering on a dictionary's items? One common solution is to grab a list of keys with the dictionary `keys` method, sort that with the list `sort` method, and then step through the result with a Python `for` loop (as for `if`, be sure to press the Enter key twice after coding the following `for` loop, and omit the outer parenthesis in the `print` in Python 2.X):

```
>>> Ks = list(D.keys())             # Unordered keys list
>>> Ks                              # A list in 2.X, "view" in 3.X: use list()
['a', 'c', 'b']

>>> Ks.sort()                       # Sorted keys list
>>> Ks
['a', 'b', 'c']

>>> for key in Ks:                  # Iterate though sorted keys
        print(key, '=>', D[key])    # <== press Enter twice here (3.X print)

a => 1
b => 2
c => 3
```

This is a three-step process, although, as we'll see in later chapters, in recent versions of Python it can be done in one step with the newer `sorted` built-in function. The `sorted` call returns the result and sorts a variety of object types, in this case sorting dictionary keys automatically:

```
>>> D
{'a': 1, 'c': 3, 'b': 2}

>>> for key in sorted(D):
        print(key, '=>', D[key])

a => 1
b => 2
c => 3
```

Besides showcasing dictionaries, this use case serves to introduce the Python `for` loop. The `for` loop is a simple and efficient way to step through all the items in a sequence and run a block of code for each item in turn. A user-defined loop variable (`key`, here) is used to reference the current item each time through. The net effect in our example is to print the unordered dictionary's keys and values, in sorted-key order.

The `for` loop, and its more general colleague the `while` loop, are the main ways we code *repetitive* tasks as statements in our scripts. Really, though, the `for` loop, like its relative the list comprehension introduced earlier, is a sequence operation. It works on any object that is a sequence and, like the list comprehension, even on some things that are not. Here, for example, it is stepping across the characters in a string, printing the uppercase version of each as it goes:

```
>>> for c in 'spam':
        print(c.upper())

S
P
A
M
```

Python's `while` loop is a more general sort of looping tool; it's not limited to stepping across sequences, but generally requires more code to do so:

```
>>> x = 4
>>> while x > 0:
        print('spam!' * x)
        x -= 1

spam!spam!spam!spam!
spam!spam!spam!
spam!spam!
spam!
```

We'll discuss looping statements, syntax, and tools in depth later in the book. First, though, I need to confess that this section has not been as forthcoming as it might have been. Really, the `for` loop, and all its cohorts that step through objects from left to right, are not just *sequence* operations, they are *iterable* operations—as the next section describes.

Iteration and Optimization

If the last section's `for` loop looks like the list comprehension expression introduced earlier, it should: both are really general iteration tools. In fact, both will work on any iterable object that follows the iteration protocol—pervasive ideas in Python that underlie all its iteration tools.

In a nutshell, an object is *iterable* if it is either a physically stored sequence in memory, or an object that generates one item at a time in the context of an iteration operation —a sort of "virtual" sequence. More formally, both types of objects are considered iterable because they support the *iteration protocol*—they respond to the `iter` call with an object that advances in response to `next` calls and raises an exception when finished producing values.

The *generator* comprehension expression we saw earlier is such an object: its values aren't stored in memory all at once, but are produced as requested, usually by iteration tools. Python *file objects* similarly iterate line by line when used by an iteration tool: file content isn't in a list, it's fetched on demand. Both are iterable objects in Python— a category that expands in 3.X to include core tools like `range` and `map`. By deferring results as needed, these tools can both save memory and minimize delays.

I'll have more to say about the iteration protocol later in this book. For now, keep in mind that every Python tool that scans an object from left to right uses the iteration protocol. This is why the `sorted` call used in the prior section works on the dictionary directly—we don't have to call the `keys` method to get a sequence because dictionaries are iterable objects, with a `next` that returns successive keys.

It may also help you to see that any list comprehension expression, such as this one, which computes the squares of a list of numbers:

```
>>> squares = [x ** 2 for x in [1, 2, 3, 4, 5]]
>>> squares
[1, 4, 9, 16, 25]
```

can always be coded as an equivalent `for` loop that builds the result list manually by appending as it goes:

```
>>> squares = []
>>> for x in [1, 2, 3, 4, 5]:        # This is what a list comprehension does
        squares.append(x ** 2)       # Both run the iteration protocol internally

>>> squares
[1, 4, 9, 16, 25]
```

Both tools leverage the iteration protocol internally and produce the same result. The list comprehension, though, and related functional programming tools like `map` and `filter`, will often run faster than a `for` loop today on some types of code (perhaps even twice as fast)—a property that could matter in your programs for large data sets. Having said that, though, I should point out that performance measures are tricky business in Python because it optimizes so much, and they may vary from release to release.

A major rule of thumb in Python is to code for simplicity and readability first and worry about performance later, after your program is working, and after you've proved that there is a genuine performance concern. More often than not, your code will be quick enough as it is. If you do need to tweak code for performance, though, Python includes tools to help you out, including the `time` and `timeit` modules for timing the speed of alternatives, and the `profile` module for isolating bottlenecks.

You'll find more on these later in this book (see especially Chapter 21's benchmarking case study) and in the Python manuals. For the sake of this preview, let's move ahead to the next core data type.

Tuples

The tuple object (pronounced "toople" or "tuhple," depending on whom you ask) is roughly like a list that cannot be changed—tuples are *sequences*, like lists, but they are *immutable*, like strings. Functionally, they're used to represent fixed collections of items: the components of a specific calendar date, for instance. Syntactically, they are normally coded in parentheses instead of square brackets, and they support arbitrary types, arbitrary nesting, and the usual sequence operations:

```
>>> T = (1, 2, 3, 4)          # A 4-item tuple
>>> len(T)                    # Length
4

>> T + (5, 6)                 # Concatenation
(1, 2, 3, 4, 5, 6)

>>> T[0]                      # Indexing, slicing, and more
1
```

Tuples also have type-specific callable methods as of Python 2.6 and 3.0, but not nearly as many as lists:

```
>>> T.index(4)                # Tuple methods: 4 appears at offset 3
3
>>> T.count(4)                # 4 appears once
1
```

The primary distinction for tuples is that they cannot be changed once created. That is, they are immutable sequences (one-item tuples like the one here require a trailing comma):

```
>>> T[0] = 2                  # Tuples are immutable
...error text omitted...
TypeError: 'tuple' object does not support item assignment

>>> T = (2,) + T[1:]          # Make a new tuple for a new value
>>> T
(2, 2, 3, 4)
```

Like lists and dictionaries, tuples support mixed types and nesting, but they don't grow and shrink because they are immutable (the parentheses enclosing a tuple's items can often be omitted, as done here; in contexts where commas don't otherwise matter, the commas are what actually builds a tuple):

```
>>> T = 'spam', 3.0, [11, 22, 33]
>>> T[1]
3.0
>>> T[2][1]
22
>>> T.append(4)
AttributeError: 'tuple' object has no attribute 'append'
```

Why Tuples?

So, why have a type that is like a list, but supports fewer operations? Frankly, tuples are not generally used as often as lists in practice, but their immutability is the whole point. If you pass a collection of objects around your program as a list, it can be changed anywhere; if you use a tuple, it cannot. That is, tuples provide a sort of integrity constraint that is convenient in programs larger than those we'll write here. We'll talk more about tuples later in the book, including an extension that builds upon them called *named tuples*. For now, though, let's jump ahead to our last major core type: the file.

Files

File objects are Python code's main interface to external files on your computer. They can be used to read and write text memos, audio clips, Excel documents, saved email messages, and whatever else you happen to have stored on your machine. Files are a core type, but they're something of an oddball—there is no specific literal syntax for creating them. Rather, to create a file object, you call the built-in open function, passing in an external filename and an optional processing mode as strings.

For example, to create a text output file, you would pass in its name and the 'w' processing mode string to write data:

```
>>> f = open('data.txt', 'w')    # Make a new file in output mode ('w' is write)
>>> f.write('Hello\n')           # Write strings of characters to it
6
>>> f.write('world\n')           # Return number of items written in Python 3.X
6
>>> f.close()                    # Close to flush output buffers to disk
```

This creates a file in the current directory and writes text to it (the filename can be a full directory path if you need to access a file elsewhere on your computer). To read back what you just wrote, reopen the file in 'r' processing mode, for reading text input —this is the default if you omit the mode in the call. Then read the file's content into a string, and display it. A file's contents are always a string in your script, regardless of the type of data the file contains:

```
>>> f = open('data.txt')          # 'r' (read) is the default processing mode
>>> text = f.read()               # Read entire file into a string
>>> text
'Hello\nworld\n'

>>> print(text)                   # print interprets control characters
Hello
world

>>> text.split()                  # File content is always a string
['Hello', 'world']
```

Other file object methods support additional features we don't have time to cover here. For instance, file objects provide more ways of reading and writing (read accepts an optional maximum byte/character size, readline reads one line at a time, and so on), as well as other tools (seek moves to a new file position). As we'll see later, though, the best way to read a file today is to *not read it at all*—files provide an *iterator* that automatically reads line by line in for loops and other contexts:

```
>>> for line in open('data.txt'): print(line)
```

We'll meet the full set of file methods later in this book, but if you want a quick preview now, run a dir call on any open file and a help on any of the method names that come back:

```
>>> dir(f)
[ ...many names omitted...
'buffer', 'close', 'closed', 'detach', 'encoding', 'errors', 'fileno', 'flush',
'isatty', 'line_buffering', 'mode', 'name', 'newlines', 'read', 'readable',
'readline', 'readlines', 'seek', 'seekable', 'tell', 'truncate', 'writable',
'write', 'writelines']

>>>help(f.seek)
...try it and see...
```

Binary Bytes Files

The prior section's examples illustrate file basics that suffice for many roles. Technically, though, they rely on either the platform's Unicode encoding default in Python 3.X, or the 8-bit byte nature of files in Python 2.X. Text files always encode strings in 3.X, and blindly write string content in 2.X. This is irrelevant for the simple ASCII data used previously, which maps to and from file bytes unchanged. But for richer types of data, file interfaces can vary depending on both content and the Python line you use.

As hinted when we met strings earlier, Python 3.X draws a sharp distinction between text and binary data in files: *text files* represent content as normal str strings and perform Unicode encoding and decoding automatically when writing and reading data, while *binary files* represent content as a special bytes string and allow you to access file content unaltered. Python 2.X supports the same dichotomy, but doesn't impose it as rigidly, and its tools differ.

For example, *binary files* are useful for processing media, accessing data created by C programs, and so on. To illustrate, Python's `struct` module can both create and unpack packed *binary data*—raw bytes that record values that are not Python objects—to be written to a file in binary mode. We'll study this technique in detail later in the book, but the concept is simple: the following creates a binary file in Python 3.X (binary files work the same in 2.X, but the "b" string literal prefix isn't required and won't be displayed):

```
>>> import struct
>>> packed = struct.pack('>i4sh', 7, b'spam', 8)    # Create packed binary data
>>> packed                                          # 10 bytes, not objects or text
b'\x00\x00\x00\x07spam\x00\x08'
>>>
>>> file = open('data.bin', 'wb')                   # Open binary output file
>>> file.write(packed)                              # Write packed binary data
10
>>> file.close()
```

Reading binary data back is essentially symmetric; not all programs need to tread so deeply into the low-level realm of bytes, but binary files make this easy in Python:

```
>>> data = open('data.bin', 'rb').read()            # Open/read binary data file
>>> data                                            # 10 bytes, unaltered
b'\x00\x00\x00\x07spam\x00\x08'
>>> data[4:8]                                       # Slice bytes in the middle
b'spam'
>>> list(data)                                      # A sequence of 8-bit bytes
[0, 0, 0, 7, 115, 112, 97, 109, 0, 8]
>>> struct.unpack('>i4sh', data)                    # Unpack into objects again
(7, b'spam', 8)
```

Unicode Text Files

Text files are used to process all sorts of text-based data, from memos to email content to JSON and XML documents. In today's broader interconnected world, though, we can't really talk about text without also asking "what kind?"—you must also know the text's Unicode encoding type if either it differs from your platform's default, or you can't rely on that default for data portability reasons.

Luckily, this is easier than it may sound. To access files containing non-ASCII *Unicode text* of the sort introduced earlier in this chapter, we simply pass in an encoding name if the text in the file doesn't match the default encoding for our platform. In this mode, Python text files automatically *encode* on writes and *decode* on reads per the encoding scheme name you provide. In *Python 3.X*:

```
>>> S = 'sp\xc4m'                                   # Non-ASCII Unicode text
>>> S
'spÄm'
>>> S[2]                                            # Sequence of characters
'Ä'

>>> file = open('unidata.txt', 'w', encoding='utf-8')   # Write/encode UTF-8 text
```

```
>>> file.write(S)                                       # 4 characters written
4
>>> file.close()

>>> text = open('unidata.txt', encoding='utf-8').read()   # Read/decode UTF-8 text
>>> text
'spÄm'
>>> len(text)                                           # 4 chars (code points)
4
```

This automatic encoding and decoding is what you normally want. Because files handle this on transfers, you may process text in memory as a simple string of characters without concern for its Unicode-encoded origins. If needed, though, you can also see what's truly stored in your file by stepping into binary mode:

```
>>> raw = open('unidata.txt', 'rb').read()              # Read raw encoded bytes
>>> raw
b'sp\xc3\x84m'
>>> len(raw)                                             # Really 5 bytes in UTF-8
5
```

You can also encode and decode manually if you get Unicode data from a source other than a file—parsed from an email message or fetched over a network connection, for example:

```
>>> text.encode('utf-8')                                # Manual encode to bytes
b'sp\xc3\x84m'
>>> raw.decode('utf-8')                                 # Manual decode to str
'spÄm'
```

This is also useful to see how text files would automatically encode the same string differently under different encoding names, and provides a way to translate data to different encodings—it's different bytes in files, but decodes to the same string in memory if you provide the proper encoding name:

```
>>> text.encode('latin-1')                              # Bytes differ in others
b'sp\xc4m'
>>> text.encode('utf-16')
b'\xff\xfes\x00p\x00\xc4\x00m\x00'

>>> len(text.encode('latin-1')), len(text.encode('utf-16'))
(4, 10)

>>> b'\xff\xfes\x00p\x00\xc4\x00m\x00'.decode('utf-16')   # But same string decoded
'spÄm'
```

This all works more or less the same in *Python 2.X*, but Unicode strings are coded and display with a leading "u," byte strings don't require or show a leading "b," and Unicode text files must be opened with codecs.open, which accepts an encoding name just like 3.X's open, and uses the special unicode string to represent content in memory. Binary file mode may seem optional in 2.X since normal files are just byte-based data, but it's required to avoid changing line ends if present (more on this later in the book):

```
>>> import codecs
>>> codecs.open('unidata.txt', encoding='utf8').read()     # 2.X: read/decode text
u'sp\xc4m'
>>> open('unidata.txt', 'rb').read()                        # 2.X: read raw bytes
'sp\xc3\x84m'
>>> open('unidata.txt').read()                              # 2.X: raw/undecoded too
'sp\xc3\x84m'
```

Although you won't generally need to care about this distinction if you deal only with
ASCII text, Python's strings and files are an asset if you deal with either binary data
(which includes most types of media) or text in internationalized character sets (which
includes most content on the Web and Internet at large today). Python also supports
non-ASCII file *names* (not just content), but it's largely automatic; tools such as walkers
and listers offer more control when needed, though we'll defer further details until
Chapter 37.

Other File-Like Tools

The open function is the workhorse for most file processing you will do in Python. For
more advanced tasks, though, Python comes with additional file-like tools: pipes,
FIFOs, sockets, keyed-access files, persistent object shelves, descriptor-based files, relational and object-oriented database interfaces, and more. Descriptor files, for instance, support file locking and other low-level tools, and sockets provide an interface
for networking and interprocess communication. We won't cover many of these topics
in this book, but you'll find them useful once you start programming Python in earnest.

Other Core Types

Beyond the core types we've seen so far, there are others that may or may not qualify
for membership in the category, depending on how broadly it is defined. *Sets*, for example, are a recent addition to the language that are neither mappings nor sequences;
rather, they are unordered collections of unique and immutable objects. You create sets
by calling the built-in set function or using new set literals and expressions in 3.X and
2.7, and they support the usual mathematical set operations (the choice of new {...}
syntax for set literals makes sense, since sets are much like the keys of a valueless dictionary):

```
>>> X = set('spam')                      # Make a set out of a sequence in 2.X and 3.X
>>> Y = {'h', 'a', 'm'}                   # Make a set with set literals in 3.X and 2.7

>>> X, Y                                  # A tuple of two sets without parentheses
({'m', 'a', 'p', 's'}, {'m', 'a', 'h'})

>>> X & Y                                 # Intersection
{'m', 'a'}
>>> X | Y                                 # Union
{'m', 'h', 'a', 'p', 's'}
>>> X - Y                                 # Difference
```

```
{'p', 's'}
>>> X > Y                              # Superset
False

>>> {n ** 2 for n in [1, 2, 3, 4]}   # Set comprehensions in 3.X and 2.7
{16, 1, 4, 9}
```

Even less mathematically inclined programmers often find sets useful for common tasks such as filtering out duplicates, isolating differences, and performing order-neutral equality tests without sorting—in lists, strings, and all other iterable objects:

```
>>> list(set([1, 2, 1, 3, 1]))      # Filtering out duplicates (possibly reordered)
[1, 2, 3]
>>> set('spam') - set('ham')        # Finding differences in collections
{'p', 's'}
>>> set('spam') == set('asmp')      # Order-neutral equality ('spam'=='asmp' False)
True
```

Sets also support in membership tests, though all other collection types in Python do too:

```
>>> 'p' in set('spam'), 'p' in 'spam', 'ham' in ['eggs', 'spam', 'ham']
(True, True, True)
```

In addition, Python recently grew a few new numeric types: *decimal* numbers, which are fixed-precision floating-point numbers, and *fraction* numbers, which are rational numbers with both a numerator and a denominator. Both can be used to work around the limitations and inherent inaccuracies of floating-point math:

```
>>> 1 / 3                            # Floating-point (add a .0 in Python 2.X)
0.3333333333333333
>>> (2/3) + (1/2)
1.1666666666666665

>>> import decimal                   # Decimals: fixed precision
>>> d = decimal.Decimal('3.141')
>>> d + 1
Decimal('4.141')

>>> decimal.getcontext().prec = 2
>>> decimal.Decimal('1.00') / decimal.Decimal('3.00')
Decimal('0.33')

>>> from fractions import Fraction   # Fractions: numerator+denominator
>>> f = Fraction(2, 3)
>>> f + 1
Fraction(5, 3)
>>> f + Fraction(1, 2)
Fraction(7, 6)
```

Python also comes with *Booleans* (with predefined True and False objects that are essentially just the integers 1 and 0 with custom display logic), and it has long supported a special placeholder object called None commonly used to initialize names and objects:

```
>>> 1 > 2, 1 < 2                        # Booleans
(False, True)
>>> bool('spam')                        # Object's Boolean value
True

>>> X = None                            # None placeholder
>>> print(X)
None
>>> L = [None] * 100                    # Initialize a list of 100 Nones
>>> L
[None, None, None, None, None, None, None, None, None, None, None, None,
None, None, None, None, None, None, None, ...a list of 100 Nones...]
```

How to Break Your Code's Flexibility

I'll have more to say about all of Python's object types later, but one merits special treatment here. The *type* object, returned by the **type** built-in function, is an object that gives the type of another object; its result differs slightly in 3.X, because types have merged with classes completely (something we'll explore in the context of "new-style" classes in Part VI). Assuming L is still the list of the prior section:

```
# In Python 2.X:
>>> type(L)                             # Types: type of L is list type object
<type 'list'>
>>> type(type(L))                       # Even types are objects
<type 'type'>

# In Python 3.X:
>>> type(L)                             # 3.X: types are classes, and vice versa
<class 'list'>
>>> type(type(L))                       # See Chapter 32 for more on class types
<class 'type'>
```

Besides allowing you to explore your objects interactively, the **type** object in its most practical application allows code to check the types of the objects it processes. In fact, there are at least three ways to do so in a Python script:

```
>>> if type(L) == type([]):            # Type testing, if you must...
        print('yes')

yes
>>> if type(L) == list:                # Using the type name
        print('yes')

yes
>>> if isinstance(L, list):            # Object-oriented tests
        print('yes')

yes
```

Now that I've shown you all these ways to do type testing, however, I am required by law to tell you that doing so is almost always the wrong thing to do in a Python program (and often a sign of an ex-C programmer first starting to use Python!). The reason why won't become completely clear until later in the book, when we start writing larger code units such as functions, but it's a (perhaps *the*) core Python concept. By checking for specific types in your code, you effectively break its flexibility—you limit it to working on just one type. Without such tests, your code may be able to work on a whole range of types.

This is related to the idea of *polymorphism* mentioned earlier, and it stems from Python's lack of type declarations. As you'll learn, in Python, we code to object *interfaces* (operations supported), not to types. That is, we care what an object *does*, not what it *is*. Not caring about specific types means that code is automatically applicable to many of them—any object with a compatible interface will work, regardless of its specific type. Although type checking is supported—and even required in some rare cases—you'll see that it's not usually the "Pythonic" way of thinking. In fact, you'll find that polymorphism is probably the key idea behind using Python well.

User-Defined Classes

We'll study *object-oriented programming* in Python—an optional but powerful feature of the language that cuts development time by supporting programming by customization—in depth later in this book. In abstract terms, though, classes define new types of objects that extend the core set, so they merit a passing glance here. Say, for example, that you wish to have a type of object that models employees. Although there is no such specific core type in Python, the following user-defined class might fit the bill:

```
>>> class Worker:
        def __init__(self, name, pay):      # Initialize when created
            self.name = name                 # self is the new object
            self.pay  = pay
        def lastName(self):
            return self.name.split()[-1]     # Split string on blanks
        def giveRaise(self, percent):
            self.pay *= (1.0 + percent)      # Update pay in place
```

This class defines a new kind of object that will have name and pay attributes (sometimes called *state information*), as well as two bits of behavior coded as functions (normally called *methods*). Calling the class like a function generates instances of our new type, and the class's methods automatically receive the instance being processed by a given method call (in the self argument):

```
>>> bob = Worker('Bob Smith', 50000)         # Make two instances
>>> sue = Worker('Sue Jones', 60000)         # Each has name and pay attrs
>>> bob.lastName()                           # Call method: bob is self
'Smith'
>>> sue.lastName()                           # sue is the self subject
'Jones'
>>> sue.giveRaise(.10)                       # Updates sue's pay
>>> sue.pay
66000.0
```

The implied "self" object is why we call this an *object-oriented* model: there is always an implied subject in functions within a class. In a sense, though, the class-based type simply builds on and uses core types—a user-defined Worker object here, for example, is just a collection of a string and a number (name and pay, respectively), plus functions for processing those two built-in objects.

The larger story of classes is that their inheritance mechanism supports software hierarchies that lend themselves to customization by *extension*. We extend software by writing new classes, not by changing what already works. You should also know that classes are an optional feature of Python, and simpler built-in types such as lists and dictionaries are often better tools than user-coded classes. This is all well beyond the bounds of our introductory object-type tutorial, though, so consider this just a preview; for full disclosure on user-defined types coded with classes, you'll have to read on. Because classes build upon other tools in Python, they are one of the major goals of this book's journey.

And Everything Else

As mentioned earlier, everything you can process in a Python script is a type of object, so our object type tour is necessarily incomplete. However, even though everything in Python is an "object," only those types of objects we've met so far are considered part of Python's core type set. Other types in Python either are objects related to program execution (like functions, modules, classes, and compiled code), which we will study later, or are implemented by imported module functions, not language syntax. The latter of these also tend to have application-specific roles—text patterns, database interfaces, network connections, and so on.

Moreover, keep in mind that the objects we've met here are objects, but not necessarily *object-oriented*—a concept that usually requires inheritance and the Python class statement, which we'll meet again later in this book. Still, Python's core objects are the workhorses of almost every Python script you're likely to meet, and they usually are the basis of larger noncore types.

Chapter Summary

And that's a wrap for our initial data type tour. This chapter has offered a brief introduction to Python's core object types and the sorts of operations we can apply to them. We've studied generic operations that work on many object types (sequence operations such as indexing and slicing, for example), as well as type-specific operations available as method calls (for instance, string splits and list appends). We've also defined some key terms, such as immutability, sequences, and polymorphism.

Along the way, we've seen that Python's core object types are more flexible and powerful than what is available in lower-level languages such as C. For instance, Python's lists and dictionaries obviate most of the work you do to support collections and searching in lower-level languages. Lists are ordered collections of other objects, and dictionaries are collections of other objects that are indexed by key instead of by position. Both dictionaries and lists may be nested, can grow and shrink on demand, and may contain objects of any type. Moreover, their space is automatically cleaned up as you go. We've also seen that strings and files work hand in hand to support a rich variety of binary and text data.

I've skipped most of the details here in order to provide a quick tour, so you shouldn't expect all of this chapter to have made sense yet. In the next few chapters we'll start to dig deeper, taking a second pass over Python's core object types that will fill in details omitted here, and give you a deeper understanding. We'll start off the next chapter with an in-depth look at Python numbers. First, though, here is another quiz to review.

Test Your Knowledge: Quiz

We'll explore the concepts introduced in this chapter in more detail in upcoming chapters, so we'll just cover the big ideas here:

1. Name four of Python's core data types.
2. Why are they called "core" data types?
3. What does "immutable" mean, and which three of Python's core types are considered immutable?
4. What does "sequence" mean, and which three types fall into that category?
5. What does "mapping" mean, and which core type is a mapping?
6. What is "polymorphism," and why should you care?

Test Your Knowledge: Answers

1. Numbers, strings, lists, dictionaries, tuples, files, and sets are generally considered to be the core object (data) types. Types, None, and Booleans are sometimes classified this way as well. There are multiple number types (integer, floating point, complex, fraction, and decimal) and multiple string types (simple strings and Unicode strings in Python 2.X, and text strings and byte strings in Python 3.X).

2. They are known as "core" types because they are part of the Python language itself and are always available; to create other objects, you generally must call functions in imported modules. Most of the core types have specific syntax for generating the objects: 'spam', for example, is an expression that makes a string and determines the set of operations that can be applied to it. Because of this, core types are hardwired into Python's syntax. In contrast, you must call the built-in open function to create a file object (even though this is usually considered a core type too).

3. An "immutable" object is an object that cannot be changed after it is created. Numbers, strings, and tuples in Python fall into this category. While you cannot

change an immutable object in place, you can always make a new one by running an expression. Bytearrays in recent Pythons offer mutability for text, but they are not normal strings, and only apply directly to text if it's a simple 8-bit kind (e.g., ASCII).

4. A "sequence" is a positionally ordered collection of objects. Strings, lists, and tuples are all sequences in Python. They share common sequence operations, such as indexing, concatenation, and slicing, but also have type-specific method calls. A related term, "iterable," means either a physical sequence, or a virtual one that produces its items on request.

5. The term "mapping" denotes an object that maps keys to associated values. Python's dictionary is the only mapping type in the core type set. Mappings do not maintain any left-to-right positional ordering; they support access to data stored by key, plus type-specific method calls.

6. "Polymorphism" means that the meaning of an operation (like a +) depends on the objects being operated on. This turns out to be a key idea (perhaps *the* key idea) behind using Python well—not constraining code to specific types makes that code automatically applicable to many types.

## CHAPTER 5

Numeric Types

This chapter begins our in-depth tour of the Python language. In Python, data takes the form of *objects*—either built-in objects that Python provides, or objects we create using Python tools and other languages such as C. In fact, objects are the basis of every Python program you will ever write. Because they are the most fundamental notion in Python programming, objects are also our first focus in this book.

In the preceding chapter, we took a quick pass over Python's core object types. Although essential terms were introduced in that chapter, we avoided covering too many specifics in the interest of space. Here, we'll begin a more careful second look at data type concepts, to fill in details we glossed over earlier. Let's get started by exploring our first data type category: Python's numeric types and operations.

Numeric Type Basics

Most of Python's number types are fairly typical and will probably seem familiar if you've used almost any other programming language in the past. They can be used to keep track of your bank balance, the distance to Mars, the number of visitors to your website, and just about any other numeric quantity.

In Python, numbers are not really a single object type, but a category of similar types. Python supports the usual numeric types (integers and floating points), as well as literals for creating numbers and expressions for processing them. In addition, Python provides more advanced numeric programming support and objects for more advanced work. A complete inventory of Python's numeric toolbox includes:

- Integer and floating-point objects
- Complex number objects
- Decimal: fixed-precision objects
- Fraction: rational number objects
- Sets: collections with numeric operations

- Booleans: true and false
- Built-in functions and modules: `round`, `math`, `random`, etc.
- Expressions; unlimited integer precision; bitwise operations; hex, octal, and binary formats
- Third-party extensions: vectors, libraries, visualization, plotting, etc.

Because the types in this list's first bullet item tend to see the most action in Python code, this chapter starts with basic numbers and fundamentals, then moves on to explore the other types on this list, which serve specialized roles. We'll also study *sets* here, which have both numeric and collection qualities, but are generally considered more the former than the latter. Before we jump into code, though, the next few sections get us started with a brief overview of how we write and process numbers in our scripts.

Numeric Literals

Among its basic types, Python provides *integers*, which are positive and negative whole numbers, and *floating-point* numbers, which are numbers with a fractional part (sometimes called "floats" for verbal economy). Python also allows us to write integers using hexadecimal, octal, and binary literals; offers a complex number type; and allows integers to have unlimited *precision*—they can grow to have as many digits as your memory space allows. Table 5-1 shows what Python's numeric types look like when written out in a program as literals or constructor function calls.

Table 5-1. Numeric literals and constructors

Literal	Interpretation
`1234, -24, 0, 99999999999999`	Integers (unlimited size)
`1.23, 1., 3.14e-10, 4E210, 4.0e+210`	Floating-point numbers
`0o177, 0x9ff, 0b101010`	Octal, hex, and binary literals in 3.X
`0177, 0o177, 0x9ff, 0b101010`	Octal, octal, hex, and binary literals in 2.X
`3+4j, 3.0+4.0j, 3J`	Complex number literals
`set('spam'), {1, 2, 3, 4}`	Sets: 2.X and 3.X construction forms
`Decimal('1.0'), Fraction(1, 3)`	Decimal and fraction extension types
`bool(X), True, False`	Boolean type and constants

In general, Python's numeric type literals are straightforward to write, but a few coding concepts are worth highlighting here:

Integer and floating-point literals

Integers are written as strings of decimal digits. Floating-point numbers have a decimal point and/or an optional signed exponent introduced by an `e` or `E` and followed by an optional sign. If you write a number with a decimal point or exponent, Python makes it a floating-point object and uses floating-point (not integer) math when the object is used in an expression. Floating-point numbers are implemented as C "doubles" in standard CPython, and therefore get as much precision as the C compiler used to build the Python interpreter gives to doubles.

Integers in Python 2.X: normal and long

In Python 2.X there are two integer types, normal (often 32 bits) and long (unlimited precision), and an integer may end in an l or L to force it to become a long integer. Because integers are automatically converted to long integers when their values overflow their allocated bits, you never need to type the letter L yourself—Python automatically converts up to long integer when extra precision is needed.

Integers in Python 3.X: a single type

In Python 3.X, the normal and long integer types have been merged—there is only integer, which automatically supports the unlimited precision of Python 2.X's separate long integer type. Because of this, integers can no longer be coded with a trailing l or L, and integers never print with this character either. Apart from this, most programs are unaffected by this change, unless they do type testing that checks for 2.X long integers.

Hexadecimal, octal, and binary literals

Integers may be coded in decimal (base 10), hexadecimal (base 16), octal (base 8), or binary (base 2), the last three of which are common in some programming domains. Hexadecimals start with a leading 0x or 0X, followed by a string of hexadecimal digits (0–9 and A–F). Hex digits may be coded in lower- or uppercase. Octal literals start with a leading 0o or 0O (zero and lower- or uppercase letter o), followed by a string of digits (0–7). In 2.X, octal literals can also be coded with just a leading 0, but not in 3.X—this original octal form is too easily confused with decimal, and is replaced by the new 0o format, which can also be used in 2.X as of 2.6. Binary literals, new as of 2.6 and 3.0, begin with a leading 0b or 0B, followed by binary digits (0–1).

Note that all of these literals produce integer objects in program code; they are just alternative syntaxes for specifying values. The built-in calls hex(*I*), oct(*I*), and bin(*I*) convert an integer to its representation string in these three bases, and int(*str, base*) converts a runtime string to an integer per a given base.

Complex numbers

Python complex literals are written as *realpart+imaginarypart*, where the *imaginarypart* is terminated with a j or J. The *realpart* is technically optional, so the *imaginarypart* may appear on its own. Internally, complex numbers are implemented as pairs of floating-point numbers, but all numeric operations perform complex math when applied to complex numbers. Complex numbers may also be created with the complex(*real, imag*) built-in call.

Coding other numeric types

As we'll see later in this chapter, there are additional numeric types at the end of Table 5-1 that serve more advanced or specialized roles. You create some of these by calling functions in imported modules (e.g., decimals and fractions), and others have literal syntax all their own (e.g., sets).

Built-in Numeric Tools

Besides the built-in number literals and construction calls shown in Table 5-1, Python provides a set of tools for processing number objects:

Expression operators
> +, -, *, /, >>, **, &, etc.

Built-in mathematical functions
> pow, abs, round, int, hex, bin, etc.

Utility modules
> random, math, etc.

We'll meet all of these as we go along.

Although numbers are primarily processed with expressions, built-ins, and modules, they also have a handful of type-specific *methods* today, which we'll meet in this chapter as well. Floating-point numbers, for example, have an `as_integer_ratio` method that is useful for the fraction number type, and an `is_integer` method to test if the number is an integer. Integers have various attributes, including a new `bit_length` method introduced in Python 3.1 that gives the number of bits necessary to represent the object's value. Moreover, as part collection and part number, *sets* also support both methods and expressions.

Since expressions are the most essential tool for most number types, though, let's turn to them next.

Python Expression Operators

Perhaps the most fundamental tool that processes numbers is the *expression*: a combination of numbers (or other objects) and operators that computes a value when executed by Python. In Python, you write expressions using the usual mathematical notation and operator symbols. For instance, to add two numbers X and Y you would say X + Y, which tells Python to apply the + operator to the values named by X and Y. The result of the expression is the sum of X and Y, another number object.

Table 5-2 lists all the operator expressions available in Python. Many are self-explanatory; for instance, the usual mathematical operators (+, -, *, /, and so on) are supported. A few will be familiar if you've used other languages in the past: % computes a division remainder, << performs a bitwise left-shift, & computes a bitwise AND result, and so on. Others are more Python-specific, and not all are numeric in nature: for example, the `is` operator tests object identity (i.e., address in memory, a strict form of equality), and `lambda` creates unnamed functions.

Table 5-2. Python expression operators and precedence

Operators	Description
yield x	Generator function send protocol
lambda args: expression	Anonymous function generation
x if y else z	Ternary selection (x is evaluated only if y is true)
x or y	Logical OR (y is evaluated only if x is false)
x and y	Logical AND (y is evaluated only if x is true)
not x	Logical negation
x in y, x not in y	Membership (iterables, sets)
x is y, x is not y	Object identity tests
x < y, x <= y, x > y, x >= y	Magnitude comparison, set subset and superset;
x == y, x != y	Value equality operators
x | y	Bitwise OR, set union
x ^ y	Bitwise XOR, set symmetric difference
x & y	Bitwise AND, set intersection
x << y, x >> y	Shift x left or right by y bits
x + y	Addition, concatenation;
x - y	Subtraction, set difference
x * y	Multiplication, repetition;
x % y	Remainder, format;
x / y, x // y	Division: true and floor
-x, +x	Negation, identity
~x	Bitwise NOT (inversion)
x ** y	Power (exponentiation)
x[i]	Indexing (sequence, mapping, others)
x[i:j:k]	Slicing
x(...)	Call (function, method, class, other callable)
x.attr	Attribute reference
(...)	Tuple, expression, generator expression
[...]	List, list comprehension
{...}	Dictionary, set, set and dictionary comprehensions

Since this book addresses both Python 2.X and 3.X, here are some notes about version differences and recent additions related to the operators in Table 5-2:

- In Python 2.X, value inequality can be written as either X != Y or X <> Y. In Python 3.X, the latter of these options is removed because it is redundant. In either version, best practice is to use X != Y for all value inequality tests.

- In Python 2.X, a backquotes expression `X` works the same as repr(X) and converts objects to display strings. Due to its obscurity, this expression is removed in Python 3.X; use the more readable str and repr built-in functions, described in "Numeric Display Formats."

- The X // Y floor division expression always truncates fractional remainders in both Python 2.X and 3.X. The X / Y expression performs true division in 3.X (retaining remainders) and classic division in 2.X (truncating for integers). See "Division: Classic, Floor, and True" on page 146.

- The syntax [...] is used for both list literals and list comprehension expressions. The latter of these performs an implied loop and collects expression results in a new list. See Chapter 4, Chapter 14, and Chapter 20 for examples.

- The syntax (...) is used for tuples and expression grouping, as well as generator expressions—a form of list comprehension that produces results on demand, instead of building a result list. See Chapter 4 and Chapter 20 for examples. The parentheses may sometimes be omitted in all three contexts. When a tuple's parentheses are omitted, the *comma* separating its items acts like a lowest-precedence operator if not otherwise significant.

- The syntax {...} is used for dictionary literals, and in Python 3.X and 2.7 for set literals and both dictionary and set comprehensions. See the set coverage in this chapter as well as Chapter 4, Chapter 8, Chapter 14, and Chapter 20 for examples.

- The yield and ternary if/else selection expressions are available in Python 2.5 and later. The former returns send(...) arguments in generators; the latter is shorthand for a multiline if statement. yield requires parentheses if not alone on the right side of an assignment statement.

- Comparison operators may be chained: X < Y < Z produces the same result as X < Y and Y < Z. See "Comparisons: Normal and Chained" on page 144 for details.

- In recent Pythons, the slice expression X[I:J:K] is equivalent to indexing with a slice object: X[slice(I, J, K)].

- In Python 2.X, magnitude comparisons of mixed types are allowed, and convert numbers to a common type, and order other mixed types according to type names. In Python 3.X, nonnumeric mixed-type magnitude comparisons are not allowed and raise exceptions; this includes sorts by proxy.

- Magnitude comparisons for dictionaries are also no longer supported in Python 3.X (though equality tests are); comparing sorted(aDict.items()) is one possible replacement.

We'll see most of the operators in Table 5-2 in action later; first, though, we need to take a quick look at the ways these operators may be combined in expressions.

Mixed operators follow operator precedence

As in most languages, in Python, you code more complex expressions by stringing together the operator expressions in Table 5-2. For instance, the sum of two multiplications might be written as a mix of variables and operators:

```
A * B + C * D
```

So, how does Python know which operation to perform first? The answer to this question lies in *operator precedence*. When you write an expression with more than one operator, Python groups its parts according to what are called *precedence rules*, and this grouping determines the order in which the expression's parts are computed. Table 5-2 is ordered by operator precedence:

- Operators lower in the table have higher precedence, and so bind more tightly in mixed expressions.
- Operators in the same row in Table 5-2 generally group from left to right when combined (except for exponentiation, which groups right to left, and comparisons, which chain left to right).

For example, if you write X + Y * Z, Python evaluates the multiplication first (Y * Z), then adds that result to X because * has higher precedence (is lower in the table) than +. Similarly, in this section's original example, both multiplications (A * B and C * D) will happen before their results are added.

Parentheses group subexpressions

You can forget about precedence completely if you're careful to group parts of expressions with parentheses. When you enclose subexpressions in parentheses, you override Python's precedence rules; Python always evaluates expressions in parentheses first before using their results in the enclosing expressions.

For instance, instead of coding X + Y * Z, you could write one of the following to force Python to evaluate the expression in the desired order:

```
(X + Y) * Z
X + (Y * Z)
```

In the first case, + is applied to X and Y first, because this subexpression is wrapped in parentheses. In the second case, the * is performed first (just as if there were no parentheses at all). Generally speaking, adding parentheses in large expressions is a good idea—it not only forces the evaluation order you want, but also aids readability.

Mixed types are converted up

Besides mixing operators in expressions, you can also mix numeric types. For instance, you can add an integer to a floating-point number:

```
40 + 3.14
```

But this leads to another question: what type is the result—integer or floating point? The answer is simple, especially if you've used almost any other language before: in mixed-type numeric expressions, Python first converts operands *up* to the type of the most complicated operand, and then performs the math on same-type operands. This behavior is similar to type conversions in the C language.

Python ranks the complexity of numeric types like so: integers are simpler than floating-point numbers, which are simpler than complex numbers. So, when an integer is mixed with a floating point, as in the preceding example, the integer is converted up to a floating-point value first, and floating-point math yields the floating-point result:

```
>>> 40 + 3.14          # Integer to float, float math/result
43.14
```

Similarly, any mixed-type expression where one operand is a complex number results in the other operand being converted up to a complex number, and the expression yields a complex result. In Python 2.X, normal integers are also converted to long integers whenever their values are too large to fit in a normal integer; in 3.X, integers subsume longs entirely.

You can force the issue by calling built-in functions to convert types manually:

```
>>> int(3.1415)        # Truncates float to integer
3
>>> float(3)           # Converts integer to float
3.0
```

However, you won't usually need to do this: because Python automatically converts up to the more complex type within an expression, the results are normally what you want.

Also, keep in mind that all these mixed-type conversions apply only when mixing *numeric* types (e.g., an integer and a floating point) in an expression, including those using numeric and comparison operators. In general, Python does not convert across any other type boundaries automatically. Adding a string to an integer, for example, results in an error, unless you manually convert one or the other; watch for an example when we meet strings in Chapter 7.

 In Python 2.X, nonnumeric mixed types can be *compared*, but no conversions are performed—mixed types compare according to a rule that seems deterministic but not aesthetically pleasing: it compares the string names of the objects' types. In 3.X, nonnumeric mixed-type magnitude comparisons are never allowed and raise exceptions. Note that this applies to comparison operators such as > only; other operators like + do not allow mixed nonnumeric types in either 3.X or 2.X.

Preview: Operator overloading and polymorphism

Although we're focusing on built-in numbers right now, all Python operators may be overloaded (i.e., implemented) by Python classes and C extension types to work on objects you create. For instance, you'll see later that objects coded with classes may be added or concatenated with x+y expressions, indexed with x[i] expressions, and so on.

Furthermore, Python itself automatically overloads some operators, such that they perform different actions depending on the type of built-in objects being processed. For example, the + operator performs addition when applied to numbers but performs concatenation when applied to sequence objects such as strings and lists. In fact, + can mean anything at all when applied to objects you define with classes.

As we saw in the prior chapter, this property is usually called *polymorphism*—a term indicating that the meaning of an operation depends on the type of the objects being operated on. We'll revisit this concept when we explore functions in Chapter 16, because it becomes a much more obvious feature in that context.

Numbers in Action

On to the code! Probably the best way to understand numeric objects and expressions is to see them in action, so with those basics in hand let's start up the interactive command line and try some simple but illustrative operations (be sure to see Chapter 3 for pointers if you need help starting an interactive session).

Variables and Basic Expressions

First of all, let's exercise some basic math. In the following interaction, we first assign two *variables* (a and b) to integers so we can use them later in a larger expression. Variables are simply names—created by you or Python—that are used to keep track of information in your program. We'll say more about this in the next chapter, but in Python:

- Variables are created when they are first assigned values.
- Variables are replaced with their values when used in expressions.
- Variables must be assigned before they can be used in expressions.
- Variables refer to objects and are never declared ahead of time.

In other words, these assignments cause the variables a and b to spring into existence automatically:

```
% python
>>> a = 3                    # Name created: not declared ahead of time
>>> b = 4
```

I've also used a *comment* here. Recall that in Python code, text after a # mark and continuing to the end of the line is considered to be a comment and is ignored by

Python. Comments are a way to write human-readable documentation for your code, and an important part of programming. I've added them to most of this book's examples to help explain the code. In the next part of the book, we'll meet a related but more functional feature—documentation strings—that attaches the text of your comments to objects so it's available after your code is loaded.

Because code you type interactively is temporary, though, you won't normally write comments in this context. If you're working along, this means you don't need to type any of the comment text from the # through to the end of the line; it's not a required part of the statements we're running this way.

Now, let's use our new integer objects in some expressions. At this point, the values of a and b are still 3 and 4, respectively. Variables like these are replaced with their values whenever they're used inside an expression, and the expression results are echoed back immediately when we're working interactively:

```
>>> a + 1, a - 1              # Addition (3 + 1), subtraction (3 – 1)
(4, 2)
>>> b * 3, b / 2              # Multiplication (4 * 3), division (4 / 2, 3.X result)
(12, 2.0)
>>> a % 2, b ** 2            # Modulus (remainder), power (4 ** 2)
(1, 16)
>>> 2 + 4.0, 2.0 ** b        # Mixed-type conversions
(6.0, 16.0)
```

Technically, the results being echoed back here are *tuples* of two values because the lines typed at the prompt contain two expressions separated by commas; that's why the results are displayed in parentheses (more on tuples later). Note that the expressions work because the variables a and b within them have been assigned values. If you use a different variable that has *not yet been assigned*, Python reports an error rather than filling in some default value:

```
>>> c * 2
Traceback (most recent call last):
  File "<stdin>", line 1, in <module>
NameError: name 'c' is not defined
```

You don't need to predeclare variables in Python, but they must have been assigned at least once before you can use them. In practice, this means you have to initialize counters to zero before you can add to them, initialize lists to an empty list before you can append to them, and so on.

Here are two slightly larger expressions to illustrate operator grouping and more about conversions, and preview a difference in the division operator in Python 3.X and 2.X:

```
>>> b / 2 + a                # Same as ((4 / 2) + 3)  [use 2.0 in 2.X]
5.0
>>> b / (2.0 + a)            # Same as (4 / (2.0 + 3))  [use print before 2.7]
0.8
```

In the first expression, there are no parentheses, so Python automatically groups the components according to its precedence rules—because / is lower in Table 5-2 than

+, it binds more tightly and so is evaluated first. The result is as if the expression had been organized with parentheses as shown in the comment to the right of the code.

Also, notice that all the numbers are *integers* in the first expression. Because of that, Python 2.X's / performs integer division and addition and will give a result of **5**, whereas Python 3.X's / performs true division, which always retains fractional remainders and gives the result **5.0** shown. If you want 2.X's integer division in 3.X, code this as **b //** **2 + a**; if you want 3.X's true division in 2.X, code this as **b / 2.0 + a** (more on division in a moment).

In the second expression, parentheses are added around the + part to force Python to evaluate it first (i.e., before the /). We also made one of the operands floating point by adding a decimal point: **2.0**. Because of the mixed types, Python converts the integer referenced by **a** to a floating-point value (**3.0**) before performing the +. If instead all the numbers in this expression were integers, integer division (**4 / 5**) would yield the truncated integer **0** in Python 2.X but the floating point **0.8** shown in Python 3.X. Again, stay tuned for formal division details.

Numeric Display Formats

If you're using Python 2.6, Python 3.0, or earlier, the result of the last of the preceding examples may look a bit odd the first time you see it:

```
>>> b / (2.0 + a)          # Pythons <= 2.6: echoes give more (or fewer) digits
0.80000000000000004

>>> print(b / (2.0 + a))   # But print rounds off digits
0.8
```

We met this phenomenon briefly in the prior chapter, and it's not present in Pythons 2.7, 3.1, and later. The full story behind this odd result has to do with the limitations of floating-point hardware and its inability to exactly represent some values in a limited number of bits. Because computer architecture is well beyond this book's scope, though, we'll finesse this by saying that your computer's floating-point hardware is doing the best it can, and neither it nor Python is in error here.

In fact, this is really just a *display* issue—the interactive prompt's automatic result echo shows more digits than the `print` statement here only because it uses a different algorithm. It's the same number in memory. If you don't want to see all the digits, use `print`; as this chapter's sidebar "str and repr Display Formats" on page 144 will explain, you'll get a user-friendly display. As of 2.7 and 3.1, Python's floating-point display logic tries to be more intelligent, usually showing fewer decimal digits, but occasionally more.

Note, however, that not all values have so many digits to display:

```
>>> 1 / 2.0
0.5
```

and that there are more ways to display the bits of a number inside your computer than using `print` and automatic echoes (the following are all run in Python 3.3, and may vary slightly in older versions):

```
>>> num = 1 / 3.0
>>> num                       # Auto-echoes
0.3333333333333333
>>> print(num)                # Print explicitly
0.3333333333333333

>>> '%e' % num                # String formatting expression
'3.333333e-01'
>>> '%4.2f' % num             # Alternative floating-point format
'0.33'
>>> '{0:4.2f}'.format(num)    # String formatting method: Python 2.6, 3.0, and later
'0.33'
```

The last three of these expressions employ *string formatting*, a tool that allows for format flexibility, which we will explore in the upcoming chapter on strings (Chapter 7). Its results are strings that are typically printed to displays or reports.

---

str and repr Display Formats

Technically, the difference between default interactive echoes and `print` corresponds to the difference between the built-in `repr` and `str` functions:

```
>>> repr('spam')      # Used by echoes: as-code form
"'spam'"
>>> str('spam')       # Used by print: user-friendly form
'spam'
```

Both of these convert arbitrary objects to their string representations: `repr` (and the default interactive echo) produces results that look as though they were code; `str` (and the `print` operation) converts to a typically more user-friendly format if available. Some objects have both—a `str` for general use, and a `repr` with extra details. This notion will resurface when we study both strings and operator overloading in classes, and you'll find more on these built-ins in general later in the book.

Besides providing print strings for arbitrary objects, the `str` built-in is also the name of the string data type, and in 3.X may be called with an encoding name to decode a Unicode string from a byte string (e.g., `str(b'xy', 'utf8')`), and serves as an alternative to the `bytes.decode` method we met in Chapter 4. We'll study the latter advanced role in Chapter 37 of this book.

Comparisons: Normal and Chained

So far, we've been dealing with standard numeric operations (addition and multiplication), but numbers, like all Python objects, can also be compared. Normal comparisons work for numbers exactly as you'd expect—they compare the relative magnitudes of their operands and return a Boolean result, which we would normally test and take action on in a larger statement and program:

```
>>> 1 < 2                    # Less than
True
>>> 2.0 >= 1                 # Greater than or equal: mixed-type 1 converted to 1.0
True
>>> 2.0 == 2.0               # Equal value
True
>>> 2.0 != 2.0               # Not equal value
False
```

Notice again how mixed types are allowed in numeric expressions (only); in the second test here, Python compares values in terms of the more complex type, float.

Interestingly, Python also allows us to *chain* multiple comparisons together to perform range tests. Chained comparisons are a sort of shorthand for larger Boolean expressions. In short, Python lets us string together magnitude comparison tests to code chained comparisons such as range tests. The expression (A < B < C), for instance, tests whether B is between A and C; it is equivalent to the Boolean test (A < B and B < C) but is easier on the eyes (and the keyboard). For example, assume the following assignments:

```
>>> X = 2
>>> Y = 4
>>> Z = 6
```

The following two expressions have identical effects, but the first is shorter to type, and it may run slightly faster since Python needs to evaluate Y only once:

```
>>> X < Y < Z                # Chained comparisons: range tests
True
>>> X < Y and Y < Z
True
```

The same equivalence holds for false results, and arbitrary chain lengths are allowed:

```
>>> X < Y > Z
False
>>> X < Y and Y > Z
False

>>> 1 < 2 < 3.0 < 4
True
>>> 1 > 2 > 3.0 > 4
False
```

You can use other comparisons in chained tests, but the resulting expressions can become nonintuitive unless you evaluate them the way Python does. The following, for instance, is false just because 1 is not equal to 2:

```
>>> 1 == 2 < 3               # Same as: 1 == 2 and 2 < 3
False                        # Not same as: False < 3 (which means 0 < 3, which is true!)
```

Python does not compare the `1 == 2` expression's `False` result to 3—this would technically mean the same as `0 < 3`, which would be `True` (as we'll see later in this chapter, `True` and `False` are just customized 1 and 0).

One last note here before we move on: chaining aside, numeric comparisons are based on magnitudes, which are generally simple—though *floating-point* numbers may not always work as you'd expect, and may require conversions or other massaging to be compared meaningfully:

```
>>> 1.1 + 2.2 == 3.3            # Shouldn't this be True?...
False
>>> 1.1 + 2.2                   # Close to 3.3, but not exactly: limited precision
3.3000000000000003
>>> int(1.1 + 2.2) == int(3.3)  # OK if convert: see also round, floor, trunc ahead
True                            # Decimals and fractions (ahead) may help here too
```

This stems from the fact that floating-point numbers cannot represent some values exactly due to their limited number of bits—a fundamental issue in numeric programming not unique to Python, which we'll learn more about later when we meet *decimals* and *fractions*, tools that can address such limitations. First, though, let's continue our tour of Python's core numeric operations, with a deeper look at division.

Division: Classic, Floor, and True

You've seen how division works in the previous sections, so you should know that it behaves slightly differently in Python 3.X and 2.X. In fact, there are actually three flavors of division, and two different division operators, one of which changes in 3.X. This story gets a bit detailed, but it's another major change in 3.X and can break 2.X code, so let's get the division operator facts straight:

X / Y

> *Classic* and *true* division. In Python 2.X, this operator performs *classic* division, truncating results for integers, and keeping remainders (i.e., fractional parts) for floating-point numbers. In Python 3.X, it performs *true* division, always keeping remainders in floating-point results, regardless of types.

X // Y

> *Floor* division. Added in Python 2.2 and available in both Python 2.X and 3.X, this operator always truncates fractional remainders down to their floor, regardless of types. Its result type depends on the types of its operands.

True division was added to address the fact that the results of the original classic division model are dependent on operand types, and so can be difficult to anticipate in a dynamically typed language like Python. Classic division was removed in 3.X because of this constraint—the / and // operators implement true and floor division in 3.X. Python 2.X defaults to classic and floor division, but you can enable true division as an option. In sum:

- *In 3.X*, the / now always performs *true* division, returning a float result that includes any remainder, regardless of operand types. The // performs *floor* division, which truncates the remainder and returns an integer for integer operands or a float if any operand is a float.
- *In 2.X*, the / does *classic* division, performing truncating integer division if both operands are integers and float division (keeping remainders) otherwise. The // does *floor* division and works as it does in 3.X, performing truncating division for integers and floor division for floats.

Here are the two operators at work in 3.X and 2.X—the first operation in each set is the crucial difference between the lines that may impact code:

```
C:\code> C:\Python33\python
>>>
>>> 10 / 4              # Differs in 3.X: keeps remainder
2.5
>>> 10 / 4.0            # Same in 3.X: keeps remainder
2.5
>>> 10 // 4             # Same in 3.X: truncates remainder
2
>>> 10 // 4.0           # Same in 3.X: truncates to floor
2.0

C:\code> C:\Python27\python
>>>
>>> 10 / 4              # This might break on porting to 3.X!
2
>>> 10 / 4.0
2.5
>>> 10 // 4             # Use this in 2.X if truncation needed
2
>>> 10 // 4.0
2.0
```

Notice that the data type of the result for // is still dependent on the operand types in 3.X: if either is a float, the result is a float; otherwise, it is an integer. Although this may seem similar to the type-dependent behavior of / in 2.X that motivated its change in 3.X, the type of the return value is much less critical than differences in the return value itself.

Moreover, because // was provided in part as a compatibility tool for programs that rely on truncating integer division (and this is more common than you might expect), it must return integers for integers. Using // instead of / in 2.X when integer truncation is required helps make code 3.X-compatible.

Supporting either Python

Although / behavior differs in 2.X and 3.X, you can still support both versions in your code. If your programs depend on truncating integer division, use // in both 2.X and 3.X as just mentioned. If your programs require floating-point results with remainders for integers, use **float** to guarantee that one operand is a float around a / when run in 2.X:

```
X = Y // Z        # Always truncates, always an int result for ints in 2.X and 3.X

X = Y / float(Z)  # Guarantees float division with remainder in either 2.X or 3.X
```

Alternatively, you can enable 3.X / division in 2.X with a __future__ import, rather than forcing it with **float** conversions:

```
C:\code> C:\Python27\python
>>> from __future__ import division      # Enable 3.X "/" behavior
>>> 10 / 4
2.5
>>> 10 // 4                              # Integer // is the same in both
2
```

This special **from** statement applies to the rest of your session when typed interactively like this, and must appear as the first executable line when used in a script file (and alas, we can import from the future in Python, but not the past; insert something about talking to "the Doc" here...).

Floor versus truncation

One subtlety: the // operator is informally called *truncating* division, but it's more accurate to refer to it as *floor* division—it truncates the result down to its floor, which means the closest whole number below the true result. The net effect is to round down, not strictly truncate, and this matters for negatives. You can see the difference for yourself with the Python **math** module (modules must be imported before you can use their contents; more on this later):

```
>>> import math
>>> math.floor(2.5)          # Closest number below value
2
>>> math.floor(-2.5)
-3
>>> math.trunc(2.5)          # Truncate fractional part (toward zero)
2
>>> math.trunc(-2.5)
-2
```

When running division operators, you only really truncate for positive results, since truncation is the same as floor; for negatives, it's a floor result (really, they are both floor, but floor is the same as truncation for positives). Here's the case for 3.X:

```
C:\code> c:\python33\python
>>> 5 / 2, 5 / -2
(2.5, -2.5)

>>> 5 // 2, 5 // -2          # Truncates to floor: rounds to first lower integer
(2, -3)                      # 2.5 becomes 2, -2.5 becomes -3

>>> 5 / 2.0, 5 / -2.0
(2.5, -2.5)
```

```
>>> 5 // 2.0, 5 // -2.0          # Ditto for floats, though result is float too
(2.0, -3.0)
```

The 2.X case is similar, but / results differ again:

```
C:code> c:\python27\python
>>> 5 / 2, 5 / -2                # Differs in 3.X
(2, -3)

>>> 5 // 2, 5 // -2              # This and the rest are the same in 2.X and 3.X
(2, -3)

>>> 5 / 2.0, 5 / -2.0
(2.5, -2.5)

>>> 5 // 2.0, 5 // -2.0
(2.0, -3.0)
```

If you really want truncation toward zero regardless of sign, you can always run a float division result through `math.trunc`, regardless of Python version (also see the `round` built-in for related functionality, and the `int` built-in, which has the same effect here but requires no import):

```
C:\code> c:\python33\python
>>> import math
>>> 5 / -2                       # Keep remainder
-2.5
>>> 5 // -2                      # Floor below result
-3
>>> math.trunc(5 / -2)           # Truncate instead of floor (same as int())
-2

C:\code> c:\python27\python
>>> import math
>>> 5 / float(-2)                # Remainder in 2.X
-2.5
>>> 5 / -2, 5 // -2              # Floor in 2.X
(-3, -3)
>>> math.trunc(5 / float(-2))    # Truncate in 2.X
-2
```

Why does truncation matter?

As a wrap-up, if you are using 3.X, here is the short story on division operators for reference:

```
>>> (5 / 2), (5 / 2.0), (5 / -2.0), (5 / -2)       # 3.X true division
(2.5, 2.5, -2.5, -2.5)

>>> (5 // 2), (5 // 2.0), (5 // -2.0), (5 // -2)   # 3.X floor division
(2, 2.0, -3.0, -3)

>>> (9 / 3), (9.0 / 3), (9 // 3), (9 // 3.0)        # Both
(3.0, 3.0, 3, 3.0)
```

For 2.X readers, division works as follows (the three bold outputs of integer division differ from 3.X):

```
>>> (5 / 2), (5 / 2.0), (5 / -2.0), (5 / -2)     # 2.X classic division (differs)
(2, 2.5, -2.5, -3)

>>> (5 // 2), (5 // 2.0), (5 // -2.0), (5 // -2)     # 2.X floor division (same)
(2, 2.0, -3.0, -3)

>>> (9 / 3), (9.0 / 3), (9 // 3), (9 // 3.0)     # Both
(3, 3.0, 3, 3.0)
```

It's possible that the nontruncating behavior of / in 3.X may break a significant number of 2.X programs. Perhaps because of a C language legacy, many programmers rely on division truncation for integers and will have to learn to use // in such contexts instead. You should do so in all new 2.X and 3.X code you write today—in the former for 3.X compatibility, and in the latter because / does not truncate in 3.X. Watch for a simple prime number while loop example in Chapter 13, and a corresponding exercise at the end of Part IV that illustrates the sort of code that may be impacted by this / change. Also stay tuned for more on the special from command used in this section; it's discussed further in Chapter 25.

Integer Precision

Division may differ slightly across Python releases, but it's still fairly standard. Here's something a bit more exotic. As mentioned earlier, Python 3.X integers support unlimited size:

```
>>> 99999999999999999999999999999999 + 1     # 3.X
100000000000000000000000000000000
```

Python 2.X has a separate type for long integers, but it automatically converts any number too large to store in a normal integer to this type. Hence, you don't need to code any special syntax to use longs, and the only way you can tell that you're using 2.X longs is that they print with a trailing "L":

```
>>> 99999999999999999999999999999999 + 1     # 2.X
100000000000000000000000000000000L
```

Unlimited-precision integers are a convenient built-in tool. For instance, you can use them to count the U.S. national debt in pennies in Python directly (if you are so inclined, and have enough memory on your computer for this year's budget). They are also why we were able to raise 2 to such large powers in the examples in Chapter 3. Here are the 3.X and 2.X cases:

```
>>> 2 ** 200
1606938044258990275541962092341162602522202993782792835301376

>>> 2 ** 200
1606938044258990275541962092341162602522202993782792835301376L
```

Because Python must do extra work to support their extended precision, integer math is usually substantially slower than normal when numbers grow large. However, if you need the precision, the fact that it's built in for you to use will likely outweigh its performance penalty.

Complex Numbers

Although less commonly used than the types we've been exploring thus far, complex numbers are a distinct core object type in Python. They are typically used in engineering and science applications. If you know what they are, you know why they are useful; if not, consider this section optional reading.

Complex numbers are represented as two floating-point numbers—the real and imaginary parts—and you code them by adding a j or J suffix to the imaginary part. We can also write complex numbers with a nonzero real part by adding the two parts with a +. For example, the complex number with a real part of 2 and an imaginary part of -3 is written 2 + -3j. Here are some examples of complex math at work:

```
>>> 1j * 1J
(-1+0j)
>>> 2 + 1j * 3
(2+3j)
>>> (2 + 1j) * 3
(6+3j)
```

Complex numbers also allow us to extract their parts as attributes, support all the usual mathematical expressions, and may be processed with tools in the standard cmath module (the complex version of the standard math module). Because complex numbers are rare in most programming domains, though, we'll skip the rest of this story here. Check Python's language reference manual for additional details.

Hex, Octal, Binary: Literals and Conversions

Python integers can be coded in hexadecimal, octal, and binary notation, in addition to the normal base-10 decimal coding we've been using so far. The first three of these may at first seem foreign to 10-fingered beings, but some programmers find them convenient alternatives for specifying values, especially when their mapping to bytes and bits is important. The coding rules were introduced briefly at the start of this chapter; let's look at some live examples here.

Keep in mind that these literals are simply an alternative syntax for specifying the value of an integer object. For example, the following literals coded in Python 3.X or 2.X produce normal integers with the specified values in all three bases. In memory, an integer's value is the same, regardless of the base we use to specify it:

```
>>> 0o1, 0o20, 0o377          # Octal literals: base 8, digits 0-7 (3.X, 2.6+)
(1, 16, 255)
>>> 0x01, 0x10, 0xFF          # Hex literals: base 16, digits 0-9/A-F (3.X, 2.X)
```

```
(1, 16, 255)
>>> 0b1, 0b10000, 0b11111111      # Binary literals: base 2, digits 0-1 (3.X, 2.6+)
(1, 16, 255)
```

Here, the octal value 0o377, the hex value 0xFF, and the binary value 0b11111111 are all decimal 255. The F digits in the hex value, for example, each mean 15 in decimal and a 4-bit 1111 in binary, and reflect powers of 16. Thus, the hex value 0xFF and others convert to decimal values as follows:

```
>>> 0xFF, (15 * (16 ** 1)) + (15 * (16 ** 0))      # How hex/binary map to decimal
(255, 255)
>>> 0x2F, (2  * (16 ** 1)) + (15 * (16 ** 0))
(47, 47)
>>> 0xF, 0b1111, (1*(2**3) + 1*(2**2) + 1*(2**1) + 1*(2**0))
(15, 15, 15)
```

Python prints integer values in decimal (base 10) by default but provides built-in functions that allow you to convert integers to other bases' digit strings, in Python-literal form—useful when programs or users expect to see values in a given base:

```
>>> oct(64), hex(64), bin(64)                      # Numbers=>digit strings
('0o100', '0x40', '0b1000000')
```

The oct function converts decimal to octal, hex to hexadecimal, and bin to binary. To go the other way, the built-in int function converts a string of digits to an integer, and an optional second argument lets you specify the numeric base—useful for numbers read from files as strings instead of coded in scripts:

```
>>> 64, 0o100, 0x40, 0b1000000                     # Digits=>numbers in scripts and strings
(64, 64, 64, 64)

>>> int('64'), int('100', 8), int('40', 16), int('1000000', 2)
(64, 64, 64, 64)

>>> int('0x40', 16), int('0b1000000', 2)     # Literal forms supported too
(64, 64)
```

The eval function, which you'll meet later in this book, treats strings as though they were Python code. Therefore, it has a similar effect, but usually runs more *slowly*—it actually compiles and runs the string as a piece of a program, and it assumes the string being run comes from a *trusted source*—a clever user might be able to submit a string that deletes files on your machine, so be careful with this call:

```
>>> eval('64'), eval('0o100'), eval('0x40'), eval('0b1000000')
(64, 64, 64, 64)
```

Finally, you can also convert integers to base-specific strings with *string formatting* method calls and expressions, which return just digits, not Python literal strings:

```
>>> '{0:o}, {1:x}, {2:b}'.format(64, 64, 64)       # Numbers=>digits, 2.6+
'100, 40, 1000000'

>>> '%o, %x, %x, %X' % (64, 64, 255, 255)          # Similar, in all Pythons
'100, 40, ff, FF'
```

String formatting is covered in more detail in Chapter 7.

Two notes before moving on. First, per the start of this chapter, Python 2.X users should remember that you can code octals with simply a *leading zero*, the original octal format in Python:

```
>>> 0o1, 0o20, 0o377        # New octal format in 2.6+ (same as 3.X)
(1, 16, 255)
>>> 01, 020, 0377           # Old octal literals in all 2.X (error in 3.X)
(1, 16, 255)
```

In 3.X, the syntax in the second of these examples generates an error. Even though it's not an error in 2.X, be careful not to begin a string of digits with a leading zero unless you really mean to code an octal value. Python 2.X will treat it as base 8, which may not work as you'd expect—010 is always decimal 8 in 2.X, not decimal 10 (despite what you may or may not think!). This, along with symmetry with the hex and binary forms, is why the octal format was changed in 3.X—you must use 0o010 in 3.X, and probably should in 2.6 and 2.7 both for clarity and forward-compatibility with 3.X.

Secondly, note that these literals can produce *arbitrarily* long integers. The following, for instance, creates an integer with hex notation and then displays it first in decimal and then in octal and binary with converters (run in 3.X here: in 2.X the decimal and octal displays have a trailing *L* to denote its separate long type, and octals display without the letter *o*):

```
>>> X = 0xFFFFFFFFFFFFFFFFFFFFFFFFFFFFFF
>>> X
5192296858534827628530496329220095
>>> oct(X)
'0o17777777777777777777777777777777777777777'
>>> bin(X)
'0b1111111111111111111111111111111111111111111111111111 ...and so on... 11111'
```

Speaking of binary digits, the next section shows tools for processing individual bits.

Bitwise Operations

Besides the normal numeric operations (addition, subtraction, and so on), Python supports most of the numeric expressions available in the C language. This includes operators that treat integers as strings of *binary bits*, and can come in handy if your Python code must deal with things like network packets, serial ports, or packed binary data produced by a C program.

We can't dwell on the fundamentals of Boolean math here—again, those who must use it probably already know how it works, and others can often postpone the topic altogether—but the basics are straightforward. For instance, here are some of Python's bitwise expression operators at work performing bitwise shift and Boolean operations on integers:

```
>>> x = 1          # 1 decimal is 0001 in bits
>>> x << 2         # Shift left 2 bits: 0100
```

```
4
>>> x | 2                    # Bitwise OR (either bit=1): 0011
3
>>> x & 1                    # Bitwise AND (both bits=1): 0001
1
```

In the first expression, a binary 1 (in base 2, 0001) is shifted left two slots to create a binary 4 (0100). The last two operations perform a binary OR to combine bits (0001| 0010 = 0011) and a binary AND to select common bits (0001&0001 = 0001). Such bit-masking operations allow us to encode and extract multiple flags and other values within a single integer.

This is one area where the binary and hexadecimal number support in Python as of 3.0 and 2.6 become especially useful—they allow us to code and inspect numbers by bit-strings:

```
>>> X = 0b0001               # Binary literals
>>> X << 2                   # Shift left
4
>>> bin(X << 2)              # Binary digits string
'0b100'

>>> bin(X | 0b010)           # Bitwise OR: either
'0b11'
>>> bin(X & 0b1)             # Bitwise AND: both
'0b1'
```

This is also true for values that begin life as hex literals, or undergo base conversions:

```
>>> X = 0xFF                 # Hex literals
>>> bin(X)
'0b11111111'
>>> X ^ 0b10101010           # Bitwise XOR: either but not both
85
>>> bin(X ^ 0b10101010)
'0b1010101'

>>> int('01010101', 2)       # Digits=>number: string to int per base
85
>>> hex(85)                  # Number=>digits: Hex digit string
'0x55'
```

Also in this department, Python 3.1 and 2.7 introduced a new integer `bit_length` method, which allows you to query the number of bits required to represent a number's value in binary. You can often achieve the same effect by subtracting 2 from the length of the `bin` string using the `len` built-in function we met in Chapter 4 (to account for the leading "0b"), though it may be less efficient:

```
>>> X = 99
>>> bin(X), X.bit_length(), len(bin(X)) - 2
('0b1100011', 7, 7)
>>> bin(256), (256).bit_length(), len(bin(256)) - 2
('0b100000000', 9, 9)
```

We won't go into much more detail on such "bit twiddling" here. It's supported if you need it, but bitwise operations are often not as important in a high-level language such as Python as they are in a low-level language such as C. As a rule of thumb, if you find yourself wanting to flip bits in Python, you should think about which language you're really coding. As we'll see in upcoming chapters, Python's lists, dictionaries, and the like provide richer—and usually better—ways to encode information than bit strings, especially when your data's audience includes readers of the human variety.

Other Built-in Numeric Tools

In addition to its core object types, Python also provides both built-in *functions* and standard library *modules* for numeric processing. The `pow` and `abs` built-in functions, for instance, compute powers and absolute values, respectively. Here are some examples of the built-in `math` module (which contains most of the tools in the C language's math library) and a few built-in functions at work in 3.3; as described earlier, some floating-point displays may show more or fewer digits in Pythons before 2.7 and 3.1:

```
>>> import math
>>> math.pi, math.e                     # Common constants
(3.141592653589793, 2.718281828459045)

>>> math.sin(2 * math.pi / 180)         # Sine, tangent, cosine
0.03489949670250097

>>> math.sqrt(144), math.sqrt(2)        # Square root
(12.0, 1.4142135623730951)

>>> pow(2, 4), 2 ** 4, 2.0 ** 4.0       # Exponentiation (power)
(16, 16, 16.0)

>>> abs(-42.0), sum((1, 2, 3, 4))       # Absolute value, summation
(42.0, 10)

>>> min(3, 1, 2, 4), max(3, 1, 2, 4)    # Minimum, maximum
(1, 4)
```

The `sum` function shown here works on a sequence of numbers, and `min` and `max` accept either a sequence or individual arguments. There are a variety of ways to drop the decimal digits of floating-point numbers. We met truncation and floor earlier; we can also round, both numerically and for display purposes:

```
>>> math.floor(2.567), math.floor(-2.567)    # Floor (next-lower integer)
(2, -3)

>>> math.trunc(2.567), math.trunc(-2.567)    # Truncate (drop decimal digits)
(2, -2)

>>> int(2.567), int(-2.567)                  # Truncate (integer conversion)
(2, -2)

>>> round(2.567), round(2.467), round(2.567, 2)   # Round (Python 3.X version)
```

```
(3, 2, 2.57)

>>> '%.1f' % 2.567, '{0:.2f}'.format(2.567)        # Round for display (Chapter 7)
('2.6', '2.57')
```

As we saw earlier, the last of these produces strings that we would usually print and supports a variety of formatting options. As also described earlier, the second-to-last test here will also output (3, 2, 2.57) prior to 2.7 and 3.1 if we wrap it in a print call to request a more user-friendly display. String formatting is still subtly different, though, even in 3.X; round rounds and drops decimal digits but still produces a floating-point number in memory, whereas string formatting produces a string, not a number:

```
>>> (1 / 3.0), round(1 / 3.0, 2), ('%.2f' % (1 / 3.0))
(0.3333333333333333, 0.33, '0.33')
```

Interestingly, there are three ways to compute *square roots* in Python: using a module function, an expression, or a built-in function (if you're interested in performance, we will revisit these in an exercise and its solution at the end of Part IV, to see which runs quicker):

```
>>> import math
>>> math.sqrt(144)              # Module
12.0
>>> 144 ** .5                   # Expression
12.0
>>> pow(144, .5)                # Built-in
12.0

>>> math.sqrt(1234567890)       # Larger numbers
35136.41828644462
>>> 1234567890 ** .5
35136.41828644462
>>> pow(1234567890, .5)
35136.41828644462
```

Notice that standard library modules such as math must be imported, but built-in functions such as abs and round are always available without imports. In other words, modules are external components, but built-in functions live in an implied namespace that Python automatically searches to find names used in your program. This namespace simply corresponds to the standard library module called builtins in Python 3.X (and __builtin__ in 2.X). There is much more about name resolution in the function and module parts of this book; for now, when you hear "module," think "import."

The standard library random module must be imported as well. This module provides an array of tools, for tasks such as picking a random floating-point number between 0 and 1, and selecting a random integer between two numbers:

```
>>> import random
>>> random.random()
0.5566014960423105
>>> random.random()             # Random floats, integers, choices, shuffles
0.051308506597373515
```

```
>>> random.randint(1, 10)
5
>>> random.randint(1, 10)
9
```

This module can also *choose* an item at random from a sequence, and *shuffle* a list of items randomly:

```
>>> random.choice(['Life of Brian', 'Holy Grail', 'Meaning of Life'])
'Holy Grail'
>>> random.choice(['Life of Brian', 'Holy Grail', 'Meaning of Life'])
'Life of Brian'

>>> suits = ['hearts', 'clubs', 'diamonds', 'spades']
>>> random.shuffle(suits)
>>> suits
['spades', 'hearts', 'diamonds', 'clubs']
>>> random.shuffle(suits)
>>> suits
['clubs', 'diamonds', 'hearts', 'spades']
```

Though we'd need additional code to make this more tangible here, the random module can be useful for shuffling cards in games, picking images at random in a slideshow GUI, performing statistical simulations, and much more. We'll deploy it again later in this book (e.g., in Chapter 20's permutations case study), but for more details, see Python's library manual.

Other Numeric Types

So far in this chapter, we've been using Python's core numeric types—integer, floating point, and complex. These will suffice for most of the number crunching that most programmers will ever need to do. Python comes with a handful of more exotic numeric types, though, that merit a brief look here.

Decimal Type

Python 2.4 introduced a new core numeric type: the decimal object, formally known as Decimal. Syntactically, you create decimals by calling a function within an imported module, rather than running a literal expression. Functionally, decimals are like floating-point numbers, but they have a fixed number of decimal points. Hence, decimals are *fixed-precision* floating-point values.

For example, with decimals, we can have a floating-point value that always retains just two decimal digits. Furthermore, we can specify how to round or truncate the extra decimal digits beyond the object's cutoff. Although it generally incurs a performance penalty compared to the normal floating-point type, the decimal type is well suited to representing fixed-precision quantities like sums of money and can help you achieve better numeric accuracy.

Decimal basics

The last point merits elaboration. As previewed briefly when we explored comparisons, floating-point math is less than exact because of the limited space used to store values. For example, the following should yield zero, but it does not. The result is close to zero, but there are not enough bits to be precise here:

```
>>> 0.1 + 0.1 + 0.1 - 0.3                      # Python 3.3
5.551115123125783e-17
```

Printing the result to produce the user-friendly display format doesn't completely help either, because the hardware related to floating-point math is inherently limited in terms of accuracy (a.k.a. *precision*). The following in 3.3 gives the same result as the previous output:

```
>>> print(0.1 + 0.1 + 0.1 - 0.3)               # Earlier Pythons (3.3. differs)
5.55111512313e-17
```

However, with decimals, the result can be dead-on:

```
>>> from decimal import Decimal
>>> Decimal('0.1') + Decimal('0.1') + Decimal('0.1') - Decimal('0.3')
Decimal('0.0')
```

As shown here, we can make decimal objects by calling the Decimal constructor function in the decimal module and passing in strings that have the desired number of decimal digits for the resulting object (using the str function to convert floating-point values to strings if needed). When decimals of different precision are mixed in expressions, Python converts up to the largest number of decimal digits automatically:

```
>>> Decimal('0.1') + Decimal('0.10') + Decimal('0.10') - Decimal('0.30')
Decimal('0.00')
```

In Pythons 2.7, 3.1, and later, it's also possible to create a decimal object from a floating-point object, with a call of the form decimal.Decimal.from_float(1.25), and recent Pythons allow floating-point numbers to be used directly. The conversion is exact but can sometimes yield a large default number of digits, unless they are fixed per the next section:

```
>>> Decimal(0.1) + Decimal(0.1) + Decimal(0.1) - Decimal(0.3)
Decimal('2.775557561565156540423631668E-17')
```

In Python 3.3 and later, the decimal module was also optimized to improve its performance radically: the reported speedup for the new version is 10X to 100X, depending on the type of program benchmarked.

Setting decimal precision globally

Other tools in the decimal module can be used to set the precision of all decimal numbers, arrange error handling, and more. For instance, a context object in this module allows for specifying precision (number of decimal digits) and rounding modes (down, ceiling, etc.). The precision is applied globally for all decimals created in the calling thread:

```
>>> import decimal
>>> decimal.Decimal(1) / decimal.Decimal(7)          # Default: 28 digits
Decimal('0.1428571428571428571428571429')

>>> decimal.getcontext().prec = 4                     # Fixed precision
>>> decimal.Decimal(1) / decimal.Decimal(7)
Decimal('0.1429')

>>> Decimal(0.1) + Decimal(0.1) + Decimal(0.1) - Decimal(0.3)   # Closer to 0
Decimal('1.110E-17')
```

Technically, significance is determined by digits input, and precision is applied on math operations. Although more subtle than we can explore in this brief overview, this property can make decimals useful as the basis for some monetary applications, and may sometimes serve as an alternative to manual rounding and string formatting:

```
>>> 1999 + 1.33          # This has more digits in memory than displayed in 3.3
2000.33
>>>
>>> decimal.getcontext().prec = 2
>>> pay = decimal.Decimal(str(1999 + 1.33))
>>> pay
Decimal('2000.33')
```

Decimal context manager

In Python 2.6 and 3.0 and later, it's also possible to reset precision temporarily by using the `with` context manager statement. The precision is reset to its original value on statement exit; in a new Python 3.3 session (per Chapter 3 the "..." here is Python's interactive prompt for continuation lines in some interfaces and requires manual indentation; IDLE omits this prompt and indents for you):

```
C:\code> C:\Python33\python
>>> import decimal
>>> decimal.Decimal('1.00') / decimal.Decimal('3.00')
Decimal('0.3333333333333333333333333333')
>>>
>>> with decimal.localcontext() as ctx:
...     ctx.prec = 2
...     decimal.Decimal('1.00') / decimal.Decimal('3.00')
...
Decimal('0.33')
>>>
>>> decimal.Decimal('1.00') / decimal.Decimal('3.00')
Decimal('0.3333333333333333333333333333')
```

Though useful, this statement requires much more background knowledge than you've obtained at this point; watch for coverage of the `with` statement in Chapter 34.

Because use of the decimal type is still relatively rare in practice, I'll defer to Python's standard library manuals and interactive help for more details. And because decimals address some of the same floating-point accuracy issues as the fraction type, let's move on to the next section to see how the two compare.

Fraction Type

Python 2.6 and 3.0 debuted a new numeric type, Fraction, which implements a *rational number* object. It essentially keeps both a numerator and a denominator explicitly, so as to avoid some of the inaccuracies and limitations of floating-point math. Like decimals, fractions do not map as closely to computer hardware as floating-point numbers. This means their performance may not be as good, but it also allows them to provide extra utility in a standard tool where required or useful.

Fraction basics

Fraction is a functional cousin to the Decimal fixed-precision type described in the prior section, as both can be used to address the floating-point type's numerical inaccuracies. It's also used in similar ways—like Decimal, Fraction resides in a module; import its constructor and pass in a numerator and a denominator to make one (among other schemes). The following interaction shows how:

```
>>> from fractions import Fraction
>>> x = Fraction(1, 3)          # Numerator, denominator
>>> y = Fraction(4, 6)          # Simplified to 2, 3 by gcd

>>> x
Fraction(1, 3)
>>> y
Fraction(2, 3)
>>> print(y)
2/3
```

Once created, Fractions can be used in mathematical expressions as usual:

```
>>> x + y
Fraction(1, 1)
>>> x - y                       # Results are exact: numerator, denominator
Fraction(-1, 3)
>>> x * y
Fraction(2, 9)
```

Fraction objects can also be created from floating-point number strings, much like decimals:

```
>>> Fraction('.25')
Fraction(1, 4)
>>> Fraction('1.25')
Fraction(5, 4)
>>>
>>> Fraction('.25') + Fraction('1.25')
Fraction(3, 2)
```

Numeric accuracy in fractions and decimals

Notice that this is different from floating-point-type math, which is constrained by the underlying limitations of floating-point hardware. To compare, here are the same operations run with floating-point objects, and notes on their limited accuracy—they may display fewer digits in recent Pythons than they used to, but they still aren't exact values in memory:

```
>>> a = 1 / 3.0                      # Only as accurate as floating-point hardware
>>> b = 4 / 6.0                      # Can lose precision over many calculations
>>> a
0.3333333333333333
>>> b
0.6666666666666666

>>> a + b
1.0
>>> a - b
-0.3333333333333333
>>> a * b
0.2222222222222222
```

This floating-point limitation is especially apparent for values that cannot be represented accurately given their limited number of bits in memory. Both Fraction and Decimal provide ways to get exact results, albeit at the cost of some speed and code verbosity. For instance, in the following example (repeated from the prior section), floating-point numbers do not accurately give the zero answer expected, but both of the other types do:

```
>>> 0.1 + 0.1 + 0.1 - 0.3            # This should be zero (close, but not exact)
5.551115123125783e-17

>>> from fractions import Fraction
>>> Fraction(1, 10) + Fraction(1, 10) + Fraction(1, 10) - Fraction(3, 10)
Fraction(0, 1)

>>> from decimal import Decimal
>>> Decimal('0.1') + Decimal('0.1') + Decimal('0.1') - Decimal('0.3')
Decimal('0.0')
```

Moreover, fractions and decimals both allow more intuitive and accurate results than floating points sometimes can, in different ways—by using rational representation and by limiting precision:

```
>>> 1 / 3                            # Use a ".0" in Python 2.X for true "/"
0.3333333333333333

>>> Fraction(1, 3)                   # Numeric accuracy, two ways
Fraction(1, 3)

>>> import decimal
>>> decimal.getcontext().prec = 2
>>> Decimal(1) / Decimal(3)
Decimal('0.33')
```

In fact, fractions both retain accuracy and automatically simplify results. Continuing the preceding interaction:

```
>>> (1 / 3) + (6 / 12)              # Use a ".0" in Python 2.X for true "/"
0.8333333333333333

>>> Fraction(6, 12)                 # Automatically simplified
Fraction(1, 2)

>>> Fraction(1, 3) + Fraction(6, 12)
Fraction(5, 6)

>>> decimal.Decimal(str(1/3)) + decimal.Decimal(str(6/12))
Decimal('0.83')

>>> 1000.0 / 1234567890
8.100000073710001e-07
>>> Fraction(1000, 1234567890)      # Substantially simpler!
Fraction(100, 123456789)
```

Fraction conversions and mixed types

To support fraction conversions, floating-point objects now have a method that yields their numerator and denominator ratio, fractions have a `from_float` method, and `float` accepts a `Fraction` as an argument. Trace through the following interaction to see how this pans out (the * in the second test is special syntax that expands a tuple into individual arguments; more on this when we study function argument passing in Chapter 18):

```
>>> (2.5).as_integer_ratio()        # float object method
(5, 2)

>>> f = 2.5
>>> z = Fraction(*f.as_integer_ratio())   # Convert float -> fraction: two args
>>> z                                      # Same as Fraction(5, 2)
Fraction(5, 2)

>>> x                                # x from prior interaction
Fraction(1, 3)
>>> x + z
Fraction(17, 6)                      # 5/2 + 1/3 = 15/6 + 2/6

>>> float(x)                         # Convert fraction -> float
0.3333333333333333
>>> float(z)
2.5
>>> float(x + z)
2.8333333333333335
>>> 17 / 6
2.8333333333333335

>>> Fraction.from_float(1.75)        # Convert float -> fraction: other way
Fraction(7, 4)
```

```
>>> Fraction(*(1.75).as_integer_ratio())
Fraction(7, 4)
```

Finally, some type mixing is allowed in expressions, though `Fraction` must sometimes be manually propagated to retain accuracy. Study the following interaction to see how this works:

```
>>> x
Fraction(1, 3)
>>> x + 2                   # Fraction + int -> Fraction
Fraction(7, 3)
>>> x + 2.0                 # Fraction + float -> float
2.3333333333333335
>>> x + (1./3)              # Fraction + float -> float
0.6666666666666666
>>> x + (4./3)
1.6666666666666665
>>> x + Fraction(4, 3)      # Fraction + Fraction -> Fraction
Fraction(5, 3)
```

Caveat: although you can convert from floating point to fraction, in some cases there is an unavoidable precision loss when you do so, because the number is inaccurate in its original floating-point form. When needed, you can simplify such results by limiting the maximum denominator value:

```
>>> 4.0 / 3
1.3333333333333333
>>> (4.0 / 3).as_integer_ratio()        # Precision loss from float
(6004799503160661, 4503599627370496)

>>> x
Fraction(1, 3)
>>> a = x + Fraction(*(4.0 / 3).as_integer_ratio())
>>> a
Fraction(22517998136852479, 13510798882111488)

>>> 22517998136852479 / 13510798882111488.    # 5 / 3 (or close to it!)
1.6666666666666667

>>> a.limit_denominator(10)                   # Simplify to closest fraction
Fraction(5, 3)
```

For more details on the `Fraction` type, experiment further on your own and consult the Python 2.6, 2.7, and 3.X library manuals and other documentation.

Sets

Besides decimals, Python 2.4 also introduced a new collection type, the *set*—an unordered collection of unique and immutable objects that supports operations corresponding to mathematical set theory. By definition, an item appears only once in a set, no matter how many times it is added. Accordingly, sets have a variety of applications, especially in numeric and database-focused work.

Because sets are collections of other objects, they share some behavior with objects such as lists and dictionaries that are outside the scope of this chapter. For example, sets are iterable, can grow and shrink on demand, and may contain a variety of object types. As we'll see, a set acts much like the keys of a valueless dictionary, but it supports extra operations.

However, because sets are unordered and do not map keys to values, they are neither sequence nor mapping types; they are a type category unto themselves. Moreover, because sets are fundamentally mathematical in nature (and for many readers, may seem more academic and be used much less often than more pervasive objects like dictionaries), we'll explore the basic utility of Python's set objects here.

Set basics in Python 2.6 and earlier

There are a few ways to make sets today, depending on which Python you use. Since this book covers all, let's begin with the case for 2.6 and earlier, which also is available (and sometimes still required) in later Pythons; we'll refine this for 2.7 and 3.X extensions in a moment. To make a set object, pass in a sequence or other iterable object to the built-in set function:

```
>>> x = set('abcde')
>>> y = set('bdxyz')
```

You get back a set object, which contains all the items in the object passed in (notice that sets do not have a positional ordering, and so are not sequences—their order is arbitrary and may vary per Python release):

```
>>> x
set(['a', 'c', 'b', 'e', 'd'])                    # Pythons <= 2.6 display format
```

Sets made this way support the common mathematical set operations with *expression* operators. Note that we can't perform the following operations on plain sequences like strings, lists, and tuples—we must create sets from them by passing them to set in order to apply these tools:

```
>>> x - y                                         # Difference
set(['a', 'c', 'e'])

>>> x | y                                         # Union
set(['a', 'c', 'b', 'e', 'd', 'y', 'x', 'z'])

>>> x & y                                         # Intersection
set(['b', 'd'])

>>> x ^ y                                         # Symmetric difference (XOR)
set(['a', 'c', 'e', 'y', 'x', 'z'])

>>> x > y, x < y                                  # Superset, subset
(False, False)
```

The notable exception to this rule is the in set membership test—this expression is also defined to work on all other collection types, where it also performs membership (or a search, if you prefer to think in procedural terms). Hence, we do not need to convert things like strings and lists to sets to run this test:

```
>>> 'e' in x                              # Membership (sets)
True

>>> 'e' in 'Camelot', 22 in [11, 22, 33]  # But works on other types too
(True, True)
```

In addition to expressions, the set object provides *methods* that correspond to these operations and more, and that support set changes—the set `add` method inserts one item, `update` is an in-place union, and `remove` deletes an item by value (run a `dir` call on any set instance or the `set` type name to see all the available methods). Assuming x and y are still as they were in the prior interaction:

```
>>> z = x.intersection(y)              # Same as x & y
>>> z
set(['b', 'd'])
>>> z.add('SPAM')                      # Insert one item
>>> z
set(['b', 'd', 'SPAM'])
>>> z.update(set(['X', 'Y']))          # Merge: in-place union
>>> z
set(['Y', 'X', 'b', 'd', 'SPAM'])
>>> z.remove('b')                      # Delete one item
>>> z
set(['Y', 'X', 'd', 'SPAM'])
```

As *iterable* containers, sets can also be used in operations such as `len`, `for` loops, and list comprehensions. Because they are unordered, though, they don't support sequence operations like indexing and slicing:

```
>>> for item in set('abc'): print(item * 3)

aaa
ccc
bbb
```

Finally, although the set expressions shown earlier generally require two sets, their method-based counterparts can often work with *any iterable type* as well:

```
>>> S = set([1, 2, 3])

>>> S | set([3, 4])            # Expressions require both to be sets
set([1, 2, 3, 4])
>>> S | [3, 4]
TypeError: unsupported operand type(s) for |: 'set' and 'list'

>>> S.union([3, 4])            # But their methods allow any iterable
set([1, 2, 3, 4])
>>> S.intersection((1, 3, 5))
set([1, 3])
>>> S.issubset(range(-5, 5))
True
```

For more details on set operations, see Python's library reference manual or a reference book. Although set operations can be coded manually in Python with other types, like lists and dictionaries (and often were in the past), Python's built-in sets use efficient algorithms and implementation techniques to provide quick and standard operation.

Set literals in Python 3.X and 2.7

If you think sets are "cool," they eventually became noticeably cooler, with new syntax for set *literals* and *comprehensions* initially added in the Python 3.X line only, but back-ported to Python 2.7 by popular demand. In these Pythons we can still use the **set** built-in to make set objects, but also a new set literal form, using the curly braces formerly reserved for dictionaries. In 3.X and 2.7, the following are equivalent:

```
set([1, 2, 3, 4])          # Built-in call (all)
{1, 2, 3, 4}               # Newer set literals (2.7, 3.X)
```

This syntax makes sense, given that sets are essentially like *valueless dictionaries*—because a set's items are unordered, unique, and immutable, the items behave much like a dictionary's keys. This operational similarity is even more striking given that dictionary key lists in 3.X are *view* objects, which support set-like behavior such as intersections and unions (see Chapter 8 for more on dictionary view objects).

Regardless of how a set is made, 3.X displays it using the new literal format. Python 2.7 *accepts* the new literal syntax, but still *displays* sets using the 2.6 display form of the prior section. In all Pythons, the **set** built-in is still required to create empty sets and to build sets from existing iterable objects (short of using set comprehensions, discussed later in this chapter), but the new literal is convenient for initializing sets of known structure.

Here's what sets look like in 3.X; it's the same in 2.7, except that set results display with 2.X's set([...]) notation, and item order may vary per version (which by definition is irrelevant in sets anyhow):

```
C:\code> c:\python33\python
>>> set([1, 2, 3, 4])              # Built-in: same as in 2.6
{1, 2, 3, 4}
>>> set('spam')                    # Add all items in an iterable
{'s', 'a', 'p', 'm'}

>>> {1, 2, 3, 4}                   # Set literals: new in 3.X (and 2.7)
{1, 2, 3, 4}
>>> S = {'s', 'p', 'a', 'm'}
>>> S
{'s', 'a', 'p', 'm'}

>>> S.add('alot')                  # Methods work as before
>>> S
{'s', 'a', 'p', 'alot', 'm'}
```

All the set processing operations discussed in the prior section work the same in 3.X, but the result sets print differently:

```
>>> S1 = {1, 2, 3, 4}
>>> S1 & {1, 3}                  # Intersection
{1, 3}
>>> {1, 5, 3, 6} | S1            # Union
{1, 2, 3, 4, 5, 6}
>>> S1 - {1, 3, 4}              # Difference
{2}
>>> S1 > {1, 3}                 # Superset
True
```

Note that {} is still a dictionary in all Pythons. *Empty* sets must be created with the set built-in, and print the same way:

```
>>> S1 - {1, 2, 3, 4}          # Empty sets print differently
set()
>>> type({})                   # Because {} is an empty dictionary
<class 'dict'>

>>> S = set()                  # Initialize an empty set
>>> S.add(1.23)
>>> S
{1.23}
```

As in Python 2.6 and earlier, sets created with 3.X/2.7 literals support the same methods, some of which allow general iterable operands that expressions do not:

```
>>> {1, 2, 3} | {3, 4}
{1, 2, 3, 4}
>>> {1, 2, 3} | [3, 4]
TypeError: unsupported operand type(s) for |: 'set' and 'list'

>>> {1, 2, 3}.union([3, 4])
{1, 2, 3, 4}
>>> {1, 2, 3}.union({3, 4})
{1, 2, 3, 4}
>>> {1, 2, 3}.union(set([3, 4]))
{1, 2, 3, 4}

>>> {1, 2, 3}.intersection((1, 3, 5))
{1, 3}
>>> {1, 2, 3}.issubset(range(-5, 5))
True
```

Immutable constraints and frozen sets

Sets are powerful and flexible objects, but they do have one constraint in both 3.X and 2.X that you should keep in mind—largely because of their implementation, sets can only contain *immutable* (a.k.a. "hashable") object types. Hence, lists and dictionaries cannot be embedded in sets, but tuples can if you need to store compound values. Tuples compare by their full values when used in set operations:

```
>>> S
{1.23}
>>> S.add([1, 2, 3])           # Only immutable objects work in a set
TypeError: unhashable type: 'list'
```

```
>>> S.add({'a':1})
TypeError: unhashable type: 'dict'
>>> S.add((1, 2, 3))
>>> S                              # No list or dict, but tuple OK
{1.23, (1, 2, 3)}

>>> S | {(4, 5, 6), (1, 2, 3)}     # Union: same as S.union(...)
{1.23, (4, 5, 6), (1, 2, 3)}
>>> (1, 2, 3) in S                 # Membership: by complete values
True
>>> (1, 4, 3) in S
False
```

Tuples in a set, for instance, might be used to represent dates, records, IP addresses, and so on (more on tuples later in this part of the book). Sets may also contain modules, type objects, and more. Sets themselves are mutable too, and so cannot be nested in other sets directly; if you need to store a set inside another set, the `frozenset` built-in call works just like `set` but creates an immutable set that cannot change and thus can be embedded in other sets.

Set comprehensions in Python 3.X and 2.7

In addition to literals, Python 3.X grew a set comprehension construct that was back-ported for use to Python 2.7 too. Like the 3.X set literal, 2.7 accepts its syntax, but displays its results in 2.X set notation. The set comprehension expression is similar in form to the list comprehension we previewed in Chapter 4, but is coded in curly braces instead of square brackets and run to make a set instead of a list. Set comprehensions run a loop and collect the result of an expression on each iteration; a loop variable gives access to the current iteration value for use in the collection expression. The result is a new set you create by running the code, with all the normal set behavior. Here is a set comprehension in 3.3 (again, result display and order differs in 2.7):

```
>>> {x ** 2 for x in [1, 2, 3, 4]}     # 3.X/2.7 set comprehension
{16, 1, 4, 9}
```

In this expression, the loop is coded on the right, and the collection expression is coded on the left (x ** 2). As for list comprehensions, we get back pretty much what this expression says: "Give me a new set containing X squared, for every X in a list." Comprehensions can also iterate across other kinds of objects, such as strings (the first of the following examples illustrates the comprehension-based way to make a set from an existing iterable):

```
>>> {x for x in 'spam'}                # Same as: set('spam')
{'m', 's', 'p', 'a'}

>>> {c * 4 for c in 'spam'}            # Set of collected expression results
{'pppp', 'aaaa', 'ssss', 'mmmm'}
>>> {c * 4 for c in 'spamham'}
{'pppp', 'aaaa', 'hhhh', 'ssss', 'mmmm'}

>>> S = {c * 4 for c in 'spam'}
```

```
>>> S | {'mmmm', 'xxxx'}
{'pppp', 'xxxx', 'mmmm', 'aaaa', 'ssss'}
>>> S & {'mmmm', 'xxxx'}
{'mmmm'}
```

Because the rest of the comprehensions story relies upon underlying concepts we're not yet prepared to address, we'll postpone further details until later in this book. In Chapter 8, we'll meet a first cousin in 3.X and 2.7, the dictionary comprehension, and I'll have much more to say about all comprehensions—list, set, dictionary, and generator—later on, especially in Chapter 14 and Chapter 20. As we'll learn there, all comprehensions support additional syntax not shown here, including nested loops and `if` tests, which can be challenging to understand until you've had a chance to study larger statements.

Why sets?

Set operations have a variety of common uses, some more practical than mathematical. For example, because items are stored only once in a set, sets can be used to *filter duplicates* out of other collections, though items may be reordered in the process because sets are unordered in general. Simply convert the collection to a set, and then convert it back again (sets work in the `list` call here because they are *iterable*, another technical artifact that we'll unearth later):

```
>>> L = [1, 2, 1, 3, 2, 4, 5]
>>> set(L)
{1, 2, 3, 4, 5}
>>> L = list(set(L))                              # Remove duplicates
>>> L
[1, 2, 3, 4, 5]

>>> list(set(['yy', 'cc', 'aa', 'xx', 'dd', 'aa']))    # But order may change
['cc', 'xx', 'yy', 'dd', 'aa']
```

Sets can be used to *isolate differences* in lists, strings, and other iterable objects too—simply convert to sets and take the difference—though again the unordered nature of sets means that the results may not match that of the originals. The last two of the following compare attribute lists of string object types in 3.X (results vary in 2.7):

```
>>> set([1, 3, 5, 7]) - set([1, 2, 4, 5, 6])      # Find list differences
{3, 7}
>>> set('abcdefg') - set('abdghij')               # Find string differences
{'c', 'e', 'f'}
>>> set('spam') - set(['h', 'a', 'm'])            # Find differences, mixed
{'p', 's'}

>>> set(dir(bytes)) - set(dir(bytearray))         # In bytes but not bytearray
{'__getnewargs__'}
>>> set(dir(bytearray)) - set(dir(bytes))
{'append', 'copy', '__alloc__', '__imul__', 'remove', 'pop', 'insert', ...more...]
```

You can also use sets to perform *order-neutral equality* tests by converting to a set before the test, because order doesn't matter in a set. More formally, two sets are *equal* if and only if every element of each set is contained in the other—that is, each is a subset of the other, regardless of order. For instance, you might use this to compare the outputs of programs that should work the same but may generate results in different order. Sorting before testing has the same effect for equality, but sets don't rely on an expensive sort, and sorts order their results to support additional magnitude tests that sets do not (greater, less, and so on):

```
>>> L1, L2 = [1, 3, 5, 2, 4], [2, 5, 3, 4, 1]
>>> L1 == L2                                       # Order matters in sequences
False
>>> set(L1) == set(L2)                             # Order-neutral equality
True
>>> sorted(L1) == sorted(L2)                       # Similar but results ordered
True
>>> 'spam' == 'asmp', set('spam') == set('asmp'), sorted('spam') == sorted('asmp')
(False, True, True)
```

Sets can also be used to keep track of where you've already been when traversing a graph or other *cyclic* structure. For example, the transitive module reloader and inheritance tree lister examples we'll study in Chapter 25 and Chapter 31, respectively, must keep track of items visited to avoid loops, as Chapter 19 discusses in the abstract. Using a list in this context is inefficient because searches require linear scans. Although recording states visited as keys in a dictionary is efficient, sets offer an alternative that's essentially equivalent (and may be more or less intuitive, depending on whom you ask).

Finally, sets are also convenient when you're dealing with large data sets (database query results, for example)—the intersection of two sets contains objects common to both categories, and the union contains all items in either set. To illustrate, here's a somewhat more realistic example of set operations at work, applied to lists of people in a hypothetical company, using 3.X/2.7 set literals and 3.X result displays (use set in 2.6 and earlier):

```
>>> engineers = {'bob', 'sue', 'ann', 'vic'}
>>> managers  = {'tom', 'sue'}

>>> 'bob' in engineers              # Is bob an engineer?
True

>>> engineers & managers            # Who is both engineer and manager?
{'sue'}

>>> engineers | managers            # All people in either category
{'bob', 'tom', 'sue', 'vic', 'ann'}

>>> engineers - managers            # Engineers who are not managers
{'vic', 'ann', 'bob'}

>>> managers - engineers            # Managers who are not engineers
{'tom'}

>>> engineers > managers            # Are all managers engineers? (superset)
False
```

```
>>> {'bob', 'sue'} < engineers          # Are both engineers? (subset)
True

>>> (managers | engineers) > managers   # All people is a superset of managers
True

>>> managers ^ engineers                # Who is in one but not both?
{'tom', 'vic', 'ann', 'bob'}

>>> (managers | engineers) - (managers ^ engineers)    # Intersection!
{'sue'}
```

You can find more details on set operations in the Python library manual and some mathematical and relational database theory texts. Also stay tuned for Chapter 8's revival of some of the set operations we've seen here, in the context of dictionary view objects in Python 3.X.

Booleans

Some may argue that the Python Boolean type, bool, is numeric in nature because its two values, True and False, are just customized versions of the integers 1 and 0 that print themselves differently. Although that's all most programmers need to know, let's explore this type in a bit more detail.

More formally, Python today has an explicit Boolean data type called bool, with the values True and False available as preassigned built-in names. Internally, the names True and False are instances of bool, which is in turn just a subclass (in the object-oriented sense) of the built-in integer type int. True and False behave exactly like the integers 1 and 0, except that they have customized printing logic—they print themselves as the words True and False, instead of the digits 1 and 0. bool accomplishes this by redefining str and repr string formats for its two objects.

Because of this customization, the output of Boolean expressions typed at the interactive prompt prints as the words True and False instead of the older and less obvious 1 and 0. In addition, Booleans make truth values more explicit in your code. For instance, an infinite loop can now be coded as while True: instead of the less intuitive while 1:. Similarly, flags can be initialized more clearly with flag = False. We'll discuss these statements further in Part III.

Again, though, for most practical purposes, you can treat True and False as though they are predefined variables set to integers 1 and 0. Most programmers had been pre-assigning True and False to 1 and 0 anyway; the bool type simply makes this standard. Its implementation can lead to curious results, though. Because True is just the integer 1 with a custom display format, True + 4 yields integer 5 in Python!

```
>>> type(True)
<class 'bool'>
>>> isinstance(True, int)
True
```

```
>>> True == 1               # Same value
True
>>> True is 1               # But a different object: see the next chapter
False
>>> True or False           # Same as: 1 or 0
True
>>> True + 4                # (Hmmm)
5
```

Since you probably won't come across an expression like the last of these in real Python code, you can safely ignore any of its deeper metaphysical implications.

We'll revisit Booleans in Chapter 9 to define Python's notion of truth, and again in Chapter 12 to see how Boolean operators like and and or work.

Numeric Extensions

Finally, although Python core numeric types offer plenty of power for most applications, there is a large library of third-party open source extensions available to address more focused needs. Because numeric programming is a popular domain for Python, you'll find a wealth of advanced tools.

For example, if you need to do serious number crunching, an optional extension for Python called *NumPy* (Numeric Python) provides advanced numeric programming tools, such as a matrix data type, vector processing, and sophisticated computation libraries. Hardcore scientific programming groups at places like Los Alamos and NASA use Python with NumPy to implement the sorts of tasks they previously coded in C++, FORTRAN, or Matlab. The combination of Python and NumPy is often compared to a free, more flexible version of Matlab—you get NumPy's performance, plus the Python language and its libraries.

Because it's so advanced, we won't talk further about NumPy in this book. You can find additional support for advanced numeric programming in Python, including graphics and plotting tools, extended precision floats, statistics libraries, and the popular *SciPy* package by searching the Web. Also note that NumPy is currently an optional extension; it doesn't come with Python and must be installed separately, though you'll probably want to do so if you care enough about this domain to look it up on the Web.

Chapter Summary

This chapter has taken a tour of Python's numeric object types and the operations we can apply to them. Along the way, we met the standard integer and floating-point types, as well as some more exotic and less commonly used types such as complex numbers, decimals, fractions, and sets. We also explored Python's expression syntax, type conversions, bitwise operations, and various literal forms for coding numbers in scripts.

Later in this part of the book, we'll continue our in-depth type tour by filling in some details about the next object type—the string. In the next chapter, however, we'll take some time to explore the mechanics of variable assignment in more detail than we have here. This turns out to be perhaps the most fundamental idea in Python, so make sure you check out the next chapter before moving on. First, though, it's time to take the usual chapter quiz.

Test Your Knowledge: Quiz

1. What is the value of the expression 2 * (3 + 4) in Python?
2. What is the value of the expression 2 * 3 + 4 in Python?
3. What is the value of the expression 2 + 3 * 4 in Python?
4. What tools can you use to find a number's square root, as well as its square?
5. What is the type of the result of the expression 1 + 2.0 + 3?
6. How can you truncate and round a floating-point number?
7. How can you convert an integer to a floating-point number?
8. How would you display an integer in octal, hexadecimal, or binary notation?
9. How might you convert an octal, hexadecimal, or binary string to a plain integer?

Test Your Knowledge: Answers

1. The value will be 14, the result of 2 * 7, because the parentheses force the addition to happen before the multiplication.
2. The value will be 10, the result of 6 + 4. Python's operator precedence rules are applied in the absence of parentheses, and multiplication has higher precedence than (i.e., happens before) addition, per Table 5-2.
3. This expression yields 14, the result of 2 + 12, for the same precedence reasons as in the prior question.
4. Functions for obtaining the square root, as well as *pi*, tangents, and more, are available in the imported math module. To find a number's square root, import math and call math.sqrt(N). To get a number's square, use either the exponent expression X ** 2 or the built-in function pow(X, 2). Either of these last two can also compute the square root when given a power of 0.5 (e.g., X ** .5).
5. The result will be a floating-point number: the integers are converted up to floating point, the most complex type in the expression, and floating-point math is used to evaluate it.
6. The int(N) and math.trunc(N) functions truncate, and the round(N, digits) function rounds. We can also compute the floor with math.floor(N) and round for display with string formatting operations.

7. The `float(I)` function converts an integer to a floating point; mixing an integer with a floating point within an expression will result in a conversion as well. In some sense, Python 3.X / division converts too—it always returns a floating-point result that includes the remainder, even if both operands are integers.

8. The `oct(I)` and `hex(I)` built-in functions return the octal and hexadecimal string forms for an integer. The `bin(I)` call also returns a number's binary digits string in Pythons 2.6, 3.0, and later. The `%` string formatting expression and `format` string method also provide targets for some such conversions.

9. The `int(S, base)` function can be used to convert from octal and hexadecimal strings to normal integers (pass in 8, 16, or 2 for the base). The `eval(S)` function can be used for this purpose too, but it's more expensive to run and can have security issues. Note that integers are always stored in binary form in computer memory; these are just display string format conversions.

## CHAPTER 6

The Dynamic Typing Interlude

In the prior chapter, we began exploring Python's core object types in depth by studying Python numeric types and operations. We'll resume our object type tour in the next chapter, but before we move on, it's important that you get a handle on what may be the most fundamental idea in Python programming and is certainly the basis of much of both the conciseness and flexibility of the Python language—dynamic typing, and the polymorphism it implies.

As you'll see here and throughout this book, in Python, we do not declare the specific types of the objects our scripts use. In fact, most programs should not even *care* about specific types; in exchange, they are naturally applicable in more contexts than we can sometimes even plan ahead for. Because dynamic typing is the root of this flexibility, and is also a potential stumbling block for newcomers, let's take a brief side trip to explore the model here.

The Case of the Missing Declaration Statements

If you have a background in compiled or statically typed languages like C, C++, or Java, you might find yourself a bit perplexed at this point in the book. So far, we've been using variables without declaring their existence or their types, and it somehow works. When we type a = 3 in an interactive session or program file, for instance, how does Python know that a should stand for an integer? For that matter, how does Python know what a is at all?

Once you start asking such questions, you've crossed over into the domain of Python's *dynamic typing* model. In Python, types are determined automatically at runtime, not in response to declarations in your code. This means that you never declare variables ahead of time (a concept that is perhaps simpler to grasp if you keep in mind that it all boils down to variables, objects, and the links between them).

Variables, Objects, and References

As you've seen in many of the examples used so far in this book, when you run an assignment statement such as a = 3 in Python, it works even if you've never told Python to use the name a as a variable, or that a should stand for an integer-type object. In the Python language, this all pans out in a very natural way, as follows:

Variable creation

A variable (also known in Python as a name), like a, is created when your code first assigns it a value. Future assignments change the value of the already created name. Technically, Python detects some names before your code runs, but you can think of it as though initial assignments make variables.

Variable types

A variable never has any type information or constraints associated with it. The notion of type lives with objects, not names. Variables are generic in nature; they always simply refer to a particular object at a particular point in time.

Variable use

When a variable appears in an expression, it is immediately replaced with the object that it currently refers to, whatever that may be. Further, all variables must be explicitly assigned before they can be used; referencing unassigned variables results in errors.

In sum, variables are created when assigned, can reference any type of object, and must be assigned before they are referenced. This means that you never need to declare names used by your script, but you must initialize names before you can update them; counters, for example, must be initialized to zero before you can add to them.

This dynamic typing model is strikingly different from the typing model of traditional languages. When you are first starting out, the model is usually easier to understand if you keep clear the distinction between names and objects. For example, when we say this to assign a variable a value:

```
>>> a = 3                    # Assign a name to an object
```

at least conceptually, Python will perform three distinct steps to carry out the request. These steps reflect the operation of all assignments in the Python language:

1. Create an object to represent the value 3.
2. Create the variable a, if it does not yet exist.
3. Link the variable a to the new object 3.

The net result will be a structure inside Python that resembles Figure 6-1. As sketched, variables and objects are stored in different parts of memory and are associated by links (the link is shown as a pointer in the figure). Variables always link to objects and never to other variables, but larger objects may link to other objects (for instance, a list object has links to the objects it contains).

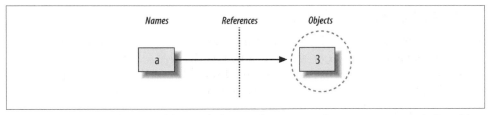

Figure 6-1. Names (a.k.a. variables) and objects after running the assignment a = 3. Variable a becomes a reference to the object 3. Internally, the variable is really a pointer to the object's memory space created by running the literal expression 3.

These links from variables to objects are called *references* in Python—that is, a reference is a kind of association, implemented as a pointer in memory.[1] Whenever the variables are later used (i.e., referenced), Python automatically follows the variable-to-object links. This is all simpler than the terminology may imply. In concrete terms:

- *Variables* are entries in a system table, with spaces for links to objects.
- *Objects* are pieces of allocated memory, with enough space to represent the values for which they stand.
- *References* are automatically followed pointers from variables to objects.

At least conceptually, each time you generate a new value in your script by running an expression, Python creates a new *object* (i.e., a chunk of memory) to represent that value. As an optimization, Python internally caches and reuses certain kinds of unchangeable objects, such as small integers and strings (each 0 is not really a new piece of memory—more on this caching behavior later). But from a logical perspective, it works as though each expression's result value is a distinct object and each object is a distinct piece of memory.

Technically speaking, objects have more structure than just enough space to represent their values. Each object also has two standard header fields: a *type designator* used to mark the type of the object, and a *reference counter* used to determine when it's OK to reclaim the object. To understand how these two header fields factor into the model, we need to move on.

Types Live with Objects, Not Variables

To see how object types come into play, watch what happens if we assign a variable multiple times:

---

1. Readers with a background in C may find Python references similar to C pointers (memory addresses). In fact, references are implemented as pointers, and they often serve the same roles, especially with objects that can be changed in place (more on this later). However, because references are always automatically dereferenced when used, you can never actually do anything useful with a reference itself; this is a feature that eliminates a vast category of C bugs. But you can think of Python references as C "void*" pointers, which are automatically followed whenever used.

```
>>> a = 3              # It's an integer
>>> a = 'spam'         # Now it's a string
>>> a = 1.23           # Now it's a floating point
```

This isn't typical Python code, but it does work—a starts out as an integer, then becomes a string, and finally becomes a floating-point number. This example tends to look especially odd to ex-C programmers, as it appears as though the *type* of a changes from integer to string when we say a = 'spam'.

However, that's not really what's happening. In Python, things work more simply. *Names* have no types; as stated earlier, types live with objects, not names. In the preceding listing, we've simply changed a to reference different objects. Because variables have no type, we haven't actually changed the type of the variable a; we've simply made the variable reference a different type of object. In fact, again, all we can ever say about a variable in Python is that it references a particular object at a particular point in time.

Objects, on the other hand, know what type they are—each object contains a header field that tags the object with its type. The integer object 3, for example, will contain the value 3, plus a designator that tells Python that the object is an integer (strictly speaking, a pointer to an object called int, the name of the integer type). The type designator of the 'spam' string object points to the string type (called str) instead. Because objects know their types, variables don't have to.

To recap, types are associated with objects in Python, not with variables. In typical code, a given variable usually will reference just one kind of object. Because this isn't a requirement, though, you'll find that Python code tends to be much more flexible than you may be accustomed to—if you use Python well, your code might work on many types automatically.

I mentioned that objects have two header fields, a type designator and a reference counter. To understand the latter of these, we need to move on and take a brief look at what happens at the end of an object's life.

Objects Are Garbage-Collected

In the prior section's listings, we assigned the variable a to different types of objects in each assignment. But when we reassign a variable, what happens to the value it was previously referencing? For example, after the following statements, what happens to the object 3?

```
>>> a = 3
>>> a = 'spam'
```

The answer is that in Python, whenever a name is assigned to a new object, the space held by the prior object is reclaimed if it is not referenced by any other name or object. This automatic reclamation of objects' space is known as *garbage collection*, and makes life much simpler for programmers of languages like Python that support it.

To illustrate, consider the following example, which sets the name x to a different object on each assignment:

```
>>> x = 42
>>> x = 'shrubbery'          # Reclaim 42 now (unless referenced elsewhere)
>>> x = 3.1415               # Reclaim 'shrubbery' now
>>> x = [1, 2, 3]            # Reclaim 3.1415 now
```

First, notice that x is set to a different type of object each time. Again, though this is not really the case, the effect is as though the type of x is changing over time. Remember, in Python types live with objects, not names. Because names are just generic references to objects, this sort of code works naturally.

Second, notice that references to objects are discarded along the way. Each time x is assigned to a new object, Python reclaims the prior object's space. For instance, when it is assigned the string 'shrubbery', the object 42 is immediately reclaimed (assuming it is not referenced anywhere else)—that is, the object's space is automatically thrown back into the free space pool, to be reused for a future object.

Internally, Python accomplishes this feat by keeping a counter in every object that keeps track of the number of references currently pointing to that object. As soon as (and exactly when) this counter drops to zero, the object's memory space is automatically reclaimed. In the preceding listing, we're assuming that each time x is assigned to a new object, the prior object's reference counter drops to zero, causing it to be reclaimed.

The most immediately tangible benefit of garbage collection is that it means you can use objects liberally without ever needing to allocate or free up space in your script. Python will clean up unused space for you as your program runs. In practice, this eliminates a substantial amount of bookkeeping code required in lower-level languages such as C and C++.

More on Python Garbage Collection

Technically speaking, Python's garbage collection is based mainly upon *reference counters*, as described here; however, it also has a component that detects and reclaims objects with *cyclic references* in time. This component can be disabled if you're sure that your code doesn't create cycles, but it is enabled by default.

Circular references are a classic issue in reference count garbage collectors. Because references are implemented as pointers, it's possible for an object to reference itself, or reference another object that does. For example, exercise 3 at the end of Part I and its solution in Appendix D show how to create a cycle easily by embedding a reference to a list within itself (e.g., L.append(L)). The same phenomenon can occur for assignments to attributes of objects created from user-defined classes. Though relatively rare, because the reference counts for such objects never drop to zero, they must be treated specially.

For more details on Python's cycle detector, see the documentation for the gc module in Python's library manual. The best news here is that garbage-collection-based memory management is implemented for you in Python, by people highly skilled at the task.

Also note that this chapter's description of Python's garbage collector applies to the standard Python (a.k.a. *CPython*) only; Chapter 2's alternative implementations such as Jython, IronPython, and PyPy may use different schemes, though the net effect in all is similar—unused space is reclaimed for you automatically, if not always as immediately.

Shared References

So far, we've seen what happens as a single variable is assigned references to objects. Now let's introduce another variable into our interaction and watch what happens to its names and objects:

```
>>> a = 3
>>> b = a
```

Typing these two statements generates the scene captured in Figure 6-2. The second command causes Python to create the variable b; the variable a is being used and not assigned here, so it is replaced with the object it references (3), and b is made to reference that object. The net effect is that the variables a and b wind up referencing the *same* object (that is, pointing to the same chunk of memory).

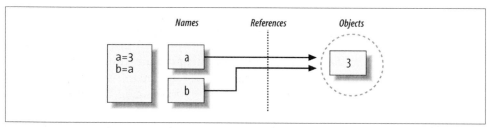

Figure 6-2. Names and objects after next running the assignment b = a. Variable b becomes a reference to the object 3. Internally, the variable is really a pointer to the object's memory space created by running the literal expression 3.

This scenario in Python—with multiple names referencing the same object—is usually called a *shared reference* (and sometimes just a *shared object*). Note that the names a and b are not linked to each other directly when this happens; in fact, there is no way to ever link a variable to another variable in Python. Rather, both variables point to the same object via their references.

Next, suppose we extend the session with one more statement:

```
>>> a = 3
>>> b = a
>>> a = 'spam'
```

As with all Python assignments, this statement simply makes a new object to represent the string value 'spam' and sets a to reference this new object. It does not, however,

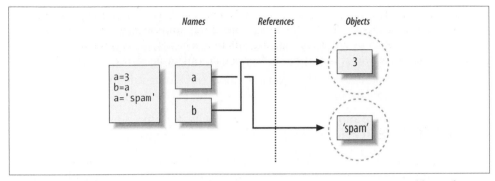

Figure 6-3. Names and objects after finally running the assignment a = 'spam'. Variable a references the new object (i.e., piece of memory) created by running the literal expression 'spam', but variable b still refers to the original object 3. Because this assignment is not an in-place change to the object 3, it changes only variable a, not b.

change the value of b; b still references the original object, the integer 3. The resulting reference structure is shown in Figure 6-3.

The same sort of thing would happen if we changed b to 'spam' instead—the assignment would change only b, not a. This behavior also occurs if there are no type differences at all. For example, consider these three statements:

```
>>> a = 3
>>> b = a
>>> a = a + 2
```

In this sequence, the same events transpire. Python makes the variable a reference the object 3 and makes b reference the same object as a, as in Figure 6-2; as before, the last assignment then sets a to a completely different object (in this case, the integer 5, which is the result of the + expression). It does not change b as a side effect. In fact, there is no way to *ever* overwrite the value of the object 3—as introduced in Chapter 4, integers are immutable and thus can never be changed in place.

One way to think of this is that, unlike in some languages, in Python variables are always pointers to objects, not labels of changeable memory areas: setting a variable to a new value does not alter the original object, but rather causes the variable to reference an entirely different object. The net effect is that assignment to a variable itself can impact only the single variable being assigned. When mutable objects and in-place changes enter the equation, though, the picture changes somewhat; to see how, let's move on.

Shared References and In-Place Changes

As you'll see later in this part's chapters, there are objects and operations that perform *in-place* object changes—Python's *mutable* types, including lists, dictionaries, and sets. For instance, an assignment to an offset in a list actually changes the list object itself in place, rather than generating a brand-new list object.

Though you must take it somewhat on faith at this point in the book, this distinction can matter much in your programs. For objects that support such in-place changes, you need to be more aware of shared references, since a change from one name may impact others. Otherwise, your objects may seem to change for no apparent reason. Given that all assignments are based on references (including function argument passing), it's a pervasive potential.

To illustrate, let's take another look at the list objects introduced in Chapter 4. Recall that lists, which do support in-place assignments to positions, are simply collections of other objects, coded in square brackets:

```
>>> L1 = [2, 3, 4]
>>> L2 = L1
```

L1 here is a list containing the objects 2, 3, and 4. Items inside a list are accessed by their positions, so L1[0] refers to object 2, the first item in the list L1. Of course, lists are also objects in their own right, just like integers and strings. After running the two prior assignments, L1 and L2 reference the same shared object, just like a and b in the prior example (see Figure 6-2). Now say that, as before, we extend this interaction to say the following:

```
>>> L1 = 24
```

This assignment simply sets L1 to a different object; L2 still references the original list. If we change this statement's syntax slightly, however, it has a radically different effect:

```
>>> L1 = [2, 3, 4]        # A mutable object
>>> L2 = L1               # Make a reference to the same object
>>> L1[0] = 24            # An in-place change

>>> L1                    # L1 is different
[24, 3, 4]
>>> L2                    # But so is L2!
[24, 3, 4]
```

Really, we haven't changed L1 itself here; we've changed a component of the *object* that L1 references. This sort of change overwrites part of the list object's value in place. Because the list object is shared by (referenced from) other variables, though, an in-place change like this doesn't affect only L1—that is, you must be aware that when you make such changes, they can impact other parts of your program. In this example, the effect shows up in L2 as well because it references the same object as L1. Again, we haven't actually changed L2, either, but its value will appear different because it refers to an object that has been overwritten in place.

This behavior only occurs for mutable objects that support in-place changes, and is usually what you want, but you should be aware of how it works, so that it's expected. It's also just the default: if you don't want such behavior, you can request that Python *copy* objects instead of making references. There are a variety of ways to copy a list, including using the built-in `list` function and the standard library `copy` module. Perhaps the most common way is to slice from start to finish (see Chapter 4 and Chapter 7 for more on slicing):

```
>>> L1 = [2, 3, 4]
>>> L2 = L1[:]          # Make a copy of L1 (or list(L1), copy.copy(L1), etc.)
>>> L1[0] = 24

>>> L1
[24, 3, 4]
>>> L2                  # L2 is not changed
[2, 3, 4]
```

Here, the change made through L1 is not reflected in L2 because L2 references a copy of the object L1 references, not the original; that is, the two variables point to different pieces of memory.

Note that this slicing technique won't work on the other major mutable core types, dictionaries and sets, because they are not sequences—to copy a dictionary or set, instead use their X.copy() method call (lists have one as of Python 3.3 as well), or pass the original object to their type names, dict and set. Also, note that the standard library copy module has a call for copying any object type generically, as well as a call for copying nested object structures—a dictionary with nested lists, for example:

```
import copy
X = copy.copy(Y)        # Make top-level "shallow" copy of any object Y
X = copy.deepcopy(Y)    # Make deep copy of any object Y: copy all nested parts
```

We'll explore lists and dictionaries in more depth, and revisit the concept of shared references and copies, in Chapter 8 and Chapter 9. For now, keep in mind that objects that can be changed in place (that is, mutable objects) are always open to these kinds of effects in any code they pass through. In Python, this includes lists, dictionaries, sets, and some objects defined with class statements. If this is not the desired behavior, you can simply copy your objects as needed.

Shared References and Equality

In the interest of full disclosure, I should point out that the garbage-collection behavior described earlier in this chapter may be more conceptual than literal for certain types. Consider these statements:

```
>>> x = 42
>>> x = 'shrubbery'     # Reclaim 42 now?
```

Because Python caches and reuses small integers and small strings, as mentioned earlier, the object 42 here is probably not literally reclaimed; instead, it will likely remain in a system table to be reused the next time you generate a 42 in your code. Most kinds of objects, though, are reclaimed immediately when they are no longer referenced; for those that are not, the caching mechanism is irrelevant to your code.

For instance, because of Python's reference model, there are two different ways to check for equality in a Python program. Let's create a shared reference to demonstrate:

```
>>> L = [1, 2, 3]
>>> M = L                    # M and L reference the same object
>>> L == M                   # Same values
True
>>> L is M                   # Same objects
True
```

The first technique here, the == operator, tests whether the two referenced objects have the same *values*; this is the method almost always used for equality checks in Python. The second method, the `is` operator, instead tests for object *identity*—it returns `True` only if both names point to the exact same object, so it is a much stronger form of equality testing and is rarely applied in most programs.

Really, `is` simply compares the pointers that implement references, and it serves as a way to detect shared references in your code if needed. It returns `False` if the names point to equivalent but different objects, as is the case when we run two different literal expressions:

```
>>> L = [1, 2, 3]
>>> M = [1, 2, 3]            # M and L reference different objects
>>> L == M                   # Same values
True
>>> L is M                   # Different objects
False
```

Now, watch what happens when we perform the same operations on small numbers:

```
>>> X = 42
>>> Y = 42                   # Should be two different objects
>>> X == Y
True
>>> X is Y                   # Same object anyhow: caching at work!
True
```

In this interaction, X and Y should be == (same value), but not `is` (same object) because we ran two different literal expressions (42). Because small integers and strings are cached and reused, though, `is` tells us they reference the same single object.

In fact, if you really want to look under the hood, you can always ask Python how many references there are to an object: the `getrefcount` function in the standard `sys` module returns the object's reference count. When I ask about the integer object `1` in the IDLE GUI, for instance, it reports 647 reuses of this same object (most of which are in IDLE's system code, not mine, though this returns 173 outside IDLE so Python must be hoarding 1s as well):

```
>>> import sys
>>> sys.getrefcount(1)       # 647 pointers to this shared piece of memory
647
```

This object caching and reuse is irrelevant to your code (unless you run the `is` check!). Because you cannot change immutable numbers or strings in place, it doesn't matter how many references there are to the same object—every reference will always see the same, unchanging value. Still, this behavior reflects one of the many ways Python optimizes its model for execution speed.

Dynamic Typing Is Everywhere

Of course, you don't really need to draw name/object diagrams with circles and arrows to use Python. When you're starting out, though, it sometimes helps you understand unusual cases if you can trace their reference structures as we've done here. If a mutable object changes out from under you when passed around your program, for example, chances are you are witnessing some of this chapter's subject matter firsthand.

Moreover, even if dynamic typing seems a little abstract at this point, you probably will care about it eventually. Because *everything* seems to work by assignment and references in Python, a basic understanding of this model is useful in many different contexts. As you'll see, it works the same in assignment statements, function arguments, for loop variables, module imports, class attributes, and more. The good news is that there is just *one* assignment model in Python; once you get a handle on dynamic typing, you'll find that it works the same everywhere in the language.

At the most practical level, dynamic typing means there is less code for you to write. Just as importantly, though, dynamic typing is also the root of Python's *polymorphism*, a concept we introduced in Chapter 4 and will revisit again later in this book. Because we do not constrain types in Python code, it is both concise and highly flexible. As you'll see, when used well, dynamic typing—and the polymorphism it implies— produces code that automatically adapts to new requirements as your systems evolve.

"Weak" References

You may occasionally see the term "weak reference" in the Python world. This is a somewhat advanced tool, but is related to the reference model we've explored here, and like the is operator, can't really be understood without it.

In short, a weak reference, implemented by the weakref standard library module, is a reference to an object that does not by itself prevent the referenced object from being garbage-collected. If the last remaining references to an object are weak references, the object is reclaimed and the weak references to it are automatically deleted (or otherwise notified).

This can be useful in dictionary-based caches of large objects, for example; otherwise, the cache's reference alone would keep the object in memory indefinitely. Still, this is really just a special-case extension to the reference model. For more details, see Python's library manual.

Chapter Summary

This chapter took a deeper look at Python's dynamic typing model—that is, the way that Python keeps track of object types for us automatically, rather than requiring us to code declaration statements in our scripts. Along the way, we learned how variables and objects are associated by references in Python; we also explored the idea of garbage collection, learned how shared references to objects can affect multiple variables, and saw how references impact the notion of equality in Python.

Because there is just one assignment model in Python, and because assignment pops up everywhere in the language, it's important that you have a handle on the model before moving on. The following quiz should help you review some of this chapter's ideas. After that, we'll resume our core object tour in the next chapter, with strings.

Test Your Knowledge: Quiz

1. Consider the following three statements. Do they change the value printed for A?

    ```
    A = "spam"
    B = A
    B = "shrubbery"
    ```

2. Consider these three statements. Do they change the printed value of A?

    ```
    A = ["spam"]
    B = A
    B[0] = "shrubbery"
    ```

3. How about these—is A changed now?

    ```
    A = ["spam"]
    B = A[:]
    B[0] = "shrubbery"
    ```

Test Your Knowledge: Answers

1. No: A still prints as "spam". When B is assigned to the string "shrubbery", all that happens is that the variable B is reset to point to the new string object. A and B initially share (i.e., reference/point to) the same single string object "spam", but two names are never linked together in Python. Thus, setting B to a different object has no effect on A. The same would be true if the last statement here were B = B + 'shrubbery', by the way—the concatenation would make a new object for its result, which would then be assigned to B only. We can never overwrite a string (or number, or tuple) in place, because strings are immutable.

2. Yes: A now prints as ["shrubbery"]. Technically, we haven't really changed either A or B; instead, we've changed part of the object they both reference (point to) by overwriting that object in place through the variable B. Because A references the same object as B, the update is reflected in A as well.

---

3. No: A still prints as `["spam"]`. The in-place assignment through B has no effect this time because the slice expression made a copy of the list object before it was assigned to B. After the second assignment statement, there are two different list objects that have the same value (in Python, we say they are `==`, but not `is`). The third statement changes the value of the list object pointed to by B, but not that pointed to by A.

## CHAPTER 7

String Fundamentals

So far, we've studied numbers and explored Python's dynamic typing model. The next major type on our in-depth core object tour is the Python *string*—an ordered collection of characters used to store and represent text- and bytes-based information. We looked briefly at strings in Chapter 4. Here, we will revisit them in more depth, filling in some of the details we skipped earlier.

This Chapter's Scope

Before we get started, I also want to clarify what we *won't* be covering here. Chapter 4 briefly previewed *Unicode* strings and files—tools for dealing with non-ASCII text. Unicode is a key tool for some programmers, especially those who work in the Internet domain. It can pop up, for example, in web pages, email content and headers, FTP transfers, GUI APIs, directory tools, and HTML, XML and JSON text.

At the same time, Unicode can be a heavy topic for programmers just starting out, and many (or most) of the Python programmers I meet today still do their jobs in blissful ignorance of the entire topic. In light of that, this book relegates most of the Unicode story to Chapter 37 of its Advanced Topics part as optional reading, and focuses on string basics here.

That is, this chapter tells only part of the string story in Python—the part that most scripts use and most programmers need to know. It explores the fundamental str string type, which handles ASCII text, and works the same regardless of which version of Python you use. Despite this intentionally limited scope, because str also handles Unicode in Python 3.X, and the separate unicode type works almost identically to str in 2.X, everything we learn here will apply directly to Unicode processing too.

Unicode: The Short Story

For readers who do care about Unicode, I'd like to also provide a quick summary of its impacts and pointers for further study. From a formal perspective, ASCII is a simple form of Unicode text, but just one of many possible encodings and alphabets. Text from non-English-speaking sources may use very different letters, and may be encoded very differently when stored in files.

As we saw in Chapter 4, Python addresses this by distinguishing between text and binary data, with distinct string object types and file interfaces for each. This support varies per Python line:

- In *Python 3.X* there are three string types: `str` is used for Unicode text (including ASCII), `bytes` is used for binary data (including encoded text), and `bytearray` is a mutable variant of `bytes`. Files work in two modes: *text*, which represents content as `str` and implements Unicode encodings, and *binary*, which deals in raw `bytes` and does no data translation.

- In *Python 2.X*, `unicode` strings represent Unicode text, `str` strings handle both 8-bit text and binary data, and `bytearray` is available in 2.6 and later as a back-port from 3.X. Normal files' content is simply bytes represented as `str`, but a `codecs` module opens Unicode text files, handles encodings, and represents content as `unicode` objects.

Despite such version differences, if and when you do need to care about Unicode you'll find that it is a relatively minor extension—once text is in memory, it's a Python string of characters that supports all the basics we'll study in this chapter. In fact, the primary distinction of Unicode often lies in the *translation* (a.k.a. *encoding*) step required to move it to and from files. Beyond that, it's largely just string processing.

Again, though, because most programmers don't need to come to grips with Unicode details up front, I've moved most of them to Chapter 37. When you're ready to learn about these more advanced string concepts, I encourage you to see both their preview in Chapter 4 and the full Unicode and bytes disclosure in Chapter 37 after reading the string fundamentals material here.

For this chapter, we'll focus on the basic string type and its operations. As you'll find, the techniques we'll study here also apply directly to the more advanced string types in Python's toolset.

String Basics

From a functional perspective, strings can be used to represent just about anything that can be encoded as text or bytes. In the text department, this includes symbols and words (e.g., your name), contents of text files loaded into memory, Internet addresses, Python source code, and so on. Strings can also be used to hold the raw bytes used for media files and network transfers, and both the encoded and decoded forms of non-ASCII Unicode text used in internationalized programs.

You may have used strings in other languages, too. Python's strings serve the same role as character arrays in languages such as C, but they are a somewhat higher-level tool than arrays. Unlike in C, in Python, strings come with a powerful set of processing tools. Also unlike languages such as C, Python has no distinct type for individual characters; instead, you just use one-character strings.

Strictly speaking, Python strings are categorized as *immutable sequences*, meaning that the characters they contain have a left-to-right positional order and that they cannot be changed in place. In fact, strings are the first representative of the larger class of objects called *sequences* that we will study here. Pay special attention to the sequence operations introduced in this chapter, because they will work the same on other sequence types we'll explore later, such as lists and tuples.

Table 7-1 previews common string literals and operations we will discuss in this chapter. Empty strings are written as a pair of quotation marks (single or double) with nothing in between, and there are a variety of ways to code strings. For processing, strings support *expression* operations such as concatenation (combining strings), slicing (extracting sections), indexing (fetching by offset), and so on. Besides expressions, Python also provides a set of string *methods* that implement common string-specific tasks, as well as *modules* for more advanced text-processing tasks such as pattern matching. We'll explore all of these later in the chapter.

Table 7-1. Common string literals and operations

Operation	Interpretation
S = ''	Empty string
S = "spam's"	Double quotes, same as single
S = 's\np\ta\x00m'	Escape sequences
S = """...multiline..."""	Triple-quoted block strings
S = r'\temp\spam'	Raw strings (no escapes)
B = b'sp\xc4m'	Byte strings in 2.6, 2.7, and 3.X (Chapter 4, Chapter 37)
U = u'sp\u00c4m'	Unicode strings in 2.X and 3.3+ (Chapter 4, Chapter 37)
S1 + S2	Concatenate, repeat
S * 3	
S[i]	Index, slice, length
S[i:j]	
len(S)	
"a %s parrot" % kind	String formatting expression
"a {0} parrot".format(kind)	String formatting method in 2.6, 2.7, and 3.X
S.find('pa')	String methods (see ahead for all 43): search,
S.rstrip()	remove whitespace,
S.replace('pa', 'xx')	replacement,
S.split(',')	split on delimiter,

Operation	Interpretation
S.isdigit()	content test,
S.lower()	case conversion,
S.endswith('spam')	end test,
'spam'.join(strlist)	delimiter join,
S.encode('latin-1')	Unicode encoding,
B.decode('utf8')	Unicode decoding, etc. (see Table 7-3)
for x in S: print(x)	Iteration, membership
'spam' in S	
[c * 2 for c in S]	
map(ord, S)	
re.match('sp(.*)am', line)	Pattern matching: library module

Beyond the core set of string tools in Table 7-1, Python also supports more advanced pattern-based string processing with the standard library's re (for "regular expression") module, introduced in Chapter 4 and Chapter 37, and even higher-level text processing tools such as XML parsers (discussed briefly in Chapter 37). This book's scope, though, is focused on the fundamentals represented by Table 7-1.

To cover the basics, this chapter begins with an overview of string literal forms and string expressions, then moves on to look at more advanced tools such as string methods and formatting. Python comes with many string tools, and we won't look at them all here; the complete story is chronicled in the Python library manual and reference books. Our goal here is to explore enough commonly used tools to give you a representative sample; methods we won't see in action here, for example, are largely analogous to those we will.

String Literals

By and large, strings are fairly easy to use in Python. Perhaps the most complicated thing about them is that there are so many ways to write them in your code:

- Single quotes: 'spa"m'
- Double quotes: "spa'm"
- Triple quotes: '''... spam ...''', """... spam ..."""
- Escape sequences: "s\tp\na\0m"
- Raw strings: r"C:\new\test.spm"
- Bytes literals in 3.X and 2.6+ (see Chapter 4, Chapter 37): b'sp\x01am'
- Unicode literals in 2.X and 3.3+ (see Chapter 4, Chapter 37): u'eggs\u0020spam'

The single- and double-quoted forms are by far the most common; the others serve specialized roles, and we're postponing further discussion of the last two advanced forms until Chapter 37. Let's take a quick look at all the other options in turn.

Single- and Double-Quoted Strings Are the Same

Around Python strings, single- and double-quote characters are interchangeable. That is, string literals can be written enclosed in either two single or two double quotes— the two forms work the same and return the same type of object. For example, the following two strings are identical, once coded:

```
>>> 'shrubbery', "shrubbery"
('shrubbery', 'shrubbery')
```

The reason for supporting both is that it allows you to embed a quote character of the other variety inside a string without escaping it with a backslash. You may embed a single-quote character in a string enclosed in double-quote characters, and vice versa:

```
>>> 'knight"s', "knight's"
('knight"s', "knight's")
```

This book generally prefers to use *single* quotes around strings just because they are marginally easier to read, except in cases where a single quote is embedded in the string. This is a purely subjective style choice, but Python displays strings this way too and most Python programmers do the same today, so you probably should too.

Note that the comma is important here. Without it, Python *automatically concatenates* adjacent string literals in any expression, although it is almost as simple to add a + operator between them to invoke concatenation explicitly (as we'll see in Chapter 12, wrapping this form in parentheses also allows it to span multiple lines):

```
>>> title = "Meaning " 'of' " Life"     # Implicit concatenation
>>> title
'Meaning of Life'
```

Adding commas between these strings would result in a tuple, not a string. Also notice in all of these outputs that Python prints strings in single quotes unless they embed one. If needed, you can also embed quote characters by escaping them with backslashes:

```
>>> 'knight\'s', "knight\"s"
("knight's", 'knight"s')
```

To understand why, you need to know how escapes work in general.

Escape Sequences Represent Special Characters

The last example embedded a quote inside a string by preceding it with a backslash. This is representative of a general pattern in strings: backslashes are used to introduce special character codings known as *escape sequences*.

Escape sequences let us embed characters in strings that cannot easily be typed on a keyboard. The character \, and one or more characters following it in the string literal, are replaced with a *single* character in the resulting string object, which has the binary value specified by the escape sequence. For example, here is a five-character string that embeds a newline and a tab:

```
>>> s = 'a\nb\tc'
```

The two characters \n stand for a single character—the binary value of the newline character in your character set (in ASCII, character code 10). Similarly, the sequence \t is replaced with the tab character. The way this string looks when printed depends on how you print it. The interactive echo shows the special characters as escapes, but print interprets them instead:

```
>>> s
'a\nb\tc'
>>> print(s)
a
b       c
```

To be completely sure how many actual characters are in this string, use the built-in len function—it returns the actual number of characters in a string, regardless of how it is coded or displayed:

```
>>> len(s)
5
```

This string is five characters long: it contains an ASCII *a*, a newline character, an ASCII *b*, and so on.

> If you're accustomed to all-ASCII text, it's tempting to think of this result as meaning 5 *bytes* too, but you probably shouldn't. Really, "bytes" has no meaning in the Unicode world. For one thing, the string object is probably larger in memory in Python.
>
> More critically, string content and length both reflect *code points* (identifying numbers) in Unicode-speak, where a single character does not necessarily map directly to a single byte, either when encoded in files or when stored in memory. This mapping might hold true for simple 7-bit ASCII text, but even this depends on both the external encoding type and the internal storage scheme used. Under UTF-16, for example, ASCII characters are multiple bytes in files, and they may be 1, 2, or 4 bytes in memory depending on how Python allocates their space. For other, non-ASCII text, whose characters' values might be too large to fit in an 8-bit byte, the character-to-byte mapping doesn't apply at all.
>
> In fact, 3.X defines str strings formally as *sequences of Unicode code points*, not bytes, to make this clear. There's more on how strings are stored internally in Chapter 37 if you care to know. For now, to be safest, think *characters* instead of *bytes* in strings. Trust me on this; as an ex-C programmer, I had to break the habit too!

Note that the original backslash characters in the preceding result are not really stored with the string in memory; they are used only to describe special character values to be stored in the string. For coding such special characters, Python recognizes a full set of escape code sequences, listed in Table 7-2.

Table 7-2. String backslash characters

Escape	Meaning
\newline	Ignored (continuation line)
\\	Backslash (stores one \)
\'	Single quote (stores ')
\"	Double quote (stores ")
\a	Bell
\b	Backspace
\f	Formfeed
\n	Newline (linefeed)
\r	Carriage return
\t	Horizontal tab
\v	Vertical tab
\xhh	Character with hex value hh (exactly 2 digits)
\ooo	Character with octal value ooo (up to 3 digits)
\0	Null: binary 0 character (doesn't end string)
\N{ id }	Unicode database ID
\uhhhh	Unicode character with 16-bit hex value
\Uhhhhhhhh	Unicode character with 32-bit hex value[a]
\other	Not an escape (keeps both \ and other)

[a] The \Uhhhh... escape sequence takes exactly eight hexadecimal digits (h); both \u and \U are recognized only in Unicode string literals in 2.X, but can be used in normal strings (which *are* Unicode) in 3.X. In a 3.X *bytes* literal, hexadecimal and octal escapes denote the byte with the given value; in a *string* literal, these escapes denote a Unicode character with the given code-point value. There is more on Unicode escapes in Chapter 37.

Some escape sequences allow you to embed absolute binary values into the characters of a string. For instance, here's a five-character string that embeds two characters with binary zero values (coded as octal escapes of one digit):

```
>>> s = 'a\0b\0c'
>>> s
'a\x00b\x00c'
>>> len(s)
5
```

In Python, a zero (null) character like this does not terminate a string the way a "null byte" typically does in C. Instead, Python keeps both the string's length and text in memory. In fact, *no* character terminates a string in Python. Here's a string that is all absolute binary escape codes—a binary 1 and 2 (coded in octal), followed by a binary 3 (coded in hexadecimal):

```
>>> s = '\001\002\x03'
>>> s
'\x01\x02\x03'
>>> len(s)
3
```

Notice that Python displays nonprintable characters in hex, regardless of how they were specified. You can freely combine absolute value escapes and the more symbolic escape types in Table 7-2. The following string contains the characters "spam", a tab and newline, and an absolute zero value character coded in hex:

```
>>> S = "s\tp\na\x00m"
>>> S
's\tp\na\x00m'
>>> len(S)
7
>>> print(S)
s       p
a m
```

This becomes more important to know when you process binary data files in Python. Because their contents are represented as strings in your scripts, it's OK to process binary files that contain any sorts of binary byte values—when opened in binary modes, files return strings of raw bytes from the external file (there's much more on files in Chapter 4, Chapter 9, and Chapter 37).

Finally, as the last entry in Table 7-2 implies, if Python does not recognize the character after a \ as being a valid escape code, it simply keeps the backslash in the resulting string:

```
>>> x = "C:\py\code"        # Keeps \ literally (and displays it as \\)
>>> x
'C:\\py\\code'
>>> len(x)
10
```

However, unless you're able to commit all of Table 7-2 to memory (and there are arguably better uses for your neurons!), you probably shouldn't rely on this behavior. To code literal backslashes explicitly such that they are retained in your strings, double them up (\\ is an escape for one \) or use raw strings; the next section shows how.

Raw Strings Suppress Escapes

As we've seen, escape sequences are handy for embedding special character codes within strings. Sometimes, though, the special treatment of backslashes for introducing escapes can lead to trouble. It's surprisingly common, for instance, to see Python newcomers in classes trying to open a file with a filename argument that looks something like this:

```
myfile = open('C:\new\text.dat', 'w')
```

thinking that they will open a file called *text.dat* in the directory *C:\new*. The problem here is that \n is taken to stand for a newline character, and \t is replaced with a tab. In effect, the call tries to open a file named *C:(newline)ew(tab)ext.dat*, with usually less-than-stellar results.

This is just the sort of thing that raw strings are useful for. If the letter *r* (uppercase or lowercase) appears just before the opening quote of a string, it turns off the escape mechanism. The result is that Python retains your backslashes literally, exactly as you type them. Therefore, to fix the filename problem, just remember to add the letter *r* on Windows:

```
myfile = open(r'C:\new\text.dat', 'w')
```

Alternatively, because two backslashes are really an escape sequence for one backslash, you can keep your backslashes by simply doubling them up:

```
myfile = open('C:\\new\\text.dat', 'w')
```

In fact, Python itself sometimes uses this doubling scheme when it prints strings with embedded backslashes:

```
>>> path = r'C:\new\text.dat'
>>> path                        # Show as Python code
'C:\\new\\text.dat'
>>> print(path)                 # User-friendly format
C:\new\text.dat
>>> len(path)                   # String length
15
```

As with numeric representation, the default format at the interactive prompt prints results as if they were code, and therefore escapes backslashes in the output. The print statement provides a more user-friendly format that shows that there is actually only one backslash in each spot. To verify this is the case, you can check the result of the built-in len function, which returns the number of characters in the string, independent of display formats. If you count the characters in the print(path) output, you'll see that there really is just 1 character per backslash, for a total of 15.

Besides directory paths on Windows, raw strings are also commonly used for regular expressions (text pattern matching, supported with the re module introduced in Chapter 4 and Chapter 37). Also note that Python scripts can usually use *forward* slashes in directory paths on Windows and Unix because Python tries to interpret paths portably (i.e., 'C:/new/text.dat' works when opening files, too). Raw strings are useful if you code paths using native Windows backslashes, though.

Despite its role, even a raw string cannot *end* in a single backslash, because the backslash escapes the following quote character—you still must escape the surrounding quote character to embed it in the string. That is, `r"...\"` is not a valid string literal—a raw string cannot end in an odd number of backslashes. If you need to end a raw string with a single backslash, you can use two and slice off the second (`r'1\nb\tc\\'[:-1]`), tack one on manually (`r'1\nb\tc' + '\\'`), or skip the raw string syntax and just double up the backslashes in a normal string (`'1\nb\\tc\\'`). All three of these forms create the same eight-character string containing three backslashes.

Triple Quotes Code Multiline Block Strings

So far, you've seen single quotes, double quotes, escapes, and raw strings in action. Python also has a triple-quoted string literal format, sometimes called a *block string*, that is a syntactic convenience for coding multiline text data. This form begins with three quotes (of either the single or double variety), is followed by any number of lines of text, and is closed with the same triple-quote sequence that opened it. Single and double quotes embedded in the string's text may be, but do not have to be, escaped—the string does not end until Python sees three unescaped quotes of the same kind used to start the literal. For example (the "..." here is Python's prompt for continuation lines outside IDLE: don't type it yourself):

```
>>> mantra = """Always look
...    on the bright
... side of life."""
>>>
>>> mantra
'Always look\n   on the bright\nside of life.'
```

This string spans three lines. As we learned in Chapter 3, in some interfaces, the interactive prompt changes to `...` on continuation lines like this, but IDLE simply drops down one line; this book shows listings in both forms, so extrapolate as needed. Either way, Python collects all the triple-quoted text into a single multiline string, with embedded newline characters (`\n`) at the places where your code has line breaks. Notice that, as in the literal, the second line in the result has leading spaces, but the third does not—what you type is truly what you get. To see the string with the newlines interpreted, print it instead of echoing:

```
>>> print(mantra)
Always look
   on the bright
side of life.
```

In fact, triple-quoted strings will retain all the enclosed text, including any to the right of your code that you might intend as *comments*. So don't do this—put your comments above or below the quoted text, or use the automatic concatenation of adjacent strings mentioned earlier, with explicit newlines if desired, and surrounding parentheses to allow line spans (again, more on this latter form when we study syntax rules in Chapter 10 and Chapter 12):

```
>>> menu = """spam        # comments here added to string!
... eggs                  # ditto
... """
>>> menu
'spam      # comments here added to string!\neggs                        # ditto\n'

>>> menu = (
... "spam\n"              # comments here ignored
... "eggs\n"              # but newlines not automatic
... )
>>> menu
'spam\neggs\n'
```

Triple-quoted strings are useful anytime you need *multiline text* in your program; for example, to embed multiline error messages or HTML, XML, or JSON code in your Python source code files. You can embed such blocks directly in your scripts by triple-quoting without resorting to external text files or explicit concatenation and newline characters.

Triple-quoted strings are also commonly used for *documentation strings*, which are string literals that are taken as comments when they appear at specific points in your file (more on these later in the book). These don't have to be triple-quoted blocks, but they usually are to allow for multiline comments.

Finally, triple-quoted strings are also sometimes used as a "horribly hackish" way to *temporarily disable* lines of code during development (OK, it's not really too horrible, and it's actually a fairly common practice today, but it wasn't the intent). If you wish to turn off a few lines of code and run your script again, simply put three quotes above and below them, like this:

```
X = 1
"""
import os                       # Disable this code temporarily
print(os.getcwd())
"""
Y = 2
```

I said this was hackish because Python really might make a string out of the lines of code disabled this way, but this is probably not significant in terms of performance. For large sections of code, it's also easier than manually adding hash marks before each line and later removing them. This is especially true if you are using a text editor that does not have support for editing Python code specifically. In Python, practicality often beats aesthetics.

Strings in Action

Once you've created a string with the literal expressions we just met, you will almost certainly want to do things with it. This section and the next two demonstrate string expressions, methods, and formatting—the first line of text-processing tools in the Python language.

Basic Operations

Let's begin by interacting with the Python interpreter to illustrate the basic string operations listed earlier in Table 7-1. You can concatenate strings using the + operator and repeat them using the * operator:

```
% python
>>> len('abc')                 # Length: number of items
3
>>> 'abc' + 'def'              # Concatenation: a new string
'abcdef'
>>> 'Ni!' * 4                  # Repetition: like "Ni!" + "Ni!" + ...
'Ni!Ni!Ni!Ni!'
```

The `len` built-in function here returns the length of a string (or any other object with a length). Formally, adding two string objects with + creates a new string object, with the contents of its operands joined, and repetition with * is like adding a string to itself a number of times. In both cases, Python lets you create arbitrarily sized strings; there's no need to predeclare anything in Python, including the sizes of data structures—you simply create string objects as needed and let Python manage the underlying memory space automatically (see Chapter 6 for more on Python's memory management "garbage collector").

Repetition may seem a bit obscure at first, but it comes in handy in a surprising number of contexts. For example, to print a line of 80 dashes, you can count up to 80, or let Python count for you:

```
>>> print('------- ...more... ---')    # 80 dashes, the hard way
>>> print('-' * 80)                     # 80 dashes, the easy way
```

Notice that operator overloading is at work here already: we're using the same + and * operators that perform addition and multiplication when using numbers. Python does the correct operation because it knows the types of the objects being added and multiplied. But be careful: the rules aren't quite as liberal as you might expect. For instance, Python doesn't allow you to mix numbers and strings in + expressions: `'abc'+9` raises an error instead of automatically converting 9 to a string.

As shown in the last row in Table 7-1, you can also iterate over strings in loops using `for` statements, which repeat actions, and test membership for both characters and substrings with the `in` expression operator, which is essentially a search. For substrings, `in` is much like the `str.find()` method covered later in this chapter, but it returns a

Boolean result instead of the substring's position (the following uses a 3.X `print` call and may leave your cursor a bit indented; in 2.X say `print c,` instead):

```
>>> myjob = "hacker"
>>> for c in myjob: print(c, end=' ')          # Step through items, print each (3.X form)
...
h a c k e r
>>> "k" in myjob                                # Found
True
>>> "z" in myjob                                # Not found
False
>>> 'spam' in 'abcspamdef'                      # Substring search, no position returned
True
```

The `for` loop assigns a variable to successive items in a sequence (here, a string) and executes one or more statements for each item. In effect, the variable `c` becomes a cursor stepping across the string's characters here. We will discuss iteration tools like these and others listed in Table 7-1 in more detail later in this book (especially in Chapter 14 and Chapter 20).

Indexing and Slicing

Because strings are defined as ordered collections of characters, we can access their components by position. In Python, characters in a string are fetched by *indexing*— providing the numeric offset of the desired component in square brackets after the string. You get back the one-character string at the specified position.

As in the C language, Python offsets start at 0 and end at one less than the length of the string. Unlike C, however, Python also lets you fetch items from sequences such as strings using *negative* offsets. Technically, a negative offset is added to the length of a string to derive a positive offset. You can also think of negative offsets as counting backward from the end. The following interaction demonstrates:

```
>>> S = 'spam'
>>> S[0], S[-2]                  # Indexing from front or end
('s', 'a')
>>> S[1:3], S[1:], S[:-1]        # Slicing: extract a section
('pa', 'pam', 'spa')
```

The first line defines a four-character string and assigns it the name S. The next line indexes it in two ways: S[0] fetches the item at offset 0 from the left—the one-character string 's'; S[-2] gets the item at offset 2 back from the end—or equivalently, at offset (4 + (–2)) from the front. In more graphic terms, offsets and slices map to cells as shown in Figure 7-1.[1]

---

1. More mathematically minded readers (and students in my classes) sometimes detect a small asymmetry here: the leftmost item is at offset 0, but the rightmost is at offset –1. Alas, there is no such thing as a distinct –0 value in Python.

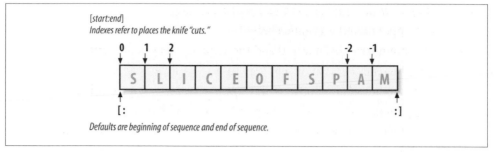

Figure 7-1. Offsets and slices: positive offsets start from the left end (offset 0 is the first item), and negatives count back from the right end (offset –1 is the last item). Either kind of offset can be used to give positions in indexing and slicing operations.

The last line in the preceding example demonstrates *slicing*, a generalized form of indexing that returns an entire *section*, not a single item. Probably the best way to think of slicing is that it is a type of *parsing* (analyzing structure), especially when applied to strings—it allows us to extract an entire *section* (substring) in a single step. Slices can be used to extract columns of data, chop off leading and trailing text, and more. In fact, we'll explore slicing in the context of text parsing later in this chapter.

The basics of slicing are straightforward. When you index a sequence object such as a string on a pair of offsets separated by a colon, Python returns a new object containing the contiguous section identified by the offset pair. The left offset is taken to be the lower bound (*inclusive*), and the right is the upper bound (*noninclusive*). That is, Python fetches all items from the lower bound up to but not including the upper bound, and returns a new object containing the fetched items. If omitted, the left and right bounds default to 0 and the length of the object you are slicing, respectively.

For instance, in the example we just saw, S[1:3] extracts the items at offsets 1 and 2: it grabs the second and third items, and stops before the fourth item at offset 3. Next, S[1:] gets *all items beyond the first*—the upper bound, which is not specified, defaults to the length of the string. Finally, S[:-1] fetches *all but the last item*—the lower bound defaults to 0, and –1 refers to the last item, noninclusive.

This may seem confusing at first glance, but indexing and slicing are simple and powerful tools to use, once you get the knack. Remember, if you're unsure about the effects of a slice, try it out interactively. In the next chapter, you'll see that it's even possible to change an entire section of another object in one step by assigning to a slice (though not for immutables like strings). Here's a summary of the details for reference:

Indexing (S[i]) fetches components at offsets:

- The first item is at offset 0.
- Negative indexes mean to count backward from the end or right.
- S[0] fetches the first item.
- S[-2] fetches the second item from the end (like S[len(S)-2]).

Slicing (S[i:j]) extracts contiguous sections of sequences:

- The upper bound is noninclusive.
- Slice boundaries default to 0 and the sequence length, if omitted.
- S[1:3] fetches items at offsets 1 up to but not including 3.
- S[1:] fetches items at offset 1 through the end (the sequence length).
- S[:3] fetches items at offset 0 up to but not including 3.
- S[:-1] fetches items at offset 0 up to but not including the last item.
- S[:] fetches items at offsets 0 through the end—making a top-level copy of S.

Extended slicing (S[i:j:k]) accepts a step (or stride) k, which defaults to +1:

- Allows for skipping items and reversing order—see the next section.

The second-to-last bullet item listed here turns out to be a very common technique: it makes a full top-level *copy* of a sequence object—an object with the same value, but a distinct piece of memory (you'll find more on copies in Chapter 9). This isn't very useful for immutable objects like strings, but it comes in handy for objects that may be changed in place, such as lists.

In the next chapter, you'll see that the syntax used to index by offset (square brackets) is used to index dictionaries by key as well; the operations look the same but have different interpretations.

Extended slicing: The third limit and slice objects

In Python 2.3 and later, slice expressions have support for an optional third index, used as a *step* (sometimes called a *stride*). The step is added to the index of each item extracted. The full-blown form of a slice is now X[I:J:K], which means "extract all the items in X, from offset I through J-1, by K." The third limit, K, defaults to +1, which is why normally all items in a slice are extracted from left to right. If you specify an explicit value, however, you can use the third limit to skip items or to reverse their order.

For instance, X[1:10:2] will fetch *every other item* in X from offsets 1–9; that is, it will collect the items at offsets 1, 3, 5, 7, and 9. As usual, the first and second limits default to 0 and the length of the sequence, respectively, so X[::2] gets every other item from the beginning to the end of the sequence:

```
>>> S = 'abcdefghijklmnop'
>>> S[1:10:2]              # Skipping items
'bdfhj'
>>> S[::2]
'acegikmo'
```

You can also use a negative stride to collect items in the opposite order. For example, the slicing expression "hello"[::-1] returns the new string "olleh"—the first two bounds default to 0 and the length of the sequence, as before, and a stride of –1 indicates that the slice should go from right to left instead of the usual left to right. The effect, therefore, is to *reverse* the sequence:

```
>>> S = 'hello'
>>> S[::-1]                        # Reversing items
'olleh'
```

With a negative stride, the meanings of the first two bounds are essentially reversed. That is, the slice S[5:1:-1] fetches the items from 2 to 5, in reverse order (the result contains items from offsets 5, 4, 3, and 2):

```
>>> S = 'abcedfg'
>>> S[5:1:-1]                      # Bounds roles differ
'fdec'
```

Skipping and reversing like this are the most common use cases for three-limit slices, but see Python's standard library manual for more details (or run a few experiments interactively). We'll revisit three-limit slices again later in this book, in conjunction with the for loop statement.

Later in the book, we'll also learn that slicing is equivalent to indexing with a *slice object*, a finding of importance to class writers seeking to support both operations:

```
>>> 'spam'[1:3]                    # Slicing syntax
'pa'
>>> 'spam'[slice(1, 3)]            # Slice objects with index syntax + object
'pa'
>>> 'spam'[::-1]
'maps'
>>> 'spam'[slice(None, None, -1)]
'maps'
```

Why You Will Care: Slices

Throughout this book, I will include common use-case sidebars (such as this one) to give you a peek at how some of the language features being introduced are typically used in real programs. Because you won't be able to make much sense of realistic use cases until you've seen more of the Python picture, these sidebars necessarily contain many references to topics not introduced yet; at most, you should consider them previews of ways that you may find these abstract language concepts useful for common programming tasks.

For instance, you'll see later that the argument words listed on a system command line used to launch a Python program are made available in the argv attribute of the built-in sys module:

```
# File echo.py
import sys
print(sys.argv)

% python echo.py -a -b -c
['echo.py', '-a', '-b', '-c']
```

Usually, you're only interested in inspecting the arguments that follow the program name. This leads to a typical application of slices: a single slice expression can be used to return all but the first item of a list. Here, sys.argv[1:] returns the desired list,

---

['-a', '-b', '-c']. You can then process this list without having to accommodate the program name at the front.

Slices are also often used to clean up lines read from input files. If you know that a line will have an end-of-line character at the end (a \n newline marker), you can get rid of it with a single expression such as line[:-1], which extracts all but the last character in the line (the lower limit defaults to 0). In both cases, slices do the job of logic that must be explicit in a lower-level language.

Having said that, calling the line.rstrip method is often preferred for stripping newline characters because this call leaves the line intact if it has no newline character at the end—a common case for files created with some text-editing tools. Slicing works if you're sure the line is properly terminated.

String Conversion Tools

One of Python's design mottos is that it refuses the temptation to guess. As a prime example, you cannot add a number and a string together in Python, even if the string looks like a number (i.e., is all digits):

```
# Python 3.X
>>> "42" + 1
TypeError: Can't convert 'int' object to str implicitly
```

```
# Python 2.X
>>> "42" + 1
TypeError: cannot concatenate 'str' and 'int' objects
```

This is by design: because + can mean both addition and concatenation, the choice of conversion would be ambiguous. Instead, Python treats this as an error. In Python, magic is generally omitted if it will make your life more complex.

What to do, then, if your script obtains a number as a text string from a file or user interface? The trick is that you need to employ conversion tools before you can treat a string like a number, or vice versa. For instance:

```
>>> int("42"), str(42)          # Convert from/to string
(42, '42')
>>> repr(42)                    # Convert to as-code string
'42'
```

The int function converts a string to a number, and the str function converts a number to its string representation (essentially, what it looks like when printed). The repr function (and the older backquotes expression, removed in Python 3.X) also converts an object to its string representation, but returns the object as a string of code that can be rerun to recreate the object. For strings, the result has quotes around it if displayed with a print statement, which differs in form between Python lines:

```
>>> print(str('spam'), repr('spam'))      # 2.X: print str('spam'), repr('spam')
spam 'spam'
```

```
>>> str('spam'), repr('spam')          # Raw interactive echo displays
('spam', "'spam'")
```

See the sidebar in Chapter 5's "str and repr Display Formats" on page 144 for more on these topics. Of these, int and str are the generally prescribed to-number and to-string conversion techniques.

Now, although you can't mix strings and number types around operators such as +, you can manually convert operands before that operation if needed:

```
>>> S = "42"
>>> I = 1
>>> S + I
TypeError: Can't convert 'int' object to str implicitly

>>> int(S) + I            # Force addition
43

>>> S + str(I)            # Force concatenation
'421'
```

Similar built-in functions handle floating-point-number conversions to and from strings:

```
>>> str(3.1415), float("1.5")
('3.1415', 1.5)

>>> text = "1.234E-10"
>>> float(text)           # Shows more digits before 2.7 and 3.1
1.234e-10
```

Later, we'll further study the built-in eval function; it runs a string containing Python expression code and so can convert a string to any kind of object. The functions int and float convert only to numbers, but this restriction means they are usually faster (and more secure, because they do not accept arbitrary expression code). As we saw briefly in Chapter 5, the string formatting expression also provides a way to convert numbers to strings. We'll discuss formatting further later in this chapter.

Character code conversions

On the subject of conversions, it is also possible to convert a single character to its underlying integer code (e.g., its ASCII byte value) by passing it to the built-in ord function—this returns the actual binary value used to represent the corresponding character in memory. The chr function performs the inverse operation, taking an integer code and converting it to the corresponding character:

```
>>> ord('s')
115
>>> chr(115)
's'
```

Technically, both of these convert characters to and from their Unicode ordinals or "code points," which are just their identifying number in the underlying character set.

For ASCII text, this is the familiar 7-bit integer that fits in a single byte in memory, but the range of code points for other kinds of Unicode text may be wider (more on character sets and Unicode in Chapter 37). You can use a loop to apply these functions to all characters in a string if required. These tools can also be used to perform a sort of string-based math. To advance to the next character, for example, convert and do the math in integer:

```
>>> S = '5'
>>> S = chr(ord(S) + 1)
>>> S
'6'
>>> S = chr(ord(S) + 1)
>>> S
'7'
```

At least for single-character strings, this provides an alternative to using the built-in int function to convert from string to integer (though this only makes sense in character sets that order items as your code expects!):

```
>>> int('5')
5
>>> ord('5') - ord('0')
5
```

Such conversions can be used in conjunction with looping statements, introduced in Chapter 4 and covered in depth in the next part of this book, to convert a string of binary digits to their corresponding integer values. Each time through the loop, multiply the current value by 2 and add the next digit's integer value:

```
>>> B = '1101'                    # Convert binary digits to integer with ord
>>> I = 0
>>> while B != '':
...     I = I * 2 + (ord(B[0]) - ord('0'))
...     B = B[1:]
...
>>> I
13
```

A left-shift operation (I << 1) would have the same effect as multiplying by 2 here. We'll leave this change as a suggested exercise, though, both because we haven't studied loops in detail yet and because the int and bin built-ins we met in Chapter 5 handle binary conversion tasks for us as of Python 2.6 and 3.0:

```
>>> int('1101', 2)           # Convert binary to integer: built-in
13
>>> bin(13)                  # Convert integer to binary: built-in
'0b1101'
```

Given enough time, Python tends to automate most common tasks!

Changing Strings I

Remember the term "immutable sequence"? As we've seen, the *immutable* part means that you cannot change a string in place—for instance, by assigning to an index:

```
>>> S = 'spam'
>>> S[0] = 'x'              # Raises an error!
TypeError: 'str' object does not support item assignment
```

How to modify text information in Python, then? To change a string, you generally need to build and assign a new string using tools such as concatenation and slicing, and then, if desired, assign the result back to the string's original name:

```
>>> S = S + 'SPAM!'        # To change a string, make a new one
>>> S
'spamSPAM!'
>>> S = S[:4] + 'Burger' + S[-1]
>>> S
'spamBurger!'
```

The first example adds a substring at the end of S, by concatenation. Really, it makes a new string and assigns it back to S, but you can think of this as "changing" the original string. The second example replaces four characters with six by slicing, indexing, and concatenating. As you'll see in the next section, you can achieve similar effects with string method calls like `replace`:

```
>>> S = 'splot'
>>> S = S.replace('pl', 'pamal')
>>> S
'spamalot'
```

Like every operation that yields a new string value, string methods generate new string objects. If you want to retain those objects, you can assign them to variable names. Generating a new string object for each string change is not as inefficient as it may sound—remember, as discussed in the preceding chapter, Python automatically garbage-collects (reclaims the space of) old unused string objects as you go, so newer objects reuse the space held by prior values. Python is usually more efficient than you might expect.

Finally, it's also possible to build up new text values with string formatting expressions. Both of the following substitute objects into a string, in a sense converting the objects to strings and changing the original string according to a format specification:

```
>>> 'That is %d %s bird!' % (1, 'dead')        # Format expression: all Pythons
That is 1 dead bird!
>>> 'That is {0} {1} bird!'.format(1, 'dead')   # Format method in 2.6, 2.7, 3.X
'That is 1 dead bird!'
```

Despite the substitution metaphor, though, the result of formatting is a new string object, not a modified one. We'll study formatting later in this chapter; as we'll find, formatting turns out to be more general and useful than this example implies. Because the second of the preceding calls is provided as a method, though, let's get a handle on string method calls before we explore formatting further.

 As previewed in Chapter 4 and to be covered in Chapter 37, Python 3.0 and 2.6 introduced a new string type known as bytearray, which *is* mutable and so may be changed in place. bytearray objects aren't really text strings; they're sequences of small, 8-bit integers. However, they support most of the same operations as normal strings and print as ASCII characters when displayed. Accordingly, they provide another option for large amounts of simple 8-bit text that must be changed frequently (richer types of Unicode text imply different techniques). In Chapter 37 we'll also see that ord and chr handle Unicode characters, too, which might not be stored in single bytes.

String Methods

In addition to expression operators, strings provide a set of *methods* that implement more sophisticated text-processing tasks. In Python, expressions and built-in functions may work across a range of types, but methods are generally *specific to object types*— string methods, for example, work only on string objects. The method sets of some types intersect in Python 3.X (e.g., many types have count and copy methods), but they are still more type-specific than other tools.

Method Call Syntax

As introduced in Chapter 4, methods are simply functions that are associated with and act upon particular objects. Technically, they are attributes attached to objects that happen to reference callable functions which always have an implied subject. In finer-grained detail, functions are packages of code, and method calls combine two operations at once—an attribute fetch and a call:

Attribute fetches
> An expression of the form *object.attribute* means "fetch the value of *attribute* in *object*."

Call expressions
> An expression of the form *function(arguments)* means "invoke the code of *function*, passing zero or more comma-separated *argument* objects to it, and return *function*'s result value."

Putting these two together allows us to call a method of an object. The method call expression:

```
object.method(arguments)
```

is evaluated from left to right—Python will first fetch the *method* of the *object* and then call it, passing in both *object* and the *arguments*. Or, in plain words, the method call expression means this:

Call *method* to process *object* with *arguments*.

If the method computes a result, it will also come back as the result of the entire method-call expression. As a more tangible example:

```
>>> S = 'spam'
>>> result = S.find('pa')        # Call the find method to look for 'pa' in string S
```

This mapping holds true for methods of both built-in types, as well as user-defined classes we'll study later. As you'll see throughout this part of the book, most objects have callable methods, and all are accessed using this same method-call syntax. To call an object method, as you'll see in the following sections, you have to go through an existing object; methods cannot be run (and make little sense) without a subject.

Methods of Strings

Table 7-3 summarizes the methods and call patterns for built-in string objects in Python 3.3; these change frequently, so be sure to check Python's standard library manual for the most up-to-date list, or run a `dir` or `help` call on any string (or the `str` type name) interactively. Python 2.X's string methods vary slightly; it includes a `decode`, for example, because of its different handling of Unicode data (something we'll discuss in Chapter 37). In this table, `S` is a string object, and optional arguments are enclosed in square brackets. String methods in this table implement higher-level operations such as splitting and joining, case conversions, content tests, and substring searches and replacements.

Table 7-3. String method calls in Python 3.3

S.capitalize()	S.ljust(width [, fill])
S.casefold()	S.lower()
S.center(width [, fill])	S.lstrip([chars])
S.count(sub [, start [, end]])	S.maketrans(x[, y[, z]])
S.encode([encoding [,errors]])	S.partition(sep)
S.endswith(suffix [, start [, end]])	S.replace(old, new [, count])
S.expandtabs([tabsize])	S.rfind(sub [,start [,end]])
S.find(sub [, start [, end]])	S.rindex(sub [, start [, end]])
S.format(fmtstr, *args, **kwargs)	S.rjust(width [, fill])
S.index(sub [, start [, end]])	S.rpartition(sep)
S.isalnum()	S.rsplit([sep[, maxsplit]])
S.isalpha()	S.rstrip([chars])
S.isdecimal()	S.split([sep [,maxsplit]])

```
S.isdigit()                          S.splitlines([keepends])

S.isidentifier()                     S.startswith(prefix [, start [, end]])

S.islower()                          S.strip([chars])

S.isnumeric()                        S.swapcase()

S.isprintable()                      S.title()

S.isspace()                          S.translate(map)

S.istitle()                          S.upper()

S.isupper()                          S.zfill(width)

S.join(iterable)
```

As you can see, there are quite a few string methods, and we don't have space to cover them all; see Python's library manual or reference texts for all the fine points. To help you get started, though, let's work through some code that demonstrates some of the most commonly used methods in action, and illustrates Python text-processing basics along the way.

String Method Examples: Changing Strings II

As we've seen, because strings are immutable, they cannot be changed in place directly. The bytearray supports in-place text changes in 2.6, 3.0, and later, but only for simple 8-bit types. We explored changes to text strings earlier, but let's take a quick second look here in the context of string methods.

In general, to make a new text value from an existing string, you construct a new string with operations such as slicing and concatenation. For example, to replace two characters in the middle of a string, you can use code like this:

```
>>> S = 'spammy'
>>> S = S[:3] + 'xx' + S[5:]          # Slice sections from S
>>> S
'spaxxy'
```

But, if you're really just out to replace a substring, you can use the string replace method instead:

```
>>> S = 'spammy'
>>> S = S.replace('mm', 'xx')          # Replace all mm with xx in S
>>> S
'spaxxy'
```

The replace method is more general than this code implies. It takes as arguments the original substring (of any length) and the string (of any length) to replace it with, and performs a global search and replace:

```
>>> 'aa$bb$cc$dd'.replace('$', 'SPAM')
'aaSPAMbbSPAMccSPAMdd'
```

In such a role, `replace` can be used as a tool to implement template replacements (e.g., in form letters). Notice that this time we simply printed the result, instead of assigning it to a name—you need to assign results to names only if you want to retain them for later use.

If you need to replace one fixed-size string that can occur at any offset, you can do a replacement again, or search for the substring with the string `find` method and then slice:

```
>>> S = 'xxxxSPAMxxxxSPAMxxxx'
>>> where = S.find('SPAM')          # Search for position
>>> where                           # Occurs at offset 4
4
>>> S = S[:where] + 'EGGS' + S[(where+4):]
>>> S
'xxxxEGGSxxxxSPAMxxxx'
```

The `find` method returns the offset where the substring appears (by default, searching from the front), or -1 if it is not found. As we saw earlier, it's a substring search operation just like the `in` expression, but `find` returns the position of a located substring.

Another option is to use `replace` with a third argument to limit it to a single substitution:

```
>>> S = 'xxxxSPAMxxxxSPAMxxxx'
>>> S.replace('SPAM', 'EGGS')       # Replace all
'xxxxEGGSxxxxEGGSxxxx'

>>> S.replace('SPAM', 'EGGS', 1)    # Replace one
'xxxxEGGSxxxxSPAMxxxx'
```

Notice that `replace` returns a new string object each time. Because strings are immutable, methods never really change the subject strings in place, even if they are called "replace"!

The fact that concatenation operations and the `replace` method generate new string objects each time they are run is actually a potential downside of using them to change strings. If you have to apply many changes to a very large string, you might be able to improve your script's performance by converting the string to an object that does support in-place changes:

```
>>> S = 'spammy'
>>> L = list(S)
>>> L
['s', 'p', 'a', 'm', 'm', 'y']
```

The built-in `list` function (an object construction call) builds a new list out of the items in any sequence—in this case, "exploding" the characters of a string into a list. Once the string is in this form, you can make multiple changes to it without generating a new copy for each change:

```
>>> L[3] = 'x'                      # Works for lists, not strings
>>> L[4] = 'x'
```

```
>>> L
['s', 'p', 'a', 'x', 'x', 'y']
```

If, after your changes, you need to convert back to a string (e.g., to write to a file), use the string `join` method to "implode" the list back into a string:

```
>>> S = ''.join(L)
>>> S
'spaxxy'
```

The `join` method may look a bit backward at first sight. Because it is a method of strings (not of lists), it is called through the desired delimiter. `join` puts the strings in a list (or other iterable) together, with the delimiter between list items; in this case, it uses an empty string delimiter to convert from a list back to a string. More generally, any string delimiter and iterable of strings will do:

```
>>> 'SPAM'.join(['eggs', 'sausage', 'ham', 'toast'])
'eggsSPAMsausageSPAMhamSPAMtoast'
```

In fact, joining substrings all at once might often run faster than concatenating them individually. Be sure to also see the earlier note about the mutable `bytearray` string available as of Python 3.0 and 2.6, described fully in Chapter 37; because it may be changed in place, it offers an alternative to this `list`/`join` combination for some kinds of 8-bit text that must be changed often.

String Method Examples: Parsing Text

Another common role for string methods is as a simple form of text *parsing*—that is, analyzing structure and extracting substrings. To extract substrings at fixed offsets, we can employ slicing techniques:

```
>>> line = 'aaa bbb ccc'
>>> col1 = line[0:3]
>>> col3 = line[8:]
>>> col1
'aaa'
>>> col3
'ccc'
```

Here, the columns of data appear at fixed offsets and so may be sliced out of the original string. This technique passes for parsing, as long as the components of your data have fixed positions. If instead some sort of delimiter separates the data, you can pull out its components by splitting. This will work even if the data may show up at arbitrary positions within the string:

```
>>> line = 'aaa bbb  ccc'
>>> cols = line.split()
>>> cols
['aaa', 'bbb', 'ccc']
```

The string `split` method chops up a string into a list of substrings, around a delimiter string. We didn't pass a delimiter in the prior example, so it defaults to whitespace—

the string is split at groups of one or more spaces, tabs, and newlines, and we get back a list of the resulting substrings. In other applications, more tangible delimiters may separate the data. This example splits (and hence parses) the string at commas, a separator common in data returned by some database tools:

```
>>> line = 'bob,hacker,40'
>>> line.split(',')
['bob', 'hacker', '40']
```

Delimiters can be longer than a single character, too:

```
>>> line = "i'mSPAMaSPAMlumberjack"
>>> line.split("SPAM")
["i'm", 'a', 'lumberjack']
```

Although there are limits to the parsing potential of slicing and splitting, both run very fast and can handle basic text-extraction chores. Comma-separated text data is part of the CSV file format; for more advanced tools on this front, see also the `csv` module in Python's standard library.

Other Common String Methods in Action

Other string methods have more focused roles—for example, to strip off whitespace at the end of a line of text, perform case conversions, test content, and test for a substring at the end or front:

```
>>> line = "The knights who say Ni!\n"
>>> line.rstrip()
'The knights who say Ni!'
>>> line.upper()
'THE KNIGHTS WHO SAY NI!\n'
>>> line.isalpha()
False
>>> line.endswith('Ni!\n')
True
>>> line.startswith('The')
True
```

Alternative techniques can also sometimes be used to achieve the same results as string methods—the in membership operator can be used to test for the presence of a substring, for instance, and length and slicing operations can be used to mimic `endswith`:

```
>>> line
'The knights who say Ni!\n'

>>> line.find('Ni') != -1          # Search via method call or expression
True
>>> 'Ni' in line
True

>>> sub = 'Ni!\n'
>>> line.endswith(sub)             # End test via method call or slice
True
```

```
>>> line[-len(sub):] == sub
True
```

See also the `format` string formatting method described later in this chapter; it provides more advanced substitution tools that combine many operations in a single step.

Again, because there are so many methods available for strings, we won't look at every one here. You'll see some additional string examples later in this book, but for more details you can also turn to the Python library manual and other documentation sources, or simply experiment interactively on your own. You can also check the `help(S.method)` results for a *method* of any string object S for more hints; as we saw in Chapter 4, running `help` on `str.method` likely gives the same details.

Note that none of the string methods accepts *patterns*—for pattern-based text processing, you must use the Python `re` standard library module, an advanced tool that was introduced in Chapter 4 but is mostly outside the scope of this text (one further brief example appears at the end of Chapter 37). Because of this limitation, though, string methods may sometimes run more quickly than the `re` module's tools.

The Original string Module's Functions (Gone in 3.X)

The history of Python's string methods is somewhat convoluted. For roughly the first decade of its existence, Python provided a standard library module called `string` that contained functions that largely mirrored the current set of string object methods. By popular demand, in Python 2.0 these functions were made available as methods of string objects. Because so many people had written so much code that relied on the original `string` module, however, it was retained for backward compatibility.

Today, you should use *only string methods*, not the original `string` module. In fact, the original module call forms of today's string methods have been removed completely from Python 3.X, and you should not use them in new code in either 2.X or 3.X. However, because you may still see the module in use in older Python 2.X code, and this text covers both Pythons 2.X and 3.X, a brief look is in order here.

The upshot of this legacy is that in Python 2.X, there technically are still two ways to invoke advanced string operations: by calling object methods, or by calling `string` module functions and passing in the objects as arguments. For instance, given a variable X assigned to a string object, calling an object method:

```
X.method(arguments)
```

is usually equivalent to calling the same operation through the `string` module (provided that you have already imported the module):

```
string.method(X, arguments)
```

Here's an example of the method scheme in action:

```
>>> S = 'a+b+c+'
>>> x = S.replace('+', 'spam')
```

```
>>> x
'aspambspamcspam'
```

To access the same operation through the `string` module in Python 2.X, you need to import the module (at least once in your process) and pass in the object:

```
>>> import string
>>> y = string.replace(S, '+', 'spam')
>>> y
'aspambspamcspam'
```

Because the module approach was the standard for so long, and because strings are such a central component of most programs, you might see both call patterns in Python 2.X code you come across.

Again, though, today you should always use method calls instead of the older module calls. There are good reasons for this, besides the fact that the module calls have gone away in 3.X. For one thing, the module call scheme requires you to import the `string` module (methods do not require imports). For another, the module makes calls a few characters longer to type (when you load the module with `import`, that is, not using `from`). And, finally, the module runs more slowly than methods (the module maps most calls back to the methods and so incurs an extra call along the way).

The original `string` module itself, without its string method equivalents, is retained in Python 3.X because it contains additional tools, including predefined string constants (e.g., `string.digits`) and a `Template` object system—a relatively obscure formatting tool that predates the string `format` method and is largely omitted here (for details, see the brief note comparing it to other formatting tools ahead, as well as Python's library manual). Unless you really want to have to change your 2.X code to use 3.X, though, you should consider any basic string operation calls in it to be just ghosts of Python past.

String Formatting Expressions

Although you can get a lot done with the string methods and sequence operations we've already met, Python also provides a more advanced way to combine string processing tasks—*string formatting* allows us to perform multiple type-specific substitutions on a string in a single step. It's never strictly required, but it can be convenient, especially when formatting text to be displayed to a program's users. Due to the wealth of new ideas in the Python world, string formatting is available in two flavors in Python today (not counting the less-used `string` module `Template` system mentioned in the prior section):

String formatting expressions: `'...%s...' % (values)`
   The original technique available since Python's inception, this form is based upon the C language's "printf" model, and sees widespread use in much existing code.

String formatting method calls: `'...{}...'.format(values)`
> A newer technique added in Python 2.6 and 3.0, this form is derived in part from a same-named tool in C#/.NET, and overlaps with string formatting expression functionality.

Since the method call flavor is newer, there is some chance that one or the other of these may become deprecated and removed over time. When 3.0 was released in 2008, the expression seemed more likely to be deprecated in later Python releases. Indeed, 3.0's documentation threatened deprecation in 3.1 and removal thereafter. This hasn't happened as of 2013 and 3.3, and now looks unlikely given the expression's wide use—in fact, it still appears even in Python's own standard library *thousands* of times today!

Naturally, this story's development depends on the future practice of Python's users. On the other hand, because both the expression and method are valid to use today and either may appear in code you'll come across, this book covers both techniques in full here. As you'll see, the two are largely *variations on a theme*, though the method has some extra features (such as thousands separators), and the expression is often more concise and seems second nature to most Python programmers.

This book itself uses both techniques in later examples for illustrative purposes. If its author has a preference, he will keep it largely classified, except to quote from Python's `import this` motto:

> There should be one—and preferably only one—obvious way to do it.

Unless the newer string formatting method is compellingly better than the original and widely used expression, its *doubling* of Python programmers' knowledge base requirements in this domain seems unwarranted—and even un-Pythonic, per the original and longstanding meaning of that term. Programmers should not have to learn two complicated tools if those tools largely overlap. You'll have to judge for yourself whether formatting merits the added language heft, of course, so let's give both a fair hearing.

Formatting Expression Basics

Since string formatting *expressions* are the original in this department, we'll start with them. Python defines the % binary operator to work on strings (you may recall that this is also the remainder of division, or modulus, operator for numbers). When applied to strings, the % operator provides a simple way to format values as strings according to a format definition. In short, the % operator provides a compact way to code multiple string substitutions all at once, instead of building and concatenating parts individually.

To format strings:

1. On the *left* of the % operator, provide a format string containing one or more embedded conversion targets, each of which starts with a % (e.g., %d).

2. On the *right* of the % operator, provide the object (or objects, embedded in a tuple) that you want Python to insert into the format string on the left in place of the conversion target (or targets).

For instance, in the formatting example we saw earlier in this chapter, the integer 1 replaces the %d in the format string on the left, and the string 'dead' replaces the %s. The result is a new string that reflects these two substitutions, which may be printed or saved for use in other roles:

```
>>> 'That is %d %s bird!' % (1, 'dead')        # Format expression
That is 1 dead bird!
```

Technically speaking, string formatting expressions are usually optional—you can generally do similar work with multiple concatenations and conversions. However, formatting allows us to combine many steps into a single operation. It's powerful enough to warrant a few more examples:

```
>>> exclamation = 'Ni'
>>> 'The knights who say %s!' % exclamation     # String substitution
'The knights who say Ni!'

>>> '%d %s %g you' % (1, 'spam', 4.0)           # Type-specific substitutions
'1 spam 4 you'

>>> '%s -- %s -- %s' % (42, 3.14159, [1, 2, 3]) # All types match a %s target
'42 -- 3.14159 -- [1, 2, 3]'
```

The first example here plugs the string 'Ni' into the target on the left, replacing the %s marker. In the second example, three values are inserted into the target string. Note that when you're inserting more than one value, you need to group the values on the right in parentheses (i.e., put them in a *tuple*). The % formatting expression operator expects either a single item or a tuple of one or more items on its right side.

The third example again inserts three values—an integer, a floating-point object, and a list object—but notice that all of the targets on the left are %s, which stands for conversion to string. As every type of object can be converted to a string (the one used when printing), every object type works with the %s conversion code. Because of this, unless you will be doing some special formatting, %s is often the only code you need to remember for the formatting expression.

Again, keep in mind that formatting always makes a new string, rather than changing the string on the left; because strings are immutable, it must work this way. As before, assign the result to a variable name if you need to retain it.

Advanced Formatting Expression Syntax

For more advanced type-specific formatting, you can use any of the conversion type codes listed in Table 7-4 in formatting expressions; they appear after the % character in substitution targets. C programmers will recognize most of these because Python string formatting supports all the usual C printf format codes (but returns the result, instead

---

of displaying it, like `printf`). Some of the format codes in the table provide alternative ways to format the same type; for instance, `%e`, `%f`, and `%g` provide alternative ways to format floating-point numbers.

Table 7-4. String formatting type codes

Code	Meaning
s	String (or any object's `str(X)` string)
r	Same as s, but uses `repr`, not `str`
c	Character (int or str)
d	Decimal (base-10 integer)
i	Integer
u	Same as d (obsolete: no longer unsigned)
o	Octal integer (base 8)
x	Hex integer (base 16)
X	Same as x, but with uppercase letters
e	Floating point with exponent, lowercase
E	Same as e, but uses uppercase letters
f	Floating-point decimal
F	Same as f, but uppercase letters
g	Floating-point e or f
G	Floating-point E or F
%	Literal % (coded as %%)

In fact, conversion targets in the format string on the expression's left side support a variety of conversion operations with a fairly sophisticated syntax all their own. The general structure of conversion targets looks like this:

```
%[(keyname)][flags][width][.precision]typecode
```

The type code characters in the first column of Table 7-4 show up at the end of this target string's format. Between the `%` and the type code character, you can do any of the following:

- Provide a *key name* for indexing the dictionary used on the right side of the expression
- List *flags* that specify things like left justification (-), numeric sign (+), a blank before positive numbers and a – for negatives (a space), and zero fills (0)
- Give a total minimum field *width* for the substituted text
- Set the number of digits (*precision*) to display after a decimal point for floating-point numbers

Both the *width* and *precision* parts can also be coded as a * to specify that they should take their values from the next item in the input values on the expression's right side (useful when this isn't known until runtime). And if you don't need any of these extra tools, a simple %s in the format string will be replaced by the corresponding value's default print string, regardless of its type.

Advanced Formatting Expression Examples

Formatting target syntax is documented in full in the Python standard manuals and reference texts, but to demonstrate common usage, let's look at a few examples. This one formats integers by default, and then in a six-character field with left justification and zero padding:

```
>>> x = 1234
>>> res = 'integers: ...%d...%-6d...%06d' % (x, x, x)
>>> res
'integers: ...1234...1234  ...001234'
```

The %e, %f, and %g formats display floating-point numbers in different ways, as the following interaction demonstrates—%E is the same as %e but the exponent is uppercase, and g chooses formats by number content (it's formally defined to use exponential format e if the exponent is less than –4 or not less than precision, and decimal format f otherwise, with a default total digits precision of 6):

```
>>> x = 1.23456789
>>> x                             # Shows more digits before 2.7 and 3.1
1.23456789

>>> '%e | %f | %g' % (x, x, x)
'1.234568e+00 | 1.234568 | 1.23457'

>>> '%E' % x
'1.234568E+00'
```

For floating-point numbers, you can achieve a variety of additional formatting effects by specifying left justification, zero padding, numeric signs, total field width, and digits after the decimal point. For simpler tasks, you might get by with simply converting to strings with a %s format expression or the str built-in function shown earlier:

```
>>> '%-6.2f | %05.2f | %+06.1f' % (x, x, x)
'1.23   | 01.23 | +001.2'

>>> '%s' % x, str(x)
('1.23456789', '1.23456789')
```

When sizes are not known until runtime, you can use a computed width and precision by specifying them with a * in the format string to force their values to be taken from the next item in the inputs to the right of the % operator—the 4 in the tuple here gives precision:

```
>>> '%f, %.2f, %.*f' % (1/3.0, 1/3.0, 4, 1/3.0)
'0.333333, 0.33, 0.3333'
```

If you're interested in this feature, experiment with some of these examples and operations on your own for more insight.

Dictionary-Based Formatting Expressions

As a more advanced extension, string formatting also allows conversion targets on the left to refer to the keys in a *dictionary* coded on the right and fetch the corresponding values. This opens the door to using formatting as a sort of template tool. We've only met dictionaries briefly thus far in Chapter 4, but here's an example that demonstrates the basics:

```
>>> '%(qty)d more %(food)s' % {'qty': 1, 'food': 'spam'}
'1 more spam'
```

Here, the (qty) and (food) in the format string on the left refer to keys in the dictionary literal on the right and fetch their associated values. Programs that generate text such as HTML or XML often use this technique—you can build up a dictionary of values and substitute them all at once with a single formatting expression that uses key-based references (notice the first comment is above the triple quote so it's not added to the string, and I'm typing this in IDLE without a "..." prompt for continuation lines):

```
>>>                                      # Template with substitution targets
>>> reply = """
Greetings...
Hello %(name)s!
Your age is %(age)s
"""
>>> values = {'name': 'Bob', 'age': 40}  # Build up values to substitute
>>> print(reply % values)                # Perform substitutions

Greetings...
Hello Bob!
Your age is 40
```

This trick is also used in conjunction with the `vars` built-in function, which returns a dictionary containing all the variables that exist in the place it is called:

```
>>> food = 'spam'
>>> qty = 10
>>> vars()
{'food': 'spam', 'qty': 10, ...plus built-in names set by Python... }
```

When used on the right side of a format operation, this allows the format string to refer to variables by name—as dictionary keys:

```
>>> '%(qty)d more %(food)s' % vars()     # Variables are keys in vars()
'10 more spam'
```

We'll study dictionaries in more depth in Chapter 8. See also Chapter 5 for examples that convert to hexadecimal and octal number strings with the %x and %o formatting expression target codes, which we won't repeat here. Additional formatting expression examples also appear ahead as comparisons to the formatting method—this chapter's next and final string topic.

String Formatting Method Calls

As mentioned earlier, Python 2.6 and 3.0 introduced a new way to format strings that is seen by some as a bit more Python-specific. Unlike formatting expressions, formatting method calls are not closely based upon the C language's "printf" model, and are sometimes more explicit in intent. On the other hand, the new technique still relies on core "printf" concepts, such as type codes and formatting specifications. Moreover, it largely overlaps with—and sometimes requires a bit more code than—formatting expressions, and in practice can be just as complex in many roles. Because of this, there is no best-use recommendation between expressions and method calls today, and most programmers would be well served by a cursory understanding of both schemes. Luckily, the two are similar enough that many core concepts overlap.

Formatting Method Basics

The string object's `format` method, available in Python 2.6, 2.7, and 3.X, is based on normal function call syntax, instead of an expression. Specifically, it uses the subject string as a template, and takes any number of arguments that represent values to be substituted according to the template.

Its use requires knowledge of functions and calls, but is mostly straightforward. Within the subject string, curly braces designate substitution targets and arguments to be inserted either by position (e.g., `{1}`), or keyword (e.g., `{food}`), or relative position in 2.7, 3.1, and later (`{}`). As we'll learn when we study argument passing in depth in Chapter 18, arguments to functions and methods may be passed by position or keyword name, and Python's ability to collect arbitrarily many positional and keyword arguments allows for such general method call patterns. For example:

```
>>> template = '{0}, {1} and {2}'                    # By position
>>> template.format('spam', 'ham', 'eggs')
'spam, ham and eggs'

>>> template = '{motto}, {pork} and {food}'          # By keyword
>>> template.format(motto='spam', pork='ham', food='eggs')
'spam, ham and eggs'

>>> template = '{motto}, {0} and {food}'             # By both
>>> template.format('ham', motto='spam', food='eggs')
'spam, ham and eggs'

>>> template = '{}, {} and {}'                        # By relative position
>>> template.format('spam', 'ham', 'eggs')           # New in 3.1 and 2.7
'spam, ham and eggs'
```

By comparison, the last section's formatting *expression* can be a bit more concise, but uses dictionaries instead of keyword arguments, and doesn't allow quite as much flexibility for value sources (which may be an asset or liability, depending on your perspective); more on how the two techniques compare ahead:

```
>>> template = '%s, %s and %s'                          # Same via expression
>>> template % ('spam', 'ham', 'eggs')
'spam, ham and eggs'

>>> template = '%(motto)s, %(pork)s and %(food)s'
>>> template % dict(motto='spam', pork='ham', food='eggs')
'spam, ham and eggs'
```

Note the use of `dict()` to make a dictionary from keyword arguments here, introduced in Chapter 4 and covered in full in Chapter 8; it's an often less-cluttered alternative to the `{...}` literal. Naturally, the subject string in the format method call can also be a literal that creates a temporary string, and arbitrary object types can be substituted at targets much like the expression's `%s` code:

```
>>> '{motto}, {0} and {food}'.format(42, motto=3.14, food=[1, 2])
'3.14, 42 and [1, 2]'
```

Just as with the `%` expression and other string methods, `format` creates and returns a new string object, which can be printed immediately or saved for further work (recall that strings are immutable, so `format` really *must* make a new object). String formatting is not just for display:

```
>>> X = '{motto}, {0} and {food}'.format(42, motto=3.14, food=[1, 2])
>>> X
'3.14, 42 and [1, 2]'

>>> X.split(' and ')
['3.14, 42', '[1, 2]']

>>> Y = X.replace('and', 'but under no circumstances')
>>> Y
'3.14, 42 but under no circumstances [1, 2]'
```

Adding Keys, Attributes, and Offsets

Like `%` formatting expressions, format calls can become more complex to support more advanced usage. For instance, format strings can name object attributes and dictionary keys—as in normal Python syntax, square brackets name dictionary keys and dots denote object attributes of an item referenced by position or keyword. The first of the following examples indexes a dictionary on the key "kind" and then fetches the attribute "platform" from the already imported `sys` module object. The second does the same, but names the objects by keyword instead of position:

```
>>> import sys

>>> 'My {1[kind]} runs {0.platform}'.format(sys, {'kind': 'laptop'})
'My laptop runs win32'
```

```
>>> 'My {map[kind]} runs {sys.platform}'.format(sys=sys, map={'kind': 'laptop'})
'My laptop runs win32'
```

Square brackets in format strings can name list (and other sequence) offsets to perform indexing, too, but only single positive offsets work syntactically within format strings, so this feature is not as general as you might think. As with % expressions, to name negative offsets or slices, or to use arbitrary expression results in general, you must run expressions outside the format string itself (note the use of *parts here to unpack a tuple's items into individual function arguments, as we did in Chapter 5 when studying fractions; more on this form in Chapter 18):

```
>>> somelist = list('SPAM')
>>> somelist
['S', 'P', 'A', 'M']

>>> 'first={0[0]}, third={0[2]}'.format(somelist)
'first=S, third=A'

>>> 'first={0}, last={1}'.format(somelist[0], somelist[-1])   # [-1] fails in fmt
'first=S, last=M'

>>> parts = somelist[0], somelist[-1], somelist[1:3]          # [1:3] fails in fmt
>>> 'first={0}, last={1}, middle={2}'.format(*parts)         # Or '{}' in 2.7/3.1+
"first=S, last=M, middle=['P', 'A']"
```

Advanced Formatting Method Syntax

Another similarity with % expressions is that you can achieve more specific layouts by adding extra syntax in the format string. For the formatting method, we use a colon after the possibly empty substitution target's identification, followed by a format specifier that can name the field size, justification, and a specific type code. Here's the formal structure of what can appear as a substitution target in a format string—its four parts are all optional, and must appear without intervening spaces:

{*fieldname component* !*conversionflag* :*formatspec*}

In this substitution target syntax:

- *fieldname* is an optional number or keyword identifying an argument, which may be omitted to use relative argument numbering in 2.7, 3.1, and later.

- *component* is a string of zero or more ".*name*" or "[*index*]" references used to fetch attributes and indexed values of the argument, which may be omitted to use the whole argument value.

- *conversionflag* starts with a ! if present, which is followed by r, s, or a to call repr, str, or ascii built-in functions on the value, respectively.

- *formatspec* starts with a : if present, which is followed by text that specifies how the value should be presented, including details such as field width, alignment, padding, decimal precision, and so on, and ends with an optional data type code.

The *formatspec* component after the colon character has a rich format all its own, and is formally described as follows (brackets denote optional components and are not coded literally):

```
[[fill]align][sign][#][0][width][,][.precision][typecode]
```

In this, *fill* can be any fill character other than { or }; *align* may be <, >, =, or ^, for left alignment, right alignment, padding after a sign character, or centered alignment, respectively; *sign* may be +, -, or space; and the , (comma) option requests a comma for a thousands separator as of Python 2.7 and 3.1. *width* and *precision* are much as in the % expression, and the *formatspec* may also contain nested {} format strings with field names only, to take values from the arguments list dynamically (much like the * in formatting expressions).

The method's *typecode* options almost completely overlap with those used in % expressions and listed previously in Table 7-4, but the format method also allows a b type code used to display integers in binary format (it's equivalent to using the bin built-in call), allows a % type code to display percentages, and uses only d for base-10 integers (i or u are not used here). Note that unlike the expression's %s, the s type code here requires a string object argument; omit the type code to accept any type generically.

See Python's library manual for more on substitution syntax that we'll omit here. In addition to the string's format method, a single object may also be formatted with the format(*object, formatspec*) built-in function (which the method uses internally), and may be customized in user-defined classes with the __format__ operator-overloading method (see Part VI).

Advanced Formatting Method Examples

As you can tell, the syntax can be complex in formatting methods. Because your best ally in such cases is often the interactive prompt here, let's turn to some examples. In the following, {0:10} means the first positional argument in a field 10 characters wide, {1:<10} means the second positional argument left-justified in a 10-character-wide field, and {0.platform:>10} means the platform attribute of the first argument right-justified in a 10-character-wide field (note again the use of dict() to make a dictionary from keyword arguments, covered in Chapter 4 and Chapter 8):

```
>>> '{0:10} = {1:10}'.format('spam', 123.4567)        # In Python 3.3
'spam       =   123.4567'

>>> '{0:>10} = {1:<10}'.format('spam', 123.4567)
'      spam = 123.4567  '

>>> '{0.platform:>10} = {1[kind]:<10}'.format(sys, dict(kind='laptop'))
'     win32 = laptop    '
```

In all cases, you can omit the argument number as of Python 2.7 and 3.1 if you're selecting them from left to right with relative autonumbering—though this makes your code less explicit, thereby negating one of the reported advantages of the formatting method over the formatting expression (see the related note ahead):

```
>>> '{:10} = {:10}'.format('spam', 123.4567)
'spam       =   123.4567'

>>> '{:>10} = {:<10}'.format('spam', 123.4567)
'      spam = 123.4567   '

>>> '{.platform:>10} = {[kind]:<10}'.format(sys, dict(kind='laptop'))
'     win32 = laptop    '
```

Floating-point numbers support the same type codes and formatting specificity in formatting method calls as in % expressions. For instance, in the following {2:g} means the third argument formatted by default according to the "g" floating-point representation, {1:.2f} designates the "f" floating-point format with just two decimal digits, and {2:06.2f} adds a field with a width of six characters and zero padding on the left:

```
>>> '{0:e}, {1:.3e}, {2:g}'.format(3.14159, 3.14159, 3.14159)
'3.141590e+00, 3.142e+00, 3.14159'

>>> '{0:f}, {1:.2f}, {2:06.2f}'.format(3.14159, 3.14159, 3.14159)
'3.141590, 3.14, 003.14'
```

Hex, octal, and binary formats are supported by the format method as well. In fact, string formatting is an alternative to some of the built-in functions that format integers to a given base:

```
>>> '{0:X}, {1:o}, {2:b}'.format(255, 255, 255)    # Hex, octal, binary
'FF, 377, 11111111'

>>> bin(255), int('11111111', 2), 0b11111111       # Other to/from binary
('0b11111111', 255, 255)

>>> hex(255), int('FF', 16), 0xFF                   # Other to/from hex
('0xff', 255, 255)

>>> oct(255), int('377', 8), 0o377                  # Other to/from octal, in 3.X
('0o377', 255, 255)                                 # 2.X prints and accepts 0377
```

Formatting parameters can either be hardcoded in format strings or taken from the arguments list dynamically by nested format syntax, much like the * syntax in formatting expressions' width and precision:

```
>>> '{0:.2f}'.format(1 / 3.0)      # Parameters hardcoded
'0.33'
>>> '%.2f' % (1 / 3.0)             # Ditto for expression
'0.33'

>>> '{0:.{1}f}'.format(1 / 3.0, 4)   # Take value from arguments
'0.3333'
>>> '%.*f' % (4, 1 / 3.0)            # Ditto for expression
'0.3333'
```

Finally, Python 2.6 and 3.0 also introduced a new built-in `format` function, which can be used to format a single item. It's a more concise alternative to the string `format` method, and is roughly similar to formatting a single item with the `%` formatting expression:

```
>>> '{0:.2f}'.format(1.2345)          # String method
'1.23'
>>> format(1.2345, '.2f')             # Built-in function
'1.23'
>>> '%.2f' % 1.2345                    # Expression
'1.23'
```

Technically, the `format` built-in runs the subject object's `__format__` method, which the `str.format` method does internally for each formatted item. It's still more verbose than the original `%` expression's equivalent here, though—which leads us to the next section.

Comparison to the % Formatting Expression

If you study the prior sections closely, you'll probably notice that at least for positional references and dictionary keys, the string `format` method looks very much like the `%` formatting expression, especially in advanced use with type codes and extra formatting syntax. In fact, in common use cases formatting expressions may be *easier* to code than formatting method calls, especially when you're using the generic `%s` print-string substitution target, and even with autonumbering of fields added in 2.7 and 3.1:

```
print('%s=%s' % ('spam', 42))          # Format expression: in all 2.X/3.X

print('{0}={1}'.format('spam', 42))    # Format method: in 3.0+ and 2.6+

print('{}={}'.format('spam', 42))      # With autonumbering: in 3.1+ and 2.7
```

As we'll see in a moment, more complex formatting tends to be a draw in terms of complexity (difficult tasks are generally difficult, regardless of approach), and some see the formatting method as redundant given the pervasiveness of the expression.

On the other hand, the formatting method also offers a few potential advantages. For example, the original `%` expression can't handle keywords, attribute references, and binary type codes, although dictionary key references in `%` format strings can often achieve similar goals. To see how the two techniques overlap, compare the following `%` expressions to the equivalent `format` method calls shown earlier:

```
>>> '%s, %s and %s' % (3.14, 42, [1, 2])          # Arbitrary types
'3.14, 42 and [1, 2]'

>>> 'My %(kind)s runs %(platform)s' % {'kind': 'laptop', 'platform': sys.platform}
'My laptop runs win32'

>>> 'My %(kind)s runs %(platform)s' % dict(kind='laptop', platform=sys.platform)
'My laptop runs win32'

>>> somelist = list('SPAM')
```

```
>>> parts = somelist[0], somelist[-1], somelist[1:3]
>>> 'first=%s, last=%s, middle=%s' % parts
"first=S, last=M, middle=['P', 'A']"
```

When more complex formatting is applied the two techniques approach parity in terms of complexity, although if you compare the following with the `format` method call equivalents listed earlier you'll again find that the % expressions tend to be a bit simpler and more concise; in Python 3.3:

```
# Adding specific formatting

>>> '%-10s = %10s' % ('spam', 123.4567)
'spam       =   123.4567'

>>> '%10s = %-10s' % ('spam', 123.4567)
'      spam = 123.4567   '

>>> '%(plat)10s = %(kind)-10s' % dict(plat=sys.platform, kind='laptop')
'     win32 = laptop    '

# Floating-point numbers

>>> '%e, %.3e, %g' % (3.14159, 3.14159, 3.14159)
'3.141590e+00, 3.142e+00, 3.14159'

>>> '%f, %.2f, %06.2f' % (3.14159, 3.14159, 3.14159)
'3.141590, 3.14, 003.14'

# Hex and octal, but not binary (see ahead)

>>> '%x, %o' % (255, 255)
'ff, 377'
```

The `format` method has a handful of advanced features that the % expression does not, but even more involved formatting still seems to be essentially a draw in terms of complexity. For instance, the following shows the same result generated with both techniques, with field sizes and justifications and various argument reference methods:

```
# Hardcoded references in both
>>> import sys

>>> 'My {1[kind]:<8} runs {0.platform:>8}'.format(sys, {'kind': 'laptop'})
'My laptop   runs    win32'

>>> 'My %(kind)-8s runs %(plat)8s' % dict(kind='laptop', plat=sys.platform)
'My laptop   runs    win32'
```

In practice, programs are less likely to hardcode references like this than to execute code that builds up a set of substitution data ahead of time (for instance, to collect input form or database data to substitute into an HTML template all at once). When we account for common practice in examples like this, the comparison between the `format` method and the % expression is even more direct:

```
# Building data ahead of time in both
>>> data = dict(platform=sys.platform, kind='laptop')

>>> 'My {kind:<8} runs {platform:>8}'.format(**data)
'My laptop   runs    win32'

>>> 'My %(kind)-8s runs %(platform)8s' % data
'My laptop   runs    win32'
```

As we'll see in Chapter 18, the **data in the method call here is special syntax that unpacks a dictionary of keys and values into individual "name=value" keyword arguments so they can be referenced by name in the format string—another unavoidable far conceptual *forward reference* to function call tools, which may be another downside of the format method in general, especially for newcomers.

As usual, though, the Python community will have to decide whether % expressions, format method calls, or a toolset with both techniques proves better over time. Experiment with these techniques on your own to get a feel for what they offer, and be sure to see the library reference manuals for Python 2.6, 3.0, and later for more details.

 String format method enhancements in Python 3.1 and 2.7: Python 3.1 and 2.7 added a thousand-separator syntax for numbers, which inserts commas between three-digit groups. To make this work, add a comma before the type code, and between the width and precision if present, as follows:

```
>>> '{0:d}'.format(999999999999)
'999999999999'
>>> '{0:,d}'.format(999999999999)
'999,999,999,999'
```

These Pythons also assign relative numbers to substitution targets automatically if they are not included explicitly, though using this extension doesn't apply in all use cases, and may negate one of the main benefits of the formatting method—its more explicit code:

```
>>> '{:,d}'.format(999999999999)
'999,999,999,999'
>>> '{:,d} {:,d}'.format(9999999, 8888888)
'9,999,999 8,888,888'
>>> '{:,.2f}'.format(296999.2567)
'296,999.26'
```

See the 3.1 release notes for more details. See also the *formats.py* comma-insertion and money-formatting function examples in Chapter 25 for a simple manual solution that can be imported and used prior to Python 3.1 and 2.7. As typical in programming, it's straightforward to implement new functionality in a callable, reusable, and customizable function of your own, rather than relying on a fixed set of built-in tools:

```
>>> from formats import commas, money
>>> '%s' % commas(999999999999)
'999,999,999,999'
>>> '%s %s' % (commas(9999999), commas(8888888))
```

```
'9,999,999 8,888,888'
>>> '%s' % money(296999.2567)
'$296,999.26'
```

And as usual, a simple function like this can be applied in more advanced
contexts too, such as the iteration tools we met in Chapter 4 and will
study fully in later chapters:

```
>>> [commas(x) for x in (9999999, 8888888)]
['9,999,999', '8,888,888']
>>> '%s %s' % tuple(commas(x) for x in (9999999, 8888888))
'9,999,999 8,888,888'
>>> ''.join(commas(x) for x in (9999999, 8888888))
'9,999,9998,888,888'
```

For better or worse, Python developers often seem to prefer adding special-case built-in tools over general development techniques—a tradeoff
explored in the next section.

Why the Format Method?

Now that I've gone to such lengths to compare and contrast the two formatting techniques, I wish to also explain why you still might want to consider using the format
method variant at times. In short, although the formatting method can sometimes require more code, it also:

- Has a handful of extra features not found in the % expression itself (though % can
  use alternatives)

- Has more flexible value reference syntax (though it may be overkill, and % often
  has equivalents)

- Can make substitution value references more explicit (though this is now optional)

- Trades an operator for a more mnemonic method name (though this is also more
  verbose)

- Does not allow different syntax for single and multiple values (though practice
  suggests this is trivial)

- As a function can be used in places an expression cannot (though a one-line function renders this moot)

Although both techniques are available today and the formatting expression is still
widely used, the format method might eventually grow in popularity and may receive
more attention from Python developers in the future. Further, with both the expression
and method in the language, *either* may appear in code you will encounter so it behooves you to understand *both*. But because the choice is currently still yours to make
in new code, let's briefly expand on the tradeoffs before closing the book on this topic.

Extra features: Special-case "batteries" versus general techniques

The method call supports a few extras that the expression does not, such as binary type
codes and (as of Python 2.7 and 3.1) thousands groupings. As we've seen, though, the

formatting expression can usually achieve the same effects in other ways. Here's the case for *binary formatting*:

```
>>> '{0:b}'.format((2 ** 16) - 1)        # Expression (only) binary format code
'1111111111111111'
>>> '%b' % ((2 ** 16) - 1)
ValueError: unsupported format character 'b'...

>>> bin((2 ** 16) - 1)                   # But other more general options work too
'0b1111111111111111'
>>> '%s' % bin((2 ** 16) - 1)            # Usable with both method and % expression
'0b1111111111111111'
>>> '{}'.format(bin((2 ** 16) - 1))      # With 2.7/3.1+ relative numbering
'0b1111111111111111'

>>> '%s' % bin((2 ** 16) - 1)[2:]        # Slice off 0b to get exact equivalent
'1111111111111111'
```

The preceding note showed that general functions could similarly stand in for the format method's *thousands groupings* option, and more fully support customization. In this case, a simple *8-line* reusable function buys us the same utility without extra special-case syntax:

```
>>> '{:,d}'.format(999999999999)         # New str.format method feature in 3.1/2.7
'999,999,999,999'

>>> '%s' % commas(999999999999)          # But % is same with simple 8-line function
'999,999,999,999'
```

See the prior note for more comma comparisons. This is essentially the same as the preceding `bin` case for binary formatting, but the `commas` function here is user-defined, not built in. As such, this technique is far more *general purpose* than precoded tools or special syntax added for a single purpose.

This case also seems indicative, perhaps, of a trend in Python (and scripting language in general) toward relying more on special-case "batteries included" tools than on general development techniques—a mindset that makes code dependent on those batteries, and seems difficult to justify unless one views software development as an end-user enterprise. To some, programmers might be better served learning how to code an algorithm to insert commas than be provided a tool that does.

We'll leave that philosophical debate aside here, but in practical terms the net effect of the trend in this case is extra syntax for you to have to both learn and remember. Given their alternatives, it's not clear that these extra features of the methods by themselves are compelling enough to be decisive.

Flexible reference syntax: Extra complexity and functional overlap

The method call also supports *key* and *attribute* references directly, which some may see as more flexible. But as we saw in earlier examples comparing dictionary-based formatting in the % expression to key and attribute references in the `format` method, the two are usually too similar to warrant a preference on these grounds. For instance, both can reference the same value multiple times:

```
>>> '{name} {job} {name}'.format(name='Bob', job='dev')
'Bob dev Bob'
>>> '%(name)s %(job)s %(name)s' % dict(name='Bob', job='dev')
'Bob dev Bob'
```

Especially in common practice, though, the expression seems just as simple, or simpler:

```
>>> D = dict(name='Bob', job='dev')
>>> '{0[name]} {0[job]} {0[name]}'.format(D)       # Method, key references
'Bob dev Bob'
>>> '{name} {job} {name}'.format(**D)              # Method, dict-to-args
'Bob dev Bob'
>>> '%(name)s %(job)s %(name)s' % D                # Expression, key references
'Bob dev Bob'
```

To be fair, the method has even more specialized substitution syntax, and other comparisons might favor either scheme in small ways. But given the overlap and extra complexity, one could argue that the format method's utility seems either a wash, or features in search of use cases. At the least, the added conceptual burden on Python programmers who may now need to know *both* tools doesn't seem clearly justified.

Explicit value references: Now optional and unlikely to be used

One use case where the `format` method is at least debatably clearer is when there are many values to be substituted into the format string. The *lister.py* classes example we'll meet in Chapter 31, for example, substitutes six items into a single string, and in this case the method's `{i}` position labels seem marginally easier to read than the expression's `%s`:

```
'\n%s<Class %s, address %s:\n%s%s%s>\n' % (...)            # Expression

'\n{0}<Class {1}, address {2}:\n{3}{4}{5}>\n'.format(...)  # Method
```

On the other hand, using dictionary *keys* in % expressions can mitigate much of this difference. This is also something of a worst-case scenario for formatting complexity, and not very common in practice; more typical use cases seem more of a tossup. Further, as of Python 3.1 and 2.7, numbering substitution targets becomes optional when relative to position, potentially subverting this purported benefit altogether:

```
>>> 'The {0} side {1} {2}'.format('bright', 'of', 'life')    # Python 3.X, 2.6+
'The bright side of life'

>>> 'The {} side {} {}'.format('bright', 'of', 'life')       # Python 3.1+, 2.7+
'The bright side of life'

>>> 'The %s side %s %s' % ('bright', 'of', 'life')           # All Pythons
'The bright side of life'
```

Given its conciseness, the second of these is likely to be preferred to the first, but seems to negate part of the method's advantage. Compare the effect on floating-point formatting, for example—the formatting expression is still more concise, and still seems less cluttered:

```
>>> '{0:f}, {1:.2f}, {2:05.2f}'.format(3.14159, 3.14159, 3.14159)
'3.141590, 3.14, 03.14'

>>> '{:f}, {:.2f}, {:06.2f}'.format(3.14159, 3.14159, 3.14159)
'3.141590, 3.14, 003.14'

>>> '%f, %.2f, %06.2f' % (3.14159, 3.14159, 3.14159)
'3.141590, 3.14, 003.14'
```

Named method and context-neutral arguments: Aesthetics versus practice

The formatting method also claims an advantage in replacing the % operator with a more mnemonic `format` method name, and not distinguishing between single and multiple substitution values. The former may make the method appear simpler to beginners at first glance ("format" may be easier to parse than multiple "%" characters), though this probably varies per reader and seems minor.

Some may see the latter difference as more significant—with the format expression, a *single* value can be given by itself, but *multiple* values must be enclosed in a tuple:

```
>>> '%.2f' % 1.2345                      # Single value
'1.23'
>>> '%.2f %s' % (1.2345, 99)             # Multiple values tuple
'1.23 99'
```

Technically, the formatting expression accepts *either* a single substitution value, or a tuple of one or more items. As a consequence, because a single item can be given either by itself or within a tuple, a tuple to be formatted must be provided as a nested tuple —a perhaps rare but plausible case:

```
>>> '%s' % 1.23                          # Single value, by itself
'1.23'
>>> '%s' % (1.23,)                       # Single value, in a tuple
'1.23'
>>> '%s' % ((1.23,),)                    # Single value that is a tuple
'(1.23,)'
```

The formatting method, on the other hand, tightens this up by accepting only general function arguments in both cases, instead of requiring a tuple both for multiple values or a single value that is a tuple:

```
>>> '{0:.2f}'.format(1.2345)             # Single value
'1.23'
>>> '{0:.2f} {1}'.format(1.2345, 99)     # Multiple values
'1.23 99'

>>> '{0}'.format(1.23)                    # Single value, by itself
'1.23'
>>> '{0}'.format((1.23,))                 # Single value that is a tuple
'(1.23,)'
```

Consequently, the method might be less confusing to beginners and cause fewer programming mistakes. This seems a fairly minor issue, though—if you *always* enclose values in a tuple and ignore the nontupled option, the expression is essentially the same as the method call here. Moreover, the method incurs a price in inflated code size to achieve its constrained usage mode. Given the expression's wide use over Python's history, this issue may be more theoretical than practical, and may not justify porting existing code to a new tool that is so similar to that it seeks to subsume.

Functions versus expressions: A minor convenience

The final rationale for the format method—it's a *function* that can appear where an expression cannot—requires more information about functions than we yet have at this point in the book, so we won't dwell on it here. Suffice it to say that both the `str.format` method and the `format` built-in function can be passed to other functions, stored in other objects, and so on. An expression like `%` cannot directly, but this may be narrow-sighted—it's trivial to wrap any expression in a one-line `def` or partial-line `lambda` once to turn it into a function with the same properties (though finding a reason to do so may be more challenging):

```
def myformat(fmt, args): return fmt % args          # See Part IV

myformat('%s %s', (88, 99))                          # Call your function object
str.format('{} {}', 88, 99)                          # Versus calling the built-in

otherfunction(myformat)                              # Your function is an object too
```

In the end, this may not be an either/or choice. While the expression still seems more pervasive in Python code, both formatting expressions and methods are available for use in Python today, and most programmers will benefit from being familiar with both techniques for years to come. That may double the work of newcomers to the language in this department, but in this bazaar of ideas we call the open source software world, there always seems to be room for more.[2]

 Plus one more: Technically speaking, there are 3 (not 2) formatting tools built into Python, if we include the obscure `string` module's `Template` tool mentioned earlier. Now that we've seen the other two, I can show you how it compares. The expression and method can be used as templating tools too, referring to substitution values by name via dictionary keys or keyword arguments:

```
>>> '%(num)i = %(title)s' % dict(num=7, title='Strings')
'7 = Strings'
```

2. See also the Chapter 31 note about a `str.format` bug (or regression) in Pythons 3.2 and 3.3 concerning generic empty substitution targets for object attributes that define no `__format__` handler. This impacted a working example from this book's prior edition. While it may be a temporary regression, it does at the least underscore that this method is still a bit of a moving target—yet another reason to question the feature redundancy it implies.

```
>>> '{num:d} = {title:s}'.format(num=7, title='Strings')
'7 = Strings'
>>> '{num} = {title}'.format(**dict(num=7, title='Strings'))
'7 = Strings'
```

The module's templating system allows values to be referenced by name too, prefixed by a $, as either dictionary keys or keywords, but does not support all the utilities of the other two methods—a limitation that yields simplicity, the prime motivation for this tool:

```
>>> import string
>>> t = string.Template('$num = $title')
>>> t.substitute({'num': 7, 'title': 'Strings'})
'7 = Strings'
>>> t.substitute(num=7, title='Strings')
'7 = Strings'
>>> t.substitute(dict(num=7, title='Strings'))
'7 = Strings'
```

See Python's manuals for more details. It's possible that you may see this alternative (as well as additional tools in the third-party domain) in Python code too; thankfully this technique is simple, and is used rarely enough to warrant its limited coverage here. The best bet for most new-comers today is to learn and use %, str.format, or both.

General Type Categories

Now that we've explored the first of Python's collection objects, the string, let's close this chapter by defining a few general type concepts that will apply to most of the types we look at from here on. With regard to built-in types, it turns out that operations work the same for all the types in the same category, so we'll only need to define most of these ideas once. We've only examined numbers and strings so far, but because they are representative of two of the three major type categories in Python, you already know more about several other types than you might think.

Types Share Operation Sets by Categories

As you've learned, strings are immutable sequences: they cannot be changed in place (the *immutable* part), and they are positionally ordered collections that are accessed by offset (the *sequence* part). It so happens that all the sequences we'll study in this part of the book respond to the same sequence operations shown in this chapter at work on strings—concatenation, indexing, iteration, and so on. More formally, there are three major type (and operation) categories in Python that have this generic nature:

Numbers (integer, floating-point, decimal, fraction, others)
    Support addition, multiplication, etc.

Sequences (strings, lists, tuples)
    Support indexing, slicing, concatenation, etc.

Mappings (dictionaries)
    Support indexing by key, etc.

I'm including the Python 3.X byte strings and 2.X Unicode strings I mentioned at the start of this chapter under the general "strings" label here (see Chapter 37). Sets are something of a category unto themselves (they don't map keys to values and are not positionally ordered sequences), and we haven't yet explored mappings on our in-depth tour (we will in the next chapter). However, many of the other types we will encounter will be similar to numbers and strings. For example, for any sequence objects X and Y:

- X + Y makes a new sequence object with the contents of both operands.
- X * N makes a new sequence object with N copies of the sequence operand X.

In other words, these operations work the same way on any kind of sequence, including strings, lists, tuples, and some user-defined object types. The only difference is that the new result object you get back is of the same type as the operands X and Y—if you concatenate lists, you get back a new list, not a string. Indexing, slicing, and other sequence operations work the same on all sequences, too; the type of the objects being processed tells Python which flavor of the task to perform.

Mutable Types Can Be Changed in Place

The immutable classification is an important constraint to be aware of, yet it tends to trip up new users. If an object type is immutable, you cannot change its value in place; Python raises an error if you try. Instead, you must run code to make a new object containing the new value. The major core types in Python break down as follows:

Immutables (numbers, strings, tuples, frozensets)
    None of the object types in the immutable category support in-place changes, though we can always run expressions to make new objects and assign their results to variables as needed.

Mutables (lists, dictionaries, sets, bytearray)
    Conversely, the mutable types can always be changed in place with operations that do not create new objects. Although such objects can be copied, in-place changes support direct modification.

Generally, immutable types give some degree of integrity by guaranteeing that an object won't be changed by another part of a program. For a refresher on why this matters, see the discussion of shared object references in Chapter 6. To see how lists, dictionaries, and tuples participate in type categories, we need to move ahead to the next chapter.

Chapter Summary

In this chapter, we took an in-depth tour of the string object type. We learned about coding string literals, and we explored string operations, including sequence expressions, string method calls, and string formatting with both expressions and method calls. Along the way, we studied a variety of concepts in depth, such as slicing, method call syntax, and triple-quoted block strings. We also defined some core ideas common to a variety of types: sequences, for example, share an entire set of operations.

In the next chapter, we'll continue our types tour with a look at the most general object collections in Python—lists and dictionaries. As you'll find, much of what you've learned here will apply to those types as well. And as mentioned earlier, in the final part of this book we'll return to Python's string model to flesh out the details of Unicode text and binary data, which are of interest to some, but not all, Python programmers. Before moving on, though, here's another chapter quiz to review the material covered here.

Test Your Knowledge: Quiz

1. Can the string `find` method be used to search a list?
2. Can a string slice expression be used on a list?
3. How would you convert a character to its ASCII integer code? How would you convert the other way, from an integer to a character?
4. How might you go about changing a string in Python?
5. Given a string S with the value `"s,pa,m"`, name two ways to extract the two characters in the middle.
6. How many characters are there in the string `"a\nb\x1f\000d"`?
7. Why might you use the `string` module instead of string method calls?

Test Your Knowledge: Answers

1. No, because methods are always type-specific; that is, they only work on a single data type. Expressions like X+Y and built-in functions like `len(X)` are generic, though, and may work on a variety of types. In this case, for instance, the `in` membership expression has a similar effect as the string `find`, but it can be used to search both strings and lists. In Python 3.X, there is some attempt to group methods by categories (for example, the mutable sequence types `list` and `bytearray` have similar method sets), but methods are still more type-specific than other operation sets.

2. Yes. Unlike methods, expressions are generic and apply to many types. In this case, the slice expression is really a sequence operation—it works on any type of se-

quence object, including strings, lists, and tuples. The only difference is that when you slice a list, you get back a new list.

3. The built-in `ord(S)` function converts from a one-character string to an integer character code; `chr(I)` converts from the integer code back to a string. Keep in mind, though, that these integers are only ASCII codes for text whose characters are drawn only from ASCII character set. In the Unicode model, text strings are really sequences of Unicode code point identifying integers, which may fall outside the 7-bit range of numbers reserved by ASCII (more on Unicode in Chapter 4 and Chapter 37).

4. Strings cannot be changed; they are immutable. However, you can achieve a similar effect by creating a new string—by concatenating, slicing, running formatting expressions, or using a method call like `replace`—and then assigning the result back to the original variable name.

5. You can slice the string using `S[2:4]`, or split on the comma and index the string using `S.split(',')[1]`. Try these interactively to see for yourself.

6. Six. The string `"a\nb\x1f\000d"` contains the characters a, newline (\n), b, binary 31 (a hex escape \x1f), binary 0 (an octal escape \000), and d. Pass the string to the built-in `len` function to verify this, and print each of its character's `ord` results to see the actual code point (identifying number) values. See Table 7-2 for more details on escapes.

7. You should never use the `string` module instead of string object method calls today —it's deprecated, and its calls are removed completely in Python 3.X. The only valid reason for using the `string` module at all today is for its other tools, such as predefined constants. You might also see it appear in what is now very old and dusty Python code (and books of the misty past—like the 1990s).

## CHAPTER 8

Lists and Dictionaries

Now that we've learned about numbers and strings, this chapter moves on to give the full story on Python's *list* and *dictionary* object types—collections of other objects, and the main workhorses in almost all Python scripts. As you'll see, both types are remarkably flexible: they can be changed in place, can grow and shrink on demand, and may contain and be nested in any other kind of object. By leveraging these types, you can build up and process arbitrarily rich information structures in your scripts.

Lists

The next stop on our built-in object tour is the Python *list*. Lists are Python's most flexible ordered collection object type. Unlike strings, lists can contain any sort of object: numbers, strings, and even other lists. Also, unlike strings, lists may be changed in place by assignment to offsets and slices, list method calls, deletion statements, and more—they are *mutable* objects.

Python lists do the work of many of the collection data structures you might have to implement manually in lower-level languages such as C. Here is a quick look at their main properties. Python lists are:

Ordered collections of arbitrary objects
> From a functional view, lists are just places to collect other objects so you can treat them as groups. Lists also maintain a left-to-right positional ordering among the items they contain (i.e., they are sequences).

Accessed by offset
> Just as with strings, you can fetch a component object out of a list by indexing the list on the object's offset. Because items in lists are ordered by their positions, you can also do tasks such as slicing and concatenation.

Variable length, heterogeneous, and arbitrarily nestable
> Unlike strings, lists can grow and shrink in place (their lengths can vary), and they can contain any sort of object, not just one-character strings (they're heterogene-

ous). Because lists can contain other complex objects, they also support arbitrary nesting; you can create lists of lists of lists, and so on.

Of the category "mutable sequence"

In terms of our type category qualifiers, lists are mutable (i.e., can be changed in place) and can respond to all the sequence operations used with strings, such as indexing, slicing, and concatenation. In fact, sequence operations work the same on lists as they do on strings; the only difference is that sequence operations such as concatenation and slicing return new lists instead of new strings when applied to lists. Because lists are mutable, however, they also support other operations that strings don't, such as deletion and index assignment operations, which change the lists in place.

Arrays of object references

Technically, Python lists contain zero or more references to other objects. Lists might remind you of arrays of pointers (addresses) if you have a background in some other languages. Fetching an item from a Python list is about as fast as indexing a C array; in fact, lists really are arrays inside the standard Python interpreter, not linked structures. As we learned in Chapter 6, though, Python always follows a reference to an object whenever the reference is used, so your program deals only with objects. Whenever you assign an object to a data structure component or variable name, Python always stores a reference to that same object, not a copy of it (unless you request a copy explicitly).

As a preview and reference, Table 8-1 summarizes common and representative list object operations. It is fairly complete for Python 3.3, but for the full story, consult the Python standard library manual, or run a `help(list)` or `dir(list)` call interactively for a complete list of list methods—you can pass in a real list, or the word `list`, which is the name of the list data type. The set of methods here is especially prone to change—in fact, two are new as of Python 3.3.

Table 8-1. Common list literals and operations

Operation	Interpretation
L = []	An empty list
L = [123, 'abc', 1.23, {}]	Four items: indexes 0..3
L = ['Bob', 40.0, ['dev', 'mgr']]	Nested sublists
L = list('spam')	List of an iterable's items, list of successive integers
L = list(range(-4, 4))	
L[i]	Index, index of index, slice, length
L[i][j]	
L[i:j]	
len(L)	
L1 + L2	Concatenate, repeat

Operation	Interpretation
`L * 3`	
`for x in L: print(x)`	Iteration, membership
`3 in L`	
`L.append(4)`	Methods: growing
`L.extend([5,6,7])`	
`L.insert(i, X)`	
`L.index(X)`	Methods: searching
`L.count(X)`	
`L.sort()`	Methods: sorting, reversing,
`L.reverse()`	copying (3.3+), clearing (3.3+)
`L.copy()`	
`L.clear()`	
`L.pop(i)`	Methods, statements: shrinking
`L.remove(X)`	
`del L[i]`	
`del L[i:j]`	
`L[i:j] = []`	
`L[i] = 3`	Index assignment, slice assignment
`L[i:j] = [4,5,6]`	
`L = [x**2 for x in range(5)]`	List comprehensions and maps (Chapter 4, Chapter 14, Chapter 20)
`list(map(ord, 'spam'))`	

When written down as a literal expression, a list is coded as a series of objects (really, expressions that return objects) in square brackets, separated by commas. For instance, the second row in Table 8-1 assigns the variable L to a four-item list. A nested list is coded as a nested square-bracketed series (row 3), and the empty list is just a square-bracket pair with nothing inside (row 1).[1]

Many of the operations in Table 8-1 should look familiar, as they are the same sequence operations we put to work on strings earlier—indexing, concatenation, iteration, and so on. Lists also respond to list-specific method calls (which provide utilities such as sorting, reversing, adding items to the end, etc.), as well as in-place change operations

---

1. In practice, you won't see many lists written out like this in list processing programs. It's more common to see code that processes lists constructed dynamically (at runtime), from user inputs, file contents, and so on. In fact, although it's important to master literal syntax, many data structures in Python are built by running program code at runtime.

(deleting items, assignment to indexes and slices, and so forth). Lists have these tools for change operations because they are a mutable object type.

Lists in Action

Perhaps the best way to understand lists is to see them at work. Let's once again turn to some simple interpreter interactions to illustrate the operations in Table 8-1.

Basic List Operations

Because they are sequences, lists support many of the same operations as strings. For example, lists respond to the + and * operators much like strings—they mean concatenation and repetition here too, except that the result is a new list, not a string:

```
% python
>>> len([1, 2, 3])                          # Length
3
>>> [1, 2, 3] + [4, 5, 6]                    # Concatenation
[1, 2, 3, 4, 5, 6]
>>> ['Ni!'] * 4                              # Repetition
['Ni!', 'Ni!', 'Ni!', 'Ni!']
```

Although the + operator works the same for lists and strings, it's important to know that it expects the *same* sort of sequence on both sides—otherwise, you get a type error when the code runs. For instance, you cannot concatenate a list and a string unless you first convert the list to a string (using tools such as str or % formatting) or convert the string to a list (the list built-in function does the trick):

```
>>> str([1, 2]) + "34"                       # Same as "[1, 2]" + "34"
'[1, 2]34'
>>> [1, 2] + list("34")                      # Same as [1, 2] + ["3", "4"]
[1, 2, '3', '4']
```

List Iteration and Comprehensions

More generally, lists respond to all the sequence operations we used on strings in the prior chapter, including iteration tools:

```
>>> 3 in [1, 2, 3]                           # Membership
True
>>> for x in [1, 2, 3]:
...     print(x, end=' ')                     # Iteration (2.X uses: print x,)
...
1 2 3
```

We will talk more formally about for iteration and the range built-ins of Table 8-1 in Chapter 13, because they are related to statement syntax. In short, for loops step through items in any sequence from left to right, executing one or more statements for each item; range produces successive integers.

The last items in Table 8-1, list comprehensions and map calls, are covered in more detail in Chapter 14 and expanded on in Chapter 20. Their basic operation is straightforward, though—as introduced in Chapter 4, list comprehensions are a way to build a new list by applying an expression to each item in a sequence (really, in any iterable), and are close relatives to for loops:

```
>>> res = [c * 4 for c in 'SPAM']          # List comprehensions
>>> res
['SSSS', 'PPPP', 'AAAA', 'MMMM']
```

This expression is functionally equivalent to a for loop that builds up a list of results manually, but as we'll learn in later chapters, list comprehensions are simpler to code and likely faster to run today:

```
>>> res = []
>>> for c in 'SPAM':                        # List comprehension equivalent
...     res.append(c * 4)
...
>>> res
['SSSS', 'PPPP', 'AAAA', 'MMMM']
```

As also introduced briefly in Chapter 4, the map built-in function does similar work, but applies a function to items in a sequence and collects all the results in a new list:

```
>>> list(map(abs, [-1, -2, 0, 1, 2]))      # Map a function across a sequence
[1, 2, 0, 1, 2]
```

Because we're not quite ready for the full iteration story, we'll postpone further details for now, but watch for a similar comprehension expression for dictionaries later in this chapter.

Indexing, Slicing, and Matrixes

Because lists are sequences, indexing and slicing work the same way for lists as they do for strings. However, the result of indexing a list is whatever type of object lives at the offset you specify, while slicing a list always returns a new list:

```
>>> L = ['spam', 'Spam', 'SPAM!']
>>> L[2]                                    # Offsets start at zero
'SPAM!'
>>> L[-2]                                   # Negative: count from the right
'Spam'
>>> L[1:]                                   # Slicing fetches sections
['Spam', 'SPAM!']
```

One note here: because you can nest lists and other object types within lists, you will sometimes need to string together index operations to go deeper into a data structure. For example, one of the simplest ways to represent matrixes (multidimensional arrays) in Python is as lists with nested sublists. Here's a basic 3 × 3 two-dimensional list-based array:

```
>>> matrix = [[1, 2, 3], [4, 5, 6], [7, 8, 9]]
```

With one index, you get an entire row (really, a nested sublist), and with two, you get an item within the row:

```
>>> matrix[1]
[4, 5, 6]
>>> matrix[1][1]
5
>>> matrix[2][0]
7
>>> matrix = [[1, 2, 3],
...           [4, 5, 6],
...           [7, 8, 9]]
>>> matrix[1][1]
5
```

Notice in the preceding interaction that lists can naturally span multiple lines if you want them to because they are contained by a pair of brackets; the "..."s here are Python's continuation line prompt (see Chapter 4 for comparable code without the "..."s, and watch for more on syntax in the next part of the book).

For more on matrixes, watch later in this chapter for a dictionary-based matrix representation, which can be more efficient when matrixes are largely empty. We'll also continue this thread in Chapter 20 where we'll write additional matrix code, especially with list comprehensions. For high-powered numeric work, the NumPy extension mentioned in Chapter 4 and Chapter 5 provides other ways to handle matrixes.

Changing Lists in Place

Because lists are mutable, they support operations that change a list object *in place*. That is, the operations in this section all modify the list object directly—overwriting its former value—without requiring that you make a new copy, as you had to for strings. Because Python deals only in object references, this distinction between changing an object in place and creating a new object matters; as discussed in Chapter 6, if you change an object in place, you might impact more than one reference to it at the same time.

Index and slice assignments

When using a list, you can change its contents by assigning to either a particular item (offset) or an entire section (slice):

```
>>> L = ['spam', 'Spam', 'SPAM!']
>>> L[1] = 'eggs'                    # Index assignment
>>> L
['spam', 'eggs', 'SPAM!']

>>> L[0:2] = ['eat', 'more']         # Slice assignment: delete+insert
>>> L                                # Replaces items 0,1
['eat', 'more', 'SPAM!']
```

Both index and slice assignments are in-place changes—they modify the subject list directly, rather than generating a new list object for the result. *Index assignment* in Python works much as it does in C and most other languages: Python replaces the single object reference at the designated offset with a new one.

Slice assignment, the last operation in the preceding example, replaces an entire section of a list in a single step. Because it can be a bit complex, it is perhaps best thought of as a combination of two steps:

1. *Deletion*. The slice you specify to the left of the = is deleted.
2. *Insertion*. The new items contained in the iterable object to the right of the = are inserted into the list on the left, at the place where the old slice was deleted.[2]

This isn't what really happens, but it can help clarify why the number of items inserted doesn't have to match the number of items deleted. For instance, given a list L of two or more items, an assignment `L[1:2]=[4,5]` replaces one item with two—Python first deletes the one-item slice at `[1:2]` (from offset 1, up to but not including offset 2), then inserts both 4 and 5 where the deleted slice used to be.

This also explains why the second slice assignment in the following is really an insert —Python replaces an empty slice at `[1:1]` with two items; and why the third is really a deletion—Python deletes the slice (the item at offset 1), and then inserts nothing:

```
>>> L = [1, 2, 3]
>>> L[1:2] = [4, 5]          # Replacement/insertion
>>> L
[1, 4, 5, 3]
>>> L[1:1] = [6, 7]          # Insertion (replace nothing)
>>> L
[1, 6, 7, 4, 5, 3]
>>> L[1:2] = []              # Deletion (insert nothing)
>>> L
[1, 7, 4, 5, 3]
```

In effect, slice assignment replaces an entire section, or "column," all at once—even if the column or its replacement is empty. Because the length of the sequence being assigned does not have to match the length of the slice being assigned to, slice assignment can be used to replace (by overwriting), expand (by inserting), or shrink (by deleting) the subject list. It's a powerful operation, but frankly, one that you may not see very often in practice. There are often more straightforward and mnemonic ways to replace, insert, and delete (concatenation, and the `insert`, `pop`, and `remove` list methods, for example), which Python programmers tend to prefer in practice.

---

2. This description requires elaboration when the value and the slice being assigned overlap: `L[2:5]=L[3:6]`, for instance, works fine because the value to be inserted is fetched before the deletion happens on the left.

On the other hand, this operation can be used as a sort of in-place concatenation at the front of the list—per the next section's method coverage, something the list's extend does more mnemonically at list end:

```
>>> L = [1]
>>> L[:0] = [2, 3, 4]          # Insert all at :0, an empty slice at front
>>> L
[2, 3, 4, 1]
>>> L[len(L):] = [5, 6, 7]     # Insert all at len(L):, an empty slice at end
>>> L
[2, 3, 4, 1, 5, 6, 7]
>>> L.extend([8, 9, 10])       # Insert all at end, named method
>>> L
[2, 3, 4, 1, 5, 6, 7, 8, 9, 10]
```

List method calls

Like strings, Python list objects also support type-specific method calls, many of which change the subject list in place:

```
>>> L = ['eat', 'more', 'SPAM!']
>>> L.append('please')              # Append method call: add item at end
>>> L
['eat', 'more', 'SPAM!', 'please']
>>> L.sort()                        # Sort list items ('S' < 'e')
>>> L
['SPAM!', 'eat', 'more', 'please']
```

Methods were introduced in Chapter 7. In brief, they are functions (really, object attributes that reference functions) that are associated with and act upon particular objects. Methods provide type-specific tools; the list methods presented here, for instance, are generally available only for lists.

Perhaps the most commonly used list method is append, which simply tacks a single item (object reference) onto the end of the list. Unlike concatenation, append expects you to pass in a single object, not a list. The effect of L.append(X) is similar to L+[X], but while the former changes L in place, the latter makes a new list.[3] The sort method orders the list's items here, but merits a section of its own.

More on sorting lists

Another commonly seen method, sort, orders a list in place; it uses Python standard comparison tests (here, string comparisons, but applicable to every object type), and

---

3. Unlike + concatenation, append doesn't have to generate new objects, so it's usually faster than + too. You can also mimic append with the clever slice assignments of the prior section: L[len(L):]=[X] is like L.append(X), and L[:0]=[X] is like appending at the front of a list. Both delete an empty slice and insert X, changing L in place quickly, like append. Both are arguably more complex than list methods, though. For instance, L.insert(0, X) can also append an item to the front of a list, and seems noticeably more mnemonic; L.insert(len(L), X) inserts one object at the end too, but unless you like typing, you might as well use L.append(X)!

by default sorts in ascending order. You can modify sort behavior by passing in *keyword arguments*—a special "name=value" syntax in function calls that specifies passing by name and is often used for giving configuration options.

In sorts, the `reverse` argument allows sorts to be made in descending instead of ascending order, and the `key` argument gives a one-argument function that returns the value to be used in sorting—the string object's standard `lower` case converter in the following (though its newer `casefold` may handle some types of Unicode text better):

```
>>> L = ['abc', 'ABD', 'aBe']
>>> L.sort()                                    # Sort with mixed case
>>> L
['ABD', 'aBe', 'abc']
>>> L = ['abc', 'ABD', 'aBe']
>>> L.sort(key=str.lower)                        # Normalize to lowercase
>>> L
['abc', 'ABD', 'aBe']
>>>
>>> L = ['abc', 'ABD', 'aBe']
>>> L.sort(key=str.lower, reverse=True)          # Change sort order
>>> L
['aBe', 'ABD', 'abc']
```

The sort `key` argument might also be useful when sorting lists of dictionaries, to pick out a sort key by indexing each dictionary. We'll study dictionaries later in this chapter, and you'll learn more about keyword function arguments in Part IV.

Comparison and sorts in 3.X: In Python 2.X, relative magnitude comparisons of differently typed objects (e.g., a string and a list) work as first noted in Chapter 5—the language defines a fixed ordering among different types, which is deterministic, if not aesthetically pleasing. That is, the ordering is based on the names of the types involved: all integers are less than all strings, for example, because `"int"` is less than `"str"`. Comparisons never automatically convert types, except when comparing numeric type objects.

In Python 3.X, this has changed: magnitude comparison of mixed types raises an exception instead of falling back on the fixed cross-type ordering. Because sorting uses comparisons internally, this means that `[1, 2, 'spam'].sort()` succeeds in Python 2.X but will raise an exception in Python 3.X. Sorting mixed-types fails by proxy.

Python 3.X also no longer supports passing in an arbitrary *comparison function* to sorts, to implement different orderings. The suggested workaround is to use the `key=`*func* keyword argument to code value transformations during the sort, and use the `reverse=True` keyword argument to change the sort order to descending. These were the typical uses of comparison functions in the past.

One warning here: beware that `append` and `sort` change the associated list object in place, but don't return the list as a result (technically, they both return a value called `None`). If you say something like `L=L.append(X)`, you won't get the modified value of L (in fact, you'll lose the reference to the list altogether!). When you use attributes such as `append` and `sort`, objects are changed as a side effect, so there's no reason to reassign.

Partly because of such constraints, sorting is also available in recent Pythons as a built-in function, which sorts any collection (not just lists) and returns a new list for the result (instead of in-place changes):

```
>>> L = ['abc', 'ABD', 'aBe']
>>> sorted(L, key=str.lower, reverse=True)          # Sorting built-in
['aBe', 'ABD', 'abc']

>>> L = ['abc', 'ABD', 'aBe']
>>> sorted([x.lower() for x in L], reverse=True)     # Pretransform items: differs!
['abe', 'abd', 'abc']
```

Notice the last example here—we can convert to lowercase prior to the sort with a list comprehension, but the result does not contain the original list's values as it does with the `key` argument. The latter is applied temporarily during the sort, instead of changing the values to be sorted altogether. As we move along, we'll see contexts in which the `sorted` built-in can sometimes be more useful than the `sort` method.

Other common list methods

Like strings, lists have other methods that perform other specialized operations. For instance, `reverse` reverses the list in-place, and the `extend` and `pop` methods insert multiple items at and delete an item from the end of the list, respectively. There is also a `reversed` built-in function that works much like `sorted` and returns a new result object, but it must be wrapped in a `list` call in both 2.X and 3.X here because its result is an iterator that produces results on demand (more on iterators later):

```
>>> L = [1, 2]
>>> L.extend([3, 4, 5])          # Add many items at end (like in-place +)
>>> L
[1, 2, 3, 4, 5]
>>> L.pop()                       # Delete and return last item (by default: –1)
5
>>> L
[1, 2, 3, 4]
>>> L.reverse()                   # In-place reversal method
>>> L
[4, 3, 2, 1]
>>> list(reversed(L))             # Reversal built-in with a result (iterator)
[1, 2, 3, 4]
```

Technically, the `extend` method always iterates through and adds each item in an *iterable* object, whereas `append` simply adds a single item as is without iterating through it —a distinction that will be more meaningful by Chapter 14. For now, it's enough to know that `extend` adds many items, and `append` adds one. In some types of programs, the list pop method is often used in conjunction with append to implement a quick last-in-first-out (LIFO) *stack* structure. The end of the list serves as the top of the stack:

```
>>> L = []
>>> L.append(1)              # Push onto stack
>>> L.append(2)
>>> L
[1, 2]
>>> L.pop()                  # Pop off stack
2
>>> L
[1]
```

The pop method also accepts an optional offset of the item to be deleted and returned (the default is the last item at offset –1). Other list methods remove an item by value (remove), insert an item at an offset (insert), count the number of occurrences (count), and search for an item's offset (index—a search for the *index of* an item, not to be confused with indexing!):

```
>>> L = ['spam', 'eggs', 'ham']
>>> L.index('eggs')          # Index of an object (search/find)
1
>>> L.insert(1, 'toast')     # Insert at position
>>> L
['spam', 'toast', 'eggs', 'ham']
>>> L.remove('eggs')         # Delete by value
>>> L
['spam', 'toast', 'ham']
>>> L.pop(1)                 # Delete by position
'toast'
>>> L
['spam', 'ham']
>>> L.count('spam')          # Number of occurrences
1
```

Note that unlike other list methods, count and index do not change the list itself, but return information about its content. See other documentation sources or experiment with these calls interactively on your own to learn more about list methods.

Other common list operations

Because lists are mutable, you can use the del statement to delete an item or section in place:

```
>>> L = ['spam', 'eggs', 'ham', 'toast']
>>> del L[0]                 # Delete one item
>>> L
['eggs', 'ham', 'toast']
>>> del L[1:]                # Delete an entire section
>>> L                        # Same as L[1:] = []
['eggs']
```

As we saw earlier, because slice assignment is a deletion plus an insertion, you can also delete a section of a list by assigning an empty list to a slice (L[i:j]=[]); Python deletes the slice named on the left, and then inserts nothing. Assigning an empty list to an index, on the other hand, just stores a reference to the empty list object in the specified slot, rather than deleting an item:

```
>>> L = ['Already', 'got', 'one']
>>> L[1:] = []
>>> L
['Already']
>>> L[0] = []
>>> L
[[]]
```

Although all the operations just discussed are typical, there may be additional list methods and operations not illustrated here. The method set, for example, may change over time, and in fact has in Python 3.3—its new `L.copy()` method makes a top-level copy of the list, much like `L[:]` and `list(L)`, but is symmetric with `copy` in sets and dictionaries. For a comprehensive and up-to-date list of type tools, you should always consult Python's manuals, Python's `dir` and `help` functions (which we first met in Chapter 4), or one of the reference texts mentioned in the preface.

And because it's such a common hurdle, I'd also like to remind you again that all the in-place change operations discussed here work only for mutable objects: they won't work on strings (or tuples, discussed in Chapter 9), no matter how hard you try. Mutability is an inherent property of each object type.

Dictionaries

Along with lists, *dictionaries* are one of the most flexible built-in data types in Python. If you think of lists as ordered collections of objects, you can think of dictionaries as unordered collections; the chief distinction is that in dictionaries, items are stored and fetched by *key*, instead of by positional offset. While lists can serve roles similar to arrays in other languages, dictionaries take the place of records, search tables, and any other sort of aggregation where item names are more meaningful than item positions.

For example, dictionaries can replace many of the searching algorithms and data structures you might have to implement manually in lower-level languages—as a highly optimized built-in type, indexing a dictionary is a very fast search operation. Dictionaries also sometimes do the work of records, structs, and symbol tables used in other languages; can be used to represent sparse (mostly empty) data structures; and much more. Here's a rundown of their main properties. Python dictionaries are:

Accessed by key, not offset position

Dictionaries are sometimes called *associative arrays* or *hashes* (especially by users of other scripting languages). They associate a set of values with keys, so you can fetch an item out of a dictionary using the key under which you originally stored it. You use the same indexing operation to get components in a dictionary as you do in a list, but the index takes the form of a key, not a relative offset.

Unordered collections of arbitrary objects

Unlike in a list, items stored in a dictionary aren't kept in any particular order; in fact, Python pseudo-randomizes their left-to-right order to provide quick lookup. Keys provide the symbolic (not physical) locations of items in a dictionary.

Variable-length, heterogeneous, and arbitrarily nestable

Like lists, dictionaries can grow and shrink in place (without new copies being made), they can contain objects of any type, and they support nesting to any depth (they can contain lists, other dictionaries, and so on). Each *key* can have just one associated *value*, but that value can be a *collection* of multiple objects if needed, and a given value can be stored under any number of keys.

Of the category "mutable mapping"

You can change dictionaries in place by assigning to indexes (they are mutable), but they don't support the sequence operations that work on strings and lists. Because dictionaries are unordered collections, operations that depend on a fixed positional order (e.g., concatenation, slicing) don't make sense. Instead, dictionaries are the only built-in, core type representatives of the *mapping* category— objects that map keys to values. Other mappings in Python are created by imported modules.

Tables of object references (hash tables)

If lists are arrays of object references that support access by position, dictionaries are unordered tables of object references that support access by key. Internally, dictionaries are implemented as hash tables (data structures that support very fast retrieval), which start small and grow on demand. Moreover, Python employs optimized hashing algorithms to find keys, so retrieval is quick. Like lists, dictionaries store object references (not copies, unless you ask for them explicitly).

For reference and preview again, Table 8-2 summarizes some of the most common and representative dictionary operations, and is relatively complete as of Python 3.3. As usual, though, see the library manual or run a `dir(dict)` or `help(dict)` call for a complete list—`dict` is the name of the type. When coded as a literal expression, a dictionary is written as a series of *key:value* pairs, separated by commas, enclosed in curly braces.[4] An empty dictionary is an empty set of braces, and you can nest dictionaries by simply coding one as a value inside another dictionary, or within a list or tuple.

---

4. As for lists, you might not see dictionaries coded in full using literals very often—programs rarely know all their data before they are run, and more typically extract it dynamically from users, files, and so on. Lists and dictionaries are grown in different ways, though. In the next section you'll see that you often build up dictionaries by assigning to new keys at runtime; this approach fails for lists, which are commonly grown with append or extend instead.

Table 8-2. Common dictionary literals and operations

Operation	Interpretation
`D = {}`	Empty dictionary
`D = {'name': 'Bob', 'age': 40}`	Two-item dictionary
`E = {'cto': {'name': 'Bob', 'age': 40}}`	Nesting
`D = dict(name='Bob', age=40)`	Alternative construction techniques:
`D = dict([('name', 'Bob'), ('age', 40)])`	keywords, key/value pairs, zipped key/value pairs, key lists
`D = dict(zip(keyslist, valueslist))`	
`D = dict.fromkeys(['name', 'age'])`	
`D['name']`	Indexing by key
`E['cto']['age']`	
`'age' in D`	Membership: key present test
`D.keys()`	Methods: all keys,
`D.values()`	all values,
`D.items()`	all key+value tuples,
`D.copy()`	copy (top-level),
`D.clear()`	clear (remove all items),
`D.update(D2)`	merge by keys,
`D.get(key, default?)`	fetch by key, if absent default (or None),
`D.pop(key, default?)`	remove by key, if absent default (or error)
`D.setdefault(key, default?)`	fetch by key, if absent set default (or None),
`D.popitem()`	remove/return any (key, value) pair; etc.
`len(D)`	Length: number of stored entries
`D[key] = 42`	Adding/changing keys
`del D[key]`	Deleting entries by key
`list(D.keys())`	Dictionary views (Python 3.X)
`D1.keys() & D2.keys()`	
`D.viewkeys(), D.viewvalues()`	Dictionary views (Python 2.7)
`D = {x: x*2 for x in range(10)}`	Dictionary comprehensions (Python 3.X, 2.7)

Dictionaries in Action

As Table 8-2 suggests, dictionaries are indexed by key, and nested dictionary entries are referenced by a series of indexes (keys in square brackets). When Python creates a dictionary, it stores its items in any left-to-right order it chooses; to fetch a value back, you supply the key with which it is associated, not its relative position. Let's go back to the interpreter to get a feel for some of the dictionary operations in Table 8-2.

Basic Dictionary Operations

In normal operation, you create dictionaries with literals and store and access items by key with indexing:

```
% python
>>> D = {'spam': 2, 'ham': 1, 'eggs': 3}     # Make a dictionary
>>> D['spam']                                 # Fetch a value by key
2
>>> D                                         # Order is "scrambled"
{'eggs': 3, 'spam': 2, 'ham': 1}
```

Here, the dictionary is assigned to the variable D; the value of the key 'spam' is the integer 2, and so on. We use the same square bracket syntax to index dictionaries by key as we did to index lists by offset, but here it means access by key, not by position.

Notice the end of this example—much like sets, the *left-to-right order* of keys in a dictionary will almost always be different from what you originally typed. This is on purpose: to implement fast key lookup (a.k.a. hashing), keys need to be reordered in memory. That's why operations that assume a fixed left-to-right order (e.g., slicing, concatenation) do not apply to dictionaries; you can fetch values only by key, not by position. Technically, the ordering is *pseudo-random*—it's not truly random (you might be able to decipher it given Python's source code and a lot of time to kill), but it's arbitrary, and might vary per release and platform, and even per interactive session in Python 3.3.

The built-in len function works on dictionaries, too; it returns the number of items stored in the dictionary or, equivalently, the length of its keys list. The dictionary in membership operator allows you to test for key existence, and the keys method returns all the keys in the dictionary. The latter of these can be useful for processing dictionaries sequentially, but you shouldn't depend on the order of the keys list. Because the keys result can be used as a normal list, however, it can always be sorted if order matters (more on sorting and dictionaries later):

```
>>> len(D)                    # Number of entries in dictionary
3
>>> 'ham' in D                # Key membership test alternative
True
>>> list(D.keys())            # Create a new list of D's keys
['eggs', 'spam', 'ham']
```

Observe the second expression in this listing. As mentioned earlier, the in membership test used for strings and lists also works on dictionaries—it checks whether a key is stored in the dictionary. Technically, this works because dictionaries define keys *iterators*, and use fast direct lookups whenever possible. Other types provide iterators that reflect their common uses; files, for example, have iterators that read line by line. We'll discuss iterators more formally in Chapter 14 and Chapter 20.

Also note the syntax of the last example in this listing. We have to enclose it in a `list` call in Python 3.X for similar reasons—keys in 3.X returns an *iterable* object, instead of a physical list. The `list` call forces it to produce all its values at once so we can print them interactively, though this call isn't required some other contexts. In 2.X, `keys` builds and returns an actual list, so the `list` call isn't even needed to display a result; more on this later in this chapter.

Changing Dictionaries in Place

Let's continue with our interactive session. Dictionaries, like lists, are mutable, so you can change, expand, and shrink them in place without making new dictionaries: simply assign a value to a key to change or create an entry. The `del` statement works here, too; it deletes the entry associated with the key specified as an index. Notice also the nesting of a list inside a dictionary in this example (the value of the key `'ham'`). All collection data types in Python can nest inside each other arbitrarily:

```
>>> D
{'eggs': 3, 'spam': 2, 'ham': 1}

>>> D['ham'] = ['grill', 'bake', 'fry']          # Change entry (value=list)
>>> D
{'eggs': 3, 'spam': 2, 'ham': ['grill', 'bake', 'fry']}

>>> del D['eggs']                                 # Delete entry
>>> D
{'spam': 2, 'ham': ['grill', 'bake', 'fry']}

>>> D['brunch'] = 'Bacon'                          # Add new entry
>>> D
{'brunch': 'Bacon', 'spam': 2, 'ham': ['grill', 'bake', 'fry']}
```

Like lists, assigning to an existing index in a dictionary changes its associated value. Unlike lists, however, whenever you assign a *new* dictionary key (one that hasn't been assigned before) you create a new entry in the dictionary, as was done in the previous example for the key `'brunch'`. This doesn't work for lists because you can only assign to existing list offsets—Python considers an offset beyond the end of a list out of bounds and raises an error. To expand a list, you need to use tools such as the **append** method or slice assignment instead.

More Dictionary Methods

Dictionary methods provide a variety of type-specific tools. For instance, the dictionary `values` and `items` methods return all of the dictionary's values and (*key,value*) pair tuples, respectively; along with `keys`, these are useful in loops that need to step through dictionary entries one by one (we'll start coding examples of such loops in the next section). As for `keys`, these two methods also return *iterable* objects in 3.X, so wrap them in a `list` call there to collect their values all at once for display:

```
>>> D = {'spam': 2, 'ham': 1, 'eggs': 3}
>>> list(D.values())
[3, 2, 1]
>>> list(D.items())
 [('eggs', 3), ('spam', 2), ('ham', 1)]
```

In realistic programs that gather data as they run, you often won't be able to predict what will be in a dictionary before the program is launched, much less when it's coded. Fetching a nonexistent key is normally an error, but the `get` method returns a default value—`None`, or a passed-in default—if the key doesn't exist. It's an easy way to fill in a default for a key that isn't present, and avoid a missing-key error when your program can't anticipate contents ahead of time:

```
>>> D.get('spam')                        # A key that is there
2
>>> print(D.get('toast'))                # A key that is missing
None
>>> D.get('toast', 88)
88
```

The `update` method provides something similar to concatenation for dictionaries, though it has nothing to do with left-to-right ordering (again, there is no such thing in dictionaries). It *merges* the keys and values of one dictionary into another, blindly overwriting values of the same key if there's a clash:

```
>>> D
{'eggs': 3, 'spam': 2, 'ham': 1}
>>> D2 = {'toast':4, 'muffin':5}         # Lots of delicious scrambled order here
>>> D.update(D2)
>>> D
{'eggs': 3, 'muffin': 5, 'toast': 4, 'spam': 2, 'ham': 1}
```

Notice how mixed up the key order is in the last result; again, that's just how dictionaries work. Finally, the dictionary `pop` method deletes a key from a dictionary and returns the value it had. It's similar to the list `pop` method, but it takes a key instead of an optional position:

```
# pop a dictionary by key
>>> D
{'eggs': 3, 'muffin': 5, 'toast': 4, 'spam': 2, 'ham': 1}
>>> D.pop('muffin')
5
>>> D.pop('toast')                       # Delete and return from a key
4
>>> D
{'eggs': 3, 'spam': 2, 'ham': 1}

# pop a list by position
>>> L = ['aa', 'bb', 'cc', 'dd']
>>> L.pop()                              # Delete and return from the end
'dd'
```

```
>>> L
['aa', 'bb', 'cc']
>>> L.pop(1)          # Delete from a specific position
'bb'
>>> L
['aa', 'cc']
```

Dictionaries also provide a **copy** method; we'll revisit this in Chapter 9, as it's a way to avoid the potential side effects of shared references to the same dictionary. In fact, dictionaries come with more methods than those listed in Table 8-2; see the Python library manual, `dir` and `help`, or other reference sources for a comprehensive list.

> *Your dictionary ordering may vary*: Don't be alarmed if your dictionaries print in a different order than shown here. As mentioned, key order is arbitrary, and might vary per release, platform, and interactive session in 3.3 (and quite possibly per day of the week, and phase of the moon!).
>
> Most of the dictionary examples in this book reflect Python 3.3's key ordering, but it has changed both since and prior to 3.0. Your Python's key order may vary, but you're not supposed to care anyhow: dictionaries are processed by key, not position. Programs shouldn't rely on the arbitrary order of keys in dictionaries, even if shown in books.
>
> There are extension types in Python's standard library that maintain insertion order among their keys—see `OrderedDict` in the `collections` module—but they are hybrids that incur extra space and speed overheads to achieve their extra utility, and are not true dictionaries. In short, keys are kept redundantly in a linked list to support sequence operations.
>
> As we'll see in Chapter 9, this module also implements a `namedtuple` that allows tuple items to be accessed by both attribute name and sequence position—a sort of tuple/class/dictionary hybrid that adds processing steps and is not a core object type in any event. Python's library manual has the full story on these and other extension types.

Example: Movie Database

Let's look at a more realistic dictionary example. In honor of Python's namesake, the following example creates a simple in-memory Monty Python movie database, as a table that maps movie release date *years* (the keys) to movie *titles* (the values). As coded, you fetch movie names by indexing on release year strings:

```
>>> table = {'1975': 'Holy Grail',          # Key: Value
...          '1979': 'Life of Brian',
...          '1983': 'The Meaning of Life'}
>>>
>>> year  = '1983'
>>> movie = table[year]                      # dictionary[Key] => Value
>>> movie
'The Meaning of Life'
```

```
>>> for year in table:                        # Same as: for year in table.keys()
...     print(year + '\t' + table[year])
...
1979    Life of Brian
1975    Holy Grail
1983    The Meaning of Life
```

The last command uses a `for` loop, which we previewed in Chapter 4 but haven't covered in detail yet. If you aren't familiar with `for` loops, this command simply iterates through each key in the table and prints a tab-separated list of keys and their values. We'll learn more about `for` loops in Chapter 13.

Dictionaries aren't sequences like lists and strings, but if you need to step through the items in a dictionary, it's easy—calling the dictionary `keys` method returns all stored *keys*, which you can iterate through with a `for`. If needed, you can index from key to *value* inside the `for` loop as you go, as was done in this code.

In fact, Python also lets you step through a dictionary's keys list without actually calling the `keys` method in most `for` loops. For any dictionary D, saying `for key in D` works the same as saying the complete `for key in D.keys()`. This is really just another instance of the *iterators* mentioned earlier, which allow the `in` membership operator to work on dictionaries as well; more on iterators later in this book.

Preview: Mapping values to keys

Notice how the prior table maps year to titles, but not vice versa. If you want to map the other way—titles to years—you can either code the dictionary differently, or use methods like `items` that give searchable sequences, though using them to best effect requires more background information than we yet have:

```
>>> table = {'Holy Grail':          '1975',      # Key=>Value (title=>year)
...          'Life of Brian':        '1979',
...          'The Meaning of Life': '1983'}
>>>
>>> table['Holy Grail']
'1975'

>>> list(table.items())                          # Value=>Key (year=>title)
[('The Meaning of Life', '1983'), ('Holy Grail', '1975'), ('Life of Brian', '1979')]
>>> [title for (title, year) in table.items() if year == '1975']
['Holy Grail']
```

The last command here is in part a preview for the *comprehension* syntax introduced in Chapter 4 and covered in full in Chapter 14. In short, it scans the dictionary's (*key, value*) tuple pairs returned by the `items` method, selecting keys having a specified value. The net effect is to index *backward*—from value to key, instead of key to value—useful if you want to store data just once and map backward only rarely (searching through sequences like this is generally much slower than a direct key index).

In fact, although dictionaries by nature map keys to values unidirectionally, there are multiple ways to map values back to keys with a bit of extra generalizable code:

```
>>> K = 'Holy Grail'
>>> table[K]                    # Key=>Value (normal usage)
'1975'

>>> V = '1975'
>>> [key for (key, value) in table.items() if value == V]      # Value=>Key
['Holy Grail']
>>> [key for key in table.keys() if table[key] == V]      # Ditto
['Holy Grail']
```

Note that both of the last two commands return a *list* of titles: in dictionaries, there's just *one* value per key, but there may be *many* keys per value. A given value may be stored under multiple keys (yielding multiple keys per value), and a value might be a collection itself (supporting multiple values per key). For more on this front, also watch for a dictionary inversion function in Chapter 32's *mapattrs.py* example—code that would surely stretch this preview past its breaking point if included here. For this chapter's purposes, let's explore more dictionary basics.

Dictionary Usage Notes

Dictionaries are fairly straightforward tools once you get the hang of them, but here are a few additional pointers and reminders you should be aware of when using them:

- **Sequence operations don't work**. Dictionaries are mappings, not sequences; because there's no notion of ordering among their items, things like concatenation (an ordered joining) and slicing (extracting a contiguous section) simply don't apply. In fact, Python raises an error when your code runs if you try to do such things.

- **Assigning to new indexes adds entries**. Keys can be created when you write a dictionary literal (embedded in the code of the literal itself), or when you assign values to new keys of an existing dictionary object individually. The end result is the same.

- **Keys need not always be strings**. Our examples so far have used strings as keys, but any other *immutable* objects work just as well. For instance, you can use integers as keys, which makes the dictionary look much like a list (when indexing, at least). Tuples may be used as dictionary keys too, allowing compound key values —such as dates and IP addresses—to have associated values. User-defined class instance objects (discussed in Part VI) can also be used as keys, as long as they have the proper protocol methods; roughly, they need to tell Python that their values are "hashable" and thus won't change, as otherwise they would be useless as fixed keys. Mutable objects such as lists, sets, and other dictionaries don't work as keys, but are allowed as values.

Using dictionaries to simulate flexible lists: Integer keys

The last point in the prior list is important enough to demonstrate with a few examples. When you use lists, it is illegal to assign to an offset that is off the end of the list:

```
>>> L = []
>>> L[99] = 'spam'
Traceback (most recent call last):
  File "<stdin>", line 1, in ?
IndexError: list assignment index out of range
```

Although you can use repetition to preallocate as big a list as you'll need (e.g., [0]*100), you can also do something that looks similar with dictionaries that does not require such space allocations. By using integer keys, dictionaries can emulate lists that seem to grow on offset assignment:

```
>>> D = {}
>>> D[99] = 'spam'
>>> D[99]
'spam'
>>> D
{99: 'spam'}
```

Here, it looks as if D is a 100-item list, but it's really a dictionary with a single entry; the value of the key 99 is the string 'spam'. You can access this structure with offsets much like a list, catching nonexistent keys with get or in tests if required, but you don't have to allocate space for all the positions you might ever need to assign values to in the future. When used like this, dictionaries are like more flexible equivalents of lists.

As another example, we might also employ integer keys in our first *movie database's* code earlier to avoid quoting the year, albeit at the expense of some expressiveness (keys cannot contain nondigit characters):

```
>>> table = {1975: 'Holy Grail',
...          1979: 'Life of Brian',         # Keys are integers, not strings
...          1983: 'The Meaning of Life'}
>>> table[1975]
'Holy Grail'
>>> list(table.items())
[(1979, 'Life of Brian'), (1983, 'The Meaning of Life'), (1975, 'Holy Grail')]
```

Using dictionaries for sparse data structures: Tuple keys

In a similar way, dictionary keys are also commonly leveraged to implement *sparse* data structures—for example, multidimensional arrays where only a few positions have values stored in them:

```
>>> Matrix = {}
>>> Matrix[(2, 3, 4)] = 88
>>> Matrix[(7, 8, 9)] = 99
>>>
>>> X = 2; Y = 3; Z = 4        # ; separates statements: see Chapter 10
>>> Matrix[(X, Y, Z)]
88
```

```
>>> Matrix
{(2, 3, 4): 88, (7, 8, 9): 99}
```

Here, we've used a dictionary to represent a three-dimensional array that is empty except for the two positions (2,3,4) and (7,8,9). The keys are *tuples* that record the coordinates of nonempty slots. Rather than allocating a large and mostly empty three-dimensional matrix to hold these values, we can use a simple two-item dictionary. In this scheme, accessing an empty slot triggers a nonexistent key exception, as these slots are not physically stored:

```
>>> Matrix[(2,3,6)]
Traceback (most recent call last):
  File "<stdin>", line 1, in ?
KeyError: (2, 3, 6)
```

Avoiding missing-key errors

Errors for nonexistent key fetches are common in sparse matrixes, but you probably won't want them to shut down your program. There are at least three ways to fill in a default value instead of getting such an error message—you can test for keys ahead of time in if statements, use a try statement to catch and recover from the exception explicitly, or simply use the dictionary get method shown earlier to provide a default for keys that do not exist. Consider the first two of these previews for statement syntax we'll begin studying in Chapter 10:

```
>>> if (2, 3, 6) in Matrix:          # Check for key before fetch
...     print(Matrix[(2, 3, 6)])     # See Chapters 10 and 12 for if/else
... else:
...     print(0)
...
0
>>> try:
...     print(Matrix[(2, 3, 6)])     # Try to index
... except KeyError:                 # Catch and recover
...     print(0)                     # See Chapters 10 and 34 for try/except
...
0
>>> Matrix.get((2, 3, 4), 0)         # Exists: fetch and return
88
>>> Matrix.get((2, 3, 6), 0)         # Doesn't exist: use default arg
0
```

Of these, the get method is the most concise in terms of coding requirements, but the if and try statements are much more general in scope; again, more on these starting in Chapter 10.

Nesting in dictionaries

As you can see, dictionaries can play many roles in Python. In general, they can replace search data structures (because indexing by key is a search operation) and can represent many types of structured information. For example, dictionaries are one of many ways to describe the properties of an item in your program's domain; that is, they can serve the same role as "records" or "structs" in other languages.

The following, for example, fills out a dictionary describing a hypothetical person, by assigning to new keys over time (if you are a Bob, my apologies for picking on your name in this book—it's easy to type!):

```
>>> rec = {}
>>> rec['name'] = 'Bob'
>>> rec['age']  = 40.5
>>> rec['job']  = 'developer/manager'
>>>
>>> print(rec['name'])
Bob
```

Especially when nested, Python's built-in data types allow us to easily represent *structured* information. The following again uses a dictionary to capture object properties, but it codes it all at once (rather than assigning to each key separately) and nests a list and a dictionary to represent structured property values:

```
>>> rec = {'name': 'Bob',
...        'jobs': ['developer', 'manager'],
...        'web':  'www.bobs.org/~Bob',
...        'home': {'state': 'Overworked', 'zip': 12345}}
```

To fetch components of nested objects, simply string together indexing operations:

```
>>> rec['name']
'Bob'
>>> rec['jobs']
['developer', 'manager']
>>> rec['jobs'][1]
'manager'
>>> rec['home']['zip']
12345
```

Although we'll learn in Part VI that *classes* (which group both data and logic) can be better in this record role, dictionaries are an easy-to-use tool for simpler requirements. For more on record representation choices, see also the upcoming sidebar "Why You Will Care: Dictionaries Versus Lists" on page 263, as well as its extension to tuples in Chapter 9 and classes in Chapter 27.

Also notice that while we've focused on a single "record" with nested data here, there's no reason we couldn't nest the record itself in a larger, enclosing *database* collection coded as a list or dictionary, though an external file or formal database interface often plays the role of top-level container in realistic programs (the following snippets both print Bob's 2-item job list if run live and provided with another record structure):

```
db = []
db.append(rec)              # A list "database"
db.append(other)
db[0]['jobs']

db = {}
```

```
db['bob'] = rec              # A dictionary "database"
db['sue'] = other
db['bob']['jobs']
```

Later in the book we'll meet tools such as Python's `shelve`, which works much the same way, but automatically maps objects to and from files to make them permanent (watch for more in this chapter's sidebar "Why You Will Care: Dictionary Interfaces" on page 271).

Other Ways to Make Dictionaries

Finally, note that because dictionaries are so useful, more ways to build them have emerged over time. In Python 2.3 and later, for example, the last two calls to the `dict` constructor (really, type name) shown here have the same effect as the literal and key-assignment forms above them:

```
{'name': 'Bob', 'age': 40}              # Traditional literal expression

D = {}                                  # Assign by keys dynamically
D['name'] = 'Bob'
D['age']  = 40

dict(name='Bob', age=40)                # dict keyword argument form

dict([('name', 'Bob'), ('age', 40)])    # dict key/value tuples form
```

All four of these forms create the same two-key dictionary, but they are useful in differing circumstances:

- The first is handy if you can spell out the entire dictionary ahead of time.
- The second is of use if you need to create the dictionary one field at a time on the fly.
- The third involves less typing than the first, but it requires all keys to be strings.
- The last is useful if you need to build up keys and values as sequences at runtime.

We met keyword arguments earlier when sorting; the third form illustrated in this code listing has become especially popular in Python code today, since it has less syntax (and hence there is less opportunity for mistakes). As suggested previously in Table 8-2, the last form in the listing is also commonly used in conjunction with the `zip` function, to combine separate lists of keys and values obtained dynamically at runtime (parsed out of a data file's columns, for instance):

```
dict(zip(keyslist, valueslist))         # Zipped key/value tuples form (ahead)
```

More on zipping dictionary keys in the next section. Provided all the key's values are the same initially, you can also create a dictionary with this special form—simply pass in a list of keys and an initial value for all of the values (the default is `None`):

```
>>> dict.fromkeys(['a', 'b'], 0)
{'a': 0, 'b': 0}
```

Although you could get by with just literals and key assignments at this point in your Python career, you'll probably find uses for all of these dictionary-creation forms as you start applying them in realistic, flexible, and dynamic Python programs.

The listings in this section document the various ways to create dictionaries in both Python 2.X and 3.X. However, there is yet another way to create dictionaries, available only in Python 3.X and 2.7: the *dictionary comprehension* expression. To see how this last form looks, we need to move on to the next and final section of this chapter.

Why You Will Care: Dictionaries Versus Lists

With all the objects in Python's core types arsenal, some readers may be puzzled over the choice between lists and dictionaries. In short, although both are flexible collections of other objects, lists assign items to *positions*, and dictionaries assign them to more mnemonic *keys*. Because of this, dictionary data often carries more meaning to human readers. For example, the nested list structure in row 3 of Table 8-1 could be used to represent a record too:

```
>>> L = ['Bob', 40.5, ['dev', 'mgr']]   # List-based "record"
>>> L[0]
'Bob'
>>> L[1]                                 # Positions/numbers for fields
40.5
>>> L[2][1]
'mgr'
```

For some types of data, the list's access-by-position makes sense—a list of employees in a company, the files in a directory, or numeric matrixes, for example. But a more symbolic record like this may be more meaningfully coded as a dictionary along the lines of row 2 in Table 8-2, with labeled fields replacing field positions (this is similar to a record we coded in Chapter 4):

```
>>> D = {'name': 'Bob', 'age': 40.5, 'jobs': ['dev', 'mgr']}
>>> D['name']
'Bob'
>>> D['age']                             # Dictionary-based "record"
40.5
>>> D['jobs'][1]                         # Names mean more than numbers
'mgr'
```

For variety, here is the same record recoded with keywords, which may seem even more readable to some human readers:

```
>>> D = dict(name='Bob', age=40.5, jobs=['dev', 'mgr'])
>>> D['name']
'Bob'
>>> D['jobs'].remove('mgr')
>>> D
{'jobs': ['dev'], 'age': 40.5, 'name': 'Bob'}
```

In practice, dictionaries tend to be best for data with labeled components, as well as structures that can benefit from quick, direct lookups by name, instead of slower linear searches. As we've seen, they also may be better for sparse collections and collections that grow at arbitrary positions.

Python programmers also have access to the *sets* we studied in Chapter 5, which are much like the keys of a valueless dictionary; they don't map keys to values, but can often be used like dictionaries for fast lookups when there is no associated value, especially in search routines:

```
>>> D = {}
>>> D['state1'] = True          # A visited-state dictionary
>>> 'state1' in D
True
>>> S = set()
>>> S.add('state1')             # Same, but with sets
>>> 'state1' in S
True
```

Watch for a rehash of this record representation thread in the next chapter, where we'll see how *tuples* and *named tuples* compare to dictionaries in this role, as well as in Chapter 27, where we'll learn how user-defined *classes* factor into this picture, combining both data and logic to process it.

Dictionary Changes in Python 3.X and 2.7

This chapter has so far focused on dictionary basics that span releases, but the dictionary's functionality has mutated in Python 3.X. If you are using Python 2.X code, you may come across some dictionary tools that either behave differently or are missing altogether in 3.X. Moreover, 3.X coders have access to additional dictionary tools not available in 2.X, apart from two back-ports to 2.7.

Specifically, dictionaries in *Python 3.X*:

- Support a new dictionary *comprehension* expression, a close cousin to list and set comprehensions
- Return set-like iterable *views* instead of lists for the methods D.keys, D.values, and D.items
- Require new coding styles for scanning by sorted keys, because of the prior point
- No longer support relative magnitude comparisons directly—compare manually instead
- No longer have the D.has_key method—the in membership test is used instead

As later back-ports from 3.X, dictionaries in *Python 2.7* (but not earlier in 2.X):

- Support item 1 in the prior list—dictionary *comprehensions*—as a direct back-port from 3.X
- Support item 2 in the prior list—set-like iterable *views*—but do so with special method names D.viewkeys, D.viewvalues, D.viewitems); their nonview methods return lists as before

Because of this overlap, some of the material in this section pertains both to 3.X and 2.7, but is presented here in the context of 3.X extensions because of its origin. With that in mind, let's take a look at what's new in dictionaries in 3.X and 2.7.

Dictionary comprehensions in 3.X and 2.7

As mentioned at the end of the prior section, dictionaries in 3.X and 2.7 can also be created with dictionary comprehensions. Like the set comprehensions we met in Chapter 5, dictionary comprehensions are available only in 3.X and 2.7 (not in 2.6 and earlier). Like the longstanding list comprehensions we met briefly in Chapter 4 and earlier in this chapter, they run an implied loop, collecting the key/value results of expressions on each iteration and using them to fill out a new dictionary. A loop variable allows the comprehension to use loop iteration values along the way.

To illustrate, a standard way to initialize a dictionary dynamically in both 2.X and 3.X is to combine its keys and values with `zip`, and pass the result to the `dict` call. The `zip` built-in function is the hook that allows us to construct a dictionary from key and value lists this way—if you cannot predict the set of keys and values in your code, you can always build them up as lists and zip them together. We'll study `zip` in detail in Chapter 13 and Chapter 14 after exploring statements; it's an iterable in 3.X, so we must wrap it in a `list` call to show its results there, but its basic usage is otherwise straightforward:

```
>>> list(zip(['a', 'b', 'c'], [1, 2, 3]))          # Zip together keys and values
[('a', 1), ('b', 2), ('c', 3)]

>>> D = dict(zip(['a', 'b', 'c'], [1, 2, 3]))      # Make a dict from zip result
>>> D
{'b': 2, 'c': 3, 'a': 1}
```

In Python 3.X and 2.7, though, you can achieve the same effect with a dictionary comprehension expression. The following builds a new dictionary with a key/value pair for every such pair in the `zip` result (it reads almost the same in Python, but with a bit more formality):

```
>>> D = {k: v for (k, v) in zip(['a', 'b', 'c'], [1, 2, 3])}
>>> D
{'b': 2, 'c': 3, 'a': 1}
```

Comprehensions actually require more code in this case, but they are also more general than this example implies—we can use them to map a single stream of values to dictionaries as well, and keys can be computed with expressions just like values:

```
>>> D = {x: x ** 2 for x in [1, 2, 3, 4]}          # Or: range(1, 5)
>>> D
{1: 1, 2: 4, 3: 9, 4: 16}

>>> D = {c: c * 4 for c in 'SPAM'}                 # Loop over any iterable
>>> D
{'S': 'SSSS', 'P': 'PPPP', 'A': 'AAAA', 'M': 'MMMM'}
```

```
>>> D = {c.lower(): c + '!' for c in ['SPAM', 'EGGS', 'HAM']}
>>> D
{'eggs': 'EGGS!', 'spam': 'SPAM!', 'ham': 'HAM!'}
```

Dictionary comprehensions are also useful for initializing dictionaries from keys lists, in much the same way as the `fromkeys` method we met at the end of the preceding section:

```
>>> D = dict.fromkeys(['a', 'b', 'c'], 0)          # Initialize dict from keys
>>> D
{'b': 0, 'c': 0, 'a': 0}

>>> D = {k:0 for k in ['a', 'b', 'c']}             # Same, but with a comprehension
>>> D
{'b': 0, 'c': 0, 'a': 0}

>>> D = dict.fromkeys('spam')                      # Other iterables, default value
>>> D
{'s': None, 'p': None, 'a': None, 'm': None}

>>> D = {k: None for k in 'spam'}
>>> D
{'s': None, 'p': None, 'a': None, 'm': None}
```

Like related tools, dictionary comprehensions support additional syntax not shown here, including nested loops and `if` clauses. Unfortunately, to truly understand dictionary comprehensions, we need to also know more about iteration statements and concepts in Python, and we don't yet have enough information to address that story well. We'll learn much more about all flavors of comprehensions (list, set, dictionary, and generator) in Chapter 14 and Chapter 20, so we'll defer further details until later. We'll also revisit the `zip` built-in we used in this section in more detail in Chapter 13, when we explore `for` loops.

Dictionary views in 3.X (and 2.7 via new methods)

In 3.X the dictionary `keys`, `values`, and `items` methods all return *view objects*, whereas in 2.X they return actual result lists. This functionality is also available in Python 2.7, but in the guise of the special, distinct method names listed at the start of this section (2.7's normal methods still return simple lists, so as to avoid breaking existing 2.X code); because of this, I'll refer to this as a 3.X feature in this section.

View objects are *iterables*, which simply means objects that generate result items one at a time, instead of producing the result list all at once in memory. Besides being iterable, dictionary views also retain the original order of dictionary components, reflect future changes to the dictionary, and may support set operations. On the other hand, because they are not lists, they do not directly support operations like indexing or the list `sort` method, and do not display their items as a normal list when printed (they do show their components as of Python 3.1 but not as a list, and are still a divergence from 2.X).

We'll discuss the notion of iterables more formally in Chapter 14, but for our purposes here it's enough to know that we have to run the results of these three methods through the `list` built-in if we want to apply list operations or display their values. For example, in Python 3.3 (other version's outputs may differ slightly):

```
>>> D = dict(a=1, b=2, c=3)
>>> D
{'b': 2, 'c': 3, 'a': 1}

>>> K = D.keys()                    # Makes a view object in 3.X, not a list
>>> K
dict_keys(['b', 'c', 'a'])
>>> list(K)                         # Force a real list in 3.X if needed
['b', 'c', 'a']

>>> V = D.values()                  # Ditto for values and items views
>>> V
dict_values([2, 3, 1])
>>> list(V)
[2, 3, 1]

>>> D.items()
dict_items([('b', 2), ('c', 3), ('a', 1)])
>>> list(D.items())
[('b', 2), ('c', 3), ('a', 1)]

>>> K[0]                            # List operations fail unless converted
TypeError: 'dict_keys' object does not support indexing
>>> list(K)[0]
'b'
```

Apart from result displays at the interactive prompt, you will probably rarely even notice this change, because looping constructs in Python automatically force iterable objects to produce one result on each iteration:

```
>>> for k in D.keys(): print(k)     # Iterators used automatically in loops
...
b
c
a
```

In addition, 3.X dictionaries still have iterators themselves, which return successive keys—as in 2.X, it's still often not necessary to call keys directly:

```
>>> for key in D: print(key)        # Still no need to call keys() to iterate
...
b
c
a
```

Unlike 2.X's list results, though, dictionary views in 3.X are not carved in stone when created—they *dynamically reflect future changes* made to the dictionary after the view object has been created:

```
>>> D = {'a': 1, 'b': 2, 'c': 3}
>>> D
{'b': 2, 'c': 3, 'a': 1}

>>> K = D.keys()
>>> V = D.values()
>>> list(K)                          # Views maintain same order as dictionary
['b', 'c', 'a']
>>> list(V)
[2, 3, 1]

>>> del D['b']                       # Change the dictionary in place
>>> D
{'c': 3, 'a': 1}

>>> list(K)                          # Reflected in any current view objects
['c', 'a']
>>> list(V)                          # Not true in 2.X! - lists detached from dict
[3, 1]
```

Dictionary views and sets

Also unlike 2.X's list results, 3.X's view objects returned by the `keys` method are *set-like* and support common set operations such as intersection and union; `values` views are not set-like, but `items` results are if their (*key, value*) pairs are unique and hashable (immutable). Given that sets behave much like valueless dictionaries (and may even be coded in curly braces like dictionaries in 3.X and 2.7), this is a logical symmetry. Per Chapter 5, set items are unordered, unique, and immutable, just like dictionary keys.

Here is what `keys` views look like when used in set operations (continuing the prior section's session); dictionary value views are never set-like, since their items are not necessarily unique or immutable:

```
>>> K, V
(dict_keys(['c', 'a']), dict_values([3, 1]))

>>> K | {'x': 4}                     # Keys (and some items) views are set-like
{'c', 'x', 'a'}

>>> V & {'x': 4}
TypeError: unsupported operand type(s) for &: 'dict_values' and 'dict'
>>> V & {'x': 4}.values()
TypeError: unsupported operand type(s) for &: 'dict_values' and 'dict_values'
```

In set operations, views may be mixed with other views, sets, and dictionaries; dictionaries are treated the same as their `keys` views in this context:

```
>>> D = {'a': 1, 'b': 2, 'c': 3}
>>> D.keys() & D.keys()              # Intersect keys views
{'b', 'c', 'a'}
>>> D.keys() & {'b'}                 # Intersect keys and set
{'b'}
>>> D.keys() & {'b': 1}              # Intersect keys and dict
{'b'}
```

```
>>> D.keys() | {'b', 'c', 'd'}        # Union keys and set
{'b', 'c', 'a', 'd'}
```

Items views are set-like too if they are hashable—that is, if they contain only immutable objects:

```
>>> D = {'a': 1}
>>> list(D.items())                   # Items set-like if hashable
[('a', 1)]
>>> D.items() | D.keys()              # Union view and view
{('a', 1), 'a'}
>>> D.items() | D                     # dict treated same as its keys
{('a', 1), 'a'}

>>> D.items() | {('c', 3), ('d', 4)}            # Set of key/value pairs
{('d', 4), ('a', 1), ('c', 3)}

>>> dict(D.items() | {('c', 3), ('d', 4)})      # dict accepts iterable sets too
{'c': 3, 'a': 1, 'd': 4}
```

See Chapter 5's coverage of sets if you need a refresher on these operations. Here, let's wrap up with three other quick coding notes for 3.X dictionaries.

Sorting dictionary keys in 3.X

First of all, because keys does not return a list in 3.X, the traditional coding pattern for scanning a dictionary by sorted keys in 2.X won't work in 3.X:

```
>>> D = {'a': 1, 'b': 2, 'c': 3}
>>> D
{'b': 2, 'c': 3, 'a': 1}

>>> Ks = D.keys()                     # Sorting a view object doesn't work!
>>> Ks.sort()
AttributeError: 'dict_keys' object has no attribute 'sort'
```

To work around this, in 3.X you must either convert to a list manually or use the sorted call (introduced in Chapter 4 and covered in this chapter) on either a keys view or the dictionary itself:

```
>>> Ks = list(Ks)                     # Force it to be a list and then sort
>>> Ks.sort()
>>> for k in Ks: print(k, D[k])       # 2.X: omit outer parens in prints
...
a 1
b 2
c 3

>>> D
{'b': 2, 'c': 3, 'a': 1}
>>> Ks = D.keys()                     # Or you can use sorted() on the keys
>>> for k in sorted(Ks): print(k, D[k])   # sorted() accepts any iterable
...                                        # sorted() returns its result
a 1
```

```
b 2
c 3
```

Of these, using the dictionary's keys iterator is probably preferable in 3.X, and works in 2.X as well:

```
>>> D
{'b': 2, 'c': 3, 'a': 1}                    # Better yet, sort the dict directly
>>> for k in sorted(D): print(k, D[k])      # dict iterators return keys
...
a 1
b 2
c 3
```

Dictionary magnitude comparisons no longer work in 3.X

Secondly, while in Python 2.X dictionaries may be compared for relative magnitude directly with <, >, and so on, in Python 3.X this no longer works. However, you can simulate it by comparing sorted keys lists manually:

```
sorted(D1.items()) < sorted(D2.items())     # Like 2.X D1 < D2
```

Dictionary equality tests (e.g., D1 == D2) still work in 3.X, though. Since we'll revisit this near the end of the next chapter in the context of comparisons at large, we'll postpone further details here.

The has_key method is dead in 3.X: Long live in!

Finally, the widely used dictionary has_key key presence test method is gone in 3.X. Instead, use the in membership expression, or a get with a default test (of these, in is generally preferred):

```
>>> D
{'b': 2, 'c': 3, 'a': 1}

>>> D.has_key('c')                                          # 2.X only: True/False
AttributeError: 'dict' object has no attribute 'has_key'

>>> 'c' in D                                                # Required in 3.X
True
>>> 'x' in D                                                # Preferred in 2.X today
False
>>> if 'c' in D: print('present', D['c'])                   # Branch on result
...
present 3

>>> print(D.get('c'))                                       # Fetch with default
3
>>> print(D.get('x'))
None
>>> if D.get('c') != None: print('present', D['c'])         # Another option
...
present 3
```

To summarize, the dictionary story changes substantially in 3.X. If you work in 2.X and care about *3.X compatibility* (or suspect that you might someday), here are some pointers. Of the 3.X changes we've met in this section:

- The first (dictionary comprehensions) can be coded only in 3.X and 2.7.
- The second (dictionary views) can be coded only in 3.X, and with special method names in 2.7.

However, the last three techniques—`sorted`, manual comparisons, and `in`—can be coded in 2.X today to ease 3.X migration in the future.

Why You Will Care: Dictionary Interfaces

Dictionaries aren't just a convenient way to store information by key in your programs —some Python extensions also present interfaces that look like and work the same as dictionaries. For instance, Python's interface to DBM access-by-key files looks much like a dictionary that must be opened. You store and fetch strings using key indexes:

```
import dbm                        # Named anydbm in Python 2.X
file = dbm.open("filename")       # Link to file
file['key'] = 'data'              # Store data by key
data = file['key']                # Fetch data by key
```

In Chapter 28, you'll see that you can store entire Python objects this way, too, if you replace `dbm` in the preceding code with `shelve` (shelves are access-by-key databases that store persistent Python objects, not just strings). For Internet work, Python's CGI script support also presents a dictionary-like interface. A call to `cgi.FieldStorage` yields a dictionary-like object with one entry per input field on the client's web page:

```
import cgi
form = cgi.FieldStorage()        # Parse form data
if 'name' in form:
    showReply('Hello, ' + form['name'].value)
```

Though dictionaries are the only core mapping type, all of these others are instances of mappings, and support most of the same operations. Once you learn dictionary interfaces, you'll find that they apply to a variety of built-in tools in Python.

For another dictionary use case, see also Chapter 9's upcoming overview of *JSON*—a language-neutral data format used for databases and data transfer. Python dictionaries, lists, and nested combinations of them can almost pass for records in this format as is, and may be easily translated to and from formal JSON text strings with Python's `json` standard library module.

Chapter Summary

In this chapter, we explored the list and dictionary types—probably the two most common, flexible, and powerful collection types you will see and use in Python code. We learned that the list type supports positionally ordered collections of arbitrary objects, and that it may be freely nested and grown and shrunk on demand. The dictionary type is similar, but it stores items by key instead of by position and does not maintain any reliable left-to-right order among its items. Both lists and dictionaries are mutable, and so support a variety of in-place change operations not available for strings: for example, lists can be grown by append calls, and dictionaries by assignment to new keys.

In the next chapter, we will wrap up our in-depth core object type tour by looking at tuples and files. After that, we'll move on to statements that code the logic that processes our objects, taking us another step toward writing complete programs. Before we tackle those topics, though, here are some chapter quiz questions to review.

Test Your Knowledge: Quiz

1. Name two ways to build a list containing five integer zeros.
2. Name two ways to build a dictionary with two keys, 'a' and 'b', each having an associated value of 0.
3. Name four operations that change a list object in place.
4. Name four operations that change a dictionary object in place.
5. Why might you use a dictionary instead of a list?

Test Your Knowledge: Answers

1. A literal expression like [0, 0, 0, 0, 0] and a repetition expression like [0] * 5 will each create a list of five zeros. In practice, you might also build one up with a loop that starts with an empty list and appends 0 to it in each iteration, with L.append(0). A list comprehension ([0 for i in range(5)]) could work here, too, but this is more work than you need to do for this answer.

2. A literal expression such as {'a': 0, 'b': 0} or a series of assignments like D = {}, D['a'] = 0, and D['b'] = 0 would create the desired dictionary. You can also use the newer and simpler-to-code dict(a=0, b=0) keyword form, or the more flexible dict([('a', 0), ('b', 0)]) key/value sequences form. Or, because all the values are the same, you can use the special form dict.fromkeys('ab', 0). In 3.X and 2.7, you can also use a dictionary comprehension: {k:0 for k in 'ab'}, though again, this may be overkill here.

3. The append and extend methods grow a list in place, the sort and reverse methods order and reverse lists, the insert method inserts an item at an offset, the remove and pop methods delete from a list by value and by position, the del statement deletes an item or slice, and index and slice assignment statements replace an item or entire section. Pick any four of these for the quiz.

4. Dictionaries are primarily changed by assignment to a new or existing key, which creates or changes the key's entry in the table. Also, the del statement deletes a

key's entry, the dictionary `update` method merges one dictionary into another in place, and `D.pop(key)` removes a key and returns the value it had. Dictionaries also have other, more exotic in-place change methods not presented in this chapter, such as `setdefault`; see reference sources for more details.

5. Dictionaries are generally better when the data is labeled (a record with field names, for example); lists are best suited to collections of unlabeled items (such as all the files in a directory). Dictionary lookup is also usually quicker than searching a list, though this might vary per program.

## CHAPTER 9

Tuples, Files, and Everything Else

This chapter rounds out our in-depth tour of the core object types in Python by exploring the *tuple*, a collection of other objects that cannot be changed, and the *file*, an interface to external files on your computer. As you'll see, the tuple is a relatively simple object that largely performs operations you've already learned about for strings and lists. The file object is a commonly used and full-featured tool for processing files on your computer. Because files are so pervasive in programming, the basic overview of files here is supplemented by larger examples in later chapters.

This chapter also concludes this part of the book by looking at properties common to all the core object types we've met—the notions of equality, comparisons, object copies, and so on. We'll also briefly explore other object types in Python's toolbox, including the None placeholder and the namedtuple hybrid; as you'll see, although we've covered all the primary built-in types, the object story in Python is broader than I've implied thus far. Finally, we'll close this part of the book by taking a look at a set of common object type pitfalls and exploring some exercises that will allow you to experiment with the ideas you've learned.

This chapter's scope—files: As in Chapter 7 on strings, our look at files here will be limited in scope to file fundamentals that most Python programmers—including newcomers to programming—need to know. In particular, *Unicode text files* were previewed in Chapter 4, but we're going to postpone full coverage of them until Chapter 37, as optional or deferred reading in the Advanced Topics part of this book.

For this chapter's purpose, we'll assume any text files used will be encoded and decoded per your platform's default, which may be UTF-8 on Windows, and ASCII or other elsewhere (and if you don't know why this matters, you probably don't need to up front). We'll also assume that filenames encode properly on the underlying platform, though we'll stick with ASCII names for portability here.

If Unicode text and files is a critical subject for you, I suggest reading the Chapter 4 preview for a quick first look, and continuing on to

Chapter 37 after you master the file basics covered here. For all others, the file coverage here will apply both to typical text and binary files of the sort we'll meet here, as well as to more advanced file-processing modes you may choose to explore later.

Tuples

The last collection type in our survey is the Python tuple. Tuples construct simple groups of objects. They work exactly like lists, except that tuples can't be changed in place (they're immutable) and are usually written as a series of items in parentheses, not square brackets. Although they don't support as many methods, tuples share most of their properties with lists. Here's a quick look at the basics. Tuples are:

Ordered collections of arbitrary objects
 Like strings and lists, tuples are positionally ordered collections of objects (i.e., they maintain a left-to-right order among their contents); like lists, they can embed any kind of object.

Accessed by offset
 Like strings and lists, items in a tuple are accessed by offset (not by key); they support all the offset-based access operations, such as indexing and slicing.

Of the category "immutable sequence"
 Like strings and lists, tuples are sequences; they support many of the same operations. However, like strings, tuples are immutable; they don't support any of the in-place change operations applied to lists.

Fixed-length, heterogeneous, and arbitrarily nestable
 Because tuples are immutable, you cannot change the size of a tuple without making a copy. On the other hand, tuples can hold any type of object, including other compound objects (e.g., lists, dictionaries, other tuples), and so support arbitrary nesting.

Arrays of object references
 Like lists, tuples are best thought of as object reference arrays; tuples store access points to other objects (references), and indexing a tuple is relatively quick.

Table 9-1 highlights common tuple operations. A tuple is written as a series of objects (technically, expressions that generate objects), separated by commas and normally enclosed in parentheses. An empty tuple is just a parentheses pair with nothing inside.

Table 9-1. Common tuple literals and operations

Operation	Interpretation
()	An empty tuple
T = (0,)	A one-item tuple (not an expression)
T = (0, 'Ni', 1.2, 3)	A four-item tuple
T = 0, 'Ni', 1.2, 3	Another four-item tuple (same as prior line)

Operation	Interpretation
T = ('Bob', ('dev', 'mgr'))	Nested tuples
T = tuple('spam')	Tuple of items in an iterable
T[i]	Index, index of index, slice, length
T[i][j]	
T[i:j]	
len(T)	
T1 + T2	Concatenate, repeat
T * 3	
for x in T: print(x)	Iteration, membership
'spam' in T	
[x ** 2 for x in T]	
T.index('Ni')	Methods in 2.6, 2.7, and 3.X: search, count
T.count('Ni')	
namedtuple('Emp', ['name', 'jobs'])	Named tuple extension type

Tuples in Action

As usual, let's start an interactive session to explore tuples at work. Notice in Table 9-1 that tuples do not have all the methods that lists have (e.g., an **append** call won't work here). They do, however, support the usual sequence operations that we saw for both strings and lists:

```
>>> (1, 2) + (3, 4)          # Concatenation
(1, 2, 3, 4)

>>> (1, 2) * 4               # Repetition
(1, 2, 1, 2, 1, 2, 1, 2)

>>> T = (1, 2, 3, 4)         # Indexing, slicing
>>> T[0], T[1:3]
(1, (2, 3))
```

Tuple syntax peculiarities: Commas and parentheses

The second and fourth entries in Table 9-1 merit a bit more explanation. Because parentheses can also enclose expressions (see Chapter 5), you need to do something special to tell Python when a single object in parentheses is a tuple object and not a simple expression. If you really want a single-item tuple, simply add a trailing comma after the single item, before the closing parenthesis:

```
>>> x = (40)                 # An integer!
>>> x
40
```

```
>>> y = (40,)                    # A tuple containing an integer
>>> y
(40,)
```

As a special case, Python also allows you to omit the opening and closing parentheses for a tuple in contexts where it isn't syntactically ambiguous to do so. For instance, the fourth line of Table 9-1 simply lists four items separated by commas. In the context of an assignment statement, Python recognizes this as a tuple, even though it doesn't have parentheses.

Now, some people will tell you to always use parentheses in your tuples, and some will tell you to never use parentheses in tuples (and still others have lives, and won't tell you what to do with your tuples!). The most common places where the parentheses are *required* for tuple literals are those where:

- *Parentheses* matter—within a function call, or nested in a larger expression.
- *Commas* matter—embedded in the literal of a larger data structure like a list or dictionary, or listed in a Python 2.X `print` statement.

In most other contexts, the enclosing parentheses are optional. For beginners, the best advice is that it's probably easier to use the parentheses than it is to remember when they are optional or required. Many programmers also find that parentheses tend to aid script readability by making the tuples more explicit and obvious.[1]

Conversions, methods, and immutability

Apart from literal syntax differences, tuple operations (the middle rows in Table 9-1) are identical to string and list operations. The only differences worth noting are that the +, *, and slicing operations return new *tuples* when applied to tuples, and that tuples don't provide the same methods you saw for strings, lists, and dictionaries. If you want to sort a tuple, for example, you'll usually have to either first convert it to a list to gain access to a sorting method call and make it a mutable object, or use the newer `sorted` built-in that accepts any sequence object (and other *iterables*—a term introduced in Chapter 4 that we'll be more formal about in the next part of this book):

```
>>> T = ('cc', 'aa', 'dd', 'bb')
>>> tmp = list(T)                    # Make a list from a tuple's items
>>> tmp.sort()                       # Sort the list
>>> tmp
['aa', 'bb', 'cc', 'dd']
>>> T = tuple(tmp)                    # Make a tuple from the list's items
>>> T
('aa', 'bb', 'cc', 'dd')

>>> sorted(T)                        # Or use the sorted built-in, and save two steps
['aa', 'bb', 'cc', 'dd']
```

---

1. A subtler factor: the comma is a sort of lowest precedence operator, but only in contexts where it's not otherwise significant. In such contexts, it's the comma that builds tuples, not the parenthesis; this makes the latter optional, but can also lead to odd, unexpected syntax errors if parentheses are omitted.

Here, the `list` and `tuple` built-in functions are used to convert the object to a list and then back to a tuple; really, both calls make new objects, but the net effect is like a conversion.

List comprehensions can also be used to convert tuples. The following, for example, makes a list from a tuple, adding 20 to each item along the way:

```
>>> T = (1, 2, 3, 4, 5)
>>> L = [x + 20 for x in T]
>>> L
[21, 22, 23, 24, 25]
```

List comprehensions are really *sequence* operations—they always build new lists, but they may be used to iterate over any sequence objects, including tuples, strings, and other lists. As we'll see later in the book, they even work on some things that are not physically stored sequences—any *iterable* objects will do, including files, which are automatically read line by line. Given this, they may be better called *iteration* tools.

Although tuples don't have the same methods as lists and strings, they do have two of their own as of Python 2.6 and 3.0—index and count work as they do for lists, but they are defined for tuple objects:

```
>>> T = (1, 2, 3, 2, 4, 2)          # Tuple methods in 2.6, 3.0, and later
>>> T.index(2)                      # Offset of first appearance of 2
1
>>> T.index(2, 2)                   # Offset of appearance after offset 2
3
>>> T.count(2)                      # How many 2s are there?
3
```

Prior to 2.6 and 3.0, tuples have no methods at all—this was an old Python convention for immutable types, which was violated years ago on grounds of practicality with strings, and more recently with both numbers and tuples.

Also, note that the rule about tuple *immutability* applies only to the top level of the tuple itself, not to its contents. A list inside a tuple, for instance, can be changed as usual:

```
>>> T = (1, [2, 3], 4)
>>> T[1] = 'spam'                   # This fails: can't change tuple itself
TypeError: object doesn't support item assignment

>>> T[1][0] = 'spam'                # This works: can change mutables inside
>>> T
(1, ['spam', 3], 4)
```

For most programs, this one-level-deep immutability is sufficient for common tuple roles. Which, coincidentally, brings us to the next section.

Why Lists and Tuples?

This seems to be the first question that always comes up when teaching beginners about tuples: why do we need tuples if we have lists? Some of the reasoning may be historic;

Python's creator is a mathematician by training, and he has been quoted as seeing a tuple as a simple association of objects and a list as a data structure that changes over time. In fact, this use of the word "tuple" derives from mathematics, as does its frequent use for a row in a relational database table.

The best answer, however, seems to be that the immutability of tuples provides some *integrity*—you can be sure a tuple won't be changed through another reference elsewhere in a program, but there's no such guarantee for lists. Tuples and other immutables, therefore, serve a similar role to "constant" declarations in other languages, though the notion of constantness is associated with objects in Python, not variables.

Tuples can also be used in places that lists cannot—for example, as dictionary keys (see the sparse matrix example in Chapter 8). Some built-in operations may also require or imply tuples instead of lists (e.g., the substitution values in a string format expression), though such operations have often been generalized in recent years to be more flexible. As a rule of thumb, lists are the tool of choice for ordered collections that might need to change; tuples can handle the other cases of fixed associations.

Records Revisited: Named Tuples

In fact, the choice of data types is even richer than the prior section may have implied —today's Python programmers can choose from an assortment of both built-in core types, and extension types built on top of them. For example, in the prior chapter's sidebar "Why You Will Care: Dictionaries Versus Lists" on page 263, we saw how to represent record-like information with both a list and a dictionary, and noted that dictionaries offer the advantage of more mnemonic keys that label data. As long as we don't require mutability, *tuples* can serve similar roles, with positions for record fields like lists:

```
>>> bob = ('Bob', 40.5, ['dev', 'mgr'])            # Tuple record
>>> bob
('Bob', 40.5, ['dev', 'mgr'])

>>> bob[0], bob[2]                                  # Access by position
('Bob', ['dev', 'mgr'])
```

As for lists, though, field numbers in tuples generally carry less information than the names of keys in a *dictionary*. Here's the same record recoded as a dictionary with named fields:

```
>>> bob = dict(name='Bob', age=40.5, jobs=['dev', 'mgr'])   # Dictionary record
>>> bob
{'jobs': ['dev', 'mgr'], 'name': 'Bob', 'age': 40.5}

>>> bob['name'], bob['jobs']                        # Access by key
('Bob', ['dev', 'mgr'])
```

In fact, we can convert parts of the dictionary to a tuple if needed:

```
>>> tuple(bob.values())                          # Values to tuple
(['dev', 'mgr'], 'Bob', 40.5)
>>> list(bob.items())                            # Items to tuple list
[('jobs', ['dev', 'mgr']), ('name', 'Bob'), ('age', 40.5)]
```

But with a bit of extra work, we can implement objects that offer *both* positional and named access to record fields. For example, the `namedtuple` utility, available in the standard library's `collections` module mentioned in Chapter 8, implements an extension type that adds logic to tuples that allows components to be accessed by both *position* and attribute *name*, and can be converted to dictionary-like form for access by *key* if desired. Attribute names come from classes and are not exactly dictionary keys, but they are similarly mnemonic:

```
>>> from collections import namedtuple              # Import extension type
>>> Rec = namedtuple('Rec', ['name', 'age', 'jobs'])  # Make a generated class
>>> bob = Rec('Bob', age=40.5, jobs=['dev', 'mgr'])   # A named-tuple record
>>> bob
Rec(name='Bob', age=40.5, jobs=['dev', 'mgr'])

>>> bob[0], bob[2]                                  # Access by position
('Bob', ['dev', 'mgr'])
>>> bob.name, bob.jobs                              # Access by attribute
('Bob', ['dev', 'mgr'])
```

Converting to a dictionary supports key-based behavior when needed:

```
>>> O = bob._asdict()                               # Dictionary-like form
>>> O['name'], O['jobs']                            # Access by key too
('Bob', ['dev', 'mgr'])
>>> O
OrderedDict([('name', 'Bob'), ('age', 40.5), ('jobs', ['dev', 'mgr'])])
```

As you can see, named tuples are a tuple/class/dictionary *hybrid*. They also represent a classic *tradeoff*. In exchange for their extra utility, they require extra code (the two startup lines in the preceding examples that import the type and make the class), and incur some performance costs to work this magic. (In short, named tuples build new classes that extend the tuple type, inserting a `property` accessor method for each named field that maps the name to its position—a technique that relies on advanced topics we'll explore in Part VIII, and uses formatted code strings instead of class annotation tools like decorators and metaclasses.) Still, they are a good example of the kind of custom data types that we can build on top of built-in types like tuples when extra utility is desired.

Named tuples are available in Python 3.X, 2.7, 2.6 (where `_asdict` returns a true dictionary), and perhaps earlier, though they rely on features relatively modern by Python standards. They are also *extensions*, not core types—they live in the standard library and fall into the same category as Chapter 5's `Fraction` and `Decimal`—so we'll delegate to the Python library manual for more details.

As a quick preview, though, both tuples and named tuples support unpacking *tuple assignment*, which we'll study formally in Chapter 13, as well as the *iteration contexts* we'll explore in Chapter 14 and Chapter 20 (notice the positional initial values here: named tuples accept these by name, position, or both):

```
>>> bob = Rec('Bob', 40.5, ['dev', 'mgr'])      # For both tuples and named tuples
>>> name, age, jobs = bob                        # Tuple assignment (Chapter 11)
>>> name, jobs
('Bob', ['dev', 'mgr'])

>>> for x in bob: print(x)                       # Iteration context (Chapters 14, 20)
...prints Bob, 40.5, ['dev', 'mgr']...
```

Tuple-unpacking assignment doesn't quite apply to dictionaries, short of fetching and converting keys and values and assuming or imposing an positional ordering on them (dictionaries are not sequences), and iteration steps through keys, not values (notice the dictionary literal form here: an alternative to `dict`):

```
>>> bob = {'name': 'Bob', 'age': 40.5, 'jobs': ['dev', 'mgr']}
>>> job, name, age = bob.values()
>>> name, job                                    # Dict equivalent (but order may vary)
('Bob', ['dev', 'mgr'])

>>> for x in bob: print(bob[x])                  # Step though keys, index values
...prints values...
>>> for x in bob.values(): print(x)              # Step through values view
...prints values...
```

Watch for a final rehash of this record representation thread when we see how user-defined *classes* compare in Chapter 27; as we'll find, classes label fields with names too, but can also provide program *logic* to process the record's data in the same package.

Files

You may already be familiar with the notion of files, which are named storage compartments on your computer that are managed by your operating system. The last major built-in object type that we'll examine on our object types tour provides a way to access those files inside Python programs.

In short, the built-in **open** function creates a Python file object, which serves as a link to a file residing on your machine. After calling **open**, you can transfer strings of data to and from the associated external file by calling the returned file object's methods.

Compared to the types you've seen so far, file objects are somewhat unusual. They are considered a core type because they are created by a built-in function, but they're not numbers, sequences, or mappings, and they don't respond to expression operators; they export only methods for common file-processing tasks. Most file methods are concerned with performing input from and output to the external file associated with a file object, but other file methods allow us to seek to a new position in the file, flush output buffers, and so on. Table 9-2 summarizes common file operations.

Table 9-2. Common file operations

Operation	Interpretation
`output = open(r'C:\spam', 'w')`	Create output file (`'w'` means write)
`input = open('data', 'r')`	Create input file (`'r'` means read)
`input = open('data')`	Same as prior line (`'r'` is the default)
`aString = input.read()`	Read entire file into a single string
`aString = input.read(N)`	Read up to next N characters (or bytes) into a string
`aString = input.readline()`	Read next line (including \n newline) into a string
`aList = input.readlines()`	Read entire file into list of line strings (with \n)
`output.write(aString)`	Write a string of characters (or bytes) into file
`output.writelines(aList)`	Write all line strings in a list into file
`output.close()`	Manual close (done for you when file is collected)
`output.flush()`	Flush output buffer to disk without closing
`anyFile.seek(N)`	Change file position to offset N for next operation
`for line in open('data'): use line`	File iterators read line by line
`open('f.txt', encoding='latin-1')`	Python 3.X Unicode text files (`str` strings)
`open('f.bin', 'rb')`	Python 3.X bytes files (`bytes` strings)
`codecs.open('f.txt', encoding='utf8')`	Python 2.X Unicode text files (`unicode` strings)
`open('f.bin', 'rb')`	Python 2.X bytes files (`str` strings)

Opening Files

To open a file, a program calls the built-in open function, with the external filename first, followed by a processing mode. The call returns a file object, which in turn has methods for data transfer:

```
afile = open(filename, mode)
afile.method()
```

The first argument to open, the external *filename*, may include a platform-specific and absolute or relative directory path prefix. Without a directory path, the file is assumed to exist in the current working directory (i.e., where the script runs). As we'll see in Chapter 37's expanded file coverage, the *filename* may also contain non-ASCII Unicode characters that Python automatically translates to and from the underlying platform's encoding, or be provided as a pre-encoded byte string.

The second argument to open, processing *mode*, is typically the string `'r'` to open for text input (the default), `'w'` to create and open for text output, or `'a'` to open for appending text to the end (e.g., for adding to logfiles). The processing mode argument can specify additional options.

- Adding a **b** to the mode string allows for *binary* data (end-of-line translations and 3.X Unicode encodings are turned off).

- Adding a **+** opens the file for *both* input and output (i.e., you can both read and write to the same file object, often in conjunction with seek operations to reposition in the file).

Both of the first two arguments to **open** must be Python strings. An optional third argument can be used to control output *buffering*—passing a zero means that output is unbuffered (it is transferred to the external file immediately on a write method call), and additional arguments may be provided for special types of files (e.g., an *encoding* for Unicode text files in Python 3.X).

We'll cover file fundamentals and explore some basic examples here, but we won't go into all file-processing mode options; as usual, consult the Python library manual for additional details.

Using Files

Once you make a file object with **open**, you can call its methods to read from or write to the associated external file. In all cases, file text takes the form of strings in Python programs; reading a file returns its content in strings, and content is passed to the write methods as strings. Reading and writing methods come in multiple flavors; Table 9-2 lists the most common. Here are a few fundamental usage notes:

File iterators are best for reading lines
> Though the reading and writing methods in the table are common, keep in mind that probably the best way to read lines from a text file today is to not read the file at all—as we'll see in Chapter 14, files also have an *iterator* that automatically reads one line at a time in a **for** loop, list comprehension, or other iteration context.

Content is strings, not objects
> Notice in Table 9-2 that data *read* from a file always comes back to your script as a string, so you'll have to convert it to a different type of Python object if a string is not what you need. Similarly, unlike with the **print** operation, Python does not add any formatting and does not convert objects to strings automatically when you *write* data to a file—you must send an already formatted string. Because of this, the tools we have already met to convert objects to and from strings (e.g., **int**, **float**, **str**, and the string formatting expression and method) come in handy when dealing with files.
>
> Python also includes advanced standard library tools for handling generic object storage (the **pickle** module), for dealing with packed binary data in files (the **struct** module), and for processing special types of content such as JSON, XML, and CSV text. We'll see these at work later in this chapter and book, but Python's manuals document them in full.

Files are buffered and seekable

By default, output files are always *buffered*, which means that text you write may not be transferred from memory to disk immediately—closing a file, or running its flush method, forces the buffered data to disk. You can avoid buffering with extra open arguments, but it may impede performance. Python files are also *random-access* on a byte offset basis—their seek method allows your scripts to jump around to read and write at specific locations.

close *is often optional: auto-close on collection*

Calling the file close method terminates your connection to the external file, releases its system resources, and flushes its buffered output to disk if any is still in memory. As discussed in Chapter 6, in Python an object's memory space is automatically reclaimed as soon as the object is no longer referenced anywhere in the program. When *file* objects are reclaimed, Python also automatically *closes* the files if they are still open (this also happens when a program shuts down). This means you don't always need to manually close your files in standard Python, especially those in simple scripts with short runtimes, and temporary files used by a single line or expression.

On the other hand, including manual close calls doesn't hurt, and may be a good habit to form, especially in long-running systems. Strictly speaking, this auto-close-on-collection feature of files is not part of the language definition—it may change over time, may not happen when you expect it to in interactive shells, and may not work the same in other Python implementations whose garbage collectors may not reclaim and close files at the same points as standard CPython. In fact, when many files are opened within loops, Pythons other than CPython may require close calls to free up system resources immediately, before garbage collection can get around to freeing objects. Moreover, close calls may sometimes be required to flush buffered output of file objects not yet reclaimed. For an alternative way to guarantee automatic file closes, also see this section's later discussion of the file object's *context manager*, used with the with/as statement in Python 2.6, 2.7, and 3.X.

Files in Action

Let's work through a simple example that demonstrates file-processing basics. The following code begins by opening a new text file for output, writing two lines (strings terminated with a newline marker, \n), and closing the file. Later, the example opens the same file again in input mode and reads the lines back one at a time with read line. Notice that the third readline call returns an empty string; this is how Python file methods tell you that you've reached the end of the file (empty lines in the file come back as strings containing just a newline character, not as empty strings). Here's the complete interaction:

```
>>> myfile = open('myfile.txt', 'w')     # Open for text output: create/empty
>>> myfile.write('hello text file\n')     # Write a line of text: string
16
```

```
>>> myfile.write('goodbye text file\n')
18
>>> myfile.close()                          # Flush output buffers to disk

>>> myfile = open('myfile.txt')             # Open for text input: 'r' is default
>>> myfile.readline()                        # Read the lines back
'hello text file\n'
>>> myfile.readline()
'goodbye text file\n'
>>> myfile.readline()                        # Empty string: end-of-file
''
```

Notice that file **write** calls return the number of characters written in Python 3.X; in 2.X they don't, so you won't see these numbers echoed interactively. This example writes each line of text, including its end-of-line terminator, \n, as a string; write methods don't add the end-of-line character for us, so we must include it to properly terminate our lines (otherwise the next write will simply extend the current line in the file).

If you want to display the file's content with end-of-line characters interpreted, read the entire file into a string *all at once* with the file object's **read** method and print it:

```
>>> open('myfile.txt').read()               # Read all at once into string
'hello text file\ngoodbye text file\n'

>>> print(open('myfile.txt').read())        # User-friendly display
hello text file
goodbye text file
```

And if you want to scan a text file line by line, *file iterators* are often your best option:

```
>>> for line in open('myfile.txt'):         # Use file iterators, not reads
...     print(line, end='')
...
hello text file
goodbye text file
```

When coded this way, the temporary file object created by **open** will automatically read and return one line on each loop iteration. This form is usually easiest to code, good on memory use, and may be faster than some other options (depending on many variables, of course). Since we haven't reached statements or iterators yet, though, you'll have to wait until Chapter 14 for a more complete explanation of this code.

 Windows users: As mentioned in Chapter 7, **open** accepts Unix-style forward slashes in place of backward slashes on Windows, so any of the following forms work for directory paths—raw strings, forward slashes, or doubled-up backslashes:

```
>>> open(r'C:\Python33\Lib\pdb.py').readline()
'#! /usr/bin/env python3\n'
>>> open('C:/Python33/Lib/pdb.py').readline()
'#! /usr/bin/env python3\n'
```

```
>>> open('C:\\Python33\\Lib\\pdb.py').readline()
'#! /usr/bin/env python3\n'
```

The raw string form in the first command is still useful to turn off accidental escapes when you can't control string content, and in other contexts.

Text and Binary Files: The Short Story

Strictly speaking, the example in the prior section uses text files. In both Python 3.X
and 2.X, file type is determined by the second argument to open, the mode string—an
included "b" means binary. Python has always supported both text and binary files,
but in Python 3.X there is a sharper distinction between the two:

- *Text files* represent content as normal str strings, perform Unicode encoding and
  decoding automatically, and perform end-of-line translation by default.

- *Binary files* represent content as a special bytes string type and allow programs to
  access file content unaltered.

In contrast, Python 2.X text files handle both 8-bit text and binary data, and a special
string type and file interface (unicode strings and codecs.open) handles Unicode text.
The differences in Python 3.X stem from the fact that simple and Unicode text have
been merged in the normal string type—which makes sense, given that all text is Unicode, including ASCII and other 8-bit encodings.

Because most programmers deal only with ASCII text, they can get by with the basic
text file interface used in the prior example, and normal strings. All strings are technically Unicode in 3.X, but ASCII users will not generally notice. In fact, text files and
strings work the same in 3.X and 2.X if your script's scope is limited to such simple
forms of text.

If you need to handle internationalized applications or byte-oriented data, though, the
distinction in 3.X impacts your code (usually for the better). In general, you must use
bytes strings for binary files, and normal str strings for text files. Moreover, because
text files implement Unicode encodings, you should not open a binary data file in text
mode—decoding its content to Unicode text will likely fail.

Let's look at an example. When you read a *binary* data file you get back a bytes object
—a sequence of small integers that represent absolute byte values (which may or may
not correspond to characters), which looks and feels almost exactly like a normal string.
In Python 3.X, and assuming an existing binary file:

```
>>> data = open('data.bin', 'rb').read()     # Open binary file: rb=read binary
>>> data                                       # bytes string holds binary data
b'\x00\x00\x00\x07spam\x00\x08'
>>> data[4:8]                                  # Act like strings
b'spam'
>>> data[4:8][0]                               # But really are small 8-bit integers
115
```

```
>>> bin(data[4:8][0])                            # Python 3.X/2.6+ bin() function
'0b1110011'
```

In addition, binary files do not perform any *end-of-line translation* on data; *text* files by default map all forms to and from \n when written and read and implement Unicode encodings on transfers in 3.X. Binary files like this one work the same in Python 2.X, but byte strings are simply normal strings and have no leading *b* when displayed, and text files must use the `codecs` module to add Unicode processing.

Per the note at the start of this chapter, though, that's as much as we're going to say about Unicode text and binary data files here, and just enough to understand upcoming examples in this chapter. Since the distinction is of marginal interest to many Python programmers, we'll defer to the files preview in Chapter 4 for a quick tour and postpone the full story until Chapter 37. For now, let's move on to some more substantial file examples to demonstrate a few common use cases.

Storing Python Objects in Files: Conversions

Our next example writes a variety of Python objects into a text file on multiple lines. Notice that it must convert objects to strings using conversion tools. Again, file data is always *strings* in our scripts, and write methods do not do any automatic to-string formatting for us (for space, I'm omitting byte-count return values from `write` methods from here on):

```
>>> X, Y, Z = 43, 44, 45                          # Native Python objects
>>> S = 'Spam'                                     # Must be strings to store in file
>>> D = {'a': 1, 'b': 2}
>>> L = [1, 2, 3]
>>>
>>> F = open('datafile.txt', 'w')                  # Create output text file
>>> F.write(S + '\n')                              # Terminate lines with \n
>>> F.write('%s,%s,%s\n' % (X, Y, Z))              # Convert numbers to strings
>>> F.write(str(L) + '$' + str(D) + '\n')          # Convert and separate with $
>>> F.close()
```

Once we have created our file, we can inspect its contents by opening it and reading it into a string (strung together as a single operation here). Notice that the interactive echo gives the exact byte contents, while the `print` operation interprets embedded end-of-line characters to render a more user-friendly display:

```
>>> chars = open('datafile.txt').read()           # Raw string display
>>> chars
"Spam\n43,44,45\n[1, 2, 3]${'a': 1, 'b': 2}\n"
>>> print(chars)                                   # User-friendly display
Spam
43,44,45
[1, 2, 3]${'a': 1, 'b': 2}
```

We now have to use other conversion tools to translate from the strings in the text file to real Python objects. As Python never converts strings to numbers (or other types of objects) automatically, this is required if we need to gain access to normal object tools like indexing, addition, and so on:

```
>>> F = open('datafile.txt')          # Open again
>>> line = F.readline()               # Read one line
>>> line
'Spam\n'
>>> line.rstrip()                     # Remove end-of-line
'Spam'
```

For this first line, we used the string rstrip method to get rid of the trailing end-of-line character; a line[:-1] slice would work, too, but only if we can be sure all lines end in the \n character (the last line in a file sometimes does not).

So far, we've read the line containing the string. Now let's grab the next line, which contains numbers, and parse out (that is, extract) the objects on that line:

```
>>> line = F.readline()               # Next line from file
>>> line                              # It's a string here
'43,44,45\n'
>>> parts = line.split(',')           # Split (parse) on commas
>>> parts
['43', '44', '45\n']
```

We used the string split method here to chop up the line on its comma delimiters; the result is a list of substrings containing the individual numbers. We still must convert from strings to integers, though, if we wish to perform math on these:

```
>>> int(parts[1])                     # Convert from string to int
44
>>> numbers = [int(P) for P in parts] # Convert all in list at once
>>> numbers
[43, 44, 45]
```

As we have learned, int translates a string of digits into an integer object, and the list comprehension expression introduced in Chapter 4 can apply the call to each item in our list all at once (you'll find more on list comprehensions later in this book). Notice that we didn't have to run rstrip to delete the \n at the end of the last part; int and some other converters quietly ignore whitespace around digits.

Finally, to convert the stored list and dictionary in the third line of the file, we can run them through eval, a built-in function that treats a string as a piece of executable program code (technically, a string containing a Python expression):

```
>>> line = F.readline()
>>> line
"[1, 2, 3]${'a': 1, 'b': 2}\n"
>>> parts = line.split('$')           # Split (parse) on $
>>> parts
['[1, 2, 3]', "{'a': 1, 'b': 2}\n"]
>>> eval(parts[0])                    # Convert to any object type
[1, 2, 3]
>>> objects = [eval(P) for P in parts] # Do same for all in list
```

```
>>> objects
[[1, 2, 3], {'a': 1, 'b': 2}]
```

Because the end result of all this parsing and converting is a list of normal Python objects instead of strings, we can now apply list and dictionary operations to them in our script.

Storing Native Python Objects: pickle

Using `eval` to convert from strings to objects, as demonstrated in the preceding code, is a powerful tool. In fact, sometimes it's *too* powerful. `eval` will happily run any Python expression—even one that might delete all the files on your computer, given the necessary permissions! If you really want to store native Python objects, but you can't trust the source of the data in the file, Python's standard library `pickle` module is ideal.

The `pickle` module is a more advanced tool that allows us to store almost any Python object in a file directly, with no to- or from-string conversion requirement on our part. It's like a super-general data formatting and parsing utility. To store a dictionary in a file, for instance, we pickle it directly:

```
>>> D = {'a': 1, 'b': 2}
>>> F = open('datafile.pkl', 'wb')
>>> import pickle
>>> pickle.dump(D, F)                        # Pickle any object to file
>>> F.close()
```

Then, to get the dictionary back later, we simply use `pickle` again to re-create it:

```
>>> F = open('datafile.pkl', 'rb')
>>> E = pickle.load(F)                        # Load any object from file
>>> E
{'a': 1, 'b': 2}
```

We get back an equivalent dictionary object, with no manual splitting or converting required. The `pickle` module performs what is known as *object serialization*—converting objects to and from strings of bytes—but requires very little work on our part. In fact, `pickle` internally translates our dictionary to a string form, though it's not much to look at (and may vary if we pickle in other data protocol modes):

```
>>> open('datafile.pkl', 'rb').read()          # Format is prone to change!
b'\x80\x03}q\x00(X\x01\x00\x00\x00bq\x01K\x02X\x01\x00\x00\x00aq\x02K\x01u.'
```

Because `pickle` can reconstruct the object from this format, we don't have to deal with it ourselves. For more on the `pickle` module, see the Python standard library manual, or import `pickle` and pass it to `help` interactively. While you're exploring, also take a look at the `shelve` module. `shelve` is a tool that uses `pickle` to store Python objects in an access-by-key filesystem, which is beyond our scope here (though you will get to see an example of `shelve` in action in Chapter 28, and other `pickle` examples in Chapter 31 and Chapter 37).

Notice that I opened the file used to store the pickled object in *binary mode*; binary mode is always required in Python 3.X, because the pickler creates and uses a **bytes** string object, and these objects imply binary-mode files (text-mode files imply **str** strings in 3.X). In earlier Pythons it's OK to use text-mode files for protocol 0 (the default, which creates ASCII text), as long as text mode is used consistently; higher protocols require binary-mode files. Python 3.X's default protocol is 3 (binary), but it creates **bytes** even for protocol 0. See Chapter 28, Chapter 31, and Chapter 37; Python's library manual; or reference books for more details on and examples of pickled data.

Python 2.X also has a **cPickle** module, which is an optimized version of **pickle** that can be imported directly for speed. Python 3.X renames this module **_pickle** and uses it automatically in **pickle**—scripts simply import **pickle** and let Python optimize itself.

Storing Python Objects in JSON Format

The prior section's **pickle** module translates nearly arbitrary Python objects to a proprietary format developed specifically for Python, and honed for performance over many years. JSON is a newer and emerging data interchange format, which is both programming-language-neutral and supported by a variety of systems. *MongoDB*, for instance, stores data in a JSON document database (using a binary JSON format).

JSON does not support as broad a range of Python object types as **pickle**, but its portability is an advantage in some contexts, and it represents another way to serialize a specific category of Python objects for storage and transmission. Moreover, because JSON is so close to Python dictionaries and lists in syntax, the translation to and from Python objects is trivial, and is automated by the **json** standard library module.

For example, a Python dictionary with nested structures is very similar to JSON data, though Python's variables and expressions support richer structuring options (any part of the following can be an arbitrary expression in Python code):

```
>>> name = dict(first='Bob', last='Smith')
>>> rec  = dict(name=name, job=['dev', 'mgr'], age=40.5)
>>> rec
{'job': ['dev', 'mgr'], 'name': {'last': 'Smith', 'first': 'Bob'}, 'age': 40.5}
```

The final dictionary format displayed here is a valid literal in Python code, and almost passes for JSON when printed as is, but the **json** module makes the translation official —here translating Python objects to and from a JSON serialized string representation in memory:

```
>>> import json
>>> json.dumps(rec)
'{"job": ["dev", "mgr"], "name": {"last": "Smith", "first": "Bob"}, "age": 40.5}'

>>> S = json.dumps(rec)
>>> S
```

```
'{"job": ["dev", "mgr"], "name": {"last": "Smith", "first": "Bob"}, "age": 40.5}'
>>> O = json.loads(S)
>>> O
{'job': ['dev', 'mgr'], 'name': {'last': 'Smith', 'first': 'Bob'}, 'age': 40.5}
>>> O == rec
True
```

It's similarly straightforward to translate Python objects to and from JSON data strings in files. Prior to being stored in a file, your data is simply Python objects; the JSON module recreates them from the JSON textual representation when it loads it from the file:

```
>>> json.dump(rec, fp=open('testjson.txt', 'w'), indent=4)
>>> print(open('testjson.txt').read())
{
    "job": [
        "dev",
        "mgr"
    ],
    "name": {
        "last": "Smith",
        "first": "Bob"
    },
    "age": 40.5
}
>>> P = json.load(open('testjson.txt'))
>>> P
{'job': ['dev', 'mgr'], 'name': {'last': 'Smith', 'first': 'Bob'}, 'age': 40.5}
```

Once you've translated from JSON text, you process the data using normal Python object operations in your script. For more details on JSON-related topics, see Python's library manuals and search the Web.

Note that strings are all *Unicode* in JSON to support text drawn from international character sets, so you'll see a leading *u* on strings after translating from JSON data in Python 2.X (but not in 3.X); this is just the syntax of Unicode objects in 2.X, as introduced Chapter 4 and Chapter 7, and covered in full in Chapter 37. Because Unicode text strings support all the usual string operations, the difference is negligible to your code while text resides in memory; the distinction matters most when transferring text to and from files, and then usually only for non-ASCII types of text where encodings come into play.

 There is also support in the Python world for translating objects to and from XML, a text format used in Chapter 37; see the web for details. For another semirelated tool that deals with formatted data files, see the standard library's csv module. It parses and creates CSV (comma-separated value) data in files and strings. This doesn't map as directly to Python objects, but is another common data exchange format:

```
>>> import csv
>>> rdr = csv.reader(open('csvdata.txt'))
```

```
>>> for row in rdr: print(row)
...
['a', 'bbb', 'cc', 'dddd']
['11', '22', '33', '44']
```

Storing Packed Binary Data: struct

One other file-related note before we move on: some advanced applications also need to deal with packed binary data, created perhaps by a C language program or a network connection. Python's standard library includes a tool to help in this domain—the struct module knows how to both compose and parse packed binary data. In a sense, this is another data-conversion tool that interprets strings in files as binary data.

We saw an overview of this tool in Chapter 4, but let's take another quick look here for more perspective. To create a packed binary data file, open it in 'wb' (write binary) mode, and pass struct a format string and some Python objects. The format string used here means pack as a 4-byte integer, a 4-character string (which must be a bytes string as of Python 3.2), and a 2-byte integer, all in big-endian form (other format codes handle padding bytes, floating-point numbers, and more):

```
>>> F = open('data.bin', 'wb')                      # Open binary output file
>>> import struct
>>> data = struct.pack('>i4sh', 7, b'spam', 8)      # Make packed binary data
>>> data
b'\x00\x00\x00\x07spam\x00\x08'
>>> F.write(data)                                   # Write byte string
>>> F.close()
```

Python creates a binary bytes data string, which we write out to the file normally—this one consists mostly of nonprintable characters printed in hexadecimal escapes, and is the same binary file we met earlier. To parse the values out to normal Python objects, we simply read the string back and unpack it using the same format string. Python extracts the values into normal Python objects—integers and a string:

```
>>> F = open('data.bin', 'rb')
>>> data = F.read()                                 # Get packed binary data
>>> data
b'\x00\x00\x00\x07spam\x00\x08'
>>> values = struct.unpack('>i4sh', data)           # Convert to Python objects
>>> values
(7, b'spam', 8)
```

Binary data files are advanced and somewhat low-level tools that we won't cover in more detail here; for more help, see the struct coverage in Chapter 37, consult the Python library manual, or import struct and pass it to the help function interactively. Also note that you can use the binary file-processing modes 'wb' and 'rb' to process a simpler binary file, such as an image or audio file, as a whole without having to unpack its contents; in such cases your code might pass it unparsed to other files or tools.

File Context Managers

You'll also want to watch for Chapter 34's discussion of the file's *context manager* support, new as of Python 3.0 and 2.6. Though more a feature of exception processing than files themselves, it allows us to wrap file-processing code in a logic layer that ensures that the file will be closed (and if needed, have its output flushed to disk) automatically on exit, instead of relying on the auto-close during garbage collection:

```
with open(r'C:\code\data.txt') as myfile:      # See Chapter 34 for details
    for line in myfile:
        ...use line here...
```

The `try/finally` statement that we'll also study in Chapter 34 can provide similar functionality, but at some cost in extra code—three extra lines, to be precise (though we can often avoid both options and let Python close files for us automatically):

```
myfile = open(r'C:\code\data.txt')
try:
    for line in myfile:
        ...use line here...
finally:
    myfile.close()
```

The `with` context manager scheme ensures release of system resources in all Pythons, and may be more useful for output files to guarantee buffer flushes; unlike the more general `try`, though, it is also limited to objects that support its protocol. Since both these options require more information than we have yet obtained, however, we'll postpone details until later in this book.

Other File Tools

There are additional, more specialized file methods shown in Table 9-2, and even more that are not in the table. For instance, as mentioned earlier, `seek` resets your current position in a file (the next read or write happens at that position), `flush` forces buffered output to be written out to disk without closing the connection (by default, files are always buffered), and so on.

The Python standard library manual and the reference books described in the preface provide complete lists of file methods; for a quick look, run a `dir` or `help` call interactively, passing in an open file object (in Python 2.X but not 3.X, you can pass in the name `file` instead). For more file-processing examples, watch for the sidebar "Why You Will Care: File Scanners" on page 400 in Chapter 13. It sketches common file-scanning loop code patterns with statements we have not covered enough yet to use here.

Also, note that although the `open` function and the file objects it returns are your main interface to external files in a Python script, there are additional file-like tools in the Python toolset. Among these:

Standard streams

Preopened file objects in the `sys` module, such as `sys.stdout` (see "Print Operations" on page 358 in Chapter 11 for details)

Descriptor files in the `os` module

Integer file handles that support lower-level tools such as file locking (see also the "x" mode in Python 3.3's `open` for exclusive creation)

Sockets, pipes, and FIFOs

File-like objects used to synchronize processes or communicate over networks

Access-by-key files known as "shelves"

Used to store unaltered and pickled Python objects directly, by key (used in Chapter 28)

Shell command streams

Tools such as `os.popen` and `subprocess.Popen` that support spawning shell commands and reading and writing to their standard streams (see Chapter 13 and Chapter 21 for examples)

The third-party open source domain offers even more file-like tools, including support for communicating with serial ports in the *PySerial* extension and interactive programs in the *pexpect* system. See applications-focused Python texts and the Web at large for additional information on file-like tools.

> *Version skew note*: In Python 2.X, the built-in name `open` is essentially a synonym for the name `file`, and you may technically open files by calling either `open` or `file` (though `open` is generally preferred for opening). In Python 3.X, the name `file` is no longer available, because of its redundancy with `open`.
>
> Python 2.X users may also use the name `file` as the file object type, in order to customize files with object-oriented programming (described later in this book). In Python 3.X, files have changed radically. The classes used to implement file objects live in the standard library module `io`. See this module's documentation or code for the classes it makes available for customization, and run a `type(F)` call on an open file `F` for hints.

Core Types Review and Summary

Now that we've seen all of Python's core built-in types in action, let's wrap up our object types tour by reviewing some of the properties they share. Table 9-3 classifies all the major types we've seen so far according to the type categories introduced earlier. Here are some points to remember:

- Objects share operations according to their category; for instance, sequence objects —strings, lists, and tuples—all share sequence operations such as concatenation, length, and indexing.

- Only mutable objects—lists, dictionaries, and sets—may be changed in place; you cannot change numbers, strings, or tuples in place.

- Files export only methods, so mutability doesn't really apply to them—their state may be changed when they are processed, but this isn't quite the same as Python core type mutability constraints.

- "Numbers" in Table 9-3 includes all number types: integer (and the distinct long integer in 2.X), floating point, complex, decimal, and fraction.

- "Strings" in Table 9-3 includes `str`, as well as `bytes` in 3.X and `unicode` in 2.X; the `bytearray` string type in 3.X, 2.6, and 2.7 is mutable.

- Sets are something like the keys of a valueless dictionary, but they don't map to values and are not ordered, so sets are neither a mapping nor a sequence type; `frozenset` is an immutable variant of `set`.

- In addition to type category operations, as of Python 2.6 and 3.0 all the types in Table 9-3 have callable methods, which are generally specific to their type.

Table 9-3. Object classifications

Object type	Category	Mutable?
Numbers (all)	Numeric	No
Strings (all)	Sequence	No
Lists	Sequence	Yes
Dictionaries	Mapping	Yes
Tuples	Sequence	No
Files	Extension	N/A
Sets	Set	Yes
Frozenset	Set	No
bytearray	Sequence	Yes

Why You Will Care: Operator Overloading

In Part VI of this book, we'll see that objects we implement with classes can pick and choose from these categories arbitrarily. For instance, if we want to provide a new kind of specialized sequence object that is consistent with built-in sequences, we can code a class that overloads things like indexing and concatenation:

```
class MySequence:
    def __getitem__(self, index):
        # Called on self[index], others
    def __add__(self, other):
        # Called on self + other
```

```
        def __iter__(self):
            # Preferred in iterations
```

and so on. We can also make the new object mutable or not by selectively implementing methods called for in-place change operations (e.g., __setitem__ is called on self[index]=value assignments). Although it's beyond this book's scope, it's also possible to implement new objects in an external language like C as C extension types. For these, we fill in C function pointer slots to choose between number, sequence, and mapping operation sets.

Object Flexibility

This part of the book introduced a number of compound object types—collections with components. In general:

- Lists, dictionaries, and tuples can hold any kind of object.
- Sets can contain any type of immutable object.
- Lists, dictionaries, and tuples can be arbitrarily nested.
- Lists, dictionaries, and sets can dynamically grow and shrink.

Because they support arbitrary structures, Python's compound object types are good at representing complex information in programs. For example, values in dictionaries may be lists, which may contain tuples, which may contain dictionaries, and so on. The nesting can be as deep as needed to model the data to be processed.

Let's look at an example of nesting. The following interaction defines a tree of nested compound sequence objects, shown in Figure 9-1. To access its components, you may include as many index operations as required. Python evaluates the indexes from left to right, and fetches a reference to a more deeply nested object at each step. Figure 9-1 may be a pathologically complicated data structure, but it illustrates the syntax used to access nested objects in general:

```
>>> L = ['abc', [(1, 2), ([3], 4)], 5]
>>> L[1]
[(1, 2), ([3], 4)]
>>> L[1][1]
([3], 4)
>>> L[1][1][0]
[3]
>>> L[1][1][0][0]
3
```

References Versus Copies

Chapter 6 mentioned that assignments always store references to objects, not copies of those objects. In practice, this is usually what you want. Because assignments can generate multiple references to the same object, though, it's important to be aware that

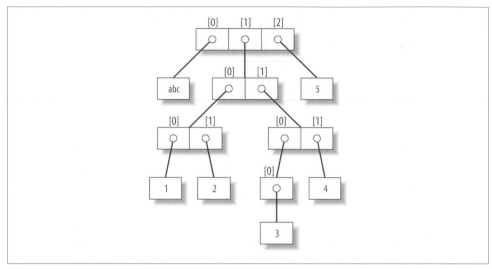

Figure 9-1. A nested object tree with the offsets of its components, created by running the literal expression ['abc', [(1, 2), ([3], 4)], 5]. Syntactically nested objects are internally represented as references (i.e., pointers) to separate pieces of memory.

changing a mutable object in place may affect other references to the same object elsewhere in your program. If you don't want such behavior, you'll need to tell Python to copy the object explicitly.

We studied this phenomenon in Chapter 6, but it can become more subtle when larger objects of the sort we've explored since then come into play. For instance, the following example creates a list assigned to X, and another list assigned to L that embeds a reference back to list X. It also creates a dictionary D that contains another reference back to list X:

```
>>> X = [1, 2, 3]
>>> L = ['a', X, 'b']            # Embed references to X's object
>>> D = {'x':X, 'y':2}
```

At this point, there are three references to the first list created: from the name X, from inside the list assigned to L, and from inside the dictionary assigned to D. The situation is illustrated in Figure 9-2.

Because lists are mutable, changing the shared list object from any of the three references also changes what the other two reference:

```
>>> X[1] = 'surprise'            # Changes all three references!
>>> L
['a', [1, 'surprise', 3], 'b']
>>> D
{'x': [1, 'surprise', 3], 'y': 2}
```

References are a higher-level analog of pointers in other languages that are always followed when used. Although you can't grab hold of the reference itself, it's possible to

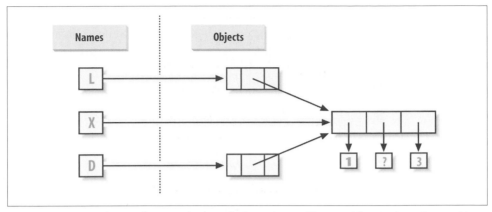

Figure 9-2. Shared object references: because the list referenced by variable X is also referenced from within the objects referenced by L and D, changing the shared list from X makes it look different from L and D, too.

store the same reference in more than one place (variables, lists, and so on). This is a feature—you can pass a large object around a program without generating expensive copies of it along the way. If you really do want copies, however, you can request them:

- Slice expressions with empty limits (L[:]) copy sequences.
- The dictionary, set, and list copy method (X.copy()) copies a dictionary, set, or list (the list's copy is new as of 3.3).
- Some built-in functions, such as list and dict make copies (list(L), dict(D), set(S)).
- The copy standard library module makes full copies when needed.

For example, say you have a list and a dictionary, and you don't want their values to be changed through other variables:

```
>>> L = [1,2,3]
>>> D = {'a':1, 'b':2}
```

To prevent this, simply assign copies to the other variables, not references to the same objects:

```
>>> A = L[:]              # Instead of A = L (or list(L))
>>> B = D.copy()          # Instead of B = D (ditto for sets)
```

This way, changes made from the other variables will change the copies, not the originals:

```
>>> A[1] = 'Ni'
>>> B['c'] = 'spam'
>>>
>>> L, D
([1, 2, 3], {'a': 1, 'b': 2})
```

```
>>> A, B
([1, 'Ni', 3], {'a': 1, 'c': 'spam', 'b': 2})
```

In terms of our original example, you can avoid the reference side effects by slicing the original list instead of simply naming it:

```
>>> X = [1, 2, 3]
>>> L = ['a', X[:], 'b']          # Embed copies of X's object
>>> D = {'x':X[:], 'y':2}
```

This changes the picture in Figure 9-2—L and D will now point to different lists than X. The net effect is that changes made through X will impact only X, not L and D; similarly, changes to L or D will not impact X.

One final note on copies: empty-limit slices and the dictionary copy method only make *top-level* copies; that is, they do not copy nested data structures, if any are present. If you need a complete, fully independent copy of a deeply nested data structure (like the various record structures we've coded in recent chapters), use the standard copy module, introduced in Chapter 6:

```
import copy
X = copy.deepcopy(Y)              # Fully copy an arbitrarily nested object Y
```

This call recursively traverses objects to copy all their parts. This is a much more rare case, though, which is why you have to say more to use this scheme. References are usually what you will want; when they are not, slices and copy methods are usually as much copying as you'll need to do.

Comparisons, Equality, and Truth

All Python objects also respond to comparisons: tests for equality, relative magnitude, and so on. Python comparisons always inspect all parts of compound objects until a result can be determined. In fact, when nested objects are present, Python automatically traverses data structures to apply comparisons from left to right, and as deeply as needed. The first difference found along the way determines the comparison result.

This is sometimes called a *recursive* comparison—the same comparison requested on the top-level objects is applied to each of the nested objects, and to each of *their* nested objects, and so on, until a result is found. Later in this book—in Chapter 19—we'll see how to write recursive functions of our own that work similarly on nested structures. For now, think about comparing all the linked pages at two websites if you want a metaphor for such structures, and a reason for writing recursive functions to process them.

In terms of core types, the recursion is automatic. For instance, a comparison of list objects compares all their components automatically until a mismatch is found or the end is reached:

```
>>> L1 = [1, ('a', 3)]            # Same value, unique objects
>>> L2 = [1, ('a', 3)]
```

```
>>> L1 == L2, L1 is L2              # Equivalent? Same object?
(True, False)
```

Here, L1 and L2 are assigned lists that are equivalent but distinct objects. As a review of what we saw in Chapter 6, because of the nature of Python references, there are two ways to test for equality:

- **The == operator tests value equivalence**. Python performs an equivalence test, comparing all nested objects recursively.

- **The is operator tests object identity**. Python tests whether the two are really the same object (i.e., live at the same address in memory).

In the preceding example, L1 and L2 pass the == test (they have equivalent values because all their components are equivalent) but fail the is check (they reference two different objects, and hence two different pieces of memory). Notice what happens for short strings, though:

```
>>> S1 = 'spam'
>>> S2 = 'spam'
>>> S1 == S2, S1 is S2
(True, True)
```

Here, we should again have two distinct objects that happen to have the same value: == should be true, and is should be false. But because Python internally caches and reuses some strings as an optimization, there really is just a single string 'spam' in memory, shared by S1 and S2; hence, the is identity test reports a true result. To trigger the normal behavior, we need to use longer strings:

```
>>> S1 = 'a longer string'
>>> S2 = 'a longer string'
>>> S1 == S2, S1 is S2
(True, False)
```

Of course, because strings are *immutable*, the object caching mechanism is irrelevant to your code—strings can't be changed in place, regardless of how many variables refer to them. If identity tests seem confusing, see Chapter 6 for a refresher on object reference concepts.

As a rule of thumb, the == operator is what you will want to use for almost all equality checks; is is reserved for highly specialized roles. We'll see cases later in the book where both operators are put to use.

Relative magnitude comparisons are also applied recursively to nested data structures:

```
>>> L1 = [1, ('a', 3)]
>>> L2 = [1, ('a', 2)]
>>> L1 < L2, L1 == L2, L1 > L2       # Less, equal, greater: tuple of results
(False, False, True)
```

Here, L1 is greater than L2 because the nested 3 is greater than 2. By now you should know that the result of the last line is really a tuple of three objects—the results of the three expressions typed (an example of a tuple without its enclosing parentheses).

More specifically, Python compares types as follows:

- *Numbers* are compared by relative magnitude, after conversion to the common highest type if needed.
- *Strings* are compared lexicographically (by the character set code point values returned by `ord`), and character by character until the end or first mismatch (`"abc"` `< "ac"`).
- *Lists* and *tuples* are compared by comparing each component from left to right, and recursively for nested structures, until the end or first mismatch (`[2] > [1, 2]`).
- *Sets* are equal if both contain the same items (formally, if each is a subset of the other), and set relative magnitude comparisons apply subset and superset tests.
- *Dictionaries* compare as equal if their sorted (`key, value`) lists are equal. Relative magnitude comparisons are not supported for dictionaries in Python 3.X, but they work in 2.X as though comparing sorted (`key, value`) lists.
- Nonnumeric mixed-type magnitude comparisons (e.g., `1 < 'spam'`) are errors in Python 3.X. They are allowed in Python 2.X, but use a fixed but arbitrary ordering rule based on type name string. By proxy, this also applies to sorts, which use comparisons internally: nonnumeric mixed-type collections cannot be sorted in 3.X.

In general, comparisons of structured objects proceed as though you had written the objects as literals and compared all their parts one at a time from left to right. In later chapters, we'll see other object types that can change the way they get compared.

Python 2.X and 3.X mixed-type comparisons and sorts

Per the last point in the preceding section's list, the change in Python 3.X for nonnumeric mixed-type comparisons applies to *magnitude* tests, not equality, but it also applies by proxy to *sorting*, which does magnitude testing internally. In Python *2.X* these all work, though mixed types compare by an arbitrary ordering:

```
c:\code> c:\python27\python
>>> 11 == '11'                          # Equality does not convert non-numbers
False
>>> 11 >= '11'                          # 2.X compares by type name string: int, str
False
>>> ['11', '22'].sort()                 # Ditto for sorts
>>> [11, '11'].sort()
```

But Python *3.X* disallows mixed-type magnitude testing, except numeric types and manually converted types:

```
c:\code> c:\python33\python
>>> 11 == '11'                          # 3.X: equality works but magnitude does not
False
>>> 11 >= '11'
TypeError: unorderable types: int() > str()
```

```
>>> ['11', '22'].sort()                      # Ditto for sorts
>>> [11, '11'].sort()
TypeError: unorderable types: str() < int()

>>> 11 > 9.123                               # Mixed numbers convert to highest type
True
>>> str(11) >= '11', 11 >= int('11')         # Manual conversions force the issue
(True, True)
```

Python 2.X and 3.X dictionary comparisons

The second-to-last point in the preceding section also merits illustration. In Python 2.X, dictionaries support magnitude comparisons, as though you were comparing sorted key/value lists:

```
C:\code> c:\python27\python
>>> D1 = {'a':1, 'b':2}
>>> D2 = {'a':1, 'b':3}
>>> D1 == D2                                  # Dictionary equality: 2.X + 3.X
False
>>> D1 < D2                                   # Dictionary magnitude: 2.X only
True
```

As noted briefly in Chapter 8, though, magnitude comparisons for dictionaries are removed in Python 3.X because they incur too much overhead when equality is desired (equality uses an optimized scheme in 3.X that doesn't literally compare sorted key/value lists):

```
C:\code> c:\python33\python
>>> D1 = {'a':1, 'b':2}
>>> D2 = {'a':1, 'b':3}
>>> D1 == D2
False
>>> D1 < D2
TypeError: unorderable types: dict() < dict()
```

The alternative in 3.X is to either write loops to compare values by key, or compare the sorted key/value lists manually—the items dictionary methods and sorted built-in suffice:

```
>>> list(D1.items())
[('b', 2), ('a', 1)]
>>> sorted(D1.items())
[('a', 1), ('b', 2)]
>>>
>>> sorted(D1.items()) < sorted(D2.items())       # Magnitude test in 3.X
True
>>> sorted(D1.items()) > sorted(D2.items())
False
```

This takes more code, but in practice, most programs requiring this behavior will develop more efficient ways to compare data in dictionaries than either this workaround or the original behavior in Python 2.X.

The Meaning of True and False in Python

Notice that the test results returned in the last two examples represent true and false values. They print as the words True and False, but now that we're using logical tests like these in earnest, I should be a bit more formal about what these names really mean.

In Python, as in most programming languages, an integer 0 represents false, and an integer 1 represents true. In addition, though, Python recognizes any empty data structure as false and any nonempty data structure as true. More generally, the notions of true and false are intrinsic properties of *every* object in Python—each object is either true or false, as follows:

- Numbers are false if zero, and true otherwise.
- Other objects are false if empty, and true otherwise.

Table 9-4 gives examples of true and false values of objects in Python.

Table 9-4. Example object truth values

Object	Value
"spam"	True
""	False
[1, 2]	True
[]	False
{'a': 1}	True
{}	False
1	True
0.0	False
None	False

As one application, because objects are true or false themselves, it's common to see Python programmers code tests like if X:, which, assuming X is a string, is the same as if X != '':. In other words, you can test the object itself to see if it contains anything, instead of comparing it to an empty, and therefore false, object of the same type (more on if statements in the next chapter).

The None object

As shown in the last row in Table 9-4, Python also provides a special object called None, which is always considered to be false. None was introduced briefly in Chapter 4; it is the only value of a special data type in Python and typically serves as an empty placeholder (much like a NULL pointer in C).

For example, recall that for lists you cannot assign to an offset unless that offset already exists—the list does not magically grow if you attempt an out-of-bounds assignment.

To preallocate a 100-item list such that you can add to any of the 100 offsets, you can fill it with None objects:

```
>>> L = [None] * 100
>>>
>>> L
[None, None, None, None, None, None, None, ... ]
```

This doesn't limit the size of the list (it can still grow and shrink later), but simply presets an initial size to allow for future index assignments. You could initialize a list with zeros the same way, of course, but best practice dictates using None if the type of the list's contents is variable or not yet known.

Keep in mind that None does not mean "undefined." That is, None is something, not nothing (despite its name!)—it is a real object and a real piece of memory that is created and given a built-in name by Python itself. Watch for other uses of this special object later in the book; as we'll learn in Part IV, it is also the default return value of functions that don't exit by running into a return statement with a result value.

The bool type

While we're on the topic of truth, also keep in mind that the Python Boolean type bool, introduced in Chapter 5, simply augments the notions of true and false in Python. As we learned in Chapter 5, the built-in words True and False are just customized versions of the integers 1 and 0—it's as if these two words have been preassigned to 1 and 0 everywhere in Python. Because of the way this new type is implemented, this is really just a minor extension to the notions of true and false already described, designed to make truth values more explicit:

- When used explicitly in truth test code, the words True and False are equivalent to 1 and 0, but they make the programmer's intent clearer.
- Results of Boolean tests run interactively print as the words True and False, instead of as 1 and 0, to make the type of result clearer.

You are not required to use only Boolean types in logical statements such as if; all objects are still inherently true or false, and all the Boolean concepts mentioned in this chapter still work as described if you use other types. Python also provides a bool built-in function that can be used to test the Boolean value of an object if you want to make this explicit (i.e., whether it is true—that is, nonzero or nonempty):

```
>>> bool(1)
True
>>> bool('spam')
True
>>> bool({})
False
```

In practice, though, you'll rarely notice the Boolean type produced by logic tests, because Boolean results are used automatically by if statements and other selection tools. We'll explore Booleans further when we study logical statements in Chapter 12.

Python's Type Hierarchies

As a summary and reference, Figure 9-3 sketches all the built-in object types available in Python and their relationships. We've looked at the most prominent of these; most of the other kinds of objects in Figure 9-3 correspond to program units (e.g., functions and modules) or exposed interpreter internals (e.g., stack frames and compiled code).

The largest point to notice here is that *everything* in a Python system is an object type and may be processed by your Python programs. For instance, you can pass a class to a function, assign it to a variable, stuff it in a list or dictionary, and so on.

Type Objects

In fact, even types themselves are an object type in Python: the type of an object is an object of type `type` (say that three times fast!). Seriously, a call to the built-in function `type(X)` returns the type object of object `X`. The practical application of this is that type objects can be used for manual type comparisons in Python `if` statements. However, for reasons introduced in Chapter 4, manual type testing is usually not the right thing to do in Python, since it limits your code's flexibility.

One note on type names: as of Python 2.2, each core type has a new built-in name added to support type customization through object-oriented subclassing: `dict`, `list`, `str`, `tuple`, `int`, `float`, `complex`, `bytes`, `type`, `set`, and more. In Python 3.X names all references classes, and in Python 2.X but not 3.X, `file` is also a type name and a synonym for `open`. Calls to these names are really object constructor calls, not simply conversion functions, though you can treat them as simple functions for basic usage.

In addition, the `types` standard library module in Python 3.X provides additional type names for types that are not available as built-ins (e.g., the type of a function; in Python 2.X but not 3.X, this module also includes synonyms for built-in type names), and it is possible to do type tests with the `isinstance` function. For example, all of the following type tests are true:

```
type([1]) == type([])        # Compare to type of another list
type([1]) == list            # Compare to list type name
isinstance([1], list)        # Test if list or customization thereof

import types                 # types has names for other types
def f(): pass
type(f) == types.FunctionType
```

Because types can be subclassed in Python today, the `isinstance` technique is generally recommended. See Chapter 32 for more on subclassing built-in types in Python 2.2 and later.

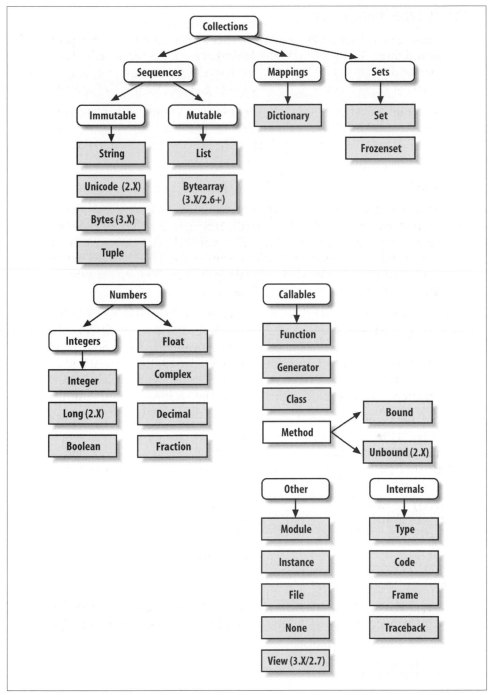

Figure 9-3. Python's major built-in object types, organized by categories. Everything is a type of object in Python, even the type of an object! Some extension types, such as named tuples, might belong in this figure too, but the criteria for inclusion in the core types set are not formal.

Also in Chapter 32, we will explore how `type(X)` and type testing in general apply to instances of user-defined *classes*. In short, in Python 3.X and for new-style classes in Python 2.X, the type of a class instance is the class from which the instance was made. For classic classes in Python 2.X, all class instances are instead of the type "instance," and we must compare instance `__class__` attributes to compare their types meaningfully. Since we're not yet equipped to tackle the subject of classes, we'll postpone the rest of this story until Chapter 32.

Other Types in Python

Besides the core objects studied in this part of the book, and the program-unit objects such as functions, modules, and classes that we'll meet later, a typical Python installation has dozens of additional object types available as linked-in C extensions or Python classes—regular expression objects, DBM files, GUI widgets, network sockets, and so on. Depending on whom you ask, the *named tuple* we met earlier in this chapter may fall in this category too (`Decimal` and `Fraction` of Chapter 5 tend to be more ambiguous).

The main difference between these extra tools and the built-in types we've seen so far is that the built-ins provide special language creation syntax for their objects (e.g., `4` for an integer, `[1,2]` for a list, the `open` function for files, and `def` and `lambda` for functions). Other tools are generally made available in standard library modules that you must first import to use, and aren't usually considered core types. For instance, to make a regular expression object, you import `re` and call `re.compile()`. See Python's library reference for a comprehensive guide to all the tools available to Python programs.

Built-in Type Gotchas

That's the end of our look at core data types. We'll wrap up this part of the book with a discussion of common problems that seem to trap new users (and the occasional expert), along with their solutions. Some of this is a review of ideas we've already covered, but these issues are important enough to warn about again here.

Assignment Creates References, Not Copies

Because this is such a central concept, I'll mention it again: shared references to mutable objects in your program can matter. For instance, in the following example, the list object assigned to the name L is referenced both from L and from inside the list assigned to the name M. Changing L in place changes what M references, too:

```
>>> L = [1, 2, 3]
>>> M = ['X', L, 'Y']            # Embed a reference to L
>>> M
['X', [1, 2, 3], 'Y']
```

```
>>> L[1] = 0                    # Changes M too
>>> M
['X', [1, 0, 3], 'Y']
```

This effect usually becomes important only in larger programs, and shared references are often exactly what you want. If objects change out from under you in unwanted ways, you can avoid sharing objects by copying them explicitly. For lists, you can always make a top-level copy by using an empty-limits slice, among other techniques described earlier:

```
>>> L = [1, 2, 3]
>>> M = ['X', L[:], 'Y']        # Embed a copy of L (or list(L), or L.copy())
>>> L[1] = 0                    # Changes only L, not M
>>> L
[1, 0, 3]
>>> M
['X', [1, 2, 3], 'Y']
```

Remember, slice limits default to 0 and the length of the sequence being sliced; if both are omitted, the slice extracts every item in the sequence and so makes a top-level copy (a new, unshared object).

Repetition Adds One Level Deep

Repeating a sequence is like adding it to itself a number of times. However, when mutable sequences are nested, the effect might not always be what you expect. For instance, in the following example X is assigned to L repeated four times, whereas Y is assigned to a list *containing* L repeated four times:

```
>>> L = [4, 5, 6]
>>> X = L * 4                   # Like [4, 5, 6] + [4, 5, 6] + ...
>>> Y = [L] * 4                 # [L] + [L] + ... = [L, L,...]

>>> X
[4, 5, 6, 4, 5, 6, 4, 5, 6, 4, 5, 6]
>>> Y
[[4, 5, 6], [4, 5, 6], [4, 5, 6], [4, 5, 6]]
```

Because L was nested in the second repetition, Y winds up embedding references back to the original list assigned to L, and so is open to the same sorts of side effects noted in the preceding section:

```
>>> L[1] = 0                    # Impacts Y but not X
>>> X
[4, 5, 6, 4, 5, 6, 4, 5, 6, 4, 5, 6]
>>> Y
[[4, 0, 6], [4, 0, 6], [4, 0, 6], [4, 0, 6]]
```

This may seem artificial and academic—until it happens unexpectedly in your code! The same solutions to this problem apply here as in the previous section, as this is really just another way to create the shared mutable object reference case—make copies when you don't want shared references:

```
>>> L = [4, 5, 6]
>>> Y = [list(L)] * 4          # Embed a (shared) copy of L
>>> L[1] = 0
>>> Y
[[4, 5, 6], [4, 5, 6], [4, 5, 6], [4, 5, 6]]
```

Even more subtly, although Y doesn't share an object with L anymore, it still embeds four references to the same copy of it. If you must avoid that sharing too, you'll want to make sure each embedded copy is unique:

```
>>> Y[0][1] = 99               # All four copies are still the same
>>> Y
[[4, 99, 6], [4, 99, 6], [4, 99, 6], [4, 99, 6]]

>>> L = [4, 5, 6]
>>> Y = [list(L) for i in range(4)]
>>> Y
[[4, 5, 6], [4, 5, 6], [4, 5, 6], [4, 5, 6]]
>>> Y[0][1] = 99
>>> Y
[[4, 99, 6], [4, 5, 6], [4, 5, 6], [4, 5, 6]]
```

If you remember that repetition, concatenation, and slicing copy only the top level of their operand objects, these sorts of cases make much more sense.

Beware of Cyclic Data Structures

We actually encountered this concept in a prior exercise: if a collection object contains a reference to itself, it's called a *cyclic object*. Python prints a [...] whenever it detects a cycle in the object, rather than getting stuck in an infinite loop (as it once did long ago):

```
>>> L = ['grail']              # Append reference to same object
>>> L.append(L)                # Generates cycle in object: [...]
>>> L
['grail', [...]]
```

Besides understanding that the three dots in square brackets represent a cycle in the object, this case is worth knowing about because it can lead to gotchas—cyclic structures may cause code of your own to fall into unexpected loops if you don't anticipate them.

For instance, some programs that walk through structured data must keep a list, dictionary, or set of *already visited* items, and check it when they're about to step into a cycle that could cause an unwanted loop. See the Part I exercise solutions in "Part I, Getting Started" on page 1465 in Appendix D for more on this problem. Also watch for general discussion of recursion in Chapter 19, as well as the *reloadall.py* program in Chapter 25 and the ListTree class in Chapter 31, for concrete examples of programs where cycle detection can matter.

The solution is knowledge: don't use cyclic references unless you really need to, and make sure you anticipate them in programs that must care. There are good reasons to create cycles, but unless you have code that knows how to handle them, objects that reference themselves may be more surprise than asset.

Immutable Types Can't Be Changed in Place

And once more for completeness: you can't change an immutable object in place. Instead, you construct a new object with slicing, concatenation, and so on, and assign it back to the original reference, if needed:

```
T = (1, 2, 3)

T[2] = 4                # Error!

T = T[:2] + (4,)        # OK: (1, 2, 4)
```

That might seem like extra coding work, but the upside is that the previous gotchas in this section can't happen when you're using immutable objects such as tuples and strings; because they can't be changed in place, they are not open to the sorts of side effects that lists are.

Chapter Summary

This chapter explored the last two major core object types—the tuple and the file. We learned that tuples support all the usual sequence operations, have just a few methods, do not allow any in-place changes because they are immutable, and are extended by the named tuple type. We also learned that files are returned by the built-in open function and provide methods for reading and writing data.

Along the way we explored how to translate Python objects to and from strings for storing in files, and we looked at the pickle, json, and struct modules for advanced roles (object serialization and binary data). Finally, we wrapped up by reviewing some properties common to all object types (e.g., shared references) and went through a list of common mistakes ("gotchas") in the object type domain.

In the next part of this book, we'll shift gears, turning to the topic of *statement syntax*—the way you code processing logic in your scripts. Along the way, this next part explores all of Python's basic procedural statements. The next chapter kicks off this topic with an introduction to Python's general syntax model, which is applicable to all statement types. Before moving on, though, take the chapter quiz, and then work through the end-of-part lab exercises to review type concepts. Statements largely just create and process objects, so make sure you've mastered this domain by working through all the exercises before reading on.

Test Your Knowledge: Quiz

1. How can you determine how large a tuple is? Why is this tool located where it is?

2. Write an expression that changes the first item in a tuple. (4, 5, 6) should become (1, 5, 6) in the process.

3. What is the default for the processing mode argument in a file open call?

4. What module might you use to store Python objects in a file without converting them to strings yourself?

5. How might you go about copying all parts of a nested structure at once?

6. When does Python consider an object true?

7. What is your quest?

Test Your Knowledge: Answers

1. The built-in len function returns the length (number of contained items) for any container object in Python, including tuples. It is a built-in function instead of a type method because it applies to many different types of objects. In general, built-in functions and expressions may span many object types; methods are specific to a single object type, though some may be available on more than one type (index, for example, works on lists and tuples).

2. Because they are immutable, you can't really change tuples in place, but you can generate a new tuple with the desired value. Given T = (4, 5, 6), you can change the first item by making a new tuple from its parts by slicing and concatenating: T = (1,) + T[1:]. (Recall that single-item tuples require a trailing comma.) You could also convert the tuple to a list, change it in place, and convert it back to a tuple, but this is more expensive and is rarely required in practice—simply use a list if you know that the object will require in-place changes.

3. The default for the processing mode argument in a file open call is 'r', for reading text input. For input text files, simply pass in the external file's name.

4. The pickle module can be used to store Python objects in a file without explicitly converting them to strings. The struct module is related, but it assumes the data is to be in packed binary format in the file; json similarly converts a limited set of Python objects to and from strings per the JSON format.

5. Import the copy module, and call copy.deepcopy(X) if you need to copy all parts of a nested structure X. This is also rarely seen in practice; references are usually the desired behavior, and shallow copies (e.g., aList[:], aDict.copy(), set(aSet)) usually suffice for most copies.

6. An object is considered true if it is either a nonzero number or a nonempty collection object. The built-in words True and False are essentially predefined to have the same meanings as integer 1 and 0, respectively.

7. Acceptable answers include "To learn Python," "To move on to the next part of the book," or "To seek the Holy Grail."

Test Your Knowledge: Part II Exercises

This session asks you to get your feet wet with built-in object fundamentals. As before, a few new ideas may pop up along the way, so be sure to flip to the answers in "Part II, Types and Operations" on page 1467 in Appendix D when you're done (or even when you're not). If you have limited time, I suggest starting with exercises 10 and 11 (the most practical of the bunch), and then working from first to last as time allows. This is all fundamental material, so try to do as many of these as you can; programming is a hands-on activity, and there is no substitute for practicing what you've read to make ideas gel.

1. *The basics.* Experiment interactively with the common type operations found in the various operation tables in this part of the book. To get started, bring up the Python interactive interpreter, type each of the following expressions, and try to explain what's happening in each case. Note that the semicolon in some of these is being used as a statement separator, to squeeze multiple statements onto a single line: for example, X=1;X assigns and then prints a variable (more on statement syntax in the next part of the book). Also remember that a comma between expressions usually builds a tuple, even if there are no enclosing parentheses: X,Y,Z is a three-item tuple, which Python prints back to you in parentheses.

```
2 ** 16
2 / 5, 2 / 5.0

"spam" + "eggs"
S = "ham"
"eggs " + S
S * 5
S[:0]
"green %s and %s" % ("eggs", S)
'green {0} and {1}'.format('eggs', S)

('x',)[0]
('x', 'y')[1]

L = [1,2,3] + [4,5,6]
L, L[:], L[:0], L[-2], L[-2:]
([1,2,3] + [4,5,6])[2:4]
[L[2], L[3]]
L.reverse(); L
L.sort(); L
L.index(4)

{'a':1, 'b':2}['b']
D = {'x':1, 'y':2, 'z':3}
D['w'] = 0
D['x'] + D['w']
D[(1,2,3)] = 4
list(D.keys()), list(D.values()), (1,2,3) in D

[[]], ["",[],(),{},None]
```

2. *Indexing and slicing.* At the interactive prompt, define a list named L that contains four strings or numbers (e.g., L=[0,1,2,3]). Then, experiment with the following boundary cases. You may never see these cases in real programs (especially not in the bizarre ways they appear here!), but they are intended to make you think about the underlying model, and some may be useful in less artificial forms—slicing out of bounds can help, for example, if a sequence is as long as you expect:

    a. What happens when you try to index out of bounds (e.g., L[4])?

    b. What about slicing out of bounds (e.g., L[-1000:100])?

    c. Finally, how does Python handle it if you try to extract a sequence in reverse, with the lower bound greater than the higher bound (e.g., L[3:1])? Hint: try assigning to this slice (L[3:1]=['?']), and see where the value is put. Do you think this may be the same phenomenon you saw when slicing out of bounds?

3. *Indexing, slicing, and del.* Define another list L with four items, and assign an empty list to one of its offsets (e.g., L[2]=[]). What happens? Then, assign an empty list to a slice (L[2:3]=[]). What happens now? Recall that slice assignment deletes the slice and inserts the new value where it used to be.

    The del statement deletes offsets, keys, attributes, and names. Use it on your list to delete an item (e.g., del L[0]). What happens if you delete an entire slice (del L[1:])? What happens when you assign a nonsequence to a slice (L[1:2]=1)?

4. *Tuple assignment.* Type the following lines:

```
>>> X = 'spam'
>>> Y = 'eggs'
>>> X, Y = Y, X
```

    What do you think is happening to X and Y when you type this sequence?

5. *Dictionary keys.* Consider the following code fragments:

```
>>> D = {}
>>> D[1] = 'a'
>>> D[2] = 'b'
```

    You've learned that dictionaries aren't accessed by offsets, so what's going on here? Does the following shed any light on the subject? (Hint: strings, integers, and tuples share which type category?)

```
>>> D[(1, 2, 3)] = 'c'
>>> D
{1: 'a', 2: 'b', (1, 2, 3): 'c'}
```

6. *Dictionary indexing.* Create a dictionary named D with three entries, for keys 'a', 'b', and 'c'. What happens if you try to index a nonexistent key (D['d'])? What does Python do if you try to assign to a nonexistent key 'd' (e.g., D['d']='spam')? How does this compare to out-of-bounds assignments and references for lists? Does this sound like the rule for variable names?

7. *Generic operations.* Run interactive tests to answer the following questions:

a. What happens when you try to use the + operator on different/mixed types (e.g., string + list, list + tuple)?

b. Does + work when one of the operands is a dictionary?

c. Does the append method work for both lists and strings? How about using the keys method on lists? (Hint: what does append assume about its subject object?)

d. Finally, what type of object do you get back when you slice or concatenate two lists or two strings?

8. *String indexing.* Define a string S of four characters: S = "spam". Then type the following expression: S[0][0][0][0][0]. Any clue as to what's happening this time? (Hint: recall that a string is a collection of characters, but Python characters are one-character strings.) Does this indexing expression still work if you apply it to a list such as ['s', 'p', 'a', 'm']? Why?

9. *Immutable types.* Define a string S of four characters again: S = "spam". Write an assignment that changes the string to "slam", using only slicing and concatenation. Could you perform the same operation using just indexing and concatenation? How about index assignment?

10. *Nesting.* Write a data structure that represents your personal information: name (first, middle, last), age, job, address, email address, and phone number. You may build the data structure with any combination of built-in object types you like (lists, tuples, dictionaries, strings, numbers). Then, access the individual components of your data structures by indexing. Do some structures make more sense than others for this object?

11. *Files.* Write a script that creates a new output file called *myfile.txt* and writes the string "Hello file world!" into it. Then write another script that opens *myfile.txt* and reads and prints its contents. Run your two scripts from the system command line. Does the new file show up in the directory where you ran your scripts? What if you add a different directory path to the filename passed to open? Note: file write methods do not add newline characters to your strings; add an explicit \n at the end of the string if you want to fully terminate the line in the file.

## PART III

Statements and Syntax

## CHAPTER 10

Introducing Python Statements

Now that you're familiar with Python's core built-in object types, this chapter begins our exploration of its fundamental statement forms. As in the previous part, we'll begin here with a general introduction to statement syntax, and we'll follow up with more details about specific statements in the next few chapters.

In simple terms, *statements* are the things you write to tell Python what your programs should do. If, as suggested in Chapter 4, programs "do things with stuff," then statements are the way you specify what sort of *things* a program does. Less informally, Python is a procedural, statement-based language; by combining statements, you specify a *procedure* that Python performs to satisfy a program's goals.

The Python Conceptual Hierarchy Revisited

Another way to understand the role of statements is to revisit the concept hierarchy introduced in Chapter 4, which talked about built-in objects and the expressions used to manipulate them. This chapter climbs the hierarchy to the next level of Python program structure:

1. Programs are composed of modules.
2. Modules contain statements.
3. *Statements contain expressions.*
4. Expressions create and process objects.

At their base, programs written in the Python language are composed of statements and expressions. Expressions process objects and are embedded in statements. Statements code the larger *logic* of a program's operation—they use and direct expressions to process the objects we studied in the preceding chapters. Moreover, statements are where objects spring into existence (e.g., in expressions within assignment statements), and some statements create entirely new kinds of objects (functions, classes, and so on). At the top, statements always exist in modules, which themselves are managed with statements.

Python's Statements

Table 10-1 summarizes Python's statement set. Each statement in Python has its own specific purpose and its own specific *syntax*—the rules that define its structure—though, as we'll see, many share common syntax patterns, and some statements' roles overlap. Table 10-1 also gives examples of each statement, when coded according to its syntax rules. In your programs, these units of code can perform actions, repeat tasks, make choices, build larger program structures, and so on.

This part of the book deals with entries in the table from the top through `break` and `continue`. You've informally been introduced to a few of the statements in Table 10-1 already; this part of the book will fill in details that were skipped earlier, introduce the rest of Python's procedural statement set, and cover the overall syntax model. Statements lower in Table 10-1 that have to do with larger program units—functions, classes, modules, and exceptions—lead to larger programming ideas, so they will each have a section of their own. More focused statements (like `del`, which deletes various components) are covered elsewhere in the book, or in Python's standard manuals.

Table 10-1. Python statements

Statement	Role	Example
Assignment	Creating references	`a, b = 'good', 'bad'`
Calls and other expressions	Running functions	`log.write("spam, ham")`
print calls	Printing objects	`print('The Killer', joke)`
if/elif/else	Selecting actions	`if "python" in text:` `    print(text)`
for/else	Iteration	`for x in mylist:` `    print(x)`
while/else	General loops	`while X > Y:` `    print('hello')`
pass	Empty placeholder	`while True:` `    pass`
break	Loop exit	`while True:` `    if exittest(): break`
continue	Loop continue	`while True:` `    if skiptest(): continue`
def	Functions and methods	`def f(a, b, c=1, *d):` `    print(a+b+c+d[0])`
return	Functions results	`def f(a, b, c=1, *d):` `    return a+b+c+d[0]`
yield	Generator functions	`def gen(n):` `    for i in n: yield i*2`

global	Namespaces	`x = 'old'`
		`def function():`
		`    global x, y; x = 'new'`

nonlocal	Namespaces (3.X)	`def outer():` `    x = 'old'`

Statement	Role	Example
| | | ```
def function():
    nonlocal x; x = 'new'
``` |
| `import` | Module access | `import sys` |
| `from` | Attribute access | `from sys import stdin` |
| `class` | Building objects | ```
class Subclass(Superclass):
    staticData = []
    def method(self): pass
``` |
| `try/except/ finally` | Catching exceptions | ```
try:
    action()
except:
    print('action error')
``` |
| `raise` | Triggering exceptions | `raise EndSearch(location)` |
| `assert` | Debugging checks | `assert X > Y, 'X too small'` |
| `with/as` | Context managers (3.X, 2.6+) | ```
with open('data') as myfile:
    process(myfile)
``` |
| `del` | Deleting references | ```
del data[k]
del data[i:j]
del obj.attr
del variable
``` |

Technically, Table 10-1 reflects Python 3.X's statements. Though sufficient as a quick preview and reference, it's not quite complete as is. Here are a few fine points about its content:

- Assignment statements come in a variety of syntax flavors, described in Chapter 11: basic, sequence, augmented, and more.

- `print` is technically neither a reserved word nor a statement in 3.X, but a built-in function call; because it will nearly always be run as an expression statement, though (and often on a line by itself), it's generally thought of as a statement type. We'll study print operations in Chapter 11.

- `yield` is also an expression instead of a statement as of 2.5; like `print`, it's typically used as an expression statement and so is included in this table, but scripts occasionally assign or otherwise use its result, as we'll see in Chapter 20. As an expression, `yield` is also a reserved word, unlike `print`.

Most of this table applies to Python 2.X, too, except where it doesn't—if you are using Python 2.X, here are a few notes for your Python, too:

- In 2.X, `nonlocal` is not available; as we'll see in Chapter 17, there are alternative ways to achieve this statement's writeable state-retention effect.

- In 2.X, `print` is a statement instead of a built-in function call, with specific syntax covered in Chapter 11.

- In 2.X, the 3.X `exec` code execution built-in function is a statement, with specific syntax; since it supports enclosing parentheses, though, you can generally use its 3.X call form in 2.X code.
```

- In 2.5, the `try`/`except` and `try`/`finally` statements were merged: the two were formerly separate statements, but we can now say both `except` and `finally` in the same `try` statement.

- In 2.5, `with`/`as` is an optional extension, and it is not available unless you explicitly turn it on by running the statement `from __future__ import with_statement` (see Chapter 34).

A Tale of Two ifs

Before we delve into the details of any of the concrete statements in Table 10-1, I want to begin our look at Python statement syntax by showing you what you are *not* going to type in Python code so you can compare and contrast it with other syntax models you might have seen in the past.

Consider the following `if` statement, coded in a C-like language:

```
if (x > y) {
    x = 1;
    y = 2;
}
```

This might be a statement in C, C++, Java, JavaScript, or similar. Now, look at the equivalent statement in the Python language:

```
if x > y:
    x = 1
    y = 2
```

The first thing that may pop out at you is that the equivalent Python statement is less, well, cluttered—that is, there are fewer syntactic components. This is by design; as a scripting language, one of Python's goals is to make programmers' lives easier by requiring less typing.

More specifically, when you compare the two syntax models, you'll notice that Python adds one new thing to the mix, and that three items that are present in the C-like language are not present in Python code.

What Python Adds

The one new syntax component in Python is the colon character (`:`). All Python *compound statements*—statements that have other statements nested inside them—follow the same general pattern of a header line terminated in a colon, followed by a nested block of code usually indented underneath the header line, like this:

```
Header line:
    Nested statement block
```

The colon is required, and omitting it is probably the most common coding mistake among new Python programmers—it's certainly one I've witnessed thousands of times

---

in Python training classes I've taught. In fact, if you are new to Python, you'll almost certainly forget the colon character very soon. You'll get an error message if you do, and most Python-friendly editors make this mistake easy to spot. Including it eventually becomes an unconscious habit (so much so that you may start typing colons in your C-like language code, too, generating many entertaining error messages from that language's compiler!).

What Python Removes

Although Python requires the extra colon character, there are three things programmers in C-like languages must include that you don't generally have to in Python.

Parentheses are optional

The first of these is the set of parentheses around the tests at the top of the statement:

```
if (x < y)
```

The parentheses here are required by the syntax of many C-like languages. In Python, though, they are not—we simply omit the parentheses, and the statement works the same way:

```
if x < y
```

Technically speaking, because every expression can be enclosed in parentheses, including them will not hurt in this Python code, and they are not treated as an error if present.

But don't do that: you'll be wearing out your keyboard needlessly, and broadcasting to the world that you're a programmer of a C-like language still learning Python (I know, because I was once, too). The "Python way" is to simply omit the parentheses in these kinds of statements altogether.

End-of-line is end of statement

The second and more significant syntax component you won't find in Python code is the semicolon. You don't need to terminate statements with semicolons in Python the way you do in C-like languages:

```
x = 1;
```

In Python, the general rule is that the end of a line automatically terminates the statement that appears on that line. In other words, you can leave off the semicolons, and it works the same way:

```
x = 1
```

There are some ways to work around this rule, as you'll see in a moment (for instance, wrapping code in a bracketed structure allows it to span lines). But, in general, you write one statement per line for the vast majority of Python code, and no semicolon is required.

Here, too, if you are pining for your C programming days (if such a state is possible) you can continue to use semicolons at the end of each statement—the language lets you get away with them if they are present, because the semicolon is also a separator when statements are combined.

But don't do that either (really!). Again, doing so tells the world that you're a programmer of a C-like language who still hasn't quite made the switch to Python coding. The Pythonic style is to leave off the semicolons altogether. Judging from students in classes, this seems a tough habit for some veteran programmers to break. But you'll get there; semicolons are useless noise in this role in Python.

End of indentation is end of block

The third and final syntax component that Python removes, and the one that may seem the most unusual to soon-to-be-ex-programmers of C-like languages (until they've used it for 10 minutes and realize it's actually a feature), is that you do not type anything explicit in your code to syntactically mark the beginning and end of a nested block of code. You don't need to include begin/end, then/endif, or braces around the nested block, as you do in C-like languages:

```
if (x > y) {
    x = 1;
    y = 2;
}
```

Instead, in Python, we consistently indent all the statements in a given single nested block the same distance to the right, and Python uses the statements' physical indentation to determine where the block starts and stops:

```
if x > y:
    x = 1
    y = 2
```

By *indentation*, I mean the blank whitespace all the way to the left of the two nested statements here. Python doesn't care *how* you indent (you may use either spaces or tabs), or *how much* you indent (you may use any number of spaces or tabs). In fact, the indentation of one nested block can be totally different from that of another. The syntax rule is only that for a given single nested block, all of its statements must be indented the same distance to the right. If this is not the case, you will get a syntax error, and your code will not run until you repair its indentation to be consistent.

Why Indentation Syntax?

The indentation rule may seem unusual at first glance to programmers accustomed to C-like languages, but it is a deliberate feature of Python, and it's one of the main ways that Python almost forces programmers to produce uniform, regular, and readable code. It essentially means that you must line up your code vertically, in columns, according to its logical structure. The net effect is to make your code more consistent and readable (unlike much of the code written in C-like languages).

To put that more strongly, aligning your code according to its logical structure is a major part of making it readable, and thus reusable and maintainable, by yourself and others. In fact, even if you never use Python after reading this book, you should get into the habit of aligning your code for readability in any block-structured language. Python underscores the issue by making this a part of its syntax, but it's an important thing to do in any programming language, and it has a huge impact on the usefulness of your code.

Your experience may vary, but when I was still doing development on a full-time basis, I was mostly paid to work on large old C++ programs that had been worked on by many programmers over the years. Almost invariably, each programmer had his or her own style for indenting code. For example, I'd often be asked to change a `while` loop coded in the C++ language that began like this:

```
while (x > 0) {
```

Before we even get into indentation, there are three or four ways that programmers can arrange these braces in a C-like language, and organizations often endure political battles and standards manuals to address the options (which seems more than a little off-topic for the problem to be solved by programming). Be that as it may, here's the scenario I often encountered in C++ code. The first person who worked on the code indented the loop four spaces:

```
while (x > 0) {
    --------;
    --------;
```

That person eventually moved on to management, only to be replaced by someone who liked to indent further to the right:

```
while (x > 0) {
    --------;
    --------;
        --------;
        --------;
```

That person later moved on to other opportunities (ending that individual's reign of coding terror...), and someone else picked up the code who liked to indent less:

```
while (x > 0) {
    --------;
    --------;
        --------;
        --------;
--------;
--------;
}
```

And so on. Eventually, the block is terminated by a closing brace (}), which of course makes this "block-structured code" (he says, sarcastically). No: in any block-structured language, Python or otherwise, if nested blocks are not indented consistently, they become very difficult for the reader to interpret, change, or reuse, because the code no longer visually reflects its logical meaning. *Readability matters*, and indentation is a major component of readability.

Here is another example that may have burned you in the past if you've done much programming in a C-like language. Consider the following statement in C:

```
if (x)
    if (y)
        statement1;
else
    statement2;
```

Which `if` does the `else` here go with? Surprisingly, the `else` is paired with the nested `if` statement (`if (y)`) in C, even though it looks visually as though it is associated with the outer `if (x)`. This is a classic pitfall in the C language, and it can lead to the reader completely misinterpreting the code and changing it incorrectly in ways that might not be uncovered until the Mars rover crashes into a giant rock!

This cannot happen in Python—because indentation is significant, the way the code looks is the way it will work. Consider an equivalent Python statement:

```
if x:
    if y:
        statement1
else:
    statement2
```

In this example, the `if` that the `else` lines up with vertically is the one it is associated with logically (the outer `if x`). In a sense, Python is a WYSIWYG language—what you see is what you get—because the way code looks is the way it runs, regardless of who coded it.

If this still isn't enough to underscore the benefits of Python's syntax, here's another anecdote. Early in my career, I worked at a successful company that developed systems software in the C language, where consistent indentation is not required. Even so, when we checked our code into source control at the end of the day, this company ran an automated script that analyzed the indentation used in the code. If the script noticed that we'd indented our code inconsistently, we received an automated email about it the next morning—and so did our managers!

The point is that even when a language doesn't require it, good programmers know that consistent use of indentation has a huge impact on code readability and quality. The fact that Python promotes this to the level of syntax is seen by most as a feature of the language.

Also keep in mind that nearly every programmer-friendly text editor has built-in support for Python's syntax model. In the IDLE Python GUI, for example, lines of code

---

are automatically indented when you are typing a nested block; pressing the Backspace key backs up one level of indentation, and you can customize how far to the right IDLE indents statements in a nested block. There is no universal standard on this: four spaces or one tab per level is common, but it's generally up to you to decide how and how much you wish to indent (unless you work at a company that's endured politics and manuals to standardize this too). Indent further to the right for further nested blocks, and less to close the prior block.

As a rule of thumb, you probably shouldn't mix tabs and spaces in the same block in Python, unless you do so consistently; use tabs or spaces in a given block, but not both (in fact, Python 3.X now issues an error for inconsistent use of tabs and spaces, as we'll see in Chapter 12). Then again, you probably shouldn't mix tabs or spaces in indentation in *any* structured language—such code can cause major readability issues if the next programmer has his or her editor set to display tabs differently than yours. C-like languages might let coders get away with this, but they shouldn't: the result can be a mangled mess.

Regardless of which language you code in, you should be indenting consistently for readability. In fact, if you weren't taught to do this earlier in your career, your teachers did you a disservice. Most programmers—especially those who must read others' code —consider it a major asset that Python elevates this to the level of syntax. Moreover, generating tabs instead of braces is no more difficult in practice for tools that must output Python code. In general, if you do what you should be doing in a C-like language anyhow, but get rid of the braces, your code will satisfy Python's syntax rules.

A Few Special Cases

As mentioned previously, in Python's syntax model:

- The end of a line terminates the statement on that line (without semicolons).
- Nested statements are blocked and associated by their physical indentation (without braces).

Those rules cover almost all Python code you'll write or see in practice. However, Python also provides some special-purpose rules that allow customization of both statements and nested statement blocks. They're not required and should be used sparingly, but programmers have found them useful in practice.

Statement rule special cases

Although statements normally appear one per line, it is possible to squeeze more than one statement onto a single line in Python by separating them with semicolons:

```
a = 1; b = 2; print(a + b)          # Three statements on one line
```

This is the only place in Python where semicolons are required: as *statement separators*. This only works, though, if the statements thus combined are not themselves compound statements. In other words, you can chain together only simple statements, like assignments, `print`s, and function calls. Compound statements like `if` tests and `while` loops must still appear on lines of their own (otherwise, you could squeeze an entire program onto one line, which probably would not make you very popular among your coworkers!).

The other special rule for statements is essentially the inverse: you can make a single statement span across *multiple lines*. To make this work, you simply have to enclose part of your statement in a bracketed pair—parentheses (`()`), square brackets (`[]`), or curly braces (`{}`). Any code enclosed in these constructs can cross multiple lines: your statement doesn't end until Python reaches the line containing the closing part of the pair. For instance, to continue a list literal:

```
mylist = [1111,
          2222,
          3333]
```

Because the code is enclosed in a square brackets pair, Python simply drops down to the next line until it encounters the closing bracket. The curly braces surrounding dictionaries (as well as set literals and dictionary and set comprehensions in 3.X and 2.7) allow them to span lines this way too, and parentheses handle tuples, function calls, and expressions. The indentation of the continuation lines does not matter, though common sense dictates that the lines should be aligned somehow for readability.

Parentheses are the catchall device—because any expression can be wrapped in them, simply inserting a left parenthesis allows you to drop down to the next line and continue your statement:

```
X = (A + B +
     C + D)
```

This technique works with compound statements, too, by the way. Anywhere you need to code a large expression, simply wrap it in parentheses to continue it on the next line:

```
if (A == 1 and
    B == 2 and
    C == 3):
        print('spam' * 3)
```

An older rule also allows for continuation lines when the prior line ends in a backslash:

```
X = A + B + \
    C + D                    # An error-prone older alternative
```

This alternative technique is dated, though, and is frowned on today because it's difficult to notice and maintain the backslashes. It's also fairly brittle and error-prone—there can be no spaces after the backslash, and accidentally omitting it can have unexpected effects if the next line is mistaken to be a new statement (in this example, "C + D" is a valid statement by itself if it's not indented). This rule is also another throwback to the C language, where it is commonly used in "#define" macros; again, when in Pythonland, do as Pythonistas do, not as C programmers do.

Block rule special case

As mentioned previously, statements in a nested block of code are normally associated by being indented the same amount to the right. As one special case here, the body of a compound statement can instead appear on the same line as the header in Python, after the colon:

```
if x > y: print(x)
```

This allows us to code single-line `if` statements, single-line `while` and `for` loops, and so on. Here again, though, this will work only if the body of the compound statement itself does not contain any compound statements. That is, only simple statements—assignments, `print`s, function calls, and the like—are allowed after the colon. Larger statements must still appear on lines by themselves. Extra parts of compound statements (such as the `else` part of an `if`, which we'll meet in the next section) must also be on separate lines of their own. Compound statement bodies can also consist of multiple simple statements separated by semicolons, but this tends to be frowned upon.

In general, even though it's not always required, if you keep all your statements on individual lines and always indent your nested blocks, your code will be easier to read and change in the future. Moreover, some code profiling and coverage tools may not be able to distinguish between multiple statements squeezed onto a single line or the header and body of a one-line compound statement. It is almost always to your advantage to keep things simple in Python. You can use the special-case exceptions to write Python code that's hard to read, but it takes a lot of work, and there are probably better ways to spend your time.

To see a prime and common exception to one of these rules in action, however (the use of a single-line `if` statement to `break` out of a loop), and to introduce more of Python's syntax, let's move on to the next section and write some real code.

A Quick Example: Interactive Loops

We'll see all these syntax rules in action when we tour Python's specific compound statements in the next few chapters, but they work the same everywhere in the Python language. To get started, let's work through a brief, realistic example that demonstrates the way that statement syntax and statement nesting come together in practice, and introduces a few statements along the way.

A Simple Interactive Loop

Suppose you're asked to write a Python program that interacts with a user in a console window. Maybe you're accepting inputs to send to a database, or reading numbers to be used in a calculation. Regardless of the purpose, you need to code a loop that reads one or more inputs from a user typing on a keyboard, and prints back a result for each. In other words, you need to write a classic read/evaluate/print loop program.

In Python, typical boilerplate code for such an interactive loop might look like this:

```
while True:
    reply = input('Enter text:')
    if reply == 'stop': break
    print(reply.upper())
```

This code makes use of a few new ideas and some we've already seen:

- The code leverages the Python `while` loop, Python's most general looping statement. We'll study the `while` statement in more detail later, but in short, it consists of the word `while`, followed by an expression that is interpreted as a true or false result, followed by a nested block of code that is repeated while the test at the top is true (the word `True` here is considered always true).

- The `input` built-in function we met earlier in the book is used here for general console input—it prints its optional argument string as a prompt and returns the user's typed reply as a string. Use `raw_input` in 2.X instead, per the upcoming note.

- A single-line `if` statement that makes use of the special rule for nested blocks also appears here: the body of the `if` appears on the header line after the colon instead of being indented on a new line underneath it. This would work either way, but as it's coded, we've saved an extra line.

- Finally, the Python `break` statement is used to exit the loop immediately—it simply jumps out of the loop statement altogether, and the program continues after the loop. Without this exit statement, the `while` would loop forever, as its test is always true.

In effect, this combination of statements essentially means "read a line from the user and print it in uppercase until the user enters the word 'stop.'" There are other ways to code such a loop, but the form used here is very common in Python code.

Notice that all three lines nested under the `while` header line are indented the same amount—because they line up vertically in a column this way, they are the block of code that is associated with the `while` test and repeated. Either the end of the source file or a lesser-indented statement will suffice to terminate the loop body block.

When this code is run, either interactively or as a script file, here is the sort of interaction we get—all of the code for this example is in *interact.py* in the book's examples package:

```
Enter text:spam
SPAM
Enter text:42
42
Enter text:stop
```

Version skew note: This example is coded for Python 3.X. If you are working in Python 2.X, the code works the same, but you must use `raw_input` instead of `input` in all of this chapter's examples, and you can omit the outer parentheses in `print` statements (though they don't hurt). In fact, if you study the *interact.py* file in the examples package, you'll see that it does this automatically—to support 2.X compatibility, it resets `input` if the running Python's major version is 2 ("input" winds up running `raw_input`):

```
import sys
if sys.version[0] == '2': input = raw_input    # 2.X compatible
```

In 3.X, `raw_input` was renamed `input`, and `print` is a built-in function instead of a statement (more on `print`s in the next chapter). Python 2.X has an `input` too, but it tries to evaluate the input string as though it were Python code, which probably won't work in this context; `eval(input())` can yield the same effect 3.X.

Doing Math on User Inputs

Our script works, but now suppose that instead of converting a text string to uppercase, we want to do some math with numeric input—squaring it, for example, perhaps in some misguided effort of an age-input program to tease its users. We might try statements like these to achieve the desired effect:

```
>>> reply = '20'
>>> reply ** 2
...error text omitted...
TypeError: unsupported operand type(s) for ** or pow(): 'str' and 'int'
```

This won't quite work in our script, though, because (as discussed in the prior part of the book) Python won't convert object types in expressions unless they are all numeric, and input from a user is always returned to our script as a *string*. We cannot raise a string of digits to a power unless we convert it manually to an integer:

```
>>> int(reply) ** 2
400
```

Armed with this information, we can now recode our loop to perform the necessary math. Type the following in a file to test it:

```
while True:
    reply = input('Enter text:')
    if reply == 'stop': break
    print(int(reply) ** 2)
print('Bye')
```

This script uses a single-line `if` statement to exit on "stop" as before, but it also converts inputs to perform the required math. This version also adds an exit message at the bottom. Because the print statement in the last line is not indented as much as the nested block of code, it is not considered part of the loop body and will run only once, after the loop is exited:

```
Enter text:2
4
Enter text:40
1600
Enter text:stop
Bye
```

 Usage note: From this point on I'll assume that this code is stored in and run from a script file, via command line, IDLE menu option, or any of the other file launching techniques we met in Chapter 3. Again, it's named *interact.py* in the book's examples. If you are entering this code interactively, though, be sure to include a blank line (i.e., press Enter twice) before the final `print` statement, to terminate the loop. This implies that you also can't cut and paste the code in its entirety into an interactive prompt: an extra blank line is required interactively, but not in script files. The final `print` doesn't quite make sense in interactive mode, though—you'll have to code it after interacting with the loop!

Handling Errors by Testing Inputs

So far so good, but notice what happens when the input is invalid:

```
Enter text:xxx
...error text omitted...
ValueError: invalid literal for int() with base 10: 'xxx'
```

The built-in `int` function raises an exception here in the face of a mistake. If we want our script to be robust, we can check the string's content ahead of time with the string object's `isdigit` method:

```
>>> S = '123'
>>> T = 'xxx'
>>> S.isdigit(), T.isdigit()
(True, False)
```

This also gives us an excuse to further nest the statements in our example. The following new version of our interactive script uses a full-blown `if` statement to work around the exception on errors:

```
while True:
    reply = input('Enter text:')
    if reply == 'stop':
        break
    elif not reply.isdigit():
        print('Bad!' * 8)
    else:
        print(int(reply) ** 2)
print('Bye')
```

We'll study the if statement in more detail in Chapter 12, but it's a fairly lightweight tool for coding logic in scripts. In its full form, it consists of the word if followed by a test and an associated block of code, one or more optional elif ("else if") tests and code blocks, and an optional else part, with an associated block of code at the bottom to serve as a default. Python runs the block of code associated with the first test that is true, working from top to bottom, or the else part if all tests are false.

The if, elif, and else parts in the preceding example are associated as part of the same statement because they all line up vertically (i.e., share the same level of indentation). The if statement spans from the word if to the start of the print statement on the last line of the script. In turn, the entire if block is part of the while loop because all of it is indented under the loop's header line. Statement nesting like this is natural once you get the hang of it.

When we run our new script, its code catches errors before they occur and prints an error message before continuing (which you'll probably want to improve in a later release), but "stop" still gets us out, and valid numbers are still squared:

```
Enter text:5
25
Enter text:xyz
Bad!Bad!Bad!Bad!Bad!Bad!Bad!Bad!
Enter text:10
100
Enter text:stop
Bye
```

Handling Errors with try Statements

The preceding solution works, but as you'll see later in the book, the most general way to handle errors in Python is to catch and recover from them completely using the Python try statement. We'll explore this statement in depth in Part VII of this book, but as a preview, using a try here can lead to code that some would see as simpler than the prior version:

```
while True:
    reply = input('Enter text:')
    if reply == 'stop': break
    try:
        num = int(reply)
    except:
        print('Bad!' * 8)
    else:
        print(num ** 2)
print('Bye')
```

This version works exactly like the previous one, but we've replaced the explicit error check with code that assumes the conversion will work and wraps it in an exception handler for cases when it doesn't. In other words, rather than detecting an error, we simply respond if one occurs.

This `try` statement is another compound statement, and follows the same pattern as `if` and `while`. It's composed of the word `try`, followed by the main block of code (the action we are trying to run), followed by an `except` part that gives the exception handler code and an `else` part to be run if no exception is raised in the `try` part. Python first runs the `try` part, then runs either the `except` part (if an exception occurs) or the `else` part (if no exception occurs).

In terms of statement nesting, because the words `try`, `except`, and `else` are all indented to the same level, they are all considered part of the same single `try` statement. Notice that the `else` part is associated with the `try` here, not the `if`. As we've seen, `else` can appear in `if` statements in Python, but it can also appear in `try` statements and loops —its indentation tells you what statement it is a part of. In this case, the `try` statement spans from the word `try` through the code indented under the word `else`, because the `else` is indented the same as `try`. The `if` statement in this code is a one-liner and ends after the `break`.

Supporting floating-point numbers

Again, we'll come back to the `try` statement later in this book. For now, be aware that because `try` can be used to intercept any error, it reduces the amount of error-checking code you have to write, and it's a very general approach to dealing with unusual cases. If we're sure that print won't fail, for instance, this example could be even more concise:

```
while True:
    reply = input('Enter text:')
    if reply == 'stop': break
    try:
        print(int(reply) ** 2)
    except:
        print('Bad!' * 8)
print('Bye')
```

And if we wanted to support input of floating-point numbers instead of just integers, for example, using `try` would be much easier than manual error testing—we could simply run a `float` call and catch its exceptions:

```
while True:
    reply = input('Enter text:')
    if reply == 'stop': break
    try:
        print(float(reply) ** 2)
    except:
        print('Bad!' * 8)
print('Bye')
```

There is no `isfloat` for strings today, so this exception-based approach spares us from having to analyze all possible floating-point syntax in an explicit error check. When coding this way, we can enter a wider variety of numbers, but errors and exits still work as before:

```
Enter text:50
2500.0
Enter text:40.5
1640.25
Enter text:1.23E-100
1.5129e-200
Enter text:spam
Bad!Bad!Bad!Bad!Bad!Bad!Bad!Bad!
Enter text:stop
Bye
```

 Python's eval call, which we used in Chapter 5 and Chapter 9 to convert data in strings and files, would work in place of float here too, and would allow input of arbitrary expressions ("2 ** 100" would be a legal, if curious, input, especially if we're assuming the program is processing ages!). This is a powerful concept that is open to the same security issues mentioned in the prior chapters. If you can't trust the source of a code string, use more restrictive conversion tools like int and float.

Python's exec, used in Chapter 3 to run code read from a file, is similar to eval (but assumes the string is a statement instead of an expression and has no result), and its compile call precompiles frequently used code strings to bytecode objects for speed. Run a help on any of these for more details; as mentioned, exec is a statement in 2.X but a function in 3.X, so see its manual entry in 2.X instead. We'll also use exec to import modules by name string in Chapter 25—an example of its more dynamic roles.

Nesting Code Three Levels Deep

Let's look at one last mutation of our code. Nesting can take us even further if we need it to—we could, for example, extend our prior integer-only script to branch to one of a set of alternatives based on the relative magnitude of a valid input:

```python
while True:
    reply = input('Enter text:')
    if reply == 'stop':
        break
    elif not reply.isdigit():
        print('Bad!' * 8)
    else:
        num = int(reply)
        if num < 20:
            print('low')
        else:
            print(num ** 2)
print('Bye')
```

This version adds an if statement nested in the else clause of another if statement, which is in turn nested in the while loop. When code is conditional or repeated like this, we simply indent it further to the right. The net effect is like that of prior versions, but we'll now print "low" for numbers less than 20:

```
Enter text:19
low
Enter text:20
400
Enter text:spam
Bad!Bad!Bad!Bad!Bad!Bad!Bad!Bad!
Enter text:stop
Bye
```

Chapter Summary

That concludes our quick look at Python statement syntax. This chapter introduced the general rules for coding statements and blocks of code. As you've learned, in Python we normally code one statement per line and indent all the statements in a nested block the same amount (indentation is part of Python's syntax). However, we also looked at a few exceptions to these rules, including continuation lines and single-line tests and loops. Finally, we put these ideas to work in an interactive script that demonstrated a handful of statements and showed statement syntax in action.

In the next chapter, we'll start to dig deeper by going over each of Python's basic procedural statements in depth. As you'll see, though, all statements follow the same general rules introduced here.

Test Your Knowledge: Quiz

1. What three things are required in a C-like language but omitted in Python?
2. How is a statement normally terminated in Python?
3. How are the statements in a nested block of code normally associated in Python?
4. How can you make a single statement span multiple lines?
5. How can you code a compound statement on a single line?
6. Is there any valid reason to type a semicolon at the end of a statement in Python?
7. What is a try statement for?
8. What is the most common coding mistake among Python beginners?

Test Your Knowledge: Answers

1. C-like languages require parentheses around the tests in some statements, semi-colons at the end of each statement, and braces around a nested block of code.
2. The end of a line terminates the statement that appears on that line. Alternatively, if more than one statement appears on the same line, they can be terminated with

semicolons; similarly, if a statement spans many lines, you must terminate it by closing a bracketed syntactic pair.

3. The statements in a nested block are all indented the same number of tabs or spaces.

4. You can make a statement span many lines by enclosing part of it in parentheses, square brackets, or curly braces; the statement ends when Python sees a line that contains the closing part of the pair.

5. The body of a compound statement can be moved to the header line after the colon, but only if the body consists of only noncompound statements.

6. Only when you need to squeeze more than one statement onto a single line of code. Even then, this only works if all the statements are noncompound, and it's discouraged because it can lead to code that is difficult to read.

7. The **try** statement is used to catch and recover from exceptions (errors) in a Python script. It's usually an alternative to manually checking for errors in your code.

8. Forgetting to type the colon character at the end of the header line in a compound statement is the most common beginner's mistake. If you're new to Python and haven't made it yet, you probably will soon!

Assignments, Expressions, and Prints

Now that we've had a quick introduction to Python statement syntax, this chapter begins our in-depth tour of specific Python statements. We'll begin with the basics: assignment statements, expression statements, and print operations. We've already seen all of these in action, but here we'll fill in important details we've skipped so far. Although they're relatively simple, as you'll see, there are optional variations for each of these statement types that will come in handy once you begin writing realistic Python programs.

Assignment Statements

We've been using the Python assignment statement for a while to assign objects to names. In its basic form, you write the *target* of an assignment on the left of an equals sign, and the *object* to be assigned on the right. The target on the left may be a name or object component, and the object on the right can be an arbitrary expression that computes an object. For the most part, assignments are straightforward, but here are a few properties to keep in mind:

- **Assignments create object references**. As discussed in Chapter 6, Python assignments store references to objects in names or data structure components. They always create references to objects instead of copying the objects. Because of that, Python variables are more like pointers than data storage areas.

- **Names are created when first assigned**. Python creates a variable name the first time you assign it a value (i.e., an object reference), so there's no need to predeclare names ahead of time. Some (but not all) data structure slots are created when assigned, too (e.g., dictionary entries, some object attributes). Once assigned, a name is replaced with the value it references whenever it appears in an expression.

- **Names must be assigned before being referenced**. It's an error to use a name to which you haven't yet assigned a value. Python raises an exception if you try, rather than returning some sort of ambiguous default value. This turns out to be crucial in Python because names are not predeclared—if Python provided default values for unassigned names used in your program instead of treating them as errors, it would be much more difficult for you to spot name typos in your code.

- **Some operations perform assignments implicitly**. In this section we're concerned with the = statement, but assignment occurs in many contexts in Python. For instance, we'll see later that module imports, function and class definitions, for loop variables, and function arguments are all implicit assignments. Because assignment works the same everywhere it pops up, all these contexts simply *bind* (i.e., assign) names to object references at runtime.

Assignment Statement Forms

Although assignment is a general and pervasive concept in Python, we are primarily interested in assignment *statements* in this chapter. Table 11-1 illustrates the different assignment statement forms in Python, and their syntax patterns.

Table 11-1. Assignment statement forms

Operation	Interpretation
spam = 'Spam'	Basic form
spam, ham = 'yum', 'YUM'	Tuple assignment (positional)
[spam, ham] = ['yum', 'YUM']	List assignment (positional)
a, b, c, d = 'spam'	Sequence assignment, generalized
a, *b = 'spam'	Extended sequence unpacking (Python 3.X)
spam = ham = 'lunch'	Multiple-target assignment
spams += 42	Augmented assignment (equivalent to spams = spams + 42)

The first form in Table 11-1 is by far the most common: binding a name (or data structure component) to a single object. In fact, you could get all your work done with this basic form alone. The other table entries represent special forms that are all optional, but that programmers often find convenient in practice:

Tuple- and list-unpacking assignments
> The second and third forms in the table are related. When you code a tuple or list on the left side of the =, Python pairs objects on the right side with targets on the left by position and assigns them from left to right. For example, in the second line of Table 11-1, the name spam is assigned the string 'yum', and the name ham is bound to the string 'YUM'. In this case Python internally may make a tuple of the items on the right, which is why this is called tuple-unpacking assignment.

Sequence assignments
> In later versions of Python, tuple and list assignments were generalized into instances of what we now call *sequence assignment*—any sequence of names can be assigned to any sequence of values, and Python assigns the items one at a time by position. We can even mix and match the types of the sequences involved. The

fourth line in Table 11-1, for example, pairs a tuple of names with a string of characters: a is assigned 's', b is assigned 'p', and so on.

Extended sequence unpacking

In Python 3.X (only), a new form of sequence assignment allows us to be more flexible in how we select portions of a sequence to assign. The fifth line in Table 11-1, for example, matches a with the first character in the string on the right and b with the rest: a is assigned 's', and b is assigned ['p', 'a', 'm']. This provides a simpler alternative to assigning the results of manual slicing operations.

Multiple-target assignments

The sixth line in Table 11-1 shows the multiple-target form of assignment. In this form, Python assigns a reference to the same object (the object farthest to the right) to all the targets on the left. In the table, the names spam and ham are both assigned references to the same string object, 'lunch'. The effect is the same as if we had coded ham = 'lunch' followed by spam = ham, as ham evaluates to the original string object (i.e., not a separate copy of that object).

Augmented assignments

The last line in Table 11-1 is an example of *augmented assignment*—a shorthand that combines an expression and an assignment in a concise way. Saying spam += 42, for example, has the same effect as spam = spam + 42, but the augmented form requires less typing and is generally quicker to run. In addition, if the subject is mutable and supports the operation, an augmented assignment may run even quicker by choosing an in-place update operation instead of an object copy. There is one augmented assignment statement for every binary expression operator in Python.

Sequence Assignments

We've already used and explored basic assignments in this book, so we'll take them as a given. Here are a few simple examples of sequence-unpacking assignments in action:

```
% python
>>> nudge = 1                  # Basic assignment
>>> wink  = 2
>>> A, B = nudge, wink         # Tuple assignment
>>> A, B                       # Like A = nudge; B = wink
(1, 2)
>>> [C, D] = [nudge, wink]     # List assignment
>>> C, D
(1, 2)
```

Notice that we really are coding two tuples in the third line in this interaction—we've just omitted their enclosing parentheses. Python pairs the values in the tuple on the right side of the assignment operator with the variables in the tuple on the left side and assigns the values one at a time.

Tuple assignment leads to a common coding trick in Python that was introduced in a solution to the exercises at the end of Part II. Because Python creates a temporary tuple that saves the original values of the variables on the right while the statement runs, unpacking assignments are also a way to *swap* two variables' values without creating a temporary variable of your own—the tuple on the right remembers the prior values of the variables automatically:

```
>>> nudge = 1
>>> wink  = 2
>>> nudge, wink = wink, nudge     # Tuples: swaps values
>>> nudge, wink                   # Like T = nudge; nudge = wink; wink = T
(2, 1)
```

In fact, the original tuple and list assignment forms in Python have been generalized to accept *any* type of sequence (really, iterable) on the right as long as it is of the same length as the sequence on the left. You can assign a tuple of values to a list of variables, a string of characters to a tuple of variables, and so on. In all cases, Python assigns items in the sequence on the right to variables in the sequence on the left by position, from left to right:

```
>>> [a, b, c] = (1, 2, 3)         # Assign tuple of values to list of names
>>> a, c
(1, 3)
>>> (a, b, c) = "ABC"             # Assign string of characters to tuple
>>> a, c
('A', 'C')
```

Technically speaking, sequence assignment actually supports any *iterable* object on the right, not just any sequence. This is a more general category that includes collections both physical (e.g., lists) and virtual (e.g., a file's lines), which was defined briefly in Chapter 4 and has popped up in passing ever since. We'll firm up this term when we explore iterables in Chapter 14 and Chapter 20.

Advanced sequence assignment patterns

Although we can mix and match sequence types around the = symbol, we must generally have the *same number* of items on the right as we have variables on the left, or we'll get an error. Python 3.X allows us to be more general with extended unpacking * syntax, described in the next section. But normally in 3.X—and always in 2.X—the number of items in the assignment target and subject must match:

```
>>> string = 'SPAM'
>>> a, b, c, d = string           # Same number on both sides
>>> a, d
('S', 'M')

>>> a, b, c = string              # Error if not
...error text omitted...
ValueError: too many values to unpack (expected 3)
```

To be more flexible, we can slice in both 2.X and 3.X. There are a variety of ways to employ slicing to make this last case work:

```
>>> a, b, c = string[0], string[1], string[2:]    # Index and slice
>>> a, b, c
('S', 'P', 'AM')

>>> a, b, c = list(string[:2]) + [string[2:]]    # Slice and concatenate
>>> a, b, c
('S', 'P', 'AM')

>>> a, b = string[:2]                             # Same, but simpler
>>> c = string[2:]
>>> a, b, c
('S', 'P', 'AM')

>>> (a, b), c = string[:2], string[2:]            # Nested sequences
>>> a, b, c
('S', 'P', 'AM')
```

As the last example in this interaction demonstrates, we can even assign *nested* sequences, and Python unpacks their parts according to their shape, as expected. In this case, we are assigning a tuple of two items, where the first item is a nested sequence (a string), exactly as though we had coded it this way:

```
>>> ((a, b), c) = ('SP', 'AM')                    # Paired by shape and position
>>> a, b, c
('S', 'P', 'AM')
```

Python pairs the first string on the right ('SP') with the first tuple on the left ((a, b)) and assigns one character at a time, before assigning the entire second string ('AM') to the variable c all at once. In this event, the sequence-nesting shape of the object on the left must match that of the object on the right. Nested sequence assignment like this is somewhat rare to see, but it can be convenient for picking out the parts of data structures with known shapes.

For example, we'll see in Chapter 13 that this technique also works in **for** loops, because loop items are assigned to the target given in the loop header:

```
for (a, b, c) in [(1, 2, 3), (4, 5, 6)]: ...      # Simple tuple assignment

for ((a, b), c) in [((1, 2), 3), ((4, 5), 6)]: ... # Nested tuple assignment
```

In a note in Chapter 18, we'll also see that this nested tuple (really, sequence) unpacking assignment form works for function argument lists in Python 2.X (though not in 3.X), because function arguments are passed by assignment as well:

```
def f(((a, b), c)): ...        # For arguments too in Python 2.X, but not 3.X
f(((1, 2), 3))
```

Sequence-unpacking assignments also give rise to another common coding idiom in Python—assigning an integer series to a set of variables:

```
>>> red, green, blue = range(3)
>>> red, blue
(0, 2)
```

This initializes the three names to the integer codes 0, 1, and 2, respectively (it's Python's equivalent of the *enumerated* data types you may have seen in other languages). To make sense of this, you need to know that the `range` built-in function generates a list of successive integers (in 3.X only, it requires a `list` around it if you wish to display its values all at once like this):

```
>>> list(range(3))                    # list() required in Python 3.X only
[0, 1, 2]
```

This call was previewed briefly in Chapter 4; because `range` is commonly used in `for` loops, we'll say more about it in Chapter 13.

Another place you may see a tuple assignment at work is for splitting a sequence into its front and the rest in loops like this:

```
>>> L = [1, 2, 3, 4]
>>> while L:
...     front, L = L[0], L[1:]        # See next section for 3.X * alternative
...     print(front, L)
...
1 [2, 3, 4]
2 [3, 4]
3 [4]
4 []
```

The tuple assignment in the loop here could be coded as the following two lines instead, but it's often more convenient to string them together:

```
...     front = L[0]
...     L = L[1:]
```

Notice that this code is using the list as a sort of stack data structure, which can often also be achieved with the `append` and `pop` methods of list objects; here, `front = L.pop(0)` would have much the same effect as the tuple assignment statement, but it would be an in-place change. We'll learn more about `while` loops, and other (often better) ways to step through a sequence with `for` loops, in Chapter 13.

Extended Sequence Unpacking in Python 3.X

The prior section demonstrated how to use manual slicing to make sequence assignments more general. In Python 3.X (but not 2.X), sequence assignment has been generalized to make this easier. In short, a single *starred name*, *X, can be used in the assignment target in order to specify a more general matching against the sequence—the starred name is assigned a list, which collects all items in the sequence not assigned to other names. This is especially handy for common coding patterns such as splitting a sequence into its "front" and "rest," as in the preceding section's last example.

Extended unpacking in action

Let's look at an example. As we've seen, sequence assignments normally require exactly as many names in the target on the left as there are items in the subject on the right. We get an error if the lengths disagree in both 2.X and 3.X (unless we manually sliced on the right, as shown in the prior section):

```
C:\code> c:\python33\python
>>> seq = [1, 2, 3, 4]

>>> a, b, c, d = seq
>>> print(a, b, c, d)
1 2 3 4

>>> a, b = seq
ValueError: too many values to unpack (expected 2)
```

In Python 3.X, though, we can use a single starred name in the target to match more generally. In the following continuation of our interactive session, a matches the first item in the sequence, and b matches the rest:

```
>>> a, *b = seq
>>> a
1
>>> b
[2, 3, 4]
```

When a starred name is used, the number of items in the target on the left need not match the length of the subject sequence. In fact, the starred name can appear anywhere in the target. For instance, in the next interaction b matches the last item in the sequence, and a matches everything before the last:

```
>>> *a, b = seq
>>> a
[1, 2, 3]
>>> b
4
```

When the starred name appears in the middle, it collects everything between the other names listed. Thus, in the following interaction a and c are assigned the first and last items, and b gets everything in between them:

```
>>> a, *b, c = seq
>>> a
1
>>> b
[2, 3]
>>> c
4
```

More generally, wherever the starred name shows up, it will be assigned a list that collects every unassigned name at that position:

```
>>> a, b, *c = seq
>>> a
```

```
1
>>> b
2
>>> c
[3, 4]
```

Naturally, like normal sequence assignment, extended sequence unpacking syntax works for any sequence types (really, again, any *iterable*), not just lists. Here it is unpacking characters in a string and a `range` (an iterable in 3.X):

```
>>> a, *b = 'spam'
>>> a, b
('s', ['p', 'a', 'm'])

>>> a, *b, c = 'spam'
>>> a, b, c
('s', ['p', 'a'], 'm')

>>> a, *b, c = range(4)
>>> a, b, c
(0, [1, 2], 3)
```

This is similar in spirit to slicing, but not exactly the same—a sequence unpacking assignment always returns a *list* for multiple matched items, whereas slicing returns a sequence of the same type as the object sliced:

```
>>> S = 'spam'

>>> S[0], S[1:]        # Slices are type-specific, * assignment always returns a list
('s', 'pam')

>>> S[0], S[1:3], S[3]
('s', 'pa', 'm')
```

Given this extension in 3.X, as long as we're processing a list the last example of the prior section becomes even simpler, since we don't have to manually slice to get the first and rest of the items:

```
>>> L = [1, 2, 3, 4]
>>> while L:
...     front, *L = L              # Get first, rest without slicing
...     print(front, L)
...
1 [2, 3, 4]
2 [3, 4]
3 [4]
4 []
```

Boundary cases

Although extended sequence unpacking is flexible, some boundary cases are worth noting. First, the starred name may match just a single item, but is always assigned a list:

```
>>> seq = [1, 2, 3, 4]
```

```
>>> a, b, c, *d = seq
>>> print(a, b, c, d)
1 2 3 [4]
```

Second, if there is nothing left to match the starred name, it is assigned an empty list, regardless of where it appears. In the following, a, b, c, and d have matched every item in the sequence, but Python assigns e an empty list instead of treating this as an error case:

```
>>> a, b, c, d, *e = seq
>>> print(a, b, c, d, e)
1 2 3 4 []

>>> a, b, *e, c, d = seq
>>> print(a, b, c, d, e)
1 2 3 4 []
```

Finally, errors can still be triggered if there is more than one starred name, if there are too few values and no star (as before), and if the starred name is not itself coded inside a sequence:

```
>>> a, *b, c, *d = seq
SyntaxError: two starred expressions in assignment

>>> a, b = seq
ValueError: too many values to unpack (expected 2)

>>> *a = seq
SyntaxError: starred assignment target must be in a list or tuple

>>> *a, = seq
>>> a
[1, 2, 3, 4]
```

A useful convenience

Keep in mind that extended sequence unpacking assignment is just a convenience. We can usually achieve the same effects with explicit indexing and slicing (and in fact must in Python 2.X), but extended unpacking is simpler to code. The common "first, rest" splitting coding pattern, for example, can be coded either way, but slicing involves extra work:

```
>>> seq
[1, 2, 3, 4]

>>> a, *b = seq                      # First, rest
>>> a, b
(1, [2, 3, 4])

>>> a, b = seq[0], seq[1:]           # First, rest: traditional
>>> a, b
(1, [2, 3, 4])
```

The also-common "rest, last" splitting pattern can similarly be coded either way, but the new extended unpacking syntax requires noticeably fewer keystrokes:

```
>>> *a, b = seq                    # Rest, last
>>> a, b
([1, 2, 3], 4)

>>> a, b = seq[:-1], seq[-1]       # Rest, last: traditional
>>> a, b
([1, 2, 3], 4)
```

Because it is not only simpler but, arguably, more natural, extended sequence unpacking syntax will likely become widespread in Python code over time.

Application to for loops

Because the loop variable in the for loop statement can be any assignment target, extended sequence assignment works here too. We met the for loop iteration tool briefly in Chapter 4 and will study it formally in Chapter 13. In Python 3.X, extended assignments may show up after the word for, where a simple variable name is more commonly used:

```
for (a, *b, c) in [(1, 2, 3, 4), (5, 6, 7, 8)]:
    ...
```

When used in this context, on each iteration Python simply assigns the next tuple of values to the tuple of names. On the first loop, for example, it's as if we'd run the following assignment statement:

```
a, *b, c = (1, 2, 3, 4)            # b gets [2, 3]
```

The names a, b, and c can be used within the loop's code to reference the extracted components. In fact, this is really not a special case at all, but just an instance of general assignment at work. As we saw earlier in this chapter, we can do the same thing with simple tuple assignment in both Python 2.X and 3.X:

```
for (a, b, c) in [(1, 2, 3), (4, 5, 6)]:       # a, b, c = (1, 2, 3), ...
```

And we can always emulate 3.X's extended assignment behavior in 2.X by manually slicing:

```
for all in [(1, 2, 3, 4), (5, 6, 7, 8)]:
    a, b, c = all[0], all[1:3], all[3]
```

Since we haven't learned enough to get more detailed about the syntax of for loops, we'll return to this topic in Chapter 13.

Multiple-Target Assignments

A multiple-target assignment simply assigns all the given names to the object all the way to the right. The following, for example, assigns the three variables a, b, and c to the string 'spam':

```
>>> a = b = c = 'spam'
>>> a, b, c
('spam', 'spam', 'spam')
```

This form is equivalent to (but easier to code than) these three assignments:

```
>>> c = 'spam'
>>> b = c
>>> a = b
```

Multiple-target assignment and shared references

Keep in mind that there is just one object here, shared by all three variables (they all wind up pointing to the same object in memory). This behavior is fine for immutable types—for example, when initializing a set of counters to zero (recall that variables must be assigned before they can be used in Python, so you must initialize counters to zero before you can start adding to them):

```
>>> a = b = 0
>>> b = b + 1
>>> a, b
(0, 1)
```

Here, changing b only changes b because numbers do not support in-place changes. As long as the object assigned is immutable, it's irrelevant if more than one name references it.

As usual, though, we have to be more cautious when initializing variables to an empty mutable object such as a list or dictionary:

```
>>> a = b = []
>>> b.append(42)
>>> a, b
([42], [42])
```

This time, because a and b reference the same object, appending to it in place through b will impact what we see through a as well. This is really just another example of the shared reference phenomenon we first met in Chapter 6. To avoid the issue, initialize mutable objects in separate statements instead, so that each creates a distinct empty object by running a distinct literal expression:

```
>>> a = []
>>> b = []                  # a and b do not share the same object
>>> b.append(42)
>>> a, b
([], [42])
```

A tuple assignment like the following has the same effect—by running two list expressions, it creates two distinct objects:

```
>>> a, b = [], []           # a and b do not share the same object
```

Augmented Assignments

Beginning with Python 2.0, the set of additional assignment statement formats listed in Table 11-2 became available. Known as *augmented assignments*, and borrowed from the C language, these formats are mostly just shorthand. They imply the combination of a binary expression and an assignment. For instance, the following two formats are roughly equivalent:

```
X = X + Y                           # Traditional form
X += Y                              # Newer augmented form
```

Table 11-2. Augmented assignment statements

X += Y	X &= Y	X -= Y	X |= Y
X *= Y	X ^= Y	X /= Y	X >>= Y
X %= Y	X <<= Y	X **= Y	X //= Y

Augmented assignment works on any type that supports the implied binary expression. For example, here are two ways to add 1 to a name:

```
>>> x = 1
>>> x = x + 1                       # Traditional
>>> x
2
>>> x += 1                          # Augmented
>>> x
3
```

When applied to a sequence such as a string, the augmented form performs concatenation instead. Thus, the second line here is equivalent to typing the longer S = S + "SPAM":

```
>>> S = "spam"
>>> S += "SPAM"                     # Implied concatenation
>>> S
'spamSPAM'
```

As shown in Table 11-2, there are analogous augmented assignment forms for every Python binary expression operator (i.e., each operator with values on the left and right side). For instance, X *= Y multiplies and assigns, X >>= Y shifts right and assigns, and so on. X //= Y (for floor division) was added in version 2.2.

Augmented assignments have three advantages:[1]

- There's less for you to type. Need I say more?
- The left side has to be evaluated only once. In X += Y, X may be a complicated object expression. In the augmented form, its code must be run only once. However, in

---

1. C/C++ programmers take note: although Python now supports statements like X += Y, it still does not have C's auto-increment/decrement operators (e.g., X++, --X). These don't quite map to the Python object model because Python has no notion of *in-place* changes to immutable objects like numbers.

the long form, X = X + Y, X appears twice and must be run twice. Because of this, augmented assignments usually run faster.

- The optimal technique is automatically chosen. That is, for objects that support in-place changes, the augmented forms automatically perform in-place change operations instead of slower copies.

The last point here requires a bit more explanation. For augmented assignments, in-place operations may be applied for mutable objects as an optimization. Recall that lists can be extended in a variety of ways. To add a single item to the end of a list, we can concatenate or call append:

```
>>> L = [1, 2]
>>> L = L + [3]              # Concatenate: slower
>>> L
[1, 2, 3]
>>> L.append(4)             # Faster, but in place
>>> L
[1, 2, 3, 4]
```

And to add a set of items to the end, we can either concatenate again or call the list extend method:[2]

```
>>> L = L + [5, 6]          # Concatenate: slower
>>> L
[1, 2, 3, 4, 5, 6]
>>> L.extend([7, 8])        # Faster, but in place
>>> L
[1, 2, 3, 4, 5, 6, 7, 8]
```

In both cases, concatenation is less prone to the side effects of shared object references but will generally run slower than the in-place equivalent. Concatenation operations must create a new object, copy in the list on the left, and then copy in the list on the right. By contrast, in-place method calls simply add items at the end of a memory block (it can be a bit more complicated than that internally, but this description suffices).

When we use augmented assignment to extend a list, we can largely forget these details —Python automatically calls the quicker extend method instead of using the slower concatenation operation implied by +:

```
>>> L += [9, 10]            # Mapped to L.extend([9, 10])
>>> L
[1, 2, 3, 4, 5, 6, 7, 8, 9, 10]
```

Note however, that because of this equivalence += for a list is not exactly the same as a + and = in all cases—for lists += allows arbitrary sequences (just like extend), but concatenation normally does not:

```
>>> L = []
>>> L += 'spam'             # += and extend allow any sequence, but + does not!
```

---

2. As suggested in Chapter 6, we can also use slice assignment (e.g., L[len(L):] = [11,12,13]), but this works roughly the same as the simpler and more mnemonic list extend method.

```
>>> L
['s', 'p', 'a', 'm']
>>> L = L + 'spam'
TypeError: can only concatenate list (not "str") to list
```

Augmented assignment and shared references

This behavior is usually what we want, but notice that it implies that the += is an *in-place* change for lists; thus, it is not exactly like + concatenation, which always makes a *new* object. As for all shared reference cases, this difference might matter if other names reference the object being changed:

```
>>> L = [1, 2]
>>> M = L                    # L and M reference the same object
>>> L = L + [3, 4]           # Concatenation makes a new object
>>> L, M                     # Changes L but not M
([1, 2, 3, 4], [1, 2])

>>> L = [1, 2]
>>> M = L
>>> L += [3, 4]              # But += really means extend
>>> L, M                     # M sees the in-place change too!
([1, 2, 3, 4], [1, 2, 3, 4])
```

This only matters for mutables like lists and dictionaries, and it is a fairly obscure case (at least, until it impacts your code!). As always, make copies of your mutable objects if you need to break the shared reference structure.

Variable Name Rules

Now that we've explored assignment statements, it's time to get more formal about the use of variable names. In Python, names come into existence when you assign values to them, but there are a few rules to follow when choosing names for the subjects of your programs:

Syntax: (underscore or letter) + (any number of letters, digits, or underscores)
>   Variable names must start with an underscore or letter, which can be followed by any number of letters, digits, or underscores. _spam, spam, and Spam_1 are legal names, but 1_Spam, spam$, and @#! are not.

Case matters: SPAM *is not the same as* spam
>   Python always pays attention to case in programs, both in names you create and in reserved words. For instance, the names X and x refer to two different variables. For portability, case also matters in the names of imported module files, even on platforms where the filesystems are case-insensitive. That way, your imports still work after programs are copied to differing platforms.

Reserved words are off-limits
>   Names you define cannot be the same as words that mean special things in the Python language. For instance, if you try to use a variable name like class, Python

will raise a syntax error, but `klass` and `Class` work fine. Table 11-3 lists the words that are currently reserved (and hence off-limits for names of your own) in Python.

Table 11-3. Python 3.X reserved words

False	class	finally	is	return
None	continue	for	lambda	try
True	def	from	nonlocal	while
and	del	global	not	with
as	elif	if	or	yield
assert	else	import	pass	
break	except	in	raise	

Table 11-3 is specific to Python 3.X. In Python 2.X, the set of reserved words differs slightly:

- `print` is a reserved word, because printing is a statement, not a built-in function (more on this later in this chapter).
- `exec` is a reserved word, because it is a statement, not a built-in function.
- `nonlocal` is not a reserved word because this statement is not available.

In older Pythons the story is also more or less the same, with a few variations:

- `with` and `as` were not reserved until 2.6, when context managers were officially enabled.
- `yield` was not reserved until Python 2.3, when generator functions came online.
- `yield` morphed from statement to expression in 2.5, but it's still a reserved word, not a built-in function.

As you can see, most of Python's reserved words are all lowercase. They are also all truly reserved—unlike names in the built-in scope that you will meet in the next part of this book, you cannot redefine reserved words by assignment (e.g., `and = 1` results in a syntax error).[3]

Besides being of mixed case, the first three entries in Table 11-3, `True`, `False`, and `None`, are somewhat unusual in meaning—they also appear in the built-in scope of Python described in Chapter 17, and they are technically names assigned to objects. In 3.X they are truly reserved in all other senses, though, and cannot be used for any other purpose in your script other than that of the objects they represent. All the other reserved words are hardwired into Python's syntax and can appear only in the specific contexts for which they are intended.

---

3. In standard CPython, at least. Alternative implementations of Python might allow user-defined variable names to be the same as Python reserved words. See Chapter 2 for an overview of alternative implementations, such as Jython.

Furthermore, because module names in `import` statements become variables in your scripts, variable name constraints extend to your *module filenames* too. For instance, you can code files called *and.py* and *my-code.py* and run them as top-level scripts, but you cannot import them: their names without the ".py" extension become *variables* in your code and so must follow all the variable rules just outlined. Reserved words are off-limits, and dashes won't work, though underscores will. We'll revisit this module idea in Part V of this book.

Python's Deprecation Protocol

It is interesting to note how reserved word changes are gradually phased into the language. When a new feature might break existing code, Python normally makes it an option and begins issuing "deprecation" warnings one or more releases before the feature is officially enabled. The idea is that you should have ample time to notice the warnings and update your code before migrating to the new release. This is not true for major new releases like 3.0 (which breaks existing code freely), but it is generally true in other cases.

For example, `yield` was an optional extension in Python 2.2, but is a standard keyword as of 2.3. It is used in conjunction with generator functions. This was one of a small handful of instances where Python broke with backward compatibility. Still, `yield` was phased in over time: it began generating deprecation warnings in 2.2 and was not enabled until 2.3.

Similarly, in Python 2.6, the words `with` and `as` become new reserved words for use in context managers (a newer form of exception handling). These two words are not reserved in 2.5, unless the context manager feature is turned on manually with a `from__future__`import (discussed later in this book). When used in 2.5, `with` and `as` generate warnings about the upcoming change—except in the version of IDLE in Python 2.5, which appears to have enabled this feature for you (that is, using these words as variable names does generate errors in 2.5, but only in its version of the IDLE GUI).

Naming conventions

Besides these rules, there is also a set of naming *conventions*—rules that are not required but are followed in normal practice. For instance, because names with two leading and trailing underscores (e.g., __name__) generally have special meaning to the Python interpreter, you should avoid this pattern for your own names. Here is a list of the conventions Python follows:

- Names that begin with a single underscore (_X) are not imported by a `from module import *` statement (described in Chapter 23).
- Names that have two leading and trailing underscores (__X__) are system-defined names that have special meaning to the interpreter.

- Names that begin with two underscores and do not end with two more (__X) are localized ("mangled") to enclosing classes (see the discussion of pseudoprivate attributes in Chapter 31).

- The name that is just a single underscore (_) retains the result of the last expression when you are working interactively.

In addition to these Python interpreter conventions, there are various other conventions that Python programmers usually follow. For instance, later in the book we'll see that class names commonly start with an uppercase letter and module names with a lowercase letter, and that the name `self`, though not reserved, usually has a special role in classes. In Chapter 17 we'll also study another, larger category of names known as the *built-ins*, which are predefined but not reserved (and so can be reassigned: `open` = `42` works, though sometimes you might wish it didn't!).

Names have no type, but objects do

This is mostly review, but remember that it's crucial to keep Python's distinction between names and objects clear. As described in Chapter 6, objects have a type (e.g., integer, list) and may be mutable or not. Names (a.k.a. variables), on the other hand, are always just references to objects; they have no notion of mutability and have no associated type information, apart from the type of the object they happen to reference at a given point in time.

Thus, it's OK to assign the same name to different kinds of objects at different times:

```
>>> x = 0            # x bound to an integer object
>>> x = "Hello"      # Now it's a string
>>> x = [1, 2, 3]    # And now it's a list
```

In later examples, you'll see that this generic nature of names can be a decided advantage in Python programming. In Chapter 17, you'll also learn that names also live in something called a *scope*, which defines where they can be used; the place where you assign a name determines where it is visible.[4]

 For additional naming suggestions, see the discussion of naming conventions in Python's semi-official style guide, known as *PEP 8*. This guide is available at *http://www.python.org/dev/peps/pep-0008*, or via a web search for "Python PEP 8." Technically, this document formalizes coding standards for Python library code.

Though useful, the usual caveats about coding standards apply here. For one thing, PEP 8 comes with more detail than you are probably ready

---

4. If you've used a more restrictive language like C++, you may be interested to know that there is no notion of C++'s `const` declaration in Python; certain objects may be *immutable*, but names can always be assigned. Python also has ways to hide names in classes and modules, but they're not the same as C++'s declarations (if hiding attributes matters to you, see the coverage of _X module names in Chapter 25, __X class names in Chapter 31, and the Private and Public class decorators example in Chapter 39).

for at this point in the book. And frankly, it has become more complex, rigid, and subjective than it may need to be—some of its suggestions are not at all universally accepted or followed by Python programmers doing real work. Moreover, some of the most prominent companies using Python today have adopted coding standards of their own that differ.

PEP 8 does codify useful rule-of-thumb Python knowledge, though, and it's a great read for Python beginners, as long as you take its recommendations as guidelines, not gospel.

Expression Statements

In Python, you can use an expression as a statement, too—that is, on a line by itself. But because the result of the expression won't be saved, it usually makes sense to do so only if the expression does something useful as a side effect. Expressions are commonly used as statements in two situations:

For calls to functions and methods
> Some functions and methods do their work without returning a value. Such functions are sometimes called *procedures* in other languages. Because they don't return values that you might be interested in retaining, you can call these functions with expression statements.

For printing values at the interactive prompt
> Python echoes back the results of expressions typed at the interactive command line. Technically, these are expression statements, too; they serve as a shorthand for typing `print` statements.

Table 11-4 lists some common expression statement forms in Python. Calls to functions and methods are coded with zero or more argument objects (really, expressions that evaluate to objects) in parentheses, after the function/method name.

Table 11-4. Common Python expression statements

Operation	Interpretation
`spam(eggs, ham)`	Function calls
`spam.ham(eggs)`	Method calls
`spam`	Printing variables in the interactive interpreter
`print(a, b, c, sep='')`	Printing operations in Python 3.X
`yield x ** 2`	Yielding expression statements

The last two entries in Table 11-4 are somewhat special cases—as we'll see later in this chapter, printing in Python 3.X is a function call usually coded on a line by itself, and the `yield` operation in generator functions (discussed in Chapter 20) is often coded as a statement as well. Both are really just instances of expression statements.

For instance, though you normally run a 3.X `print` call on a line by itself as an expression statement, it returns a value like any other function call (its return value is `None`, the default return value for functions that don't return anything meaningful):

```
>>> x = print('spam')       # print is a function call expression in 3.X
spam
>>> print(x)                # But it is coded as an expression statement
None
```

Also keep in mind that although expressions can appear as statements in Python, statements cannot be used as expressions. A statement that is not an expression must generally appear on a line all by itself, not nested in a larger syntactic structure. For example, Python doesn't allow you to embed assignment statements (=) in other expressions. The rationale for this is that it avoids common coding mistakes; you can't accidentally change a variable by typing = when you really mean to use the == equality test. You'll see how to code around this restriction when you meet the Python `while` loop in Chapter 13.

Expression Statements and In-Place Changes

This brings up another mistake that is common in Python work. Expression statements are often used to run list methods that change a list in place:

```
>>> L = [1, 2]
>>> L.append(3)             # Append is an in-place change
>>> L
[1, 2, 3]
```

However, it's not unusual for Python newcomers to code such an operation as an assignment statement instead, intending to assign L to the larger list:

```
>>> L = L.append(4)         # But append returns None, not L
>>> print(L)                # So we lose our list!
None
```

This doesn't quite work, though. Calling an in-place change operation such as `append`, `sort`, or `reverse` on a list always changes the list in place, but these methods do not return the list they have changed; instead, they return the `None` object. Thus, if you assign such an operation's result back to the variable name, you effectively lose the list (and it is probably garbage-collected in the process!).

The moral of the story is, don't do this—call in-place change operations without assigning their results. We'll revisit this phenomenon in the section "Common Coding Gotchas" on page 463 because it can also appear in the context of some looping statements we'll meet in later chapters.

Print Operations

In Python, `print` prints things—it's simply a programmer-friendly interface to the standard output stream.

Technically, printing converts one or more objects to their textual representations, adds some minor formatting, and sends the resulting text to either standard output or another file-like stream. In a bit more detail, `print` is strongly bound up with the notions of files and streams in Python:

File object methods

In Chapter 9, we learned about file object methods that write text (e.g., `file.write(str)`). Printing operations are similar, but more focused—whereas file write methods write strings to arbitrary files, `print` writes objects to the `stdout` stream by default, with some automatic formatting added. Unlike with file methods, there is no need to convert objects to strings when using print operations.

Standard output stream

The standard output stream (often known as `stdout`) is simply a default place to send a program's text output. Along with the standard input and error streams, it's one of three data connections created when your script starts. The standard output stream is usually mapped to the window where you started your Python program, unless it's been redirected to a file or pipe in your operating system's shell.

Because the standard output stream is available in Python as the `stdout` file object in the built-in `sys` module (i.e., `sys.stdout`), it's possible to emulate `print` with file write method calls. However, `print` is noticeably easier to use and makes it easy to print text to other files and streams.

Printing is also one of the most visible places where Python 3.X and 2.X have diverged. In fact, this divergence is usually the first reason that most 2.X code won't run unchanged under 3.X. Specifically, the way you code print operations depends on which version of Python you use:

- In Python 3.X, printing is a *built-in function*, with keyword arguments for special modes.
- In Python 2.X, printing is a *statement* with specific syntax all its own.

Because this book covers both 3.X and 2.X, we will look at each form in turn here. If you are fortunate enough to be able to work with code written for just one version of Python, feel free to pick the section that is relevant to you. Because your needs may change, however, it probably won't hurt to be familiar with both cases. Moreover, users of recent Python 2.X releases can also import and use 3.X's flavor of printing in their Pythons if desired—both for its extra functionality and to ease future migration to 3.X.

The Python 3.X print Function

Strictly speaking, printing is not a separate statement form in 3.X. Instead, it is simply an instance of the *expression statement* we studied in the preceding section.

The print built-in function is normally called on a line of its own, because it doesn't return any value we care about (technically, it returns None, as we saw in the preceding section). Because it is a normal function, though, printing in 3.X uses *standard function-call syntax*, rather than a special statement form. And because it provides special operation modes with keyword arguments, this form is both more general and supports future enhancements better.

By comparison, Python 2.X print statements have somewhat ad hoc syntax to support extensions such as end-of-line suppression and target files. Further, the 2.X statement does not support separator specification at all; in 2.X, you wind up building strings ahead of time more often than you do in 3.X. Rather than adding yet more ad hoc syntax, Python 3.X's print takes a single, general approach that covers them all.

Call format

Syntactically, calls to the 3.X print function have the following form (the flush argument is new as of Python 3.3):

```
print([object, ...][, sep=' '][, end='\n'][, file=sys.stdout][, flush=False])
```

In this formal notation, items in square brackets are optional and may be omitted in a given call, and values after = give argument defaults. In English, this built-in function prints the textual representation of one or more objects separated by the string sep and followed by the string end to the stream file, flushing buffered output or not per flush.

The sep, end, file, and (in 3.3 and later) flush parts, if present, must be given as *keyword arguments*—that is, you must use a special "name=value" syntax to pass the arguments by name instead of position. Keyword arguments are covered in depth in Chapter 18, but they're straightforward to use. The keyword arguments sent to this call may appear in any left-to-right order following the objects to be printed, and they control the print operation:

- sep is a string inserted between each object's text, which defaults to a single space if not passed; passing an empty string suppresses separators altogether.

- end is a string added at the end of the printed text, which defaults to a \n newline character if not passed. Passing an empty string avoids dropping down to the next output line at the end of the printed text—the next print will keep adding to the end of the current output line.

- file specifies the file, standard stream, or other file-like object to which the text will be sent; it defaults to the sys.stdout standard output stream if not passed. Any object with a file-like write(*string*) method may be passed, but real files should be already opened for output.

- `flush`, added in 3.3, defaults to `False`. It allows prints to mandate that their text be flushed through the output stream immediately to any waiting recipients. Normally, whether printed output is buffered in memory or not is determined by `file`; passing a true value to `flush` forcibly flushes the stream.

The textual representation of each `object` to be printed is obtained by passing the object to the `str` built-in call (or its equivalent inside Python); as we've seen, this built-in returns a "user friendly" display string for any object.[5] With no arguments at all, the `print` function simply prints a newline character to the standard output stream, which usually displays a blank line.

The 3.X print function in action

Printing in 3.X is probably simpler than some of its details may imply. To illustrate, let's run some quick examples. The following prints a variety of object types to the default standard output stream, with the default separator and end-of-line formatting added (these are the defaults because they are the most common use case):

```
C:\code> c:\python33\python
>>> print()                                    # Display a blank line

>>> x = 'spam'
>>> y = 99
>>> z = ['eggs']
>>>
>>> print(x, y, z)                             # Print three objects per defaults
spam 99 ['eggs']
```

There's no need to convert objects to strings here, as would be required for file write methods. By default, `print` calls add a space between the objects printed. To suppress this, send an empty string to the `sep` keyword argument, or send an alternative separator of your choosing:

```
>>> print(x, y, z, sep='')                     # Suppress separator
spam99['eggs']
>>>
>>> print(x, y, z, sep=', ')                   # Custom separator
spam, 99, ['eggs']
```

Also by default, `print` adds an end-of-line character to terminate the output line. You can suppress this and avoid the line break altogether by passing an empty string to the `end` keyword argument, or you can pass a different terminator of your own including a `\n` character to break the line manually if desired (the second of the following is two statements on one line, separated by a semicolon):

---

5. Technically, printing uses the equivalent of `str` in the internal implementation of Python, but the effect is the same. Besides this to-string conversion role, `str` is also the name of the string data type and can be used to decode Unicode strings from raw bytes with an extra encoding argument, as we'll learn in Chapter 37; this latter role is an advanced usage that we can safely ignore here.

```
>>> print(x, y, z, end='')                      # Suppress line break
spam 99 ['eggs']>>>
>>>
>>> print(x, y, z, end=''); print(x, y, z)       # Two prints, same output line
spam 99 ['eggs']spam 99 ['eggs']
>>> print(x, y, z, end='...\n')                  # Custom line end
spam 99 ['eggs']...
>>>
```

You can also combine keyword arguments to specify both separators and end-of-line strings—they may appear in any order but must appear after all the objects being printed:

```
>>> print(x, y, z, sep='...', end='!\n')         # Multiple keywords
spam...99...['eggs']!
>>> print(x, y, z, end='!\n', sep='...')         # Order doesn't matter
spam...99...['eggs']!
```

Here is how the `file` keyword argument is used—it directs the printed text to an open output file or other compatible object for the duration of the single `print` (this is really a form of stream redirection, a topic we will revisit later in this section):

```
>>> print(x, y, z, sep='...', file=open('data.txt', 'w'))   # Print to a file
>>> print(x, y, z)                                          # Back to stdout
spam 99 ['eggs']
>>> print(open('data.txt').read())                          # Display file text
spam...99...['eggs']
```

Finally, keep in mind that the separator and end-of-line options provided by print operations are just conveniences. If you need to display more specific formatting, don't print this way. Instead, build up a more complex string ahead of time or within the `print` itself using the string tools we met in Chapter 7, and print the string all at once:

```
>>> text = '%s: %-.4f, %05d' % ('Result', 3.14159, 42)
>>> print(text)
Result: 3.1416, 00042
>>> print('%s: %-.4f, %05d' % ('Result', 3.14159, 42))
Result: 3.1416, 00042
```

As we'll see in the next section, almost everything we've just seen about the 3.X `print` function also applies directly to 2.X `print` statements—which makes sense, given that the function was intended to both emulate and improve upon 2.X printing support.

The Python 2.X print Statement

As mentioned earlier, printing in Python 2.X uses a statement with unique and specific syntax, rather than a built-in function. In practice, though, 2.X printing is mostly a variation on a theme; with the exception of separator strings (which are supported in 3.X but not 2.X) and flushes on prints (available as of 3.3 only), everything we can do with the 3.X `print` function has a direct translation to the 2.X `print` statement.

Statement forms

Table 11-5 lists the `print` statement's forms in Python 2.X and gives their Python 3.X `print` function equivalents for reference. Notice that the *comma* is significant in `print` statements—it separates objects to be printed, and a trailing comma suppresses the end-of-line character normally added at the end of the printed text (not to be confused with tuple syntax!). The `>>` syntax, normally used as a bitwise right-shift operation, is used here as well, to specify a target output stream other than the `sys.stdout` default.

Table 11-5. Python 2.X print statement forms

Python 2.X statement	Python 3.X equivalent	Interpretation
`print x, y`	`print(x, y)`	Print objects' textual forms to `sys.stdout`; add a space between the items and an end-of-line at the end
`print x, y,`	`print(x, y, end='')`	Same, but don't add end-of-line at end of text
`print >> afile, x, y`	`print(x, y, file=afile)`	Send text to `afile.write`, not to `sys.stdout.write`

The 2.X print statement in action

Although the 2.X `print` statement has more unique syntax than the 3.X function, it's similarly easy to use. Let's turn to some basic examples again. The 2.X `print` statement adds a space between the items separated by commas and by default adds a line break at the end of the current output line:

```
C:\code> c:\python27\python
>>> x = 'a'
>>> y = 'b'
>>> print x, y
a b
```

This formatting is just a default; you can choose to use it or not. To suppress the line break so you can add more text to the current line later, end your `print` statement with a comma, as shown in the second line of Table 11-5 (the following uses a semicolon to separate two statements on one line again):

```
>>> print x, y,; print x, y
a b a b
```

To suppress the space between items, again, don't print this way. Instead, build up an output string using the string concatenation and formatting tools covered in Chapter 7, and print the string all at once:

```
>>> print x + y
ab
>>> print '%s...%s' % (x, y)
a...b
```

As you can see, apart from their special syntax for usage modes, 2.X `print` statements are roughly as simple to use as 3.X's function. The next section uncovers the way that files are specified in 2.X `print`s.

Print Stream Redirection

In both Python 3.X and 2.X, printing sends text to the standard output stream by default. However, it's often useful to send it elsewhere—to a text file, for example, to save results for later use or testing purposes. Although such redirection can be accomplished in system shells outside Python itself, it turns out to be just as easy to redirect a script's streams from within the script.

The Python "hello world" program

Let's start off with the usual (and largely pointless) language benchmark—the "hello world" program. To print a "hello world" message in Python, simply print the string per your version's print operation:

```
>>> print('hello world')          # Print a string object in 3.X
hello world
```

```
>>> print 'hello world'           # Print a string object in 2.X
hello world
```

Because expression results are echoed on the interactive command line, you often don't even need to use a `print` statement there—simply type the expressions you'd like to have printed, and their results are echoed back:

```
>>> 'hello world'                 # Interactive echoes
'hello world'
```

This code isn't exactly an earth-shattering piece of software mastery, but it serves to illustrate printing behavior. Really, the `print` operation is just an ergonomic feature of Python—it provides a simple interface to the `sys.stdout` object, with a bit of default formatting. In fact, if you enjoy working harder than you must, you can also code print operations this way (per Chapters 4 and 9, a 3.X-only return value is omitted here):

```
>>> import sys                    # Printing the hard way
>>> sys.stdout.write('hello world\n')
hello world
```

This code explicitly calls the `write` method of `sys.stdout`—an attribute preset when Python starts up to an open file object connected to the output stream. The `print` operation hides most of those details, providing a simple tool for simple printing tasks.

Manual stream redirection

So, why did I just show you the hard way to print? The `sys.stdout` print equivalent turns out to be the basis of a common technique in Python. In general, `print` and `sys.stdout` are directly related as follows. This statement:

```
    print(X, Y)                         # Or, in 2.X: print X, Y
```

is equivalent to the longer:

```
    import sys
    sys.stdout.write(str(X) + ' ' + str(Y) + '\n')
```

which manually performs a string conversion with `str`, adds a separator and newline with `+`, and calls the output stream's `write` method. Which would you rather code? (He says, hoping to underscore the programmer-friendly nature of prints...)

Obviously, the long form isn't all that useful for printing by itself. However, it is useful to know that this is exactly what `print` operations do because it is possible to *reassign* `sys.stdout` to something different from the standard output stream. In other words, this equivalence provides a way of making your `print` operations send their text to other places. For example:

```
    import sys
    sys.stdout = open('log.txt', 'a')     # Redirects prints to a file
    ...
    print(x, y, x)                        # Shows up in log.txt
```

Here, we reset `sys.stdout` to a manually opened file named *log.txt*, located in the script's working directory and opened in append mode (so we add to its current content). After the reset, every `print` operation anywhere in the program will write its text to the end of the file *log.txt* instead of to the original output stream. The `print` operations are happy to keep calling `sys.stdout`'s `write` method, no matter what `sys.stdout` happens to refer to. Because there is just one `sys` module in your process, assigning `sys.stdout` this way will redirect every `print` anywhere in your program.

In fact, as the sidebar "Why You Will Care: print and stdout" on page 368 will explain, you can even reset `sys.stdout` to an object that isn't a file at all, as long as it has the expected interface: a method named `write` to receive the printed text string argument. When that object is a *class*, printed text can be routed and processed arbitrarily per a `write` method you code yourself.

This trick of resetting the output stream might be more useful for programs originally coded with `print` statements. If you know that output should go to a file to begin with, you can always call file write methods instead. To redirect the output of a `print`-based program, though, resetting `sys.stdout` provides a convenient alternative to changing every `print` statement or using system shell-based redirection syntax.

In other roles, streams may be reset to objects that display them in pop-up windows in GUIs, colorize then in IDEs like IDLE, and so on. It's a general technique.

Automatic stream redirection

Although redirecting printed text by assigning `sys.stdout` is a useful tool, a potential problem with the last section's code is that there is no direct way to restore the original output stream should you need to switch back after printing to a file. Because

---

`sys.stdout` is just a normal file object, though, you can always save it and restore it if needed:[6]

```
C:\code> c:\python33\python
>>> import sys
>>> temp = sys.stdout              # Save for restoring later
>>> sys.stdout = open('log.txt', 'a')    # Redirect prints to a file
>>> print('spam')                  # Prints go to file, not here
>>> print(1, 2, 3)
>>> sys.stdout.close()             # Flush output to disk
>>> sys.stdout = temp              # Restore original stream

>>> print('back here')            # Prints show up here again
back here
>>> print(open('log.txt').read())  # Result of earlier prints
spam
1 2 3
```

As you can see, though, manual saving and restoring of the original output stream like this involves quite a bit of extra work. Because this crops up fairly often, a `print` extension is available to make it unnecessary.

In 3.X, the `file` keyword allows a single `print` call to send its text to the `write` method of a file (or file-like object), without actually resetting `sys.stdout`. Because the redirection is temporary, normal `print` calls keep printing to the original output stream. In 2.X, a `print` statement that begins with a `>>` followed by an output file object (or other compatible object) has the same effect. For example, the following again sends printed text to a file named *log.txt*:

```
log = open('log.txt', 'a')        # 3.X
print(x, y, z, file=log)          # Print to a file-like object
print(a, b, c)                    # Print to original stdout

log = open('log.txt', 'a')        # 2.X
print >> log, x, y, z             # Print to a file-like object
print a, b, c                     # Print to original stdout
```

These redirected forms of `print` are handy if you need to print to *both* files and the standard output stream in the same program. If you use these forms, however, be sure to give them a file object (or an object that has the same `write` method as a file object), not a file's name string. Here is the technique in action:

```
C:\code> c:\python33\python
>>> log = open('log.txt', 'w')
>>> print(1, 2, 3, file=log)      # For 2.X: print >> log, 1, 2, 3
>>> print(4, 5, 6, file=log)
>>> log.close()
>>> print(7, 8, 9)                # For 2.X: print 7, 8, 9
```

---

6. In both 2.X and 3.X you may also be able to use the __stdout__ attribute in the sys module, which refers to the original value sys.stdout had at program startup time. You still need to restore sys.stdout to sys.__stdout__ to go back to this original stream value, though. See the sys module documentation for more details.

```
7 8 9
>>> print(open('log.txt').read())
1 2 3
4 5 6
```

These extended forms of `print` are also commonly used to print error messages to the standard error stream, available to your script as the preopened file object `sys.stderr`. You can either use its file `write` methods and format the output manually, or print with redirection syntax:

```
>>> import sys
>>> sys.stderr.write(('Bad!' * 8) + '\n')
Bad!Bad!Bad!Bad!Bad!Bad!Bad!Bad!

>>> print('Bad!' * 8, file=sys.stderr)        # In 2.X: print >> sys.stderr, 'Bad!' * 8
Bad!Bad!Bad!Bad!Bad!Bad!Bad!Bad!
```

Now that you know all about print redirections, the equivalence between printing and file `write` methods should be fairly obvious. The following interaction prints both ways in 3.X, then redirects the output to an external file to verify that the same text is printed:

```
>>> X = 1; Y = 2
>>> print(X, Y)                                           # Print: the easy way
1 2
>>> import sys                                            # Print: the hard way
>>> sys.stdout.write(str(X) + ' ' + str(Y) + '\n')
1 2
4
>>> print(X, Y, file=open('temp1', 'w'))                  # Redirect text to file

>>> open('temp2', 'w').write(str(X) + ' ' + str(Y) + '\n')  # Send to file manually
4
>>> print(open('temp1', 'rb').read())                     # Binary mode for bytes
b'1 2\r\n'
>>> print(open('temp2', 'rb').read())
b'1 2\r\n'
```

As you can see, unless you happen to enjoy typing, print operations are usually the best option for displaying text. For another example of the equivalence between prints and file writes, watch for a 3.X `print` function emulation example in Chapter 18; it uses this code pattern to provide a general 3.X `print` function equivalent for use in Python 2.X.

Version-Neutral Printing

Finally, if you need your prints to work on *both* Python lines, you have some options. This is true whether you're writing 2.X code that strives for 3.X compatibility, or 3.X code that aims to support 2.X too.

2to3 converter

For one, you can code 2.X `print` statements and let 3.X's `2to3` conversion script translate them to 3.X function calls automatically. See the Python 3.X manuals for more details about this script; it attempts to translate 2.X code to run under 3.X—a useful tool, but perhaps more than you want to make just your print operations version-neutral. A related tool named 3to2 attempts to do the inverse: convert 3.X code to run on 2.X; see Appendix C for more information.

Importing from __future__

Alternatively, you can code 3.X print function calls in code to be run by 2.X, by enabling the function call variant with a statement like the following coded at the top of a script, or anywhere in an interactive session:

```
from __future__ import print_function
```

This statement changes 2.X to support 3.X's print functions exactly. This way, you can use 3.X print features and won't have to change your prints if you later migrate to 3.X. Two usage notes here:

- This statement is simply *ignored* if it appears in code run by 3.X—it doesn't hurt if included in 3.X code for 2.X compatibility.

- This statement must appear at the top of *each file* that prints in 2.X—because it modifies that parser for a single file only, it's not enough to import another file that includes this statement.

Neutralizing display differences with code

Also keep in mind that simple prints, like those in the first row of Table 11-5, work in *either* version of Python—because any expression may be enclosed in parentheses, we can always pretend to be calling a 3.X print function in 2.X by adding outer parentheses. The main downside to this is that it makes a *tuple* out of your printed objects if there are more than one, or none—they will print with extra enclosing parentheses. In 3.X, for example, any number of objects may be listed in the call's parentheses:

```
C:\code> c:\python33\python
>>> print('spam')                      # 3.X print function call syntax
spam
>>> print('spam', 'ham', 'eggs')       # These are multiple arguments
spam ham eggs
```

The first of these works the same in 2.X, but the second generates a tuple in the output:

```
C:\code> c:\python27\python
>>> print('spam')                      # 2.X print statement, enclosing parens
spam
>>> print('spam', 'ham', 'eggs')       # This is really a tuple object!
('spam', 'ham', 'eggs')
```

The same applies when there are *no* objects printed to force a line-feed: 2.X shows a tuple, unless you print an empty string:

```
c:\code> py -2
>> print()                             # This is just a line-feed on 3.X
```

```
()
>>> print('')                          # This is a line-feed in both 2.X and 3.X
```

Strictly speaking, outputs may in some cases differ in more than just extra enclosing parentheses in 2.X. If you look closely at the preceding results, you'll notice that the strings also print with *enclosing quotes* in 2.X only. This is because objects may print differently when *nested* in another object than they do as top-level items. Technically, nested appearances display with `repr` and top-level objects with `str`—the two alternative display formats we noted in Chapter 5.

Here this just means extra quotes around strings nested in the tuple that is created for printing multiple parenthesized items in 2.X. Displays of nested objects can differ much more for other object types, though, and especially for class objects that define alternative displays with *operator overloading*—a topic we'll cover in Part VI in general and Chapter 30 in particular.

To be truly portable without enabling 3.X prints everywhere, and to sidestep display difference for nested appearances, you can always format the print string as a single object to unify displays across versions, using the string formatting expression or method call, or other string tools that we studied in Chapter 7:

```
>>> print('%s %s %s' % ('spam', 'ham', 'eggs'))
spam ham eggs
>>> print('{0} {1} {2}'.format('spam', 'ham', 'eggs'))
spam ham eggs
>>> print('answer: ' + str(42))
answer: 42
```

Of course, if you can use 3.X exclusively you can forget such mappings entirely, but many Python programmers will at least encounter, if not write, 2.X code and systems for some time to come. We'll use both __future__ and version-neutral code to achieve 2.X/3.X portability in many examples in this book.

 I use Python 3.X `print` function calls throughout this book. I'll often make prints version-neutral, and will usually warn you when the results may differ in 2.X, but I sometimes don't, so please consider this note a blanket warning. If you see extra parentheses in your printed text in 2.X, either drop the parentheses in your `print` statements, import 3.X prints from the __future__, recode your prints using the version-neutral scheme outlined here, or learn to love superfluous text.

Why You Will Care: print and stdout

The equivalence between the `print` operation and writing to `sys.stdout` is important. It makes it possible to reassign `sys.stdout` to any user-defined object that provides the same `write` method as files. Because the `print` statement just sends text to the `sys.stdout.write` method, you can capture printed text in your programs by assigning `sys.stdout` to an object whose `write` method processes the text in arbitrary ways.

For instance, you can send printed text to a GUI window, or tee it off to multiple destinations, by defining an object with a `write` method that does the required routing. You'll see an example of this trick when we study classes in Part VI of this book, but abstractly, it looks like this:

```
class FileFaker:
    def write(self, string):
        # Do something with printed text in string

import sys
sys.stdout = FileFaker()
print(someObjects)                  # Sends to class write method
```

This works because `print` is what we will call in the next part of this book a *polymorphic* operation—it doesn't care what `sys.stdout` is, only that it has a method (i.e., interface) called `write`. This redirection to objects is made even simpler with the `file` keyword argument in 3.X and the `>>` extended form of `print` in 2.X, because we don't need to reset `sys.stdout` explicitly—normal prints will still be routed to the `stdout` stream:

```
myobj = FileFaker()                    # 3.X: Redirect to object for one print
print(someObjects, file=myobj)         # Does not reset sys.stdout

myobj = FileFaker()                    # 2.X: same effect
print >> myobj, someObjects            # Does not reset sys.stdout
```

Python's 3.X's built-in `input` function (named `raw_input` in 2.X) reads from the `sys.stdin` file, so you can intercept read requests in a similar way, using classes that implement file-like `read` methods instead. See the `input` and `while` loop example in Chapter 10 for more background on this function.

Notice that because printed text goes to the `stdout` stream, it's also the way to print HTML reply pages in CGI scripts used on the Web, and enables you to redirect Python script input and output at the operating system's shell command line as usual:

```
python script.py < inputfile > outputfile
python script.py | filterProgram
```

Python's print operation redirection tools are essentially pure-Python alternatives to these shell syntax forms. See other resources for more on CGI scripts and shell syntax.

Chapter Summary

In this chapter, we began our in-depth look at Python statements by exploring assignments, expressions, and print operations. Although these are generally simple to use, they have some alternative forms that, while optional, are often convenient in practice —augmented assignment statements and the redirection form of `print` operations, for example, allow us to avoid some manual coding work. Along the way, we also studied the syntax of variable names, stream redirection techniques, and a variety of common mistakes to avoid, such as assigning the result of an `append` method call back to a variable.

In the next chapter, we'll continue our statement tour by filling in details about the `if` statement, Python's main selection tool; there, we'll also revisit Python's syntax model in more depth and look at the behavior of Boolean expressions. Before we move on, though, the end-of-chapter quiz will test your knowledge of what you've learned here.

Test Your Knowledge: Quiz

1. Name three ways that you can assign three variables to the same value.
2. Why might you need to care when assigning three variables to a mutable object?
3. What's wrong with saying `L = L.sort()`?
4. How might you use the `print` operation to send text to an external file?

Test Your Knowledge: Answers

1. You can use multiple-target assignments (`A = B = C = 0`), sequence assignment (`A, B, C = 0, 0, 0`), or multiple assignment statements on three separate lines (`A = 0`, `B = 0`, and `C = 0`). With the latter technique, as introduced in Chapter 10, you can also string the three separate statements together on the same line by separating them with semicolons (`A = 0; B = 0; C = 0`).

2. If you assign them this way:

    ```
    A = B = C = []
    ```

    all three names reference the same object, so changing it in place from one (e.g., `A.append(99)`) will affect the others. This is true only for in-place changes to mutable objects like lists and dictionaries; for immutable objects such as numbers and strings, this issue is irrelevant.

3. The list `sort` method is like `append` in that it makes an in-place change to the subject list—it returns `None`, not the list it changes. The assignment back to L sets L to `None`, not to the sorted list. As discussed both earlier and later in this book (e.g., Chapter 8), a newer built-in function, `sorted`, sorts any sequence and returns a new list with the sorting result; because this is not an in-place change, its result can be meaningfully assigned to a name.

4. To print to a file for a single `print` operation, you can use 3.X's `print(X, file=F)` call form, use 2.X's extended `print >> file, X` statement form, or assign `sys.stdout` to a manually opened file before the `print` and restore the original after. You can also redirect all of a program's printed text to a file with special syntax in the system shell, but this is outside Python's scope.

if Tests and Syntax Rules

This chapter presents the Python `if` statement, which is the main statement used for selecting from alternative actions based on test results. Because this is our first in-depth look at *compound statements*—statements that embed other statements—we will also explore the general concepts behind the Python statement syntax model here in more detail than we did in the introduction in Chapter 10. Because the `if` statement introduces the notion of tests, this chapter will also deal with Boolean expressions, cover the "ternary" `if` expression, and fill in some details on truth tests in general.

if Statements

In simple terms, the Python `if` statement selects actions to perform. Along with its expression counterpart, it's the primary selection tool in Python and represents much of the *logic* a Python program possesses. It's also our first compound statement. Like all compound Python statements, the `if` statement may contain other statements, including other `if`s. In fact, Python lets you combine statements in a program sequentially (so that they execute one after another), and in an arbitrarily nested fashion (so that they execute only under certain conditions such as selections and loops).

General Format

The Python `if` statement is typical of `if` statements in most procedural languages. It takes the form of an `if` test, followed by one or more optional `elif` ("else if") tests and a final optional `else` block. The tests and the `else` part each have an associated block of nested statements, indented under a header line. When the `if` statement runs, Python executes the block of code associated with the first test that evaluates to true, or the `else` block if all tests prove false. The general form of an `if` statement looks like this:

```
if test1:              # if test
    statements1        # Associated block
elif test2:            # Optional elifs
    statements2
```

```
else:                    # Optional else
    statements3
```

Basic Examples

To demonstrate, let's look at a few simple examples of the if statement at work. All parts are optional, except the initial if test and its associated statements. Thus, in the simplest case, the other parts are omitted:

```
>>> if 1:
...     print('true')
...
true
```

Notice how the prompt changes to ... for continuation lines when you're typing interactively in the basic interface used here; in IDLE, you'll simply drop down to an indented line instead (hit Backspace to back up). A blank line (which you can get by pressing Enter twice) terminates and runs the entire statement. Remember that 1 is Boolean true (as we'll see later, the word True is its equivalent), so this statement's test always succeeds. To handle a false result, code the else:

```
>>> if not 1:
...     print('true')
... else:
...     print('false')
...
false
```

Multiway Branching

Now here's an example of a more complex if statement, with all its optional parts present:

```
>>> x = 'killer rabbit'
>>> if x == 'roger':
...     print("shave and a haircut")
... elif x == 'bugs':
...     print("what's up doc?")
... else:
...     print('Run away! Run away!')
...
Run away! Run away!
```

This multiline statement extends from the if line through the block nested under the else. When it's run, Python executes the statements nested under the first test that is true, or the else part if all tests are false (in this example, they are). In practice, both the elif and else parts may be omitted, and there may be more than one statement nested in each section. Note that the words if, elif, and else are associated by the fact that they line up vertically, with the same indentation.

If you've used languages like C or Pascal, you might be interested to know that there is no `switch` or `case` statement in Python that selects an action based on a variable's value. Instead, you usually code *multiway branching* as a series of `if`/`elif` tests, as in the prior example, and occasionally by indexing dictionaries or searching lists. Because dictionaries and lists can be built at runtime dynamically, they are sometimes more flexible than hardcoded `if` logic in your script:

```
>>> choice = 'ham'
>>> print({'spam':  1.25,          # A dictionary-based 'switch'
...        'ham':   1.99,          # Use has_key or get for default
...        'eggs':  0.99,
...        'bacon': 1.10}[choice])
1.99
```

Although it may take a few moments for this to sink in the first time you see it, this dictionary is a multiway branch—indexing on the key `choice` branches to one of a set of values, much like a `switch` in C. An almost equivalent but more verbose Python `if` statement might look like the following:

```
>>> if choice == 'spam':          # The equivalent if statement
...     print(1.25)
... elif choice == 'ham':
...     print(1.99)
... elif choice == 'eggs':
...     print(0.99)
... elif choice == 'bacon':
...     print(1.10)
... else:
...     print('Bad choice')
...
1.99
```

Though it's perhaps more readable, the potential downside of an `if` like this is that, short of constructing it as a string and running it with tools like the prior chapter's `eval` or `exec`, you cannot construct it at runtime as easily as a dictionary. In more dynamic programs, data structures offer added flexibility.

Handling switch defaults

Notice the `else` clause on the `if` here to handle the default case when no key matches. As we saw in Chapter 8, dictionary defaults can be coded with `in` expressions, `get` method calls, or exception catching with the `try` statement introduced in the preceding chapter. All of the same techniques can be used here to code a default action in a dictionary-based multiway branch. As a review in the context of this use case, here's the `get` scheme at work with defaults:

```
>>> branch = {'spam': 1.25,
...           'ham':  1.99,
...           'eggs': 0.99}

>>> print(branch.get('spam', 'Bad choice'))
1.25
```

```
>>> print(branch.get('bacon', 'Bad choice'))
Bad choice
```

An `in` membership test in an `if` statement can have the same default effect:

```
>>> choice = 'bacon'
>>> if choice in branch:
...     print(branch[choice])
... else:
...     print('Bad choice')
...
Bad choice
```

And the `try` statement is a general way to handle defaults by catching and handling the exceptions they'd otherwise trigger (for more on exceptions, see Chapter 11's overview and Part VII's full treatment):

```
>>> try:
...     print(branch[choice])
... except KeyError:
...     print('Bad choice')
...
Bad choice
```

Handling larger actions

Dictionaries are good for associating values with keys, but what about the more complicated actions you can code in the statement blocks associated with `if` statements? In Part IV, you'll learn that dictionaries can also contain *functions* to represent more complex branch actions and implement general jump tables. Such functions appear as dictionary values, they may be coded as function names or inline `lambda`s, and they are called by adding parentheses to trigger their actions. Here's an abstract sampler, but stay tuned for a rehash of this topic in Chapter 19 after we've learned more about function definition:

```
def function(): ...
def default(): ...

branch = {'spam': lambda: ...,          # A table of callable function objects
          'ham':  function,
          'eggs': lambda: ...}

branch.get(choice, default)()
```

Although dictionary-based multiway branching is useful in programs that deal with more dynamic data, most programmers will probably find that coding an `if` statement is the most straightforward way to perform multiway branching. As a rule of thumb in coding, when in doubt, err on the side of simplicity and readability; it's the "Pythonic" way.

Python Syntax Revisited

I introduced Python's syntax model in Chapter 10. Now that we're stepping up to larger statements like `if`, this section reviews and expands on the syntax ideas introduced earlier. In general, Python has a simple, statement-based syntax. However, there are a few properties you need to know about:

- **Statements execute one after another, until you say otherwise**. Python normally runs statements in a file or nested block in order from first to last as a *sequence*, but statements like `if` (as well as loops and exceptions) cause the interpreter to jump around in your code. Because Python's path through a program is called the *control flow*, statements such as `if` that affect it are often called *control-flow statements*.

- **Block and statement boundaries are detected automatically**. As we've seen, there are no braces or "begin/end" delimiters around blocks of code in Python; instead, Python uses the indentation of statements under a header to group the statements in a nested block. Similarly, Python statements are not normally terminated with semicolons; rather, the end of a line usually marks the end of the statement coded on that line. As a special case, statements can span lines and be combined on a line with special syntax.

- **Compound statements = header + ":" + indented statements**. All Python *compound statements*—those with nested statements—follow the same pattern: a header line terminated with a colon, followed by one or more nested statements, usually indented under the header. The indented statements are called a *block* (or sometimes, a suite). In the `if` statement, the `elif` and `else` clauses are part of the `if`, but they are also header lines with nested blocks of their own. As a special case, blocks can show up on the same line as the header if they are simple noncompound code.

- **Blank lines, spaces, and comments are usually ignored**. Blank lines are both optional and ignored in files (but not at the interactive prompt, when they terminate compound statements). Spaces inside statements and expressions are almost always ignored (except in string literals, and when used for indentation). Comments are always ignored: they start with a # character (not inside a string literal) and extend to the end of the current line.

- **Docstrings are ignored but are saved and displayed by tools**. Python supports an additional comment form called documentation strings (*docstrings* for short), which, unlike # comments, are retained at runtime for inspection. Docstrings are simply strings that show up at the top of program files and some statements. Python ignores their contents, but they are automatically attached to objects at runtime and may be displayed with documentation tools like PyDoc. Docstrings are part of Python's larger documentation strategy and are covered in the last chapter in this part of the book.

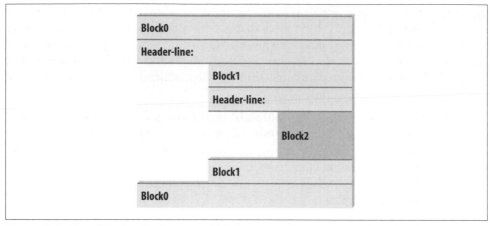

Figure 12-1. Nested blocks of code: a nested block starts with a statement indented further to the right and ends with either a statement that is indented less, or the end of the file.

As you've seen, there are no variable type declarations in Python; this fact alone makes for a much simpler language syntax than what you may be used to. However, for most new users the lack of the braces and semicolons used to mark blocks and statements in many other languages seems to be the most novel syntactic feature of Python, so let's explore what this means in more detail.

Block Delimiters: Indentation Rules

As introduced in Chapter 10, Python detects block boundaries automatically, by line *indentation*—that is, the empty space to the left of your code. All statements indented the same distance to the right belong to the same block of code. In other words, the statements within a block line up vertically, as in a column. The block ends when the end of the file or a lesser-indented line is encountered, and more deeply nested blocks are simply indented further to the right than the statements in the enclosing block. Compound statement bodies can appear on the header's line in some cases we'll explore later, but most are indented under it.

For instance, Figure 12-1 demonstrates the block structure of the following code:

```
x = 1
if x:
    y = 2
    if y:
        print('block2')
    print('block1')
print('block0')
```

This code contains three blocks: the first (the top-level code of the file) is not indented at all, the second (within the outer `if` statement) is indented four spaces, and the third (the `print` statement under the nested `if`) is indented eight spaces.

In general, top-level (unnested) code must start in column 1. Nested blocks can start in any column; indentation may consist of any number of spaces and tabs, as long as it's the same for all the statements in a given single block. That is, Python doesn't care *how* you indent your code; it only cares that it's done consistently. Four spaces or one tab per indentation level are common conventions, but there is no absolute standard in the Python world.

Indenting code is quite natural in practice. For example, the following (arguably silly) code snippet demonstrates common indentation errors in Python code:

```
  x = 'SPAM'                          # Error: first line indented
if 'rubbery' in 'shrubbery':
    print(x * 8)
        x += 'NI'                     # Error: unexpected indentation
        if x.endswith('NI'):
            x *= 2
          print(x)                    # Error: inconsistent indentation
```

The properly indented version of this code looks like the following—even for an artificial example like this, proper indentation makes the code's intent much more apparent:

```
x = 'SPAM'
if 'rubbery' in 'shrubbery':
    print(x * 8)                      # Prints 8 "SPAM"
    x += 'NI'
    if x.endswith('NI'):
        x *= 2
        print(x)                      # Prints "SPAMNISPAMNI"
```

It's important to know that the only major place in Python where whitespace matters is where it's used to the left of your code, for indentation; in most other contexts, space can be coded or not. However, indentation is really part of Python syntax, not just a stylistic suggestion: all the statements within any given single block must be indented to the same level, or Python reports a syntax error. This is intentional—because you don't need to explicitly mark the start and end of a nested block of code, some of the syntactic clutter found in other languages is unnecessary in Python.

As described in Chapter 10, making indentation part of the syntax model also enforces consistency, a crucial component of readability in structured programming languages like Python. Python's syntax is sometimes described as "what you see is what you get" —the indentation of each line of code unambiguously tells readers what it is associated with. This uniform and consistent appearance makes Python code easier to maintain and reuse.

Indentation is simpler in practice than its details might initially imply, and it makes your code reflect its logical structure. Consistently indented code always satisfies Python's rules. Moreover, most text editors (including IDLE) make it easy to follow Python's indentation model by automatically indenting code as you type it.

Avoid mixing tabs and spaces: New error checking in 3.X

One rule of thumb: although you can use spaces or tabs to indent, it's usually not a good idea to *mix* the two within a block—use one or the other. Technically, tabs count for enough spaces to move the current column number up to a multiple of 8, and your code will work if you mix tabs and spaces consistently. However, such code can be difficult to change. Worse, mixing tabs and spaces makes your code difficult to read completely apart from Python's syntax rules—tabs may look very different in the next programmer's editor than they do in yours.

In fact, Python 3.X issues an error, for these very reasons, when a script mixes tabs and spaces for indentation inconsistently within a block (that is, in a way that makes it dependent on a tab's equivalent in spaces). Python 2.X allows such scripts to run, but it has a -t command-line flag that will warn you about inconsistent tab usage and a -tt flag that will issue errors for such code (you can use these switches in a command line like python -t main.py in a system shell window). Python 3.X's error case is equivalent to 2.X's -tt switch.

Statement Delimiters: Lines and Continuations

A statement in Python normally ends at the end of the line on which it appears. When a statement is too long to fit on a single line, though, a few special rules may be used to make it span multiple lines:

- **Statements may span multiple lines if you're continuing an open syntactic pair**. Python lets you continue typing a statement on the next line if you're coding something enclosed in a (), {}, or [] pair. For instance, expressions in parentheses and dictionary and list literals can span any number of lines; your statement doesn't end until the Python interpreter reaches the line on which you type the closing part of the pair (a), }, or]). *Continuation lines*—lines 2 and beyond of the statement —can start at any indentation level you like, but you should try to make them align vertically for readability if possible. This open pairs rule also covers set and dictionary comprehensions in Python 3.X and 2.7.

- **Statements may span multiple lines if they end in a backslash**. This is a somewhat outdated feature that's not generally recommended, but if a statement needs to span multiple lines, you can also add a backslash (a \ not embedded in a string literal or comment) at the end of the prior line to indicate you're continuing on the next line. Because you can also continue by adding parentheses around most constructs, backslashes are rarely used today. This approach is also error-prone: accidentally forgetting a \ usually generates a syntax error and might even cause the next line to be silently mistaken (i.e., without warning) for a new statement, with unexpected results.

- **Special rules for string literals**. As we learned in Chapter 7, triple-quoted string blocks are designed to span multiple lines normally. We also learned in Chapter 7 that adjacent string literals are implicitly concatenated; when it's used in conjunction with the open pairs rule mentioned earlier, wrapping this construct in parentheses allows it to span multiple lines.

- **Other rules**. There are a few other points to mention with regard to statement delimiters. Although it is uncommon, you can terminate a statement with a semi-colon—this convention is sometimes used to squeeze more than one simple (non-compound) statement onto a single line. Also, comments and blank lines can appear anywhere in a file; comments (which begin with a # character) terminate at the end of the line on which they appear.

A Few Special Cases

Here's what a continuation line looks like using the open syntactic pairs rule just described. Delimited constructs, such as lists in square brackets, can span across any number of lines:

```
L = ["Good",
     "Bad",
     "Ugly"]                    # Open pairs may span lines
```

This also works for anything in parentheses (expressions, function arguments, function headers, tuples, and generator expressions), as well as anything in curly braces (dictionaries and, in 3.X and 2.7, set literals and set and dictionary comprehensions). Some of these are tools we'll study in later chapters, but this rule naturally covers most constructs that span lines in practice.

If you like using backslashes to continue lines, you can, but it's not common practice in Python:

```
if a == b and c == d and    \
   d == e and f == g:
   print('olde')                # Backslashes allow continuations...
```

Because any expression can be enclosed in parentheses, you can usually use the open pairs technique instead if you need your code to span multiple lines—simply wrap a part of your statement in parentheses:

```
if (a == b and c == d and
    d == e and e == f):
    print('new')                # But parentheses usually do too, and are obvious
```

In fact, backslashes are generally frowned on by most Python developers, because they're too easy to not notice and too easy to omit altogether. In the following, x is assigned 10 with the backslash, as intended; if the backslash is accidentally omitted, though, x is assigned 6 instead, and *no error is reported* (the +4 is a valid expression statement by itself).

In a real program with a more complex assignment, this could be the source of a very nasty bug:[1]

```
x = 1 + 2 + 3 \              # Omitting the \ makes this very different!
+4
```

As another special case, Python allows you to write more than one noncompound statement (i.e., statements without nested statements) on the same line, separated by semicolons. Some coders use this form to save program file real estate, but it usually makes for more readable code if you stick to one statement per line for most of your work:

```
x = 1; y = 2; print(x)          # More than one simple statement
```

As we learned in Chapter 7, triple-quoted string literals span lines too. In addition, if two string literals appear next to each other, they are concatenated as if a + had been added between them—when used in conjunction with the open pairs rule, wrapping in parentheses allows this form to span multiple lines. For example, the first of the following inserts newline characters at line breaks and assigns S to '\naaaa\nbbbb \ncccc', and the second implicitly concatenates and assigns S to 'aaaabbbbcccc'; as we also saw in Chapter 7, # comments are ignored in the second form, but included in the string in the first:

```
S = """
aaaa
bbbb
cccc"""

S = ('aaaa'
     'bbbb'                      # Comments here are ignored
     'cccc')
```

Finally, Python lets you move a compound statement's body up to the header line, provided the body contains just simple (noncompound) statements. You'll most often see this used for simple if statements with a single test and action, as in the interactive loops we coded in Chapter 10:

```
if 1: print('hello')            # Simple statement on header line
```

You can combine some of these special cases to write code that is difficult to read, but I don't recommend it; as a rule of thumb, try to keep each statement on a line of its own, and indent all but the simplest of blocks. Six months down the road, you'll be happy you did.

Truth Values and Boolean Tests

The notions of comparison, equality, and truth values were introduced in Chapter 9. Because the if statement is the first statement we've looked at that actually uses test

---

1. Candidly, it was a bit surprising that backslash continuations were not removed in Python 3.0, given the broad scope of its other changes! See the 3.0 changes tables in Appendix C for a list of 3.0 removals; some seem fairly innocuous in comparison with the dangers inherent in backslash continuations. Then again, this book's goal is Python instruction, not populist outrage, so the best advice I can give is simply: don't do this. You should generally avoid backslash continuations in new Python code, even if you developed the habit in your C programming days.

results, we'll expand on some of these ideas here. In particular, Python's Boolean operators are a bit different from their counterparts in languages like C. In Python:

- All objects have an inherent Boolean true or false value.
- Any nonzero number or nonempty object is true.
- Zero numbers, empty objects, and the special object None are considered false.
- Comparisons and equality tests are applied recursively to data structures.
- Comparisons and equality tests return True or False (custom versions of 1 and 0).
- Boolean and and or operators return a true or false operand object.
- Boolean operators stop evaluating ("short circuit") as soon as a result is known.

The if statement takes action on truth values, but Boolean operators are used to combine the results of other tests in richer ways to produce new truth values. More formally, there are three Boolean expression operators in Python:

X and Y
    Is true if both X and Y are true

X or Y
    Is true if either X or Y is true

not X
    Is true if X is false (the expression returns True or False)

Here, X and Y may be any truth value, or any expression that returns a truth value (e.g., an equality test, range comparison, and so on). Boolean operators are typed out as words in Python (instead of C's &&, ||, and !). Also, Boolean and and or operators return a true or false *object* in Python, not the values True or False. Let's look at a few examples to see how this works:

```
>>> 2 < 3, 3 < 2          # Less than: return True or False (1 or 0)
(True, False)
```

Magnitude comparisons such as these return True or False as their truth results, which, as we learned in Chapter 5 and Chapter 9, are really just custom versions of the integers 1 and 0 (they print themselves differently but are otherwise the same).

On the other hand, the and and or operators always return an object—either the object on the *left* side of the operator or the object on the *right*. If we test their results in if or other statements, they will be as expected (remember, every object is inherently true or false), but we won't get back a simple True or False.

For or tests, Python evaluates the operand objects from left to right and returns the first one that is true. Moreover, Python stops at the first true operand it finds. This is usually called *short-circuit evaluation*, as determining a result short-circuits (terminates) the rest of the expression as soon as the result is known:

```
>>> 2 or 3, 3 or 2        # Return left operand if true
(2, 3)                    # Else, return right operand (true or false)
```

```
>>> [] or 3
3
>>> [] or {}
{}
```

In the first line of the preceding example, both operands (2 and 3) are true (i.e., are nonzero), so Python always stops and returns the one on the left—it determines the result because true or anything is always true. In the other two tests, the left operand is false (an empty object), so Python simply evaluates and returns the object on the right—which may happen to have either a true or a false value when tested.

Python and operations also stop as soon as the result is known; however, in this case Python evaluates the operands from left to right and stops if the left operand is a *false* object because it determines the result—false and anything is always false:

```
>>> 2 and 3, 3 and 2      # Return left operand if false
(3, 2)                    # Else, return right operand (true or false)
>>> [] and {}
[]
>>> 3 and []
[]
```

Here, both operands are true in the first line, so Python evaluates both sides and returns the object on the right. In the second test, the left operand is false ([]), so Python stops and returns it as the test result. In the last test, the left side is true (3), so Python evaluates and returns the object on the right—which happens to be a false [].

The end result of all this is the same as in C and most other languages—you get a value that is logically true or false if tested in an if or while according to the normal definitions of or and and. However, in Python Booleans return either the left or the right *object*, not a simple integer flag.

This behavior of and and or may seem esoteric at first glance, but see this chapter's sidebar "Why You Will Care: Booleans" on page 384 for examples of how it is sometimes used to advantage in coding by Python programmers. The next section also shows a common way to leverage this behavior, and its more mnemonic replacement in recent versions of Python.

The if/else Ternary Expression

One common role for the prior section's Boolean operators is to code an expression that runs the same as an if statement. Consider the following statement, which sets A to either Y or Z, based on the truth value of X:

```
if X:
    A = Y
else:
    A = Z
```

Sometimes, though, the items involved in such a statement are so simple that it seems like overkill to spread them across four lines. At other times, we may want to nest such a construct in a larger statement instead of assigning its result to a variable. For these reasons (and, frankly, because the C language has a similar tool), Python 2.5 introduced a new expression format that allows us to say the same thing in one expression:

```
A = Y if X else Z
```

This expression has the exact same effect as the preceding four-line `if` statement, but it's simpler to code. As in the statement equivalent, Python runs expression Y only if X turns out to be true, and runs expression Z only if X turns out to be false. That is, it *short-circuits*, just like the Boolean operators described in the prior section, running just Y or Z but not both. Here are some examples of it in action:

```
>>> A = 't' if 'spam' else 'f'          # For strings, nonempty means true
>>> A
't'
>>> A = 't' if '' else 'f'
>>> A
'f'
```

Prior to Python 2.5 (and after 2.5, if you insist), the same effect can often be achieved by a careful combination of the `and` and `or` operators, because they return either the object on the left side or the object on the right as the preceding section described:

```
A = ((X and Y) or Z)
```

This works, but there is a catch—you have to be able to assume that Y will be Boolean true. If that is the case, the effect is the same: the `and` runs first and returns Y if X is true; if X if false the `and` skips Y, and the `or` simply returns Z. In other words, we get "if X then Y else Z." This is equivalent to the ternary form:

```
A = Y if X else Z
```

The `and`/`or` combination form also seems to require a "moment of great clarity" to understand the first time you see it, and it's no longer required as of 2.5—use the equivalent and more robust and mnemonic `if`/`else` expression when you need this structure, or use a full `if` statement if the parts are nontrivial.

As a side note, using the following expression in Python is similar because the `bool` function will translate X into the equivalent of integer `1` or `0`, which can then be used as offsets to pick true and false values from a list:

```
A = [Z, Y][bool(X)]
```

For example:

```
>>> ['f', 't'][bool('')]
'f'
>>> ['f', 't'][bool('spam')]
't'
```

However, this isn't exactly the same, because Python will not *short-circuit*—it will always run both Z and Y, regardless of the value of X. Because of such complexities, you're better off using the simpler and more easily understood `if`/`else` expression as of Python 2.5 and later. Again, though, you should use even that sparingly, and only if its parts are all fairly simple; otherwise, you're better off coding the full `if` statement form to make changes easier in the future. Your coworkers will be happy you did.

Still, you may see the `and`/`or` version in code written prior to 2.5 (and in Python code written by ex–C programmers who haven't quite let go of their dark coding pasts).[2]

Why You Will Care: Booleans

One common way to use the somewhat unusual behavior of Python Boolean operators is to select from a set of objects with an `or`. A statement such as this:

```
X = A or B or C or None
```

assigns `X` to the first nonempty (that is, true) object among `A`, `B`, and `C`, or to `None` if all of them are empty. This works because the `or` operator returns one of its two objects, and it turns out to be a fairly common coding paradigm in Python: to select a nonempty object from among a fixed-size set, simply string them together in an `or` expression. In simpler form, this is also commonly used to designate a default—the following sets `X` to `A` if `A` is true (or nonempty), and to `default` otherwise:

```
X = A or default
```

It's also important to understand the short-circuit evaluation of Boolean operators and the `if`/`else`, because it may prevent actions from running. Expressions on the right of a Boolean operator, for example, might call functions that perform substantial or important work, or have side effects that won't happen if the short-circuit rule takes effect:

```
if f1() or f2(): ...
```

Here, if `f1` returns a true (or nonempty) value, Python will never run `f2`. To guarantee that both functions will be run, call them before the `or`:

```
tmp1, tmp2 = f1(), f2()
if tmp1 or tmp2: ...
```

You've already seen another application of this behavior in this chapter: because of the way Booleans work, the expression `((A and B) or C)` can be used to emulate an `if` statement—almost (see this chapter's discussion of this form for details).

We met additional Boolean use cases in prior chapters. As we saw in Chapter 9, because all objects are inherently true or false, it's common and easier in Python to test an object directly (`if X:`) than to compare it to an empty value (`if X != '':`). For a string, the two tests are equivalent. As we also saw in Chapter 5, the preset Boolean values `True` and `False` are the same as the integers `1` and `0` and are useful for initializing variables

---

2. In fact, Python's `Y if X else Z` has a slightly different order than C's `X ? Y : Z`, and uses more readable words. Its differing order was reportedly chosen in response to analysis of common usage patterns in Python code. According to the Python folklore, this order was also chosen in part to discourage ex–C programmers from overusing it! Remember, simple is better than complex, in Python and elsewhere. If you have to work at packing logic into expressions like this, statements are probably your better bet.

(X = False), for loop tests (while True:), and for displaying results at the interactive prompt.

Also watch for related discussion in operator overloading in Part VI: when we define new object types with classes, we can specify their Boolean nature with either the __bool__ or __len__ methods (__bool__ is named __nonzero__ in 2.7). The latter of these is tried if the former is absent and designates false by returning a length of zero—an empty object is considered false.

Finally, and as a preview, other tools in Python have roles similar to the or chains at the start of this sidebar: the filter call and list comprehensions we'll meet later can be used to select true values when the set of candidates isn't known until runtime (though they evaluate all values and return all that are true), and the any and all built-ins can be used to test if any or all items in a collection are true (though they don't select an item):

```
>>> L = [1, 0, 2, 0, 'spam', '', 'ham', []]
>>> list(filter(bool, L))              # Get true values
[1, 2, 'spam', 'ham']
>>> [x for x in L if x]                # Comprehensions
[1, 2, 'spam', 'ham']
>>> any(L), all(L)                     # Aggregate truth
(True, False)
```

As seen in Chapter 9, the bool function here simply returns its argument's true or false value, as though it were tested in an if. Watch for more on these related tools in Chapter 14, Chapter 19, and Chapter 20.

Chapter Summary

In this chapter, we studied the Python if statement. Additionally, because this was our first compound and logical statement, we reviewed Python's general syntax rules and explored the operation of truth values and tests in more depth than we were able to previously. Along the way, we also looked at how to code multiway branching in Python, learned about the if/else expression introduced in Python 2.5, and explored some common ways that Boolean values crop up in code.

The next chapter continues our look at procedural statements by expanding on the while and for loops. There, we'll learn about alternative ways to code loops in Python, some of which may be better than others. Before that, though, here is the usual chapter quiz.

Test Your Knowledge: Quiz

1. How might you code a multiway branch in Python?
2. How can you code an if/else statement as an expression in Python?
3. How can you make a single statement span many lines?

4. What do the words `True` and `False` mean?

Test Your Knowledge: Answers

1. An `if` statement with multiple `elif` clauses is often the most straightforward way to code a multiway branch, though not necessarily the most concise or flexible. Dictionary indexing can often achieve the same result, especially if the dictionary contains callable functions coded with `def` statements or `lambda` expressions.

2. In Python 2.5 and later, the expression form `Y if X else Z` returns Y if X is true, or Z otherwise; it's the same as a four-line `if` statement. The `and`/`or` combination (`((X and Y) or Z)`) can work the same way, but it's more obscure and requires that the Y part be true.

3. Wrap up the statement in an open syntactic pair ((), [], or {}), and it can span as many lines as you like; the statement ends when Python sees the closing (right) half of the pair, and lines 2 and beyond of the statement can begin at any indentation level. Backslash continuations work too, but are broadly discouraged in the Python world.

4. `True` and `False` are just custom versions of the integers `1` and `0`, respectively: they always stand for Boolean true and false values in Python. They're available for use in truth tests and variable initialization, and are printed for expression results at the interactive prompt. In all these roles, they serve as a more mnemonic and hence readable alternative to `1` and `0`.

while and for Loops

This chapter concludes our tour of Python procedural statements by presenting the language's two main *looping* constructs—statements that repeat an action over and over. The first of these, the `while` statement, provides a way to code general loops. The second, the `for` statement, is designed for stepping through the items in a sequence or other iterable object and running a block of code for each.

We've seen both of these informally already, but we'll fill in additional usage details here. While we're at it, we'll also study a few less prominent statements used within loops, such as `break` and `continue`, and cover some built-ins commonly used with loops, such as `range`, `zip`, and `map`.

Although the `while` and `for` statements covered here are the primary syntax provided for coding repeated actions, there are additional looping operations and concepts in Python. Because of that, the iteration story is continued in the next chapter, where we'll explore the related ideas of Python's *iteration protocol* (used by the `for` loop) and *list comprehensions* (a close cousin to the `for` loop). Later chapters explore even more exotic iteration tools such as *generators*, `filter`, and `reduce`. For now, though, let's keep things simple.

while Loops

Python's `while` statement is the most general iteration construct in the language. In simple terms, it repeatedly executes a block of (normally indented) statements as long as a test at the top keeps evaluating to a true value. It is called a "loop" because control keeps looping back to the start of the statement until the test becomes false. When the test becomes false, control passes to the statement that follows the `while` block. The net effect is that the loop's body is executed repeatedly while the test at the top is true. If the test is false to begin with, the body never runs and the `while` statement is skipped.

General Format

In its most complex form, the `while` statement consists of a header line with a test expression, a body of one or more normally indented statements, and an optional `else` part that is executed if control exits the loop without a `break` statement being encountered. Python keeps evaluating the test at the top and executing the statements nested in the loop body until the test returns a false value:

```
while test:              # Loop test
    statements           # Loop body
else:                    # Optional else
    statements           # Run if didn't exit loop with break
```

Examples

To illustrate, let's look at a few simple `while` loops in action. The first, which consists of a `print` statement nested in a `while` loop, just prints a message forever. Recall that `True` is just a custom version of the integer `1` and always stands for a Boolean true value; because the test is always true, Python keeps executing the body forever, or until you stop its execution. This sort of behavior is usually called an *infinite loop*—it's not really immortal, but you may need a Ctrl-C key combination to forcibly terminate one:

```
>>> while True:
...     print('Type Ctrl-C to stop me!')
```

The next example keeps slicing off the first character of a string until the string is empty and hence false. It's typical to test an object directly like this instead of using the more verbose equivalent (`while x != '':`). Later in this chapter, we'll see other ways to step through the items in a string more easily with a `for` loop.

```
>>> x = 'spam'
>>> while x:                   # While x is not empty
...     print(x, end=' ')      # In 2.X use print x,
...     x = x[1:]              # Strip first character off x
...
spam pam am m
```

Note the `end=' '` keyword argument used here to place all outputs on the same line separated by a space; see Chapter 11 if you've forgotten why this works as it does. This may leave your input prompt in an odd state at the end of your output; type Enter to reset. Python 2.X readers: also remember to use a trailing comma instead of `end` in the `print`s like this.

The following code counts from the value of `a` up to, but not including, `b`. We'll also see an easier way to do this with a Python `for` loop and the built-in `range` function later:

```
>>> a=0; b=10
>>> while a < b:               # One way to code counter loops
...     print(a, end=' ')
...     a += 1                 # Or, a = a + 1
```

```
...
0 1 2 3 4 5 6 7 8 9
```

Finally, notice that Python doesn't have what some languages call a "do until" loop statement. However, we can simulate one with a test and break at the bottom of the loop body, so that the loop's body is always run at least once:

```
while True:
    ...loop body...
    if exitTest(): break
```

To fully understand how this structure works, we need to move on to the next section and learn more about the break statement.

break, continue, pass, and the Loop else

Now that we've seen a few Python loops in action, it's time to take a look at two simple statements that have a purpose only when nested inside loops—the break and continue statements. While we're looking at oddballs, we will also study the loop else clause here because it is intertwined with break, and Python's empty placeholder statement, pass (which is not tied to loops per se, but falls into the general category of simple one-word statements). In Python:

break
: Jumps out of the closest enclosing loop (past the entire loop statement)

continue
: Jumps to the top of the closest enclosing loop (to the loop's header line)

pass
: Does nothing at all: it's an empty statement placeholder

Loop else block
: Runs if and only if the loop is exited normally (i.e., without hitting a break)

General Loop Format

Factoring in break and continue statements, the general format of the while loop looks like this:

```
while test:
    statements
    if test: break        # Exit loop now, skip else if present
    if test: continue     # Go to test at top of loop now
else:
    statements            # Run if we didn't hit a 'break'
```

break and continue statements can appear anywhere inside the while (or for) loop's body, but they are usually coded further nested in an if test to take action in response to some condition.

Let's turn to a few simple examples to see how these statements come together in practice.

pass

Simple things first: the `pass` statement is a no-operation placeholder that is used when the syntax requires a statement, but you have nothing useful to say. It is often used to code an empty body for a compound statement. For instance, if you want to code an infinite loop that does nothing each time through, do it with a `pass`:

```
while True: pass                        # Type Ctrl-C to stop me!
```

Because the body is just an empty statement, Python gets stuck in this loop. `pass` is roughly to statements as `None` is to objects—an explicit nothing. Notice that here the `while` loop's body is on the same line as the header, after the colon; as with `if` statements, this only works if the body isn't a compound statement.

This example does nothing forever. It probably isn't the most useful Python program ever written (unless you want to warm up your laptop computer on a cold winter's day!); frankly, though, I couldn't think of a better `pass` example at this point in the book.

We'll see other places where `pass` makes more sense later—for instance, to ignore exceptions caught by `try` statements, and to define empty `class` objects with attributes that behave like "structs" and "records" in other languages. A `pass` is also sometime coded to mean "to be filled in later," to stub out the bodies of functions temporarily:

```
def func1():
    pass                        # Add real code here later

def func2():
    pass
```

We can't leave the body empty without getting a syntax error, so we say `pass` instead.

> Version skew note: Python 3.X (but not 2.X) allows *ellipses* coded as `...` (literally, three consecutive dots) to appear any place an expression can. Because ellipses do nothing by themselves, this can serve as an alternative to the `pass` statement, especially for code to be filled in later—a sort of Python "TBD":
>
> ```
> def func1():
>     ...                 # Alternative to pass
>
> def func2():
>     ...
>
> func1()                 # Does nothing if called
> ```
>
> Ellipses can also appear on the same line as a statement header and may be used to initialize variable names if no specific type is required:
>
> ```
> def func1(): ...        # Works on same line too
> def func2(): ...
> ```

```
>>> X = ...                    # Alternative to None
>>> X
Ellipsis
```

This notation is new in Python 3.X—and goes well beyond the original intent of ... in slicing extensions—so time will tell if it becomes widespread enough to challenge pass and None in these roles.

continue

The continue statement causes an immediate jump to the top of a loop. It also sometimes lets you avoid statement nesting. The next example uses continue to skip odd numbers. This code prints all even numbers less than 10 and greater than or equal to 0. Remember, 0 means false and % is the remainder of division (modulus) operator, so this loop counts down to 0, skipping numbers that aren't multiples of 2—it prints 8 6 4 2 0:

```
x = 10
while x:
    x = x-1                    # Or, x -= 1
    if x % 2 != 0: continue    # Odd? -- skip print
    print(x, end=' ')
```

Because continue jumps to the top of the loop, you don't need to nest the print statement here inside an if test; the print is only reached if the continue is not run. If this sounds similar to a "go to" in other languages, it should. Python has no "go to" statement, but because continue lets you jump about in a program, many of the warnings about readability and maintainability you may have heard about "go to" apply. continue should probably be used sparingly, especially when you're first getting started with Python. For instance, the last example might be clearer if the print were nested under the if:

```
x = 10
while x:
    x = x-1
    if x % 2 == 0:             # Even? -- print
        print(x, end=' ')
```

Later in this book, we'll also learn that raised and caught exceptions can also emulate "go to" statements in limited and structured ways; stay tuned for more on this technique in Chapter 36 where we will learn how to use it to break out of multiple nested loops, a feat not possible with the next section's topic alone.

break

The break statement causes an immediate exit from a loop. Because the code that follows it in the loop is not executed if the break is reached, you can also sometimes avoid nesting by including a break. For example, here is a simple interactive loop (a variant

---

of a larger example we studied in Chapter 10) that inputs data with `input` (known as `raw_input` in Python 2.X) and exits when the user enters "stop" for the name request:

```
>>> while True:
...     name = input('Enter name:')           # Use raw_input() in 2.X
...     if name == 'stop': break
...     age  = input('Enter age: ')
...     print('Hello', name, '=>', int(age) ** 2)
...
Enter name:bob
Enter age: 40
Hello bob => 1600
Enter name:sue
Enter age: 30
Hello sue => 900
Enter name:stop
```

Notice how this code converts the `age` input to an integer with `int` before raising it to the second power; as you'll recall, this is necessary because `input` returns user input as a string. In Chapter 36, you'll see that `input` also raises an exception at end-of-file (e.g., if the user types Ctrl-Z on Windows or Ctrl-D on Unix); if this matters, wrap `input` in `try` statements.

Loop else

When combined with the loop `else` clause, the `break` statement can often eliminate the need for the search status flags used in other languages. For instance, the following piece of code determines whether a positive integer `y` is prime by searching for factors greater than 1:

```
x = y // 2                          # For some y > 1
while x > 1:
    if y % x == 0:                  # Remainder
        print(y, 'has factor', x)
        break                       # Skip else
    x -= 1
else:                               # Normal exit
    print(y, 'is prime')
```

Rather than setting a flag to be tested when the loop is exited, it inserts a `break` where a factor is found. This way, the loop `else` clause can assume that it will be executed only if no factor is found; if you don't hit the `break`, the number is prime. Trace through this code to see how this works.

The loop `else` clause is also run if the body of the loop is never executed, as you don't run a `break` in that event either; in a `while` loop, this happens if the test in the header is false to begin with. Thus, in the preceding example you still get the "is prime" message if `x` is initially less than or equal to 1 (for instance, if `y` is 2).

This example determines primes, but only informally so. Numbers less than 2 are not considered prime by the strict mathematical definition. To be really picky, this code also fails for negative numbers and succeeds for floating-point numbers with no decimal digits. Also note that its code must use // instead of / in Python 3.X because of the migration of / to "true division," as described in Chapter 5 (we need the initial division to truncate remainders, not retain them!). If you want to experiment with this code, be sure to see the exercise at the end of Part IV, which wraps it in a function for reuse.

More on the loop else

Because the loop `else` clause is unique to Python, it tends to perplex some newcomers (and go unused by some veterans; I've met some who didn't even know there *was* an `else` on loops!). In general terms, the loop `else` simply provides explicit syntax for a common coding scenario—it is a coding structure that lets us catch the "other" way out of a loop, without setting and checking flags or conditions.

Suppose, for instance, that we are writing a loop to search a list for a value, and we need to know whether the value was found after we exit the loop. We might code such a task this way (this code is intentionally abstract and incomplete; x is a sequence and match is a tester function to be defined):

```
found = False
while x and not found:
    if match(x[0]):            # Value at front?
        print('Ni')
        found = True
    else:
        x = x[1:]              # Slice off front and repeat
if not found:
    print('not found')
```

Here, we initialize, set, and later test a flag to determine whether the search succeeded or not. This is valid Python code, and it does work; however, this is exactly the sort of structure that the loop `else` clause is there to handle. Here's an `else` equivalent:

```
while x:                       # Exit when x empty
    if match(x[0]):
        print('Ni')
        break                  # Exit, go around else
    x = x[1:]
else:
    print('Not found')         # Only here if exhausted x
```

This version is more concise. The flag is gone, and we've replaced the `if` test at the loop end with an `else` (lined up vertically with the word `while`). Because the `break` inside the main part of the `while` exits the loop and goes around the `else`, this serves as a more structured way to catch the search-failure case.

Some readers might have noticed that the prior example's else clause could be replaced with a test for an empty x after the loop (e.g., if not x:). Although that's true in this example, the else provides explicit syntax for this coding pattern (it's more obviously a search-failure clause here), and such an explicit empty test may not apply in some cases. The loop else becomes even more useful when used in conjunction with the for loop—the topic of the next section—because sequence iteration is not under your control.

Why You Will Care: Emulating C while Loops

The section on expression statements in Chapter 11 stated that Python doesn't allow statements such as assignments to appear in places where it expects an expression. That is, each statement must generally appear on a line by itself, not nested in a larger construct. That means this common C language coding pattern won't work in Python:

```
while ((x = next(obj)) != NULL) {...process x...}
```

C assignments return the value assigned, but Python assignments are just statements, not expressions. This eliminates a notorious class of C errors: you can't accidentally type = in Python when you mean ==. If you need similar behavior, though, there are at least three ways to get the same effect in Python while loops without embedding assignments in loop tests. You can move the assignment into the loop body with a break:

```
while True:
    x = next(obj)
    if not x: break
    ...process x...
```

or move the assignment into the loop with tests:

```
x = True
while x:
    x = next(obj)
    if x:
        ...process x...
```

or move the first assignment outside the loop:

```
x = next(obj)
while x:
    ...process x...
    x = next(obj)
```

Of these three coding patterns, the first may be considered by some to be the least structured, but it also seems to be the simplest and is the most commonly used. A simple Python for loop may replace such C loops as well and be more Pythonic, but C doesn't have a directly analogous tool:

```
for x in obj: ...process x...
```

---

for Loops

The for loop is a generic iterator in Python: it can step through the items in any ordered sequence or other iterable object. The for statement works on strings, lists, tuples, and other built-in iterables, as well as new user-defined objects that we'll learn how to create later with classes. We met for briefly in Chapter 4 and in conjunction with sequence object types; let's expand on its usage more formally here.

General Format

The Python for loop begins with a header line that specifies an assignment target (or targets), along with the object you want to step through. The header is followed by a block of (normally indented) statements that you want to repeat:

```
for target in object:        # Assign object items to target
    statements               # Repeated loop body: use target
else:                        # Optional else part
    statements               # If we didn't hit a 'break'
```

When Python runs a for loop, it assigns the items in the iterable object to the target one by one and executes the loop body for each. The loop body typically uses the assignment target to refer to the current item in the sequence as though it were a cursor stepping through the sequence.

The name used as the assignment target in a for header line is usually a (possibly new) variable in the scope where the for statement is coded. There's not much unique about this name; it can even be changed inside the loop's body, but it will automatically be set to the next item in the sequence when control returns to the top of the loop again. After the loop this variable normally still refers to the last item visited, which is the last item in the sequence unless the loop exits with a break statement.

The for statement also supports an optional else block, which works exactly as it does in a while loop—it's executed if the loop exits without running into a break statement (i.e., if all items in the sequence have been visited). The break and continue statements introduced earlier also work the same in a for loop as they do in a while. The for loop's complete format can be described this way:

```
for target in object:        # Assign object items to target
    statements
    if test: break           # Exit loop now, skip else
    if test: continue        # Go to top of loop now
else:
    statements               # If we didn't hit a 'break'
```

Examples

Let's type a few for loops interactively now, so you can see how they are used in practice.

Basic usage

As mentioned earlier, a `for` loop can step across any kind of sequence object. In our first example, for instance, we'll assign the name x to each of the three items in a list in turn, from left to right, and the `print` statement will be executed for each. Inside the `print` statement (the loop body), the name x refers to the current item in the list:

```
>>> for x in ["spam", "eggs", "ham"]:
...     print(x, end=' ')
...
spam eggs ham
```

The next two examples compute the sum and product of all the items in a list. Later in this chapter and later in the book we'll meet tools that apply operations such as + and * to items in a list automatically, but it's often just as easy to use a `for`:

```
>>> sum = 0
>>> for x in [1, 2, 3, 4]:
...     sum = sum + x
...
>>> sum
10
>>> prod = 1
>>> for item in [1, 2, 3, 4]: prod *= item
...
>>> prod
24
```

Other data types

Any sequence works in a `for`, as it's a generic tool. For example, `for` loops work on strings and tuples:

```
>>> S = "lumberjack"
>>> T = ("and", "I'm", "okay")

>>> for x in S: print(x, end=' ')        # Iterate over a string
...
l u m b e r j a c k

>>> for x in T: print(x, end=' ')        # Iterate over a tuple
...
and I'm okay
```

In fact, as we'll learn in the next chapter when we explore the notion of "iterables," `for` loops can even work on some objects that are not sequences—files and dictionaries work, too.

Tuple assignment in for loops

If you're iterating through a sequence of tuples, the loop target itself can actually be a *tuple* of targets. This is just another case of the tuple-unpacking assignment we studied

---

in Chapter 11 at work. Remember, the for loop assigns items in the sequence object to the target, and assignment works the same everywhere:

```
>>> T = [(1, 2), (3, 4), (5, 6)]
>>> for (a, b) in T:                    # Tuple assignment at work
...     print(a, b)
...
1 2
3 4
5 6
```

Here, the first time through the loop is like writing (a,b) = (1,2), the second time is like writing (a,b) = (3,4), and so on. The net effect is to automatically unpack the current tuple on each iteration.

This form is commonly used in conjunction with the zip call we'll meet later in this chapter to implement parallel traversals. It also makes regular appearances in conjunction with SQL databases in Python, where query result tables are returned as sequences of sequences like the list used here—the outer list is the database table, the nested tuples are the rows within the table, and tuple assignment extracts columns.

Tuples in for loops also come in handy to iterate through *both* keys and values in dictionaries using the items method, rather than looping through the keys and indexing to fetch the values manually:

```
>>> D = {'a': 1, 'b': 2, 'c': 3}
>>> for key in D:
...     print(key, '=>', D[key])        # Use dict keys iterator and index
...
a => 1
c => 3
b => 2

>>> list(D.items())
[('a', 1), ('c', 3), ('b', 2)]

>>> for (key, value) in D.items():
...     print(key, '=>', value)         # Iterate over both keys and values
...
a => 1
c => 3
b => 2
```

It's important to note that tuple assignment in for loops isn't a special case; any assignment target works syntactically after the word for. We can always assign manually within the loop to unpack:

```
>>> T
[(1, 2), (3, 4), (5, 6)]

>>> for both in T:
...     a, b = both                     # Manual assignment equivalent
...     print(a, b)                     # 2.X: prints with enclosing tuple "()"
...
```

```
1 2
3 4
5 6
```

But tuples in the loop header save us an extra step when iterating through sequences of sequences. As suggested in Chapter 11, even *nested* structures may be automatically unpacked this way in a `for`:

```
>>> ((a, b), c) = ((1, 2), 3)          # Nested sequences work too
>>> a, b, c
(1, 2, 3)

>>> for ((a, b), c) in [((1, 2), 3), ((4, 5), 6)]: print(a, b, c)
...
1 2 3
4 5 6
```

Even this is not a special case, though—the `for` loop simply runs the sort of assignment we ran just before it, on each iteration. Any nested sequence structure may be unpacked this way, simply because *sequence assignment* is so generic:

```
>>> for ((a, b), c) in [([1, 2], 3), ['XY', 6]]: print(a, b, c)
...
1 2 3
X Y 6
```

Python 3.X extended sequence assignment in for loops

In fact, because the loop variable in a `for` loop can be any assignment target, we can also use Python 3.X's extended sequence-unpacking assignment syntax here to extract items and sections of sequences within sequences. Really, this isn't a special case either, but simply a new assignment form in 3.X, as discussed in Chapter 11; because it works in assignment statements, it automatically works in `for` loops.

Consider the tuple assignment form introduced in the prior section. A tuple of values is assigned to a tuple of names on each iteration, exactly like a simple assignment statement:

```
>>> a, b, c = (1, 2, 3)                          # Tuple assignment
>>> a, b, c
(1, 2, 3)

>>> for (a, b, c) in [(1, 2, 3), (4, 5, 6)]:      # Used in for loop
...         print(a, b, c)
...
1 2 3
4 5 6
```

In Python 3.X, because a sequence can be assigned to a more general set of names with a starred name to collect multiple items, we can use the same syntax to extract parts of nested sequences in the `for` loop:

```
>>> a, *b, c = (1, 2, 3, 4)                       # Extended seq assignment
>>> a, b, c
```

```
(1, [2, 3], 4)
>>> for (a, *b, c) in [(1, 2, 3, 4), (5, 6, 7, 8)]:
...     print(a, b, c)
...
1 [2, 3] 4
5 [6, 7] 8
```

In practice, this approach might be used to pick out multiple columns from rows of data represented as nested sequences. In Python 2.X starred names aren't allowed, but you can achieve similar effects by slicing. The only difference is that slicing returns a type-specific result, whereas starred names always are assigned lists:

```
>>> for all in [(1, 2, 3, 4), (5, 6, 7, 8)]:          # Manual slicing in 2.X
...     a, b, c = all[0], all[1:3], all[3]
...     print(a, b, c)
...
1 (2, 3) 4
5 (6, 7) 8
```

See Chapter 11 for more on this assignment form.

Nested for loops

Now let's look at a for loop that's a bit more sophisticated than those we've seen so far. The next example illustrates statement nesting and the loop else clause in a for. Given a list of objects (items) and a list of keys (tests), this code searches for each key in the objects list and reports on the search's outcome:

```
>>> items = ["aaa", 111, (4, 5), 2.01]      # A set of objects
>>> tests = [(4, 5), 3.14]                   # Keys to search for
>>>
>>> for key in tests:                        # For all keys
...     for item in items:                   # For all items
...         if item == key:                  # Check for match
...             print(key, "was found")
...             break
...     else:
...         print(key, "not found!")
...
(4, 5) was found
3.14 not found!
```

Because the nested if runs a break when a match is found, the loop else clause can assume that if it is reached, the search has failed. Notice the nesting here. When this code runs, there are two loops going at the same time: the outer loop scans the keys list, and the inner loop scans the items list for each key. The nesting of the loop else clause is critical; it's indented to the same level as the header line of the inner for loop, so it's associated with the inner loop, not the if or the outer for.

This example is illustrative, but it may be easier to code if we employ the in operator to test membership. Because in implicitly scans an object looking for a match (at least logically), it replaces the inner loop:

```
>>> for key in tests:                      # For all keys
...     if key in items:                    # Let Python check for a match
...         print(key, "was found")
...     else:
...         print(key, "not found!")
...
(4, 5) was found
3.14 not found!
```

In general, it's a good idea to let Python do as much of the work as possible (as in this solution) for the sake of brevity and performance.

The next example is similar, but builds a list as it goes for later use instead of printing. It performs a typical data-structure task with a `for`—collecting common items in two sequences (strings)—and serves as a rough set intersection routine. After the loop runs, `res` refers to a list that contains all the items found in `seq1` and `seq2`:

```
>>> seq1 = "spam"
>>> seq2 = "scam"
>>>
>>> res = []                                # Start empty
>>> for x in seq1:                          # Scan first sequence
...     if x in seq2:                        # Common item?
...         res.append(x)                    # Add to result end
...
>>> res
['s', 'a', 'm']
```

Unfortunately, this code is equipped to work only on two specific variables: `seq1` and `seq2`. It would be nice if this loop could somehow be generalized into a tool you could use more than once. As you'll see, that simple idea leads us to *functions*, the topic of the next part of the book.

This code also exhibits the classic *list comprehension* pattern—collecting a results list with an iteration and optional filter test—and could be coded more concisely too:

```
>>> [x for x in seq1 if x in seq2]          # Let Python collect results
['s', 'a', 'm']
```

But you'll have to read on to the next chapter for the rest of this story.

Why You Will Care: File Scanners

In general, loops come in handy anywhere you need to repeat an operation or process something more than once. Because *files* contain multiple characters and lines, they are one of the more typical use cases for loops. To load a file's contents into a string all at once, you simply call the file object's `read` method:

```
file = open('test.txt', 'r')       # Read contents into a string
print(file.read())
```

But to load a file in smaller pieces, it's common to code either a `while` loop with breaks on end-of-file, or a `for` loop. To read by *characters*, either of the following codings will suffice:

```
file = open('test.txt')
while True:
    char = file.read(1)        # Read by character
    if not char: break         # Empty string means end-of-file
    print(char)

for char in open('test.txt').read():
    print(char)
```

The for loop here also processes each character, but it loads the file into memory all at once (and assumes it fits!). To read by *lines* or *blocks* instead, you can use while loop code like this:

```
file = open('test.txt')
while True:
    line = file.readline()     # Read line by line
    if not line: break
    print(line.rstrip())       # Line already has a \n

file = open('test.txt', 'rb')
while True:
    chunk = file.read(10)      # Read byte chunks: up to 10 bytes
    if not chunk: break
    print(chunk)
```

You typically read binary data in blocks. To read text files *line by line*, though, the for loop tends to be easiest to code and the quickest to run:

```
for line in open('test.txt').readlines():
    print(line.rstrip())

for line in open('test.txt'):      # Use iterators: best for text input
    print(line.rstrip())
```

Both of these versions work in both Python 2.X and 3.X. The first uses the file read lines method to load a file all at once into a line-string list, and the last example here relies on file *iterators* to automatically read one line on each loop iteration.

The last example is also generally the *best* option for text files—besides its simplicity, it works for arbitrarily large files because it doesn't load the entire file into memory all at once. The iterator version may also be the quickest, though I/O performance may vary per Python line and release.

File readlines calls can still be useful, though—to *reverse* a file's lines, for example, assuming its content can fit in memory. The reversed built-in accepts a sequence, but not an arbitrary iterable that generates values; in other words, a list works, but a file object doesn't:

```
for line in reversed(open('test.txt').readlines()): ...
```

In some 2.X Python code, you may also see the name open replaced with file and the file object's older xreadlines method used to achieve the same effect as the file's automatic line iterator (it's like readlines but doesn't load the file into memory all at once). Both file and xreadlines are removed in Python 3.X, because they are redundant. You should generally avoid them in new 2.X code too—use file iterators and open call in recent 2.X releases—but they may pop up in older code and resources.

See the library manual for more on the calls used here, and Chapter 14 for more on file line iterators. Also watch for the sidebar "Why You Will Care: Shell Commands and More" on page 411 in this chapter; it applies these same file tools to the `os.popen` command-line launcher to read program output. There's more on reading files in Chapter 37 too; as we'll see there, text and binary files have slightly different semantics in 3.X.

Loop Coding Techniques

The `for` loop we just studied subsumes most counter-style loops. It's generally simpler to code and often quicker to run than a `while`, so it's the first tool you should reach for whenever you need to step through a sequence or other iterable. In fact, as a general rule, you should *resist the temptation to count things in Python*—its iteration tools automate much of the work you do to loop over collections in lower-level languages like C.

Still, there are situations where you will need to iterate in more specialized ways. For example, what if you need to visit every second or third item in a list, or change the list along the way? How about traversing more than one sequence in parallel, in the same `for` loop? What if you need indexes too?

You can always code such unique iterations with a `while` loop and manual indexing, but Python provides a set of built-ins that allow you to specialize the iteration in a `for`:

- The built-in `range` function (available since Python 0.X) produces a series of successively higher integers, which can be used as indexes in a `for`.
- The built-in `zip` function (available since Python 2.0) returns a series of parallel-item tuples, which can be used to traverse multiple sequences in a `for`.
- The built-in `enumerate` function (available since Python 2.3) generates both the values and indexes of items in an iterable, so we don't need to count manually.
- The built-in `map` function (available since Python 1.0) can have a similar effect to `zip` in Python 2.X, though this role is removed in 3.X.

Because `for` loops may run quicker than `while`-based counter loops, though, it's to your advantage to use tools like these that allow you to use `for` whenever possible. Let's look at each of these built-ins in turn, in the context of common use cases. As we'll see, their usage may differ slightly between 2.X and 3.X, and some of their applications are more valid than others.

Counter Loops: range

Our first loop-related function, `range`, is really a general tool that can be used in a variety of contexts. We met it briefly in Chapter 4. Although it's used most often to generate indexes in a `for`, you can use it anywhere you need a series of integers. In

Python 2.X range creates a physical *list*; in 3.X, range is an *iterable* that generates items on demand, so we need to wrap it in a list call to display its results all at once in 3.X only:

```
>>> list(range(5)), list(range(2, 5)), list(range(0, 10, 2))
([0, 1, 2, 3, 4], [2, 3, 4], [0, 2, 4, 6, 8])
```

With one argument, range generates a list of integers from zero up to but not including the argument's value. If you pass in two arguments, the first is taken as the lower bound. An optional third argument can give a *step*; if it is used, Python adds the step to each successive integer in the result (the step defaults to +1). Ranges can also be nonpositive and nonascending, if you want them to be:

```
>>> list(range(-5, 5))
[-5, -4, -3, -2, -1, 0, 1, 2, 3, 4]

>>> list(range(5, -5, -1))
[5, 4, 3, 2, 1, 0, -1, -2, -3, -4]
```

We'll get more formal about iterables like this one in Chapter 14. There, we'll also see that Python 2.X has a cousin named xrange, which is like its range but doesn't build the result list in memory all at once. This is a space optimization, which is subsumed in 3.X by the generator behavior of its range.

Although such range results may be useful all by themselves, they tend to come in most handy within for loops. For one thing, they provide a simple way to repeat an action a specific number of times. To print three lines, for example, use a range to generate the appropriate number of integers:

```
>>> for i in range(3):
...     print(i, 'Pythons')
...
0 Pythons
1 Pythons
2 Pythons
```

Note that for loops force results from range automatically in 3.X, so we don't need to use a list wrapper here in 3.X (in 2.X we get a temporary list unless we call xrange instead).

Sequence Scans: while and range Versus for

The range call is also sometimes used to iterate over a sequence indirectly, though it's often not the best approach in this role. The easiest and generally fastest way to step through a sequence exhaustively is always with a simple for, as Python handles most of the details for you:

```
>>> X = 'spam'
>>> for item in X: print(item, end=' ')          # Simple iteration
...
s p a m
```

Internally, the `for` loop handles the details of the iteration automatically when used this way. If you really need to take over the indexing logic explicitly, you can do it with a `while` loop:

```
>>> i = 0
>>> while i < len(X):                          # while loop iteration
...     print(X[i], end=' ')
...     i += 1
...
s p a m
```

You can also do manual indexing with a `for`, though, if you use `range` to generate a list of indexes to iterate through. It's a multistep process, but it's sufficient to generate offsets, rather than the items at those offsets:

```
>>> X
'spam'
>>> len(X)                                     # Length of string
4
>>> list(range(len(X)))                        # All legal offsets into X
[0, 1, 2, 3]
>>>
>>> for i in range(len(X)): print(X[i], end=' ')   # Manual range/len iteration
...
s p a m
```

Note that because this example is stepping over a list of *offsets* into X, not the actual *items* of X, we need to index back into X within the loop to fetch each item. If this seems like overkill, though, it's because it is: there's really no reason to work this hard in this example.

Although the `range`/`len` combination suffices in this role, it's probably not the best option. It may run slower, and it's also more work than we need to do. Unless you have a special indexing requirement, you're better off using the simple `for` loop form in Python:

```
>>> for item in X: print(item, end=' ')        # Use simple iteration if you can
```

As a general rule, use `for` instead of `while` whenever possible, and don't use `range` calls in `for` loops except as a last resort. This simpler solution is almost always better. Like every good rule, though, there are plenty of exceptions—as the next section demonstrates.

Sequence Shufflers: range and len

Though not ideal for simple sequence scans, the coding pattern used in the prior example does allow us to do more specialized sorts of traversals when required. For example, some algorithms can make use of sequence reordering—to generate alternatives in searches, to test the effect of different value orderings, and so on. Such cases may require offsets in order to pull sequences apart and put them back together, as in the following; the range's integers provide a repeat count in the first, and a position for slicing in the second:

```
>>> S = 'spam'
>>> for i in range(len(S)):          # For repeat counts 0..3
...     S = S[1:] + S[:1]            # Move front item to end
...     print(S, end=' ')
...
pams amsp mspa spam

>>> S
'spam'
>>> for i in range(len(S)):          # For positions 0..3
...     X = S[i:] + S[:i]            # Rear part + front part
...     print(X, end=' ')
...
spam pams amsp mspa
```

Trace through these one iteration at a time if they seem confusing. The second creates the same results as the first, though in a different order, and doesn't change the original variable as it goes. Because both slice to obtain parts to concatenate, they also work on any type of sequence, and return sequences of the same type as that being shuffled—if you shuffle a list, you create reordered lists:

```
>>> L = [1, 2, 3]
>>> for i in range(len(L)):
...     X = L[i:] + L[:i]           # Works on any sequence type
...     print(X, end=' ')
...
[1, 2, 3] [2, 3, 1] [3, 1, 2]
```

We'll make use of code like this to test functions with different argument orderings in Chapter 18, and will extend it to functions, generators, and more complete permutations in Chapter 20—it's a widely useful tool.

Nonexhaustive Traversals: range Versus Slices

Cases like that of the prior section are valid applications for the range/len combination. We might also use this technique to skip items as we go:

```
>>> S = 'abcdefghijk'
>>> list(range(0, len(S), 2))
[0, 2, 4, 6, 8, 10]

>>> for i in range(0, len(S), 2): print(S[i], end=' ')
...
a c e g i k
```

Here, we visit every *second* item in the string S by stepping over the generated range list. To visit every third item, change the third range argument to be 3, and so on. In effect, using range this way lets you skip items in loops while still retaining the simplicity of the for loop construct.

In most cases, though, this is also probably not the "best practice" technique in Python today. If you really mean to skip items in a sequence, the extended three-limit form of the *slice expression*, presented in Chapter 7, provides a simpler route to the same goal. To visit every second character in S, for example, slice with a stride of 2:

```
>>> S = 'abcdefghijk'
>>> for c in S[::2]: print(c, end=' ')
...
a c e g i k
```

The result is the same, but substantially easier for you to write and for others to read. The potential advantage to using range here instead is space: slicing makes a copy of the string in both 2.X and 3.X, while range in 3.X and xrange in 2.X do not create a list; for very large strings, they may save memory.

Changing Lists: range Versus Comprehensions

Another common place where you may use the range/len combination with for is in loops that change a list as it is being traversed. Suppose, for example, that you need to add 1 to every item in a list (maybe you're giving everyone a raise in an employee database list). You can try this with a simple for loop, but the result probably won't be exactly what you want:

```
>>> L = [1, 2, 3, 4, 5]

>>> for x in L:
...     x += 1                   # Changes x, not L
...
>>> L
[1, 2, 3, 4, 5]
>>> x
6
```

This doesn't quite work—it changes the loop variable x, not the list L. The reason is somewhat subtle. Each time through the loop, x refers to the next integer already pulled out of the list. In the first iteration, for example, x is integer 1. In the next iteration, the loop body sets x to a different object, integer 2, but it does not update the list where 1 originally came from; it's a piece of memory separate from the list.

To really change the list as we march across it, we need to use indexes so we can assign an updated value to each position as we go. The range/len combination can produce the required indexes for us:

```
>>> L = [1, 2, 3, 4, 5]

>>> for i in range(len(L)):      # Add one to each item in L
...     L[i] += 1                # Or L[i] = L[i] + 1
...
>>> L
[2, 3, 4, 5, 6]
```

When coded this way, the list is changed as we proceed through the loop. There is no way to do the same with a simple `for x in L:`–style loop, because such a loop iterates through actual items, not list positions. But what about the equivalent `while` loop? Such a loop requires a bit more work on our part, and might run more slowly depending on your Python (it does on 2.7 and 3.3, though less so on 3.3—we'll see how to verify this in Chapter 21):

```
>>> i = 0
>>> while i < len(L):
...     L[i] += 1
...     i += 1
...
>>> L
[3, 4, 5, 6, 7]
```

Here again, though, the `range` solution may not be ideal either. A list comprehension expression of the form:

```
[x + 1 for x in L]
```

likely runs faster today and would do similar work, albeit without changing the original list in place (we could assign the expression's new list object result back to L, but this would not update any other references to the original list). Because this is such a central looping concept, we'll save a complete exploration of list comprehensions for the next chapter, and continue this story there.

Parallel Traversals: zip and map

Our next loop coding technique extends a loop's scope. As we've seen, the `range` built-in allows us to traverse sequences with `for` in a nonexhaustive fashion. In the same spirit, the built-in `zip` function allows us to use `for` loops to visit multiple sequences *in parallel*—not overlapping in time, but during the same loop. In basic operation, `zip` takes one or more sequences as arguments and returns a series of tuples that pair up parallel items taken from those sequences. For example, suppose we're working with two lists (a list of names and addresses paired by position, perhaps):

```
>>> L1 = [1,2,3,4]
>>> L2 = [5,6,7,8]
```

To combine the items in these lists, we can use `zip` to create a list of tuple pairs. Like `range`, `zip` is a list in Python 2.X, but an iterable object in 3.X where we must wrap it in a `list` call to display all its results at once (again, there's more on iterables coming up in the next chapter):

```
>>> zip(L1, L2)
<zip object at 0x026523C8>
>>> list(zip(L1, L2))            # list() required in 3.X, not 2.X
[(1, 5), (2, 6), (3, 7), (4, 8)]
```

Such a result may be useful in other contexts as well, but when wedded with the for loop, it supports parallel iterations:

```
>>> for (x, y) in zip(L1, L2):
...     print(x, y, '--', x+y)
...
1 5 -- 6
2 6 -- 8
3 7 -- 10
4 8 -- 12
```

Here, we step over the result of the `zip` call—that is, the pairs of items pulled from the two lists. Notice that this `for` loop again uses the tuple assignment form we met earlier to unpack each tuple in the `zip` result. The first time through, it's as though we ran the assignment statement `(x, y) = (1, 5)`.

The net effect is that we scan both L1 *and* L2 in our loop. We could achieve a similar effect with a `while` loop that handles indexing manually, but it would require more typing and would likely run more slowly than the `for/zip` approach.

Strictly speaking, the `zip` function is more general than this example suggests. For instance, it accepts any type of sequence (really, any iterable object, including files), and it accepts more than two arguments. With three arguments, as in the following example, it builds a list of three-item tuples with items from each sequence, essentially projecting by columns (technically, we get an N-ary tuple for N arguments):

```
>>> T1, T2, T3 = (1,2,3), (4,5,6), (7,8,9)
>>> T3
(7, 8, 9)
>>> list(zip(T1, T2, T3))          # Three tuples for three arguments
[(1, 4, 7), (2, 5, 8), (3, 6, 9)]
```

Moreover, `zip` truncates result tuples at the length of the shortest sequence when the argument lengths differ. In the following, we zip together two strings to pick out characters in parallel, but the result has only as many tuples as the length of the shortest sequence:

```
>>> S1 = 'abc'
>>> S2 = 'xyz123'
>>>
>>> list(zip(S1, S2))              # Truncates at len(shortest)
[('a', 'x'), ('b', 'y'), ('c', 'z')]
```

map equivalence in Python 2.X

In Python 2.X only, the related built-in `map` function pairs items from sequences in a similar fashion when passed `None` for its function argument, but it pads shorter sequences with `None` if the argument lengths differ instead of truncating to the shortest length:

```
>>> S1 = 'abc'
>>> S2 = 'xyz123'

>>> map(None, S1, S2)                  # 2.X only: pads to len(longest)
[('a', 'x'), ('b', 'y'), ('c', 'z'), (None, '1'), (None, '2'), (None,'3')]
```

This example is using a degenerate form of the `map` built-in, which is no longer supported in 3.X. Normally, `map` takes a function and one or more sequence arguments and collects the results of calling the function with parallel items taken from the sequence(s).

We'll study `map` in detail in Chapter 19 and Chapter 20, but as a brief example, the following maps the built-in `ord` function across each item in a string and collects the results (like `zip`, `map` is a value generator in 3.X and so must be passed to `list` to collect all its results at once in 3.X only):

```
>>> list(map(ord, 'spam'))
[115, 112, 97, 109]
```

This works the same as the following loop statement, but `map` is often quicker, as Chapter 21 will show:

```
>>> res = []
>>> for c in 'spam': res.append(ord(c))
>>> res
[115, 112, 97, 109]
```

 Version skew note: The degenerate form of `map` using a function argument of `None` is no longer supported in Python 3.X, because it largely overlaps with `zip` (and was, frankly, a bit at odds with `map`'s function-application purpose). In 3.X, either use `zip` or write loop code to pad results yourself. In fact, we'll see how to write such loop code in Chapter 20, after we've had a chance to study some additional iteration concepts.

Dictionary construction with zip

Let's look at another `zip` use case. Chapter 8 suggested that the `zip` call used here can also be handy for generating dictionaries when the sets of keys and values must be computed at runtime. Now that we're becoming proficient with `zip`, let's explore more fully how it relates to dictionary construction. As you've learned, you can always create a dictionary by coding a dictionary literal, or by assigning to keys over time:

```
>>> D1 = {'spam':1, 'eggs':3, 'toast':5}
>>> D1
{'eggs': 3, 'toast': 5, 'spam': 1}

>>> D1 = {}
>>> D1['spam']  = 1
>>> D1['eggs']  = 3
>>> D1['toast'] = 5
```

What to do, though, if your program obtains dictionary keys and values in *lists* at runtime, after you've coded your script? For example, say you had the following keys and values lists, collected from a user, parsed from a file, or obtained from another dynamic source:

```
>>> keys = ['spam', 'eggs', 'toast']
>>> vals = [1, 3, 5]
```

One solution for turning those lists into a dictionary would be to `zip` the lists and step through them in parallel with a `for` loop:

```
>>> list(zip(keys, vals))
[('spam', 1), ('eggs', 3), ('toast', 5)]

>>> D2 = {}
>>> for (k, v) in zip(keys, vals): D2[k] = v
...
>>> D2
{'eggs': 3, 'toast': 5, 'spam': 1}
```

It turns out, though, that in Python 2.2 and later you can skip the `for` loop altogether and simply pass the zipped keys/values lists to the built-in `dict` constructor call:

```
>>> keys = ['spam', 'eggs', 'toast']
>>> vals = [1, 3, 5]

>>> D3 = dict(zip(keys, vals))
>>> D3
{'eggs': 3, 'toast': 5, 'spam': 1}
```

The built-in name `dict` is really a type name in Python (you'll learn more about type names, and subclassing them, in Chapter 32). Calling it achieves something like a list-to-dictionary conversion, but it's really an object construction request.

In the next chapter we'll explore the related but richer concept, the list comprehension, which builds lists in a single expression; we'll also revisit Python 3.X and 2.7 dictionary comprehensions, an alternative to the `dict` call for zipped key/value pairs:

```
>>> {k: v for (k, v) in zip(keys, vals)}
{'eggs': 3, 'toast': 5, 'spam': 1}
```

Generating Both Offsets and Items: enumerate

Our final loop helper function is designed to support dual usage modes. Earlier, we discussed using `range` to generate the offsets of items in a string, rather than the items at those offsets. In some programs, though, we need both: the item to use, plus an offset as we go. Traditionally, this was coded with a simple `for` loop that also kept a counter of the current offset:

```
>>> S = 'spam'
>>> offset = 0
>>> for item in S:
...     print(item, 'appears at offset', offset)
...     offset += 1
...
s appears at offset 0
p appears at offset 1
a appears at offset 2
m appears at offset 3
```

This works, but in all recent Python 2.X and 3.X releases (since 2.3) a new built-in named enumerate does the job for us—its net effect is to give loops a counter "for free," without sacrificing the simplicity of automatic iteration:

```
>>> S = 'spam'
>>> for (offset, item) in enumerate(S):
...     print(item, 'appears at offset', offset)
...
s appears at offset 0
p appears at offset 1
a appears at offset 2
m appears at offset 3
```

The enumerate function returns a *generator object*—a kind of object that supports the iteration protocol that we will study in the next chapter and will discuss in more detail in the next part of the book. In short, it has a method called by the next built-in function, which returns an (*index, value*) tuple each time through the loop. The for steps through these tuples automatically, which allows us to unpack their values with tuple assignment, much as we did for zip:

```
>>> E = enumerate(S)
>>> E
<enumerate object at 0x0000000002A8B900>
>>> next(E)
(0, 's')
>>> next(E)
(1, 'p')
>>> next(E)
(2, 'a')
```

We don't normally see this machinery because all iteration contexts—including list comprehensions, the subject of Chapter 14—run the iteration protocol automatically:

```
>>> [c * i for (i, c) in enumerate(S)]
['', 'p', 'aa', 'mmm']

>>> for (i, l) in enumerate(open('test.txt')):
...     print('%s) %s' % (i, l.rstrip()))
...
0) aaaaaa
1) bbbbbb
2) cccccc
```

To fully understand iteration concepts like enumerate, zip, and list comprehensions, though, we need to move on to the next chapter for a more formal dissection.

Why You Will Care: Shell Commands and More

An earlier sidebar showed loops applied to files. As briefly noted in Chapter 9, Python's related os.popen call also gives a file-like interface, for reading the outputs of spawned *shell commands*. Now that we've studied looping statements in full, here's an example of this tool in action—to run a shell command and read its standard output text, pass the command as a string to os popen, and read text from the file-like object it returns

---

(if this triggers a Unicode encoding issue on your computer, Chapter 25's discussion of currency symbols may apply):

```
>>> import os
>>> F = os.popen('dir')              # Read line by line
>>> F.readline()
' Volume in drive C has no label.\n'
>>> F = os.popen('dir')              # Read by sized blocks
>>> F.read(50)
' Volume in drive C has no label.\n Volume Serial Nu'

>>> os.popen('dir').readlines()[0]   # Read all lines: index
' Volume in drive C has no label.\n'
>>> os.popen('dir').read()[:50]      # Read all at once: slice
' Volume in drive C has no label.\n Volume Serial Nu'

>>> for line in os.popen('dir'):     # File line iterator loop
...     print(line.rstrip())
...
 Volume in drive C has no label.
 Volume Serial Number is D093-D1F7
...and so on...
```

This runs a `dir` directory listing on Windows, but any program that can be started with a command line can be launched this way. We might use this scheme, for example, to display the output of the windows `systeminfo` command—`os.system` simply runs a shell command, but `os.popen` also connects to its streams; both of the following show the shell command's output in a simple console window, but the first might not in a GUI interface such as IDLE:

```
>>> os.system('systeminfo')
...output in console, popup in IDLE...
0
>>> for line in os.popen('systeminfo'): print(line.rstrip())

Host Name:              MARK-VAIO
OS Name:                Microsoft Windows 7 Professional
OS Version:             6.1.7601 Service Pack 1 Build 7601
...lots of system information text...
```

And once we have a command's output in text form, any string processing tool or technique applies—including display formatting and content parsing:

```
# Formatted, limited display
>>> for (i, line) in enumerate(os.popen('systeminfo')):
...     if i == 4: break
...     print('%05d) %s' % (i, line.rstrip()))
...
00000)
00001) Host Name:              MARK-VAIO
00002) OS Name:                Microsoft Windows 7 Professional
00003) OS Version:             6.1.7601 Service Pack 1 Build 7601

# Parse for specific lines, case neutral
>>> for line in os.popen('systeminfo'):
...     parts = line.split(':')
...     if parts and parts[0].lower() == 'system type':
...         print(parts[1].strip())
```

```
...
x64-based PC
```

We'll see os.popen in action again in Chapter 21, where we'll deploy it to read the results of a constructed command line that times code alternatives, and in Chapter 25, where it will be used to compare outputs of scripts being tested.

Tools like os.popen and os.system (and the subprocess module not shown here) allow you to leverage every command-line program on your computer, but you can also write emulators with in-process code. For example, simulating the Unix awk utility's ability to strip columns out of text files is almost trivial in Python, and can become a reusable function in the process:

```
# awk emulation: extract column 7 from whitespace-delimited file
for val in [line.split()[6] for line in open('input.txt')]:
    print(val)

# Same, but more explicit code that retains result
col7 = []
for line in open('input.txt'):
    cols = line.split()
    col7.append(cols[6])
for item in col7:  print(item)

# Same, but a reusable function (see next part of book)
def awker(file, col):
    return [line.rstrip().split()[col-1] for line in open(file)]

print(awker('input.txt', 7))            # List of strings
print(','.join(awker('input.txt', 7))) # Put commas between
```

By itself, though, Python provides file-like access to a wide variety of data—including the text returned by *websites* and their pages identified by URL, though we'll have to defer to Part V for more on the package import used here, and other resources for more on such tools in general (e.g., this works in 2.X, but uses urllib instead of urllib.request, and returns text strings):

```
>>> from urllib.request import urlopen
>>> for line in urlopen('http://home.rmi.net/~lutz'):
...     print(line)
...
b'<HTML>\n'
b'\n'
b'<HEAD>\n'
b"<TITLE>Mark Lutz's Book Support Site</TITLE>\n"
...etc...
```

Chapter Summary

In this chapter, we explored Python's looping statements as well as some concepts related to looping in Python. We looked at the while and for loop statements in depth, and we learned about their associated else clauses. We also studied the break and continue statements, which have meaning only inside loops, and met several built-in tools commonly used in for loops, including range, zip, map, and enumerate, although some of the details regarding their roles as iterables in Python 3.X were intentionally cut short.

In the next chapter, we continue the iteration story by discussing list comprehensions and the iteration protocol in Python—concepts strongly related to for loops. There, we'll also give the rest of the picture behind the iterable tools we met here, such as range and zip, and study some of the subtleties of their operation. As always, though, before moving on let's exercise what you've picked up here with a quiz.

Test Your Knowledge: Quiz

1. What are the main functional differences between a while and a for?
2. What's the difference between break and continue?
3. When is a loop's else clause executed?
4. How can you code a counter-based loop in Python?
5. What can a range be used for in a for loop?

Test Your Knowledge: Answers

1. The while loop is a general looping statement, but the for is designed to iterate across items in a sequence or other iterable. Although the while can imitate the for with counter loops, it takes more code and might run slower.

2. The break statement exits a loop immediately (you wind up below the entire while or for loop statement), and continue jumps back to the top of the loop (you wind up positioned just before the test in while or the next item fetch in for).

3. The else clause in a while or for loop will be run once as the loop is exiting, if the loop exits normally (without running into a break statement). A break exits the loop immediately, skipping the else part on the way out (if there is one).

4. Counter loops can be coded with a while statement that keeps track of the index manually, or with a for loop that uses the range built-in function to generate successive integer offsets. Neither is the preferred way to work in Python, if you need to simply step across all the items in a sequence. Instead, use a simple for loop instead, without range or counters, whenever possible; it will be easier to code and usually quicker to run.

5. The range built-in can be used in a for to implement a fixed number of repetitions, to scan by offsets instead of items at offsets, to skip successive items as you go, and to change a list while stepping across it. None of these roles requires range, and most have alternatives—scanning actual items, three-limit slices, and list comprehensions are often better solutions today (despite the natural inclinations of ex–C programmers to want to count things!).

Iterations and Comprehensions

In the prior chapter we met Python's two looping statements, `while` and `for`. Although they can handle most repetitive tasks programs need to perform, the need to iterate over sequences is so common and pervasive that Python provides additional tools to make it simpler and more efficient. This chapter begins our exploration of these tools. Specifically, it presents the related concepts of Python's *iteration protocol*, a method-call model used by the `for` loop, and fills in some details on *list comprehensions*, which are a close cousin to the `for` loop that applies an expression to items in an iterable.

Because these tools are related to both the `for` loop and functions, we'll take a two-pass approach to covering them in this book, along with a postscript:

- This chapter introduces their basics in the context of looping tools, serving as something of a continuation of the prior chapter.

- Chapter 20 revisits them in the context of function-based tools, and extends the topic to include built-in and user-defined *generators*.

- Chapter 30 also provides a shorter final installment in this story, where we'll learn about user-defined iterable objects coded with *classes*.

In this chapter, we'll also sample additional iteration tools in Python, and touch on the new iterables available in Python 3.X—where the notion of iterables grows even more pervasive.

One note up front: some of the concepts presented in these chapters may seem advanced at first glance. With practice, though, you'll find that these tools are useful and powerful. Although never strictly required, because they've become commonplace in Python code, a basic understanding can also help if you must read programs written by others.

Iterations: A First Look

In the preceding chapter, I mentioned that the `for` loop can work on any sequence type in Python, including lists, tuples, and strings, like this:

```
>>> for x in [1, 2, 3, 4]: print(x ** 2, end=' ')          # In 2.X: print x ** 2,
...
1 4 9 16

>>> for x in (1, 2, 3, 4): print(x ** 3, end=' ')
...
1 8 27 64

>>> for x in 'spam': print(x * 2, end=' ')
...
ss pp aa mm
```

Actually, the `for` loop turns out to be even more generic than this—it works on any *iterable object*. In fact, this is true of all iteration tools that scan objects from left to right in Python, including `for` loops, the list comprehensions we'll study in this chapter, `in` membership tests, the `map` built-in function, and more.

The concept of "iterable objects" is relatively recent in Python, but it has come to permeate the language's design. It's essentially a generalization of the notion of sequences—an object is considered *iterable* if it is either a physically stored sequence, or an object that produces one result at a time in the context of an iteration tool like a `for` loop. In a sense, iterable objects include both physical sequences and *virtual sequences* computed on demand.

> *Terminology* in this topic tends to be a bit loose. The terms "iterable" and "iterator" are sometimes used interchangeably to refer to an object that supports iteration in general. For clarity, this book has a very strong preference for using the term *iterable* to refer to an object that supports the `iter` call, and *iterator* to refer to an object returned by an iterable on `iter` that supports the `next(I)` call. Both these calls are defined ahead.
>
> That convention is not universal in either the Python world or this book, though; "iterator" is also sometimes used for tools that iterate. Chapter 20 extends this category with the term "generator"—which refers to objects that automatically support the iteration protocol, and hence are iterable—even though all iterables generate results!

The Iteration Protocol: File Iterators

One of the easiest ways to understand the iteration protocol is to see how it works with a built-in type such as the file. In this chapter, we'll be using the following input file to demonstrate:

```
>>> print(open('script2.py').read())
import sys
```

```
print(sys.path)
x = 2
print(x ** 32)

>>> open('script2.py').read()
'import sys\nprint(sys.path)\nx = 2\nprint(x ** 32)\n'
```

Recall from Chapter 9 that open file objects have a method called `readline`, which reads one line of text from a file at a time—each time we call the `readline` method, we advance to the next line. At the end of the file, an empty string is returned, which we can detect to break out of the loop:

```
>>> f = open('script2.py')        # Read a four-line script file in this directory
>>> f.readline()                  # readline loads one line on each call
'import sys\n'
>>> f.readline()
'print(sys.path)\n'
>>> f.readline()
'x = 2\n'
>>> f.readline()                  # Last lines may have a \n or not
'print(x ** 32)\n'
>>> f.readline()                  # Returns empty string at end-of-file
''
```

However, files also have a method named __next__ in 3.X (and next in 2.X) that has a nearly identical effect—it returns the next line from a file each time it is called. The only noticeable difference is that __next__ raises a built-in `StopIteration` exception at end-of-file instead of returning an empty string:

```
>>> f = open('script2.py')        # __next__ loads one line on each call too
>>> f.__next__()                  # But raises an exception at end-of-file
'import sys\n'
>>> f.__next__()                  # Use f.next() in 2.X, or next(f) in 2.X or 3.X
'print(sys.path)\n'
>>> f.__next__()
'x = 2\n'
>>> f.__next__()
'print(x ** 32)\n'
>>> f.__next__()
Traceback (most recent call last):
  File "<stdin>", line 1, in <module>
StopIteration
```

This interface is most of what we call the *iteration protocol* in Python. Any object with a __next__ method to advance to a next result, which raises `StopIteration` at the end of the series of results, is considered an iterator in Python. Any such object may also be stepped through with a `for` loop or other iteration tool, because all iteration tools normally work internally by calling __next__ on each iteration and catching the `StopIteration` exception to determine when to exit. As we'll see in a moment, for some objects the full protocol includes an additional first step to call iter, but this isn't required for files.

The net effect of this magic is that, as mentioned in Chapter 9 and Chapter 13, the best way to read a text file line by line today is to *not read it at all*—instead, allow the `for` loop to automatically call `__next__` to advance to the next line on each iteration. The file object's iterator will do the work of automatically loading lines as you go. The following, for example, reads a file line by line, printing the uppercase version of each line along the way, without ever explicitly reading from the file at all:

```
>>> for line in open('script2.py'):          # Use file iterators to read by lines
...     print(line.upper(), end='')          # Calls __next__, catches StopIteration
...
IMPORT SYS
PRINT(SYS.PATH)
X = 2
PRINT(X ** 32)
```

Notice that the `print` uses `end=''` here to suppress adding a `\n`, because line strings already have one (without this, our output would be double-spaced; in 2.X, a trailing comma works the same as the end). This is considered the *best* way to read text files line by line today, for three reasons: it's the simplest to code, might be the quickest to run, and is the best in terms of memory usage. The older, original way to achieve the same effect with a `for` loop is to call the file `readlines` method to load the file's content into memory as a list of line strings:

```
>>> for line in open('script2.py').readlines():
...     print(line.upper(), end='')
...
IMPORT SYS
PRINT(SYS.PATH)
X = 2
PRINT(X ** 32)
```

This `readlines` technique still works but is not considered the best practice today and performs poorly in terms of memory usage. In fact, because this version really does load the entire file into memory all at once, it will not even work for files too big to fit into the memory space available on your computer. By contrast, because it reads one line at a time, the iterator-based version is immune to such memory-explosion issues. The iterator version might run quicker too, though this can vary per release

As mentioned in the prior chapter's sidebar, "Why You Will Care: File Scanners" on page 400, it's also possible to read a file line by line with a `while` loop:

```
>>> f = open('script2.py')
>>> while True:
...     line = f.readline()
...     if not line: break
...     print(line.upper(), end='')
...
...same output...
```

However, this may run slower than the iterator-based `for` loop version, because iterators run at C language speed inside Python, whereas the `while` loop version runs Python byte code through the Python virtual machine. Anytime we trade Python code for C code, speed tends to increase. This is not an absolute truth, though, especially in Python 3.X; we'll see timing techniques later in Chapter 21 for measuring the relative speed of alternatives like these.[1]

 Version skew note: In Python 2.X, the iteration method is named X.next() instead of X.__next__(). For portability, a next(X) built-in function is also available in both Python 3.X and 2.X (2.6 and later), and calls X.__next__() in 3.X and X.next() in 2.X. Apart from method names, iteration works the same in 2.X and 3.X in all other ways. In 2.6 and 2.7, simply use X.next() or next(X) for manual iterations instead of 3.X's X.__next__(); prior to 2.6, use X.next() calls instead of next(X).

Manual Iteration: iter and next

To simplify manual iteration code, Python 3.X also provides a built-in function, next, that automatically calls an object's __next__ method. Per the preceding note, this call also is supported on Python 2.X for portability. Given an iterator object X, the call next(X) is the same as X.__next__() on 3.X (and X.next() on 2.X), but is noticeably simpler and more version-neutral. With files, for instance, either form may be used:

```
>>> f = open('script2.py')
>>> f.__next__()                        # Call iteration method directly
'import sys\n'
>>> f.__next__()
'print(sys.path)\n'

>>> f = open('script2.py')
>>> next(f)                             # The next(f) built-in calls f.__next__() in 3.X
'import sys\n'
>>> next(f)                             # next(f) => [3.X: f.__next__()], [2.X: f.next()]
'print(sys.path)\n'
```

Technically, there is one more piece to the iteration protocol alluded to earlier. When the for loop begins, it first obtains an iterator from the iterable object by passing it to the iter built-in function; the object returned by iter in turn has the required next method. The iter function internally runs the __iter__ method, much like next and __next__.

---

1. Spoiler alert: the file iterator still appears to be slightly faster than readlines and at least 30% faster than the while loop in both 2.7 and 3.3 on tests I've run with this chapter's code on a 1,000-line file (while is twice as slow on 2.7). The usual benchmarking caveats apply—this is true only for my Pythons, my computer, and my test file, and Python 3.X complicates such analyses by rewriting I/O libraries to support Unicode text and be less system-dependent. Chapter 21 covers tools and techniques you can use to time these loop statements on your own.

The full iteration protocol

As a more formal definition, Figure 14-1 sketches this full iteration protocol, used by every iteration tool in Python, and supported by a wide variety of object types. It's really based on *two objects*, used in two distinct steps by iteration tools:

- The *iterable* object you request iteration for, whose `__iter__` is run by `iter`
- The *iterator* object returned by the iterable that actually produces values during the iteration, whose `__next__` is run by `next` and raises `StopIteration` when finished producing results

These steps are orchestrated automatically by iteration tools in most cases, but it helps to understand these two objects' roles. For example, in some cases these two objects are the *same* when only a single scan is supported (e.g., files), and the *iterator* object is often temporary, used internally by the iteration tool.

Moreover, some objects are *both* an iteration context tool (they iterate) and an iterable object (their results are iterable)—including Chapter 20's generator expressions, and `map` and `zip` in Python 3.X. As we'll see ahead, more tools become iterables in 3.X—including `map`, `zip`, `range`, and some dictionary methods—to avoid constructing result lists in memory all at once.

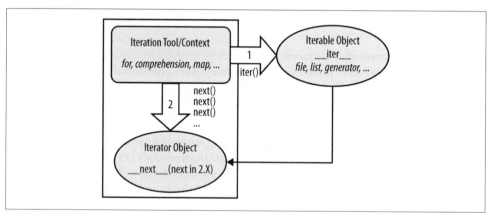

Figure 14-1. The Python iteration protocol, used by for loops, comprehensions, maps, and more, and supported by files, lists, dictionaries, Chapter 20's generators, and more. Some objects are both iteration context and iterable object, such as generator expressions and 3.X's flavors of some tools (such as map and zip). Some objects are both iterable and iterator, returning themselves for the iter() call, which is then a no-op.

In actual code, the protocol's first step becomes obvious if we look at how `for` loops internally process built-in sequence types such as lists:

```
>>> L = [1, 2, 3]
>>> I = iter(L)                 # Obtain an iterator object from an iterable
>>> I.__next__()                # Call iterator's next to advance to next item
1
```

```
>>> I.__next__()                    # Or use I.next() in 2.X, next(I) in either line
2
>>> I.__next__()
3
>>> I.__next__()
...error text omitted...
StopIteration
```

This initial step is not required for files, because a file object is its own iterator. Because they support just one iteration (they can't seek backward to support multiple active scans), files have their own __next__ method and do not need to return a different object that does:

```
>>> f = open('script2.py')
>>> iter(f) is f
True
>>> iter(f) is f.__iter__()
True
>>> f.__next__()
'import sys\n'
```

Lists and many other built-in objects, though, are not their own iterators because they do support multiple open iterations—for example, there may be multiple iterations in nested loops all at different positions. For such objects, we must call `iter` to start iterating:

```
>>> L = [1, 2, 3]
>>> iter(L) is L
False
>>> L.__next__()
AttributeError: 'list' object has no attribute '__next__'

>>> I = iter(L)
>>> I.__next__()
1
>>> next(I)                         # Same as I.__next__()
2
```

Manual iteration

Although Python iteration tools call these functions automatically, we can use them to apply the iteration protocol *manually*, too. The following interaction demonstrates the equivalence between automatic and manual iteration:[2]

```
>>> L = [1, 2, 3]
>>>
>>> for X in L:                     # Automatic iteration
...     print(X ** 2, end=' ')      # Obtains iter, calls __next__, catches exceptions
...
...
1 4 9
```

---

2. Technically speaking, the for loop calls the internal equivalent of I.__next__, instead of the next(I) used here, though there is rarely any difference between the two. Your manual iterations can generally use either call scheme.

```
>>> I = iter(L)                    # Manual iteration: what for loops usually do
>>> while True:
...     try:                       # try statement catches exceptions
...         X = next(I)            # Or call I.__next__ in 3.X
...     except StopIteration:
...         break
...     print(X ** 2, end=' ')
...
1 4 9
```

To understand this code, you need to know that **try** statements run an action and catch exceptions that occur while the action runs (we met exceptions briefly in Chapter 11 but will explore them in depth in Part VII). I should also note that **for** loops and other iteration contexts can sometimes work differently for user-defined classes, repeatedly indexing an object instead of running the iteration protocol, but prefer the iteration protocol if it's used. We'll defer that story until we study class operator overloading in Chapter 30.

Other Built-in Type Iterables

Besides files and physical sequences like lists, other types have useful iterators as well. The classic way to step through the keys of a *dictionary*, for example, is to request its keys list explicitly:

```
>>> D = {'a':1, 'b':2, 'c':3}
>>> for key in D.keys():
...     print(key, D[key])
...
a 1
b 2
c 3
```

In recent versions of Python, though, dictionaries are iterables with an iterator that automatically returns one key at a time in an iteration context:

```
>>> I = iter(D)
>>> next(I)
'a'
>>> next(I)
'b'
>>> next(I)
'c'
>>> next(I)
Traceback (most recent call last):
  File "<stdin>", line 1, in <module>
StopIteration
```

The net effect is that we no longer need to call the **keys** method to step through dictionary keys—the **for** loop will use the iteration protocol to grab one key each time through:

```
>>> for key in D:
...      print(key, D[key])
...
a 1
b 2
c 3
```

We can't delve into their details here, but other Python object types also support the iteration protocol and thus may be used in for loops too. For instance, *shelves* (an access-by-key filesystem for Python objects) and the results from os.popen (a tool for reading the output of shell commands, which we met in the preceding chapter) are iterable as well:

```
>>> import os
>>> P = os.popen('dir')
>>> P.__next__()
' Volume in drive C has no label.\n'
>>> P.__next__()
' Volume Serial Number is D093-D1F7\n'
>>> next(P)
TypeError: _wrap_close object is not an iterator
```

Notice that popen objects themselves support a P.next() method in Python 2.X. In 3.X, they support the P.__next__() method, but not the next(P) built-in. Since the latter is defined to call the former, this may seem unusual, though both calls work correctly if we use the full iteration protocol employed automatically by for loops and other iteration contexts, with its top-level iter call (this performs internal steps required to also support next calls for this object):

```
>>> P = os.popen('dir')
>>> I = iter(P)
>>> next(I)
' Volume in drive C has no label.\n'
>>> I.__next__()
' Volume Serial Number is D093-D1F7\n'
```

Also in the systems domain, the standard directory walker in Python, os.walk, is similarly iterable, but we'll save an example until Chapter 20's coverage of this tool's basis —generators and yield.

The iteration protocol also is the reason that we've had to wrap some results in a list call to see their values all at once. Objects that are iterable return results one at a time, not in a physical list:

```
>>> R = range(5)
>>> R                          # Ranges are iterables in 3.X
range(0, 5)
>>> I = iter(R)                # Use iteration protocol to produce results
>>> next(I)
0
>>> next(I)
1
>>> list(range(5))             # Or use list to collect all results at once
[0, 1, 2, 3, 4]
```

Note that the `list` call here is not required in 2.X (where `range` builds a real list), and is not needed in 3.X for contexts where iteration happens automatically (such as within `for` loops). It is needed for displaying values here in 3.X, though, and may also be required when list-like behavior or multiple scans are required for objects that produce results on demand in 2.X or 3.X (more on this ahead).

Now that you have a better understanding of this protocol, you should be able to see how it explains why the `enumerate` tool introduced in the prior chapter works the way it does:

```
>>> E = enumerate('spam')          # enumerate is an iterable too
>>> E
<enumerate object at 0x00000000029B7678>
>>> I = iter(E)
>>> next(I)                        # Generate results with iteration protocol
(0, 's')
>>> next(I)                        # Or use list to force generation to run
(1, 'p')
>>> list(enumerate('spam'))
[(0, 's'), (1, 'p'), (2, 'a'), (3, 'm')]
```

We don't normally see this machinery because `for` loops run it for us automatically to step through results. In fact, everything that scans left to right in Python employs the iteration protocol in the same way—including the topic of the next section.

List Comprehensions: A First Detailed Look

Now that we've seen how the iteration protocol works, let's turn to one of its most common use cases. Together with `for` loops, list comprehensions are one of the most prominent contexts in which the iteration protocol is applied.

In the previous chapter, we learned how to use `range` to change a list as we step across it:

```
>>> L = [1, 2, 3, 4, 5]

>>> for i in range(len(L)):
...     L[i] += 10
...
>>> L
[11, 12, 13, 14, 15]
```

This works, but as I mentioned there, it may not be the optimal "best practice" approach in Python. Today, the list comprehension expression makes many such prior coding patterns obsolete. Here, for example, we can replace the loop with a single expression that produces the desired result list:

```
>>> L = [x + 10 for x in L]
>>> L
[21, 22, 23, 24, 25]
```

The net result is similar, but it requires less coding on our part and is likely to run substantially faster. The list comprehension isn't exactly the same as the for loop statement version because it makes a *new* list object (which might matter if there are multiple references to the original list), but it's close enough for most applications and is a common and convenient enough approach to merit a closer look here.

List Comprehension Basics

We met the list comprehension briefly in Chapter 4. Syntactically, its syntax is derived from a construct in set theory notation that applies an operation to each item in a set, but you don't have to know set theory to use this tool. In Python, most people find that a list comprehension simply looks like a backward for loop.

To get a handle on the syntax, let's dissect the prior section's example in more detail:

```
L = [x + 10 for x in L]
```

List comprehensions are written in square brackets because they are ultimately a way to construct a new list. They begin with an arbitrary expression that we make up, which uses a loop variable that we make up (x + 10). That is followed by what you should now recognize as the header of a for loop, which names the loop variable, and an iterable object (for x in L).

To run the expression, Python executes an iteration across L inside the interpreter, assigning x to each item in turn, and collects the results of running the items through the expression on the left side. The result list we get back is exactly what the list comprehension says—a new list containing x + 10, for every x in L.

Technically speaking, list comprehensions are never really required because we can always build up a list of expression results manually with for loops that append results as we go:

```
>>> res = []
>>> for x in L:
...     res.append(x + 10)
...
>>> res
[31, 32, 33, 34, 35]
```

In fact, this is exactly what the list comprehension does internally.

However, list comprehensions are more concise to write, and because this code pattern of building up result lists is so common in Python work, they turn out to be very useful in many contexts. Moreover, depending on your Python and code, list comprehensions might run much faster than manual for loop statements (often roughly twice as fast) because their iterations are performed at C language speed inside the interpreter, rather than with manual Python code. Especially for larger data sets, there is often a major performance advantage to using this expression.

Using List Comprehensions on Files

Let's work through another common application of list comprehensions to explore them in more detail. Recall that the file object has a `readlines` method that loads the file into a list of line strings all at once:

```
>>> f = open('script2.py')
>>> lines = f.readlines()
>>> lines
['import sys\n', 'print(sys.path)\n', 'x = 2\n', 'print(x ** 32)\n']
```

This works, but the lines in the result all include the newline character (\n) at the end. For many programs, the newline character gets in the way—we have to be careful to avoid double-spacing when printing, and so on. It would be nice if we could get rid of these newlines all at once, wouldn't it?

Anytime we start thinking about performing an operation on each item in a sequence, we're in the realm of list comprehensions. For example, assuming the variable `lines` is as it was in the prior interaction, the following code does the job by running each line in the list through the string `rstrip` method to remove whitespace on the right side (a `line[:-1]` slice would work, too, but only if we can be sure all lines are properly \n terminated, and this may not always be the case for the last line in a file):

```
>>> lines = [line.rstrip() for line in lines]
>>> lines
['import sys', 'print(sys.path)', 'x = 2', 'print(x ** 32)']
```

This works as planned. Because list comprehensions are an iteration context just like `for` loop statements, though, we don't even have to open the file ahead of time. If we open it inside the expression, the list comprehension will automatically use the iteration protocol we met earlier in this chapter. That is, it will read one line from the file at a time by calling the file's next handler method, run the line through the `rstrip` expression, and add it to the result list. Again, we get what we ask for—the `rstrip` result of a line, for every line in the file:

```
>>> lines = [line.rstrip() for line in open('script2.py')]
>>> lines
['import sys', 'print(sys.path)', 'x = 2', 'print(x ** 32)']
```

This expression does a lot implicitly, but we're getting a lot of work for free here—Python scans the file by lines and builds a list of operation results automatically. It's also an efficient way to code this operation: because most of this work is done inside the Python interpreter, it may be faster than an equivalent `for` statement, and won't load a file into memory all at once like some other techniques. Again, especially for large files, the advantages of list comprehensions can be significant.

Besides their efficiency, list comprehensions are also remarkably expressive. In our example, we can run any string operation on a file's lines as we iterate. To illustrate, here's the list comprehension equivalent to the file iterator uppercase example we met earlier, along with a few other representative operations:

```
>>> [line.upper() for line in open('script2.py')]
['IMPORT SYS\n', 'PRINT(SYS.PATH)\n', 'X = 2\n', 'PRINT(X ** 32)\n']

>>> [line.rstrip().upper() for line in open('script2.py')]
['IMPORT SYS', 'PRINT(SYS.PATH)', 'X = 2', 'PRINT(X ** 32)']

>>> [line.split() for line in open('script2.py')]
[['import', 'sys'], ['print(sys.path)'], ['x', '=', '2'], ['print(x', '**', '32)']]

>>> [line.replace(' ', '!') for line in open('script2.py')]
['import!sys\n', 'print(sys.path)\n', 'x!=!2\n', 'print(x!**!32)\n']

>>> [('sys' in line, line[:5]) for line in open('script2.py')]
[(True, 'impor'), (True, 'print'), (False, 'x = 2'), (False, 'print')]
```

Recall that the method *chaining* in the second of these examples works because string methods return a new string, to which we can apply another string method. The last of these shows how we can also collect *multiple* results, as long as they're wrapped in a collection like a tuple or list.

 One fine point here: recall from Chapter 9 that file objects *close* themselves automatically when garbage-collected if still open. Hence, these list comprehensions will also automatically close the file when their temporary file object is garbage-collected after the expression runs. Outside CPython, though, you may want to code these to close manually if this is run in a loop, to ensure that file resources are freed immediately. See Chapter 9 for more on file close calls if you need a refresher on this.

Extended List Comprehension Syntax

In fact, list comprehensions can be even richer in practice, and even constitute a sort of *iteration mini-language* in their fullest forms. Let's take a quick look at their syntax tools here.

Filter clauses: if

As one particularly useful extension, the `for` loop nested in a comprehension expression can have an associated `if` clause to *filter out* of the result items for which the test is not true.

For example, suppose we want to repeat the prior section's file-scanning example, but we need to collect only lines that begin with the letter *p* (perhaps the first character on each line is an action code of some sort). Adding an `if` filter clause to our expression does the trick:

```
>>> lines = [line.rstrip() for line in open('script2.py') if line[0] == 'p']
>>> lines
['print(sys.path)', 'print(x ** 32)']
```

Here, the if clause checks each line read from the file to see whether its first character is *p*; if not, the line is omitted from the result list. This is a fairly big expression, but it's easy to understand if we translate it to its simple for loop statement equivalent. In general, we can always translate a list comprehension to a for statement by appending as we go and further indenting each successive part:

```
>>> res = []
>>> for line in open('script2.py'):
...         if line[0] == 'p':
...             res.append(line.rstrip())
...
>>> res
['print(sys.path)', 'print(x ** 32)']
```

This for statement equivalent works, but it takes up four lines instead of one and may run slower. In fact, you can squeeze a substantial amount of logic into a list comprehension when you need to—the following works like the prior but selects only lines that *end in a digit* (before the newline at the end), by filtering with a more sophisticated expression on the right side (replace [-1] with [-1:] for files with blank lines):

```
>>> [line.rstrip() for line in open('script2.py') if line.rstrip()[-1].isdigit()]
['x = 2']
```

As another if filter example, the first result in the following gives the total lines in a text file, and the second strips whitespace on both ends to *omit blank lines* in the tally in just one line of code (this file, not included, contains lines describing typos found in the first draft of this book by my proofreader):

```
>>> fname = r'd:\books\5e\lp5e\draft1typos.txt'
>>> len(open(fname).readlines())                        # All lines
263
>>> len([line for line in open(fname) if line.strip() != ''])   # Nonblank lines
185
```

Nested loops: for

List comprehensions can become even more complex if we need them to—for instance, they may contain *nested loops*, coded as a series of for clauses. In fact, their full syntax allows for any number of for clauses, each of which can have an optional associated if clause.

For example, the following builds a list of the concatenation of x + y for every x in one string and every y in another. It effectively collects all the *ordered combinations* of the characters in two strings:

```
>>> [x + y for x in 'abc' for y in 'lmn']
['al', 'am', 'an', 'bl', 'bm', 'bn', 'cl', 'cm', 'cn']
```

Again, one way to understand this expression is to convert it to statement form by indenting its parts. The following is an equivalent, but likely slower, alternative way to achieve the same effect:

```
>>> res = []
>>> for x in 'abc':
...     for y in 'lmn':
...         res.append(x + y)
...
>>> res
['al', 'am', 'an', 'bl', 'bm', 'bn', 'cl', 'cm', 'cn']
```

Beyond this complexity level, though, list comprehension expressions can often become too compact for their own good. In general, they are intended for simple types of iterations; for more involved work, a simpler for statement structure will probably be easier to understand and modify in the future. As usual in programming, if something is difficult for you to understand, it's probably not a good idea.

Because comprehensions are generally best taken in multiple doses, we'll cut this story short here for now. We'll revisit list comprehensions in Chapter 20 in the context of functional programming tools, and will define their syntax more formally and explore additional examples there. As we'll find, comprehensions turn out to be just as related to *functions* as they are to looping *statements*.

 A blanket qualification for all *performance claims* in this book, list comprehension or other: the relative speed of code depends much on the exact code tested and Python used, and is prone to change from release to release.

For example, in CPython 2.7 and 3.3 today, list comprehensions can still be twice as fast as corresponding for loops on some tests, but just marginally quicker on others, and perhaps even slightly slower on some when if filter clauses are used.

We'll see how to time code in Chapter 21, and will learn how to interpret the file *listcomp-speed.txt* in the book examples package, which times this chapter's code. For now, keep in mind that absolutes in performance benchmarks are as elusive as consensus in open source projects!

Other Iteration Contexts

Later in the book, we'll see that user-defined classes can implement the iteration protocol too. Because of this, it's sometimes important to know which built-in tools make use of it—any tool that employs the iteration protocol will automatically work on any built-in type or user-defined class that provides it.

So far, I've been demonstrating iterators in the context of the for loop statement, because this part of the book is focused on statements. Keep in mind, though, that *every* built-in tool that scans from left to right across objects uses the iteration protocol. This includes the for loops we've seen:

```
>>> for line in open('script2.py'):        # Use file iterators
...     print(line.upper(), end='')
```

```
...
IMPORT SYS
PRINT(SYS.PATH)
X = 2
PRINT(X ** 32)
```

But also much more. For instance, list comprehensions and the `map` built-in function use the same protocol as their `for` loop cousin. When applied to a file, they both leverage the file object's iterator automatically to scan line by line, fetching an iterator with `__iter__` and calling `__next__` each time through:

```
>>> uppers = [line.upper() for line in open('script2.py')]
>>> uppers
['IMPORT SYS\n', 'PRINT(SYS.PATH)\n', 'X = 2\n', 'PRINT(X ** 32)\n']

>>> map(str.upper, open('script2.py'))        # map is itself an iterable in 3.X
<map object at 0x00000000029476D8>
>>> list(map(str.upper, open('script2.py')))
['IMPORT SYS\n', 'PRINT(SYS.PATH)\n', 'X = 2\n', 'PRINT(X ** 32)\n']
```

We introduced the `map` call used here briefly in the preceding chapter (and in passing in Chapter 4); it's a built-in that applies a function call to each item in the passed-in iterable object. `map` is similar to a list comprehension but is more limited because it requires a function instead of an arbitrary expression. It also *returns* an iterable object itself in Python 3.X, so we must wrap it in a `list` call to force it to give us all its values at once; more on this change later in this chapter. Because `map`, like the list comprehension, is related to both `for` loops and functions, we'll also explore both again in Chapter 19 and Chapter 20.

Many of Python's other built-ins process iterables, too. For example, `sorted` sorts items in an iterable; `zip` combines items from iterables; `enumerate` pairs items in an iterable with relative positions; `filter` selects items for which a function is true; and `reduce` runs pairs of items in an iterable through a function. All of these *accept* iterables, and `zip`, `enumerate`, and `filter` also *return* an iterable in Python 3.X, like `map`. Here they are in action running the file's iterator automatically to read line by line:

```
>>> sorted(open('script2.py'))
['import sys\n', 'print(sys.path)\n', 'print(x ** 32)\n', 'x = 2\n']

>>> list(zip(open('script2.py'), open('script2.py')))
[('import sys\n', 'import sys\n'), ('print(sys.path)\n', 'print(sys.path)\n'),
('x = 2\n', 'x = 2\n'), ('print(x ** 32)\n', 'print(x ** 32)\n')]

>>> list(enumerate(open('script2.py')))
[(0, 'import sys\n'), (1, 'print(sys.path)\n'), (2, 'x = 2\n'),
(3, 'print(x ** 32)\n')]

>>> list(filter(bool, open('script2.py')))        # nonempty=True
['import sys\n', 'print(sys.path)\n', 'x = 2\n', 'print(x ** 32)\n']

>>> import functools, operator
>>> functools.reduce(operator.add, open('script2.py'))
'import sys\nprint(sys.path)\nx = 2\nprint(x ** 32)\n'
```

All of these are iteration tools, but they have unique roles. We met `zip` and `enumerate` in the prior chapter; `filter` and `reduce` are in Chapter 19's functional programming domain, so we'll defer their details for now; the point to notice here is their use of the iteration protocol for files and other iterables.

We first saw the `sorted` function used here at work in Chapter 4, and we used it for dictionaries in Chapter 8. `sorted` is a built-in that employs the iteration protocol—it's like the original list `sort` method, but it returns the new sorted list as a result and runs on any iterable object. Notice that, unlike `map` and others, `sorted` returns an actual *list* in Python 3.X instead of an iterable.

Interestingly, the iteration protocol is even more pervasive in Python today than the examples so far have demonstrated—essentially *everything* in Python's built-in toolset that scans an object from left to right is defined to use the iteration protocol on the subject object. This even includes tools such as the `list` and `tuple` built-in functions (which build new objects from iterables), and the string `join` method (which makes a new string by putting a substring between strings contained in an iterable). Consequently, these will also work on an open file and automatically read one line at a time:

```
>>> list(open('script2.py'))
['import sys\n', 'print(sys.path)\n', 'x = 2\n', 'print(x ** 32)\n']

>>> tuple(open('script2.py'))
('import sys\n', 'print(sys.path)\n', 'x = 2\n', 'print(x ** 32)\n')

>>> '&&'.join(open('script2.py'))
'import sys\n&&print(sys.path)\n&&x = 2\n&&print(x ** 32)\n'
```

Even some tools you might not expect fall into this category. For example, sequence assignment, the `in` membership test, slice assignment, and the list's `extend` method also leverage the iteration protocol to scan, and thus read a file by lines automatically:

```
>>> a, b, c, d = open('script2.py')          # Sequence assignment
>>> a, d
('import sys\n', 'print(x ** 32)\n')

>>> a, *b = open('script2.py')               # 3.X extended form
>>> a, b
('import sys\n', ['print(sys.path)\n', 'x = 2\n', 'print(x ** 32)\n'])

>>> 'y = 2\n' in open('script2.py')          # Membership test
False
>>> 'x = 2\n' in open('script2.py')
True

>>> L = [11, 22, 33, 44]                     # Slice assignment
>>> L[1:3] = open('script2.py')
>>> L
[11, 'import sys\n', 'print(sys.path)\n', 'x = 2\n', 'print(x ** 32)\n', 44]

>>> L = [11]
>>> L.extend(open('script2.py'))             # list.extend method
```

```
>>> L
[11, 'import sys\n', 'print(sys.path)\n', 'x = 2\n', 'print(x ** 32)\n']
```

Per Chapter 8 extend iterates automatically, but append does not—use the latter (or similar) to add an iterable to a list without iterating, with the potential to be iterated across later:

```
>>> L = [11]
>>> L.append(open('script2.py'))            # list.append does not iterate
>>> L
[11, <_io.TextIOWrapper name='script2.py' mode='r' encoding='cp1252'>]
>>> list(L[1])
['import sys\n', 'print(sys.path)\n', 'x = 2\n', 'print(x ** 32)\n']
```

Iteration is a broadly supported and powerful model. Earlier, we saw that the built-in dict call accepts an iterable zip result, too (see Chapter 8 and Chapter 13). For that matter, so does the set call, as well as the newer set and dictionary comprehension expressions in Python 3.X and 2.7, which we met in Chapter 4, Chapter 5, and Chapter 8:

```
>>> set(open('script2.py'))
{'print(x ** 32)\n', 'import sys\n', 'print(sys.path)\n', 'x = 2\n'}

>>> {line for line in open('script2.py')}
{'print(x ** 32)\n', 'import sys\n', 'print(sys.path)\n', 'x = 2\n'}

>>> {ix: line for ix, line in enumerate(open('script2.py'))}
{0: 'import sys\n', 1: 'print(sys.path)\n', 2: 'x = 2\n', 3: 'print(x ** 32)\n'}
```

In fact, both set and dictionary comprehensions support the extended syntax of list comprehensions we met earlier in this chapter, including if tests:

```
>>> {line for line in open('script2.py') if line[0] == 'p'}
{'print(x ** 32)\n', 'print(sys.path)\n'}
>>> {ix: line for (ix, line) in enumerate(open('script2.py')) if line[0] == 'p'}
{1: 'print(sys.path)\n', 3: 'print(x ** 32)\n'}
```

Like the list comprehension, both of these scan the file line by line and pick out lines that begin with the letter *p*. They also happen to build sets and dictionaries in the end, but we get a lot of work "for free" by combining file iteration and comprehension syntax. Later in the book we'll meet a relative of comprehensions—generator expressions—that deploys the same syntax and works on iterables too, but is also iterable itself:

```
>>> list(line.upper() for line in open('script2.py'))        # See Chapter 20
['IMPORT SYS\n', 'PRINT(SYS.PATH)\n', 'X = 2\n', 'PRINT(X ** 32)\n']
```

Other built-in functions support the iteration protocol as well, but frankly, some are harder to cast in interesting examples related to files! For example, the sum call computes the sum of all the numbers in any iterable; the any and all built-ins return True if any or all items in an iterable are True, respectively; and max and min return the largest and smallest item in an iterable, respectively. Like reduce, all of the tools in the following examples accept any iterable as an argument and use the iteration protocol to scan it, but return a single result:

```
>>> sum([3, 2, 4, 1, 5, 0])          # sum expects numbers only
15
>>> any(['spam', '', 'ni'])
True
>>> all(['spam', '', 'ni'])
False
>>> max([3, 2, 5, 1, 4])
5
>>> min([3, 2, 5, 1, 4])
1
```

Strictly speaking, the max and min functions can be applied to files as well—they automatically use the iteration protocol to scan the file and pick out the lines with the highest and lowest string values, respectively (though I'll leave valid use cases to your imagination):

```
>>> max(open('script2.py'))          # Line with max/min string value
'x = 2\n'
>>> min(open('script2.py'))
'import sys\n'
```

There's one last iteration context that's worth mentioning, although it's mostly a preview: in Chapter 18, we'll learn that a special *arg form can be used in function calls to unpack a collection of values into individual arguments. As you can probably predict by now, this accepts any iterable, too, including files (see Chapter 18 for more details on this call syntax; Chapter 20 for a section that extends this idea to generator expressions; and Chapter 11 for tips on using the following's 3.X print in 2.X as usual):

```
>>> def f(a, b, c, d): print(a, b, c, d, sep='&')
...
>>> f(1, 2, 3, 4)
1&2&3&4
>>> f(*[1, 2, 3, 4])                 # Unpacks into arguments
1&2&3&4
>>>
>>> f(*open('script2.py'))           # Iterates by lines too!
import sys
&print(sys.path)
&x = 2
&print(x ** 32)
```

In fact, because this argument-unpacking syntax in calls accepts iterables, it's also possible to use the zip built-in to *unzip* zipped tuples, by making prior or nested zip results arguments for another zip call (warning: you probably shouldn't read the following example if you plan to operate heavy machinery anytime soon!):

```
>>> X = (1, 2)
>>> Y = (3, 4)
>>>
>>> list(zip(X, Y))                  # Zip tuples: returns an iterable
[(1, 3), (2, 4)]
```

```
>>>
>>> A, B = zip(*zip(X, Y))          # Unzip a zip!
>>> A
(1, 2)
>>> B
(3, 4)
```

Still other tools in Python, such as the `range` built-in and dictionary view objects, *return* iterables instead of processing them. To see how these have been absorbed into the iteration protocol in Python 3.X as well, we need to move on to the next section.

New Iterables in Python 3.X

One of the fundamental distinctions of Python 3.X is its stronger emphasis on iterators than 2.X. This, along with its Unicode model and mandated new-style classes, is one of 3.X's most sweeping changes.

Specifically, in addition to the iterators associated with built-in types such as files and dictionaries, the dictionary methods `keys`, `values`, and `items` return iterable objects in Python 3.X, as do the built-in functions `range`, `map`, `zip`, and `filter`. As shown in the prior section, the last three of these functions both return iterables and process them. All of these tools produce results on demand in Python 3.X, instead of constructing result lists as they do in 2.X.

Impacts on 2.X Code: Pros and Cons

Although this saves memory space, it can impact your coding styles in some contexts. In various places in this book so far, for example, we've had to wrap up some function and method call results in a `list(...)` call in order to force them to produce all their results at once for *display*:

```
>>> zip('abc', 'xyz')          # An iterable in Python 3.X (a list in 2.X)
<zip object at 0x000000000294C308>

>>> list(zip('abc', 'xyz'))          # Force list of results in 3.X to display
[('a', 'x'), ('b', 'y'), ('c', 'z')]
```

A similar conversion is required if we wish to apply list or *sequence operations* to most iterables that generate items on demand—to index, slice, or concatenate the iterable itself, for example. The list results for these tools in 2.X support such operations directly:

```
>>> Z = zip((1, 2), (3, 4))          # Unlike 2.X lists, cannot index, etc.
>>> Z[0]
TypeError: 'zip' object is not subscriptable
```

As we'll see in more detail in Chapter 20, conversion to lists may also be more subtly required to support *multiple iterations* for newly iterable tools that support just one scan such as `map` and `zip`—unlike their 2.X list forms, their values in 3.X are exhausted after a single pass:

```
>>> M = map(lambda x: 2 ** x, range(3))
>>> for i in M: print(i)
...
1
2
4
>>> for i in M: print(i)          # Unlike 2.X lists, one pass only (zip too)
...
>>>
```

Such conversion isn't required in 2.X, because functions like `zip` return lists of results. In 3.X, though, they return iterable objects, producing results on demand. This may break 2.X code, and means extra typing is required to display the results at the interactive prompt (and possibly in some other contexts), but it's an asset in larger programs—delayed evaluation like this conserves memory and avoids pauses while large result lists are computed. Let's take a quick look at some of the new 3.X iterables in action.

The range Iterable

We studied the `range` built-in's basic behavior in the preceding chapter. In 3.X, it returns an iterable that generates numbers in the range on demand, instead of building the result list in memory. This subsumes the older 2.X `xrange` (see the upcoming version skew note), and you must use `list(range(...))` to force an actual range list if one is needed (e.g., to display results):

```
C:\code> c:\python33\python
>>> R = range(10)                 # range returns an iterable, not a list
>>> R
range(0, 10)

>>> I = iter(R)                   # Make an iterator from the range iterable
>>> next(I)                       # Advance to next result
0                                 # What happens in for loops, comprehensions, etc.
>>> next(I)
1
>>> next(I)
2

>>> list(range(10))               # To force a list if required
[0, 1, 2, 3, 4, 5, 6, 7, 8, 9]
```

Unlike the list returned by this call in 2.X, `range` objects in 3.X support only iteration, indexing, and the `len` function. They do not support any other sequence operations (use `list(...)` if you require more list tools):

```
>>> len(R)                        # range also does len and indexing, but no others
10
>>> R[0]
0
```

```
>>> R[-1]
9

>>> next(I)                        # Continue taking from iterator, where left off
3
>>> I.__next__()                   # .next() becomes .__next__(), but use new next()
4
```

 Version skew note: As first mentioned in the preceding chapter, Python 2.X also has a built-in called xrange, which is like range but produces items on demand instead of building a list of results in memory all at once. Since this is exactly what the new iterator-based range does in Python 3.X, xrange is no longer available in 3.X—it has been subsumed. You may still both see and use it in 2.X code, though, especially since range builds result lists there and so is not as efficient in its memory usage.

As noted in the prior chapter, the file.xreadlines() method used to minimize memory use in 2.X has been dropped in Python 3.X for similar reasons, in favor of file iterators.

The map, zip, and filter Iterables

Like range, the map, zip, and filter built-ins also become iterables in 3.X to conserve space, rather than producing a result list all at once in memory. All three not only process iterables, as in 2.X, but also return iterable results in 3.X. Unlike range, though, they are their own iterators—after you step through their results once, they are exhausted. In other words, you can't have multiple iterators on their results that maintain different positions in those results.

Here is the case for the map built-in we met in the prior chapter. As with other iterables, you can force a list with list(...) if you really need one, but the default behavior can save substantial space in memory for large result sets:

```
>>> M = map(abs, (-1, 0, 1))       # map returns an iterable, not a list
>>> M
<map object at 0x00000000029B75C0>
>>> next(M)                        # Use iterator manually: exhausts results
1                                  # These do not support len() or indexing
>>> next(M)
0
>>> next(M)
1
>>> next(M)
StopIteration

>>> for x in M: print(x)           # map iterator is now empty: one pass only
...

>>> M = map(abs, (-1, 0, 1))       # Make a new iterable/iterator to scan again
>>> for x in M: print(x)           # Iteration contexts auto call next()
```

```
...
1
0
1
>>> list(map(abs, (-1, 0, 1)))          # Can force a real list if needed
[1, 0, 1]
```

The `zip` built-in, introduced in the prior chapter, is an iteration context itself, but also returns an iterable with an iterator that works the same way:

```
>>> Z = zip((1, 2, 3), (10, 20, 30))    # zip is the same: a one-pass iterator
>>> Z
<zip object at 0x0000000002951108>

>>> list(Z)
[(1, 10), (2, 20), (3, 30)]

>>> for pair in Z: print(pair)          # Exhausted after one pass
...

>>> Z = zip((1, 2, 3), (10, 20, 30))
>>> for pair in Z: print(pair)          # Iterator used automatically or manually
...
(1, 10)
(2, 20)
(3, 30)

>>> Z = zip((1, 2, 3), (10, 20, 30))    # Manual iteration (iter() not needed)
>>> next(Z)
(1, 10)
>>> next(Z)
(2, 20)
```

The `filter` built-in, which we met briefly in Chapter 12 and will study in the next part of this book, is also analogous. It returns items in an iterable for which a passed-in function returns `True` (as we've learned, in Python `True` includes nonempty objects, and `bool` returns an object's truth value):

```
>>> filter(bool, ['spam', '', 'ni'])
<filter object at 0x00000000029B7B70>
>>> list(filter(bool, ['spam', '', 'ni']))
['spam', 'ni']
```

Like most of the tools discussed in this section, `filter` both *accepts* an iterable to process and *returns* an iterable to generate results in 3.X. It can also generally be emulated by extended list comprehension syntax that automatically tests truth values:

```
>>> [x for x in ['spam', '', 'ni'] if bool(x)]
['spam', 'ni']
>>> [x for x in ['spam', '', 'ni'] if x]
['spam', 'ni']
```

Multiple Versus Single Pass Iterators

It's important to see how the `range` object differs from the built-ins described in this section—it supports `len` and indexing, it is not its own iterator (you make one with `iter` when iterating manually), and it supports multiple iterators over its result that remember their positions independently:

```
>>> R = range(3)                    # range allows multiple iterators
>>> next(R)
TypeError: range object is not an iterator

>>> I1 = iter(R)
>>> next(I1)
0
>>> next(I1)
1
>>> I2 = iter(R)                     # Two iterators on one range
>>> next(I2)
0
>>> next(I1)                         # I1 is at a different spot than I2
2
```

By contrast, in 3.X `zip`, `map`, and `filter` do not support multiple active iterators on the same result; because of this the `iter` call is optional for stepping through such objects' results—their `iter` is themselves (in 2.X these built-ins return multiple-scan lists so the following does not apply):

```
>>> Z = zip((1, 2, 3), (10, 11, 12))
>>> I1 = iter(Z)
>>> I2 = iter(Z)                     # Two iterators on one zip
>>> next(I1)
(1, 10)
>>> next(I1)
(2, 11)
>>> next(I2)                         # (3.X) I2 is at same spot as I1!
(3, 12)

>>> M = map(abs, (-1, 0, 1))         # Ditto for map (and filter)
>>> I1 = iter(M); I2 = iter(M)
>>> print(next(I1), next(I1), next(I1))
1 0 1
>>> next(I2)                         # (3.X) Single scan is exhausted!
StopIteration

>>> R = range(3)                     # But range allows many iterators
>>> I1, I2 = iter(R), iter(R)
>>> [next(I1), next(I1), next(I1)]
[0 1 2]
>>> next(I2)                         # Multiple active scans, like 2.X lists
0
```

When we code our own iterable objects with classes later in the book (Chapter 30), we'll see that multiple iterators are usually supported by returning new objects for the `iter` call; a single iterator generally means an object returns itself. In Chapter 20, we'll also find that *generator functions and expressions* behave like `map` and `zip` instead of `range` in this regard, supporting just a single active iteration scan. In that chapter, we'll see some subtle implications of one-shot iterators in loops that attempt to scan multiple times—code that formerly treated these as lists may fail without manual list conversions.

Dictionary View Iterables

Finally, as we saw briefly in Chapter 8, in Python 3.X the dictionary `keys`, `values`, and `items` methods return iterable *view* objects that generate result items one at a time, instead of producing result lists all at once in memory. Views are also available in 2.7 as an option, but under special method names to avoid impacting existing code. View items maintain the same physical ordering as that of the dictionary and reflect changes made to the underlying dictionary. Now that we know more about iterables here's the rest of this story—in Python 3.3 (your key order may vary):

```
>>> D = dict(a=1, b=2, c=3)
>>> D
{'a': 1, 'b': 2, 'c': 3}

>>> K = D.keys()                         # A view object in 3.X, not a list
>>> K
dict_keys(['a', 'b', 'c'])

>>> next(K)                              # Views are not iterators themselves
TypeError: dict_keys object is not an iterator

>>> I = iter(K)                          # View iterables have an iterator,
>>> next(I)                              # which can be used manually,
'a'                                      # but does not support len(), index
>>> next(I)
'b'

>>> for k in D.keys(): print(k, end=' ') # All iteration contexts use auto
...
a b c
```

As for all iterables that produce values on request, you can always force a 3.X dictionary view to build a real list by passing it to the `list` built-in. However, this usually isn't required except to display results interactively or to apply list operations like indexing:

```
>>> K = D.keys()
>>> list(K)                              # Can still force a real list if needed
['a', 'b', 'c']

>>> V = D.values()                       # Ditto for values() and items() views
>>> V
dict_values([1, 2, 3])
>>> list(V)                              # Need list() to display or index as list
[1, 2, 3]

>>> V[0]
```

```
TypeError: 'dict_values' object does not support indexing
>>> list(V)[0]
1

>>> list(D.items())
[('a', 1), ('b', 2), ('c', 3)]

>>> for (k, v) in D.items(): print(k, v, end=' ')
...
a 1 b 2 c 3
```

In addition, 3.X dictionaries still are iterables themselves, with an iterator that returns successive keys. Thus, it's not often necessary to call keys directly in this context:

```
>>> D                                    # Dictionaries still produce an iterator
{'a': 1, 'b': 2, 'c': 3}                 # Returns next key on each iteration
>>> I = iter(D)
>>> next(I)
'a'
>>> next(I)
'b'

>>> for key in D: print(key, end=' ')    # Still no need to call keys() to iterate
...                                      # But keys is an iterable in 3.X too!
a b c
```

Finally, remember again that because keys no longer returns a list, the traditional coding pattern for scanning a dictionary by sorted keys won't work in 3.X. Instead, convert keys views first with a list call, or use the sorted call on either a keys view or the dictionary itself, as follows. We saw this in Chapter 8, but it's important enough to 2.X programmers making the switch to demonstrate again:

```
>>> D
{'a': 1, 'b': 2, 'c': 3}
>>> for k in sorted(D.keys()): print(k, D[k], end=' ')
...
a 1 b 2 c 3
>>> for k in sorted(D): print(k, D[k], end=' ')      # "Best practice" key sorting
...
a 1 b 2 c 3
```

Other Iteration Topics

As mentioned in this chapter's introduction, there is more coverage of both list comprehensions and iterables in Chapter 20, in conjunction with functions, and again in Chapter 30 when we study classes. As you'll see later:

- User-defined functions can be turned into iterable *generator functions*, with yield statements.

- List comprehensions morph into iterable *generator expressions* when coded in parentheses.

- User-defined classes are made iterable with __iter__ or __getitem__ *operator over-loading*.

In particular, user-defined iterables defined with classes allow arbitrary objects and operations to be used in any of the iteration contexts we've met in this chapter. By supporting just a single operation—*iteration*—objects may be used in a wide variety of contexts and tools.

Chapter Summary

In this chapter, we explored concepts related to looping in Python. We took our first substantial look at the *iteration protocol* in Python—a way for nonsequence objects to take part in iteration loops—and at *list comprehensions*. As we saw, a list comprehension is an expression similar to a for loop that applies another expression to all the items in any iterable object. Along the way, we also saw other built-in iteration tools at work and studied recent iteration additions in Python 3.X.

This wraps up our tour of specific procedural statements and related tools. The next chapter closes out this part of the book by discussing documentation options for Python code. Though a bit of a diversion from the more detailed aspects of coding, documentation is also part of the general syntax model, and it's an important component of well-written programs. In the next chapter, we'll also dig into a set of exercises for this part of the book before we turn our attention to larger structures such as functions. As usual, though, let's first exercise what we've learned here with a quiz.

Test Your Knowledge: Quiz

1. How are for loops and iterable objects related?
2. How are for loops and list comprehensions related?
3. Name four iteration contexts in the Python language.
4. What is the best way to read line by line from a text file today?
5. What sort of weapons would you expect to see employed by the Spanish Inquisition?

Test Your Knowledge: Answers

1. The for loop uses the *iteration protocol* to step through items in the iterable object across which it is iterating. It first fetches an iterator from the iterable by passing the object to iter, and then calls this iterator object's __next__ method in 3.X on each iteration and catches the StopIteration exception to determine when to stop looping. The method is named next in 2.X, and is run by the next built-in function in both 3.x and 2.X. Any object that supports this model works in a for loop and

in all other iteration contexts. For some objects that are their own iterator, the initial `iter` call is extraneous but harmless.

2. Both are iteration tools and contexts. List comprehensions are a concise and often efficient way to perform a common `for` loop task: collecting the results of applying an expression to all items in an iterable object. It's always possible to translate a list comprehension to a `for` loop, and part of the list comprehension expression looks like the header of a `for` loop syntactically.

3. Iteration contexts in Python include the `for` loop; list comprehensions; the `map` built-in function; the `in` membership test expression; and the built-in functions `sorted`, `sum`, `any`, and `all`. This category also includes the `list` and `tuple` built-ins, string `join` methods, and sequence assignments, all of which use the iteration protocol (see answer #1) to step across iterable objects one item at a time.

4. The best way to read lines from a text file today is to not read it explicitly at all: instead, open the file within an iteration context tool such as a `for` loop or list comprehension, and let the iteration tool automatically scan one line at a time by running the file's next handler method on each iteration. This approach is generally best in terms of coding simplicity, memory space, and possibly execution speed requirements.

5. I'll accept any of the following as correct answers: fear, intimidation, nice red uniforms, a comfy chair, and soft pillows.

The Documentation Interlude

This part of the book concludes with a look at techniques and tools used for documenting Python code. Although Python code is designed to be readable, a few well-placed human-accessible comments can do much to help others understand the workings of your programs. As we'll see, Python includes both syntax and tools to make documentation easier. In particular, the *PyDoc* system covered here can render a module's internal documentation as either plain text in a shell, or HTML in a web browser.

Although this is something of a tools-related concept, this topic is presented here partly because it involves Python's syntax model, and partly as a resource for readers struggling to understand Python's toolset. For the latter purpose, I'll also expand here on documentation pointers first given in Chapter 4. As usual, because this chapter closes out its part, it also ends with some warnings about common pitfalls and a set of exercises for this part of the text, in addition to its chapter quiz.

Python Documentation Sources

By this point in the book, you're probably starting to realize that Python comes with an amazing amount of prebuilt functionality—built-in functions and exceptions, predefined object attributes and methods, standard library modules, and more. And we've really only scratched the surface of each of these categories.

One of the first questions that bewildered beginners often ask is: how do I find information on all the built-in tools? This section provides hints on the various documentation sources available in Python. It also presents *documentation strings* (docstrings) and the *PyDoc* system that makes use of them. These topics are somewhat peripheral to the core language itself, but they become essential knowledge as soon as your code reaches the level of the examples and exercises in this part of the book.

As summarized in Table 15-1, there are a variety of places to look for information on Python, with generally increasing verbosity. Because documentation is such a crucial tool in practical programming, we'll explore each of these categories in the sections that follow.

Table 15-1. Python documentation sources

Form	Role
# comments	In-file documentation
The dir function	Lists of attributes available in objects
Docstrings: __doc__	In-file documentation attached to objects
PyDoc: the help function	Interactive help for objects
PyDoc: HTML reports	Module documentation in a browser
Sphinx third-party tool	Richer documentation for larger projects
The standard manual set	Official language and library descriptions
Web resources	Online tutorials, examples, and so on
Published books	Commercially polished reference texts

Comments

As we've learned, hash-mark comments are the most basic way to document your code. Python simply ignores all the text following a # (as long as it's not inside a string literal), so you can follow this character with any words and descriptions meaningful to programmers. Such comments are accessible only in your source files, though; to code comments that are more widely available, you'll need to use docstrings.

In fact, current best practice generally dictates that docstrings are best for larger functional documentation (e.g., "my file does this"), and # comments are best limited to smaller code documentation (e.g., "this strange expression does that") and are best limited in scope to a statement or small group of statements within a script or function. More on docstrings in a moment; first, let's see how to explore objects.

The dir Function

As we've also seen, the built-in `dir` function is an easy way to grab a list of all the attributes available inside an object (i.e., its methods and simpler data items). It can be called with no arguments to list variables in the caller's scope. More usefully, it can also be called on any object that has attributes, including imported modules and built-in types, as well as the name of a data type. For example, to find out what's available in a *module* such as the standard library's `sys`, import it and pass it to `dir`:

```
>>> import sys
>>> dir(sys)
['__displayhook__', ...more names omitted..., 'winver']
```

These results are from Python 3.3, and I'm omitting most returned names because they vary slightly elsewhere; run this on your own for a better look. In fact, there are currently 78 attributes in `sys`, though we generally care only about the 69 that do not have leading double underscores (two usually means interpreter-related) or the 62 that have no leading underscore at all (one underscore usually means informal implementation private)—a prime example of the preceding chapter's list comprehension at work:

```
>>> len(dir(sys))                                    # Number names in sys
78
>>> len([x for x in dir(sys) if not x.startswith('__')])    # Non __X names only
69
>>> len([x for x in dir(sys) if not x[0] == '_'])    # Non underscore names
62
```

To find out what attributes are provided in objects of *built-in types*, run `dir` on a literal or an existing instance of the desired type. For example, to see list and string attributes, you can pass empty objects:

```
>>> dir([])
['__add__', '__class__', '__contains__', ...more..., 'append', 'clear', 'copy',
'count', 'extend', 'index', 'insert', 'pop', 'remove', 'reverse', 'sort']

>>> dir('')
['__add__', '__class__', '__contains__', ...more..., 'split', 'splitlines',
'startswith', 'strip', 'swapcase', 'title', 'translate', 'upper', 'zfill']
```

The `dir` results for any built-in type include a set of attributes that are related to the implementation of that type (technically, operator overloading methods); much as in modules they all begin and end with double underscores to make them distinct, and you can safely ignore them at this point in the book (they are used for OOP). For instance, there are 45 list attributes, but only 11 that correspond to named methods:

```
>>> len(dir([])), len([x for x in dir([]) if not x.startswith('__')])
(45, 11)
>>> len(dir('')), len([x for x in dir('') if not x.startswith('__')])
(76, 44)
```

In fact, to filter out double-underscored items that are not of common program interest, run the same list comprehensions but print the attributes. For instance, here are the named attributes in lists and dictionaries in Python 3.3:

```
>>> [a for a in dir(list) if not a.startswith('__')]
['append', 'clear', 'copy', 'count', 'extend', 'index', 'insert', 'pop',
'remove', 'reverse', 'sort']

>>> [a for a in dir(dict) if not a.startswith('__')]
['clear', 'copy', 'fromkeys', 'get', 'items', 'keys', 'pop', 'popitem',
'setdefault', 'update', 'values']
```

This may seem like a lot to type to get an attribute list, but beginning in the next chapter we'll learn how to wrap such code in an importable and reusable *function* so we don't need to type it again:

```
>>> def dir1(x): return [a for a in dir(x) if not a.startswith('__')]    # See Part IV
...
>>> dir1(tuple)
['count', 'index']
```

Notice that you can list built-in type attributes by passing a type name to `dir` instead of a literal:

```
>>> dir(str) == dir('')            # Same result, type name or literal
True
>>> dir(list) == dir([])
True
```

This works because names like `str` and `list` that were once type converter functions are actually names of types in Python today; calling one of these invokes its constructor to generate an instance of that type. Part VI will have more to say about constructors and operator overloading methods when we discuss classes.

The `dir` function serves as a sort of memory-jogger—it provides a list of attribute names, but it does not tell you anything about what those names mean. For such extra information, we need to move on to the next documentation source.

 Some IDEs for Python work, including IDLE, have features that list attributes on objects automatically within their GUIs, and can be viewed as alternatives to `dir`. IDLE, for example, will list an object's attributes in a pop-up selection window when you type a period after the object's name and pause or press Tab. This is mostly meant as an autocomplete feature, though, not an information source. Chapter 3 has more on IDLE.

Docstrings: __doc__

Besides # comments, Python supports documentation that is automatically attached to objects and retained at runtime for inspection. Syntactically, such comments are coded as strings at the tops of module files and function and class statements, before any other executable code (# comments, including Unix-style #! lines are OK before them). Python automatically stuffs the text of these strings, known informally as *docstrings*, into the __doc__ attributes of the corresponding objects.

User-defined docstrings

For example, consider the following file, *docstrings.py*. Its docstrings appear at the beginning of the file and at the start of a function and a class within it. Here, I've used triple-quoted block strings for multiline comments in the file and the function, but any sort of string will work; single- or double-quoted one-liners like those in the class are fine, but don't allow multiple-line text. We haven't studied the `def` or `class` statements in detail yet, so ignore everything about them here except the strings at their tops:

```
"""
Module documentation
Words Go Here
"""
```

```
spam = 40

def square(x):
    """
    function documentation
    can we have your liver then?
    """
    return x ** 2          # square

class Employee:
    "class documentation"
    pass

print(square(4))
print(square.__doc__)
```

The whole point of this documentation protocol is that your comments are *retained* for inspection in __doc__ attributes after the file is imported. Thus, to display the docstrings associated with the module and its objects, we simply import the file and print their __doc__ attributes, where Python has saved the text:

```
>>> import docstrings
16

    function documentation
    can we have your liver then?

>>> print(docstrings.__doc__)

Module documentation
Words Go Here

>>> print(docstrings.square.__doc__)

    function documentation
    can we have your liver then?

>>> print(docstrings.Employee.__doc__)
    class documentation
```

Note that you will generally want to use print to print docstrings; otherwise, you'll get a single string with embedded \n newline characters.

You can also attach docstrings to *methods* of classes (covered in Part VI), but because these are just def statements nested in class statements, they're not a special case. To fetch the docstring of a method function inside a class within a module, you would simply extend the path to go through the class: module.class.method.__doc__ (we'll see an example of method docstrings in Chapter 29).

Docstring standards and priorities

As mentioned earlier, common practice today recommends hash-mark comments for only smaller-scale documentation about an expression, statement, or small group of statements. Docstrings are better used for higher-level and broader functional documentation for a file, function, or class, and have become an expected part of Python software. Beyond these guidelines, though, you still must decide what to write.

Although some companies have internal standards, there is no broad standard about what should go into the text of a docstring. There have been various markup language and template proposals (e.g., HTML or XML), but they don't seem to have caught on in the Python world. Frankly, convincing Python programmers to document their code using handcoded HTML is probably not going to happen in our lifetimes. That may be too much to ask, but this doesn't apply to documenting code in general.

Documentation tends to have a lower priority among some programmers than it should. Too often, if you get any comments in a file at all, you count yourself lucky (and even better if it's accurate and up to date). I strongly encourage you to document your code liberally—it really is an important part of well-written programs. When you do, though, there is presently no standard on the structure of docstrings; if you want to use them, anything goes today. Just as for writing code itself, it's up to you to create documentation content and keep it up to date, but common sense is probably your best ally on this task too.

Built-in docstrings

As it turns out, built-in modules and objects in Python use similar techniques to attach documentation above and beyond the attribute lists returned by dir. For example, to see an actual human-readable description of a built-in module, import it and print its __doc__ string:

```
>>> import sys
>>> print(sys.__doc__)
This module provides access to some objects used or maintained by the
interpreter and to functions that interact strongly with the interpreter.

Dynamic objects:

argv -- command line arguments; argv[0] is the script pathname if known
path -- module search path; path[0] is the script directory, else ''
modules -- dictionary of loaded modules
...more text omitted...
```

Functions, classes, and methods within built-in modules have attached descriptions in their __doc__ attributes as well:

```
>>> print(sys.getrefcount.__doc__)
getrefcount(object) -> integer

Return the reference count of object.  The count returned is generally
one higher than you might expect, because it includes the (temporary)
reference as an argument to getrefcount().
```

You can also read about built-in functions via their docstrings:

```
>>> print(int.__doc__)
int(x[, base]) -> integer
```

```
Convert a string or number to an integer, if possible.  A floating
point argument will be truncated towards zero (this does not include a
...more text omitted...
```

```
>>> print(map.__doc__)
map(func, *iterables) --> map object
```

```
Make an iterator that computes the function using arguments from
each of the iterables.  Stops when the shortest iterable is exhausted.
```

You can get a wealth of information about built-in tools by inspecting their docstrings this way, but you don't have to—the `help` function, the topic of the next section, does this automatically for you.

PyDoc: The help Function

The docstring technique proved to be so useful that Python eventually added a tool that makes docstrings even easier to display. The standard *PyDoc* tool is Python code that knows how to extract docstrings and associated structural information and format them into nicely arranged reports of various types. Additional tools for extracting and formatting docstrings are available in the open source domain (including tools that may support structured text—search the Web for pointers), but Python ships with PyDoc in its standard library.

There are a variety of ways to launch PyDoc, including command-line script options that can save the resulting documentation for later viewing (described both ahead and in the Python library manual). Perhaps the two most prominent PyDoc interfaces are the built-in `help` function and the PyDoc GUI- and web-based HTML report interfaces. We met the `help` function briefly in Chapter 4; it invokes PyDoc to generate a simple textual report for any Python object. In this mode, help text looks much like a "man-page" on Unix-like systems, and in fact pages the same way as a Unix "more" outside GUIs like IDLE when there are multiple pages of text—press the space bar to move to the next page, Enter to go to the next line, and Q to quit:

```
>>> import sys
>>> help(sys.getrefcount)
Help on built-in function getrefcount in module sys:
```

```
getrefcount(...)
    getrefcount(object) -> integer
```

```
    Return the reference count of object.  The count returned is generally
    one higher than you might expect, because it includes the (temporary)
    reference as an argument to getrefcount().
```

Note that you do not have to import sys in order to call `help`, but you do have to import sys to get help on sys this way; it expects an object reference to be passed in. In Pythons

3.3 and 2.7, you can get help for a module you have not imported by quoting the module's name as a string—for example, help('re'), help('email.message')—but support for this and other modes may differ across Python versions.

For larger objects such as modules and classes, the help display is broken down into multiple sections, the preambles of which are shown here. Run this interactively to see the full report (I'm running this on 3.3):

```
>>> help(sys)
Help on built-in module sys:

NAME
    sys

MODULE REFERENCE
    http://docs.python.org/3.3/library/sys
    ...more omitted...

DESCRIPTION
    This module provides access to some objects used or maintained by the
    interpreter and to functions that interact strongly with the interpreter.
    ...more omitted...

FUNCTIONS
    __displayhook__ = displayhook(...)
        displayhook(object) -> None
    ...more omitted...

DATA
    __stderr__ = <_io.TextIOWrapper name='<stderr>' mode='w' encoding='cp4...
    __stdin__ = <_io.TextIOWrapper name='<stdin>' mode='r' encoding='cp437...
    __stdout__ = <_io.TextIOWrapper name='<stdout>' mode='w' encoding='cp4...
    ...more omitted...

FILE
    (built-in)
```

Some of the information in this report is docstrings, and some of it (e.g., function call patterns) is structural information that PyDoc gleans automatically by inspecting objects' internals, when available.

Besides modules, you can also use help on built-in functions, methods, and types. Usage varies slightly across Python versions, but to get help for a *built-in type*, try either the type name (e.g., dict for dictionary, str for string, list for list); an actual object of the type (e.g., {}, '', []); or a method of an actual object or type name (e.g., str.join, 's'.join).[1] You'll get a large display that describes all the methods available for that type or the usage of that method:

```
>>> help(dict)
Help on class dict in module builtins:

class dict(object)
 |  dict() -> new empty dictionary.
 |  dict(mapping) -> new dictionary initialized from a mapping object's
 ...more omitted...

>>> help(str.replace)
Help on method_descriptor:

replace(...)
    S.replace (old, new[, count]) -> str

    Return a copy of S with all occurrences of substring
    ...more omitted...

>>> help(''.replace)
...similar to prior result...

>>> help(ord)
Help on built-in function ord in module builtins:

ord(...)
    ord(c) -> integer

    Return the integer ordinal of a one-character string.
```

Finally, the help function works just as well on your modules as it does on built-ins. Here it is reporting on the *docstrings.py* file we coded earlier. Again, some of this is docstrings, and some is information automatically extracted by inspecting objects' structures:

```
>>> import docstrings
>>> help(docstrings.square)
Help on function square in module docstrings:

square(x)
    function documentation
    can we have your liver then?

>>> help(docstrings.Employee)
Help on class Employee in module docstrings:
```

---

1. Note that asking for help on an actual *string object* directly (e.g., help('')) doesn't work in recent Pythons: you usually get no help, because strings are interpreted specially—as a request for help on an unimported module, for instance (see earlier). You must use the str type name in this context, though both other types of actual objects (help([])) and string method names referenced through actual objects (help(''.join)) work fine (at least in Python 3.3—this has been prone to change over time). There is also an interactive help mode, which you start by typing just help().

```
class Employee(builtins.object)
 |  class documentation
 |
 ...more omitted...

>>> help(docstrings)
Help on module docstrings:

NAME
    docstrings

DESCRIPTION
    Module documentation
    Words Go Here

CLASSES
    builtins.object
        Employee

    class Employee(builtins.object)
     |  class documentation
     |
     ...more omitted...

FUNCTIONS
    square(x)
        function documentation
        can we have your liver then?

DATA
    spam = 40

FILE
    c:\code\docstrings.py
```

PyDoc: HTML Reports

The text displays of the help function are adequate in many contexts, especially at the interactive prompt. To readers who've grown accustomed to richer presentation mediums, though, they may seem a bit primitive. This section presents the HTML-based flavor of PyDoc, which renders module documentation more graphically for viewing in a web browser, and can even open one automatically for you. The way this is run has changed as of Python 3.3:

- *Prior to 3.3*, Python ships with a simple GUI desktop client for submitting search requests. This client launches a web browser to view documentation produced by an automatically started local server.

- *As of 3.3*, the former GUI client is replaced by an all-browser interface scheme, which combines both search and display in a web page that communicates with an automatically started local server.

- *Python 3.2* straddles this fence, supporting both the original GUI client scheme, as well as the newer all-browser mode mandated as of 3.3.

Because this book's audience is both users of the latest-and-greatest as well as the masses still using older tried-and-true Pythons, we'll explore both schemes here. As we do, keep in mind that the way these schemes differ pertains only to the top level of their user interfaces. Their documentation displays are nearly identical, and under either regime PyDoc can also be used to generate both text in a console, and HTML files for later viewing in whatever manner you wish.

Python 3.2 and later: PyDoc's all-browser mode

As of Python 3.3 the original GUI client mode of PyDoc, present in 2.X and earlier 3.X releases, is no longer available. This mode is present through Python 3.2 with the "Module Docs" Start button entry on Windows 7 and earlier, and via the `pydoc -g` command line. This GUI mode was reportedly deprecated in 3.2, though you had to look closely to notice—it works fine and without warning on 3.2 on my machine.

In 3.3, though, this mode goes away altogether, and is replaced with a `pydoc -b` command line, which instead spawns both a locally running documentation server, as well as a web browser that functions as both search engine client and page display. The browser is initially opened on a module index page with enhanced functionality. There are additional ways to use PyDoc (e.g., to save the HTML page to a file for later viewing, as described ahead), so this is a relatively minor operational change.

To launch the newer browser-only mode of PyDoc in Python 3.2 and later, a command-line like any of the following suffice: they all use the -m Python command-line argument for convenience to locate PyDoc's module file on your module import search path. The first assumes Python is on your system path; the second employs Python 3.3's new Windows launcher; and the third gives the full path to your Python if the other two schemes won't work. See Appendix A for more on -m, and Appendix B for coverage of the Windows launcher.

```
c:\code> python -m pydoc -b
Server ready at http://localhost:62135/
Server commands: [b]rowser, [q]uit
server> q
Server stopped

c:\code> py -3 -m pydoc -b
Server ready at http://localhost:62144/
Server commands: [b]rowser, [q]uit
server> q
Server stopped

c:\code> C:\python33\python -m pydoc -b
Server ready at http://localhost:62153/
Server commands: [b]rowser, [q]uit
server> q
Server stopped
```

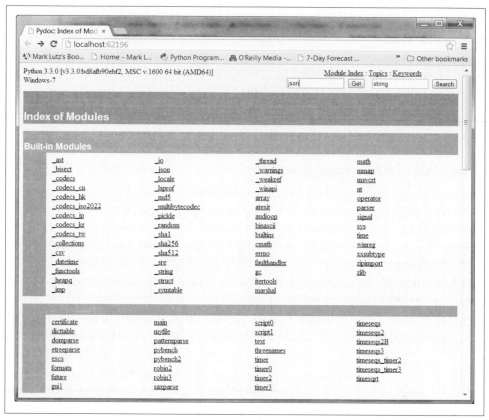

Figure 15-1. The top-level index start page of the all-browser PyDoc HTML interface in Python 3.2 and later, which as of 3.3 replaces the former GUI client in earlier Pythons.

However you run this command line, the effect is to start PyDoc as a locally running *web server* on a dedicated (but by default arbitrary unused) port, and pop up a web browser to act as *client*, displaying a page giving links to documentation for all the modules importable on your module search path (including the directory where PyDoc is launched). PyDoc's top-level web page interface is captured in Figure 15-1.

Besides the module index, PyDoc's web page also includes input fields at the top to request a specific module's documentation page (*Get*) and search for related entries (*Search*), which stand in for the prior interface's GUI client fields. You can also click on this page's links to go to the *Module Index* (the start page), *Topics* (general Python subjects), and *Keywords* (overviews of statements and some expressions).

Notice that the index page in Figure 15-1 lists both *modules* and top-level *scripts* in the current directory—the book's *C:\code*, where PyDoc was started by the earlier command lines. PyDoc is mostly intended for documenting importable modules, but can sometimes be used to show documentation for scripts too. A selected file must be imported in order to render its documentation, and as we've learned, importing runs a file's code. Modules normally just define tools when run, so this is usually irrelevant.

If you ask for documentation for a top-level script file, though, the shell window where you launched PyDoc serves as the script's standard input and output for any user interaction. The net effect is that the documentation page for a script will appear after it *runs*, and after its printed output shows up in the shell window. This may work better for some scripts than others, though; interactive input, for example, may interleave oddly with PyDoc's own server command prompts.

Once you get past the new start page in Figure 15-1, the documentation pages for specific modules are essentially the same in both the newer all-browser mode and the earlier GUI-client scheme, apart from the additional input fields at the top of page in the former. For instance, Figure 15-2 shows the new documentation display pages—opened on two user-defined modules we'll be writing in the next part of this book, as part of Chapter 21's benchmarking case study. In either scheme, documentation pages contain automatically created hyperlinks that allow you to click your way through the documentation of related components in your application. For instance, you'll find links to open imported modules' pages too.

Because of the similarity in their display pages, the next section on pre-3.2 PyDoc and its screen shots largely apply after 3.2 too, so be sure to read ahead for additional notes even if you're using more recent Python. In effect, 3.3's PyDoc simply cuts out the pre-3.2 GUI client "middleman," while retaining its browser and server.

PyDoc in Python 3.3 also still supports other former usage modes. For instance, `pydoc -p port` can be used to set its PyDoc server port, and `pydoc -w module` still writes a module's HTML documentation to a file named `module.html` for later viewing. Only the `pydoc -g` GUI client mode is removed and replaced by `pydoc -b`. You can also run PyDoc to generate a plain-text form of the documentation (its Unix "manpage" flavor shown earlier in this chapter)—the following command line is equivalent to the `help` call at an interactive Python prompt:

```
c:\code> py -3 -m pydoc timeit          # Command-line text help

c:\code> py -3
>>> help("timeit")                      # Interactive prompt text help
```

As an interactive system, your best bet is to take PyDoc's web-based interface for a test drive, so we'll cut its usage details short here; see Python's manuals for additional details and command-line options. Also note that PyDoc's server and browser functionality come largely "for free" from tools that automate such utility in the portable modules of Python's standard library (e.g., `webbrowser`, `http.server`). Consult PyDoc's Python code in the standard library file *pydoc.py* for additional details and inspiration.

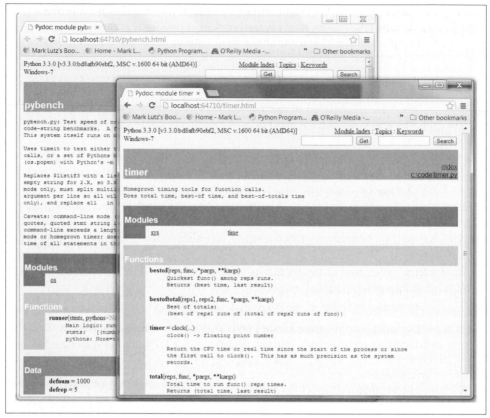

Figure 15-2. PyDoc's module display page in Python 3.2 and later with input fields at the top, displaying two modules we will be coding in the next part of this book (Chapter 21).

Changing PyDoc's Colors

You won't be able to tell in the paper version of this book, but if you have an ebook or start PyDoc live, you'll notice that it chooses colors that may or may not be to your liking. Unfortunately, there presently is no easy way to customize PyDoc's colors. They are hardcoded deep in its source code, and can't be passed in as arguments to functions or command lines, or changed in configuration files or global variables in the PyDoc module itself.

Except that, in an open source system, you can always change the code—PyDoc lives in the file *pydoc.py* in Python's standard library, which is directory *C:\Python33\Lib* on Windows for Python 3.3. Its colors are hardcoded RGB value hex strings embedded throughout its code. For instance, its string `'#eeaa77'` specifies 2-byte (16-bit) values for red, green, and blue levels (decimal 238, 170, and 119), yielding a shade of orange for function banners. The string `'#ee77aa'` similarly renders the dark pinkish color used in nine places, including class and index page banners.

To tailor, search for these color value strings and replace them with your preferences. In IDLE, an Edit/Find for regular expression #\w{6} will locate color strings (this matches six alphanumeric characters after a # per Python's `re` module pattern syntax; see the library manual for details).

To pick colors, in most programs with color selection dialogs you can map to and from RGB values; the book's examples include a GUI script *setcolor.py* that does the same. In my copy of PyDoc, I replaced all #ee77aa with #008080 (teal) to banish the dark pink. Replacing #ffc8d8 with #c0c0c0 (grey) does similar for the light pink background of class docstrings.

Such surgery isn't for the faint of heart—PyDoc's file is currently 2,600 lines long—but makes for a fair exercise in code maintenance. Be cautious when replacing colors like #ffffff and #000000 (white and black), and be sure to make a backup copy of *py-doc.py* first so you have a fallback. This file uses tools we haven't yet met, but you can safely ignore the rest of its code while you make your tactical changes.

Be sure to watch for PyDoc changes on the configurations front; this seems a prime candidate for improvement. In fact, there already is an effort under way: issue 10716 on the Python developers' list seeks to make PyDoc more user-customizable by changing it to support *CSS style sheets*. If successful, this may allow users to make color and other display choices in external CSS files instead of PyDoc's source code.

On the other hand, this is currently not planned to appear until Python 3.4, and will require PyDoc's users to also be proficient with CSS code—which unfortunately has a nontrivial structure all its own that many people using Python may not understand well enough to change. As I write this, for example, the proposed PyDoc CSS file is already 234 lines of code that probably won't mean much to people not already familiar with web development (and it hardly seems reasonable to ask them to learn a web development tool just to tailor PyDoc!).

Today's PyDoc in 3.3 already supports a CSS style sheet that offers some customization options, but only half-heartedly, and ships with one that is empty. Until this is hashed out, code changes seem the best option. In any event, CSS style sheets are well beyond this Python book's scope—see the Web for details, and check future Python release notes for PyDoc developments.

Python 3.2 and earlier: GUI client

This section documents the original GUI client mode of PyDoc, for readers using 3.2 and earlier, and gives some addition PyDoc context in general. It builds on the basics covered in the prior section, which aren't repeated here, so be sure to at least scan the prior section if you're using an older Python.

As mentioned, through Python 3.2, PyDoc provides a top-level GUI interface—a simple but portable Python/tkinter script for submitting requests—as well as a documentation server. Requests in the client are routed to the server, which produces reports displayed in a popped-up web browser. Apart from your having to submit search requests, this process is largely automatic.

Figure 15-3. The PyDoc top-level search engine GUI client in 3.2 and earlier: type the name of a module you want documentation for, press Enter, select the module, and then press "go to selected" (or omit the module name and press "open browser" to see all available modules).

To start PyDoc in this mode, you generally first launch the search engine GUI captured in Figure 15-3. You can start this either by selecting the Module Docs item in Python's Start button menu on Windows 7 and earlier, or by launching the *pydoc.py* script in Python's standard library directory with a -g command-line argument: it lives in *Lib* on Windows, but you can use Python's -m flag to avoid typing script paths here too:

```
c:\code> c:\python32\python -m pydoc -g      # Explicit Python path
c:\code> py -3.2 -m pydoc -g                 # Windows 3.3+ launcher version
```

Enter the name of a module you're interested in, and press the Enter key; PyDoc will march down your module import search path (sys.path), looking for the requested module and references to it.

Once you've found a promising entry, select it and click "go to selected." PyDoc will spawn a web browser on your machine to display the report rendered in HTML format. Figure 15-4 shows the information PyDoc displays for the built-in glob module. Notice the hyperlinks in the *Modules* section of this page—you can click these to jump to the PyDoc pages for related (imported) modules. For larger pages, PyDoc also generates hyperlinks to sections within the page.

Like the help function interface, the GUI interface works on user-defined modules as well as built-ins. Figure 15-5 shows the page generated for our *docstrings.py* module file coded earlier.

Make sure that the directory containing your module is on your module import search path—as mentioned, PyDoc must be able to import a file to render its documentation. This includes the current working directory—PyDoc might not check the directory it was launched from (which is probably meaningless when started from the Windows Start button anyhow), so you may need to extend your PYTHONPATH setting to get this to

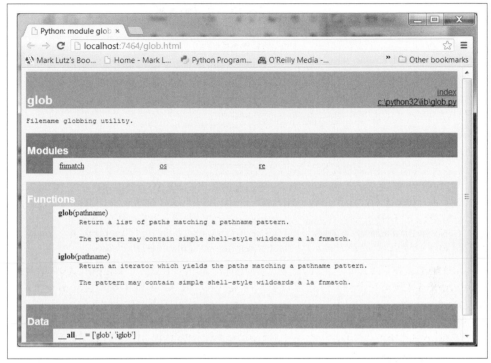

Figure 15-4. When you find a module in the Figure 15-3 GUI (such as this built-in standard library module) and press "go to selected," the module's documentation is rendered in HTML and displayed in a web browser window like this one.

work. On Pythons 3.2 and 2.7, I had to add "." to my PYTHONPATH to get PyDoc's GUI client mode to look in the directory it was started from by command line:

```
c:\code> set PYTHONPATH=.;%PYTYONPATH%
c:\code> py -3.2 -m pydoc -g
```

This setting was also required to see the current directory for the new all-browser pydoc -b mode in 3.2. However, Python 3.3 automatically includes "." in its index list, so no path setting is required to view files in the directory where PyDoc is started—a minor but noteworthy improvement.

PyDoc can be customized and launched in various ways we won't cover here; see its entry in Python's standard library manual for more details. The main thing to take away from this section is that PyDoc essentially gives you implementation reports "for free" —if you are good about using docstrings in your files, PyDoc does all the work of collecting and formatting them for display. PyDoc helps only for objects like functions and modules, but it provides an easy way to access a middle level of documentation for such tools—its reports are more useful than raw attribute lists, and less exhaustive than the standard manuals.

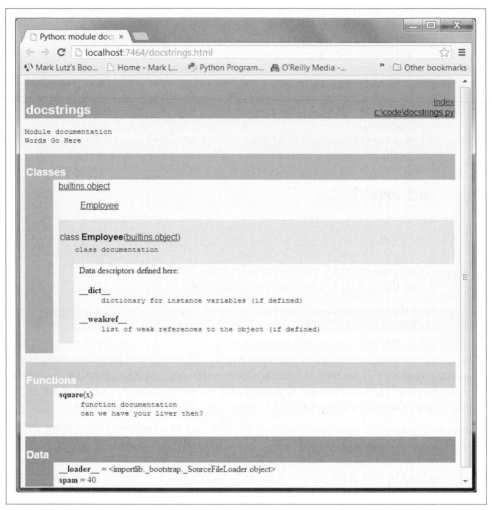

Figure 15-5. PyDoc can serve up documentation pages for both built-in and user-coded modules on the module search path. Here is the page for a user-defined module, showing all its documentation strings (docstrings) extracted from the source file.

PyDoc can also be run to save the HTML documentation for a module in a file for later viewing or printing; see the preceding section for pointers. Also, note that PyDoc might not work well if run on *scripts* that read from standard input—PyDoc imports the target module to inspect its contents, and there may be no connection for standard input text when it is run in GUI mode, especially if run from the Windows Start button. Modules that can be imported without immediate input requirements will always work under PyDoc, though. See also the preceding section's notes regarding scripts in PyDoc's -b mode in 3.2 and later; launching PyDoc's GUI mode by command line works the same —you interact in the launch window.

PyDoc GUI client trick of the day: If you press the "open browser" button in Figure 15-3's window, PyDoc will produce an index page containing a hyperlink to every module you can possibly import on your computer. This includes Python standard library modules, modules of installed third-party extensions, user-defined modules on your import search path, and even statically or dynamically linked-in C-coded modules. Such information is hard to come by otherwise without writing code that inspects all module sources. On Python 3.2, you'll want to do this immediately after the GUI opens, as it may not fully work after searches. Also note that in PyDoc's all-browser –b interface in 3.2 and later, you get the same index functionality on its top-level start page of Figure 15-1.

Beyond docstrings: Sphinx

If you're looking for a way to document your Python system in a more sophisticated way, you may wish to check out *Sphinx* (currently at *http://sphinx-doc.org*). Sphinx is used by the standard Python documentation described in the next section, and many other projects. It uses simple *reStructuredText* as its markup language, and inherits much from the *Docutils* suite of reStructuredText parsing and translating tools.

Among other things, Sphinx supports a variety of output formats (HTML including Windows HTML Help, LaTeX for printable PDF versions, manual pages, and plain text); extensive and automatic cross-references; hierarchical structure with automatic links to relatives; automatic indexes; automatic code highlighting using *Pygments* (itself a notable Python tool); and more. This is probably overkill for smaller programs where docstrings and PyDoc may suffice, but can yield professional-grade documentation for large projects. See the Web for more details on Sphinx and its related tools.

The Standard Manual Set

For the complete and most up-to-date description of the language and its toolset, Python's standard manuals stand ready to serve. Python's manuals ship in HTML and other formats, and they are installed with the Python system on Windows—they are available in your Start button's menu for Python on Windows 7 and earlier, and they can also be opened from the Help menu within IDLE. You can also fetch the manual set separately from *http://www.python.org* in a variety of formats, or read it online at that site (follow the Documentation link). On Windows, the manuals are a compiled help file to support searches, and the online versions at the Python website include a web-based search page.

When opened, the Windows format of the manuals displays a root page like that in Figure 15-6, showing the local copy on Windows. The two most important entries here are most likely the *Library Reference* (which documents built-in types, functions, exceptions, and standard library modules) and the *Language Reference* (which provides

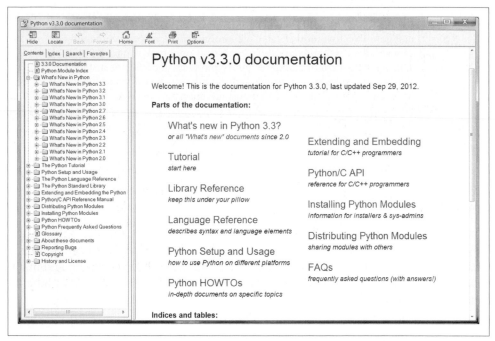

Figure 15-6. Python's standard manual set, available online at http://www.python.org, from IDLE's Help menu, and in the Windows 7 and earlier Start button menu. It's a searchable help file on Windows, and there is a search engine for the online version. Of these, the Library Reference is the one you'll want to use most of the time.

a formal description of language-level details). The tutorial listed on this page also provides a brief introduction for newcomers, which you're probably already beyond.

Of notable interest, the *What's New* documents in this standard manual set chronicle Python changes made in each release beginning with Python 2.0, which came out in late 2000—useful for those porting older Python code, or older Python skills. These documents are especially useful for uncovering additional details on the differences in the Python 2.X and 3.X language lines covered in this book, as well as in their standard libraries.

Web Resources

At the official Python website (*http://www.python.org*), you'll find links to various Python resources, some of which cover special topics or domains. Click the Documentation link to access an online tutorial and the Beginners Guide to Python. The site also lists non-English Python resources, and introductions scaled to different target audiences.

Today you will also find numerous Python wikis, blogs, websites, and a host of other resources on the Web at large. To sample the online community, try searching for a term like "Python programming" in Google, or search on any topic of interest; chances are good you'll find ample material to browse.

Published Books

As a final resource, you can choose from a collection of professionally edited and published reference books for Python. Bear in mind that books tend to lag behind the cutting edge of Python changes, partly because of the work involved in writing, and partly because of the natural delays built into the publishing cycle. Usually, by the time a book comes out, it's three or more months behind the current Python state (trust me on that—my books have a nasty habit of falling out of date in minor ways between the time I write them and the time they hit the shelves!). Unlike standard manuals, books are also generally not free.

Still, for many, the convenience and quality of a professionally published text is worth the cost. Moreover, Python changes so slowly that books are usually still relevant years after they are published, especially if their authors post updates on the Web. See the preface for pointers to other Python books.

Common Coding Gotchas

Before the programming exercises for this part of the book, let's run through some of the most common mistakes beginners make when coding Python statements and programs. Many of these are warnings I've thrown out earlier in this part of the book, collected here for ease of reference. You'll learn to avoid these pitfalls once you've gained a bit of Python coding experience, but a few words now might help you avoid falling into some of these traps initially:

- **Don't forget the colons**. Always remember to type a `:` at the end of compound statement headers—the first line of an `if`, `while`, `for`, etc. You'll probably forget at first (I did, and so have most of my roughly 4,000 Python students over the years), but you can take some comfort from the fact that it will soon become an unconscious habit.

- **Start in column 1**. Be sure to start top-level (unnested) code in column 1. That includes unnested code typed into module files, as well as unnested code typed at the interactive prompt.

- **Blank lines matter at the interactive prompt**. Blank lines in compound statements are always irrelevant and ignored in module files, but when you're typing code at the interactive prompt, they end the statement. In other words, blank lines tell the interactive command line that you've finished a compound statement; if you want to continue, don't hit the Enter key at the `...` prompt (or in IDLE) until you're really done. This also means you can't paste multiline code at this prompt; it must run one full statement at a time.

- **Indent consistently**. Avoid mixing tabs and spaces in the indentation of a block, unless you know what your text editor does with tabs. Otherwise, what you see in your editor may not be what Python sees when it counts tabs as a number of spaces. This is true in any block-structured language, not just Python—if the next programmer has tabs set differently, it will be difficult or impossible to understand the structure of your code. It's safer to use all tabs or all spaces for each block.

- **Don't code C in Python**. A reminder for C/C++ programmers: you don't need to type parentheses around tests in `if` and `while` headers (e.g., `if (X==1):`). You can, if you like (any expression can be enclosed in parentheses), but they are fully superfluous in this context. Also, do not terminate all your statements with semicolons; it's technically legal to do this in Python as well, but it's totally useless unless you're placing more than one statement on a single line (the end of a line normally terminates a statement). And remember, don't embed assignment statements in `while` loop tests, and don't use {} around blocks (indent your nested code blocks consistently instead).

- **Use simple `for` loops instead of `while` or `range`**. Another reminder: a simple `for` loop (e.g., `for x in seq:`) is almost always simpler to code and often quicker to run than a `while`- or `range`-based counter loop. Because Python handles indexing internally for a simple `for`, it can sometimes be faster than the equivalent `while`, though this can vary per code and Python. For code simplicity alone, though, avoid the temptation to count things in Python!

- **Beware of mutables in assignments**. I mentioned this in Chapter 11: you need to be careful about using mutables in a multiple-target assignment (`a = b = []`), as well as in an augmented assignment (`a += [1, 2]`). In both cases, in-place changes may impact other variables. See Chapter 11 for details if you've forgotten why this is true.

- **Don't expect results from functions that change objects in place**. We encountered this one earlier, too: in-place change operations like the `list.append` and `list.sort` methods introduced in Chapter 8 do not return values (other than `None`), so you should call them without assigning the result. It's not uncommon for beginners to say something like `mylist = mylist.append(X)` to try to get the result of an `append`, but what this actually does is assign `mylist` to `None`, not to the modified list (in fact, you'll lose your reference to the list altogether).

  A more devious example of this pops up in Python 2.X code when trying to step through dictionary items in a sorted fashion. It's fairly common to see code like `for k in D.keys().sort():`. This almost works—the `keys` method builds a keys list, and the `sort` method orders it—but because the `sort` method returns `None`, the loop fails because it is ultimately a loop over `None` (a nonsequence). This fails even sooner in Python 3.X, because dictionary keys are views, not lists! To code this correctly, either use the newer `sorted` built-in function, which returns the sorted list, or split the method calls out to statements: `Ks = list(D.keys())`, then `Ks.sort()`, and finally, `for k in Ks:`. This, by the way, is one case where you may still want to call the keys method explicitly for looping, instead of relying on the dictionary iterators—iterators do not sort.

- **Always use parentheses to call a function**. You must add parentheses after a function name to call it, whether it takes arguments or not (e.g., use function(), not function). In the next part of this book, we'll learn that functions are simply objects that have a special operation—a call that you trigger with the parentheses. They can be referenced like any other object without triggering a call.

  In classes, this problem seems to occur most often with files; it's common to see beginners type file.close to close a file, rather than file.close(). Because it's legal to reference a function without calling it, the first version with no parentheses succeeds silently, but it does not close the file!

- **Don't use extensions or paths in imports and reloads**. Omit directory paths and file extensions in import statements—say import mod, not import mod.py. We discussed module basics in Chapter 3 and will continue studying modules in Part V. Because modules may have other extensions besides *.py* (*.pyc*, for instance), hardcoding a particular extension is not only illegal syntax, it doesn't make sense. Python picks an extension automatically, and any platform-specific directory path syntax comes from module search path settings, not the import statement.

- **And other pitfalls in other parts**. Be sure to also see the built-in type warnings at the end of the prior part, as they may qualify as coding issues too. There are additional "gotchas" that crop up commonly in Python coding—losing a built-in function by reassigning its name, hiding a library module by using its name for one of your own, changing mutable argument defaults, and so on—but we don't have enough background to cover them yet. To learn more about both what you should and shouldn't do in Python, you'll have to read on; later parts extend the set of "gotchas" and fixes we've added to here.

Chapter Summary

This chapter took us on a tour of program documentation—both documentation we write ourselves for our own programs, and documentation available for tools we use. We met docstrings, explored the online and manual resources for Python reference, and learned how PyDoc's help function and web page interfaces provide extra sources of documentation. Because this is the last chapter in this part of the book, we also reviewed common coding mistakes to help you avoid them.

In the next part of this book, we'll start applying what we already know to larger program constructs. Specifically, the next part takes up the topic of *functions*—a tool used to group statements for reuse. Before moving on, however, be sure to work through the set of lab exercises for this part of the book that appear at the end of this chapter. And even before that, let's run through this chapter's quiz.

Test Your Knowledge: Quiz

1. When should you use documentation strings instead of hash-mark comments?
2. Name three ways you can view documentation strings.
3. How can you obtain a list of the available attributes in an object?
4. How can you get a list of all available modules on your computer?
5. Which Python book should you purchase after this one?

Test Your Knowledge: Answers

1. Documentation strings (docstrings) are considered best for larger, functional documentation, describing the use of modules, functions, classes, and methods in your code. Hash-mark comments are today best limited to smaller-scale documentation about arcane expressions or statements at strategic points on your code. This is partly because docstrings are easier to find in a source file, but also because they can be extracted and displayed by the PyDoc system.

2. You can see docstrings by printing an object's __doc__ attribute, by passing it to PyDoc's `help` function, and by selecting modules in PyDoc's HTML-based user interfaces—either the `-g` GUI client mode in Python 3.2 and earlier, or the `-b` all-browser mode in Python 3.2 and later (and required as of 3.3). Both run a client/server system that displays documentation in a popped-up web browser. PyDoc can also be run to save a module's documentation in an HTML file for later viewing or printing.

3. The built-in `dir(X)` function returns a list of all the attributes attached to any object. A list comprehension of the form `[a for a in dir(X) if not a.starts with('__')]` can be used to filter out internals names with underscores (we'll learn how to wrap this in a function in the next part of the book to make it easier to use).

4. In Python 3.2 and earlier, you can run the PyDoc GUI interface, and select "open browser"; this opens a web page containing a link to every module available to your programs. This GUI mode no longer works as of Python 3.3. In Python 3.2 and later, you get the same functionality by running PyDoc's newer all-browser mode with a `-b` command-line switch; the top-level start page displayed in a web browser in this newer mode has the same index page listing all available modules.

5. Mine, of course. (Seriously, there are hundreds today; the preface lists a few recommended follow-up books, both for reference and for application tutorials, and you should browse for books that fit your needs.)

Test Your Knowledge: Part III Exercises

Now that you know how to code basic program logic, the following exercises will ask you to implement some simple tasks with statements. Most of the work is in exercise 4, which lets you explore coding alternatives. There are always many ways to arrange statements, and part of learning Python is learning which arrangements work better than others. You'll eventually gravitate naturally toward what experienced Python programmers call "best practice," but best practice takes practice.

See "Part III, Statements and Syntax" on page 1473 in Appendix D for the solutions.

1. *Coding basic loops*. This exercise asks you to experiment with `for` loops.

   a. Write a `for` loop that prints the ASCII code of each character in a string named S. Use the built-in function `ord(character)` to convert each character to an ASCII integer. This function technically returns a Unicode code point in Python 3.X, but if you restrict its content to ASCII characters, you'll get back ASCII codes. (Test it interactively to see how it works.)

   b. Next, change your loop to compute the *sum* of the ASCII codes of all the characters in a string.

   c. Finally, modify your code again to return a new list that *contains* the ASCII codes of each character in the string. Does the expression `map(ord, S)` have a similar effect? How about `[ord(c) for c in S]`? Why? (Hint: see Chapter 14.)

2. *Backslash characters*. What happens on your machine when you type the following code interactively?

   ```
   for i in range(50):
       print('hello %d\n\a' % i)
   ```

   Beware that if it's run outside of the IDLE interface this example may beep at you, so you may not want to run it in a crowded room! IDLE prints odd characters instead of beeping—spoiling much of the joke (see the backslash escape characters in Table 7-2).

3. *Sorting dictionaries*. In Chapter 8, we saw that dictionaries are unordered collections. Write a `for` loop that prints a dictionary's items in sorted (ascending) order. (Hint: use the dictionary `keys` and list `sort` methods, or the newer `sorted` built-in function.)

4. *Program logic alternatives*. Consider the following code, which uses a `while` loop and `found` flag to search a list of powers of 2 for the value of 2 raised to the fifth power (32). It's stored in a module file called *power.py*.

   ```
   L = [1, 2, 4, 8, 16, 32, 64]
   X = 5

   found = False
   i = 0
   while not found and i < len(L):
   ```

```
    if 2 ** X == L[i]:
        found = True
    else:
        i = i+1

if found:
    print('at index', i)
else:
    print(X, 'not found')
```

```
C:\book\tests> python power.py
at index 5
```

As is, the example doesn't follow normal Python coding techniques. Follow the steps outlined here to improve it (for all the transformations, you may either type your code interactively or store it in a script file run from the system command line —using a file makes this exercise much easier):

a. First, rewrite this code with a `while` loop `else` clause to eliminate the `found` flag and final `if` statement.

b. Next, rewrite the example to use a `for` loop with an `else` clause, to eliminate the explicit list-indexing logic. (Hint: to get the index of an item, use the list `index` method—`L.index(X)` returns the offset of the first `X` in list `L`.)

c. Next, remove the loop completely by rewriting the example with a simple `in` operator membership expression. (See Chapter 8 for more details, or type this to test: `2 in [1,2,3]`.)

d. Finally, use a `for` loop and the list `append` method to generate the powers-of-2 list (`L`) instead of hardcoding a list literal.

Deeper thoughts:

e. Do you think it would improve performance to move the `2 ** X` expression outside the loops? How would you code that?

f. As we saw in exercise 1, Python includes a `map(function, list)` tool that can generate a powers-of-2 list, too: `map(lambda x: 2 ** x, range(7))`. Try typing this code interactively; we'll meet `lambda` more formally in the next part of this book, especially in Chapter 19. Would a list comprehension help here (see Chapter 14)?

5. *Code maintenance.* If you haven't already done so, experiment with making the code changes suggested in this chapter's sidebar "Changing PyDoc's Colors" on page 456. Much of the work of real software development is in changing existing code, so the sooner you begin doing so, the better. For reference, my edited copy of PyDoc is in the book's examples package, named *mypydoc.py*; to see how it differs, you can run a file compare (`fc` on Windows) with the original *pydoc.py* in 3.3 (also included, lest it change radically in 3.4 as the sidebar describes). If PyDoc is more easily customized by the time you read these words, customize

colors per its current convention instead; if this involves changing a CSS file, let's hope the procedure will be well documented in Python's manuals.

Functions and Generators

Function Basics

In Part III, we studied basic procedural statements in Python. Here, we'll move on to explore a set of additional statements and expressions that we can use to create functions of our own.

In simple terms, a *function* is a device that groups a set of statements so they can be run more than once in a program—a packaged procedure invoked by name. Functions also can compute a result value and let us specify parameters that serve as function inputs and may differ each time the code is run. Coding an operation as a function makes it a generally useful tool, which we can use in a variety of contexts.

More fundamentally, functions are the alternative to programming by *cutting and pasting*—rather than having multiple redundant copies of an operation's code, we can factor it into a single function. In so doing, we reduce our future work radically: if the operation must be changed later, we have only one copy to update in the function, not many scattered throughout the program.

Functions are also the most basic program structure Python provides for maximizing *code reuse*, and lead us to the larger notions of program *design*. As we'll see, functions let us split complex systems into manageable parts. By implementing each part as a function, we make it both reusable and easier to code.

Table 16-1 previews the primary function-related tools we'll study in this part of the book—a set that includes call expressions, two ways to make functions (`def` and `lambda`), two ways to manage scope visibility (`global` and `nonlocal`), and two ways to send results back to callers (`return` and `yield`).

Table 16-1. Function-related statements and expressions

Statement or expression	Examples
Call expressions	`myfunc('spam', 'eggs', meat=ham, *rest)`
`def`	```def printer(message):``` ``` print('Hello ' + message)```
`return`	```def adder(a, b=1, *c):``` ``` return a + b + c[0]```

Statement or expression	Examples
| global | ```
x = 'old'
def changer():
    global x; x = 'new'
``` |
| nonlocal (3.X) | ```
def outer():
    x = 'old'
    def changer():
        nonlocal x; x = 'new'
``` |
| yield | ```
def squares(x):
    for i in range(x): yield i ** 2
``` |
| lambda | ```
funcs = [lambda x: x**2, lambda x: x**3]
``` |

Why Use Functions?

Before we get into the details, let's establish a clear picture of what functions are all about. Functions are a nearly universal program-structuring device. You may have come across them before in other languages, where they may have been called *subroutines* or *procedures*. As a brief introduction, functions serve two primary development roles:

Maximizing code reuse and minimizing redundancy

As in most programming languages, Python functions are the simplest way to package logic you may wish to use in more than one place and more than one time. Up until now, all the code we've been writing has run immediately. Functions allow us to group and generalize code to be used arbitrarily many times later. Because they allow us to code an operation in a single place and use it in many places, Python functions are the most basic *factoring* tool in the language: they allow us to reduce code redundancy in our programs, and thereby reduce maintenance effort.

Procedural decomposition

Functions also provide a tool for splitting systems into pieces that have well-defined roles. For instance, to make a pizza from scratch, you would start by mixing the dough, rolling it out, adding toppings, baking it, and so on. If you were programming a pizza-making robot, functions would help you divide the overall "make pizza" task into chunks—one function for each subtask in the process. It's easier to implement the smaller tasks in isolation than it is to implement the entire process at once. In general, functions are about *procedure*—how to do something, rather than what you're doing it to. We'll see why this distinction matters in Part VI, when we start making new objects with classes.

In this part of the book, we'll explore the tools used to code functions in Python: function basics, scope rules, and argument passing, along with a few related concepts such as generators and functional tools. Because its importance begins to become more apparent at this level of coding, we'll also revisit the notion of polymorphism, which was introduced earlier in the book. As you'll see, functions don't imply much new syntax, but they do lead us to some bigger programming ideas.

Coding Functions

Although it wasn't made very formal, we've already used some functions in earlier chapters. For instance, to make a file object, we called the built-in open function; similarly, we used the len built-in function to ask for the number of items in a collection object.

In this chapter, we will explore how to write *new* functions in Python. Functions we write behave the same way as the built-ins we've already seen: they are called in expressions, are passed values, and return results. But writing new functions requires the application of a few additional ideas that haven't yet been introduced. Moreover, functions behave very differently in Python than they do in compiled languages like C. Here is a brief introduction to the main concepts behind Python functions, all of which we will study in this part of the book:

- **def is executable code**. Python functions are written with a new statement, the def. Unlike functions in compiled languages such as C, def is an executable statement—your function does not exist until Python reaches and runs the def. In fact, it's legal (and even occasionally useful) to nest def statements inside if statements, while loops, and even other defs. In typical operation, def statements are coded in module files and are naturally run to generate functions when the module file they reside in is first imported.

- **def creates an object and assigns it to a name**. When Python reaches and runs a def statement, it generates a new function object and assigns it to the function's name. As with all assignments, the function name becomes a reference to the function object. There's nothing magic about the name of a function—as you'll see, the function object can be assigned to other names, stored in a list, and so on. Function objects may also have arbitrary user-defined *attributes* attached to them to record data.

- **lambda creates an object but returns it as a result**. Functions may also be created with the lambda expression, a feature that allows us to *in-line* function definitions in places where a def statement won't work syntactically. This is a more advanced concept that we'll defer until Chapter 19.

- **return sends a result object back to the caller**. When a function is called, the caller stops until the function finishes its work and returns control to the caller. Functions that compute a value send it back to the caller with a return statement; the returned value becomes the result of the function call. A return without a value simply returns to the caller (and sends back None, the default result).

- **yield sends a result object back to the caller, but remembers where it left off**. Functions known as *generators* may also use the yield statement to send back a value and suspend their state such that they may be resumed later, to produce a series of results over time. This is another advanced topic covered later in this part of the book.

- **global declares module-level variables that are to be assigned**. By default, all names assigned in a function are local to that function and exist only while the function runs. To assign a name in the enclosing module, functions need to list it in a `global` statement. More generally, names are always looked up in *scopes*—places where variables are stored—and assignments bind names to scopes.

- **nonlocal declares enclosing function variables that are to be assigned**. Similarly, the `nonlocal` statement added in Python 3.X allows a function to assign a name that exists in the scope of a syntactically enclosing `def` statement. This allows enclosing functions to serve as a place to retain *state*—information remembered between function calls—without using shared global names.

- **Arguments are passed by assignment (object reference)**. In Python, arguments are passed to functions by assignment (which, as we've learned, means by object reference). As you'll see, in Python's model the caller and function share objects by references, but there is no name aliasing. Changing an argument name within a function does not also change the corresponding name in the caller, but changing passed-in mutable objects in place can change objects shared by the caller, and serve as a function result.

- **Arguments are passed by position, unless you say otherwise**. Values you pass in a function call match argument names in a function's definition from left to right by default. For flexibility, function *calls* can also pass arguments by name with *name=value* keyword syntax, and unpack arbitrarily many arguments to send with `*pargs` and `**kargs` starred-argument notation. Function *definitions* use the same two forms to specify argument defaults, and collect arbitrarily many arguments received.

- **Arguments, return values, and variables are not declared**. As with everything in Python, there are no type constraints on functions. In fact, nothing about a function needs to be declared ahead of time: you can pass in arguments of any type, return any kind of object, and so on. As one consequence, a single function can often be applied to a variety of object types—any objects that sport a compatible *interface* (methods and expressions) will do, regardless of their specific types.

If some of the preceding words didn't sink in, don't worry—we'll explore all of these concepts with real code in this part of the book. Let's get started by expanding on some of these ideas and looking at a few examples.

def Statements

The `def` statement creates a function object and assigns it to a name. Its general format is as follows:

```
def name(arg1, arg2,... argN):
    statements
```

As with all compound Python statements, def consists of a header line followed by a block of statements, usually indented (or a simple statement after the colon). The statement block becomes the function's *body*—that is, the code Python executes each time the function is later called.

The def header line specifies a function *name* that is assigned the function object, along with a list of zero or more *arguments* (sometimes called *parameters*) in parentheses. The argument names in the header are assigned to the objects passed in parentheses at the point of call.

Function bodies often contain a return statement:

```
def name(arg1, arg2,... argN):
    ...
    return value
```

The Python return statement can show up anywhere in a function body; when reached, it ends the function call and sends a result back to the caller. The return statement consists of an optional object value expression that gives the function's result. If the value is omitted, return sends back a None.

The return statement itself is optional too; if it's not present, the function exits when the control flow falls off the end of the function body. Technically, a function without a return statement also returns the None object automatically, but this return value is usually ignored at the call.

Functions may also contain yield statements, which are designed to produce a series of values over time, but we'll defer discussion of these until we survey generator topics in Chapter 20.

def Executes at Runtime

The Python def is a true executable statement: when it runs, it creates a new function object and assigns it to a name. (Remember, all we have in Python is *runtime*; there is no such thing as a separate compile time.) Because it's a statement, a def can appear anywhere a statement can—even nested in other statements. For instance, although defs normally are run when the module enclosing them is imported, it's also completely legal to nest a function def inside an if statement to select between alternative definitions:

```
if test:
    def func():        # Define func this way
        ...
else:
    def func():        # Or else this way
        ...
...
func()                 # Call the version selected and built
```

One way to understand this code is to realize that the `def` is much like an = statement: it simply assigns a name at runtime. Unlike in compiled languages such as C, Python functions do not need to be fully defined before the program runs. More generally, `def`s are not evaluated until they are reached and run, and the code *inside* `def`s is not evaluated until the functions are later called.

Because function definition happens at runtime, there's nothing special about the function name. What's important is the object to which it refers:

```
othername = func        # Assign function object
othername()             # Call func again
```

Here, the function was assigned to a different name and called through the new name. Like everything else in Python, functions are just *objects*; they are recorded explicitly in memory at program execution time. In fact, besides calls, functions allow arbitrary *attributes* to be attached to record information for later use:

```
def func(): ...         # Create function object
func()                  # Call object
func.attr = value       # Attach attributes
```

A First Example: Definitions and Calls

Apart from such runtime concepts (which tend to seem most unique to programmers with backgrounds in traditional compiled languages), Python functions are straightforward to use. Let's code a first real example to demonstrate the basics. As you'll see, there are two sides to the function picture: a *definition* (the `def` that creates a function) and a *call* (an expression that tells Python to run the function's body).

Definition

Here's a definition typed interactively that defines a function called `times`, which returns the product of its two arguments:

```
>>> def times(x, y):     # Create and assign function
...     return x * y     # Body executed when called
...
```

When Python reaches and runs this `def`, it creates a new function object that packages the function's code and assigns the object to the name `times`. Typically, such a statement is coded in a module file and runs when the enclosing file is imported; for something this small, though, the interactive prompt suffices.

Calls

The `def` statement makes a function but does not call it. After the `def` has run, you can call (run) the function in your program by adding parentheses after the function's name.

The parentheses may optionally contain one or more object arguments, to be passed (assigned) to the names in the function's header:

```
>>> times(2, 4)          # Arguments in parentheses
8
```

This expression passes two arguments to `times`. As mentioned previously, arguments are passed by assignment, so in this case the name `x` in the function header is assigned the value `2`, `y` is assigned the value `4`, and the function's body is run. For this function, the body is just a `return` statement that sends back the result as the value of the call expression. The returned object was printed here interactively (as in most languages, `2 * 4` is `8` in Python), but if we needed to use it later we could instead assign it to a variable. For example:

```
>>> x = times(3.14, 4)   # Save the result object
>>> x
12.56
```

Now, watch what happens when the function is called a third time, with very different kinds of objects passed in:

```
>>> times('Ni', 4)       # Functions are "typeless"
'NiNiNiNi'
```

This time, our function means something completely different (Monty Python reference again intended). In this third call, a string and an integer are passed to `x` and `y`, instead of two numbers. Recall that `*` works on both numbers and sequences; because we never declare the types of variables, arguments, or return values in Python, we can use `times` to either *multiply* numbers or *repeat* sequences.

In other words, what our `times` function means and does depends on what we pass into it. This is a core idea in Python (and perhaps the key to using the language well), which merits a bit of expansion here.

Polymorphism in Python

As we just saw, the very meaning of the expression `x * y` in our simple `times` function depends completely upon the kinds of objects that `x` and `y` are—thus, the same function can perform multiplication in one instance and repetition in another. Python leaves it up to the *objects* to do something reasonable for the syntax. Really, `*` is just a dispatch mechanism that routes control to the objects being processed.

This sort of type-dependent behavior is known as *polymorphism*, a term we first met in Chapter 4 that essentially means that the meaning of an operation depends on the objects being operated upon. Because it's a dynamically typed language, polymorphism runs rampant in Python. In fact, *every* operation is a polymorphic operation in Python: printing, indexing, the `*` operator, and much more.

This is deliberate, and it accounts for much of the language's conciseness and flexibility. A single function, for instance, can generally be applied to a whole category of object types automatically. As long as those objects support the expected *interface* (a.k.a. protocol), the function can process them. That is, if the objects passed into a function have the expected methods and expression operators, they are plug-and-play compatible with the function's logic.

Even in our simple `times` function, this means that *any* two objects that support a * will work, no matter what they may be, and no matter when they are coded. This function will work on two numbers (performing multiplication), or a string and a number (performing repetition), or any other combination of objects supporting the expected interface—even class-based objects we have not even imagined yet.

Moreover, if the objects passed in do *not* support this expected interface, Python will detect the error when the * expression is run and raise an exception automatically. It's therefore usually pointless to code error checking ourselves. In fact, doing so would limit our function's utility, as it would be restricted to work only on objects whose types we test for.

This turns out to be a crucial philosophical difference between Python and statically typed languages like C++ and Java: in Python, your code is *not supposed to care* about specific data types. If it does, it will be limited to working on just the types you anticipated when you wrote it, and it will not support other compatible object types that may be coded in the future. Although it is possible to test for types with tools like the `type` built-in function, doing so breaks your code's flexibility. By and large, we code to object *interfaces* in Python, not data types.[1]

Of course, some programs have unique requirements, and this polymorphic model of programming means we have to test our code to detect errors, rather than providing type declarations a compiler can use to detect some types of errors for us ahead of time. In exchange for an initial bit of testing, though, we radically reduce the amount of code we have to write and radically increase our code's flexibility. As you'll learn, it's a net win in practice.

A Second Example: Intersecting Sequences

Let's look at a second function example that does something a bit more useful than multiplying arguments and further illustrates function basics.

In Chapter 13, we coded a `for` loop that collected items held in common in two strings. We noted there that the code wasn't as useful as it could be because it was set up to work only on specific variables and could not be rerun later. Of course, we could copy

---

1. This polymorphic behavior has in recent years come to also be known as *duck typing*—the essential idea being that your code is not supposed to care if an object is a *duck*, only that it *quacks*. Anything that quacks will do, duck or not, and the implementation of quacks is up to the object, a principle which will become even more apparent when we study classes in Part VI. Graphic metaphor to be sure, though this is really just a new label for an older idea, and use cases for quacking software would seem limited in the tangible world (he says, bracing for emails from militant ornithologists...).

---

the code and paste it into each place where it needs to be run, but this solution is neither good nor general—we'd still have to edit each copy to support different sequence names, and changing the algorithm would then require changing multiple copies.

Definition

By now, you can probably guess that the solution to this dilemma is to package the for loop inside a function. Doing so offers a number of advantages:

- Putting the code in a function makes it a tool that you can run as many times as you like.
- Because callers can pass in arbitrary arguments, functions are general enough to work on any two sequences (or other iterables) you wish to intersect.
- When the logic is packaged in a function, you have to change code in only one place if you ever need to change the way the intersection works.
- Coding the function in a module file means it can be imported and reused by any program run on your machine.

In effect, wrapping the code in a function makes it a general intersection utility:

```
def intersect(seq1, seq2):
    res = []                  # Start empty
    for x in seq1:            # Scan seq1
        if x in seq2:         # Common item?
            res.append(x)     # Add to end
    return res
```

The transformation from the simple code of Chapter 13 to this function is straightforward; we've just nested the original logic under a def header and made the objects on which it operates passed-in parameter names. Because this function computes a result, we've also added a return statement to send a result object back to the caller.

Calls

Before you can call a function, you have to make it. To do this, run its def statement, either by typing it interactively or by coding it in a module file and importing the file. Once you've run the def, you can call the function by passing any two sequence objects in parentheses:

```
>>> s1 = "SPAM"
>>> s2 = "SCAM"
>>> intersect(s1, s2)         # Strings
['S', 'A', 'M']
```

Here, we've passed in two strings, and we get back a list containing the characters in common. The algorithm the function uses is simple: "for every item in the first argument, if that item is also in the second argument, append the item to the result." It's a little shorter to say that in Python than in English, but it works out the same.

To be fair, our intersect function is fairly slow (it executes nested loops), isn't really mathematical intersection (there may be duplicates in the result), and isn't required at all (as we've seen, Python's set data type provides a built-in intersection operation). Indeed, the function could be replaced with a single list comprehension expression, as it exhibits the classic loop collector code pattern:

```
>>> [x for x in s1 if x in s2]
['S', 'A', 'M']
```

As a function basics example, though, it does the job—this single piece of code can apply to an entire range of object types, as the next section explains. In fact, we'll improve and extend this to support arbitrarily many operands in Chapter 18, after we learn more about argument passing modes.

Polymorphism Revisited

Like all good functions in Python, intersect is polymorphic. That is, it works on arbitrary types, as long as they support the expected object interface:

```
>>> x = intersect([1, 2, 3], (1, 4))      # Mixed types
>>> x                                       # Saved result object
[1]
```

This time, we passed in different types of objects to our function—a list and a tuple (mixed types)—and it still picked out the common items. Because you don't have to specify the types of arguments ahead of time, the intersect function happily iterates through any kind of sequence objects you send it, as long as they support the expected interfaces.

For intersect, this means that the first argument has to support the for loop, and the second has to support the in membership test. Any two such objects will work, regardless of their specific types—that includes physically stored sequences like strings and lists; all the iterable objects we met in Chapter 14, including files and dictionaries; and even any class-based objects we code that apply operator overloading techniques we'll discuss later in the book.[2]

Here again, if we pass in objects that do not support these interfaces (e.g., numbers), Python will automatically detect the mismatch and raise an exception for us—which is exactly what we want, and the best we could do on our own if we coded explicit type

---

2. This code will always work if we intersect files' contents obtained with file.readlines(). It may not work to intersect lines in open input files directly, though, depending on the file object's implementation of the in operator or general iteration. Files must generally be rewound (e.g., with a file.seek(0) or another open) after they have been read to end-of-file once, and so are single-pass iterators. As we'll see in Chapter 30 when we study operator overloading, objects implement the in operator either by providing the specific __contains__ method or by supporting the general iteration protocol with the __iter__ or older __getitem__ methods; classes can code these methods arbitrarily to define what iteration means for their data.

tests. By not coding type tests and allowing Python to detect the mismatches for us, we both reduce the amount of code we need to write and increase our code's flexibility.

Local Variables

Probably the most interesting part of this example, though, is its names. It turns out that the variable `res` inside `intersect` is what in Python is called a *local variable*—a name that is visible only to code inside the function `def` and that exists only while the function runs. In fact, because all names *assigned* in any way inside a function are classified as local variables by default, nearly all the names in `intersect` are local variables:

- `res` is obviously assigned, so it is a local variable.
- Arguments are passed by assignment, so `seq1` and `seq2` are, too.
- The `for` loop assigns items to a variable, so the name `x` is also local.

All these local variables appear when the function is called and disappear when the function exits—the `return` statement at the end of `intersect` sends back the result *object*, but the *name* `res` goes away. Because of this, a function's variables won't remember values between calls; although the object returned by a function lives on, retaining other sorts of state information requires other sorts of techniques. To fully explore the notion of locals and state, though, we need to move on to the scopes coverage of Chapter 17.

Chapter Summary

This chapter introduced the core ideas behind function definition—the syntax and operation of the `def` and `return` statements, the behavior of function call expressions, and the notion and benefits of polymorphism in Python functions. As we saw, a `def` statement is executable code that creates a function object at runtime; when the function is later called, objects are passed into it by assignment (recall that assignment means object reference in Python, which, as we learned in Chapter 6, really means pointer internally), and computed values are sent back by `return`. We also began exploring the concepts of local variables and scopes in this chapter, but we'll save all the details on those topics for Chapter 17. First, though, a quick quiz.

Test Your Knowledge: Quiz

1. What is the point of coding functions?
2. At what time does Python create a function?
3. What does a function return if it has no `return` statement in it?
4. When does the code nested inside the function definition statement run?

5. What's wrong with checking the types of objects passed into a function?

Test Your Knowledge: Answers

1. Functions are the most basic way of avoiding code *redundancy* in Python—factoring code into functions means that we have only one copy of an operation's code to update in the future. Functions are also the basic unit of code *reuse* in Python —wrapping code in functions makes it a reusable tool, callable in a variety of programs. Finally, functions allow us to divide a complex system into manageable parts, each of which may be developed individually.

2. A function is created when Python reaches and runs the def statement; this statement creates a function object and assigns it the function's name. This normally happens when the enclosing module file is imported by another module (recall that imports run the code in a file from top to bottom, including any defs), but it can also occur when a def is typed interactively or nested in other statements, such as ifs.

3. A function returns the None object by default if the control flow falls off the end of the function body without running into a return statement. Such functions are usually called with expression statements, as assigning their None results to variables is generally pointless. A return statement with no expression in it also returns None.

4. The function body (the code nested inside the function definition statement) is run when the function is later called with a call expression. The body runs anew each time the function is called.

5. Checking the types of objects passed into a function effectively breaks the function's flexibility, constraining the function to work on specific types only. Without such checks, the function would likely be able to process an entire range of object types—any objects that support the interface expected by the function will work. (The term *interface* means the set of methods and expression operators the function's code runs.)

Scopes

Chapter 16 introduced basic function definitions and calls. As we saw, Python's core function model is simple to use, but even simple function examples quickly led us to questions about the meaning of variables in our code. This chapter moves on to present the details behind Python's *scopes*—the places where variables are defined and looked up. Like module files, scopes help prevent name clashes across your program's code: names defined in one program unit don't interfere with names in another.

As we'll see, the place where a name is assigned in our code is crucial to determining what the name means. We'll also find that scope usage can have a major impact on program maintenance effort; overuse of *globals*, for example, is a generally bad thing. On the plus side, we'll learn that scopes can provide a way to retain *state information* between function calls, and offer an alternative to classes in some roles.

Python Scope Basics

Now that you're ready to start writing your own functions, we need to get more formal about what names mean in Python. When you use a name in a program, Python creates, changes, or looks up the name in what is known as a *namespace*—a place where names live. When we talk about the search for a name's value in relation to code, the term *scope* refers to a namespace: that is, the location of a name's assignment in your source code determines the scope of the name's visibility to your code.

Just about everything related to names, including scope classification, happens at assignment time in Python. As we've seen, names in Python spring into existence when they are first assigned values, and they must be assigned before they are used. Because names are not declared ahead of time, Python uses the location of the assignment of a name to associate it with (i.e., *bind* it to) a particular namespace. In other words, the place where you assign a name in your source code determines the namespace it will live in, and hence its scope of visibility.

Besides packaging code for reuse, functions add an extra namespace layer to your programs to minimize the potential for collisions among variables of the same name—*by default, all names assigned inside a function are associated with that function's namespace, and no other*. This rule means that:

- Names assigned inside a `def` can only be seen by the code within that `def`. You cannot even refer to such names from outside the function.

- Names assigned inside a `def` do not clash with variables outside the `def`, even if the same names are used elsewhere. A name `X` assigned outside a given `def` (i.e., in a different `def` or at the top level of a module file) is a completely different variable from a name `X` assigned inside that `def`.

In all cases, the scope of a variable (where it can be used) is always determined by where it is assigned in your source code and has nothing to do with which functions call which. In fact, as we'll learn in this chapter, variables may be assigned in three different places, corresponding to three different scopes:

- If a variable is assigned inside a `def`, it is *local* to that function.
- If a variable is assigned in an enclosing `def`, it is *nonlocal* to nested functions.
- If a variable is assigned outside all `def`s, it is *global* to the entire file.

We call this *lexical scoping* because variable scopes are determined entirely by the locations of the variables in the source code of your program files, not by function calls.

For example, in the following module file, the `X = 99` assignment creates a *global* variable named `X` (visible everywhere in this file), but the `X = 88` assignment creates a *local* variable `X` (visible only within the `def` statement):

```
X = 99                      # Global (module) scope X

def func():
    X = 88                  # Local (function) scope X: a different variable
```

Even though both variables are named `X`, their scopes make them different. The net effect is that function scopes help to avoid name clashes in your programs and help to make functions more self-contained program units—their code need not be concerned with names used elsewhere.

Scope Details

Before we started writing functions, all the code we wrote was at the top level of a module (i.e., not nested in a `def`), so the names we used either lived in the module itself or were built-ins predefined by Python (e.g., `open`). Technically, the interactive prompt is a module named `__main__` that prints results and doesn't save its code; in all other ways, though, it's like the top level of a module file.

Functions, though, provide nested namespaces (scopes) that localize the names they use, such that names inside a function won't clash with those outside it (in a module or another function). Functions define a *local scope* and modules define a *global scope* with the following properties:

- **The enclosing module is a global scope**. Each module is a global scope—that is, a namespace in which variables created (assigned) at the top level of the module file live. Global variables become attributes of a module object to the outside world after imports but can also be used as simple variables within the module file itself.

- **The global scope spans a single file only**. Don't be fooled by the word "global" here—names at the top level of a file are global to code within that single file only. There is really no notion of a single, all-encompassing global file-based scope in Python. Instead, names are partitioned into modules, and you must always import a module explicitly if you want to be able to use the names its file defines. When you hear "global" in Python, think "module."

- **Assigned names are local unless declared global or nonlocal**. By default, all the names assigned inside a function definition are put in the local scope (the namespace associated with the function call). If you need to assign a name that lives at the top level of the module enclosing the function, you can do so by declaring it in a `global` statement inside the function. If you need to assign a name that lives in an enclosing `def`, as of Python 3.X you can do so by declaring it in a `nonlocal` statement.

- **All other names are enclosing function locals, globals, or built-ins**. Names not assigned a value in the function definition are assumed to be *enclosing* scope locals, defined in a physically surrounding `def` statement; *globals* that live in the enclosing module's namespace; or *built-ins* in the predefined built-ins module Python provides.

- **Each call to a function creates a new local scope**. Every time you call a function, you create a new local scope—that is, a namespace in which the names created inside that function will usually live. You can think of each `def` statement (and `lambda` expression) as defining a new local scope, but the local scope actually corresponds to a function *call*. Because Python allows functions to call themselves to loop—an advanced technique known as *recursion* and noted briefly in Chapter 9 when we explored comparisons—each active call receives its own copy of the function's local variables. Recursion is useful in functions we write as well, to process structures whose shapes can't be predicted ahead of time; we'll explore it more fully in Chapter 19.

There are a few subtleties worth underscoring here. First, keep in mind that code typed at the *interactive command prompt* lives in a module, too, and follows the normal scope rules: they are global variables, accessible to the entire interactive session. You'll learn more about modules in the next part of this book.

Also note that *any type of assignment* within a function classifies a name as local. This includes = statements, module names in `import`, function names in `def`, function argument names, and so on. If you assign a name in any way within a `def`, it will become a local to that function by default.

Conversely, *in-place changes* to objects do not classify names as locals; only actual name assignments do. For instance, if the name L is assigned to a list at the top level of a module, a statement L = X within a function will classify L as a local, but L.append(X) will not. In the latter case, we are changing the list object that L references, not L itself —L is found in the global scope as usual, and Python happily modifies it without requiring a global (or nonlocal) declaration. As usual, it helps to keep the distinction between names and objects clear: changing an object is not an assignment to a name.

Name Resolution: The LEGB Rule

If the prior section sounds confusing, it really boils down to three simple rules. Within a def statement:

- Name *assignments* create or change local names by default.
- Name *references* search at most four scopes: local, then enclosing functions (if any), then global, then built-in.
- Names declared in global and nonlocal statements map assigned names to enclosing module and function scopes, respectively.

In other words, all names assigned inside a function def statement (or a lambda, an expression we'll meet later) are locals by default. Functions can freely use names assigned in syntactically enclosing functions and the global scope, but they must declare such nonlocals and globals in order to change them.

Python's name-resolution scheme is sometimes called the *LEGB rule*, after the scope names:

- When you use an unqualified name inside a function, Python searches up to four scopes—the local (*L*) scope, then the local scopes of any enclosing (*E*) defs and lambdas, then the global (*G*) scope, and then the built-in (*B*) scope—and stops at the first place the name is found. If the name is not found during this search, Python reports an error.
- When you assign a name in a function (instead of just referring to it in an expression), Python always creates or changes the name in the local scope, unless it's declared to be global or nonlocal in that function.
- When you assign a name outside any function (i.e., at the top level of a module file, or at the interactive prompt), the local scope is the same as the global scope— the module's namespace.

Because names must be assigned before they can be used (as we learned in Chapter 6), there are no automatic components in this model: assignments always determine name scopes unambiguously. Figure 17-1 illustrates Python's four scopes. Note that the second scope lookup layer, *E*—the scopes of enclosing defs or lambdas—can technically correspond to more than one lookup level. This case only comes into play when you nest functions within functions, and is enhanced by the nonlocal statement in 3.X.[1]

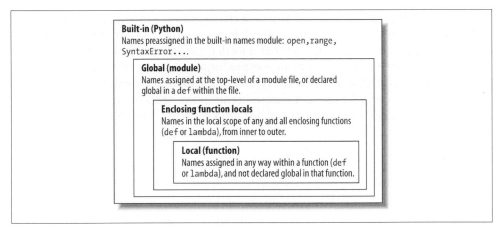

Built-in (Python)
Names preassigned in the built-in names module: open, range, SyntaxError....

Global (module)
Names assigned at the top-level of a module file, or declared global in a def within the file.

Enclosing function locals
Names in the local scope of any and all enclosing functions (def or lambda), from inner to outer.

Local (function)
Names assigned in any way within a function (def or lambda), and not declared global in that function.

Figure 17-1. The LEGB scope lookup rule. When a variable is referenced, Python searches for it in this order: in the local scope, in any enclosing functions' local scopes, in the global scope, and finally in the built-in scope. The first occurrence wins. The place in your code where a variable is assigned usually determines its scope. In Python 3.X, nonlocal declarations can also force names to be mapped to enclosing function scopes, whether assigned or not.

Also keep in mind that these rules apply only to simple *variable* names (e.g., spam). In Parts V and VI, we'll see that qualified *attribute* names (e.g., *object*.spam) live in particular objects and follow a completely different set of lookup rules than those covered here. References to attribute names following periods (.) search one or more *objects*, not scopes, and in fact may invoke something called *inheritance* in Python's OOP model; more on this in Part VI of this book.

Other Python scopes: Preview

Though obscure at this point in the book, there are technically three more scopes in Python—temporary loop variables in some comprehensions, exception reference variables in some try handlers, and local scopes in class statements. The first two of these are special cases that rarely impact real code, and the third falls under the LEGB umbrella rule.

Most statement blocks and other constructs do not localize the names used within them, with the following version-specific exceptions (whose variables are not available to, but also will not clash with, surrounding code, and which involve topics covered in full later):

---

1. The scope lookup rule was called the "LGB rule" in the first edition of this book. The enclosing def "E" layer was added later in Python to obviate the task of passing in enclosing scope names explicitly with default arguments—a topic usually of marginal interest to Python beginners that we'll defer until later in this chapter. Since this scope is now addressed by the nonlocal statement in Python 3.X, the lookup rule might be better named "LNGB" today, but backward compatibility matters in books, too. The present form of this acronym also does not account for the newer obscure scopes of some comprehensions and exception handlers, but acronyms longer than four letters tend to defeat their purpose!

- *Comprehension variables*—the variable X used to refer to the current iteration item in a comprehension expression such as [X for X in I]. Because they might clash with other names and reflect internal state in generators, in 3.X, such variables are local to the expression itself in all comprehension forms: generator, list, set, and dictionary. In 2.X, they are local to generator expressions and set and dictionary comprehensions, but not to list comprehensions that map their names to the scope outside the expression. By contrast, for loop statements never localize their variables to the statement block in any Python. See Chapter 20 for more details and examples.

- *Exception variables*—the variable X used to reference the raised exception in a try statement handler clause such as except E as X. Because they might defer garbage collection's memory recovery, in 3.X, such variables are local to that except block, and in fact are removed when the block is exited (even if you've used it earlier in your code!). In 2.X, these variables live on after the try statement. See Chapter 34 for additional information.

These contexts augment the LEGB rule, rather than modifying it. Variables assigned in a comprehension, for example, are simply bound to a further nested and special-case scope; other names referenced within these expressions follow the usual LEGB lookup rules.

It's also worth noting that the class statement we'll meet in Part VI creates a new *local* scope too for the names assigned inside the top level of its block. As for def, names assigned inside a class don't clash with names elsewhere, and follow the LEGB lookup rule, where the class block is the "L" level. Like modules and imports, these names also morph into class object attributes after the class statements ends.

Unlike functions, though, class names are not created per call: class object calls generate *instances*, which inherit names assigned in the class and record per-object state as attributes. As we'll also learn in Chapter 29, although the LEGB rule is used to resolve names used in both the top level of a class itself as well as the top level of method functions nested within it, classes themselves are *skipped* by scope lookups—their names must be fetched as object attributes. Because Python searches enclosing functions for referenced names, but not enclosing classes, the LEGB rule still applies to OOP code.

Scope Example

Let's step through a larger example that demonstrates scope ideas. Suppose we wrote the following code in a module file:

```
# Global scope
X = 99                    # X and func assigned in module: global

def func(Y):              # Y and Z assigned in function: locals
    # Local scope
    Z = X + Y             # X is a global
```

```
        return Z

    func(1)                    # func in module: result=100
```

This module and the function it contains use a number of names to do their business. Using Python's scope rules, we can classify the names as follows:

Global names: `X`, `func`
> `X` is global because it's assigned at the top level of the module file; it can be referenced inside the function as a simple unqualified variable without being declared global. `func` is global for the same reason; the `def` statement assigns a function object to the name `func` at the top level of the module.

Local names: `Y`, `Z`
> `Y` and `Z` are local to the function (and exist only while the function runs) because they are both assigned values in the function definition: `Z` by virtue of the `=` statement, and `Y` because arguments are always passed by assignment.

The underlying rationale for this name-segregation scheme is that local variables serve as *temporary* names that you need only while a function is running. For instance, in the preceding example, the argument `Y` and the addition result `Z` exist only inside the function; these names don't interfere with the enclosing module's namespace (or any other function, for that matter). In fact, local variables are removed from memory when the function call exits, and objects they reference may be *garbage-collected* if not referenced elsewhere. This is an automatic, internal step, but it helps minimize memory requirements.

The local/global distinction also makes functions easier to understand, as most of the names a function uses appear in the function itself, not at some arbitrary place in a module. Also, because you can be sure that local names will not be changed by some remote function in your program, they tend to make programs easier to debug and modify. Functions are self-contained units of software.

The Built-in Scope

We've been talking about the built-in scope in the abstract, but it's a bit simpler than you may think. Really, the built-in scope is just a built-in module called `builtins`, but you have to import `builtins` to query built-ins because the name `builtins` is not itself built in…

No, I'm serious! The built-in scope is implemented as a standard library module named `builtins` in 3.X, but that name itself is not placed in the built-in scope, so you have to import it in order to inspect it. Once you do, you can run a `dir` call to see which names are predefined. In Python 3.3 (see ahead for 2.X usage):

```
>>> import builtins
>>> dir(builtins)
['ArithmeticError', 'AssertionError', 'AttributeError', 'BaseException',
'BlockingIOError', 'BrokenPipeError', 'BufferError', 'BytesWarning',
```

```
...many more names omitted...
'ord', 'pow', 'print', 'property', 'quit', 'range', 'repr', 'reversed',
'round', 'set', 'setattr', 'slice', 'sorted', 'staticmethod', 'str', 'sum',
'super', 'tuple', 'type', 'vars', 'zip']
```

The names in this list constitute the built-in scope in Python; roughly the first half are built-in exceptions, and the second half are built-in functions. Also in this list are the special names None, True, and False, though they are treated as reserved words in 3.X. Because Python automatically searches this module last in its LEGB lookup, you get all the names in this list "for free"—that is, you can use them without importing any modules. Thus, there are really two ways to refer to a built-in function—by taking advantage of the LEGB rule, or by manually importing the builtins module:

```
>>> zip                          # The normal way
<class 'zip'>

>>> import builtins              # The hard way: for customizations
>>> builtins.zip
<class 'zip'>

>>> zip is builtins.zip          # Same object, different lookups
True
```

The second of these approaches is sometimes useful in advanced ways we'll meet in this chapter's sidebars.

Redefining built-in names: For better or worse

The careful reader might also notice that because the LEGB lookup procedure takes the *first* occurrence of a name that it finds, names in the local scope may override variables of the same name in both the global and built-in scopes, and global names may override built-ins. A function can, for instance, create a local variable called open by assigning to it:

```
def hider():
    open = 'spam'                # Local variable, hides built-in here
    ...
    open('data.txt')             # Error: this no longer opens a file in this scope!
```

However, this will hide the built-in function called open that lives in the built-in (outer) scope, such that the name open will no longer work within the function to open files—it's now a string, not the opener function. This isn't a problem if you don't need to open files in this function, but triggers an error if you attempt to open through this name.

This can even occur more simply at the interactive prompt, which works as a global, module scope:

```
>>> open = 99                    # Assign in global scope, hides built-in here too
```

Now, there is nothing inherently *wrong* with using a built-in name for variables of your own, as long as you don't need the original built-in version. After all, if these were truly off limits, we would need to memorize the entire built-in names list and treat all its names as reserved. With over 140 names in this module in 3.3, that would be far too restrictive and daunting:

```
>>> len(dir(builtins)), len([x for x in dir(builtins) if not x.startswith('__')])
(148, 142)
```

In fact, there are times in advanced programming where you may really *want* to replace a built-in name by redefining it in your code—to define a custom open that verifies access attempts, for instance (see this chapter's sidebar "Breaking the Universe in Python 2.X" on page 494 for more on this thread).

Still, redefining a built-in name is often a bug, and a nasty one at that, because Python will not issue a warning message about it. Tools like *PyChecker* (see the Web) can warn you of such mistakes, but knowledge may be your best defense on this point: don't redefine a built-in name you need. If you accidentally reassign a built-in name at the interactive prompt this way, you can either restart your session or run a del *name* statement to remove the redefinition from your scope, thereby restoring the original in the built-in scope.

Note that functions can similarly hide global variables of the same name with locals, but this is more broadly useful, and in fact is much of the point of local scopes—because they minimize the potential for name clashes, your functions are self-contained namespace scopes:

```
X = 88                          # Global X

def func():
    X = 99                      # Local X: hides global, but we want this here

func()
print(X)                        # Prints 88: unchanged
```

Here, the assignment within the function creates a local X that is a completely different variable from the global X in the module outside the function. As one consequence, though, there is no way to *change* a name outside a function without adding a global (or nonlocal) declaration to the def, as described in the next section.

Version skew note: Actually, the tongue twisting gets a bit worse. The Python 3.X builtins module used here is named __builtin__ in Python 2.X. In addition, the name __builtins__ (with the *s*) is preset in most global scopes, including the interactive session, to reference the module known as builtins in 3.X and __builtin__ in 2.X, so you can often use __builtins__ without an import but cannot run an import on that name itself—it's a preset variable, not a module's name.

That is, in 3.X builtins is __builtins__ is True after you import builtins, and in 2.X __builtin__ is __builtins__ is True after you import __builtin__. The upshot is that we can usually inspect the built-in scope by simply running dir(__builtins__) with no import in both 3.X and

2.X, but we are advised to use `builtins` for real work and customization in 3.X, and `__builtin__` for the same in 2.X. Who said documenting this stuff was easy?

Breaking the Universe in Python 2.X

Here's another thing you can do in Python that you probably shouldn't—because the names `True` and `False` in 2.X are just variables in the built-in scope and are not reserved, it's possible to reassign them with a statement like `True = False`. Don't worry: you won't actually break the logical consistency of the universe in so doing! This statement merely redefines the word `True` for the single scope in which it appears to return `False`. All other scopes still find the originals in the built-in scope.

For more fun, though, in Python 2.X you could say `__builtin__.True = False`, to reset `True` to `False` for the entire Python process. This works because there is only one built-in scope module in a program, shared by all its clients. Alas, this type of assignment has been disallowed in Python 3.X, because `True` and `False` are treated as actual reserved words, just like `None`. In 2.X, though, it sends IDLE into a strange panic state that resets the user code process (in other words, don't try this at home, kids).

This technique can be useful, however, both to illustrate the underlying namespace model, and for tool writers who must change built-ins such as `open` to customized functions. By reassigning a function's name in the built-in scope, you reset it to your customization for every module in the process. If you do, you'll probably also need to remember the original version to call from your customization—in fact, we'll see one way to achieve this for a custom `open` in the sidebar "Why You Will Care: Customizing open" on page 517 after we've had a chance to explore nested scope closures and state retention options.

Also, note again that third-party tools such as PyChecker, and others such as PyLint, will warn about common programming mistakes, including accidental assignment to built-in names (this is usually known as "shadowing" a built-in in such tools). It's not a bad idea to run your first few Python programs through tools like these to see what they point out.

The global Statement

The `global` statement and its `nonlocal` 3.X cousin are the only things that are remotely like declaration statements in Python. They are not type or size declarations, though; they are *namespace declarations*. The `global` statement tells Python that a function plans to change one or more global names—that is, names that live in the enclosing module's scope (namespace).

We've talked about `global` in passing already. Here's a summary:

- Global names are variables assigned at the top level of the enclosing module file.

- Global names must be declared only if they are assigned within a function.
- Global names may be referenced within a function without being declared.

In other words, global allows us to *change* names that live outside a def at the top level of a module file. As we'll see later, the nonlocal statement is almost identical but applies to names in the enclosing def's local scope, rather than names in the enclosing module.

The global statement consists of the keyword global, followed by one or more names separated by commas. All the listed names will be mapped to the enclosing module's scope when assigned or referenced within the function body. For instance:

```
X = 88                      # Global X

def func():
    global X
    X = 99                  # Global X: outside def

func()
print(X)                    # Prints 99
```

We've added a global declaration to the example here, such that the X inside the def now refers to the X outside the def; they are the same variable this time, so changing X inside the function changes the X outside it. Here is a slightly more involved example of global at work:

```
y, z = 1, 2                 # Global variables in module
def all_global():
    global x                # Declare globals assigned
    x = y + z               # No need to declare y, z: LEGB rule
```

Here, x, y, and z are all globals inside the function all_global. y and z are global because they aren't assigned in the function; x is global because it was listed in a global statement to map it to the module's scope explicitly. Without the global here, x would be considered local by virtue of the assignment.

Notice that y and z are not declared global; Python's LEGB lookup rule finds them in the module automatically. Also, notice that x does not even exist in the enclosing module before the function runs; in this case, the first assignment in the function creates x in the module.

Program Design: Minimize Global Variables

Functions in general, and global variables in particular, raise some larger design questions. How should our functions communicate? Although some of these will become more apparent when you begin writing larger functions of your own, a few guidelines up front might spare you from problems later. In general, functions should rely on arguments and return values instead of globals, but I need to explain why.

By default, names assigned in functions are locals, so if you want to change names outside functions you have to write extra code (e.g., global statements). This is deliberate—as is common in Python, you have to say more to do the potentially "wrong" thing. Although there are times when globals are useful, variables assigned in a def are local by default because that is normally the best policy. Changing globals can lead to well-known software engineering problems: because the variables' values are dependent on the order of calls to arbitrarily distant functions, programs can become difficult to debug, or to understand at all.

Consider this module file, for example, which is presumably imported and used elsewhere:

```
X = 99
def func1():
    global X
    X = 88

def func2():
    global X
    X = 77
```

Now, imagine that it is your job to modify or reuse this code. What will the value of X be here? Really, that question has no meaning unless it's qualified with a point of reference in *time*—the value of X is timing-dependent, as it depends on which function was called last (something we can't tell from this file alone).

The net effect is that to understand this code, you have to trace the flow of control through the *entire program*. And, if you need to reuse or modify the code, you have to keep the entire program in your head all at once. In this case, you can't really use one of these functions without bringing along the other. They are dependent on—that is, *coupled* with—the global variable. This is the problem with globals: they generally make code more difficult to understand and reuse than code consisting of self-contained functions that rely on locals.

On the other hand, short of using tools like nested scope closures or object-oriented programming with classes, global variables are probably the most straightforward way in Python to retain shared *state information*—information that a function needs to remember for use the next time it is called. Local variables disappear when the function returns, but globals do not. As we'll see later, other techniques can achieve this, too, and allow for multiple copies of the retained information, but they are generally more complex than pushing values out to the global scope for retention in simple use cases where this applies.

Moreover, some programs designate a single module to collect globals; as long as this is expected, it is not as harmful. Programs that use multithreading to do parallel processing in Python also commonly depend on global variables—they become shared memory between functions running in parallel threads, and so act as a communication device.[2]

For now, though, especially if you are relatively new to programming, avoid the temptation to use globals whenever you can—they tend to make programs difficult to understand and reuse, and won't work for cases where one copy of saved data is not enough. Try to communicate with passed-in arguments and return values instead. Six months from now, both you and your coworkers may be happy you did.

Program Design: Minimize Cross-File Changes

Here's another scope-related design issue: although we *can* change variables in another file directly, we usually shouldn't. Module files were introduced in Chapter 3 and are covered in more depth in the next part of this book. To illustrate their relationship to scopes, consider these two module files:

```
# first.py
X = 99                      # This code doesn't know about second.py

# second.py
import first
print(first.X)              # OK: references a name in another file
first.X = 88                # But changing it can be too subtle and implicit
```

The first defines a variable X, which the second prints and then changes by assignment. Notice that we must import the first module into the second file to get to its variable at all—as we've learned, each module is a self-contained namespace (package of variables), and we must import one module to see inside it from another. That's the main point about modules: by segregating variables on a per-file basis, they avoid name collisions across files, in much the same way that local variables avoid name clashes across functions.

Really, though, in terms of this chapter's topic, the global scope of a module file *becomes* the attribute namespace of the module object once it is imported—importers automatically have access to all of the file's global variables, because a file's global scope morphs into an object's attribute namespace when it is imported.

After importing the first module, the second module prints its variable and then assigns it a new value. Referencing the module's variable to print it is fine—this is how modules are linked together into a larger system normally. The problem with the assignment to `first.X`, however, is that it is far too implicit: whoever's charged with maintaining or reusing the first module probably has no clue that some arbitrarily far-removed module on the import chain can change X out from under him or her at runtime. In fact, the

---

2. *Multithreading* runs function calls in parallel with the rest of the program and is supported by Python's standard library modules `_thread`, `threading`, and `queue` (`thread`, `threading`, and `Queue` in Python 2.X). Because all threaded functions run in the same process, global scopes often serve as one form of shared memory between them (threads may share both names in global scopes, as well as objects in a process's memory space). Threading is commonly used for long-running tasks in GUIs, to implement nonblocking operations in general and to maximize CPU capacity. It is also beyond this book's scope; see the Python library manual, as well as the follow-up texts listed in the preface (such as O'Reilly's *Programming Python*), for more details.

second module may be in a completely different directory, and so difficult to notice at all.

Although such cross-file variable changes are always possible in Python, they are usually much more subtle than you will want. Again, this sets up too strong a *coupling* between the two files—because they are both dependent on the value of the variable X, it's difficult to understand or reuse one file without the other. Such implicit cross-file dependencies can lead to inflexible code at best, and outright bugs at worst.

Here again, the best prescription is generally to not do this—the best way to communicate across file boundaries is to call functions, passing in arguments and getting back return values. In this specific case, we would probably be better off coding an *accessor function* to manage the change:

```
# first.py
X = 99

def setX(new):          # Accessor make external changes explit
    global X            # And can manage access in a single place
    X = new

# second.py
import first
first.setX(88)          # Call the function instead of changing directly
```

This requires more code and may seem like a trivial change, but it makes a huge difference in terms of readability and maintainability—when a person reading the first module by itself sees a function, that person will know that it is a point of *interface* and will expect the change to the X. In other words, it removes the element of surprise that is rarely a good thing in software projects. Although we cannot prevent cross-file changes from happening, common sense dictates that they should be minimized unless widely accepted across the program.

 When we meet classes in Part VI, we'll see similar techniques for coding attribute accessors. Unlike modules, classes can also intercept attribute fetches automatically with operator overloading, even when accessors aren't used by their clients.

Other Ways to Access Globals

Interestingly, because global-scope variables morph into the attributes of a loaded module object, we can emulate the `global` statement by importing the enclosing module and assigning to its attributes, as in the following example module file. Code in this file imports the enclosing module, first by name, and then by indexing the `sys.modules` loaded modules table (more on this table in Chapter 22 and Chapter 25):

```
# thismod.py

var = 99                        # Global variable == module attribute
```

```
def local():
    var = 0                                      # Change local var

def glob1():
    global var                                   # Declare global (normal)
    var += 1                                      # Change global var

def glob2():
    var = 0                                      # Change local var
    import thismod                               # Import myself
    thismod.var += 1                             # Change global var

def glob3():
    var = 0                                      # Change local var
    import sys                                   # Import system table
    glob = sys.modules['thismod']                # Get module object (or use __name__)
    glob.var += 1                                 # Change global var

def test():
    print(var)
    local(); glob1(); glob2(); glob3()
    print(var)
```

When run, this adds 3 to the global variable (only the first function does not impact it):

```
>>> import thismod
>>> thismod.test()
99
102
>>> thismod.var
102
```

This works, and it illustrates the equivalence of globals to module attributes, but it's much more work than using the global statement to make your intentions explicit.

As we've seen, global allows us to change names in a module outside a function. It has a close relative named nonlocal that can be used to change names in enclosing functions, too—but to understand how that can be useful, we first need to explore enclosing functions in general.

Scopes and Nested Functions

So far, I've omitted one part of Python's scope rules on purpose, because it's relatively uncommon to encounter it in practice. However, it's time to take a deeper look at the letter *E* in the LEGB lookup rule. The *E* layer was added in Python 2.2; it takes the form of the local scopes of any and all enclosing function's local scopes. Enclosing scopes are sometimes also called *statically nested scopes*. Really, the nesting is a lexical one— nested scopes correspond to physically and syntactically nested code structures in your program's source code text.

Nested Scope Details

With the addition of nested function scopes, variable lookup rules become slightly more complex. Within a function:

- **A reference** (X) looks for the name X first in the current local scope (function); then in the local scopes of any lexically enclosing functions in your source code, from inner to outer; then in the current global scope (the module file); and finally in the built-in scope (the module `builtins`). `global` declarations make the search begin in the global (module file) scope instead.

- **An assignment** (X = value) creates or changes the name X in the current local scope, by default. If X is declared *global* within the function, the assignment creates or changes the name X in the enclosing module's scope instead. If, on the other hand, X is declared *nonlocal* within the function in 3.X (only), the assignment changes the name X in the closest enclosing function's local scope.

Notice that the `global` declaration still maps variables to the enclosing module. When nested functions are present, variables in enclosing functions may be referenced, but they require 3.X `nonlocal` declarations to be changed.

Nested Scope Examples

To clarify the prior section's points, let's illustrate with some real code. Here is what an enclosing function scope looks like (type this into a script file or at the interactive prompt to run it live):

```
X = 99                  # Global scope name: not used

def f1():
    X = 88              # Enclosing def local
    def f2():
        print(X)        # Reference made in nested def
    f2()

f1()                    # Prints 88: enclosing def local
```

First off, this is legal Python code: the `def` is simply an executable statement, which can appear anywhere any other statement can—including nested in another `def`. Here, the nested `def` runs while a call to the function `f1` is running; it generates a function and assigns it to the name `f2`, a local variable within `f1`'s local scope. In a sense, `f2` is a temporary function that lives only during the execution of (and is visible only to code in) the enclosing `f1`.

But notice what happens inside `f2`: when it prints the variable X, it refers to the X that lives in the enclosing `f1` function's local scope. Because functions can access names in all physically enclosing `def` statements, the X in `f2` is automatically mapped to the X in `f1`, by the LEGB lookup rule.

This enclosing scope lookup works even if the enclosing function has already returned. For example, the following code defines a function that makes and *returns* another function, and represents a more common usage pattern:

```
def f1():
    X = 88
    def f2():
        print(X)          # Remembers X in enclosing def scope
    return f2             # Return f2 but don't call it

action = f1()            # Make, return function
action()                 # Call it now: prints 88
```

In this code, the call to `action` is really running the function we named `f2` when `f1` ran. This works because functions are objects in Python like everything else, and can be passed back as return values from other functions. Most importantly, `f2` remembers the enclosing scope's X in `f1`, even though `f1` is no longer active—which leads us to the next topic.

Factory Functions: Closures

Depending on whom you ask, this sort of behavior is also sometimes called a *closure* or a *factory* function—the former describing a *functional programming* technique, and the latter denoting a *design pattern*. Whatever the label, the function object in question remembers values in enclosing scopes regardless of whether those scopes are still present in memory. In effect, they have attached packets of memory (a.k.a. *state retention*), which are local to each copy of the nested function created, and often provide a simple alternative to classes in this role.

A simple function factory

Factory functions (a.k.a. closures) are sometimes used by programs that need to generate event handlers on the fly in response to conditions at runtime. For instance, imagine a GUI that must define actions according to user inputs that cannot be anticipated when the GUI is built. In such cases, we need a function that creates and returns another function, with information that may vary per function made.

To illustrate this in simple terms, consider the following function, typed at the interactive prompt (and shown here without the "..." continuation-line prompts, per the presentation note ahead):

```
>>> def maker(N):
        def action(X):             # Make and return action
            return X ** N          # action retains N from enclosing scope
        return action
```

This defines an outer function that simply generates and returns a nested function, without calling it—maker makes action, but simply returns action without running it. If we call the outer function:

```
>>> f = maker(2)                        # Pass 2 to argument N
>>> f
<function maker.<locals>.action at 0x0000000002A4A158>
```

what we get back is a reference to the generated nested function—the one created when the nested def runs. If we now call what we got back from the outer function:

```
>>> f(3)                                # Pass 3 to X, N remembers 2: 3 ** 2
9
>>> f(4)                                # 4 ** 2
16
```

we invoke the nested function—the one called action within maker. In other words, we're calling the nested function that maker created and passed back.

Perhaps the most unusual part of this, though, is that the nested function *remembers* integer 2, the value of the variable N in maker, even though maker has returned and exited by the time we call action. In effect, N from the enclosing local scope is retained as state information attached to the generated action, which is why we get back its argument squared when it is later called.

Just as important, if we now call the outer function again, we get back a *new* nested function with *different* state information attached. That is, we get the argument cubed instead of squared when calling the new function, but the original still squares as before:

```
>>> g = maker(3)                        # g remembers 3, f remembers 2
>>> g(4)                                # 4 ** 3
64
>>> f(4)                                # 4 ** 2
16
```

This works because each call to a factory function like this gets its *own* set of state information. In our case, the function we assign to name g remembers 3, and f remembers 2, because each has its own state information retained by the variable N in maker.

This is a somewhat advanced technique that you may not see very often in most code, and may be popular among programmers with backgrounds in functional programming languages. On the other hand, enclosing scopes are often employed by the lambda function-creation expressions we'll expand on later in this chapter—because they are expressions, they are almost always nested within a def. For example, a lambda would serve in place of a def in our example:

```
>>> def maker(N):
        return lambda X: X ** N          # lambda functions retain state too

>>> h = maker(3)
>>> h(4)                                 # 4 ** 3 again
64
```

For a more tangible example of closures at work, see the upcoming sidebar "Why You Will Care: Customizing open" on page 517. It uses similar techniques to store information for later use in an enclosing scope.

Presentation note: In this chapter, I've started listing interactive examples without the "..." *continuation-line prompts* that may or may not appear in your interface (they do at the shell, but not in IDLE). This convention will be followed from this point on to make larger code examples a bit easier to cut and paste from an ebook or other. I'm assuming that by now you understand indentation rules and have had your fair share of typing Python code, and some functions and classes ahead may be too large for rote input.

I'm also listing more and more code alone or in *files*, and switching between these and interactive input arbitrarily; when you see a ">>>" prompt, the code is typed interactively, and can generally be cut and pasted into your Python shell if you omit the ">>>" itself. If this fails, you can still run by pasting line by line, or editing in a file.

Closures versus classes, round 1

To some, *classes*, described in full in Part VI of this book, may seem better at state retention like this, because they make their memory more explicit with attribute assignments. Classes also directly support additional tools that closure functions do not, such as customization by inheritance and operator overloading, and more naturally implement multiple behaviors in the form of methods. Because of such distinctions, classes may be better at implementing more complete objects.

Still, closure functions often provide a lighter-weight and viable alternative when retaining state is the only goal. They provide for per-call localized storage for data required by a single nested function. This is especially true when we add the 3.X `nonlocal` statement described ahead to allow enclosing scope state changes (in 2.X, enclosing scopes are read-only, and so have more limited uses).

From a broader perspective, there are multiple ways for Python functions to retain state between calls. Although the values of normal local variables go away when a function returns, values can be retained from call to call in global variables; in class instance attributes; in the enclosing scope references we've met here; and in argument defaults and function attributes. Some might include mutable default arguments to this list too (though others may wish they didn't).

We'll preview class-based alternatives and meet function attributes later in this chapter, and get the full story on arguments and defaults in Chapter 18. To help us judge how defaults compete on state retention, though, the next section gives enough of an introduction to get us started.

Closures can also be created when a `class` is nested in a `def`: the values of the enclosing function's local names are retained by references within the class, or one of its method functions. See Chapter 29 for more on nested classes. As we'll see in later examples (e.g., Chapter 39's decorators), the outer `def` in such code serves a similar role: it becomes a class factory, and provides state retention for the nested class.

Retaining Enclosing Scope State with Defaults

In early versions of Python (prior to 2.2), the sort of code in the prior section failed because nested `def`s did not do anything about scopes—a reference to a variable within `f2` in the following would search only the local (`f2`), then global (the code outside `f1`), and then built-in scopes. Because it skipped the scopes of enclosing functions, an error would result. To work around this, programmers typically used *default argument values* to pass in and remember the objects in an enclosing scope:

```python
def f1():
    x = 88
    def f2(x=x):            # Remember enclosing scope X with defaults
        print(x)
    f2()

f1()                        # Prints 88
```

This coding style works in all Python releases, and you'll still see this pattern in some existing Python code. In fact, it's still *required* for loop variables, as we'll see in a moment, which is why it remains worth studying today. In short, the syntax `arg=val` in a `def` header means that the argument `arg` will default to the value `val` if no real value is passed to `arg` in a call. This syntax is used here to explicitly assign enclosing scope state to be retained.

Specifically, in the modified `f2` here, the `x=x` means that the argument `x` will default to the value of `x` in the enclosing scope—because the second `x` is evaluated before Python steps into the nested `def`, it still refers to the `x` in `f1`. In effect, the default argument remembers what `x` was in `f1`: the object `88`.

That's fairly complex, and it depends entirely on the timing of default value evaluations. In fact, the nested scope lookup rule was added to Python to make defaults unnecessary for this role—today, Python automatically remembers any values required in the enclosing scope for use in nested `def`s.

Of course, the best prescription for much code is simply to avoid nesting `def`s within `def`s, as it will make your programs much simpler—in the *Pythonic* view, flat is generally better than nested. The following is an equivalent of the prior example that avoids nesting altogether. Notice the forward reference in this code—it's OK to call a function defined after the function that calls it, as long as the second `def` runs before the first function is actually called. Code inside a `def` is never evaluated until the function is actually called:

```
>>> def f1():
        x = 88                      # Pass x along instead of nesting
        f2(x)                       # Forward reference OK

>>> def f2(x):
        print(x)                    # Flat is still often better than nested!

>>> f1()
88
```

If you avoid nesting this way, you can almost forget about the nested scopes concept in Python. On the other hand, the nested functions of closure (factory) functions are fairly common in modern Python code, as are lambda functions—which almost naturally appear nested in defs and often rely on the nested scopes layer, as the next section explains.

Nested scopes, defaults, and lambdas

Although they see increasing use in defs these days, you may be more likely to care about nested function scopes when you start coding or reading lambda expressions. We've met lambda briefly and won't cover it in depth until Chapter 19, but in short, it's an expression that generates a new function to be called later, much like a def statement. Because it's an expression, though, it can be used in places that def cannot, such as within list and dictionary literals.

Like a def, a lambda expression also introduces a new local scope for the function it creates. Thanks to the enclosing scopes lookup layer, lambdas can see all the variables that live in the functions in which they are coded. Thus, the following code—a variation on the factory we saw earlier—works, but only because the nested scope rules are applied:

```
def func():
    x = 4
    action = (lambda n: x ** n)         # x remembered from enclosing def
    return action

x = func()
print(x(2))                             # Prints 16, 4 ** 2
```

Prior to the introduction of nested function scopes, programmers used defaults to pass values from an enclosing scope into lambdas, just as for defs. For instance, the following works on all Pythons:

```
def func():
    x = 4
    action = (lambda n, x=x: x ** n)    # Pass x in manually
    return action
```

Because lambdas are expressions, they naturally (and even normally) nest inside enclosing defs. Hence, they were perhaps the biggest initial beneficiaries of the addition of enclosing function scopes in the lookup rules; in most cases, it is no longer necessary to pass values into lambdas with defaults.

Loop variables may require defaults, not scopes

There is one notable exception to the rule I just gave (and a reason why I've shown you the otherwise dated default argument technique we just saw): if a lambda or def defined within a function is nested inside a loop, and the nested function references an enclosing scope variable that is changed by that loop, all functions generated within the loop will have the same value—the value the referenced variable had in the *last* loop iteration. In such cases, you must still use defaults to save the variable's *current* value instead.

This may seem a fairly obscure case, but it can come up in practice more often than you may think, especially in code that generates callback handler functions for a number of widgets in a GUI—for instance, handlers for button-clicks for all the buttons in a row. If these are created in a loop, you may need to be careful to save state with defaults, or all your buttons' callbacks may wind up doing the same thing.

Here's an illustration of this phenomenon reduced to simple code: the following attempts to build up a list of functions that each remember the current variable i from the enclosing scope:

```
>>> def makeActions():
        acts = []
        for i in range(5):                # Tries to remember each i
            acts.append(lambda x: i ** x)  # But all remember same last i!
        return acts

>>> acts = makeActions()
>>> acts[0]
<function makeActions.<locals>.<lambda> at 0x0000000002A4A400>
```

This doesn't quite work, though—because the enclosing scope variable is looked up when the nested functions are later *called*, they all effectively remember the same value: the value the loop variable had on the *last* loop iteration. That is, when we pass a power argument of 2 in each of the following calls, we get back 4 to the power of 2 for each function in the list, because i is the same in all of them—4:

```
>>> acts[0](2)                # All are 4 ** 2, 4=value of last i
16
>>> acts[1](2)                # This should be 1 ** 2 (1)
16
>>> acts[2](2)                # This should be 2 ** 2 (4)
16
>>> acts[4](2)                # Only this should be 4 ** 2 (16)
16
```

This is the one case where we still have to explicitly retain enclosing scope values with default arguments, rather than enclosing scope references. That is, to make this sort of code work, we must pass in the *current* value of the enclosing scope's variable with a default. Because defaults are evaluated when the nested function is *created* (not when it's later *called*), each remembers its own value for `i`:

```
>>> def makeActions():
        acts = []
        for i in range(5):              # Use defaults instead
            acts.append(lambda x, i=i: i ** x)    # Remember current i
        return acts

>>> acts = makeActions()
>>> acts[0](2)                          # 0 ** 2
0
>>> acts[1](2)                          # 1 ** 2
1
>>> acts[2](2)                          # 2 ** 2
4
>>> acts[4](2)                          # 4 ** 2
16
```

This seems an implementation artifact that is prone to change, and may become more important as you start writing larger programs. We'll talk more about defaults in Chapter 18 and `lambda`s in Chapter 19, so you may also want to return and review this section later.[3]

Arbitrary scope nesting

Before ending this discussion, we should note that scopes may nest arbitrarily, but only enclosing function `def` statements (not classes, described in Part VI) are searched when names are referenced:

```
>>> def f1():
        x = 99
        def f2():
            def f3():
                print(x)        # Found in f1's local scope!
            f3()
        f2()

>>> f1()
99
```

Python will search the local scopes of *all* enclosing `def`s, from inner to outer, after the referencing function's local scope and before the module's global scope or built-ins. However, this sort of code is even less likely to pop up in practice. Again, in Python, we say *flat is better than nested*, and this still holds generally true even with the addition

---

3. In the section "Function Gotchas" on page 656, we'll also see that there is a similar issue with using mutable objects like lists and dictionaries for default arguments (e.g., `def f(a=[])`)—because defaults are implemented as single objects attached to functions, mutable defaults retain state from call to call, rather then being initialized anew on each call. Depending on whom you ask, this is either considered a feature that supports another way to implement state retention, or a strange corner of the language; more on this at the end of Chapter 21.

of nested scope closures. Except in limited contexts, your life (and the lives of your coworkers) will generally be better if you minimize nested function definitions.

The nonlocal Statement in 3.X

In the prior section we explored the way that nested functions can *reference* variables in an enclosing function's scope, even if that function has already returned. It turns out that, in Python 3.X (though not in 2.X), we can also *change* such enclosing scope variables, as long as we declare them in `nonlocal` statements. With this statement, nested `def`s can have both read and write access to names in enclosing functions. This makes nested scope closures more useful, by providing changeable state information.

The `nonlocal` statement is similar in both form and role to `global`, covered earlier. Like `global`, `nonlocal` declares that a name will be changed in an enclosing scope. Unlike `global`, though, `nonlocal` applies to a name in an enclosing function's scope, not the global module scope outside all `def`s. Also unlike `global`, `nonlocal` names must already exist in the enclosing function's scope when declared—they can exist only in enclosing functions and cannot be created by a first assignment in a nested `def`.

In other words, `nonlocal` both allows assignment to names in enclosing function scopes and limits scope lookups for such names to enclosing `def`s. The net effect is a more direct and reliable implementation of changeable state information, for contexts that do not desire or need classes with attributes, inheritance, and multiple behaviors.

nonlocal Basics

Python 3.X introduces a new `nonlocal` statement, which has meaning only inside a function:

```
def func():
    nonlocal name1, name2, ...          # OK here

>>> nonlocal X
SyntaxError: nonlocal declaration not allowed at module level
```

This statement allows a nested function to change one or more names defined in a syntactically enclosing function's scope. In Python 2.X, when one function `def` is nested in another, the nested function can reference any of the names defined by assignment in the enclosing `def`'s scope, but it cannot change them. In 3.X, declaring the enclosing scopes' names in a `nonlocal` statement enables nested functions to assign and thus change such names as well.

This provides a way for enclosing functions to provide *writeable* state information, remembered when the nested function is later called. Allowing the state to change makes it more useful to the nested function (imagine a counter in the enclosing scope, for instance). In 2.X, programmers usually achieve similar goals by using classes or other schemes. Because nested functions have become a more common coding pattern for state retention, though, nonlocal makes it more generally applicable.

Besides allowing names in enclosing defs to be changed, the nonlocal statement also forces the issue for references—much like the global statement, nonlocal causes searches for the names listed in the statement to begin in the enclosing defs' scopes, not in the local scope of the declaring function. That is, nonlocal also means "skip my local scope entirely."

In fact, the names listed in a nonlocal *must* have been previously defined in an enclosing def when the nonlocal is reached, or an error is raised. The net effect is much like global: global means the names reside in the enclosing module, and nonlocal means they reside in an enclosing def. nonlocal is even more strict, though—scope search is restricted to *only* enclosing defs. That is, nonlocal names can appear only in enclosing defs, not in the module's global scope or built-in scopes outside the defs.

The addition of nonlocal does not alter name reference scope rules in general; they still work as before, per the "LEGB" rule described earlier. The nonlocal statement mostly serves to allow names in enclosing scopes to be changed rather than just referenced. However, both global and nonlocal statements do tighten up and even restrict the lookup rules somewhat, when coded in a function:

- global makes scope lookup begin in the enclosing module's scope and allows names there to be assigned. Scope lookup continues on to the built-in scope if the name does not exist in the module, but assignments to global names always create or change them in the module's scope.

- nonlocal restricts scope lookup to just enclosing defs, requires that the names already exist there, and allows them to be assigned. Scope lookup does not continue on to the global or built-in scopes.

In Python 2.X, references to enclosing def scope names are allowed, but not assignment. However, you can still use classes with explicit attributes to achieve the same changeable state information effect as nonlocals (and you may be better off doing so in some contexts); globals and function attributes can sometimes accomplish similar goals as well. More on this in a moment; first, let's turn to some working code to make this more concrete.

nonlocal in Action

On to some examples, all run in 3.X. References to enclosing def scopes work in 3X as they do in 2.X—in the following, tester builds and returns the function nested, to be called later, and the state reference in nested maps the local scope of tester using the normal scope lookup rules:

```
C:\code> c:\python33\python

>>> def tester(start):
```

```
            state = start                # Referencing nonlocals works normally
            def nested(label):
                print(label, state)      # Remembers state in enclosing scope
            return nested

>>> F = tester(0)
>>> F('spam')
spam 0
>>> F('ham')
ham 0
```

Changing a name in an enclosing def's scope is not allowed by default, though; this is the normal case in 2.X as well:

```
>>> def tester(start):
        state = start
        def nested(label):
            print(label, state)
            state += 1                   # Cannot change by default (never in 2.X)
        return nested

>>> F = tester(0)
>>> F('spam')
UnboundLocalError: local variable 'state' referenced before assignment
```

Using nonlocal for changes

Now, under 3.X, if we declare state in the tester scope as nonlocal within nested, we get to change it inside the nested function, too. This works even though tester has returned and exited by the time we call the returned nested function through the name F:

```
>>> def tester(start):
        state = start                    # Each call gets its own state
        def nested(label):
            nonlocal state               # Remembers state in enclosing scope
            print(label, state)
            state += 1                   # Allowed to change it if nonlocal
        return nested

>>> F = tester(0)
>>> F('spam')                            # Increments state on each call
spam 0
>>> F('ham')
ham 1
>>> F('eggs')
eggs 2
```

As usual with enclosing scope references, we can call the tester factory (closure) function multiple times to get multiple copies of its state in memory. The state object in the enclosing scope is essentially attached to the nested function object returned; each call makes a new, distinct state object, such that updating one function's state won't impact the other. The following continues the prior listing's interaction:

```
>>> G = tester(42)                    # Make a new tester that starts at 42
>>> G('spam')
spam 42

>>> G('eggs')                         # My state information updated to 43
eggs 43

>>> F('bacon')                        # But F's is where it left off: at 3
bacon 3                               # Each call has different state information
```

In this sense, Python's nonlocals are more functional than function locals typical in some other languages: in a closure function, nonlocals are *per-call, multiple copy data.*

Boundary cases

Though useful, nonlocals come with some subtleties to be aware of. First, unlike the global statement, nonlocal names really *must* have previously been assigned in an enclosing def's scope when a nonlocal is evaluated, or else you'll get an error—you cannot create them dynamically by assigning them anew in the enclosing scope. In fact, they are checked at function definition time before either an enclosing or nested function is called:

```
>>> def tester(start):
        def nested(label):
            nonlocal state            # Nonlocals must already exist in enclosing def!
            state = 0
            print(label, state)
        return nested

SyntaxError: no binding for nonlocal 'state' found

>>> def tester(start):
        def nested(label):
            global state              # Globals don't have to exist yet when declared
            state = 0                 # This creates the name in the module now
            print(label, state)
        return nested

>>> F = tester(0)
>>> F('abc')
abc 0
>>> state
0
```

Second, nonlocal restricts the scope lookup to just enclosing defs; nonlocals are not looked up in the enclosing module's global scope or the built-in scope outside all defs, even if they are already there:

```
>>> spam = 99
>>> def tester():
        def nested():
            nonlocal spam            # Must be in a def, not the module!
            print('Current=', spam)
            spam += 1
```

```
        return nested

    SyntaxError: no binding for nonlocal 'spam' found
```

These restrictions make sense once you realize that Python would not otherwise generally know which enclosing scope to create a brand-new name in. In the prior listing, should spam be assigned in tester, or the module outside? Because this is ambiguous, Python must resolve nonlocals at function *creation* time, not function *call* time.

Why nonlocal? State Retention Options

Given the extra complexity of nested functions, you might wonder what the fuss is about. Although it's difficult to see in our small examples, state information becomes crucial in many programs. While functions can return results, their local variables won't normally retain other values that must live on between calls. Moreover, many applications require such values to differ per context of use.

As mentioned earlier, there are a variety of ways to "remember" information across function and method calls in Python. While there are tradeoffs for all, nonlocal does improve this story for enclosing scope references—the nonlocal statement allows multiple copies of *changeable* state to be retained in memory. It addresses simple state-retention needs where classes may not be warranted and global variables do not apply, though function attributes can often serve similar roles more portably. Let's review the options to see how they stack up.

State with nonlocal: 3.X only

As we saw in the prior section, the following code allows state to be retained and modified in an enclosing scope. Each call to tester creates a self-contained *package of changeable information*, whose names do not clash with any other part of the program:

```
>>> def tester(start):
        state = start                  # Each call gets its own state
        def nested(label):
            nonlocal state             # Remembers state in enclosing scope
            print(label, state)
            state += 1                 # Allowed to change it if nonlocal
        return nested

>>> F = tester(0)
>>> F('spam')                          # State visible within closure only
spam 0
>>> F.state
AttributeError: 'function' object has no attribute 'state'
```

We need to declare variables nonlocal only if they must be changed (other enclosing scope name references are automatically retained as usual), and nonlocal names are still not visible outside the enclosing function.

Unfortunately, this code works in Python 3.X only. If you are using Python 2.X, other options are available, depending on your goals. The next three sections present some alternatives. Some of the code in these sections uses tools we haven't covered yet and is intended partially as preview, but we'll keep the examples simple here so that you can compare and contrast along the way.

State with Globals: A Single Copy Only

One common prescription for achieving the `nonlocal` effect in 2.X and earlier is to simply move the state out to the *global scope* (the enclosing module):

```
>>> def tester(start):
        global state                  # Move it out to the module to change it
        state = start                 # global allows changes in module scope
        def nested(label):
            global state
            print(label, state)
            state += 1
        return nested
```

```
>>> F = tester(0)
>>> F('spam')                         # Each call increments shared global state
spam 0
>>> F('eggs')
eggs 1
```

This works in this case, but it requires `global` declarations in both functions and is prone to name collisions in the global scope (what if "state" is already being used?). A worse, and more subtle, problem is that it only allows for a *single shared copy* of the state information in the module scope—if we call `tester` again, we'll wind up resetting the module's `state` variable, such that prior calls will see their `state` overwritten:

```
>>> G = tester(42)                    # Resets state's single copy in global scope
>>> G('toast')
toast 42

>>> G('bacon')
bacon 43

>>> F('ham')                          # But my counter has been overwritten!
ham 44
```

As shown earlier, when you are using `nonlocal` and nested function closures instead of `global`, each call to `tester` remembers its own unique copy of the `state` object.

State with Classes: Explicit Attributes (Preview)

The other prescription for changeable state information in 2.X and earlier is to use *classes with attributes* to make state information access more explicit than the implicit magic of scope lookup rules. As an added benefit, each instance of a class gets a fresh copy of the state information, as a natural byproduct of Python's object model. Classes also support inheritance, multiple behaviors, and other tools.

We haven't explored classes in detail yet, but as a brief preview for comparison, the following is a reformulation of the earlier tester/nested functions as a class, which records state in objects explicitly as they are created. To make sense of this code, you need to know that a def within a class like this works exactly like a normal def, except that the function's self argument automatically receives the implied subject of the call (an instance object created by calling the class itself). The function named __init__ is run automatically when the class is called:

```
>>> class tester:                          # Class-based alternative (see Part VI)
        def __init__(self, start):         # On object construction,
            self.state = start             # save state explicitly in new object
        def nested(self, label):
            print(label, self.state)       # Reference state explicitly
            self.state += 1                # Changes are always allowed

>>> F = tester(0)                          # Create instance, invoke __init__
>>> F.nested('spam')                       # F is passed to self
spam 0
>>> F.nested('ham')
ham 1
```

In classes, we save *every* attribute explicitly, whether it's changed or just referenced, and they are available outside the class. As for nested functions and nonlocal, the class alternative supports multiple copies of the retained data:

```
>>> G = tester(42)                         # Each instance gets new copy of state
>>> G.nested('toast')                      # Changing one does not impact others
toast 42
>>> G.nested('bacon')
bacon 43

>>> F.nested('eggs')                       # F's state is where it left off
eggs 2
>>> F.state                                # State may be accessed outside class
3
```

With just slightly more magic—which we'll delve into later in this book—we could also make our class objects look like callable functions using operator overloading. __call__ intercepts direct calls on an instance, so we don't need to call a named method:

```
>>> class tester:
        def __init__(self, start):
            self.state = start
        def __call__(self, label):         # Intercept direct instance calls
            print(label, self.state)       # So .nested() not required
            self.state += 1

>>> H = tester(99)
>>> H('juice')                             # Invokes __call__
juice 99
```

```
>>> H('pancakes')
pancakes 100
```

Don't sweat the details in this code too much at this point in the book; it's mostly a preview, intended for general comparison to closures only. We'll explore classes in depth in Part VI, and will look at specific operator overloading tools like __call__ in Chapter 30. The point to notice here is that classes can make state information more obvious, by leveraging explicit attribute assignment instead of implicit scope lookups. In addition, class attributes are always changeable and don't require a nonlocal statement, and classes are designed to scale up to implementing richer objects with many attributes and behaviors.

While using classes for state information is generally a good rule of thumb to follow, they might also be *overkill* in cases like this, where state is a single counter. Such trivial state cases are more common than you might think; in such contexts, nested defs are sometimes more lightweight than coding classes, especially if you're not familiar with OOP yet. Moreover, there are some scenarios in which nested defs may actually work *better* than classes—stay tuned for the description of *method decorators* in Chapter 39 for an example that is far beyond this chapter's already well-stretched scope!

State with Function Attributes: 3.X and 2.X

As a portable and often simpler state-retention option, we can also sometimes achieve the same effect as nonlocals with *function attributes*—user-defined names attached to functions directly. When you attach user-defined attributes to nested functions generated by enclosing factory functions, they can also serve as per-call, multiple copy, and writeable state, just like nonlocal scope closures and class attributes. Such user-defined attribute names won't clash with names Python creates itself, and as for nonlocal, need be used only for state variables that must be *changed*; other scope references are retained and work normally.

Crucially, this scheme is *portable*—like classes, but unlike nonlocal, function attributes work in both Python 3.X and 2.X. In fact, they've been available since 2.1, much longer than 3.X's nonlocal. Because factory functions make a new function on each call anyhow, this does not require extra objects—the new function's attributes become per-call state in much the same way as nonlocals, and are similarly associated with the generated function in memory.

Moreover, function attributes allow state variables to be accessed *outside* the nested function, like class attributes; with nonlocal, state variables can be seen directly only within the nested def. If you need to access a call counter externally, it's a simple function attribute fetch in this model.

Here's a final version of our example based on this technique—it replaces a nonlocal with an attribute attached to the nested function. This scheme may not seem as intuitive to some at first glance; you access state though the function's name instead of as simple variables, and must initialize after the nested `def`. Still, it's far more portable, allows state to be accessed externally, and saves a line by not requiring a `nonlocal` declaration:

```
>>> def tester(start):
        def nested(label):
            print(label, nested.state)      # nested is in enclosing scope
            nested.state += 1               # Change attr, not nested itself
        nested.state = start                # Initial state after func defined
        return nested

>>> F = tester(0)
>>> F('spam')                               # F is a 'nested' with state attached
spam 0
>>> F('ham')
ham 1
>>> F.state                                 # Can access state outside functions too
2
```

Because each call to the outer function produces a new nested function object, this scheme supports multiple copy *per-call* changeable data just like nonlocal closures and classes—a usage mode that global variables cannot provide:

```
>>> G = tester(42)                          # G has own state, doesn't overwrite F's
>>> G('eggs')
eggs 42
>>> F('ham')
ham 2

>>> F.state                                 # State is accessible and per-call
3
>>> G.state
43
>>> F is G                                  # Different function objects
False
```

This code relies on the fact that the function name `nested` is a local variable in the `tester` scope enclosing `nested`; as such, it can be referenced freely inside `nested`. This code also relies on the fact that changing an object in place is not an assignment to a name; when it increments `nested.state`, it is changing part of the object `nested` references, not the name `nested` itself. Because we're not really assigning a name in the enclosing scope, no `nonlocal` declaration is required.

Function attributes are supported in both Python 3.X and 2.X; we'll explore them further in Chapter 19. Importantly, we'll see there that Python uses naming conventions in both 2.X and 3.X that ensure that the arbitrary names you assign as function attributes won't clash with names related to internal implementation, making the name-space equivalent to a scope. Subjective factors aside, function attributes' utility does overlap with the newer `nonlocal` in 3.X, making the latter technically redundant and far less portable.

State with mutables: Obscure ghost of Pythons past?

On a related note, it's also possible to change a *mutable* object in the enclosing scope in 2.X and 3.X without declaring its name nonlocal. The following, for example, works the same as the previous version, is just as portable, and provides changeable per-call state:

```
def tester(start):
    def nested(label):
        print(label, state[0])          # Leverage in-place mutable change
        state[0] += 1                     # Extra syntax, deep magic?
    state = [start]
    return nested
```

This leverages the mutability of lists, and like function attributes, relies on the fact that in-place object changes do not classify a name as local. This is perhaps more obscure than either function attributes or 3.X's nonlocal, though—a technique that predates even function attributes, and seems to lie today somewhere on the spectrum from clever hack to dark magic! You're probably better off using named function attributes than lists and numeric offsets this way, though this may show up in code you must use.

To summarize: globals, nonlocals, classes, and function attributes all offer changeable state-retention options. Globals support only single-copy shared data; nonlocals can be changed in 3.X only; classes require a basic knowledge of OOP; and both classes and function attributes provide portable solutions that allow state to be accessed directly from outside the stateful callable object itself. As usual, the best tool for your program depends upon your program's goals.

We'll revisit all the state options introduced here in Chapter 39 in a more realistic context—decorators, a tool that by nature involves multilevel state retention. State options have additional selection factors (e.g., performance), which we'll have to leave unexplored here for space (we'll learn how to time code speed in Chapter 21). For now, it's time to move on to explore argument passing modes.

Why You Will Care: Customizing open

For another example of closures at work, consider changing the built-in open call to a custom version, as suggested in this chapter's earlier sidebar "Breaking the Universe in Python 2.X" on page 494 If the custom version needs to call the original, it must save it before changing it, and retain it for later use—a classic state retention scenario. Moreover, if we wish to support multiple customizations to the same function, globals won't do: we need per-customizer state.

The following, coded for Python 3.X in file *makeopen.py*, is one way to achieve this (in 2.X, change the built-in scope name and prints). It uses a nested scope closure to remember a value for later use, without relying on global variables—which can clash and allow just one value, and without using a class—that may require more code than is warranted here:

```
import builtins
```

```
def makeopen(id):
    original = builtins.open
    def custom(*pargs, **kargs):
        print('Custom open call %r:' % id , pargs, kargs)
        return original(*pargs, **kargs)
    builtins.open = custom
```

To change open for every module in a process, this code reassigns it in the built-in scope to a custom version coded with a nested def, after saving the original in the enclosing scope so the customization can call it later. This code is also partially preview, as it relies on *starred-argument* forms to collect and later unpack arbitrary positional and keyword arguments meant for open—a topic coming up in the next chapter. Much of the magic here, though, is nested scope closures: the custom open found by the scope lookup rules retains the original for later use:

```
>>> F = open('script2.py')              # Call built-in open in builtins
>>> F.read()
'import sys\nprint(sys.path)\nx = 2\nprint(x ** 32)\n'

>>> from makeopen import makeopen       # Import open resetter function
>>> makeopen('spam')                    # Custom open calls built-in open

>>> F = open('script2.py')              # Call custom open in builtins
Custom open call 'spam': ('script2.py',) {}
>>> F.read()
'import sys\nprint(sys.path)\nx = 2\nprint(x ** 32)\n'
```

Because each customization remembers the former built-in scope version in its own enclosing scope, they can even be *nested* naturally in ways that global variables cannot support—each call to the makeopen closure function remembers its own versions of id and original, so multiple customizations may be run:

```
>>> makeopen('eggs')                    # Nested customizers work too!
>>> F = open('script2.py')              # Because each retains own state
Custom open call 'eggs': ('script2.py',) {}
Custom open call 'spam': ('script2.py',) {}
>>> F.read()
'import sys\nprint(sys.path)\nx = 2\nprint(x ** 32)\n'
```

As is, our function simply adds possibly nested call tracing to a built-in function, but the general technique may have other applications. A class-based equivalent to this may require more code because it would need to save the id and original values explicitly in object attributes—but requires more background knowledge than we yet have, so consider this a Part VI preview only:

```
import builtins

class makeopen:                         # See Part VI: call catches self()
    def __init__(self, id):
        self.id = id
        self.original = builtins.open
        builtins.open = self
    def __call__(self, *pargs, **kargs):
        print('Custom open call %r:' % self.id, pargs, kargs)
        return self.original(*pargs, **kargs)
```

The point to notice here is that classes may be more explicit but also may take extra code when state retention is the only goal. We'll see additional closure use cases later, especially when exploring *decorators* in Chapter 39, where we'll find the closures are actually preferred to classes in certain roles.

Chapter Summary

In this chapter, we studied one of two key concepts related to functions: *scopes*, which determine how variables are looked up when used. As we learned, variables are considered local to the function definitions in which they are assigned, unless they are specifically declared to be global or nonlocal. We also explored some more advanced scope concepts here, including nested function scopes and function attributes. Finally, we looked at some general design ideas, such as the need to avoid globals and cross-file changes.

In the next chapter, we're going to continue our function tour with the second key function-related concept: argument passing. As we'll find, arguments are passed into a function by assignment, but Python also provides tools that allow functions to be flexible in how items are passed. Before we move on, let's take this chapter's quiz to review the scope concepts we've covered here.

Test Your Knowledge: Quiz

1. What is the output of the following code, and why?

   ```
   >>> X = 'Spam'
   >>> def func():
           print(X)

   >>> func()
   ```

2. What is the output of this code, and why?

   ```
   >>> X = 'Spam'
   >>> def func():
           X = 'NI!'

   >>> func()
   >>> print(X)
   ```

3. What does this code print, and why?

   ```
   >>> X = 'Spam'
   >>> def func():
           X = 'NI'
           print(X)

   >>> func()
   >>> print(X)
   ```

4. What output does this code produce? Why?

```
>>> X = 'Spam'
>>> def func():
        global X
        X = 'NI'

>>> func()
>>> print(X)
```

5. What about this code—what's the output, and why?

```
>>> X = 'Spam'
>>> def func():
        X = 'NI'
        def nested():
            print(X)
        nested()

>>> func()
>>> X
```

6. How about this example: what is its output in Python 3.X, and why?

```
>>> def func():
        X = 'NI'
        def nested():
            nonlocal X
            X = 'Spam'
        nested()
        print(X)

>>> func()
```

7. Name three or more ways to retain state information in a Python function.

Test Your Knowledge: Answers

1. The output here is `'Spam'`, because the function references a global variable in the enclosing module (because it is not assigned in the function, it is considered global).

2. The output here is `'Spam'` again because assigning the variable inside the function makes it a local and effectively hides the global of the same name. The `print` statement finds the variable unchanged in the global (module) scope.

3. It prints `'NI'` on one line and `'Spam'` on another, because the reference to the variable within the function finds the assigned local and the reference in the `print` statement finds the global.

4. This time it just prints `'NI'` because the global declaration forces the variable assigned inside the function to refer to the variable in the enclosing global scope.

5. The output in this case is again `'NI'` on one line and `'Spam'` on another, because the `print` statement in the nested function finds the name in the enclosing function's local scope, and the display at the end finds the variable in the global scope.

6. This example prints `'Spam'`, because the `nonlocal` statement (available in Python 3.X but not 2.X) means that the assignment to X inside the nested function changes X in the enclosing function's local scope. Without this statement, this assignment would classify X as local to the nested function, making it a different variable; the code would then print `'NI'` instead.

7. Although the values of local variables go away when a function returns, you can make a Python function retain state information by using shared global variables, enclosing function scope references within nested functions, or using default argument values. Function attributes can sometimes allow state to be attached to the function itself, instead of looked up in scopes. Another alternative, using classes and OOP, sometimes supports state retention better than any of the scope-based techniques because it makes it explicit with attribute assignments; we'll explore this option in Part VI.

Arguments

Chapter 17 explored the details behind Python's *scopes*—the places where variables are defined and looked up. As we learned, the place where a name is defined in our code determines much of its meaning. This chapter continues the function story by studying the concepts in Python *argument passing*—the way that objects are sent to functions as inputs. As we'll see, arguments (a.k.a. parameters) are assigned to names in a function, but they have more to do with object references than with variable scopes. We'll also find that Python provides extra tools, such as keywords, defaults, and arbitrary argument collectors and extractors that allow for wide flexibility in the way arguments are sent to a function, and we'll put them to work in examples.

Argument-Passing Basics

Earlier in this part of the book, I noted that arguments are passed by *assignment*. This has a few ramifications that aren't always obvious to newcomers, which I'll expand on in this section. Here is a rundown of the key points in passing arguments to functions:

- **Arguments are passed by automatically assigning objects to local variable names**. Function arguments—references to (possibly) shared objects sent by the caller—are just another instance of Python assignment at work. Because references are implemented as pointers, all arguments are, in effect, passed by pointer. Objects passed as arguments are never automatically copied.

- **Assigning to argument names inside a function does not affect the caller**. Argument names in the function header become new, local names when the function runs, in the scope of the function. There is no aliasing between function argument names and variable names in the scope of the caller.

- **Changing a mutable object argument in a function may impact the caller**. On the other hand, as arguments are simply assigned to passed-in objects, functions can change passed-in mutable objects in place, and the results may affect the caller. Mutable arguments can be input and output for functions.

For more details on *references*, see Chapter 6; everything we learned there also applies to function arguments, though the assignment to argument names is automatic and implicit.

Python's pass-by-assignment scheme isn't quite the same as C++'s reference parameters option, but it turns out to be very similar to the argument-passing model of the C language (and others) in practice:

- **Immutable arguments are effectively passed "by value."** Objects such as integers and strings are passed by object reference instead of by copying, but because you can't change immutable objects in place anyhow, the effect is much like making a copy.

- **Mutable arguments are effectively passed "by pointer."** Objects such as lists and dictionaries are also passed by object reference, which is similar to the way C passes arrays as pointers—mutable objects can be changed in place in the function, much like C arrays.

Of course, if you've never used C, Python's argument-passing mode will seem simpler still—it involves just the assignment of objects to names, and it works the same whether the objects are mutable or not.

Arguments and Shared References

To illustrate argument-passing properties at work, consider the following code:

```
>>> def f(a):              # a is assigned to (references) the passed object
        a = 99             # Changes local variable a only

>>> b = 88
>>> f(b)                   # a and b both reference same 88 initially
>>> print(b)               # b is not changed
88
```

In this example the variable a is assigned the object 88 at the moment the function is called with f(b), but a lives only within the called function. Changing a inside the function has no effect on the place where the function is called; it simply resets the local variable a to a completely different object.

That's what is meant by a lack of name *aliasing*—assignment to an argument name inside a function (e.g., a=99) does not magically change a variable like b in the scope of the function call. Argument names may share passed objects initially (they are essentially pointers to those objects), but only temporarily, when the function is first called. As soon as an argument name is reassigned, this relationship ends.

At least, that's the case for assignment to argument *names* themselves. When arguments are passed *mutable* objects like lists and dictionaries, we also need to be aware that in-place changes to such *objects* may live on after a function exits, and hence impact callers. Here's an example that demonstrates this behavior:

```
>>> def changer(a, b):        # Arguments assigned references to objects
        a = 2                 # Changes local name's value only
        b[0] = 'spam'         # Changes shared object in place

>>> X = 1
>>> L = [1, 2]                # Caller:
>>> changer(X, L)             # Pass immutable and mutable objects
>>> X, L                      # X is unchanged, L is different!
(1, ['spam', 2])
```

In this code, the changer function assigns values to argument a itself, and to a component of the *object* referenced by argument b. These two assignments within the function are only slightly different in syntax but have radically different results:

- Because a is a local variable name in the function's scope, the first assignment has no effect on the caller—it simply changes the local variable a to reference a completely different object, and does not change the binding of the name X in the caller's scope. This is the same as in the prior example.

- Argument b is a local variable name, too, but it is passed a mutable object (the list that L references in the caller's scope). As the second assignment is an in-place object change, the result of the assignment to b[0] in the function impacts the value of L after the function returns.

Really, the second assignment statement in changer doesn't change b—it changes part of the object that b currently references. This in-place change impacts the caller only because the changed object outlives the function call. The name L hasn't changed either —it still references the same, changed object—but it seems as though L differs after the call because the value it references has been modified within the function. In effect, the list name L serves as both input to and output from the function.

Figure 18-1 illustrates the name/object bindings that exist immediately after the function has been called, and before its code has run.

If this example is still confusing, it may help to notice that the effect of the automatic assignments of the passed-in arguments is the same as running a series of simple assignment statements. In terms of the first argument, the assignment has no effect on the caller:

```
>>> X = 1
>>> a = X                     # They share the same object
>>> a = 2                     # Resets 'a' only, 'X' is still 1
>>> print(X)
1
```

The assignment through the second argument does affect a variable at the call, though, because it is an in-place object change:

```
>>> L = [1, 2]
>>> b = L                     # They share the same object
>>> b[0] = 'spam'             # In-place change: 'L' sees the change too
>>> print(L)
['spam', 2]
```

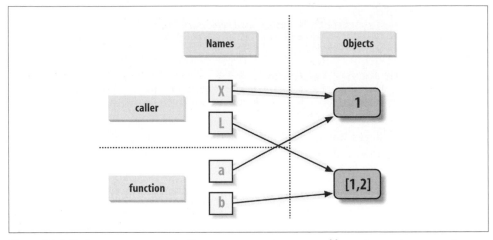

Figure 18-1. References: arguments. Because arguments are passed by assignment, argument names in the function may share objects with variables in the scope of the call. Hence, in-place changes to mutable arguments in a function can impact the caller. Here, a and b in the function initially reference the objects referenced by variables X and L when the function is first called. Changing the list through variable b makes L appear different after the call returns.

If you recall our discussions about shared mutable objects in Chapter 6 and Chapter 9, you'll recognize the phenomenon at work: changing a mutable object in place can impact other references to that object. Here, the effect is to make one of the arguments work like both an input and an output of the function.

Avoiding Mutable Argument Changes

This behavior of in-place changes to mutable arguments isn't a bug—it's simply the way argument passing works in Python, and turns out to be widely useful in practice. Arguments are normally passed to functions by reference because that is what we normally want. It means we can pass large objects around our programs without making multiple copies along the way, and we can easily update these objects as we go. In fact, as we'll see in Part VI, Python's class model *depends* upon changing a passed-in "self" argument in place, to update object state.

If we don't want in-place changes within functions to impact objects we pass to them, though, we can simply make explicit copies of mutable objects, as we learned in Chapter 6. For function arguments, we can always copy the list at the point of call, with tools like list, list.copy as of 3.3, or an empty slice:

```
L = [1, 2]
changer(X, L[:])          # Pass a copy, so our 'L' does not change
```

We can also copy within the function itself, if we never want to change passed-in objects, regardless of how the function is called:

```
def changer(a, b):
    b = b[:]                # Copy input list so we don't impact caller
    a = 2
    b[0] = 'spam'           # Changes our list copy only
```

Both of these copying schemes don't stop the function from changing the object—they just prevent those changes from impacting the caller. To really prevent changes, we can always convert to immutable objects to force the issue. Tuples, for example, raise an exception when changes are attempted:

```
L = [1, 2]
changer(X, tuple(L))      # Pass a tuple, so changes are errors
```

This scheme uses the built-in tuple function, which builds a new tuple out of all the items in a sequence (really, any iterable). It's also something of an extreme—because it forces the function to be written to never change passed-in arguments, this solution might impose more limitations on the function than it should, and so should generally be avoided (you never know when changing arguments might come in handy for other calls in the future). Using this technique will also make the function lose the ability to call any list-specific methods on the argument, including methods that do not change the object in place.

The main point to remember here is that functions might update mutable objects like lists and dictionaries passed into them. This isn't necessarily a problem if it's expected, and often serves useful purposes. Moreover, functions that change passed-in mutable objects in place are probably designed and intended to do so—the change is likely part of a well-defined API that you shouldn't violate by making copies.

However, you do have to be aware of this property—if objects change out from under you unexpectedly, check whether a called function might be responsible, and make copies when objects are passed if needed.

Simulating Output Parameters and Multiple Results

We've already discussed the return statement and used it in a few examples. Here's another way to use this statement: because return can send back any sort of object, it can return *multiple values* by packaging them in a tuple or other collection type. In fact, although Python doesn't support what some languages label "call by reference" argument passing, we can usually simulate it by returning tuples and assigning the results back to the original argument names in the caller:

```
>>> def multiple(x, y):
        x = 2                  # Changes local names only
        y = [3, 4]
        return x, y            # Return multiple new values in a tuple

>>> X = 1
>>> L = [1, 2]
>>> X, L = multiple(X, L)      # Assign results to caller's names
```

```
>>> X, L
(2, [3, 4])
```

It looks like the code is returning two values here, but it's really just one—a two-item tuple with the optional surrounding parentheses omitted. After the call returns, we can use tuple assignment to unpack the parts of the returned tuple. (If you've forgotten why this works, flip back to "Tuples" in Chapter 4 and Chapter 9, and "Assignment Statements" in Chapter 11.) The net effect of this coding pattern is to both send back multiple results and simulate the *output parameters* of other languages by explicit assignments. Here, X and L change after the call, but only because the code said so.

 Unpacking arguments in Python 2.X: The preceding example unpacks a tuple returned by the function with tuple assignment. In Python 2.X, it's also possible to automatically unpack tuples in arguments passed *to* a function. In 2.X (only), a function defined by this header:

> ```
> def f((a, (b, c))):
> ```

can be called with tuples that match the expected structure: f((1, (2, 3))) assigns a, b, and c to 1, 2, and 3, respectively. Naturally, the passed tuple can also be an object created before the call (f(T)). This def syntax is no longer supported in Python 3.X. Instead, code this function as:

> ```
> def f(T): (a, (b, c)) = T
> ```

to unpack in an explicit assignment statement. This explicit form works in both 3.X and 2.X. Argument unpacking is reportedly an obscure and rarely used feature in Python 2.X (except in code that uses it!). Moreover, a function header in 2.X supports only the *tuple* form of sequence assignment; more general sequence assignments (e.g., def f((a, [b, c])):) fail on syntax errors in 2.X as well and require the explicit assignment form mandated in 3.X. Conversely, arbitrary sequences in the call successfully match tuples in the header (e.g., f((1, [2, 3])), f((1, "ab"))).

Tuple unpacking argument syntax is also disallowed by 3.X in lambda function argument lists: see the Chapter 20 sidebar "Why You Will Care: List Comprehensions and map" on page 590 for a lambda unpacking example. Somewhat asymmetrically, tuple unpacking assignment is still automatic in 3.X for loops targets; see Chapter 13 for examples.

Special Argument-Matching Modes

As we've just seen, arguments are always passed by *assignment* in Python; names in the def header are assigned to passed-in objects. On top of this model, though, Python provides additional tools that alter the way the argument objects in a call are *matched* with argument names in the header prior to assignment. These tools are all optional, but they allow us to write functions that support more flexible calling patterns, and you may encounter some libraries that require them.

By default, arguments are matched by *position*, from left to right, and you must pass exactly as many arguments as there are argument names in the function header. However, you can also specify matching by name, provide default values, and use collectors for extra arguments.

Argument Matching Basics

Before we go into the syntactic details, I want to stress that these special modes are optional and deal only with matching objects to names; the underlying passing mechanism after the matching takes place is still assignment. In fact, some of these tools are intended more for people writing libraries than for application developers. But because you may stumble across these modes even if you don't code them yourself, here's a synopsis of the available tools:

Positionals: matched from left to right
> The normal case, which we've mostly been using so far, is to match passed argument values to argument names in a function header by position, from left to right.

Keywords: matched by argument name
> Alternatively, callers can specify which argument in the function is to receive a value by using the argument's name in the call, with the `name=value` syntax.

Defaults: specify values for optional arguments that aren't passed
> Functions themselves can specify default values for arguments to receive if the call passes too few values, again using the `name=value` syntax.

Varargs collecting: collect arbitrarily many positional or keyword arguments
> Functions can use special arguments preceded with one or two * characters to collect an arbitrary number of possibly extra arguments. This feature is often referred to as *varargs*, after a variable-length argument list tool in the C language; in Python, the arguments are collected in a normal object.

Varargs unpacking: pass arbitrarily many positional or keyword arguments
> Callers can also use the * syntax to unpack argument collections into separate arguments. This is the inverse of a * in a function header—in the header it means collect arbitrarily many arguments, while in the call it means unpack arbitrarily many arguments, and pass them individually as discrete values.

Keyword-only arguments: arguments that must be passed by name
> In Python 3.X (but not 2.X), functions can also specify arguments that must be passed by name with keyword arguments, not by position. Such arguments are typically used to define configuration options in addition to actual arguments.

Argument Matching Syntax

Table 18-1 summarizes the syntax that invokes the special argument-matching modes.

Table 18-1. Function argument-matching forms

Syntax	Location	Interpretation
func(value)	Caller	Normal argument: matched by position
func(name=value)	Caller	Keyword argument: matched by name
func(*iterable)	Caller	Pass all objects in *iterable* as individual positional arguments
func(**dict)	Caller	Pass all key/value pairs in *dict* as individual keyword arguments
def func(name)	Function	Normal argument: matches any passed value by position or name
def func(name=value)	Function	Default argument value, if not passed in the call
def func(*name)	Function	Matches and collects remaining positional arguments in a tuple
def func(**name)	Function	Matches and collects remaining keyword arguments in a dictionary
def func(*other, name)	Function	Arguments that must be passed by keyword only in calls (3.X)
def func(*, name=value)	Function	Arguments that must be passed by keyword only in calls (3.X)

These special matching modes break down into function calls and definitions as follows:

- In a *function call* (the first four rows of the table), simple values are matched by position, but using the name=value form tells Python to match by name to arguments instead; these are called *keyword arguments*. Using a *iterable or **dict in a call allows us to package up arbitrarily many positional or keyword objects in sequences (and other iterables) and dictionaries, respectively, and unpack them as separate, individual arguments when they are passed to the function.

- In a *function header* (the rest of the table), a simple name is matched by position or name depending on how the caller passes it, but the name=value form specifies a *default value*. The *name form collects any extra unmatched positional arguments in a tuple, and the **name form collects extra keyword arguments in a dictionary. In Python 3.X, any normal or defaulted argument names following a *name or a bare * are *keyword-only* arguments and must be passed by keyword in calls.

Of these, keyword arguments and defaults are probably the most commonly used in Python code. We've informally used both of these earlier in this book:

- We've already used *keywords* to specify options to the 3.X print function, but they are more general—keywords allow us to label any argument with its name, to make calls more informational.

- We met *defaults* earlier, too, as a way to pass in values from the enclosing function's scope, but they are also more general—they allow us to make any argument optional, providing its default value in a function definition.

As we'll see, the combination of defaults in a function header and keywords in a call further allows us to pick and choose which defaults to override.

In short, special argument-matching modes let you be fairly liberal about how many arguments must be passed to a function. If a function specifies defaults, they are used if you pass *too few* arguments. If a function uses the * variable argument list forms, you can seemingly pass *too many* arguments; the * names collect the extra arguments in data structures for processing in the function.

The Gritty Details

If you choose to use and combine the special argument-matching modes, Python will ask you to follow these ordering rules among the modes' optional components:

- In a function *call*, arguments must appear in this order: any positional arguments (value); followed by a combination of any keyword arguments (name=value) and the *iterable form; followed by the **dict form.

- In a function *header*, arguments must appear in this order: any normal arguments (name); followed by any default arguments (name=value); followed by the *name (or * in 3.X) form; followed by any name or name=value keyword-only arguments (in 3.X); followed by the **name form.

In both the call and header, the **args form must appear last if present. If you mix arguments in any other order, you will get a syntax error because the combinations can be ambiguous. The steps that Python internally carries out to match arguments before assignment can roughly be described as follows:

1. Assign nonkeyword arguments by position.
2. Assign keyword arguments by matching names.
3. Assign extra nonkeyword arguments to *name tuple.
4. Assign extra keyword arguments to **name dictionary.
5. Assign default values to unassigned arguments in header.

After this, Python checks to make sure each argument is passed just one value; if not, an error is raised. When all matching is complete, Python assigns argument names to the objects passed to them.

The actual matching algorithm Python uses is a bit more complex (it must also account for keyword-only arguments in 3.X, for instance), so we'll defer to Python's standard language manual for a more exact description. It's not required reading, but tracing Python's matching algorithm may help you to understand some convoluted cases, especially when modes are mixed.

In Python 3.X only, argument names in a function header can also have *annotation* values, specified as `name:value` (or `name:value=default` when defaults are present). This is simply additional syntax for arguments and does not augment or change the argument-ordering rules described here. The function itself can also have an annotation value, given as `def f()->value`. Python attaches annotation values to the function object. See the discussion of function annotation in Chapter 19 for more details.

Keyword and Default Examples

This is all simpler in code than the preceding descriptions may imply. If you don't use any special matching syntax, Python matches names by position from left to right, like most other languages. For instance, if you define a function that requires three arguments, you must call it with three arguments:

```
>>> def f(a, b, c): print(a, b, c)

>>> f(1, 2, 3)
1 2 3
```

Here, we pass by position—a is matched to 1, b is matched to 2, and so on (this works the same in Python 3.X and 2.X, but extra tuple parentheses are displayed in 2.X because we're using 3.X print calls again).

Keywords

In Python, though, you can be more specific about what goes where when you call a function. Keyword arguments allow us to match by *name*, instead of by position. Using the same function:

```
>>> f(c=3, b=2, a=1)
1 2 3
```

The c=3 in this call, for example, means send 3 to the argument named c. More formally, Python matches the name c in the call to the argument named c in the function definition's header, and then passes the value 3 to that argument. The net effect of this call is the same as that of the prior call, but notice that the left-to-right order of the arguments no longer matters when keywords are used because arguments are matched by name, not by position. It's even possible to combine positional and keyword arguments in a single call. In this case, all positionals are matched first from left to right in the header, before keywords are matched by name:

```
>>> f(1, c=3, b=2)          # a gets 1 by position, b and c passed by name
1 2 3
```

When most people see this the first time, they wonder why one would use such a tool. Keywords typically have two roles in Python. First, they make your calls a bit more self-documenting (assuming that you use better argument names than a, b, and c!). For example, a call of this form:

```
func(name='Bob', age=40, job='dev')
```

is much more meaningful than a call with three naked values separated by commas, especially in larger programs—the keywords serve as labels for the data in the call. The second major use of keywords occurs in conjunction with defaults, which we turn to next.

Defaults

We talked about defaults in brief earlier, when discussing nested function scopes. In short, defaults allow us to make selected function arguments optional; if not passed a value, the argument is assigned its default before the function runs. For example, here is a function that requires one argument and defaults two:

```
>>> def f(a, b=2, c=3): print(a, b, c)        # a required, b and c optional
```

When we call this function, we must provide a value for a, either by position or by keyword; however, providing values for b and c is optional. If we don't pass values to b and c, they default to 2 and 3, respectively:

```
>>> f(1)                 # Use defaults
1 2 3
>>> f(a=1)
1 2 3
```

If we pass two values, only c gets its default, and with three values, no defaults are used:

```
>>> f(1, 4)              # Override defaults
1 4 3
>>> f(1, 4, 5)
1 4 5
```

Finally, here is how the keyword and default features interact. Because they subvert the normal left-to-right positional mapping, keywords allow us to essentially skip over arguments with defaults:

```
>>> f(1, c=6)            # Choose defaults
1 2 6
```

Here, a gets 1 by position, c gets 6 by keyword, and b, in between, defaults to 2.

Be careful not to confuse the special name=value syntax in a function header and a function call; in the *call* it means a match-by-name keyword argument, while in the *header* it specifies a default for an optional argument. In both cases, this is not an assignment statement (despite its appearance); it is special syntax for these two contexts, which modifies the default argument-matching mechanics.

Combining keywords and defaults

Here is a slightly larger example that demonstrates keywords and defaults in action. In the following, the caller must always pass at least two arguments (to match spam and eggs), but the other two are optional. If they are omitted, Python assigns `toast` and `ham` to the defaults specified in the header:

```
def func(spam, eggs, toast=0, ham=0):    # First 2 required
    print((spam, eggs, toast, ham))

func(1, 2)                              # Output: (1, 2, 0, 0)
func(1, ham=1, eggs=0)                  # Output: (1, 0, 0, 1)
func(spam=1, eggs=0)                    # Output: (1, 0, 0, 0)
func(toast=1, eggs=2, spam=3)           # Output: (3, 2, 1, 0)
func(1, 2, 3, 4)                        # Output: (1, 2, 3, 4)
```

Notice again that when keyword arguments are used in the call, the order in which the arguments are listed doesn't matter; Python matches by name, not by position. The caller must supply values for `spam` and `eggs`, but they can be matched by position or by name. Again, keep in mind that the form `name=value` means different things in the call and the `def`: a keyword in the call and a default in the header.

 Beware mutable defaults: As footnoted in the prior chapter, if you code a default to be a mutable object (e.g., `def f(a=[])`), the same, *single* mutable object is reused every time the function is later called—even if it is changed in place within the function. The net effect is that the argument's default retains its value from the prior call, and is not reset to its original value coded in the `def` header. To reset anew on each call, move the assignment into the function body instead. Mutable defaults allow state retention, but this is often a surprise. Since this is such a common trap, we'll postpone further exploration until this part's "gotchas" list at the end of Chapter 21.

Arbitrary Arguments Examples

The last two matching extensions, `*` and `**`, are designed to support functions that take *any number* of arguments. Both can appear in either the function definition or a function call, and they have related purposes in the two locations.

Headers: Collecting arguments

The first use, in the function definition, collects unmatched *positional* arguments into a tuple:

```
>>> def f(*args): print(args)
```

When this function is called, Python collects all the positional arguments into a new *tuple* and assigns the variable `args` to that tuple. Because it is a normal tuple object, it can be indexed, stepped through with a `for` loop, and so on:

```
>>> f()
()
>>> f(1)
(1,)
```

```
>>> f(1, 2, 3, 4)
(1, 2, 3, 4)
```

The ** feature is similar, but it only works for *keyword* arguments—it collects them into a new *dictionary*, which can then be processed with normal dictionary tools. In a sense, the ** form allows you to convert from keywords to dictionaries, which you can then step through with keys calls, dictionary iterators, and the like (this is roughly what the dict call does when passed keywords, but it *returns* the new dictionary):

```
>>> def f(**args): print(args)

>>> f()
{}
>>> f(a=1, b=2)
{'a': 1, 'b': 2}
```

Finally, function headers can combine normal arguments, the *, and the ** to implement wildly flexible call signatures. For instance, in the following, 1 is passed to a by position, 2 and 3 are collected into the pargs positional tuple, and x and y wind up in the kargs keyword dictionary:

```
>>> def f(a, *pargs, **kargs): print(a, pargs, kargs)

>>> f(1, 2, 3, x=1, y=2)
1 (2, 3) {'y': 2, 'x': 1}
```

Such code is rare, but shows up in functions that need to support multiple call patterns (for backward compatibility, for instance). In fact, these features can be combined in even more complex ways that may seem ambiguous at first glance—an idea we will revisit later in this chapter. First, though, let's see what happens when * and ** are coded in function calls instead of definitions.

Calls: Unpacking arguments

In all recent Python releases, we can use the * syntax when we call a function, too. In this context, its meaning is the inverse of its meaning in the function definition—it unpacks a collection of arguments, rather than building a collection of arguments. For example, we can pass four arguments to a function in a tuple and let Python unpack them into individual arguments:

```
>>> def func(a, b, c, d): print(a, b, c, d)

>>> args = (1, 2)
>>> args += (3, 4)
>>> func(*args)                        # Same as func(1, 2, 3, 4)
1 2 3 4
```

Similarly, the ** syntax in a function call unpacks a dictionary of key/value pairs into separate keyword arguments:

```
>>> args = {'a': 1, 'b': 2, 'c': 3}
>>> args['d'] = 4
```

```
>>> func(**args)                          # Same as func(a=1, b=2, c=3, d=4)
1 2 3 4
```

Again, we can combine normal, positional, and keyword arguments in the call in very flexible ways:

```
>>> func(*(1, 2), **{'d': 4, 'c': 3})      # Same as func(1, 2, d=4, c=3)
1 2 3 4
>>> func(1, *(2, 3), **{'d': 4})           # Same as func(1, 2, 3, d=4)
1 2 3 4
>>> func(1, c=3, *(2,), **{'d': 4})        # Same as func(1, 2, c=3, d=4)
1 2 3 4
>>> func(1, *(2, 3), d=4)                  # Same as func(1, 2, 3, d=4)
1 2 3 4
>>> func(1, *(2,), c=3, **{'d':4})         # Same as func(1, 2, c=3, d=4)
1 2 3 4
```

This sort of code is convenient when you cannot predict the number of arguments that will be passed to a function when you write your script; you can build up a collection of arguments at runtime instead and call the function generically this way. Again, don't confuse the */** starred-argument syntax in the function header and the function call —in the *header* it collects any number of arguments, while in the *call* it unpacks any number of arguments. In both, one star means positionals, and two applies to keywords.

> As we saw in Chapter 14, the *pargs form in a call is an *iteration context*, so technically it accepts any iterable object, not just tuples or other sequences as shown in the examples here. For instance, a file object works after the *, and unpacks its lines into individual arguments (e.g., func(*open('fname'))). Watch for additional examples of this utility in Chapter 20, after we study generators.
>
> This generality is supported in both Python 3.X and 2.X, but it holds true only for *calls*—a *pargs in a call allows any iterable, but the same form in a def header always bundles extra arguments into a *tuple*. This header behavior is similar in spirit and syntax to the * in Python 3.X extended sequence unpacking assignment forms we met in Chapter 11 (e.g., x, *y = z), though that star usage always creates lists, not tuples.

Applying functions generically

The prior section's examples may seem academic (if not downright esoteric), but they are used more often than you might expect. Some programs need to call arbitrary functions in a generic fashion, without knowing their names or arguments ahead of time. In fact, the real power of the special "varargs" call syntax is that you don't need to know how many arguments a function call requires before you write a script. For example, you can use if logic to select from a set of functions and argument lists, and call any of them generically (functions in some of the following examples are hypothetical):

```
if sometest:
    action, args = func1, (1,)           # Call func1 with one arg in this case
else:
    action, args = func2, (1, 2, 3)      # Call func2 with three args here
...etc...
action(*args)                            # Dispatch generically
```

This leverages both the * form, and the fact that functions are objects that may be both referenced by, and called through, any variable. More generally, this varargs call syntax is useful anytime you cannot predict the arguments list. If your user selects an arbitrary function via a user interface, for instance, you may be unable to hardcode a function call when writing your script. To work around this, simply build up the arguments list with sequence operations, and call it with starred-argument syntax to unpack the arguments:

```
>>> ...define or import func3...
>>> args = (2,3)
>>> args += (4,)
>>> args
(2, 3, 4)
>>> func3(*args)
```

Because the arguments list is passed in as a tuple here, the program can build it at runtime. This technique also comes in handy for functions that test or time other functions. For instance, in the following code we support any function with any arguments by passing along whatever arguments were sent in (this is file *tracer0.py* in the book examples package):

```
def tracer(func, *pargs, **kargs):      # Accept arbitrary arguments
    print('calling:', func.__name__)
    return func(*pargs, **kargs)         # Pass along arbitrary arguments

def func(a, b, c, d):
    return a + b + c + d

print(tracer(func, 1, 2, c=3, d=4))
```

This code uses the built-in __name__ attribute attached to every function (as you might expect, it's the function's name string), and uses stars to collect and then unpack the arguments intended for the traced function. In other words, when this code is run, arguments are intercepted by the tracer and then *propagated* with varargs call syntax:

```
calling: func
10
```

For another example of this technique, see the preview near the end of the preceding chapter, where it was used to reset the built-in open function. We'll code additional examples of such roles later in this book; see especially the sequence timing examples in Chapter 21 and the various decorator utilities we will code in Chapter 39. It's a common technique in general tools.

The defunct apply built-in (Python 2.X)

Prior to Python 3.X, the effect of the *args and **args varargs call syntax could be achieved with a built-in function named apply. This original technique has been removed in 3.X because it is now redundant (3.X cleans up many such dusty tools that have been subsumed over the years). It's still available in all Python 2.X releases, though, and you may come across it in older 2.X code.

In short, the following are equivalent prior to Python 3.X:

```
func(*pargs, **kargs)          # Newer call syntax: func(*sequence, **dict)
apply(func, pargs, kargs)      # Defunct built-in: apply(func, sequence, dict)
```

For example, consider the following function, which accepts any number of positional or keyword arguments:

```
>>> def echo(*args, **kwargs): print(args, kwargs)

>>> echo(1, 2, a=3, b=4)
(1, 2) {'a': 3, 'b': 4}
```

In Python 2.X, we can call it generically with apply, or with the call syntax that is now required in 3.X:

```
>>> pargs = (1, 2)
>>> kargs = {'a':3, 'b':4}

>>> apply(echo, pargs, kargs)
(1, 2) {'a': 3, 'b': 4}

>>> echo(*pargs, **kargs)
(1, 2) {'a': 3, 'b': 4}
```

Both forms work for built-in functions in 2.X too (notice 2.X's trailing L for its long integers):

```
>>> apply(pow, (2, 100))
1267650600228229401496703205376L
>>> pow(*(2, 100))
1267650600228229401496703205376L
```

The unpacking call syntax form is newer than the apply function, is preferred in general, and is required in 3.X. (Technically, it was added in 2.0, was documented as deprecated in 2.3, is still usable without warning in 2.7, and is gone in 3.0 and later.) Apart from its symmetry with the * collector forms in def headers, and the fact that it requires fewer keystrokes, the newer call syntax also allows us to pass along additional arguments without having to manually extend argument sequences or dictionaries:

```
>>> echo(0, c=5, *pargs, **kargs)      # Normal, keyword, *sequence, **dictionary
(0, 1, 2) {'a': 3, 'c': 5, 'b': 4}
```

That is, the call syntax form is *more general*. Since it's required in 3.X, you should now disavow all knowledge of apply (unless, of course, it appears in 2.X code you must use or maintain...).

Python 3.X Keyword-Only Arguments

Python 3.X generalizes the ordering rules in function headers to allow us to specify *keyword-only arguments*—arguments that must be passed by keyword only and will never be filled in by a positional argument. This is useful if we want a function to both process any number of arguments and accept possibly optional configuration options.

Syntactically, keyword-only arguments are coded as named arguments that may appear after *args in the arguments list. All such arguments must be passed using keyword syntax in the call. For example, in the following, a may be passed by name or position, b collects any extra positional arguments, and c must be passed by keyword only. In 3.X:

```
>>> def kwonly(a, *b, c):
        print(a, b, c)

>>> kwonly(1, 2, c=3)
1 (2,) 3
>>> kwonly(a=1, c=3)
1 () 3
>>> kwonly(1, 2, 3)
TypeError: kwonly() missing 1 required keyword-only argument: 'c'
```

We can also use a * character by itself in the arguments list to indicate that a function does not accept a variable-length argument list but still expects all arguments following the * to be passed as keywords. In the next function, a may be passed by position or name again, but b and c must be keywords, and no extra positionals are allowed:

```
>>> def kwonly(a, *, b, c):
        print(a, b, c)

>>> kwonly(1, c=3, b=2)
1 2 3
>>> kwonly(c=3, b=2, a=1)
1 2 3
>>> kwonly(1, 2, 3)
TypeError: kwonly() takes 1 positional argument but 3 were given
>>> kwonly(1)
TypeError: kwonly() missing 2 required keyword-only arguments: 'b' and 'c'
```

You can still use defaults for keyword-only arguments, even though they appear after the * in the function header. In the following code, a may be passed by name or position, and b and c are optional but must be passed by keyword if used:

```
>>> def kwonly(a, *, b='spam', c='ham'):
        print(a, b, c)

>>> kwonly(1)
1 spam ham
>>> kwonly(1, c=3)
1 spam 3
>>> kwonly(a=1)
1 spam ham
>>> kwonly(c=3, b=2, a=1)
1 2 3
```

```
>>> kwonly(1, 2)
TypeError: kwonly() takes 1 positional argument but 2 were given
```

In fact, keyword-only arguments with defaults are optional, but those without defaults effectively become *required keywords* for the function:

```
>>> def kwonly(a, *, b, c='spam'):
        print(a, b, c)

>>> kwonly(1, b='eggs')
1 eggs spam
>>> kwonly(1, c='eggs')
TypeError: kwonly() missing 1 required keyword-only argument: 'b'
>>> kwonly(1, 2)
TypeError: kwonly() takes 1 positional argument but 2 were given

>>> def kwonly(a, *, b=1, c, d=2):
        print(a, b, c, d)

>>> kwonly(3, c=4)
3 1 4 2
>>> kwonly(3, c=4, b=5)
3 5 4 2
>>> kwonly(3)
TypeError: kwonly() missing 1 required keyword-only argument: 'c'
>>> kwonly(1, 2, 3)
TypeError: kwonly() takes 1 positional argument but 3 were given
```

Ordering rules

Finally, note that keyword-only arguments must be specified after a single star, not two —named arguments cannot appear after the **args arbitrary keywords form, and a ** can't appear by itself in the arguments list. Both attempts generate a syntax error:

```
>>> def kwonly(a, **pargs, b, c):
SyntaxError: invalid syntax
>>> def kwonly(a, **, b, c):
SyntaxError: invalid syntax
```

This means that in a function *header*, keyword-only arguments must be coded before the **args arbitrary keywords form and after the *args arbitrary positional form, when both are present. Whenever an argument name appears before *args, it is a possibly default positional argument, not keyword-only:

```
>>> def f(a, *b, **d, c=6): print(a, b, c, d)     # Keyword-only before **!
SyntaxError: invalid syntax

>>> def f(a, *b, c=6, **d): print(a, b, c, d)     # Collect args in header

>>> f(1, 2, 3, x=4, y=5)                          # Default used
1 (2, 3) 6 {'y': 5, 'x': 4}

>>> f(1, 2, 3, x=4, y=5, c=7)                     # Override default
1 (2, 3) 7 {'y': 5, 'x': 4}
```

```
>>> f(1, 2, 3, c=7, x=4, y=5)                    # Anywhere in keywords
1 (2, 3) 7 {'y': 5, 'x': 4}

>>> def f(a, c=6, *b, **d): print(a, b, c, d)    # c is not keyword-only here!

>>> f(1, 2, 3, x=4)
1 (3,) 2 {'x': 4}
```

In fact, similar ordering rules hold true in function *calls*: when keyword-only arguments are passed, they must appear before a **args form. The keyword-only argument can be coded either before or after the *args, though, and may be included in **args:

```
>>> def f(a, *b, c=6, **d): print(a, b, c, d)    # KW-only between * and **

>>> f(1, *(2, 3), **dict(x=4, y=5))              # Unpack args at call
1 (2, 3) 6 {'y': 5, 'x': 4}

>>> f(1, *(2, 3), **dict(x=4, y=5), c=7)         # Keywords before **args!
SyntaxError: invalid syntax

>>> f(1, *(2, 3), c=7, **dict(x=4, y=5))         # Override default
1 (2, 3) 7 {'y': 5, 'x': 4}

>>> f(1, c=7, *(2, 3), **dict(x=4, y=5))         # After or before *
1 (2, 3) 7 {'y': 5, 'x': 4}

>>> f(1, *(2, 3), **dict(x=4, y=5, c=7))         # Keyword-only in **
1 (2, 3) 7 {'y': 5, 'x': 4}
```

Trace through these cases on your own, in conjunction with the general argument-ordering rules described formally earlier. They may appear to be worst cases in the artificial examples here, but they can come up in real practice, especially for people who write libraries and tools for other Python programmers to use.

Why keyword-only arguments?

So why care about keyword-only arguments? In short, they make it easier to allow a function to accept both any number of positional arguments to be processed, and configuration options passed as keywords. While their use is optional, without keyword-only arguments extra work may be required to provide defaults for such options and to verify that no superfluous keywords were passed.

Imagine a function that processes a set of passed-in objects and allows a tracing flag to be passed:

```
process(X, Y, Z)            # Use flag's default
process(X, Y, notify=True)  # Override flag default
```

Without keyword-only arguments we have to use both *args and **args and manually inspect the keywords, but with keyword-only arguments less code is required. The following guarantees that no positional argument will be incorrectly matched against notify and requires that it be a keyword if passed:

```
def process(*args, notify=False): ...
```

Since we're going to see a more realistic example of this later in this chapter, in "Emulating the Python 3.X print Function," I'll postpone the rest of this story until then. For an additional example of keyword-only arguments in action, see the iteration options timing case study in Chapter 21. And for additional function definition enhancements in Python 3.X, stay tuned for the discussion of function annotation syntax in Chapter 19.

The min Wakeup Call!

OK—it's time for something more realistic. To make this chapter's concepts more concrete, let's work through an exercise that demonstrates a practical application of argument-matching tools.

Suppose you want to code a function that is able to compute the minimum value from an arbitrary set of arguments and an arbitrary set of object data types. That is, the function should accept zero or more arguments, as many as you wish to pass. Moreover, the function should work for all kinds of Python object types: numbers, strings, lists, lists of dictionaries, files, and even None. (To be fair, Python 3.X users don't need to support dictionaries, because their dictionaries don't support direct comparisons; see Chapters 8 and 9.)

The first requirement provides a natural example of how the * feature can be put to good use—we can collect arguments into a tuple and step over each of them in turn with a simple for loop. The second part of the problem definition is easy: because every object type supports comparisons, we don't have to specialize the function per type (an application of *polymorphism*); we can simply compare objects blindly and let Python worry about what sort of comparison to perform according to the objects being compared.

Full Credit

The following file shows three ways to code this operation, at least one of which was suggested by a student in one of my courses (this example is often a group exercise to circumvent dozing after lunch):

- The first function fetches the first argument (args is a tuple) and traverses the rest by slicing off the first (there's no point in comparing an object to itself, especially if it might be a large structure).
- The second version lets Python pick off the first and rest of the arguments automatically, and so avoids an index and slice.
- The third converts from a tuple to a list with the built-in list call and employs the list sort method.

The **sort** method is coded in C, so it can be quicker than the other approaches at times, but the linear scans of the first two techniques may make them faster much of the time.[1] The file *mins.py* contains the code for all three solutions:

```
def min1(*args):
    res = args[0]
    for arg in args[1:]:
        if arg < res:
            res = arg
    return res

def min2(first, *rest):
    for arg in rest:
        if arg < first:
            first = arg
    return first

def min3(*args):
    tmp = list(args)            # Or, in Python 2.4+: return sorted(args)[0]
    tmp.sort()
    return tmp[0]

print(min1(3, 4, 1, 2))
print(min2("bb", "aa"))
print(min3([2,2], [1,1], [3,3]))
```

All three solutions produce the same result when the file is run. Try typing a few calls interactively to experiment with these on your own:

```
% python mins.py
1
aa
[1, 1]
```

Notice that none of these three variants tests for the case where no arguments are passed in. They could, but there's no point in doing so here—in all three solutions, Python will automatically raise an exception if no arguments are passed in. The first variant raises an exception when we try to fetch item 0, the second when Python detects an argument list mismatch, and the third when we try to return item 0 at the end.

This is exactly what we want to happen—because these functions support any data type, there is no valid sentinel value that we could pass back to designate an error, so we may as well let the exception be raised. There are exceptions to this rule (e.g., you

---

1. Actually, this is fairly complicated. The Python **sort** routine is coded in C and uses a highly optimized algorithm that attempts to take advantage of partial ordering in the items to be sorted. It's named "timsort" after Tim Peters, its creator, and in its documentation it claims to have "supernatural performance" at times (pretty good, for a sort!). Still, sorting is an inherently exponential operation (it must chop up the sequence and put it back together many times), and the other versions simply perform one linear left-to-right scan. The net effect is that sorting is quicker if the arguments are partially ordered, but is likely to be slower otherwise (this still holds true in test runs in 3.3). Even so, Python performance can change over time, and the fact that sorting is implemented in the C language can help greatly; for an exact analysis, you should time the alternatives with the **time** or **timeit** modules—we'll see how in Chapter 21.

might test for errors yourself if you'd rather avoid actions run before reaching the code that triggers an error automatically), but in general it's better to assume that arguments will work in your functions' code and let Python raise errors for you when they do not.

Bonus Points

You can get bonus points here for changing these functions to compute the *maximum*, rather than minimum, values. This one's easy: the first two versions only require changing < to >, and the third simply requires that we return tmp[-1] instead of tmp[0]. For an extra point, be sure to set the function name to "max" as well (though this part is strictly optional).

It's also possible to generalize a single function to compute either a minimum *or* a maximum value, by evaluating comparison expression strings with a tool like the eval built-in function (see the library manual, and various appearances here, especially in Chapter 10) or passing in an arbitrary comparison function. The file *minmax.py* shows how to implement the latter scheme:

```
def minmax(test, *args):
    res = args[0]
    for arg in args[1:]:
        if test(arg, res):
            res = arg
    return res

def lessthan(x, y): return x < y          # See also: lambda, eval
def grtrthan(x, y): return x > y

print(minmax(lessthan, 4, 2, 1, 5, 6, 3))      # Self-test code
print(minmax(grtrthan, 4, 2, 1, 5, 6, 3))

% python minmax.py
1
6
```

Functions are another kind of object that can be passed into a function like this one. To make this a max (or other) function, for example, we simply pass in the right sort of test function. This may seem like extra work, but the main point of generalizing functions this way—instead of cutting and pasting to change just a single character—is that we'll only have one version to change in the future, not two.

The Punch Line...

Of course, all this was just a coding exercise. There's really no reason to code min or max functions, because both are built-ins in Python! We met them briefly in Chapter 5 in conjunction with numeric tools, and again in Chapter 14 when exploring iteration contexts. The built-in versions work almost exactly like ours, but they're coded in C for optimal speed and accept either a single iterable or multiple arguments. Still, though it's superfluous in this context, the general coding pattern we used here might be useful in other scenarios.

Generalized Set Functions

Let's look at a more useful example of special argument-matching modes at work. At the end of Chapter 16, we wrote a function that returned the intersection of two sequences (it picked out items that appeared in both). Here is a version that intersects an arbitrary number of sequences (one or more) by using the varargs matching form *args to collect all the passed-in arguments. Because the arguments come in as a tuple, we can process them in a simple for loop. Just for fun, we'll code a union function that also accepts an arbitrary number of arguments to collect items that appear in any of the operands:

```
def intersect(*args):
    res = []
    for x in args[0]:                  # Scan first sequence
        if x in res: continue          # Skip duplicates
        for other in args[1:]:         # For all other args
            if x not in other: break   # Item in each one?
        else:                          # No: break out of loop
            res.append(x)              # Yes: add items to end
    return res

def union(*args):
    res = []
    for seq in args:                   # For all args
        for x in seq:                  # For all nodes
            if not x in res:
                res.append(x)          # Add new items to result
    return res
```

Because these are tools potentially worth reusing (and they're too big to retype interactively), we'll store the functions in a module file called *inter2.py* (if you've forgotten how modules and imports work, see the introduction in Chapter 3, or stay tuned for in-depth coverage in Part V). In both functions, the arguments passed in at the call come in as the args tuple. As in the original intersect, both work on any kind of sequence. Here, they are processing strings, mixed types, and more than two sequences:

```
% python
>>> from inter2 import intersect, union
>>> s1, s2, s3 = "SPAM", "SCAM", "SLAM"

>>> intersect(s1, s2), union(s1, s2)        # Two operands
(['S', 'A', 'M'], ['S', 'P', 'A', 'M', 'C'])

>>> intersect([1, 2, 3], (1, 4))            # Mixed types
[1]

>>> intersect(s1, s2, s3)                   # Three operands
['S', 'A', 'M']
```

```
>>> union(s1, s2, s3)
['S', 'P', 'A', 'M', 'C', 'L']
```

To test more thoroughly, the following codes a function to apply the two tools to arguments in different orders using a simple shuffling technique that we saw in Chapter 13—it slices to move the first to the end on each loop, uses a * to unpack arguments, and sorts so results are comparable:

```
>>> def tester(func, items, trace=True):
        for i in range(len(items)):
            items = items[1:] + items[:1]
            if trace: print(items)
            print(sorted(func(*items)))

>>> tester(intersect, ('a', 'abcdefg', 'abdst', 'albmcnd'))
('abcdefg', 'abdst', 'albmcnd', 'a')
['a']
('abdst', 'albmcnd', 'a', 'abcdefg')
['a']
('albmcnd', 'a', 'abcdefg', 'abdst')
['a']
('a', 'abcdefg', 'abdst', 'albmcnd')
['a']

>>> tester(union, ('a', 'abcdefg', 'abdst', 'albmcnd'), False)
['a', 'b', 'c', 'd', 'e', 'f', 'g', 'l', 'm', 'n', 's', 't']
['a', 'b', 'c', 'd', 'e', 'f', 'g', 'l', 'm', 'n', 's', 't']
['a', 'b', 'c', 'd', 'e', 'f', 'g', 'l', 'm', 'n', 's', 't']
['a', 'b', 'c', 'd', 'e', 'f', 'g', 'l', 'm', 'n', 's', 't']

>>> tester(intersect, ('ba', 'abcdefg', 'abdst', 'albmcnd'), False)
['a', 'b']
['a', 'b']
['a', 'b']
['a', 'b']
```

The argument scrambling here doesn't generate all possible argument orders (that would require a full permutation, and 24 orderings for 4 arguments), but suffices to check if argument order impacts results here. If you test these further, you'll notice that *duplicates* won't appear in either intersection or union results, which qualify them as set operations from a mathematical perspective:

```
>>> intersect([1, 2, 1, 3], (1, 1, 4))
[1]
>>> union([1, 2, 1, 3], (1, 1, 4))
[1, 2, 3, 4]
>>> tester(intersect, ('ababa', 'abcdefga', 'aaaab'), False)
['a', 'b']
['a', 'b']
['a', 'b']
```

These are still far from optimal from an algorithmic perspective, but due to the following note, we'll leave further improvements to this code as suggested exercise. Also notice that the argument scrambling in our tester function might be a generally useful tool, and the tester would be simpler if we delegated this to another function, one that would be free to create or generate argument combinations as it saw fit:

```
>>> def tester(func, items, trace=True):
        for args in scramble(items):
            ...use args...
```

In fact we will—watch for this example to be revised in Chapter 20 to address this last point, after we've learned how to code user-defined *generators*. We'll also recode the set operations one last time in Chapter 32 and a solution to a Part VI exercise as *classes* that extend the list object with methods.

 Because Python now has a *set object type* (described in Chapter 5), none of the set-processing examples in this book are strictly required anymore; they are included just as demonstrations of coding techniques, and are today instructional only. Because it's constantly improving and growing, Python has an uncanny way of conspiring to make my book examples obsolete over time!

Emulating the Python 3.X print Function

To round out the chapter, let's look at one last example of argument matching at work. The code you'll see here is intended for use in Python 2.X or earlier (it works in 3.X, too, but is pointless there): it uses both the `*args` arbitrary positional tuple and the `**args` arbitrary keyword-arguments dictionary to simulate most of what the Python 3.X print function does. Python might have offered code like this as an *option* in 3.X rather than removing the 2.X print entirely, but 3.X chose a clean break with the past instead.

As we learned in Chapter 11, this isn't actually required, because 2.X programmers can always enable the 3.X print function with an import of this form (available in 2.6 and 2.7):

```
from __future__ import print_function
```

To demonstrate argument matching in general, though, the following file, *print3.py*, does the same job in a small amount of reusable code, by building up the print string and routing it per configuration arguments:

```
#!python
"""
Emulate most of the 3.X print function for use in 2.X (and 3.X).
Call signature: print3(*args, sep=' ', end='\n', file=sys.stdout)
"""

import sys

def print3(*args, **kargs):
    sep  = kargs.get('sep', ' ')          # Keyword arg defaults
```

```
end  = kargs.get('end', '\n')
file = kargs.get('file', sys.stdout)
output = ''
first  = True
for arg in args:
    output += ('' if first else sep) + str(arg)
    first = False
file.write(output + end)
```

To test it, import this into another file or the interactive prompt, and use it like the 3.X print function. Here is a test script, *testprint3.py* (notice that the function must be called "print3", because "print" is a reserved word in 2.X):

```
from print3 import print3
print3(1, 2, 3)
print3(1, 2, 3, sep='')                               # Suppress separator
print3(1, 2, 3, sep='...')
print3(1, [2], (3,), sep='...')                       # Various object types

print3(4, 5, 6, sep='', end='')                       # Suppress newline
print3(7, 8, 9)
print3()                                              # Add newline (or blank line)

import sys
print3(1, 2, 3, sep='??', end='.\n', file=sys.stderr)    # Redirect to file
```

When this is run under 2.X, we get the same results as 3.X's print function:

```
C:\code> c:\python27\python testprint3.py
1 2 3
123
1...2...3
1...[2]...(3,)
4567 8 9

1??2??3.
```

Although pointless in 3.X, the results are identical when run there. As usual, the generality of Python's design allows us to prototype or develop concepts in the Python language itself. In this case, argument-matching tools are as flexible in Python code as they are in Python's internal implementation.

Using Keyword-Only Arguments

It's interesting to notice that this example could be coded with Python 3.X keyword-only arguments, described earlier in this chapter, to automatically validate configuration arguments. The following variant, in the file *print3_alt1.py*, illustrates:

```
#!python3
"Use 3.X only keyword-only args"
import sys

def print3(*args, sep=' ', end='\n', file=sys.stdout):
    output = ''
```

```
    first  = True
    for arg in args:
        output += ('' if first else sep) + str(arg)
        first = False
    file.write(output + end)
```

This version works the same as the original, and it's a prime example of how keyword-only arguments come in handy. The original version assumes that all positional arguments are to be printed, and all keywords are for options only. That's almost sufficient, but any extra keyword arguments are silently ignored. A call like the following, for instance, will generate an exception correctly with the keyword-only form:

```
>>> print3(99, name='bob')
TypeError: print3() got an unexpected keyword argument 'name'
```

but will silently ignore the name argument in the original version. To detect superfluous keywords manually, we could use dict.pop() to delete fetched entries, and check if the dictionary is not empty. The following version, in the file *print3_alt2.py*, is equivalent to the keyword-only version—it triggers a built-in exception with a raise statement, which works just as though Python had done so (we'll study this in more detail in Part VII):

```
#!python
"Use 2.X/3.X keyword args deletion with defaults"
import sys

def print3(*args, **kargs):
    sep  = kargs.pop('sep', ' ')
    end  = kargs.pop('end', '\n')
    file = kargs.pop('file', sys.stdout)
    if kargs: raise TypeError('extra keywords: %s' % kargs)
    output = ''
    first  = True
    for arg in args:
        output += ('' if first else sep) + str(arg)
        first = False
    file.write(output + end)
```

This works as before, but it now catches extraneous keyword arguments, too:

```
>>> print3(99, name='bob')
TypeError: extra keywords: {'name': 'bob'}
```

This version of the function runs under Python 2.X, but it requires four more lines of code than the keyword-only version. Unfortunately, the extra code is unavoidable in this case—the keyword-only version works on 3.X only, which negates most of the reason that I wrote this example in the first place: a 3.X emulator that only works on 3.X isn't incredibly useful! In programs written to run on 3.X only, though, keyword-only arguments can simplify a specific category of functions that accept both arguments and options. For another example of 3.X keyword-only arguments, be sure to see the iteration timing case study in Chapter 21.

Chapter Summary

In this chapter, we studied the second of two key concepts related to functions: *arguments*—how objects are passed into a function. As we learned, arguments are passed into a function by assignment, which means by object reference (which really means by pointer). We also studied some more advanced extensions, including default and keyword arguments, tools for using arbitrarily many arguments, and keyword-only arguments in 3.X. Finally, we saw how mutable arguments can exhibit the same behavior as other shared references to objects—unless the object is explicitly copied when it's sent in, changing a passed-in mutable in a function can impact the caller.

The next chapter continues our look at functions by exploring some more advanced function-related ideas: function annotations, recursion, `lambda`s, and functional tools such as `map` and `filter`. Many of these concepts stem from the fact that functions are normal objects in Python, and so support some advanced and very flexible processing modes. Before diving into those topics, however, take this chapter's quiz to review the argument ideas we've studied here.

Test Your Knowledge: Quiz

In most of this quiz's questions, results may vary slightly in 2.X—with enclosing parentheses and commas when multiple values are printed. To match the 3.X answers exactly in 2.X, import `print_function` from __future__ before starting.

1. What is the output of the following code, and why?

    ```
    >>> def func(a, b=4, c=5):
            print(a, b, c)

    >>> func(1, 2)
    ```

2. What is the output of this code, and why?

    ```
    >>> def func(a, b, c=5):
            print(a, b, c)

    >>> func(1, c=3, b=2)
    ```

3. How about this code: what is its output, and why?

    ```
    >>> def func(a, *pargs):
            print(a, pargs)

    >>> func(1, 2, 3)
    ```

4. What does this code print, and why?

    ```
    >>> def func(a, **kargs):
            print(a, kargs)

    >>> func(a=1, c=3, b=2)
    ```

5. What gets printed by this, and why?

    ```
    >>> def func(a, b, c=3, d=4): print(a, b, c, d)

    >>> func(1, *(5, 6))
    ```

6. One last time: what is the output of this code, and why?

    ```
    >>> def func(a, b, c): a = 2; b[0] = 'x'; c['a'] = 'y'

    >>> l=1; m=[1]; n={'a':0}
    ```

```
>>> func(l, m,  n)
>>> l, m, n
```

Test Your Knowledge: Answers

1. The output here is 1 2 5, because 1 and 2 are passed to a and b by position, and c is omitted in the call and defaults to 5.

2. The output this time is 1 2 3: 1 is passed to a by position, and b and c are passed 2 and 3 by name (the left-to-right order doesn't matter when keyword arguments are used like this).

3. This code prints 1 (2, 3), because 1 is passed to a and the *pargs collects the remaining positional arguments into a new tuple object. We can step through the extra positional arguments tuple with any iteration tool (e.g., for arg in pargs: ...).

4. This time the code prints 1 {'b': 2, 'c': 3}, because 1 is passed to a by name and the **kargs collects the remaining keyword arguments into a dictionary. We could step through the extra keyword arguments dictionary by key with any iteration tool (e.g., for key in kargs: ...). Note that the order of the dictionary's keys may vary per Python and other variables.

5. The output here is 1 5 6 4: the 1 matches a by position, 5 and 6 match b and c by *name positionals (6 overrides c's default), and d defaults to 4 because it was not passed a value.

6. This displays (1, ['x'], {'a': 'y'})—the first assignment in the function doesn't impact the caller, but the second two do because they change passed-in mutable objects in place.

Advanced Function Topics

This chapter introduces a collection of more advanced function-related topics: recursive functions, function attributes and annotations, the `lambda` expression, and functional programming tools such as `map` and `filter`. These are all somewhat advanced tools that, depending on your job description, you may not encounter on a regular basis. Because of their roles in some domains, though, a basic understanding can be useful; `lambda`s, for instance, are regular customers in GUIs, and functional programming techniques are increasingly common in Python code.

Part of the art of using functions lies in the interfaces between them, so we will also explore some general function design principles here. The next chapter continues this advanced theme with an exploration of generator functions and expressions and a revival of list comprehensions in the context of the functional tools we will study here.

Function Design Concepts

Now that we've had a chance to study function basics in Python, let's begin this chapter with a few words of context. When you start using functions in earnest, you're faced with choices about how to glue components together—for instance, how to decompose a task into purposeful functions (known as *cohesion*), how your functions should communicate (called *coupling*), and so on. You also need to take into account concepts such as the size of your functions, because they directly impact code usability. Some of this falls into the category of structured analysis and design, but it applies to Python code as to any other.

We introduced some ideas related to function and module coupling in Chapter 17 when studying scopes, but here is a review of a few general guidelines for readers new to function design principles:

- **Coupling: use arguments for inputs and return for outputs**. Generally, you should strive to make a function independent of things outside of it. Arguments and `return` statements are often the best ways to isolate external dependencies to a small number of well-known places in your code.

- **Coupling: use global variables only when truly necessary**. Global variables (i.e., names in the enclosing module) are usually a poor way for functions to communicate. They can create dependencies and timing issues that make programs difficult to debug, change, and reuse.

- **Coupling: don't change mutable arguments unless the caller expects it**. Functions can change parts of passed-in mutable objects, but (as with global variables) this creates a tight coupling between the caller and callee, which can make a function too specific and brittle.

- **Cohesion: each function should have a single, unified purpose**. When designed well, each of your functions should do one thing—something you can summarize in a simple declarative sentence. If that sentence is very broad (e.g., "this function implements my whole program"), or contains lots of conjunctions (e.g., "this function gives employee raises *and* submits a pizza order"), you might want to think about splitting it into separate and simpler functions. Otherwise, there is no way to reuse the code behind the steps mixed together in the function.

- **Size: each function should be relatively small**. This naturally follows from the preceding goal, but if your functions start spanning multiple pages on your display, it's probably time to split them. Especially given that Python code is so concise to begin with, a long or deeply nested function is often a symptom of design problems. Keep it simple, and keep it short.

- **Coupling: avoid changing variables in another module file directly**. We introduced this concept in Chapter 17, and we'll revisit it in the next part of the book when we focus on modules. For reference, though, remember that changing variables across file boundaries sets up a coupling between modules similar to how global variables couple functions—the modules become difficult to understand and reuse. Use accessor functions whenever possible, instead of direct assignment statements.

Figure 19-1 summarizes the ways functions can talk to the outside world; inputs may come from items on the left side, and results may be sent out in any of the forms on the right. Good function designers prefer to use only arguments for inputs and `return` statements for outputs, whenever possible.

Of course, there are plenty of exceptions to the preceding design rules, including some related to Python's OOP support. As you'll see in Part VI, Python classes *depend* on changing a passed-in mutable object—class functions set attributes of an automatically passed-in argument called `self` to change per-object state information (e.g., `self.name='bob'`). Moreover, if classes are not used, global variables are often the most straightforward way for functions in modules to retain single-copy state between calls. Side effects are usually dangerous only if they're unexpected.

In general though, you should strive to minimize external dependencies in functions and other program components. The more *self-contained* a function is, the easier it will be to understand, reuse, and modify.

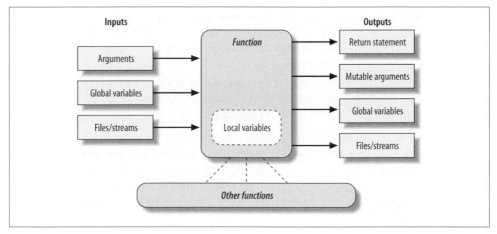

Figure 19-1. Function execution environment. Functions may obtain input and produce output in a variety of ways, though functions are usually easier to understand and maintain if you use arguments for input and return statements and anticipated mutable argument changes for output. In Python 3.X only, outputs may also take the form of declared nonlocal names that exist in an enclosing function scope.

Recursive Functions

We mentioned recursion in relation to comparisons of core types in Chapter 9. While discussing scope rules near the start of Chapter 17, we also briefly noted that Python supports *recursive functions*—functions that call themselves either directly or indirectly in order to loop. In this section, we'll explore what this looks like in our functions' code.

Recursion is a somewhat advanced topic, and it's relatively rare to see in Python, partly because Python's procedural statements include simpler looping structures. Still, it's a useful technique to know about, as it allows programs to traverse structures that have arbitrary and unpredictable shapes and depths—planning travel routes, analyzing language, and crawling links on the Web, for example. Recursion is even an alternative to simple loops and iterations, though not necessarily the simplest or most efficient one.

Summation with Recursion

Let's look at some examples. To sum a list (or other sequence) of numbers, we can either use the built-in sum function or write a more custom version of our own. Here's what a custom summing function might look like when coded with recursion:

```
>>> def mysum(L):
        if not L:
            return 0
        else:
            return L[0] + mysum(L[1:])        # Call myself recursively
```

```
>>> mysum([1, 2, 3, 4, 5])
15
```

At each level, this function calls itself recursively to compute the sum of the *rest* of the list, which is later added to the item at the *front*. The recursive loop ends and zero is returned when the list becomes empty. When using recursion like this, each open level of call to the function has its own copy of the function's local scope on the runtime call stack—here, that means L is different in each level.

If this is difficult to understand (and it often is for new programmers), try adding a print of L to the function and run it again, to trace the current list at each call level:

```
>>> def mysum(L):
        print(L)                          # Trace recursive levels
        if not L:                         # L shorter at each level
            return 0
        else:
            return L[0] + mysum(L[1:])

>>> mysum([1, 2, 3, 4, 5])
[1, 2, 3, 4, 5]
[2, 3, 4, 5]
[3, 4, 5]
[4, 5]
[5]
[]
15
```

As you can see, the list to be summed grows smaller at each recursive level, until it becomes empty—the termination of the recursive loop. The sum is computed as the recursive calls unwind on returns.

Coding Alternatives

Interestingly, we can use Python's if/else ternary expression (described in Chapter 12) to save some code real estate here. We can also generalize for any summable type (which is easier if we assume at least one item in the input, as we did in Chapter 18's minimum value example) and use Python 3.X's extended sequence assignment to make the first/rest unpacking simpler (as covered in Chapter 11):

```
def mysum(L):
    return 0 if not L else L[0] + mysum(L[1:])          # Use ternary expression

def mysum(L):
    return L[0] if len(L) == 1 else L[0] + mysum(L[1:])  # Any type, assume one

def mysum(L):
    first, *rest = L
    return first if not rest else first + mysum(rest)    # Use 3.X ext seq assign
```

The latter two of these fail for empty lists but allow for sequences of any object type that supports +, not just numbers:

```
>>> mysum([1])                               # mysum([]) fails in last 2
1
>>> mysum([1, 2, 3, 4, 5])
15
>>> mysum(('s', 'p', 'a', 'm'))              # But various types now work
'spam'
>>> mysum(['spam', 'ham', 'eggs'])
'spamhameggs'
```

Run these on your own for more insight. If you study these three variants, you'll find that:

- The latter two also work on a single string argument (e.g., mysum('spam')), because strings are sequences of one-character strings.

- The third variant works on arbitrary iterables, including open input files (mysum(open(*name*))), but the others do not because they index (Chapter 14 illustrates extended sequence assignment on files).

- The function header def mysum(first, *rest), although similar to the third variant, wouldn't work at all, because it expects individual arguments, not a single iterable.

Keep in mind that recursion can be direct, as in the examples so far, or *indirect*, as in the following (a function that calls another function, which calls back to its caller). The net effect is the same, though there are two function calls at each level instead of one:

```
>>> def mysum(L):
        if not L: return 0
        return nonempty(L)                   # Call a function that calls me

>>> def nonempty(L):
        return L[0] + mysum(L[1:])           # Indirectly recursive

>>> mysum([1.1, 2.2, 3.3, 4.4])
11.0
```

Loop Statements Versus Recursion

Though recursion works for summing in the prior sections' examples, it's probably overkill in this context. In fact, recursion is not used nearly as often in Python as in more esoteric languages like Prolog or Lisp, because Python emphasizes simpler procedural statements like loops, which are usually more natural. The while, for example, often makes things a bit more concrete, and it doesn't require that a function be defined to allow recursive calls:

```
>>> L = [1, 2, 3, 4, 5]
>>> sum = 0
>>> while L:
        sum += L[0]
        L = L[1:]
```

```
>>> sum
15
```

Better yet, for loops iterate for us automatically, making recursion largely extraneous in many cases (and, in all likelihood, less efficient in terms of memory space and execution time):

```
>>> L = [1, 2, 3, 4, 5]
>>> sum = 0
>>> for x in L: sum += x

>>> sum
15
```

With looping statements, we don't require a fresh copy of a local scope on the call stack for each iteration, and we avoid the speed costs associated with function calls in general. (Stay tuned for Chapter 21's timer case study for ways to compare the execution times of alternatives like these.)

Handling Arbitrary Structures

On the other hand, recursion—or equivalent explicit stack-based algorithms we'll meet shortly—can be required to traverse arbitrarily shaped structures. As a simple example of recursion's role in this context, consider the task of computing the sum of all the numbers in a nested sublists structure like this:

```
[1, [2, [3, 4], 5], 6, [7, 8]]                    # Arbitrarily nested sublists
```

Simple looping statements won't work here because this is not a linear iteration. Nested looping statements do not suffice either, because the sublists may be nested to arbitrary depth and in an arbitrary shape—there's no way to know how many nested loops to code to handle all cases. Instead, the following code accommodates such general nesting by using recursion to visit sublists along the way:

```
# file sumtree.py

def sumtree(L):
    tot = 0
    for x in L:                      # For each item at this level
        if not isinstance(x, list):
            tot += x                 # Add numbers directly
        else:
            tot += sumtree(x)        # Recur for sublists
    return tot

L = [1, [2, [3, 4], 5], 6, [7, 8]]   # Arbitrary nesting
print(sumtree(L))                    # Prints 36

# Pathological cases
print(sumtree([1, [2, [3, [4, [5]]]]]))   # Prints 15 (right-heavy)
print(sumtree([[[[[1], 2], 3], 4], 5]))   # Prints 15 (left-heavy)
```

Trace through the test cases at the bottom of this script to see how recursion traverses their nested lists.

Recursion versus queues and stacks

It sometimes helps to understand that internally, Python implements recursion by pushing information on a call stack at each recursive call, so it remembers where it must return and continue later. In fact, it's generally possible to implement recursive-style procedures without recursive calls, by using an explicit stack or queue of your own to keep track of remaining steps.

For instance, the following computes the same sums as the prior example, but uses an explicit list to schedule when it will visit items in the subject, instead of issuing recursive calls; the item at the front of the list is always the next to be processed and summed:

```
def sumtree(L):                            # Breadth-first, explicit queue
    tot = 0
    items = list(L)                        # Start with copy of top level
    while items:
        front = items.pop(0)               # Fetch/delete front item
        if not isinstance(front, list):
            tot += front                   # Add numbers directly
        else:
            items.extend(front)            # <== Append all in nested list
    return tot
```

Technically, this code traverses the list in *breadth-first* fashion by levels, because it adds nested lists' contents to the end of the list, forming a first-in-first-out *queue*. To emulate the traversal of the recursive call version more closely, we can change it to perform *depth-first* traversal simply by adding the content of nested lists to the front of the list, forming a last-in-first-out *stack*:

```
def sumtree(L):                            # Depth-first, explicit stack
    tot = 0
    items = list(L)                        # Start with copy of top level
    while items:
        front = items.pop(0)               # Fetch/delete front item
        if not isinstance(front, list):
            tot += front                   # Add numbers directly
        else:
            items[:0] = front              # <== Prepend all in nested list
    return tot
```

For more on the last two examples (and another variant), see file *sumtree2.py* in the book's examples. It adds items list tracing so you can watch it grow in both schemes, and can show numbers as they are visited so you see the search order. For instance, the breadth-first and depth-first variants visit items in the same three test lists used for the recursive version in the following orders, respectively (sums are shown last):

```
c:\code> sumtree2.py
1, 6, 2, 5, 7, 8, 3, 4, 36
1, 2, 3, 4, 5, 15
```

```
5, 4, 3, 2, 1, 15
----------------------------------------
1, 2, 3, 4, 5, 6, 7, 8, 36
1, 2, 3, 4, 5, 15
1, 2, 3, 4, 5, 15
----------------------------------------
```

In general, though, once you get the hang of recursive calls, they are more natural than the explicit scheduling lists they automate, and are generally preferred unless you need to traverse structure in specialized ways. Some programs, for example, perform a *best-first* search that requires an explicit search queue ordered by relevance or other criteria. If you think of a web crawler that scores pages visited by content, the applications may start to become clearer.

Cycles, paths, and stack limits

As is, these programs suffice for our example, but larger recursive applications can sometimes require a bit more infrastructure than shown here: they may need to avoid cycles or repeats, record paths taken for later use, and expand stack space when using recursive calls instead of explicit queues or stacks.

For instance, neither the recursive call nor the explicit queue/stack examples in this section do anything about avoiding *cycles*—visiting a location already visited. That's not required here, because we're traversing strictly hierarchical list object trees. If data can be a cyclic graph, though, both these schemes will fail: the recursive call version will fall into an infinite recursive loop (and may run out of call-stack space), and the others will fall into simple infinite loops, re-adding the same items to their lists (and may or may not run out of general memory). Some programs also need to avoid repeated processing for a state reached more than once, even if that wouldn't lead to a loop.

To do better, the recursive call version could simply keep and pass a set, dictionary, or list of states visited so far and check for repeats as it goes. We will use this scheme in later recursive examples in this book:

```
if state not in visited:
    visited.add(state)          # x.add(state), x[state]=True, or x.append(state)
    ...proceed...
```

The nonrecursive alternatives could similarly avoid adding states already visited with code like the following. Note that checking for duplicates already on the items list would avoid scheduling a state twice, but would not prevent revisiting a state traversed earlier and hence removed from that list:

```
visited.add(front)
...proceed...
items.extend([x for x in front if x not in visited])
```

This model doesn't quite apply to this section's use case that simply adds numbers in lists, but larger applications will be able to identify repeated states—a URL of a previously visited web page, for instance. In fact, we'll use such techniques to avoid cycles and repeats in later examples listed in the next section.

Some programs may also need to record complete *paths* for each state followed so they can report solutions when finished. In such cases, each item in the nonrecursive scheme's stack or queue may be a full path list that suffices for a record of states visited, and contains the next item to explore at either end.

Also note that standard Python limits the *depth* of its runtime call stack—crucial to recursive call programs—to trap infinite recursion errors. To expand it, use the **sys** module:

```
>>> sys.getrecursionlimit()          # 1000 calls deep default
1000
>>> sys.setrecursionlimit(10000)     # Allow deeper nesting
>>> help(sys.setrecursionlimit)      # Read more about it
```

The maximum allowed setting can vary per platform. This isn't required for programs that use stacks or queues to avoid recursive calls and gain more control over the traversal process.

More recursion examples

Although this section's example is artificial, it is representative of a larger class of programs; inheritance trees and module import chains, for example, can exhibit similarly general structures, and computing structures such as permutations can require arbitrarily many nested loops. In fact, we will use recursion again in such roles in more realistic examples later in this book:

- In Chapter 20's *permute.py*, to shuffle arbitrary sequences
- In Chapter 25's *reloadall.py*, to traverse import chains
- In Chapter 29's *classtree.py*, to traverse class inheritance trees
- In Chapter 31's *lister.py*, to traverse class inheritance trees again
- In Appendix D's solutions to two exercises at the end of this part of the book: countdowns and factorials

The second and third of these will also detect states already visited to avoid cycles and repeats. Although simple loops should generally be preferred to recursion for linear iterations on the grounds of simplicity and efficiency, we'll find that recursion is essential in scenarios like those in these later examples.

Moreover, you sometimes need to be aware of the potential of *unintended* recursion in your programs. As you'll also see later in the book, some operator overloading methods in classes such as __setattr__ and __getattribute__ and even __repr__ have the potential to recursively loop if used incorrectly. Recursion is a powerful tool, but it tends to be best when both understood and expected!

Function Objects: Attributes and Annotations

Python functions are more flexible than you might think. As we've seen in this part of the book, functions in Python are much more than code-generation specifications for a compiler—Python functions are full-blown *objects*, stored in pieces of memory all their own. As such, they can be freely passed around a program and called indirectly. They also support operations that have little to do with calls at all—attribute storage and annotation.

Indirect Function Calls: "First Class" Objects

Because Python functions are objects, you can write programs that process them generically. Function objects may be assigned to other names, passed to other functions, embedded in data structures, returned from one function to another, and more, as if they were simple numbers or strings. Function objects also happen to support a special operation: they can be called by listing arguments in parentheses after a function expression. Still, functions belong to the same general category as other objects.

This is usually called a *first-class object model*; it's ubiquitous in Python, and a necessary part of functional programming. We'll explore this programming mode more fully in this and the next chapter; because its motif is founded on the notion of applying functions, functions must be treated as data.

We've seen some of these generic use cases for functions in earlier examples, but a quick review helps to underscore the object model. For example, there's really nothing special about the name used in a def statement: it's just a variable assigned in the current scope, as if it had appeared on the left of an = sign. After a def runs, the function name is simply a reference to an object—you can *reassign* that object to other names freely and call it through any reference:

```
>>> def echo(message):          # Name echo assigned to function object
        print(message)

>>> echo('Direct call')         # Call object through original name
Direct call

>>> x = echo                    # Now x references the function too
>>> x('Indirect call!')         # Call object through name by adding ()
Indirect call!
```

Because arguments are passed by assigning objects, it's just as easy to *pass* functions to other functions as arguments. The callee may then call the passed-in function just by adding arguments in parentheses:

```
>>> def indirect(func, arg):
        func(arg)               # Call the passed-in object by adding ()

>>> indirect(echo, 'Argument call!')   # Pass the function to another function
Argument call!
```

You can even stuff function objects into data structures, as though they were integers or strings. The following, for example, *embeds* the function twice in a list of tuples, as a sort of actions table. Because Python compound types like these can contain any sort of object, there's no special case here, either:

```
>>> schedule = [ (echo, 'Spam!'), (echo, 'Ham!') ]
>>> for (func, arg) in schedule:
        func(arg)                        # Call functions embedded in containers

Spam!
Ham!
```

This code simply steps through the schedule list, calling the echo function with one argument each time through (notice the tuple-unpacking assignment in the for loop header, introduced in Chapter 13). As we saw in Chapter 17's examples, functions can also be created and *returned* for use elsewhere—the *closure* created in this mode also retains state from the enclosing scope:

```
>>> def make(label):                     # Make a function but don't call it
        def echo(message):
            print(label + ':' + message)
        return echo

>>> F = make('Spam')                     # Label in enclosing scope is retained
>>> F('Ham!')                            # Call the function that make returned
Spam:Ham!
>>> F('Eggs!')
Spam:Eggs!
```

Python's universal first-class object model and lack of type declarations make for an incredibly flexible programming language.

Function Introspection

Because they are objects, we can also process functions with normal object tools. In fact, functions are more flexible than you might expect. For instance, once we make a function, we can call it as usual:

```
>>> def func(a):
        b = 'spam'
        return b * a

>>> func(8)
'spamspamspamspamspamspamspamspam'
```

But the call expression is just one operation defined to work on function objects. We can also inspect their attributes generically (the following is run in Python 3.3, but 2.X results are similar):

```
>>> func.__name__
'func'
>>> dir(func)
['__annotations__', '__call__', '__class__', '__closure__', '__code__',
```

```
...more omitted: 34 total...
'__repr__', '__setattr__', '__sizeof__', '__str__', '__subclasshook__']
```

Introspection tools allow us to explore implementation details too—functions have attached *code objects*, for example, which provide details on aspects such as the functions' local variables and arguments:

```
>>> func.__code__
<code object func at 0x00000000021A6030, file "<stdin>", line 1>

>>> dir(func.__code__)
['__class__', '__delattr__', '__dir__', '__doc__', '__eq__', '__format__', '__ge__',
...more omitted: 37 total...
'co_argcount', 'co_cellvars', 'co_code', 'co_consts', 'co_filename',
'co_firstlineno', 'co_flags', 'co_freevars', 'co_kwonlyargcount', 'co_lnotab',
'co_name', 'co_names', 'co_nlocals', 'co_stacksize', 'co_varnames']

>>> func.__code__.co_varnames
('a', 'b')
>>> func.__code__.co_argcount
1
```

Tool writers can make use of such information to manage functions (in fact, we will too in Chapter 39, to implement validation of function arguments in decorators).

Function Attributes

Function objects are not limited to the system-defined attributes listed in the prior section, though. As we learned in Chapter 17, it's been possible to attach arbitrary *user-defined* attributes to them as well since Python 2.1:

```
>>> func
<function func at 0x000000000296A1E0>
>>> func.count = 0
>>> func.count += 1
>>> func.count
1
>>> func.handles = 'Button-Press'
>>> func.handles
'Button-Press'
>>> dir(func)
['__annotations__', '__call__', '__class__', '__closure__', '__code__',
...and more: in 3.X all others have double underscores so your names won't clash...
__str__', '__subclasshook__', 'count', 'handles']
```

Python's own implementation-related data stored on functions follows naming conventions that prevent them from clashing with the more arbitrary attribute names you might assign yourself. In 3.X, all function internals' names have leading and trailing double underscores ("__X__"); 2.X follows the same scheme, but also assigns some names that begin with "func_X":

```
c:\code> py -3
>>> def f(): pass
```

```
>>> dir(f)
...run on your own to see...
>>> len(dir(f))
34
>>> [x for x in dir(f) if not x.startswith('__')]
[]

c:\code> py -2
>>> def f(): pass

>>> dir(f)
...run on your own to see...
>>> len(dir(f))
31
>>> [x for x in dir(f) if not x.startswith('__')]
['func_closure', 'func_code', 'func_defaults', 'func_dict', 'func_doc',
 'func_globals', 'func_name']
```

If you're careful not to name attributes the same way, you can safely use the function's namespace as though it were your own namespace or scope.

As we saw in that chapter, such attributes can be used to attach *state information* to function objects directly, instead of using other techniques such as globals, nonlocals, and classes. Unlike nonlocals, such attributes are accessible anywhere the function itself is, even from outside its code.

In a sense, this is also a way to emulate "static locals" in other languages—variables whose names are local to a function, but whose values are retained after a function exits. Attributes are related to objects instead of scopes (and must be referenced through the function name within its code), but the net effect is similar.

Moreover, as we learned in Chapter 17, when attributes are attached to functions generated by other *factory* functions, they also support multiple copy, per-call, and writeable state retention, much like nonlocal closures and class instance attributes.

Function Annotations in 3.X

In Python 3.X (but not 2.X), it's also possible to attach *annotation information*—arbitrary user-defined data about a function's arguments and result—to a function object. Python provides special syntax for specifying annotations, but it doesn't do anything with them itself; annotations are completely optional, and when present are simply attached to the function object's __annotations__ attribute for use by other tools. For instance, such a tool might use annotations in the context of error testing.

We met Python 3.X's keyword-only arguments in the preceding chapter; annotations generalize function header syntax further. Consider the following nonannotated function, which is coded with three arguments and returns a result:

```
>>> def func(a, b, c):
        return a + b + c
```

```
>>> func(1, 2, 3)
6
```

Syntactically, function annotations are coded in def header lines, as arbitrary expressions associated with arguments and return values. For arguments, they appear after a colon immediately following the argument's name; for return values, they are written after a -> following the arguments list. This code, for example, annotates all three of the prior function's arguments, as well as its return value:

```
>>> def func(a: 'spam', b: (1, 10), c: float) -> int:
        return a + b + c

>>> func(1, 2, 3)
6
```

Calls to an annotated function work as usual, but when annotations are present Python collects them in a *dictionary* and attaches it to the function object itself. Argument names become keys, the return value annotation is stored under key "return" if coded (which suffices because this reserved word can't be used as an argument name), and the values of annotation keys are assigned to the results of the annotation expressions:

```
>>> func.__annotations__
{'c': <class 'float'>, 'b': (1, 10), 'a': 'spam', 'return': <class 'int'>}
```

Because they are just Python objects attached to a Python object, annotations are straightforward to process. The following annotates just two of three arguments and steps through the attached annotations generically:

```
>>> def func(a: 'spam', b, c: 99):
        return a + b + c

>>> func(1, 2, 3)
6
>>> func.__annotations__
{'c': 99, 'a': 'spam'}

>>> for arg in func.__annotations__:
        print(arg, '=>', func.__annotations__[arg])

c => 99
a => spam
```

There are two fine points to note here. First, you can still use *defaults* for arguments if you code annotations—the annotation (and its : character) appear before the default (and its = character). In the following, for example, a: 'spam' = 4 means that argument a defaults to 4 and is annotated with the string 'spam':

```
>>> def func(a: 'spam' = 4, b: (1, 10) = 5, c: float = 6) -> int:
        return a + b + c

>>> func(1, 2, 3)
6
>>> func()                          # 4 + 5 + 6  (all defaults)
15
```

```
>>> func(1, c=10)                       # 1 + 5 + 10  (keywords work normally)
16
>>> func.__annotations__
{'c': <class 'float'>, 'b': (1, 10), 'a': 'spam', 'return': <class 'int'>}
```

Second, note that the *blank spaces* in the prior example are all optional—you can use spaces between components in function headers or not, but omitting them might degrade your code's readability to some observers (and probably improve it to others!):

```
>>> def func(a:'spam'=4, b:(1,10)=5, c:float=6)->int:
        return a + b + c

>>> func(1, 2)                          # 1 + 2 + 6
9
>>> func.__annotations__
{'c': <class 'float'>, 'b': (1, 10), 'a': 'spam', 'return': <class 'int'>}
```

Annotations are a new feature in 3.X, and some of their potential uses remain to be uncovered. It's easy to imagine annotations being used to specify constraints for argument types or values, though, and larger APIs might use this feature as a way to register function interface information.

In fact, we'll see a potential application in Chapter 39, where we'll look at annotations as an alternative to *function decorator arguments*—a more general concept in which information is coded outside the function header and so is not limited to a single role. Like Python itself, annotation is a tool whose roles are shaped by your imagination.

Finally, note that annotations work only in `def` statements, not `lambda` expressions, because `lambda`'s syntax already limits the utility of the functions it defines. Coincidentally, this brings us to our next topic.

Anonymous Functions: lambda

Besides the `def` statement, Python also provides an expression form that generates function objects. Because of its similarity to a tool in the Lisp language, it's called `lambda`.[1] Like `def`, this expression creates a function to be called later, but it returns the function instead of assigning it to a name. This is why `lambda`s are sometimes known as *anonymous* (i.e., unnamed) functions. In practice, they are often used as a way to inline a function definition, or to defer execution of a piece of code.

---

1. The `lambda` tends to intimidate people more than it should. This reaction seems to stem from the name "lambda" itself—a name that comes from the Lisp language, which got it from lambda calculus, which is a form of symbolic logic. In Python, though, it's really just a keyword that introduces the expression syntactically. Obscure mathematical heritage aside, `lambda` is simpler to use than you may think: it's simply an alternative way to code a function, albeit without full statements, decorators, or 3.X annotations.

lambda Basics

The `lambda`'s general form is the keyword `lambda`, followed by one or more arguments (exactly like the arguments list you enclose in parentheses in a `def` header), followed by an expression after a colon:

```
lambda argument1, argument2,... argumentN : expression using arguments
```

Function objects returned by running `lambda` expressions work exactly the same as those created and assigned by `def`s, but there are a few differences that make `lambda`s useful in specialized roles:

- **`lambda` is an expression, not a statement**. Because of this, a `lambda` can appear in places a `def` is not allowed by Python's syntax—inside a list literal or a function call's arguments, for example. With `def`, functions can be referenced by name but must be created elsewhere. As an expression, `lambda` returns a value (a new function) that can optionally be assigned a name. In contrast, the `def` statement always assigns the new function to the name in the header, instead of returning it as a result.

- **`lambda`'s body is a single expression, not a block of statements**. The `lambda`'s body is similar to what you'd put in a `def` body's `return` statement; you simply type the result as a naked expression, instead of explicitly returning it. Because it is limited to an expression, a `lambda` is less general than a `def`—you can only squeeze so much logic into a `lambda` body without using statements such as `if`. This is by design, to limit program nesting: `lambda` is designed for coding simple functions, and `def` handles larger tasks.

Apart from those distinctions, `def`s and `lambda`s do the same sort of work. For instance, we've seen how to make a function with a `def` statement:

```
>>> def func(x, y, z): return x + y + z

>>> func(2, 3, 4)
9
```

But you can achieve the same effect with a `lambda` expression by explicitly assigning its result to a name through which you can later call the function:

```
>>> f = lambda x, y, z: x + y + z
>>> f(2, 3, 4)
9
```

Here, `f` is assigned the function object the `lambda` expression creates; this is how `def` works, too, but its assignment is automatic.

Defaults work on `lambda` arguments, just like in a `def`:

```
>>> x = (lambda a="fee", b="fie", c="foe": a + b + c)
>>> x("wee")
'weefiefoe'
```

The code in a `lambda` body also follows the same scope lookup rules as code inside a `def`. `lambda` expressions introduce a local scope much like a nested `def`, which automatically sees names in enclosing functions, the module, and the built-in scope (via the LEGB rule, and per Chapter 17):

```
>>> def knights():
        title = 'Sir'
        action = (lambda x: title + ' ' + x)    # Title in enclosing def scope
        return action                            # Return a function object

>>> act = knights()
>>> msg = act('robin')                           # 'robin' passed to x
>>> msg
'Sir robin'

>>> act                                          # act: a function, not its result
<function knights.<locals>.<lambda> at 0x00000000029CA488>
```

In this example, prior to Release 2.2, the value for the name `title` would typically have been passed in as a default argument value instead; flip back to the scopes coverage in Chapter 17 if you've forgotten why.

Why Use lambda?

Generally speaking, `lambda` comes in handy as a sort of function shorthand that allows you to embed a function's definition within the code that uses it. They are entirely optional—you can always use `def` instead, and *should* if your function requires the power of full statements that the `lambda`'s expression cannot easily provide—but they tend to be simpler coding constructs in scenarios where you just need to embed small bits of executable code inline at the place it is to be used.

For instance, we'll see later that callback handlers are frequently coded as inline `lambda` expressions embedded directly in a registration call's arguments list, instead of being defined with a `def` elsewhere in a file and referenced by name (see the sidebar "Why You Will Care: lambda Callbacks" on page 573 for an example).

`lambda` is also commonly used to code *jump tables*, which are lists or dictionaries of actions to be performed on demand. For example:

```
L = [lambda x: x ** 2,            # Inline function definition
     lambda x: x ** 3,
     lambda x: x ** 4]            # A list of three callable functions

for f in L:
    print(f(2))                   # Prints 4, 8, 16

print(L[0](3))                    # Prints 9
```

The `lambda` expression is most useful as a shorthand for `def`, when you need to stuff small pieces of executable code into places where statements are illegal syntactically. The preceding code snippet, for example, builds up a list of three functions by embedding `lambda` expressions inside a list literal; a `def` won't work inside a list literal like this because it is a statement, not an expression. The equivalent `def` coding would require temporary function names (which might clash with others) and function definitions outside the context of intended use (which might be hundreds of lines away):

```
def f1(x): return x ** 2
def f2(x): return x ** 3          # Define named functions
def f3(x): return x ** 4

L = [f1, f2, f3]                  # Reference by name

for f in L:
    print(f(2))                   # Prints 4, 8, 16

print(L[0](3))                    # Prints 9
```

Multiway branch switches: The finale

In fact, you can do the same sort of thing with dictionaries and other data structures in Python to build up more general sorts of action tables. Here's another example to illustrate, at the interactive prompt:

```
>>> key = 'got'
>>> {'already': (lambda: 2 + 2),
     'got':     (lambda: 2 * 4),
     'one':     (lambda: 2 ** 6)}[key]()
8
```

Here, when Python makes the temporary dictionary, each of the nested `lambda`s generates and leaves behind a function to be called later. Indexing by key fetches one of those functions, and parentheses force the fetched function to be called. When coded this way, a dictionary becomes a more general multiway branching tool than what I could fully show you in Chapter 12's coverage of `if` statements.

To make this work without `lambda`, you'd need to instead code three `def` statements somewhere else in your file, outside the dictionary in which the functions are to be used, and reference the functions by name:

```
>>> def f1(): return 2 + 2

>>> def f2(): return 2 * 4

>>> def f3(): return 2 ** 6

>>> key = 'one'
>>> {'already': f1, 'got': f2, 'one': f3}[key]()
64
```

This works, too, but your `def`s may be arbitrarily far away in your file, even if they are just little bits of code. The *code proximity* that `lambda`s provide is especially useful for functions that will only be used in a single context—if the three functions here are not useful anywhere else, it makes sense to embed their definitions within the dictionary as `lambda`s. Moreover, the `def` form requires you to make up names for these little functions that may clash with other names in this file (perhaps unlikely, but always possible).[2]

`lambda`s also come in handy in function-call argument lists as a way to inline temporary function definitions not used anywhere else in your program; we'll see some examples of such other uses later in this chapter, when we study `map`.

How (Not) to Obfuscate Your Python Code

The fact that the body of a `lambda` has to be a single expression (not a series of statements) would seem to place severe limits on how much logic you can pack into a `lambda`. If you know what you're doing, though, you can code most statements in Python as expression-based equivalents.

For example, if you want to *print* from the body of a lambda function, simply say `print(X)` in Python 3.X where this becomes a call expression instead of a statement, or say `sys.stdout.write(str(X)+'\n')` in either Python 2.X or 3.X to make sure it's an expression portably (recall from Chapter 11 that this is what `print` really does). Similarly, to nest *selection* logic in a `lambda`, you can use the `if`/`else` ternary expression introduced in Chapter 12, or the equivalent but trickier `and`/`or` combination also described there. As you learned earlier, the following statement:

```
if a:
    b
else:
    c
```

can be emulated by either of these roughly equivalent expressions:

```
b if a else c
((a and b) or c)
```

Because expressions like these can be placed inside a `lambda`, they may be used to implement selection logic within a `lambda` function:

```
>>> lower = (lambda x, y: x if x < y else y)
>>> lower('bb', 'aa')
'aa'
>>> lower('aa', 'bb')
'aa'
```

---

2. A student once noted that you could skip the dispatch table dictionary in such code if the function name is the same as its string lookup key—run an `eval(funcname)()` to kick off the call. While true in this case and sometimes useful, as we saw earlier (e.g., Chapter 10), `eval` is relatively slow (it must compile and run code), and insecure (you must trust the string's source). More fundamentally, jump tables are generally subsumed by polymorphic method dispatch in Python: calling a method does the "right thing" based on the type of object. To see why, stay tuned for Part VI.

Furthermore, if you need to perform *loops* within a `lambda`, you can also embed things like `map` calls and list comprehension expressions—tools we met in earlier chapters and will revisit in this and the next chapter:

```
>>> import sys
>>> showall = lambda x: list(map(sys.stdout.write, x))     # 3.X: must use list
>>> t = showall(['spam\n', 'toast\n', 'eggs\n'])            # 3.X: can use print
spam
toast
eggs
>>> showall = lambda x: [sys.stdout.write(line) for line in x]
>>> t = showall(('bright\n', 'side\n', 'of\n', 'life\n'))
bright
side
of
life
>>> showall = lambda x: [print(line, end='') for line in x]   # Same: 3.X only
>>> showall = lambda x: print(*x, sep='', end='')             # Same: 3.X only
```

There is a limit to emulating statements with expressions: you can't directly achieve an assignment statement's effect, for instance, though tools like the `setattr` built-in, the `__dict__` of namespaces, and methods that change mutable objects in place can sometimes stand in, and functional programming techniques can take you deep into the dark realm of convoluted expression.

Now that I've shown you these tricks, I am required to ask you to please only use them as a last resort. Without due care, they can lead to unreadable (a.k.a. *obfuscated*) Python code. In general, simple is better than complex, explicit is better than implicit, and full statements are better than arcane expressions. That's why `lambda` is limited to expressions. If you have larger logic to code, use `def`; `lambda` is for small pieces of inline code. On the other hand, you may find these techniques useful in moderation.

Scopes: lambdas Can Be Nested Too

`lambda`s are the main beneficiaries of nested function scope lookup (the *E* in the LEGB scope rule we studied in Chapter 17). As a review, in the following the `lambda` appears inside a `def`—the typical case—and so can access the value that the name x had in the enclosing function's scope at the time that the enclosing function was called:

```
>>> def action(x):
        return (lambda y: x + y)      # Make and return function, remember x

>>> act = action(99)
>>> act
<function action.<locals>.<lambda> at 0x00000000029CA2F0>
>>> act(2)                            # Call what action returned
101
```

What wasn't illustrated in the prior discussion of nested function scopes is that a `lambda` also has access to the names in any enclosing `lambda`. This case is somewhat obscure, but imagine if we recoded the prior `def` with a `lambda`:

```
>>> action = (lambda x: (lambda y: x + y))
>>> act = action(99)
>>> act(3)
102
>>> ((lambda x: (lambda y: x + y))(99))(4)
103
```

Here, the nested `lambda` structure makes a function that makes a function when called. In both cases, the nested `lambda`'s code has access to the variable `x` in the enclosing `lambda`. This works, but it seems fairly convoluted code; in the interest of readability, nested `lambda`s are generally best avoided.

Why You Will Care: lambda Callbacks

Another very common application of `lambda` is to define inline callback functions for Python's `tkinter` GUI API (this module is named `Tkinter` in Python 2.X). For example, the following creates a button that prints a message on the console when pressed, assuming `tkinter` is available on your computer (it is by default on Windows, Mac, Linux, and other OSs):

```
import sys
from tkinter import Button, mainloop   # Tkinter in 2.X
x = Button(
        text='Press me',
        command=(lambda:sys.stdout.write('Spam\n')))  # 3.X: print()
x.pack()
mainloop()  # This may be optional in console mode
```

Here, we register the callback handler by passing a function generated with a `lambda` to the `command` keyword argument. The advantage of `lambda` over `def` here is that the code that handles a button press is right here, embedded in the button-creation call.

In effect, the `lambda` *defers* execution of the handler until the event occurs: the `write` call happens on button presses, not when the button is created, and effectively "knows" the string it should write when the event occurs.

Because the nested function scope rules apply to `lambda`s as well, they are also easier to use as callback handlers, as of Python 2.2—they automatically see names in the functions in which they are coded and no longer require passed-in defaults in most cases. This is especially handy for accessing the special `self` instance argument that is a local variable in enclosing class method functions (more on classes in Part VI):

```
class MyGui:
    def makewidgets(self):
        Button(command=(lambda: self.onPress("spam")))
    def onPress(self, message):
        ...use message...
```

In early versions of Python, even `self` had to be passed in to a `lambda` with defaults. As we'll see later, class objects with `__call__` and *bound methods* often serve in callback roles too—watch for coverage of these in Chapter 30 and Chapter 31.

Functional Programming Tools

By most definitions, today's Python blends support for multiple programming paradigms: procedural (with its basic statements), object-oriented (with its classes), and functional. For the latter of these, Python includes a set of built-ins used for *functional programming*—tools that apply functions to sequences and other iterables. This set includes tools that call functions on an iterable's items (map); filter out items based on a test function (`filter`); and apply functions to pairs of items and running results (`reduce`).

Though the boundaries are sometimes a bit grey, by most definitions Python's functional programming arsenal also includes the *first-class object* model explored earlier, the nested scope *closures* and anonymous function *lambdas* we met earlier in this part of the book, the *generators* and *comprehensions* we'll be expanding on in the next chapter, and perhaps the function and class *decorators* of this book's final part. For our purposes here, let's wrap up this chapter with a quick survey of built-in functions that apply other functions to iterables automatically.

Mapping Functions over Iterables: map

One of the more common things programs do with lists and other sequences is apply an operation to each item and collect the results—selecting columns in database tables, incrementing pay fields of employees in a company, parsing email attachments, and so on. Python has multiple tools that make such collection-wide operations easy to code. For instance, updating all the counters in a list can be done easily with a `for` loop:

```
>>> counters = [1, 2, 3, 4]
>>>
>>> updated = []
>>> for x in counters:
        updated.append(x + 10)          # Add 10 to each item

>>> updated
[11, 12, 13, 14]
```

But because this is such a common operation, Python also provides built-ins that do most of the work for you. The `map` function applies a passed-in function to each item in an iterable object and returns a list containing all the function call results. For example:

```
>>> def inc(x): return x + 10           # Function to be run

>>> list(map(inc, counters))            # Collect results
[11, 12, 13, 14]
```

We met `map` briefly in Chapter 13 and Chapter 14, as a way to apply a built-in function to items in an iterable. Here, we make more general use of it by passing in a *user-defined* function to be applied to each item in the list—map calls `inc` on each list item and collects all the return values into a new list. Remember that map is an iterable in

Python 3.X, so a `list` call is used to force it to produce all its results for display here; this isn't necessary in 2.X (see Chapter 14 if you've forgotten this requirement).

Because `map` expects a function to be passed in and applied, it also happens to be one of the places where `lambda` commonly appears:

```
>>> list(map((lambda x: x + 3), counters))      # Function expression
[4, 5, 6, 7]
```

Here, the function adds 3 to each item in the `counters` list; as this little function isn't needed elsewhere, it was written inline as a `lambda`. Because such uses of `map` are equivalent to `for` loops, with a little extra code you can always code a general mapping utility yourself:

```
>>> def mymap(func, seq):
        res = []
        for x in seq: res.append(func(x))
        return res
```

Assuming the function `inc` is still as it was when it was shown previously, we can map it across a sequence (or other iterable) with either the built-in or our equivalent:

```
>>> list(map(inc, [1, 2, 3]))          # Built-in is an iterable
[11, 12, 13]
>>> mymap(inc, [1, 2, 3])              # Ours builds a list (see generators)
[11, 12, 13]
```

However, as `map` is a built-in, it's always available, always works the same way, and has some performance benefits (as we'll prove in Chapter 21, it's faster than a manually coded `for` loop in some usage modes). Moreover, `map` can be used in more advanced ways than shown here. For instance, given multiple sequence arguments, it sends items taken from sequences in parallel as distinct arguments to the function:

```
>>> pow(3, 4)                          # 3**4
81
>>> list(map(pow, [1, 2, 3], [2, 3, 4]))   # 1**2, 2**3, 3**4
[1, 8, 81]
```

With multiple sequences, `map` expects an N-argument function for N sequences. Here, the `pow` function takes two arguments on each call—one from each sequence passed to `map`. It's not much extra work to simulate this multiple-sequence generality in code, too, but we'll postpone doing so until later in the next chapter, after we've met some additional iteration tools.

The `map` call is similar to the list comprehension expressions we studied in Chapter 14 and will revisit in the next chapter from a functional perspective:

```
>>> list(map(inc, [1, 2, 3, 4]))
[11, 12, 13, 14]
>>> [inc(x) for x in [1, 2, 3, 4]]     # Use () parens to generate items instead
[11, 12, 13, 14]
```

In some cases, `map` may be faster to run than a list comprehension (e.g., when mapping a built-in function), and it may also require less coding. On the other hand, because `map` applies a *function* call to each item instead of an arbitrary *expression*, it is a somewhat less general tool, and often requires extra helper functions or `lambda`s. Moreover, wrapping a comprehension in parentheses instead of square brackets creates an object that *generates* values on request to save memory and increase responsiveness, much like `map` in 3.X—a topic we'll take up in the next chapter.

Selecting Items in Iterables: filter

The `map` function is a primary and relatively straightforward representative of Python's functional programming toolset. Its close relatives, `filter` and `reduce`, select an iterable's items based on a test function and apply functions to item pairs, respectively.

Because it also returns an iterable, `filter` (like `range`) requires a `list` call to display all its results in 3.X. For example, the following `filter` call picks out items in a sequence that are greater than zero:

```
>>> list(range(-5, 5))                          # An iterable in 3.X
[-5, -4, -3, -2, -1, 0, 1, 2, 3, 4]

>>> list(filter((lambda x: x > 0), range(-5, 5)))    # An iterable in 3.X
[1, 2, 3, 4]
```

We met `filter` briefly earlier in a Chapter 12 sidebar, and while exploring 3.X iterables in Chapter 14. Items in the sequence or iterable for which the function returns a true result are added to the result list. Like `map`, this function is roughly equivalent to a `for` loop, but it is built-in, concise, and often fast:

```
>>> res = []
>>> for x in range(-5, 5):              # The statement equivalent
        if x > 0:
            res.append(x)

>>> res
[1, 2, 3, 4]
```

Also like `map`, `filter` can be emulated by *list comprehension* syntax with often-simpler results (especially when it can avoid creating a new function), and with a similar *generator expression* when delayed production of results is desired—though we'll save the rest of this story for the next chapter:

```
>>> [x for x in range(-5, 5) if x > 0]          # Use () to generate items
[1, 2, 3, 4]
```

Combining Items in Iterables: reduce

The functional `reduce` call, which is a simple built-in function in 2.X but lives in the `functools` module in 3.X, is more complex. It accepts an iterable to process, but it's not an iterable itself—it returns a single result. Here are two `reduce` calls that compute the sum and product of the items in a list:

```
>>> from functools import reduce                    # Import in 3.X, not in 2.X
>>> reduce((lambda x, y: x + y), [1, 2, 3, 4])
10
>>> reduce((lambda x, y: x * y), [1, 2, 3, 4])
24
```

At each step, reduce passes the current sum or product, along with the next item from the list, to the passed-in lambda function. By default, the first item in the sequence initializes the starting value. To illustrate, here's the for loop equivalent to the first of these calls, with the addition hardcoded inside the loop:

```
>>> L = [1,2,3,4]
>>> res = L[0]
>>> for x in L[1:]:
        res = res + x

>>> res
10
```

Coding your own version of reduce is actually fairly straightforward. The following function emulates most of the built-in's behavior and helps demystify its operation in general:

```
>>> def myreduce(function, sequence):
        tally = sequence[0]
        for next in sequence[1:]:
            tally = function(tally, next)
        return tally

>>> myreduce((lambda x, y: x + y), [1, 2, 3, 4, 5])
15
>>> myreduce((lambda x, y: x * y), [1, 2, 3, 4, 5])
120
```

The built-in reduce also allows an optional third argument placed before the items in the sequence to serve as a default result when the sequence is empty, but we'll leave this extension as a suggested exercise.

If this coding technique has sparked your interest, you might also be interested in the standard library operator module, which provides functions that correspond to built-in expressions and so comes in handy for some uses of functional tools (see Python's library manual for more details on this module):

```
>>> import operator, functools
>>> functools.reduce(operator.add, [2, 4, 6])       # Function-based +
12
>>> functools.reduce((lambda x, y: x + y), [2, 4, 6])
12
```

Together, map, filter, and reduce support powerful functional programming techniques. As mentioned, many observers would also extend the functional programming toolset in Python to include nested function scope closures (a.k.a. factory functions) and the anonymous function lambda—both discussed earlier—as well as *generators* and *comprehensions*, topics we will return to in the next chapter.

Chapter Summary

This chapter took us on a tour of advanced function-related concepts: recursive functions; function annotations; `lambda` expression functions; functional tools such as `map`, `filter`, and `reduce`; and general function design ideas. The next chapter continues the advanced topics motif with a look at generators and a reprisal of iterables and list comprehensions—tools that are just as related to functional programming as to looping statements. Before you move on, though, make sure you've mastered the concepts covered here by working through this chapter's quiz.

Test Your Knowledge: Quiz

1. How are `lambda` expressions and `def` statements related?
2. What's the point of using `lambda`?
3. Compare and contrast `map`, `filter`, and `reduce`.
4. What are function annotations, and how are they used?
5. What are recursive functions, and how are they used?
6. What are some general design guidelines for coding functions?
7. Name three or more ways that functions can communicate results to a caller.

Test Your Knowledge: Answers

1. Both `lambda` and `def` create function objects to be called later. Because `lambda` is an expression, though, it returns a function object instead of assigning it to a name, and it can be used to nest a function definition in places where a `def` will not work syntactically. A `lambda` allows for only a single implicit return value expression, though; because it does not support a block of statements, it is not ideal for larger functions.

2. `lambda`s allow us to "inline" small units of executable code, defer its execution, and provide it with state in the form of default arguments and enclosing scope variables. Using a `lambda` is never required; you can always code a `def` instead and reference the function by name. `lambda`s come in handy, though, to embed small pieces of deferred code that are unlikely to be used elsewhere in a program. They commonly appear in callback-based programs such as GUIs, and they have a natural affinity with functional tools like `map` and `filter` that expect a processing function.

3. These three built-in functions all apply another function to items in a sequence (or other iterable) object and collect results. `map` passes each item to the function and collects all results, `filter` collects items for which the function returns a `True` value, and `reduce` computes a single value by applying the function to an accumulator

and successive items. Unlike the other two, `reduce` is available in the `functools` module in 3.X, not the built-in scope; `reduce` is a built-in in 2.X.

4. Function annotations, available in 3.X (3.0 and later), are syntactic embellishments of a function's arguments and result, which are collected into a dictionary assigned to the function's `__annotations__` attribute. Python places no semantic meaning on these annotations, but simply packages them for potential use by other tools.

5. Recursive functions call themselves either directly or indirectly in order to loop. They may be used to traverse arbitrarily shaped structures, but they can also be used for iteration in general (though the latter role is often more simply and efficiently coded with looping statements). Recursion can often be simulated or replaced by code that uses explicit stacks or queues to have more control over traversals.

6. Functions should generally be small and as self-contained as possible, have a single unified purpose, and communicate with other components through input arguments and return values. They may use mutable arguments to communicate results too if changes are expected, and some types of programs imply other communication mechanisms.

7. Functions can send back results with `return` statements, by changing passed-in mutable arguments, and by setting global variables. Globals are generally frowned upon (except for very special cases, like multithreaded programs) because they can make code more difficult to understand and use. `return` statements are usually best, but changing mutables is fine (and even useful), if expected. Functions may also communicate results with system devices such as files and sockets, but these are beyond our scope here.

Comprehensions and Generations

This chapter continues the advanced function topics theme, with a reprisal of the comprehension and iteration concepts previewed in Chapter 4 and introduced in Chapter 14. Because *comprehensions* are as much related to the prior chapter's *functional* tools (e.g., `map` and `filter`) as they are to `for` loops, we'll revisit them in this context here. We'll also take a second look at iterables in order to study *generator functions* and their *generator expression* relatives—user-defined ways to produce results on demand.

Iteration in Python also encompasses user-defined *classes*, but we'll defer that final part of this story until Part VI, when we study operator overloading. As this is the last pass we'll make over built-in iteration tools, though, we will summarize the various tools we've met thus far. The next chapter continues this thread by timing the relative performance of these tools as a larger case study. Before that, though, let's continue the comprehensions and iterations story, and extend it to include value generators.

List Comprehensions and Functional Tools

As mentioned early in this book, Python supports the procedural, object-oriented, and function programming paradigms. In fact, Python has a host of tools that most would consider *functional* in nature, which we enumerated in the preceding chapter—closures, generators, lambdas, comprehensions, maps, decorators, function objects, and more. These tools allow us to apply and combine functions in powerful ways, and often offer state retention and coding solutions that are alternatives to classes and OOP.

For instance, the prior chapter explored tools such as `map` and `filter`—key members of Python's early functional programming toolset inspired by the Lisp language—that map operations over iterables and collect results. Because this is such a common task in Python coding, Python eventually sprouted a new expression—the *list comprehension*—that is even more flexible than the tools we just studied.

Per Python history, list comprehensions were originally inspired by a similar tool in the functional programming language Haskell, around the time of Python 2.0. In short, list comprehensions apply an arbitrary *expression* to items in an iterable, rather than applying a function. Accordingly, they can be more general tools. In later releases, the comprehension was extended to other roles—sets, dictionaries, and even the value generator expressions we'll explore in this chapter. It's not just for lists anymore.

We first met list comprehensions in Chapter 4's preview, and studied them further in Chapter 14, in conjunction with looping statements. Because they're also related to functional programming tools like the `map` and `filter` calls, though, we'll resurrect the topic here for one last look. Technically, this feature is not tied to functions—as we'll see, list comprehensions can be a more general tool than `map` and `filter`—but it is sometimes best understood by analogy to function-based alternatives.

List Comprehensions Versus map

Let's work through an example that demonstrates the basics. As we saw in Chapter 7, Python's built-in `ord` function returns the integer code point of a single character (the `chr` built-in is the converse—it returns the character for an integer code point). These happen to be ASCII codes if your characters fall into the ASCII character set's 7-bit code point range:

```
>>> ord('s')
115
```

Now, suppose we wish to collect the ASCII codes of *all* characters in an entire string. Perhaps the most straightforward approach is to use a simple `for` loop and append the results to a list:

```
>>> res = []
>>> for x in 'spam':
        res.append(ord(x))              # Manual results collection

>>> res
[115, 112, 97, 109]
```

Now that we know about `map`, though, we can achieve similar results with a single function call without having to manage list construction in the code:

```
>>> res = list(map(ord, 'spam'))        # Apply function to sequence (or other)
>>> res
[115, 112, 97, 109]
```

However, we can get the same results from a list comprehension expression—while `map` maps a *function* over an iterable, list comprehensions map an *expression* over a sequence or other iterable:

```
>>> res = [ord(x) for x in 'spam']      # Apply expression to sequence (or other)
>>> res
[115, 112, 97, 109]
```

List comprehensions collect the results of applying an arbitrary expression to an iterable of values and return them in a new list. Syntactically, list comprehensions are enclosed in square brackets—to remind you that they construct lists. In their simple form, within the brackets you code an expression that names a variable followed by what looks like a for loop header that names the same variable. Python then collects the expression's results for each iteration of the implied loop.

The effect of the preceding example is similar to that of the manual for loop and the map call. List comprehensions become more convenient, though, when we wish to apply an arbitrary expression to an iterable instead of a function:

```
>>> [x ** 2 for x in range(10)]
[0, 1, 4, 9, 16, 25, 36, 49, 64, 81]
```

Here, we've collected the squares of the numbers 0 through 9 (we're just letting the interactive prompt print the resulting list object; assign it to a variable if you need to retain it). To do similar work with a map call, we would probably need to invent a little function to implement the square operation. Because we won't need this function elsewhere, we'd typically (but not necessarily) code it inline, with a lambda, instead of using a def statement elsewhere:

```
>>> list(map((lambda x: x ** 2), range(10)))
[0, 1, 4, 9, 16, 25, 36, 49, 64, 81]
```

This does the same job, and it's only a few keystrokes longer than the equivalent list comprehension. It's also only marginally more complex (at least, once you understand the lambda). For more advanced kinds of expressions, though, list comprehensions will often require considerably less typing. The next section shows why.

Adding Tests and Nested Loops: filter

List comprehensions are even more general than shown so far. For instance, as we learned in Chapter 14, you can code an if clause after the for to add selection logic. List comprehensions with if clauses can be thought of as analogous to the filter built-in discussed in the preceding chapter—they skip an iterable's items for which the if clause is not true.

To demonstrate, following are both schemes picking up even numbers from 0 to 4; like the map list comprehension alternative of the prior section, the filter version here must invent a little lambda function for the test expression. For comparison, the equivalent for loop is shown here as well:

```
>>> [x for x in range(5) if x % 2 == 0]
[0, 2, 4]

>>> list(filter((lambda x: x % 2 == 0), range(5)))
[0, 2, 4]

>>> res = []
>>> for x in range(5):
        if x % 2 == 0:
            res.append(x)
```

```
>>> res
[0, 2, 4]
```

All of these use the modulus (remainder of division) operator, %, to detect even numbers: if there is no remainder after dividing a number by 2, it must be even. The `filter` call here is not much longer than the list comprehension either. However, we can combine an `if` clause and an arbitrary expression in our list comprehension, to give it the effect of a `filter` *and* a `map`, in a single expression:

```
>>> [x ** 2 for x in range(10) if x % 2 == 0]
[0, 4, 16, 36, 64]
```

This time, we collect the squares of the even numbers from 0 through 9: the `for` loop skips numbers for which the attached `if` clause on the right is false, and the expression on the left computes the squares. The equivalent `map` call would require a lot more work on our part—we would have to combine `filter` selections with `map` iteration, making for a noticeably more complex expression:

```
>>> list( map((lambda x: x**2), filter((lambda x: x % 2 == 0), range(10))) )
[0, 4, 16, 36, 64]
```

Formal comprehension syntax

In fact, list comprehensions are more general still. In their simplest form, you must always code an accumulation expression and a single `for` clause:

```
[ expression for target in iterable ]
```

Though all other parts are optional, they allow richer iterations to be expressed—you can code any number of nested `for` loops in a list comprehension, and each may have an optional associated `if` test to act as a filter. The general structure of list comprehensions looks like this:

```
[ expression for target1 in iterable1 if condition1
             for target2 in iterable2 if condition2 ...
             for targetN in iterableN if conditionN ]
```

This same syntax is inherited by *set* and *dictionary* comprehensions as well as the *generator expressions* coming up, though these use different enclosing characters (curly braces or often-optional parentheses), and the dictionary comprehension begins with two expressions separated by a colon (for key and value).

We experimented with the `if` filter clause in the previous section. When `for` clauses are *nested* within a list comprehension, they work like equivalent nested `for` loop statements. For example:

```
>>> res = [x + y for x in [0, 1, 2] for y in [100, 200, 300]]
>>> res
[100, 200, 300, 101, 201, 301, 102, 202, 302]
```

This has the same effect as this substantially more verbose equivalent:

```
>>> res = []
>>> for x in [0, 1, 2]:
```

```
        for y in [100, 200, 300]:
            res.append(x + y)

>>> res
[100, 200, 300, 101, 201, 301, 102, 202, 302]
```

Although list comprehensions construct list results, remember that they can iterate over any sequence or other iterable type. Here's a similar bit of code that traverses strings instead of lists of numbers, and so collects concatenation results:

```
>>> [x + y for x in 'spam' for y in 'SPAM']
['sS', 'sP', 'sA', 'sM', 'pS', 'pP', 'pA', 'pM',
 'aS', 'aP', 'aA', 'aM', 'mS', 'mP', 'mA', 'mM']
```

Each `for` clause can have an associated `if` filter, no matter how deeply the loops are nested—though use cases for the following sort of code, apart from perhaps multidimensional arrays, start to become more and more difficult to imagine at this level:

```
>>> [x + y for x in 'spam' if x in 'sm' for y in 'SPAM' if y in ('P', 'A')]
['sP', 'sA', 'mP', 'mA']

>>> [x + y + z for x in 'spam' if x in 'sm'
               for y in 'SPAM' if y in ('P', 'A')
               for z in '123'  if z > '1']
['sP2', 'sP3', 'sA2', 'sA3', 'mP2', 'mP3', 'mA2', 'mA3']
```

Finally, here is a similar list comprehension that illustrates the effect of attached `if` selections on nested `for` clauses applied to numeric objects rather than strings:

```
>>> [(x, y) for x in range(5) if x % 2 == 0 for y in range(5) if y % 2 == 1]
[(0, 1), (0, 3), (2, 1), (2, 3), (4, 1), (4, 3)]
```

This expression combines even numbers from 0 through 4 with odd numbers from 0 through 4. The `if` clauses filter out items in each iteration. Here is the equivalent statement-based code:

```
>>> res = []
>>> for x in range(5):
        if x % 2 == 0:
            for y in range(5):
                if y % 2 == 1:
                    res.append((x, y))

>>> res
[(0, 1), (0, 3), (2, 1), (2, 3), (4, 1), (4, 3)]
```

Recall that if you're confused about what a complex list comprehension does, you can always nest the list comprehension's `for` and `if` clauses inside each other like this—indenting each clause successively further to the right—to derive the equivalent statements. The result is longer, but perhaps clearer in intent to some human readers on first glance, especially those more familiar with basic statements.

The map and filter equivalent of this last example would be wildly complex and deeply nested, so I won't even try showing it here. I'll leave its coding as an exercise for Zen masters, ex–Lisp programmers, and the criminally insane!

Example: List Comprehensions and Matrixes

Not all list comprehensions are so artificial, of course. Let's look at one more application to stretch a few synapses. As we saw in Chapter 4 and Chapter 8, one basic way to code matrixes (a.k.a. multidimensional arrays) in Python is with nested list structures. The following, for example, defines two 3 × 3 matrixes as lists of nested lists:

```
>>> M = [[1, 2, 3],
         [4, 5, 6],
         [7, 8, 9]]

>>> N = [[2, 2, 2],
         [3, 3, 3],
         [4, 4, 4]]
```

Given this structure, we can always index rows, and columns within rows, using normal index operations:

```
>>> M[1]                # Row 2
[4, 5, 6]

>>> M[1][2]             # Row 2, item 3
6
```

List comprehensions are powerful tools for processing such structures, though, because they automatically scan rows and columns for us. For instance, although this structure stores the matrix by rows, to collect the second *column* we can simply iterate across the rows and pull out the desired column, or iterate through positions in the rows and index as we go:

```
>>> [row[1] for row in M]             # Column 2
[2, 5, 8]

>>> [M[row][1] for row in (0, 1, 2)]             # Using offsets
[2, 5, 8]
```

Given positions, we can also easily perform tasks such as pulling out a *diagonal*. The first of the following expressions uses range to generate the list of offsets and then indexes with the row and column the same, picking out M[0][0], then M[1][1], and so on. The second scales the column index to fetch M[0][2], M[1][1], etc. (we assume the matrix has the same number of rows and columns):

```
>>> [M[i][i] for i in range(len(M))]             # Diagonals
[1, 5, 9]
>>> [M[i][len(M)-1-i] for i in range(len(M))]
[3, 5, 7]
```

Changing such a matrix *in place* requires assignment to offsets (use range twice if shapes differ):

```
>>> L = [[1, 2, 3], [4, 5, 6]]
>>> for i in range(len(L)):
        for j in range(len(L[i])):          # Update in place
            L[i][j] += 10

>>> L
[[11, 12, 13], [14, 15, 16]]
```

We can't really do the same with list comprehensions, as they make *new lists*, but we could always assign their results to the original name for a similar effect. For example, we can apply an operation to every item in a matrix, producing results in either a simple vector or a matrix of the same shape:

```
>>> [col + 10 for row in M for col in row]      # Assign to M to retain new value
[11, 12, 13, 14, 15, 16, 17, 18, 19]

>>> [[col + 10 for col in row] for row in M]
[[11, 12, 13], [14, 15, 16], [17, 18, 19]]
```

To understand these, translate to their simple statement form equivalents that follow —indent parts that are further to the right in the expression (as in the first loop in the following), and make a new list when comprehensions are nested on the left (like the second loop in the following). As its statement equivalent makes clearer, the second expression in the preceding works because the row iteration is an outer loop: for each row, it runs the nested column iteration to build up one row of the result matrix:

```
>>> res = []
>>> for row in M:                           # Statement equivalents
        for col in row:                     # Indent parts further right
            res.append(col + 10)

>>> res
[11, 12, 13, 14, 15, 16, 17, 18, 19]

>>> res = []
>>> for row in M:
        tmp = []                            # Left-nesting starts new list
        for col in row:
            tmp.append(col + 10)
        res.append(tmp)

>>> res
[[11, 12, 13], [14, 15, 16], [17, 18, 19]]
```

Finally, with a bit of creativity, we can also use list comprehensions to combine values of *multiple matrixes*. The following first builds a flat list that contains the result of multiplying the matrixes pairwise, and then builds a nested list structure having the same values by nesting list comprehensions again:

```
>>> M
[[1, 2, 3], [4, 5, 6], [7, 8, 9]]
```

```
>>> N
[[2, 2, 2], [3, 3, 3], [4, 4, 4]]

>>> [M[row][col] * N[row][col] for row in range(3) for col in range(3)]
[2, 4, 6, 12, 15, 18, 28, 32, 36]

>>> [[M[row][col] * N[row][col] for col in range(3)] for row in range(3)]
[[2, 4, 6], [12, 15, 18], [28, 32, 36]]
```

This last expression works because the row iteration is an outer loop again; it's equivalent to this statement-based code:

```
res = []
for row in range(3):
    tmp = []
    for col in range(3):
        tmp.append(M[row][col] * N[row][col])
    res.append(tmp)
```

And for more fun, we can use `zip` to pair items to be multiplied—the following comprehension and loop statement forms both produce the same list-of-lists pairwise multiplication result as the last preceding example (and because `zip` is a generator of values in 3.X, this isn't as inefficient as it may seem):

```
[[col1 * col2 for (col1, col2) in zip(row1, row2)] for (row1, row2) in zip(M, N)]

res = []
for (row1, row2) in zip(M, N):
    tmp = []
    for (col1, col2) in zip(row1, row2):
        tmp.append(col1 * col2)
    res.append(tmp)
```

Compared to their statement equivalents, the list comprehension versions here require only one line of code, might run substantially faster for large matrixes, and just might make your head explode! Which brings us to the next section.

Don't Abuse List Comprehensions: KISS

With such generality, list comprehensions can quickly become, well, incomprehensible, especially when nested. Some programming tasks are inherently complex, and we can't sugarcoat them to make them any simpler than they are (see the upcoming permutations for a prime example). Tools like comprehensions are powerful solutions when used wisely, and there's nothing inherently wrong with using them in your scripts.

At the same time, code like that of the prior section may push the complexity envelope more than it should—and, frankly, tends to disproportionately pique the interest of those holding the darker and misguided assumption that code obfuscation somehow implies talent. Because such tools tend to appeal to some people more than they probably should, I need to be clear about their scope here.

This book demonstrates advanced comprehensions to teach, but in the real world, using complicated and tricky code where not warranted is both bad engineering and bad software citizenship. To repurpose a line from the first chapter: programming is not about being clever and obscure—it's about how clearly your program communicates its purpose.

Or, to quote from Python's `import this` motto:

> Simple is better than complex.

Writing complicated comprehension code may be a fun academic recreation, but it doesn't have a place in programs that others will someday need to understand.

Consequently, my advice is to use simple `for` loops when getting started with Python, and comprehensions or `map` in isolated cases where they are easy to apply. The "keep it simple" rule applies here as always: code conciseness is a much less important goal than code readability. If you have to translate code to statements to understand it, it should probably be statements in the first place. In other words, the age-old acronym *KISS* still applies: Keep It Simple—followed either by a word that is today too sexist (Sir), or another that is too colorful for a family-oriented book like this...

On the other hand: performance, conciseness, expressiveness

However, in this case, there is currently a substantial *performance* advantage to the extra complexity: based on tests run under Python today, `map` calls can be twice as fast as equivalent `for` loops, and list comprehensions are often faster than `map` calls. This speed difference can vary per usage pattern and Python, but is generally due to the fact that `map` and list comprehensions run at C language speed inside the interpreter, which is often much faster than stepping through Python `for` loop bytecode within the PVM.

In addition, list comprehensions offer a code *conciseness* that's compelling and even warranted when that reduction in size doesn't also imply a reduction in meaning for the next programmer. Moreover, many find the *expressiveness* of comprehensions to be a powerful ally. Because `map` and list comprehensions are both expressions, they also can show up syntactically in places that `for` loop statements cannot, such as in the bodies of `lambda` functions, within list and dictionary literals, and more.

Because of this, list comprehensions and `map` calls are worth knowing and using for simpler kinds of iterations, especially if your application's speed is an important consideration. Still, because `for` loops make logic more explicit, they are generally recommended on the grounds of simplicity, and often make for more straightforward code. When used, you should try to keep your `map` calls and list comprehensions simple; for more complex tasks, use full statements instead.

As I've stated before, *performance* generalizations like those just given here can depend on call patterns, as well as changes and optimizations in Python itself. Recent Python releases have sped up the simple **for** loop statement, for example. On some code, though, list comprehensions are still substantially faster than **for** loops and even faster than **map**, though **map** can still win when the alternatives must apply a function call, built-in functions or otherwise. At least until this story changes arbitrarily—to time these alternatives yourself, see tools in the standard library's **time** module or in the newer **timeit** module added in Release 2.4, or stay tuned for the extended coverage of both of these in the next chapter, where we'll prove the prior paragraph's claims.

Why You Will Care: List Comprehensions and map

Here are some more realistic examples of list comprehensions and **map** in action. We solved the first with list comprehensions in Chapter 14, but we'll revive it here to add **map** alternatives. Recall that the file **readlines** method returns lines with \n end-of-line characters at the ends (the following assumes a 3-line text file in the current directory):

```
>>> open('myfile').readlines()
['aaa\n', 'bbb\n', 'ccc\n']
```

If you don't want the end-of-line characters, you can slice them off all the lines in a single step with a list comprehension or a **map** call (**map** results are iterables in Python 3.X, so we must run them through **list** to display all their results at once):

```
>>> [line.rstrip() for line in open('myfile').readlines()]
['aaa', 'bbb', 'ccc']

>>> [line.rstrip() for line in open('myfile')]
['aaa', 'bbb', 'ccc']

>>> list(map((lambda line: line.rstrip()), open('myfile')))
['aaa', 'bbb', 'ccc']
```

The last two of these make use of *file iterators*; as we saw in Chapter 14, this means that you don't need a method call to read lines in iteration contexts such as these. The **map** call is slightly longer than the list comprehension, but neither has to manage result list construction explicitly.

A list comprehension can also be used as a sort of column projection operation. Python's standard SQL *database* API returns query results as a sequence of sequences like the following—the list is the table, tuples are rows, and items in tuples are column values:

```
>>> listoftuple = [('bob', 35, 'mgr'), ('sue', 40, 'dev')]
```

A **for** loop could pick up all the values from a selected column manually, but **map** and list comprehensions can do it in a single step, and faster:

```
>>> [age for (name, age, job) in listoftuple]
[35, 40]
```

```
>>> list(map((lambda row: row[1]), listoftuple))
[35, 40]
```

The first of these makes use of *tuple assignment* to unpack row tuples in the list, and the second uses indexing. In Python 2.X (but not in 3.X—see the note on 2.X argument unpacking in Chapter 18), map can use tuple unpacking on its argument, too:

```
# 2.X only
>>> list(map((lambda (name, age, job): age), listoftuple))
[35, 40]
```

See other books and resources for more on Python's database API.

Besides the distinction between running functions versus expressions, the biggest difference between map and list comprehensions in Python 3.X is that map is an *iterable*, generating results on demand. To achieve the same memory economy and execution time division, list comprehensions must be coded as *generator expressions*—one of the major topics this chapter turns to next.

Generator Functions and Expressions

Python today supports procrastination much more than it did in the past—it provides tools that produce results only when needed, instead of all at once. We've seen this at work in built-in tools: files that read lines on request, and functions like map and zip that produce items on demand in 3.X. Such laziness isn't confined to Python itself, though. In particular, two language constructs delay result creation whenever possible in user-defined operations:

- *Generator functions* (available since 2.3) are coded as normal def statements, but use yield statements to return results one at a time, suspending and resuming their state between each.

- *Generator expressions* (available since 2.4) are similar to the list comprehensions of the prior section, but they return an object that produces results on demand instead of building a result list.

Because neither constructs a result list all at once, they save memory space and allow computation time to be split across result requests. As we'll see, both of these ultimately perform their delayed-results magic by implementing the *iteration protocol* we studied in Chapter 14.

These features are not new (generator functions were available as an option as early as Python 2.2), and are fairly common in Python code today. Python's notion of generators owes much to other programming languages, especially Icon. Though they may initially seem unusual if you're accustomed to simpler programming models, you'll probably find generators to be a powerful tool where applicable. Moreover, because they are a natural extension to the function, comprehension, and iteration ideas we've already explored, you already know more about coding generators than you might expect.

Generator Functions: yield Versus return

In this part of the book, we've learned about coding normal functions that receive input parameters and send back a single result immediately. It is also possible, however, to write functions that may send back a value and later be resumed, picking up where they left off. Such functions, available in both Python 2.X and 3.X, are known as *generator functions* because they generate a sequence of values over time.

Generator functions are like normal functions in most respects, and in fact are coded with normal `def` statements. However, when created, they are compiled specially into an object that supports the iteration protocol. And when called, they don't return a result: they return a result generator that can appear in any iteration context. We studied iterables in Chapter 14, and Figure 14-1 gave a formal and graphic summary of their operation. Here, we'll revisit them to see how they relate to generators.

State suspension

Unlike normal functions that return a value and exit, generator functions automatically suspend and resume their execution and state around the point of value generation. Because of that, they are often a useful alternative to both computing an entire series of values up front and manually saving and restoring state in classes. The *state* that generator functions retain when they are suspended includes both their code location, and their entire local scope. Hence, their *local variables* retain information between results, and make it available when the functions are resumed.

The chief code difference between generator and normal functions is that a generator *yields* a value, rather than *returning* one—the `yield` statement suspends the function and sends a value back to the caller, but retains enough state to enable the function to resume from where it left off. When resumed, the function continues execution immediately after the last `yield` run. From the function's perspective, this allows its code to produce a series of values over time, rather than computing them all at once and sending them back in something like a list.

Iteration protocol integration

To truly understand generator functions, you need to know that they are closely bound up with the notion of the iteration protocol in Python. As we've seen, iterator objects define a `__next__` method (next in 2.X), which either returns the next item in the iteration, or raises the special `StopIteration` exception to end the iteration. An iterable object's iterator is fetched initially with the `iter` built-in function, though this step is a no-op for objects that are their own iterator.

Python `for` loops, and all other iteration contexts, use this iteration protocol to step through a sequence or value generator, if the protocol is supported (if not, iteration falls back on repeatedly indexing sequences instead). Any object that supports this interface works in all iteration tools.

To support this protocol, functions containing a yield statement are compiled specially as *generators*—they are not normal functions, but rather are built to return an object with the expected iteration protocol methods. When later called, they return a generator object that supports the iteration interface with an automatically created method named __next__ to start or resume execution.

Generator functions may also have a return statement that, along with falling off the end of the def block, simply terminates the generation of values—technically, by raising a StopIteration exception after any normal function exit actions. From the caller's perspective, the generator's __next__ method resumes the function and runs until either the next yield result is returned or a StopIteration is raised.

The net effect is that generator functions, coded as def statements containing yield statements, are automatically made to support the iteration object protocol and thus may be used in any iteration context to produce results over time and on demand.

 As noted in Chapter 14, in Python 2.X, iterator objects define a method named next instead of __next__. This includes the generator objects we are using here. In 3.X this method is renamed to __next__. The next built-in function is provided as a convenience and portability tool: next(I) is the same as I.__next__() in 3.X and I.next() in 2.6 and 2.7. Prior to 2.6, programs simply call I.next() instead to iterate manually.

Generator functions in action

To illustrate generator basics, let's turn to some code. The following code defines a generator function that can be used to generate the squares of a series of numbers over time:

```
>>> def gensquares(N):
        for i in range(N):
            yield i ** 2          # Resume here later
```

This function yields a value, and so returns to its caller, each time through the loop; when it is resumed, its prior state is restored, including the last values of its variables i and N, and control picks up again immediately after the yield statement. For example, when it's used in the body of a for loop, the first iteration starts the function and gets its first result; thereafter, control returns to the function after its yield statement each time through the loop:

```
>>> for i in gensquares(5):           # Resume the function
        print(i, end=' : ')           # Print last yielded value

0 : 1 : 4 : 9 : 16 :
>>>
```

To end the generation of values, functions either use a return statement with no value or simply allow control to fall off the end of the function body.[1]

To most people, this process seems a bit implicit (if not magical) on first encounter. It's actually quite tangible, though. If you really want to see what is going on inside the for, call the generator function directly:

```
>>> x = gensquares(4)
>>> x
<generator object gensquares at 0x000000000292CA68>
```

You get back a *generator object* that supports the iteration protocol we met in Chapter 14—the generator function was compiled to return this automatically. The returned generator object in turn has a __next__ method that starts the function or resumes it from where it last yielded a value, and raises a StopIteration exception when the end of the series of values is reached and the function returns. For convenience, the next(X) built-in calls an object's X.__next__() method for us in 3.X (and X.next() in 2.X):

```
>>> next(x)                      # Same as x.__next__() in 3.X
0
>>> next(x)                      # Use x.next() or next() in 2.X
1
>>> next(x)
4
>>> next(x)
9
>>> next(x)
Traceback (most recent call last):
  File "<stdin>", line 1, in <module>
StopIteration
```

As we learned in Chapter 14, for loops (and other iteration contexts) work with generators in the same way—by calling the __next__ method repeatedly, until an exception is caught. For a generator, the result is to produce yielded values over time. If the object to be iterated over does not support this protocol, for loops instead use the indexing protocol to iterate.

Notice that the top-level iter call of the iteration protocol isn't required here because generators are their own iterator, supporting just one active iteration scan. To put that another way generators return themselves for iter, because they support next directly. This also holds true in the generator expressions we'll meet later in this chapter (more on this ahead):

```
>>> y = gensquares(5)            # Returns a generator which is its own iterator
>>> iter(y) is y                 # iter() is not required: a no-op here
True
```

---

1. Technically, Python treats return statement values in generator functions as syntax errors in 2.X, and in all 3.X prior to 3.3. As of 3.3, a return statement value is allowed and attached to the StopIteration object, but the value is ignored in automatic iterations contexts, and using this makes code incompatible with all prior releases.

```
>>> next(y)                        # Can run next()immediately
0
```

Why generator functions?

Given the simple examples we're using to illustrate fundamentals, you might be wondering just why you'd ever care to code a generator at all. In this section's example, for instance, we could also simply build the list of yielded values all at once:

```
>>> def buildsquares(n):
        res = []
        for i in range(n): res.append(i ** 2)
        return res

>>> for x in buildsquares(5): print(x, end=' : ')

0 : 1 : 4 : 9 : 16 :
```

For that matter, we could use any of the for loop, map, or list comprehension techniques:

```
>>> for x in [n ** 2 for n in range(5)]:
        print(x, end=' : ')

0 : 1 : 4 : 9 : 16 :

>>> for x in map((lambda n: n ** 2), range(5)):
        print(x, end=' : ')

0 : 1 : 4 : 9 : 16 :
```

However, generators can be better in terms of both memory use and performance in larger programs. They allow functions to avoid doing all the work up front, which is especially useful when the result lists are large or when it takes a lot of computation to produce each value. Generators distribute the time required to produce the series of values among loop iterations.

Moreover, for more advanced uses, generators can provide a simpler alternative to manually saving the state between iterations in class objects—with generators, variables accessible in the function's scopes are saved and restored automatically.[2] We'll discuss class-based iterables in more detail in Part VI.

Generator functions are also much more broadly focused than implied so far. They can operate on and return any type of object, and as *iterables* may appear in any of

---

2. Interestingly, generator functions are also something of a "poor man's" *multithreading* device—they interleave a function's work with that of its caller, by dividing its operation into steps run between yields. Generators are not threads, though: the program is explicitly directed to and from the function within a single thread of control. In one sense, threading is more general (producers can run truly independently and post results to a queue), but generators may be simpler to code. See the footnote in Chapter 17 for a brief introduction to Python multithreading tools. Note that because control is routed explicitly at yield and next calls, generators are also not *backtracking*, but are more strongly related to *coroutines*—formal concepts that are both beyond this chapter's scope.

Chapter 14's iteration contexts, including `tuple` calls, enumerations, and dictionary comprehensions:

```
>>> def ups(line):
        for sub in line.split(','):          # Substring generator
            yield sub.upper()

>>> tuple(ups('aaa,bbb,ccc'))                 # All iteration contexts
('AAA', 'BBB', 'CCC')

>>> {i: s for (i, s) in enumerate(ups('aaa,bbb,ccc'))}
{0: 'AAA', 1: 'BBB', 2: 'CCC'}
```

In a moment we'll see the same assets for generator expressions—a tool that trades function flexibility for comprehension conciseness. Later in this chapter we'll also see that generators can sometimes make the impossible possible, by producing components of result sets that would be far too large to create all at once. First, though, let's explore some advanced generator function features.

Extended generator function protocol: send versus next

In Python 2.5, a `send` method was added to the generator function protocol. The `send` method advances to the next item in the series of results, just like `__next__`, but also provides a way for the caller to communicate with the generator, to affect its operation.

Technically, `yield` is now an expression form that returns the item passed to `send`, not a statement (though it can be called either way—as `yield X`, or `A = (yield X)`). The expression must be enclosed in parentheses unless it's the only item on the right side of the assignment statement. For example, `X = yield Y` is OK, as is `X = (yield Y) + 42`.

When this extra protocol is used, values are sent into a generator G by calling `G.send(value)`. The generator's code is then resumed, and the `yield` expression in the generator returns the value passed to `send`. If the regular `G.__next__()` method (or its `next(G)` equivalent) is called to advance, the `yield` simply returns `None`. For example:

```
>>> def gen():
        for i in range(10):
            X = yield i
            print(X)

>>> G = gen()
>>> next(G)             # Must call next() first, to start generator
0
>>> G.send(77)          # Advance, and send value to yield expression
77
1
>>> G.send(88)
88
2
>>> next(G)             # next() and X.__next__() send None
None
3
```

The send method can be used, for example, to code a generator that its caller can terminate by sending a termination code, or redirect by passing a new position in data being processed inside the generator.

In addition, generators in 2.5 and later also support a throw(*type*) method to raise an exception inside the generator at the latest yield, and a close method that raises a special GeneratorExit exception inside the generator to terminate the iteration entirely. These are advanced features that we won't delve into in more detail here; see reference texts and Python's standard manuals for more information, and watch for more on exceptions in Part VII.

Note that while Python 3.X provides a next(X) convenience built-in that calls the X.__next__() method of an object, other generator methods, like send, must be called as methods of generator objects directly (e.g., G.send(X)). This makes sense if you realize that these extra methods are implemented on built-in generator objects only, whereas the __next__ method applies to all iterable objects—both built-in types and user-defined classes.

Also note that Python 3.3 introduces an extension to yield—a from clause—that allows generators to delegate to nested generators. Since this is an extension to what is already a fairly advanced topic, we'll delegate this topic itself to a sidebar, and move on here to a tool that's close enough to be called a twin.

Generator Expressions: Iterables Meet Comprehensions

Because the delayed evaluation of generator functions was so useful, it eventually spread to other tools. In both Python 2.X and 3.X, the notions of iterables and list comprehensions are combined in a new tool: *generator expressions*. Syntactically, generator expressions are just like normal list comprehensions, and support all their syntax —including if filters and loop nesting—but they are enclosed in parentheses instead of square brackets (like tuples, their enclosing parentheses are often optional):

```
>>> [x ** 2 for x in range(4)]          # List comprehension: build a list
[0, 1, 4, 9]

>>> (x ** 2 for x in range(4))          # Generator expression: make an iterable
<generator object <genexpr> at 0x00000000029A8288>
```

In fact, at least on a functionality basis, coding a list comprehension is essentially the same as wrapping a generator expression in a list built-in call to force it to produce all its results in a list at once:

```
>>> list(x ** 2 for x in range(4))      # List comprehension equivalence
[0, 1, 4, 9]
```

Operationally, however, generator expressions are very different: instead of building the result list in memory, they return a *generator object*—an automatically created iterable. This iterable object in turn supports the *iteration protocol* to yield one piece of the result list at a time in any iteration context. The iterable object also retains generator state while active—the variable x in the preceding expressions, along with the generator's code location.

The net effect is much like that of generator functions, but in the context of a comprehension *expression*: we get back an object that remembers where it left off after each part of its result is returned. Also like generator functions, looking under the hood at the protocol that these objects automatically support can help demystify them; the iter call is again not required at the top here, for reasons we'll expand on ahead:

```
>>> G = (x ** 2 for x in range(4))
>>> iter(G) is G                        # iter(G) optional: __iter__ returns self
True
>>> next(G)                             # Generator objects: automatic methods
0
>>> next(G)
1
>>> next(G)
4
>>> next(G)
9
>>> next(G)
Traceback (most recent call last):
  File "<stdin>", line 1, in <module>
StopIteration

>>> G
<generator object <genexpr> at 0x00000000029A8318>
```

Again, we don't typically see the next iterator machinery under the hood of a generator expression like this because for loops trigger it for us automatically:

```
>>> for num in (x ** 2 for x in range(4)):      # Calls next() automatically
        print('%s, %s' % (num, num / 2.0))

0, 0.0
1, 0.5
4, 2.0
9, 4.5
```

As we've already learned, every iteration context does this—including for loops; the sum, map, and sorted built-in functions; list comprehensions; and other iteration contexts we learned about in Chapter 14, such as the any, all, and list built-in functions. As *iterables*, generator expressions can appear in any of these iteration contexts, just like the result of a generator function call.

For example, the following deploys generator expressions in the string join method call and tuple assignment, iteration contexts both. In the first test here, join runs the generator and joins the substrings it produces with nothing between—to simply concatenate:

```
>>> ''.join(x.upper() for x in 'aaa,bbb,ccc'.split(','))
'AAABBBCCC'

>>> a, b, c = (x + '\n' for x in 'aaa,bbb,ccc'.split(','))
```

```
>>> a, c
('aaa\n', 'ccc\n')
```

Notice how the join call in the preceding doesn't require *extra* parentheses around the generator. Syntactically, parentheses are *not required* around a generator expression that is the sole item already enclosed in parentheses used for other purposes—like those of a function call. Parentheses are required in all other cases, however, even if they seem extra, as in the second call to sorted that follows:

```
>>> sum(x ** 2 for x in range(4))          # Parens optional
14
>>> sorted(x ** 2 for x in range(4))       # Parens optional
[0, 1, 4, 9]
>>> sorted((x ** 2 for x in range(4)), reverse=True)   # Parens required
[9, 4, 1, 0]
```

Like the often-optional parentheses in tuples, there is no widely accepted rule on this, though a generator expression does not have as clear a role as a fixed collection of other objects as a tuple, making extra parentheses seem perhaps more spurious here.

Why generator expressions?

Just like generator functions, generator expressions are a *memory-space* optimization—they do not require the entire result list to be constructed all at once, as the square-bracketed list comprehension does. Also like generator functions, they divide the work of results production into smaller *time slices*—they yield results in piecemeal fashion, instead of making the caller wait for the full set to be created in a single call.

On the other hand, generator expressions may also run slightly *slower* than list comprehensions in practice, so they are probably best used only for very large result sets, or applications that cannot wait for full results generation. A more authoritative statement about performance, though, will have to await the timing scripts we'll code in the next chapter.

Though more subjective, generator expressions offer *coding* advantages too—as the next sections show.

Generator expressions versus map

One way to see the coding benefits of generator expressions is to compare them to other functional tools, as we did for list comprehensions. For example, generator expressions often are equivalent to 3.X map calls, because both generate result items on request. Like list comprehensions, though, generator expressions may be simpler to code when the operation applied is not a function call. In 2.X, map makes temporary lists and generator expressions do not, but the same coding comparisons apply:

```
>>> list(map(abs, (-1, -2, 3, 4)))        # Map function on tuple
[1, 2, 3, 4]
>>> list(abs(x) for x in (-1, -2, 3, 4))  # Generator expression
[1, 2, 3, 4]
```

```
>>> list(map(lambda x: x * 2, (1, 2, 3, 4)))        # Nonfunction case
[2, 4, 6, 8]
>>> list(x * 2 for x in (1, 2, 3, 4))               # Simpler as generator?
[2, 4, 6, 8]
```

The same holds true for text-processing use cases like the join call we saw earlier—a list comprehension makes an extra temporary list of results, which is completely *pointless* in this context because the list is not retained, and map loses simplicity points compared to generator expression syntax when the operation being applied is not a call:

```
>>> line = 'aaa,bbb,ccc'
>>> ''.join([x.upper() for x in line.split(',')])   # Makes a pointless list
'AAABBBCCC'

>>> ''.join(x.upper() for x in line.split(','))     # Generates results
'AAABBBCCC'
>>> ''.join(map(str.upper, line.split(',')))        # Generates results
'AAABBBCCC'

>>> ''.join(x * 2 for x in line.split(','))         # Simpler as generator?
'aaaaaabbbbbbcccccc'
>>> ''.join(map(lambda x: x * 2, line.split(',')))
'aaaaaabbbbbbcccccc'
```

Both map and generator expressions can also be arbitrarily *nested*, which supports general use in programs, and requires a list call or other iteration context to start the process of producing results. For example, the list comprehension in the following produces the same result as the 3.X map and generator equivalents that follow it, but makes two physical lists; the others generate just one integer at a time with nested generators, and the generator expression form may more clearly reflect its intent:

```
>>> [x * 2 for x in [abs(x) for x in (-1, -2, 3, 4)]]     # Nested comprehensions
[2, 4, 6, 8]

>>> list(map(lambda x: x * 2, map(abs, (-1, -2, 3, 4))))   # Nested maps
[2, 4, 6, 8]

>>> list(x * 2 for x in (abs(x) for x in (-1, -2, 3, 4)))  # Nested generators
[2, 4, 6, 8]
```

Although the effect of all three of these is to combine operations, the generators do so without making multiple temporary lists. In 3.X, the next example both nests *and* combines generators—the nested generator expression is activated by map, which in turn is only activated by list.

```
>>> import math
>>> list(map(math.sqrt, (x ** 2 for x in range(4))))       # Nested combinations
[0.0, 1.0, 2.0, 3.0]
```

Technically speaking, the range on the right in the preceding is a value generator in 3.X too, activated by the generator expression itself—*three levels* of value generation, which produce individual values from inner to outer only on request, and which "just works" because of Python's iteration tools and protocol. In fact, generator nestings can be arbitrarily mixed and deep, though some may be more valid than others:

```
>>> list(map(abs, map(abs, map(abs, (-1, 0, 1)))))        # Nesting gone bad?
[1, 0, 1]
>>> list(abs(x) for x in (abs(x) for x in (abs(x) for x in (-1, 0, 1))))
[1, 0, 1]
```

These last examples illustrate how general generators can be, but are also coded in an intentionally complex form to underscore that generator expressions have the same potential for abuse as the list comprehensions discussed earlier—as usual, you should keep them simple unless they must be complex, a theme we'll revisit later in this chapter.

When used well, though, generator expressions combine the expressiveness of list comprehensions with the space and time benefits of other iterables. Here, for example, *nonnested* approaches provide simpler solutions but still leverage generators' strengths —per a Python motto, flat is generally better than nested:

```
>>> list(abs(x) * 2 for x in (-1, -2, 3, 4))        # Unnested equivalents
[2, 4, 6, 8]
>>> list(math.sqrt(x ** 2) for x in range(4))        # Flat is often better
[0.0, 1.0, 2.0, 3.0]
>>> list(abs(x) for x in (-1, 0, 1))
[1, 0, 1]
```

Generator expressions versus filter

Generator expressions also support all the usual list comprehension syntax—including `if` clauses, which work like the `filter` call we met earlier. Because `filter` is an iterable in 3.X that generates its results on request, a generator expression with an `if` clause is operationally equivalent (in 2.X, `filter` produces a temporary list that the generator does not, but the code comparisons again apply). Again, the `join` in the following suffices to force all forms to produce their results:

```
>>> line = 'aa bbb c'
>>> ''.join(x for x in line.split() if len(x) > 1)        # Generator with 'if'
'aabbb'
>>> ''.join(filter(lambda x: len(x) > 1, line.split()))        # Similar to filter
'aabbb'
```

The generator seems marginally simpler than the `filter` here. As for list comprehensions, though, adding processing steps to `filter` results requires a `map` too, which makes `filter` noticeably more complex than a generator expression:

```
>>> ''.join(x.upper() for x in line.split() if len(x) > 1)
'AABBB'
>>> ''.join(map(str.upper, filter(lambda x: len(x) > 1, line.split())))
'AABBB'
```

In effect, generator expressions do for 3.X iterables like `map` and `filter` what list comprehensions do for the 2.X list-builder flavors of these calls—they provide more general coding structures that do not rely on functions, but still delay results production. Also like list comprehensions, there is always a statement-based equivalent to a generator expression, though it sometimes renders substantially more code:

```
>>> ''.join(x.upper() for x in line.split() if len(x) > 1)
'AABBB'

>>> res = ''
>>> for x in line.split():          # Statement equivalent?
        if len(x) > 1:              # This is also a join
            res += x.upper()

>>> res
'AABBB'
```

In this case, though, the statement form isn't quite the same—it cannot produce items one at a time, and it's also emulating the effect of the `join` that forces results to be produced all at once. The true equivalent to a generator expression would be a generator function with a `yield`, as the next section shows.

Generator Functions Versus Generator Expressions

Let's recap what we've covered so far in this section:

Generator functions

A function `def` statement that contains a `yield` statement is turned into a generator function. When called, it returns a new *generator object* with automatic retention of local scope and code position; an automatically created `__iter__` method that simply returns itself; and an automatically created `__next__` method (next in 2.X) that starts the function or resumes it where it last left off, and raises `StopItera tion` when finished producing results.

Generator expressions

A comprehension expression enclosed in parentheses is known as a generator expression. When run, it returns a new *generator object* with the same automatically created method interface and state retention as a generator function call's results —with an `__iter__` method that simply returns itself; and a `_next__` method (next in 2.X) that starts the implied loop or resumes it where it last left off, and raises `StopIteration` when finished producing results.

The net effect is to produce results on demand in iteration contexts that employ these interfaces automatically.

As implied by some of the preceding sections, the same iteration can often be coded with *either* a generator function or a generator expression. The following generator expression, for example, repeats each character in a string four times:

```
>>> G = (c * 4 for c in 'SPAM')     # Generator expression
>>> list(G)                         # Force generator to produce all results
['SSSS', 'PPPP', 'AAAA', 'MMMM']
```

The equivalent generator function requires slightly more code, but as a multiple-statement function it will be able to code more logic and use more state information if needed. In fact, this is essentially the same as the prior chapter's tradeoff between lambda and def—expression conciseness versus statement power:

```
>>> def timesfour(S):                # Generator function
        for c in S:
            yield c * 4

>>> G = timesfour('spam')
>>> list(G)                          # Iterate automatically
['ssss', 'pppp', 'aaaa', 'mmmm']
```

To clients, the two are more similar than different. Both expressions and functions support both automatic and manual iteration—the prior list call iterates automatically, and the following iterate manually:

```
>>> G = (c * 4 for c in 'SPAM')
>>> I = iter(G)                      # Iterate manually (expression)
>>> next(I)
'SSSS'
>>> next(I)
'PPPP'

>>> G = timesfour('spam')
>>> I = iter(G)                      # Iterate manually (function)
>>> next(I)
'ssss'
>>> next(I)
'pppp'
```

In either case, Python automatically creates a generator object, which has both the methods required by the iteration protocol, and state retention for variables in the generator's code and its current code location. Notice how we make new generators here to iterate again—as explained in the next section, generators are one-shot iterators.

First, though, here's the true statement-based equivalent of expression at the end of the prior section: a function that yields values—though the difference is irrelevant if the code using it produces all results with a tool like join:

```
>>> line = 'aa bbb c'

>>> ''.join(x.upper() for x in line.split() if len(x) > 1)     # Expression
'AABBB'

>>> def gensub(line):                                          # Function
        for x in line.split():
            if len(x) > 1:
                yield x.upper()

>>> ''.join(gensub(line))                                      # But why generate?
'AABBB'
```

Though generators have valid roles, in cases like this the use of generators over the simple statement equivalent shown earlier may be difficult to justify, except on stylistic grounds. On the other hand, trading four lines for one may to many seem fairly compelling stylistic grounds!

Generators Are Single-Iteration Objects

A subtle but important point: both generator functions and generator expressions are their own iterators and thus support just *one active iteration*—unlike some built-in types, you can't have multiple iterators of either positioned at different locations in the set of results. Because of this, a generator's iterator is the generator itself; in fact, as suggested earlier, calling `iter` on a generator expression or function is an optional no-op:

```
>>> G = (c * 4 for c in 'SPAM')
>>> iter(G) is G                          # My iterator is myself: G has __next__
True
```

If you iterate over the results stream manually with multiple iterators, they will all point to the same position:

```
>>> G = (c * 4 for c in 'SPAM')          # Make a new generator
>>> I1 = iter(G)                          # Iterate manually
>>> next(I1)
'SSSS'
>>> next(I1)
'PPPP'
>>> I2 = iter(G)                          # Second iterator at same position!
>>> next(I2)
'AAAA'
```

Moreover, once any iteration runs to completion, all are exhausted—we have to make a new generator to start again:

```
>>> list(I1)                              # Collect the rest of I1's items
['MMMM']
>>> next(I2)                              # Other iterators exhausted too
StopIteration

>>> I3 = iter(G)                          # Ditto for new iterators
>>> next(I3)
StopIteration

>>> I3 = iter(c * 4 for c in 'SPAM')     # New generator to start over
>>> next(I3)
'SSSS'
```

The same holds true for generator functions—the following `def` statement-based equivalent supports just one active iterator and is exhausted after one pass:

```
>>> def timesfour(S):
        for c in S:
            yield c * 4
```

```
>>> G = timesfour('spam')          # Generator functions work the same way
>>> iter(G) is G
True
>>> I1, I2 = iter(G), iter(G)
>>> next(I1)
'ssss'
>>> next(I1)
'pppp'
>>> next(I2)                        # I2 at same position as I1
'aaaa'
```

This is different from the behavior of some built-in types, which support multiple iterators and passes and reflect their in-place changes in active iterators:

```
>>> L = [1, 2, 3, 4]
>>> I1, I2 = iter(L), iter(L)
>>> next(I1)
1
>>> next(I1)
2
>>> next(I2)                        # Lists support multiple iterators
1
>>> del L[2:]                       # Changes reflected in iterators
>>> next(I1)
StopIteration
```

Though not readily apparent in these simple examples, this can matter in your code: if you wish to scan a generator's values multiple times, you must either create a new generator for each scan or build a rescannable list out of its values—a single generator's values will be consumed and exhausted after a single pass. See this chapter's sidebar "Why You Will Care: One-Shot Iterations" on page 621 for a prime example of the sort of code that must accommodate this generator property.

When we begin coding class-based iterables in Part VI, we'll also see that it's up to us to decide how many iterations we wish to support for our objects, if any. In general, objects that wish to support multiple scans will return supplemental class objects instead of themselves. The next section previews more of this model.

The Python 3.3 yield from Extension

Python 3.3 introduces extended syntax for the yield statement that allows delegation to a subgenerator with a from *generator* clause. In simple cases, it's the equivalent to a yielding for loop—the list here in the following forces the generator to produce all its values, and the comprehension in parentheses is a generator expression, covered in this chapter:

```
>>> def both(N):
        for i in range(N): yield i
        for i in (x ** 2 for x in range(N)): yield i

>>> list(both(5))
[0, 1, 2, 3, 4, 0, 1, 4, 9, 16]
```

The new 3.3 syntax makes this arguably more concise and explicit, and supports all the usual generator usage contexts:

```
>>> def both(N):
        yield from range(N)
        yield from (x ** 2 for x in range(N))

>>> list(both(5))
[0, 1, 2, 3, 4, 0, 1, 4, 9, 16]

>>> ' : '.join(str(i) for i in both(5))
'0 : 1 : 2 : 3 : 4 : 0 : 1 : 4 : 9 : 16'
```

In more advanced roles, however, this extension allows subgenerators to receive *sent* and *thrown* values directly from the calling scope, and return a final value to the outer generator. The net effect is to allow such generators to be split into multiple subgenerators much as a single function can be split into multiple subfunctions.

Since this is only available in 3.3 and later, and is beyond this chapter's generator coverage in general, we'll defer to Python 3.3's manuals for additional details. For an additional `yield from` example, also see the solution to this part's Exercise 11 described at the end of Chapter 21.

Generation in Built-in Types, Tools, and Classes

Finally, although we've focused on coding value generators ourselves in this section, don't forget that many built-in types behave in similar ways—as we saw in Chapter 14, for example, *dictionaries* are iterables with iterators that produce keys on each iteration:

```
>>> D = {'a':1, 'b':2, 'c':3}
>>> x = iter(D)
>>> next(x)
'c'
>>> next(x)
'b'
```

Like the values produced by handcoded generators, dictionary keys may be iterated over both manually and with automatic iteration tools including `for` loops, `map` calls, list comprehensions, and the many other contexts we met in Chapter 14:

```
>>> for key in D:
        print(key, D[key])

c 3
b 2
a 1
```

As we've also seen, for *file* iterators, Python simply loads lines from the file on demand:

```
>>> for line in open('temp.txt'):
        print(line, end='')
```

```
Tis but
a flesh wound.
```

While built-in type iterables are bound to a specific type of value generation, the concept is similar to the multipurpose generators we code with expressions and functions. Iteration contexts like `for` loops accept any iterable that has the expected methods, whether user-defined or built-in.

Generators and library tools: Directory walkers

Though beyond this book's scope, many Python standard library tools generate values today too, including email parsers, and the standard *directory walker*—which at each level of a tree yields a tuple of the current directory, its subdirectories, and its files:

```
>>> import os
>>> for (root, subs, files) in os.walk('.'):     # Directory walk generator
        for name in files:                        # A Python 'find' operation
            if name.startswith('call'):
                print(root, name)

. callables.py
.\dualpkg callables.py
```

In fact, `os.walk` is coded as a recursive function in Python in its *os.py* standard library file, in *C:\Python33\Lib* on Windows. Because it uses `yield` (and in 3.3 `yield from` instead of a `for` loop) to return results, it's a normal generator function, and hence an iterable object:

```
>>> G = os.walk(r'C:\code\pkg')
>>> iter(G) is G                       # Single-scan iterator: iter(G) optional
True
>>> I = iter(G)
>>> next(I)
('C:\\code\\pkg', ['__pycache__'], ['eggs.py', 'eggs.pyc', 'main.py', ...etc...])
>>> next(I)
('C:\\code\\pkg\\__pycache__', [], ['eggs.cpython-33.pyc', ...etc...])
>>> next(I)
StopIteration
```

By yielding results as it goes, the walker does not require its clients to wait for an entire tree to be scanned. See Python's manuals and follow-up books such as *Programming Python* for more on this tool. Also see Chapter 14 and others for `os.popen`—a related iterable used to run a shell command and read its output.

Generators and function application

In Chapter 18, we noted that starred arguments can unpack an *iterable* into individual arguments. Now that we've seen generators, we can also see what this means in code. In both 3.X and 2.X (though 2.X's `range` is a list):

```
>>> def f(a, b, c): print('%s, %s, and %s' % (a, b, c))

>>> f(0, 1, 2)                         # Normal positionals
```

```
0, 1, and 2
>>> f(*range(3))                        # Unpack range values: iterable in 3.X
0, 1, and 2
>>> f(*(i for i in range(3)))           # Unpack generator expression values
0, 1, and 2
```

This applies to dictionaries and views too (though `dict.values` is also a list in 2.X, and order is arbitrary when passing values by position):

```
>>> D = dict(a='Bob', b='dev', c=40.5); D
{'b': 'dev', 'c': 40.5, 'a': 'Bob'}
>>> f(a='Bob', b='dev', c=40.5)         # Normal keywords
Bob, dev, and 40.5
>>> f(**D)                              # Unpack dict: key=value
Bob, dev, and 40.5
>>> f(*D)                               # Unpack keys iterator
b, c, and a
>>> f(*D.values())                      # Unpack view iterator: iterable in 3.X
dev, 40.5, and Bob
```

Because the built-in `print` function in 3.X prints all its variable number of arguments, this also makes the following three forms equivalent—the latter using a * to unpack the results forced from a generator expression (though the second also creates a list of return values, and the first may leave your cursor at the end of the output line in some shells, but not in the IDLE GUI):

```
>>> for x in 'spam': print(x.upper(), end=' ')
S P A M

>>> list(print(x.upper(), end=' ') for x in 'spam')
S P A M [None, None, None, None]

>>> print(*(x.upper() for x in 'spam'))
S P A M
```

See Chapter 14 for an additional example that unpacks a file's lines by iterator into arguments.

Preview: User-defined iterables in classes

Although beyond the scope of this chapter, it is also possible to implement arbitrary user-defined generator objects with *classes* that conform to the iteration protocol. Such classes define a special __iter__ method run by the `iter` built-in function, which in turn returns an object having a __next__ method (`next` in 2.X) run by the `next` built-in function:

```
class SomeIterable:
    def __init__(...): ...       # On iter(): return self or supplemental object
    def __next__(...): ...       # On next(): coded here, or in another class
```

As the prior section suggested, these classes usually return their objects directly for single-iteration behavior, or a supplemental object with scan-specific state for multiple-scan support.

Alternatively, a user-defined iterable class's method functions can sometimes use yield to transform themselves into generators, with an automatically created __next__ method—a common application of yield we'll meet in Chapter 30 that is both wildly implicit and potentially useful! A __getitem__ indexing method is also available as a fallback option for iteration, though this is often not as flexible as the __iter__ and __next__ scheme (but has advantages for coding sequences).

The instance objects created from such a class are considered iterable and may be used in for loops and all other iteration contexts. With classes, though, we have access to richer logic and data structuring options, such as inheritance, that other generator constructs cannot offer by themselves. By coding methods, classes also can make iteration behavior much more *explicit* than the "magic" generator objects associated with built-in types and generator functions and expressions (though classes wield some magic of their own).

Hence, the iterator and generator story won't really be complete until we've seen how it maps to classes, too. For now, we'll have to settle for postponing its conclusion—and its final sequel—until we study class-based iterables in Chapter 30.

Example: Generating Scrambled Sequences

To demonstrate the power of iteration tools in action, let's turn to some more complete use case examples. In Chapter 18, we wrote a testing function that scrambled the order of arguments used to test generalized intersection and union functions. There, I noted that this might be better coded as a generator of values. Now that we've learned how to write generators, this serves to illustrate a practical application.

One note up front: because they slice and concatenate objects, all the examples in the section (including the permutations at the end) work only on *sequences* like strings and list, not on arbitrary *iterables* like files, maps, and other generators. That is, some of these examples will *be* generators themselves, producing values on request, but they cannot process generators as their inputs. Generalization for broader categories is left as an open issue, though the code here will suffice unchanged if you wrap nonsequence generators in list calls before passing them in.

Scrambling sequences

As coded in Chapter 18, we can reorder a sequence with slicing and concatenation, moving the front item to the end on each loop; *slicing* instead of indexing the item allows + to work for arbitrary sequence types:

```
>>> L, S = [1, 2, 3], 'spam'
>>> for i in range(len(S)):            # For repeat counts 0..3
        S = S[1:] + S[:1]              # Move front item to the end
        print(S, end=' ')

pams amsp mspa spam
```

```
>>> for i in range(len(L)):
        L = L[1:] + L[:1]                    # Slice so any sequence type works
        print(L, end=' ')

[2, 3, 1] [3, 1, 2] [1, 2, 3]
```

Alternatively, as we saw in Chapter 13, we get the same results by moving an entire front section to the end, though the order of the results varies slightly:

```
>>> for i in range(len(S)):                  # For positions 0..3
        X = S[i:] + S[:i]                     # Rear part + front part (same effect)
        print(X, end=' ')

spam pams amsp mspa
```

Simple functions

As is, this code works on specific named variables only. To generalize, we can turn it into a *simple function* to work on any object passed to its argument and return a result; since the first of these exhibits the classic list comprehension pattern, we can save some work by coding it as such in the second:

```
>>> def scramble(seq):
        res = []
        for i in range(len(seq)):
            res.append(seq[i:] + seq[:i])
        return res

>>> scramble('spam')
['spam', 'pams', 'amsp', 'mspa']

>>> def scramble(seq):
        return [seq[i:] + seq[:i] for i in range(len(seq))]

>>> scramble('spam')
['spam', 'pams', 'amsp', 'mspa']

>>> for x in scramble((1, 2, 3)):
        print(x, end=' ')

(1, 2, 3) (2, 3, 1) (3, 1, 2)
```

We could use recursion here as well, but it's probably overkill in this context.

Generator functions

The preceding section's simple approach works, but must build an entire result list in memory all at once (not great on memory usage if it's massive), and requires the caller to wait until the entire list is complete (less than ideal if this takes a substantial amount of time). We can do better on both fronts by translating this to a *generator function* that yields one result at a time, using either coding scheme:

```
>>> def scramble(seq):
        for i in range(len(seq)):
```

```
        seq = seq[1:] + seq[:1]              # Generator function
        yield seq                            # Assignments work here

>>> def scramble(seq):
        for i in range(len(seq)):            # Generator function
            yield seq[i:] + seq[:i]          # Yield one item per iteration

>>> list(scramble('spam'))                   # list() generates all results
['spam', 'pams', 'amsp', 'mspa']
>>> list(scramble((1, 2, 3)))                # Any sequence type works
[(1, 2, 3), (2, 3, 1), (3, 1, 2)]
>>>
>>> for x in scramble((1, 2, 3)):            # for loops generate results
        print(x, end=' ')


(1, 2, 3) (2, 3, 1) (3, 1, 2)
```

Generator functions retain their local scope state while active, minimize memory space requirements, and divide the work into shorter time slices. As full functions, they are also very general. Importantly, for loops and other iteration tools work the same whether stepping through a real list or a generator of values—the function can select between the two schemes freely, and even change strategies in the future.

Generator expressions

As we've seen, *generator expressions*—comprehensions in parentheses instead of square brackets—also generate values on request and retain their local state. They're not as flexible as full functions, but because they yield their values automatically, expressions can often be more concise in specific use cases like this:

```
>>> S
'spam'
>>> G = (S[i:] + S[:i] for i in range(len(S)))   # Generator expression equivalent
>>> list(G)
['spam', 'pams', 'amsp', 'mspa']
```

Notice that we can't use the assignment statement of the first generator function version here, because generator expressions cannot contain statements. This makes them a bit narrower in scope; in many cases, though, expressions can do similar work, as shown here. To generalize a generator expression for an arbitrary subject, wrap it in a *simple function* that takes an argument and returns a generator that uses it:

```
>>> F = lambda seq: (seq[i:] + seq[:i] for i in range(len(seq)))
>>> F(S)
<generator object <genexpr> at 0x00000000029883F0>
>>>
>>> list(F(S))
['spam', 'pams', 'amsp', 'mspa']
>>> list(F([1, 2, 3]))
[[1, 2, 3], [2, 3, 1], [3, 1, 2]]

>>> for x in F((1, 2, 3)):
        print(x, end=' ')
```

```
(1, 2, 3) (2, 3, 1) (3, 1, 2)
```

Tester client

Finally, we can use either the generator function or its expression equivalent in Chapter 18's *tester* to produce scrambled arguments—the sequence scrambling function becomes a tool we can use in other contexts:

```
# file scramble.py

def scramble(seq):
    for i in range(len(seq)):           # Generator function
        yield seq[i:] + seq[:i]         # Yield one item per iteration

scramble2 = lambda seq: (seq[i:] + seq[:i] for i in range(len(seq)))
```

And by moving the values generation out to an external tool, the tester becomes simpler:

```
>>> from scramble import scramble
>>> from inter2 import intersect, union
>>>
>>> def tester(func, items, trace=True):
        for args in scramble(items):        # Use generator (or: scramble2(items))
            if trace: print(args)
            print(sorted(func(*args)))

>>> tester(intersect, ('aab', 'abcde', 'ababab'))
('aab', 'abcde', 'ababab')
['a', 'b']
('abcde', 'ababab', 'aab')
['a', 'b']
('ababab', 'aab', 'abcde')
['a', 'b']

>>> tester(intersect, ([1, 2], [2, 3, 4], [1, 6, 2, 7, 3]), False)
[2]
[2]
[2]
```

Permutations: All possible combinations

These techniques have many other real-world applications—consider generating attachments in an email message or points to be plotted in a GUI. Moreover, other types of sequence scrambles serve central roles in other applications, from searches to mathematics. As is, our sequence scrambler is a simple reordering, but some programs warrant the more exhaustive set of all possible orderings we get from *permutations*—produced using recursive functions in both list-builder and generator forms by the following module file:

```
# File permute.py

def permute1(seq):
    if not seq:                          # Shuffle any sequence: list
```

```
        return [seq]                              # Empty sequence
    else:
        res = []
        for i in range(len(seq)):
            rest = seq[:i] + seq[i+1:]            # Delete current node
            for x in permute1(rest):              # Permute the others
                res.append(seq[i:i+1] + x)        # Add node at front
        return res

def permute2(seq):
    if not seq:                                   # Shuffle any sequence: generator
        yield seq                                 # Empty sequence
    else:
        for i in range(len(seq)):
            rest = seq[:i] + seq[i+1:]            # Delete current node
            for x in permute2(rest):              # Permute the others
                yield seq[i:i+1] + x              # Add node at front
```

Both of these functions produce the same results, though the second defers much of its
work until it is asked for a result. This code is a bit advanced, especially the second of
these functions (and to some Python newcomers might even be categorized as cruel
and inhumane punishment!). Still, as I'll explain in a moment, there are cases where
the generator approach can be highly useful.

Study and test this code for more insight, and add prints to trace if it helps. If it's still
a mystery, try to make sense of the first version first; remember that generator functions
simply return objects with methods that handle next operations run by for loops at
each level, and don't produce any results until iterated; and trace through some of the
following examples to see how they're handled by this code.

Permutations produce more orderings than the original shuffler—for N items, we get
N! (factorial) results instead of just N (24 for 4: 4 * 3 * 2 * 1). In fact, that's why we need
recursion here: the number of nested loops is arbitrary, and depends on the length of
the sequence permuted:

```
>>> from scramble import scramble
>>> from permute import permute1, permute2

>>> list(scramble('abc'))                         # Simple scrambles: N
['abc', 'bca', 'cab']

>>> permute1('abc')                               # Permutations larger: N!
['abc', 'acb', 'bac', 'bca', 'cab', 'cba']
>>> list(permute2('abc'))                         # Generate all combinations
['abc', 'acb', 'bac', 'bca', 'cab', 'cba']

>>> G = permute2('abc')                           # Iterate (iter() not needed)
>>> next(G)
'abc'
>>> next(G)
'acb'
>>> for x in permute2('abc'): print(x)            # Automatic iteration
...prints six lines...
```

The list and generator versions' results are the same, though the generator minimizes both space usage and delays for results. For larger items, the set of all permutations is much larger than the simpler scrambler's:

```
>>> permute1('spam') == list(permute2('spam'))
True
>>> len(list(permute2('spam'))), len(list(scramble('spam')))
(24, 4)

>>> list(scramble('spam'))
['spam', 'pams', 'amsp', 'mspa']
>>> list(permute2('spam'))
['spam', 'spma', 'sapm', 'samp', 'smpa', 'smap', 'psam', 'psma', 'pasm', 'pams',
 'pmsa', 'pmas', 'aspm', 'asmp', 'apsm', 'apms', 'amsp', 'amps', 'mspa', 'msap',
 'mpsa', 'mpas', 'masp', 'maps']
```

Per Chapter 19, there are nonrecursive alternatives here too, using explicit stacks or queues, and other sequence orderings are common (e.g., fixed-size subsets and combinations that filter out duplicates of differing order), but these require coding extensions we'll forgo here. See the book *Programming Python* for more on this theme, or experiment further on your own.

Don't Abuse Generators: EIBTI

Generators are a somewhat advanced tool, and might be better treated as an optional topic, but for the fact that they permeate the Python language, especially in 3.X. In fact, they seem less optional to this book's audience than Unicode (which was exiled to Part VIII). As we've seen, fundamental built-in tools such as range, map, dictionary keys, and even files are now generators, so you must be familiar with the concept even if you don't write new generators of your own. Moreover, user-defined generators are increasingly common in Python code that you might come across today—in the Python standard library, for instance.

In general, the same cautions I gave for list comprehensions apply here as well: don't complicate your code with user-defined generators if they are not warranted. Especially for smaller programs and data sets, there may be no good reason to use these tools. In such cases, simple lists of results will suffice, will be easier to understand, will be garbage-collected automatically, and may be produced quicker (and they are today: see the next chapter). Advanced tools like generators that rely on implicit "magic" can be fun to experiment with, but they have no place in real code that must be used by others except when clearly justified.

Or, to quote from Python's import this motto again:

> Explicit is better than implicit.

The acronym for this, *EIBTI*, is one of Python's core guidelines, and for good reason: the more explicit your code is about its behavior, the more likely it is that the next programmer will be able to understand it. This applies directly to generators, whose implicit behavior may very well be more difficult for some to grasp than less obscure alternatives. Always: keep it simple unless it must be complicated!

On the other hand: Space and time, conciseness, expressiveness

That being said, there are specific use cases that generators can address well. They can reduce memory footprint in some programs, reduce delays in others, and can occasionally make the impossible possible. Consider, for example, a program that must produce all possible permutations of a nontrivial sequence. Since the number of combinations is a *factorial* that explodes exponentially, the preceding `permute1` recursive list-builder function will either introduce a noticeable and perhaps interminable pause or fail completely due to memory requirements, whereas the `permute2` recursive generator will not—it returns each individual result quickly, and can handle very large result sets:

```
>>> import math
>>> math.factorial(10)                  # 10 * 9 * 8 * 7 * 6 * 5 * 4 * 3 * 2 * 1
3628800
>>> from permute import permute1, permute2
>>> seq = list(range(10))
>>> p1 = permute1(seq)                   # 37 seconds on a 2GHz quad-core machine
                                         # Creates a list of 3.6M numbers
>>> len(p1), p1[0], p1[1]
(3628800, [0, 1, 2, 3, 4, 5, 6, 7, 8, 9], [0, 1, 2, 3, 4, 5, 6, 7, 9, 8])
```

In this case, the list builder pauses for 37 seconds on my computer to build a 3.6-million-item list, but the generator can begin returning results immediately:

```
>>> p2 = permute2(seq)                   # Returns generator immediately
>>> next(p2)                             # And produces each result quickly on request
[0, 1, 2, 3, 4, 5, 6, 7, 8, 9]
>>> next(p2)
[0, 1, 2, 3, 4, 5, 6, 7, 9, 8]

>>> p2 = list(permute2(seq))             # About 28 seconds, though still impractical
>>> p1 == p2                             # Same set of results generated
True
```

Naturally, we might be able to optimize the list builder's code to run quicker (e.g., an explicit stack instead of recursion might change its performance), but for larger sequences, it's not an option at all—at just 50 items, the number of permutations precludes building a results list, and would take far too long for mere mortals like us (and larger values will overflow the preset recursion stack depth limit: see the preceding chapter). The generator, however, is still viable—it is able to produce individual results immediately:

```
>>> math.factorial(50)
30414093201713378043612608166064768844377641568960512000000000000
>>> p3 = permute2(list(range(50)))
>>> next(p3)                             # permute1 is not an option here!
[0, 1, 2, 3, 4, 5, 6, 7, 8, 9, 10, 11, 12, 13, 14, 15, 16, 17, 18, 19, 20, 21, 22,
```

```
    23, 24, 25, 26, 27, 28, 29, 30, 31, 32, 33, 34, 35, 36, 37, 38, 39, 40, 41, 42, 43,
    44, 45, 46, 47, 48, 49]
```

For more fun—and to yield results that are more variable and less obviously deterministic—we could also use Python's `random` module of Chapter 5 to randomly shuffle the sequence to be permuted before the permuter begins its work. (In fact, we might be able to use the random shuffler as a permutation generator in general, as long as we either can assume that it won't repeat shuffles during the time we consume them, or test its results against prior shuffles to avoid repeats—and hope that we do not live in the strange universe where a random sequence repeats the same result an infinite number of times!). In the following, each `permute2` and `next` call returns immediately as before, but a `permute1` hangs:

```
>>> import random
>>> math.factorial(20)                 # permute1 is not an option here
2432902008176640000
>>> seq = list(range(20))

>>> random.shuffle(seq)                 # Shuffle sequence randomly first
>>> p = permute2(seq)
>>> next(p)
[10, 17, 4, 14, 11, 3, 16, 19, 12, 8, 6, 5, 2, 15, 18, 7, 1, 0, 13, 9]
>>> next(p)
[10, 17, 4, 14, 11, 3, 16, 19, 12, 8, 6, 5, 2, 15, 18, 7, 1, 0, 9, 13]

>>> random.shuffle(seq)
>>> p = permute2(seq)
>>> next(p)
[16, 1, 5, 14, 15, 12, 0, 2, 6, 19, 10, 17, 11, 18, 13, 7, 4, 9, 8, 3]
>>> next(p)
[16, 1, 5, 14, 15, 12, 0, 2, 6, 19, 10, 17, 11, 18, 13, 7, 4, 9, 3, 8]
```

The main point here is that generators can sometimes produce results from large solution sets when list builders cannot. Then again, it's not clear how common such use cases may be in the real world, and this doesn't necessarily justify the *implicit* flavor of value generation that we get with generator functions and expressions. As we'll see in Part VI, value generation can also be coded as iterable objects with *classes*. Class-based iterables can produce items on request too, and are far more *explicit* than the magic objects and methods produced for generator functions and expressions.

Part of programming is finding a balance among tradeoffs like these, and there are no absolute rules here. While the benefits of generators may sometimes justify their use, maintainability should always be a top priority too. Like comprehensions, generators also offer an *expressiveness* and *code economy* that's hard to resist if you understand how they work—but you'll want to weigh this against the frustration of coworkers who might not.

Example: Emulating zip and map with Iteration Tools

To help you evaluate their roles further, let's take a quick look at one more example of generators in action that illustrates just how expressive they can be. Once you know about comprehensions, generators, and other iteration tools, it turns out that emulating many of Python's functional built-ins is both straightforward and instructive. For example, we've already seen how the built-in `zip` and `map` functions combine iterables and project functions across them, respectively. With multiple iterable arguments, `map` projects the function across items taken from each iterable in much the same way that `zip` pairs them up (3.X's `map` truncates shorter iterables; 2.X pads them with `None`):

```
>>> S1 = 'abc'
>>> S2 = 'xyz123'
>>> list(zip(S1, S2))                    # zip pairs items from iterables
[('a', 'x'), ('b', 'y'), ('c', 'z')]

# zip pairs items, truncates at shortest
>>> list(zip([-2, -1, 0, 1, 2]))         # Single sequence: 1-ary tuples
[(-2,), (-1,), (0,), (1,), (2,)]
>>> list(zip([1, 2, 3], [2, 3, 4, 5]))   # N sequences: N-ary tuples
[(1, 2), (2, 3), (3, 4)]

# map passes paired items to function, truncates
>>> list(map(abs, [-2, -1, 0, 1, 2]))    # Single sequence: 1-ary function
[2, 1, 0, 1, 2]
>>> list(map(pow, [1, 2, 3], [2, 3, 4, 5]))   # N sequences: N-ary function, 3.X
[1, 8, 81]

# map and zip accept arbitrary iterables
>>> list(map(lambda x, y: x + y, open('script2.py'), open('script2.py')))
['import sys\nimport sys\n', 'print(sys.path)\nprint(sys.path)\n', ...etc...]

>>> [x + y for (x, y) in zip(open('script2.py'), open('script2.py'))]
['import sys\nimport sys\n', 'print(sys.path)\nprint(sys.path)\n', ...etc...]
```

Though they're being used for different purposes, if you study these examples long enough, you might notice a relationship between `zip` results and mapped function arguments that our next example can exploit.

Coding your own map(func, ...)

Although the `map` and `zip` built-ins are fast and convenient, it's always possible to emulate them in code of our own. In the preceding chapter, for example, we saw a function that emulated the `map` built-in for a single sequence (or other iterable) argument. It doesn't take much more work to allow for multiple sequences, as the built-in does:

```
# map(func, seqs...) workalike with zip

def mymap(func, *seqs):
    res = []
    for args in zip(*seqs):
        res.append(func(*args))
```

```
        return res
    print(mymap(abs, [-2, -1, 0, 1, 2]))
    print(mymap(pow, [1, 2, 3], [2, 3, 4, 5]))
```

This version relies heavily upon the special *args argument-passing syntax—it collects multiple sequence (really, iterable) arguments, unpacks them as zip arguments to combine, and then unpacks the paired zip results as arguments to the passed-in function. That is, we're using the fact that the zipping is essentially a nested operation in mapping. The test code at the bottom applies this to both one and two sequences to produce this output—the same we would get with the built-in map (this code is in file *mymap.py* in the book's examples if you want to run it live):

```
[2, 1, 0, 1, 2]
[1, 8, 81]
```

Really, though, the prior version exhibits the classic *list comprehension pattern*, building a list of operation results within a for loop. We can code our map more concisely as an equivalent one-line list comprehension:

```
# Using a list comprehension

def mymap(func, *seqs):
    return [func(*args) for args in zip(*seqs)]

print(mymap(abs, [-2, -1, 0, 1, 2]))
print(mymap(pow, [1, 2, 3], [2, 3, 4, 5]))
```

When this is run the result is the same as before, but the code is more concise and might run faster (more on performance in the section "Timing Iteration Alternatives" on page 629). Both of the preceding mymap versions build result lists all at once, though, and this can waste memory for larger lists. Now that we know about *generator functions and expressions*, it's simple to recode both these alternatives to produce results on demand instead:

```
# Using generators: yield and (...)

def mymap(func, *seqs):
    for args in zip(*seqs):
        yield func(*args)

def mymap(func, *seqs):
    return (func(*args) for args in zip(*seqs))
```

These versions produce the same results but return generators designed to support the iteration protocol—the first yields one result at a time, and the second returns a generator expression's result to do the same. They produce the same results if we wrap them in list calls to force them to produce their values all at once:

```
print(list(mymap(abs, [-2, -1, 0, 1, 2])))
print(list(mymap(pow, [1, 2, 3], [2, 3, 4, 5])))
```

No work is really done here until the `list` calls force the generators to run, by activating the iteration protocol. The generators returned by these functions themselves, as well as that returned by the Python 3.X flavor of the `zip` built-in they use, produce results only on demand.

Coding your own zip(...) and map(None, ...)

Of course, much of the magic in the examples shown so far lies in their use of the `zip` built-in to pair arguments from multiple sequences or iterables. Our `map` workalikes are also really emulating the behavior of the Python 3.X `map`—they truncate at the length of the shortest argument, and they do not support the notion of padding results when lengths differ, as `map` does in Python 2.X with a `None` argument:

```
C:code> c:\python27\python
>>> map(None, [1, 2, 3], [2, 3, 4, 5])
[(1, 2), (2, 3), (3, 4), (None, 5)]
>>> map(None, 'abc', 'xyz123')
[('a', 'x'), ('b', 'y'), ('c', 'z'), (None, '1'), (None, '2'), (None, '3')]
```

Using iteration tools, we can code workalikes that emulate both truncating `zip` and 2.X's padding `map`—these turn out to be nearly the same in code:

```
# zip(seqs...) and 2.X map(None, seqs...) workalikes

def myzip(*seqs):
    seqs = [list(S) for S in seqs]
    res  = []
    while all(seqs):
        res.append(tuple(S.pop(0) for S in seqs))
    return res

def mymapPad(*seqs, pad=None):
    seqs = [list(S) for S in seqs]
    res  = []
    while any(seqs):
        res.append(tuple((S.pop(0) if S else pad) for S in seqs))
    return res

S1, S2 = 'abc', 'xyz123'
print(myzip(S1, S2))
print(mymapPad(S1, S2))
print(mymapPad(S1, S2, pad=99))
```

Both of the functions coded here work on any type of *iterable* object, because they run their arguments through the `list` built-in to force result generation (e.g., files would work as arguments, in addition to sequences like strings). Notice the use of the `all` and `any` built-ins here—these return `True` if all and any items in an iterable are `True` (or equivalently, nonempty), respectively. These built-ins are used to stop looping when any or all of the listified arguments become empty after deletions.

Also note the use of the Python 3.X *keyword-only* argument, pad; unlike the 2.X map, our version will allow any pad object to be specified (if you're using 2.X, use a

**kargs form to support this option instead; see Chapter 18 for details). When these functions are run, the following results are printed—a zip, and two padding maps:

```
[('a', 'x'), ('b', 'y'), ('c', 'z')]
[('a', 'x'), ('b', 'y'), ('c', 'z'), (None, '1'), (None, '2'), (None, '3')]
[('a', 'x'), ('b', 'y'), ('c', 'z'), (99, '1'), (99, '2'), (99, '3')]
```

These functions aren't amenable to list comprehension translation because their loops are too specific. As before, though, while our zip and map workalikes currently build and return result lists, it's just as easy to turn them into *generators* with yield so that they each return one piece of their result set at a time. The results are the same as before, but we need to use list again to force the generators to yield their values for display:

```python
# Using generators: yield

def myzip(*seqs):
    seqs = [list(S) for S in seqs]
    while all(seqs):
        yield tuple(S.pop(0) for S in seqs)

def mymapPad(*seqs, pad=None):
    seqs = [list(S) for S in seqs]
    while any(seqs):
        yield tuple((S.pop(0) if S else pad) for S in seqs)

S1, S2 = 'abc', 'xyz123'
print(list(myzip(S1, S2)))
print(list(mymapPad(S1, S2)))
print(list(mymapPad(S1, S2, pad=99)))
```

Finally, here's an alternative implementation of our zip and map emulators—rather than deleting arguments from lists with the pop method, the following versions do their job by calculating the minimum and maximum *argument lengths*. Armed with these lengths, it's easy to code nested list comprehensions to step through argument index ranges:

```python
# Alternate implementation with lengths

def myzip(*seqs):
    minlen = min(len(S) for S in seqs)
    return [tuple(S[i] for S in seqs) for i in range(minlen)]

def mymapPad(*seqs, pad=None):
    maxlen = max(len(S) for S in seqs)
    index  = range(maxlen)
    return [tuple((S[i] if len(S) > i else pad) for S in seqs) for i in index]

S1, S2 = 'abc', 'xyz123'
print(myzip(S1, S2))
print(mymapPad(S1, S2))
print(mymapPad(S1, S2, pad=99))
```

Because these use len and indexing, they assume that arguments are *sequences* or similar, not arbitrary iterables, much like our earlier sequence scramblers and permuters.

The outer comprehensions here step through argument index ranges, and the inner comprehensions (passed to tuple) step through the passed-in sequences to pull out arguments in parallel. When they're run, the results are as before.

Most strikingly, generators and iterators seem to run rampant in this example. The arguments passed to min and max are generator expressions, which run to completion before the nested comprehensions begin iterating. Moreover, the nested list comprehensions employ two levels of delayed evaluation—the Python 3.X range built-in is an iterable, as is the generator expression argument to tuple.

In fact, no results are produced here until the square brackets of the list comprehensions request values to place in the result list—they force the comprehensions and generators to run. To turn these functions themselves into generators instead of list builders, use parentheses instead of square brackets again. Here's the case for our zip:

```
# Using generators: (...)

def myzip(*seqs):
    minlen = min(len(S) for S in seqs)
    return (tuple(S[i] for S in seqs) for i in range(minlen))

S1, S2 = 'abc', 'xyz123'
print(list(myzip(S1, S2)))          # Go!... [('a', 'x'), ('b', 'y'), ('c', 'z')]
```

In this case, it takes a list call to activate the generators and other iterables to produce their results. Experiment with these on your own for more details. Developing further coding alternatives is left as a suggested exercise (see also the sidebar "Why You Will Care: One-Shot Iterations" on page 621 for investigation of one such option).

 Watch for more yield examples in Chapter 30, where we'll use it in conjunction with the __iter__ operator overloading method to implement user-defined iterable objects in an automated fashion. The state retention of local variables in this role serves as an alternative to class attributes in the same spirit as the closure functions of Chapter 17; as we'll see, though, this technique *combines* classes and functional tools instead of posing a paradigm alternative.

Why You Will Care: One-Shot Iterations

In Chapter 14, we saw how some built-ins (like map) support only a single traversal and are empty after it occurs, and I promised to show you an example of how that can become subtle but important in practice. Now that we've studied a few more iteration topics, I can make good on this promise. Consider the following clever alternative coding for this chapter's zip emulation examples, adapted from one in Python's manuals at the time I wrote these words:

```
def myzip(*args):
    iters = map(iter, args)
    while iters:
```

```
    res = [next(i) for i in iters]
    yield tuple(res)
```

Because this code uses `iter` and `next`, it works on any type of iterable. Note that there is no reason to catch the `StopIteration` raised by the `next(i)` inside the comprehension here when any one of the arguments' iterators is exhausted—allowing it to pass ends this generator function and has the same effect that a `return` statement would. The `while iters:` suffices to loop if at least one argument is passed, and avoids an infinite loop otherwise (the list comprehension would always return an empty list).

This code works fine in Python 2.X as is:

```
>>> list(myzip('abc', 'lmnop'))
[('a', 'l'), ('b', 'm'), ('c', 'n')]
```

But it falls into an infinite loop and fails in Python 3.X, because the 3.X `map` returns a one-shot iterable object instead of a list as in 2.X. In 3.X, as soon as we've run the list comprehension inside the loop once, `iters` will be exhausted but still `True` (and `res` will be `[]`) forever. To make this work in 3.X, we need to use the `list` built-in function to create an object that can support multiple iterations:

```
def myzip(*args):
    iters = list(map(iter, args))        # Allow multiple scans
    ...rest as is...
```

Run this on your own to trace its operation. The lesson here: wrapping `map` calls in `list` calls in 3.X is not just for display!

Comprehension Syntax Summary

We've been focusing on list comprehensions and generators in this chapter, but keep in mind that there are two other comprehension expression forms available in both 3.X and 2.7: set and dictionary comprehensions. We met these briefly in Chapter 5 and Chapter 8, but with our new knowledge of comprehensions and generators, you should now be able to grasp these extensions in full:

- For *sets*, the new literal form `{1, 3, 2}` is equivalent to `set([1, 3, 2])`, and the new set comprehension syntax `{f(x) for x in S if P(x)}` is like the generator expression `set(f(x) for x in S if P(x))`, where `f(x)` is an arbitrary expression.

- For *dictionaries*, the new dictionary comprehension syntax `{key: val for (key, val) in zip(keys, vals)}` works like the form `dict(zip(keys, vals))`, and `{x: f(x) for x in items}` is like the generator expression `dict((x, f(x)) for x in items)`.

Here's a summary of all the comprehension alternatives in 3.X and 2.7. The last two are new and are not available in 2.6 and earlier:

```
>>> [x * x for x in range(10)]                # List comprehension: builds list
[0, 1, 4, 9, 16, 25, 36, 49, 64, 81]          # Like list(generator expr)
```

```
>>> (x * x for x in range(10))            # Generator expression: produces items
<generator object at 0x009E7328>          # Parens are often optional

>>> {x * x for x in range(10)}            # Set comprehension, 3.X and 2.7
{0, 1, 4, 81, 64, 9, 16, 49, 25, 36}      # {x, y} is a set in these versions too

>>> {x: x * x for x in range(10)}         # Dictionary comprehension, 3.X and 2.7
{0: 0, 1: 1, 2: 4, 3: 9, 4: 16, 5: 25, 6: 36, 7: 49, 8: 64, 9: 81}
```

Scopes and Comprehension Variables

Now that we've seen all comprehension forms, be sure to also review Chapter 17's overview of the localization of loop variables in these expressions. *Python 3.X* localizes loop variables in all four forms—temporary loop variable names in generator, set, dictionary, and list comprehensions are local to the expression. They don't clash with names outside, but are also not available there, and work differently than the **for** loop iteration statement:

```
c:\code> py -3
>>> (X for X in range(5))
<generator object <genexpr> at 0x00000000028E4798>
>>> X
NameError: name 'X' is not defined

>>> X = 99
>>> [X for X in range(5)]           # 3.X: generator, set, dict, and list localize
[0, 1, 2, 3, 4]
>>> X
99

>>> Y = 99
>>> for Y in range(5): pass         # But loop statements do not localize names

>>> Y
4
```

As mentioned in Chapter 17, 3.X variables assigned in a comprehension are really a further nested special-case scope; other names referenced within these expressions follow the usual LEGB rules. In the following generator, for example, Z is localized in the comprehension, but Y and X are found in the enclosing local and global scopes as usual:

```
>>> X = 'aaa'
>>> def func():
        Y = 'bbb'
        print(''.join(Z for Z in X + Y))        # Z comprehension, Y local, X global

>>> func()
aaabbb
```

Python 2.X is the same in this regard, except that *list comprehension* variables are not localized—they work just like **for** loops and keep their last iteration values, but are also open to unexpected clashes with outside names. Generator, set, and dictionary forms localize names as in 3.X:

```
c:\code> py -2
>>> (X for X in range(5))
<generator object <genexpr> at 0x0000000002147EE8>
>>> X
NameError: name 'X' is not defined

>>> X = 99
>>> [X for X in range(5)]          # 2.X: List does not localize its names, like for
[0, 1, 2, 3, 4]
>>> X
4

>>> Y = 99
>>> for Y in range(5): pass        # for loops do not localize names in 2.X or 3.X

>>> Y
4
```

If you care about version portability, and symmetry with the **for** loop statement, use unique names for variables in comprehension expressions as a rule of thumb. The 2.X behavior makes sense given that a generator object is discarded after it finishes producing results, but a list comprehension is equivalent to a **for** loop—though this analogy doesn't hold for the set and dictionary forms that localize their names in both Pythons, and are, somewhat coincidentally, the topic of the next section.

Comprehending Set and Dictionary Comprehensions

In a sense, set and dictionary comprehensions are just syntactic sugar for passing generator expressions to the type names. Because both accept any iterable, a generator works well here:

```
>>> {x * x for x in range(10)}                  # Comprehension
{0, 1, 4, 81, 64, 9, 16, 49, 25, 36}
>>> set(x * x for x in range(10))               # Generator and type name
{0, 1, 4, 81, 64, 9, 16, 49, 25, 36}

>>> {x: x * x for x in range(10)}
{0: 0, 1: 1, 2: 4, 3: 9, 4: 16, 5: 25, 6: 36, 7: 49, 8: 64, 9: 81}
>>> dict((x, x * x) for x in range(10))
{0: 0, 1: 1, 2: 4, 3: 9, 4: 16, 5: 25, 6: 36, 7: 49, 8: 64, 9: 81}

>>> x                                           # Loop variable localized in 2.X + 3.X
NameError: name 'x' is not defined
```

As for list comprehensions, though, we can always build the result objects with manual code, too. Here are statement-based equivalents of the last two comprehensions (though they differ in that name localization, per the prior section):

```
>>> res = set()
>>> for x in range(10):                         # Set comprehension equivalent
```

```
        res.add(x * x)

>>> res
{0, 1, 4, 81, 64, 9, 16, 49, 25, 36}

>>> res = {}
>>> for x in range(10):                    # Dict comprehension equivalent
        res[x] = x * x

>>> res
{0: 0, 1: 1, 2: 4, 3: 9, 4: 16, 5: 25, 6: 36, 7: 49, 8: 64, 9: 81}

>>> x       # Localized in comprehension expressions, but not in loop statements
9
```

Notice that although both set and dictionary comprehensions accept and scan iterables, they have no notion of *generating* results on demand—both forms build complete objects all at once. If you mean to produce keys and values upon request, a generator expression is more appropriate:

```
>>> G = ((x, x * x) for x in range(10))
>>> next(G)
(0, 0)
>>> next(G)
(1, 1)
```

Extended Comprehension Syntax for Sets and Dictionaries

Like list comprehensions and generator expressions, both set and dictionary comprehensions support nested associated if clauses to filter items out of the result—the following collect squares of even items (i.e., items having no remainder for division by 2) in a range:

```
>>> [x * x for x in range(10) if x % 2 == 0]        # Lists are ordered
[0, 4, 16, 36, 64]
>>> {x * x for x in range(10) if x % 2 == 0}        # But sets are not
{0, 16, 4, 64, 36}
>>> {x: x * x for x in range(10) if x % 2 == 0}     # Neither are dict keys
{0: 0, 8: 64, 2: 4, 4: 16, 6: 36}
```

Nested for loops work as well, though the unordered and no-duplicates nature of both types of objects can make the results a bit less straightforward to decipher:

```
>>> [x + y for x in [1, 2, 3] for y in [4, 5, 6]]    # Lists keep duplicates
[5, 6, 7, 6, 7, 8, 7, 8, 9]
>>> {x + y for x in [1, 2, 3] for y in [4, 5, 6]}    # But sets do not
{8, 9, 5, 6, 7}
>>> {x: y for x in [1, 2, 3] for y in [4, 5, 6]}     # Neither do dict keys
{1: 6, 2: 6, 3: 6}
```

Like list comprehensions, the set and dictionary varieties can also iterate over any type of iterable—lists, strings, files, ranges, and anything else that supports the iteration protocol:

```
>>> {x + y for x in 'ab' for y in 'cd'}
{'ac', 'bd', 'bc', 'ad'}

>>> {x + y: (ord(x), ord(y)) for x in 'ab' for y in 'cd'}
{'ac': (97, 99), 'bd': (98, 100), 'bc': (98, 99), 'ad': (97, 100)}

>>> {k * 2 for k in ['spam', 'ham', 'sausage'] if k[0] == 's'}
{'sausagesausage', 'spamspam'}

>>> {k.upper(): k * 2 for k in ['spam', 'ham', 'sausage'] if k[0] == 's'}
{'SAUSAGE': 'sausagesausage', 'SPAM': 'spamspam'}
```

For more details, experiment with these tools on your own. They may or may not have a performance advantage over the generator or `for` loop alternatives, but we would have to time their performance explicitly to be sure—which seems a natural segue to the next chapter.

Chapter Summary

This chapter wrapped up our coverage of built-in comprehension and iteration tools. It explored list comprehensions in the context of functional tools, and presented generator functions and expressions as additional iteration protocol tools. As a finale, we also summarized the four forms of comprehension in Python today—list, generator, set, and dictionary. Though we've now seen all the built-in iteration tools, the subject will resurface when we study user-defined iterable class objects in Chapter 30.

The next chapter is something of a continuation of the theme of this one—it rounds out this part of the book with a case study that times the performance of the tools we've studied here, and serves as a more realistic example at the midpoint in this book. Before we move ahead to benchmarking comprehensions and generators, though, this chapter's quizzes give you a chance to review what you've learned about them here.

Test Your Knowledge: Quiz

1. What is the difference between enclosing a list comprehension in square brackets and parentheses?
2. How are generators and iterators related?
3. How can you tell if a function is a generator function?
4. What does a `yield` statement do?
5. How are `map` calls and list comprehensions related? Compare and contrast the two.

Test Your Knowledge: Answers

1. List comprehensions in square brackets produce the result list all at once in memory. When they are enclosed in parentheses instead, they are actually generator

expressions—they have a similar meaning but do not produce the result list all at once. Instead, generator expressions return a generator object, which yields one item in the result at a time when used in an iteration context.

2. Generators are iterable objects that support the iteration protocol automatically—they have an iterator with a __next__ method (next in 2.X) that repeatedly advances to the next item in a series of results and raises an exception at the end of the series. In Python, we can code generator functions with def and yield, generator expressions with parenthesized comprehensions, and generator objects with classes that define a special method named __iter__ (discussed later in the book).

3. A generator function has a yield statement somewhere in its code. Generator functions are otherwise identical to normal functions syntactically, but they are compiled specially by Python so as to return an iterable generator object when called. That object retains state and code location between values.

4. When present, this statement makes Python compile the function specially as a generator; when called, the function returns a generator object that supports the iteration protocol. When the yield statement is run, it sends a result back to the caller and suspends the function's state; the function can then be resumed after the last yield statement, in response to a next built-in or __next__ method call issued by the caller. In more advanced roles, the generator send method similarly resumes the generator, but can also pass a value that shows up as the yield expression's value. Generator functions may also have a return statement, which terminates the generator.

5. The map call is similar to a list comprehension—both produce a series of values, by collecting the results of applying an operation to each item in a sequence or other iterable, one item at a time. The primary difference is that map applies a function call to each item, and list comprehensions apply arbitrary expressions. Because of this, list comprehensions are more general; they can apply a function call expression like map, but map requires a function to apply other kinds of expressions. List comprehensions also support extended syntax such as nested for loops and if clauses that subsume the filter built-in. In Python 3.X, map also differs in that it produces a *generator* of values; the list comprehension materializes the result list in memory all at once. In 2.X, both tools create result lists.

The Benchmarking Interlude

Now that we know about coding functions and iteration tools, we're going to take a short side trip to put both of them to work. This chapter closes out the function part of this book with a larger case study that times the relative performance of the iteration tools we've met so far.

Along the way, this case study surveys Python's code timing tools, discusses benchmarking techniques in general, and allows us to explore code that's a bit more realistic and useful than most of what we've seen up to this point. We'll also measure the speed of current Python implementations—a data point that may or may not be significant, depending on the type of code you write.

Finally, because this is the last chapter in this part of the book, we'll close with the usual sets of "gotchas" and exercises to help you start coding the ideas you've read about. First, though, let's have some fun with a tangible Python application.

Timing Iteration Alternatives

We've met quite a few iteration alternatives in this book. Like much in programming, they represent tradeoffs—in terms of both subjective factors like expressiveness, and more objective criteria such as performance. Part of your job as a programmer and engineer is selecting tools based on factors like these.

In terms of performance, I've mentioned a few times that list comprehensions sometimes have a speed advantage over for loop statements, and that map calls can be faster or slower than both depending on call patterns. The generator functions and expressions of the preceding chapter tend to be slightly slower than list comprehensions, though they minimize memory space requirements and don't delay the caller for result generation when there are many results to generate.

All that is generally true today, but relative performance can vary over time because Python's internals are constantly being changed and optimized, and code structure can influence speed arbitrarily. If you want to verify their performance for yourself, you need to time these alternatives on your own computer and your own version of Python.

Timing Module: Homegrown

Luckily, Python makes it easy to time code. For example, to get the total time taken to run multiple calls to a function with arbitrary positional arguments, the following first-cut function might suffice:

```
# File timer0.py
import time
def timer(func, *args):                        # Simplistic timing function
    start = time.clock()
    for i in range(1000):
        func(*args)
    return time.clock() - start                 # Total elapsed time in seconds
```

This works—it fetches time values from Python's `time` module, and subtracts the system start time from the stop time after running 1,000 calls to the passed-in function with the passed-in arguments. On my computer in Python 3.3:

```
>>> from timer0 import timer
>>> timer(pow, 2, 1000)                         # Time to call pow(2, 1000) 1000 times
0.00296260674205626
>>> timer(str.upper, 'spam')                    # Time to call 'spam'.upper() 1000 times
0.0005165746166859719
```

Though simple, this timer is also fairly limited, and deliberately exhibits some classic mistakes in both function design and benchmarking. Among these, it:

- Doesn't support *keyword* arguments in the tested function call
- Hardcodes the *repetitions* count
- Charges the cost of `range` to the tested function's time
- Always uses `time.clock`, which might not be best outside Windows
- Doesn't give callers a way to verify that the tested function actually *worked*
- Only gives *total* time, which might fluctuate on some heavily loaded machines

In other words, timing code is more complex than you might expect! To be more general and accurate, let's expand this into still simple but more useful timer utility functions we can use both to see how iteration alternative options stack up now, and apply to other timing needs in the future. These functions are coded in a module file so they can be used in a variety of programs, and have docstrings giving some basic details that PyDoc can display on request—see Figure 15-2 in Chapter 15 for a screenshot of the documentation pages rendered for the timing modules we're coding here:

```
# File timer.py
"""
Homegrown timing tools for function calls.
Does total time, best-of time, and best-of-totals time
"""
```

```
import time, sys
timer = time.clock if sys.platform[:3] == 'win' else time.time

def total(reps, func, *pargs, **kargs):
    """
    Total time to run func() reps times.
    Returns (total time, last result)
    """
    repslist = list(range(reps))           # Hoist out, equalize 2.x, 3.x
    start = timer()                         # Or perf_counter/other in 3.3+
    for i in repslist:
        ret = func(*pargs, **kargs)
    elapsed = timer() - start
    return (elapsed, ret)

def bestof(reps, func, *pargs, **kargs):
    """
    Quickest func() among reps runs.
    Returns (best time, last result)
    """
    best = 2 ** 32                          # 136 years seems large enough
    for i in range(reps):                   # range usage not timed here
        start = timer()
        ret = func(*pargs, **kargs)
        elapsed = timer() - start           # Or call total() with reps=1
        if elapsed < best: best = elapsed   # Or add to list and take min()
    return (best, ret)

def bestoftotal(reps1, reps2, func, *pargs, **kargs):
    """
    Best of totals:
    (best of reps1 runs of (total of reps2 runs of func))
    """
    return bestof(reps1, total, reps2, func, *pargs, **kargs)
```

Operationally, this module implements both *total* time and *best* time calls, and a nested *best of totals* that combines the other two. In each, it times a call to any function with any positional and keyword arguments passed individually, by fetching the start time, calling the function, and subtracting the start time from the stop time. Points to notice about how this version addresses the shortcomings of its predecessor:

- Python's time module gives access to the current time, with precision that varies per platform. On Windows its clock function is claimed to give microsecond granularity and so is very accurate. Because the time function may be better on Unix, this script selects between them automatically based on the platform string in the sys module; it starts with "win" if running in Windows. See also the sidebar "New Timer Calls in 3.3" on page 633 on other time options in 3.3 and later not used here for portability; we will also be timing Python 2.X where these newer calls are not available, and their results on Windows appear similar in 3.3 in any event.

- The range call is hoisted out of the timing loop in the total function, so its construction cost is not charged to the timed function in Python 2.X. In 3.X range is an iterable, so this step is neither required nor harmful, but we still run the result through `list` so its traversal cost is the same in both 2.X and 3.X. This doesn't apply to the `bestof` function, since no `range` factors are charged to the test's time.

- The `reps` count is passed in as an argument, before the test function and its arguments, to allow repetition to vary per call.

- Any number of both positional and keyword *arguments* are collected with *starred-argument* syntax, so they must be sent individually, not in a sequence or dictionary. If needed, callers can unpack argument collections into individual arguments with stars in the call, as done by the `bestoftotal` function at the end. See Chapter 18 for a refresher if this code doesn't make sense.

- The first function in this module returns *total* elapsed time for all calls in a tuple, along with the timed function's final return value so callers can verify its operation.

- The second function does similar, but returns the *best* (minimum) time among all calls instead of the total—more useful if you wish to filter out the impacts of other activity on your computer, but less for tests that run too quickly to produce substantial runtimes.

- To address the prior point, the last function in this file runs nested total tests within a best-of test, to get the *best-of-totals* time. The nested total operation can make runtimes more useful, but we still get the best-of filter. This function's code may be easier to understand if you remember that every function is a passable object, even the testing functions themselves.

From a larger perspective, because these functions are coded in a module file, they become generally useful tools anywhere we wish to import them. Modules and imports were introduced in Chapter 3, and you'll learn more about them in the next part of this book; for now, simply import the module and call the function to use one of this file's timers. In simple usage, this module is similar to its predecessor, but will be more robust in larger contexts. In Python 3.3 again:

```
>>> import timer
>>> timer.total(1000, pow, 2, 1000)[0]          # Compare to timer0 results above
0.0029542985410557776
>>> timer.total(1000, str.upper, 'spam')        # Returns (time, last call's result)
(0.000504845391709686, 'SPAM')

>>> timer.bestof(1000, str.upper, 'spam')       # 1/1000 as long as total time
(4.887177027512735e-07, 'SPAM')
>>> timer.bestof(1000, pow, 2, 1000000)[0]
0.00393515497972885

>>> timer.bestof(50, timer.total, 1000, str.upper, 'spam')
(0.0005468751145372153, (0.0005004469323637295, 'SPAM'))
>>> timer.bestoftotal(50, 1000, str.upper, 'spam')
(0.000566912540591602, (0.0005195069228989269, 'SPAM'))
```

The last two calls here calculate the *best-of-totals* times—the lowest time among 50 runs, each of which computes the total time to call `str.upper` 1,000 times (roughly corresponding to the total times at the start of this listing). The function used in the last call is really just a convenience that maps to the call form preceding it; both return the best-of tuple, which embeds the last total call's result tuple.

Compare these last two results to the following generator-based alternative:

```
>>> min(timer.total(1000, str.upper, 'spam') for i in range(50))
(0.0005155971812769167, 'SPAM')
```

Taking the min of an iteration of total results this way has a similar effect because the times in the result tuples dominate comparisons made by min (they are leftmost in the tuple). We could use this in our module too (and will in later variations); it varies slightly by omitting a very small overhead in the best-of function's code and not nesting result tuples, though either result suffices for relative comparisons. As is, the best-of function must pick a high initial lowest time value—though 136 years is probably longer than most of the tests you're likely to run!

```
>>> (((( 2 ** 32) / 60) / 60) / 24) / 365          # Plus a few extra days
136.19251953323186
>>> (((( 2 ** 32) // 60) // 60) // 24) // 365      # Floor: see Chapter 5
136
```

New Timer Calls in 3.3

This section uses the time module's clock and time calls because they apply to all readers of this book. Python 3.3 introduces new interfaces in this module that are designed to be more portable. Specifically, the behavior of this module's clock and time calls varies per platform, but its new perf_counter and process_time functions have well-defined and platform-neutral semantics:

- time.perf_counter() returns the value in fractional seconds of a performance counter, defined as a clock with the highest available resolution to measure a short duration. It includes time elapsed during sleep states and is system-wide.

- time.process_time() returns the value in fractional seconds of the sum of the system and user CPU time of the current process. It does not include time elapsed during sleep, and is process-wide by definition.

For both of these calls, the reference point of the returned value is undefined, so that only the *difference* between the results of consecutive calls is valid. The perf_counter call can be thought of as wall time, and as of Python 3.3 is used by default for benchmarking in the timeit module discussed ahead; process_time gives CPU time portably.

The time.clock call is still usable on Windows today, as shown in this book. It is documented as being deprecated in 3.3's manuals, but issues no warning when used there —meaning it may or may not become officially deprecated in later releases. If needed, you can detect a Python 3.3 or later with code like this, which I opted to not use for the sake of brevity and timer comparability:

```
if sys.version_info[0] >= 3 and sys.version_info[1] >= 3:
    timer = time.perf_counter       # or process_time
else:
    timer = time.clock if sys.platform[:3] == 'win' else time.time
```

Alternatively, the following code would also add portability and insulate you from future deprecations, though it depends on exception topics we haven't studied in full yet, and its choices may also make cross-version speed comparisons invalid—timers may differ in resolution!

```
try:
    timer = time.perf_counter      # or process_time
except AttributeError:
    timer = time.clock if sys.platform[:3] == 'win' else time.time
```

If I were writing this book for Python 3.3+ readers only, I'd use the new and apparently improved calls here, and you should in your work too if they apply to you. The newer calls won't work for users of any other Pythons, though, and that's still the majority of the Python world today. It would be easier to pretend that the past doesn't matter, but that would not only be evasive of reality, it might also be just plain rude.

Timing Script

Now, to time iteration tool speed (our original goal), run the following script—it uses the timer module we wrote to time the relative speeds of the list construction techniques we've studied:

```
# File timeseqs.py
"Test the relative speed of iteration tool alternatives."

import sys, timer                              # Import timer functions
reps = 10000
repslist = list(range(reps))                  # Hoist out, list in both 2.X/3.X

def forLoop():
    res = []
    for x in repslist:
        res.append(abs(x))
    return res

def listComp():
    return [abs(x) for x in repslist]

def mapCall():
    return list(map(abs, repslist))           # Use list() here in 3.X only!
  # return map(abs, repslist)

def genExpr():
    return list(abs(x) for x in repslist)     # list() required to force results

def genFunc():
    def gen():
        for x in repslist:
            yield abs(x)
    return list(gen())                         # list() required to force results

print(sys.version)
```

```
for test in (forLoop, listComp, mapCall, genExpr, genFunc):
    (bestof, (total, result)) = timer.bestoftotal(5, 1000, test)
    print ('%-9s: %.5f => [%s...%s]' %
           (test.__name__, bestof, result[0], result[-1]))
```

This script tests five alternative ways to build lists of results. As shown, its reported times reflect on the order of 10 million steps for each of the five test functions—each builds a list of 10,000 items 1,000 times. This process is repeated 5 times to get the best-of time for each of the 5 test functions, yielding a whopping 250 million total steps for the script at large (impressive but reasonable on most machines these days).

Notice how we have to run the results of the generator expression and function through the built-in `list` call to force them to yield all of their values; if we did not, in both 2.X and 3.X we would just produce generators that never do any real work. In Python 3.X only we must do the same for the `map` result, since it is now an iterable object as well; for 2.X, the `list` around `map` must be removed manually to avoid charging an extra list construction overhead per test (though its impact seems negligible in most tests).

In a similar way, the inner loops' `range` result is hoisted out to the top of the module to remove its construction cost from total time, and wrapped in a `list` call so that its traversal cost isn't skewed by being a generator in 3.X only (much as we did in the timer module too). This may be overshadowed by the cost of the inner iterations loop, but it's best to remove as many variables as we can.

Also notice how the code at the bottom steps through a tuple of five function objects and prints the `__name__` of each: as we've seen, this is a built-in attribute that gives a function's name.[1]

Timing Results

When the script of the prior section is run under *Python 3.3*, I get these results on my Windows 7 laptop—`map` is slightly faster than list comprehensions, both are quicker than `for` loops, and generator expressions and functions place in the middle (times here are total time in seconds):

```
C:\code> c:\python33\python timeseqs.py
3.3.0 (v3.3.0:bd8afb90ebf2, Sep 29 2012, 10:57:17) [MSC v.1600 64 bit (AMD64)]
forLoop  : 1.33290 => [0...9999]
listComp : 0.69658 => [0...9999]
mapCall  : 0.56483 => [0...9999]
genExpr  : 1.08457 => [0...9999]
genFunc  : 1.07623 => [0...9999]
```

---

1. A preview: notice how we must pass functions into the timer manually here. In Chapter 39 and Chapter 40 we'll see *decorator*-based timer alternatives with which timed functions are called normally, but require extra "@" syntax where defined. Decorators may be more useful to instrument functions with timing logic when they are already being used within a larger system, and don't as easily support the more isolated test call patterns assumed here—when decorated, *every* call to the function runs the timing logic, which is either a plus or minus depending on your goals.

If you study this code and its output long enough, you'll notice that generator expressions run slower than list comprehensions today. Although wrapping a generator expression in a `list` call makes it *functionally* equivalent to a square-bracketed list comprehension, the internal *implementations* of the two expressions appear to differ (though we're also effectively timing the `list` call for the generator test):

```
return [abs(x) for x in repslist]          # 0.69 seconds
return list(abs(x) for x in repslist)      # 1.08 seconds: differs internally
```

Though the exact cause would require deeper analysis (and possibly source code study), this seems to make sense given that the generator expression must do extra work to save and restore its state during value production; the list comprehension does not, and runs quicker by a small constant here and in later tests.

Interestingly, when I ran this on Windows Vista under Python 3.0 for the fourth edition of this book, and on Windows XP with Python 2.5 for the third, the results were relatively similar—list comprehensions were nearly twice as fast as equivalent `for` loop statements, and `map` was slightly quicker than list comprehensions when mapping a function such as the `abs` (absolute value) built-in this way. Python 2.5's absolute times were roughly four to five times slower than the current 3.3 output, but this likely reflects quicker laptops much more than any improvements in Python.

In fact, most of the *Python 2.7* results for this script are slightly quicker than 3.3 on this same machine today—I removed the `list` call from the `map` test in the following to avoid creating the results list twice in that test, though it adds only a very small constant time if left in:

```
c:\code> c:\python27\python timeseqs.py
2.7.3 (default, Apr 10 2012, 23:24:47) [MSC v.1500 64 bit (AMD64)]
forLoop  : 1.24902 => [0...9999]
listComp : 0.66970 => [0...9999]
mapCall  : 0.57018 => [0...9999]
genExpr  : 0.90339 => [0...9999]
genFunc  : 0.90542 => [0...9999]
```

For comparison, following are the same tests' speed results under the current *PyPy*, the optimized Python implementation discussed in Chapter 2, whose current 1.9 release implements the Python 2.7 language. PyPy is roughly 10X (an order of magnitude) quicker here; it will do even better when we revisit Python version comparisons later in this chapter using tools with different code structures (though it will lose on a few other tests as well):

```
c:\code> c:\PyPy\pypy-1.9\pypy.exe timeseqs.py
2.7.2 (341e1e3821ff, Jun 07 2012, 15:43:00)
[PyPy 1.9.0 with MSC v.1500 32 bit]
forLoop  : 0.10106 => [0...9999]
listComp : 0.05629 => [0...9999]
mapCall  : 0.10022 => [0...9999]
genExpr  : 0.17234 => [0...9999]
genFunc  : 0.17519 => [0...9999]
```

On PyPy alone, list comprehensions beat map in this test, but the fact that all of PyPy's results are so much quicker today seems the larger point here. On CPython, map is still quickest so far.

The impact of function calls: map

Watch what happens, though, if we change this script to perform an inline operation on each iteration, such as addition, instead of calling a built-in function like abs (the omitted parts of the following file are the same as before, and I put list back in around map for testing on 3.3 only):

```
# File timeseqs2.py (differing parts)
...
def forLoop():
    res = []
    for x in repslist:
        res.append(x + 10)
    return res

def listComp():
    return [x + 10 for x in repslist]

def mapCall():
    return list(map((lambda x: x + 10), repslist))        # list() in 3.X only

def genExpr():
    return list(x + 10 for x in repslist)                 # list() in 2.X + 3.X

def genFunc():
    def gen():
        for x in repslist:
            yield x + 10
    return list(gen())                                    # list in 2.X + 3.X
...
```

Now the need to call a user-defined function for the map call makes it slower than the for loop statements, despite the fact that the looping statements version is larger in terms of code—or equivalently, the removal of function calls may make the others quicker (more on this in an upcoming note). On Python 3.3:

```
c:\code> c:\python33\python timeseqs2.py
3.3.0 (v3.3.0:bd8afb90ebf2, Sep 29 2012, 10:57:17) [MSC v.1600 64 bit (AMD64)]
forLoop  : 1.35136 => [10...10009]
listComp : 0.73730 => [10...10009]
mapCall  : 1.68588 => [10...10009]
genExpr  : 1.10963 => [10...10009]
genFunc  : 1.11074 => [10...10009]
```

These results have also been consistent in CPython. The prior edition's Python 3.0 results on a slower machine were again relatively similar, though about twice as slow due to test machine differences (Python 2.5 results on an even slower machine were again four to five times as slow as the current results).

Because the interpreter optimizes so much internally, performance analysis of Python code like this is a very tricky affair. Without numbers, though, it's virtually impossible to guess which method will perform the best—the best you can do is time your own code, on your computer, with your version of Python.

In this case, what we can say for certain is that on this Python, using a user-defined function in map calls seems to slow performance substantially (though + may also be slower than a trivial abs), and that list comprehensions run quickest in this case (though slower than map in some others). List comprehensions seem consistently twice as fast as for loops, but even this must be qualified—the list comprehension's relative speed might be affected by its extra syntax (e.g., if filters), Python changes, and usage modes we did not time here.

As I've mentioned before, however, performance should not be your primary concern when writing Python code—the first thing you should do to optimize Python code is to not optimize Python code! Write for *readability and simplicity* first, then optimize later, if and only if needed. It could very well be that any of the five alternatives is quick enough for the data sets your program needs to process; if so, program clarity should be the chief goal.

 For deeper truth, change this code to apply a simple user-defined function in all five iteration techniques timed. For instance (from *time-seqs2B.py* of the book's examples):

```
def F(x): return x
def listComp():
    return [F(x) for x in repslist]
def mapCall():
    return list(map(F, repslist))
```

The results, in file *timeseqs-results.txt*, are then relatively similar to using a built-in function like abs—at least in CPython, map is quickest. More generally, among the five iteration techniques, map is fastest today if all five call any *function*, built in or not, but slowest when the others do not.

That is, map appears to be slower simply *because it requires function calls*, and function calls are relatively slow in general. Since map can't avoid calling functions, it can lose simply by association! The other iteration tools win because they can operate without function calls. We'll prove this finding in tests run under the timeit module ahead.

Timing Module Alternatives

The timing module of the preceding section works, but it could be a bit more user-friendly. Most obviously, its functions require passing in a repetitions count as a first argument, and provide no default for it—a minor point, perhaps, but less than ideal in a general-purpose tool. We could also leverage the min technique we saw earlier to simplify the return value slightly and remove a minor overhead charge.

The following implements an alternative timer module that addresses these points, allowing the repeat count to be passed in as a keyword argument named _reps:

```
# File timer2.py (2.X and 3.X)
"""
total(spam, 1, 2, a=3, b=4, _reps=1000) calls and times spam(1, 2, a=3, b=4)
_reps times, and returns total time for all runs, with final result.

bestof(spam, 1, 2, a=3, b=4, _reps=5) runs best-of-N timer to attempt to
filter out system load variation, and returns best time among _reps tests.

bestoftotal(spam, 1, 2, a=3, b=4, _reps1=5, _reps=1000) runs best-of-totals
test, which takes the best among _reps1 runs of (the total of _reps runs);
"""

import time, sys
timer = time.clock if sys.platform[:3] == 'win' else time.time

def total(func, *pargs, **kargs):
    _reps = kargs.pop('_reps', 1000)      # Passed-in or default reps
    repslist = list(range(_reps))         # Hoist range out for 2.X lists
    start = timer()
    for i in repslist:
        ret = func(*pargs, **kargs)
    elapsed = timer() - start
    return (elapsed, ret)

def bestof(func, *pargs, **kargs):
    _reps = kargs.pop('_reps', 5)
    best = 2 ** 32
    for i in range(_reps):
        start = timer()
        ret = func(*pargs, **kargs)
        elapsed = timer() - start
        if elapsed < best: best = elapsed
    return (best, ret)

def bestoftotal(func, *pargs, **kargs):
    _reps1 = kargs.pop('_reps1', 5)
    return min(total(func, *pargs, **kargs) for i in range(_reps1))
```

This module's docstring at the top of the file describes its intended usage. It uses dictionary pop operations to remove the _reps argument from arguments intended for the test function and provide it with a default (it has an unusual name to avoid clashing with real keyword arguments meant for the function being timed).

Notice how the best of totals here uses the min and generator scheme we saw earlier instead of nested calls, in part because this simplifies results and avoids a minor time overhead in the prior version (whose code fetches best of time *after* total time has been computed), but also because it must support *two* distinct repetition keywords with defaults—total and bestof can't both use the same argument name. Add argument prints in the code if it would help to trace its operation.

To test with this new timer module, you can change the timing scripts as follows, or use the precoded version in the book's examples file *timeseqs_timer2.py*; the results are essentially the same as before (this is primarily just an API change), so I won't list them again here:

```
import sys, timer2
...
for test in (forLoop, listComp, mapCall, genExpr, genFunc):
    (total, result) = timer2.bestoftotal(test, _reps1=5, _reps=1000)

# Or:
#   (total, result) = timer2.bestoftotal(test)
#   (total, result) = timer2.bestof(test, _reps=5)
#   (total, result) = timer2.total(test, _reps=1000)
#   (bestof, (total, result)) = timer2.bestof(timer2.total, test, _reps=5)

    print ('%-9s: %.5f => [%s...%s]' %
              (test.__name__, total, result[0], result[-1]))
```

You can also run a few interactive tests as we did for the original version—the results are again essentially the same as before, but we pass in the repetition counts as keywords that provide defaults if omitted; in Python 3.3:

```
>>> from timer2 import total, bestof, bestoftotal
>>> total(pow, 2, 1000)[0]                          # 2 ** 1000, 1K dflt reps
0.0029562534118596773
>>> total(pow, 2, 1000, _reps=1000)[0]              # 2 ** 1000, 1K reps
0.0029733585316193967
>>> total(pow, 2, 1000, _reps=1000000)[0]           # 2 ** 1000, 1M reps
1.2451676814889865

>>> bestof(pow, 2, 100000)[0]                       # 2 ** 100K, 5 dflt reps
0.0007550688578703557
>>> bestof(pow, 2, 1000000, _reps=30)[0]            # 2 ** 1M, best of 30
0.004040229286800923

>>> bestoftotal(str.upper, 'spam', _reps1=30, _reps=1000)   # Best of 30, tot of 1K
(0.0004945823198454491, 'SPAM')
>>> bestof(total, str.upper, 'spam', _reps=30)      # Nested calls work too
(0.0005463863968202531, (0.0004994694969298052, 'SPAM'))
```

To see how keywords are supported now, define a function with more arguments and pass some by name:

```
>>> def spam(a, b, c, d): return a + b + c + d

>>> total(spam, 1, 2, c=3, d=4, _reps=1000)
(0.0009730369554290519, 10)
>>> bestof(spam, 1, 2, c=3, d=4, _reps=1000)
(9.774353202374186e-07, 10)
>>> bestoftotal(spam, 1, 2, c=3, d=4, _reps1=1000, _reps=1000)
(0.00037289161070930277, 10)
>>> bestoftotal(spam, *(1, 2), _reps1=1000, _reps=1000, **dict(c=3, d=4))
(0.00037289161070930277, 10)
```

Using keyword-only arguments in 3.X

One last point on this thread: we can also make use of Python 3.X *keyword-only argu-ments* here to simplify the timer module's code. As we learned in Chapter 18, keyword-only arguments are ideal for configuration options such as our functions' _reps argu-ment. They must be coded after a * and before a ** in the function *header*, and in a function *call* they must be passed by keyword and appear before the ** if used. The following is a keyword-only-based alternative to the prior module. Though simpler, it compiles and runs under Python 3.X only, not 2.X:

```
# File timer3.py (3.X only)
"""
Same usage as timer2.py, but uses 3.X keyword-only default arguments
instead of dict pops for simpler code.  No need to hoist range() out
of tests in 3.X: always a generator in 3.X, and this can't run on 2.X.
"""
import time, sys
timer = time.clock if sys.platform[:3] == 'win' else time.time

def total(func, *pargs, _reps=1000, **kargs):
    start = timer()
    for i in range(_reps):
        ret = func(*pargs, **kargs)
    elapsed = timer() - start
    return (elapsed, ret)

def bestof(func, *pargs, _reps=5, **kargs):
    best = 2 ** 32
    for i in range(_reps):
        start = timer()
        ret = func(*pargs, **kargs)
        elapsed = timer() - start
        if elapsed < best: best = elapsed
    return (best, ret)

def bestoftotal(func, *pargs, _reps1=5, **kargs):
    return min(total(func, *pargs, **kargs) for i in range(_reps1))
```

This version is used the same way as the prior version and produces identical results, so I won't relist its outputs on the same tests here; experiment on your own as you wish. If you do, pay attention to the argument ordering rules in calls. A former bes tof that ran total, for instance, called like this:

```
(elapsed, ret) = total(func, *pargs, _reps=1, **kargs)
```

See Chapter 18 for more on keyword-only arguments in 3.X; they can simplify code for configurable tools like this one but are not backward compatible with 2.X Pythons. If you want to compare 2.X and 3.X speed, or support programmers using either Python line, the prior version is likely a better choice.

Also keep in mind that for trivial functions like some of those tested for the prior version, the costs of the timer's code may sometimes be as significant as those of a simple timed function, so you should not take timer results too absolutely. The timer's results can help you judge *relative* speeds of coding alternatives, though, and may be more meaningful for operations that run longer or are repeated often.

Other Suggestions

For more insight, try modifying the repetition counts used by these modules, or explore the alternative `timeit` module in Python's standard library, which automates timing of code, supports command-line usage modes, and finesses some platform-specific issues —in fact, we'll put it to work in the next section.

You might also want to look at the `profile` standard library module for a complete source code profiler tool. We'll learn more about it in Chapter 36 in the context of development tools for large projects. In general, you should profile code to isolate bottlenecks before recoding and timing alternatives as we've done here.

You might try modifying or emulating the timing script to measure the speed of the 3.X and 2.7 *set and dictionary comprehensions* shown in the preceding chapter, and their `for` loop equivalents. Using them is less common in Python programs than building lists of results, so we'll leave this task in the suggested exercise column (please, no wagering...); the next section will partly spoil the surprise.

Finally, keep the timing module we wrote here filed away for future reference—we'll repurpose it to measure performance of alternative numeric square root operations in an *exercise* at the end of this chapter. If you're interested in pursuing this topic further, we'll also experiment with techniques for timing dictionary comprehensions versus `for` loops interactively in the exercises.

Timing Iterations and Pythons with timeit

The preceding section used homegrown timing functions to compare code speed. As mentioned there, the standard library also ships with a module named `timeit` that can be used in similar ways, but offers added flexibility and may better insulate clients from some platform differences.

As usual in Python, it's important to understand fundamental principles like those illustrated in the prior section. Python's "batteries included" approach means you'll usually find precoded options as well, though you still need to know the ideas underlying them to use them properly. Indeed, this module is a prime example of this—it seems to have had a history of being misused by people who don't yet understand the principles it embodies. Now that we've learned the basics, though, let's move ahead to a tool that can automate much of our work.

Basic timeit Usage

Let's start with this module's fundamentals before leveraging them in larger scripts. With `timeit`, tests are specified by either *callable objects* or *statement strings*; the latter can hold multiple statements if they use ; separators or \n characters for line breaks, and spaces or tabs to indent statements in nested blocks (e.g., \n\t). Tests may also give setup actions, and can be launched from both *command lines* and *API calls*, and from both scripts and the interactive prompt.

Interactive usage and API calls

For example, the `timeit` module's `repeat` call returns a list giving the total time taken to run a test a `number` of times, for each of `repeat` runs—the `min` of this list yields the best time among the runs, and helps filter out system load fluctuations that can otherwise skew timing results artificially high.

The following shows this call in action, timing a list comprehension on two versions of *CPython* and the optimized *PyPy* implementation of Python described in Chapter 2 (it currently supports Python 2.7 code). The results here give the best total time in seconds among 5 runs that each execute the code string 1,000 times; the code string itself constructs a 1,000-item list of integers each time through (see Appendix B for the Windows launcher used for variety in the first two of these commands):

```
c:\code> py -3
Python 3.3.0 (v3.3.0:bd8afb90ebf2, Sep 29 2012, 10:57:17) [MSC v.1600 64 bit...
>>> import timeit
>>> min(timeit.repeat(stmt="[x ** 2 for x in range(1000)]", number=1000, repeat=5))
0.5062382371756811

c:\code> py -2
Python 2.7.3 (default, Apr 10 2012, 23:24:47) [MSC v.1500 64 bit (AMD64)] on win32
>>> import timeit
>>> min(timeit.repeat(stmt="[x ** 2 for x in range(1000)]", number=1000, repeat=5))
0.0708020004193198

c:\code> c:\pypy\pypy-1.9\pypy.exe
Python 2.7.2 (341e1e3821ff, Jun 07 2012, 15:43:00)
[PyPy 1.9.0 with MSC v.1500 32 bit] on win32
>>>> import timeit
>>>> min(timeit.repeat(stmt="[x ** 2 for x in range(1000)]", number=1000, repeat=5))
0.0059330329674303905
```

You'll notice that PyPy checks in at 10X faster than CPython 2.7 here, and a whopping 100X faster than CPython 3.3, despite the fact that PyPy is a potentially slower 32-bit build. This is a small artificial benchmark, of course, but seems arguably stunning nonetheless, and reflects a relative speed ranking that is generally supported by other tests run in this book (though as we'll see, CPython still beats PyPy on some types of code).

This particular test measures the speed of both a list comprehension and integer math. The latter varies between lines: CPython 3.X has a single integer type, and CPython 2.X has both short and long integers. This may explain part of the *size* of the difference, but the results are valid nonetheless. Noninteger tests yield similar rankings (e.g., a floating-point test in the solutions to this part's exercises), and integer math matters— the one and two order of magnitude (power of 10) speedups here will be realized by many real programs, because integers and iterations are ubiquitous in Python code.

These results also differ from the preceding section's relative version speeds, where CPython 2.7 was slightly quicker than 3.3, and PyPy was 10X quicker overall, a figure affirmed by most other tests in this book too. Apart from the different type of code being timed here, the different coding structure inside `timeit` may have an effect too— for code strings like those tested here, `timeit` builds, compiles, and executes a function `def` statement string that embeds the test string, thereby avoiding a function call per inner loop. As we'll see in the next section, though, this appears irrelevant from a relative-speed perspective.

Command-line usage

The `timeit` module has reasonable defaults and can be also run as a script, either by explicit filename or automatically located on the module search path with Python's –m flag (see Appendix A). All the following run Python (a.k.a. CPython) 3.3. In this mode `timeit` reports the average time for a *single* -n loop, in either microseconds (labeled "usec"), milliseconds ("msec"), or seconds ("sec"); to compare results here to the total time values reported by other tests, multiply by the number of loops run— 500 usec here * 1,000 loops is 500 msec, or half a second in total time:

```
c:\code> C:\python33\Lib\timeit.py -n 1000 "[x ** 2 for x in range(1000)]"
1000 loops, best of 3: 506 usec per loop

c:\code> python -m timeit -n 1000 "[x ** 2 for x in range(1000)]"
1000 loops, best of 3: 504 usec per loop

c:\code> py -3 -m timeit -n 1000 -r 5 "[x ** 2 for x in range(1000)]"
1000 loops, best of 5: 505 usec per loop
```

As an example, we can use command lines to verify that choice of timer call doesn't impact cross-version speed comparisons run in this chapter so far—3.3 uses its new calls by default, and that might matter if timer precision differs widely. To prove that this is irrelevant, the following uses the -c flag to force `timeit` to use `time.clock` in all versions, an option that 3.3's manuals call deprecated, but required to even the score with prior versions (I'm setting my system path to include PyPy here for command brevity):

```
c:\code> set PATH=%PATH%;C:\pypy\pypy-1.9

c:\code> py -3 -m timeit -n 1000 -r 5 -c "[x ** 2 for x in range(1000)]"
1000 loops, best of 5: 502 usec per loop
c:\code> py -2 -m timeit -n 1000 -r 5 -c "[x ** 2 for x in range(1000)]"
```

```
1000 loops, best of 5: 70.6 usec per loop
c:\code> pypy -m timeit -n 1000 -r 5 -c  "[x ** 2 for x in range(1000)]"
1000 loops, best of 5: 5.44 usec per loop

C:\code> py -3 -m timeit -n 1000 -r 5 -c "[abs(x) for x in range(10000)]"
1000 loops, best of 5: 815 usec per loop
C:\code> py -2 -m timeit -n 1000 -r 5 -c "[abs(x) for x in range(10000)]"
1000 loops, best of 5: 700 usec per loop
C:\code> pypy -m timeit -n 1000 -r 5 -c  "[abs(x) for x in range(10000)]"
1000 loops, best of 5: 61.7 usec per loop
```

These results are essentially the same as those for earlier tests in this chapter on the same types of code. When applying x ** 2, CPython 2.7 and PyPy are again 10X and 100X faster than CPython 3.3, respectively, showing that timer choice isn't a factor. For the abs(x) we timed under the homegrown timer earlier (*timeseqs.py*), these two Pythons are faster than 3.3 by a small constant and 10X just as before, implying that timeit's different code structure doesn't impact relative comparisons—the type of code being tested fully determines the size of speed differences.

Subtle point: notice that the results of the last three of these tests, which mimic tests run for the homegrown timer earlier, are basically the same as before, but seem to incur a small net overhead for range usage differences—it was a prebuilt list formerly, but here is either a 3.X generator or a 2.X list built anew on each inner total loop. In other words, we're not timing the exact same thing, but the relative speeds of the Pythons tested are the same.

Timing multiline statements

To time larger multiline sections of code in *API call* mode, use line breaks and tabs or spaces to satisfy Python's syntax; code read from a source file already will. Because you pass Python string objects to a Python function in this mode, there are no shell considerations, though be careful to escape nested quotes if needed. The following, for instance, times Chapter 13 loop alternatives in Python 3.3; you can use the same pattern to time the file-line-reader alternatives in Chapter 14:

```
c:\code> py -3
>>> import timeit
>>> min(timeit.repeat(number=10000, repeat=3,
        stmt="L = [1, 2, 3, 4, 5]\nfor i in range(len(L)): L[i] += 1"))
0.013972927971318l4

>>> min(timeit.repeat(number=10000, repeat=3,
        stmt="L = [1, 2, 3, 4, 5]\ni=0\nwhile i < len(L):\n\tL[i] += 1\n\ti += 1"))
0.015452276471516813

>>> min(timeit.repeat(number=10000, repeat=3,
        stmt="L = [1, 2, 3, 4, 5]\nM = [x + 1 for x in L]"))
0.009464995838568635
```

To run multiline statements like these in *command-line* mode, appease your shell by passing each statement line as a separate argument, with whitespace for indentation—

`timeit` concatenates all the lines together with a newline character between them, and later reindents for its own statement nesting purposes. Leading spaces may work better for indentation than tabs in this mode, and be sure to quote the code arguments if required by your shell:

```
c:\code> py -3 -m timeit -n 1000 -r 3 "L = [1,2,3,4,5]" "i=0" "while i < len(L):"
"    L[i] += 1" "    i += 1"
1000 loops, best of 3: 1.54 usec per loop

c:\code> py -3 -m timeit -n 1000 -r 3 "L = [1,2,3,4,5]" "M = [x + 1 for x in L]"
1000 loops, best of 3: 0.959 usec per loop
```

Other usage modes: Setup, totals, and objects

The `timeit` module also allows you to provide *setup* code that is run in the main statement's scope, but whose time is not charged to the main statement's total—potentially useful for initialization code you wish to exclude from total time, such as imports of required modules, test function definition, and test data creation. Because they're run in the same scope, any names created by setup code are available to the main test statement; names defined in the interactive shell generally are not.

To specify setup code, use a `-s` in command-line mode (or many of these for multiline setups) and a `setup` argument string in API call mode. This can focus tests more sharply, as in the following, which splits list initialization off to a setup statement to time just iteration. As a rule of thumb, though, the more code you include in a test statement, the more applicable its results will generally be to realistic code:

```
c:\code> python -m timeit -n 1000 -r 3 "L = [1,2,3,4,5]" "M = [x + 1 for x in L]"
1000 loops, best of 3: 0.956 usec per loop

c:\code> python -m timeit -n 1000 -r 3 -s "L = [1,2,3,4,5]" "M = [x + 1 for x in L]"
1000 loops, best of 3: 0.775 usec per loop
```

Here's a setup example in API call mode: I used the following type of code to time the sort-based option in Chapter 18's minimum value example—ordered ranges sort much faster than random numbers, and are faster sorted than scanned linearly in the example's code under 3.3 (adjacent strings are concatenated here):

```
>>> from timeit import repeat

>>> min(repeat(number=1000, repeat=3,
setup='from mins import min1, min2, min3\n'
      'vals=list(range(1000))',
stmt= 'min3(*vals)'))
0.0387865921275079

>>> min(repeat(number=1000, repeat=3,
setup='from mins import min1, min2, min3\n'
      'import random\nvals=[random.random() for i in range(1000)]',
stmt= 'min3(*vals)'))
0.275656482278373
```

With `timeit`, you can also ask for just total time, use the module's class API, time callable objects instead of strings, accept automatic loop counts, and use class-based techniques and additional command-line switches and API argument options we don't have space to show here—consult Python's library manual for more details:

```
c:\code> py -3
>>> import timeit
>>> timeit.timeit(stmt='[x ** 2 for x in range(1000)]', number=1000)   # Total time
0.5238125259325834

>>> timeit.Timer(stmt='[x ** 2 for x in range(1000)]').timeit(1000)     # Class API
0.5282652329644009

>>> timeit.repeat(stmt='[x ** 2 for x in range(1000)]', number=1000, repeat=3)
[0.5299034147194845, 0.5082454007998365, 0.5095136232504416]

>>> def testcase():
        y = [x ** 2 for x in range(1000)]       # Callable objects or code strings

>>> min(timeit.repeat(stmt=testcase, number=1000, repeat=3))
0.5073828140463377
```

Benchmark Module and Script: timeit

Rather than go into more details on this module, let's study a program that deploys it to time both coding alternatives and Python versions. The following file, *pybench.py*, is set up to time a set of statements coded in scripts that import and use it, under either the version running its code or all Python versions named in a list. It uses some application-level tools described ahead. Because it mostly applies ideas we've already learned and is amply documented, though, I'm going to list this as mostly self-study material, and an exercise in reading Python code.

```
"""
pybench.py: Test speed of one or more Pythons on a set of simple
code-string benchmarks.  A function, to allow stmts to vary.
This system itself runs on both 2.X and 3.X, and may spawn both.

Uses timeit to test either the Python running this script by API
calls, or a set of Pythons by reading spawned command-line outputs
(os.popen) with Python's -m flag to find timeit on module search path.

Replaces $listif3 with a list() around generators for 3.X and an
empty string for 2.X, so 3.X does same work as 2.X.  In command-line
mode only, must split multiline statements into one separate quoted
argument per line so all will be run (else might run/time first line
only), and replace all \t in indentation with 4 spaces for uniformity.

Caveats: command-line mode (only) may fail if test stmt embeds double
quotes, quoted stmt string is incompatible with shell in general, or
command-line exceeds a length limit on platform's shell--use API call
mode or homegrown timer; does not yet support a setup statement: as is,
time of all statements in the test stmt are charged to the total time.
"""
```

```
import sys, os, timeit
defnum, defrep= 1000, 5     # May vary per stmt

def runner(stmts, pythons=None, tracecmd=False):
    """
    Main logic: run tests per input lists, caller handles usage modes.
    stmts:   [(number?, repeat?, stmt-string)], replaces $listif3 in stmt
    pythons: None=this python only, or [(ispy3?, python-executable-path)]
    """
    print(sys.version)
    for (number, repeat, stmt) in stmts:
        number = number or defnum
        repeat = repeat or defrep   # 0=default

        if not pythons:
            # Run stmt on this python: API call
            # No need to split lines or quote here
            ispy3 = sys.version[0] == '3'
            stmt  = stmt.replace('$listif3', 'list' if ispy3 else '')
            best  = min(timeit.repeat(stmt=stmt, number=number, repeat=repeat))
            print('%.4f  [%r]' % (best, stmt[:70]))

        else:
            # Run stmt on all pythons: command line
            # Split lines into quoted arguments
            print('-' * 80)
            print('[%r]' % stmt)
            for (ispy3, python) in pythons:
                stmt1 = stmt.replace('$listif3', 'list' if ispy3 else '')
                stmt1 = stmt1.replace('\t', ' ' * 4)
                lines = stmt1.split('\n')
                args  = ' '.join('"%s"' % line for line in lines)
                cmd = '%s -m timeit -n %s -r %s %s' % (python, number, repeat, args)
                print(python)
                if tracecmd: print(cmd)
                print('\t' + os.popen(cmd).read().rstrip())
```

This file is really only half the picture, though. Testing scripts use this module's function, passing in concrete though variable lists of statements and Pythons to be tested,
as appropriate for the usage mode desired. For example, the following script, *py-
bench_cases.py*, tests a handful of statements and Pythons, and allows command-line
arguments to determine part of its operation: -a tests all listed Pythons instead of just
one, and an added -t traces constructed command lines so you can see how multiline
statements and indentation are handled per the command-line formats shown earlier
(see both files' docstrings for details):

```
"""
pybench_cases.py: Run pybench on a set of pythons and statements.

Select modes by editing this script or using command-line arguments (in
sys.argv): e.g., run a "C:\python27\python pybench_cases.py" to test just
one specific version on stmts, "pybench_cases.py -a" to test all pythons
listed, or a "py -3 pybench_cases.py -a -t" to trace command lines too.
```

```
"""

import pybench, sys

pythons = [                                                    # (ispy3?, path)
    (1, 'C:\python33\python'),
    (0, 'C:\python27\python'),
    (0, 'C:\pypy\pypy-1.9\pypy')
]

stmts = [                                                      # (num,rpt,stmt)
    (0, 0, "[x ** 2 for x in range(1000)]"),                   # Iterations
    (0, 0, "res=[]\nfor x in range(1000): res.append(x ** 2)"),  # \n=multistmt
    (0, 0, "$listif3(map(lambda x: x ** 2, range(1000)))"),    # \n\t=indent
    (0, 0, "list(x ** 2 for x in range(1000))"),               # $=list or ''
    (0, 0, "s = 'spam' * 2500\nx = [s[i] for i in range(10000)]"),  # String ops
    (0, 0, "s = '?'\nfor i in range(10000): s += '?'"),
]

tracecmd = '-t' in sys.argv                           # -t: trace command lines?
pythons  = pythons if '-a' in sys.argv else None      # -a: all in list, else one?
pybench.runner(stmts, pythons, tracecmd)
```

Benchmark Script Results

Here is this script's output when run to test a *specific version* (the Python running the script)—this mode uses direct API calls, not command lines, with total time listed in the left column, and the statement tested on the right. I'm again using the 3.3 Windows launcher in the first two of these tests to time *CPython* 3.3 and 2.7, and am running release 1.9 of the *PyPy* implementation in the third:

```
c:\code> py -3 pybench_cases.py
3.3.0 (v3.3.0:bd8afb90ebf2, Sep 29 2012, 10:57:17) [MSC v.1600 64 bit (AMD64)]
0.5015  ['[x ** 2 for x in range(1000)]']
0.5655  ['res=[]\nfor x in range(1000): res.append(x ** 2)']
0.6044  ['list(map(lambda x: x ** 2, range(1000)))']
0.5425  ['list(x ** 2 for x in range(1000))']
0.8746  ["s = 'spam' * 2500\nx = [s[i] for i in range(10000)]"]
2.8060  ["s = '?'\nfor i in range(10000): s += '?'"]

c:\code> py -2 pybench_cases.py
2.7.3 (default, Apr 10 2012, 23:24:47) [MSC v.1500 64 bit (AMD64)]
0.0696  ['[x ** 2 for x in range(1000)]']
0.1285  ['res=[]\nfor x in range(1000): res.append(x ** 2)']
0.1636  ['(map(lambda x: x ** 2, range(1000)))']
0.0952  ['list(x ** 2 for x in range(1000))']
0.6143  ["s = 'spam' * 2500\nx = [s[i] for i in range(10000)]"]
2.0657  ["s = '?'\nfor i in range(10000): s += '?'"]

c:\code> c:\pypy\pypy-1.9\pypy pybench_cases.py
2.7.2 (341e1e3821ff, Jun 07 2012, 15:43:00)
[PyPy 1.9.0 with MSC v.1500 32 bit]
0.0059  ['[x ** 2 for x in range(1000)]']
0.0102  ['res=[]\nfor x in range(1000): res.append(x ** 2)']
```

```
0.0099  ['(map(lambda x: x ** 2, range(1000)))']
0.0156  ['list(x ** 2 for x in range(1000))']
0.1298  ["s = 'spam' * 2500\nx = [s[i] for i in range(10000)]"]
5.5242  ["s = '?'\nfor i in range(10000): s += '?'"]
```

The following shows this script's output when run to test *multiple Python versions* for each statement string. In this mode the script itself is run by Python 3.3, but it launches shell command lines that start other Pythons to run the `timeit` module on the test statement strings. This mode must split, format, and quote multiline statements for use in command lines according to `timeit` expectations and shell requirements.

This mode also relies on the `-m` Python command-line flag to locate `timeit` on the module search path and run it as a script, and the `os.popen` and `sys.argv` standard library tools to run a shell command and inspect command-line arguments, respectively. See Python manuals and other sources for more on these calls; `os.popen` is also mentioned briefly in the files coverage of Chapter 9, and demonstrated in the loops coverage in Chapter 13. Run with a `-t` flag to watch the command lines run:

```
c:\code> py -3 pybench_cases.py -a
3.3.0 (v3.3.0:bd8afb90ebf2, Sep 29 2012, 10:57:17) [MSC v.1600 64 bit (AMD64)]
--------------------------------------------------------------------------------
['[x ** 2 for x in range(1000)]']
C:\python33\python
        1000 loops, best of 5: 499 usec per loop
C:\python27\python
        1000 loops, best of 5: 71.4 usec per loop
C:\pypy\pypy-1.9\pypy
        1000 loops, best of 5: 5.71 usec per loop
--------------------------------------------------------------------------------
['res=[]\nfor x in range(1000): res.append(x ** 2)']
C:\python33\python
        1000 loops, best of 5: 562 usec per loop
C:\python27\python
        1000 loops, best of 5: 130 usec per loop
C:\pypy\pypy-1.9\pypy
        1000 loops, best of 5: 9.81 usec per loop
--------------------------------------------------------------------------------
['$listif3(map(lambda x: x ** 2, range(1000)))']
C:\python33\python
        1000 loops, best of 5: 599 usec per loop
C:\python27\python
        1000 loops, best of 5: 161 usec per loop
C:\pypy\pypy-1.9\pypy
        1000 loops, best of 5: 9.45 usec per loop
--------------------------------------------------------------------------------
['list(x ** 2 for x in range(1000))']
C:\python33\python
        1000 loops, best of 5: 540 usec per loop
C:\python27\python
        1000 loops, best of 5: 92.3 usec per loop
C:\pypy\pypy-1.9\pypy
        1000 loops, best of 5: 15.1 usec per loop
--------------------------------------------------------------------------------
["s = 'spam' * 2500\nx = [s[i] for i in range(10000)]"]
```

```
C:\python33\python
        1000 loops, best of 5: 873 usec per loop
C:\python27\python
        1000 loops, best of 5: 614 usec per loop
C:\pypy\pypy-1.9\pypy
        1000 loops, best of 5: 118 usec per loop
----------------------------------------------------------------------
["s = '?'\nfor i in range(10000): s += '?'"]
C:\python33\python
        1000 loops, best of 5: 2.81 msec per loop
C:\python27\python
        1000 loops, best of 5: 1.94 msec per loop
C:\pypy\pypy-1.9\pypy
        1000 loops, best of 5: 5.68 msec per loop
```

As you can see, in most of these tests, CPython 2.7 is still quicker than CPython 3.3, and PyPy is noticeably faster than both of them—except on the last test where PyPy is twice as slow as CPython, presumably due to memory management differences. On the other hand, timing results are often relative at best. In addition to other general timing caveats mentioned in this chapter:

- `timeit` may skew results in ways beyond our scope to explore here (e.g., garbage collection).
- There is a baseline overhead, which differs per Python version, that is ignored here (but appears trivial).
- This script runs very small statements that may or may not reflect real-world code (but are still valid).
- Results may occasionally vary in ways that seem random (using process time may help here).
- All results here are highly prone to change over time (in each new Python release, in fact!).

In other words, you should draw your own conclusions from these numbers, and run these tests on your Pythons and machines for results more relevant to your needs. To time the baseline overhead of each Python, run `timeit` with no statement argument, or equivalently, with a `pass` statement.

More Fun with Benchmarks

For more insight, try running the script on other Python versions and other statement test strings. The file *pybench_cases2.py* in this book's examples distribution adds more tests to see how CPython 3.3 compares to 3.2, how PyPy's 2.0 beta stacks up against its current release, and how additional use cases fare.

A win for map and a rare loss for PyPy

For example, the following tests in *pybench_cases2.py* measure the impact of charging other iteration operations with a function call, which improves map's chances of winning the day per this chapter's earlier note—map usually loses by its association with function calls in general:

```
# pybench_cases2.py

pythons += [
    (1, 'C:\python32\python'),
    (0, 'C:\pypy\pypy-2.0-beta1\pypy')]

stmts += [
# Use function calls: map wins
    (0, 0, "[ord(x) for x in 'spam' * 2500]"),
    (0, 0, "res=[]\nfor x in 'spam' * 2500: res.append(ord(x))"),
    (0, 0, "$listif3(map(ord, 'spam' * 2500))"),
    (0, 0, "list(ord(x) for x in 'spam' * 2500)"),
# Set and dicts
    (0, 0, "{x ** 2 for x in range(1000)}"),
    (0, 0, "s=set()\nfor x in range(1000): s.add(x ** 2)"),
    (0, 0, "{x: x ** 2 for x in range(1000)}"),
    (0, 0, "d={}\nfor x in range(1000): d[x] = x ** 2"),
# Pathological: 300k digits
    (1, 1, "len(str(2**1000000))")]   # Pypy loses on this today
```

Here is the script's results on these statement tests on CPython 3.X, showing how map is quickest when function calls level the playing field (it lost earlier when the other tests ran an inline x ** 2):

```
c:\code> py -3 pybench_cases2.py
3.3.0 (v3.3.0:bd8afb90ebf2, Sep 29 2012, 10:57:17) [MSC v.1600 64 bit (AMD64)]
0.7237  ["[ord(x) for x in 'spam' * 2500]"]
1.3471  ["res=[]\nfor x in 'spam' * 2500: res.append(ord(x))"]
0.6160  ["list(map(ord, 'spam' * 2500))"]
1.1244  ["list(ord(x) for x in 'spam' * 2500)"]
0.5446  ['{x ** 2 for x in range(1000)}']
0.6053  ['s=set()\nfor x in range(1000): s.add(x ** 2)']
0.5278  ['{x: x ** 2 for x in range(1000)}']
0.5414  ['d={}\nfor x in range(1000): d[x] = x ** 2']
1.8933  ['len(str(2**1000000))']
```

As before, on these tests today 2.X clocks in faster than 3.X and PyPy is faster still on all of these tests but the last—which it loses by a full order of magnitude (10X), though it wins all the other tests here by the same degree. However, if you run file tests precoded in *pybench_cases2.py* you'll see that PyPy also loses to CPython when reading files line by line, as for the following test tuple on the stmts list:

```
(0, 0, "f=open('C:/Python33/Lib/pdb.py')\nfor line in f: x=line\nf.close()"),
```

This test opens and reads a 60K, 1,675-line text file line by line using file iterators. Its input loop presumably dominates overall test time. On this test, CPython 2.7 is twice as fast as 3.3, but PyPy is again an order of magnitude slower than CPython in general.

You can find this case in the *pybench_cases2* results files, or verify interactively or by command line (this is just what *pybench* does internally):

```
c:\code> py -3 -m timeit -n 1000 -r 5 "f=open('C:/Python33/Lib/pdb.py')"
 "for line in f: x=line" "f.close()"

>>> import timeit
>>> min(timeit.repeat(number=1000, repeat=5,
     stmt="f=open('C:/Python33/Lib/pdb.py')\nfor line in f: x=line\nf.close()"))
```

For another example that measures both list comprehensions and PyPy's current file speed, see the file *listcomp-speed.txt* in the book examples package; it uses direct PyPy command lines to run code from Chapter 14 with similar results: PyPy's line input is slower today by roughly a factor of 10.

I'll omit other Pythons' output here both for space and because these findings could very well change by the time you read these words. As usual, different types of code can exhibit different types of performance. While PyPy may optimize much algorithmic code, it may or may not optimize yours. You can find additional results in the book's examples package, but you may be better served by running these tests on your own to verify these findings today or observe their possibly different results in the future.

The impact of function calls revisited

As suggested earlier, map also wins for added *user-defined* functions—the following tests prove the earlier note's claim that map wins the race in CPython if *any* function must be applied by its alternatives:

```
stmts = [
    (0, 0, "def f(x): return x\n[f(x) for x in 'spam' * 2500]"),
    (0, 0, "def f(x): return x\nres=[]\nfor x in 'spam' * 2500: res.append(f(x))"),
    (0, 0, "def f(x): return x\n$listif3(map(f, 'spam' * 2500))"),
    (0, 0, "def f(x): return x\nlist(f(x) for x in 'spam' * 2500)")]

c:\code> py -3 pybench_cases2.py
3.3.0 (v3.3.0:bd8afb90ebf2, Sep 29 2012, 10:57:17) [MSC v.1600 64 bit (AMD64)]
1.5400  ["def f(x): return x\n[f(x) for x in 'spam' * 2500]"]
2.0506  ["def f(x): return x\nres=[]\nfor x in 'spam' * 2500: res.append(f(x))"]
1.2489  ["def f(x): return x\nlist(map(f, 'spam' * 2500))"]
1.6526  ["def f(x): return x\nlist(f(x) for x in 'spam' * 2500)"]
```

Compare this with the preceding section's ord tests; though user-defined functions may be slower than built-ins, the larger speed hit today seems to be functions in general, whether they are built-in or not. Notice that the total time here includes the cost of making a helper function, though only one for every 10,000 inner loop repetitions—a negligible factor per both common sense and additional tests run.

Comparing techniques: Homegrown versus batteries

For perspective, let's see how this section's timeit-based results compare to the homegrown-based timer results of the prior section, by running the file *timeseqs3.py* in this

book's examples package—it uses the homegrown timer but performs the same x **
2 operation and uses the same repetition counts as *pybench_cases.py*:

```
c:\code> py -3 timeseqs3.py
3.3.0 (v3.3.0:bd8afb90ebf2, Sep 29 2012, 10:57:17) [MSC v.1600 64 bit (AMD64)]
forLoop  : 0.55022 => [0...998001]
listComp : 0.48787 => [0...998001]
mapCall  : 0.59499 => [0...998001]
genExpr  : 0.52773 => [0...998001]
genFunc  : 0.52603 => [0...998001]

c:\code> py -3 pybench_cases.py
3.3.0 (v3.3.0:bd8afb90ebf2, Sep 29 2012, 10:57:17) [MSC v.1600 64 bit (AMD64)]
0.5015  ['[x ** 2 for x in range(1000)]']
0.5657  ['res=[]\nfor x in range(1000): res.append(x ** 2)']
0.6025  ['list(map(lambda x: x ** 2, range(1000)))']
0.5404  ['list(x ** 2 for x in range(1000))']
0.8711  ["s = 'spam' * 2500\nx = [s[i] for i in range(10000)]"]
2.8009  ["s = '?'\nfor i in range(10000): s += '?'"]
```

The homegrown timer results are very similar to the *pybench*-based results of this section that use `timeit`, though it's not entirely apples-to-apples—the homegrown timer-based *timeseqs3.py* incurs a function call per its middle totals loop and a slight overhead in best of logic of the timer itself, but also uses a prebuilt list instead of a 3.X `range` generator in its inner loop, which seems to make it slightly net faster on comparable tests (and I'd call this example a "sanity check," but I'm not sure the term applies in benchmarking!).

Room for improvement: Setup

Like most software, this section's program is open-ended and could be expanded arbitrarily. As one example, the files *pybench2.py* and *pybench2_cases.py* in the book's examples package add support for `timeit`'s *setup* statement option described earlier, in both API call and command-line modes.

This feature was omitted initially for brevity, and frankly, because my tests didn't seem to require it—timing more code gives a more complete picture when comparing Pythons, and setup actions cost the same when timing alternatives on a single Python. Even so, it's sometimes useful to provide setup code that is run once in the tested code's scope, but whose time is not charged to the statement's total—a module import, object initialization, or helper function definition, for example.

I won't list these two files in whole, but here are their important varying bits as an example of software evolution at work—as for the test statement, the setup code statement is passed as is in API call mode, but is split and space-indented in command-line mode and passed with one -s argument per line ("$listif3" isn't used because setup code is not timed):

```
# pybench2.py
...
def runner(stmts, pythons=None, tracecmd=False):
```

```
    for (number, repeat, setup, stmt) in stmts:
        if not pythons:
            ...
            best = min(timeit.repeat(
                            setup=setup, stmt=stmt, number=number, repeat=repeat))
        else:
            setup = setup.replace('\t', ' ' * 4)
            setup = ' '.join('-s "%s"' % line for line in setup.split('\n'))
            ...
            for (ispy3, python) in pythons:
                ...
                cmd = '%s -m timeit -n %s -r %s %s %s' % \
                            (python, number, repeat, setup, args)
```

```
# pybench2_cases.py
import pybench2, sys
...
stmts = [                                               # (num,rpt,setup,stmt)
    (0, 0, "", "[x ** 2 for x in range(1000)]"),
    (0, 0, "", "res=[]\nfor x in range(1000): res.append(x ** 2)"),

    (0, 0, "def f(x):\n\treturn x",
           "[f(x) for x in 'spam' * 2500]"),
    (0, 0, "def f(x):\n\treturn x",
           "res=[]\nfor x in 'spam' * 2500:\n\tres.append(f(x))"),

    (0, 0, "L = [1, 2, 3, 4, 5]", "for i in range(len(L)): L[i] += 1"),
    (0, 0, "L = [1, 2, 3, 4, 5]", "i=0\nwhile i < len(L):\n\tL[i] += 1\n\ti += 1")]
...
pybench2.runner(stmts, pythons, tracecmd)
```

Run this script with the -a and -t command-line flags to see how command lines are constructed for setup code. For instance, the following test specification tuple generates the command line that follows it for 3.3—not nice to look at, perhaps, but sufficient to pass lines from Windows to `timeit`, to be concatenated with line breaks between and inserted into a generated timing function with appropriate reindentation:

```
    (0, 0, "def f(x):\n\treturn x",
           "res=[]\nfor x in 'spam' * 2500:\n\tres.append(f(x))")

C:\python33\python -m timeit -n 1000 -r 5 -s "def f(x):" -s "    return x" "res=[]"
    "for x in 'spam' * 2500:" "    res.append(f(x))"
```

In API call mode, code strings are passed unchanged, because there's no need to placate a shell, and embedded tabs and end-of-line characters suffice. Experiment on your own to uncover more about Python code alternatives' speed. You may eventually run into shell limitations for larger sections of code in command-line mode, but both our home-grown timer and *pybench*'s `timeit`-based API call mode support more arbitrary code. Benchmarks can be great sport, but we'll have to leave future improvements as suggested exercises.

Other Benchmarking Topics: pystones

This chapter has focused on code timing fundamentals that you can use on your own code, that apply to Python benchmarking in general, and that served as a common use case for developing larger examples for this book. Benchmarking Python is a broader and richer domain than so far implied, though. If you're interested in pursuing this topic further, search the Web for links. Among the topics you'll find:

- *pystone.py*—a program designed for measuring Python speed across a range of code that ships with Python in its *Lib\test* directory
- *http://speed.python.org*—a project site for coordinating work on common Python benchmarks
- *http://speed.pypy.org*—the PyPy benchmarking site that the preceding bullet is partially emulating

The *pystone* test, for example, is based on a C language benchmark program that was translated to Python by Python original creator Guido van Rossum. It provides another way to measure the relative speeds of Python implementations, and seems to generally support our findings here:

```
c:\Python33\Lib\test> cd C:\python33\lib\test
c:\Python33\Lib\test> py -3 pystone.py
Pystone(1.1) time for 50000 passes = 0.685303
This machine benchmarks at 72960.4 pystones/second

c:\Python33\Lib\test> cd c:\python27\lib\test
c:\Python27\Lib\test> py -2 pystone.py
Pystone(1.1) time for 50000 passes = 0.463547
This machine benchmarks at 107864 pystones/second

c:\Python27\Lib\test> c:\pypy\pypy-1.9\pypy pystone.py
Pystone(1.1) time for 50000 passes = 0.099975
This machine benchmarks at 500125 pystones/second
```

Since it's time to wrap up this chapter, this will have to suffice as independent confirmation of our tests' results. Analyzing the meaning of pystone's results is left as suggested exercise; its code is not identical across 3.X and 2.X, but appears to differ today only in terms of print operations and an initialization of a global. Also keep in mind that benchmarking is just one of many aspects of Python code analysis; for pointers on options in related domains (e.g., testing), see Chapter 36's review of Python development tools.

Function Gotchas

Now that we've reached the end of the function story, let's review some common pitfalls. Functions have some jagged edges that you might not expect. They're all relatively

---

obscure, and a few have started to fall away from the language completely in recent releases, but most have been known to trip up new users.

Local Names Are Detected Statically

As you know, Python classifies names assigned in a function as *locals* by default; they live in the function's scope and exist only while the function is running. What you may not realize is that Python detects locals statically, when it compiles the def's code, rather than by noticing assignments as they happen at runtime. This leads to one of the most common oddities posted on the Python newsgroup by beginners.

Normally, a name that isn't assigned in a function is looked up in the enclosing module:

```
>>> X = 99

>>> def selector():          # X used but not assigned
        print(X)             # X found in global scope

>>> selector()
99
```

Here, the X in the function resolves to the X in the module. But watch what happens if you add an assignment to X after the reference:

```
>>> def selector():
        print(X)             # Does not yet exist!
        X = 88               # X classified as a local name (everywhere)
                             # Can also happen for "import X", "def X"...
>>> selector()
UnboundLocalError: local variable 'X' referenced before assignment
```

You get the name usage error shown here, but the reason is subtle. Python reads and compiles this code when it's typed interactively or imported from a module. While compiling, Python sees the assignment to X and decides that X will be a local name everywhere in the function. But when the function is actually run, because the assignment hasn't yet happened when the print executes, Python says you're using an undefined name. According to its name rules, it should say this; the local X is used before being assigned. In fact, any assignment in a function body makes a name local. Imports, =, nested defs, nested classes, and so on are all susceptible to this behavior.

The problem occurs because assigned names are treated as locals everywhere in a function, not just after the statements where they're assigned. Really, the previous example is ambiguous: was the intention to print the global X and create a local X, or is this a real programming error? Because Python treats X as a local everywhere, it's seen as an error; if you mean to print the global X, you need to declare it in a global statement:

```
>>> def selector():
        global X             # Force X to be global (everywhere)
        print(X)
        X = 88
```

```
>>> selector()
99
```

Remember, though, that this means the assignment also changes the global X, not a local X. Within a function, you can't use both local and global versions of the same simple name. If you really meant to print the global and then set a local of the same name, you'd need to import the enclosing module and use module attribute notation to get to the global version:

```
>>> X = 99
>>> def selector():
        import __main__          # Import enclosing module
        print(__main__.X)        # Qualify to get to global version of name
        X = 88                   # Unqualified X classified as local
        print(X)                 # Prints local version of name

>>> selector()
99
88
```

Qualification (the .X part) fetches a value from a namespace object. The interactive namespace is a module called __main__, so __main__.X reaches the global version of X. If that isn't clear, check out Chapter 17.

In recent versions Python has improved on this story somewhat by issuing for this case the more specific "unbound local" error message shown in the example listing (it used to simply raise a generic name error); this gotcha is still present in general, though.

Defaults and Mutable Objects

As noted briefly in Chapter 17 and Chapter 18, mutable values for default arguments can retain state between calls, though this is often unexpected. In general, default argument values are evaluated and saved once when a def statement is run, not each time the resulting function is later called. Internally, Python saves one object per default argument attached to the function itself.

That's usually what you want—because defaults are evaluated at def time, it lets you save values from the enclosing scope, if needed (functions defined within loops by factories may even depend on this behavior—see ahead). But because a default retains an object between calls, you have to be careful about changing mutable defaults. For instance, the following function uses an empty list as a default value, and then changes it in place each time the function is called:

```
>>> def saver(x=[]):          # Saves away a list object
        x.append(1)           # Changes same object each time!
        print(x)

>>> saver([2])                # Default not used
[2, 1]
>>> saver()                   # Default used
[1]
```

```
>>> saver()                         # Grows on each call!
[1, 1]
>>> saver()
[1, 1, 1]
```

Some see this behavior as a feature—because mutable default arguments retain their state between function calls, they can serve some of the same roles as *static* local function variables in the C language. In a sense, they work much like global variables, but their names are local to the functions and so will not clash with names elsewhere in a program.

To other observers, though, this seems like a gotcha, especially the first time they run into it. There are better ways to retain state between calls in Python (e.g., using the nested scope closures we met in this part and the classes we will study in Part VI).

Moreover, mutable defaults are tricky to remember (and to understand at all). They depend upon the timing of default object construction. In the prior example, there is just one list object for the default value—the one created when the def is executed. You don't get a new list every time the function is called, so the list grows with each new append; it is not reset to empty on each call.

If that's not the behavior you want, simply make a copy of the default at the start of the function body, or move the default value expression into the function body. As long as the value resides in code that's actually executed each time the function runs, you'll get a new object each time through:

```
>>> def saver(x=None):
        if x is None:           # No argument passed?
            x = []              # Run code to make a new list each time
        x.append(1)             # Changes new list object
        print(x)

>>> saver([2])
[2, 1]
>>> saver()                     # Doesn't grow here
[1]
>>> saver()
[1]
```

By the way, the if statement in this example could *almost* be replaced by the assignment x = x or [], which takes advantage of the fact that Python's or returns one of its operand objects: if no argument was passed, x would default to None, so the or would return the new empty list on the right.

However, this isn't exactly the same. If an empty list were passed in, the or expression would cause the function to extend and return a newly created list, rather than extending and returning the passed-in list like the if version. (The expression becomes [] or [], which evaluates to the new empty list on the right; see the section "Truth Tests" if you don't recall why.) Real program requirements may call for either behavior.

Today, another way to achieve the value retention effect of mutable defaults in a possibly less confusing way is to use the *function attributes* we discussed in Chapter 19:

```
>>> def saver():
        saver.x.append(1)
        print(saver.x)

>>> saver.x = []
>>> saver()
[1]
>>> saver()
[1, 1]
>>> saver()
[1, 1, 1]
```

The function name is global to the function itself, but it need not be declared because it isn't changed directly within the function. This isn't used in exactly the same way, but when coded like this, the attachment of an object to the function is much more explicit (and arguably less magical).

Functions Without returns

In Python functions, `return` (and `yield`) statements are optional. When a function doesn't return a value explicitly, the function exits when control falls off the end of the function body. Technically, all functions return a value; if you don't provide a `return` statement, your function returns the None object automatically:

```
>>> def proc(x):
        print(x)                     # No return is a None return

>>> x = proc('testing 123...')
testing 123...
>>> print(x)
None
```

Functions such as this without a `return` are Python's equivalent of what are called "procedures" in some languages. They're usually invoked as statements, and the None results are ignored, as they do their business without computing a useful result.

This is worth knowing, because Python won't tell you if you try to use the result of a function that doesn't return one. As we noted in Chapter 11, for instance, assigning the result of a list `append` method won't raise an error, but you'll get back None, not the modified list:

```
>>> list = [1, 2, 3]
>>> list = list.append(4)            # append is a "procedure"
>>> print(list)                      # append changes list in place
None
```

Chapter 15's section "Common Coding Gotchas" on page 463 discusses this more broadly. In general, any functions that do their business as a side effect are usually designed to be run as statements, not expressions.

Miscellaneous Function Gotchas

Here are two additional function-related gotchas—mostly reviews, but common enough to reiterate.

Enclosing scopes and loop variables: Factory functions

We described this gotcha in Chapter 17's discussion of enclosing function scopes, but as a reminder: when coding factory functions (a.k.a. closures), be careful about relying on enclosing function scope lookup for variables that are changed by enclosing loops —when a generated function is later called, all such references will remember the value of the *last* loop iteration in the enclosing function's scope. In this case, you must use defaults to save loop variable values instead of relying on automatic lookup in enclosing scopes. See "Loop variables may require defaults, not scopes" on page 506 in Chapter 17 for more details on this topic.

Hiding built-ins by assignment: Shadowing

Also in Chapter 17, we saw how it's possible to reassign built-in names in a closer local or global scope; the reassignment effectively hides and replaces that built-in's name for the remainder of the scope where the assignment occurs. This means you won't be able to use the original built-in value for the name. As long as you don't need the built-in value of the name you're assigning, this isn't an issue—many names are built in, and they may be freely reused. However, if you reassign a built-in name your code relies on, you may have problems. So either don't do that, or use tools like *PyChecker* that can warn you if you do. The good news is that the built-ins you commonly use will soon become second nature, and Python's error trapping will alert you early in testing if your built-in name is not what you think it is.

Chapter Summary

This chapter rounded out our look at functions and built-in iteration tools with a larger case study that measured the performance of iteration alternatives and Pythons, and closed with a review of common function-related mistakes to help you avoid pitfalls. The iteration story has one last sequel in Part VI, where we'll learn how to code user-defined iterable objects that generate values with classes and `__iter__`, in Chapter 30's operator overloading coverage.

This concludes the functions part of this book. In the next part, we will expand on what we already know about *modules*—files of tools that form the topmost organizational unit in Python, and the structure in which our functions always live. After that, we will explore classes, tools that are largely packages of functions with special first arguments. As we'll see, user-defined classes can implement objects that tap into the iteration protocol, just like the generators and iterables we met here. In fact, everything we have learned in this part of the book will apply when functions pop up later in the context of class methods.

Before moving on to modules, though, be sure to work through this chapter's quiz and the exercises for this part of the book, to practice what we've learned about functions here.

Test Your Knowledge: Quiz

1. What conclusions can you draw from this chapter about the relative speed of Python iteration tools?
2. What conclusions can you draw from this chapter about the relative speed of the Pythons timed?

Test Your Knowledge: Answers

1. In general, list comprehensions are usually the quickest of the bunch; map beats list comprehensions in Python only when all tools must call functions; for loops tend to be slower than comprehensions; and generator functions and expressions are slower than comprehensions by a constant factor. Under PyPy, some of these findings differ; map often turns in a different relative performance, for example, and list comprehensions seem always quickest, perhaps due to function-level optimizations.

   At least that's the case today on the Python versions tested, on the test machine used, and for the type of code timed—these results may vary if any of these three variables differ. Use the homegrown timer or standard library timeit to test your use cases for more relevant results. Also keep in mind that iteration is just one component of a program's time: more code gives a more complete picture.

2. In general, PyPy 1.9 (implementing Python 2.7) is typically faster than CPython 2.7, and CPython 2.7 is often faster than CPython 3.3. In most cases timed, PyPy is some 10X faster than CPython, and CPython 2.7 is often a small constant faster than CPython 3.3. In cases that use integer math, CPython 2.7 can be 10X faster than CPython 3.3, and PyPy can be 100X faster than 3.3. In other cases (e.g., string operations and file iterators), PyPy can be slower than CPython by 10X, though timeit and memory management differences may influence some results. The *pystone* benchmark confirms these relative rankings, though the sizes of the differences it reports differ due to the code timed.

   At least that's the case today on the Python versions tested, on the test machine used, and for the type of code timed—these results may vary if any of these three variables differ. Use the homegrown timer or standard library timeit to test your use cases for more relevant results. This is especially true when timing Python implementations, which may be arbitrarily optimized in each new release.

Test Your Knowledge: Part IV Exercises

In these exercises, you're going to start coding more sophisticated programs. Be sure to check the solutions in "Part IV, Functions and Generators" on page 1475 in Appendix D, and be sure to start writing your code in module files. You won't want to retype these exercises if you make a mistake.

1. *The basics.* At the Python interactive prompt, write a function that prints its single argument to the screen and call it interactively, passing a variety of object types: string, integer, list, dictionary. Then, try calling it without passing any argument. What happens? What happens when you pass two arguments?

2. *Arguments.* Write a function called `adder` in a Python module file. The function should accept two arguments and return the sum (or concatenation) of the two. Then, add code at the bottom of the file to call the `adder` function with a variety of object types (two strings, two lists, two floating points), and run this file as a script from the system command line. Do you have to print the call statement results to see results on your screen?

3. *varargs.* Generalize the `adder` function you wrote in the last exercise to compute the sum of an arbitrary number of arguments, and change the calls to pass more or fewer than two arguments. What type is the return value sum? (Hints: a slice such as `S[:0]` returns an empty sequence of the same type as `S`, and the `type` built-in function can test types; but see the manually coded `min` examples in Chapter 18 for a simpler approach.) What happens if you pass in arguments of different types? What about passing in dictionaries?

4. *Keywords.* Change the `adder` function from exercise 2 to accept and sum/concatenate three arguments: `def adder(good, bad, ugly)`. Now, provide default values for each argument, and experiment with calling the function interactively. Try passing one, two, three, and four arguments. Then, try passing keyword arguments. Does the call `adder(ugly=1, good=2)` work? Why? Finally, generalize the new `adder` to accept and sum/concatenate an *arbitrary* number of keyword arguments. This is similar to what you did in exercise 3, but you'll need to iterate over a dictionary, not a tuple. (Hint: the `dict.keys` method returns a list you can step through with a `for` or `while`, but be sure to wrap it in a `list` call to index it in 3.X; `dict.values` may help here too.)

5. *Dictionary tools.* Write a function called `copyDict(dict)` that copies its dictionary argument. It should return a new dictionary containing all the items in its argument. Use the dictionary `keys` method to iterate (or, in Python 2.2 and later, step over a dictionary's keys without calling `keys`). Copying sequences is easy (`X[:]` makes a top-level copy); does this work for dictionaries, too? As explained in this exercise's solution, because dictionaries now come with similar tools, this and the next exercise are just coding exercises but still serve as representative function examples.

6. *Dictionary tools.* Write a function called `addDict(dict1, dict2)` that computes the union of two dictionaries. It should return a new dictionary containing all the items in both its arguments (which are assumed to be dictionaries). If the same key appears in both arguments, feel free to pick a value from either. Test your function by writing it in a file and running the file as a script. What happens if you pass lists instead of dictionaries? How could you generalize your function to handle this case, too? (Hint: see the `type` built-in function used earlier.) Does the order of the arguments passed in matter?

7. *More argument-matching examples.* First, define the following six functions (either interactively or in a module file that can be imported):

```
def f1(a, b): print(a, b)          # Normal args
def f2(a, *b): print(a, b)         # Positional varargs

def f3(a, **b): print(a, b)        # Keyword varargs

def f4(a, *b, **c): print(a, b, c) # Mixed modes

def f5(a, b=2, c=3): print(a, b, c) # Defaults

def f6(a, b=2, *c): print(a, b, c)  # Defaults and positional varargs
```

Now, test the following calls interactively, and try to explain each result; in some cases, you'll probably need to fall back on the matching algorithm shown in Chapter 18. Do you think mixing matching modes is a good idea in general? Can you think of cases where it would be useful?

```
>>> f1(1, 2)
>>> f1(b=2, a=1)

>>> f2(1, 2, 3)
>>> f3(1, x=2, y=3)
>>> f4(1, 2, 3, x=2, y=3)

>>> f5(1)
>>> f5(1, 4)

>>> f6(1)
>>> f6(1, 3, 4)
```

8. *Primes revisited.* Recall the following code snippet from Chapter 13, which simplistically determines whether a positive integer is prime:

```
x = y // 2                     # For some y > 1
while x > 1:
    if y % x == 0:             # Remainder
        print(y, 'has factor', x)
        break                  # Skip else
    x -= 1
else:                          # Normal exit
    print(y, 'is prime')
```

Package this code as a reusable function in a module file (y should be a passed-in argument), and add some calls to the function at the bottom of your file. While you're at it, experiment with replacing the first line's // operator with / to see how true division changes the / operator in Python 3.X and breaks this code (refer back to Chapter 5 if you need a reminder). What can you do about negatives, and the values 0 and 1? How about speeding this up? Your outputs should look something like this:

```
13 is prime
13.0 is prime
15 has factor 5
15.0 has factor 5.0
```

9. *Iterations and comprehensions.* Write code to build a new list containing the square roots of all the numbers in this list: [2, 4, 9, 16, 25]. Code this as a for loop first, then as a map call, then as a list comprehension, and finally as a generator expression. Use the sqrt function in the built-in math module to do the calculation (i.e., import math and say math.sqrt(x)). Of the four, which approach do you like best?

10. *Timing tools.* In Chapter 5, we saw three ways to compute square roots: math.sqrt(X), X ** .5, and pow(X, .5). If your programs run a lot of these, their relative performance might become important. To see which is quickest, repurpose the *timerseqs.py* script we wrote in this chapter to time each of these three tools. Use the bestof or bestoftotal functions in one of this chapter's timer modules to test (you can use either the original, the 3.X-only keyword-only variant, or the 2.X/3.X version, and may use Python's timeit module as well). You might also want to repackage the testing code in this script for better reusability—by passing a test functions tuple to a general tester function, for example (for this exercise a copy-and-modify approach is fine). Which of the three square root tools seems to run fastest on your machine and Python in general? Finally, how might you go about interactively timing the speed of dictionary comprehensions versus for loops?

11. *Recursive functions.* Write a simple recursion function named countdown that prints numbers as it counts down to zero. For example, a call countdown(5) will print: 5 4 3 2 1 stop. There's no obvious reason to code this with an explicit stack or queue, but what about a nonfunction approach? Would a generator make sense here?

12. *Computing factorials.* Finally, a computer science classic (but demonstrative nonetheless). We employed the notion of factorials in Chapter 20's coverage of permutations: N!, computed as N*(N-1)*(N-2)*...1. For instance, 6! is 6*5*4*3*2*1, or 720. Code and time four functions that, for a call fact(N), each return N!. Code these four functions (1) as a recursive countdown per Chapter 19; (2) using the functional reduce call per Chapter 19; (3) with a simple iterative counter loop per Chapter 13; and (4) using the math.factorial library tool per Chapter 20. Use Chapter 21's timeit to time each of your functions. What conclusions can you draw from your results?

Modules and Packages

Modules: The Big Picture

This chapter begins our in-depth look at the Python *module*—the highest-level program organization unit, which packages program code and data for reuse, and provides self-contained namespaces that minimize variable name clashes across your programs. In concrete terms, modules typically correspond to Python program files. Each file is a module, and modules import other modules to use the names they define. Modules might also correspond to extensions coded in external languages such as C, Java, or C#, and even to directories in package imports. Modules are processed with two statements and one important function:

`import`
> Lets a client (importer) fetch a module as a whole

`from`
> Allows clients to fetch particular names from a module

`imp.reload` *(reload in 2.X)*
> Provides a way to reload a module's code without stopping Python

Chapter 3 introduced module fundamentals, and we've been using them ever since. The goal here is to expand on the core module concepts you're already familiar with, and move on to explore more advanced module usage. This first chapter reviews module basics, and offers a general look at the role of modules in overall program structure. In the chapters that follow, we'll dig into the coding details behind the theory.

Along the way, we'll flesh out module details omitted so far—you'll learn about reloads, the `__name__` and `__all__` attributes, package imports, relative import syntax, 3.3 namespace packages, and so on. Because modules and classes are really just glorified *namespaces*, we'll formalize namespace concepts here as well.

Why Use Modules?

In short, modules provide an easy way to organize components into a system by serving as self-contained packages of variables known as *namespaces*. All the names defined at the top level of a module file become attributes of the imported module object. As we saw in the last part of this book, imports give access to names in a module's global scope. That is, the module file's global scope *morphs* into the module object's attribute namespace when it is imported. Ultimately, Python's modules allow us to link individual files into a larger program system.

More specifically, modules have at least three roles:

Code reuse

As discussed in Chapter 3, modules let you save code in files permanently. Unlike code you type at the Python interactive prompt, which goes away when you exit Python, code in module files is *persistent*—it can be reloaded and rerun as many times as needed. Just as importantly, modules are a place to define names, known as *attributes*, which may be referenced by multiple external clients. When used well, this supports a *modular* program design that groups functionality into reusable units.

System namespace partitioning

Modules are also the highest-level program organization unit in Python. Although they are fundamentally just packages of names, these packages are also *self-contained*—you can never see a name in another file, unless you explicitly import that file. Much like the local scopes of functions, this helps avoid name clashes across your programs. In fact, you can't avoid this feature—everything "lives" in a module, both the code you run and the objects you create are always implicitly enclosed in modules. Because of that, modules are natural tools for grouping system components.

Implementing shared services or data

From an operational perspective, modules are also useful for implementing components that are shared across a system and hence require only a *single copy*. For instance, if you need to provide a global object that's used by more than one function or file, you can code it in a module that can then be imported by many clients.

At least that's the abstract story—for you to truly understand the role of modules in a Python system, we need to digress for a moment and explore the general structure of a Python program.

Python Program Architecture

So far in this book, I've sugarcoated some of the complexity in my descriptions of Python programs. In practice, programs usually involve more than just one file. For all but the simplest scripts, your programs will take the form of *multifile* systems—as the code timing programs of the preceding chapter illustrate. Even if you can get by with coding a single file yourself, you will almost certainly wind up using external files that someone else has already written.

This section introduces the general *architecture* of Python programs—the way you divide a program into a collection of source files (a.k.a. modules) and link the parts into a whole. As we'll see, Python fosters a modular program structure that groups functionality into coherent and reusable units, in ways that are natural, and almost automatic. Along the way, we'll also explore the central concepts of Python modules, imports, and object attributes.

How to Structure a Program

At a base level, a Python program consists of text files containing Python *statements*, with one main *top-level* file, and zero or more supplemental files known as *modules*.

Here's how this works. The top-level (a.k.a. script) file contains the main flow of control of your program—this is the file you run to launch your application. The module files are libraries of tools used to collect components used by the top-level file, and possibly elsewhere. Top-level files use tools defined in module files, and modules use tools defined in other modules.

Although they are files of code too, module files generally don't do anything when run directly; rather, they define tools intended for use in other files. A file *imports* a module to gain access to the tools it defines, which are known as its *attributes*—variable names attached to objects such as functions. Ultimately, we import modules and access their attributes to use their tools.

Imports and Attributes

Let's make this a bit more concrete. Figure 22-1 sketches the structure of a Python program composed of three files: *a.py*, *b.py*, and *c.py*. The file *a.py* is chosen to be the top-level file; it will be a simple text file of statements, which is executed from top to bottom when launched. The files *b.py* and *c.py* are modules; they are simple text files of statements as well, but they are not usually launched directly. Instead, as explained previously, modules are normally imported by other files that wish to use the tools the modules define.

For instance, suppose the file *b.py* in Figure 22-1 defines a function called `spam`, for external use. As we learned when studying functions in Part IV, *b.py* will contain a Python `def` statement to generate the function, which you can later run by passing zero or more values in parentheses after the function's name:

```
def spam(text):              # File b.py
    print(text, 'spam')
```

Now, suppose *a.py* wants to use `spam`. To this end, it might contain Python statements such as the following:

```
import b                     # File a.py
b.spam('gumby')              # Prints "gumby spam"
```

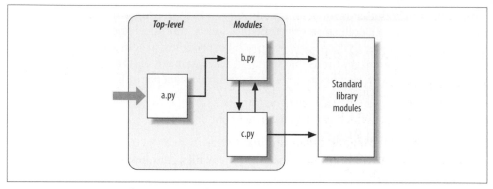

Figure 22-1. Program architecture in Python. A program is a system of modules. It has one top-level script file (launched to run the program), and multiple module files (imported libraries of tools). Scripts and modules are both text files containing Python statements, though the statements in modules usually just create objects to be used later. Python's standard library provides a collection of precoded modules.

The first of these, a Python `import` statement, gives the file *a.py* access to everything defined by top-level code in the file *b.py*. The code `import b` roughly means:

> Load the file *b.py* (unless it's already loaded), and give me access to all its attributes through the name `b`.

To satisfy such goals, `import` (and, as you'll see later, `from`) statements execute and load other files on request. More formally, in Python, cross-file module linking is not resolved until such `import` statements are executed at *runtime*; their net effect is to assign module names—simple variables like `b`—to loaded module objects. In fact, the module name used in an `import` statement serves two purposes: it identifies the external *file* to be loaded, but it also becomes a *variable* assigned to the loaded module.

Similarly, objects *defined* by a module are also created at runtime, as the `import` is executing: `import` literally runs statements in the target file one at a time to create its contents. Along the way, every name assigned at the top-level of the file becomes an attribute of the module, accessible to importers. For example, the second of the statements in *a.py* calls the function `spam` defined in the module `b`—created by running its `def` statement during the import—using object attribute notation. The code `b.spam` means:

> Fetch the value of the name `spam` that lives within the object `b`.

This happens to be a callable function in our example, so we pass a string in parentheses (`'gumby'`). If you actually type these files, save them, and run *a.py*, the words "gumby spam" will be printed.

As we've seen, the `object.attribute` notation appears throughout Python code—most objects have useful attributes that are fetched with the "." operator. Some reference callable objects like functions that take action (e.g., a salary computer), and others are simple data values that denote more static objects and properties (e.g., a person's name).

The notion of importing is also completely general throughout Python. Any file can import tools from any other file. For instance, the file *a.py* may import *b.py* to call its function, but *b.py* might also import *c.py* to leverage different tools defined there. Import chains can go as deep as you like: in this example, the module a can import b, which can import c, which can import b again, and so on.

Besides serving as the highest organizational structure, modules (and module packages, described in Chapter 24) are also the highest level of *code reuse* in Python. Coding components in module files makes them useful in your original program, and in any other programs you may write later. For instance, if after coding the program in Figure 22-1 we discover that the function b.spam is a general-purpose tool, we can reuse it in a completely different program; all we have to do is import the file *b.py* again from the other program's files.

Standard Library Modules

Notice the rightmost portion of Figure 22-1. Some of the modules that your programs will import are provided by Python itself and are not files you will code.

Python automatically comes with a large collection of utility modules known as the *standard library*. This collection, over 200 modules large at last count, contains platform-independent support for common programming tasks: operating system interfaces, object persistence, text pattern matching, network and Internet scripting, GUI construction, and much more. None of these tools are part of the Python language itself, but you can use them by importing the appropriate modules on any standard Python installation. Because they are standard library modules, you can also be reasonably sure that they will be available and will work portably on most platforms on which you will run Python.

This book's examples employ a few of the standard library's modules—timeit, sys, and os in last chapter's code, for instance—but we'll really only scratch the surface of the libraries story here. For a complete look, you should browse the standard Python library reference manual, available either online at *http://www.python.org*, or with your Python installation (via IDLE or Python's Start button menu on some Windows). The *PyDoc* tool discussed in Chapter 15 is another way to explore standard library modules.

Because there are so many modules, this is really the only way to get a feel for what tools are available. You can also find tutorials on Python library tools in commercial books that cover application-level programming, such as O'Reilly's *Programming Python*, but the manuals are free, viewable in any web browser (in HTML format), viewable in other formats (e.g., Windows help), and updated each time Python is re-released. See Chapter 15 for more pointers.

How Imports Work

The prior section talked about importing modules without really explaining what happens when you do so. Because imports are at the heart of program structure in Python, this section goes into more formal detail on the import operation to make this process less abstract.

Some C programmers like to compare the Python module import operation to a C `#include`, but they really shouldn't—in Python, imports are not just textual insertions of one file into another. They are really runtime operations that perform three distinct steps the first time a program imports a given file:

1. *Find* the module's file.
2. *Compile* it to byte code (if needed).
3. *Run* the module's code to build the objects it defines.

To better understand module imports, we'll explore these steps in turn. Bear in mind that all three of these steps are carried out only the *first time* a module is imported during a program's execution; later imports of the same module in a program run bypass all of these steps and simply fetch the already loaded module object in memory. Technically, Python does this by storing loaded modules in a table named `sys.mod ules` and checking there at the start of an import operation. If the module is not present, a three-step process begins.

1. Find It

First, Python must locate the module file referenced by an `import` statement. Notice that the `import` statement in the prior section's example names the file without a *.py* extension and without its directory path: it just says `import b`, instead of something like `import c:\dir1\b.py`. Path and extension details are omitted on purpose; instead, Python uses a standard *module search path* and known file types to locate the module file corresponding to an `import` statement.[1] Because this is the main part of the import operation that programmers must know about, we'll return to this topic in a moment.

---

1. It's syntactically illegal to include path and extension details in a standard `import`. However, *package imports*, which we'll discuss in Chapter 24, allow `import` statements to include part of the directory path leading to a file as a set of period-separated names. Package imports, though, still rely on the normal module search path to locate the leftmost directory in a package path (i.e., they are relative to a directory in the search path). They also cannot make use of any platform-specific directory syntax in the `import` statements; such syntax only works on the search path. Also, note that module file search path issues are not as relevant when you run *frozen executables* (discussed in Chapter 2), which typically embed byte code in the binary image.

2. Compile It (Maybe)

After finding a source code file that matches an `import` statement by traversing the module search path, Python next compiles it to byte code, if necessary. We discussed byte code briefly in Chapter 2, but it's a bit richer than explained there. During an import operation Python checks both file modification times and the byte code's Python version number to decide how to proceed. The former uses file "timestamps," and the latter uses either a "magic" number embedded in the byte code or a filename, depending on the Python release being used. This step chooses an action as follows:

Compile

If the byte code file is *older* than the source file (i.e., if you've changed the source) or was created by a different Python *version*, Python automatically regenerates the byte code when the program is run.

As discussed ahead, this model is modified somewhat in Python 3.2 and later—byte code files are segregated in a *__pycache__* subdirectory and named with their Python version to avoid contention and recompiles when multiple Pythons are installed. This obviates the need to check version numbers in the byte code, but the timestamp check is still used to detect changes in the source.

Don't compile

If, on the other hand, Python finds a *.pyc* byte code file that is *not older* than the corresponding *.py* source file and was created by the same Python version, it skips the source-to-byte-code compile step.

In addition, if Python finds only a byte code file on the search path and no source, it simply loads the byte code directly; this means you can ship a program as just byte code files and avoid sending source. In other words, the compile step is *bypassed* if possible to speed program startup.

Notice that compilation happens when a file is being imported. Because of this, you will not usually see a *.pyc* byte code file for the *top-level* file of your program, unless it is also imported elsewhere —only imported files leave behind *.pyc* files on your machine. The byte code of top-level files is used internally and discarded; byte code of imported files is saved in files to speed future imports.

Top-level files are often designed to be executed directly and not imported at all. Later, we'll see that it is possible to design a file that serves both as the top-level code of a program and as a module of tools to be imported. Such a file may be both executed and imported, and thus does generate a *.pyc*. To learn how this works, watch for the discussion of the special `__name__` attribute and `__main__` in Chapter 25.

3. Run It

The final step of an import operation executes the byte code of the module. All statements in the file are run in turn, from top to bottom, and any assignments made to names during this step generate attributes of the resulting module object. This is how the tools defined by the module's code are created. For instance, `def` statements in a file are run at import time to create functions and assign attributes within the module to those functions. The functions can then be called later in the program by the file's importers.

Because this last import step actually runs the file's code, if any top-level code in a module file does real work, you'll see its results at import time. For example, top-level `print` statements in a module show output when the file is imported. Function `def` statements simply define objects for later use.

As you can see, import operations involve quite a bit of work—they search for files, possibly run a compiler, and run Python code. Because of this, any given module is imported only *once* per process by default. Future imports skip all three import steps and reuse the already loaded module in memory. If you need to import a file again after it has already been loaded (for example, to support dynamic end-user customizations), you have to force the issue with an `imp.reload` call—a tool we'll meet in the next chapter.[2]

Byte Code Files: __pycache__ in Python 3.2+

As mentioned briefly, the way that Python stores files to retain the byte code that results from compiling your source has changed in Python 3.2 and later. First of all, if Python cannot write a file to save this on your computer for any reason, your program still runs fine—Python simply creates and uses the byte code in memory and discards it on exit. To speed startups, though, it will try to save byte code in a file in order to skip the compile step next time around. The way it does this varies per Python version:

In Python 3.1 and earlier (including all of Python 2.X)
Byte code is stored in files in the *same* directory as the corresponding source files, normally with the filename extension *.pyc* (e.g., *module.pyc*). Byte code files are also stamped internally with the version of Python that created them (known as a "magic" field to developers) so Python knows to *recompile* when this differs in the version of Python running your program. For instance, if you upgrade to a new Python whose byte code differs, all your byte code files will be recompiled automatically due to a version number mismatch, even if you haven't changed your source code.

In Python 3.2 and later
Byte code is instead stored in files in a subdirectory named *__pycache__*, which Python creates if needed, and which is located in the directory containing the corresponding source files. This helps avoid *clutter* in your source directories by segregating the byte code files in their own directory. In addition, although byte code

---

2. As described earlier, Python keeps already imported modules in the built-in `sys.modules` dictionary so it can keep track of what's been loaded. In fact, if you want to see which modules are loaded, you can import `sys` and print `list(sys.modules.keys())`. There's more on other uses for this internal table in Chapter 25.

files still get the *.pyc* extension as before, they are given more descriptive names that include text identifying the *version* of Python that created them (e.g., *module.cpython-32.pyc*). This avoids contention and *recompiles*: because each version of Python installed can have its own uniquely named version of byte code files in the *__pycache__* subdirectory, running under a given version doesn't overwrite the byte code of another, and doesn't require recompiles. Technically, byte code filenames also include the *name* of the Python that created them, so CPython, Jython, and other implementations mentioned in the preface and Chapter 2 can coexist on the same machine without stepping on each other's work (once they support this model).

In *both* models, Python always recreates the byte code file if you've changed the source code file since the last compile, but version differences are handled differently—by magic numbers and replacement prior to 3.2, and by filenames that allow for multiple copies in 3.2 and later.

Byte Code File Models in Action

The following is a quick example of these two models in action under 2.X and 3.3. I've omitted much of the text displayed by the `dir` directory listing on Windows here to save space, and the script used here isn't listed because it is not relevant to this discussion (it's from Chapter 2, and simply prints two values). *Prior to 3.2*, byte code files show up alongside their source files after being created by import operations:

```
c:\code\py2x> dir
10/31/2012  10:58 AM                      39 script0.py

c:\code\py2x> C:\python27\python
>>> import script0
hello world
1267650600228229401496703205376
>>> ^Z

c:\code\py2x> dir
10/31/2012  10:58 AM                      39 script0.py
10/31/2012  11:00 AM                     154 script0.pyc
```

However, in *3.2 and later* byte code files are saved in the *__pycache__* subdirectory and include versions and Python implementation details in their names to avoid clutter and contention among the Pythons on your computer:

```
c:\code\py2x> cd ..\py3x
c:\code\py3x> dir
10/31/2012  10:58 AM                      39 script0.py

c:\code\py3x> C:\python33\python
>>> import script0
hello world
1267650600228229401496703205376
>>> ^Z
```

```
c:\code\py3x> dir
10/31/2012  10:58 AM                    39 script0.py
10/31/2012  11:00 AM    <DIR>           __pycache__

c:\code\py3x> dir __pycache__
10/31/2012  11:00 AM                   184 script0.cpython-33.pyc
```

Crucially, under the model used in 3.2 and later, importing the same file with a different Python creates a *different* byte code file, instead of overwriting the *single* file as done by the pre-3.2 model—in the newer model, each Python version and implementation has its own byte code files, ready to be loaded on the next program run (earlier Pythons will happily continue using their scheme on the same machine):

```
c:\code\py3x> C:\python32\python
>>> import script0
hello world
1267650600228229401496703205376
>>> ^Z

c:\code\py3x> dir __pycache__
10/31/2012  12:28 PM                   178 script0.cpython-32.pyc
10/31/2012  11:00 AM                   184 script0.cpython-33.pyc
```

Python 3.2's newer byte code file model is probably superior, as it avoids recompiles when there is more than one Python on your machine—a common case in today's mixed 2.X/3.X world. On the other hand, it is not without potential incompatibilities in programs that rely on the prior file and directory structure. This may be a compatibility issue in some tools programs, for instance, though most well-behaved tools should work as before. See Python 3.2's "What's New?" document for details on potential impacts.

Also keep in mind that this process is completely *automatic*—it's a side effect of running programs—and most programmers probably won't care about or even notice the difference, apart from faster startups due to fewer recompiles.

The Module Search Path

As mentioned earlier, the part of the import procedure that most programmers *will* need to care about is usually the first—locating the file to be imported (the "find it" part). Because you may need to tell Python where to look to find files to import, you need to know how to tap into its search path in order to extend it.

In many cases, you can rely on the automatic nature of the module import search path and won't need to configure this path at all. If you want to be able to import user-defined files across directory boundaries, though, you will need to know how the search path works in order to customize it. Roughly, Python's module search path is composed of the concatenation of these major components, some of which are preset for you and some of which you can tailor to tell Python where to look:

1. The home directory of the program
2. PYTHONPATH directories (if set)
3. Standard library directories
4. The contents of any *.pth* files (if present)
5. The *site-packages* home of third-party extensions

Ultimately, the concatenation of these four components becomes `sys.path`, a mutable list of directory name strings that I'll expand upon later in this section. The first and third elements of the search path are defined automatically. Because Python searches the concatenation of these components from first to last, though, the *second* and *fourth* elements can be used to extend the path to include your own source code directories. Here is how Python uses each of these path components:

Home directory (automatic)
> Python first looks for the imported file in the home directory. The meaning of this entry depends on how you are running the code. When you're running a *program*, this entry is the directory containing your program's top-level script file. When you're working *interactively*, this entry is the directory in which you are working (i.e., the current working directory).

> Because this directory is always searched first, if a program is located entirely in a single directory, all of its imports will work automatically with no path configuration required. On the other hand, because this directory is searched first, its files will also override modules of the same name in directories elsewhere on the path; be careful not to accidentally hide library modules this way if you need them in your program, or use package tools we'll meet later that can partially sidestep this issue.

PYTHONPATH *directories (configurable)*
> Next, Python searches all directories listed in your PYTHONPATH environment variable setting, from left to right (assuming you have set this at all: it's not preset for you). In brief, PYTHONPATH is simply a list of user-defined and platform-specific names of directories that contain Python code files. You can add all the directories from which you wish to be able to import, and Python will extend the module search path to include all the directories your PYTHONPATH lists.

> Because Python searches the home directory first, this setting is only important when importing files across directory boundaries—that is, if you need to import a file that is stored in a *different* directory from the file that imports it. You'll probably want to set your PYTHONPATH variable once you start writing substantial programs, but when you're first starting out, as long as you save all your module files in the directory in which you're working (i.e., the home directory, like the *C:\code* used in this book) your imports will work without you needing to worry about this setting at all.

Standard library directories (automatic)

Next, Python automatically searches the directories where the standard library modules are installed on your machine. Because these are always searched, they normally do not need to be added to your PYTHONPATH or included in path files (discussed next).

.pth path file directories (configurable)

Next, a lesser-used feature of Python allows users to add directories to the module search path by simply listing them, one per line, in a text file whose name ends with a *.pth* suffix (for "path"). These path configuration files are a somewhat advanced installation-related feature; we won't cover them fully here, but they provide an alternative to PYTHONPATH settings.

In short, text files of directory names dropped in an appropriate directory can serve roughly the same role as the PYTHONPATH environment variable setting. For instance, if you're running Windows and Python 3.3, a file named *myconfig.pth* may be placed at the top level of the Python install directory (*C:\Python33*) or in the *site-packages* subdirectory of the standard library there (*C:\Python33\Lib\site-packages*) to extend the module search path. On Unix-like systems, this file might be located in *usr/local/lib/python3.3/site-packages* or */usr/local/lib/site-python* instead.

When such a file is present, Python will add the directories listed on each line of the file, from first to last, near the end of the module search path list—currently, after PYTHONPATH and standard libraries, but before the *site-packages* directory where third-party extensions are often installed. In fact, Python will collect the directory names in all the *.pth* path files it finds and will filter out any duplicates and nonexistent directories. Because they are files rather than shell settings, path files can apply to all users of an installation, instead of just one user or shell. Moreover, for some users and applications, text files may be simpler to code than environment settings.

This feature is more sophisticated than I've described here. For more details, consult the Python library manual, and especially its documentation for the standard library module `site`—this module allows the locations of Python libraries and path files to be configured, and its documentation describes the expected locations of path files in general. I recommend that beginners use PYTHONPATH or perhaps a single *.pth* file, and then only if you must import across directories. Path files are used more often by third-party libraries, which commonly install a path file in Python's *site-packages*, described next.

The Lib\site-packages directory of third-party extensions (automatic)

Finally, Python automatically adds the *site-packages* subdirectory of its standard library to the module search path. By convention, this is the place that most third-party extensions are installed, often automatically by the `distutils` utility described in an upcoming sidebar. Because their install directory is always part of the module search path, clients can import the modules of such extensions without any path settings.

Configuring the Search Path

The net effect of all of this is that both the PYTHONPATH and path file components of the search path allow you to tailor the places where imports look for files. The way you set environment variables and where you store path files varies per platform. For instance, on Windows, you might use your Control Panel's System icon to set PYTHONPATH to a list of directories separated by semicolons, like this:

```
c:\pycode\utilities;d:\pycode\package1
```

Or you might instead create a text file called *C:\Python33\pydirs.pth*, which looks like this:

```
c:\pycode\utilities
d:\pycode\package1
```

These settings are analogous on other platforms, but the details can vary too widely for us to cover in this chapter. See Appendix A for pointers on extending your module search path with PYTHONPATH or *.pth* files on various platforms.

Search Path Variations

This description of the module search path is accurate, but generic; the exact configuration of the search path is prone to changing across platforms, Python releases, and even Python implementations. Depending on your platform, additional directories may automatically be added to the module search path as well.

For instance, some Pythons may add an entry for the *current working directory*—the directory from which you launched your program—in the search path before the PYTHONPATH directories. When you're launching from a command line, the current working directory may not be the same as the home directory of your top-level file (i.e., the directory where your program file resides), which is always added. Because the current working directory can vary each time your program runs, you normally shouldn't depend on its value for import purposes. See Chapter 3 for more on launching programs from command lines.[3]

To see how your Python configures the module search path on your platform, you can always inspect sys.path—the topic of the next section.

The sys.path List

If you want to see how the module search path is truly configured on your machine, you can always inspect the path as Python knows it by printing the built-in sys.path

---

3. Also watch for Chapter 24's discussion of the new *relative import syntax* and search rules in Python 3.X; they modify the search path for from statements in files inside packages when "." characters are used (e.g., from . import string). By default, a package's own directory is not automatically searched by imports in Python 3.X, unless such relative imports are used by files in the package itself.

list (that is, the `path` attribute of the standard library module `sys`). This list of directory name strings is the actual search path within Python; on imports, Python searches each directory in this list from left to right, and uses the first file match it finds.

Really, `sys.path` *is* the module search path. Python configures it at program startup, automatically merging the home directory of the top-level file (or an empty string to designate the current working directory), any `PYTHONPATH` directories, the contents of any *.pth* file paths you've created, and all the standard library directories. The result is a list of directory name strings that Python searches on each import of a new file.

Python exposes this list for two good reasons. First, it provides a way to verify the search path settings you've made—if you don't see your settings somewhere in this list, you need to recheck your work. For example, here is what my module search path looks like on Windows under Python 3.3, with my `PYTHONPATH` set to `C:\code` and a *C: \Python33\mypath.pth* path file that lists `C:\Users\mark`. The empty string at the front means current directory, and my two settings are merged in; the rest are standard library directories and files and the *site-packages* home for third-party extensions:

```
>>> import sys
>>> sys.path
['', 'C:\\code', 'C:\\Windows\\system32\\python33.zip', 'C:\\Python33\\DLLs',
'C:\\Python33\\lib', 'C:\\Python33', 'C:\\Users\\mark',
'C:\\Python33\\lib\\site-packages']
```

Second, if you know what you're doing, this list provides a way for scripts to tailor their search paths manually. As you'll see by example later in this part of the book, by *modifying* the `sys.path` list, you can modify the search path for all future imports made in a program's run. Such changes last only for the duration of the script, however; `PYTHONPATH` and *.pth* files offer more permanent ways to modify the path—the first per user, and the second per installation.

On the other hand, some programs really *do* need to change `sys.path`. Scripts that run on web servers, for example, often run as the user "nobody" to limit machine access. Because such scripts cannot usually depend on "nobody" to have set `PYTHONPATH` in any particular way, they often set `sys.path` manually to include required source directories, prior to running any import statements. A `sys.path.append` or `sys.path.insert` will often suffice, though will endure for a single program run only.

Module File Selection

Keep in mind that filename extensions (e.g., *.py*) are omitted from `import` statements intentionally. Python chooses the first file it can find on the search path that matches the imported name. In fact, imports are the point of interface to a host of external components—source code, multiple flavors of byte code, compiled extensions, and more. Python automatically selects any type that matches a module's name.

Module sources

For example, an `import` statement of the form `import b` might today load or resolve to:

- A source code file named *b.py*
- A byte code file named *b.pyc*
- An optimized byte code file named *b.pyo* (a less common format)
- A directory named *b*, for package imports (described in Chapter 24)
- A compiled extension module, coded in C, C++, or another language, and dynamically linked when imported (e.g., *b.so* on Linux, or *b.dll* or *b.pyd* on Cygwin and Windows)
- A compiled built-in module coded in C and statically linked into Python
- A ZIP file component that is automatically extracted when imported
- An in-memory image, for frozen executables
- A Java class, in the Jython version of Python
- A .NET component, in the IronPython version of Python

C extensions, Jython, and package imports all extend imports beyond simple files. To importers, though, differences in the loaded file type are completely irrelevant, both when importing and when fetching module attributes. Saying `import b` gets whatever module `b` is, according to your module search path, and `b.attr` fetches an item in the module, be it a Python variable or a linked-in C function. Some standard modules we will use in this book are actually coded in C, not Python; because they look just like Python-coded module files, their clients don't have to care.

Selection priorities

If you have both a *b.py* and a *b.so* in different directories, Python will always load the one found in the first (leftmost) directory of your module search path during the left-to-right search of `sys.path`. But what happens if it finds both a *b.py* and a *b.so* in the *same* directory? In this case, Python follows a standard picking order, though this order is not guaranteed to stay the same over time or across implementations. In general, you should not depend on which type of file Python will choose within a given directory—make your module names distinct, or configure your module search path to make your module selection preferences explicit.

Import hooks and ZIP files

Normally, imports work as described in this section—they find and load files on your machine. However, it is possible to redefine much of what an import operation does in Python, using what are known as *import hooks*. These hooks can be used to make imports do various useful things, such as loading files from archives, performing decryption, and so on.

In fact, Python itself makes use of these hooks to enable files to be directly imported from ZIP archives: archived files are automatically extracted at import time when a *.zip* file is selected from the module import search path. One of the standard library directories in the earlier `sys.path` display, for example, is a *.zip* file today. For more details, see the Python standard library manual's description of the built-in `__import__` function, the customizable tool that `import` statements actually run.

 Also see Python 3.3's "What's New?" document for updates on this front that we'll mostly omit here for space. In short, in this version and later, the `__import__` function is now implemented by `importlib.__import__`, in part to unify and more clearly expose its implementation.

The latter of these calls is also wrapped by `importlib.import_module`—a tool that, per Python's current manuals, is generally preferred over `__import__` for direct calls to import by name string, a technique discussed in Chapter 25. Both calls still work today, though the `__import__` function supports customizing imports by replacement in the built-in scope (see Chapter 17), and other techniques support similar roles. See the Python library manuals for more details.

Optimized byte code files

Finally, Python also supports the notion of *.pyo* optimized byte code files, created and run with the `-O` Python command-line flag, and automatically generated by some install tools. Because these run only slightly faster than normal *.pyc* files (typically 5 percent faster), however, they are infrequently used. The PyPy system (see Chapter 2 and Chapter 21), for example, provides more substantial speedups. See Appendix A and Chapter 36 for more on *.pyo* files.

Third-Party Software: distutils

This chapter's description of module search path settings is targeted mainly at user-defined source code that you write on your own. Third-party extensions for Python typically use the `distutils` tools in the standard library to automatically install themselves, so no path configuration is required to use their code.

Systems that use `distutils` generally come with a *setup.py* script, which is run to install them; this script imports and uses `distutils` modules to place such systems in a directory that is automatically part of the module search path (usually in the *Lib\site-packages* subdirectory of the Python install tree, wherever that resides on the target machine).

For more details on distributing and installing with `distutils`, see the Python standard manual set; its use is beyond the scope of this book (for instance, it also provides ways to automatically compile C-coded extensions on the target machine). Also check out the third-party open source *eggs* system, which adds dependency checking for installed Python software.

Note: as this fifth edition is being written, there is some talk of deprecating `distutils` and replacing it with a newer `distutils2` package in the Python standard library. The status of this is unclear—it was anticipated in 3.3 but did not appear—so be sure to see Python's "What's New" documents for updates on this front that may emerge after this book is released.

Chapter Summary

In this chapter, we covered the basics of modules, attributes, and imports and explored the operation of `import` statements. We learned that imports find the designated file on the module search path, compile it to byte code, and execute all of its statements to generate its contents. We also learned how to configure the search path to be able to import from directories other than the home directory and the standard library directories, primarily with `PYTHONPATH` settings.

As this chapter demonstrated, the import operation and modules are at the heart of program architecture in Python. Larger programs are divided into multiple files, which are linked together at runtime by imports. Imports in turn use the module search path to locate files, and modules define attributes for external use.

Of course, the whole point of imports and modules is to provide a structure to your program, which divides its logic into self-contained software components. Code in one module is isolated from code in another; in fact, no file can ever see the names defined in another, unless explicit `import` statements are run. Because of this, modules minimize name collisions between different parts of your program.

You'll see what this all means in terms of actual statements and code in the next chapter. Before we move on, though, let's run through the chapter quiz.

Test Your Knowledge: Quiz

1. How does a module source code file become a module object?
2. Why might you have to set your `PYTHONPATH` environment variable?
3. Name the five major components of the module import search path.
4. Name four file types that Python might load in response to an import operation.
5. What is a namespace, and what does a module's namespace contain?

Test Your Knowledge: Answers

1. A module's source code file automatically becomes a module object when that module is imported. Technically, the module's source code is run during the im-

port, one statement at a time, and all the names assigned in the process become attributes of the module object.

2. You only need to set PYTHONPATH to import from directories other than the one in which you are working (i.e., the current directory when working interactively, or the directory containing your top-level file). In practice, this will be a common case for nontrivial programs.

3. The five major components of the module import search path are the top-level script's home directory (the directory containing it), all directories listed in the PYTHONPATH environment variable, the standard library directories, all directories listed in *.pth* path files located in standard places, and the *site-packages* root directory for third-party extension installs. Of these, programmers can customize PYTHONPATH and *.pth* files.

4. Python might load a source code (*.py*) file, a byte code (*.pyc* or *.pyo*) file, a C extension module (e.g., a *.so* file on Linux or a *.dll* or *.pyd* file on Windows), or a directory of the same name for package imports. Imports may also load more exotic things such as ZIP file components, Java classes under the Jython version of Python, .NET components under IronPython, and statically linked C extensions that have no files present at all. In fact, with import hooks, imports can load arbitrary items.

5. A namespace is a self-contained package of variables, which are known as the *attributes* of the namespace object. A module's namespace contains all the names assigned by code at the top level of the module file (i.e., not nested in def or class statements). Technically, a module's global scope *morphs* into the module object's attributes namespace. A module's namespace may also be altered by assignments from other files that import it, though this is generally frowned upon (see Chapter 17 for more on the downsides of cross-file changes).

Module Coding Basics

Now that we've looked at the larger ideas behind modules, let's turn to some examples of modules in action. Although some of the early topics in this chapter will be review for linear readers who have already applied them in previous chapters' examples, we'll find that they quickly lead us to further details surrounding Python's modules that we haven't yet met, such as nesting, reloads, scopes, and more.

Python modules are easy to *create*; they're just files of Python program code created with a text editor. You don't need to write special syntax to tell Python you're making a module; almost any text file will do. Because Python handles all the details of finding and loading modules, modules are also easy to *use*; clients simply import a module, or specific names a module defines, and use the objects they reference.

Module Creation

To define a module, simply use your text editor to type some Python code into a text file, and save it with a ".py" extension; any such file is automatically considered a Python module. All the names assigned at the top level of the module become its *attributes* (names associated with the module object) and are exported for clients to use —they morph from variable to module object attribute automatically.

For instance, if you type the following `def` into a file called *module1.py* and import it, you create a module object with one attribute—the name `printer`, which happens to be a reference to a function object:

```
def printer(x):              # Module attribute
    print(x)
```

Module Filenames

Before we go on, I should say a few more words about module filenames. You can call modules just about anything you like, but module filenames should end in a *.py* suffix if you plan to import them. The *.py* is technically optional for top-level files that will be run but not imported, but adding it in all cases makes your files' types more obvious and allows you to import any of your files in the future.

Because module names become variable names inside a Python program (without the *.py*), they should also follow the normal variable name rules outlined in Chapter 11. For instance, you can create a module file named *if.py*, but you cannot import it because `if` is a reserved word—when you try to run `import if`, you'll get a syntax error. In fact, both the names of module *files* and the names of *directories* used in package imports (discussed in the next chapter) must conform to the rules for variable names presented in Chapter 11; they may, for instance, contain only letters, digits, and underscores. Package directories also cannot contain platform-specific syntax such as spaces in their names.

When a module is imported, Python maps the internal module name to an external filename by adding a directory path from the module search path to the front, and a *.py* or other extension at the end. For instance, a module named M ultimately maps to some external file *<directory>\M.<extension>* that contains the module's code.

Other Kinds of Modules

As mentioned in the preceding chapter, it is also possible to create a Python module by writing code in an external language such as C, C++, and others (e.g., Java, in the Jython implementation of the language). Such modules are called *extension modules*, and they are generally used to wrap up external libraries for use in Python scripts. When imported by Python code, extension modules look and feel the same as modules coded as Python source code files—they are accessed with `import` statements, and they provide functions and objects as module attributes. Extension modules are beyond the scope of this book; see Python's standard manuals or advanced texts such as *Programming Python* for more details.

Module Usage

Clients can use the simple module file we just wrote by running an `import` or `from` statement. Both statements find, compile, and run a module file's code, if it hasn't yet been loaded. The chief difference is that `import` fetches the module as a whole, so you must qualify to fetch its names; in contrast, `from` fetches (or copies) specific *names* out of the module.

Let's see what this means in terms of code. All of the following examples wind up calling the `printer` function defined in the prior section's *module1.py* module file, but in different ways.

The import Statement

In the first example, the name `module1` serves two different purposes—it identifies an external file to be loaded, and it becomes a variable in the script, which references the module object after the file is loaded:

```
>>> import module1                      # Get module as a whole (one or more)
>>> module1.printer('Hello world!')     # Qualify to get names
Hello world!
```

The `import` statement simply lists one or more names of modules to load, separated by commas. Because it gives a name that refers to the *whole module* object, we must go through the module name to fetch its attributes (e.g., `module1.printer`).

The from Statement

By contrast, because `from` copies *specific names* from one file over to another scope, it allows us to use the copied names directly in the script without going through the module (e.g., `printer`):

```
>>> from module1 import printer        # Copy out a variable (one or more)
>>> printer('Hello world!')            # No need to qualify name
Hello world!
```

This form of `from` allows us to list one or more names to be copied out, separated by commas. Here, it has the same effect as the prior example, but because the imported name is copied into the scope where the `from` statement appears, using that name in the script requires less typing—we can use it directly instead of naming the enclosing module. In fact, we must; `from` doesn't assign the name of the module itself.

As you'll see in more detail later, the `from` statement is really just a minor extension to the `import` statement—it imports the module file as usual (running the full three-step procedure of the preceding chapter), but adds an extra step that copies one or more names (not objects) out of the file. The entire file is loaded, but you're given names for more direct access to its parts.

The from * Statement

Finally, the next example uses a special form of `from`: when we use a * instead of specific names, we get copies of *all names* assigned at the top level of the referenced module. Here again, we can then use the copied name `printer` in our script without going through the module name:

```
>>> from module1 import *              # Copy out _all_ variables
>>> printer('Hello world!')
Hello world!
```

Technically, both `import` and `from` statements invoke the same import operation; the `from` * form simply adds an extra step that copies all the names in the module into the importing scope. It essentially collapses one module's namespace into another; again, the net effect is less typing for us. Note that only * works in this context; you can't use pattern matching to select a subset of names (though you could with more work and a loop through a module's __dict__, discussed ahead).

And that's it—modules really are simple to use. To give you a better understanding of what really happens when you define and use modules, though, let's move on to look at some of their properties in more detail.

> In Python 3.X, the `from ...*` statement form described here can be used *only* at the top level of a module file, not within a function. Python 2.X allows it to be used within a function, but issues a warning anyhow. It's rare to see this statement used inside a function in practice; when present, it makes it impossible for Python to detect variables statically, before the function runs. Best practice in all Pythons recommends listing *all* your imports at the top of a module file; it's not required, but makes them easier to spot.

Imports Happen Only Once

One of the most common questions people seem to ask when they start using modules is, "Why won't my imports keep working?" They often report that the first import works fine, but later imports during an interactive session (or program run) seem to have no effect. In fact, they're not supposed to. This section explains why.

Modules are loaded and run on the first `import` or `from`, and only the first. This is on purpose—because importing is an expensive operation, by default Python does it just once per file, per process. Later import operations simply fetch the already loaded module object.

Initialization code

As one consequence, because top-level code in a module file is usually executed only once, you can use it to initialize variables. Consider the file *simple.py*, for example:

```
print('hello')
spam = 1                    # Initialize variable
```

In this example, the `print` and = statements run the first time the module is imported, and the variable `spam` is initialized at import time:

```
% python
>>> import simple           # First import: loads and runs file's code
hello
>>> simple.spam             # Assignment makes an attribute
1
```

Second and later imports don't rerun the module's code; they just fetch the already created module object from Python's internal modules table. Thus, the variable `spam` is not reinitialized:

```
>>> simple.spam = 2        # Change attribute in module
>>> import simple          # Just fetches already loaded module
>>> simple.spam            # Code wasn't rerun: attribute unchanged
2
```

Of course, sometimes you really *want* a module's code to be rerun on a subsequent import. We'll see how to do this with Python's `reload` function later in this chapter.

import and from Are Assignments

Just like `def`, `import` and `from` are *executable statements*, not compile-time declarations. They may be nested in `if` tests, to select among options; appear in function `def`s, to be loaded only on calls (subject to the preceding note); be used in `try` statements, to provide defaults; and so on. They are not resolved or run until Python reaches them while executing your program. In other words, imported modules and names are not available until their associated `import` or `from` statements run.

Changing mutables in modules

Also, like `def`, the `import` and `from` are *implicit assignments*:

- `import` assigns an entire module object to a single name.
- `from` assigns one or more names to objects of the same names in another module.

All the things we've already discussed about assignment apply to module access, too. For instance, names copied with a `from` become references to shared objects; as with function arguments, reassigning a copied name has no effect on the module from which it was copied, but changing a shared *mutable object* through a copied name can also change it in the module from which it was imported. To illustrate, consider the following file, *small.py*:

```
x = 1
y = [1, 2]
```

When importing with `from`, we copy names to the importer's scope that initially share objects referenced by the module's names:

```
% python
>>> from small import x, y      # Copy two names out
>>> x = 42                      # Changes local x only
>>> y[0] = 42                   # Changes shared mutable in place
```

Here, `x` is not a shared mutable object, but `y` is. The names `y` in the importer and the importee both reference the same list object, so changing it from one place changes it in the other:

```
>>> import small                # Get module name (from doesn't)
>>> small.x                     # Small's x is not my x
1
>>> small.y                     # But we share a changed mutable
[42, 2]
```

For more background on this, see Chapter 6. And for a graphical picture of what from assignments do with references, flip back to Figure 18-1 (function argument passing), and mentally replace "caller" and "function" with "imported" and "importer." The effect is the same, except that here we're dealing with names in modules, not functions. Assignment works the same everywhere in Python.

Cross-file name changes

Recall from the preceding example that the assignment to x in the interactive session changed the name x in that scope only, not the x in the file—there is no link from a name copied with from back to the file it came from. To really change a global name in another file, you must use import:

```
% python
>>> from small import x, y          # Copy two names out
>>> x = 42                          # Changes my x only

>>> import small                    # Get module name
>>> small.x = 42                    # Changes x in other module
```

This phenomenon was introduced in Chapter 17. Because changing variables in other modules like this is a common source of confusion (and often a bad design choice), we'll revisit this technique again later in this part of the book. Note that the change to y[0] in the prior session is different; it changes an *object*, not a name, and the name in both modules references the same, changed object.

import and from Equivalence

Notice in the prior example that we have to execute an import statement after the from to access the small module name at all. from only copies names from one module to another; it does not assign the module name itself. At least conceptually, a from statement like this one:

```
from module import name1, name2        # Copy these two names out (only)
```

is equivalent to this statement sequence:

```
import module                   # Fetch the module object
name1 = module.name1            # Copy names out by assignment
name2 = module.name2
del module                      # Get rid of the module name
```

Like all assignments, the from statement creates new variables in the importer, which initially refer to objects of the same names in the imported file. Only the *names* are copied out, though, not the objects they reference, and not the name of the module itself. When we use the from * form of this statement (from module import *), the equivalence is the same, but all the top-level names in the module are copied over to the importing scope this way.

Notice that the first step of the `from` runs a normal `import` operation, with all the semantics outlined in the preceding chapter. Because of this, the `from` always imports the *entire* module into memory if it has not yet been imported, regardless of how many names it copies out of the file. There is no way to load just part of a module file (e.g., just one function), but because modules are byte code in Python instead of machine code, the performance implications are generally negligible.

Potential Pitfalls of the from Statement

Because the `from` statement makes the location of a variable more implicit and obscure (`name` is less meaningful to the reader than `module.name`), some Python users recommend using `import` instead of `from` most of the time. I'm not sure this advice is warranted, though; `from` is commonly and widely used, without too many dire consequences. In practice, in realistic programs, it's often convenient not to have to type a module's name every time you wish to use one of its tools. This is especially true for large modules that provide many attributes—the standard library's `tkinter` GUI module, for example.

It is true that the `from` statement has the potential to corrupt namespaces, at least in principle—if you use it to import variables that happen to have the same names as existing variables in your scope, your variables will be silently overwritten. This problem doesn't occur with the simple `import` statement because you must always go through a module's name to get to its contents (`module.attr` will not clash with a variable named `attr` in your scope). As long as you understand and expect that this can happen when using `from`, though, this isn't a major concern in practice, especially if you list the imported names explicitly (e.g., `from module import x, y, z`).

On the other hand, the `from` statement has more serious issues when used in conjunction with the `reload` call, as imported names might reference prior versions of objects. Moreover, the `from module import *` form really *can* corrupt namespaces and make names difficult to understand, especially when applied to more than one file—in this case, there is no way to tell which module a name came from, short of searching the external source files. In effect, the `from *` form collapses one namespace into another, and so defeats the namespace partitioning feature of modules. We will explore these issues in more detail in the section "Module Gotchas" on page 770 (see Chapter 25).

Probably the best real-world advice here is to generally prefer `import` to `from` for simple modules, to explicitly list the variables you want in most `from` statements, and to limit the `from *` form to just one import per file. That way, any undefined names can be assumed to live in the module referenced with the `from *`. Some care is required when using the `from` statement, but armed with a little knowledge, most programmers find it to be a convenient way to access modules.

When import is required

The only time you really *must* use `import` instead of `from` is when you must use the same name defined in two different modules. For example, if two files define the same name differently:

```
# M.py
def func():
    ...do something...
```

```
# N.py
def func():
    ...do something else...
```

and you must use both versions of the name in your program, the `from` statement will fail—you can have only one assignment to the name in your scope:

```
# O.py
from M import func
from N import func        # This overwrites the one we fetched from M
func()                    # Calls N.func only!
```

An `import` will work here, though, because including the name of the enclosing module makes the two names unique:

```
# O.py
import M, N               # Get the whole modules, not their names
M.func()                  # We can call both names now
N.func()                  # The module names make them unique
```

This case is unusual enough that you're unlikely to encounter it very often in practice. If you do, though, `import` allows you to avoid the name collision. Another way out of this dilemma is using the `as` extension, which we'll cover in Chapter 25 but is simple enough to introduce here:

```
# O.py
from M import func as mfunc    # Rename uniquely with "as"
from N import func as nfunc
mfunc(); nfunc()               # Calls one or the other
```

The `as` extension works in both `import` and `from` as a simple renaming tool (it can also be used to give a shorter synonym for a long module name in `import`); more on this form in Chapter 25.

Module Namespaces

Modules are probably best understood as simply packages of names—i.e., places to define names you want to make visible to the rest of a system. Technically, modules usually correspond to files, and Python creates a module object to contain all the names assigned in a module file. But in simple terms, modules are just namespaces (places where names are created), and the names that live in a module are called its *attributes*. This section expands on the details behind this model.

Files Generate Namespaces

I've mentioned that files *morph* into namespaces, but how does this actually happen? The short answer is that every name that is assigned a value at the top level of a module file (i.e., not nested in a function or class body) becomes an attribute of that module.

For instance, given an assignment statement such as X = 1 at the top level of a module file *M.py*, the name X becomes an attribute of M, which we can refer to from outside the module as M.X. The name X also becomes a global variable to other code inside *M.py*, but we need to consider the notion of module loading and scopes a bit more formally to understand why:

- **Module statements run on the first import**. The first time a module is imported anywhere in a system, Python creates an empty module object and executes the statements in the module file one after another, from the top of the file to the bottom.

- **Top-level assignments create module attributes**. During an import, statements at the top level of the file not nested in a def or class that assign names (e.g., =, def) create attributes of the module object; assigned names are stored in the module's namespace.

- **Module namespaces can be accessed via the attribute __dict__ or dir(M)**. Module namespaces created by imports are dictionaries; they may be accessed through the built-in __dict__ attribute associated with module objects and may be inspected with the dir function. The dir function is roughly equivalent to the sorted keys list of an object's __dict__ attribute, but it includes inherited names for classes, may not be complete, and is prone to changing from release to release.

- **Modules are a single scope (local is global)**. As we saw in Chapter 17, names at the top level of a module follow the same reference/assignment rules as names in a function, but the local and global scopes are the same—or, more formally, they follow the LEGB scope rule we met in Chapter 17, but without the *L* and *E* lookup layers.

  Crucially, though, the module's global *scope* becomes an attribute dictionary of a module *object* after the module has been loaded. Unlike function scopes, where the local namespace exists only while the function runs, a module file's scope becomes a module object's attribute namespace and *lives on* after the import, providing a source of tools to importers.

Here's a demonstration of these ideas. Suppose we create the following module file in a text editor and call it *module2.py*:

```
print('starting to load...')
import sys
name = 42

def func(): pass
```

```
class klass: pass

print('done loading.')
```

The first time this module is imported (or run as a program), Python executes its statements from top to bottom. Some statements create names in the module's namespace as a side effect, but others do actual work while the import is going on. For instance, the two `print` statements in this file execute at import time:

```
>>> import module2
starting to load...
done loading.
```

Once the module is loaded, its scope becomes an attribute namespace in the module object we get back from `import`. We can then access attributes in this namespace by qualifying them with the name of the enclosing module:

```
>>> module2.sys
<module 'sys' (built-in)>

>>> module2.name
42

>>> module2.func
<function func at 0x000000000222E7B8>

>>> module2.klass
<class 'module2.klass'>
```

Here, `sys`, `name`, `func`, and `klass` were all assigned while the module's statements were being run, so they are attributes after the import. We'll talk about classes in Part VI, but notice the `sys` attribute—`import` statements really *assign* module objects to names, and any type of assignment to a name at the top level of a file generates a module attribute.

Namespace Dictionaries: __dict__

In fact, internally, module namespaces are stored as *dictionary* objects. These are just normal dictionaries with all the usual methods. When needed—for instance, to write tools that list module content generically as we will in Chapter 25—we can access a module's namespace dictionary through the module's __dict__ attribute. Continuing the prior section's example (remember to wrap this in a `list` call in Python 3.X—it's a view object there, and contents may vary outside 3.3 used here):

```
>>> list(module2.__dict__.keys())
['__loader__', 'func', 'klass', '__builtins__', '__doc__', '__file__', '__name__',
'name', '__package__', 'sys', '__initializing__', '__cached__']
```

The names we assigned in the module file become dictionary keys internally, so some of the names here reflect top-level assignments in our file. However, Python also adds some names in the module's namespace for us; for instance, __file__ gives the name of the file the module was loaded from, and __name__ gives its name as known to importers (without the *.py* extension and directory path). To see just the names your code assigns, filter out the double-underscore names as we've done before, in Chapter 15's `dir` coverage and Chapter 17's built-in scope coverage:

```
>>> list(name for name in module2.__dict__.keys() if not name.startswith('__'))
['func', 'klass', 'name', 'sys']
>>> list(name for name in module2.__dict__ if not name.startswith('__'))
['func', 'sys', 'name', 'klass']
```

This time we're filtering with a *generator* instead of a list comprehension, and can omit the `.keys()` because dictionaries generate their keys automatically though implicitly; the effect is the same. We'll see similar __dict__ dictionaries on *class*-related objects in Part VI too. In both cases, attribute fetch is similar to dictionary indexing, though only the former kicks off inheritance in classes:

```
>>> module2.name, module2.__dict__['name']
(42, 42)
```

Attribute Name Qualification

Speaking of attribute fetch, now that you're becoming more familiar with modules, we should firm up the notion of name qualification more formally too. In Python, you can access the attributes of any object that has attributes using the *qualification* (a.k.a. attribute fetch) syntax *object.attribute*.

Qualification is really an expression that returns the value assigned to an attribute name associated with an object. For example, the expression module2.sys in the previous example fetches the value assigned to sys in module2. Similarly, if we have a built-in list object L, L.append returns the append method object associated with that list.

It's important to keep in mind that attribute qualification has nothing to do with the scope rules we studied in Chapter 17; it's an independent concept. When you use qualification to access names, you give Python an explicit object from which to fetch the specified names. The LEGB scope rule applies only to bare, unqualified names—it may be used for the leftmost name in a name path, but later names after dots search specific objects instead. Here are the rules:

Simple variables
> X means search for the name X in the current scopes (following the LEGB rule of Chapter 17).

Qualification
> X.Y means find X in the current scopes, then search for the attribute Y in the object X (not in scopes).

Qualification paths
> X.Y.7 means look up the name Y in the object X, then look up Z in the object X.Y.

Generality

Qualification works on all objects with attributes: modules, classes, C extension types, etc.

In Part VI, we'll see that attribute qualification means a bit more for classes—it's also the place where something called *inheritance* happens—but in general, the rules outlined here apply to all names in Python.

Imports Versus Scopes

As we've learned, it is never possible to access names defined in another module file without first importing that file. That is, you never automatically get to see names in another file, regardless of the structure of imports or function calls in your program. A variable's meaning is always determined by the locations of assignments in your source code, and attributes are always requested of an object explicitly.

For example, consider the following two simple modules. The first, *moda.py*, defines a variable X global to code in its file only, along with a function that changes the global X in this file:

```
X = 88                  # My X: global to this file only
def f():
    global X            # Change this file's X
    X = 99              # Cannot see names in other modules
```

The second module, *modb.py*, defines its own global variable X and imports and calls the function in the first module:

```
X = 11                  # My X: global to this file only

import moda             # Gain access to names in moda
moda.f()                # Sets moda.X, not this file's X
print(X, moda.X)
```

When run, `moda.f` changes the X in `moda`, not the X in `modb`. The global scope for `moda.f` is always the file enclosing it, regardless of which module it is ultimately called from:

```
% python modb.py
11 99
```

In other words, import operations never give upward visibility to code in imported files —an imported file cannot see names in the importing file. More formally:

- Functions can never see names in other functions, unless they are physically enclosing.
- Module code can never see names in other modules, unless they are explicitly imported.

Such behavior is part of the *lexical scoping* notion—in Python, the scopes surrounding a piece of code are completely determined by the code's physical position in your file. Scopes are never influenced by function calls or module imports.[1]

Namespace Nesting

In some sense, although imports do not nest namespaces upward, they do nest downward. That is, although an imported module never has direct access to names in a file that imports it, using attribute qualification paths it is possible to descend into arbitrarily nested modules and access their attributes. For example, consider the next three files. *mod3.py* defines a single global name and attribute by assignment:

```
X = 3
```

mod2.py in turn defines its own X, then imports mod3 and uses qualification to access the imported module's attribute:

```
X = 2
import mod3

print(X, end=' ')          # My global X
print(mod3.X)              # mod3's X
```

mod1.py also defines its own X, then imports mod2, and fetches attributes in both the first and second files:

```
X = 1
import mod2

print(X, end=' ')          # My global X
print(mod2.X, end=' ')     # mod2's X
print(mod2.mod3.X)         # Nested mod3's X
```

Really, when mod1 imports mod2 here, it sets up a two-level namespace nesting. By using the path of names mod2.mod3.X, it can descend into mod3, which is nested in the imported mod2. The net effect is that mod1 can see the Xs in all three files, and hence has access to all three global scopes:

```
% python mod1.py
2 3
1 2 3
```

The reverse, however, is not true: mod3 cannot see names in mod2, and mod2 cannot see names in mod1. This example may be easier to grasp if you don't think in terms of namespaces and scopes, but instead focus on the objects involved. Within mod1, mod2 is just a name that refers to an object with attributes, some of which may refer to other

---

1. Some languages act differently and provide for *dynamic scoping*, where scopes really may depend on runtime calls. This tends to make code trickier, though, because the meaning of a variable can differ over time. In Python, scopes more simply correspond to the text of your program.

objects with attributes (`import` is an assignment). For paths like `mod2.mod3.X`, Python simply evaluates from left to right, fetching attributes from objects along the way.

Note that `mod1` can say `import mod2`, and then `mod2.mod3.X`, but it cannot say `import mod2.mod3`—this syntax invokes something called *package* (directory) imports, described in the next chapter. Package imports also create module namespace nesting, but their `import` statements are taken to reflect directory trees, not simple file import chains.

Reloading Modules

As we've seen, a module's code is run only once per process by default. To force a module's code to be reloaded and rerun, you need to ask Python to do so explicitly by calling the `reload` built-in function. In this section, we'll explore how to use reloads to make your systems more dynamic. In a nutshell:

- Imports (via both `import` and `from` statements) load and run a module's code only the first time the module is imported in a process.

- Later imports use the already loaded module object without reloading or rerunning the file's code.

- The `reload` function forces an already loaded module's code to be reloaded and rerun. Assignments in the file's new code change the existing module object in place.

Why care about reloading modules? In short, *dynamic customization*: the `reload` function allows parts of a program to be changed without stopping the whole program. With `reload`, the effects of changes in components can be observed immediately. Reloading doesn't help in every situation, but where it does, it makes for a much shorter development cycle. For instance, imagine a database program that must connect to a server on startup; because program changes or customizations can be tested immediately after reloads, you need to connect only once while debugging. Long-running servers can update themselves this way, too.

Because Python is interpreted (more or less), it already gets rid of the compile/link steps you need to go through to get a C program to run: modules are loaded dynamically when imported by a running program. Reloading offers a further performance advantage by allowing you to also change parts of running programs without stopping.

Though beyond this book's scope, note that `reload` currently only works on modules written in Python; compiled extension modules coded in a language such as C can be dynamically loaded at runtime, too, but they can't be reloaded (though most users probably prefer to code customizations in Python anyhow!).

Version skew note: In Python 2.X, `reload` is available as a built-in function. In Python 3.X, it has been moved to the `imp` standard library module—it's known as `imp.reload` in 3.X. This simply means that an extra `import` or `from` statement is required to load this tool in 3.X only. Readers using 2.X can ignore these imports in this book's examples, or use them anyhow—2.X also has a `reload` in its `imp` module to ease migration to 3.X. Reloading works the same regardless of its packaging.

reload Basics

Unlike `import` and `from`:

- `reload` is a function in Python, not a statement.
- `reload` is passed an existing module object, not a new name.
- `reload` lives in a module in Python 3.X and must be imported itself.

Because `reload` expects an object, a module must have been previously imported successfully before you can reload it (if the import was unsuccessful due to a syntax or other error, you may need to repeat it before you can reload the module). Furthermore, the syntax of `import` statements and `reload` calls differs: as a function reloads require parentheses, but import statements do not. Abstractly, reloading looks like this:

```
import module                    # Initial import
...use module.attributes...
...                              # Now, go change the module file
...
from imp import reload           # Get reload itself (in 3.X)
reload(module)                   # Get updated exports
...use module.attributes...
```

The typical usage pattern is that you import a module, then change its source code in a text editor, and then reload it. This can occur when working interactively, but also in larger programs that reload periodically.

When you call `reload`, Python rereads the module file's source code and reruns its top-level statements. Perhaps the most important thing to know about `reload` is that it changes a module object *in place*; it does not delete and re-create the module object. Because of that, every reference to an entire module *object* anywhere in your program is automatically affected by a reload. Here are the details:

- **reload runs a module file's new code in the module's current namespace**. Rerunning a module file's code overwrites its existing namespace, rather than deleting and re-creating it.
- **Top-level assignments in the file replace names with new values**. For instance, rerunning a `def` statement replaces the prior version of the function in the module's namespace by reassigning the function name.

- **Reloads impact all clients that use `import` to fetch modules**. Because clients that use `import` qualify to fetch attributes, they'll find new values in the module object after a reload.

- **Reloads impact future `from` clients only**. Clients that used `from` to fetch attributes in the past won't be affected by a reload; they'll still have references to the old objects fetched before the reload.

- **Reloads apply to a single module only**. You must run them on each module you wish to update, unless you use code or tools that apply reloads transitively.

reload Example

To demonstrate, here's a more concrete example of `reload` in action. In the following, we'll change and reload a module file without stopping the interactive Python session. Reloads are used in many other scenarios, too (see the sidebar "Why You Will Care: Module Reloads" on page 703), but we'll keep things simple for illustration here. First, in the text editor of your choice, write a module file named *changer.py* with the following contents:

```
message = "First version"
def printer():
    print(message)
```

This module creates and exports two names—one bound to a string, and another to a function. Now, start the Python interpreter, import the module, and call the function it exports. The function will print the value of the global `message` variable:

```
% python
>>> import changer
>>> changer.printer()
First version
```

Keeping the interpreter active, now edit the module file in another window:

```
...modify changer.py without stopping Python...
% notepad changer.py
```

Change the global `message` variable, as well as the `printer` function body:

```
message = "After editing"
def printer():
    print('reloaded:', message)
```

Then, return to the Python window and reload the module to fetch the new code. Notice in the following interaction that importing the module again has no effect; we get the original message, even though the file's been changed. We have to call `reload` in order to get the new version:

```
...back to the Python interpreter...
>>> import changer
>>> changer.printer()            # No effect: uses loaded module
First version
>>> from imp import reload
```

```
>>> reload(changer)                          # Forces new code to load/run
<module 'changer' from '.\\changer.py'>
>>> changer.printer()                         # Runs the new version now
reloaded: After editing
```

Notice that `reload` actually *returns* the module object for us—its result is usually ignored, but because expression results are printed at the interactive prompt, Python shows a default `<module 'name'...>` representation.

Two final notes here: first, if you use `reload`, you'll probably want to pair it with `import` instead of `from`, as the latter isn't updated by reload operations—leaving your names in a state that's strange enough to warrant postponing further elaboration until this part's "gotchas" at the end of Chapter 25. Second, `reload` by itself updates only a *single* module, but it's straightforward to code a function that applies it transitively to related modules—an extension we'll save for a case study near the end of Chapter 25.

Why You Will Care: Module Reloads

Besides allowing you to reload (and hence rerun) modules at the interactive prompt, module reloads are also useful in larger systems, especially when the cost of restarting the entire application is prohibitive. For instance, game servers and systems that must connect to servers over a network on startup are prime candidates for dynamic reloads.

They're also useful in GUI work (a widget's callback action can be changed while the GUI remains active), and when Python is used as an embedded language in a C or C++ program (the enclosing program can request a reload of the Python code it runs, without having to stop). See *Programming Python* for more on reloading GUI callbacks and embedded Python code.

More generally, reloads allow programs to provide highly dynamic interfaces. For instance, Python is often used as a *customization* language for larger systems—users can customize products by coding bits of Python code onsite, without having to recompile the entire product (or even having its source code at all). In such worlds, the Python code already adds a dynamic flavor by itself.

To be even more dynamic, though, such systems can automatically reload the Python customization code periodically at runtime. That way, users' changes are picked up while the system is running; there is no need to stop and restart each time the Python code is modified. Not all systems require such a dynamic approach, but for those that do, module reloads provide an easy-to-use dynamic customization tool.

Chapter Summary

This chapter delved into the essentials of module coding tools—the `import` and `from` statements, and the `reload` call. We learned how the `from` statement simply adds an extra step that copies names out of a file after it has been imported, and how `reload` forces a file to be imported again without stopping and restarting Python. We also surveyed namespace concepts, saw what happens when imports are nested, explored the way files become module namespaces, and learned about some potential pitfalls of the `from` statement.

Although we've already seen enough to handle module files in our programs, the next chapter extends our coverage of the import model by presenting *package imports*—a way for our `import` statements to specify part of the directory path leading to the desired module. As we'll see, package imports give us a hierarchy that is useful in larger systems and allow us to break conflicts between same-named modules. Before we move on, though, here's a quick quiz on the concepts presented here.

Test Your Knowledge: Quiz

1. How do you make a module?
2. How is the `from` statement related to the `import` statement?
3. How is the `reload` function related to imports?
4. When must you use `import` instead of `from`?
5. Name three potential pitfalls of the `from` statement.
6. What…is the airspeed velocity of an unladen swallow?

Test Your Knowledge: Answers

1. To create a module, you simply write a text file containing Python statements; every source code file is automatically a module, and there is no syntax for declaring one. Import operations load module files into module objects in memory. You can also make a module by writing code in an external language like C or Java, but such extension modules are beyond the scope of this book.

2. The `from` statement imports an entire module, like the `import` statement, but as an extra step it also copies one or more variables from the imported module into the scope where the `from` appears. This enables you to use the imported names directly (`name`) instead of having to go through the module (`module.name`).

3. By default, a module is imported only once per process. The `reload` function forces a module to be imported again. It is mostly used to pick up new versions of a module's source code during development, and in dynamic customization scenarios.

4. You must use `import` instead of `from` only when you need to access the same name in two different modules; because you'll have to specify the names of the enclosing modules, the two names will be unique. The `as` extension can render `from` usable in this context as well.

5. The `from` statement can obscure the meaning of a variable (which module it is defined in), can have problems with the `reload` call (names may reference prior versions of objects), and can corrupt namespaces (it might silently overwrite names

you are using in your scope). The `from` * form is worse in most regards—it can seriously corrupt namespaces and obscure the meaning of variables, so it is probably best used sparingly.

6. What do you mean? An African or European swallow?

Module Packages

So far, when we've imported modules, we've been loading files. This represents typical module usage, and it's probably the technique you'll use for most imports you'll code early on in your Python career. However, the module import story is a bit richer than I have thus far implied.

In addition to a module name, an import can name a directory path. A directory of Python code is said to be a *package*, so such imports are known as *package imports*. In effect, a package import turns a directory on your computer into another Python namespace, with attributes corresponding to the subdirectories and module files that the directory contains.

This is a somewhat advanced feature, but the hierarchy it provides turns out to be handy for organizing the files in a large system and tends to simplify module search path settings. As we'll see, package imports are also sometimes required to resolve import ambiguities when multiple program files of the same name are installed on a single machine.

Because it is relevant to code in packages only, we'll also introduce Python's recent *relative imports* model and syntax here. As we'll see, this model modifies search paths in 3.X, and extends the `from` statement for imports within packages in both 2.X and 3.X. This model can make such intrapackage imports more explicit and succinct, but comes with some tradeoffs that can impact your programs.

Finally, for readers using Python 3.3 and later, its new *namespace package* model—which allows packages to span multiple directories and requires no initialization file—is also introduced here. This new-style package model is optional and can be used in concert with the original (now known as "regular") package model, but it upends some of the original model's basic ideas and rules. Because of that, we'll explore regular packages here first for all readers, and present namespace packages last as an optional topic.

Package Import Basics

At a base level, package imports are straightforward—in the place where you have been naming a simple file in your `import` statements, you can instead list a *path* of names separated by periods:

```
import dir1.dir2.mod
```

The same goes for `from` statements:

```
from dir1.dir2.mod import x
```

The "dotted" path in these statements is assumed to correspond to a path through the directory hierarchy on your computer, leading to the file *mod.py* (or similar; the extension may vary). That is, the preceding statements indicate that on your machine there is a directory *dir1*, which has a subdirectory *dir2*, which contains a module file *mod.py* (or similar).

Furthermore, these imports imply that *dir1* resides within some container directory *dir0*, which is a component of the normal Python module search path. In other words, these two `import` statements imply a directory structure that looks something like this (shown with Windows backslash separators):

```
dir0\dir1\dir2\mod.py            # Or mod.pyc, mod.so, etc.
```

The container directory *dir0* needs to be added to your module search path unless it's the home directory of the top-level file, exactly as if *dir1* were a simple module file.

More formally, the leftmost component in a package import path is still *relative* to a directory included in the `sys.path` module search path list we explored in Chapter 22. From there down, though, the import statements in your script explicitly give the directory paths leading to modules in packages.

Packages and Search Path Settings

If you use this feature, keep in mind that the directory paths in your import statements can be only variables separated by periods. You cannot use any platform-specific path syntax in your import statements, such as `C:\dir1`, `My Documents.dir2`, or `../dir1`—these do not work syntactically. Instead, use any such platform-specific syntax in your module search path settings to name the container directories.

For instance, in the prior example, *dir0*—the directory name you add to your module search path—can be an arbitrarily long and platform-specific directory path leading up to *dir1*. You cannot use an invalid statement like this:

```
import C:\mycode\dir1\dir2\mod        # Error: illegal syntax
```

But you can add *C:\mycode* to your `PYTHONPATH` variable or a *.pth* file, and say this in your script:

```
import dir1.dir2.mod
```

In effect, entries on the module search path provide platform-specific directory path *prefixes*, which lead to the leftmost names in `import` and `from` statements. These import statements themselves provide the remainder of the directory path in a platform-neutral fashion.[1]

As for simple file imports, you don't need to add the container directory *dir0* to your module search path if it's already there—per Chapter 22, it will be if it's the home directory of the top-level file, the directory you're working in interactively, a standard library directory, or the *site-packages* third-party install root. One way or another, though, your module search path must include all the directories containing leftmost components in your code's package import statements.

Package __init__.py Files

If you choose to use package imports, there is one more constraint you must follow: at least until Python 3.3, each directory named within the path of a package import statement must contain a file named *__init__.py*, or your package imports will fail. That is, in the example we've been using, both *dir1* and *dir2* must contain a file called *__init__.py*; the container directory *dir0* does not require such a file because it's not listed in the `import` statement itself.

More formally, for a directory structure such as this:

```
dir0\dir1\dir2\mod.py
```

and an `import` statement of the form:

```
import dir1.dir2.mod
```

the following rules apply:

- *dir1* and *dir2* both must contain an *__init__.py* file.
- *dir0*, the container, does not require an *__init__.py* file; this file will simply be ignored if present.
- *dir0*, not *dir0\dir1*, must be listed on the module search path `sys.path`.

To satisfy the first two of these rules, package creators must create files of the sort we'll explore here. To satisfy the latter of these, *dir0* must be an automatic path component (the home, libraries, or *site-packages* directories), or be given in `PYTHONPATH` or *.pth* file settings or manual `sys.path` changes.

---

1. The dot path syntax was chosen partly for platform neutrality, but also because paths in `import` statements become real nested object paths. This syntax also means that you may get odd error messages if you forget to omit the *.py* in your `import` statements. For example, `import mod.py` is assumed to be a directory path import—it loads *mod.py*, then tries to load a *mod\py.py*, and ultimately issues a potentially confusing "No module named py" error message. As of Python 3.3 this error message has been improved to say "No module named 'm.py'; m is not a package."

The net effect is that this example's directory structure should be as follows, with indentation designating directory nesting:

```
dir0\                                    # Container on module search path
    dir1\
        __init__.py
        dir2\
            __init__.py
            mod.py
```

The *__init__.py* files can contain Python code, just like normal module files. Their names are special because their code is run automatically the first time a Python program imports a directory, and thus serves primarily as a hook for performing initialization steps required by the package. These files can also be completely empty, though, and sometimes have additional roles—as the next section explains.

 As we'll see near the end of this chapter, the requirement of packages to have a file named *__init__.py* has been lifted as of Python 3.3. In that release and later, directories of modules with no such file may be imported as single-directory *namespace packages*, which work the same but run no initialization-time code file. Prior to Python 3.3, though, and in all of Python 2.X, packages still require *__init__.py* files. As described ahead, in 3.3 and later these files also provide a performance advantage when used.

Package initialization file roles

In more detail, the *__init__.py* file serves as a hook for package initialization-time actions, declares a directory as a Python package, generates a module namespace for a directory, and implements the behavior of `from *` (i.e., `from .. import *`) statements when used with directory imports:

Package initialization
> The first time a Python program imports through a directory, it automatically runs all the code in the directory's *__init__.py* file. Because of that, these files are a natural place to put code to initialize the state required by files in a package. For instance, a package might use its initialization file to create required data files, open connections to databases, and so on. Typically, *__init__.py* files are not meant to be useful if executed directly; they are run automatically when a package is first accessed.

Module usability declarations
> Package *__init__.py* files are also partly present to declare that a directory is a Python package. In this role, these files serve to prevent directories with common names from unintentionally hiding true modules that appear later on the module search path. Without this safeguard, Python might pick a directory that has nothing to do with your code, just because it appears nested in an earlier directory on the search path. As we'll see later, Python 3.3's namespace packages obviate much of

this role, but achieve a similar effect algorithmically by scanning ahead on the path to find later files.

Module namespace initialization

In the package import model, the directory paths in your script become real nested object paths after an import. For instance, in the preceding example, after the import the expression `dir1.dir2` works and returns a module object whose namespace contains all the names assigned by *dir2*'s *__init__.py* initialization file. Such files provide a namespace for module objects created for directories, which would otherwise have no real associated module file.

`from` * *statement behavior*

As an advanced feature, you can use `__all__` lists in *__init__.py* files to define what is exported when a directory is imported with the `from` * statement form. In an *__init__.py* file, the `__all__` list is taken to be the list of submodule names that should be automatically imported when `from` * is used on the package (directory) name. If `__all__` is not set, the `from` * statement does not automatically load submodules nested in the directory; instead, it loads just names defined by assignments in the directory's *__init__.py* file, including any submodules explicitly imported by code in this file. For instance, the statement `from submodule import X` in a directory's *__init__.py* makes the name X available in that directory's namespace. (We'll see additional roles for `__all__` in Chapter 25: it serves to declare `from` * exports of simple files as well.)

You can also simply leave these files empty, if their roles are beyond your needs (and frankly, they are often empty in practice). They must exist, though, for your directory imports to work at all.

 Don't confuse package *__init__.py* files with the class `__init__` constructor methods we'll meet in the next part of the book. The former are files of code run when imports first step through a package directory in a program run, while the latter are called when an instance is created. Both have initialization roles, but they are otherwise very different.

Package Import Example

Let's actually code the example we've been talking about to show how initialization files and paths come into play. The following three files are coded in a directory *dir1* and its subdirectory *dir2*—comments give the pathnames of these files:

```
# dir1\__init__.py
print('dir1 init')
x = 1

# dir1\dir2\__init__.py
print('dir2 init')
y = 2
```

```
# dir1\dir2\mod.py
print('in mod.py')
z = 3
```

Here, *dir1* will be either an immediate subdirectory of the one we're working in (i.e., the home directory), or an immediate subdirectory of a directory that is listed on the module search path (technically, on `sys.path`). Either way, *dir1*'s container does not need an *__init__.py* file.

`import` statements run each directory's initialization file the first time that directory is traversed, as Python descends the path; `print` statements are included here to trace their execution:

```
C:\code> python             # Run in dir1's container directory
>>> import dir1.dir2.mod    # First imports run init files
dir1 init
dir2 init
in mod.py
>>>
>>> import dir1.dir2.mod    # Later imports do not
```

Just like module files, an already imported directory may be passed to `reload` to force reexecution of that single item. As shown here, `reload` accepts a dotted pathname to reload nested directories and files:

```
>>> from imp import reload    # from needed in 3.X only
>>> reload(dir1)
dir1 init
<module 'dir1' from '.\\dir1\\__init__.py'>
>>>
>>> reload(dir1.dir2)
dir2 init
<module 'dir1.dir2' from '.\\dir1\\dir2\\__init__.py'>
```

Once imported, the path in your `import` statement becomes a *nested object path* in your script. Here, `mod` is an object nested in the object `dir2`, which in turn is nested in the object `dir1`:

```
>>> dir1
<module 'dir1' from '.\\dir1\\__init__.py'>
>>> dir1.dir2
<module 'dir1.dir2' from '.\\dir1\\dir2\\__init__.py'>
>>> dir1.dir2.mod
<module 'dir1.dir2.mod' from '.\\dir1\\dir2\\mod.py'>
```

In fact, each directory name in the path becomes a variable assigned to a module object whose namespace is initialized by all the assignments in that directory's *__init__.py* file. `dir1.x` refers to the variable x assigned in *dir1__init__.py*, much as `mod.z` refers to the variable z assigned in *mod.py*:

```
>>> dir1.x
1
>>> dir1.dir2.y
2
```

```
>>> dir1.dir2.mod.z
3
```

from Versus import with Packages

import statements can be somewhat inconvenient to use with packages, because you may have to retype the paths frequently in your program. In the prior section's example, for instance, you must retype and rerun the full path from dir1 each time you want to reach z. If you try to access dir2 or mod directly, you'll get an error:

```
>>> dir2.mod
NameError: name 'dir2' is not defined
>>> mod.z
NameError: name 'mod' is not defined
```

It's often more convenient, therefore, to use the from statement with packages to avoid retyping the paths at each access. Perhaps more importantly, if you ever restructure your directory tree, the from statement requires just one path update in your code, whereas imports may require many. The import as extension, discussed formally in the next chapter, can also help here by providing a shorter synonym for the full path, and a renaming tool when the same name appears in multiple modules:

```
C:\code> python
>>> from dir1.dir2 import mod            # Code path here only
dir1 init
dir2 init
in mod.py
>>> mod.z                                # Don't repeat path
3
>>> from dir1.dir2.mod import z
>>> z
3
>>> import dir1.dir2.mod as mod          # Use shorter name (see Chapter 25)
>>> mod.z
3
>>> from dir1.dir2.mod import z as modz  # Ditto if names clash (see Chapter 25)
>>> modz
3
```

Why Use Package Imports?

If you're new to Python, make sure that you've mastered simple modules before stepping up to packages, as they are a somewhat more advanced feature. They do serve useful roles, though, especially in larger programs: they make imports more informative, serve as an organizational tool, simplify your module search path, and can resolve ambiguities.

First of all, because package imports give some directory information in program files, they both make it easier to locate your files and serve as an organizational tool. Without package paths, you must often resort to consulting the module search path to find files.

Moreover, if you organize your files into subdirectories for functional areas, package imports make it more obvious what role a module plays, and so make your code more readable. For example, a normal import of a file in a directory somewhere on the module search path, like this:

```
import utilities
```

offers much less information than an import that includes the path:

```
import database.client.utilities
```

Package imports can also greatly simplify your PYTHONPATH and *.pth* file search path settings. In fact, if you use explicit package imports for all your cross-directory imports, and you make those package imports relative to a common root directory where all your Python code is stored, you really only need a single entry on your search path: the common root. Finally, package imports serve to resolve ambiguities by making explicit exactly which files you want to import—and resolve conflicts when the same module name appears in more than one place. The next section explores this role in more detail.

A Tale of Three Systems

The only time package imports are actually *required* is to resolve ambiguities that may arise when multiple programs with same-named files are installed on a single machine. This is something of an install issue, but it can also become a concern in general practice —especially given the tendency of developers to use simple and similar names for module files. Let's turn to a hypothetical scenario to illustrate.

Suppose that a programmer develops a Python program that contains a file called *utilities.py* for common utility code, and a top-level file named *main.py* that users launch to start the program. All over this program, its files say import utilities to load and use the common code. When the program is shipped, it arrives as a single *.tar* or *.zip* file containing all the program's files, and when it is installed, it unpacks all its files into a single directory named *system1* on the target machine:

```
system1\
    utilities.py        # Common utility functions, classes
    main.py             # Launch this to start the program
    other.py            # Import utilities to load my tools
```

Now, suppose that a second programmer develops a different program with files also called *utilities.py* and *main.py*, and again uses import utilities throughout the program to load the common code file. When this second system is fetched and installed on the same computer as the first system, its files will unpack into a new directory called *system2* somewhere on the receiving machine—ensuring that they do not overwrite same-named files from the first system:

```
system2\
    utilities.py        # Common utilities
    main.py             # Launch this to run
    other.py            # Imports utilities
```

So far, there's no problem: both systems can coexist and run on the same computer. In fact, you won't even need to configure the module search path to use these programs on your computer—because Python always searches the home directory first (that is, the directory containing the top-level file), imports in either system's files will automatically see all the files in that system's directory. For instance, if you click on *system1\main.py*, all imports will search *system1* first. Similarly, if you launch *system2\main.py*, *system2* will be searched first instead. Remember, module search path settings are only needed to import across directory boundaries.

However, suppose that after you've installed these two programs on your machine, you decide that you'd like to use some of the code in each of the *utilities.py* files in a system of your own. It's common utility code, after all, and Python code by nature "wants" to be reused. In this case, you'd like to be able to say the following from code that you're writing in a third directory to load one of the two files:

```
import utilities
utilities.func('spam')
```

Now the problem starts to materialize. To make this work at all, you'll have to set the module search path to include the directories containing the *utilities.py* files. But which directory do you put first in the path—*system1* or *system2*?

The problem is the *linear* nature of the search path. It is always scanned from left to right, so no matter how long you ponder this dilemma, you will always get just one *utilities.py*—from the directory listed first (leftmost) on the search path. As is, you'll never be able to import it from the other directory at all.

You could try changing `sys.path` within your script before each import operation, but that's both extra work and highly error prone. And changing `PYTHONPATH` before each Python program run is too tedious, and won't allow you to use both versions in a single file in an event. By default, you're stuck.

This is the issue that packages actually fix. Rather than installing programs in independent directories listed on the module search path individually, you can package and install them as *subdirectories* under a common root. For instance, you might organize all the code in this example as an install hierarchy that looks like this:

```
root\
    system1\
        __init__.py
        utilities.py
        main.py
        other.py
    system2\
        __init__.py
        utilities.py
        main.py
        other.py
    system3\                    # Here or elsewhere
        __init__.py             # Need __init__.py here only if imported elsewhere
        myfile.py               # Your new code here
```

Now, add just the common root directory to your search path. If your code's imports are all relative to this common root, you can import *either* system's utility file with a package import—the enclosing directory name makes the path (and hence, the module reference) unique. In fact, you can import *both* utility files in the same module, as long as you use an `import` statement and repeat the full path each time you reference the utility modules:

```
import system1.utilities
import system2.utilities
system1.utilities.function('spam')
system2.utilities.function('eggs')
```

The names of the enclosing directories here make the module references unique.

Note that you have to use `import` instead of `from` with packages only if you need to access the *same* attribute name in two or more paths. If the name of the called function here were different in each path, you could use `from` statements to avoid repeating the full package path whenever you call one of the functions, as described earlier; the `as` extension in `from` can also be used to provide unique synonyms.

Also, notice in the install hierarchy shown earlier that *__init__.py* files were added to the *system1* and *system2* directories to make this work, but not to the *root* directory. Only directories listed within `import` statements in your code require these files; as we've seen, they are run automatically the first time the Python process imports through a package directory.

Technically, in this case the *system3* directory doesn't have to be under *root*—just the packages of code from which you will import. However, because you never know when your own modules might be useful in other programs, you might as well place them under the common *root* directory as well to avoid similar name-collision problems in the future.

Finally, notice that both of the two original systems' imports will keep working unchanged. Because their *home* directories are searched first, the addition of the common root on the search path is irrelevant to code in *system1* and *system2*; they can keep saying just `import utilities` and expect to find their own files when run as programs —though not when used as packages in 3.X, as the next section explains. If you're careful to unpack all your Python systems under a common root like this, path configuration also becomes simple: you'll only need to add the common root directory once.

Why You Will Care: Module Packages

Because packages are a standard part of Python, it's common to see larger third-party extensions shipped as sets of package directories, rather than flat lists of modules. The *win32all* Windows extensions package for Python, for instance, was one of the first to jump on the package bandwagon. Many of its utility modules reside in packages imported with paths. For instance, to load client-side COM tools, you use a statement like this:

```
from win32com.client import constants, Dispatch
```

This line fetches names from the `client` module of the `win32com` package—an install subdirectory.

Package imports are also pervasive in code run under the Jython Java-based implementation of Python, because Java libraries are organized into hierarchies as well. In recent Python releases, the email and XML tools are likewise organized into package subdirectories in the standard library, and Python 3.X groups even more related modules into packages—including tkinter GUI tools, HTTP networking tools, and more. The following imports access various standard library tools in 3.X (2.X usage may vary):

```
from email.message import Message
from tkinter.filedialog import askopenfilename
from http.server import CGIHTTPRequestHandler
```

Whether you create package directories or not, you will probably import from them eventually.

Package Relative Imports

The coverage of package imports so far has focused mostly on importing package files from *outside* the package. Within the package itself, imports of same-package files can use the same full path syntax as imports from outside the package—and as we'll see, sometimes should. However, package files can also make use of special *intrapackage* search rules to simplify `import` statements. That is, rather than listing package import paths, imports within the package can be *relative* to the package.

The way this works is version-dependent: Python 2.X implicitly searches package directories first on imports, while 3.X requires explicit relative import syntax in order to import from the package directory. This 3.X change can enhance code readability by making same-package imports more obvious, but it's also incompatible with 2.X and may break some programs.

If you're starting out in Python with version 3.X, your focus in this section will likely be on its new import syntax and model. If you've used other Python packages in the past, though, you'll probably also be interested in how the 3.X model differs. Let's begin our tour with the latter perspective on this topic.

 As we'll learn in this section, use of package relative imports can actually *limit your files' roles*. In short, they can no longer be used as executable program files in both 2.X and 3.X. Because of this, normal package import paths may be a better option in many cases. Still, this feature has found its way into many a Python file, and merits a review by most Python programmers to better understand both its tradeoffs and motivation.

Changes in Python 3.X

The way import operations in packages work has changed slightly in Python 3.X. This change applies only to imports within files when files are used as part of a package directory; imports in other usage modes work as before. For *imports in packages*, though, Python 3.X introduces two changes:

- It modifies the module import search path semantics to skip the package's own directory by default. Imports check only paths on the `sys.path` search path. These are known as *absolute* imports.

- It extends the syntax of `from` statements to allow them to explicitly request that imports search the package's directory only, with leading dots. This is known as *relative* import syntax.

These changes are fully present in Python 3.X. The new `from` statement relative syntax is also available in Python 2.X, but the default absolute search path change must be enabled as an option there. Enabling this can break 2.X programs, but is available for 3.X forward compatibility.

The impact of this change is that in 3.X (and optionally in 2.X), you must generally use special `from` dotted syntax to import modules located in the *same* package as the importer, unless your imports list a complete path relative to a package root on `sys.path`, or your imports are relative to the always-searched home directory of the program's top-level file (which is usually the current working directory).

By default, though, your package directory is not automatically searched, and intra-package imports made by files in a directory used as a package will fail without the special `from` syntax. As we'll see, in 3.X this can affect the way you will structure imports or directories for modules meant for use in both top-level programs and importable packages. First, though, let's take a more detailed look at how this all works.

Relative Import Basics

In both Python 3.X and 2.X, `from` statements can now use leading dots (".") to specify that they require modules located within the same package (known as package *relative imports*), instead of modules located elsewhere on the module import search path (called *absolute imports*). That is:

- *Imports with dots*: In both Python 3.X and 2.X, you can use leading dots in `from` statements' module names to indicate that imports should be *relative-only* to the containing package—such imports will search for modules inside the package directory only and will not look for same-named modules located elsewhere on the import search path (`sys.path`). The net effect is that package modules override outside modules.

- *Imports without dots*: In Python 2.X, normal imports in a package's code without leading dots currently default to a *relative-then-absolute* search path order—that is, they search the package's own directory first. However, in Python 3.X, normal imports within a package are *absolute-only* by default—in the absence of any special dot syntax, imports skip the containing package itself and look elsewhere on the `sys.path` search path.

For example, in both Python 3.X and 2.X a statement of the form:

```
from . import spam                          # Relative to this package
```

instructs Python to import a module named `spam` located in the same package directory as the file in which this statement appears. Similarly, this statement:

```
from .spam import name
```

means "from a module named `spam` located in the same package as the file that contains this statement, import the variable `name`."

The behavior of a statement *without* the leading dot depends on which version of Python you use. In 2.X, such an import will still default to the original *relative-then-absolute* search path order (i.e., searching the package's directory first), unless a statement of the following form is included at the top of the importing file (as its first executable statement):

```
from __future__ import absolute_import      # Use 3.X relative import model in 2.X
```

If present, this statement enables the Python 3.X *absolute-only* search path change. In 3.X, and in 2.X when enabled, an import without a leading dot in the module name always causes Python to skip the relative components of the module import search path and look instead in the absolute directories that `sys.path` contains. For instance, in 3.X's model, a statement of the following form will always find a `string` module somewhere on `sys.path`, instead of a module of the same name in the package:

```
import string                               # Skip this package's version
```

By contrast, without the `from __future__` statement in 2.X, if there's a local `string` module in the package, it will be imported instead. To get the same behavior in 3.X, and in 2.X when the absolute import change is enabled, run a statement of the following form to force a relative import:

```
from . import string                        # Searches this package only
```

This statement works in both Python 2.X and 3.X today. The only difference in the 3.X model is that it is *required* in order to load a module that is located in the same package directory as the file in which this appears, when the file is being used as part of a package (and unless full package paths are spelled out).

Notice that leading dots can be used to force relative imports only with the `from` statement, not with the `import` statement. In Python 3.X, the `import modname` statement is always absolute-only, skipping the containing package's directory. In 2.X, this statement form still performs relative imports, searching the package's directory first. `from` statements without leading dots behave the same as `import` statements—absolute-only in 3.X (skipping the package directory), and relative-then-absolute in 2.X (searching the package directory first).

Other dot-based relative reference patterns are possible, too. Within a module file located in a package directory named *mypkg*, the following alternative import forms work as described:

```
from .string import name1, name2      # Imports names from mypkg.string
from . import string                  # Imports mypkg.string
from .. import string                 # Imports string sibling of mypkg
```

To understand these latter forms better, and to justify all this added complexity, we need to take a short detour to explore the rationale behind this change.

Why Relative Imports?

Besides making intrapackage imports more explicit, this feature is designed in part to allow scripts to resolve ambiguities that can arise when a same-named file appears in multiple places on the module search path. Consider the following package directory:

```
mypkg\
    __init__.py
    main.py
    string.py
```

This defines a package named `mypkg` containing modules named `mypkg.main` and `mypkg.string`. Now, suppose that the `main` module tries to import a module named `string`. In Python 2.X and earlier, Python will first look in the *mypkg* directory to perform a *relative* import. It will find and import the *string.py* file located there, assigning it to the name `string` in the `mypkg.main` module's namespace.

It could be, though, that the intent of this import was to load the Python standard library's `string` module instead. Unfortunately, in these versions of Python, there's no straightforward way to ignore `mypkg.string` and look for the standard library's `string` module located on the module search path. Moreover, we cannot resolve this with full package import paths, because we cannot depend on any extra package directory structure above the standard library being present on every machine.

In other words, simple imports in packages can be both ambiguous and error-prone. Within a package, it's not clear whether an `import spam` statement refers to a module within or outside the package. As one consequence, a local module or package can hide another hanging directly off of `sys.path`, whether intentionally or not.

In practice, Python users can avoid reusing the names of standard library modules they need for modules of their own (if you need the standard `string`, don't name a new module `string`!). But this doesn't help if a package accidentally hides a standard module; moreover, Python might add a new standard library module in the future that has the same name as a module of your own. Code that relies on relative imports is also less easy to understand, because the reader may be confused about which module is intended to be used. It's better if the resolution can be made explicit in code.

The relative imports solution in 3.X

To address this dilemma, imports run within packages have changed in Python 3.X to be absolute-only (and can be made so as an option in 2.X). Under this model, an `import` statement of the following form in our example file *mypkg/main.py* will always find a `string` module *outside* the package, via an absolute import search of `sys.path`:

```
import string                          # Imports string outside package (absolute)
```

A `from` import without leading-dot syntax is considered absolute as well:

```
from string import name                # Imports name from string outside package
```

If you really want to import a module from your package without giving its full path from the package root, though, relative imports are still possible if you use the dot syntax in the `from` statement:

```
from . import string                   # Imports mypkg.string here (relative)
```

This form imports the `string` module relative to the current package only and is the relative equivalent to the prior `import` example's absolute form (both load a module as a whole). When this special relative syntax is used, the package's directory is the only directory searched.

We can also copy specific names from a module with relative syntax:

```
from .string import name1, name2       # Imports names from mypkg.string
```

This statement again refers to the `string` module relative to the current package. If this code appears in our `mypkg.main` module, for example, it will import `name1` and `name2` from `mypkg.string`.

In effect, the "." in a relative import is taken to stand for the package directory *containing* the file in which the import appears. An additional leading dot performs the relative import starting from the *parent* of the current package. For example, this statement:

```
from .. import spam                    # Imports a sibling of mypkg
```

will load a sibling of `mypkg`—i.e., the `spam` module located in the package's own container directory, next to `mypkg`. More generally, code located in some module `A.B.C` can use any of these forms:

```
from . import D                        # Imports A.B.D    (. means A.B)
from .. import E                       # Imports A.E      (.. means A)

from .D import X                       # Imports A.B.D.X  (. means A.B)
from ..E import X                       # Imports A.E.X    (.. means A)
```

Relative imports versus absolute package paths

Alternatively, a file can sometimes name its own package explicitly in an absolute import statement, relative to a directory on `sys.path`. For example, in the following, `mypkg` will be found in an absolute directory on `sys.path`:

```
from mypkg import string          # Imports mypkg.string (absolute)
```

However, this relies on both the configuration and the order of the module search path settings, while relative import dot syntax does not. In fact, this form requires that the directory immediately containing `mypkg` be included in the module search path. It probably is if `mypkg` is the package root (or else the package couldn't be used from the outside in the first place!), but this directory may be nested in a much larger package tree. If `mypkg` isn't the package's root, absolute import statements must list all the directories below the package's root entry in `sys.path` when naming packages explicitly like this:

```
from system.section.mypkg import string     # system container on sys.path only
```

In large or deep packages, that could be substantially more work to code than a dot:

```
from . import string              # Relative import syntax
```

With this latter form, the containing package is searched automatically, regardless of the search path settings, search path order, and directory nesting. On the other hand, the full-path absolute form will work regardless of how the file is being used—as part of a program or package—as we'll explore ahead.

The Scope of Relative Imports

Relative imports can seem a bit perplexing on first encounter, but it helps if you remember a few key points about them:

- **Relative imports apply to imports within packages only**. Keep in mind that this feature's module search path change applies only to import statements within module files used as part of a package—that is, *intrapackage* imports. Normal imports in files not used as part of a package still work exactly as described earlier, automatically searching the directory containing the top-level script first.

- **Relative imports apply to the `from` statement only**. Also remember that this feature's new syntax applies only to `from` statements, not `import` statements. It's detected by the fact that the module name in a `from` begins with one or more dots (periods). Module names that contain embedded dots but don't have a leading dot are package imports, not relative imports.

In other words, package relative imports in 3.X really boil down to just the removal of 2.X's inclusive search path behavior for packages, along with the addition of special `from` syntax to explicitly request that relative package-only behavior be used. If you coded your package imports in the past so that they did not depend upon 2.X's implicit relative lookup (e.g., by always spelling out full paths from a package root), this change is largely a moot point. If you didn't, you'll need to update your package files to use the new `from` syntax for local package files, or full absolute paths.

Module Lookup Rules Summary

With packages and relative imports, the module search story in Python 3.X that we have seen so far can be summarized as follows:

- Basic modules with simple names (e.g., A) are located by searching each directory on the `sys.path` list, from left to right. This list is constructed from both system defaults and user-configurable settings described in Chapter 22.

- Packages are simply directories of Python modules with a special _init_.py file, which enables A.B.C directory path syntax in imports. In an import of A.B.C, for example, the directory named A is located relative to the normal module import search of `sys.path`, B is another package subdirectory within A, and C is a module or other importable item within B.

- Within a package's files, normal `import` and `from` statements use the same `sys.path` search rule as imports elsewhere. Imports in packages using `from` statements and leading *dots*, however, are relative to the package; that is, only the package directory is checked, and the normal `sys.path` lookup is not used. In `from .` `import A`, for example, the module search is restricted to the directory containing the file in which this statement appears.

Python 2.X works the same, except that normal imports without dots also automatically search the *package directory* first before proceeding on to *sys.path*.

In sum, Python imports select between *relative* (in the containing directory) and *absolute* (in a directory on `sys.path`) resolutions as follows:

Dotted imports: `from .` `import m,` `from .m import x`
  Are *relative-only* in both 2.X and 3.X

Nondotted imports: `import m,` `from m import x`
  Are *relative-then-absolute* in 2.X, and *absolute-only* in 3.X

As we'll see later, Python 3.3 adds another flavor to modules—*namespace packages*—which is largely disjointed from the package-relative story we're covering here. This newer model supports package-relative imports too, and is simply a different way to construct a package. It augments the import search procedure to allow package content to be spread across multiple simple directories as a last-resort resolution. Thereafter, though, the composite package behaves the same in terms of relative import rules.

Relative Imports in Action

But enough theory: let's run some simple code to demonstrate the concepts behind relative imports.

Imports outside packages

First of all, as mentioned previously, this feature does not impact imports outside a package. Thus, the following finds the standard library `string` module as expected:

```
C:\code> c:\Python33\python
>>> import string
>>> string
<module 'string' from 'C:\\Python33\\lib\\string.py'>
```

But if we add a module of the same name in the directory we're working in, it is selected instead, because the first entry on the module search path is the current working directory (CWD):

```
# code\string.py
print('string' * 8)
```

```
C:\code> c:\Python33\python
>>> import string
stringstringstringstringstringstringstringstring
>>> string
<module 'string' from '.\\string.py'>
```

In other words, normal imports are still relative to the "home" directory (the top-level script's container, or the directory you're working in). In fact, package relative import syntax is not even allowed in code that is not in a file being used as part of a package:

```
>>> from . import string
SystemError: Parent module '' not loaded, cannot perform relative import
```

In this section, code entered at the interactive prompt behaves the same as it would if run in a top-level *script*, because the first entry on `sys.path` is either the interactive working directory or the directory containing the top-level file. The only difference is that the start of `sys.path` is an absolute directory, not an empty string:

```
# code\main.py
import string                                     # Same code but in a file
print(string)
```

```
C:\code> C:\python33\python main.py               # Equivalent results in 2.X
stringstringstringstringstringstringstringstring
<module 'string' from 'c:\\code\\string.py'>
```

Similarly, a `from . import string` in this nonpackage file fails the same as it does at the interactive prompt—programs and packages are different file usage modes.

Imports within packages

Now, let's get rid of the local `string` module we coded in the CWD and build a package directory there with two modules, including the required but empty *test\pkg __init__.py* file. Package roots in this section are located in the CWD added automatically to `sys.path`, so we don't need to set `PYTHONPATH`. I'll also largely omit empty *__init__.py* files and most error message text for space (and non-Windows readers will have to pardon the shell commands here, and translate for your platform):

```
C:\code> del string*               # del __pycache__\string* for bytecode in 3.2+
C:\code> mkdir pkg
c:\code> notepad pkg\__init__.py

# code\pkg\spam.py
import eggs                         # <== Works in 2.X but not 3.X!
print(eggs.X)

# code\pkg\eggs.py
X = 99999
import string
print(string)
```

The first file in this package tries to import the second with a normal `import` statement. Because this is taken to be relative in 2.X but absolute in 3.X, it fails in the latter. That is, 2.X searches the containing package first, but 3.X does not. This is the *incompatible behavior* you have to be aware of in 3.X:

```
C:\code> c:\Python27\python
>>> import pkg.spam
<module 'string' from 'C:\Python27\lib\string.pyc'>
99999

C:\code> c:\Python33\python
>>> import pkg.spam
ImportError: No module named 'eggs'
```

To make this work in *both* 2.X and 3.X, change the first file to use the special relative import syntax, so that its import searches the package directory in 3.X too:

```
# code\pkg\spam.py
from . import eggs                  # <== Use package relative import in 2.X or 3.X
print(eggs.X)

# code\pkg\eggs.py
X = 99999
import string
print(string)

C:\code> c:\Python27\python
>>> import pkg.spam
<module 'string' from 'C:\Python27\lib\string.pyc'>
99999

C:\code> c:\Python33\python
>>> import pkg.spam
<module 'string' from 'C:\\Python33\\lib\\string.py'>
99999
```

Imports are still relative to the CWD

Notice in the preceding example that the package modules still have access to standard library modules like `string`—their normal imports are still relative to the entries on the module search path. In fact, if you add a `string` module to the CWD again, imports in a package will find it there instead of in the standard library. Although you can skip the package directory with an absolute import in 3.X, you still can't skip the home directory of the program that imports the package:

```
# code\string.py
print('string' * 8)

# code\pkg\spam.py
from . import eggs
print(eggs.X)

# code\pkg\eggs.py
X = 99999
import string                      # <== Gets string in CWD, not Python lib!
print(string)

C:\code> c:\Python33\python        # Same result in 2.X
>>> import pkg.spam
stringstringstringstringstringstringstringstring
<module 'string' from '.\\string.py'>
99999
```

Selecting modules with relative and absolute imports

To show how this applies to imports of standard library modules, reset the package again. Get rid of the local `string` module, and define a new one inside the package itself:

```
C:\code> del string*               # del __pycache__\string* for bytecode in 3.2+

# code\pkg\spam.py
import string                      # <== Relative in 2.X, absolute in 3.X
print(string)

# code\pkg\string.py
print('Ni' * 8)
```

Now, which version of the `string` module you get depends on which Python you use. As before, 3.X interprets the import in the first file as absolute and skips the package, but 2.X does not—another example of the *incompatible behavior* in 3.X:

```
C:\code> c:\Python33\python
>>> import pkg.spam
<module 'string' from 'C:\\Python33\\lib\\string.py'>

C:\code> c:\Python27\python
>>> import pkg.spam
NiNiNiNiNiNiNiNi
<module 'pkg.string' from 'pkg\string.py'>
```

Using relative import syntax in 3.X forces the package to be searched again, as it is in 2.X—by using absolute or relative import syntax in 3.X, you can either skip or select the package directory explicitly. In fact, *this is the use case that the 3.X model addresses*:

```
# code\pkg\spam.py
from . import string          # <== Relative in both 2.X and 3.X
print(string)

# code\pkg\string.py
print('Ni' * 8)

C:\code> c:\Python33\python
>>> import pkg.spam
NiNiNiNiNiNiNiNi
<module 'pkg.string' from '.\\pkg\\string.py'>

C:\code> c:\Python27\python
>>> import pkg.spam
NiNiNiNiNiNiNiNi
<module 'pkg.string' from 'pkg\string.py'>
```

Relative imports search packages only

It's also important to note that relative import syntax is really *a binding declaration*, not just a preference. If we delete the *string.py* file and any associated byte code in this example now, the relative import in *spam.py fails* in both 3.X and 2.X, instead of falling back on the standard library (or any other) version of this module:

```
# code\pkg\spam.py
from . import string          # <== Fails in both 2.X and 3.X if no string.py here!

C:\code> del pkg\string*

C:\code> C:\python33\python
>>> import pkg.spam
ImportError: cannot import name string

C:\code> C:\python27\python
>>> import pkg.spam
ImportError: cannot import name string
```

Modules referenced by relative imports must exist in the package directory.

Imports are still relative to the CWD, again

Although absolute imports let you skip package modules this way, they still rely on other components of `sys.path`. For one last test, let's define two `string` modules of our own. In the following, there is one module by that name in the CWD, one in the package, and another in the standard library:

```
# code\string.py
print('string' * 8)

# code\pkg\spam.py
```

```
from . import string              # <== Relative in both 2.X and 3.X
print(string)

# code\pkg\string.py
print('Ni' * 8)
```

When we import the `string` module with relative import syntax like this, we get the version in the package in both 2.X and 3.X, as desired:

```
C:\code> c:\Python33\python       # Same result in 2.X
>>> import pkg.spam
NiNiNiNiNiNiNiNi
<module 'pkg.string' from '.\\pkg\\string.py'>
```

When absolute syntax is used, though, the module we get varies per version again. 2.X interprets this as relative to the package first, but 3.X makes it "absolute," which in this case really just means it skips the package and loads the version relative to the CWD —*not* the version in the standard library:

```
# code\string.py
print('string' * 8)

# code\pkg\spam.py
import string                     # <== Relative in 2.X, "absolute" in 3.X: CWD!
print(string)

# code\pkg\string.py
print('Ni' * 8)

C:\code> c:\Python33\python
>>> import pkg.spam
stringstringstringstringstringstringstringstring
<module 'string' from '.\\string.py'>

C:\code> c:\Python27\python
>>> import pkg.spam
NiNiNiNiNiNiNiNi
<module 'pkg.string' from 'pkg\string.pyc'>
```

As you can see, although packages can explicitly request modules within their own directories with dots, their "absolute" imports are otherwise still relative to the rest of the normal module search path. In this case, a file in the program using the package hides the standard library module the package may want. The change in 3.X simply allows package code to select files either inside or outside the package (i.e., relatively or absolutely). Because import resolution can depend on an enclosing context that may not be foreseen, though, absolute imports in 3.X are not a guarantee of finding a module in the standard library.

Experiment with these examples on your own for more insight. In practice, this is not usually as ad hoc as it might seem: you can generally structure your imports, search paths, and module names to work the way you wish during development. You should keep in mind, though, that imports in larger systems may depend upon context of use, and the module import protocol is part of a successful library's design.

Pitfalls of Package-Relative Imports: Mixed Use

Now that you've learned about package-relative imports, you should also keep in mind that they may not always be your best option. Absolute package imports, with a complete directory path relative to a directory on `sys.path`, are still sometimes preferred over both implicit package-relative imports in Python 2.X, and explicit package-relative import dot syntax in both Python 2.X and 3.X. This issue may seem obscure, but will likely become important fairly soon after you start coding packages of your own.

As we've seen, Python 3.X's relative import syntax and absolute search rule default make intrapackage imports explicit and thus easier to notice and maintain, and allow explicit choice in some name conflict scenarios. However, there are also two major ramifications of this model that you should be aware of:

- In both Python 3.X and 2.X, use of package-relative import statements implicitly binds a file to a package directory and role, and precludes it from being used in other ways.
- In Python 3.X, the new relative search rule change means that a file can no longer serve as both script and package module as easily as it could in 2.X.

These constraint's causes are a bit subtle, but because the following are simultaneously true:

- Python 3.X and 2.X do not allow `from .` relative syntax to be used unless the importer is being used as part of a package (i.e., is being imported from somewhere else).
- Python 3.X does not search a package module's own directory for imports, unless `from .` relative syntax is used (or the module is in the current working directory or main script's home directory).

Use of relative imports prevents you from creating directories that serve as both executable programs and externally importable packages in 3.X and 2.X. Moreover, some files can no longer serve as both script and package module in 3.X as they could in 2.X. In terms of import statements, the rules pan out as follows—the first is for *package* mode only in both Pythons, and the second is for *program* mode only in 3.X:

```
from . import mod      # Not allowed in nonpackage mode in both 2.X and 3.X
import mod             # Does not search file's own directory in package mode in 3.X
```

The net effect is that for files to be used in either 2.X or 3.X, you may need to *choose* a single usage mode—*package* (with relative imports) or *program* (with simple imports), and isolate true package module files in a subdirectory apart from top-level script files.

Alternatively, you can attempt manual `sys.path` changes (a generally brittle and error-prone task), or always use full package paths in absolute imports instead of either package-relative syntax or simple imports, and assume the package root is on the module search path:

```
from system.section.mypkg import mod    # Works in both program and package mode
```

Of all these schemes, the last—full package path imports—may be the most portable and functional, but we need to turn to more concrete code to see why.

The issue

For example, in Python 2.X it's common to use the same *single directory* as both program and package, using normal undotted imports. This relies on the script's home directory to resolve imports when used as a program, and the 2.X relative-then-absolute rule to resolve intrapackage imports when used as a package. This won't quite work in 3.X, though—in package mode, plain imports do not load modules in the same directory anymore, unless that directory also happens to be the same as the main file's container or the current working directory (and hence, be on `sys.path`).

Here's what this looks like in action, stripped to a bare minimum of code (for brevity in this section I again omit *__init__.py* package directory files required prior to Python 3.3, and for variety use the 3.3 Windows launcher covered in Appendix B):

```
# code\pkg\main.py
import spam

# code\pkg\spam.py
import eggs                    # <== Works if in "." = home of main script file

# code\pkg\eggs.py
print('Eggs' * 4)             # But won't load this file when used as pkg in 3.X!

c:\code> python pkg\main.py    # OK as program, in both 2.X and 3.X
EggsEggsEggsEggs
c:\code> python pkg\spam.py
EggsEggsEggsEggs

c:\code> py -2                 # OK as package in 2.X: relative-then-absolute
>>> import pkg.spam            # 2.X: plain imports search package directory first
EggsEggsEggsEggs

C:\code> py -3                 # But 3.X fails to find file here: absolute only
>>> import pkg.spam            # 3.X: plain imports search only CWD plus sys.path
ImportError: No module named 'eggs'
```

Your next step might be to add the required *relative import* syntax for 3.X use, but it won't help here. The following retains the single directory for both a main top-level script and package modules, and adds the required dots—in both 2.X and 3.X this now works when the directory is imported as a package, but fails when it is used as a program directory (including attempts to run a module as a script directly):

```
# code\pkg\main.py
import spam

# code\pkg\spam.py
from . import eggs             # <== Not a package if main file here (even if me)!

# code\pkg\eggs.py
```

```
print('Eggs' * 4)
```

```
c:\code> python                          # OK as package but not program in both 3.X and 2.X
>>> import pkg.spam
EggsEggsEggsEggs
```

```
c:\code> python pkg\main.py
SystemError: ... cannot perform relative import
c:\code> python pkg\spam.py
SystemError: ... cannot perform relative import
```

Fix 1: Package subdirectories

In a mixed-use case like this, one solution is to isolate all but the main files used only by the program in a *subdirectory*—this way, your intrapackage imports still work in all Pythons, you can use the top directory as a standalone program, and the nested directory still serves as a package for use from other programs:

```
# code\pkg\main.py
import sub.spam                          # <== Works if move modules to pkg below main file

# code\pkg\sub\spam.py
from . import eggs                       # Package relative works now: in subdirectory

# code\pkg\sub\eggs.py
print('Eggs' * 4)

c:\code> python pkg\main.py              # From main script: same result in 2.X and 3.X
EggsEggsEggsEggs

c:\code> python                          # From elsewhere: same result in 2.X and 3.X
>>> import pkg.sub.spam
EggsEggsEggsEggs
```

The potential downside of this scheme is that you won't be able to run package modules directly to test them with embedded self-test code, though tests can be coded separately in their parent directory instead:

```
c:\code> py -3 pkg\sub\spam.py           # But individual modules can't be run to test
SystemError: ... cannot perform relative import
```

Fix 2: Full path absolute import

Alternatively, *full path package import* syntax would address this case too—it requires the directory above the package root to be in your path, though this is probably not an *extra* requirement for a realistic software package. Most Python packages will either require this setting, or arrange for it to be handled automatically with install tools (such as *distutils*, which may store a package's code in a directory on the default module search path such as the *site-packages* root; see Chapter 22 for more details):

```
# code\pkg\main.py
import spam
```

```
# code\pkg\spam.py
import pkg.eggs                    # <== Full package paths work in all cases, 2.X+3.X

# code\pkg\eggs.py
print('Eggs' * 4)

c:\code> set PYTHONPATH=C:\code
c:\code> python pkg\main.py        # From main script: Same result in 2.X and 3.X
EggsEggsEggsEggs

c:\code> python                    # From elsewhere: Same result in 2.X and 3.X
>>> import pkg.spam
EggsEggsEggsEggs
```

Unlike the subdirectory fix, full path absolute imports like these also allow you to run your modules standalone to test:

```
c:\code> python pkg\spam.py        # Individual modules are runnable too in 2.X and 3.X
EggsEggsEggsEggs
```

Example: Application to module self-test code (preview)

To summarize, here's another typical example of the issue and its full path resolution. This uses a common technique we'll expand on in the next chapter, but the idea is simple enough to include as a preview here (though you may want to review this again later—the coverage makes more sense here).

Consider the following two modules in a package directory, the second of which includes *self-test* code. In short, a module's __name__ attribute is the string "__main__" when it is being run as a top-level script, but not when it is being imported, which allows it to be used as *both* module and script:

```
# code\dualpkg\m1.py
def somefunc():
    print('m1.somefunc')

# code\dualpkg\m2.py
...import m1 here...                # Replace me with a real import statement

def somefunc():
    m1.somefunc()
    print('m2.somefunc')

if __name__ == '__main__':
    somefunc()                     # Self-test or top-level script usage mode code
```

The second of these needs to import the first where the "...import m1 here..." placeholder appears. Replacing this line with a relative import statement works when the file is used as a package, but is not allowed in nonpackage mode by either 2.X or 3.X (results and error messages are omitted here for space; see the file *dualpkg\results.txt* in the book's examples for the full listing):

```
# code\dualpkg\m2.py
from . import m1
```

```
c:\code> py -3
>>> import dualpkg.m2              # OK
C:\code> py -2
>>> import dualpkg.m2              # OK

c:\code> py -3 dualpkg\m2.py       # Fails!
c:\code> py -2 dualpkg\m2.py       # Fails!
```

Conversely, a simple import statement works in nonpackage mode in both 2.X and 3.X, but fails in package mode in 3.X only, because such statements do not search the package directory in 3.X:

```
# code\dualpkg\m2.py
import m1

c:\code> py -3
>>> import dualpkg.m2              # Fails!
c:\code> py -2
>>> import dualpkg.m2              # OK

c:\code> py -3 dualpkg\m2.py       # OK
c:\code> py -2 dualpkg\m2.py       # OK
```

And finally, using full package paths works again in both usage modes and Pythons, as long as the package's root is on the module search path (as it must be to be used elsewhere):

```
# code\dualpkg\m2.py
import dualpkg.m1 as m1            # And: set PYTHONPATH=c:\code

c:\code> py -3
>>> import dualpkg.m2              # OK
C:\code> py -2
>>> import dualpkg.m2              # OK

c:\code> py -3 dualpkg\m2.py       # OK
c:\code> py -2 dualpkg\m2.py       # OK
```

In sum, unless you're willing and able to isolate your modules in subdirectories below scripts, full package path imports are probably preferable to package-relative imports —though they're more typing, they handle all cases, and they work the same in 2.X and 3.X. There may be additional workarounds that involve extra tasks (e.g., manually setting sys.path in your code), but we'll skip them here because they are more obscure and rely on import semantics, which is error-prone; full package imports rely only on the basic package mechanism.

Naturally, the extent to which this may impact your modules can vary per package; absolute imports may also require changes when directories are reorganized, and relative imports may become invalid if a local module is relocated.

Be sure to also watch for future Python changes on this front. Although this book covers Python up to 3.3 only, at this writing, there is talk in a PEP of possibly addressing some package issues in *Python 3.4*, perhaps even allowing relative imports to be used in program mode. On the other hand, this initiative's scope and outcome is uncertain and would work only on 3.4 and later; the full path solution given here is version-neutral; and 3.4 is more than a year away in any event. That is, you can wait for a change to a 3.X change that limited functionality, or simply use tried-and-true full package paths.

Python 3.3 Namespace Packages

Now that you've learned all about package and package-relative imports, I need to explain that there's a new option that modifies some of the ideas we just covered. At least abstractly, as of release 3.3 Python has four import models. From original to newest:

Basic module imports: `import mod`, `from mod import attr`
> The original model: imports of files and their contents, relative to the `sys.path` module search path

Package imports: `import dir1.dir2.mod`, `from dir1.mod import attr`
> Imports that give directory path extensions relative to the `sys.path` module search path, where each package is contained in a single directory and has an initialization file, in *Python 2.X and 3.X*

Package-relative imports: `from . import mod` *(relative)*, `import mod` *(absolute)*
> The model used for intrapackage imports of the prior section, with its relative or absolute lookup schemes for dotted and nondotted imports, available but differing in *Python 2.X and 3.X*

Namespace packages: `import splitdir.mod`
> The new namespace package model that we'll survey here, which allows packages to span multiple directories, and requires no initialization file, introduced in *Python 3.3*

The first two of these are self-contained, but the third tightens up the search order and extends syntax for intrapackage imports, and the fourth upends some of the core notions and requirements of the prior package model. In fact, Python 3.3 (and later) now has two flavors of packages:

- The original model, now known as *regular packages*
- The alternative model, known as *namespace packages*

This is similar in spirit to the "classic" and "new style" class model dichotomy we'll meet in the next part of this book, though the new is more an addition to the old here. The original and new package models are not mutually exclusive, and can be used

---

simultaneously in the same program. In fact, the new namespace package model works as something of a *fallback option*, recognized only if normal modules and regular packages of the same name are not present on the module search path.

The *rationale* for namespace packages is rooted in package *installation* goals that may seem obscure unless you are responsible for such tasks, and is better addressed by this feature's PEP document. In short, though, they resolve a potential for collision of multiple *__init__.py* files when package parts are merged, by removing this file completely. Moreover, by providing standard support for packages that can be split across multiple directories and located in multiple `sys.path` entries, namespace packages both enhance install flexibility and provide a common mechanism to replace the multiple incompatible solutions that have arisen to address this goal.

Though too early to judge their uptake, average Python users may find namespace packages to be a useful and alternative extension to the regular package model—one that does not require initialization files, and allows any directory of code to be used as an importable package. To see why, let's move on to the details.

Namespace Package Semantics

A namespace package is not fundamentally different from a regular package; it is just a different way of creating packages. Moreover, they are still relative to `sys.path` at the top level: the leftmost component of a dotted namespace package path must still be located in an entry on the normal module search path.

In terms of physical structure, though, the two can differ substantially. Regular packages still *must* have an *__init__.py* file that is run automatically, and reside in a single directory as before. By contrast, new-style namespace packages *cannot* contain an *__init__.py*, and may span multiple directories that are collected at import time. In fact, *none* of the directories that make up a namespace package can have an *__init__.py*, but the content nested within each of them is treated as a single package.

The import algorithm

To truly understand namespace packages, we have to look under the hood to see how the import operation works in 3.3. During imports, Python still iterates over each directory in the module search path—defined by `sys.path` for the leftmost components of absolute imports, and by a package's location for relative imports and components nested in package paths—just as in 3.2 and earlier. In 3.3, though, while looking for an imported module or package named `spam`, for each *directory* in the module search path, Python tests for a wider variety of matching criteria, in the following order:

1. If *directory*\spam__init__.py is found, a regular package is imported and returned.
2. If *directory*\spam.{py, pyc, *or other module extension*} is found, a simple module is imported and returned.

3. If *directory*\spam is found and is a directory, it is recorded and the scan continues with the next directory in the search path.

4. If none of the above was found, the scan continues with the next directory in the search path.

If the search path scan completes without returning a module or package by steps 1 or 2, and at least one directory was recorded by step 3, then a *namespace package* is created.

The creation of the namespace package happens immediately, and is not deferred until a sublevel import occurs. The new namespace package has a __path__ attribute set to an iterable of the directory path strings that were found and recorded during the scan by step 3, but does not have a __file__.

The __path__ attribute is then used in later, deeper accesses to search all package components—each recorded entry on a namespace package's __path__ is searched whenever further nested items are requested, much like the sole directory of a regular package.

Viewed another way, the __path__ attribute of a namespace package serves the same role for lower-level components that sys.path does at the top for the leftmost component of package import paths; it becomes the "parent path" for accessing lower items using the same four-step procedure just sketched.

The net result is that a namespace package is a sort of *virtual concatenation* of directories located via possibly multiple module search path entries. Once a namespace package is created, though, there is no functional difference between it and a regular package; it supports everything we've learned for regular packages, including package-relative import syntax.

Impacts on Regular Packages: Optional __init__.py

As one consequence of this new import procedure, as of Python 3.3 packages no longer require *__init__.py* files—when a single-directory package does not have this file, it will be treated as a single-directory namespace package, and no warning will be issued. This is a major relaxation of prior rules, but a commonly requested change; many packages require no initialization code, and it seemed extraneous to have to create an empty initialization file in such cases. This is finally no longer required as of 3.3.

At the same time, the original regular package model is still fully supported, and automatically runs code in *__init__.py* as before as an *initialization hook*. Moreover, when it's known that a package will never be a portion of a split namespace package, there is a *performance advantage* to coding it as a regular package with an *__init__.py*. Creation and loading of a regular package occurs immediately when it is located along the path. With namespace packages, all entries in the path must be scanned before the package is created. More formally, regular packages stop the prior section's algorithm at step 1; namespace packages do not.

Per this change's PEP, there is no plan to remove support of regular packages—at least, that's the story today; change is always a possibility in open source projects (indeed, the prior edition quoted plans on string formatting and relative imports in 2.X that were later abandoned), so as usual, be sure to watch for future developments on this front. Given the performance advantage and auto-initialization code of regular packages, though, it seems unlikely that they would be removed altogether.

Namespace Packages in Action

To see how namespace packages work, consider the following two modules and nested directory structure—with two subdirectories named sub located in different parent directories, dir1 and dir2:

```
C:\code\ns\dir1\sub\mod1.py
C:\code\ns\dir2\sub\mod2.py
```

If we add both dir1 and dir2 to the module search path, sub becomes a namespace package spanning both, with the two module files available under that name even though they live in separate physical directories. Here's the files' contents and the required path settings on Windows: there are no *__init__.py* files here—in fact there *cannot be* in namespace packages, as this is their chief physical differentiation:

```
c:\code> mkdir ns\dir1\sub          # Two dirs of same name in different dirs
c:\code> mkdir ns\dir2\sub          # And similar outside Windows

c:\code> type ns\dir1\sub\mod1.py   # Module files in different directories
print(r'dir1\sub\mod1')

c:\code> type ns\dir2\sub\mod2.py
print(r'dir2\sub\mod2')

c:\code> set PYTHONPATH=C:\code\ns\dir1;C:\code\ns\dir2
```

Now, when imported directly in 3.3 and later, the namespace package is the *virtual concatenation* of its individual directory components, and allows further nested parts to be accessed through its single, composite name with normal imports:

```
c:\code> C:\Python33\python
>>> import sub
>>> sub                             # Namespace packages: nested search paths
<module 'sub' (namespace)>
>>> sub.__path__
_NamespacePath(['C:\\code\\ns\\dir1\\sub', 'C:\\code\\ns\\dir2\\sub'])

>>> from sub import mod1
dir1\sub\mod1
>>> import sub.mod2                  # Content from two different directories
dir2\sub\mod2

>>> mod1
<module 'sub.mod1' from 'C:\\code\\ns\\dir1\\sub\\mod1.py'>
```

```
>>> sub.mod2
<module 'sub.mod2' from 'C:\\code\\ns\\dir2\\sub\\mod2.py'>
```

This is also true if we import through the namespace package name *immediately*—
because the namespace package is made when first reached, the timing of path extensions is irrelevant:

```
c:\code> C:\Python33\python
>>> import sub.mod1
dir1\sub\mod1
>>> import sub.mod2                        # One package spanning two directories
dir2\sub\mod2

>>> sub.mod1
<module 'sub.mod1' from 'C:\\code\\ns\\dir1\\sub\\mod1.py'>
>>> sub.mod2
<module 'sub.mod2' from 'C:\\code\\ns\\dir2\\sub\\mod2.py'>

>>> sub
<module 'sub' (namespace)>
>>> sub.__path__
_NamespacePath(['C:\\code\\ns\\dir1\\sub', 'C:\\code\\ns\\dir2\\sub'])
```

Interestingly, *relative imports* work in namespace packages too—in the following, the
relative import statement references a file in the package, even though the referenced
file resides in a *different directory*:

```
c:\code> type ns\dir1\sub\mod1.py
from . import mod2                         # And "from . import string" still fails
print(r'dir1\sub\mod1')

c:\code> C:\Python33\python
>>> import sub.mod1                        # Relative import of mod2 in another dir
dir2\sub\mod2
dir1\sub\mod1
>>> import sub.mod2                        # Already imported module not rerun
>>> sub.mod2
<module 'sub.mod2' from 'C:\\code\\ns\\dir2\\sub\\mod2.py'>
```

As you can see, namespace packages are like ordinary single-directory packages in every
way, except for having a split physical storage—which is why *single directory* namespaces packages without *__init__.py* files are exactly like regular packages, but with no
initialization logic to be run.

Namespace Package Nesting

Namespace packages even support arbitrary *nesting*—once a package namespace package is created, it serves essentially the same role at its level that sys.path does at the
top, becoming the "parent path" for lower levels. Continuing the prior section's example:

```
c:\code> mkdir ns\dir2\sub\lower          # Further nested components
c:\code> type  ns\dir2\sub\lower\mod3.py
```

```
      print(r'dir2\sub\lower\mod3')

c:\code> C:\Python33\python
>>> import sub.lower.mod3                      # Namespace pkg nested in namespace pkg
dir2\sub\lower\mod3

c:\code> C:\Python33\python
>>> import sub                                 # Same effect if accessed incrementally
>>> import sub.mod2
dir2\sub\mod2
>>> import sub.lower.mod3
dir2\sub\lower\mod3

>>> sub.lower                                  # A single-directory namespace pkg
<module 'sub.lower' (namespace)>
>>> sub.lower.__path__
_NamespacePath(['C:\\code\\ns\\dir2\\sub\\lower'])
```

In the preceding, sub is a namespace package split across two directories, and
sub.lower is a single-directory namespace package nested within the portion of sub
physically located in dir2. sub.lower is also the namespace package equivalent of a
regular package with no __init__.py.

This nesting behavior holds true whether the lower component is a module, regular
package, or another namespace package—by serving as new import search paths,
namespace packages allow all three to be nested within them freely:

```
c:\code> mkdir ns\dir1\sub\pkg
C:\code> type  ns\dir1\sub\pkg\__init__.py
      print(r'dir1\sub\pkg\__init__.py')

c:\code> C:\Python33\python
>>> import sub.mod2                            # Nested module
dir2\sub\mod2
>>> import sub.pkg                             # Nested regular package
dir1\sub\pkg\__init__.py
>>> import sub.lower.mod3                      # Nested namespace package
dir2\sub\lower\mod3

>>> sub                                        # Modules, packages,and namespaces
<module 'sub' (namespace)>
>>> sub.mod2
<module 'sub.mod2' from 'C:\\code\\ns\\dir2\\sub\\mod2.py'>
>>> sub.pkg
<module 'sub.pkg' from 'C:\\code\\ns\\dir1\\sub\\pkg\\__init__.py'>
>>> sub.lower
<module 'sub.lower' (namespace)>
>>> sub.lower.mod3
<module 'sub.lower.mod3' from 'C:\\code\\ns\\dir2\\sub\\lower\\mod3.py'>
```

Trace through this example's files and directories for more insight. As you can see,
namespace packages integrate seamlessly into the former import models, and extend
it with new functionality.

Files Still Have Precedence over Directories

As explained earlier, part of the purpose of _init_.py files in regular packages is to declare the directory as a package—it tells Python to use the directory, rather than skipping ahead to a possible file of the same name later on the path. This avoids inadvertently choosing a noncode subdirectory that accidentally appears early on the path, over a desired module of the same name.

Because namespace packages do not require these special files, they would seem to invalidate this safeguard. This isn't the case, though—because the namespace algorithm outlined earlier continues scanning the path after a namespace directory has been found, files later on the path still have priority over earlier directories with no _init_.py. For example, consider the following directories and modules:

```
c:\code> mkdir ns2
c:\code> mkdir ns3
c:\code> mkdir    ns3\dir
c:\code> notepad ns3\dir\ns2.py
c:\code> type    ns3\dir\ns2.py
print(r'ns3\dir\ns2.py!')
```

The ns2 directory here cannot be imported in Python 3.2 and earlier—it's not a regular package, as it lacks an _init_.py initialization file. This directory can be imported under 3.3, though—it's a namespace package directory in the current working directory, which is always the *first* item on the sys.path module search path irrespective of PYTHONPATH settings:

```
c:\code> set PYTHONPATH=
c:\code> py -3.2
>>> import ns2
ImportError: No module named ns2

c:\code> py -3.3
>>> import ns2
>>> ns2                          # A single-directory namespace package in CWD
<module 'ns2' (namespace)>
>>> ns2.__path__
_NamespacePath(['.\\ns2'])
```

But watch what happens when the directory containing a file of the same name as a namespace directory is added *later* on the search path, via PYTHONPATH settings—the file is used instead, because Python keeps searching later path entries after a namespace package directory is found. It stops searching only when a module or regular package is located, or the path has been completely scanned. Namespace packages are returned only if nothing else was found along the way:

```
c:\code> set PYTHONPATH=C:\code\ns3\dir
c:\code> py -3.3
>>> import ns2                        # Use later module file, not same-named directory!
ns3\dir\ns2.py!
>>> ns2
<module 'ns2' from 'C:\\code\\ns3\\dir\\ns2.py'>
```

```
>>> import sys
>>> sys.path[:2]          # First '' means current working directory, CWD
['', 'C:\\code\\ns3\\dir']
```

In fact, setting the path to include a module works the same as it does in earlier Pythons, even if a same-named namespace directory appears earlier on the path; namespace packages are used in 3.3 only in cases that would be errors in earlier Pythons:

```
c:\code> py -3.2
>>> import ns2
ns3\dir\ns2.py!
>>> ns2
<module 'ns2' from 'C:\code\ns3\dir\ns2.py'>
```

This is also why *none* of the directories in a namespace package is allowed to have a *__init__.py* file: as soon as the import algorithm finds one that does, it returns a regular package immediately, and abandons the path search and the namespace package. Put more formally, the import algorithm chooses a namespace package only at the *end* of the path scan, and stops at steps 1 or 2 if either a regular package or module file is found sooner.

The net effect is that both module files *and* regular packages anywhere on the module search path have precedence over namespace package directories. In the following, for example, a namespace package called sub exists as the concatenation of same-named directories under dir1 and dir2 on the path:

```
c:\code> mkdir ns4\dir1\sub
c:\code> mkdir ns4\dir2\sub
c:\code> set PYTHONPATH=c:\code\ns4\dir1;c:\code\ns4\dir2
c:\code> py -3
>>> import sub
>>> sub
<module 'sub' (namespace)>
>>> sub.__path__
_NamespacePath(['c:\\code\\ns4\\dir1\\sub', 'c:\\code\\ns4\\dir2\\sub'])
```

Much like a module file, though, a *regular package* added in the rightmost path entry takes priority over same-named namespace package directories too—the import path scan starts recording a namespace package tentatively in dir1 as before, but abandons it when the regular package is detected in dir2:

```
c:\code> notepad ns4\dir2\sub\__init__.py
c:\code> py -3
>>> import sub                    # Use later reg. package, not same-named directory!
>>> sub
<module 'sub' from 'c:\\code\\ns4\\dir2\\sub\\__init__.py'>
```

Though a useful extension, because namespace packages are available only to readers using Python 3.3 (and later) I'm going to defer to Python's manuals for more details on the subject. See especially this change's PEP document for this change's rationale, additional details, and more comprehensive examples.

Chapter Summary

This chapter introduced Python's *package import* model—an optional but useful way to explicitly list part of the directory path leading up to your modules. Package imports are still relative to a directory on your module import search path, but your script gives the rest of the path to the module explicitly.

As we've seen, packages not only make imports more meaningful in larger systems, but also simplify import search path settings if all cross-directory imports are relative to a common root directory, and resolve ambiguities when there is more than one module of the same name—including the name of the enclosing directory in a package import helps distinguish between them.

Because it's relevant only to code in packages, we also explored the newer *relative import* model here—a way for imports in package files to select modules in the same package explicitly using leading dots in a `from`, instead of relying on an older and error-prone implicit package search rule. Finally, we surveyed Python 3.3 *namespace packages*, which allow a logical package to span multiple physical directories as a fallback option of import searches, and remove the initialization file requirements of the prior model.

In the next chapter, we will survey a handful of more advanced module-related topics, such as the `__name__` usage mode variable and name-string imports. As usual, though, let's close out this chapter first with a short quiz to review what you've learned here.

Test Your Knowledge: Quiz

1. What is the purpose of an *__init__.py* file in a module package directory?
2. How can you avoid repeating the full package path every time you reference a package's content?
3. Which directories require *__init__.py* files?
4. When must you use `import` instead of `from` with packages?
5. What is the difference between `from mypkg import spam` and `from . import spam`?
6. What is a namespace package?

Test Your Knowledge: Answers

1. The *__init__.py* file serves to declare and initialize a regular module package; Python automatically runs its code the first time you import through a directory in a process. Its assigned variables become the attributes of the module object created in memory to correspond to that directory. It is also not optional until 3.3 and later—you can't import through a directory with package syntax unless it contains this file.

2. Use the `from` statement with a package to copy names out of the package directly, or use the `as` extension with the `import` statement to rename the path to a shorter synonym. In both cases, the path is listed in only one place, in the `from` or `import` statement.

3. In Python 3.2 and earlier, each directory listed in an executed `import` or `from` statement must contain an *__init__.py* file. Other directories, including the directory that contains the leftmost component of a package path, do not need to include this file.

4. You must use `import` instead of `from` with packages only if you need to access the same name defined in more than one path. With `import`, the path makes the references unique, but `from` allows only one version of any given name (unless you also use the `as` extension to rename).

5. In Python 3.X, `from mypkg import spam` is an *absolute* import—the search for mypkg skips the package directory and the module is located in an absolute directory in `sys.path`. A statement `from . import spam`, on the other hand, is a *relative* import —spam is looked up relative to the package in which this statement is contained only. In Python 2.X, the absolute import searches the package directory first before proceeding to `sys.path`; relative imports work as described.

6. A *namespace package* is an extension to the import model, available in Python 3.3 and later, that corresponds to one or more directories that do not have *__init__.py* files. When Python finds these during an import search, and does not find a simple module or regular package first, it creates a namespace package that is the virtual concatenation of all found directories having the requested module name. Further nested components are looked up in all the namespace package's directories. The effect is similar to a regular package, but content may be split across multiple directories.

Advanced Module Topics

This chapter concludes this part of the book with a collection of more advanced module-related topics—data hiding, the `_future_` module, the `_name_` variable, `sys.path` changes, listing tools, importing modules by name string, transitive reloads, and so on—along with the standard set of gotchas and exercises related to what we've covered in this part of the book.

Along the way, we'll build some larger and more useful tools than we have so far that combine functions and modules. Like functions, modules are more effective when their interfaces are well defined, so this chapter also briefly reviews module design concepts, some of which we have explored in prior chapters.

Despite the word "advanced" used in this chapter's title for symmetry, this is mostly a grab-bag assortment of additional module topics. Because some of the topics discussed here are widely used—especially the `_name_` trick—be sure to browse here before moving on to classes in the next part of the book.

Module Design Concepts

Like functions, modules present design tradeoffs: you have to think about which functions go in which modules, module communication mechanisms, and so on. All of this will become clearer when you start writing bigger Python systems, but here are a few general ideas to keep in mind:

- **You're always in a module in Python**. There's no way to write code that doesn't live in some module. As mentioned briefly in Chapter 17 and Chapter 21, even code typed at the interactive prompt really goes in a built-in module called `_main_`; the only unique things about the interactive prompt are that code runs and is discarded immediately, and expression results are printed automatically.

- **Minimize module coupling: global variables**. Like functions, modules work best if they're written to be closed boxes. As a rule of thumb, they should be as independent of global variables used within other modules as possible, except for functions and classes imported from them. The only things a module should share with the outside world are the tools it uses, and the tools it defines.

- **Maximize module cohesion: unified purpose**. You can minimize a module's couplings by maximizing its cohesion; if all the components of a module share a general purpose, you're less likely to depend on external names.

- **Modules should rarely change other modules' variables**. We illustrated this with code in Chapter 17, but it's worth repeating here: it's perfectly OK to use globals defined in another module (that's how clients import services, after all), but changing globals in another module is often a symptom of a design problem. There are exceptions, of course, but you should try to communicate results through devices such as function arguments and return values, not cross-module changes. Otherwise, your globals' values become dependent on the order of arbitrarily remote assignments in other files, and your modules become harder to understand and reuse.

As a summary, Figure 25-1 sketches the environment in which modules operate. Modules contain variables, functions, classes, and other modules (if imported). Functions have local variables of their own, as do classes—objects that live within modules and which we'll begin studying in the next chapter. As we saw in Part IV, functions can nest, too, but all are ultimately contained by modules at the top.

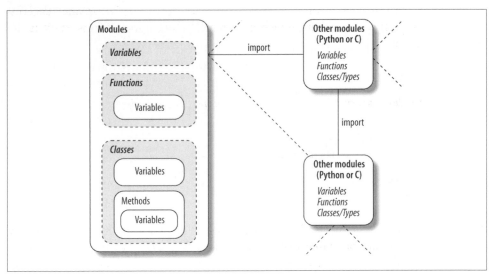

Figure 25-1. Module execution environment. Modules are imported, but modules also import and use other modules, which may be coded in Python or another language such as C. Modules in turn contain variables, functions, and classes to do their work, and their functions and classes may contain variables and other items of their own. At the top, though, programs are just sets of modules.

Data Hiding in Modules

As we've seen, a Python module exports all the names assigned at the top level of its file. There is no notion of declaring which names should and shouldn't be visible outside the module. In fact, there's no way to prevent a client from changing names inside a module if it wants to.

In Python, data hiding in modules is a convention, not a syntactical constraint. If you want to break a module by trashing its names, you can, but fortunately, I've yet to meet a programmer for whom this was a life goal. Some purists object to this liberal attitude toward data hiding, claiming that it means Python can't implement encapsulation. However, encapsulation in Python is more about packaging than about restricting. We'll expand this idea in the next part in relation to classes, which also have no privacy syntax but can often emulate its effect in code.

Minimizing from * Damage: _X and __all__

As a special case, you can prefix names with a single underscore (e.g., _X) to prevent them from being copied out when a client imports a module's names with a from * statement. This really is intended only to minimize namespace pollution; because from * copies out all names, the importer may get more than it's bargained for (including names that overwrite names in the importer). Underscores aren't "private" declarations: you can still see and change such names with other import forms, such as the import statement:

```
# unders.py
a, _b, c, _d = 1, 2, 3, 4

>>> from unders import *          # Load non _X names only
>>> a, c
(1, 3)
>>> _b
NameError: name '_b' is not defined

>>> import unders                 # But other importers get every name
>>> unders._b
2
```

Alternatively, you can achieve a hiding effect similar to the _X naming convention by assigning a list of variable name strings to the variable __all__ at the top level of the module. When this feature is used, the from * statement will copy out only those names listed in the __all__ list. In effect, this is the converse of the _X convention: __all__ identifies names to be copied, while _X identifies names *not* to be copied. Python looks for an __all__ list in the module first and copies its names irrespective of any underscores; if __all__ is not defined, from * copies all names without a single leading underscore:

```
# alls.py
__all__ = ['a', '_c']             # __all__ has precedence over _X
```

```
        a, b, _c, _d = 1, 2, 3, 4

        >>> from alls import *            # Load __all__ names only
        >>> a, _c
        (1, 3)
        >>> b
        NameError: name 'b' is not defined

        >>> from alls import a, b, _c, _d      # But other importers get every name
        >>> a, b, _c, _d
        (1, 2, 3, 4)

        >>> import alls
        >>> alls.a, alls.b, alls._c, alls._d
        (1, 2, 3, 4)
```

Like the _X convention, the __all__ list has meaning only to the from * statement form and does not amount to a privacy declaration: other import statements can still access all names, as the last two tests show. Still, module writers can use either technique to implement modules that are well behaved when used with from *. See also the discussion of __all__ lists in package __init__.py files in Chapter 24; there, these lists declare submodules to be automatically loaded for a from * on their container.

Enabling Future Language Features: __future__

Changes to the language that may potentially break existing code are usually introduced gradually in Python. They often initially appear as optional extensions, which are disabled by default. To turn on such extensions, use a special import statement of this form:

```
        from __future__ import featurename
```

When used in a script, this statement must appear as the first executable statement in the file (possibly following a docstring or comment), because it enables special compilation of code on a per-module basis. It's also possible to submit this statement at the interactive prompt to experiment with upcoming language changes; the feature will then be available for the remainder of the interactive session.

For example, in this book we've seen how to use this statement in Python 2.X to activate 3.X true division in Chapter 5, 3.X print calls in Chapter 11, and 3.X absolute imports for packages in Chapter 24. Prior editions of this book used this statement form to demonstrate generator functions, which required a keyword that was not yet enabled by default (they use a featurename of generators).

All of these changes have the potential to break existing code in Python 2.X, so they were phased in gradually or offered as optional extensions, enabled with this special import. At the same time, some are available to allow you to write code that is forward compatible with later releases you may port to someday.

For a list of futurisms you may import and turn on this way, run a dir call on the __future__ module after importing it, or see its library manual entry. Per its documentation, none of its feature names will ever be removed, so it's safe to leave in a __future__ import even in code run by a version of Python where the feature is present normally.

Mixed Usage Modes: __name__ and __main__

Our next module-related trick lets you both import a file as a module and run it as a standalone program, and is widely used in Python files. It's actually so simple that some miss the point at first: each module has a built-in attribute called __name__, which Python creates and assigns automatically as follows:

- If the file is being run as a top-level program file, __name__ is set to the string "__main__" when it starts.

- If the file is being imported instead, __name__ is set to the module's name as known by its clients.

The upshot is that a module can test its own __name__ to determine whether it's being run or imported. For example, suppose we create the following module file, named *runme.py*, to export a single function called `tester`:

```
def tester():
    print("It's Christmas in Heaven...")

if __name__ == '__main__':          # Only when run
    tester()                        # Not when imported
```

This module defines a function for clients to import and use as usual:

```
c:\code> python
>>> import runme
>>> runme.tester()
It's Christmas in Heaven...
```

But the module also includes code at the bottom that is set up to call the function automatically when this file is run as a program:

```
c:\code> python runme.py
It's Christmas in Heaven...
```

In effect, a module's __name__ variable serves as a *usage mode flag*, allowing its code to be leveraged as *both* an importable library and a top-level script. Though simple, you'll see this hook used in the majority of the Python program files you are likely to encounter in the wild—both for testing and dual usage.

For instance, perhaps the most common way you'll see the __name__ test applied is for *self-test* code. In short, you can package code that tests a module's exports in the module itself by wrapping it in a __name__ test at the bottom of the file. This way, you can use the file in clients by *importing it*, but also test its logic by *running* it from the system shell or via another launching scheme.

Coding self-test code at the bottom of a file under the __name__ test is probably the most common and simplest unit-testing protocol in Python. It's much more convenient than retyping all your tests at the interactive prompt. (Chapter 36 will discuss other commonly used options for testing Python code—as you'll see, the unittest and doctest standard library modules provide more advanced testing tools.)

In addition, the __name__ trick is also commonly used when you're writing files that can be used both as command-line utilities and as tool libraries. For instance, suppose you write a file-finder script in Python. You can get more mileage out of your code if you package it in functions and add a __name__ test in the file to automatically call those functions when the file is run standalone. That way, the script's code becomes reusable in other programs.

Unit Tests with __name__

In fact, we've already seen a prime example in this book of an instance where the __name__ check could be useful. In the section on arguments in Chapter 18, we coded a script that computed the minimum value from the set of arguments sent in (this was the file *minmax.py* in "The min Wakeup Call!"):

```
def minmax(test, *args):
    res = args[0]
    for arg in args[1:]:
        if test(arg, res):
            res = arg
    return res

def lessthan(x, y): return x < y
def grtrthan(x, y): return x > y

print(minmax(lessthan, 4, 2, 1, 5, 6, 3))      # Self-test code
print(minmax(grtrthan, 4, 2, 1, 5, 6, 3))
```

This script includes self-test code at the bottom, so we can test it without having to retype everything at the interactive command line each time we run it. The problem with the way it is currently coded, however, is that the output of the self-test call will appear every time this file is imported from another file to be used as a tool—not exactly a user-friendly feature! To improve it, we can wrap up the self-test call in a __name__ check, so that it will be launched only when the file is run as a top-level script, not when it is imported (this new version of the module file is renamed *minmax2.py* here):

```
print('I am:', __name__)

def minmax(test, *args):
    res = args[0]
    for arg in args[1:]:
        if test(arg, res):
            res = arg
    return res
```

```
def lessthan(x, y): return x < y
def grtrthan(x, y): return x > y

if __name__ == '__main__':
    print(minmax(lessthan, 4, 2, 1, 5, 6, 3))     # Self-test code
    print(minmax(grtrthan, 4, 2, 1, 5, 6, 3))
```

We're also printing the value of __name__ at the top here to trace its value. Python creates and assigns this usage-mode variable as soon as it starts loading a file. When we run this file as a top-level script, its name is set to __main__, so its self-test code kicks in automatically:

```
c:\code> python minmax2.py
I am: __main__
1
6
```

If we import the file, though, its name is not __main__, so we must explicitly call the function to make it run:

```
c:\code> python
>>> import minmax2
I am: minmax2
>>> minmax2.minmax(minmax2.lessthan, 's', 'p', 'a', 'a')
'a'
```

Again, regardless of whether this is used for testing, the net effect is that we get to use our code in *two different roles*—as a library module of tools, or as an executable program.

 Per Chapter 24's discussion of package relative imports, this section's technique can also have some implications for imports run by files that are also used as package components in 3.X, but can still be leveraged with absolute package path imports and other techniques. See the prior chapter's discussion and example for more details.

Example: Dual Mode Code

Here's a more substantial module example that demonstrates another way that the prior section's __name__ trick is commonly employed. The following module, *formats.py*, defines string formatting utilities for importers, but also checks its name to see if it is being run as a top-level script; if so, it tests and uses arguments listed on the system command line to run a canned or passed-in test. In Python, the `sys.argv` list contains *command-line arguments*—it is a list of strings reflecting words typed on the command line, where the first item is always the name of the script being run. We used this in Chapter 21's benchmark tool as switches, but leverage it as a general input mechanism here:

```
#!python
"""
```

```
File: formats.py (2.X and 3.X)
Various specialized string display formatting utilities.
Test me with canned self-test or command-line arguments.
To do: add parens for negative money, add more features.
"""

def commas(N):
    """
    Format positive integer-like N for display with
    commas between digit groupings: "xxx,yyy,zzz".
    """
    digits = str(N)
    assert digits.isdigit()
    result = ''
    while digits:
        digits, last3 = digits[:-3], digits[-3:]
        result = (last3 + ',' + result) if result else last3
    return result

def money(N, numwidth=0, currency='$'):
    """
    Format number N for display with commas, 2 decimal digits,
    leading $ and sign, and optional padding: "$  -xxx,yyy.zz".
    numwidth=0 for no space padding, currency='' to omit symbol,
    and non-ASCII for others (e.g., pound=u'\xA3' or u'\u00A3').
    """
    sign   = '-' if N < 0 else ''
    N      = abs(N)
    whole  = commas(int(N))
    fract  = ('%.2f' % N)[-2:]
    number = '%s%s.%s' % (sign, whole, fract)
    return '%s%*s' % (currency, numwidth, number)

if __name__ == '__main__':
    def selftest():
        tests  = 0, 1         # fails: -1, 1.23
        tests += 12, 123, 1234, 12345, 123456, 1234567
        tests += 2 ** 32, 2 ** 100
        for test in tests:
            print(commas(test))

        print('')
        tests  = 0, 1, -1, 1.23, 1., 1.2, 3.14159
        tests += 12.34, 12.344, 12.345, 12.346
        tests += 2 ** 32, (2 ** 32 + .2345)
        tests += 1.2345, 1.2, 0.2345
        tests += -1.2345, -1.2, -0.2345
        tests += -(2 ** 32), -(2**32 + .2345)
        tests += (2 ** 100), -(2 ** 100)
        for test in tests:
            print('%s [%s]' % (money(test, 17), test))

    import sys
    if len(sys.argv) == 1:
        selftest()
```

```
    else:
        print(money(float(sys.argv[1]), int(sys.argv[2])))
```

This file works identically in Python 2.X and 3.X. When run directly, it tests itself as before, but it uses options on the command line to control the test behavior. Run this file directly with no command-line arguments on your own to see what its self-test code prints—it's too extensive to list in full here:

```
c:\code> python formats.py
0
1
12
123
1,234
12,345
123,456
1,234,567
...etc...
```

To test specific strings, pass them in on the command line along with a minimum field width; the script's __main__ code passes them on to its money function, which in turn runs commas:

```
C:\code> python formats.py 999999999 0
$999,999,999.00
C:\code> python formats.py -999999999 0
$-999,999,999.00

C:\code> python formats.py 123456789012345 0
$123,456,789,012,345.00
C:\code> python formats.py -123456789012345 25
$   -123,456,789,012,345.00

C:\code> python formats.py 123.456 0
$123.46
C:\code> python formats.py -123.454 0
$-123.45
```

As before, because this code is instrumented for dual-mode usage, we can also import its tools normally to reuse them as library components in scripts, modules, and the interactive prompt:

```
>>> from formats import money, commas
>>> money(123.456)
'$123.46'
>>> money(-9999999.99, 15)
'$   -9,999,999.99'
>>> X = 99999999999999999999
>>> '%s (%s)' % (commas(X), X)
'99,999,999,999,999,999,999 (99999999999999999999)'
```

You can use command-line arguments in ways similar to this example to provide general input to scripts that may also package their code as functions and classes for reuse by importers. For more advanced command-line processing, see "Python Command-

Line Arguments" on page 1432 in Appendix A, and the `getopt`, `optparse`, and `arg parse` modules' documentation in Python's standard library manual. In some scenarios, you might also use the built-in `input` function, used in Chapter 3 and Chapter 10, to prompt the shell user for test inputs instead of pulling them from the command line. For more on the `assert` statement used here, see Chapter 34.

 Also see Chapter 7's discussion of the new `{,d}` string format method syntax added in Python 2.7 and 3.1; this formatting extension separates thousands groups with commas much like the code here. The module listed here, though, adds money formatting, can be changed, and serves as a manual alternative for comma insertions in earlier Pythons.

Currency Symbols: Unicode in Action

This module's `money` function defaults to dollars, but supports other currency symbols by allowing you to pass in non-ASCII Unicode characters. The Unicode ordinal with hexadecimal value 00A3, for example, is the pound symbol, and 00A5 is the yen. You can code these in a variety of forms, as:

- The character's decoded Unicode code point ordinal (integer) in a *text string*, with either Unicode or hex escapes (for 2.X compatibility, use a leading u in such string literals in Python 3.3)

- The character's raw encoded form in a *byte string* that is decoded before passed, with hex escapes (for 3.X compatibility, use a leading b in such string literals in Python 2.X)

- The actual character itself in your program's text, along with a source code encoding declaration

We previewed Unicode in Chapter 4 and will get into more details in Chapter 37, but its basic requirements here are fairly simple, and serve as a decent use case. To test alternative currencies, I typed the following in a file, *formats_currency.py*, because it was too much to reenter interactively on changes:

```
from __future__ import print_function # 2.X
from formats import money
X = 54321.987

print(money(X), money(X, 0, ''))
print(money(X, currency=u'\xA3'), money(X, currency=u'\u00A5'))
print(money(X, currency=b'\xA3'.decode('latin-1')))

print(money(X, currency=u'\u20AC'), money(X, 0, b'\xA4'.decode('iso-8859-15')))
print(money(X, currency=b'\xA4'.decode('latin-1')))
```

The following gives this test file's output in Python 3.3 in IDLE, and in other contexts configured properly. It works the same in 2.X because it prints and codes strings portably. Per Chapter 11, a `__future__` import enables 3.X `print` calls in 2.X. And as introduced in Chapter 4, 3.X b'...' bytes literals are taken as simple strings in 2.X, and 2.X u'...' Unicode literals as treated as normal strings in 3.X as of 3.3.

```
$54,321.99 54,321.99
£54,321.99 ¥54,321.99
£54,321.99
€54,321.99 €54,321.99
¤54,321.99
```

If this works on your computer, you can probably skip the next few paragraphs. Depending on your interface and system settings, though, getting this to run and display properly may require additional steps. On my machine, it behaves correctly when Python and the display medium are in sync, but the euro and generic currency symbols in the last two lines fail with errors in a basic Command Prompt on Windows.

Specifically, this test script always runs and produces the output shown in the *IDLE GUI* in both 3.X and 2.X, because Unicode-to-glyph mappings are handled well. It also works as advertised in 3.X on Windows if you *redirect* the output to a file and open it with Notepad, because 3.X encodes content on this platform in a default Windows format that Notepad understands:

```
c:\code> formats_currency.py > temp
c:\code> notepad temp
```

However, this doesn't work in 2.X, because Python tries to encode printed text as ASCII by default. To show all the non-ASCII characters in a Windows Command Prompt window directly, on some computers you may need to change the Windows *code page* (used to render characters) as well as Python's PYTHONIOENCODING environment variable (used as the encoding of text in standard streams, including the translation of characters to bytes when they are printed) to a common Unicode format such as UTF-8:

```
c:\code> chcp 65001              # Console matches Python
c:\code> set PYTHONIOENCODING=utf-8     # Python matches console
c:\code> formats_currency.py > temp     # Both 3.X and 2.X write UTF-8 text
c:\code> type temp               # Console displays it properly
c:\code> notepad temp            # Notepad recognizes UTF-8 too
```

You may not need to take these steps on some platforms and even on some Windows distributions. I did because my laptop's code page is set to 437 (U.S. characters), but your code pages may vary.

Subtly, the only reason this test works on Python 2.X at all is because 2.X allows normal and Unicode strings to be *mixed*, as long as the normal string is all 7-bit ASCII characters. On 3.3, the 2.X u'...' Unicode literal is supported for compatibility, but taken the same as normal '...' strings, which are always Unicode (removing the leading u makes the test work in 3.0 through 3.2 too, but breaks 2.X compatibility):

```
c:\code> py -2
>>> print u'\xA5' + '1', '%s2' % u'\u00A3'    # 2.X: unicode/str mix for ASCII str
¥1 £2

c:\code> py -3
```

```
>>> print(u'\xA5' + '1', '%s2' % u'\u00A3')    # 3.X: str is Unicode, u'' optional
¥1 £2
>>> print('\xA5' + '1', '%s2' % '\u00A3')
¥1 £2
```

Again, there's much more on Unicode in Chapter 37—a topic many see as peripheral, but which can crop up even in relatively simple contexts like this! The takeaway point here is that, operational issues aside, a carefully coded script can often manage to support Unicode in both 3.X and 2.X.

Docstrings: Module Documentation at Work

Finally, because this example's main file uses the *docstring* feature introduced in Chapter 15, we can use the `help` function or PyDoc's GUI/browser modes to explore its tools as well—modules are almost automatically general-purpose tools. Here's `help` at work; Figure 25-2 gives the PyDoc view on our file.

```
>>> import formats
>>> help(formats)
Help on module formats:

NAME
    formats

DESCRIPTION
    File: formats.py (2.X and 3.X)
    Various specialized string display formatting utilities.
    Test me with canned self-test or command-line arguments.
    To do: add parens for negative money, add more features.

FUNCTIONS
    commas(N)
        Format positive integer-like N for display with
        commas between digit groupings: "xxx,yyy,zzz".

    money(N, numwidth=0, currency='$')
        Format number N for display with commas, 2 decimal digits,
        leading $ and sign, and optional padding: "$  -xxx,yyy.zz".
        numwidth=0 for no space padding, currency='' to omit symbol,
        and non-ASCII for others (e.g., pound=u'£' or u'£').

FILE
    c:\code\formats.py
```

Changing the Module Search Path

Let's return to more general module topics. In Chapter 22, we learned that the module search path is a list of directories that can be customized via the environment variable PYTHONPATH, and possibly via *.pth* files. What I haven't shown you until now is how a Python program itself can actually change the search path by changing the built-in

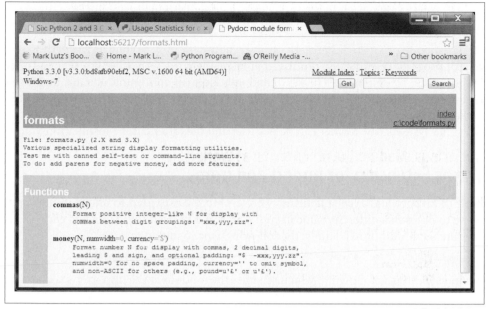

Figure 25-2. PyDoc's view of formats.py, obtained by running a "py –3 -m pydoc –b" command line in 3.2 and later and clicking on the file's index entry (see Chapter 15)

`sys.path` list. Per Chapter 22, `sys.path` is initialized on startup, but thereafter you can delete, append, and reset its components however you like:

```
>>> import sys
>>> sys.path
['', 'c:\\temp', 'C:\\Windows\\system32\\python33.zip', ...more deleted...]

>>> sys.path.append('C:\\sourcedir')        # Extend module search path
>>> import string                           # All imports search the new dir last
```

Once you've made such a change, it will impact all future imports anywhere while a Python program runs, as all importers share the same single `sys.path` list (there's only one copy of a given module in memory during a program's run—that's why `reload` exists). In fact, this list may be changed arbitrarily:

```
>>> sys.path = [r'd:\temp']                    # Change module search path
>>> sys.path.append('c:\\lp5e\\examples')      # For this run (process) only
>>> sys.path.insert(0, '..')
>>> sys.path
['..', 'd:\\temp', 'c:\\lp5e\\examples']
>>> import string
Traceback (most recent call last):
  File "<stdin>", line 1, in <module>
ImportError: No module named 'string'
```

Thus, you can use this technique to dynamically configure a search path inside a Python program. Be careful, though: if you delete a critical directory from the path, you may lose access to critical utilities. In the prior example, for instance, we no longer have access to the `string` module because we deleted the Python source library's directory from the path!

Also, remember that such `sys.path` settings endure for only as long as the Python session or program (technically, *process*) that made them runs; they are not retained after Python exits. By contrast, `PYTHONPATH` and *.pth* file path configurations live in the operating system instead of a running Python program, and so are more global: they are picked up by every program on your machine and live on after a program completes. On some systems, the former can be per-user and the latter can be installation-wide.

The as Extension for import and from

Both the `import` and `from` statements were eventually extended to allow an imported name to be given a different name in your script. We've used this extension earlier, but here are some additional details: the following `import` statement:

```
import modulename as name              # And use name, not modulename
```

is equivalent to the following, which renames the module in the importer's scope only (it's still known by its original name to other files):

```
import modulename
name = modulename
del modulename                         # Don't keep original name
```

After such an `import`, you can—and in fact must—use the name listed after the `as` to refer to the module. This works in a `from` statement, too, to assign a name imported from a file to a different name in the importer's scope; as before you get only the new name you provide, not its original:

```
from modulename import attrname as name     # And use name, not attrname
```

As discussed in Chapter 23, this extension is commonly used to provide *short synonyms* for longer names, and to avoid *name clashes* when you are already using a name in your script that would otherwise be overwritten by a normal `import` statement:

```
import reallylongmodulename as name         # Use shorter nickname
name.func()

from module1 import utility as util1        # Can have only 1 "utility"
from module2 import utility as util2
util1(); util2()
```

It also comes in handy for providing a short, simple name for an entire directory path and avoiding name collisions when using the *package import* feature described in Chapter 24:

```
import dir1.dir2.mod as mod                 # Only list full path once
mod.func()

from dir1.dir2.mod import func as modfunc   # Rename to make unique if needed
modfunc()
```

This is also something of a hedge against name changes: if a new release of a library renames a module or tool your code uses extensively, or provides a new alternative you'd rather use instead, you can simply rename it to its prior name on import to avoid breaking your code:

```
import newname as oldname
from library import newname as oldname
...and keep happily using oldname until you have time to update all your code...
```

For example, this approach can address some 3.X library changes (e.g., 3.X's tkinter versus 2.X's Tkinter), though they're often substantially more than just a new name!

Example: Modules Are Objects

Because modules expose most of their interesting properties as built-in attributes, it's easy to write programs that manage other programs. We usually call such manager programs *metaprograms* because they work on top of other systems. This is also referred to as *introspection*, because programs can see and process object internals. Introspection is a somewhat advanced feature, but it can be useful for building programming tools.

For instance, to get to an attribute called name in a module called M, we can use attribute qualification or index the module's attribute dictionary, exposed in the built-in __dict__ attribute we met in Chapter 23. Python also exports the list of all loaded modules as the sys.modules dictionary and provides a built-in called getattr that lets us fetch attributes from their string names—it's like saying object.attr, but attr is an expression that yields a string at runtime. Because of that, all the following expressions reach the same attribute and object:[1]

```
M.name                    # Qualify object by attribute
M.__dict__['name']        # Index namespace dictionary manually
sys.modules['M'].name     # Index loaded-modules table manually
getattr(M, 'name')        # Call built-in fetch function
```

By exposing module internals like this, Python helps you build programs about programs. For example, here is a module named *mydir.py* that puts these ideas to work to implement a customized version of the built-in dir function. It defines and exports a function called listing, which takes a module object as an argument and prints a formatted listing of the module's namespace sorted by name:

---

1. As we saw briefly in "Other Ways to Access Globals" in Chapter 17, because a function can access its enclosing module by going through the sys.modules table like this, it can also be used to emulate the effect of the global statement. For instance, the effect of global X; X=0 can be simulated (albeit with much more typing!) by saying this inside a function: import sys; glob=sys.modules[__name__]; glob.X=0. Remember, each module gets a __name__ attribute for free; it's visible as a global name inside the functions within the module. This trick provides another way to change both local and global variables of the same name inside a function.

```
#!python
"""
mydir.py: a module that lists the namespaces of other modules
"""
from __future__ import print_function  # 2.X compatibility

seplen = 60
sepchr = '-'

def listing(module, verbose=True):
    sepline = sepchr * seplen
    if verbose:
        print(sepline)
        print('name:', module.__name__, 'file:', module.__file__)
        print(sepline)

    count = 0
    for attr in sorted(module.__dict__):          # Scan namespace keys (or enumerate)
        print('%02d) %s' % (count, attr), end = ' ')
        if attr.startswith('__'):
            print('<built-in name>')              # Skip __file__, etc.
        else:
            print(getattr(module, attr))          # Same as .__dict__[attr]
        count += 1

    if verbose:
        print(sepline)
        print(module.__name__, 'has %d names' % count)
        print(sepline)

if __name__ == '__main__':
    import mydir
    listing(mydir)                                # Self-test code: list myself
```

Notice the docstring at the top; as in the prior *formats.py* example, because we may want to use this as a general tool, the docstring provides functional information accessible via `help` and GUI/browser mode of PyDoc—a tool that uses similar introspection tools to do its job. A *self-test* is also provided at the bottom of this module, which narcissistically imports and lists itself. Here's the sort of output produced in Python 3.3; this script works on 2.X too (where it may list fewer names) because it prints from the __future__:

```
c:\code> py -3 mydir.py
------------------------------------------------------------
name: mydir file: c:\code\mydir.py
------------------------------------------------------------
00) __builtins__ <built-in name>
01) __cached__ <built-in name>
02) __doc__ <built-in name>
03) __file__ <built-in name>
04) __initializing__ <built-in name>
05) __loader__ <built-in name>
06) __name__ <built-in name>
07) __package__ <built-in name>
```

```
08) listing <function listing at 0x000000000295B488>
09) print_function _Feature((2, 6, 0, 'alpha', 2), (3, 0, 0, 'alpha', 0), 65536)
10) sepchr -
11) seplen 60
------------------------------------------------------------
mydir has 12 names
------------------------------------------------------------
```

To use this as a tool for listing other modules, simply pass the modules in as objects to this file's function. Here it is listing attributes in the `tkinter` GUI module in the standard library (a.k.a. `Tkinter` in Python 2.X); it will technically work on any object with `__name__`, `__file__`, and `__dict__` attributes:

```
>>> import mydir
>>> import tkinter
>>> mydir.listing(tkinter)
------------------------------------------------------------
name: tkinter file: C:\Python33\lib\tkinter\__init__.py
------------------------------------------------------------
00) ACTIVE active
01) ALL all
02) ANCHOR anchor
03) ARC arc
04) At <function At at 0x0000000002BD41E0>
...many more names omitted...
156) image_types <function image_types at 0x0000000002BE2378>
157) mainloop <function mainloop at 0x0000000002BCBBF8>
158) sys <module 'sys' (built-in)>
159) wantobjects 1
160) warnings <module 'warnings' from 'C:\\Python33\\lib\\warnings.py'>
------------------------------------------------------------
tkinter has 161 names
------------------------------------------------------------
```

We'll meet `getattr` and its relatives again later. The point to notice here is that `mydir` is a program that lets you browse other programs. Because Python exposes its internals, you can process objects generically.[2]

Importing Modules by Name String

The module name in an `import` or `from` statement is a hardcoded variable name. Sometimes, though, your program will get the name of a module to be imported as a string at runtime—from a user selection in a GUI, or a parse of an XML document, for instance. Unfortunately, you can't use `import` statements directly to load a module given its name as a string—Python expects a variable name that's taken literally and not evaluated, not a string or expression. For instance:

---

2. You can preload tools such as `mydir.listing` and the reloader we'll meet in a moment into the interactive namespace by importing them in the file referenced by the PYTHONSTARTUP environment variable. Because code in the startup file runs in the interactive namespace (module `__main__`), importing common tools in the startup file can save you some typing. See Appendix A for more details.

```
>>> import 'string'
  File "<stdin>", line 1
    import "string"
                  ^
SyntaxError: invalid syntax
```

It also won't work to simply assign the string to a variable name:

```
x = 'string'
import x
```

Here, Python will try to import a file *x.py*, not the `string` module—the name in an `import` statement both becomes a variable assigned to the loaded module and identifies the external file literally.

Running Code Strings

To get around this, you need to use special tools to load a module dynamically from a string that is generated at runtime. The most general approach is to construct an `import` statement as a string of Python code and pass it to the `exec` built-in function to run (`exec` is a statement in Python 2.X, but it can be used exactly as shown here—the parentheses are simply ignored):

```
>>> modname = 'string'
>>> exec('import ' + modname)        # Run a string of code
>>> string                           # Imported in this namespace
<module 'string' from 'C:\\Python33\\lib\\string.py'>
```

We met the `exec` function (and its cousin for expressions, `eval`) earlier, in Chapter 3 and Chapter 10. It compiles a string of code and passes it to the Python interpreter to be executed. In Python, the byte code compiler is available at runtime, so you can write programs that construct and run other programs like this. By default, `exec` runs the code in the current scope, but you can get more specific by passing in optional namespace dictionaries if needed. It also has security issues noted earlier in the book, which may be minor in a code string you are building yourself.

Direct Calls: Two Options

The only real drawback to `exec` here is that it must compile the `import` statement each time it runs, and compiling can be slow. Precompiling to byte code with the `compile` built-in may help for code strings run many times, but in most cases it's probably simpler and may run quicker to use the built-in `__import__` function to load from a name string instead, as noted in Chapter 22. The effect is similar, but `__import__` returns the module object, so assign it to a name here to keep it:

```
>>> modname = 'string'
>>> string = __import__(modname)
>>> string
<module 'string' from 'C:\\Python33\\lib\\string.py'>
```

As also noted in Chapter 22, the newer call `importlib.import_module` does the same work, and is generally preferred in more recent Pythons for direct calls to import by name string—at least per the current "official" policy stated in Python's manuals:

```
>>> import importlib
>>> modname = 'string'
>>> string = importlib.import_module(modname)
>>> string
<module 'string' from 'C:\\Python33\\lib\\string.py'>
```

The `import_module` call takes a module name string, and an optional second argument that gives the *package* used as the anchor point for resolving relative imports, which defaults to `None`. This call works the same as `__import__` in its basic roles, but see Python's manuals for more details.

Though both calls still work, in Pythons where both are available, the original `__import__` is generally intended for customizing import operations by reassignment in the built-in scope (and any future changes in "official" policy are beyond the scope of this book!).

Example: Transitive Module Reloads

This section develops a module tool that ties together and applies some earlier topics, and serves as a larger case study to close out this chapter and part. We studied module reloads in Chapter 23, as a way to pick up changes in code without stopping and restarting a program. When you reload a module, though, Python reloads only that particular module's file; it doesn't automatically reload modules that the file being reloaded happens to import.

For example, if you reload some module A, and A imports modules B and C, the reload applies only to A, not to B and C. The statements inside A that import B and C are rerun during the reload, but they just fetch the already loaded B and C module objects (assuming they've been imported before). In actual yet abstract code, here's the file *A.py*:

```
# A.py
import B          # Not reloaded when A is!
import C          # Just an import of an already loaded module: no-ops

% python
>>> . . .
>>> from imp import reload
>>> reload(A)
```

By default, this means that you cannot depend on reloads to pick up changes in all the modules in your program transitively—instead, you must use multiple `reload` calls to update the subcomponents independently. This can require substantial work for large systems you're testing interactively. You can design your systems to reload their subcomponents automatically by adding `reload` calls in parent modules like A, but this complicates the modules' code.

A Recursive Reloader

A better approach is to write a general tool to do transitive reloads automatically by scanning modules' __dict__ namespace attributes and checking each item's type to find nested modules to reload. Such a utility function could call itself *recursively* to navigate arbitrarily shaped and deep import dependency chains. Module __dict__ attributes were introduced in Chapter 23 and employed earlier in this chapter, and the type call was presented in Chapter 9; we just need to combine the two tools.

The module *reloadall.py* listed next defines a reload_all function that automatically reloads a module, every module that the module imports, and so on, all the way to the bottom of each import chain. It uses a dictionary to keep track of already reloaded modules, recursion to walk the import chains, and the standard library's types module, which simply predefines type results for built-in types. The visited dictionary technique works to avoid cycles here when imports are recursive or redundant, because module objects are immutable and so can be dictionary keys; as we learned in Chapter 5 and Chapter 8, a *set* would offer similar functionality if we use visited.add(module) to insert:

```python
#!python
"""
reloadall.py: transitively reload nested modules (2.X + 3.X).
Call reload_all with one or more imported module module objects.
"""

import types
from imp import reload                                 # from required in 3.X

def status(module):
    print('reloading ' + module.__name__)

def tryreload(module):
    try:
        reload(module)                                 # 3.3 (only?) fails on some
    except:
        print('FAILED: %s' % module)

def transitive_reload(module, visited):
    if not module in visited:                          # Trap cycles, duplicates
        status(module)                                 # Reload this module
        tryreload(module)                              # And visit children
        visited[module] = True
        for attrobj in module.__dict__.values():       # For all attrs
            if type(attrobj) == types.ModuleType:      # Recur if module
                transitive_reload(attrobj, visited)

def reload_all(*args):
    visited = {}                                       # Main entry point
    for arg in args:                                   # For all passed in
        if type(arg) == types.ModuleType:
            transitive_reload(arg, visited)
```

```
def tester(reloader, modname):              # Self-test code
    import importlib, sys                    # Import on tests only
    if len(sys.argv) > 1: modname = sys.argv[1]   # command line (or passed)
    module  = importlib.import_module(modname)    # Import by name string
    reloader(module)                         # Test passed-in reloader

if __name__ == '__main__':
    tester(reload_all, 'reloadall')          # Test: reload myself?
```

Besides namespace dictionaries, this script makes use of other tools we've studied here: it includes a __name__ test to launch self-test code when run as a top-level script only, and its tester function uses sys.argv to inspect command-line arguments and impor tlib to import a module by name string passed in as a function or command-line argument. One curious bit: notice how this code must wrap the basic reload call in a try statement to catch exceptions—in Python 3.3, reloads sometimes fail due to a rewrite of the import machinery. The try was previewed in Chapter 10, and is covered in full in Part VII.

Testing recursive reloads

Now, to leverage this utility for normal use, import its reload_all function and pass it an already loaded module object—just as you would for the built-in reload function. When the file runs standalone, its self-test code calls reload_all automatically, reloading its own module by default if no command-line arguments are used. In this mode, the module must import itself because its own name is not defined in the file without an import. This code works in both 3.X and 2.X because we've used + and % instead of a comma in the prints, though the set of modules used and thus reloaded may vary across lines:

```
C:\code> c:\Python33\python reloadall.py
reloading reloadall
reloading types

c:\code> C:\Python27\python reloadall.py
reloading reloadall
reloading types
```

With a command-line argument, the tester instead reloads the given module by its name string—here, the benchmark module we coded in Chapter 21. Note that we give a module name in this mode, not a filename (as for import statements, don't include the .py extension); the script ultimately imports the module using the module search path as usual:

```
c:\code> reloadall.py pybench
reloading pybench
reloading timeit
reloading itertools
reloading sys
reloading time
reloading gc
reloading os
```

```
reloading errno
reloading ntpath
reloading stat
reloading genericpath
reloading copyreg
```

Perhaps most commonly, we can also deploy this module at the interactive prompt—here, in 3.3 for some standard library modules. Notice how os is imported by tkinter, but tkinter reaches sys before os can (if you want to test this on Python 2.X, substitute Tkinter for tkinter):

```
>>> from reloadall import reload_all
>>> import os, tkinter
>>> reload_all(os)                        # Normal usage mode
reloading os
reloading ntpath
reloading stat
reloading sys
reloading genericpath
reloading errno
reloading copyreg

>>> reload_all(tkinter)
reloading tkinter
reloading _tkinter
reloading warnings
reloading sys
reloading linecache
reloading tokenize
reloading builtins
FAILED: <module 'builtins'>
reloading re
...etc...
reloading os
reloading ntpath
reloading stat
reloading genericpath
reloading errno
...etc...
```

And finally here is a session that shows the effect of normal versus transitive reloads—changes made to the two nested files are not picked up by reloads, unless the transitive utility is used:

```
import b        # File a.py
X = 1

import c        # File b.py
Y = 2

Z = 3           # File c.py

C:\code> py -3
>>> import a
>>> a.X, a.b.Y, a.b.c.Z
```

```
(1, 2, 3)
```

 # Without stopping Python, change all three files' assignment values and save

```
>>> from imp import reload
>>> reload(a)                              # Built-in reload is top level only
<module 'a' from '.\\a.py'>
>>> a.X, a.b.Y, a.b.c.Z
(111, 2, 3)

>>> from reloadall import reload_all
>>> reload_all(a)                          # Normal usage mode
reloading a
reloading b
reloading c
>>> a.X, a.b.Y, a.b.c.Z                     # Reloads all nested modules too
(111, 222, 333)
```

Study the reloader's code and results for more on its operation. The next section exercises its tools further.

Alternative Codings

For all the recursion fans in the audience, the following lists an alternative *recursive* coding for the function in the prior section—it uses a *set* instead of a dictionary to detect cycles, is marginally more *direct* because it eliminates a top-level loop, and serves to illustrate recursive function techniques in general (compare with the original to see how this differs). This version also gets some of its work for free from the original, though the order in which it reloads modules might vary if namespace dictionary order does too:

```
"""
reloadall2.py: transitively reload nested modules (alternative coding)
"""

import types
from imp import reload                                 # from required in 3.X
from reloadall import status, tryreload, tester

def transitive_reload(objects, visited):
    for obj in objects:
        if type(obj) == types.ModuleType and obj not in visited:
            status(obj)
            tryreload(obj)                              # Reload this, recur to attrs
            visited.add(obj)
            transitive_reload(obj.__dict__.values(), visited)

def reload_all(*args):
    transitive_reload(args, set())

if __name__ == '__main__':
    tester(reload_all, 'reloadall2')                    # Test code: reload myself?
```

As we saw in Chapter 19, there is usually an *explicit stack* or queue equivalent to most recursive functions, which may be preferable in some contexts. The following is one such transitive reloader; it uses a generator expression to filter out nonmodules and modules already visited in the current module's namespace. Because it both pops and adds items at the end of its list, it is stack based, though the order of both pushes and dictionary values influences the order in which it reaches and reloads modules—it visits submodules in namespace dictionaries from right to left, unlike the left-to-right order of the recursive versions (trace through the code to see how). We could change this, but dictionary order is arbitrary anyhow.

```
"""
reloadall3.py: transitively reload nested modules (explicit stack)
"""

import types
from imp import reload                          # from required in 3.X
from reloadall import status, tryreload, tester

def transitive_reload(modules, visited):
    while modules:
        next = modules.pop()                    # Delete next item at end
        status(next)                            # Reload this, push attrs
        tryreload(next)
        visited.add(next)
        modules.extend(x for x in next.__dict__.values()
            if type(x) == types.ModuleType and x not in visited)

def reload_all(*modules):
    transitive_reload(list(modules), set())

if __name__ == '__main__':
    tester(reload_all, 'reloadall3')            # Test code: reload myself?
```

If the recursion and nonrecursion used in this example is confusing, see the discussion of recursive functions in Chapter 19 for background on the subject.

Testing reload variants

To prove that these work the same, let's test all three of our reloader variants. Thanks to their common testing function, we can run all three from a command line both with no arguments to test the module reloading itself, and with the name of a module to be reloaded listed on the command line (in **sys.argv**):

```
c:\code> reloadall.py
reloading reloadall
reloading types

c:\code> reloadall2.py
reloading reloadall2
reloading types

c:\code> reloadall3.py
```

```
reloading reloadall3
reloading types
```

Though it's hard to see here, we really are testing the individual reloader alternatives —each of these tests shares a common `tester` function, but passes it the `reload_all` from its own file. Here are the variants reloading the 3.X `tkinter` GUI module and all the modules its imports reach:

```
c:\code> reloadall.py tkinter
reloading tkinter
reloading _tkinter
reloading tkinter._fix
...etc...
c:\code> reloadall2.py tkinter
reloading tkinter
reloading tkinter.constants
reloading tkinter._fix
...etc...
c:\code> reloadall3.py tkinter
reloading tkinter
reloading sys
reloading tkinter.constants
...etc...
```

All three work on both Python 3.X and 2.X too—they're careful to unify prints with formatting, and avoid using version-specific tools (though you must use 2.X module names like `Tkinter`, and I'm using the 3.3 Windows launcher here to run per Appendix B):

```
c:\code> py -2 reloadall.py
reloading reloadall
reloading types

c:\code> py -2 reloadall2.py Tkinter
reloading Tkinter
reloading _tkinter
reloading FixTk
...etc...
```

As usual we can test interactively, too, by importing and calling either a module's main reload entry point with a module object, or the testing function with a reloader function and module name string:

```
C:\code> py -3
>>> import reloadall, reloadall2, reloadall3
>>> import tkinter
>>> reloadall.reload_all(tkinter)                       # Normal use case
reloading tkinter
reloading tkinter._fix
reloading os
...etc...
>>> reloadall.tester(reloadall2.reload_all, 'tkinter')  # Testing utility
reloading tkinter
reloading tkinter._fix
reloading os
```

```
...etc...
>>> reloadall.tester(reloadall3.reload_all, 'reloadall3')    # Mimic self-test code
reloading reloadall3
reloading types
```

Finally, if you look at the output of `tkinter` reloads earlier, you may notice that each of the three variants may produce results in a different *order*; they all depend on namespace dictionary ordering, and the last also relies on the order in which items are added to its stack. In fact, under Python 3.3, the reload order for a given reloader can vary from run to run. To ensure that all three are reloading the same modules irrespective of the order in which they do so, we can use sets (or sorts) to test for order-neutral equality of their printed messages—obtained here by running shell commands with the `os.popen` utility we met in Chapter 13 and used in Chapter 21:

```
>>> import os
>>> res1 = os.popen('reloadall.py tkinter').readlines()
>>> res2 = os.popen('reloadall2.py tkinter').readlines()
>>> res3 = os.popen('reloadall3.py tkinter').readlines()
>>> res1[:3]
['reloading tkinter\n', 'reloading sys\n', 'reloading tkinter._fix\n']

>>> res1 == res2, res2 == res3
(False, False)
>>> set(res1) == set(res2), set(res2) == set(res3)
(True, True)
```

Run these scripts, study their code, and experiment on your own for more insight; these are the sort of importable tools you might want to add to your own source code library. Watch for a similar testing technique in the coverage of class tree listers in Chapter 31, where we'll apply it to passed *class* objects and extend it further.

Also keep in mind that all three variants reload only modules that were loaded with `import` statements—since names copied with `from` statements do not cause a module to be nested and referenced in the importer's namespace, their containing module is not reloaded. More fundamentally, the transitive reloaders rely on the fact that module reloads update module objects *in place*, such that all references to those modules in any scope will see the updated version automatically. Because they copy names out, `from` importers are not updated by reloads—transitive or not—and supporting this may require either source code analysis, or customization of the import operation (see Chapter 22 for pointers).

Tool impacts like this are perhaps another reason to prefer `import` to `from`—which brings us to the end of this chapter and part, and the standard set of warnings for this part's topic.

Module Gotchas

In this section, we'll take a look at the usual collection of boundary cases that can make life interesting for Python beginners. Some are review here, and a few are so obscure that coming up with representative examples can be a challenge, but most illustrate something important about the language.

Module Name Clashes: Package and Package-Relative Imports

If you have two modules of the same name, you may only be able to import one of them —by default, the one whose directory is leftmost in the sys.path module search path will always be chosen. This isn't an issue if the module you prefer is in your top-level script's directory; since that is always first in the module path, its contents will be located first automatically. For cross-directory imports, however, the linear nature of the module search path means that same-named files can clash.

To fix, either avoid same-named files or use the package imports feature of Chapter 24. If you need to get to both same-named files, structure your source files in subdirectories, such that package import directory names make the module references unique. As long as the enclosing package directory names are unique, you'll be able to access either or both of the same-named modules.

Note that this issue can also crop up if you accidentally use a name for a module of your own that happens to be the same as a standard library module you need—your local module in the program's home directory (or another directory early in the module path) can hide and replace the library module.

To fix, either avoid using the same name as another module you need or store your modules in a package directory and use Python 3.X's package-relative import model, available in 2.X as an option. In this model, normal imports skip the package directory (so you'll get the library's version), but special dotted import statements can still select the local version of the module if needed.

Statement Order Matters in Top-Level Code

As we've seen, when a module is first imported (or reloaded), Python executes its statements one by one, from the top of the file to the bottom. This has a few subtle implications regarding forward references that are worth underscoring here:

- Code at the *top level* of a module file (not nested in a function) runs as soon as Python reaches it during an import; because of that, it cannot reference names assigned *lower* in the file.

- Code inside a *function* body doesn't run until the function is called; because names in a function aren't resolved until the function actually runs, they can usually reference names *anywhere* in the file.

Generally, forward references are only a concern in top-level module code that executes immediately; functions can reference names arbitrarily. Here's a file that illustrates forward reference dos and don'ts:

```
func1()                              # Error: "func1" not yet assigned

def func1():
    print(func2())                   # OK: "func2" looked up later

func1()                              # Error: "func2" not yet assigned

def func2():
    return "Hello"

func1()                              # OK: "func1" and "func2" assigned
```

When this file is imported (or run as a standalone program), Python executes its statements from top to bottom. The first call to func1 fails because the func1 def hasn't run yet. The call to func2 inside func1 works as long as func2's def has been reached by the time func1 is called—and it hasn't when the second top-level func1 call is run. The last call to func1 at the bottom of the file works because func1 and func2 have both been assigned.

Mixing defs with top-level code is not only difficult to read, it's also dependent on statement ordering. As a rule of thumb, if you need to mix immediate code with defs, put your defs at the top of the file and your top-level code at the bottom. That way, your functions are guaranteed to be defined and assigned by the time Python runs the code that uses them.

from Copies Names but Doesn't Link

Although it's commonly used, the from statement is the source of a variety of potential gotchas in Python. As we've learned, the from statement is really an assignment to names in the importer's scope—a name-copy operation, not a name aliasing. The implications of this are the same as for all assignments in Python, but they're subtle, especially given that the code that shares the objects lives in different files. For instance, suppose we define the following module, *nested1.py*:

```
# nested1.py
X = 99
def printer(): print(X)
```

If we import its two names using from in another module, *nested2.py*, we get copies of those names, not links to them. Changing a name in the importer resets only the binding of the local version of that name, not the name in *nested1.py*:

```
# nested2.py
from nested1 import X, printer     # Copy names out
X = 88                             # Changes my "X" only!
printer()                          # nested1's X is still 99

% python nested2.py
99
```

If we use `import` to get the whole module and then assign to a qualified name, however, we change the name in *nested1.py*. Attribute qualification directs Python to a name in the module object, rather than a name in the importer, *nested3.py*:

```
# nested3.py
import nested1              # Get module as a whole
nested1.X = 88             # OK: change nested1's X
nested1.printer()

% python nested3.py
88
```

from * Can Obscure the Meaning of Variables

I mentioned this earlier but saved the details for here. Because you don't list the variables you want when using the `from module import *` statement form, it can accidentally overwrite names you're already using in your scope. Worse, it can make it difficult to determine where a variable comes from. This is especially true if the `from *` form is used on more than one imported file.

For example, if you use `from *` on three modules in the following, you'll have no way of knowing what a raw function call really means, short of searching all three external module files—all of which may be in other directories:

```
>>> from module1 import *     # Bad: may overwrite my names silently
>>> from module2 import *     # Worse: no way to tell what we get!
>>> from module3 import *
>>> . . .

>>> func()                    # Huh???
```

The solution again is not to do this: try to explicitly list the attributes you want in your `from` statements, and restrict the `from *` form to at most one imported module per file. That way, any undefined names must by deduction be in the module named in the single `from *`. You can avoid the issue altogether if you always use `import` instead of `from`, but that advice is too harsh; like much else in programming, `from` is a convenient tool if used wisely. Even this example isn't an absolute evil—it's OK for a program to use this technique to collect names in a single space for convenience, as long as it's well known.

reload May Not Impact from Imports

Here's another `from`-related gotcha: as discussed previously, because `from` copies (assigns) names when run, there's no link back to the modules where the names came from. Names imported with `from` simply become references to objects, which happen to have been referenced by the same names in the importee when the `from` ran.

Because of this behavior, reloading the importee has no effect on clients that import its names using `from`. That is, the client's names will still reference the original objects fetched with `from`, even if the names in the original module are later reset:

```
from module import X          # X may not reflect any module reloads!
. . .
from imp import reload
reload(module)                # Changes module, but not my names
X                             # Still references old object
```

To make reloads more effective, use `import` and name qualification instead of `from`. Because qualifications always go back to the module, they will find the new bindings of module names after reloading has updated the module's content *in place*:

```
import module                 # Get module, not names
. . .
from imp import reload
reload(module)                # Changes module in place
module.X                      # Get current X: reflects module reloads
```

As a related consequence, our transitive reloader earlier in this chapter doesn't apply to names fetched with `from`, only `import`; again, if you're going to use reloads, you're probably better off with `import`.

reload, from, and Interactive Testing

In fact, the prior gotcha is even more subtle than it appears. Chapter 3 warned that it's usually better not to launch programs with imports and reloads because of the complexities involved. Things get even worse when `from` is brought into the mix. Python beginners most often stumble onto its issues in scenarios like this—imagine that after opening a module file in a text edit window, you launch an interactive session to load and test your module with `from`:

```
from module import function
function(1, 2, 3)
```

Finding a bug, you jump back to the edit window, make a change, and try to reload the module this way:

```
from imp import reload
reload(module)
```

This doesn't work, because the `from` statement assigned only the name `function`, not `module`. To refer to the module in a `reload`, you have to first bind its name with an `import` statement at least once:

```
from imp import reload
import module
reload(module)
function(1, 2, 3)
```

However, this doesn't quite work either—`reload` updates the module object in place, but as discussed in the preceding section, names like `function` that were copied out of the module in the past still refer to the *old objects*; in this instance, `function` is still the original version of the function. To really get the new function, you must refer to it as `module.function` after the `reload`, or rerun the `from`:

```
from imp import reload
import module
reload(module)
from module import function        # Or give up and use module.function()
function(1, 2, 3)
```

Now, the new version of the function will finally run, but it seems an awful lot of work to get there.

As you can see, there are problems inherent in using `reload` with `from`: not only do you have to remember to reload after imports, but you also have to remember to rerun your `from` statements after reloads. This is complex enough to trip up even an expert once in a while. In fact, the situation has gotten even worse in Python 3.X, because you must also remember to import `reload` itself!

The short story is that you should not expect `reload` and `from` to play together nicely. Again, the best policy is not to combine them at all—use `reload` with `import`, or launch your programs other ways, as suggested in Chapter 3: using the Run→Run Module menu option in IDLE, file icon clicks, system command lines, or the `exec` built-in function.

Recursive from Imports May Not Work

I saved the most bizarre (and, thankfully, obscure) gotcha for last. Because imports execute a file's statements from top to bottom, you need to be careful when using modules that import each other. This is often called *recursive* imports, but the recursion doesn't really occur (in fact, *circular* may be a better term here)—such imports won't get stuck in infinite importing loops. Still, because the statements in a module may not all have been run when it imports another module, some of its names may not yet exist.

If you use `import` to fetch the module as a whole, this probably doesn't matter; the module's names won't be accessed until you later use qualification to fetch their values, and by that time the module is likely complete. But if you use `from` to fetch specific names, you must bear in mind that you will only have access to names in that module that have already been assigned when a recursive import is kicked off.

For instance, consider the following modules, `recur1` and `recur2`. `recur1` assigns a name X, and then imports `recur2` before assigning the name Y. At this point, `recur2` can fetch `recur1` as a whole with an `import`—it already exists in Python's internal modules table, which makes it importable, and also prevents the imports from looping. But if `recur2` uses `from`, it will be able to see only the name X; the name Y, which is assigned below the `import` in `recur1`, doesn't yet exist, so you get an error:

```
# recur1.py
X = 1
```

```
    import recur2                            # Run recur2 now if it doesn't exist
    Y = 2

    # recur2.py
    from recur1 import X                      # OK: "X" already assigned
    from recur1 import Y                      # Error: "Y" not yet assigned

    C:\code> py -3
    >>> import recur1
    Traceback (most recent call last):
      File "<stdin>", line 1, in <module>
      File ".\recur1.py", line 2, in <module>
        import recur2
      File ".\recur2.py", line 2, in <module>
        from recur1 import Y
    ImportError: cannot import name Y
```

Python avoids rerunning recur1's statements when they are imported recursively from recur2 (otherwise the imports would send the script into an infinite loop that might require a Ctrl-C solution or worse), but recur1's namespace is incomplete when it's imported by recur2.

The solution? Don't use from in recursive imports (no, really!). Python won't get stuck in a cycle if you do, but your programs will once again be dependent on the order of the statements in the modules. In fact, there are two ways out of this gotcha:

- You can usually eliminate import cycles like this by careful design—maximizing cohesion and minimizing coupling are good first steps.
- If you can't break the cycles completely, postpone module name accesses by using import and attribute qualification (instead of from and direct names), or by running your froms either inside functions (instead of at the top level of the module) or near the bottom of your file to defer their execution.

There is additional perspective on this issue in the exercises at the end of this chapter —which we've officially reached.

Chapter Summary

This chapter surveyed some more advanced module-related concepts. We studied data hiding techniques, enabling new language features with the __future__ module, the __name__ usage mode variable, transitive reloads, importing by name strings, and more. We also explored and summarized module design issues, wrote some more substantial programs, and looked at common mistakes related to modules to help you avoid them in your code.

The next chapter begins our look at Python's *class*—its object-oriented programming tool. Much of what we've covered in the last few chapters will apply there, too: classes live in modules and are namespaces as well, but they add an extra component to attribute lookup called *inheritance search*. As this is the last chapter in this part of the book, however, before we dive into that topic, be sure to work through this part's set of lab exercises. And before that, here is this chapter's quiz to review the topics covered here.

Test Your Knowledge: Quiz

1. What is significant about variables at the top level of a module whose names begin with a single underscore?
2. What does it mean when a module's __name__ variable is the string "__main__"?
3. If the user interactively types the name of a module to test, how can your code import it?
4. How is changing sys.path different from setting PYTHONPATH to modify the module search path?
5. If the module __future__ allows us to import from the future, can we also import from the past?

Test Your Knowledge: Answers

1. Variables at the top level of a module whose names begin with a single underscore are *not* copied out to the importing scope when the from * statement form is used. They can still be accessed by an import or the normal from statement form, though. The __all__ list is similar, but the logical converse; its contents are the only names that *are* copied out on a from *.
2. If a module's __name__ variable is the string "__main__", it means that the file is being executed as a top-level script instead of being imported from another file in the program. That is, the file is being used as a program, not a library. This usage mode variable supports dual-mode code and tests.
3. User input usually comes into a script as a string; to import the referenced module given its string name, you can build and run an import statement with exec, or pass the string name in a call to the __import__ or importlib.import_module.
4. Changing sys.path only affects one running program (process), and is temporary —the change goes away when the program ends. PYTHONPATH settings live in the operating system—they are picked up globally by all your programs on a machine, and changes to these settings endure after programs exit.
5. No, we can't import from the past in Python. We can install (or stubbornly use) an older version of the language, but the latest Python is generally the best Python (at least within lines—see 2.X longevity!).

Test Your Knowledge: Part V Exercises

See "Part V, Modules and Packages" on page 1485 in Appendix D for the solutions.

1. *Import basics.* Write a program that counts the lines and characters in a file (similar in spirit to part of what *wc* does on Unix). With your text editor, code a Python module called *mymod.py* that exports three top-level names:

   - A `countLines(name)` function that reads an input file and counts the number of lines in it (hint: `file.readlines` does most of the work for you, and `len` does the rest, though you could count with `for` and file iterators to support massive files too).

   - A `countChars(name)` function that reads an input file and counts the number of characters in it (hint: `file.read` returns a single string, which may be used in similar ways).

   - A `test(name)` function that calls both counting functions with a given input filename. Such a filename generally might be passed in, hardcoded, input with the `input` built-in function, or pulled from a command line via the `sys.argv` list shown in this chapter's *formats.py* and *reloadall.py* examples; for now, you can assume it's a passed-in function argument.

   All three `mymod` functions should expect a filename string to be passed in. If you type more than two or three lines per function, you're working much too hard—use the hints I just gave!

   Next, test your module interactively, using `import` and attribute references to fetch your exports. Does your `PYTHONPATH` need to include the directory where you created *mymod.py*? Try running your module on itself: for example, `test("mymod.py")`. Note that `test` opens the file twice; if you're feeling ambitious, you may be able to improve this by passing an open file object into the two count functions (hint: `file.seek(0)` is a file rewind).

2. `from/from *`. Test your `mymod` module from exercise 1 interactively by using `from` to load the exports directly, first by name, then using the `from *` variant to fetch everything.

3. *__main__*. Add a line in your `mymod` module that calls the `test` function automatically only when the module is run as a script, not when it is imported. The line you add will probably test the value of `__name__` for the string `"__main__"`, as shown in this chapter. Try running your module from the system command line; then, import the module and test its functions interactively. Does it still work in both modes?

4. *Nested imports.* Write a second module, *myclient.py*, that imports `mymod` and tests its functions; then run `myclient` from the system command line. If `myclient` uses `from` to fetch from `mymod`, will `mymod`'s functions be accessible from the top level of `myclient`? What if it imports with `import` instead? Try coding both variations in

`myclient` and test interactively by importing `myclient` and inspecting its `__dict__` attribute.

5. *Package imports.* Import your file from a package. Create a subdirectory called *mypkg* nested in a directory on your module import search path, copy or move the *mymod.py* module file you created in exercise 1 or 3 into the new directory, and try to import it with a package import of the form `import mypkg.mymod` and call its functions. Try to fetch your counter functions with a `from` too.

   You'll need to add an *__init__.py* file in the directory your module was moved to make this go, but it should work on all major Python platforms (that's part of the reason Python uses "." as a path separator). The package directory you create can be simply a subdirectory of the one you're working in; if it is, it will be found via the home directory component of the search path, and you won't have to configure your path. Add some code to your *__init__.py*, and see if it runs on each import.

6. *Reloads.* Experiment with module reloads: perform the tests in Chapter 23's *changer.py* example, changing the called function's message and/or behavior repeatedly, without stopping the Python interpreter. Depending on your system, you might be able to edit `changer` in another window, or suspend the Python interpreter and edit in the same window (on Unix, a Ctrl-Z key combination usually suspends the current process, and an `fg` command later resumes it, though a text edit window probably works just as well).

7. *Circular imports.* In the section on recursive (a.k.a. circular) import gotchas, importing `recur1` raised an error. But if you restart Python and import `recur2` interactively, the error doesn't occur—test this and see for yourself. Why do you think it works to import `recur2`, but not `recur1`? (Hint: Python stores new modules in the built-in `sys.modules` table—a dictionary—before running their code; later imports fetch the module from this table first, whether the module is "complete" yet or not.) Now, try running `recur1` as a top-level script file: **python recur1.py**. Do you get the same error that occurs when `recur1` is imported interactively? Why? (Hint: when modules are run as programs, they aren't imported, so this case has the same effect as importing `recur2` interactively; `recur2` is the first module imported.) What happens when you run `recur2` as a script? Circular imports are uncommon and rarely this bizarre in practice. On the other hand, if you can understand why they are a potential problem, you know a lot about Python's import semantics.

Classes and OOP

OOP: The Big Picture

So far in this book, we've been using the term "object" generically. Really, the code written up to this point has been *object-based*—we've passed objects around our scripts, used them in expressions, called their methods, and so on. For our code to qualify as being truly *object-oriented* (OO), though, our objects will generally need to also participate in something called an *inheritance hierarchy*.

This chapter begins our exploration of the Python *class*—a coding structure and device used to implement new kinds of objects in Python that support inheritance. Classes are Python's main object-oriented programming (OOP) tool, so we'll also look at OOP basics along the way in this part of the book. OOP offers a different and often more effective way of programming, in which we factor code to minimize redundancy, and write new programs by *customizing* existing code instead of changing it in place.

In Python, classes are created with a new statement: the `class`. As you'll see, the objects defined with classes can look a lot like the built-in types we studied earlier in the book. In fact, classes really just apply and extend the ideas we've already covered; roughly, they are packages of functions that use and process built-in object types. Classes, though, are designed to create and manage new objects, and support *inheritance*—a mechanism of code customization and reuse above and beyond anything we've seen so far.

One note up front: in Python, OOP is entirely optional, and you don't need to use classes just to get started. You can get plenty of work done with simpler constructs such as functions, or even simple top-level script code. Because using classes well requires some up-front planning, they tend to be of more interest to people who work in *strategic* mode (doing long-term product development) than to people who work in *tactical* mode (where time is in very short supply).

Still, as you'll see in this part of the book, classes turn out to be one of the most useful tools Python provides. When used well, classes can actually cut development time radically. They're also employed in popular Python tools like the tkinter GUI API, so most Python programmers will usually find at least a working knowledge of class basics helpful.

Why Use Classes?

Remember when I told you that programs "do things with stuff" in Chapter 4 and Chapter 10? In simple terms, classes are just a way to define new sorts of *stuff*, reflecting real objects in a program's domain. For instance, suppose we decide to implement that hypothetical pizza-making robot we used as an example in Chapter 16. If we implement it using classes, we can model more of its real-world structure and relationships. Two aspects of OOP prove useful here:

Inheritance
> Pizza-making robots are kinds of robots, so they possess the usual robot-y properties. In OOP terms, we say they "inherit" properties from the general category of all robots. These common properties need to be implemented only once for the general case and can be reused in part or in full by all types of robots we may build in the future.

Composition
> Pizza-making robots are really collections of components that work together as a team. For instance, for our robot to be successful, it might need arms to roll dough, motors to maneuver to the oven, and so on. In OOP parlance, our robot is an example of composition; it contains other objects that it activates to do its bidding. Each component might be coded as a class, which defines its own behavior and relationships.

General OOP ideas like inheritance and composition apply to any application that can be decomposed into a set of objects. For example, in typical GUI systems, interfaces are written as collections of widgets—buttons, labels, and so on—which are all drawn when their container is drawn (*composition*). Moreover, we may be able to write our own custom widgets—buttons with unique fonts, labels with new color schemes, and the like—which are specialized versions of more general interface devices (*inheritance*).

From a more concrete programming perspective, classes are Python program units, just like functions and modules: they are another compartment for packaging logic and data. In fact, classes also define new namespaces, much like modules. But, compared to other program units we've already seen, classes have three critical distinctions that make them more useful when it comes to building new objects:

Multiple instances
> Classes are essentially factories for generating one or more objects. Every time we call a class, we generate a new object with a distinct namespace. Each object generated from a class has access to the class's attributes *and* gets a namespace of its own for data that varies per object. This is similar to the per-call state retention of Chapter 17's closure functions, but is explicit and natural in classes, and is just one of the things that classes do. Classes offer a complete programming solution.

Customization via inheritance

Classes also support the OOP notion of inheritance; we can extend a class by re-defining its attributes outside the class itself in new software components coded as subclasses. More generally, classes can build up namespace hierarchies, which define names to be used by objects created from classes in the hierarchy. This supports multiple customizable behaviors more directly than other tools.

Operator overloading

By providing special protocol methods, classes can define objects that respond to the sorts of operations we saw at work on built-in types. For instance, objects made with classes can be sliced, concatenated, indexed, and so on. Python provides hooks that classes can use to intercept and implement any built-in type operation.

At its base, the mechanism of OOP in Python is largely just *two bits of magic*: a special first argument in functions (to receive the subject of a call) and inheritance attribute search (to support programming by customization). Other than this, the model is largely just functions that ultimately process built-in types. While not radically new, though, OOP adds an extra layer of structure that supports better programming than flat procedural models. Along with the functional tools we met earlier, it represents a major abstraction step above computer hardware that helps us build more sophisticated programs.

OOP from 30,000 Feet

Before we see what this all means in terms of code, I'd like to say a few words about the general ideas behind OOP. If you've never done anything object-oriented in your life before now, some of the terminology in this chapter may seem a bit perplexing on the first pass. Moreover, the motivation for these terms may be elusive until you've had a chance to study the ways that programmers apply them in larger systems. OOP is as much an experience as a technology.

Attribute Inheritance Search

The good news is that OOP is much simpler to understand and use in Python than in other languages, such as C++ or Java. As a dynamically typed scripting language, Python removes much of the syntactic clutter and complexity that clouds OOP in other tools. In fact, much of the OOP story in Python boils down to this expression:

```
object.attribute
```

We've been using this expression throughout the book to access module attributes, call methods of objects, and so on. When we say this to an object that is derived from a `class` statement, however, the expression kicks off a *search* in Python—it searches a tree of linked objects, looking for the first appearance of *attribute* that it can find. When classes are involved, the preceding Python expression effectively translates to the following in natural language:

Find the first occurrence of *attribute* by looking in *object*, then in all classes above it, from bottom to top and left to right.

In other words, attribute fetches are simply tree searches. The term *inheritance* is applied because objects lower in a tree inherit attributes attached to objects higher in that tree. As the search proceeds from the bottom up, in a sense, the objects linked into a tree are the union of all the attributes defined in all their tree parents, all the way up the tree.

In Python, this is all very literal: we really do build up trees of linked objects with code, and Python really does climb this tree at runtime searching for attributes every time we use the *object.attribute* expression. To make this more concrete, Figure 26-1 sketches an example of one of these trees.

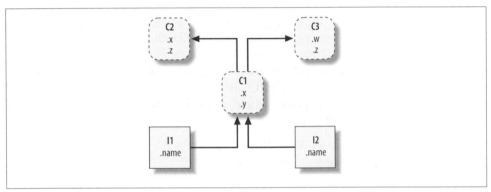

Figure 26-1. A class tree, with two instances at the bottom (I1 and I2), a class above them (C1), and two superclasses at the top (C2 and C3). All of these objects are namespaces (packages of variables), and the inheritance search is simply a search of the tree from bottom to top looking for the lowest occurrence of an attribute name. Code implies the shape of such trees.

In this figure, there is a tree of five objects labeled with variables, all of which have attached attributes, ready to be searched. More specifically, this tree links together three *class objects* (the ovals C1, C2, and C3) and two *instance objects* (the rectangles I1 and I2) into an inheritance search tree. Notice that in the Python object model, classes and the instances you generate from them are two distinct object types:

Classes
> Serve as instance factories. Their attributes provide behavior—data and functions —that is inherited by all the instances generated from them (e.g., a function to compute an employee's salary from pay and hours).

Instances
> Represent the concrete items in a program's domain. Their attributes record data that varies per specific object (e.g., an employee's Social Security number).

In terms of search trees, an instance inherits attributes from its class, and a class inherits attributes from all classes above it in the tree.

In Figure 26-1, we can further categorize the ovals by their relative positions in the tree. We usually call classes higher in the tree (like C2 and C3) *superclasses*; classes lower in the tree (like C1) are known as *subclasses*. These terms refer to both relative tree positions and roles. Superclasses provide behavior shared by all their subclasses, but because the search proceeds from the bottom up, subclasses may override behavior defined in their superclasses by redefining superclass names lower in the tree.[1]

As these last few words are really the crux of the matter of software customization in OOP, let's expand on this concept. Suppose we build up the tree in Figure 26-1, and then say this:

```
I2.w
```

Right away, this code invokes inheritance. Because this is an *object.attribute* expression, it triggers a search of the tree in Figure 26-1—Python will search for the attribute w by looking in I2 and above. Specifically, it will search the linked objects in this order:

```
I2, C1, C2, C3
```

and stop at the first attached w it finds (or raise an error if w isn't found at all). In this case, w won't be found until C3 is searched because it appears only in that object. In other words, I2.w resolves to C3.w by virtue of the automatic search. In OOP terminology, I2 "inherits" the attribute w from C3.

Ultimately, the two instances inherit four attributes from their classes: w, x, y, and z. Other attribute references will wind up following different paths in the tree. For example:

- I1.x and I2.x both find x in C1 and stop because C1 is lower than C2.
- I1.y and I2.y both find y in C1 because that's the only place y appears.
- I1.z and I2.z both find z in C2 because C2 is further to the left than C3.
- I2.name finds name in I2 without climbing the tree at all.

Trace these searches through the tree in Figure 26-1 to get a feel for how inheritance searches work in Python.

The first item in the preceding list is perhaps the most important to notice—because C1 redefines the attribute x lower in the tree, it effectively *replaces* the version above it in C2. As you'll see in a moment, such redefinitions are at the heart of software customization in OOP—by redefining and replacing the attribute, C1 effectively customizes what it inherits from its superclasses.

---

1. In other literature and circles, you may also occasionally see the terms *base classes* and *derived classes* used to describe superclasses and subclasses, respectively. Python people and this book tend to use the latter terms.

Classes and Instances

Although they are technically two separate object types in the Python model, the classes and instances we put in these trees are almost identical—each type's main purpose is to serve as another kind of *namespace*—a package of variables, and a place where we can attach attributes. If classes and instances therefore sound like modules, they should; however, the objects in class trees also have automatically searched links to other namespace objects, and classes correspond to statements, not entire files.

The primary difference between classes and instances is that classes are a kind of *factory* for generating instances. For example, in a realistic application, we might have an `Employee` class that defines what it means to be an employee; from that class, we generate actual `Employee` instances. This is another difference between classes and modules—we only ever have one instance of a given module in memory (that's why we have to reload a module to get its new code), but with classes, we can make as many instances as we need.

Operationally, classes will usually have functions attached to them (e.g., `computeSalary`), and the instances will have more basic data items used by the class's functions (e.g., `hoursWorked`). In fact, the object-oriented model is not that different from the classic data-processing model of *programs* plus *records*—in OOP, instances are like records with "data," and classes are the "programs" for processing those records. In OOP, though, we also have the notion of an inheritance hierarchy, which supports software customization better than earlier models.

Method Calls

In the prior section, we saw how the attribute reference `I2.w` in our example class tree was translated to `C3.w` by the inheritance search procedure in Python. Perhaps just as important to understand as the inheritance of attributes, though, is what happens when we try to call *methods*—functions attached to classes as attributes.

If this `I2.w` reference is a *function* call, what it really means is "call the `C3.w` function to process `I2`." That is, Python will automatically map the call `I2.w()` into the call `C3.w(I2)`, passing in the instance as the first argument to the inherited function.

In fact, whenever we call a function attached to a class in this fashion, an instance of the class is always implied. This implied subject or context is part of the reason we refer to this as an *object-oriented* model—there is always a subject object when an operation is run. In a more realistic example, we might invoke a method called `giveRaise` attached as an attribute to an `Employee` class; such a call has no meaning unless qualified with the employee to whom the raise should be given.

As we'll see later, Python passes in the implied instance to a special first argument in the method, called `self` by convention. Methods go through this argument to process the subject of the call. As we'll also learn, methods can be called through either an instance—`bob.giveRaise()`—or a class—`Employee.giveRaise(bob)`—and both forms serve purposes in our scripts. These calls also illustrate both of the key ideas in OOP: to run a `bob.giveRaise()` method call, Python:

1. Looks up `giveRaise` from `bob`, by inheritance search
2. Passes `bob` to the located `giveRaise` function, in the special `self` argument

When you call `Employee.giveRaise(bob)`, you're just performing both steps yourself. This description is technically the default case (Python has additional method types we'll meet later), but it applies to the vast majority of the OOP code written in the language. To see how methods receive their subjects, though, we need to move on to some code.

Coding Class Trees

Although we are speaking in the abstract here, there is tangible code behind all these ideas, of course. We construct trees and their objects with `class` statements and class calls, which we'll meet in more detail later. In short:

- Each `class` statement generates a new class object.
- Each time a class is called, it generates a new instance object.
- Instances are automatically linked to the classes from which they are created.
- Classes are automatically linked to their superclasses according to the way we list them in parentheses in a `class` header line; the left-to-right order there gives the order in the tree.

To build the tree in Figure 26-1, for example, we would run Python code of the following form. Like function definition, classes are normally coded in module files and are run during an import (I've omitted the guts of the `class` statements here for brevity):

```
class C2: ...                    # Make class objects (ovals)
class C3: ...
class C1(C2, C3): ...            # Linked to superclasses (in this order)

I1 = C1()                        # Make instance objects (rectangles)
I2 = C1()                        # Linked to their classes
```

Here, we build the three class objects by running three `class` statements, and make the two instance objects by calling the class `C1` twice, as though it were a function. The instances remember the class they were made from, and the class `C1` remembers its listed superclasses.

Technically, this example is using something called *multiple inheritance*, which simply means that a class has more than one superclass above it in the class tree—a useful technique when you wish to combine multiple tools. In Python, if there is more than one superclass listed in parentheses in a `class` statement (like `C1`'s here), their left-to-right order gives the order in which those superclasses will be searched for attributes by inheritance. The leftmost version of a name is used by default, though you can always choose a name by asking for it from the class it lives in (e.g., C3.z).

Because of the way inheritance searches proceed, the object to which you attach an attribute turns out to be crucial—it determines the name's scope. Attributes attached to instances pertain only to those single instances, but attributes attached to classes are shared by all their subclasses and instances. Later, we'll study the code that hangs attributes on these objects in depth. As we'll find:

- Attributes are usually attached to classes by assignments made at the top level in class statement blocks, and not nested inside function def statements there.

- Attributes are usually attached to instances by assignments to the special argument passed to functions coded inside classes, called self.

For example, classes provide behavior for their instances with method functions we create by coding def statements inside class statements. Because such nested defs assign names within the class, they wind up attaching attributes to the class object that will be inherited by all instances and subclasses:

```
class C2: ...                    # Make superclass objects
class C3: ...

class C1(C2, C3):                # Make and link class C1
    def setname(self, who):      # Assign name: C1.setname
        self.name = who          # Self is either I1 or I2

I1 = C1()                        # Make two instances
I2 = C1()
I1.setname('bob')                # Sets I1.name to 'bob'
I2.setname('sue')                # Sets I2.name to 'sue'
print(I1.name)                   # Prints 'bob'
```

There's nothing syntactically unique about def in this context. Operationally, though, when a def appears inside a class like this, it is usually known as a *method*, and it automatically receives a special first argument—called self by convention—that provides a handle back to the instance to be processed. Any values you pass to the method yourself go to arguments after self (here, to who).[2]

Because classes are factories for multiple instances, their methods usually go through this automatically passed-in self argument whenever they need to fetch or set attributes of the particular instance being processed by a method call. In the preceding code, self is used to store a name in one of two instances.

Like simple variables, attributes of classes and instances are not declared ahead of time, but spring into existence the first time they are assigned values. When a method assigns to a self attribute, it creates or changes an attribute in an instance at the bottom of the

---

[2]. If you've ever used C++ or Java, you'll recognize that Python's self is the same as the this pointer, but self is always explicit in both headers and bodies of Python methods to make attribute accesses more obvious: a name has fewer possible meanings.

class tree (i.e., one of the rectangles in Figure 26-1) because `self` automatically refers to the instance being processed—the subject of the call.

In fact, because all the objects in class trees are just namespace objects, we can fetch or set any of their attributes by going through the appropriate names. Saying `C1.setname` is as valid as saying `I1.setname`, as long as the names `C1` and `I1` are in your code's scopes.

Operator Overloading

As currently coded, our `C1` class doesn't attach a `name` attribute to an instance until the `setname` method is called. Indeed, referencing `I1.name` before calling `I1.setname` would produce an undefined name error. If a class wants to guarantee that an attribute like `name` is always set in its instances, it more typically will fill out the attribute at construction time, like this:

```
class C2: ...                   # Make superclass objects
class C3: ...

class C1(C2, C3):
    def __init__(self, who):    # Set name when constructed
        self.name = who         # Self is either I1 or I2

I1 = C1('bob')                  # Sets I1.name to 'bob'
I2 = C1('sue')                  # Sets I2.name to 'sue'
print(I1.name)                  # Prints 'bob'
```

If it's coded or inherited, Python automatically calls a method named `__init__` each time an instance is generated from a class. The new instance is passed in to the `self` argument of `__init__` as usual, and any values listed in parentheses in the class call go to arguments two and beyond. The effect here is to initialize instances when they are made, without requiring extra method calls.

The `__init__` method is known as the *constructor* because of when it is run. It's the most commonly used representative of a larger class of methods called *operator overloading methods*, which we'll discuss in more detail in the chapters that follow. Such methods are inherited in class trees as usual and have double underscores at the start and end of their names to make them distinct. Python runs them automatically when instances that support them appear in the corresponding operations, and they are mostly an alternative to using simple method calls. They're also optional: if omitted, the operations are not supported. If no `__init__` is present, class calls return an empty instance, without initializing it.

For example, to implement set intersection, a class might either provide a method named `intersect`, or overload the `&` expression operator to dispatch to the required logic by coding a method named `__and__`. Because the operator scheme makes instances look and feel more like built-in types, it allows some classes to provide a consistent and natural interface, and be compatible with code that expects a built-in type. Still, apart from the `__init__` constructor—which appears in most realistic classes—many programs may be better off with simpler named methods unless their objects are similar to built-ins. A `giveRaise` may make sense for an `Employee`, but a & might not.

OOP Is About Code Reuse

And that, along with a few syntax details, is most of the OOP story in Python. Of course, there's a bit more to it than just inheritance. For example, operator overloading is much more general than I've described so far—classes may also provide their own implementations of operations such as indexing, fetching attributes, printing, and more. By and large, though, OOP is about looking up attributes in trees with a special first argument in functions.

So why would we be interested in building and searching trees of objects? Although it takes some experience to see how, when used well, classes support code *reuse* in ways that other Python program components cannot. In fact, this is their highest purpose. With classes, we code by customizing existing software, instead of either changing existing code in place or starting from scratch for each new project. This turns out to be a powerful paradigm in realistic programming.

At a fundamental level, classes are really just packages of functions and other names, much like modules. However, the automatic attribute inheritance search that we get with classes supports customization of software above and beyond what we can do with modules and functions. Moreover, classes provide a natural structure for code that packages and localizes logic and names, and so aids in debugging.

For instance, because methods are simply functions with a special first argument, we can mimic some of their behavior by manually passing objects to be processed to simple functions. The participation of methods in class inheritance, though, allows us to naturally customize existing software by coding subclasses with new method definitions, rather than changing existing code in place. There is really no such concept with modules and functions.

Polymorphism and classes

As an example, suppose you're assigned the task of implementing an employee database application. As a Python OOP programmer, you might begin by coding a general superclass that defines default behaviors common to all the kinds of employees in your organization:

```
class Employee:                     # General superclass
    def computeSalary(self): ...    # Common or default behaviors
    def giveRaise(self): ...
    def promote(self): ...
    def retire(self): ...
```

Once you've coded this general behavior, you can specialize it for each specific kind of employee to reflect how the various types differ from the norm. That is, you can code subclasses that customize just the bits of behavior that differ per employee type; the rest of the employee types' behavior will be inherited from the more general class. For example, if engineers have a unique salary computation rule (perhaps it's not hours times rate), you can replace just that one method in a subclass:

```
class Engineer(Employee):              # Specialized subclass
    def computeSalary(self): ...       # Something custom here
```

Because the `computeSalary` version here appears lower in the class tree, it will replace (override) the general version in `Employee`. You then create instances of the kinds of employee classes that the real employees belong to, to get the correct behavior:

```
bob = Employee()                       # Default behavior
sue = Employee()                       # Default behavior
tom = Engineer()                       # Custom salary calculator
```

Notice that you can make instances of any class in a tree, not just the ones at the bottom —the class you make an instance from determines the level at which the attribute search will begin, and thus which versions of the methods it will employ.

Ultimately, these three instance objects might wind up embedded in a larger container object—for instance, a list, or an instance of another class—that represents a department or company using the composition idea mentioned at the start of this chapter. When you later ask for these employees' salaries, they will be computed according to the classes from which the objects were made, due to the principles of the inheritance search:

```
company = [bob, sue, tom]              # A composite object
for emp in company:
    print(emp.computeSalary())         # Run this object's version: default or custom
```

This is yet another instance of the idea of *polymorphism* introduced in Chapter 4 and expanded in Chapter 16. Recall that polymorphism means that the meaning of an operation depends on the object being operated on. That is, code shouldn't care about what an object *is*, only about what it *does*. Here, the method `computeSalary` is located by inheritance search in each object before it is called. The net effect is that we automatically run the correct version for the object being processed. Trace the code to see why.[3]

In other applications, polymorphism might also be used to hide (i.e., *encapsulate*) interface differences. For example, a program that processes data streams might be coded to expect objects with input and output methods, without caring what those methods actually do:

```
def processor(reader, converter, writer):
    while True:
        data = reader.read()
```

---

3. The company list in this example could be a database if stored in a file with Python object pickling, introduced in Chapter 9, to make the employees persistent. Python also comes with a module named `shelve`, which allows the pickled representation of class instances to be stored in an access-by-key filesystem; we'll deploy it in Chapter 28.

```
            if not data: break
            data = converter(data)
            writer.write(data)
```

By passing in instances of subclasses that specialize the required `read` and `write` method interfaces for various data sources, we can reuse the `processor` function for any data source we need to use, both now and in the future:

```
class Reader:
    def read(self): ...              # Default behavior and tools
    def other(self): ...
class FileReader(Reader):
    def read(self): ...              # Read from a local file
class SocketReader(Reader):
    def read(self): ...              # Read from a network socket
...
processor(FileReader(...),   Converter, FileWriter(...))
processor(SocketReader(...), Converter, TapeWriter(...))
processor(FtpReader(...),    Converter, XmlWriter(...))
```

Moreover, because the internal implementations of those `read` and `write` methods have been factored into single locations, they can be changed without impacting code such as this that uses them. The `processor` function might even be a class itself to allow the conversion logic of `converter` to be filled in by inheritance, and to allow readers and writers to be embedded by composition (we'll see how this works later in this part of the book).

Programming by customization

Once you get used to programming this way (by software customization), you'll find that when it's time to write a new program, much of your work may already be done —your task largely becomes one of mixing together existing superclasses that already implement the behavior required by your program. For example, someone else might have written the `Employee`, `Reader`, and `Writer` classes in this section's examples for use in completely different programs. If so, you get all of that person's code "for free."

In fact, in many application domains, you can fetch or purchase collections of superclasses, known as *frameworks*, that implement common programming tasks as classes, ready to be mixed into your applications. These frameworks might provide database interfaces, testing protocols, GUI toolkits, and so on. With frameworks, you often simply code a subclass that fills in an expected method or two; the framework classes higher in the tree do most of the work for you. Programming in such an OOP world is just a matter of combining and specializing already debugged code by writing subclasses of your own.

Of course, it takes a while to learn how to leverage classes to achieve such OOP utopia. In practice, object-oriented work also entails substantial design work to fully realize the code reuse benefits of classes—to this end, programmers have begun cataloging common OOP structures, known as *design patterns*, to help with design issues. The actual code you write to do OOP in Python, though, is so simple that it will not in itself pose an additional obstacle to your OOP quest. To see why, you'll have to move on to Chapter 27.

Chapter Summary

We took an abstract look at classes and OOP in this chapter, taking in the big picture before we dive into syntax details. As we've seen, OOP is mostly about an argument named `self`, and a search for attributes in trees of linked objects called inheritance. Objects at the bottom of the tree inherit attributes from objects higher up in the tree —a feature that enables us to program by customizing code, rather than changing it or starting from scratch. When used well, this model of programming can cut development time radically.

The next chapter will begin to fill in the coding details behind the picture painted here. As we get deeper into Python classes, though, keep in mind that the OOP model in Python is very simple; as we've seen here, it's really just about looking up attributes in object trees and a special function argument. Before we move on, here's a quick quiz to review what we've covered here.

Test Your Knowledge: Quiz

1. What is the main point of OOP in Python?
2. Where does an inheritance search look for an attribute?
3. What is the difference between a class object and an instance object?
4. Why is the first argument in a class's method function special?
5. What is the `__init__` method used for?
6. How do you create a class instance?
7. How do you create a class?
8. How do you specify a class's superclasses?

Test Your Knowledge: Answers

1. OOP is about code reuse—you factor code to minimize redundancy and program by customizing what already exists instead of changing code in place or starting from scratch.
2. An inheritance search looks for an attribute first in the instance object, then in the class the instance was created from, then in all higher superclasses, progressing from the bottom to the top of the object tree, and from left to right (by default). The search stops at the first place the attribute is found. Because the lowest version of a name found along the way wins, class hierarchies naturally support customization by extension in new subclasses.

3. Both class and instance objects are namespaces (packages of variables that appear as attributes). The main difference between them is that classes are a kind of factory for creating multiple instances. Classes also support operator overloading methods, which instances inherit, and treat any functions nested in the class as methods for processing instances.

4. The first argument in a class's method function is special because it always receives the instance object that is the implied subject of the method call. It's usually called `self` by convention. Because method functions always have this implied subject and object context by default, we say they are "object-oriented" (i.e., designed to process or change objects).

5. If the `__init__` method is coded or inherited in a class, Python calls it automatically each time an instance of that class is created. It's known as the constructor method; it is passed the new instance implicitly, as well as any arguments passed explicitly to the class name. It's also the most commonly used operator overloading method. If no `__init__` method is present, instances simply begin life as empty namespaces.

6. You create a class instance by calling the class name as though it were a function; any arguments passed into the class name show up as arguments two and beyond in the `__init__` constructor method. The new instance remembers the class it was created from for inheritance purposes.

7. You create a class by running a `class` statement; like function definitions, these statements normally run when the enclosing module file is imported (more on this in the next chapter).

8. You specify a class's superclasses by listing them in parentheses in the `class` statement, after the new class's name. The left-to-right order in which the classes are listed in the parentheses gives the left-to-right inheritance search order in the class tree.

Class Coding Basics

Now that we've talked about OOP in the abstract, it's time to see how this translates to actual code. This chapter begins to fill in the syntax details behind the class model in Python.

If you've never been exposed to OOP in the past, classes can seem somewhat complicated if taken in a single dose. To make class coding easier to absorb, we'll begin our detailed exploration of OOP by taking a first look at some basic classes in action in this chapter. We'll expand on the details introduced here in later chapters of this part of the book, but in their basic form, Python classes are easy to understand.

In fact, classes have just three primary distinctions. At a base level, they are mostly just namespaces, much like the modules we studied in Part V. Unlike modules, though, classes also have support for generating multiple objects, for namespace inheritance, and for operator overloading. Let's begin our `class` statement tour by exploring each of these three distinctions in turn.

Classes Generate Multiple Instance Objects

To understand how the multiple objects idea works, you have to first understand that there are two kinds of objects in Python's OOP model: *class* objects and *instance* objects. Class objects provide default behavior and serve as factories for instance objects. Instance objects are the real objects your programs process—each is a namespace in its own right, but inherits (i.e., has automatic access to) names in the class from which it was created. Class objects come from statements, and instances come from calls; each time you call a class, you get a new instance of that class.

This object-generation concept is very different from most of the other program constructs we've seen so far in this book. In effect, classes are essentially *factories* for generating multiple instances. By contrast, only one copy of each module is ever imported into a single program. In fact, this is why `reload` works as it does, updating a single-instance shared object in place. With classes, each instance can have its own, independent data, supporting multiple versions of the object that the class models.

In this role, class instances are similar to the per-call state of the *closure* (a.k.a. factory) functions of Chapter 17, but this is a natural part of the class model, and state in classes is explicit attributes instead of implicit scope references. Moreover, this is just part of what classes do—they also support customization by inheritance, operator overloading, and multiple behaviors via methods. Generally speaking, classes are a more complete programming tool, though OOP and *function programming* are not mutually exclusive paradigms. We may combine them by using functional tools in methods, by coding methods that are themselves generators, by writing user-defined iterators (as we'll see in Chapter 30), and so on.

The following is a quick summary of the bare essentials of Python OOP in terms of its two object types. As you'll see, Python classes are in some ways similar to both `def`s and modules, but they may be quite different from what you're used to in other languages.

Class Objects Provide Default Behavior

When we run a `class` statement, we get a class object. Here's a rundown of the main properties of Python classes:

- **The class statement creates a class object and assigns it a name**. Just like the function `def` statement, the Python `class` statement is an *executable* statement. When reached and run, it generates a new class object and assigns it to the name in the `class` header. Also, like `def`s, `class` statements typically run when the files they are coded in are first imported.

- **Assignments inside class statements make class attributes**. Just like in module files, top-level assignments within a `class` statement (not nested in a `def`) generate attributes in a class object. Technically, the `class` statement defines a local scope that *morphs* into the attribute namespace of the class object, just like a module's global scope. After running a `class` statement, class attributes are accessed by name qualification: *object.name*.

- **Class attributes provide object state and behavior**. Attributes of a class object record state information and behavior to be shared by all instances created from the class; function `def` statements nested inside a `class` generate *methods*, which process instances.

Instance Objects Are Concrete Items

When we call a class object, we get an instance object. Here's an overview of the key points behind class instances:

- **Calling a class object like a function makes a new instance object**. Each time a class is called, it creates and returns a new instance object. Instances represent concrete items in your program's domain.

- **Each instance object inherits class attributes and gets its own namespace**.
  Instance objects created from classes are new namespaces; they start out empty
  but inherit attributes that live in the class objects from which they were generated.
- **Assignments to attributes of self in methods make per-instance attributes**.
  Inside a class's method functions, the first argument (called self by convention)
  references the instance object being processed; assignments to attributes of self
  create or change data in the instance, not the class.

The end result is that classes define common, shared data and behavior, and generate
instances. Instances reflect concrete application entities, and record per-instance data
that may vary per object.

A First Example

Let's turn to a real example to show how these ideas work in practice. To begin, let's
define a class named FirstClass by running a Python class statement interactively:

```
>>> class FirstClass:                    # Define a class object
        def setdata(self, value):        # Define class's methods
            self.data = value            # self is the instance
        def display(self):
            print(self.data)             # self.data: per instance
```

We're working interactively here, but typically, such a statement would be run when
the module file it is coded in is imported. Like functions created with defs, this class
won't even exist until Python reaches and runs this statement.

Like all compound statements, the class starts with a header line that lists the class
name, followed by a body of one or more nested and (usually) indented statements.
Here, the nested statements are defs; they define functions that implement the behavior
the class means to export.

As we learned in Part IV, def is really an assignment. Here, it assigns function objects
to the names setdata and display in the class statement's scope, and so generates
attributes attached to the class—FirstClass.setdata and FirstClass.display. In fact,
any name assigned at the top level of the class's nested block becomes an attribute of
the class.

Functions inside a class are usually called *methods*. They're coded with normal defs,
and they support everything we've learned about functions already (they can have defaults, return values, yield items on request, and so on). But in a method function, the
first argument automatically receives an implied instance object when called—the subject of the call. We need to create a couple of instances to see how this works:

```
>>> x = FirstClass()                     # Make two instances
>>> y = FirstClass()                     # Each is a new namespace
```

By *calling* the class this way (notice the parentheses), we generate instance objects,
which are just namespaces that have access to their classes' attributes. Properly speak-

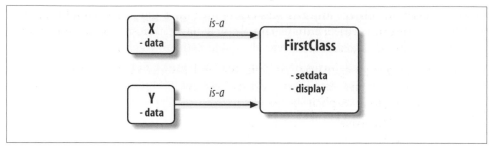

Figure 27-1. Classes and instances are linked namespace objects in a class tree that is searched by inheritance. Here, the "data" attribute is found in instances, but "setdata" and "display" are in the class above them.

ing, at this point, we have three objects: two instances and a class. Really, we have three linked namespaces, as sketched in Figure 27-1. In OOP terms, we say that x "is a" FirstClass, as is y—they both inherit names attached to the class.

The two instances start out empty but have links back to the class from which they were generated. If we qualify an instance with the name of an attribute that lives in the class object, Python fetches the name from the class by inheritance search (unless it also lives in the instance):

```
>>> x.setdata("King Arthur")          # Call methods: self is x
>>> y.setdata(3.14159)                 # Runs: FirstClass.setdata(y, 3.14159)
```

Neither x nor y has a `setdata` attribute of its own, so to find it, Python follows the link from instance to class. And that's about all there is to inheritance in Python: it happens at attribute qualification time, and it just involves looking up names in linked objects —here, by following the is-a links in Figure 27-1.

In the `setdata` function inside `FirstClass`, the value passed in is assigned to `self.data`. Within a method, `self`—the name given to the leftmost argument by convention—automatically refers to the instance being processed (x or y), so the assignments store values in the instances' namespaces, not the class's; that's how the `data` names in Figure 27-1 are created.

Because classes can generate multiple instances, methods must go through the `self` argument to get to the instance to be processed. When we call the class's `display` method to print `self.data`, we see that it's different in each instance; on the other hand, the name `display` itself is the same in x and y, as it comes (is inherited) from the class:

```
>>> x.display()                        # self.data differs in each instance
King Arthur
>>> y.display()                        # Runs: FirstClass.display(y)
3.14159
```

Notice that we stored different object types in the `data` member in each instance—a string and a floating-point number. As with everything else in Python, there are no declarations for instance attributes (sometimes called *members*); they spring into existence the first time they are assigned values, just like simple variables. In fact, if we were to call `display` on one of our instances *before* calling `setdata`, we would trigger an undefined name error—the attribute named `data` doesn't even exist in memory until it is assigned within the `setdata` method.

As another way to appreciate how dynamic this model is, consider that we can change instance attributes in the class itself, by assigning to `self` in methods, or *outside* the class, by assigning to an explicit instance object:

```
>>> x.data = "New value"          # Can get/set attributes
>>> x.display()                   # Outside the class too
New value
```

Although less common, we could even generate an entirely *new* attribute in the instance's namespace by assigning to its name outside the class's method functions:

```
>>> x.anothername = "spam"        # Can set new attributes here too!
```

This would attach a new attribute called `anothername`, which may or may not be used by any of the class's methods, to the instance object x. Classes usually create all of the instance's attributes by assignment to the `self` argument, but they don't have to— programs can fetch, change, or create attributes on any objects to which they have references.

It usually doesn't make sense to add data that the class cannot use, and it's possible to prevent this with extra "privacy" code based on attribute access operator overloading, as we'll discuss later in this book (see Chapter 30 and Chapter 39). Still, free attribute access translates to less syntax, and there are cases where it's even useful—for example, in coding data records of the sort we'll see later in this chapter.

Classes Are Customized by Inheritance

Let's move on to the second major distinction of classes. Besides serving as factories for generating multiple instance objects, classes also allow us to make changes by introducing new components (called *subclasses*), instead of changing existing components in place.

As we've seen, instance objects generated from a class inherit the class's attributes. Python also allows classes to inherit from other classes, opening the door to coding *hierarchies* of classes that specialize behavior—by redefining attributes in subclasses that appear lower in the hierarchy, we override the more general definitions of those attributes higher in the tree. In effect, the further down the hierarchy we go, the more specific the software becomes. Here, too, there is no parallel with modules, whose attributes live in a single, flat namespace that is not as amenable to customization.

In Python, instances inherit from classes, and classes inherit from superclasses. Here are the key ideas behind the machinery of attribute inheritance:

- **Superclasses are listed in parentheses in a class header**. To make a class inherit attributes from another class, just list the other class in parentheses in the new `class` statement's header line. The class that inherits is usually called a *subclass*, and the class that is inherited from is its *superclass*.

- **Classes inherit attributes from their superclasses**. Just as instances inherit the attribute names defined in their classes, classes inherit all of the attribute names defined in their superclasses; Python finds them automatically when they're accessed, if they don't exist in the subclasses.

- **Instances inherit attributes from all accessible classes**. Each instance gets names from the class it's generated from, as well as all of that class's superclasses. When looking for a name, Python checks the instance, then its class, then all superclasses.

- **Each *object.attribute* reference invokes a new, independent search**. Python performs an independent search of the class tree for each attribute fetch expression. This includes references to instances and classes made outside `class` statements (e.g., X.*attr*), as well as references to attributes of the `self` instance argument in a class's method functions. Each `self`.*attr* expression in a method invokes a new search for *attr* in `self` and above.

- **Logic changes are made by subclassing, not by changing superclasses**. By redefining superclass names in subclasses lower in the hierarchy (class tree), subclasses replace and thus customize inherited behavior.

The net effect—and the main purpose of all this searching—is that classes support factoring and customization of code better than any other language tool we've seen so far. On the one hand, they allow us to minimize code redundancy (and so reduce maintenance costs) by factoring operations into a single, shared implementation; on the other, they allow us to program by customizing what already exists, rather than changing it in place or starting from scratch.

 Strictly speaking, Python's *inheritance* is a bit richer than described here, when we factor in new-style descriptors and metaclasses—advanced topics we'll study later—but we can safely restrict our scope to instances and their classes, both at this point in the book and in most Python application code. We'll define inheritance formally in Chapter 40.

A Second Example

To illustrate the role of inheritance, this next example builds on the previous one. First, we'll define a new class, `SecondClass`, that inherits all of `FirstClass`'s names and provides one of its own:

```
>>> class SecondClass(FirstClass):          # Inherits setdata
        def display(self):                   # Changes display
            print('Current value = "%s"' % self.data)
```

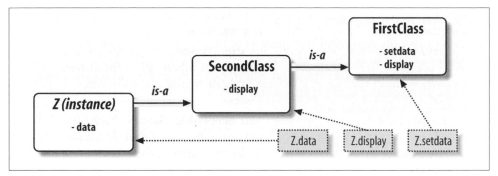

Figure 27-2. Specialization: overriding inherited names by redefining them in extensions lower in the class tree. Here, SecondClass redefines and so customizes the "display" method for its instances.

SecondClass defines the display method to print with a different format. By defining an attribute with the same name as an attribute in FirstClass, SecondClass effectively replaces the display attribute in its superclass.

Recall that inheritance searches proceed upward from instances to subclasses to superclasses, stopping at the first appearance of the attribute name that it finds. In this case, since the display name in SecondClass will be found before the one in First Class, we say that SecondClass *overrides* FirstClass's display. Sometimes we call this act of replacing attributes by redefining them lower in the tree *overloading*.

The net effect here is that SecondClass specializes FirstClass by changing the behavior of the display method. On the other hand, SecondClass (and any instances created from it) still inherits the setdata method in FirstClass verbatim. Let's make an instance to demonstrate:

```
>>> z = SecondClass()
>>> z.setdata(42)          # Finds setdata in FirstClass
>>> z.display()            # Finds overridden method in SecondClass
Current value = "42"
```

As before, we make a SecondClass instance object by calling it. The setdata call still runs the version in FirstClass, but this time the display attribute comes from Second Class and prints a custom message. Figure 27-2 sketches the namespaces involved.

Now, here's a crucial thing to notice about OOP: the specialization introduced in SecondClass is completely *external* to FirstClass. That is, it doesn't affect existing or future FirstClass objects, like the x from the prior example:

```
>>> x.display()            # x is still a FirstClass instance (old message)
New value
```

Rather than *changing* FirstClass, we *customized* it. Naturally, this is an artificial example, but as a rule, because inheritance allows us to make changes like this in external components (i.e., in subclasses), classes often support extension and reuse better than functions or modules can.

Classes Are Attributes in Modules

Before we move on, remember that there's nothing magic about a class name. It's just a variable assigned to an object when the `class` statement runs, and the object can be referenced with any normal expression. For instance, if our `FirstClass` were coded in a module file instead of being typed interactively, we could import it and use its name normally in a `class` header line:

```
from modulename import FirstClass      # Copy name into my scope
class SecondClass(FirstClass):          # Use class name directly
    def display(self): ...
```

Or, equivalently:

```
import modulename                       # Access the whole module
class SecondClass(modulename.FirstClass):   # Qualify to reference
    def display(self): ...
```

Like everything else, class names always live within a module, so they must follow all the rules we studied in Part V. For example, more than one class can be coded in a single module file—like other statements in a module, `class` statements are run during imports to define names, and these names become distinct module attributes. More generally, each module may arbitrarily mix any number of variables, functions, and classes, and all names in a module behave the same way. The file *food.py* demonstrates:

```
# food.py
var = 1                    # food.var
def func(): ...            # food.func
class spam: ...            # food.spam
class ham:  ...            # food.ham
class eggs: ...            # food.eggs
```

This holds true even if the module and class happen to have the same name. For example, given the following file, *person.py*:

```
class person: ...
```

we need to go through the module to fetch the class as usual:

```
import person             # Import module
x = person.person()       # Class within module
```

Although this path may look redundant, it's required: `person.person` refers to the `person` class inside the `person` module. Saying just `person` gets the module, not the class, unless the `from` statement is used:

```
from person import person    # Get class from module
x = person()                 # Use class name
```

As with any other variable, we can never see a class in a file without first importing and somehow fetching it from its enclosing file. If this seems confusing, don't use the same name for a module and a class within it. In fact, common convention in Python dictates that class names should begin with an *uppercase* letter, to help make them more distinct:

```
import person                          # Lowercase for modules
x = person.Person()                    # Uppercase for classes
```

Also, keep in mind that although classes and modules are both namespaces for attaching attributes, they correspond to very different source code structures: a module reflects an entire *file*, but a class is a *statement* within a file. We'll say more about such distinctions later in this part of the book.

Classes Can Intercept Python Operators

Let's move on to the third and final major difference between classes and modules: operator overloading. In simple terms, *operator overloading* lets objects coded with classes intercept and respond to operations that work on built-in types: addition, slicing, printing, qualification, and so on. It's mostly just an automatic dispatch mechanism —expressions and other built-in operations route control to implementations in classes. Here, too, there is nothing similar in modules: modules can implement function calls, but not the behavior of expressions.

Although we could implement all class behavior as method functions, operator overloading lets objects be more tightly integrated with Python's object model. Moreover, because operator overloading makes our own objects act like built-ins, it tends to foster object interfaces that are more consistent and easier to learn, and it allows class-based objects to be processed by code written to expect a built-in type's interface. Here is a quick rundown of the main ideas behind overloading operators:

- **Methods named with double underscores (_X_) are special hooks**. In Python classes we implement operator overloading by providing specially named methods to intercept operations. The Python language defines a fixed and unchangeable mapping from each of these operations to a specially named method.

- **Such methods are called automatically when instances appear in built-in operations**. For instance, if an instance object inherits an __add__ method, that method is called whenever the object appears in a + expression. The method's return value becomes the result of the corresponding expression.

- **Classes may override most built-in type operations**. There are dozens of special operator overloading method names for intercepting and implementing nearly every operation available for built-in types. This includes expressions, but also basic operations like printing and object creation.

- **There are no defaults for operator overloading methods, and none are required**. If a class does not define or inherit an operator overloading method, it just means that the corresponding operation is not supported for the class's instances. If there is no __add__, for example, + expressions raise exceptions.

- **New-style classes have some defaults, but not for common operations**. In Python 3.X, and so-called "new style" classes in 2.X that we'll define later, a root class named object does provide defaults for some __X__ methods, but not for many, and not for most commonly used operations.

- **Operators allow classes to integrate with Python's object model**. By overloading type operations, the user-defined objects we implement with classes can act just like built-ins, and so provide consistency as well as compatibility with expected interfaces.

Operator overloading is an optional feature; it's used primarily by people developing tools for other Python programmers, not by application developers. And, candidly, you probably *shouldn't* use it just because it seems clever or "cool." Unless a class needs to mimic built-in type interfaces, it should usually stick to simpler named methods. Why would an employee database application support expressions like * and +, for example? Named methods like giveRaise and promote would usually make more sense.

Because of this, we won't go into details on every operator overloading method available in Python in this book. Still, there is one operator overloading method you are likely to see in almost every realistic Python class: the __init__ method, which is known as the *constructor* method and is used to initialize objects' state. You should pay special attention to this method, because __init__, along with the self argument, turns out to be a key requirement to reading and understanding most OOP code in Python.

A Third Example

On to another example. This time, we'll define a subclass of the prior section's Second Class that implements three specially named attributes that Python will call automatically:

- __init__ is run when a new instance object is created: self is the new ThirdClass object.[1]
- __add__ is run when a ThirdClass instance appears in a + expression.
- __str__ is run when an object is printed (technically, when it's converted to its print string by the str built-in function or its Python internals equivalent).

Our new subclass also defines a normally named method called mul, which changes the instance object in place. Here's the new subclass:

```
>>> class ThirdClass(SecondClass):              # Inherit from SecondClass
        def __init__(self, value):              # On "ThirdClass(value)"
            self.data = value
        def __add__(self, other):               # On "self + other"
            return ThirdClass(self.data + other)
        def __str__(self):                      # On "print(self)", "str()"
            return '[ThirdClass: %s]' % self.data
```

---

1. Not to be confused with the *__init__.py* files in module packages! The method here is a class constructor function used to initialize the newly created instance, not a module package. See Chapter 24 for more details.

```
        def mul(self, other):                          # In-place change: named
            self.data *= other

>>> a = ThirdClass('abc')              # __init__ called
>>> a.display()                        # Inherited method called
Current value = "abc"
>>> print(a)                           # __str__: returns display string
[ThirdClass: abc]

>>> b = a + 'xyz'                      # __add__: makes a new instance
>>> b.display()                        # b has all ThirdClass methods
Current value = "abcxyz"
>>> print(b)                           # __str__: returns display string
[ThirdClass: abcxyz]

>>> a.mul(3)                           # mul: changes instance in place
>>> print(a)
[ThirdClass: abcabcabc]
```

ThirdClass "is a" SecondClass, so its instances inherit the customized display method from SecondClass of the preceding section. This time, though, ThirdClass creation calls pass an argument (e.g., "abc"). This argument is passed to the value argument in the __init__ constructor and assigned to self.data there. The net effect is that Third Class arranges to set the data attribute automatically at construction time, instead of requiring setdata calls after the fact.

Further, ThirdClass objects can now show up in + expressions and print calls. For +, Python passes the instance object on the left to the self argument in __add__ and the value on the right to other, as illustrated in Figure 27-3; whatever __add__ returns becomes the result of the + expression (more on its result in a moment).

For print, Python passes the object being printed to self in __str__; whatever string this method returns is taken to be the print string for the object. With __str__ (or its more broadly relevant twin __repr__, which we'll meet and use in the next chapter), we can use a normal print to display objects of this class, instead of calling the special display method.

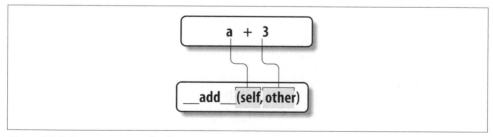

Figure 27-3. In operator overloading, expression operators and other built-in operations performed on class instances are mapped back to specially named methods in the class. These special methods are optional and may be inherited as usual. Here, a + expression triggers the __add__ method.

Specially named methods such as __init__, __add__, and __str__ are inherited by subclasses and instances, just like any other names assigned in a class. If they're not coded in a class, Python looks for such names in all its superclasses, as usual. Operator overloading method names are also not built-in or reserved words; they are just attributes that Python looks for when objects appear in various contexts. Python usually calls them automatically, but they may occasionally be called by your code as well. For example, the __init__ method is often called manually to trigger initialization steps in a superclass, as we'll see in the next chapter.

Returning results, or not

Some operator overloading methods like __str__ require results, but others are more flexible. For example, notice how the __add__ method makes and returns a *new* instance object of its class, by calling ThirdClass with the result value—which in turn triggers __init__ to initialize the result. This is a common convention, and explains why b in the listing has a display method; it's a ThirdClass object too, because that's what + returns for this class's objects. This essentially propagates the type.

By contrast, mul *changes* the current instance object in place, by reassigning the self attribute. We could overload the * expression to do the latter, but this would be too different from the behavior of * for built-in types such as numbers and strings, for which it always makes new objects. Common practice dictates that overloaded operators should work the same way that built-in operator implementations do. Because operator overloading is really just an expression-to-method dispatch mechanism, though, you can interpret operators any way you like in your own class objects.

Why Use Operator Overloading?

As a class designer, you can choose to use operator overloading or not. Your choice simply depends on how much you want your object to look and feel like built-in types. As mentioned earlier, if you omit an operator overloading method and do not inherit it from a superclass, the corresponding operation will not be supported for your instances; if it's attempted, an exception will be raised (or, in some cases like printing, a standard default will be used).

Frankly, many operator overloading methods tend to be used only when you are implementing objects that are mathematical in nature; a vector or matrix class may overload the addition operator, for example, but an employee class likely would not. For simpler classes, you might not use overloading at all, and would rely instead on explicit method calls to implement your objects' behavior.

On the other hand, you might decide to use operator overloading if you need to pass a user-defined object to a function that was coded to expect the operators available on a built-in type like a list or a dictionary. Implementing the same operator set in your class will ensure that your objects support the same expected object interface and so are compatible with the function. Although we won't cover every operator overloading method in this book, we'll survey additional common operator overloading techniques in action in Chapter 30.

One overloading method we will use often here is the __init__ constructor method, used to initialize newly created instance objects, and present in almost every realistic class. Because it allows classes to fill out the attributes in their new instances immediately, the constructor is useful for almost every kind of class you might code. In fact, even though instance attributes are not declared in Python, you can usually find out which attributes an instance will have by inspecting its class's __init__ method.

Of course, there's nothing wrong with experimenting with interesting language tools, but they don't always translate to production code. With time and experience, you'll find these programming patterns and guidelines to be natural and nearly automatic.

The World's Simplest Python Class

We've begun studying class statement syntax in detail in this chapter, but I'd again like to remind you that the basic inheritance model that classes produce is very simple —all it really involves is searching for attributes in trees of linked objects. In fact, we can create a class with nothing in it at all. The following statement makes a class with no attributes attached, an empty namespace object:

```
>>> class rec: pass          # Empty namespace object
```

We need the no-operation pass placeholder statement (discussed in Chapter 13) here because we don't have any methods to code. After we make the class by running this statement interactively, we can start attaching attributes to the class by assigning names to it completely outside of the original class statement:

```
>>> rec.name = 'Bob'          # Just objects with attributes
>>> rec.age  = 40
```

And, after we've created these attributes by assignment, we can fetch them with the usual syntax. When used this way, a class is roughly similar to a "struct" in C, or a "record" in Pascal. It's basically an object with field names attached to it (as we'll see ahead, doing similar with dictionary keys requires extra characters):

```
>>> print(rec.name)          # Like a C struct or a record
Bob
```

Notice that this works even though there are *no instances* of the class yet; classes are objects in their own right, even without instances. In fact, they are just self-contained namespaces; as long as we have a reference to a class, we can set or change its attributes anytime we wish. Watch what happens when we do create two instances, though:

```
>>> x = rec()                # Instances inherit class names
>>> y = rec()
```

These instances begin their lives as completely empty namespace objects. Because they remember the class from which they were made, though, they will obtain the attributes we attached to the class by inheritance:

```
>>> x.name, y.name                 # name is stored on the class only
('Bob', 'Bob')
```

Really, these instances have no attributes of their own; they simply fetch the name attribute from the class object where it is stored. If we do assign an attribute to an instance, though, it creates (or changes) the attribute in that object, and no other—crucially, attribute *references* kick off inheritance searches, but attribute *assignments* affect only the objects in which the assignments are made. Here, this means that x gets its own name, but y still inherits the name attached to the class above it:

```
>>> x.name = 'Sue'                 # But assignment changes x only
>>> rec.name, x.name, y.name
('Bob', 'Sue', 'Bob')
```

In fact, as we'll explore in more detail in Chapter 29, the attributes of a namespace object are usually implemented as dictionaries, and class inheritance trees are (generally speaking) just dictionaries with links to other dictionaries. If you know where to look, you can see this explicitly.

For example, the __dict__ attribute is the namespace dictionary for most class-based objects. Some classes may also (or instead) define attributes in __slots__, an advanced and seldom-used feature that we'll note in Chapter 28, but largely postpone until Chapter 31 and Chapter 32. Normally, __dict__ literally is an instance's attribute namespace.

To illustrate, the following was run in Python 3.3; the order of names and set of __X__ internal names present can vary from release to release, and we filter out built-ins with a generator expression as we've done before, but the names we assigned are present in all:

```
>>> list(rec.__dict__.keys())
['age', '__module__', '__qualname__', '__weakref__', 'name', '__dict__', '__doc__']

>>> list(name for name in rec.__dict__ if not name.startswith('__'))
['age', 'name']
>>> list(x.__dict__.keys())
['name']
>>> list(y.__dict__.keys())          # list() not required in Python 2.X
[]
```

Here, the class's namespace dictionary shows the name and age attributes we assigned to it, x has its own name, and y is still empty. Because of this model, an attribute can often be fetched by *either* dictionary indexing or attribute notation, but only if it's present on the object in question—attribute notation kicks off inheritance search, but indexing looks in the single object *only* (as we'll see later, both have valid roles):

```
>>> x.name, x.__dict__['name']      # Attributes present here are dict keys
('Sue', 'Sue')
```

```
>>> x.age                          # But attribute fetch checks classes too
40
>>> x.__dict__['age']              # Indexing dict does not do inheritance
KeyError: 'age'
```

To facilitate inheritance search on attribute fetches, each instance has a link to its class that Python creates for us—it's called __class__, if you want to inspect it:

```
>>> x.__class__                    # Instance to class link
<class '__main__.rec'>
```

Classes also have a __bases__ attribute, which is a tuple of references to their superclass objects—in this example just the implied object root class in Python 3.X we'll explore later (you'll get an empty tuple in 2.X instead):

```
>>> rec.__bases__                  # Class to superclasses link, () in 2.X
(<class 'object'>,)
```

These two attributes are how class trees are literally represented in memory by Python. Internal details like these are not required knowledge—class trees are implied by the code you run, and their search is normally automatic—but they can often help demystify the model.

The main point to take away from this look under the hood is that Python's class model is extremely dynamic. Classes and instances are just namespace objects, with attributes created on the fly by assignment. Those assignments usually happen within the `class` statements you code, but they can occur anywhere you have a reference to one of the objects in the tree.

Even *methods*, normally created by a `def` nested in a `class`, can be created completely independently of any class object. The following, for example, defines a simple function outside of any class that takes one argument:

```
>>> def uppername(obj):
        return obj.name.upper()    # Still needs a self argument (obj)
```

There is nothing about a class here yet—it's a simple function, and it can be called as such at this point, provided we pass in an object `obj` with a `name` attribute, whose value in turn has an `upper` method—our class instances happen to fit the expected interface, and kick off string uppercase conversion:

```
>>> uppername(x)                   # Call as a simple function
'SUE'
```

If we assign this simple function to an attribute of our class, though, it becomes a *method*, callable through any instance, as well as through the class name itself as long as we pass in an instance manually—a technique we'll leverage further in the next chapter:[2]

```
>>> rec.method = uppername         # Now it's a class's method!

>>> x.method()                     # Run  method to process x
'SUE'
```

```
>>> y.method()                    # Same, but pass y to self
'BOB'

>>> rec.method(x)                 # Can call through instance or class
'SUE'
```

Normally, classes are filled out by `class` statements, and instance attributes are created by assignments to `self` attributes in method functions. The point again, though, is that they don't have to be; OOP in Python really is mostly about looking up attributes in linked namespace objects.

Records Revisited: Classes Versus Dictionaries

Although the simple classes of the prior section are meant to illustrate class model basics, the techniques they employ can also be used for real work. For example, Chapter 8 and Chapter 9 showed how to use dictionaries, tuples, and lists to record properties of entities in our programs, generically called *records*. It turns out that classes can often serve better in this role—they package information like dictionaries, but can also bundle processing logic in the form of methods. For reference, here is an example for tuple- and dictionary-based records we used earlier in the book (using one of many dictionary coding techniques):

```
>>> rec = ('Bob', 40.5, ['dev', 'mgr'])     # Tuple-based record
>>> print(rec[0])
Bob

>>> rec = {}
>>> rec['name'] = 'Bob'                       # Dictionary-based record
>>> rec['age']  = 40.5                        # Or {...}, dict(n=v), etc.
>>> rec['jobs'] = ['dev', 'mgr']
>>>
>>> print(rec['name'])
Bob
```

This code emulates tools like records in other languages. As we just saw, though, there are also multiple ways to do the same with classes. Perhaps the simplest is this—trading keys for attributes:

```
>>> class rec: pass

>>> rec.name = 'Bob'                          # Class-based record
>>> rec.age  = 40.5
>>> rec.jobs = ['dev', 'mgr']
```

2. In fact, this is one of the reasons the `self` argument *must* always be explicit in Python methods—because methods can be created as simple functions independent of a class, they need to make the implied instance argument explicit. They can be called as either functions or methods, and Python can neither guess nor assume that a simple function might eventually become a class's method. The main reason for the explicit `self` argument, though, is to make the meanings of names more obvious: names not referenced through `self` are simple variables mapped to scopes, while names referenced through `self` with attribute notation are obviously instance attributes.

```
>>>
>>> print(rec.name)
Bob
```

This code has substantially less syntax than the dictionary equivalent. It uses an empty `class` statement to generate an empty namespace object. Once we make the empty class, we fill it out by assigning class attributes over time, as before.

This works, but a new `class` statement will be required for each distinct record we will need. Perhaps more typically, we can instead generate *instances* of an empty class to represent each distinct entity:

```
>>> class rec: pass

>>> pers1 = rec()                          # Instance-based records
>>> pers1.name = 'Bob'
>>> pers1.jobs = ['dev', 'mgr']
>>> pers1.age  = 40.5
>>>
>>> pers2 = rec()
>>> pers2.name = 'Sue'
>>> pers2.jobs = ['dev', 'cto']
>>>
>>> pers1.name, pers2.name
('Bob', 'Sue')
```

Here, we make two records from the same class. Instances start out life empty, just like classes. We then fill in the records by assigning to attributes. This time, though, there are two separate objects, and hence two separate `name` attributes. In fact, instances of the same class don't even have to have the same set of attribute names; in this example, one has a unique `age` name. Instances really are distinct namespaces, so each has a distinct attribute dictionary. Although they are normally filled out consistently by a class's methods, they are more flexible than you might expect.

Finally, we might instead code a more full-blown class to implement the record *and* its processing—something that data-oriented dictionaries do not directly support:

```
>>> class Person:
        def __init__(self, name, jobs, age=None):     # class = data + logic
            self.name = name
            self.jobs = jobs
            self.age  = age
        def info(self):
            return (self.name, self.jobs)

>>> rec1 = Person('Bob', ['dev', 'mgr'], 40.5)         # Construction calls
>>> rec2 = Person('Sue', ['dev', 'cto'])
>>>
>>> rec1.jobs, rec2.info()                             # Attributes + methods
(['dev', 'mgr'], ('Sue', ['dev', 'cto']))
```

This scheme also makes multiple instances, but the class is not empty this time: we've added *logic* (methods) to initialize instances at construction time and collect attributes into a tuple on request. The constructor imposes some consistency on instances here by always setting the name, job, and age attributes, even though the latter can be omitted when an object is made. Together, the class's methods and instance attributes create a *package*, which combines both *data* and *logic*.

We could further extend this code by adding logic to compute salaries, parse names, and so on. Ultimately, we might link the class into a larger hierarchy to inherit and customize an existing set of methods via the automatic attribute search of classes, or perhaps even store instances of the class in a file with Python object pickling to make them persistent. In fact, we *will*—in the next chapter, we'll expand on this analogy between classes and records with a more realistic running example that demonstrates class basics in action.

To be fair to other tools, in this form, the two class construction calls above more closely resemble dictionaries made all at once, but still seem less cluttered and provide extra processing methods. In fact, the class's construction calls more closely resemble Chapter 9's *named tuples*—which makes sense, given that named tuples really *are* classes with extra logic to map attributes to tuple offsets:

```
>>> rec = dict(name='Bob', age=40.5, jobs=['dev', 'mgr'])        # Dictionaries

>>> rec = {'name': 'Bob', 'age': 40.5, 'jobs': ['dev', 'mgr']}

>>> rec = Rec('Bob', 40.5, ['dev', 'mgr'])                       # Named tuples
```

In the end, although types like dictionaries and tuples are flexible, classes allow us to add behavior to objects in ways that built-in types and simple functions do not directly support. Although we can store functions in dictionaries, too, using them to process implied instances is nowhere near as natural and structured as it is in classes. To see this more clearly, let's move ahead to the next chapter.

Chapter Summary

This chapter introduced the basics of coding classes in Python. We studied the syntax of the class statement, and we saw how to use it to build up a class inheritance tree. We also studied how Python automatically fills in the first argument in method functions, how attributes are attached to objects in a class tree by simple assignment, and how specially named operator overloading methods intercept and implement built-in operations for our instances (e.g., expressions and printing).

Now that we've learned all about the mechanics of coding classes in Python, the next chapter turns to a larger and more realistic example that ties together much of what we've learned about OOP so far, and introduces some new topics. After that, we'll continue our look at class coding, taking a second pass over the model to fill in some of the details that were omitted here to keep things simple. First, though, let's work through a quiz to review the basics we've covered so far.

Test Your Knowledge: Quiz

1. How are classes related to modules?
2. How are instances and classes created?
3. Where and how are class attributes created?
4. Where and how are instance attributes created?
5. What does `self` mean in a Python class?
6. How is operator overloading coded in a Python class?
7. When might you want to support operator overloading in your classes?
8. Which operator overloading method is most commonly used?
9. What are two key concepts required to understand Python OOP code?

Test Your Knowledge: Answers

1. Classes are always nested inside a module; they are attributes of a module object. Classes and modules are both namespaces, but classes correspond to statements (not entire files) and support the OOP notions of multiple instances, inheritance, and operator overloading (modules do not). In a sense, a module is like a single-instance class, without inheritance, which corresponds to an entire file of code.

2. Classes are made by running `class` statements; instances are created by calling a class as though it were a function.

3. Class attributes are created by assigning attributes to a class object. They are normally generated by top-level assignments nested in a `class` statement—each name assigned in the `class` statement block becomes an attribute of the class object (technically, the `class` statement's local scope morphs into the class object's attribute namespace, much like a module). Class attributes can also be created, though, by assigning attributes to the class anywhere a reference to the class object exists—even outside the `class` statement.

4. Instance attributes are created by assigning attributes to an instance object. They are normally created within a class's method functions coded inside the `class` statement, by assigning attributes to the `self` argument (which is always the implied instance). Again, though, they may be created by assignment anywhere a reference to the instance appears, even outside the `class` statement. Normally, all instance attributes are initialized in the `__init__` constructor method; that way, later method calls can assume the attributes already exist.

5. `self` is the name commonly given to the first (leftmost) argument in a class's method function; Python automatically fills it in with the instance object that is the implied subject of the method call. This argument need not be called `self` (though this is a very strong convention); its position is what is significant. (Ex-C++ or Java programmers might prefer to call it `this` because in those languages

that name reflects the same idea; in Python, though, this argument must always be explicit.)

6. Operator overloading is coded in a Python class with specially named methods; they all begin and end with double underscores to make them unique. These are not built-in or reserved names; Python just runs them automatically when an instance appears in the corresponding operation. Python itself defines the mappings from operations to special method names.

7. Operator overloading is useful to implement objects that resemble built-in types (e.g., sequences or numeric objects such as matrixes), and to mimic the built-in type interface expected by a piece of code. Mimicking built-in type interfaces enables you to pass in class instances that also have state information (i.e., attributes that remember data between operation calls). You shouldn't use operator overloading when a simple named method will suffice, though.

8. The __init__ constructor method is the most commonly used; almost every class uses this method to set initial values for instance attributes and perform other startup tasks.

9. The special self argument in method functions and the __init__ constructor method are the two cornerstones of OOP code in Python; if you get these, you should be able to read the text of most OOP Python code—apart from these, it's largely just packages of functions. The inheritance search matters too, of course, but self represents the automatic object argument, and __init__ is widespread.

CHAPTER 28

A More Realistic Example

We'll dig into more class syntax details in the next chapter. Before we do, though, I'd like to show you a more realistic example of classes in action that's more practical than what we've seen so far. In this chapter, we're going to build a set of classes that do something more concrete—recording and processing information about people. As you'll see, what we call *instances* and *classes* in Python programming can often serve the same roles as *records* and *programs* in more traditional terms.

Specifically, in this chapter we're going to code two classes:

- `Person`—a class that creates and processes information about people
- `Manager`—a customization of `Person` that modifies inherited behavior

Along the way, we'll make instances of both classes and test out their functionality. When we're done, I'll show you a nice example use case for classes—we'll store our instances in a *shelve* object-oriented database, to make them permanent. That way, you can use this code as a template for fleshing out a full-blown personal database written entirely in Python.

Besides actual utility, though, our aim here is also *educational*: this chapter provides a tutorial on object-oriented programming in Python. Often, people grasp the last chapter's class syntax on paper, but have trouble seeing how to get started when confronted with having to code a new class from scratch. Toward this end, we'll take it one step at a time here, to help you learn the basics; we'll build up the classes gradually, so you can see how their features come together in complete programs.

In the end, our classes will still be relatively small in terms of code, but they will demonstrate *all* of the main ideas in Python's OOP model. Despite its syntax details, Python's class system really is largely just a matter of searching for an attribute in a tree of objects, along with a special first argument for functions.

Step 1: Making Instances

OK, so much for the design phase—let's move on to implementation. Our first task is to start coding the main class, `Person`. In your favorite text editor, open a new file for the code we'll be writing. It's a fairly strong convention in Python to begin module names with a lowercase letter and class names with an uppercase letter; like the name of `self` arguments in methods, this is not required by the language, but it's so common that deviating might be confusing to people who later read your code. To conform, we'll call our new module file *person.py* and our class within it `Person`, like this:

```
# File person.py (start)
```

```
class Person:                           # Start a class
```

All our work will be done in this file until later in this chapter. We can code any number of functions and classes in a single module file in Python, and this one's *person.py* name might not make much sense if we add unrelated components to it later. For now, we'll assume everything in it will be `Person`-related. It probably should be anyhow—as we've learned, modules tend to work best when they have a single, *cohesive* purpose.

Coding Constructors

Now, the first thing we want to do with our `Person` class is record basic information about people—to fill out record fields, if you will. Of course, these are known as instance object *attributes* in Python-speak, and they generally are created by assignment to `self` attributes in a class's method functions. The normal way to give instance attributes their first values is to assign them to `self` in the `__init__` *constructor method*, which contains code run automatically by Python each time an instance is created. Let's add one to our class:

```
# Add record field initialization
```

```
class Person:
    def __init__(self, name, job, pay):    # Constructor takes three arguments
        self.name = name                   # Fill out fields when created
        self.job  = job                    # self is the new instance object
        self.pay  = pay
```

This is a very common coding pattern: we pass in the data to be attached to an instance as arguments to the constructor method and assign them to `self` to retain them permanently. In OO terms, `self` is the newly created instance object, and `name`, `job`, and `pay` become *state information*—descriptive data saved on an object for later use. Although other techniques (such as enclosing scope reference closures) can save details, too, instance attributes make this very explicit and easy to understand.

Notice that the argument names appear *twice* here. This code might even seem a bit redundant at first, but it's not. The `job` argument, for example, is a local variable in the scope of the `__init__` function, but `self.job` is an attribute of the instance that's the implied subject of the method call. They are two different variables, which happen to have the same name. By assigning the job local to the `self.job` attribute with `self.job=job`, we save the passed-in `job` on the instance for later use. As usual in Python, where a name is assigned, or what object it is assigned to, determines what it means.

Speaking of arguments, there's really nothing magical about `__init__`, apart from the fact that it's called automatically when an instance is made and has a special first argument. Despite its weird name, it's a normal function and supports all the features of functions we've already covered. We can, for example, provide *defaults* for some of its arguments, so they need not be provided in cases where their values aren't available or useful.

To demonstrate, let's make the `job` argument optional—it will default to None, meaning the person being created is not (currently) employed. If `job` defaults to None, we'll probably want to default **pay** to 0, too, for consistency (unless some of the people you know manage to get paid without having jobs!). In fact, we have to specify a default for **pay** because according to Python's syntax rules and Chapter 18, any arguments in a function's header after the first default must all have defaults, too:

```
# Add defaults for constructor arguments

class Person:
    def __init__(self, name, job=None, pay=0):          # Normal function args
        self.name = name
        self.job  = job
        self.pay  = pay
```

What this code means is that we'll need to pass in a name when making Persons, but `job` and `pay` are now optional; they'll default to None and 0 if omitted. The `self` argument, as usual, is filled in by Python automatically to refer to the instance object—assigning values to attributes of `self` attaches them to the new instance.

Testing As You Go

This class doesn't do much yet—it essentially just fills out the fields of a new record—but it's a real working class. At this point we could add more code to it for more features, but we won't do that yet. As you've probably begun to appreciate already, programming in Python is really a matter of *incremental prototyping*—you write some code, test it, write more code, test again, and so on. Because Python provides both an interactive session and nearly immediate turnaround after code changes, it's more natural to test as you go than to write a huge amount of code to test all at once.

Before adding more features, then, let's test what we've got so far by making a few instances of our class and displaying their attributes as created by the constructor. We could do this interactively, but as you've also probably surmised by now, interactive testing has its limits—it gets tedious to have to reimport modules and retype test cases each time you start a new testing session. More commonly, Python programmers use the interactive prompt for simple one-off tests but do more substantial testing by writing code at the bottom of the file that contains the objects to be tested, like this:

```
# Add incremental self-test code

class Person:
    def __init__(self, name, job=None, pay=0):
        self.name = name
        self.job  = job
        self.pay  = pay

bob = Person('Bob Smith')                        # Test the class
sue = Person('Sue Jones', job='dev', pay=100000) # Runs __init__ automatically
print(bob.name, bob.pay)                         # Fetch attached attributes
print(sue.name, sue.pay)                         # sue's and bob's attrs differ
```

Notice here that the bob object accepts the defaults for job and pay, but sue provides values explicitly. Also note how we use *keyword arguments* when making sue; we could pass by position instead, but the keywords may help remind us later what the data is, and they allow us to pass the arguments in any left-to-right order we like. Again, despite its unusual name, __init__ is a normal function, supporting everything you already know about functions—including both defaults and pass-by-name keyword arguments.

When this file runs as a script, the test code at the bottom makes two instances of our class and prints two attributes of each (name and pay):

```
C:\code> person.py
Bob Smith 0
Sue Jones 100000
```

You can also type this file's test code at Python's interactive prompt (assuming you import the Person class there first), but coding canned tests inside the module file like this makes it much easier to rerun them in the future.

Although this is fairly simple code, it's already demonstrating something important. Notice that bob's name is not sue's, and sue's pay is not bob's. Each is an independent record of information. Technically, bob and sue are both *namespace objects*—like all class instances, they each have their own independent copy of the state information created by the class. Because each instance of a class has its own set of self attributes, classes are a natural for recording information for multiple objects this way; just like built-in types such as lists and dictionaries, classes serve as a sort of *object factory*.

Other Python program structures, such as functions and modules, have no such concept. Chapter 17's closure functions come close in terms of per-call state, but don't have the multiple methods, inheritance, and larger structure we get from classes.

Using Code Two Ways

As is, the test code at the bottom of the file works, but there's a big catch—its top-level print statements run both when the file is run as a script and when it is imported as a module. This means if we ever decide to import the class in this file in order to use it somewhere else (and we will soon in this chapter), we'll see the output of its test code every time the file is imported. That's not very good software citizenship, though: client programs probably don't care about our internal tests and won't want to see our output mixed in with their own.

Although we could split the test code off into a separate file, it's often more convenient to code tests in the same file as the items to be tested. It would be better to arrange to run the test statements at the bottom *only* when the file is run for testing, not when the file is imported. That's exactly what the module __name__ check is designed for, as you learned in the preceding part of this book. Here's what this addition looks like—add the require test and indent your self-test code:

```
# Allow this file to be imported as well as run/tested

class Person:
    def __init__(self, name, job=None, pay=0):
        self.name = name
        self.job  = job
        self.pay  = pay

if __name__ == '__main__':                          # When run for testing only
    # self-test code
    bob = Person('Bob Smith')
    sue = Person('Sue Jones', job='dev', pay=100000)
    print(bob.name, bob.pay)
    print(sue.name, sue.pay)
```

Now, we get exactly the behavior we're after—running the file as a top-level script tests it because its __name__ is __main__, but importing it as a library of classes later does not:

```
C:\code> person.py
Bob Smith 0
Sue Jones 100000

C:\code> python
Python 3.3.0 (v3.3.0:bd8afb90ebf2, Sep 29 2012, 10:57:17) ...
>>> import person
>>>
```

When imported, the file now defines the class, but does not use it. When run directly, this file creates two instances of our class as before, and prints two attributes of each; again, because each instance is an independent namespace object, the values of their attributes differ.

Version Portability: Prints

All of this chapter's code works on both Python 2.X and 3.X, but I'm running it under Python 3.X, and a few of its outputs use 3.X print function calls with multiple arguments. As explained in Chapter 11, this means that some of its outputs may vary slightly under Python 2.X. If you run under 2.X the code will work as is, but you'll notice

parentheses around some output lines because the extra parentheses in a `print` turn
multiple items into a tuple in 2.X only:

```
C:\code> c:\python27\python person.py
('Bob Smith', 0)
('Sue Jones', 100000)
```

If this difference is the sort of detail that might keep you awake at nights, simply remove
the parentheses to use 2.X `print` statements, or add an import of Python 3.X's print
function at the top of your script, as shown in Chapter 11 (I'd add this everywhere here,
but it's a bit distracting):

```
from __future__ import print_function
```

You can also avoid the extra parentheses portably by using formatting to yield a single
object to print. Either of the following works in both 2.X and 3.X, though the method
form is newer:

```
print('{0} {1}'.format(bob.name, bob.pay))     # Format method
print('%s %s' % (bob.name, bob.pay))           # Format expression
```

As also described in Chapter 11, such formatting may be required in some cases, because objects *nested* in a tuple may print differently than those printed as top-level
objects—the former prints with `__repr__` and the latter with `__str__` (operator overloading methods discussed further in this chapter as well as Chapter 30).

To sidestep this issue, this edition codes displays with `__repr__` (the fallback in all cases,
including nesting and the interactive prompt) instead of `__str__` (the default for prints)
so that all object appearances print the same in 3.X and 2.X, even those in superfluous
tuple parentheses!

Step 2: Adding Behavior Methods

Everything looks good so far—at this point, our class is essentially a record *factory*; it
creates and fills out fields of records (attributes of instances, in more Pythonic terms).
Even as limited as it is, though, we can still run some operations on its objects. Although
classes add an extra layer of structure, they ultimately do most of their work by embedding and processing basic *core data types* like lists and strings. In other words, if
you already know how to use Python's simple core types, you already know much of
the Python class story; classes are really just a minor structural extension.

For example, the `name` field of our objects is a simple string, so we can extract last names
from our objects by splitting on spaces and indexing. These are all core data type operations, which work whether their subjects are embedded in class instances or not:

```
>>> name = 'Bob Smith'          # Simple string, outside class
>>> name.split()                # Extract last name
['Bob', 'Smith']
>>> name.split()[-1]            # Or [1], if always just two parts
'Smith'
```

Similarly, we can give an object a pay raise by updating its pay field—that is, by changing its state information in place with an assignment. This task also involves basic operations that work on Python's core objects, regardless of whether they are standalone or embedded in a class structure (I'm formatting the result in the following to mask the fact that different Pythons print a different number of decimal digits):

```
>>> pay = 100000          # Simple variable, outside class
>>> pay *= 1.10           # Give a 10% raise
>>> print('%.2f' % pay)   # Or: pay = pay * 1.10, if you like to type
110000.00                 # Or: pay = pay + (pay * .10), if you _really_ do!
```

To apply these operations to the `Person` objects created by our script, simply do to `bob.name` and `sue.pay` what we just did to `name` and `pay`. The operations are the same, but the subjects are attached as attributes to objects created from our class:

```
# Process embedded built-in types: strings, mutability

class Person:
    def __init__(self, name, job=None, pay=0):
        self.name = name
        self.job  = job
        self.pay  = pay

if __name__ == '__main__':
    bob = Person('Bob Smith')
    sue = Person('Sue Jones', job='dev', pay=100000)
    print(bob.name, bob.pay)
    print(sue.name, sue.pay)
    print(bob.name.split()[-1])    # Extract object's last name
    sue.pay *= 1.10                # Give this object a raise
    print('%.2f' % sue.pay)
```

We've added the last three lines here; when they're run, we extract bob's last name by using basic string and list operations on his name field, and give sue a pay raise by modifying her pay attribute in place with basic number operations. In a sense, sue is also a *mutable* object—her state changes in place just like a list after an append call. Here's the new version's output:

```
Bob Smith 0
Sue Jones 100000
Smith
110000.00
```

The preceding code works as planned, but if you show it to a veteran software developer he or she will probably tell you that its general approach is not a great idea in practice. Hardcoding operations like these *outside* of the class can lead to maintenance problems in the future.

For example, what if you've hardcoded the last-name-extraction formula at many different places in your program? If you ever need to change the way it works (to support a new name structure, for instance), you'll need to hunt down and update *every* occurrence. Similarly, if the pay-raise code ever changes (e.g., to require approval or database updates), you may have multiple copies to modify. Just finding all the appearances of such code may be problematic in larger programs—they may be scattered across many files, split into individual steps, and so on. In a prototype like this, frequent change is almost guaranteed.

Coding Methods

What we really want to do here is employ a software design concept known as *encapsulation*—wrapping up operation logic behind interfaces, such that each operation is coded only once in our program. That way, if our needs change in the future, there is just one copy to update. Moreover, we're free to change the single copy's internals almost arbitrarily, without breaking the code that uses it.

In Python terms, we want to code operations on objects in a class's *methods*, instead of littering them throughout our program. In fact, this is one of the things that classes are very good at—*factoring* code to remove *redundancy* and thus optimize maintainability. As an added bonus, turning operations into methods enables them to be applied to any instance of the class, not just those that they've been hardcoded to process.

This is all simpler in code than it may sound in theory. The following achieves encapsulation by moving the two operations from code outside the class to methods inside the class. While we're at it, let's change our self-test code at the bottom to use the new methods we're creating, instead of hardcoding operations:

```python
# Add methods to encapsulate operations for maintainability

class Person:
    def __init__(self, name, job=None, pay=0):
        self.name = name
        self.job  = job
        self.pay  = pay
    def lastName(self):                            # Behavior methods
        return self.name.split()[-1]               # self is implied subject
    def giveRaise(self, percent):
        self.pay = int(self.pay * (1 + percent))   # Must change here only

if __name__ == '__main__':
    bob = Person('Bob Smith')
    sue = Person('Sue Jones', job='dev', pay=100000)
    print(bob.name, bob.pay)
    print(sue.name, sue.pay)
    print(bob.lastName(), sue.lastName())          # Use the new methods
    sue.giveRaise(.10)                             # instead of hardcoding
    print(sue.pay)
```

As we've learned, *methods* are simply normal functions that are attached to classes and designed to process instances of those classes. The instance is the subject of the method call and is passed to the method's `self` argument automatically.

The transformation to the methods in this version is straightforward. The new `last Name` method, for example, simply does to `self` what the previous version hardcoded for bob, because self is the implied subject when the method is called. lastName also returns the result, because this operation is a called function now; it computes a value for its caller to use arbitrarily, even if it is just to be printed. Similarly, the new giveRaise method just does to self what we did to sue before.

When run now, our file's output is similar to before—we've mostly just *refactored* the code to allow for easier changes in the future, not altered its behavior:

```
Bob Smith 0
Sue Jones 100000
Smith Jones
110000
```

A few coding details are worth pointing out here. First, notice that sue's pay is now still an *integer* after a pay raise—we convert the math result back to an integer by calling the int built-in within the method. Changing the value to either int or float is probably not a significant concern for this demo: integer and floating-point objects have the same interfaces and can be mixed within expressions. Still, we may need to address truncation and rounding issues in a real system—money probably is significant to Persons!

As we learned in Chapter 5, we might handle this by using the round(N, 2) built-in to round and retain cents, using the decimal type to fix precision, or storing monetary values as full floating-point numbers and displaying them with a %.2f or {0:.2f} formatting string to show cents as we did earlier. For now, we'll simply truncate any cents with int. For another idea, also see the money function in the *formats.py* module of Chapter 25; you could import this tool to show pay with commas, cents, and currency signs.

Second, notice that we're also printing sue's last name this time—because the last-name logic has been encapsulated in a method, we get to use it on *any instance* of the class. As we've seen, Python tells a method which instance to process by automatically passing it in to the first argument, usually called self. Specifically:

- In the first call, bob.lastName(), bob is the implied subject passed to self.
- In the second call, sue.lastName(), sue goes to self instead.

Trace through these calls to see how the instance winds up in self—it's a key concept. The net effect is that the method fetches the name of the implied subject each time. The same happens for giveRaise. We could, for example, give bob a raise by calling giveRaise for both instances this way, too. Unfortunately for bob, though, his zero starting pay will prevent him from getting a raise as the program is currently coded— nothing times anything is nothing, something we may want to address in a future 2.0 release of our software.

Finally, notice that the giveRaise method assumes that percent is passed in as a floating-point number between zero and one. That may be too radical an assumption in the real world (a 1000% raise would probably be a bug for most of us!); we'll let it pass for this prototype, but we might want to test or at least document this in a future iteration of this code. Stay tuned for a rehash of this idea in a later chapter in this book, where we'll code something called *function decorators* and explore Python's `assert` statement—alternatives that can do the validity test for us automatically during development. In Chapter 39, for example, we'll write a tool that lets us validate with strange incantations like the following:

```
@rangetest(percent=(0.0, 1.0))                    # Use decorator to validate
def giveRaise(self, percent):
    self.pay = int(self.pay * (1 + percent))
```

Step 3: Operator Overloading

At this point, we have a fairly full-featured class that generates and initializes instances, along with two new bits of behavior for processing instances in the form of methods. So far, so good.

As it stands, though, testing is still a bit less convenient than it needs to be—to trace our objects, we have to manually fetch and print *individual attributes* (e.g., `bob.name`, `sue.pay`). It would be nice if displaying an instance all at once actually gave us some useful information. Unfortunately, the default display format for an instance object isn't very good—it displays the object's class name, and its address in memory (which is essentially useless in Python, except as a unique identifier).

To see this, change the last line in the script to `print(sue)` so it displays the object as a whole. Here's what you'll get—the output says that `sue` is an "object" in 3.X, and an "instance" in 2.X as coded:

```
Bob Smith 0
Sue Jones 100000
Smith Jones
<__main__.Person object at 0x00000000029A0668>
```

Providing Print Displays

Fortunately, it's easy to do better by employing *operator overloading*—coding methods in a class that intercept and process built-in operations when run on the class's instances. Specifically, we can make use of what are probably the second most commonly used operator overloading methods in Python, after `__init__`: the `__repr__` method we'll deploy here, and its `__str__` twin introduced in the preceding chapter.

These methods are run automatically every time an instance is converted to its print string. Because that's what printing an object does, the net transitive effect is that printing an object displays whatever is returned by the object's `__str__` or `__repr__` method, if the object either defines one itself or inherits one from a superclass. Double-underscored names are inherited just like any other.

Technically, `__str__` is preferred by `print` and `str`, and `__repr__` is used as a fallback for these roles and in all other contexts. Although the two can be used to implement

---

different displays in different contexts, coding just __repr__ alone suffices to give a single display in all cases—prints, nested appearances, and interactive echoes. This still allows clients to provide an alternative display with __str__, but for limited contexts only; since this is a self-contained example, this is a moot point here.

The __init__ constructor method we've already coded is, strictly speaking, operator overloading too—it is run automatically at construction time to initialize a newly created instance. Constructors are so common, though, that they almost seem like a special case. More focused methods like __repr__ allow us to tap into specific operations and provide *specialized behavior* when our objects are used in those contexts.

Let's put this into code. The following extends our class to give a custom display that lists attributes when our class's instances are displayed as a whole, instead of relying on the less useful default display:

```
# Add __repr__ overload method for printing objects

class Person:
    def __init__(self, name, job=None, pay=0):
        self.name = name
        self.job  = job
        self.pay  = pay
    def lastName(self):
        return self.name.split()[-1]
    def giveRaise(self, percent):
        self.pay = int(self.pay * (1 + percent))
    def __repr__(self):                                    # Added method
        return '[Person: %s, %s]' % (self.name, self.pay)  # String to print

if __name__ == '__main__':
    bob = Person('Bob Smith')
    sue = Person('Sue Jones', job='dev', pay=100000)
    print(bob)
    print(sue)
    print(bob.lastName(), sue.lastName())
    sue.giveRaise(.10)
    print(sue)
```

Notice that we're doing string % formatting to build the display string in __repr__ here; at the bottom, classes use built-in type objects and operations like these to get their work done. Again, everything you've already learned about both built-in types and functions applies to class-based code. Classes largely just add an additional layer of *structure* that packages functions and data together and supports extensions.

We've also changed our self-test code to print objects directly, instead of printing individual attributes. When run, the output is more coherent and meaningful now; the "[...]" lines are returned by our new __repr__, run automatically by print operations:

```
[Person: Bob Smith, 0]
[Person: Sue Jones, 100000]
Smith Jones
[Person: Sue Jones, 110000]
```

Design note: as we'll learn in Chapter 30, the __repr__ method is often used to provide an as-code low-level display of an object when present, and __str__ is reserved for more user-friendly informational displays like ours here. Sometimes classes provide both a __str__ for user-friendly displays and a __repr__ with extra details for developers to view. Because printing runs __str__ and the interactive prompt echoes results with __repr__, this can provide both target audiences with an appropriate display.

Since __repr__ applies to more display cases, including nested appearances, and because we're not interested in displaying two different formats, the all-inclusive __repr__ is sufficient for our class. Here, this also means that our custom display will be used in 2.X if we list both bob and sue in a 3.X print call—a technically nested appearance, per the sidebar in "Version Portability: Prints" on page 821.

Step 4: Customizing Behavior by Subclassing

At this point, our class captures much of the OOP machinery in Python: it makes instances, provides behavior in methods, and even does a bit of operator overloading now to intercept print operations in __repr__. It effectively packages our data and logic together into a single, self-contained *software component*, making it easy to locate code and straightforward to change it in the future. By allowing us to encapsulate behavior, it also allows us to factor that code to avoid redundancy and its associated maintenance headaches.

The only major OOP concept it does not yet capture is *customization by inheritance*. In some sense, we're already doing inheritance, because instances inherit methods from their classes. To demonstrate the real power of OOP, though, we need to define a superclass/subclass relationship that allows us to extend our software and replace bits of inherited behavior. That's the main idea behind OOP, after all; by fostering a coding model based upon customization of work already done, it can dramatically cut development time.

Coding Subclasses

As a next step, then, let's put OOP's methodology to use and customize our Person class by extending our software hierarchy. For the purpose of this tutorial, we'll define a subclass of Person called Manager that replaces the inherited giveRaise method with a more specialized version. Our new class begins as follows:

```
class Manager(Person):                    # Define a subclass of Person
```

This code means that we're defining a new class named Manager, which inherits from and may add customizations to the superclass Person. In plain terms, a Manager is almost like a Person (admittedly, a very long journey for a very small joke...), but Manager has a custom way to give raises.

For the sake of argument, let's assume that when a Manager gets a raise, it receives the passed-in percentage as usual, but also gets an extra bonus that defaults to 10%. For instance, if a Manager's raise is specified as 10%, it will really get 20%. (Any relation to Persons living or dead is, of course, strictly coincidental.) Our new method begins as follows; because this redefinition of giveRaise will be closer in the class tree to Manager instances than the original version in Person, it effectively replaces, and thereby customizes, the operation. Recall that according to the inheritance search rules, the *lowest* version of the name wins:[1]

```
class Manager(Person):                      # Inherit Person attrs
    def giveRaise(self, percent, bonus=.10): # Redefine to customize
```

Augmenting Methods: The Bad Way

Now, there are two ways we might code this Manager customization: a good way and a bad way. Let's start with the *bad way*, since it might be a bit easier to understand. The bad way is to cut and paste the code of giveRaise in Person and modify it for Manager, like this:

```
class Manager(Person):
    def giveRaise(self, percent, bonus=.10):
        self.pay = int(self.pay * (1 + percent + bonus))   # Bad: cut and paste
```

This works as advertised—when we later call the giveRaise method of a Manager instance, it will run this custom version, which tacks on the extra bonus. So what's wrong with something that runs correctly?

The problem here is a very general one: anytime you copy code with cut and paste, you essentially *double* your maintenance effort in the future. Think about it: because we copied the original version, if we ever have to change the way raises are given (and we probably will), we'll have to change the code in *two* places, not one. Although this is a small and artificial example, it's also representative of a universal issue—anytime you're tempted to program by copying code this way, you probably want to look for a better approach.

Augmenting Methods: The Good Way

What we really want to do here is somehow *augment* the original giveRaise, instead of replacing it altogether. The *good way* to do that in Python is by calling to the original version directly, with augmented arguments, like this:

```
class Manager(Person):
    def giveRaise(self, percent, bonus=.10):
        Person.giveRaise(self, percent + bonus)            # Good: augment original
```

---

[1] And no offense to any managers in the audience, of course. I once taught a Python class in New Jersey, and nobody laughed at this joke, among others. The organizers later told me it was a group of managers evaluating Python.

This code leverages the fact that a class's method can always be called either through an *instance* (the usual way, where Python sends the instance to the `self` argument automatically) or through the *class* (the less common scheme, where you must pass the instance manually). In more symbolic terms, recall that a normal method call of this form:

```
instance.method(args...)
```

is automatically translated by Python into this equivalent form:

```
class.method(instance, args...)
```

where the class containing the method to be run is determined by the inheritance search rule applied to the method's name. You can code *either* form in your script, but there is a slight asymmetry between the two—you must remember to pass along the instance manually if you call through the class directly. The method always needs a subject instance one way or another, and Python provides it automatically only for calls made through an instance. For calls through the class name, you need to send an instance to `self` yourself; for code inside a method like `giveRaise`, `self` already *is* the subject of the call, and hence the instance to pass along.

Calling through the class directly effectively subverts inheritance and kicks the call higher up the class tree to run a specific version. In our case, we can use this technique to invoke the default `giveRaise` in `Person`, even though it's been redefined at the `Manager` level. In some sense, we *must* call through `Person` this way, because a `self.giveRaise()` inside `Manager`'s `giveRaise` code would loop—since `self` already is a `Manager`, `self.giveRaise()` would resolve again to `Manager.giveRaise`, and so on and so forth *recursively* until available memory is exhausted.

This "good" version may seem like a small difference in code, but it can make a huge difference for future *code maintenance*—because the `giveRaise` logic lives in just one place now (`Person`'s method), we have only one version to change in the future as needs evolve. And really, this form captures our intent more directly anyhow—we want to perform the standard `giveRaise` operation, but simply tack on an extra bonus. Here's our entire module file with this step applied:

```python
# Add customization of one behavior in a subclass

class Person:
    def __init__(self, name, job=None, pay=0):
        self.name = name
        self.job  = job
        self.pay  = pay
    def lastName(self):
        return self.name.split()[-1]
    def giveRaise(self, percent):
        self.pay = int(self.pay * (1 + percent))
    def __repr__(self):
        return '[Person: %s, %s]' % (self.name, self.pay)

class Manager(Person):
```

```
        def giveRaise(self, percent, bonus=.10):        # Redefine at this level
            Person.giveRaise(self, percent + bonus)      # Call Person's version

    if __name__ == '__main__':
        bob = Person('Bob Smith')
        sue = Person('Sue Jones', job='dev', pay=100000)
        print(bob)
        print(sue)
        print(bob.lastName(), sue.lastName())
        sue.giveRaise(.10)
        print(sue)
        tom = Manager('Tom Jones', 'mgr', 50000)          # Make a Manager: __init__
        tom.giveRaise(.10)                                # Runs custom version
        print(tom.lastName())                             # Runs inherited method
        print(tom)                                        # Runs inherited __repr__
```

To test our Manager subclass customization, we've also added self-test code that makes a Manager, calls its methods, and prints it. When we make a Manager, we pass in a name, and an optional job and pay as before—because Manager had no __init__ constructor, it inherits that in Person. Here's the new version's output:

```
[Person: Bob Smith, 0]
[Person: Sue Jones, 100000]
Smith Jones
[Person: Sue Jones, 110000]
Jones
[Person: Tom Jones, 60000]
```

Everything looks good here: bob and sue are as before, and when tom the Manager is given a 10% raise, he really gets 20% (his pay goes from $50K to $60K), because the customized giveRaise in Manager is run for him only. Also notice how printing tom as a whole at the end of the test code displays the nice format defined in Person's __repr__: Manager objects get this, lastName, and the __init__ constructor method's code "for free" from Person, by inheritance.

What About super?

To extend inherited methods, the examples in this chapter simply call the original through the superclass name: Person.giveRaise(...). This is the traditional and simplest scheme in Python, and the one used in most of this book.

Java programmers may especially be interested to know that Python also has a super built-in function that allows calling back to a superclass's methods more generically—but it's cumbersome to use in 2.X; differs in form between 2.X and 3.X; relies on unusual semantics in 3.X; works unevenly with Python's operator overloading; and does not always mesh well with traditionally coded multiple inheritance, where a single superclass call won't suffice.

In its defense, the super call has a valid use case too—cooperative same-named method dispatch in multiple inheritance trees—but it relies on the "MRO" ordering of classes, which many find esoteric and artificial; unrealistically assumes universal deployment to be used reliably; does not fully support method replacement and varying argument lists; and to many observers seems an obscure solution to a use case that is rare in real Python code.

Because of these downsides, this book prefers to call superclasses by explicit name instead of **super**, recommends the same policy for newcomers, and defers presenting **super** until Chapter 32. It's usually best judged after you learn the simpler, and generally more traditional and "Pythonic" ways of achieving the same goals, especially if you're new to OOP. Topics like MROs and cooperative multiple inheritance dispatch seem a lot to ask of beginners—and others.

And to any Java programmers in the audience: I suggest resisting the temptation to use Python's **super** until you've had a chance to study its subtle implications. Once you step up to multiple inheritance, it's not what you think it is, and more than you probably expect. The class it invokes may not be the superclass at all, and can even vary per context. Or to paraphrase a movie line: Python's **super** is like a box of chocolates—*you never know what you're going to get!*

Polymorphism in Action

To make this acquisition of inherited behavior even more striking, we can add the following code at the end of our file temporarily:

```
if __name__ == '__main__':
    ...
    print('--All three--')
    for obj in (bob, sue, tom):         # Process objects generically
        obj.giveRaise(.10)              # Run this object's giveRaise
        print(obj)                      # Run the common __repr__
```

Here's the resulting output, with its new parts highlighted in bold:

```
[Person: Bob Smith, 0]
[Person: Sue Jones, 100000]
Smith Jones
[Person: Sue Jones, 110000]
Jones
[Person: Tom Jones, 60000]
--All three--
[Person: Bob Smith, 0]
[Person: Sue Jones, 121000]
[Person: Tom Jones, 72000]
```

In the added code, object is *either* a Person or a Manager, and Python runs the appropriate giveRaise automatically—our original version in Person for bob and sue, and our customized version in Manager for tom. Trace the method calls yourself to see how Python selects the right giveRaise method for each object.

This is just Python's notion of *polymorphism*, which we met earlier in the book, at work again—what giveRaise does depends on what you do it to. Here, it's made all the more obvious when it selects from code we've written ourselves in classes. The practical effect in this code is that sue gets another 10% but tom gets another 20%, because giveRaise is dispatched based upon the object's type. As we've learned, polymorphism is at the heart of Python's flexibility. Passing any of our three objects to a function that calls a giveRaise method, for example, would have the same effect: the appropriate version would be run automatically, depending on which type of object was passed.

On the other hand, printing runs the *same __repr__* for all three objects, because it's coded just once in Person. Manager both specializes and applies the code we originally wrote in Person. Although this example is small, it's already leveraging OOP's talent for code customization and reuse; with classes, this almost seems automatic at times.

Inherit, Customize, and Extend

In fact, classes can be even more flexible than our example implies. In general, classes can *inherit*, *customize*, or *extend* existing code in superclasses. For example, although we're focused on customization here, we can also add unique methods to Manager that are not present in Person, if Managers require something completely different (Python namesake reference intended). The following snippet illustrates. Here, giveRaise redefines a superclass's method to customize it, but someThingElse defines something new to extend:

```
class Person:
    def lastName(self): ...
    def giveRaise(self): ...
    def __repr__(self): ...

class Manager(Person):                          # Inherit
    def giveRaise(self, ...): ...               # Customize
    def someThingElse(self, ...): ...           # Extend

tom = Manager()
tom.lastName()              # Inherited verbatim
tom.giveRaise()             # Customized version
tom.someThingElse()         # Extension here
print(tom)                  # Inherited overload method
```

Extra methods like this code's someThingElse *extend* the existing software and are available on Manager objects only, not on Persons. For the purposes of this tutorial, however, we'll limit our scope to customizing some of Person's behavior by redefining it, not adding to it.

OOP: The Big Idea

As is, our code may be small, but it's fairly functional. And really, it already illustrates the main point behind OOP in general: in OOP, we program by *customizing* what has already been done, rather than copying or changing existing code. This isn't always an obvious win to newcomers at first glance, especially given the extra coding requirements of classes. But overall, the programming style implied by classes can cut development time radically compared to other approaches.

For instance, in our example we could theoretically have implemented a custom `giv eRaise` operation without subclassing, but none of the other options yield code as optimal as ours:

- Although we could have simply coded `Manager` *from scratch* as new, independent code, we would have had to reimplement all the behaviors in `Person` that are the same for `Manager`s.

- Although we could have simply *changed* the existing `Person` class in place for the requirements of `Manager`'s `giveRaise`, doing so would probably break the places where we still need the original `Person` behavior.

- Although we could have simply *copied* the `Person` class in its entirety, renamed the copy to `Manager`, and changed its `giveRaise`, doing so would introduce code redundancy that would double our work in the future—changes made to `Person` in the future would not be picked up automatically, but would have to be manually propagated to `Manager`'s code. As usual, the cut-and-paste approach may seem quick now, but it doubles your work in the future.

The *customizable hierarchies* we can build with classes provide a much better solution for software that will evolve over time. No other tools in Python support this development mode. Because we can tailor and extend our prior work by coding new subclasses, we can leverage what we've already done, rather than starting from scratch each time, breaking what already works, or introducing multiple copies of code that may all have to be updated in the future. When done right, OOP is a powerful programmer's ally.

Step 5: Customizing Constructors, Too

Our code works as it is, but if you study the current version closely, you may be struck by something a bit odd—it seems pointless to have to provide a `mgr` job name for `Manager` objects when we create them: this is already implied by the class itself. It would be better if we could somehow fill in this value automatically when a `Manager` is made.

The trick we need to improve on this turns out to be the *same* as the one we employed in the prior section: we want to customize the constructor logic for `Manager`s in such a way as to provide a job name automatically. In terms of code, we want to redefine an `__init__` method in `Manager` that provides the `mgr` string for us. And as in `giveRaise` customization, we also want to run the original `__init__` in `Person` by calling through the class name, so it still initializes our objects' state information attributes.

The following extension to *person.py* will do the job—we've coded the new `Manager` constructor and changed the call that creates `tom` to not pass in the `mgr` job name:

```
# File person.py
# Add customization of constructor in a subclass

class Person:
    def __init__(self, name, job=None, pay=0):
        self.name = name
```

```
            self.job  = job
            self.pay  = pay
        def lastName(self):
            return self.name.split()[-1]
        def giveRaise(self, percent):
            self.pay = int(self.pay * (1 + percent))
        def __repr__(self):
            return '[Person: %s, %s]' % (self.name, self.pay)

    class Manager(Person):
        def __init__(self, name, pay):               # Redefine constructor
            Person.__init__(self, name, 'mgr', pay)  # Run original with 'mgr'
        def giveRaise(self, percent, bonus=.10):
            Person.giveRaise(self, percent + bonus)

    if __name__ == '__main__':
        bob = Person('Bob Smith')
        sue = Person('Sue Jones', job='dev', pay=100000)
        print(bob)
        print(sue)
        print(bob.lastName(), sue.lastName())
        sue.giveRaise(.10)
        print(sue)
        tom = Manager('Tom Jones', 50000)            # Job name not needed:
        tom.giveRaise(.10)                           # Implied/set by class
        print(tom.lastName())
        print(tom)
```

Again, we're using the same technique to augment the __init__ constructor here that
we used for giveRaise earlier—running the superclass version by calling through the
class name directly and passing the self instance along explicitly. Although the constructor has a strange name, the effect is identical. Because we need Person's construction logic to run too (to initialize instance attributes), we really have to call it this way;
otherwise, instances would not have any attributes attached.

Calling superclass constructors from redefinitions this way turns out to be a very common coding pattern in Python. By itself, Python uses inheritance to look for and call
only *one* __init__ method at construction time—the *lowest* one in the class tree. If you
need higher __init__ methods to be run at construction time (and you usually do), you
must call them manually, and usually through the superclass's name. The upside to
this is that you can be explicit about which argument to pass up to the superclass's
constructor and can choose to *not* call it at all: not calling the superclass constructor
allows you to replace its logic altogether, rather than augmenting it.

The output of this file's self-test code is the same as before—we haven't changed what
it does, we've simply restructured to get rid of some logical redundancy:

```
[Person: Bob Smith, 0]
[Person: Sue Jones, 100000]
Smith Jones
[Person: Sue Jones, 110000]
Jones
[Person: Tom Jones, 60000]
```

OOP Is Simpler Than You May Think

In this complete form, and despite their relatively small sizes, our classes capture nearly all the important concepts in Python's OOP machinery:

- Instance creation—filling out instance attributes
- Behavior methods—encapsulating logic in a class's methods
- Operator overloading—providing behavior for built-in operations like printing
- Customizing behavior—redefining methods in subclasses to specialize them
- Customizing constructors—adding initialization logic to superclass steps

Most of these concepts are based upon just three simple ideas: the inheritance search for attributes in object trees, the special `self` argument in methods, and operator overloading's automatic dispatch to methods.

Along the way, we've also made our code easy to change in the future, by harnessing the class's propensity for factoring code to reduce *redundancy*. For example, we wrapped up logic in methods and called back to superclass methods from extensions to avoid having multiple copies of the same code. Most of these steps were a natural outgrowth of the structuring power of classes.

By and large, that's all there is to OOP in Python. Classes certainly can become larger than this, and there are some more advanced class concepts, such as decorators and metaclasses, which we will meet in later chapters. In terms of the basics, though, our classes already do it all. In fact, if you've grasped the workings of the classes we've written, most OOP Python code should now be within your reach.

Other Ways to Combine Classes

Having said that, I should also tell you that although the basic mechanics of OOP are simple in Python, some of the art in larger programs lies in the way that classes are put together. We're focusing on *inheritance* in this tutorial because that's the mechanism the Python language provides, but programmers sometimes combine classes in other ways, too.

For example, a common coding pattern involves nesting objects inside each other to build up *composites*. We'll explore this pattern in more detail in Chapter 31, which is really more about design than about Python. As a quick example, though, we could use this composition idea to code our `Manager` extension by *embedding* a `Person`, instead of inheriting from it.

The following alternative, coded in file *person-composite.py*, does so by using the `__get attr__` operator overloading method to intercept undefined attribute fetches and delegate them to the embedded object with the `getattr` built-in. The `getattr` call was introduced in Chapter 25—it's the same as `X.Y` attribute fetch notation and thus performs inheritance, but the attribute name Y is a runtime string—and __getattr__ is covered in full in Chapter 30, but its basic usage is simple enough to leverage here.

By combining these tools, the giveRaise method here still achieves customization, by changing the argument passed along to the embedded object. In effect, Manager becomes a controller layer that passes calls *down* to the embedded object, rather than *up* to superclass methods:

```
# File person-composite.py
# Embedding-based Manager alternative

class Person:
    ...same...

class Manager:
    def __init__(self, name, pay):
        self.person = Person(name, 'mgr', pay)        # Embed a Person object
    def giveRaise(self, percent, bonus=.10):
        self.person.giveRaise(percent + bonus)        # Intercept and delegate
    def __getattr__(self, attr):
        return getattr(self.person, attr)             # Delegate all other attrs
    def __repr__(self):
        return str(self.person)                       # Must overload again (in 3.X)

if __name__ == '__main__':
    ...same...
```

The output of this version is the same as the prior, so I won't list it again. The more important point here is that this Manager alternative is representative of a general coding pattern usually known as *delegation*—a composite-based structure that manages a wrapped object and propagates method calls to it.

This pattern works in our example, but it requires about twice as much code and is less well suited than inheritance to the kinds of direct customizations we meant to express (in fact, no reasonable Python programmer would code this example this way in practice, except perhaps those writing general tutorials!). Manager isn't really a Person here, so we need extra code to manually dispatch method calls to the embedded object; operator overloading methods like __repr__ must be redefined (in 3.X, at least, as noted in the upcoming sidebar "Catching Built-in Attributes in 3.X" on page 839); and adding new Manager behavior is less straightforward since state information is one level removed.

Still, *object embedding*, and design patterns based upon it, can be a very good fit when embedded objects require more limited interaction with the container than direct customization implies. A controller layer, or *proxy*, like this alternative Manager, for example, might come in handy if we want to adapt a class to an expected interface it does not support, or trace or validate calls to another object's methods (indeed, we will use a nearly identical coding pattern when we study *class decorators* later in the book).

Moreover, a hypothetical Department class like the following could *aggregate* other objects in order to treat them as a set. Replace the self-test code at the bottom of the *person.py* file temporarily to try this on your own; the file *person-department.py* in the book's examples does:

```
# File person-department.py
# Aggregate embedded objects into a composite

class Person:
    ...same...

class Manager(Person):
    ...same...

class Department:
    def __init__(self, *args):
        self.members = list(args)
    def addMember(self, person):
        self.members.append(person)
    def giveRaises(self, percent):
        for person in self.members:
            person.giveRaise(percent)
    def showAll(self):
        for person in self.members:
            print(person)

if __name__ == '__main__':
    bob = Person('Bob Smith')
    sue = Person('Sue Jones', job='dev', pay=100000)
    tom = Manager('Tom Jones', 50000)

    development = Department(bob, sue)        # Embed objects in a composite
    development.addMember(tom)
    development.giveRaises(.10)               # Runs embedded objects' giveRaise
    development.showAll()                     # Runs embedded objects' __repr__
```

When run, the department's `showAll` method lists all of its contained objects after updating their state in true polymorphic fashion with `giveRaises`:

```
[Person: Bob Smith, 0]
[Person: Sue Jones, 110000]
[Person: Tom Jones, 60000]
```

Interestingly, this code uses both inheritance *and* composition—`Department` is a composite that embeds and controls other objects to aggregate, but the embedded `Person` and `Manager` objects themselves use inheritance to customize. As another example, a GUI might similarly use *inheritance* to customize the behavior or appearance of labels and buttons, but also *composition* to build up larger packages of embedded widgets, such as input forms, calculators, and text editors. The class structure to use depends on the objects you are trying to model—in fact, the ability to model real-world entities this way is one of OOP's strengths.

Design issues like composition are explored in Chapter 31, so we'll postpone further investigations for now. But again, in terms of the basic mechanics of OOP in Python, our `Person` and `Manager` classes already tell the entire story. Now that you've mastered the basics of OOP, though, developing general tools for applying it more easily in your scripts is often a natural next step—and the topic of the next section.

Catching Built-in Attributes in 3.X

An implementation note: in Python 3.X—and in 2.X when 3.X's "new style" classes are enabled—the alternative delegation-based `Manager` class of the file *person-composite.py* that we coded in this chapter will not be able to intercept and delegate operator overloading method attributes like `__repr__` without redefining them itself. Although we know that `__repr__` is the only such name used in our specific example, this is a general issue for delegation-based classes.

Recall that built-in operations like printing and addition implicitly invoke operator overloading methods such as `__repr__` and `__add__`. In 3.X's new-style classes, built-in operations like these do not route their implicit attribute fetches through generic attribute managers: neither `__getattr__` (run for undefined attributes) nor its cousin `__getattribute__` (run for all attributes) is invoked. This is why we have to redefine `__repr__` redundantly in the alternative `Manager`, in order to ensure that printing is routed to the embedded `Person` object in 3.X.

Comment out this method to see this live—the `Manager` instance prints with a default in 3.X, but still uses `Person`'s `__repr__` in 2.X. In fact, the `__repr__` in `Manager` isn't required in 2.X at all, as it's coded to use 2.X normal and default (a.k.a. "*classic*") classes:

```
c:\code> py -3 person-composite.py
[Person: Bob Smith, 0]
...etc...
<__main__.Manager object at 0x00000000029AA8D0>

c:\code> py -2 person-composite.py
[Person: Bob Smith, 0]
...etc...
[Person: Tom Jones, 60000]
```

Technically, this happens because built-in operations begin their implicit search for method names at the *instance* in 2.X's default *classic* classes, but start at the *class* in 3.X's mandated *new-style* classes, skipping the instance entirely. By contrast, explicit by-name attribute fetches are always routed to the instance first in both models. In 2.X classic classes, built-ins route attributes this way too—printing, for example, routes `__repr__` through `__getattr__`. This is why commenting out `Manager`'s `__repr__` has no effect in 2.X: the call is delegated to `Person`. New-style classes also inherit a default for `__repr__` from their automatic `object` superclass that would foil `__getattr__`, but the new-style `__getattribute__` doesn't intercept the name either.

This is a change, but isn't a show-stopper—delegation-based new-style classes can generally redefine operator overloading methods to delegate them to wrapped objects, either manually or via tools or superclasses. This topic is too advanced to explore further in this tutorial, though, so don't sweat the details too much here. Watch for it to be revisited in Chapter 31 and Chapter 32 (the latter of which defines new-style classes more formally); to impact examples again in the attribute management coverage of

---

Chapter 38 and the `Private` class decorator in Chapter 39 (the last of these also codes workarounds); and to be a special-case factor in a nearly formal *inheritance* definition in Chapter 40. In a language like Python that supports both attribute interception and operator overloading, the impacts of this change can be as broad as this spread implies!

Step 6: Using Introspection Tools

Let's make one final tweak before we throw our objects onto a database. As they are, our classes are complete and demonstrate most of the basics of OOP in Python. They still have two remaining issues we probably should iron out, though, before we go live with them:

- First, if you look at the display of the objects as they are right now, you'll notice that when you print `tom` the `Manager`, the display labels him as a `Person`. That's not technically incorrect, since `Manager` is a kind of customized and specialized `Person`. Still, it would be more accurate to display an object with the most specific (that is, *lowest*) class possible: the one an object is made from.

- Second, and perhaps more importantly, the current display format shows *only* the attributes we include in our `__repr__`, and that might not account for future goals. For example, we can't yet verify that `tom`'s job name has been set to `mgr` correctly by `Manager`'s constructor, because the `__repr__` we coded for `Person` does not print this field. Worse, if we ever expand or otherwise change the set of attributes assigned to our objects in `__init__`, we'll have to remember to also update `__repr__` for new names to be displayed, or it will become out of sync over time.

The last point means that, yet again, we've made potential extra work for ourselves in the future by introducing *redundancy* in our code. Because any disparity in `__repr__` will be reflected in the program's output, this redundancy may be more obvious than the other forms we addressed earlier; still, avoiding extra work in the future is generally *a good thing*.

Special Class Attributes

We can address both issues with Python's *introspection tools*—special attributes and functions that give us access to some of the internals of objects' implementations. These tools are somewhat advanced and generally used more by people writing tools for other programmers to use than by programmers developing applications. Even so, a basic knowledge of some of these tools is useful because they allow us to write code that processes classes in generic ways. In our code, for example, there are two hooks that can help us out, both of which were introduced near the end of the preceding chapter and used in earlier examples:

- The built-in *instance.*`__class__` attribute provides a link from an instance to the class from which it was created. Classes in turn have a `__name__`, just like modules, and a __bases__ sequence that provides access to superclasses. We can use these here to print the name of the class from which an instance is made rather than one we've hardcoded.

- The built-in *object.*__dict__ attribute provides a dictionary with one key/value pair for every attribute attached to a namespace object (including modules, classes, and instances). Because it is a dictionary, we can fetch its keys list, index by key, iterate over its keys, and so on, to process all attributes generically. We can use this here to print every attribute in any instance, not just those we hardcode in custom displays, much as we did in Chapter 25's module tools.

We met the first of these categories in the prior chapter, but here's a quick review at Python's interactive prompt with the latest versions of our *person.py* classes. Notice how we load Person at the interactive prompt with a from statement here—class names live in and are imported from modules, exactly like function names and other variables:

```
>>> from person import Person
>>> bob = Person('Bob Smith')
>>> bob                                    # Show bob's __repr__ (not __str__)
[Person: Bob Smith, 0]
>>> print(bob)                             # Ditto: print => __str__ or __repr__
[Person: Bob Smith, 0]

>>> bob.__class__                          # Show bob's class and its name
<class 'person.Person'>
>>> bob.__class__.__name__
'Person'

>>> list(bob.__dict__.keys())             # Attributes are really dict keys
['pay', 'job', 'name']                    # Use list to force list in 3.X

>>> for key in bob.__dict__:
        print(key, '=>', bob.__dict__[key])   # Index manually

pay => 0
job => None
name => Bob Smith

>>> for key in bob.__dict__:
        print(key, '=>', getattr(bob, key))   # obj.attr, but attr is a var

pay => 0
job => None
name => Bob Smith
```

As noted briefly in the prior chapter, some attributes accessible from an instance might not be stored in the __dict__ dictionary if the instance's class defines __slots__: an optional and relatively obscure feature of new-style classes (and hence all classes in Python 3.X) that stores attributes sequentially in the instance; may preclude an instance __dict__ altogether; and which we won't study in full until Chapter 31 and Chapter 32. Since slots really belong to classes instead of instances, and since they are rarely

used in any event, we can reasonably ignore them here and focus on the normal
__dict__.

As we do, though, keep in mind that some programs may need to catch exceptions for
a missing __dict__, or use hasattr to test or getattr with a default if its users might
deploy slots. As we'll see in Chapter 32, the next section's code won't fail if used by a
class with slots (its lack of them is enough to guarantee a __dict__) but slots—and other
"virtual" attributes—won't be reported as instance data.

A Generic Display Tool

We can put these interfaces to work in a superclass that displays accurate class names
and formats all attributes of an instance of any class. Open a new file in your text editor
to code the following—it's a new, independent module named *classtools.py* that implements just such a class. Because its __repr__ display overload uses generic introspection tools, it will work on *any instance*, regardless of the instance's attributes set.
And because this is a class, it automatically becomes a general formatting tool: thanks
to inheritance, it can be mixed into *any class* that wishes to use its display format. As
an added bonus, if we ever want to change how instances are displayed we need only
change this class, as every class that inherits its __repr__ will automatically pick up the
new format when it's next run:

```
# File classtools.py (new)
"Assorted class utilities and tools"

class AttrDisplay:
    """
    Provides an inheritable display overload method that shows
    instances with their class names and a name=value pair for
    each attribute stored on the instance itself (but not attrs
    inherited from its classes). Can be mixed into any class,
    and will work on any instance.
    """
    def gatherAttrs(self):
        attrs = []
        for key in sorted(self.__dict__):
            attrs.append('%s=%s' % (key, getattr(self, key)))
        return ', '.join(attrs)

    def __repr__(self):
        return '[%s: %s]' % (self.__class__.__name__, self.gatherAttrs())

if __name__ == '__main__':

    class TopTest(AttrDisplay):
        count = 0
        def __init__(self):
            self.attr1 = TopTest.count
            self.attr2 = TopTest.count+1
            TopTest.count += 2
```

```
class SubTest(TopTest):
    pass

X, Y = TopTest(), SubTest()          # Make two instances
print(X)                             # Show all instance attrs
print(Y)                             # Show lowest class name
```

Notice the docstrings here—because this is a general-purpose tool, we want to add some functional documentation for potential users to read. As we saw in Chapter 15, docstrings can be placed at the top of simple functions and modules, and also at the start of classes and any of their methods; the help function and the PyDoc tool extract and display these automatically. We'll revisit docstrings for classes in Chapter 29.

When run directly, this module's self-test makes two instances and prints them; the __repr__ defined here shows the instance's class, and all its attributes names and values, in sorted attribute name order. This output is the same in Python 3.X and 2.X because each object's display is a single constructed string:

```
C:\code> classtools.py
[TopTest: attr1=0, attr2=1]
[SubTest: attr1=2, attr2=3]
```

Another design note here: because this class uses __repr__ instead of __str__ its displays are used in all contexts, but its clients also won't have the option of providing an alternative low-level display—they can still add a __str__, but this applies to print and str only. In a more general tool, using __str__ instead limits a display's scope, but leaves clients the option of adding a __repr__ for a secondary display at interactive prompts and nested appearances. We'll follow this alternative policy when we code expanded versions of this class in Chapter 31; for this demo, we'll stick with the all-inclusive __repr__.

Instance Versus Class Attributes

If you study the classtools module's self-test code long enough, you'll notice that its class displays only *instance attributes*, attached to the self object at the bottom of the inheritance tree; that's what self's __dict__ contains. As an intended consequence, we don't see attributes inherited by the instance from classes above it in the tree (e.g., count in this file's self-test code—a class attribute used as an instance counter). Inherited class attributes are attached to the class only, not copied down to instances.

If you ever do wish to include inherited attributes too, you can climb the __class__ link to the instance's class, use the __dict__ there to fetch class attributes, and then iterate through the class's __bases__ attribute to climb to even higher superclasses, repeating as necessary. If you're a fan of simple code, running a built-in dir call on the instance instead of using __dict__ and climbing would have much the same effect, since dir results include inherited names in the sorted results list. In Python 2.7:

```
>>> from person import Person          # 2.X: keys is list, dir shows less
>>> bob = Person('Bob Smith')
```

```
>>> bob.__dict__.keys()                    # Instance attrs only
['pay', 'job', 'name']

>>> dir(bob)                                # Plus inherited attrs in classes
['__doc__', '__init__', '__module__', '__repr__', 'giveRaise', 'job', 'lastName',
'name', 'pay']
```

If you're using Python 3.X, your output will vary, and may be more than you bargained for; here's the 3.3 result for the last two statements (keys list order can vary per run):

```
>>> list(bob.__dict__.keys())              # 3.X keys is a view, not a list
['name', 'job', 'pay']

>>> dir(bob)                                # 3.X includes class type methods
['__class__', '__delattr__', '__dict__', '__dir__', '__doc__', '__eq__',
'__format__', '__ge__', '__getattribute__', '__gt__', '__hash__', '__init__',
...more omitted: 31 attrs...
'__setattr__', '__sizeof__', '__str__', '__subclasshook__', '__weakref__',
'giveRaise', 'job', 'lastName', 'name', 'pay']
```

The code and output here varies between Python 2.X and 3.X, because 3.X's `dict.keys` is not a list, and 3.X's `dir` returns extra class-type implementation attributes. Technically, `dir` returns more in 3.X because classes are all "new style" and inherit a large set of operator overloading names from the class type. In fact, as usual you'll probably want to filter out most of the _X_ names in the 3.X `dir` result, since they are internal implementation details and not something you'd normally want to display:

```
>>> len(dir(bob))
31
>>> list(name for name in dir(bob) if not name.startswith('__'))
['giveRaise', 'job', 'lastName', 'name', 'pay']
```

In the interest of space, we'll leave optional display of inherited class attributes with either tree climbs or `dir` as suggested experiments for now. For more hints on this front, though, watch for the *classtree.py* inheritance tree climber we will write in Chapter 29, and the *lister.py* attribute listers and climbers we'll code in Chapter 31.

Name Considerations in Tool Classes

One last subtlety here: because our `AttrDisplay` class in the `classtools` module is a general tool designed to be mixed into other arbitrary classes, we have to be aware of the potential for unintended *name collisions* with client classes. As is, I've assumed that client subclasses may want to use both its `__repr__` and `gatherAttrs`, but the latter of these may be more than a subclass expects—if a subclass innocently defines a `gatherAttrs` name of its own, it will likely break our class, because the lower version in the subclass will be used instead of ours.

To see this for yourself, add a `gatherAttrs` to `TopTest` in the file's self-test code; unless the new method is identical, or intentionally customizes the original, our tool class will no longer work as planned—`self.gatherAttrs` within `AttrDisplay` searches anew from the `TopTest` instance:

```
class TopTest(AttrDisplay):
    ....
    def gatherAttrs(self):              # Replaces method in AttrDisplay!
        return 'Spam'
```

This isn't necessarily bad—sometimes we want other methods to be available to subclasses, either for direct calls or for customization this way. If we really meant to provide a `__repr__` only, though, this is less than ideal.

To minimize the chances of name collisions like this, Python programmers often prefix methods not meant for external use with a *single underscore*: `_gatherAttrs` in our case. This isn't foolproof (what if another class defines `_gatherAttrs`, too?), but it's usually sufficient, and it's a common Python naming convention for methods internal to a class.

A better and less commonly used solution would be to use *two underscores* at the front of the method name only: `__gatherAttrs` for us. Python automatically expands such names to include the enclosing class's name, which makes them truly unique when looked up by the inheritance search. This is a feature usually called *pseudoprivate class attributes*, which we'll expand on in Chapter 31 and deploy in an expanded version of this class there. For now, we'll make both our methods available.

Our Classes' Final Form

Now, to use this generic tool in our classes, all we need to do is import it from its module, mix it in by inheritance in our top-level class, and get rid of the more specific `__repr__` we coded before. The new display overload method will be inherited by instances of `Person`, as well as `Manager`; `Manager` gets `__repr__` from `Person`, which now obtains it from the `AttrDisplay` coded in another module. Here is the final version of our *person.py* file with these changes applied:

```
# File classtools.py (new)
...as listed earlier...

# File person.py (final)
"""
Record and process information about people.
Run this file directly to test its classes.
"""

from classtools import AttrDisplay          # Use generic display tool

class Person(AttrDisplay):                   # Mix in a repr at this level
    """
    Create and process person records
    """
    def __init__(self, name, job=None, pay=0):
        self.name = name
        self.job  = job
        self.pay  = pay
```

```
    def lastName(self):                              # Assumes last is last
        return self.name.split()[-1]

    def giveRaise(self, percent):                    # Percent must be 0..1
        self.pay = int(self.pay * (1 + percent))

class Manager(Person):
    """
    A customized Person with special requirements
    """
    def __init__(self, name, pay):
        Person.__init__(self, name, 'mgr', pay)      # Job name is implied

    def giveRaise(self, percent, bonus=.10):
        Person.giveRaise(self, percent + bonus)

if __name__ == '__main__':
    bob = Person('Bob Smith')
    sue = Person('Sue Jones', job='dev', pay=100000)
    print(bob)
    print(sue)
    print(bob.lastName(), sue.lastName())
    sue.giveRaise(.10)
    print(sue)
    tom = Manager('Tom Jones', 50000)
    tom.giveRaise(.10)
    print(tom.lastName())
    print(tom)
```

As this is the final revision, we've added a few *comments* here to document our work
—docstrings for functional descriptions and # for smaller notes, per best-practice conventions, as well as *blank lines* between methods for readability—a generally good style
choice when classes or methods grow large, which I resisted earlier for these small
classes, in part to save space and keep the code more compact.

When we run this code now, we see all the attributes of our objects, not just the ones
we hardcoded in the original __repr__. And our final issue is resolved: because AttrDis
play takes class names off the self instance directly, each object is shown with the name
of its closest (lowest) class—tom displays as a Manager now, not a Person, and we can
finally verify that his job name has been correctly filled in by the Manager constructor:

```
C:\code> person.py
[Person: job=None, name=Bob Smith, pay=0]
[Person: job=dev, name=Sue Jones, pay=100000]
Smith Jones
[Person: job=dev, name=Sue Jones, pay=110000]
Jones
[Manager: job=mgr, name=Tom Jones, pay=60000]
```

This is the more useful display we were after. From a larger perspective, though, our
attribute display class has become a *general tool*, which we can mix into any class by
inheritance to leverage the display format it defines. Further, all its clients will auto-

matically pick up future changes in our tool. Later in the book, we'll meet even more powerful class tool concepts, such as decorators and metaclasses; along with Python's many introspection tools, they allow us to write code that augments and manages classes in structured and maintainable ways.

Step 7 (Final): Storing Objects in a Database

At this point, our work is almost complete. We now have a *two-module system* that not only implements our original design goals for representing people, but also provides a general attribute display tool we can use in other programs in the future. By coding functions and classes in module files, we've ensured that they naturally support reuse. And by coding our software as classes, we've ensured that it naturally supports extension.

Although our classes work as planned, though, the objects they create are not real database records. That is, if we kill Python, our instances will disappear—they're transient objects in memory and are not stored in a more permanent medium like a file, so they won't be available in future program runs. It turns out that it's easy to make instance objects more permanent, with a Python feature called *object persistence*— making objects live on after the program that creates them exits. As a final step in this tutorial, let's make our objects permanent.

Pickles and Shelves

Object persistence is implemented by three standard library modules, available in every Python:

pickle
> Serializes arbitrary Python objects to and from a string of bytes

dbm *(named* anydbm *in Python 2.X)*
> Implements an access-by-key filesystem for storing strings

shelve
> Uses the other two modules to store Python objects on a file by key

We met these modules very briefly in Chapter 9 when we studied file basics. They provide powerful data storage options. Although we can't do them complete justice in this tutorial or book, they are simple enough that a brief introduction is enough to get you started.

The pickle module

The pickle module is a sort of super-general object formatting and deformatting tool: given a nearly arbitrary Python object in memory, it's clever enough to convert the object to a string of bytes, which it can use later to reconstruct the original object in memory. The pickle module can handle almost any object you can create—lists, dictionaries, nested combinations thereof, and class instances. The latter are especially useful things to pickle, because they provide both data (attributes) and behavior (methods); in fact, the combination is roughly equivalent to "records" and "programs." Because `pickle` is so general, it can replace extra code you might otherwise write to create and parse custom text file representations for your objects. By storing an object's pickle string on a file, you effectively make it permanent and persistent: simply load and unpickle it later to re-create the original object.

The shelve module

Although it's easy to use `pickle` by itself to store objects in simple flat files and load them from there later, the `shelve` module provides an extra layer of structure that allows you to store pickled objects by *key*. `shelve` translates an object to its pickled string with `pickle` and stores that string under a key in a `dbm` file; when later loading, `shelve` fetches the pickled string by key and re-creates the original object in memory with `pickle`. This is all quite a trick, but to your script a shelve[2] of pickled objects looks just like a *dictionary*—you index by key to fetch, assign to keys to store, and use dictionary tools such as `len`, `in`, and `dict.keys` to get information. Shelves automatically map dictionary operations to objects stored in a file.

In fact, to your script the only coding difference between a shelve and a normal dictionary is that you must *open* shelves initially and must *close* them after making changes. The net effect is that a shelve provides a simple database for storing and fetching native Python objects by keys, and thus makes them persistent across program runs. It does not support query tools such as SQL, and it lacks some advanced features found in enterprise-level databases (such as true transaction processing), but native Python objects stored on a shelve may be processed with the full power of the Python language once they are fetched back by key.

Storing Objects on a Shelve Database

Pickling and shelves are somewhat advanced topics, and we won't go into all their details here; you can read more about them in the standard library manuals, as well as application-focused books such as the *Programming Python* follow-up text. This is all simpler in Python than in English, though, so let's jump into some code.

Let's write a new script that throws objects of our classes onto a shelve. In your text editor, open a new file we'll call *makedb.py*. Since this is a new file, we'll need to import our classes in order to create a few instances to store. We used `from` to load a class at the interactive prompt earlier, but really, as with functions and other variables, there are two ways to load a class from a file (class names are variables like any other, and not at all magic in this context):

---

2. Yes, we use "shelve" as a noun in Python, much to the chagrin of a variety of editors I've worked with over the years, both electronic and human.

```
import person                                 # Load class with import
bob = person.Person(...)                      # Go through module name

from person import Person                      # Load class with from
bob = Person(...)                              # Use name directly
```

We'll use from to load in our script, just because it's a bit less to type. To keep this simple, copy or retype in our new script the self-test lines from *person.py* that make instances of our classes, so we have something to store (this is a simple demo, so we won't worry about the test-code redundancy here). Once we have some instances, it's almost trivial to store them on a shelve. We simply import the shelve module, open a new shelve with an external filename, assign the objects to keys in the shelve, and close the shelve when we're done because we've made changes:

```
# File makedb.py: store Person objects on a shelve database

from person import Person, Manager            # Load our classes
bob = Person('Bob Smith')                     # Re-create objects to be stored
sue = Person('Sue Jones', job='dev', pay=100000)
tom = Manager('Tom Jones', 50000)

import shelve
db = shelve.open('persondb')                  # Filename where objects are stored
for obj in (bob, sue, tom):                   # Use object's name attr as key
    db[obj.name] = obj                        # Store object on shelve by key
db.close()                                    # Close after making changes
```

Notice how we assign objects to the shelve using their own names as keys. This is just for convenience; in a shelve, the *key* can be any string, including one we might create to be unique using tools such as process IDs and timestamps (available in the os and time standard library modules). The only rule is that the keys must be strings and should be unique, since we can store just one object per key, though that object can be a list, dictionary, or other object containing many objects itself.

In fact, the *values* we store under keys can be Python objects of almost any sort—built-in types like strings, lists, and dictionaries, as well as user-defined class instances, and nested combinations of all of these and more. For example, the name and job attributes of our objects could be nested dictionaries and lists as in earlier incarnations in this book (though this would require a bit of redesign to the current code).

That's all there is to it—if this script has no output when run, it means it probably worked; we're not printing anything, just creating and storing objects in a file-based database.

```
C:\code> makedb.py
```

Exploring Shelves Interactively

At this point, there are one or more real files in the current directory whose names all start with "persondb". The actual files created can vary per platform, and just as in the built-in open function, the filename in shelve.open() is relative to the current working directory unless it includes a directory path. Wherever they are stored, these files implement a keyed-access file that contains the pickled representation of our three Python objects. Don't delete these files—they are your database, and are what you'll need to copy or transfer when you back up or move your storage.

You can look at the shelve's files if you want to, either from Windows Explorer or the Python shell, but they are binary hash files, and most of their content makes little sense outside the context of the shelve module. With Python 3.X and no extra software installed, our database is stored in three files (in 2.X, it's just one file, *persondb*, because the bsddb extension module is preinstalled with Python for shelves; in 3.X, bsddb is an optional third-party open source add-on).

For example, Python's standard library glob module allows us to get directory listings in Python code to verify the files here, and we can open the files in text or binary mode to explore strings and bytes:

```
>>> import glob
>>> glob.glob('person*')
['person-composite.py', 'person-department.py', 'person.py', 'person.pyc',
'persondb.bak', 'persondb.dat', 'persondb.dir']

>>> print(open('persondb.dir').read())
'Sue Jones', (512, 92)
'Tom Jones', (1024, 91)
'Bob Smith', (0, 80)

>>> print(open('persondb.dat','rb').read())
b'\x80\x03cperson\nPerson\nq\x00)\x81q\x01}q\x02(X\x03\x00\x00\x00jobq\x03NX\x03\x00
...more omitted...
```

This content isn't impossible to decipher, but it can vary on different platforms and doesn't exactly qualify as a user-friendly database interface! To verify our work better, we can write another script, or poke around our shelve at the interactive prompt. Because shelves are Python objects containing Python objects, we can process them with normal Python syntax and development modes. Here, the interactive prompt effectively becomes a *database client*:

```
>>> import shelve
>>> db = shelve.open('persondb')          # Reopen the shelve

>>> len(db)                               # Three 'records' stored
3
>>> list(db.keys())                       # keys is the index
['Sue Jones', 'Tom Jones', 'Bob Smith']   # list() to make a list in 3.X

>>> bob = db['Bob Smith']                 # Fetch bob by key
>>> bob                                   # Runs __repr__ from AttrDisplay
[Person: job=None, name=Bob Smith, pay=0]

>>> bob.lastName()                        # Runs lastName from Person
'Smith'
```

```
>>> for key in db:                                      # Iterate, fetch, print
        print(key, '=>', db[key])

Sue Jones => [Person: job=dev, name=Sue Jones, pay=100000]
Tom Jones => [Manager: job=mgr, name=Tom Jones, pay=50000]
Bob Smith => [Person: job=None, name=Bob Smith, pay=0]

>>> for key in sorted(db):
        print(key, '=>', db[key])                       # Iterate by sorted keys

Bob Smith => [Person: job=None, name=Bob Smith, pay=0]
Sue Jones => [Person: job=dev, name=Sue Jones, pay=100000]
Tom Jones => [Manager: job=mgr, name=Tom Jones, pay=50000]
```

Notice that we don't have to import our Person or Manager classes here in order to load or use our stored objects. For example, we can call bob's lastName method freely, and get his custom print display format automatically, even though we don't have his Person class in our scope here. This works because when Python pickles a class instance, it records its self instance attributes, along with the name of the class it was created from and the module where the class lives. When bob is later fetched from the shelve and unpickled, Python will automatically reimport the class and link bob to it.

The upshot of this scheme is that class instances automatically acquire all their class behavior when they are loaded in the future. We have to import our classes only to make new instances, not to process existing ones. Although a deliberate feature, this scheme has somewhat mixed consequences:

- The *downside* is that classes and their module's files must be *importable* when an instance is later loaded. More formally, pickleable classes must be coded at the top level of a module file accessible from a directory listed on the sys.path module search path (and shouldn't live in the topmost script files' module __main__ unless they're always in that module when used). Because of this external module file requirement, some applications choose to pickle simpler objects such as dictionaries or lists, especially if they are to be transferred across the Internet.

- The *upside* is that changes in a class's source code file are automatically picked up when instances of the class are loaded again; there is often no need to update stored objects themselves, since updating their class's code changes their behavior.

Shelves also have well-known limitations (the database suggestions at the end of this chapter mention a few of these). For simple object storage, though, shelves and pickles are remarkably easy-to-use tools.

Updating Objects on a Shelve

Now for one last script: let's write a program that updates an instance (record) each time it runs, to prove the point that our objects really are *persistent*—that their current values are available every time a Python program runs. The following file, *updatedb.py*, prints the database and gives a raise to one of our stored objects each time. If you trace through what's going on here, you'll notice that we're getting a lot of utility "for free"—printing our objects automatically employs the general __repr__ overloading method, and we give raises by calling the giveRaise method we wrote earlier. This all "just works" for objects based on OOP's inheritance model, even when they live in a file:

```
# File updatedb.py: update Person object on database

import shelve
db = shelve.open('persondb')            # Reopen shelve with same filename

for key in sorted(db):                  # Iterate to display database objects
    print(key, '\t=>', db[key])         # Prints with custom format

sue = db['Sue Jones']                   # Index by key to fetch
sue.giveRaise(.10)                      # Update in memory using class's method
db['Sue Jones'] = sue                   # Assign to key to update in shelve
db.close()                              # Close after making changes
```

Because this script prints the database when it starts up, we have to run it at least twice to see our objects change. Here it is in action, displaying all records and increasing sue's pay each time it is run (it's a pretty good script for sue...something to schedule to run regularly as a cron job perhaps?):

```
C:\code> updatedb.py
Bob Smith       => [Person: job=None, name=Bob Smith, pay=0]
Sue Jones       => [Person: job=dev, name=Sue Jones, pay=100000]
Tom Jones       => [Manager: job=mgr, name=Tom Jones, pay=50000]

C:\code> updatedb.py
Bob Smith       => [Person: job=None, name=Bob Smith, pay=0]
Sue Jones       => [Person: job=dev, name=Sue Jones, pay=110000]
Tom Jones       => [Manager: job=mgr, name=Tom Jones, pay=50000]

C:\code> updatedb.py
Bob Smith       => [Person: job=None, name=Bob Smith, pay=0]
Sue Jones       => [Person: job=dev, name=Sue Jones, pay=121000]
Tom Jones       => [Manager: job=mgr, name=Tom Jones, pay=50000]

C:\code> updatedb.py
Bob Smith       => [Person: job=None, name=Bob Smith, pay=0]
Sue Jones       => [Person: job=dev, name=Sue Jones, pay=133100]
Tom Jones       => [Manager: job=mgr, name=Tom Jones, pay=50000]
```

Again, what we see here is a product of the shelve and pickle tools we get from Python, and of the behavior we coded in our classes ourselves. And once again, we can verify our script's work at the interactive prompt—the shelve's equivalent of a database client:

```
C:\code> python
>>> import shelve
>>> db = shelve.open('persondb')        # Reopen database
>>> rec = db['Sue Jones']               # Fetch object by key
>>> rec
[Person: job=dev, name=Sue Jones, pay=146410]
```

```
>>> rec.lastName()
'Jones'
>>> rec.pay
146410
```

For another example of object persistence in this book, see the sidebar in Chapter 31 titled "Why You Will Care: Classes and Persistence" on page 941. It stores a somewhat larger composite object in a flat file with `pickle` instead of `shelve`, but the effect is similar. For more details and examples for both pickles and shelves, see also Chapter 9 (file basics) and Chapter 37 (3.X string tool changes), other books, and Python's manuals.

Future Directions

And that's a wrap for this tutorial. At this point, you've seen all the basics of Python's OOP machinery in action, and you've learned ways to avoid redundancy and its associated maintenance issues in your code. You've built full-featured classes that do real work. As an added bonus, you've made them real database records by storing them in a Python shelve, so their information lives on persistently.

There is much more we could explore here, of course. For example, we could extend our classes to make them more realistic, add new kinds of behavior to them, and so on. Giving a raise, for instance, should in practice verify that pay increase rates are between zero and one—an extension we'll add when we meet decorators later in this book. You might also mutate this example into a personal contacts database, by changing the state information stored on objects, as well as the classes' methods used to process it. We'll leave this a suggested exercise open to your imagination.

We could also expand our scope to use tools that either come with Python or are freely available in the open source world:

GUIs

As is, we can only process our database with the interactive prompt's command-based interface, and scripts. We could also work on expanding our object database's usability by adding a desktop graphical user interface for browsing and updating its records. GUIs can be built portably with either Python's `tkinter` (Tkinter in 2.X) standard library support, or third-party toolkits such as WxPython and PyQt. `tkinter` ships with Python, lets you build simple GUIs quickly, and is ideal for learning GUI programming techniques; WxPython and PyQt tend to be more complex to use but often produce higher-grade GUIs in the end.

Websites

Although GUIs are convenient and fast, the Web is hard to beat in terms of accessibility. We might also implement a website for browsing and updating records, instead of or in addition to GUIs and the interactive prompt. Websites can be constructed with either basic CGI scripting tools that come with Python, or full-featured third-party web frameworks such as Django, TurboGears, Pylons, web2Py, Zope, or Google's App Engine. On the Web, your data can still be stored in a shelve, pickle file, or other Python-based medium; the scripts that process it are simply run automatically on a server in response to requests from web browsers and other clients, and they produce HTML to interact with a user, either directly or by interfacing with framework APIs. Rich Internet application (RIA) systems such as Silverlight and pyjamas also attempt to combine GUI-like interactivity with web-based deployment.

Web services

Although web clients can often parse information in the replies from websites (a technique colorfully known as "screen scraping"), we might go further and provide a more direct way to fetch records on the Web via a web services interface such as SOAP or XML-RPC calls—APIs supported by either Python itself or the third-party open source domain, which generally map data to and from XML format for transmission. To Python scripts, such APIs return data more directly than text embedded in the HTML of a reply page.

Databases

If our database becomes higher-volume or critical, we might eventually move it from shelves to a more full-featured storage mechanism such as the open source ZODB object-oriented database system (OODB), or a more traditional SQL-based relational database system such as MySQL, Oracle, or PostgreSQL. Python itself comes with the in-process SQLite database system built-in, but other open source options are freely available on the Web. ZODB, for example, is similar to Python's `shelve` but addresses many of its limitations, better supporting larger databases, concurrent updates, transaction processing, and automatic write-through on in-memory changes (shelves can cache objects and flush to disk at close time with their `writeback` option, but this has limitations: see other resources). SQL-based systems like MySQL offer enterprise-level tools for database storage and may be directly used from a Python script. As we saw in Chapter 9, MongoDB offers an alternative approach that stores JSON documents, which closely parallel Python dictionaries and lists, and are language neutral, unlike `pickle` data.

ORMs

If we do migrate to a relational database system for storage, we don't have to sacrifice Python's OOP tools. Object-relational mappers (ORMs) like SQLObject and SQLAlchemy can automatically map relational tables and rows to and from Python classes and instances, such that we can process the stored data using normal Python class syntax. This approach provides an alternative to OODBs like `shelve` and ZODB and leverages the power of both relational databases and Python's class model.

While I hope this introduction whets your appetite for future exploration, all of these topics are of course far beyond the scope of this tutorial and this book at large. If you want to explore any of them on your own, see the Web, Python's standard library manuals, and application-focused books such as *Programming Python*. In the latter I pick up this example where we've stopped here, showing how to add both a GUI and a website on top of the database to allow for browsing and updating instance records. I hope to see you there eventually, but first, let's return to class fundamentals and finish up the rest of the core Python language story.

Chapter Summary

In this chapter, we explored all the fundamentals of Python classes and OOP in action, by building upon a simple but real example, step by step. We added constructors, methods, operator overloading, customization with subclasses, and introspection-based tools, and we met other concepts such as composition, delegation, and polymorphism along the way.

In the end, we took objects created by our classes and made them persistent by storing them on a shelve object database—an easy-to-use system for saving and retrieving native Python objects by key. While exploring class basics, we also encountered multiple ways to factor our code to reduce redundancy and minimize future maintenance costs. Finally, we briefly previewed ways to extend our code with application-programming tools such as GUIs and databases, covered in follow-up books.

In the next chapters of this part of the book, we'll return to our study of the details behind Python's class model and investigate its application to some of the design concepts used to combine classes in larger programs. Before we move ahead, though, let's work through this chapter's quiz to review what we covered here. Since we've already done a lot of hands-on work in this chapter, we'll close with a set of mostly theory-oriented questions designed to make you trace through some of the code and ponder some of the bigger ideas behind it.

Test Your Knowledge: Quiz

1. When we fetch a `Manager` object from the shelve and print it, where does the display format logic come from?

2. When we fetch a `Person` object from a shelve without importing its module, how does the object know that it has a `giveRaise` method that we can call?

3. Why is it so important to move processing into methods, instead of hardcoding it outside the class?

4. Why is it better to customize by subclassing rather than copying the original and modifying?

5. Why is it better to call back to a superclass method to run default actions, instead of copying and modifying its code in a subclass?

6. Why is it better to use tools like `__dict__` that allow objects to be processed generically than to write more custom code for each type of class?

7. In general terms, when might you choose to use object embedding and composition instead of inheritance?

8. What would you have to change if the objects coded in this chapter used a dictionary for names and a list for jobs, as in similar examples earlier in this book?

9. How might you modify the classes in this chapter to implement a personal contacts database in Python?

Test Your Knowledge: Answers

1. In the final version of our classes, Manager ultimately inherits its __repr__ printing method from AttrDisplay in the separate classtools module and two levels up in the class tree. Manager doesn't have one itself, so the inheritance search climbs to its Person superclass; because there is no __repr__ there either, the search climbs higher and finds it in AttrDisplay. The class names listed in parentheses in a class statement's header line provide the links to higher superclasses.

2. Shelves (really, the pickle module they use) automatically relink an instance to the class it was created from when that instance is later loaded back into memory. Python reimports the class from its module internally, creates an instance with its stored attributes, and sets the instance's __class__ link to point to its original class. This way, loaded instances automatically obtain all their original methods (like lastName, giveRaise, and __repr__), even if we have not imported the instance's class into our scope.

3. It's important to move processing into methods so that there is only one copy to change in the future, and so that the methods can be run on any instance. This is Python's notion of *encapsulation*—wrapping up logic behind interfaces, to better support future code maintenance. If you don't do so, you create code redundancy that can multiply your work effort as the code evolves in the future.

4. Customizing with subclasses reduces development effort. In OOP, we code by *customizing* what has already been done, rather than copying or changing existing code. This is the real "big idea" in OOP—because we can easily extend our prior work by coding new subclasses, we can leverage what we've already done. This is much better than either starting from scratch each time, or introducing multiple redundant copies of code that may all have to be updated in the future.

5. Copying and modifying code *doubles* your potential work effort in the future, regardless of the context. If a subclass needs to perform default actions coded in a superclass method, it's much better to call back to the original through the superclass's name than to copy its code. This also holds true for superclass constructors. Again, copying code creates redundancy, which is a major issue as code evolves.

6. Generic tools can avoid hardcoded solutions that must be kept in sync with the rest of the class as it evolves over time. A generic __repr__ print method, for example, need not be updated each time a new attribute is added to instances in an

__init__ constructor. In addition, a generic `print` method inherited by all classes appears and need be modified in only one place—changes in the generic version are picked up by all classes that inherit from the generic class. Again, eliminating code *redundancy* cuts future development effort; that's one of the primary assets classes bring to the table.

7. Inheritance is best at coding extensions based on direct customization (like our `Manager` specialization of `Person`). Composition is well suited to scenarios where multiple objects are aggregated into a whole and directed by a controller layer class. Inheritance passes calls *up* to reuse, and composition passes *down* to delegate. Inheritance and composition are not mutually exclusive; often, the objects embedded in a controller are themselves customizations based upon inheritance.

8. Not much since this was really a first-cut prototype, but the `lastName` method would need to be updated for the new namc formal; the `Person` constructor would have change the job default to an empty list; and the `Manager` class would probably need to pass along a job list in its constructor instead of a single string (self-test code would change as well, of course). The good news is that these changes would need to be made in just one place—in our classes, where such details are encapsulated. The database scripts should work as is, as shelves support arbitrarily nested data.

9. The classes in this chapter could be used as boilerplate "template" code to implement a variety of types of databases. Essentially, you can repurpose them by modifying the constructors to record different attributes and providing whatever methods are appropriate for the target application. For instance, you might use attributes such as `name`, `address`, `birthday`, `phone`, `email`, and so on for a contacts database, and methods appropriate for this purpose. A method named `sendmail`, for example, might use Python's standard library `smptlib` module to send an email to one of the contacts automatically when called (see Python's manuals or application-level books for more details on such tools). The `AttrDisplay` tool we wrote here could be used verbatim to print your objects, because it is intentionally generic. Most of the shelve database code here can be used to store your objects, too, with minor changes.

Class Coding Details

If you haven't quite gotten all of Python OOP yet, don't worry; now that we've had a first tour, we're going to dig a bit deeper and study the concepts introduced earlier in further detail. In this and the following chapter, we'll take another look at class mechanics. Here, we're going to study classes, methods, and inheritance, formalizing and expanding on some of the coding ideas introduced in Chapter 27. Because the class is our last namespace tool, we'll summarize Python's namespace and scope concepts as well.

The next chapter continues this in-depth second pass over class mechanics by covering one specific aspect: operator overloading. Besides presenting additional details, this chapter and the next also give us an opportunity to explore some larger classes than those we have studied so far.

Content note: if you've been reading linearly, some of this chapter will be review and summary of topics introduced in the preceding chapter's case study, revisited here by language topics with smaller and more self-contained examples for readers new to OOP. Others may be tempted to skip some of this chapter, but be sure to see the namespace coverage here, as it explains some subtleties in Python's class model.

The class Statement

Although the Python `class` statement may seem similar to tools in other OOP languages on the surface, on closer inspection, it is quite different from what some programmers are used to. For example, as in C++, the `class` statement is Python's main OOP tool, but unlike in C++, Python's `class` is not a declaration. Like a `def`, a `class` statement is an object builder, and an implicit assignment—when run, it generates a class object and stores a reference to it in the name used in the header. Also like a `def`, a `class` statement is true executable code—your class doesn't exist until Python reaches and runs the `class` statement that defines it. This typically occurs while importing the module it is coded in, but not before.

General Form

`class` is a compound statement, with a body of statements typically indented appearing under the header. In the header, superclasses are listed in parentheses after the class name, separated by commas. Listing more than one superclass leads to multiple inheritance, which we'll discuss more formally in Chapter 31. Here is the statement's general form:

```
class name(superclass,...):      # Assign to name
    attr = value                 # Shared class data
    def method(self,...):        # Methods
        self.attr = value        # Per-instance data
```

Within the `class` statement, any assignments generate class attributes, and specially named methods overload operators; for instance, a function called __init__ is called at instance object construction time, if defined.

Example

As we've seen, classes are mostly just *namespaces*—that is, tools for defining names (i.e., attributes) that export data and logic to clients. A `class` statement effectively defines a namespace. Just as in a module file, the statements nested in a `class` statement body create its attributes. When Python executes a `class` statement (not a call to a class), it runs all the statements in its body, from top to bottom. Assignments that happen during this process create names in the class's local scope, which become attributes in the associated class object. Because of this, classes resemble both *modules* and *functions*:

- Like functions, `class` statements are local scopes where names created by nested assignments live.
- Like names in a module, names assigned in a `class` statement become attributes in a class object.

The main distinction for classes is that their namespaces are also the basis of *inheritance* in Python; reference attributes that are not found in a class or instance object are fetched from other classes.

Because `class` is a compound statement, any sort of statement can be nested inside its body—`print`, assignments, `if`, `def`, and so on. All the statements inside the `class` statement run when the `class` statement itself runs (not when the class is later called to make an instance). Typically, assignment statements inside the `class` statement make data attributes, and nested `def`s make method attributes. In general, though, any type of name assignment at the top level of a `class` statement creates a same-named attribute of the resulting class object.

For example, assignments of simple nonfunction objects to class attributes produce *data attributes*, shared by all instances:

```
>>> class SharedData:
        spam = 42                  # Generates a class data attribute

>>> x = SharedData()              # Make two instances
>>> y = SharedData()
>>> x.spam, y.spam                # They inherit and share 'spam' (a.k.a. SharedData.spam)
(42, 42)
```

Here, because the name spam is assigned at the top level of a class statement, it is attached to the class and so will be shared by all instances. We can change it by going through the class name, and we can refer to it through either instances or the class:[1]

```
>>> SharedData.spam = 99
>>> x.spam, y.spam, SharedData.spam
(99, 99, 99)
```

Such class attributes can be used to manage information that spans all the instances—a counter of the number of instances generated, for example (we'll expand on this idea by example in Chapter 32). Now, watch what happens if we assign the name spam through an instance instead of the class:

```
>>> x.spam = 88
>>> x.spam, y.spam, SharedData.spam
(88, 99, 99)
```

Assignments to instance attributes create or change the names in the instance, rather than in the shared class. More generally, inheritance searches occur only on attribute *references*, not on assignment: assigning to an object's attribute always changes that object, and no other.[2] For example, y.spam is looked up in the class by inheritance, but the assignment to x.spam attaches a name to x itself.

Here's a more comprehensive example of this behavior that stores the same name in two places. Suppose we run the following class:

```
class MixedNames:                          # Define class
    data = 'spam'                          # Assign class attr
    def __init__(self, value):             # Assign method name
        self.data = value                  # Assign instance attr
    def display(self):
        print(self.data, MixedNames.data)  # Instance attr, class attr
```

---

1. If you've used C++ you may recognize this as similar to the notion of C++'s "static" data members—members that are stored in the class, independent of instances. In Python, it's nothing special: all class attributes are just names assigned in the class statement, whether they happen to reference functions (C++'s "methods") or something else (C++'s "members"). In Chapter 32, we'll also meet Python static methods (akin to those in C++), which are just self-less functions that usually process class attributes.

2. Unless the class has redefined the attribute assignment operation to do something unique with the __setattr__ operator overloading method (discussed in Chapter 30), or uses advanced attribute tools such as *properties* and *descriptors* (discussed in Chapter 32 and Chapter 38). Much of this chapter presents the normal case, which suffices at this point in the book, but as we'll see later, Python hooks allow programs to deviate from the norm often.

This class contains two defs, which bind class attributes to method functions. It also contains an = assignment statement; because this assignment assigns the name data inside the class, it lives in the class's local scope and becomes an attribute of the class object. Like all class attributes, this data is inherited and shared by all instances of the class that don't have data attributes of their own.

When we make instances of this class, the name data is attached to those instances by the assignment to self.data in the constructor method:

```
>>> x = MixedNames(1)          # Make two instance objects
>>> y = MixedNames(2)          # Each has its own data
>>> x.display(); y.display()   # self.data differs, MixedNames.data is the same
1 spam
2 spam
```

The net result is that data lives in two places: in the instance objects (created by the self.data assignment in __init__), and in the class from which they inherit names (created by the data assignment in the class). The class's display method prints both versions, by first qualifying the self instance, and then the class.

By using these techniques to store attributes in different objects, we determine their scope of visibility. When attached to classes, names are shared; in instances, names record per-instance data, not shared behavior or data. Although inheritance searches look up names for us, we can always get to an attribute anywhere in a tree by accessing the desired object directly.

In the preceding example, for instance, specifying x.data or self.data will return an instance name, which normally hides the same name in the class; however, Mixed Names.data grabs the class's version of the name explicitly. The next section describes one of the most common roles for such coding patterns, and explains more about the way we deployed it in the prior chapter.

Methods

Because you already know about functions, you also know about methods in classes. Methods are just function objects created by def statements nested in a class statement's body. From an abstract perspective, methods provide behavior for instance objects to inherit. From a programming perspective, methods work in exactly the same way as simple functions, with one crucial exception: a method's first argument always receives the instance object that is the implied subject of the method call.

In other words, Python automatically maps instance method calls to a class's method functions as follows. Method calls made through an instance, like this:

```
instance.method(args...)
```

are automatically translated to class method function calls of this form:

```
class.method(instance, args...)
```

where Python determines the class by locating the method name using the inheritance search procedure. In fact, both call forms are valid in Python.

Besides the normal inheritance of method attribute names, the special first argument is the only real magic behind method calls. In a class's method, the first argument is usually called self by convention (technically, only its position is significant, not its name). This argument provides methods with a hook back to the instance that is the subject of the call—because classes generate many instance objects, they need to use this argument to manage data that varies per instance.

C++ programmers may recognize Python's self argument as being similar to C++'s this pointer. In Python, though, self is always explicit in your code: methods must always go through self to fetch or change attributes of the instance being processed by the current method call. This explicit nature of self is by design—the presence of this name makes it obvious that you are using instance attribute names in your script, not names in the local or global scope.

Method Example

To clarify these concepts, let's turn to an example. Suppose we define the following class:

```
class NextClass:                    # Define class
    def printer(self, text):        # Define method
        self.message = text         # Change instance
        print(self.message)         # Access instance
```

The name printer references a function object; because it's assigned in the class statement's scope, it becomes a class object attribute and is inherited by every instance made from the class. Normally, because methods like printer are designed to process instances, we call them through instances:

```
>>> x = NextClass()                 # Make instance
>>> x.printer('instance call')      # Call its method
instance call
>>> x.message                       # Instance changed
'instance call'
```

When we call the method by qualifying an instance like this, printer is first located by inheritance, and then its self argument is automatically assigned the instance object (x); the text argument gets the string passed at the call ('instance call'). Notice that because Python automatically passes the first argument to self for us, we only actually have to pass in one argument. Inside printer, the name self is used to access or set per-instance data because it refers back to the instance currently being processed.

As we've seen, though, methods may be called in one of two ways—through an instance, or through the class itself. For example, we can also call printer by going through the class name, provided we pass an instance to the self argument explicitly:

```
>>> NextClass.printer(x, 'class call')        # Direct class call
class call
>>> x.message                                 # Instance changed again
'class call'
```

Calls routed through the instance and the class have the exact same effect, as long as we pass the same instance object ourselves in the class form. By default, in fact, you get an error message if you try to call a method without any instance:

```
>>> NextClass.printer('bad call')
TypeError: unbound method printer() must be called with NextClass instance...
```

Calling Superclass Constructors

Methods are normally called through instances. Calls to methods through a class, though, do show up in a variety of special roles. One common scenario involves the constructor method. The __init__ method, like all attributes, is looked up by inheritance. This means that at construction time, Python locates and calls just *one* __init__. If subclass constructors need to guarantee that superclass construction-time logic runs, too, they generally must call the superclass's __init__ method explicitly through the class:

```
class Super:
    def __init__(self, x):
        ...default code...

class Sub(Super):
    def __init__(self, x, y):
        Super.__init__(self, x)          # Run superclass __init__
        ...custom code...                # Do my init actions

I = Sub(1, 2)
```

This is one of the few contexts in which your code is likely to call an operator over-loading method directly. Naturally, you should call the superclass constructor this way only if you really *want* it to run—without the call, the subclass replaces it completely. For a more realistic illustration of this technique in action, see the Manager class example in the prior chapter's tutorial.[3]

Other Method Call Possibilities

This pattern of calling methods through a class is the general basis of extending—instead of completely replacing—inherited method behavior. It requires an explicit instance to be passed because all methods do by default. Technically, this is because methods are *instance methods* in the absence of any special code.

---

3. On a related note, you can also code multiple __init__ methods within the same class, but only the last definition will be used; see Chapter 31 for more details on multiple method definitions.

In Chapter 32, we'll also meet a newer option added in Python 2.2, *static methods*, that allow you to code methods that do not expect instance objects in their first arguments. Such methods can act like simple instanceless functions, with names that are local to the classes in which they are coded, and may be used to manage class data. A related concept we'll meet in the same chapter, the *class method*, receives a class when called instead of an instance and can be used to manage per-class data, and is implied in metaclasses.

These are both advanced and usually optional extensions, though. Normally, an instance must always be passed to a method—whether automatically when it is called through an instance, or manually when you call through a class.

 Per the sidebar "What About super?" on page 831 in Chapter 28, Python also has a **super** built-in function that allows calling back to a superclass's methods more generically, but we'll defer its presentation until Chapter 32 due to its downsides and complexities. See the aforementioned sidebar for more details; this call has well-known tradeoffs in basic usage, and an esoteric advanced use case that requires universal deployment to be most effective. Because of these issues, this book prefers to call superclasses by explicit name instead of **super** as a policy; if you're new to Python, I recommend the same approach for now, especially for your first pass over OOP. Learn the simple way now, so you can compare it to others later.

Inheritance

Of course, the whole point of the namespace created by the **class** statement is to support name inheritance. This section expands on some of the mechanisms and roles of attribute inheritance in Python.

As we've seen, in Python, inheritance happens when an object is qualified, and it involves searching an attribute definition tree—one or more namespaces. Every time you use an expression of the form *object.attr* where *object* is an instance or class object, Python searches the namespace tree from bottom to top, beginning with *object*, looking for the first *attr* it can find. This includes references to **self** attributes in your methods. Because lower definitions in the tree override higher ones, inheritance forms the basis of specialization.

Attribute Tree Construction

Figure 29-1 summarizes the way namespace trees are constructed and populated with names. Generally:

- Instance attributes are generated by assignments to **self** attributes in methods.
- Class attributes are created by statements (assignments) in **class** statements.

- Superclass links are made by listing classes in parentheses in a **class** statement header.

The net result is a tree of attribute namespaces that leads from an instance, to the class it was generated from, to all the superclasses listed in the **class** header. Python searches upward in this tree, from instances to superclasses, each time you use qualification to fetch an attribute name from an instance object.[4]

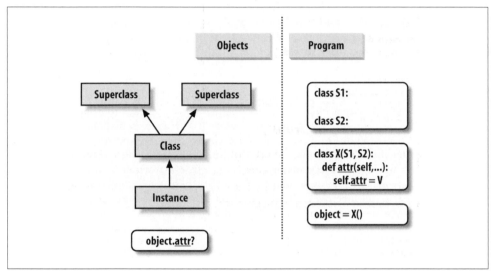

Figure 29-1. Program code creates a tree of objects in memory to be searched by attribute inheritance. Calling a class creates a new instance that remembers its class, running a class statement creates a new class, and superclasses are listed in parentheses in the class statement header. Each attribute reference triggers a new bottom-up tree search—even references to self attributes within a class's methods.

Specializing Inherited Methods

The tree-searching model of inheritance just described turns out to be a great way to specialize systems. Because inheritance finds names in subclasses before it checks superclasses, subclasses can replace default behavior by redefining their superclasses'

---

4. Two fine points here: first, this description isn't 100% complete, because we can also create instance and class attributes by assigning them to objects outside **class** statements—but that's a much less common and sometimes more error-prone approach (changes aren't isolated to **class** statements). In Python, all attributes are always accessible by default. We'll talk more about attribute name *privacy* in Chapter 30 when we study __setattr__, in Chapter 31 when we meet _X names, and again in Chapter 39, where we'll implement it with a class decorator.

Second, as also noted in Chapter 27, the full *inheritance* story grows more convoluted when advanced topics such as *metaclasses* and *descriptors* are added to the mix—and we're deferring a formal definition until Chapter 40 for this reason. In common usage, though, it's simply a way to redefine, and hence customize, behavior coded in classes.

attributes. In fact, you can build entire systems as hierarchies of classes, which you extend by adding new external subclasses rather than changing existing logic in place.

The idea of redefining inherited names leads to a variety of specialization techniques. For instance, subclasses may *replace* inherited attributes completely, *provide* attributes that a superclass expects to find, and *extend* superclass methods by calling back to the superclass from an overridden method. We've already seen some of these patterns in action; here's a self-contained example of extension at work:

```
>>> class Super:
        def method(self):
            print('in Super.method')

>>> class Sub(Super):
        def method(self):                          # Override method
            print('starting Sub.method')           # Add actions here
            Super.method(self)                     # Run default action
            print('ending Sub.method')
```

Direct superclass method calls are the crux of the matter here. The Sub class replaces Super's method function with its own specialized version, but within the replacement, Sub calls back to the version exported by Super to carry out the default behavior. In other words, Sub.method just extends Super.method's behavior, rather than replacing it completely:

```
>>> x = Super()                              # Make a Super instance
>>> x.method()                               # Runs Super.method
in Super.method

>>> x = Sub()                                # Make a Sub instance
>>> x.method()                               # Runs Sub.method, calls Super.method
starting Sub.method
in Super.method
ending Sub.method
```

This extension coding pattern is also commonly used with constructors; see the section "Methods" on page 862 for an example.

Class Interface Techniques

Extension is only one way to interface with a superclass. The file shown in this section, *specialize.py*, defines multiple classes that illustrate a variety of common techniques:

Super
: Defines a method function and a delegate that expects an action in a subclass.

Inheritor
: Doesn't provide any new names, so it gets everything defined in Super.

Replacer
: Overrides Super's method with a version of its own.

Extender

Customizes Super's method by overriding and calling back to run the default.

Provider

Implements the action method expected by Super's delegate method.

Study each of these subclasses to get a feel for the various ways they customize their common superclass. Here's the file:

```python
class Super:
    def method(self):
        print('in Super.method')          # Default behavior
    def delegate(self):
        self.action()                      # Expected to be defined

class Inheritor(Super):                    # Inherit method verbatim
    pass

class Replacer(Super):                     # Replace method completely
    def method(self):
        print('in Replacer.method')

class Extender(Super):                     # Extend method behavior
    def method(self):
        print('starting Extender.method')
        Super.method(self)
        print('ending Extender.method')

class Provider(Super):                     # Fill in a required method
    def action(self):
        print('in Provider.action')

if __name__ == '__main__':
    for klass in (Inheritor, Replacer, Extender):
        print('\n' + klass.__name__ + '...')
        klass().method()
    print('\nProvider...')
    x = Provider()
    x.delegate()
```

A few things are worth pointing out here. First, notice how the self-test code at the end of this example creates instances of three different classes in a for loop. Because classes are objects, you can store them in a tuple and create instances generically with no extra syntax (more on this idea later). Classes also have the special __name__ attribute, like modules; it's preset to a string containing the name in the class header. Here's what happens when we run the file:

```
% python specialize.py

Inheritor...
in Super.method

Replacer...
in Replacer.method
```

```
Extender...
starting Extender.method
in Super.method
ending Extender.method

Provider...
in Provider.action
```

Abstract Superclasses

Of the prior example's classes, `Provider` may be the most crucial to understand. When we call the `delegate` method through a `Provider` instance, *two* independent inheritance searches occur:

1. On the initial `x.delegate` call, Python finds the `delegate` method in `Super` by searching the `Provider` instance and above. The instance `x` is passed into the method's `self` argument as usual.

2. Inside the `Super.delegate` method, `self.action` invokes a new, independent inheritance search of `self` and above. Because `self` references a `Provider` instance, the `action` method is located in the `Provider` subclass.

This "filling in the blanks" sort of coding structure is typical of OOP frameworks. In a more realistic context, the method filled in this way might handle an event in a GUI, provide data to be rendered as part of a web page, process a tag's text in an XML file, and so on—your subclass provides specific actions, but the framework handles the rest of the overall job.

At least in terms of the `delegate` method, the superclass in this example is what is sometimes called an *abstract superclass*—a class that expects parts of its behavior to be provided by its subclasses. If an expected method is not defined in a subclass, Python raises an undefined name exception when the inheritance search fails.

Class coders sometimes make such subclass requirements more obvious with `assert` statements, or by raising the built-in `NotImplementedError` exception with `raise` statements. We'll study statements that may trigger exceptions in depth in the next part of this book; as a quick preview, here's the `assert` scheme in action:

```
class Super:
    def delegate(self):
        self.action()
    def action(self):
        assert False, 'action must be defined!'      # If this version is called

>>> X = Super()
>>> X.delegate()
AssertionError: action must be defined!
```

We'll meet `assert` in Chapter 33 and Chapter 34; in short, if its first expression evaluates to false, it raises an exception with the provided error message. Here, the expression is always false so as to trigger an error message if a method is not redefined, and inheritance locates the version here. Alternatively, some classes simply raise a `NotImplemen` `tedError` exception directly in such method stubs to signal the mistake:

```
class Super:
    def delegate(self):
        self.action()
    def action(self):
        raise NotImplementedError('action must be defined!')

>>> X = Super()
>>> X.delegate()
NotImplementedError: action must be defined!
```

For instances of subclasses, we still get the exception unless the subclass provides the expected method to replace the default in the superclass:

```
>>> class Sub(Super): pass

>>> X = Sub()
>>> X.delegate()
NotImplementedError: action must be defined!

>>> class Sub(Super):
        def action(self): print('spam')

>>> X = Sub()
>>> X.delegate()
spam
```

For a somewhat more realistic example of this section's concepts in action, see the "Zoo animal hierarchy" exercise (Exercise 8) at the end of Chapter 32, and its solution in "Part VI, Classes and OOP" on page 1489 in Appendix D. Such taxonomies are a traditional way to introduce OOP, but they're a bit removed from most developers' job descriptions (with apologies to any readers who happen to work at the zoo!).

Abstract superclasses in Python 3.X and 2.6+: Preview

As of Python 2.6 and 3.0, the prior section's abstract superclasses (a.k.a. "abstract base classes"), which require methods to be filled in by subclasses, may also be implemented with special class syntax. The way we code this varies slightly depending on the version. In Python 3.X, we use a keyword argument in a `class` header, along with special `@` decorator syntax, both of which we'll study in detail later in this book:

```
from abc import ABCMeta, abstractmethod

class Super(metaclass=ABCMeta):
    @abstractmethod
    def method(self, ...):
        pass
```

But in Python 2.6 and 2.7, we use a class attribute instead:

```
class Super:
    __metaclass__ = ABCMeta
    @abstractmethod
    def method(self, ...):
        pass
```

Either way, the effect is the same—we can't make an instance unless the method is defined lower in the class tree. In 3.X, for example, here is the special syntax equivalent of the prior section's example:

```
>>> from abc import ABCMeta, abstractmethod
>>>
>>> class Super(metaclass=ABCMeta):
        def delegate(self):
            self.action()
        @abstractmethod
        def action(self):
            pass

>>> X = Super()
TypeError: Can't instantiate abstract class Super with abstract methods action

>>> class Sub(Super): pass

>>> X = Sub()
TypeError: Can't instantiate abstract class Sub with abstract methods action

>>> class Sub(Super):
        def action(self): print('spam')

>>> X = Sub()
>>> X.delegate()
spam
```

Coded this way, a class with an abstract method cannot be instantiated (that is, we cannot create an instance by calling it) unless all of its abstract methods have been defined in subclasses. Although this requires more code and extra knowledge, the potential advantage of this approach is that errors for missing methods are issued when we attempt to make an instance of the class, not later when we try to call a missing method. This feature may also be used to define an expected interface, automatically verified in client classes.

Unfortunately, this scheme also relies on two advanced language tools we have not met yet—*function decorators*, introduced in Chapter 32 and covered in depth in Chapter 39, as well as *metaclass declarations*, mentioned in Chapter 32 and covered in Chapter 40—so we will finesse other facets of this option here. See Python's standard manuals for more on this, as well as precoded abstract superclasses Python provides.

Namespaces: The Conclusion

Now that we've examined class and instance objects, the Python namespace story is complete. For reference, I'll quickly summarize all the rules used to resolve names here. The first things you need to remember are that qualified and unqualified names are treated differently, and that some scopes serve to initialize object namespaces:

- Unqualified names (e.g., X) deal with scopes.
- Qualified attribute names (e.g., *object*.X) use object namespaces.
- Some scopes initialize object namespaces (for modules and classes).

These concepts sometimes interact—in *object*.X, for example, object is looked up per scopes, and then X is looked up in the result objects. Since scopes and namespaces are essential to understanding Python code, let's summarize the rules in more detail.

Simple Names: Global Unless Assigned

As we've learned, unqualified simple names follow the LEGB lexical scoping rule outlined when we explored functions in Chapter 17:

Assignment (X = value)
> Makes names local by default: creates or changes the name X in the current local scope, unless declared global (or nonlocal in 3.X).

Reference (X)
> Looks for the name X in the current local scope, then any and all enclosing functions, then the current global scope, then the built-in scope, per the LEGB rule. Enclosing classes are not searched: class names are fetched as object attributes instead.

Also per Chapter 17, some special-case constructs localize names further (e.g., variables in some comprehensions and try statement clauses), but the vast majority of names follow the LEGB rule.

Attribute Names: Object Namespaces

We've also seen that qualified attribute names refer to attributes of specific objects and obey the rules for modules and classes. For class and instance objects, the reference rules are augmented to include the inheritance search procedure:

Assignment (object.X = value)
> Creates or alters the attribute name X in the namespace of the *object* being qualified, and none other. Inheritance-tree climbing happens only on attribute reference, not on attribute assignment.

Reference (object.X)

> For class-based objects, searches for the attribute name X in *object*, then in all accessible classes above it, using the inheritance search procedure. For nonclass objects such as modules, fetches X from *object* directly.

As noted earlier, the preceding captures the normal and typical case. These attribute rules can vary in classes that utilize more advanced tools, especially for new-style classes —an option in 2.X and the standard in 3.X, which we'll explore in Chapter 32. For example, reference inheritance can be richer than implied here when metaclasses are deployed, and classes which leverage attribute management tools such as properties, descriptors, and __setattr__ can intercept and route attribute assignments arbitrarily.

In fact, some inheritance *is* run on assignment too, to locate descriptors with a __set__ method in new-style classes; such tools override the normal rules for both reference and assignment. We'll explore attribute management tools in depth in Chapter 38, and formalize inheritance and its use of descriptors in Chapter 40. For now, most readers should focus on the normal rules given here, which cover most Python application code.

The "Zen" of Namespaces: Assignments Classify Names

With distinct search procedures for qualified and unqualified names, and multiple lookup layers for both, it can sometimes be difficult to tell where a name will wind up going. In Python, the place where you *assign* a name is crucial—it fully determines the scope or object in which a name will reside. The file *manynames.py* illustrates how this principle translates to code and summarizes the namespace ideas we have seen throughout this book (sans obscure special-case scopes like comprehensions):

```
# File manynames.py

X = 11                      # Global (module) name/attribute (X, or manynames.X)

def f():
    print(X)                # Access global X (11)

def g():
    X = 22                  # Local (function) variable (X, hides module X)
    print(X)

class C:
    X = 33                  # Class attribute (C.X)
    def m(self):
        X = 44              # Local variable in method (X)
        self.X = 55         # Instance attribute (instance.X)
```

This file assigns the same name, X, five times—illustrative, though not exactly best practice! Because this name is assigned in five different locations, though, all five Xs in this program are completely different variables. From top to bottom, the assignments to X here generate: a module attribute (11), a local variable in a function (22), a class attribute (33), a local variable in a method (44), and an instance attribute (55). Although all five are named X, the fact that they are all assigned at different places in the source code or to different objects makes all of these unique variables.

You should take the time to study this example carefully because it collects ideas we've been exploring throughout the last few parts of this book. When it makes sense to you, you will have achieved Python namespace enlightenment. Or, you can run the code and see what happens—here's the remainder of this source file, which makes an instance and prints all the Xs that it can fetch:

```
# manynames.py, continued

if __name__ == '__main__':
    print(X)              # 11: module (a.k.a. manynames.X outside file)
    f()                   # 11: global
    g()                   # 22: local
    print(X)              # 11: module name unchanged

    obj = C()             # Make instance
    print(obj.X)          # 33: class name inherited by instance

    obj.m()               # Attach attribute name X to instance now
    print(obj.X)          # 55: instance
    print(C.X)            # 33: class (a.k.a. obj.X if no X in instance)

    #print(C.m.X)         # FAILS: only visible in method
    #print(g.X)           # FAILS: only visible in function
```

The outputs that are printed when the file is run are noted in the comments in the code; trace through them to see which variable named X is being accessed each time. Notice in particular that we can go through the class to fetch its attribute (C.X), but we can never fetch local variables in functions or methods from outside their def statements. Locals are visible only to other code within the def, and in fact only live in memory while a call to the function or method is executing.

Some of the names defined by this file are visible *outside the file* to other modules too, but recall that we must always import before we can access names in another file—name segregation is the main point of modules, after all:

```
# otherfile.py

import manynames

X = 66
print(X)                    # 66: the global here
print(manynames.X)          # 11: globals become attributes after imports

manynames.f()               # 11: manynames's X, not the one here!
manynames.g()               # 22: local in other file's function

print(manynames.C.X)        # 33: attribute of class in other module
I = manynames.C()
print(I.X)                  # 33: still from class here
```

```
    I.m()
    print(I.X)                      # 55: now from instance!
```

Notice here how `manynames.f()` prints the X in `manynames`, not the X assigned in this file —scopes are always determined by the position of assignments in your source code (i.e., lexically) and are never influenced by what imports what or who imports whom. Also, notice that the instance's own X is not created until we call `I.m()`—attributes, like all variables, spring into existence when assigned, and not before. Normally we create instance attributes by assigning them in class __init__ constructor methods, but this isn't the only option.

Finally, as we learned in Chapter 17, it's also possible for a function to *change* names outside itself, with `global` and (in Python 3.X) `nonlocal` statements—these statements provide write access, but also modify assignment's namespace binding rules:

```
    X = 11                          # Global in module

    def g1():
        print(X)                    # Reference global in module (11)

    def g2():
        global X
        X = 22                      # Change global in module

    def h1():
        X = 33                      # Local in function
        def nested():
            print(X)                # Reference local in enclosing scope (33)

    def h2():
        X = 33                      # Local in function
        def nested():
            nonlocal X              # Python 3.X statement
            X = 44                  # Change local in enclosing scope
```

Of course, you generally shouldn't use the same name for every variable in your script —but as this example demonstrates, even if you do, Python's namespaces will work to keep names used in one context from accidentally clashing with those used in another.

Nested Classes: The LEGB Scopes Rule Revisited

The preceding example summarized the effect of nested functions on scopes, which we studied in Chapter 17. It turns out that classes can be nested too—a useful coding pattern in some types of programs, with scope implications that follow naturally from what you already know, but that may not be obvious on first encounter. This section illustrates the concept by example.

Though they are normally coded at the top level of a module, classes also sometimes appear nested in functions that generate them—a variation on the "factory function" (a.k.a. *closure*) theme in Chapter 17, with similar state retention roles. There we noted that `class` statements introduce new local scopes much like function `def` statements, which follow the same LEGB scope lookup rule as function definitions.

This rule applies both to the top level of the class itself, as well as to the top level of method functions nested within it. Both form the *L* layer in this rule—they are normal local scopes, with access to their names, names in any enclosing functions, globals in the enclosing module, and built-ins. Like modules, the class's local scope *morphs* into an attribute namespace after the `class` statement is run.

Although classes have access to enclosing functions' scopes, though, they do not act as enclosing scopes to code nested within the class: Python searches enclosing functions for referenced names, but *never* any enclosing classes. That is, a class *is* a local scope and has access *to* enclosing local scopes, but it does not *serve* as an enclosing local scope to further nested code. Because the search for names used in method functions skips the enclosing class, class attributes must be fetched as object attributes using inheritance.

For example, in the following `nester` function, all references to X are routed to the global scope except the last, which picks up a local scope redefinition (the section's code is in file *classscope.py*, and the output of each example is described in its last two comments):

```
X = 1

def nester():
    print(X)                    # Global: 1
    class C:
        print(X)                # Global: 1
        def method1(self):
            print(X)            # Global: 1
        def method2(self):
            X = 3               # Hides global
            print(X)            # Local: 3
    I = C()
    I.method1()
    I.method2()

print(X)                        # Global: 1
nester()                        # Rest: 1, 1, 1, 3
print('-'*40)
```

Watch what happens, though, when we reassign the same name in nested function layers: the redefinitions of X create locals that hide those in enclosing scopes, just as for simple nested functions; the enclosing class layer does not change this rule, and in fact is irrelevant to it:

```
X = 1

def nester():
    X = 2                       # Hides global
    print(X)                    # Local: 2
    class C:
        print(X)                # In enclosing def (nester): 2
```

```
        def method1(self):
            print(X)              # In enclosing def (nester): 2
        def method2(self):
            X = 3                 # Hides enclosing (nester)
            print(X)              # Local: 3
    I = C()
    I.method1()
    I.method2()

print(X)                          # Global: 1
nester()                          # Rest: 2, 2, 2, 3
print('-'*40)
```

And here's what happens when we reassign the same name at multiple stops along the way: assignments in the local scopes of both functions and classes hide globals or enclosing function locals of the same name, regardless of the nesting involved:

```
X = 1

def nester():
    X = 2                        # Hides global
    print(X)                     # Local: 2
    class C:
        X = 3                    # Class local hides nester's: C.X or I.X (not scoped)
        print(X)                 # Local: 3
        def method1(self):
            print(X)             # In enclosing def (not 3 in class!): 2
            print(self.X)        # Inherited class local: 3
        def method2(self):
            X = 4                # Hides enclosing (nester, not class)
            print(X)             # Local: 4
            self.X = 5           # Hides class
            print(self.X)        # Located in instance: 5
    I = C()
    I.method1()
    I.method2()

print(X)                         # Global: 1
nester()                         # Rest: 2, 3, 2, 3, 4, 5
print('-'*40)
```

Most importantly, the lookup rules for simple names like X never search enclosing class statements—just defs, modules, and built-ins (it's the LEGB rule, not CLEGB!). In method1, for example, X is found in a def outside the enclosing class that has the same name in its local scope. To get to names assigned in the class (e.g., methods), we must fetch them as class or instance object attributes, via self.X in this case.

Believe it or not, we'll see use cases for this nested classes coding pattern later in this book, especially in some of Chapter 39's *decorators*. In this role, the enclosing function usually both serves as a class factory and provides retained state for later use in the enclosed class or its methods.

Namespace Dictionaries: Review

In Chapter 23, we learned that module namespaces have a concrete implementation as dictionaries, exposed with the built-in __dict__ attribute. In Chapter 27 and Chapter 28, we learned that the same holds true for class and instance objects—attribute qualification is mostly a dictionary indexing operation internally, and attribute inheritance is largely a matter of searching linked dictionaries. In fact, within Python, instance and class objects are mostly just dictionaries with links between them. Python exposes these dictionaries, as well as their links, for use in advanced roles (e.g., for coding tools).

We put some of these tools to work in the prior chapter, but to summarize and help you better understand how attributes work internally, let's work through an interactive session that traces the way namespace dictionaries grow when classes are involved. Now that we know more about methods and superclasses, we can also embellish the coverage here for a better look. First, let's define a superclass and a subclass with methods that will store data in their instances:

```
>>> class Super:
        def hello(self):
            self.data1 = 'spam'

>>> class Sub(Super):
        def hola(self):
            self.data2 = 'eggs'
```

When we make an instance of the subclass, the instance starts out with an empty namespace dictionary, but it has links back to the class for the inheritance search to follow. In fact, the inheritance tree is explicitly available in special attributes, which you can inspect. Instances have a __class__ attribute that links to their class, and classes have a __bases__ attribute that is a tuple containing links to higher superclasses (I'm running this on Python 3.3; your name formats, internal attributes, and key orders may vary):

```
>>> X = Sub()
>>> X.__dict__                      # Instance namespace dict
{}
>>> X.__class__                     # Class of instance
<class '__main__.Sub'>
>>> Sub.__bases__                   # Superclasses of class
(<class '__main__.Super'>,)
>>> Super.__bases__                 # () empty tuple in Python 2.X
(<class 'object'>,)
```

As classes assign to self attributes, they populate the instance objects—that is, attributes wind up in the instances' attribute namespace dictionaries, not in the classes'. An instance object's namespace records data that can vary from instance to instance, and self is a hook into that namespace:

```
>>> Y = Sub()
```

```
>>> X.hello()
>>> X.__dict__
{'data1': 'spam'}

>>> X.hola()
>>> X.__dict__
{'data2': 'eggs', 'data1': 'spam'}

>>> list(Sub.__dict__.keys())
['__qualname__', '__module__', '__doc__', 'hola']
>>> list(Super.__dict__.keys())
['__module__', 'hello', '__dict__', '__qualname__', '__doc__', '__weakref__']

>>> Y.__dict__
{}
```

Notice the extra underscore names in the class dictionaries; Python sets these automatically, and we can filter them out with the generator expressions we saw in Chapter 27 and Chapter 28 that we won't repeat here. Most are not used in typical programs, but there are tools that use some of them (e.g., __doc__ holds the docstrings discussed in Chapter 15).

Also, observe that Y, a second instance made at the start of this series, still has an empty namespace dictionary at the end, even though X's dictionary has been populated by assignments in methods. Again, each instance has an independent namespace dictionary, which starts out empty and can record completely different attributes than those recorded by the namespace dictionaries of other instances of the same class.

Because attributes are actually dictionary keys inside Python, there are really two ways to fetch and assign their values—by qualification, or by key indexing:

```
>>> X.data1, X.__dict__['data1']
('spam', 'spam')

>>> X.data3 = 'toast'
>>> X.__dict__
{'data2': 'eggs', 'data3': 'toast', 'data1': 'spam'}

>>> X.__dict__['data3'] = 'ham'
>>> X.data3
'ham'
```

This equivalence applies only to attributes actually attached to the *instance*, though. Because attribute fetch qualification also performs an inheritance search, it can access *inherited* attributes that namespace dictionary indexing cannot. The inherited attribute X.hello, for instance, cannot be accessed by X.__dict__['hello'].

Experiment with these special attributes on your own to get a better feel for how namespaces actually do their attribute business. Also try running these objects through the dir function we met in the prior two chapters—dir(X) is similar to X.__dict__.keys(), but dir sorts its list and includes some inherited and built-in attributes. Even if you will never use these in the kinds of programs you write, seeing that they are just normal dictionaries can help solidify namespaces in general.

 In Chapter 32, we'll learn also about *slots*, a somewhat advanced new-style class feature that stores attributes in instances, but not in their namespace dictionaries. It's tempting to treat these as class attributes, and indeed, they appear in class namespaces where they manage the per-instance values. As we'll see, though, slots may prevent a __dict__ from being created in the instance entirely—a potential that generic tools must sometimes account for by using storage-neutral tools such as dir and getattr.

Namespace Links: A Tree Climber

The prior section demonstrated the special __class__ and __bases__ instance and class attributes, without really explaining why you might care about them. In short, these attributes allow you to inspect inheritance hierarchies within your own code. For example, they can be used to display a class tree, as in the following Python 3.X and 2.X example:

```python
#!python
"""
classtree.py: Climb inheritance trees using namespace links,
displaying higher superclasses with indentation for height
"""

def classtree(cls, indent):
    print('.' * indent + cls.__name__)      # Print class name here
    for supercls in cls.__bases__:           # Recur to all superclasses
        classtree(supercls, indent+3)        # May visit super > once

def instancetree(inst):
    print('Tree of %s' % inst)               # Show instance
    classtree(inst.__class__, 3)             # Climb to its class

def selftest():
    class A:        pass
    class B(A):     pass
    class C(A):     pass
    class D(B,C):   pass
    class E:        pass
    class F(D,E):   pass
    instancetree(B())
    instancetree(F())

if __name__ == '__main__': selftest()
```

The classtree function in this script is *recursive*—it prints a class's name using __name__, then climbs up to the superclasses by calling itself. This allows the function to traverse arbitrarily shaped class trees; the recursion climbs to the top, and stops at root superclasses that have empty __bases__ attributes. When using recursion, each active level of a function gets its own copy of the local scope; here, this means that cls and indent are different at each classtree level.

Most of this file is self-test code. When run standalone in Python 2.X, it builds an empty class tree, makes two instances from it, and prints their class tree structures:

```
C:\code> c:\python27\python classtree.py
Tree of <__main__.B instance at 0x00000000022C3A88>
...B
......A
Tree of <__main__.F instance at 0x00000000022C3A88>
...F
......D
.........B
............A
.........C
............A
......E
```

When run by Python 3.X, the tree includes the implied object superclass that is auto-matically added above standalone root (i.e., topmost) classes, because all classes are "new style" in 3.X—more on this change in Chapter 32:

```
C:\code> c:\python33\python classtree.py
Tree of <__main__.selftest.<locals>.B object at 0x00000000029216A0>
...B
......A
.........object
Tree of <__main__.selftest.<locals>.F object at 0x00000000029216A0>
...F
......D
.........B
............A
...............object
.........C
............A
...............object
......E
.........object
```

Here, indentation marked by periods is used to denote class tree height. Of course, we could improve on this output format, and perhaps even sketch it in a GUI display. Even as is, though, we can import these functions anywhere we want a quick display of a physical class tree:

```
C:\code> c:\python33\python
>>> class Emp: pass

>>> class Person(Emp): pass

>>> bob = Person()

>>> import classtree
>>> classtree.instancetree(bob)
```

```
Tree of <__main__.Person object at 0x000000000298B6D8>
...Person
......Emp
.........object
```

Regardless of whether you will ever code or use such tools, this example demonstrates one of the many ways that you can make use of special attributes that expose interpreter internals. You'll see another when we code the *lister.py* general-purpose class display tools in Chapter 31's section "Multiple Inheritance: "Mix-in" Classes" on page 956 —there, we will extend this technique to also display attributes in each object in a class tree and function as a common superclass.

In the last part of this book, we'll revisit such tools in the context of Python tool building at large, to code tools that implement attribute privacy, argument validation, and more. While not in every Python programmer's job description, access to internals enables powerful development tools.

Documentation Strings Revisited

The last section's example includes a docstring for its module, but remember that docstrings can be used for class components as well. Docstrings, which we covered in detail in Chapter 15, are string literals that show up at the top of various structures and are automatically saved by Python in the corresponding objects' __doc__ attributes. This works for module files, function defs, and classes and methods.

Now that we know more about classes and methods, the following file, *docstr.py*, provides a quick but comprehensive example that summarizes the places where docstrings can show up in your code. All of these can be triple-quoted blocks or simpler one-liner literals like those here:

```python
"I am: docstr.__doc__"

def func(args):
    "I am: docstr.func.__doc__"
    pass

class spam:
    "I am: spam.__doc__ or docstr.spam.__doc__ or self.__doc__"
    def method(self):
        "I am: spam.method.__doc__ or self.method.__doc__"
        print(self.__doc__)
        print(self.method.__doc__)
```

The main advantage of documentation strings is that they stick around at runtime. Thus, if it's been coded as a docstring, you can qualify an object with its __doc__ attribute to fetch its documentation (printing the result interprets line breaks if it's a multiline string):

```python
>>> import docstr
>>> docstr.__doc__
```

```
'I am: docstr.__doc__'
>>> docstr.func.__doc__
'I am: docstr.func.__doc__'
>>> docstr.spam.__doc__
'I am: spam.__doc__ or docstr.spam.__doc__ or self.__doc__'
>>> docstr.spam.method.__doc__
'I am: spam.method.__doc__ or self.method.__doc__'

>>> x = docstr.spam()
>>> x.method()
I am: spam.__doc__ or docstr.spam.__doc__ or self.__doc__
I am: spam.method.__doc__ or self.method.__doc__
```

A discussion of the *PyDoc* tool, which knows how to format all these strings in reports and web pages, appears in Chapter 15. Here it is running its `help` function on our code under Python 2.X (Python 3.X shows additional attributes inherited from the implied `object` superclass in the new-style class model—run this on your own to see the 3.X extras, and watch for more about this difference in Chapter 32):

```
>>> help(docstr)
Help on module docstr:

NAME
    docstr - I am: docstr.__doc__

FILE
    c:\code\docstr.py

CLASSES
    spam

    class spam
     |  I am: spam.__doc__ or docstr.spam.__doc__ or self.__doc__
     |
     |  Methods defined here:
     |
     |  method(self)
     |      I am: spam.method.__doc__ or self.method.__doc__

FUNCTIONS
    func(args)
        I am: docstr.func.__doc__
```

Documentation strings are available at runtime, but they are less flexible syntactically than # comments, which can appear anywhere in a program. Both forms are useful tools, and any program documentation is good (as long as it's accurate, of course!). As stated before, the Python "best practice" rule of thumb is to use docstrings for functional documentation (what your objects do) and hash-mark comments for more micro-level documentation (how arcane bits of code work).

Classes Versus Modules

Finally, let's wrap up this chapter by briefly comparing the topics of this book's last two parts: modules and classes. Because they're both about namespaces, the distinction can be confusing. In short:

- Modules
    - Implement data/logic packages
    - Are created with Python files or other-language extensions
    - Are used by being imported
    - Form the top-level in Python program structure
- Classes
    - Implement new full-featured objects
    - Are created with `class` statements
    - Are used by being called
    - Always live within a module

Classes also support extra features that modules don't, such as operator overloading, multiple instance generation, and inheritance. Although both classes and modules are namespaces, you should be able to tell by now that they are very different things. We need to move ahead to see just how different classes can be.

Chapter Summary

This chapter took us on a second, more in-depth tour of the OOP mechanisms of the Python language. We learned more about classes, methods, and inheritance, and we wrapped up the namespaces and scopes story in Python by extending it to cover its application to classes. Along the way, we looked at some more advanced concepts, such as abstract superclasses, class data attributes, namespace dictionaries and links, and manual calls to superclass methods and constructors.

Now that we've learned all about the mechanics of coding classes in Python, Chapter 30 turns to a specific facet of those mechanics: *operator overloading*. After that we'll explore common design patterns, looking at some of the ways that classes are commonly used and combined to optimize code reuse. Before you read ahead, though, be sure to work through the usual chapter quiz to review what we've covered here.

Test Your Knowledge: Quiz

1. What is an abstract superclass?
2. What happens when a simple assignment statement appears at the top level of a `class` statement?

3. Why might a class need to manually call the __init__ method in a superclass?

4. How can you augment, instead of completely replacing, an inherited method?

5. How does a class's local scope differ from that of a function?

6. What...was the capital of Assyria?

Test Your Knowledge: Answers

1. An abstract superclass is a class that calls a method, but does not inherit or define it—it expects the method to be filled in by a subclass. This is often used as a way to generalize classes when behavior cannot be predicted until a more specific subclass is coded. OOP frameworks also use this as a way to dispatch to client-defined, customizable operations.

2. When a simple assignment statement (X = Y) appears at the top level of a `class` statement, it attaches a data attribute to the class (`Class.X`). Like all class attributes, this will be shared by all instances; data attributes are not callable method functions, though.

3. A class must manually call the __init__ method in a superclass if it defines an __init__ constructor of its own and still wants the superclass's construction code to run. Python itself automatically runs just *one* constructor—the lowest one in the tree. Superclass constructors are usually called through the class name, passing in the `self` instance manually: `Superclass.__init__(self, ...)`.

4. To augment instead of completely replacing an inherited method, redefine it in a subclass, but call back to the superclass's version of the method manually from the new version of the method in the subclass. That is, pass the `self` instance to the superclass's version of the method manually: `Superclass.method(self, ...)`.

5. A class is a local scope and has access to enclosing local scopes, but it does not serve as an enclosing local scope to further nested code. Like modules, the class local scope morphs into an attribute namespace after the `class` statement is run.

6. Ashur (or Qalat Sherqat), Calah (or Nimrud), the short-lived Dur Sharrukin (or Khorsabad), and finally Nineveh.

Operator Overloading

This chapter continues our in-depth survey of class mechanics by focusing on operator overloading. We looked briefly at operator overloading in prior chapters; here, we'll fill in more details and look at a handful of commonly used overloading methods. Although we won't demonstrate each of the many operator overloading methods available, those we will code here are a representative sample large enough to uncover the possibilities of this Python class feature.

The Basics

Really "operator overloading" simply means *intercepting* built-in operations in a class's methods—Python automatically invokes your methods when instances of the class appear in built-in operations, and your method's return value becomes the result of the corresponding operation. Here's a review of the key ideas behind overloading:

- Operator overloading lets classes intercept normal Python operations.
- Classes can overload all Python expression operators.
- Classes can also overload built-in operations such as printing, function calls, attribute access, etc.
- Overloading makes class instances act more like built-in types.
- Overloading is implemented by providing specially named methods in a class.

In other words, when certain specially named methods are provided in a class, Python automatically calls them when instances of the class appear in their associated expressions. Your class provides the behavior of the corresponding operation for instance objects created from it.

As we've learned, operator overloading methods are never required and generally don't have defaults (apart from a handful that some classes get from `object`); if you don't code or inherit one, it just means that your class does not support the corresponding operation. When used, though, these methods allow classes to emulate the interfaces of built-in objects, and so appear more consistent.

Constructors and Expressions: __init__ and __sub__

As a review, consider the following simple example: its `Number` class, coded in the file *number.py*, provides a method to intercept instance construction (`__init__`), as well as one for catching subtraction expressions (`__sub__`). Special methods such as these are the hooks that let you tie into built-in operations:

```
# File number.py

class Number:
    def __init__(self, start):          # On Number(start)
        self.data = start
    def __sub__(self, other):           # On instance - other
        return Number(self.data - other) # Result is a new instance

>>> from number import Number          # Fetch class from module
>>> X = Number(5)                      # Number.__init__(X, 5)
>>> Y = X - 2                          # Number.__sub__(X, 2)
>>> Y.data                             # Y is new Number instance
3
```

As we've already learned, the `__init__` constructor method seen in this code is the most commonly used operator overloading method in Python; it's present in most classes, and used to initialize the newly created instance object using any arguments passed to the class name. The `__sub__` method plays the binary operator role that `__add__` did in Chapter 27's introduction, intercepting subtraction expressions and returning a new instance of the class as its result (and running `__init__` along the way).

We've already studied `__init__` and basic binary operators like `__sub__` in some depth, so we won't rehash their usage further here. In this chapter, we will tour some of the other tools available in this domain and look at example code that applies them in common use cases.

 Technically, instance creation first triggers the `__new__` method, which creates and returns the new instance object, which is then passed into `__init__` for initialization. Since `__new__` has a built-in implementation and is redefined in only very limited roles, though, nearly all Python classes initialize by defining an `__init__` method. We'll see one use case for `__new__` when we study *metaclasses* in Chapter 40; though rare, it is sometimes also used to customize creation of instances of immutable types.

Common Operator Overloading Methods

Just about everything you can do to built-in objects such as integers and lists has a corresponding specially named method for overloading in classes. Table 30-1 lists a few of the most common; there are many more. In fact, many overloading methods come in multiple versions (e.g., `__add__`, `__radd__`, and `__iadd__` for addition), which is one reason there are so many. See other Python books, or the Python language reference manual, for an exhaustive list of the special method names available.

Table 30-1. Common operator overloading methods

Method	Implements	Called for
__init__	Constructor	Object creation: X = Class(args)
__del__	Destructor	Object reclamation of X
__add__	Operator +	X + Y, X += Y if no __iadd__
__or__	Operator | (bitwise OR)	X | Y, X |= Y if no __ior__
__repr__, __str__	Printing, conversions	print(X), repr(X), str(X)
__call__	Function calls	X(*args, **kargs)
__getattr__	Attribute fetch	X.undefined
__setattr__	Attribute assignment	X.any = value
__delattr__	Attribute deletion	del X.any
__getattribute__	Attribute fetch	X.any
__getitem__	Indexing, slicing, iteration	X[key], X[i:j], for loops and other iterations if no __iter__
__setitem__	Index and slice assignment	X[key] = value, X[i:j] = iterable
__delitem__	Index and slice deletion	del X[key], del X[i:j]
__len__	Length	len(X), truth tests if no __bool__
__bool__	Boolean tests	bool(X), truth tests (named __nonzero__ in 2.X)
__lt__, __gt__, __le__, __ge__, __eq__, __ne__	Comparisons	X < Y, X > Y, X <= Y, X >= Y, X == Y, X != Y (or else __cmp__ in 2.X only)
__radd__	Right-side operators	Other + X
__iadd__	In-place augmented operators	X += Y (or else __add__)
__iter__, __next__	Iteration contexts	I=iter(X), next(I); for loops, in if no __contains__, all comprehensions, map(F,X), others (__next__ is named next in 2.X)
__contains__	Membership test	item in X (any iterable)
__index__	Integer value	hex(X), bin(X), oct(X), O[X], O[X:] (replaces 2.X __oct__, __hex__)
__enter__, __exit__	Context manager (Chapter 34)	with obj as var:
__get__, __set__, __delete__	Descriptor attributes (Chapter 38)	X.attr, X.attr = value, del X.attr
__new__	Creation (Chapter 40)	Object creation, before __init__

All overloading methods have names that start and end with two underscores to keep them distinct from other names you define in your classes. The mappings from special method names to expressions or operations are predefined by the Python language, and documented in full in the standard language manual and other reference resources. For example, the name __add__ always maps to + expressions by Python language definition, regardless of what an __add__ method's code actually does.

Operator overloading methods may be inherited from superclasses if not defined, just like any other methods. Operator overloading methods are also all optional—if you don't code or inherit one, that operation is simply unsupported by your class, and attempting it will raise an exception. Some built-in operations, like printing, have defaults (inherited from the implied object class in Python 3.X), but most built-ins fail for class instances if no corresponding operator overloading method is present.

Most overloading methods are used only in advanced programs that require objects to behave like built-ins, though the __init__ constructor we've already met tends to appear in most classes. Let's explore some of the additional methods in Table 30-1 by example.

> Although expressions trigger operator methods, be careful not to assume that there is a speed advantage to cutting out the middleman and calling the operator method directly. In fact, calling the operator method directly might *be twice as slow*, presumably because of the overhead of a function call, which Python avoids or optimizes in built-in cases.
>
> Here's the story for len and __len__ using Appendix B's Windows launcher and Chapter 21's timing techniques on Python 3.3 and 2.7: in both, calling __len__ directly takes twice as long:
>
> ```
> c:\code> py -3 -m timeit -n 1000 -r 5
>                      -s "L = list(range(100))" "x = L.__len__()"
> 1000 loops, best of 5: 0.134 usec per loop
>
> c:\code> py -3 -m timeit -n 1000 -r 5
>                      -s "L = list(range(100))" "x = len(L)"
> 1000 loops, best of 5: 0.063 usec per loop
>
> c:\code> py -2 -m timeit -n 1000 -r 5
>                      -s "L = list(range(100))" "x = L.__len__()"
> 1000 loops, best of 5: 0.117 usec per loop
>
> c:\code> py -2 -m timeit -n 1000 -r 5
>                      -s "L = list(range(100))" "x = len(L)"
> 1000 loops, best of 5: 0.0596 usec per loop
> ```
>
> This is not as artificial as it may seem—I've actually come across recommendations for using the slower alternative in the name of speed at a noted research institution!

Indexing and Slicing: __getitem__ and __setitem__

Our first method set allows your classes to mimic some of the behaviors of sequences and mappings. If defined in a class (or inherited by it), the __getitem__ method is called automatically for instance-indexing operations. When an instance X appears in an indexing expression like X[i], Python calls the __getitem__ method inherited by the instance, passing X to the first argument and the index in brackets to the second argument.

For example, the following class returns the square of an index value—atypical perhaps, but illustrative of the mechanism in general:

```
>>> class Indexer:
        def __getitem__(self, index):
            return index ** 2

>>> X = Indexer()
>>> X[2]                          # X[i] calls X.__getitem__(i)
4

>>> for i in range(5):
        print(X[i], end=' ')      # Runs __getitem__(X, i) each time

0 1 4 9 16
```

Intercepting Slices

Interestingly, in addition to indexing, __getitem__ is also called for *slice expressions*—always in 3.X, and conditionally in 2.X if you don't provide more specific slicing methods. Formally speaking, built-in types handle slicing the same way. Here, for example, is slicing at work on a built-in list, using upper and lower bounds and a stride (see Chapter 7 if you need a refresher on slicing):

```
>>> L = [5, 6, 7, 8, 9]
>>> L[2:4]                        # Slice with slice syntax: 2..(4-1)
[7, 8]
>>> L[1:]
[6, 7, 8, 9]
>>> L[:-1]
[5, 6, 7, 8]
>>> L[::2]
[5, 7, 9]
```

Really, though, slicing bounds are bundled up into a *slice object* and passed to the list's implementation of indexing. In fact, you can always pass a slice object manually—slice syntax is mostly syntactic sugar for indexing with a slice object:

```
>>> L[slice(2, 4)]                # Slice with slice objects
[7, 8]
>>> L[slice(1, None)]
[6, 7, 8, 9]
>>> L[slice(None, -1)]
[5, 6, 7, 8]
>>> L[slice(None, None, 2)]
[5, 7, 9]
```

This matters in classes with a __getitem__ method—in 3.X, the method will be called both for basic indexing (with an index) and for slicing (with a slice object). Our previous class won't handle slicing because its math assumes integer indexes are passed, but the following class will. When called for *indexing*, the argument is an integer as before:

```
>>> class Indexer:
        data = [5, 6, 7, 8, 9]
        def __getitem__(self, index):      # Called for index or slice
            print('getitem:', index)
            return self.data[index]         # Perform index or slice

>>> X = Indexer()
>>> X[0]                                    # Indexing sends __getitem__ an integer
getitem: 0
5
>>> X[1]
getitem: 1
6
>>> X[-1]
getitem: -1
9
```

When called for *slicing*, though, the method receives a slice object, which is simply passed along to the embedded list indexer in a new index expression:

```
>>> X[2:4]                                  # Slicing sends __getitem__ a slice object
getitem: slice(2, 4, None)
[7, 8]
>>> X[1:]
getitem: slice(1, None, None)
[6, 7, 8, 9]
>>> X[:-1]
getitem: slice(None, -1, None)
[5, 6, 7, 8]
>>> X[::2]
getitem: slice(None, None, 2)
[5, 7, 9]
```

Where needed, __getitem__ can test the type of its argument, and extract slice object bounds—slice objects have attributes start, stop, and step, any of which can be None if omitted:

```
>>> class Indexer:
        def __getitem__(self, index):
            if isinstance(index, int):               # Test usage mode
                print('indexing', index)
            else:
                print('slicing', index.start, index.stop, index.step)

>>> X = Indexer()
>>> X[99]
indexing 99
>>> X[1:99:2]
slicing 1 99 2
>>> X[1:]
slicing 1 None None
```

If used, the __setitem__ index assignment method similarly intercepts both index and slice assignments—in 3.X (and usually in 2.X) it receives a slice object for the latter, which may be passed along in another index assignment or used directly in the same way:

```
class IndexSetter:
    def __setitem__(self, index, value):      # Intercept index or slice assignment
        ...
        self.data[index] = value              # Assign index or slice
```

In fact, __getitem__ may be called automatically in even more contexts than indexing and slicing—it's also an *iteration* fallback option, as we'll see in a moment. First, though, let's take a quick look at 2.X's flavor of these operations for 2.X readers, and clarify a potential point of confusion in this category.

Slicing and Indexing in Python 2.X

In Python 2.X only, classes can also define __getslice__ and __setslice__ methods to intercept slice fetches and assignments specifically. If defined, these methods are passed the bounds of the slice expression, and are preferred over __getitem__ and __setitem__ for two-limit slices. In all other cases, though, this context works the same as in 3.X; for example, a slice object is still created and passed to __getitem__ if no __getslice__ is found or a three-limit extended slice form is used:

```
C:\code> c:\python27\python
>>> class Slicer:
        def __getitem__(self, index):   print index
        def __getslice__(self, i, j):    print i, j
        def __setslice__(self, i, j,seq): print i, j,seq

>>> Slicer()[1]          # Runs __getitem__ with int, like 3.X
1
>>> Slicer()[1:9]        # Runs __getslice__ if present, else __getitem__
1 9
>>> Slicer()[1:9:2]      # Runs __getitem__ with slice(), like 3.X!
slice(1, 9, 2)
```

These slice-specific methods are *removed* in 3.X, so even in 2.X you should generally use __getitem__ and __setitem__ instead and allow for both indexes and slice objects as arguments—both for forward compatibility, and to avoid having to handle two- and three-limit slices differently. In most classes, this works without any special code, because indexing methods can manually pass along the slice object in the square brackets of another index expression, as in the prior section's example. See the section "Membership: __contains__, __iter__, and __getitem__" on page 906 for another example of slice interception at work.

But 3.X's __index__ Is Not Indexing!

On a related note, don't confuse the (perhaps unfortunately named) __index__ method in Python 3.X for index interception—this method returns an *integer value* for an instance when needed and is used by built-ins that convert to digit strings (and in retrospect, might have been better named *__asindex__*):

```
>>> class C:
        def __index__(self):
            return 255

>>> X = C()
>>> hex(X)              # Integer value
'0xff'
>>> bin(X)
'0b11111111'
>>> oct(X)
'0o377'
```

Although this method does not intercept instance indexing like __getitem__, it is also used in contexts that require an integer—*including* indexing:

```
>>> ('C' * 256)[255]
'C'
>>> ('C' * 256)[X]       # As index (not X[i])
'C'
>>> ('C' * 256)[X:]      # As index (not X[i:])
'C'
```

This method works the same way in Python 2.X, except that it is not called for the hex and oct built-in functions; use __hex__ and __oct__ in 2.X (only) instead to intercept these calls.

Index Iteration: __getitem__

Here's a hook that isn't always obvious to beginners, but turns out to be surprisingly useful. In the absence of more-specific iteration methods we'll get to in the next section, the for statement works by repeatedly indexing a sequence from zero to higher indexes, until an out-of-bounds IndexError exception is detected. Because of that, __geti tem__ also turns out to be one way to overload iteration in Python—if this method is defined, for loops call the class's __getitem__ each time through, with successively higher offsets.

It's a case of "code one, get one free"—any built-in or user-defined object that responds to indexing also responds to for loop iteration:

```
>>> class StepperIndex:
        def __getitem__(self, i):
            return self.data[i]

>>> X = StepperIndex()           # X is a StepperIndex object
>>> X.data = "Spam"
```

```
>>>
>>> X[1]                               # Indexing calls __getitem__
'p'
>>> for item in X:                     # for loops call __getitem__
        print(item, end=' ')           # for indexes items 0..N

S p a m
```

In fact, it's really a case of "code one, get a bunch free." Any class that supports `for` loops automatically supports all *iteration contexts* in Python, many of which we've seen in earlier chapters (iteration contexts were presented in Chapter 14). For example, the `in` membership test, list comprehensions, the `map` built-in, list and tuple assignments, and type constructors will also call __getitem__ automatically, if it's defined:

```
>>> 'p' in X                           # All call __getitem__ too
True

>>> [c for c in X]                     # List comprehension
['S', 'p', 'a', 'm']

>>> list(map(str.upper, X))            # map calls (use list() in 3.X)
['S', 'P', 'A', 'M']

>>> (a, b, c, d) = X                   # Sequence assignments
>>> a, c, d
('S', 'a', 'm')

>>> list(X), tuple(X), ''.join(X)      # And so on...
(['S', 'p', 'a', 'm'], ('S', 'p', 'a', 'm'), 'Spam')

>>> X
<__main__.StepperIndex object at 0x000000000297B630>
```

In practice, this technique can be used to create objects that provide a sequence interface and to add logic to built-in sequence type operations; we'll revisit this idea when extending built-in types in Chapter 32.

Iterable Objects: __iter__ and __next__

Although the __getitem__ technique of the prior section works, it's really just a fallback for iteration. Today, all iteration contexts in Python will try the __iter__ method first, before trying __getitem__. That is, they prefer the *iteration protocol* we learned about in Chapter 14 to repeatedly indexing an object; only if the object does not support the iteration protocol is indexing attempted instead. Generally speaking, you should prefer __iter__ too—it supports general iteration contexts better than __getitem__ can.

Technically, iteration contexts work by passing an iterable object to the `iter` built-in function to invoke an __iter__ method, which is expected to return an iterator object. If it's provided, Python then repeatedly calls this iterator object's __next__ method to produce items until a `StopIteration` exception is raised. A `next` built-in function is also available as a convenience for manual iterations—next(I) is the same as I.__next__(). For a review of this model's essentials, see Figure 14-1 in Chapter 14.

This iterable object interface is given priority and attempted first. Only if no such __iter__ method is found, Python falls back on the __getitem__ scheme and repeatedly indexes by offsets as before, until an IndexError exception is raised.

 Version skew note: As described in Chapter 14, if you are using Python 2.X, the I.__next__() iterator method just described is named I.next() in your Python, and the next(I) built-in is present for portability—it calls I.next() in 2.X and I.__next__() in 3.X. Iteration works the same in 2.X in all other respects.

User-Defined Iterables

In the __iter__ scheme, classes implement user-defined iterables by simply implementing the iteration protocol introduced in Chapter 14 and elaborated in Chapter 20. For example, the following file uses a class to define a user-defined iterable that generates squares on demand, instead of all at once (per the preceding note, in Python 2.X define next instead of __next__, and print with a trailing comma as usual):

```
# File squares.py

class Squares:
    def __init__(self, start, stop):      # Save state when created
        self.value = start - 1
        self.stop  = stop
    def __iter__(self):                    # Get iterator object on iter
        return self
    def __next__(self):                    # Return a square on each iteration
        if self.value == self.stop:        # Also called by next built-in
            raise StopIteration
        self.value += 1
        return self.value ** 2
```

When imported, its instances can appear in iteration contexts just like built-ins:

```
% python
>>> from squares import Squares
>>> for i in Squares(1, 5):          # for calls iter, which calls __iter__
        print(i, end=' ')            # Each iteration calls __next__

1 4 9 16 25
```

Here, the iterator object returned by __iter__ is simply the instance self, because the __next__ method is part of this class itself. In more complex scenarios, the iterator object may be defined as a separate class and object with its own state information to support multiple active iterations over the same data (we'll see an example of this in a moment). The end of the iteration is signaled with a Python **raise** statement—introduced in Chapter 29 and covered in full in the next part of this book, but which simply raises an exception as if Python itself had done so. Manual iterations work the same on user-defined iterables as they do on built-in types as well:

```
>>> X = Squares(1, 5)              # Iterate manually: what loops do
>>> I = iter(X)                    # iter calls __iter__
>>> next(I)                        # next calls __next__ (in 3.X)
1
>>> next(I)
4
...more omitted...
>>> next(I)
25
>>> next(I)                        # Can catch this in try statement
StopIteration
```

An equivalent coding of this iterable with __getitem__ might be less natural, because the for would then iterate through all offsets zero and higher; the offsets passed in would be only indirectly related to the range of values produced (0..N would need to map to start..stop). Because __iter__ objects retain explicitly managed state between next calls, they can be more general than __getitem__.

On the other hand, iterables based on __iter__ can sometimes be more complex and less functional than those based on __getitem__. They are really designed for iteration, not random indexing—in fact, they don't overload the indexing expression at all, though you can collect their items in a sequence such as a list to enable other operations:

```
>>> X = Squares(1, 5)
>>> X[1]
TypeError: 'Squares' object does not support indexing
>>> list(X)[1]
4
```

Single versus multiple scans

The __iter__ scheme is also the implementation for all the other iteration contexts we saw in action for the __getitem__ method—membership tests, type constructors, sequence assignment, and so on. Unlike our prior __getitem__ example, though, we also need to be aware that a class's __iter__ may be designed for a *single traversal* only, not many. Classes choose scan behavior explicitly in their code.

For example, because the current Squares class's __iter__ always returns self with just one copy of iteration state, it is a one-shot iteration; once you've iterated over an instance of that class, it's empty. Calling __iter__ again on the same instance returns self again, in whatever state it may have been left. You generally need to make a new iterable instance object for each new iteration:

```
>>> X = Squares(1, 5)              # Make an iterable with state
>>> [n for n in X]                 # Exhausts items: __iter__ returns self
[1, 4, 9, 16, 25]
>>> [n for n in X]                 # Now it's empty: __iter__ returns same self
[]
```

```
>>> [n for n in Squares(1, 5)]        # Make a new iterable object
[1, 4, 9, 16, 25]
>>> list(Squares(1, 3))               # A new object for each new __iter__ call
[1, 4, 9]
```

To support multiple iterations more directly, we could also recode this example with an extra class or other technique, as we will in a moment. As is, though, by creating a *new instance* for each iteration, you get a fresh copy of iteration state:

```
>>> 36 in Squares(1, 10)              # Other iteration contexts
True
>>> a, b, c = Squares(1, 3)           # Each calls __iter__ and then __next__
>>> a, b, c
(1, 4, 9)
>>> ':'.join(map(str, Squares(1, 5)))
'1:4:9:16:25'
```

Just like single-scan built-ins such as map, converting to a *list* supports multiple scans as well, but adds time and space performance costs, which may or may not be significant to a given program:

```
>>> X = Squares(1, 5)
>>> tuple(X), tuple(X)                # Iterator exhausted in second tuple()
((1, 4, 9, 16, 25), ())

>>> X = list(Squares(1, 5))
>>> tuple(X), tuple(X)
((1, 4, 9, 16, 25), (1, 4, 9, 16, 25))
```

We'll improve this to support multiple scans more directly ahead, after a bit of compare-and-contrast.

Classes versus generators

Notice that the preceding example would probably be simpler if it was coded with *generator functions or expressions*—tools introduced in Chapter 20 that automatically produce iterable objects and retain local variable state between iterations:

```
>>> def gsquares(start, stop):
        for i in range(start, stop + 1):
            yield i ** 2

>>> for i in gsquares(1, 5):
        print(i, end=' ')

1 4 9 16 25

>>> for i in (x ** 2 for x in range(1, 6)):
        print(i, end=' ')

1 4 9 16 25
```

Unlike classes, generator functions and expressions implicitly save their state and create the methods required to conform to the iteration protocol—with obvious advantages

---

in code conciseness for simpler examples like these. On the other hand, the class's more explicit attributes and methods, extra structure, inheritance hierarchies, and support for multiple behaviors may be better suited for richer use cases.

Of course, for this artificial example, you could in fact skip both techniques and simply use a for loop, map, or a list comprehension to build the list all at once. Barring performance data to the contrary, the best and fastest way to accomplish a task in Python is often also the simplest:

```
>>> [x ** 2 for x in range(1, 6)]
[1, 4, 9, 16, 25]
```

However, classes may be better at modeling more complex iterations, especially when they can benefit from the assets of classes in general. An iterable that produces items in a complex database or web service result, for example, might be able to take fuller advantage of classes. The next section explores another use case for classes in user-defined iterables.

Multiple Iterators on One Object

Earlier, I mentioned that the iterator object (with a __next__) produced by an iterable may be defined as a separate class with its own state information to more directly support multiple active iterations over the same data. Consider what happens when we step across a built-in type like a string:

```
>>> S = 'ace'
>>> for x in S:
        for y in S:
            print(x + y, end=' ')

aa ac ae ca cc ce ea ec ee
```

Here, the outer loop grabs an iterator from the string by calling iter, and each nested loop does the same to get an independent iterator. Because each active iterator has its own state information, each loop can maintain its own position in the string, regardless of any other active loops. Moreover, we're not required to make a new string or convert to a list each time; the single string object itself supports multiple scans.

We saw related examples earlier, in Chapter 14 and Chapter 20. For instance, generator functions and expressions, as well as built-ins like map and zip, proved to be single-iterator objects, thus supporting a single active scan. By contrast, the range built-in, and other built-in types like lists, support multiple active iterators with independent positions.

When we code user-defined iterables with classes, it's up to us to decide whether we will support a single active iteration or many. To achieve the multiple-iterator effect, __iter__ simply needs to define a new stateful object for the iterator, instead of returning self for each iterator request.

The following `SkipObject` class, for example, defines an iterable object that skips every other item on iterations. Because its iterator object is created anew from a supplemental class for each iteration, it supports multiple active loops directly (this is file *skipper.py* in the book's examples):

```
#!python3
# File skipper.py

class SkipObject:
    def __init__(self, wrapped):                    # Save item to be used
        self.wrapped = wrapped
    def __iter__(self):
        return SkipIterator(self.wrapped)           # New iterator each time

class SkipIterator:
    def __init__(self, wrapped):
        self.wrapped = wrapped                      # Iterator state information
        self.offset  = 0
    def __next__(self):
        if self.offset >= len(self.wrapped):        # Terminate iterations
            raise StopIteration
        else:
            item = self.wrapped[self.offset]        # else return and skip
            self.offset += 2
            return item

if __name__ == '__main__':
    alpha = 'abcdef'
    skipper = SkipObject(alpha)                     # Make container object
    I = iter(skipper)                               # Make an iterator on it
    print(next(I), next(I), next(I))                # Visit offsets 0, 2, 4

    for x in skipper:                # for calls __iter__ automatically
        for y in skipper:            # Nested fors call __iter__ again each time
            print(x + y, end=' ')    # Each iterator has its own state, offset
```

A quick portability note: as is, this is 3.X-only code. To make it 2.X compatible, import the 3.X `print` function, and either use `next` instead of `__next__` for 2.X-only use, or alias the two names in the class's scope for dual 2.X/3.X usage (file *skipper_2x.py* in the book's examples does):

```
#!python
from __future__ import print_function          # 2.X/3.X compatibility
...
class SkipIterator:
    ...
    def __next__(self):
        ...
    next = __next__                             # 2.X/3.X compatibility
```

When the appropriate version is run in either Python, this example works like the nested loops with built-in strings. Each active loop has its own position in the string because each obtains an independent iterator object that records its own state information:

```
% python skipper.py
a c e
aa ac ae ca cc ce ea ec ee
```

By contrast, our earlier `Squares` example supports just one active iteration, unless we call `Squares` again in nested loops to obtain new objects. Here, there is just one `SkipOb ject` iterable, with multiple iterator objects created from it.

Classes versus slices

As before, we could achieve similar results with built-in tools—for example, slicing with a third bound to skip items:

```
>>> S = 'abcdef'
>>> for x in S[::2]:
        for y in S[::2]:              # New objects on each iteration
            print(x + y, end=' ')

aa ac ae ca cc ce ea ec ee
```

This isn't quite the same, though, for two reasons. First, each slice expression here will *physically store* the result list all at once in memory; iterables, on the other hand, produce just one value at a time, which can save substantial space for large result lists. Second, slices produce *new objects*, so we're not really iterating over the same object in multiple places here. To be closer to the class, we would need to make a single object to step across by slicing ahead of time:

```
>>> S = 'abcdef'
>>> S = S[::2]
>>> S
'ace'
>>> for x in S:
        for y in S:                   # Same object, new iterators
            print(x + y, end=' ')

aa ac ae ca cc ce ea ec ee
```

This is more similar to our class-based solution, but it still stores the slice result in memory all at once (there is no generator form of built-in slicing today), and it's only equivalent for this particular case of skipping every other item.

Because user-defined iterables coded with classes can do anything a class can do, they are much more general than this example may imply. Though such generality is not required in all applications, user-defined iterables are a powerful tool—they allow us to make arbitrary objects look and feel like the other sequences and iterables we have met in this book. We could use this technique with a database object, for example, to support iterations over large database fetches, with multiple cursors into the same query result.

Coding Alternative: __iter__ plus yield

And now, for something completely implicit—but potentially useful nonetheless. In some applications, it's possible to minimize coding requirements for user-defined iterables by *combining* the __iter__ method we're exploring here and the `yield` generator function statement we studied in Chapter 20. Because generator functions *automatically* save local variable state and create required iterator methods, they fit this role well, and complement the state retention and other utility we get from classes.

As a review, recall that any function that contains a `yield` statement is turned into a generator function. When called, it returns a new *generator object* with automatic retention of local scope and code position, an automatically created __iter__ method that simply returns itself, and an automatically created __next__ method (next in 2.X) that starts the function or resumes it where it last left off:

```
>>> def gen(x):
        for i in range(x): yield i ** 2

>>> G = gen(5)              # Create a generator with __iter__ and __next__
>>> G.__iter__() == G       # Both methods exist on the same object
True
>>> I = iter(G)             # Runs __iter__: generator returns itself
>>> next(I), next(I)        # Runs __next__ (next in 2.X)
(0, 1)
>>> list(gen(5))            # Iteration contexts automatically run iter and next
[0, 1, 4, 9, 16]
```

This is still true even if the generator function with a `yield` happens to be a method named __iter__: whenever invoked by an iteration context tool, such a method will return a new generator object with the requisite __next__. As an added bonus, generator functions coded as methods in classes have access to saved state in *both* instance attributes and local scope variables.

For example, the following class is equivalent to the initial `Squares` user-defined iterable we coded earlier in *squares.py*.

```
# File squares_yield.py

class Squares:                              # __iter__ + yield generator
    def __init__(self, start, stop):        # __next__ is automatic/implied
        self.start = start
        self.stop  = stop
    def __iter__(self):
        for value in range(self.start, self.stop + 1):
            yield value ** 2
```

There's no need to alias next to __next__ for 2.X compatibility here, because this method is now automated and implied by the use of `yield`. As before, `for` loops and other iteration tools iterate through instances of this class automatically:

```
% python
>>> from squares_yield import Squares
>>> for i in Squares(1, 5): print(i, end=' ')
```

```
1 4 9 16 25
```

And as usual, we can look under the hood to see how this actually works in iteration contexts. Running our class instance through `iter` obtains the result of calling `__iter__` as usual, but in this case the result is a generator object with an automatically created `__next__` of the same sort we always get when calling a generator function that contains a `yield`. The only difference here is that the generator function is automatically called on iter. Invoking the result object's next interface produces results on demand:

```
>>> S = Squares(1, 5)          # Runs __init__: class saves instance state
>>> S
<squares_yield.Squares object at 0x000000000294B630>

>>> I = iter(S)                # Runs __iter__: returns a generator
>>> I
<generator object __iter__ at 0x00000000029A8CF0>
>>> next(I)
1
>>> next(I)                    # Runs generator's __next__
4
...etc...
>>> next(I)                    # Generator has both instance and local scope state
StopIteration
```

It may also help to notice that we could name the generator method something other than `__iter__` and call manually to iterate—`Squares(1,5).gen()`, for example. Using the `__iter__` name invoked automatically by iteration tools simply skips a manual attribute fetch and call step:

```
class Squares:                 # Non __iter__ equivalent (squares_manual.py)
    def __init__(...):
        ...
    def gen(self):
        for value in range(self.start, self.stop + 1):
            yield value ** 2

% python
>>> from squares_manual import Squares
>>> for i in Squares(1, 5).gen(): print(i, end=' ')
...same results...

>>> S = Squares(1, 5)
>>> I = iter(S.gen())          # Call generator manually for iterable/iterator
>>> next(I)
...same results...
```

Coding the generator as `__iter__` instead cuts out the middleman in your code, though both schemes ultimately wind up creating a new generator object for each iteration:

- With `__iter__`, iteration triggers `__iter__`, which returns a new generator with `__next__`.

- Without `__iter__`, your code calls to make a generator, which returns itself for `__iter__`.

See Chapter 20 for more on `yield` and generators if this is puzzling, and compare it with the more explicit `__next__` version in *squares.py* earlier. You'll notice that this new *squares_yield.py* version is 4 lines shorter (7 versus 11). In a sense, this scheme reduces class coding requirements much like the closure functions of Chapter 17, but in this case does so with a *combination* of functional and OOP techniques, instead of an alternative to classes. For example, the generator method still leverages `self` attributes.

This may also very well seem like one too many levels of *magic* to some observers—it relies on both the iteration protocol and the object creation of generators, both of which are highly implicit (in contradiction of longstanding Python themes: see `import this`). Opinions aside, it's important to understand the non-`yield` flavor of class iterables too, because it's explicit, general, and sometimes broader in scope.

Still, the `__iter__`/yield technique may prove effective in cases where it applies. It also comes with a substantial advantage—as the next section explains.

Multiple iterators with yield

Besides its code conciseness, the user-defined class iterable of the prior section based upon the `__iter__`/yield combination has an important added bonus—it also supports *multiple active iterators* automatically. This naturally follows from the fact that each call to `__iter__` is a call to a generator function, which returns a new generator with its own copy of the local scope for state retention:

```
% python
>>> from squares_yield import Squares     # Using the __iter__/yield Squares
>>> S = Squares(1, 5)
>>> I = iter(S)
>>> next(I); next(I)
1
4
>>> J = iter(S)                            # With yield, multiple iterators automatic
>>> next(J)
1
>>> next(I)                                # I is independent of J: own local state
9
```

Although generator functions are single-scan iterables, the implicit calls to `__iter__` in iteration contexts make new generators supporting new independent scans:

```
>>> S = Squares(1, 3)
>>> for i in S:                            # Each for calls __iter__
        for j in S:
            print('%s:%s' % (i, j), end=' ')

1:1 1:4 1:9 4:1 4:4 4:9 9:1 9:4 9:9
```

To do the same without `yield` requires a supplemental class that stores iterator state explicitly and manually, using techniques of the preceding section (and grows to 15 lines: 8 more than with `yield`):

```
# File squares_nonyield.py

class Squares:
    def __init__(self, start, stop):          # Non-yield generator
        self.start = start                      # Multiscans: extra object
        self.stop  = stop
    def __iter__(self):
        return SquaresIter(self.start, self.stop)

class SquaresIter:
    def __init__(self, start, stop):
        self.value = start - 1
        self.stop  = stop
    def __next__(self):
        if self.value == self.stop:
            raise StopIteration
        self.value += 1
        return self.value ** 2
```

This works the same as the `yield` multiscan version, but with more, and more explicit, code:

```
% python
>>> from squares_nonyield import Squares
>>> for i in Squares(1, 5): print(i, end=' ')

1 4 9 16 25
>>>
>>> S = Squares(1, 5)
>>> I = iter(S)
>>> next(I); next(I)
1
4
>>> J = iter(S)                       # Multiple iterators without yield
>>> next(J)
1
>>> next(I)
9

>>> S = Squares(1, 3)
>>> for i in S:                       # Each for calls __iter__
        for j in S:
            print('%s:%s' % (i, j), end=' ')

1:1 1:4 1:9 4:1 4:4 4:9 9:1 9:4 9:9
```

Finally, the generator-based approach could similarly remove the need for an extra iterator class in the prior item-skipper example of file *skipper.py*, thanks to its automatic methods and local variable state retention (and checks in at 9 lines versus the original's 16):

```
# File skipper_yield.py

class SkipObject:                               # Another __iter__ + yield generator
    def __init__(self, wrapped):                # Instance scope retained normally
        self.wrapped = wrapped                  # Local scope state saved auto
    def __iter__(self):
        offset = 0
        while offset < len(self.wrapped):
            item = self.wrapped[offset]
            offset += 2
            yield item
```

This works the same as the non-`yield` multiscan version, but with less, and less explicit, code:

```
% python
>>> from skipper_yield import SkipObject
>>> skipper = SkipObject('abcdef')
>>> I = iter(skipper)
>>> next(I); next(I); next(I)
'a'
'c'
'e'
>>> for x in skipper:                           # Each for calls __iter__: new auto generator
        for y in skipper:
            print(x + y, end=' ')

aa ac ae ca cc ce ea ec ee
```

Of course, these are all artificial examples that could be replaced with simpler tools like comprehensions, and their code may or may not scale up in kind to more realistic tasks. Study these alternatives to see how they compare. As so often in programming, the best tool for the job will likely be the best tool for your job!

Membership: __contains__, __iter__, and __getitem__

The iteration story is even richer than we've seen thus far. Operator overloading is often *layered*: classes may provide specific methods, or more general alternatives used as fallback options. For example:

- Comparisons in Python 2.X use specific methods such as __lt__ for "less than" if present, or else the general __cmp__. Python 3.X uses only specific methods, not __cmp__, as discussed later in this chapter.

- Boolean tests similarly try a specific __bool__ first (to give an explicit True/False result), and if it's absent fall back on the more general __len__ (a nonzero length means True). As we'll also see later in this chapter, Python 2.X works the same but uses the name __nonzero__ instead of __bool__.

In the iterations domain, classes can implement the `in` membership operator as an iteration, using either the __iter__ or __getitem__ methods. To support more specific membership, though, classes may code a __contains__ method—when present, this

method is preferred over __iter__, which is preferred over __getitem__. The __con
tains__ method should define membership as applying to keys for a *mapping* (and can
use quick lookups), and as a search for *sequences*.

Consider the following class, whose file has been instrumented for dual 2.X/3.X usage
using the techniques described earlier. It codes all three methods and tests membership
and various iteration contexts applied to an instance. Its methods print trace messages
when called:

```python
# File contains.py
from __future__ import print_function          # 2.X/3.X compatibility

class Iters:
    def __init__(self, value):
        self.data = value

    def __getitem__(self, i):                   # Fallback for iteration
        print('get[%s]:' % i, end='')           # Also for index, slice
        return self.data[i]

    def __iter__(self):                         # Preferred for iteration
        print('iter=> ', end='')                # Allows only one active iterator
        self.ix = 0
        return self

    def __next__(self):
        print('next:', end='')
        if self.ix == len(self.data): raise StopIteration
        item = self.data[self.ix]
        self.ix += 1
        return item

    def __contains__(self, x):                  # Preferred for 'in'
        print('contains: ', end='')
        return x in self.data
    next = __next__                             # 2.X/3.X compatibility

if __name__ == '__main__':
    X = Iters([1, 2, 3, 4, 5])                  # Make instance
    print(3 in X)                               # Membership
    for i in X:                                 # for loops
        print(i, end=' | ')

    print()
    print([i ** 2 for i in X])                  # Other iteration contexts
    print( list(map(bin, X)) )

    I = iter(X)                                 # Manual iteration (what other contexts do)
    while True:
        try:
            print(next(I), end=' @ ')
        except StopIteration:
            break
```

As is, the class in this file has an __iter__ that supports multiple scans, but only a single scan can be active at any point in time (e.g., nested loops won't work), because each iteration attempt resets the scan cursor to the front. Now that you know about yield in iteration methods, you should be able to tell that the following is equivalent but allows multiple active scans—and judge for yourself whether its more implicit nature is worth the nested-scan support and six lines shaved (this is in file *contains_yield.py*):

```python
class Iters:
    def __init__(self, value):
        self.data = value

    def __getitem__(self, i):          # Fallback for iteration
        print('get[%s]:' % i, end='')  # Also for index, slice
        return self.data[i]

    def __iter__(self):                # Preferred for iteration
        print('iter=> next:', end='')  # Allows multiple active iterators
        for x in self.data:            # no __next__ to alias to next
            yield x
            print('next:', end='')

    def __contains__(self, x):         # Preferred for 'in'
        print('contains: ', end='')
        return x in self.data
```

On both Python 3.X and 2.X, when either version of this file runs its output is as follows —the specific __contains__ intercepts membership, the general __iter__ catches other iteration contexts such that __next__ (whether explicitly coded or implied by yield) is called repeatedly, and __getitem__ is never called:

```
contains: True
iter=> next:1 | next:2 | next:3 | next:4 | next:5 | next:
iter=> next:next:next:next:next:next:[1, 4, 9, 16, 25]
iter=> next:next:next:next:next:next:['Ob1', 'Ob10', 'Ob11', 'Ob100', 'Ob101']
iter=> next:1 @ next:2 @ next:3 @ next:4 @ next:5 @ next:
```

Watch what happens to this code's output if we comment out its __contains__ method, though—membership is now routed to the general __iter__ instead:

```
iter=> next:next:next:True
iter=> next:1 | next:2 | next:3 | next:4 | next:5 | next:
iter=> next:next:next:next:next:next:[1, 4, 9, 16, 25]
iter=> next:next:next:next:next:next:['Ob1', 'Ob10', 'Ob11', 'Ob100', 'Ob101']
iter=> next:1 @ next:2 @ next:3 @ next:4 @ next:5 @ next:
```

And finally, here is the output if both __contains__ and __iter__ are commented out —the indexing __getitem__ fallback is called with successively higher indexes until it raises IndexError, for membership and other iteration contexts:

```
get[0]:get[1]:get[2]:True
get[0]:1 | get[1]:2 | get[2]:3 | get[3]:4 | get[4]:5 | get[5]:
get[0]:get[1]:get[2]:get[3]:get[4]:get[5]:[1, 4, 9, 16, 25]
get[0]:get[1]:get[2]:get[3]:get[4]:get[5]:['Ob1', 'Ob10', 'Ob11', 'Ob100','Ob101']
get[0]:1 @ get[1]:2 @ get[2]:3 @ get[3]:4 @ get[4]:5 @ get[5]:
```

As we've seen, the __getitem__ method is even more general: besides iterations, it also intercepts explicit indexing as well as slicing. Slice expressions trigger __getitem__ with a slice object containing bounds, both for built-in types and user-defined classes, so slicing is automatic in our class:

```
>>> from contains import Iters
>>> X = Iters('spam')
>>> X[0]                              # Indexing
get[0]:'s'                            # __getitem__(0)

>>> 'spam'[1:]                        # Slice syntax
'pam'
>>> 'spam'[slice(1, None)]            # Slice object
'pam'

>>> X[1:]                             # __getitem__(slice(..))
get[slice(1, None, None)]:'pam'
>>> X[:-1]
get[slice(None, -1, None)]:'spa'

>>> list(X)                           # And iteration too!
iter=> next:next:next:next:next:['s', 'p', 'a', 'm']
```

In more realistic iteration use cases that are not sequence-oriented, though, the __iter__ method may be easier to write since it must not manage an integer index, and __contains__ allows for membership optimization as a special case.

Attribute Access: __getattr__ and __setattr__

In Python, classes can also intercept basic attribute access (a.k.a. qualification) when needed or useful. Specifically, for an *object* created from a class, the dot operator expression *object.attribute* can be implemented by your code too, for reference, assignment, and deletion contexts. We saw a limited example in this category in Chapter 28, but will review and expand on the topic here.

Attribute Reference

The __getattr__ method intercepts attribute references. It's called with the attribute name as a string whenever you try to qualify an instance with an *undefined* (nonexistent) attribute name. It is *not* called if Python can find the attribute using its inheritance tree search procedure.

Because of its behavior, __getattr__ is useful as a hook for responding to attribute requests in a generic fashion. It's commonly used to delegate calls to embedded (or "wrapped") objects from a proxy controller object—of the sort introduced in Chapter 28's introduction to *delegation*. This method can also be used to adapt classes to an interface, or add *accessors* for data attributes after the fact—logic in a method that validates or computes an attribute after it's already being used with simple dot notation.

The basic mechanism underlying these goals is straightforward—the following class catches attribute references, computing the value for one dynamically, and triggering an error for others unsupported with the `raise` statement described earlier in this chapter for iterators (and fully covered in Part VII):

```
>>> class Empty:
        def __getattr__(self, attrname):          # On self.undefined
            if attrname == 'age':
                return 40
            else:
                raise AttributeError(attrname)
>>> X = Empty()
>>> X.age
40
>>> X.name
...error text omitted...
AttributeError: name
```

Here, the `Empty` class and its instance `X` have no real attributes of their own, so the access to `X.age` gets routed to the `__getattr__` method; `self` is assigned the instance (`X`), and `attrname` is assigned the undefined attribute name string (`'age'`). The class makes `age` look like a real attribute by returning a real value as the result of the `X.age` qualification expression (`40`). In effect, `age` becomes a *dynamically computed* attribute—its value is formed by running code, not fetching an object.

For attributes that the class doesn't know how to handle, `__getattr__` raises the built-in `AttributeError` exception to tell Python that these are bona fide undefined names; asking for `X.name` triggers the error. You'll see `__getattr__` again when we see delegation and properties at work in the next two chapters; let's move on to related tools here.

Attribute Assignment and Deletion

In the same department, the `__setattr__` intercepts *all* attribute assignments. If this method is defined or inherited, `self.attr = value` becomes `self.__setattr__('attr', value)`. Like `__getattr__`, this allows your class to catch attribute changes, and validate or transform as desired.

This method is a bit trickier to use, though, because assigning to any `self` attributes within `__setattr__` calls `__setattr__` again, potentially causing an infinite *recursion loop* (and a fairly quick stack overflow exception!). In fact, this applies to all `self` attribute assignments anywhere in the class—all are routed to `__setattr__`, even those in other methods, and those to names other than that which may have triggered `__setattr__` in the first place. Remember, this catches *all* attribute assignments.

If you wish to use this method, you can avoid loops by coding instance attribute assignments as assignments to attribute dictionary keys. That is, use `self.__dict__['name'] = x`, not `self.name = x`; because you're not assigning to `__dict__` itself, this avoids the loop:

```
>>> class Accesscontrol:
        def __setattr__(self, attr, value):
            if attr == 'age':
                self.__dict__[attr] = value + 10        # Not self.name=val or setattr
            else:
                raise AttributeError(attr + ' not allowed')

>>> X = Accesscontrol()
>>> X.age = 40                                          # Calls __setattr__
>>> X.age
50
>>> X.name = 'Bob'
...text omitted...
AttributeError: name not allowed
```

If you change the __dict__ assignment in this to either of the following, it triggers the infinite recursion loop and exception—both dot notation and its setattr built-in function (the assignment analog of getattr) fail when age is assigned outside the class:

```
self.age = value + 10                       # Loops
setattr(self, attr, value + 10)             # Loops (attr is 'age')
```

An assignment to another name within the class triggers a recursive __setattr__ call too, though in this class ends less dramatically in the manual AttributeError exception:

```
self.other = 99                             # Recurs but doesn't loop: fails
```

It's also possible to avoid recursive loops in a class that uses __setattr__ by routing any attribute assignments to a higher superclass with a call, instead of assigning keys in __dict__:

```
self.__dict__[attr] = value + 10            # OK: doesn't loop
object.__setattr__(self, attr, value + 10)  # OK: doesn't loop (new-style only)
```

Because the object form requires use of new-style classes in 2.X, though, we'll postpone details on this form until Chapter 38's deeper look at attribute management at large.

A third attribute management method, __delattr__, is passed the attribute name string and invoked on all attribute deletions (i.e., del object.attr). Like __setattr__, it must avoid recursive loops by routing attribute deletions with the using class through __dict__ or a superclass.

 As we'll learn in Chapter 32, attributes implemented with new-style class features such as *slots* and *properties* are not physically stored in the instance's __dict__ namespace dictionary (and slots may even preclude its existence entirely!). Because of this, code that wishes to support such attributes should code __setattr__ to assign with the object.__setattr__ scheme shown here, not by self.__dict__ indexing unless it's known that subject classes store all their data in the instance itself. In Chapter 38 we'll also see that the new-style __getattribute__

has similar requirements. This change is mandated in Python 3.X, but also applies to 2.X if new-style classes are used.

Other Attribute Management Tools

These three attribute-access overloading methods allow you to control or specialize access to attributes in your objects. They tend to play highly specialized roles, some of which we'll explore later in this book. For another example of __getattr__ at work, see Chapter 28's *person-composite.py*. And for future reference, keep in mind that there are other ways to manage attribute access in Python:

- The __getattribute__ method intercepts *all* attribute fetches, not just those that are undefined, but when using it you must be more cautious than with __getattr__ to avoid loops.
- The property built-in function allows us to associate methods with fetch and set operations on a *specific* class attribute.
- *Descriptors* provide a protocol for associating __get__ and __set__ methods of a class with accesses to a *specific* class attribute.
- *Slots* attributes are declared in classes but create implicit storage in each instance.

Because these are somewhat advanced tools not of interest to every Python programmer, we'll defer a look at properties until Chapter 32 and detailed coverage of all the attribute management techniques until Chapter 38.

Emulating Privacy for Instance Attributes: Part 1

As another use case for such tools, the following code—file *private0.py*—generalizes the previous example, to allow each subclass to have its own list of private names that cannot be *assigned* to its instances (and uses a user-defined exception class, which you'll have to take on faith until Part VII):

```python
class PrivateExc(Exception): pass              # More on exceptions in Part VII

class Privacy:
    def __setattr__(self, attrname, value):    # On self.attrname = value
        if attrname in self.privates:
            raise PrivateExc(attrname, self)   # Make, raise user-define except
        else:
            self.__dict__[attrname] = value    # Avoid loops by using dict key

class Test1(Privacy):
    privates = ['age']

class Test2(Privacy):
    privates = ['name', 'pay']
    def __init__(self):
        self.__dict__['name'] = 'Tom'          # To do better, see Chapter 39!
```

```
if __name__ == '__main__':
    x = Test1()
    y = Test2()

    x.name = 'Bob'      # Works
    #y.name = 'Sue'     # Fails
    print(x.name)

    y.age  = 30         # Works
    #x.age  = 40        # Fails
    print(y.age)
```

In fact, this is a first-cut solution for an implementation of *attribute privacy* in Python —disallowing changes to attribute names outside a class. Although Python doesn't support private declarations per se, techniques like this can emulate much of their purpose.

This is a partial—and even clumsy—solution, though; to make it more effective, we must augment it to allow classes to set their private attributes more naturally, without having to go through __dict__ each time, as the constructor must do here to avoid triggering __setattr__ and an exception. A better and more complete approach might require a wrapper ("proxy") class to check for private attribute accesses made outside the class only, and a __getattr__ to validate attribute fetches too.

We'll postpone a more complete solution to attribute privacy until Chapter 39, where we'll use *class decorators* to intercept and validate attributes more generally. Even though privacy can be emulated this way, though, it almost never is in practice. Python programmers are able to write large OOP frameworks and applications without private declarations—an interesting finding about access controls in general that is beyond the scope of our purposes here.

Still, catching attribute references and assignments is generally a useful technique; it supports *delegation*, a design technique that allows controller objects to wrap up embedded objects, add new behaviors, and route other operations back to the wrapped objects. Because they involve design topics, we'll revisit delegation and wrapper classes in the next chapter.

String Representation: __repr__ and __str__

Our next methods deal with display formats—a topic we've already explored in prior chapters, but will summarize and formalize here. As a review, the following code exercises the __init__ constructor and the __add__ overload method, both of which we've already seen (+ is an in-place operation here, just to show that it can be; per Chapter 27, a named method may be preferred). As we've learned, the default display of instance objects for a class like this is neither generally useful nor aesthetically pretty:

```
>>> class adder:
        def __init__(self, value=0):
            self.data = value                    # Initialize data
```

```
        def __add__(self, other):
            self.data += other                      # Add other in place (bad form?)

    >>> x = adder()                                 # Default displays
    >>> print(x)
    <__main__.adder object at 0x00000000029736D8>
    >>> x
    <__main__.adder object at 0x00000000029736D8>
```

But coding or inheriting string representation methods allows us to customize the display—as in the following, which defines a __repr__ method in a subclass that returns a string representation for its instances.

```
    >>> class addrepr(adder):                       # Inherit __init__, __add__
            def __repr__(self):                     # Add string representation
                return 'addrepr(%s)' % self.data    # Convert to as-code string

    >>> x = addrepr(2)                              # Runs __init__
    >>> x + 1                                       # Runs __add__ (x.add() better?)
    >>> x                                           # Runs __repr__
    addrepr(3)
    >>> print(x)                                    # Runs __repr__
    addrepr(3)
    >>> str(x), repr(x)                             # Runs __repr__ for both
    ('addrepr(3)', 'addrepr(3)')
```

If defined, __repr__ (or its close relative, __str__) is called automatically when class instances are printed or converted to strings. These methods allow you to define a better display format for your objects than the default instance display. Here, __repr__ uses basic string formatting to convert the managed self.data object to a more human-friendly string for display.

Why Two Display Methods?

So far, what we've seen is largely review. But while these methods are generally straightforward to use, their roles and behavior have some subtle implications both for design and coding. In particular, Python provides two display methods to support alternative displays for different audiences:

- __str__ is tried first for the print operation and the str built-in function (the internal equivalent of which print runs). It generally should return a user-friendly display.

- __repr__ is used in all other contexts: for interactive echoes, the repr function, and nested appearances, as well as by print and str if no __str__ is present. It should generally return an as-code string that could be used to re-create the object, or a detailed display for developers.

That is, __repr__ is used everywhere, except by print and str when a __str__ is defined. This means you can code a __repr__ to define a single display format used everywhere, and may code a __str__ to either support print and str exclusively, or to provide an alternative display for them.

As noted in Chapter 28, general tools may also prefer __str__ to leave other classes the option of adding an alternative __repr__ display for use in other contexts, as long as print and str displays suffice for the tool. Conversely, a general tool that codes a __repr__ still leaves clients the option of adding alternative displays with a __str__ for print and str. In other words, if you code either, the other is available for an additional display. In cases where the choice isn't clear, __str__ is generally preferred for larger user-friendly displays, and __repr__ for lower-level or as-code displays and all-inclusive roles.

Let's write some code to illustrate these two methods' distinctions in more concrete terms. The prior example in this section showed how __repr__ is used as the fallback option in many contexts. However, while printing falls back on __repr__ if no __str__ is defined, the inverse is not true—other contexts, such as interactive echoes, use __repr__ only and don't try __str__ at all:

```
>>> class addstr(adder):
        def __str__(self):                        # __str__ but no __repr__
            return '[Value: %s]' % self.data       # Convert to nice string

>>> x = addstr(3)
>>> x + 1
>>> x                                              # Default __repr__
<__main__.addstr object at 0x00000000029738D0>
>>> print(x)                                       # Runs __str__
[Value: 4]
>>> str(x), repr(x)
('[Value: 4]', '<__main__.addstr object at 0x00000000029738D0>')
```

Because of this, __repr__ may be best if you want a *single* display for all contexts. By defining both methods, though, you can support different displays in different contexts —for example, an end-user display with __str__, and a low-level display for programmers to use during development with __repr__. In effect, __str__ simply overrides __repr__ for more user-friendly display contexts:

```
>>> class addboth(adder):
        def __str__(self):
            return '[Value: %s]' % self.data       # User-friendly string
        def __repr__(self):
            return 'addboth(%s)' % self.data        # As-code string

>>> x = addboth(4)
>>> x + 1
>>> x                                              # Runs __repr__
addboth(5)
>>> print(x)                                       # Runs __str__
[Value: 5]
>>> str(x), repr(x)
('[Value: 5]', 'addboth(5)')
```

Display Usage Notes

Though generally simple to use, I should mention three usage notes regarding these methods here. First, keep in mind that __str__ and __repr__ must both return *strings*; other result types are not converted and raise errors, so be sure to run them through a to-string converter (e.g., str or %) if needed.

Second, depending on a container's string-conversion logic, the user-friendly display of __str__ might only apply when objects appear at the top level of a print operation; objects *nested* in larger objects might still print with their __repr__ or its default. The following illustrates both of these points:

```
>>> class Printer:
        def __init__(self, val):
            self.val = val
        def __str__(self):              # Used for instance itself
            return str(self.val)        # Convert to a string result

>>> objs = [Printer(2), Printer(3)]
>>> for x in objs: print(x)            # __str__ run when instance printed
                                       # But not when instance is in a list!

2
3
>>> print(objs)
[<__main__.Printer object at 0x000000000297AB38>, <__main__.Printer obj...etc...>]
>>> objs
[<__main__.Printer object at 0x000000000297AB38>, <__main__.Printer obj...etc...>]
```

To ensure that a custom display is run in all contexts regardless of the container, code __repr__, not __str__; the former is run in all cases if the latter doesn't apply, including nested appearances:

```
>>> class Printer:
        def __init__(self, val):
            self.val = val
        def __repr__(self):             # __repr__ used by print if no __str__
            return str(self.val)        # __repr__ used if echoed or nested

>>> objs = [Printer(2), Printer(3)]
>>> for x in objs: print(x)            # No __str__: runs __repr__


2
3
>>> print(objs)                        # Runs __repr__, not __str__
[2, 3]
>>> objs
[2, 3]
```

Third, and perhaps most subtle, the display methods also have the potential to trigger infinite *recursion loops* in rare contexts—because some objects' displays include displays of other objects, it's not impossible that a display may trigger a display of an object being displayed, and thus loop. This is rare and obscure enough to skip here, but watch for an example of this looping potential to appear for these methods in a note near the end of the next chapter in its *listinherited.py* example's class, where __repr__ can loop.

In practice, __str__, and its more inclusive relative __repr__, seem to be the second most commonly used operator overloading methods in Python scripts, behind __init__. Anytime you can print an object and see a custom display, one of these two tools is probably in use. For additional examples of these tools at work and the design tradeoffs they imply, see Chapter 28's case study and Chapter 31's class lister mix-ins, as well as their role in Chapter 35's exception classes, where __str__ is required over __repr__.

Right-Side and In-Place Uses: __radd__ and __iadd__

Our next group of overloading methods extends the functionality of binary operator methods such as __add__ and __sub__ (called for + and -), which we've already seen. As mentioned earlier, part of the reason there are so many operator overloading methods is because they come in multiple flavors—for every binary expression, we can implement a *left*, *right*, and *in-place* variant. Though defaults are also applied if you don't code all three, your objects' roles dictate how many variants you'll need to code.

Right-Side Addition

For instance, the __add__ methods coded so far technically do not support the use of instance objects on the right side of the + operator:

```
>>> class Adder:
        def __init__(self, value=0):
            self.data = value
        def __add__(self, other):
            return self.data + other

>>> x = Adder(5)
>>> x + 2
7
>>> 2 + x
TypeError: unsupported operand type(s) for +: 'int' and 'Adder'
```

To implement more general expressions, and hence support *commutative*-style operators, code the __radd__ method as well. Python calls __radd__ only when the object on the right side of the + is your class instance, but the object on the left is not an instance of your class. The __add__ method for the object on the left is called instead in all other cases (all of this section's five Commuter classes are coded in file *commuter.py* in the book's examples, along with a self-test):

```
class Commuter1:
    def __init__(self, val):
        self.val = val
    def __add__(self, other):
        print('add', self.val, other)
```

```
            return self.val + other
        def __radd__(self, other):
            print('radd', self.val, other)
            return other + self.val

>>> from commuter import Commuter1
>>> x = Commuter1(88)
>>> y = Commuter1(99)

>>> x + 1                           # __add__: instance + noninstance
add 88 1
89
>>> 1 + y                           # __radd__: noninstance + instance
radd 99 1
100
>>> x + y                           # __add__: instance + instance, triggers __radd__
add 88 <commuter.Commuter1 object at 0x00000000029B39E8>
radd 99 88
187
```

Notice how the order is reversed in __radd__: self is really on the right of the +, and other is on the left. Also note that x and y are instances of the same class here; when instances of different classes appear mixed in an expression, Python prefers the class of the one on the left. When we add the two instances together, Python runs __add__, which in turn triggers __radd__ by simplifying the left operand.

Reusing __add__ in __radd__

For truly commutative operations that do not require special-casing by position, it is also sometimes sufficient to reuse __add__ for __radd__: either by calling __add__ directly; by swapping order and re-adding to trigger __add__ indirectly; or by simply assigning __radd__ to be an alias for __add__ at the top level of the class statement (i.e., in the class's scope). The following alternatives implement all three of these schemes, and return the same results as the original—though the last saves an extra call or dispatch and hence may be quicker (in all, __radd__ is run when self is on the right side of a +):

```
class Commuter2:
    def __init__(self, val):
        self.val = val
    def __add__(self, other):
        print('add', self.val, other)
        return self.val + other
    def __radd__(self, other):
        return self.__add__(other)                  # Call __add__ explicitly

class Commuter3:
    def __init__(self, val):
        self.val = val
    def __add__(self, other):
        print('add', self.val, other)
        return self.val + other
    def __radd__(self, other):
```

```
        return self + other                      # Swap order and re-add

class Commuter4:
    def __init__(self, val):
        self.val = val
    def __add__(self, other):
        print('add', self.val, other)
        return self.val + other
    __radd__ = __add__                            # Alias: cut out the middleman
```

In all these, right-side instance appearances trigger the single, shared __add__ method, passing the right operand to self, to be treated the same as a left-side appearance. Run these on your own for more insight; their returned values are the same as the original.

Propagating class type

In more realistic classes where the class type may need to be propagated in results, things can become trickier: type testing may be required to tell whether it's safe to convert and thus avoid nesting. For instance, without the isinstance test in the following, we could wind up with a Commuter5 whose val is another Commuter5 when two instances are added and __add__ triggers __radd__:

```
class Commuter5:                                 # Propagate class type in results
    def __init__(self, val):
        self.val = val
    def __add__(self, other):
        if isinstance(other, Commuter5):         # Type test to avoid object nesting
            other = other.val
        return Commuter5(self.val + other)       # Else + result is another Commuter
    def __radd__(self, other):
        return Commuter5(other + self.val)
    def __str__(self):
        return '<Commuter5: %s>' % self.val
```

```
>>> from commuter import Commuter5
>>> x = Commuter5(88)
>>> y = Commuter5(99)
>>> print(x + 10)                   # Result is another Commuter instance
<Commuter5: 98>
>>> print(10 + y)
<Commuter5: 109>

>>> z = x + y                       # Not nested: doesn't recur to __radd__
>>> print(z)
<Commuter5: 187>
>>> print(z + 10)
<Commuter5: 197>
>>> print(z + z)
<Commuter5: 374>
>>> print(z + z + 1)
<Commuter5: 375>
```

The need for the isinstance type test here is very subtle—uncomment, run, and trace to see why it's required. If you do, you'll see that the last part of the preceding test

---

winds up differing and nesting objects—which still do the math correctly, but kick off pointless recursive calls to simplify their values, and extra constructor calls build results:

```
>>> z = x + y                          # With isinstance test commented-out
>>> print(z)
<Commuter5: <Commuter5: 187>>
>>> print(z + 10)
<Commuter5: <Commuter5: 197>>
>>> print(z + z)
<Commuter5: <Commuter5: <Commuter5: <Commuter5: 374>>>>
>>> print(z + z + 1)
<Commuter5: <Commuter5: <Commuter5: <Commuter5: 375>>>>
```

To test, the rest of *commuter.py* looks and runs like this—classes can appear in tuples naturally:

```
#!python
from __future__ import print_function        # 2.X/3.X compatibility
...classes defined here...

if __name__ == '__main__':
    for klass in (Commuter1, Commuter2, Commuter3, Commuter4, Commuter5):
        print('-' * 60)
        x = klass(88)
        y = klass(99)
        print(x + 1)
        print(1 + y)
        print(x + y)


c:\code> commuter.py
------------------------------------------------------------
add 88 1
89
radd 99 1
100
add 88 <__main__.Commuter1 object at 0x000000000297F2B0>
radd 99 88
187
------------------------------------------------------------
...etc...
```

There are too many coding variations to explore here, so experiment with these classes on your own for more insight; aliasing __radd__ to __add__ in Commuter5, for example, saves a line, but doesn't prevent object nesting without isinstance. See also Python's manuals for a discussion of other options in this domain; for example, classes may also return the special NotImplemented object for unsupported operands to influence method selection (this is treated as though the method were not defined).

In-Place Addition

To also implement += in-place augmented addition, code either an __iadd__ or an __add__. The latter is used if the former is absent. In fact, the prior section's Commuter

---

classes already support += for this reason—Python runs __add__ and assigns the result manually. The __iadd__ method, though, allows for more efficient in-place changes to be coded where applicable:

```
>>> class Number:
        def __init__(self, val):
            self.val = val
        def __iadd__(self, other):          # __iadd__ explicit: x += y
            self.val += other               # Usually returns self
            return self

>>> x = Number(5)
>>> x += 1
>>> x += 1
>>> x.val
7
```

For mutable objects, this method can often specialize for quicker in-place changes:

```
>>> y = Number([1])                         # In-place change faster than +
>>> y += [2]
>>> y += [3]
>>> y.val
[1, 2, 3]
```

The normal __add__ method is run as a fallback, but may not be able optimize in-place cases:

```
>>> class Number:
        def __init__(self, val):
            self.val = val
        def __add__(self, other):           # __add__ fallback: x = (x + y)
            return Number(self.val + other) # Propagates class type

>>> x = Number(5)
>>> x += 1
>>> x += 1                                  # And += does concatenation here
>>> x.val
7
```

Though we've focused on + here, keep in mind that *every* binary operator has similar right-side and in-place overloading methods that work the same (e.g., __mul__, __rmul__, and __imul__). Still, right-side methods are an advanced topic and tend to be fairly uncommon in practice; you only code them when you need operators to be commutative, and then only if you need to support such operators at all. For instance, a Vector class may use these tools, but an Employee or Button class probably would not.

Call Expressions: __call__

On to our next overloading method: the __call__ method is called when your instance is called. No, this isn't a circular definition—if defined, Python runs a __call__ method for function call expressions applied to your instances, passing along whatever positional or keyword arguments were sent. This allows instances to conform to a function-based API:

```
>>> class Callee:
        def __call__(self, *pargs, **kargs):        # Intercept instance calls
            print('Called:', pargs, kargs)          # Accept arbitrary arguments

>>> C = Callee()
>>> C(1, 2, 3)                                       # C is a callable object
Called: (1, 2, 3) {}
>>> C(1, 2, 3, x=4, y=5)
Called: (1, 2, 3) {'y': 5, 'x': 4}
```

More formally, all the argument-passing modes we explored in Chapter 18 are supported by the __call__ method—whatever is passed to the instance is passed to this method, along with the usual implied instance argument. For example, the method definitions:

```
class C:
    def __call__(self, a, b, c=5, d=6): ...          # Normals and defaults

class C:
    def __call__(self, *pargs, **kargs): ...         # Collect arbitrary arguments

class C:
    def __call__(self, *pargs, d=6, **kargs): ...    # 3.X keyword-only argument
```

all match all the following instance calls:

```
X = C()
X(1, 2)                                              # Omit defaults
X(1, 2, 3, 4)                                        # Positionals
X(a=1, b=2, d=4)                                     # Keywords
X(*[1, 2], **dict(c=3, d=4))                         # Unpack arbitrary arguments
X(1, *(2,), c=3, **dict(d=4))                        # Mixed modes
```

See Chapter 18 for a refresher on function arguments. The net effect is that classes and instances with a __call__ support the exact same argument syntax and semantics as normal functions and methods.

Intercepting call expression like this allows class instances to emulate the look and feel of things like functions, but also retain state information for use during calls. We saw an example similar to the following while exploring scopes in Chapter 17, but you should now be familiar enough with operator overloading to understand this pattern better:

```
>>> class Prod:
        def __init__(self, value):                   # Accept just one argument
            self.value = value
        def __call__(self, other):
            return self.value * other

>>> x = Prod(2)                                      # "Remembers" 2 in state
>>> x(3)                                             # 3 (passed) * 2 (state)
6
```

```
>>> x(4)
8
```

In this example, the __call__ may seem a bit gratuitous at first glance. A simple method can provide similar utility:

```
>>> class Prod:
        def __init__(self, value):
            self.value = value
        def comp(self, other):
            return self.value * other

>>> x = Prod(3)
>>> x.comp(3)
9
>>> x.comp(4)
12
```

However, __call__ can become more useful when interfacing with APIs (i.e., libraries) that expect functions—it allows us to code objects that conform to an expected function call interface, but also retain state information, and other class assets such as inheritance. In fact, it may be the third most commonly used operator overloading method, behind the __init__ constructor and the __str__ and __repr__ display-format alternatives.

Function Interfaces and Callback-Based Code

As an example, the tkinter GUI toolkit (named Tkinter in Python 2.X) allows you to register functions as event handlers (a.k.a. *callbacks*)—when events occur, tkinter calls the registered objects. If you want an event handler to retain state between events, you can register either a class's *bound method*, or an *instance* that conforms to the expected interface with __call__.

In the prior section's code, for example, both x.comp from the second example and x from the first can pass as function-like objects this way. Chapter 17's *closure functions* with state in enclosing scopes can achieve similar effects, but don't provide as much support for multiple operations or customization.

I'll have more to say about bound methods in the next chapter, but for now, here's a hypothetical example of __call__ applied to the GUI domain. The following class defines an object that supports a function-call interface, but also has state information that remembers the color a button should change to when it is later pressed:

```
class Callback:
    def __init__(self, color):          # Function + state information
        self.color = color
    def __call__(self):                  # Support calls with no arguments
        print('turn', self.color)
```

Now, in the context of a GUI, we can register instances of this class as event handlers for buttons, even though the GUI expects to be able to invoke event handlers as simple functions with no arguments:

```
# Handlers
cb1 = Callback('blue')                  # Remember blue
cb2 = Callback('green')                 # Remember green

B1 = Button(command=cb1)                # Register handlers
B2 = Button(command=cb2)
```

When the button is later pressed, the instance object is called as a simple function with no arguments, exactly like in the following calls. Because it retains state as instance attributes, though, it remembers what to do—it becomes a *stateful function* object:

```
# Events
cb1()                                   # Prints 'turn blue'
cb2()                                   # Prints 'turn green'
```

In fact, many consider such classes to be the best way to retain state information in the Python language (per generally accepted Pythonic principles, at least). With OOP, the state remembered is made explicit with attribute assignments. This is different than other state retention techniques (e.g., global variables, enclosing function scope references, and default mutable arguments), which rely on more limited or implicit behavior. Moreover, the added structure and customization in classes goes beyond state retention.

On the other hand, tools such as closure functions are useful in basic state retention roles too, and 3.X's `nonlocal` statement makes enclosing scopes a viable alternative in more programs. We'll revisit such tradeoffs when we start coding substantial decorators in Chapter 39, but here's a quick *closure* equivalent:

```
def callback(color):                    # Enclosing scope versus attrs
    def oncall():
        print('turn', color)
    return oncall

cb3 = callback('yellow')                # Handler to be registered
cb3()                                   # On event: prints 'turn yellow'
```

Before we move on, there are two other ways that Python programmers sometimes tie information to a callback function like this. One option is to use default arguments in `lambda` functions:

```
cb4 = (lambda color='red': 'turn ' + color)  # Defaults retain state too
print(cb4())
```

The other is to use *bound methods* of a class— a bit of a preview, but simple enough to introduce here. A bound method object is a kind of object that remembers both the `self` instance and the referenced function. This object may therefore be called later as a simple function without an instance:

```
class Callback:
    def __init__(self, color):                    # Class with state information
        self.color = color
    def changeColor(self):                         # A normal named method
        print('turn', self.color)

cb1 = Callback('blue')
cb2 = Callback('yellow')

B1 = Button(command=cb1.changeColor)              # Bound method: reference, don't call
B2 = Button(command=cb2.changeColor)              # Remembers function + self pair
```

In this case, when this button is later pressed it's as if the GUI does this, which invokes the instance's changeColor method to process the object's state information, instead of the instance itself:

```
cb1 = Callback('blue')
obj = cb1.changeColor                              # Registered event handler
obj()                                              # On event prints 'turn blue'
```

Note that a lambda is not required here, because a bound method reference by itself already defers a call until later. This technique is simpler, but perhaps less general than overloading calls with __call__. Again, watch for more about bound methods in the next chapter.

You'll also see another __call__ example in Chapter 32, where we will use it to implement something known as a *function decorator*—a callable object often used to add a layer of logic on top of an embedded function. Because __call__ allows us to attach state information to a callable object, it's a natural implementation technique for a function that must remember to call another function when called itself. For more __call__ examples, see the state retention preview examples in Chapter 17, and the more advanced decorators and metaclasses of Chapter 39 and Chapter 40.

Comparisons: __lt__, __gt__, and Others

Our next batch of overloading methods supports comparisons. As suggested in Table 30-1, classes can define methods to catch all six comparison operators: <, >, <=, >=, ==, and !=. These methods are generally straightforward to use, but keep the following qualifications in mind:

- Unlike the __add__/__radd__ pairings discussed earlier, there are no right-side variants of comparison methods. Instead, reflective methods are used when only one operand supports comparison (e.g., __lt__ and __gt__ are each other's reflection).

- There are no implicit relationships among the comparison operators. The truth of == does not imply that != is false, for example, so both __eq__ and __ne__ should be defined to ensure that both operators behave correctly.

- In Python 2.X, a __cmp__ method is used by all comparisons if no more specific comparison methods are defined; it returns a number that is less than, equal to, or greater than zero, to signal less than, equal, and greater than results for the comparison of its two arguments (`self` and another operand). This method often uses the `cmp(x, y)` built-in to compute its result. Both the `__cmp__` method and the `cmp` built-in function are removed in Python 3.X: use the more specific methods instead.

We don't have space for an in-depth exploration of comparison methods, but as a quick introduction, consider the following class and test code:

```
class C:
    data = 'spam'
    def __gt__(self, other):          # 3.X and 2.X version
        return self.data > other
    def __lt__(self, other):
        return self.data < other

X = C()
print(X > 'ham')                       # True  (runs __gt__)
print(X < 'ham')                       # False (runs __lt__)
```

When run under Python 3.X or 2.X, the prints at the end display the expected results noted in their comments, because the class's methods intercept and implement comparison expressions. Consult Python's manuals and other reference resources for more details in this category; for example, `__lt__` is used for sorts in Python3.X, and as for binary expression operators, these methods can also return `NotImplemented` for unsupported arguments.

The `__cmp__` Method in Python 2.X

In Python 2.X only, the `__cmp__` method is used as a fallback if more specific methods are not defined: its integer result is used to evaluate the operator being run. The following produces the same result as the prior section's code under 2.X, for example, but fails in 3.X because `__cmp__` is no longer used:

```
class C:
    data = 'spam'                      # 2.X only
    def __cmp__(self, other):          # __cmp__ not used in 3.X
        return cmp(self.data, other)   # cmp not defined in 3.X

X = C()
print(X > 'ham')                       # True  (runs __cmp__)
print(X < 'ham')                       # False (runs __cmp__)
```

Notice that this fails in 3.X because `__cmp__` is no longer special, not because the `cmp` built-in function is no longer present. If we change the prior class to the following to try to simulate the `cmp` call, the code still works in 2.X but fails in 3.X:

```
class C:
    data = 'spam'
    def __cmp__(self, other):
        return (self.data > other) - (self.data < other)
```

So why, you might be asking, did I just show you a comparison method that is no longer supported in 3.X? While it would be easier to erase history entirely, this book is designed to support both 2.X and 3.X readers. Because __cmp__ may appear in code 2.X readers must reuse or maintain, it's fair game in this book. Moreover, __cmp__ was removed more abruptly than the __getslice__ method described earlier, and so may endure longer. If you use 3.X, though, or care about running your code under 3.X in the future, don't use __cmp__ anymore: use the more specific comparison methods instead.

Boolean Tests: __bool__ and __len__

The next set of methods is truly useful (yes, pun intended!). As we've learned, every object is inherently true or false in Python. When you code classes, you can define what this means for your objects by coding methods that give the True or False values of instances on request. The names of these methods differ per Python line; this section starts with the 3.X story, then shows 2.X's equivalent.

As mentioned briefly earlier, in Boolean contexts, Python first tries __bool__ to obtain a direct Boolean value; if that method is missing, Python tries __len__ to infer a truth value from the object's length. The first of these generally uses object state or other information to produce a Boolean result. In 3.X:

```
>>> class Truth:
        def __bool__(self): return True

>>> X = Truth()
>>> if X: print('yes!')

yes!

>>> class Truth:
        def __bool__(self): return False

>>> X = Truth()
>>> bool(X)
False
```

If this method is missing, Python falls back on length because a nonempty object is considered true (i.e., a nonzero length is taken to mean the object is true, and a zero length means it is false):

```
>>> class Truth:
        def __len__(self): return 0

>>> X = Truth()
>>> if not X: print('no!')

no!
```

If *both* methods are present Python prefers __bool__ over __len__, because it is more specific:

```
>>> class Truth:
        def __bool__(self): return True        # 3.X tries __bool__ first
        def __len__(self): return 0            # 2.X tries __len__ first

>>> X = Truth()
>>> if X: print('yes!')

yes!
```

If neither truth method is defined, the object is vacuously considered true (though any potential implications for more metaphysically inclined readers are strictly coincidental):

```
>>> class Truth:
        pass

>>> X = Truth()
>>> bool(X)
True
```

At least that's the Truth in 3.X. These examples won't generate exceptions in 2.X, but some of their results there may look a bit odd (and trigger an existential crisis or two) unless you read the next section.

Boolean Methods in Python 2.X

Alas, it's not nearly as dramatic as billed—Python 2.X users simply use __nonzero__ instead of __bool__ in all of the preceding section's code. Python 3.X renamed the 2.X __nonzero__ method to __bool__, but Boolean tests work the same otherwise; both 3.X and 2.X use __len__ as a fallback.

Subtly, if you don't use the 2.X name, the first test in the prior section will work the same for you anyhow, but only because __bool__ is not recognized as a special method name in 2.X, and objects are considered true by default! To witness this version difference live, you need to return False:

```
C:\code> c:\python33\python
>>> class C:
        def __bool__(self):
            print('in bool')
            return False

>>> X = C()
>>> bool(X)
in bool
False
>>> if X: print(99)

in bool
```

This works as advertised in 3.X. In 2.X, though, __bool__ is ignored and the object is always considered true by default:

```
C:\code> c:\python27\python
>>> class C:
        def __bool__(self):
            print('in bool')
            return False

>>> X = C()
>>> bool(X)
True
>>> if X: print(99)

99
```

The short story here: in 2.X, use __nonzero__ for Boolean values, or return 0 from the
__len__ fallback method to designate false:

```
C:\code> c:\python27\python
>>> class C:
        def __nonzero__(self):
            print('in nonzero')
            return False            # Returns int (or True/False, same as 1/0)

>>> X = C()
>>> bool(X)
in nonzero
False
>>> if X: print(99)

in nonzero
```

But keep in mind that __nonzero__ works in 2.X only; if used in 3.X it will be silently
ignored and the object will be classified as true by default—just like using 3.X's
__bool__ in 2.X!

And now that we've managed to cross over into the realm of philosophy, let's move on
to look at one last overloading context: *object demise*.

Object Destruction: __del__

It's time to close out this chapter—and learn how to do the same for our class objects.
We've seen how the __init__ *constructor* is called whenever an instance is generated
(and noted how __new__ is run first to make the object). Its counterpart, the *destructor* method __del__, is run automatically when an instance's space is being reclaimed
(i.e., at "garbage collection" time):

```
>>> class Life:
        def __init__(self, name='unknown'):
            print('Hello ' + name)
            self.name = name
        def live(self):
            print(self.name)
        def __del__(self):
            print('Goodbye ' + self.name)
```

```
>>> brian = Life('Brian')
Hello Brian
>>> brian.live()
Brian
>>> brian = 'loretta'
Goodbye Brian
```

Here, when `brian` is assigned a string, we lose the last reference to the `Life` instance and so trigger its destructor method. This works, and it may be useful for implementing some cleanup activities, such as terminating a server connection. However, destructors are not as commonly used in Python as in some OOP languages, for a number of reasons that the next section describes.

Destructor Usage Notes

The destructor method works as documented, but it has some well-known caveats and a few outright dark corners that make it somewhat rare to see in Python code:

- *Need*: For one thing, destructors may not be as useful in Python as they are in some other OOP languages. Because Python automatically reclaims all *memory space* held by an instance when the instance is reclaimed, destructors are not necessary for space management. In the current CPython implementation of Python, you also don't need to close *file objects* held by the instance in destructors because they are automatically closed when reclaimed. As mentioned in Chapter 9, though, it's still sometimes best to run file close methods anyhow, because this autoclose behavior may vary in alternative Python implementations (e.g., Jython).

- *Predictability*: For another, you cannot always easily predict when an instance will be reclaimed. In some cases, there may be lingering references to your objects in system tables that prevent destructors from running when your program expects them to be triggered. Python also does not guarantee that destructor methods will be called for objects that still exist when the interpreter exits.

- *Exceptions*: In fact, `__del__` can be tricky to use for even more subtle reasons. Exceptions raised within it, for example, simply print a warning message to `sys.stderr` (the standard error stream) rather than triggering an exception event, because of the unpredictable context under which it is run by the garbage collector —it's not always possible to know where such an exception should be delivered.

- *Cycles*: In addition, cyclic (a.k.a. circular) references among objects may prevent garbage collection from happening when you expect it to. An optional cycle detector, enabled by default, can automatically collect such objects eventually, but only if they do not have `__del__` methods. Since this is relatively obscure, we'll ignore further details here; see Python's standard manuals' coverage of both `__del__` and the `gc` garbage collector module for more information.

Because of these downsides, it's often better to code termination activities in an explicitly called method (e.g., `shutdown`). As described in the next part of the book, the

---

`try`/`finally` statement also supports termination actions, as does the `with` statement for objects that support its context manager model.

Chapter Summary

That's as many overloading examples as we have space for here. Most of the other operator overloading methods work similarly to the ones we've explored, and all are just hooks for intercepting built-in type operations. Some overloading methods, for example, have unique argument lists or return values, but the general usage pattern is the same. We'll see a few others in action later in the book:

- Chapter 34 uses __enter__ and __exit__ in `with` statement context managers.
- Chapter 38 uses the __get__ and __set__ class descriptor fetch/set methods.
- Chapter 40 uses the __new__ object creation method in the context of metaclasses.

In addition, some of the methods we've studied here, such as __call__ and __str__, will be employed by later examples in this book. For complete coverage, though, I'll defer to other documentation sources—see Python's standard language manual or reference books for details on additional overloading methods.

In the next chapter, we leave the realm of class mechanics behind to explore common design patterns—the ways that classes are commonly used and combined to optimize code reuse. After that, we'll survey a handful of advanced topics and move on to exceptions, the last core subject of this book. Before you read on, though, take a moment to work through the chapter quiz below to review the concepts we've covered.

Test Your Knowledge: Quiz

1. What two operator overloading methods can you use to support iteration in your classes?
2. What two operator overloading methods handle printing, and in what contexts?
3. How can you intercept slice operations in a class?
4. How can you catch in-place addition in a class?
5. When should you provide operator overloading?

Test Your Knowledge: Answers

1. Classes can support iteration by defining (or inheriting) __getitem__ or __iter__. In all iteration contexts, Python tries to use __iter__ first, which returns an object that supports the iteration protocol with a __next__ method: if no __iter__ is found by inheritance search, Python falls back on the __getitem__ indexing method,

which is called repeatedly, with successively higher indexes. If used, the `yield` statement can create the `__next__` method automatically.

2. The `__str__` and `__repr__` methods implement object print displays. The former is called by the `print` and `str` built-in functions; the latter is called by `print` and `str` if there is no `__str__`, and always by the `repr` built-in, interactive echoes, and nested appearances. That is, `__repr__` is used everywhere, except by `print` and `str` when a `__str__` is defined. A `__str__` is usually used for user-friendly displays; `__repr__` gives extra details or the object's as-code form.

3. Slicing is caught by the `__getitem__` indexing method: it is called with a slice object, instead of a simple integer index, and slice objects may be passed on or inspected as needed. In Python 2.X, `__getslice__` (defunct in 3.X) may be used for two-limit slices as well.

4. In-place addition tries `__iadd__` first, and `__add__` with an assignment second. The same pattern holds true for all binary operators. The `__radd__` method is also available for right-side addition.

5. When a class naturally matches, or needs to emulate, a built-in type's interfaces. For example, collections might imitate sequence or mapping interfaces, and callables might be coded for use with an API that expects a function. You generally shouldn't implement expression operators if they don't naturally map to your objects naturally and logically, though—use normally named methods instead.

Designing with Classes

So far in this part of the book, we've concentrated on using Python's OOP tool, the class. But OOP is also about *design issues*—that is, how to use classes to model useful objects. This chapter will touch on a few core OOP ideas and present some additional examples that are more realistic than many shown so far.

Along the way, we'll code some common OOP design patterns in Python, such as inheritance, composition, delegation, and factories. We'll also investigate some design-focused class concepts, such as pseudoprivate attributes, multiple inheritance, and bound methods.

One note up front: some of the design terms mentioned here require more explanation than I can provide in this book. If this material sparks your curiosity, I suggest exploring a text on OOP design or design patterns as a next step. As we'll see, the good news is that Python makes many traditional design patterns trivial.

Python and OOP

Let's begin with a review—Python's implementation of OOP can be summarized by three ideas:

Inheritance
> Inheritance is based on attribute lookup in Python (in X.name expressions).

Polymorphism
> In X.method, the meaning of method depends on the type (class) of subject object X.

Encapsulation
> Methods and operators implement behavior, though data hiding is a convention by default.

By now, you should have a good feel for what inheritance is all about in Python. We've also talked about Python's polymorphism a few times already; it flows from Python's lack of type declarations. Because attributes are always resolved at runtime, objects that implement the same interfaces are automatically interchangeable; clients don't need to know what sorts of objects are implementing the methods they call.

Encapsulation means packaging in Python—that is, hiding implementation details behind an object's interface. It does not mean enforced privacy, though that can be implemented with code, as we'll see in Chapter 39. Encapsulation is available and useful in Python nonetheless: it allows the implementation of an object's interface to be changed without impacting the users of that object.

Polymorphism Means Interfaces, Not Call Signatures

Some OOP languages also define polymorphism to mean overloading functions based on the type signatures of their arguments—the number passed and/or their types. Because there are no type declarations in Python, this concept doesn't really apply; as we've seen, polymorphism in Python is based on object *interfaces*, not types.

If you're pining for your C++ days, you can try to overload methods by their argument lists, like this:

```
class C:
    def meth(self, x):
        ...
    def meth(self, x, y, z):
        ...
```

This code will run, but because the def simply assigns an object to a name in the class's scope, the *last* definition of the method function is the only one that will be retained. Put another way, it's just as if you say X = 1 and then X = 2; X will be 2. Hence, there can be only one definition of a method name.

If they are truly required, you can always code type-based selections using the type-testing ideas we met in Chapter 4 and Chapter 9, or the argument list tools introduced in Chapter 18:

```
class C:
    def meth(self, *args):
        if len(args) == 1:             # Branch on number arguments
            ...
        elif type(arg[0]) == int:      # Branch on argument types (or isinstance())
            ...
```

You normally shouldn't do this, though—it's not the Python way. As described in Chapter 16, you should write your code to expect only an object *interface*, not a specific data *type*. That way, it will be useful for a broader category of types and applications, both now and in the future:

```
class C:
    def meth(self, x):
        x.operation()                  # Assume x does the right thing
```

It's also generally considered better to use distinct method *names* for distinct operations, rather than relying on call signatures (no matter what language you code in).

Although Python's object model is straightforward, much of the art in OOP is in the way we combine classes to achieve a program's goals. The next section begins a tour of some of the ways larger programs use classes to their advantage.

OOP and Inheritance: "Is-a" Relationships

We've explored the mechanics of inheritance in depth already, but I'd now like to show you an example of how it can be used to model real-world relationships. From a *programmer's* point of view, inheritance is kicked off by attribute qualifications, which trigger searches for names in instances, their classes, and then any superclasses. From a *designer's* point of view, inheritance is a way to specify set membership: a class defines a set of properties that may be inherited and customized by more specific sets (i.e., subclasses).

To illustrate, let's put that pizza-making robot we talked about at the start of this part of the book to work. Suppose we've decided to explore alternative career paths and open a pizza restaurant (not bad, as career paths go). One of the first things we'll need to do is hire employees to serve customers, prepare the food, and so on. Being engineers at heart, we've decided to build a robot to make the pizzas; but being politically and cybernetically correct, we've also decided to make our robot a full-fledged employee with a salary.

Our pizza shop team can be defined by the four classes in the following Python 3.X and 2.X example file, *employees.py*. The most general class, `Employee`, provides common behavior such as bumping up salaries (`giveRaise`) and printing (`__repr__`). There are two kinds of employees, and so two subclasses of `Employee`—`Chef` and `Server`. Both override the inherited `work` method to print more specific messages. Finally, our pizza robot is modeled by an even more specific class—`PizzaRobot` is a kind of `Chef`, which is a kind of `Employee`. In OOP terms, we call these relationships "is-a" links: a robot is a chef, which is an employee. Here's the *employees.py* file:

```
# File employees.py (2.X + 3.X)
from __future__ import print_function

class Employee:
    def __init__(self, name, salary=0):
        self.name   = name
        self.salary = salary
    def giveRaise(self, percent):
        self.salary = self.salary + (self.salary * percent)
    def work(self):
        print(self.name, "does stuff")
    def __repr__(self):
        return "<Employee: name=%s, salary=%s>" % (self.name, self.salary)

class Chef(Employee):
```

```
        def __init__(self, name):
            Employee.__init__(self, name, 50000)
        def work(self):
            print(self.name, "makes food")

    class Server(Employee):
        def __init__(self, name):
            Employee.__init__(self, name, 40000)
        def work(self):
            print(self.name, "interfaces with customer")

    class PizzaRobot(Chef):
        def __init__(self, name):
            Chef.__init__(self, name)
        def work(self):
            print(self.name, "makes pizza")

    if __name__ == "__main__":
        bob = PizzaRobot('bob')          # Make a robot named bob
        print(bob)                       # Run inherited __repr__
        bob.work()                       # Run type-specific action
        bob.giveRaise(0.20)              # Give bob a 20% raise
        print(bob); print()

        for klass in Employee, Chef, Server, PizzaRobot:
            obj = klass(klass.__name__)
            obj.work()
```

When we run the self-test code included in this module, we create a pizza-making robot named bob, which inherits names from three classes: PizzaRobot, Chef, and Employee. For instance, printing bob runs the Employee.__repr__ method, and giving bob a raise invokes Employee.giveRaise because that's where the inheritance search finds that method:

```
c:\code> python employees.py
<Employee: name=bob, salary=50000>
bob makes pizza
<Employee: name=bob, salary=60000.0>

Employee does stuff
Chef makes food
Server interfaces with customer
PizzaRobot makes pizza
```

In a class hierarchy like this, you can usually make instances of any of the classes, not just the ones at the bottom. For instance, the for loop in this module's self-test code creates instances of all four classes; each responds differently when asked to work because the work method is different in each. bob the robot, for example, gets work from the most specific (i.e., lowest) PizzaRobot class.

Of course, these classes just *simulate* real-world objects; work prints a message for the time being, but it could be expanded to do real work later (see Python's interfaces to devices such as serial ports, Arduino boards, and the Raspberry Pi if you're taking this section much too literally!).

OOP and Composition: "Has-a" Relationships

The notion of composition was introduced in Chapter 26 and Chapter 28. From a *programmer's* point of view, composition involves embedding other objects in a container object, and activating them to implement container methods. To a *designer*, composition is another way to represent relationships in a problem domain. But, rather than set membership, composition has to do with components—parts of a whole.

Composition also reflects the relationships between parts, called "has-a" relationships. Some OOP design texts refer to composition as *aggregation*, or distinguish between the two terms by using aggregation to describe a weaker dependency between container and contained. In this text, a "composition" simply refers to a collection of embedded objects. The composite class generally provides an interface all its own and implements it by directing the embedded objects.

Now that we've implemented our employees, let's put them in the pizza shop and let them get busy. Our pizza shop is a composite object: it has an oven, and it has employees like servers and chefs. When a customer enters and places an order, the components of the shop spring into action—the server takes the order, the chef makes the pizza, and so on. The following example—file *pizzashop.py*—runs the same on Python 3.X and 2.X and simulates all the objects and relationships in this scenario:

```
# File pizzashop.py (2.X + 3.X)
from __future__ import print_function
from employees import PizzaRobot, Server

class Customer:
    def __init__(self, name):
        self.name = name
    def order(self, server):
        print(self.name, "orders from", server)
    def pay(self, server):
        print(self.name, "pays for item to", server)

class Oven:
    def bake(self):
        print("oven bakes")

class PizzaShop:
    def __init__(self):
        self.server = Server('Pat')          # Embed other objects
        self.chef   = PizzaRobot('Bob')      # A robot named bob
        self.oven   = Oven()

    def order(self, name):
        customer = Customer(name)            # Activate other objects
        customer.order(self.server)          # Customer orders from server
```

```
            self.chef.work()
            self.oven.bake()
            customer.pay(self.server)

    if __name__ == "__main__":
        scene = PizzaShop()                    # Make the composite
        scene.order('Homer')                   # Simulate Homer's order
        print('...')
        scene.order('Shaggy')                  # Simulate Shaggy's order
```

The PizzaShop class is a container and controller; its constructor makes and embeds instances of the employee classes we wrote in the prior section, as well as an Oven class defined here. When this module's self-test code calls the PizzaShop order method, the embedded objects are asked to carry out their actions in turn. Notice that we make a new Customer object for each order, and we pass on the embedded Server object to Customer methods; customers come and go, but the server is part of the pizza shop composite. Also notice that employees are still involved in an inheritance relationship; composition and inheritance are complementary tools.

When we run this module, our pizza shop handles two orders—one from Homer, and then one from Shaggy:

```
c:\code> python pizzashop.py
Homer orders from <Employee: name=Pat, salary=40000>
Bob makes pizza
oven bakes
Homer pays for item to <Employee: name=Pat, salary=40000>
...
Shaggy orders from <Employee: name=Pat, salary=40000>
Bob makes pizza
oven bakes
Shaggy pays for item to <Employee: name=Pat, salary=40000>
```

Again, this is mostly just a toy simulation, but the objects and interactions are representative of composites at work. As a rule of thumb, classes can represent just about any objects and relationships you can express in a sentence; just replace *nouns* with classes (e.g., Oven), and *verbs* with methods (e.g., bake), and you'll have a first cut at a design.

Stream Processors Revisited

For a composition example that may be a bit more tangible than pizza-making robots, recall the generic data stream processor function we partially coded in the introduction to OOP in Chapter 26:

```
def processor(reader, converter, writer):
    while True:
        data = reader.read()
        if not data: break
        data = converter(data)
        writer.write(data)
```

Rather than using a simple function here, we might code this as a class that uses composition to do its work in order to provide more structure and support inheritance. The following 3.X/2.X file, *streams.py*, demonstrates one way to code the class:

```
class Processor:
    def __init__(self, reader, writer):
        self.reader = reader
        self.writer = writer

    def process(self):
        while True:
            data = self.reader.readline()
            if not data: break
            data = self.converter(data)
            self.writer.write(data)

    def converter(self, data):
        assert False, 'converter must be defined'        # Or raise exception
```

This class defines a converter method that it expects subclasses to fill in; it's an example of the *abstract superclass* model we outlined in Chapter 29 (more on assert in Part VII—it simply raises an exception if its test is false). Coded this way, reader and writer objects are embedded within the class instance (*composition*), and we supply the conversion logic in a subclass rather than passing in a converter function (*inheritance*). The file *converters.py* shows how:

```
from streams import Processor

class Uppercase(Processor):
    def converter(self, data):
        return data.upper()

if __name__ == '__main__':
    import sys
    obj = Uppercase(open('trispam.txt'), sys.stdout)
    obj.process()
```

Here, the Uppercase class inherits the stream-processing loop logic (and anything else that may be coded in its superclasses). It needs to define only what is unique about it —the data conversion logic. When this file is run, it makes and runs an instance that reads from the file *trispam.txt* and writes the uppercase equivalent of that file to the stdout stream:

```
c:\code> type trispam.txt
spam
Spam
SPAM!

c:\code> python converters.py
SPAM
SPAM
SPAM!
```

To process different sorts of streams, pass in different sorts of objects to the class construction call. Here, we use an output file instead of a stream:

```
C:\code> python
>>> import converters
>>> prog = converters.Uppercase(open('trispam.txt'), open('trispamup.txt', 'w'))
>>> prog.process()

C:\code> type trispamup.txt
SPAM
SPAM
SPAM!
```

But, as suggested earlier, we could also pass in arbitrary objects coded as classes that define the required input and output method interfaces. Here's a simple example that passes in a writer class that wraps up the text inside HTML tags:

```
C:\code> python
>>> from converters import Uppercase
>>>
>>> class HTMLize:
        def write(self, line):
            print('<PRE>%s</PRE>' % line.rstrip())

>>> Uppercase(open('trispam.txt'), HTMLize()).process()
<PRE>SPAM</PRE>
<PRE>SPAM</PRE>
<PRE>SPAM!</PRE>
```

If you trace through this example's control flow, you'll see that we get *both* uppercase conversion (by inheritance) and HTML formatting (by composition), even though the core processing logic in the original `Processor` superclass knows nothing about either step. The processing code only cares that writers have a `write` method and that a method named `convert` is defined; it doesn't care what those methods do when they are called. Such polymorphism and encapsulation of logic is behind much of the power of classes in Python.

As is, the `Processor` superclass only provides a file-scanning loop. In more realistic work, we might extend it to support additional programming tools for its subclasses, and, in the process, turn it into a full-blown application *framework*. Coding such a tool once in a superclass enables you to reuse it in all of your programs. Even in this simple example, because so much is packaged and inherited with classes, all we had to code was the HTML formatting step; the rest was free.

For another example of composition at work, see exercise 9 at the end of Chapter 32 and its solution in "Part VI, Classes and OOP" on page 1489 in Appendix D; it's similar to the pizza shop example. We've focused on inheritance in this book because that is the main tool that the Python language itself provides for OOP. But, in practice, composition may be used as much as inheritance as a way to structure classes, especially in larger systems. As we've seen, inheritance and composition are often complementary (and sometimes alternative) techniques. Because composition is a design issue outside the scope of the Python language and this book, though, I'll defer to other resources for more on this topic.

Why You Will Care: Classes and Persistence

I've mentioned Python's `pickle` and `shelve` object persistence support a few times in this part of the book because it works especially well with class instances. In fact, these tools are often compelling enough to motivate the use of classes in general—by pickling or shelving a class instance, we get data storage that contains both data and logic combined.

For example, besides allowing us to simulate real-world interactions, the pizza shop classes developed in this chapter could also be used as the basis of a persistent restaurant database. Instances of classes can be stored away on disk in a single step using Python's `pickle` or `shelve` modules. We used shelves to store instances of classes in the OOP tutorial in Chapter 28, but the object pickling interface is remarkably easy to use as well:

```python
import pickle
object = SomeClass()
file   = open(filename, 'wb')    # Create external file
pickle.dump(object, file)        # Save object in file

import pickle
file   = open(filename, 'rb')
object = pickle.load(file)       # Fetch it back later
```

Pickling converts in-memory objects to serialized byte streams (in Python, strings), which may be stored in files, sent across a network, and so on; unpickling converts back from byte streams to identical in-memory objects. Shelves are similar, but they automatically pickle objects to an access-by-key database, which exports a dictionary-like interface:

```python
import shelve
object = SomeClass()
dbase  = shelve.open(filename)
dbase['key'] = object            # Save under key

import shelve
dbase  = shelve.open(filename)
object = dbase['key']            # Fetch it back later
```

In our pizza shop example, using classes to model employees means we can get a simple database of employees and shops with little extra work—pickling such instance objects to a file makes them persistent across Python program executions:

```python
>>> from pizzashop import PizzaShop
>>> shop = PizzaShop()
>>> shop.server, shop.chef
(<Employee: name=Pat, salary=40000>, <Employee: name=Bob, salary=50000>)
>>> import pickle
>>> pickle.dump(shop, open('shopfile.pkl', 'wb'))
```

This stores an entire composite `shop` object in a file all at once. To bring it back later in another session or program, a single step suffices as well. In fact, objects restored this way retain both state and behavior:

```
>>> import pickle
>>> obj = pickle.load(open('shopfile.pkl', 'rb'))
>>> obj.server, obj.chef
(<Employee: name=Pat, salary=40000>, <Employee: name=Bob, salary=50000>)

>>> obj.order('LSP')
LSP orders from <Employee: name=Pat, salary=40000>
Bob makes pizza
oven bakes
LSP pays for item to <Employee: name=Pat, salary=40000>
```

This just runs a simulation as is, but we might extend the shop to keep track of inventory, revenue, and so on—saving it to its file after changes would retain its updated state. See the standard library manual and related coverage in Chapter 9, Chapter 28, and Chapter 37 for more on pickles and shelves.

OOP and Delegation: "Wrapper" Proxy Objects

Beside inheritance and composition, object-oriented programmers often speak of *delegation*, which usually implies controller objects that embed other objects to which they pass off operation requests. The controllers can take care of administrative activities, such as logging or validating accesses, adding extra steps to interface components, or monitoring active instances.

In a sense, delegation is a special form of composition, with a single embedded object managed by a *wrapper* (sometimes called a *proxy*) class that retains most or all of the embedded object's interface. The notion of proxies sometimes applies to other mechanisms too, such as function calls; in delegation, we're concerned with proxies for *all* of an object's behavior, including method calls and other operations.

This concept was introduced by example in Chapter 28, and in Python is often implemented with the __getattr__ method hook we studied in Chapter 30. Because this operator overloading method intercepts accesses to nonexistent attributes, a wrapper class can use __getattr__ to route arbitrary accesses to a wrapped object. Because this method allows attribute requests to be routed generically, the wrapper class retains the interface of the wrapped object and may add additional operations of its own.

By way of review, consider the file *trace.py* (which runs the same in 2.X and 3.X):

```
class Wrapper:
    def __init__(self, object):
        self.wrapped = object                    # Save object
    def __getattr__(self, attrname):
        print('Trace: ' + attrname)              # Trace fetch
        return getattr(self.wrapped, attrname)   # Delegate fetch
```

Recall from Chapter 30 that __getattr__ gets the attribute name as a string. This code makes use of the getattr built-in function to fetch an attribute from the wrapped object by name string—getattr(X,N) is like X.N, except that N is an expression that evaluates to a string at runtime, not a variable. In fact, getattr(X,N) is similar to X.__dict__[N], but the former also performs an inheritance search, like X.N, while the latter does not (see Chapter 22 and Chapter 29 for more on the __dict__ attribute).

You can use the approach of this module's wrapper class to manage access to any object with attributes—lists, dictionaries, and even classes and instances. Here, the Wrapper class simply prints a trace message on each attribute access and delegates the attribute request to the embedded wrapped object:

```
>>> from trace import Wrapper
>>> x = Wrapper([1, 2, 3])           # Wrap a list
>>> x.append(4)                      # Delegate to list method
Trace: append
>>> x.wrapped                        # Print my member
[1, 2, 3, 4]

>>> x = Wrapper({'a': 1, 'b': 2})    # Wrap a dictionary
>>> list(x.keys())                   # Delegate to dictionary method
Trace: keys
['a', 'b']
```

The net effect is to augment the entire interface of the wrapped object, with additional code in the Wrapper class. We can use this to log our method calls, route method calls to extra or custom logic, adapt a class to a new interface, and so on.

We'll revive the notions of wrapped objects and delegated operations as one way to extend built-in types in the next chapter. If you are interested in the delegation design pattern, also watch for the discussions in Chapter 32 and Chapter 39 of *function decorators*, a strongly related concept designed to augment a specific function or method call rather than the entire interface of an object, and *class decorators*, which serve as a way to automatically add such delegation-based wrappers to all instances of a class.

 Version skew note: As we saw by example in Chapter 28, delegation of object interfaces by general *proxies* has changed substantially in 3.X when wrapped objects implement operator overloading methods. Technically, this is a *new-style class* difference, and can appear in 2.X code too if it enables this option; per the next chapter, it's mandatory in 3.X and thus often considered a 3.X change.

In Python 2.X's default classes, operator overloading methods run by built-in operations are routed through generic attribute interception methods like __getattr__. Printing a wrapped object directly, for example, calls this method for __repr__ or __str__, which then passes the call on to the wrapped object. This pattern holds for __iter__, __add__, and the other operator methods of the prior chapter.

In Python 3.X, this no longer happens: printing does not trigger __getattr__ (or its __getattribute__ cousin we'll study in the next chapter) and a default display is used instead. In 3.X, new-style classes look up methods invoked implicitly by built-in operations in classes and skip the normal instance lookup entirely. Explicit name attribute fetches are routed to __getattr__ the same way in both 2.X and 3.X, but built-in operation method lookup differs in ways that may impact some delegation-based tools.

We'll return to this issue in the next chapter as a new-style class change, and see it live in Chapter 38 and Chapter 39, in the context of managed attributes and decorators. For now, keep in mind that for delegation coding patterns, you may need to redefine operator overloading methods in wrapper classes (either by hand, by tools, or by superclasses) if they are used by embedded objects and you want them to be intercepted in new-style classes.

Pseudoprivate Class Attributes

Besides larger structuring goals, class designs often must address name usage too. In Chapter 28's case study, for example, we noted that methods defined within a general tool class might be modified by subclasses if exposed, and noted the tradeoffs of this policy—while it supports method customization and direct calls, it's also open to accidental replacements.

In Part V, we learned that every name assigned at the top level of a module file is exported. By default, the same holds for classes—data hiding is a convention, and clients may fetch or change attributes in any class or instance to which they have a reference. In fact, attributes are all "public" and "virtual," in C++ terms; they're all accessible everywhere and are looked up dynamically at runtime.[1]

That said, Python today does support the notion of name "mangling" (i.e., expansion) to localize some names in classes. Mangled names are sometimes misleadingly called "private attributes," but really this is just a way to *localize* a name to the class that created it—name mangling does not prevent access by code outside the class. This feature is mostly intended to avoid namespace collisions in instances, not to restrict access to names in general; mangled names are therefore better called "pseudoprivate" than "private."

Pseudoprivate names are an advanced and entirely optional feature, and you probably won't find them very useful until you start writing general tools or larger class hierarchies for use in multiprogrammer projects. In fact, they are not always used even when they probably should be—more commonly, Python programmers code internal names with a single underscore (e.g., _X), which is just an informal convention to let you know that a name shouldn't generally be changed (it means nothing to Python itself).

---

1. This tends to scare people with a C++ background disproportionately. In Python, it's even possible to change or completely delete a class's method at runtime. On the other hand, almost nobody ever does this in practical programs. As a scripting language, Python is more about enabling than restricting. Also, recall from our discussion of operator overloading in Chapter 30 that __getattr__ and __setattr__ can be used to emulate privacy, but are generally not used for this purpose in practice. More on this when we code a more realistic privacy decorator in Chapter 39.

Because you may see this feature in other people's code, though, you need to be somewhat aware of it, even if you don't use it yourself. And once you learn its advantages and contexts of use, you may find this feature to be more useful in your own code than some programmers realize.

Name Mangling Overview

Here's how name mangling works: within a class statement only, any names that *start* with two underscores but don't *end* with two underscores are automatically expanded to include the name of the enclosing class at their front. For instance, a name like __X within a class named Spam is changed to _Spam__X automatically: the original name is prefixed with a single underscore and the enclosing class's name. Because the modified name contains the name of the enclosing class, it's generally unique; it won't clash with similar names created by other classes in a hierarchy.

Name mangling happens only for names that appear inside a class statement's code, and then only for names that begin with two leading underscores. It works for *every* name preceded with double underscores, though—both class attributes (including method names) and instance attribute names assigned to self. For example, in a class named Spam, a method named __meth is mangled to _Spam__meth, and an instance attribute reference self.__X is transformed to self._Spam__X.

Despite the mangling, as long as the class uses the double underscore version everywhere it refers to the name, all its references will still work. Because more than one class may add attributes to an instance, though, this mangling helps avoid clashes—but we need to move on to an example to see how.

Why Use Pseudoprivate Attributes?

One of the main issues that the pseudoprivate attribute feature is meant to alleviate has to do with the way instance attributes are stored. In Python, all instance attributes wind up in the *single* instance object at the bottom of the class tree, and are shared by all class-level method functions the instance is passed into. This is different from the C++ model, where each class gets its own space for data members it defines.

Within a class's method in Python, whenever a method assigns to a self attribute (e.g., self.*attr* = *value*), it changes or creates an attribute in the instance (recall that inheritance searches happen only on reference, not on assignment). Because this is true even if multiple classes in a hierarchy assign to the same attribute, collisions are possible.

For example, suppose that when a programmer codes a class, it is assumed that the class owns the attribute name X in the instance. In this class's methods, the name is set, and later fetched:

```
class C1:
    def meth1(self): self.X = 88      # I assume X is mine
    def meth2(self): print(self.X)
```

Suppose further that another programmer, working in isolation, makes the same assumption in another class:

```
class C2:
    def metha(self): self.X = 99        # Me too
    def methb(self): print(self.X)
```

Both of these classes work by themselves. The problem arises if the two classes are ever mixed together in the same class tree:

```
class C3(C1, C2): ...
I = C3()                                # Only 1 X in I!
```

Now, the value that each class gets back when it says self.X will depend on which class assigned it last. Because all assignments to self.X refer to the same single instance, there is only one X attribute—I.X—no matter how many classes use that attribute name.

This isn't a problem if it's expected, and indeed, this is how classes communicate—the instance is shared memory. To guarantee that an attribute belongs to the class that uses it, though, prefix the name with double underscores everywhere it is used in the class, as in this 2.X/3.X file, *pseudoprivate.py*:

```
class C1:
    def meth1(self): self.__X = 88      # Now X is mine
    def meth2(self): print(self.__X)    # Becomes _C1__X in I
class C2:
    def metha(self): self.__X = 99      # Me too
    def methb(self): print(self.__X)    # Becomes _C2__X in I

class C3(C1, C2): pass
I = C3()                                # Two X names in I

I.meth1(); I.metha()
print(I.__dict__)
I.meth2(); I.methb()
```

When thus prefixed, the X attributes will be expanded to include the names of their classes before being added to the instance. If you run a dir call on I or inspect its namespace dictionary after the attributes have been assigned, you'll see the expanded names, _C1_X and _C2_X, but not X. Because the expansion makes the names more unique within the instance, the class coders can be fairly safe in assuming that they truly own any names that they prefix with two underscores:

```
% python pseudoprivate.py
{'_C2__X': 99, '_C1__X': 88}
88
99
```

This trick can avoid potential name collisions in the instance, but note that it does not amount to true privacy. If you know the name of the enclosing class, you can still access either of these attributes anywhere you have a reference to the instance by using the fully expanded name (e.g., I._C1__X = 77). Moreover, names could still collide if unknowing programmers use the expanded naming pattern explicitly (unlikely, but not impossible). On the other hand, this feature makes it less likely that you will *accidentally* step on a class's names.

Pseudoprivate attributes are also useful in larger frameworks or tools, both to avoid introducing new method names that might accidentally hide definitions elsewhere in the class tree and to reduce the chance of internal methods being replaced by names defined lower in the tree. If a method is intended for use only within a class that may be mixed into other classes, the double underscore prefix virtually ensures that the method won't interfere with other names in the tree, especially in multiple-inheritance scenarios:

```
class Super:
    def method(self): ...          # A real application method

class Tool:
    def __method(self): ...        # Becomes _Tool__method
    def other(self): self.__method()  # Use my internal method

class Sub1(Tool, Super): ...
    def actions(self): self.method()  # Runs Super.method as expected

class Sub2(Tool):
    def __init__(self): self.method = 99  # Doesn't break Tool.__method
```

We met multiple inheritance briefly in Chapter 26 and will explore it in more detail later in this chapter. Recall that superclasses are searched according to their left-to-right order in `class` header lines. Here, this means `Sub1` prefers `Tool` attributes to those in `Super`. Although in this example we could force Python to pick the application class's methods first by switching the order of the superclasses listed in the `Sub1` class header, pseudoprivate attributes resolve the issue altogether. Pseudoprivate names also prevent subclasses from accidentally redefining the internal method's names, as in `Sub2`.

Again, I should note that this feature tends to be of use primarily for larger, multiprogrammer projects, and then only for selected names. Don't be tempted to clutter your code unnecessarily; only use this feature for names that truly need to be controlled by a single class. Although useful in some general class-based tools, for simpler programs, it's probably overkill.

For more examples that make use of the __X naming feature, see the *lister.py* mix-in classes introduced later in this chapter in the multiple inheritance section, as well as the discussion of `Private` class decorators in Chapter 39.

If you care about privacy in general, you might want to review the emulation of private instance attributes sketched in the section "Attribute Access: __getattr__ and __setattr__" on page 909 in Chapter 30, and watch for the more complete `Private` class decorator we'll build with delegation in Chapter 39. Although it's possible to emulate true access controls in Python classes, this is rarely done in practice, even for large systems.

Methods Are Objects: Bound or Unbound

Methods in general, and bound methods in particular, simplify the implementation of many design goals in Python. We met bound methods briefly while studying `__call__` in Chapter 30. The full story, which we'll flesh out here, turns out to be more general and flexible than you might expect.

In Chapter 19, we learned how functions can be processed as normal objects. Methods are a kind of object too, and can be used generically in much the same way as other objects—they can be assigned to names, passed to functions, stored in data structures, and so on—and like simple functions, qualify as "first class" objects. Because a class's methods can be accessed from an instance or a class, though, they actually come in two flavors in Python:

Unbound (class) method objects: no `self`
> Accessing a function attribute of a class by qualifying the *class* returns an unbound method object. To call the method, you must provide an instance object explicitly as the first argument. In Python 3.X, an unbound method is the same as a simple function and can be called through the class's name; in 2.X it's a distinct type and cannot be called without providing an instance.

Bound (instance) method objects: `self` *+ function pairs*
> Accessing a function attribute of a class by qualifying an *instance* returns a bound method object. Python automatically packages the instance with the function in the bound method object, so you don't need to pass an instance to call the method.

Both kinds of methods are full-fledged objects; they can be transferred around a program at will, just like strings and numbers. Both also require an instance in their first argument when run (i.e., a value for `self`). This is why we've had to pass in an instance explicitly when calling superclass methods from subclass methods in previous examples (including this chapter's *employees.py*); technically, such calls produce *unbound* method objects along the way.

When calling a *bound* method object, Python provides an instance for you automatically—the instance used to create the bound method object. This means that bound method objects are usually interchangeable with simple function objects, and makes them especially useful for interfaces originally written for functions (see the sidebar "Why You Will Care: Bound Method Callbacks" on page 953 for a realistic use case in GUIs).

To illustrate in simple terms, suppose we define the following class:

```
class Spam:
    def doit(self, message):
        print(message)
```

Now, in normal operation, we make an instance and call its method in a single step to print the passed-in argument:

```
object1 = Spam()
object1.doit('hello world')
```

Really, though, a *bound* method object is generated along the way, just before the method call's parentheses. In fact, we can fetch a bound method without actually calling it. An *object.name* expression evaluates to an object as all expressions do. In the following, it returns a bound method object that packages the instance (`object1`) with the method function (`Spam.doit`). We can assign this bound method pair to another name and then call it as though it were a simple function:

```
object1 = Spam()
x = object1.doit         # Bound method object: instance+function
x('hello world')         # Same effect as object1.doit('...')
```

On the other hand, if we qualify the class to get to `doit`, we get back an *unbound* method object, which is simply a reference to the function object. To call this type of method, we must pass in an instance as the leftmost argument—there isn't one in the expression otherwise, and the method expects it:

```
object1 = Spam()
t = Spam.doit            # Unbound method object (a function in 3.X: see ahead)
t(object1, 'howdy')      # Pass in instance (if the method expects one in 3.X)
```

By extension, the same rules apply within a class's method if we reference `self` attributes that refer to functions in the class. A `self.method` expression is a bound method object because `self` is an instance object:

```
class Eggs:
    def m1(self, n):
        print(n)
    def m2(self):
        x = self.m1          # Another bound method object
        x(42)                # Looks like a simple function

Eggs().m2()                  # Prints 42
```

Most of the time, you call methods immediately after fetching them with attribute qualification, so you don't always notice the method objects generated along the way. But if you start writing code that calls objects generically, you need to be careful to treat unbound methods specially—they normally require an explicit instance object to be passed in.

 For an optional exception to this rule, see the discussion of *static and class methods* in the next chapter, and the brief mention of one in the next section. Like bound methods, static methods can masquerade as basic functions because they do not expect instances when called. Formally speaking, Python supports three kinds of class-level methods— instance, static, and class—and 3.X allows simple functions in classes, too. Chapter 40's metaclass methods are distinct too, but they are essentially class methods with less scope.

Unbound Methods Are Functions in 3.X

In Python 3.X, the language has dropped the notion of *unbound methods*. What we describe as an unbound method here is treated as a *simple function* in 3.X. For most purposes, this makes no difference to your code; either way, an instance will be passed to a method's first argument when it's called through an instance.

Programs that do explicit type testing might be impacted, though—if you print the type of an instance-less class-level method, it displays "unbound method" in 2.X, and "function" in 3.X.

Moreover, in 3.X it is OK to call a method without an instance, as long as the method does not expect one and you call it only through the *class* and never through an instance. That is, Python 3.X will pass along an instance to methods only for through-instance calls. When calling through a class, you must pass an instance manually only if the method expects one:

```
C:\code> c:\python33\python
>>> class Selfless:
        def __init__(self, data):
            self.data = data
        def selfless(arg1, arg2):            # A simple function in 3.X
            return arg1 + arg2
        def normal(self, arg1, arg2):        # Instance expected when called
            return self.data + arg1 + arg2

>>> X = Selfless(2)
>>> X.normal(3, 4)                    # Instance passed to self automatically: 2+(3+4)
9
>>> Selfless.normal(X, 3, 4)          # self expected by method: pass manually
9
>>> Selfless.selfless(3, 4)           # No instance: works in 3.X, fails in 2.X!
7
```

The last test in this fails in 2.X, because unbound methods require an instance to be passed by default; it works in 3.X because such methods are treated as simple functions not requiring an instance. Although this removes some potential error trapping in 3.X (what if a programmer accidentally forgets to pass an instance?), it allows a class's methods to be used as simple functions as long as they are not passed and do not expect a "self" instance argument.

The following two calls still fail in both 3.X and 2.X, though—the first (calling through an instance) automatically passes an instance to a method that does not expect one, while the second (calling through a class) does not pass an instance to a method that does expect one (error message text here is per 3.3):

```
>>> X.selfless(3, 4)
TypeError: selfless() takes 2 positional arguments but 3 were given

>>> Selfless.normal(3, 4)
TypeError: normal() missing 1 required positional argument: 'arg2'
```

Because of this change, the `staticmethod` built-in function and decorator described in the next chapter is not needed in 3.X for methods without a `self` argument that are called only through the *class* name, and never through an instance—such methods are run as simple functions, without receiving an instance argument. In 2.X, such calls are errors unless an instance is passed manually or the method is marked as being static (more on static methods in the next chapter).

It's important to be aware of the differences in behavior in 3.X, but bound methods are generally more important from a practical perspective anyway. Because they pair together the instance and function in a single object, they can be treated as callables generically. The next section demonstrates what this means in code.

 For a more visual illustration of unbound method treatment in Python 3.X and 2.X, see also the *lister.py* example in the multiple inheritance section later in this chapter. Its classes print the value of methods fetched from both instances and classes, in both versions of Python—as unbound methods in 2.X and simple functions in 3.X. Also note that this change is inherent in 3.X itself, not the new-style class model it mandates.

Bound Methods and Other Callable Objects

As mentioned earlier, bound methods can be processed as generic objects, just like simple functions—they can be passed around a program arbitrarily. Moreover, because bound methods combine both a function and an instance in a single package, they can be treated like any other callable object and require no special syntax when invoked. The following, for example, stores four bound method objects in a list and calls them later with normal call expressions:

```
>>> class Number:
        def __init__(self, base):
            self.base = base
        def double(self):
            return self.base * 2
        def triple(self):
            return self.base * 3

>>> x = Number(2)                              # Class instance objects
>>> y = Number(3)                              # State + methods
>>> z = Number(4)
>>> x.double()                                 # Normal immediate calls
4

>>> acts = [x.double, y.double, y.triple, z.double]   # List of bound methods
>>> for act in acts:                           # Calls are deferred
        print(act())                           # Call as though functions

4
6
```

```
9
8
```

Like simple functions, bound method objects have introspection information of their own, including attributes that give access to the instance object and method function they pair. Calling the bound method simply dispatches the pair:

```
>>> bound = x.double
>>> bound.__self__, bound.__func__
(<__main__.Number object at 0x...etc...>, <function Number.double at 0x...etc...>)
>>> bound.__self__.base
2
>>> bound()                      # Calls bound.__func__(bound.__self__, ...)
4
```

Other callables

In fact, bound methods are just one of a handful of callable object types in Python. As the following demonstrates, simple functions coded with a def or lambda, instances that inherit a __call__, and bound instance methods can all be treated and called the same way:

```
>>> def square(arg):
        return arg ** 2                   # Simple functions (def or lambda)

>>> class Sum:
        def __init__(self, val):          # Callable instances
            self.val = val
        def __call__(self, arg):
            return self.val + arg

>>> class Product:
        def __init__(self, val):          # Bound methods
            self.val = val
        def method(self, arg):
            return self.val * arg

>>> sobject = Sum(2)
>>> pobject = Product(3)
>>> actions = [square, sobject, pobject.method]  # Function, instance, method

>>> for act in actions:                    # All three called same way
        print(act(5))                      # Call any one-arg callable

25
7
15
>>> actions[-1](5)                         # Index, comprehensions, maps
15
>>> [act(5) for act in actions]
[25, 7, 15]
>>> list(map(lambda act: act(5), actions))
[25, 7, 15]
```

Technically speaking, classes belong in the callable objects category too, but we normally call them to generate instances rather than to do actual work—a single action is better coded as a simple function than a class with a constructor, but the class here serves to illustrate its callable nature:

```
>>> class Negate:
        def __init__(self, val):          # Classes are callables too
            self.val = -val               # But called for object, not work
        def __repr__(self):               # Instance print format
            return str(self.val)

>>> actions = [square, sobject, pobject.method, Negate]    # Call a class too
>>> for act in actions:
        print(act(5))

25
7
15
-5
>>> [act(5) for act in actions]          # Runs __repr__ not __str__!
[25, 7, 15, -5]

>>> table = {act(5): act for act in actions}    # 3.X/2.7 dict comprehension
>>> for (key, value) in table.items():
        print('{0:2} => {1}'.format(key, value))   # 2.6+/3.X str.format

25 => <function square at 0x0000000002987400>
15 => <bound method Product.method of <__main__.Product object at ...etc...>>
-5 => <class '__main__.Negate'>
 7 => <__main__.Sum object at 0x000000000298BE48>
```

As you can see, bound methods, and Python's callable objects model in general, are some of the many ways that Python's design makes for an incredibly flexible language.

You should now understand the method object model. For other examples of bound methods at work, see the upcoming sidebar "Why You Will Care: Bound Method Callbacks" on page 953 as well as the prior chapter's discussion of callback handlers in the section on the method __call__.

Why You Will Care: Bound Method Callbacks

Because bound methods automatically pair an instance with a class's method function, you can use them anywhere a simple function is expected. One of the most common places you'll see this idea put to work is in code that registers methods as event callback handlers in the tkinter GUI interface (named Tkinter in Python 2.X) we've met before. As review, here's the simple case:

```
def handler():
    ...use globals or closure scopes for state...
...
widget = Button(text='spam', command=handler)
```

To register a handler for button click events, we usually pass a callable object that takes no arguments to the command keyword argument. Function names (and lambdas) work

---

here, and so do class-level methods—though they must be bound methods if they expect an instance when called:

```
class MyGui:
    def handler(self):
        ...use self.attr for state...
    def makewidgets(self):
        b = Button(text='spam', command=self.handler)
```

Here, the event handler is `self.handler`—a bound method object that remembers both `self` and `MyGui.handler`. Because `self` will refer to the original instance when `handler` is later invoked on events, the method will have access to instance attributes that can retain state between events, as well as class-level methods. With simple functions, state normally must be retained in global variables or enclosing function scopes instead.

See also the discussion of `__call__` operator overloading in Chapter 30 for another way to make classes compatible with function-based APIs, and `lambda` in Chapter 19 for another tool often used in callback roles. As noted in the former of these, you don't generally need to wrap a bound method in a `lambda`; the bound method in the preceding example already defers the call (note that there are no parentheses to trigger one), so adding a lambda here would be pointless!

Classes Are Objects: Generic Object Factories

Sometimes, class-based designs require objects to be created in response to conditions that can't be predicted when a program is written. The factory design pattern allows such a deferred approach. Due in large part to Python's flexibility, factories can take multiple forms, some of which don't seem special at all.

Because classes are also "first class" objects, it's easy to pass them around a program, store them in data structures, and so on. You can also pass classes to functions that generate arbitrary kinds of objects; such functions are sometimes called *factories* in OOP design circles. Factories can be a major undertaking in a strongly typed language such as C++ but are almost trivial to implement in Python.

For example, the call syntax we met in Chapter 18 can call any class with any number of positional or keyword constructor arguments in one step to generate any sort of instance:[2]

```
def factory(aClass, *pargs, **kargs):      # Varargs tuple, dict
    return aClass(*pargs, **kargs)         # Call aClass (or apply in 2.X only)

class Spam:
```

---

2. Actually, this syntax can invoke any callable object, including functions, classes, and methods. Hence, the `factory` function here can also run any callable object, not just a class (despite the argument name). Also, as we learned in Chapter 18, Python 2.X has an alternative to `aClass(*pargs, **kargs)`: the `apply(aClass, pargs, kargs)` built-in call, which has been removed in Python 3.X because of its redundancy and limitations.

```
        def doit(self, message):
            print(message)

class Person:
    def __init__(self, name, job=None):
        self.name = name
        self.job  = job

object1 = factory(Spam)                     # Make a Spam object
object2 = factory(Person, "Arthur", "King") # Make a Person object
object3 = factory(Person, name='Brian')     # Ditto, with keywords and default
```

In this code, we define an object generator function called `factory`. It expects to be passed a class object (any class will do) along with one or more arguments for the class's constructor. The function uses special "varargs" call syntax to call the function and return an instance.

The rest of the example simply defines two classes and generates instances of both by passing them to the `factory` function. And that's the only factory function you'll ever need to write in Python; it works for any class and any constructor arguments. If you run this live (*factory.py*), your objects will look like this:

```
>>> object1.doit(99)
99
>>> object2.name, object2.job
('Arthur', 'King')
>>> object3.name, object3.job
('Brian', None)
```

By now, you should know that everything is a "first class" object in Python—including classes, which are usually just compiler input in languages like C++. It's natural to pass them around this way. As mentioned at the start of this part of the book, though, only objects *derived* from classes do full OOP in Python.

Why Factories?

So what good is the `factory` function (besides providing an excuse to illustrate first-class class objects in this book)? Unfortunately, it's difficult to show applications of this design pattern without listing much more code than we have space for here. In general, though, such a factory might allow code to be insulated from the details of dynamically configured object construction.

For instance, recall the `processor` example presented in the abstract in Chapter 26, and then again as a composition example earlier in this chapter. It accepts reader and writer objects for processing arbitrary data streams. The original version of this example manually passed in instances of specialized classes like `FileWriter` and `SocketReader` to customize the data streams being processed; later, we passed in hardcoded file, stream, and formatter objects. In a more dynamic scenario, external devices such as configuration files or GUIs might be used to configure the streams.

In such a dynamic world, we might not be able to hardcode the creation of stream interface objects in our scripts, but might instead create them at runtime according to the contents of a configuration file.

Such a file might simply give the string name of a stream class to be imported from a module, plus an optional constructor call argument. Factory-style functions or code might come in handy here because they would allow us to fetch and pass in classes that are not hardcoded in our program ahead of time. Indeed, those classes might not even have existed at all when we wrote our code:

```
classname = ...parse from config file...
classarg  = ...parse from config file...

import streamtypes                          # Customizable code
aclass = getattr(streamtypes, classname)    # Fetch from module
reader = factory(aclass, classarg)          # Or aclass(classarg)
processor(reader, ...)
```

Here, the `getattr` built-in is again used to fetch a module attribute given a string name (it's like saying *obj.attr*, but *attr* is a string). Because this code snippet assumes a single constructor argument, it doesn't strictly need `factory`—we could make an instance with just `aclass(classarg)`. The factory function may prove more useful in the presence of unknown argument lists, however, and the general factory coding pattern can improve the code's flexibility.

Multiple Inheritance: "Mix-in" Classes

Our last design pattern is one of the most useful, and will serve as a subject for a more realistic example to wrap up this chapter and point toward the next. As a bonus, the code we'll write here may be a useful tool.

Many class-based designs call for combining disparate sets of methods. As we've seen, in a **class** statement, more than one superclass can be listed in parentheses in the header line. When you do this, you leverage *multiple inheritance*—the class and its instances inherit names from *all* the listed superclasses.

When searching for an attribute, Python's inheritance search traverses all superclasses in the class header from left to right until a match is found. Technically, because any of the superclasses may have superclasses of its own, this search can be a bit more complex for larger class trees:

- In *classic* classes (the default until Python 3.0), the attribute search in all cases proceeds depth-first all the way to the top of the inheritance tree, and then from left to right. This order is usually called *DFLR*, for its depth-first, left-to-right path.
- In *new-style* classes (optional in 2.X and standard in 3.X), the attribute search is usually as before, but in diamond patterns proceeds across by tree levels before moving up, in a more breadth-first fashion. This order is usually called the new-

style *MRO*, for method resolution order, though it's used for all attributes, not just methods.

The second of these search rules is explained fully in the new-style class discussion in the next chapter. Though difficult to understand without the next chapter's code (and somewhat rare to create yourself), *diamond* patterns appear when multiple classes in a tree share a common superclass; the new-style search order is designed to visit such a shared superclass just once, and after all its subclasses. In either model, though, when a class has multiple superclasses, they are searched from left to right according to the order listed in the `class` statement header lines.

In general, multiple inheritance is good for modeling objects that belong to more than one set. For instance, a person may be an engineer, a writer, a musician, and so on, and inherit properties from all such sets. With multiple inheritance, objects obtain the union of the behavior in all their superclasses. As we'll see ahead, multiple inheritance also allows classes to function as general packages of mixable attributes.

Though a useful pattern, multiple inheritance's chief downside is that it can pose a *conflict* when the same method (or other attribute) name is defined in more than one superclass. When this occurs, the conflict is resolved either automatically by the inheritance search order, or manually in your code:

- *Default*: By default, inheritance chooses the *first* occurrence of an attribute it finds when an attribute is referenced normally—by `self.method()`, for example. In this mode, Python chooses the lowest and leftmost in classic classes, and in nondiamond patterns in all classes; new-style classes may choose an option to the right before one above in diamonds.

- *Explicit*: In some class models, you may sometimes need to *select* an attribute explicitly by referencing it through its class name—with `superclass.method(self)`, for instance. Your code breaks the conflict and overrides the search's default—to select an option to the right of or above the inheritance search's default.

This is an issue only when the *same name* appears in multiple superclasses, and you do not wish to use the first one inherited. Because this isn't as common an issue in typical Python code as it may sound, we'll defer details on this topic until we study new-style classes and their MRO and `super` tools in the next chapter, and revisit this as a "gotcha" at the end of that chapter. First, though, the next section demonstrates a practical use case for multiple inheritance-based tools.

Coding Mix-in Display Classes

Perhaps the most common way multiple inheritance is used is to "mix in" general-purpose methods from superclasses. Such superclasses are usually called *mix-in classes* —they provide methods you add to application classes by inheritance. In a sense, mix-in classes are similar to modules: they provide packages of methods for use in their client subclasses. Unlike simple functions in modules, though, methods in mix-in classes also can participate in inheritance hierarchies, and have access to the self instance for using state information and other methods in their trees.

For example, as we've seen, Python's default way to print a class instance object isn't incredibly useful:

```
>>> class Spam:
        def __init__(self):                 # No __repr__ or __str__
            self.data1 = "food"

>>> X = Spam()
>>> print(X)                                 # Default: class name + address (id)
<__main__.Spam object at 0x00000000029CA908>  # Same in 2.X, but says "instance"
```

As you saw in both Chapter 28's case study and Chapter 30's operator overloading coverage, you can provide a __str__ or __repr__ method to implement a custom string representation of your own. But, rather than coding one of these in each and every class you wish to print, why not code it once in a general-purpose tool class and inherit it in all your classes?

That's what mix-ins are for. Defining a display method in a mix-in superclass once enables us to reuse it anywhere we want to see a custom display format—even in classes that may already have another superclass. We've already seen tools that do related work:

- Chapter 28's AttrDisplay class formatted instance attributes in a generic __repr__ method, but it did not climb class trees and was utilized in single-inheritance mode only.
- Chapter 29's *classtree.py* module defined functions for climbing and sketching class trees, but it did not display object attributes along the way and was not architected as an inheritable class.

Here, we're going to revisit these examples' techniques and expand upon them to code a set of three mix-in classes that serve as generic display tools for listing instance attributes, inherited attributes, and attributes on all objects in a class tree. We'll also use our tools in multiple-inheritance mode and deploy coding techniques that make classes better suited to use as generic tools.

Unlike Chapter 28, we'll also code this with a __str__ instead of a __repr__. This is partially a style issue and limits their role to print and str, but the displays we'll be developing will be rich enough to be categorized as more user-friendly than as-code. This policy also leaves client classes the option of coding an alternative lower-level display for interactive echoes and nested appearances with a __repr__. Using __repr__ here would still allow an alternative __str__, but the *nature* of the displays we'll be implementing more strongly suggests a __str__ role. See Chapter 30 for a review of these distinctions.

Listing instance attributes with __dict__

Let's get started with the simple case—listing attributes attached to an instance. The following class, coded in the file *listinstance.py*, defines a mix-in called ListInstance that overloads the __str__ method for all classes that include it in their header lines. Because this is coded as a class, ListInstance is a generic tool whose formatting logic can be used for instances of any subclass client:

```python
#!python
# File listinstance.py (2.X + 3.X)

class ListInstance:
    """
    Mix-in class that provides a formatted print() or str() of instances via
    inheritance of __str__ coded here;  displays instance attrs only;  self is
    instance of lowest class;  __X names avoid clashing with client's attrs
    """
    def __attrnames(self):
        result = ''
        for attr in sorted(self.__dict__):
            result += '\t%s=%s\n' % (attr, self.__dict__[attr])
        return result

    def __str__(self):
        return '<Instance of %s, address %s:\n%s>' % (
                        self.__class__.__name__,       # My class's name
                        id(self),                      # My address
                        self.__attrnames())            # name=value list

if __name__ == '__main__':
    import testmixin
    testmixin.tester(ListInstance)
```

All the code in this section runs in both Python 2.X and 3.X. A coding note: this code exhibits a classic comprehension pattern, and you could save some program real estate by implementing the __attrnames method here more concisely with a *generator expression* that is triggered by the string join method, but it's arguably less clear—expressions that wrap lines like this should generally make you consider simpler coding alternatives:

```python
    def __attrnames(self):
        return ''.join('\t%s=%s\n' % (attr, self.__dict__ [attr])
                            for attr in sorted(self.__dict__))
```

ListInstance uses some previously explored tricks to extract the instance's class name and attributes:

- Each instance has a built-in __class__ attribute that references the class from which it was created, and each class has a __name__ attribute that references the name in the header, so the expression self.__class__.__name__ fetches the name of an instance's class.

- This class does most of its work by simply scanning the instance's attribute dictionary (remember, it's exported in __dict__) to build up a string showing the names and values of all instance attributes. The dictionary's keys are sorted to finesse any ordering differences across Python releases.

In these respects, ListInstance is similar to Chapter 28's attribute display; in fact, it's largely just a variation on a theme. Our class here uses two additional techniques, though:

- It displays the instance's memory address by calling the id built-in function, which returns any object's address (by definition, a unique object identifier, which will be useful in later mutations of this code).

- It uses the *pseudoprivate* naming pattern for its worker method: __attrnames. As we learned earlier in this chapter, Python automatically localizes any such name to its enclosing class by expanding the attribute name to include the class name (in this case, it becomes _ListInstance__attrnames). This holds true for both class attributes (like methods) and instance attributes attached to self. As noted in Chapter 28's first-cut version, this behavior is useful in a general tool like this, as it ensures that its names don't clash with any names used in its client subclasses.

Because ListInstance defines a __str__ operator overloading method, instances derived from this class display their attributes automatically when printed, giving a bit more information than a simple address. Here is the class in action, in single-inheritance mode, mixed in to the previous section's class (this code works the same in both Python 3.X and 2.X, though 2.X default repr displays use the label "instance" instead of "object"):

```
>>> from listinstance import ListInstance
>>> class Spam(ListInstance):            # Inherit a __str__ method
        def __init__(self):
            self.data1 = 'food'

>>> x = Spam()
>>> print(x)                             # print() and str() run __str__
<Instance of Spam, address 43034496:
        data1=food
>
```

You can also fetch and save the listing output as a string without printing it with str, and interactive echoes still use the default format because we've left __repr__ as an option for clients:

```
>>> display = str(x)                     # Print this to interpret escapes
>>> display
'<Instance of Spam, address 43034496:\n\tdata1=food\n>'

>>> x                                    # The __repr__ still is a default
<__main__.Spam object at 0x000000000290A780>
```

The `ListInstance` class is useful for any classes you write—even classes that already have one or more superclasses. This is where *multiple inheritance* comes in handy: by adding `ListInstance` to the list of superclasses in a class header (i.e., mixing it in), you get its `__str__` "for free" while still inheriting from the existing superclass(es). The file *testmixin0.py* demonstrates with a first-cut testing script:

```
# File testmixin0.py
from listinstance import ListInstance      # Get lister tool class

class Super:
    def __init__(self):                     # Superclass __init__
        self.data1 = 'spam'                 # Create instance attrs
    def ham(self):
        pass

class Sub(Super, ListInstance):             # Mix in ham and a __str__
    def __init__(self):                     # Listers have access to self
        Super.__init__(self)
        self.data2 = 'eggs'                 # More instance attrs
        self.data3 = 42
    def spam(self):                         # Define another method here
        pass

if __name__ == '__main__':
    X = Sub()
    print(X)                                # Run mixed-in __str__
```

Here, `Sub` inherits names from both `Super` and `ListInstance`; it's a composite of its own names and names in both its superclasses. When you make a `Sub` instance and print it, you automatically get the custom representation mixed in from `ListInstance` (in this case, this script's output is the same under both Python 3.X and 2.X, except for object addresses, which can naturally vary per process):

```
c:\code> python testmixin0.py
<Instance of Sub, address 44304144:
        data1=spam
        data2=eggs
        data3=42
>
```

This *testmixin0* testing script works, but it hardcodes the tested class's name in the code, and makes it difficult to experiment with alternatives—as we will in a moment. To be more flexible, we can borrow a page from Chapter 25's module reloaders, and pass in the object to be tested, as in the following improved test script, *testmixin*—the one actually used by all the lister class modules' self-test code. In this context the object passed in to the tester is a mix-in *class* instead of a function, but the principle is similar: everything qualifies as a passable "first class" object in Python:

```
#!python
# File testmixin.py (2.X + 3.X)
"""
Generic lister mixin tester: similar to transitive reloader in
Chapter 25, but passes a class object to tester (not function),
```

and testByNames adds loading of both module and class by name strings here, in keeping with Chapter 31's factories pattern.
"""

```
import importlib

def tester(listerclass, sept=False):

    class Super:
        def __init__(self):              # Superclass __init__
            self.data1 = 'spam'          # Create instance attrs
        def ham(self):
            pass

    class Sub(Super, listerclass):       # Mix in ham and a __str__
        def __init__(self):              # Listers have access to self
            Super.__init__(self)
            self.data2 = 'eggs'          # More instance attrs
            self.data3 = 42
        def spam(self):                  # Define another method here
            pass

    instance = Sub()                     # Return instance with lister's __str__
    print(instance)                      # Run mixed-in __str__ (or via str(x))
    if sept: print('-' * 80)

def testByNames(modname, classname, sept=False):
    modobject   = importlib.import_module(modname)   # Import by namestring
    listerclass = getattr(modobject, classname)      # Fetch attr by namestring
    tester(listerclass, sept)

if __name__ == '__main__':
    testByNames('listinstance',  'ListInstance',  True)      # Test all three here
    testByNames('listinherited', 'ListInherited', True)
    testByNames('listtree',      'ListTree',      False)
```

While it's at it, this script also adds the ability to specify test module and class by *name string*, and leverages this in its self-test code—an application of the factory pattern's mechanics described earlier. Here is the new script in action, being run by the lister module that imports it to test its own class (with the same results in 2.X and 3.X again); we can run the test script itself too, but that mode tests the two lister variants, which we have yet to see (or code!):

```
c:\code> python listinstance.py
<Instance of Sub, address 43256968:
        data1=spam
        data2=eggs
        data3=42
>

c:\code> python testmixin.py
<Instance of Sub, address 43977584:
        data1=spam
        data2=eggs
        data3=42
```

```
>
...and tests of two other lister classes coming up...
```

The ListInstance class we've coded so far works in any class it's mixed into because self refers to an instance of the subclass that pulls this class in, whatever that may be. Again, in a sense, mix-in classes are the class equivalent of modules—packages of methods useful in a variety of clients. For example, here is ListInstance working again in single-inheritance mode on a different class's instances, loaded with import, and displaying attributes assigned outside the class:

```
>>> import listinstance
>>> class C(listinstance.ListInstance): pass

>>> x = C()
>>> x.a, x.b, x.c = 1, 2, 3
>>> print(x)
<Instance of C, address 43230824:
        a=1
        b=2
        c=3
>
```

Besides the utility they provide, mix-ins optimize code maintenance, like all classes do. For example, if you later decide to extend ListInstance's __str__ to also print all the class attributes that an instance inherits, you're safe; because it's an inherited method, changing __str__ automatically updates the display of each subclass that imports the class and mixes it in. And since it's now officially "later," let's move on to the next section to see what such an extension might look like.

Listing inherited attributes with dir

As it is, our ListerInstance mix-in displays instance attributes only (i.e., names attached to the instance object itself). It's trivial to extend the class to display all the attributes accessible from an instance, though—both its own and those it inherits from its classes. The trick is to use the dir built-in function instead of scanning the instance's __dict__ dictionary; the latter holds instance attributes only, but the former also collects all inherited attributes in Python 2.2 and later.

The following mutation codes this scheme; I've coded this in its own module to facilitate simple testing, but if existing clients were to use this version instead they would pick up the new display automatically (and recall from Chapter 25 that an import's as clause can rename a new version to a prior name being used):

```
#!python
# File listinherited.py (2.X + 3.X)

class ListInherited:
    """
    Use dir() to collect both instance attrs and names inherited from
    its classes;  Python 3.X shows more names than 2.X because of the
    implied object superclass in the new-style class model;  getattr()
```

```
                fetches inherited names not in self.__dict__;  use __str__, not
                __repr__, or else this loops when printing bound methods!
                """

            def __attrnames(self):
                result = ''
                for attr in dir(self):                          # Instance dir()
                    if attr[:2] == '__' and attr[-2:] == '__':   # Skip internals
                        result += '\t%s\n' % attr
                    else:
                        result += '\t%s=%s\n' % (attr, getattr(self, attr))
                return result

            def __str__(self):
                return '<Instance of %s, address %s:\n%s>' % (
                                  self.__class__.__name__,       # My class's name
                                  id(self),                      # My address
                                  self.__attrnames())            # name=value list

    if __name__ == '__main__':
        import testmixin
        testmixin.tester(ListInherited)
```

Notice that this code skips __X__ names' values; most of these are internal names that
we don't generally care about in a generic listing like this. This version also must use
the `getattr` built-in function to fetch attributes by name string instead of using instance
attribute dictionary indexing—`getattr` employs the inheritance search protocol, and
some of the names we're listing here are not stored on the instance itself.

To test the new version, run its file directly—it passes the class it defines to the *test-
mixin.py* file's test function to be used as a mix-in in a subclass. This output of this test
and lister class varies per release, though, because `dir` results differ. In Python 2.X, we
get the following; notice the name mangling at work in the lister's method name (I
truncated some of the full value displays to fit on this page):

```
c:\code> c:\python27\python listinherited.py
<Instance of Sub, address 35161352:
        _ListInherited__attrnames=<bound method Sub.__attrnames of <test...more...>>
        __doc__
        __init__
        __module__
        __str__
        data1=spam
        data2=eggs
        data3=42
        ham=<bound method Sub.ham of <testmixin.Sub instance at 0x00000...more...>>
        spam=<bound method Sub.spam of <testmixin.Sub instance at 0x00000...more...>>
>
```

In Python 3.X, more attributes are displayed because all classes are "new style" and
inherit names from the implied `object` superclass; more on this in Chapter 32. Because
so many names are inherited from the default superclass, I've omitted many here—
there are 32 in total in 3.3. Run this on your own for the full listing:

```
c:\code> c:\python33\python listinherited.py
<Instance of Sub, address 43253152:
    _ListInherited__attrnames=<bound method Sub.__attrnames of <test...more...>>
    __class__
    __delattr__
    __dict__
    __dir__
    __doc__
    __eq__
    ...more names omitted 32 total...
    __repr__
    __setattr__
    __sizeof__
    __str__
    __subclasshook__
    __weakref__
    data1=spam
    data2=eggs
    data3=42
    ham=<bound method Sub.ham of <testmixin.tester.<locals>.Sub ...more...>>
    spam=<bound method Sub.spam of <testmixin.tester.<locals>.Sub ...more...>>
>
```

As one possible improvement to address the proliferation of inherited built-in names
and long values here, the following alternative for __attrnames in file *listinherited2.py*
of the book example's package groups the double-underscore names separately, and
minimizes line wrapping for large attribute values; notice how it escapes a % with %% so
that just one remains for the final formatting operation at the end:

```
    def __attrnames(self, indent=' '*4):
        result = 'Unders%s\n%s%%s\nOthers%s\n' % ('-'*77, indent, '-'*77)
        unders = []
        for attr in dir(self):                          # Instance dir()
            if attr[:2] == '__' and attr[-2:] == '__':  # Skip internals
                unders.append(attr)
            else:
                display = str(getattr(self, attr))[:82-(len(indent) + len(attr))]
                result += '%s%s=%s\n' % (indent, attr, display)
        return result % ', '.join(unders)
```

With this change, the class's test output is a bit more sophisticated, but also more
concise and usable:

```
c:\code> c:\python27\python listinherited2.py
<Instance of Sub, address 36299208:
Unders-----------------------------------------------------------------------------
    __doc__, __init__, __module__, __str__
Others-----------------------------------------------------------------------------
    _ListInherited__attrnames=<bound method Sub.__attrnames of <testmixin.Sub insta
    data1=spam
    data2=eggs
    data3=42
    ham=<bound method Sub.ham of <testmixin.Sub instance at 0x000000000229E1C8>>
    spam=<bound method Sub.spam of <testmixin.Sub instance at 0x000000000229E1C8>>
>
```

```
c:\code> c:\python33\python listinherited2.py
<Instance of Sub, address 43318912:
Unders----------------------------------------------------------------------
    __class__, __delattr__, __dict__, __dir__, __doc__, __eq__, __format__, __ge__,
__getattribute__, __gt__, __hash__, __init__, __le__, __lt__, __module__, __ne__,
__new__, __qualname__, __reduce__, __reduce_ex__, __repr__, __setattr__, __sizeof__,
__str__, __subclasshook__, __weakref__
Others----------------------------------------------------------------------
    _ListInherited__attrnames=<bound method Sub.__attrnames of <testmixin.tester.<l
    data1=spam
    data2=eggs
    data3=42
    ham=<bound method Sub.ham of <testmixin.tester.<locals>.Sub object at 0x0000000
    spam=<bound method Sub.spam of <testmixin.tester.<locals>.Sub object at 0x00000
>
```

Display format is an open-ended problem (e.g., Python's standard pprint "pretty printer" module may offer options here too), so we'll leave further polishing as a suggested exercise. The tree lister of the next section may be more useful in any event.

 Looping in __repr__: One caution here—now that we're displaying inherited methods too, we have to use __str__ instead of __repr__ to overload printing. With __repr__, this code will fall into *recursive loops* —displaying the value of a method triggers the __repr__ of the method's class, in order to display the class. That is, if the lister's __repr__ tries to display a method, displaying the method's class will trigger the lister's __repr__ again. Subtle, but true! Change __str__ to __repr__ here to see this for yourself. If you must use __repr__ in such a context, you can avoid the loops by using isinstance to compare the type of attribute values against types.MethodType in the standard library, to know which items to skip.

Listing attributes per object in class trees

Let's code one last extension. As it is, our latest lister includes inherited names, but doesn't give any sort of designation of the classes from which the names are acquired. As we saw in the *classtree.py* example near the end of Chapter 29, though, it's straightforward to climb class inheritance trees in code. The following mix-in class, coded in the file *listtree.py*, makes use of this same technique to display attributes grouped by the classes they live in—it sketches the full *physical class tree*, displaying attributes attached to each object along the way. The reader must still infer attribute inheritance, but this gives substantially more detail than a simple flat list:

```
#!python
# File listtree.py (2.X + 3.X)

class ListTree:
    """
    Mix-in that returns an __str__ trace of the entire class tree and all
```

```
        its objects' attrs at and above self;  run by print(), str() returns
        constructed string;  uses __X attr names to avoid impacting clients;
        recurses to superclasses explicitly, uses str.format() for clarity;
        """
        def __attrnames(self, obj, indent):
            spaces = ' ' * (indent + 1)
            result = ''
            for attr in sorted(obj.__dict__):
                if attr.startswith('__') and attr.endswith('__'):
                    result += spaces + '{0}\n'.format(attr)
                else:
                    result += spaces + '{0}={1}\n'.format(attr, getattr(obj, attr))
            return result

        def __listclass(self, aClass, indent):
            dots = '.' * indent
            if aClass in self.__visited:
                return '\n{0}<Class {1}:, address {2}: (see above)>\n'.format(
                             dots,
                             aClass.__name__,
                             id(aClass))
            else:
                self.__visited[aClass] = True
                here  = self.__attrnames(aClass, indent)
                above = ''
                for super in aClass.__bases__:
                    above += self.__listclass(super, indent+4)
                return '\n{0}<Class {1}, address {2}:\n{3}{4}{5}>\n'.format(
                             dots,
                             aClass.__name__,
                             id(aClass),
                             here, above,
                             dots)

        def __str__(self):
            self.__visited = {}
            here  = self.__attrnames(self, 0)
            above = self.__listclass(self.__class__, 4)
            return '<Instance of {0}, address {1}:\n{2}{3}>'.format(
                             self.__class__.__name__,
                             id(self),
                             here, above)

if __name__ == '__main__':
    import testmixin
    testmixin.tester(ListTree)
```

This class achieves its goal by traversing the inheritance tree—from an instance's
__class__ to its class, and then from the class's __bases__ to all superclasses recursively,
scanning each object's attribute __dict__ along the way. Ultimately, it concatenates
each tree portion's string as the recursion unwinds.

It can take a while to understand recursive programs like this, but given the arbitrary
shape and depth of class trees, we really have no choice here (apart from explicit stack

equivalents of the sorts we met in Chapter 19 and Chapter 25, which tend to be no simpler, and which we'll omit here for space and time). This class is coded to keep its business as explicit as possible, though, to maximize clarity.

For example, you could replace the __listclass method's loop statement in the first of the following with the implicitly run generator expression in the second, but the second seems unnecessarily convoluted in this context—*recursive calls* embedded in a *generator expression*—and has no obvious performance advantage, especially given this program's limited scope (neither alternative makes a temporary list, though the first may create more temporary results depending on the internal implementation of strings, concatenation, and join—something you'd need to time with Chapter 21's tools to determine):

```
        above = ''
        for super in aClass.__bases__:
            above += self.__listclass(super, indent+4)
```

...*or*...

```
        above = ''.join(
                self.__listclass(super, indent+4) for super in aClass.__bases__)
```

You could also code the else clause in __listclass like the following, as in the prior edition of this book—an alternative that embeds everything in the format arguments list; relies on the fact that the join call kicks off the generator expression and its recursive calls *before* the format operation even begins building up the result text; and seems more difficult to understand, despite the fact that I wrote it (never a good sign!):

```
        self.__visited[aClass] = True
        genabove = (self.__listclass(c, indent+4) for c in aClass.__bases__)
        return '\n{0}<Class {1}, address {2}:\n{3}{4}{5}>\n'.format(
                    dots,
                    aClass.__name__,
                    id(aClass),
                    self.__attrnames(aClass, indent),    # Runs before format!
                    ''.join(genabove),
                    dots)
```

As always, explicit is better than implicit, and your code can be as big a factor in this as the tools it uses.

Also notice how this version uses the Python 3.X and 2.6/2.7 string format method instead of % formatting expressions, in an effort to make substitutions arguably clearer; when many substitutions are applied like this, explicit argument numbers may make the code easier to decipher. In short, in this version we exchange the first of the following lines for the second:

```
        return '<Instance of %s, address %s:\n%s%s>' % (...)        # Expression
        return '<Instance of {0}, address {1}:\n{2}{3}>'.format(...)   # Method
```

This policy has an unfortunate downside in 3.2 and 3.3 too, but we have to run the code to see why.

Running the tree lister

Now, to test, run this class's module file as before; it passes the `ListTree` class to *testmixin.py* to be mixed in with a subclass in the test function. The file's tree-sketcher output in Python 2.X is as follows:

```
c:\code> c:\python27\python listtree.py
<Instance of Sub, address 36690632:
 _ListTree__visited={}
 data1=spam
 data2=eggs
 data3=42

....<Class Sub, address 36652616:
    __doc__
    __init__
    __module__
    spam=<unbound method Sub.spam>

........<Class Super, address 36652712:
        __doc__
        __init__
        __module__
        ham=<unbound method Super.ham>
........>

........<Class ListTree, address 30795816:
        _ListTree__attrnames=<unbound method ListTree.__attrnames>
        _ListTree__listclass=<unbound method ListTree.__listclass>
        __doc__
        __module__
        __str__
........>
....>
>
```

Notice in this output how methods are *unbound* now under 2.X, because we fetch them from *classes* directly. In the previous section's version they displayed as *bound* methods, because `ListInherited` fetched these from *instances* with `getattr` instead (the first version indexed the instance `__dict__` and did not display inherited methods on classes at all). Also observe how the lister's `__visited` table has its name mangled in the instance's attribute dictionary; unless we're very unlucky, this won't clash with other data there. Some of the lister class's methods are mangled for pseudoprivacy as well.

Under Python 3.X in the following, we again get extra attributes which may vary within the 3.X line, and extra superclasses—as we'll learn in the next chapter, all top-level classes inherit from the built-in `object` class automatically in 3.X; Python 2.X classes do so manually if they desire new-style class behavior. Also notice that the attributes that were unbound methods in 2.X are simple *functions* in 3.X, as described earlier in this chapter (and that again, I've deleted most built-in attributes in `object` to save space here; run this on your own for the complete listing):

```
c:\code> c:\python33\python listtree.py
<Instance of Sub, address 44277488:
 _ListTree__visited={}
data1=spam
data2=eggs
data3=42

....<Class Sub, address 36990264:
     __doc__
     __init__
     __module__
     __qualname__
     spam=<function tester.<locals>.Sub.spam at 0x0000000002A3C840>

........<Class Super, address 36989352:
         __dict__
         __doc__
         __init__
         __module__
         __qualname__
         __weakref__
         ham=<function tester.<locals>.Super.ham at 0x0000000002A3C730>

............<Class object, address 506770624:
             __class__
             __delattr__
             __dir__
             __doc__
             __eq__
             ...more omitted: 22 total...
             __repr__
             __setattr__
             __sizeof__
             __str__
             __subclasshook__
............>
........>

........<Class ListTree, address 36988440:
         _ListTree__attrnames=<function ListTree.__attrnames at 0x0000000002A3C158>
         _ListTree__listclass=<function ListTree.__listclass at 0x0000000002A3C1E0>
         __dict__
         __doc__
         __module__
         __qualname__
         __str__
         __weakref__

............<Class object:, address 506770624: (see above)>
........>
....>
>
```

This version avoids listing the same class object twice by keeping a table of classes
visited so far (this is why an object's `id` is included—to serve as a key for a previously

---

displayed item in the report). Like the transitive module reloader of Chapter 25, a dictionary works to avoid repeats in the output because class objects are hashable and thus may be dictionary keys; a set would provide similar functionality.

Technically, *cycles* are not generally possible in class inheritance trees—a class must already have been defined to be named as a superclass, and Python raises an exception as it should if you attempt to create a cycle later by __bases__ changes—but the visited mechanism here avoids relisting a class twice:

```
>>> class C: pass
>>> class B(C): pass
>>> C.__bases__ = (B,)          # Deep, dark magic!
TypeError: a __bases__ item causes an inheritance cycle
```

Usage variation: Showing underscore name values

This version also takes care to avoid displaying large internal objects by skipping __X__ names again. If you comment out the code that treats these names specially:

```
        for attr in sorted(obj.__dict__):
#            if attr.startswith('__') and attr.endswith('__'):
#                result += spaces + '{0}\n'.format(attr)
#            else:
                result += spaces + '{0}={1}\n'.format(attr, getattr(obj, attr))
```

then their values will display normally. Here's the output in 2.X with this temporary change made, giving the values of every attribute in the class tree:

```
c:\code> c:\python27\python listtree.py
<Instance of Sub, address 35750408:
 _ListTree__visited={}
 data1=spam
 data2=eggs
 data3=42

....<Class Sub, address 36353608:
    __doc__=None
    __init__=<unbound method Sub.__init__>
    __module__=testmixin
    spam=<unbound method Sub.spam>

........<Class Super, address 36353704:
        __doc__=None
        __init__=<unbound method Super.__init__>
        __module__=testmixin
        ham=<unbound method Super.ham>
........>

........<Class ListTree, address 31254568:
        _ListTree__attrnames=<unbound method ListTree.__attrnames>
        _ListTree__listclass=<unbound method ListTree.__listclass>
        __doc__=
    Mix-in that returns an __str__ trace of the entire class tree and all
    its objects' attrs at and above self;  run by print(), str() returns
```

```
constructed string;  uses __X attr names to avoid impacting clients;
recurses to superclasses explicitly, uses str.format() for clarity;

        __module__ = __main__
        __str__=<unbound method ListTree.__str__>
........>
....>
>
```

This test's output is much larger in 3.X and may justify isolating underscore names in general as we did earlier. In fact, this test may not even work in some currently recent 3.X releases as is:

```
c:\code> c:\python33\python listtree.py
  ...etc...
  File "listtree.py", line 18, in __attrnames
    result += spaces + '{0}={1}\n'.format(attr, getattr(obj, attr))
TypeError: Type method_descriptor doesn't define __format__
```

I debated recoding to work around this issue, but it serves as a fair example of debugging requirements and techniques in a dynamic open source project like Python. Per the following note, the str.format call no longer supports certain object types that are the values of built-in attribute names—yet another reason these names are probably better skipped.

> *Debugging a str.format issue*: In 3.X, running the commented-out version works in 3.0 and 3.1, but there seems to be a bug, or at least a regression, here in 3.2 and 3.3—these Pythons fail with an exception because five built-in methods in object do not define a __format__ expected by str.format, and the default in object is apparently no longer applied correctly in such cases with empty and generic formatting targets. To see this live, it's enough to run simplified code that isolates the problem:
>
> ```
> c:\code> py -3.1
> >>> '{0}'.format(object.__reduce__)
> "<method '__reduce__' of 'object' objects>"
> c:\code> py -3.3
> >>> '{0}'.format(object.__reduce__)
> TypeError: Type method_descriptor doesn't define __format__
> ```
>
> Per both prior behavior and current Python documentation, empty targets like this are supposed to convert the object to its str print string (see both the original PEP 3101 and the 3.3 language reference manual). Oddly, the {0} and {0:s} string targets both now fail, but the {0!s} forced str conversion target works, as does manual str preconversion —apparently reflecting a change for a type-specific case that neglected perhaps more common generic usage modes:
>
> ```
> c:\code> py -3.3
> >>> '{0:s}'.format(object.__reduce__)
> TypeError: Type method_descriptor doesn't define __format__
> >>> '{0!s}'.format(object.__reduce__)
> "<method '__reduce__' of 'object' objects>"
> ```

```
>>> '{0}'.format(str(object._reduce_))
"<method '_reduce_' of 'object' objects>"
```

To fix, wrap the format call in a try statement to catch the exception; use % formatting expressions instead of the str.format method; use one of the aforementioned still-working str.format usage modes and hope it does not change too; or wait for a repair of this in a later 3.X release. Here's the recommended workaround using the tried-and-true % (it's also noticeably shorter, but I won't repeat Chapter 7's comparisons here):

```
c:\code> py -3.3
>>> '%s' % object._reduce_
"<method '_reduce_' of 'object' objects>"
```

To apply this in the tree lister's code, change the first of these to its follower:

```
result += spaces + '{0}={1}\n'.format(attr, getattr(obj, attr))
result += spaces + '%s=%s\n' % (attr, getattr(obj, attr))
```

Python 2.X has the same regression in 2.7 but not 2.6—inherited from the 3.2 change, apparently—but does not show object methods in this chapter's example. Since this example generates too much output in 3.X anyhow, it's a moot point here, but is a decent example of real-world coding. Unfortunately, using newer features like str.format sometimes puts your code in the awkward position of *beta tester* in the current 3.X line!

Usage variation: Running on larger modules

For more fun, uncomment the underscore handler lines to enable them again, and try mixing this class into something more substantial, like the Button class of Python's tkinter GUI toolkit module. In general, you'll want to name ListTree first (leftmost) in a class header, so its _str_ is picked up; Button has one, too, and the leftmost superclass is always searched first in multiple inheritance.

The output of the following is fairly massive (20K characters and 330 lines in 3.X—and 38K if you forget to uncomment the underscore detection!), so run this code on your own to see the full listing. Notice how our lister's _visited dictionary attribute mixes harmlessly with those created by tkinter itself. If you're using Python 2.X, also recall that you should use Tkinter for the module name instead of tkinter:

```
>>> from listtree import ListTree
>>> from tkinter import Button              # Both classes have a _str_
>>> class MyButton(ListTree, Button): pass  # ListTree first: use its _str_

>>> B = MyButton(text='spam')
>>> open('savetree.txt', 'w').write(str(B)) # Save to a file for later viewing
20513
>>> len(open('savetree.txt').readlines())   # Lines in the file
330
>>> print(B)                                # Print the display here
<Instance of MyButton, address 43363688:
```

```
_ListTree__visited={}
_name=43363688
_tclCommands=[]
_w=.43363688
children={}
master=.
...much more omitted...
>
>>> S = str(B)                                    # Or print just the first part
>>> print(S[:1000])
```

Experiment arbitrarily on your own. The main point here is that OOP is all about code reuse, and mix-in classes are a powerful example. Like almost everything else in programming, multiple inheritance can be a useful device when applied well. In practice, though, it is an advanced feature and can become complicated if used carelessly or excessively. We'll revisit this topic as a gotcha at the end of the next chapter.

Collector module

Finally, to make importing our tools even easier, we can provide a collector module that combines them in a single namespace—importing just the following gives access to all three lister mix-ins at once:

```
# File lister.py
# Collect all three listers in one module for convenience

from listinstance  import ListInstance
from listinherited import ListInherited
from listtree      import ListTree

Lister = ListTree  # Choose a default lister
```

Importers can use the individual class names as is, or alias them to a common name used in subclasses that can be modified in the import statement:

```
>>> import lister
>>> lister.ListInstance                           # Use a specific lister
<class 'listinstance.ListInstance'>
>>> lister.Lister                                 # Use Lister default
<class 'listtree.ListTree'>

>>> from lister import Lister                      # Use Lister default
>>> Lister
<class 'listtree.ListTree'>

>>> from lister import ListInstance as Lister     # Use Lister alias
>>> Lister
<class 'listinstance.ListInstance'>
```

Python often makes flexible tool APIs nearly automatic.

Room for improvement: MRO, slots, GUIs

Like most software, there's much more we could do here. The following gives some pointers on extensions you may wish to explore. Some are interesting projects, and two serve as segue to the next chapter, but for space will have to remain in the suggested exercise category here.

General ideas: GUIs, built-ins

Grouping double-underscore names as we did earlier may help reduce the size of the tree display, though some like __init__ are user-defined and may merit special treatment. Sketching the tree in a GUI might be a natural next step too—the tkinter toolkit that we utilized in the prior section's lister examples ships with Python and provides basic but easy support, and others offer richer but more complex alternatives. See the notes at the end of Chapter 28's case study for more pointers in this department.

Physical trees versus inheritance: using the MRO (preview)

In the next chapter, we'll also meet the new-style class model, which modifies the search order for one special multiple inheritance case (diamonds). There, we'll also study the class.__mro__ new-style class object attribute—a tuple giving the class tree search order used by inheritance, known as the new-style MRO.

As is, our ListTree tree lister sketches the *physical shape* of the inheritance tree, and expects the viewer to infer from this where an attribute is inherited from. This was its goal, but a general object viewer might also use the MRO tuple to automatically associate an attribute with the class from which it is *inherited*—by scanning the new-style MRO (or the classic classes' DFLR ordering) for each inherited attribute in a dir result, we can simulate Python's inheritance search, and map attributes to their source objects in the physical class tree displayed.

In fact, we *will* write code that comes very close to this idea in the next chapter's mapattrs module, and reuse this example's test classes there to demonstrate the idea, so stay tuned for an epilogue to this story. This might be used instead of or in addition to displaying attribute physical locations in __attrnames here; both forms might be useful data for programmers to see. This approach is also one way to deal with slots, the topic of the next note.

Virtual data: slots, properties, and more (preview)

Because they scan instance __dict__ namespace dictionaries, the ListInstance and ListTree classes presented here raise some subtle design issues. In Python classes, some names associated with instance data may not be stored at the instance itself. This includes topics presented in the next chapter such as new-style properties, slots, and descriptors, but also attributes dynamically computed in all classes with tools like __getattr__. None of these "virtual" attributes' names are stored in an instance's namespace dictionary, so none will be displayed as part of an instance's own data.

Of these, *slots* seem the most strongly associated with an instance; they store data on instances, even though their names don't appear in instance namespace dictionaries. Properties and descriptors are associated with instances too, but they don't reserve space in the instance, their computed nature is much more explicit, and they may seem closer to class-level methods than instance data.

As we'll see in the next chapter, slots function like instance attributes, but are created and managed by automatically created items in classes. They are a relatively infrequently used new-style class option, where instance attributes are declared in a `__slots__` class attribute, and not physically stored in an instance's `__dict__`; in fact, slots may suppress a `__dict__` entirely. Because of this, tools that display instances by scanning their namespaces alone won't directly associate the instance with attributes stored in slots. As is, `ListTree` displays slots as class attributes wherever they appear (though not at the instance), and `ListInstance` doesn't display them at all.

Though this will make more sense after we study this feature in the next chapter, it impacts code here and similar tools. For example, if in *textmixin.py* we assign `__slots__=['data1']` in `Super` and `__slots__=['data3']` in `Sub`, only the `data2` attribute is displayed in the instance by these two lister classes. `ListTree` also displays `data1` and `data3`, but as attributes of the `Super` and `Sub` *class* objects and with a special format for their values (technically, they are class-level descriptors, another new-style tool introduced in the next chapter).

As the next chapter will explain, to show slot attributes as instance names, tools generally need to use `dir` to get a list of all attributes—both physically present and inherited—and then use either `getattr` to fetch their values from the instance, or fetch values from their inheritance source via `__dict__` in tree scans and accept the display of the implementations of some at classes. Because `dir` includes the names of inherited "virtual" attributes—including both slots and properties—they would be included in the instance set. As we'll also find, the MRO might assist here to map `dir` attribute to their sources, or restrict instance displays to names coded in user-defined classes by filtering out names inherited from the built-in `object`.

`ListInherited` is immune to most of this, because it already displays the full `dir` results set, which include both `__dict__` names and all classes' `__slots__` names, though its display is of marginal use as is. A `ListTree` variant using the `dir` technique along with the MRO sequence to map attributes to classes would apply to slots too, because slots-based names appear in class's `__dict__` results individually as slot management tools, though not in the instance `__dict__`.

Alternatively, as a policy we could simply let our code handle slot-based attributes as it currently does, rather than complicating it for a rarely used, advanced feature that's even questionable practice today. Slots and normal instance attributes are different kinds of names. In fact, displaying slots names as attributes of classes instead of instances is technically more accurate—as we'll see in the next chapter their implementation is at classes, though their space is at instances.

Ultimately, attempting to collect all the "virtual" attributes associated with a class may be a bit of a pipe dream anyhow. Techniques like those outlined here may address slots and properties, but some attributes are *entirely* dynamic, with no physical basis at all: those computed on fetch by generic method such as __get attr__ are not data in the classic sense. Tools that attempt to display data in a wildly dynamic language like Python must come with the caveat that some data is *ethereal at best*![3]

We'll also make a minor extension to this section's code in the exercises at the end of this part of the book, to list superclass names in parentheses at the start of instance displays, so keep it filed for future reference for now. To better understand the last of the preceding two points, we need to wrap up this chapter and move on to the next and last in this part of the book.

Other Design-Related Topics

In this chapter, we've studied inheritance, composition, delegation, multiple inheritance, bound methods, and factories—all common patterns used to combine classes in Python programs. We've really only scratched the surface here in the design patterns domain, though. Elsewhere in this book you'll find coverage of other design-related topics, such as:

- *Abstract superclasses* (Chapter 29)
- *Decorators* (Chapter 32 and Chapter 39)
- *Type subclasses* (Chapter 32)
- *Static and class methods* (Chapter 32)
- *Managed attributes* (Chapter 32 and Chapter 38)
- *Metaclasses* (Chapter 32 and Chapter 40)

For more details on design patterns, though, we'll delegate to other resources on OOP at large. Although patterns are important in OOP work and are often more natural in Python than other languages, they are not specific to Python itself, and a subject that's often best acquired by experience.

Chapter Summary

In this chapter, we sampled common ways to use and combine classes to optimize their reusability and factoring benefits—what are usually considered design issues that are

---

3. Some dynamic and proxy objects based on __getattr__ and the like can also use the __dir__ operator overloading method to manually publish an attributes list for dir calls. Because this is optional, though, general tools cannot rely on their client classes to do so. See *Python Pocket Reference, 5th Edition* for more on the __dir__ method.

often independent of any particular programming language (though Python can make them easier to implement). We studied *delegation* (wrapping objects in proxy classes), *composition* (controlling embedded objects), and *inheritance* (acquiring behavior from other classes), as well as some more esoteric concepts such as pseudoprivate attributes, multiple inheritance, bound methods, and factories.

The next chapter ends our look at classes and OOP by surveying more advanced class-related topics. Some of its material may be of more interest to tool writers than application programmers, but it still merits a review by most people who will do OOP in Python—if not for your code, then for the code of others you may need to understand. First, though, here's another quick chapter quiz to review.

Test Your Knowledge: Quiz

1. What is multiple inheritance?
2. What is delegation?
3. What is composition?
4. What are bound methods?
5. What are pseudoprivate attributes used for?

Test Your Knowledge: Answers

1. Multiple inheritance occurs when a class inherits from more than one superclass; it's useful for mixing together multiple packages of class-based code. The left-to-right order in `class` statement headers determines the general order of attribute searches.
2. Delegation involves wrapping an object in a proxy class, which adds extra behavior and passes other operations to the wrapped object. The proxy retains the interface of the wrapped object.
3. Composition is a technique whereby a controller class embeds and directs a number of objects, and provides an interface all its own; it's a way to build up larger structures with classes.
4. Bound methods combine an instance and a method function; you can call them without passing in an instance object explicitly because the original instance is still available.
5. Pseudoprivate attributes (whose names begin but do not end with two leading underscores: _X) are used to localize names to the enclosing class. This includes both class attributes like methods defined inside the class, and `self` instance attributes assigned inside the class's methods. Such names are expanded to include the class name, which makes them generally unique.

Advanced Class Topics

This chapter concludes our look at OOP in Python by presenting a few more advanced class-related topics: we will survey subclassing built-in types, "new style" class changes and extensions, static and class methods, slots and properties, function and class decorators, the MRO and the **super** call, and more.

As we've seen, Python's OOP model is, at its core, relatively simple, and some of the topics presented in this chapter are so advanced and optional that you may not encounter them very often in your Python applications-programming career. In the interest of completeness, though—and because you never know when an "advanced" topic may crop up in code you use—we'll round out our discussion of classes with a brief look at these advanced tools for OOP work.

As usual, because this is the last chapter in this part of the book, it ends with a section on class-related "gotchas," and the set of lab exercises for this part. I encourage you to work through the exercises to help cement the ideas we've studied here. I also suggest working on or studying larger OOP Python projects as a supplement to this book. As with much in computing, the benefits of OOP tend to become more apparent with practice.

 Content notes: This chapter collects advanced class topics, but some are too large for this chapter to cover well. Topics such as properties, descriptors, decorators, and metaclasses are mentioned only briefly here, and given a fuller treatment in the *final part* of this book, after exceptions. Be sure to look ahead for more complete examples and extended coverage of some of the subjects that fall into this chapter's category.

You'll also notice that this is the *largest* chapter in this book—I'm assuming that readers courageous enough to take on this chapter's topics are ready to roll up their sleeves and explore its in-depth coverage. If you're not looking for advanced OOP topics, you may wish to skip ahead to chapter-end materials, and come back here when you confront these tools in the code of your programming future.

Extending Built-in Types

Besides implementing new kinds of objects, classes are sometimes used to extend the functionality of Python's built-in types to support more exotic data structures. For instance, to add queue insert and delete methods to lists, you can code classes that wrap (embed) a list object and export insert and delete methods that process the list specially, like the delegation technique we studied in Chapter 31. As of Python 2.2, you can also use inheritance to specialize built-in types. The next two sections show both techniques in action.

Extending Types by Embedding

Do you remember those set functions we wrote in Chapter 16 and Chapter 18? Here's what they look like brought back to life as a Python class. The following example (the file *setwrapper.py*) implements a new set object type by moving some of the set functions to methods and adding some basic operator overloading. For the most part, this class just wraps a Python list with extra set operations. But because it's a class, it also supports multiple instances and customization by inheritance in subclasses. Unlike our earlier functions, using classes here allows us to make multiple self-contained set objects with preset data and behavior, rather than passing lists into functions manually:

```
class Set:
    def __init__(self, value = []):       # Constructor
        self.data = []                    # Manages a list
        self.concat(value)

    def intersect(self, other):           # other is any sequence
        res = []                          # self is the subject
        for x in self.data:
            if x in other:                # Pick common items
                res.append(x)
        return Set(res)                   # Return a new Set

    def union(self, other):               # other is any sequence
        res = self.data[:]                # Copy of my list
        for x in other:                   # Add items in other
            if not x in res:
                res.append(x)
        return Set(res)

    def concat(self, value):              # value: list, Set...
        for x in value:                   # Removes duplicates
            if not x in self.data:
                self.data.append(x)

    def __len__(self):          return len(self.data)       # len(self), if self
    def __getitem__(self, key): return self.data[key]       # self[i], self[i:j]
    def __and__(self, other):   return self.intersect(other) # self & other
    def __or__(self, other):    return self.union(other)    # self | other
```

```
    def __repr__(self):      return 'Set:' + repr(self.data)   # print(self),...
    def __iter__(self):      return iter(self.data)            # for x in self,...
```

To use this class, we make instances, call methods, and run defined operators as usual:

```
from setwrapper import Set
x = Set([1, 3, 5, 7])
print(x.union(Set([1, 4, 7])))          # prints Set:[1, 3, 5, 7, 4]
print(x | Set([1, 4, 6]))               # prints Set:[1, 3, 5, 7, 4, 6]
```

Overloading operations such as indexing and iteration also enables instances of our Set class to often masquerade as real lists. Because you will interact with and extend this class in an exercise at the end of this chapter, I won't say much more about this code until Appendix D.

Extending Types by Subclassing

Beginning with Python 2.2, all the built-in types in the language can now be subclassed directly. Type-conversion functions such as list, str, dict, and tuple have become built-in type names—although transparent to your script, a type-conversion call (e.g., list('spam')) is now really an invocation of a type's object constructor.

This change allows you to customize or extend the behavior of built-in types with user-defined class statements: simply subclass the new type names to customize them. Instances of your type subclasses can generally be used anywhere that the original built-in type can appear. For example, suppose you have trouble getting used to the fact that Python list offsets begin at 0 instead of 1. Not to worry—you can always code your own subclass that customizes this core behavior of lists. The file *typesubclass.py* shows how:

```
# Subclass built-in list type/class
# Map 1..N to 0..N-1; call back to built-in version.

class MyList(list):
    def __getitem__(self, offset):
        print('(indexing %s at %s)' % (self, offset))
        return list.__getitem__(self, offset - 1)

if __name__ == '__main__':
    print(list('abc'))
    x = MyList('abc')                   # __init__ inherited from list
    print(x)                            # __repr__ inherited from list

    print(x[1])                         # MyList.__getitem__
    print(x[3])                         # Customizes list superclass method

    x.append('spam'); print(x)          # Attributes from list superclass
    x.reverse();      print(x)
```

In this file, the MyList subclass extends the built-in list's __getitem__ indexing method only, to map indexes 1 to N back to the required 0 to N–1. All it really does is decrement the submitted index and call back to the superclass's version of indexing, but it's enough to do the trick:

```
% python typesubclass.py
['a', 'b', 'c']
['a', 'b', 'c']
(indexing ['a', 'b', 'c'] at 1)
a
(indexing ['a', 'b', 'c'] at 3)
c
['a', 'b', 'c', 'spam']
['spam', 'c', 'b', 'a']
```

This output also includes tracing text the class prints on indexing. Of course, whether changing indexing this way is a good idea in general is *another issue*—users of your MyList class may very well be confused by such a core departure from Python sequence behavior! The ability to customize built-in types this way can be a powerful asset, though.

For instance, this coding pattern gives rise to an alternative way to code a set—as a subclass of the built-in list type, rather than a standalone class that manages an embedded list object as shown in the prior section. As we learned in Chapter 5, Python today comes with a powerful built-in set object, along with literal and comprehension syntax for making new sets. Coding one yourself, though, is still a great way to learn about type subclassing in general.

The following class, coded in the file *setsubclass.py*, customizes lists to add just methods and operators related to set processing. Because all other behavior is inherited from the built-in list superclass, this makes for a shorter and simpler alternative—everything not defined here is routed to list directly:

```
from __future__ import print_function      # 2.X compatibility

class Set(list):
    def __init__(self, value = []):        # Constructor
        list.__init__(self)                # Customizes list
        self.concat(value)                 # Copies mutable defaults

    def intersect(self, other):            # other is any sequence
        res = []                           # self is the subject
        for x in self:
            if x in other:                 # Pick common items
                res.append(x)
        return Set(res)                    # Return a new Set

    def union(self, other):                # other is any sequence
        res = Set(self)                    # Copy me and my list
        res.concat(other)
        return res

    def concat(self, value):               # value: list, Set, etc.
        for x in value:                    # Removes duplicates
            if not x in self:
```

```
                self.append(x)

        def __and__(self, other): return self.intersect(other)
        def __or__(self, other):  return self.union(other)
        def __repr__(self):       return 'Set:' + list.__repr__(self)

if __name__ == '__main__':
    x = Set([1,3,5,7])
    y = Set([2,1,4,5,6])
    print(x, y, len(x))
    print(x.intersect(y), y.union(x))
    print(x & y, x | y)
    x.reverse(); print(x)
```

Here is the output of the self-test code at the end of this file. Because subclassing core types is a somewhat advanced feature with a limited target audience, I'll omit further details here, but I invite you to trace through these results in the code to study its behavior (which is the same on Python 3.X and 2.X):

```
% python setsubclass.py
Set:[1, 3, 5, 7] Set:[2, 1, 4, 5, 6] 4
Set:[1, 5] Set:[2, 1, 4, 5, 6, 3, 7]
Set:[1, 5] Set:[1, 3, 5, 7, 2, 4, 6]
Set:[7, 5, 3, 1]
```

There are more efficient ways to implement sets with dictionaries in Python, which replace the nested linear search scans in the set implementations shown here with more direct dictionary index operations (hashing) and so run much quicker. For more details, see the continuation of this thread in the follow-up book *Programming Python*. Again, if you're interested in sets, also take another look at the **set** object type we explored in Chapter 5; this type provides extensive set operations as built-in tools. Set implementations are fun to experiment with, but they are no longer strictly required in Python today.

For another type subclassing example, explore the implementation of the **bool** type in Python 2.3 and later. As mentioned earlier in the book, **bool** is a subclass of **int** with two instances (**True** and **False**) that behave like the integers **1** and **0** but inherit custom string-representation methods that display their names.

The "New Style" Class Model

In release 2.2, Python introduced a new flavor of classes, known as *new-style* classes; classes following the original and traditional model became known as *classic* classes when compared to the new kind. In 3.X the class story has merged, but it remains split for Python 2.X users and code:

- In *Python 3.X*, all classes are automatically what were formerly called "new style," whether they explicitly inherit from **object** or not. Coding the **object** superclass is optional and implied.

- In *Python 2.X*, classes must explicitly inherit from `object` (or another built-in type) to be considered "new style" and enable and obtain all new-style behavior. Classes without this are "classic."

Because all classes are automatically new-style in 3.X, the features of new-style classes are simply normal class features in that line. I've opted to keep their descriptions in this section separate, however, in deference to users of Python 2.X code—classes in such code acquire new-style features and behavior only when they are derived from `object`.

In other words, when Python 3.X users see descriptions of "new style" topics in this book, they should take them to be descriptions of existing properties of their classes. For 2.X readers, these are a set of optional changes and extensions that you may choose to enable or not, unless the code you must use already employs them.

In Python 2.X, the identifying *syntactic* difference for new-style classes is that they are derived from either a built-in type, such as `list`, or a special built-in class known as `object`. The built-in name `object` is provided to serve as a superclass for new-style classes if no other built-in type is appropriate to use:

```
class newstyle(object):            # 2.X explicit new-style derivation
    ...normal class code...        # Not required in 3.X: automatic
```

Any class derived from `object`, or any other built-in type, is automatically treated as a new-style class. That is, as long as a built-in type is somewhere in its superclass tree, a 2.X class acquires new-style class behavior and extensions. Classes not derived from built-ins such as `object` are considered classic.

Just How New Is New-Style?

As we'll see, new-style classes come with profound differences that impact programs broadly, especially when code leverages their added advanced features. In fact, at least in terms of its OOP support, these changes on some levels transform Python into a *different language altogether*—one that's mandated in the 3.X line, one that's optional in 2.X only if ignored by every programmer, and one that borrows much more from (and is often as complex as) other languages in this domain.

New-style classes stem in part from an attempt to merge the notion of *class* with that of *type* around the time of Python 2.2, though they went unnoticed by many until they were escalated to required knowledge in 3.X. You'll need to judge the success of that merging for yourself, but as we'll see, there are still distinctions in the model—now between *class* and *metaclass*—and one of its side effects is to make normal classes more powerful but also substantially more complex. The new-style inheritance algorithm formalized in Chapter 40, for example, grows in complexity by at least a factor of 2.

Still, some programmers using straightforward application code may notice only slight divergence from traditional "classic" classes. After all, we've managed to get to this point in this book writing substantial class examples, with mostly just passing mentions of this change. Moreover, the classic class model still available in 2.X works exactly as it has for some two decades.[1]

However, because they modify core class behaviors, new-style classes had to be introduced in Python 2.X as a distinct tool so as to avoid impacting any existing code that depends on the prior model. For example, some subtle differences, such as diamond pattern inheritance search and the interaction of built-in operations and managed attribute methods such as __getattr__ can cause some existing code to fail if left unchanged. Using optional extensions in the new model such as slots can have the same effect.

The class model split is removed in Python 3.X, which *mandates* new-style classes, but it still exists for readers using 2.X, or reusing the vast amount of existing 2.X code in production use. Because this has been an optional extension in 2.X, code written for that line may use either class model.

The next two top-level sections provide overviews of the ways in which new-style classes differ and the new tools they provide. These topics represent potential changes to some Python 2.X readers, but simply additional advanced class topics to many Python 3.X readers. If you're in the latter group, you'll find full coverage here, though some of it is presented in the context of changes—which you can accept as features, but only if you never must deal with any of the millions of lines of existing 2.X code.

New-Style Class Changes

New-style classes differ from classic classes in a number of ways, some of which are subtle but can impact both existing 2.X code and common coding styles. As preview and summary, here are some of the most prominent ways they differ:

Attribute fetch for built-ins: instance skipped
   The __getattr__ and __getattribute__ generic attribute interception methods are still run for attributes accessed by explicit name, but no longer for attributes implicitly fetched by built-in operations. They are not called for __X__ operator overloading method names in built-in contexts only—the search for such names begins at classes, not instances. This breaks or complicates objects that serve as *proxies* for another object's interface, if wrapped objects implement operator overloading.

---

1. As a data point, the book *Programming Python*, a 1,600-page applications programming follow-up to this book that uses 3.X exclusively, neither uses nor needs to accommodate any of the new-style class tools of this chapter, and still manages to build significant programs for GUIs, websites, systems programming, databases, and text. It's mostly straightforward code that leverages built-in types and libraries to do its work, not obscure and esoteric OOP extensions. When it does use classes, they are relatively simple, providing structure and code factoring. That book's code is also probably more representative of real-world programming than some in this language tutorial text—which suggests that many of Python's advanced OOP tools may be artificial, having more to do with language design than practical program goals. Then again, that book has the luxury of restricting its toolset to such code; as soon as your coworker finds a way to use an arcane language feature, all bets are off!

Such methods must be redefined for the sake of differing built-ins dispatch in new-style classes.

Classes and types merged: type testing

Classes are now types, and types are now classes. In fact, the two are essentially synonyms, though the *metaclasses* that now subsume types are still somewhat distinct from normal classes. The `type(I)` built-in returns the class an instance is made from, instead of a generic instance type, and is normally the same as `I.__class__`. Moreover, classes are instances of the `type` class, and `type` may be subclassed to customize class creation with metaclasses coded with `class` statements. This can impact code that tests types or otherwise relies on the prior type model.

Automatic `object` root class: defaults

All new-style classes (and hence types) inherit from `object`, which comes with a small set of default operator overloading methods (e.g., `__repr__`). In 3.X, this class is added automatically above the user-defined root (i.e., *topmost*) classes in a tree, and need not be listed as a superclass explicitly. This can affect code that assumes the absence of method defaults and root classes.

Inheritance search order: MRO and diamonds

Diamond patterns of multiple inheritance have a slightly different search order—roughly, at diamonds they are searched across before up, and more breadth-first than depth-first. This attribute search order, known as the MRO, can be traced with a new `__mro__` attribute available on new-style classes. The new search order largely applies only to diamond class trees, though the new model's implied `object` root itself forms a diamond in all multiple inheritance trees. Code that relies on the prior order will not work the same.

Inheritance algorithm: Chapter 40

The algorithm used for inheritance in new-style classes is substantially more complex than the depth-first model of classic classes, incorporating special cases for descriptors, metaclasses, and built-ins. We won't be able to formalize this until Chapter 40 after we've studied metaclasses and descriptors in more depth, but it can impact code that does not anticipate its extra convolutions.

New advanced tools: code impacts

New-style classes have a set of new class tools, including *slots*, *properties*, *descriptors*, `super`, and the `__getattribute__` method. Most of these have very specific tool-building purposes. Their use can also impact or break existing code, though; slots, for example, sometimes prevent creation of an instance namespace dictionary altogether, and generic attribute handlers may require different coding.

We'll explore the *extensions* noted in the last of these items in a later top-level section of its own, and will defer formal inheritance algorithm coverage until Chapter 40 as noted. Because the other items on this list have the potential to break traditional Python code, though, let's take a closer look at each in turn here.

Content note: Keep in mind that *new-style class changes* apply to *both* 3.X and 2.X, even though they are an option in the latter. This chapter and book sometimes label features as *3.X changes* to contrast with traditional 2.X code, but some are technically introduced by new-style classes—which are mandated in 3.X, but can show up in 2.X code too. For space, this distinction is called out often but not dogmatically here. Complicating this distinction, some 3.X class-related changes owe to new-style classes (e.g., skipping __getattr__ for operator methods) but some do not (e.g., replacing unbound methods with functions). Moreover, many 2.X programmers stick to classic classes, ignoring what they view as a 3.X feature. New-style classes are not new, though, and apply to both Pythons—if they appear in 2.X code, they're required reading for 2.X users too.

Attribute Fetch for Built-ins Skips Instances

We introduced this new-style class change in sidebars in both Chapter 28 and Chapter 31 because of their impact on prior examples and topics. In new-style classes (and hence all classes in 3.X), the generic instance attribute interception methods __getattr__ and __getattribute__ are no longer called by built-in operations for __X__ operator overloading method names—the search for such names begins at classes, not instances. Attributes accessed by explicit name, however, are routed through these methods, even if they are __X__ names. Hence, this is primarily a change to the behavior of built-in operations.

More formally, if a class defines a __getitem__ index overload method and X is an instance of this class, then an index expression like X[I] is roughly equivalent to X.__getitem__(I) for classic classes, but type(X).__getitem__(X, I) for new-style classes—the latter beginning its search in the class, and thus skipping a __getattr__ step from the instance for an undefined name.

Technically, this method search for built-in operations like X[I] uses normal inheritance beginning at the class level, and inspects only the *namespace dictionaries* of all the classes from which X derives—a distinction that can matter in the *metaclass* model we'll meet later in this chapter and focus on in Chapter 40, where classes may acquire behavior differently. The instance, however, is omitted by built-ins' search.

Why the lookup change?

You can find formal rationales for this change elsewhere; this book is disinclined to parrot justifications for a change that breaks many working programs. But this is imagined as both an *optimization* path and a solution to a seemingly obscure *call pattern* issue. The former rationale is supported by the frequency of built-in operations. If every +, for example, requires extra steps at the instance, it can degrade program speed —especially so given the new-style model's many attribute-level extensions.

The latter rationale is more obscure, and is described in Python manuals; in short, it reflects a conundrum introduced by the *metaclass* model. Because classes are now instances of metaclasses, and because metaclasses can define built-in operator methods to process the classes they generate, a method call run for a class must skip the class itself and look one level higher to pick up a method that processes the class, rather than selecting the class's own version. Its own version would result in an unbound method call, because the class's own method processes lower instances. This is just the usual unbound method model we discussed in the prior chapter, but is potentially aggravated by the fact that classes can acquire type behavior from metaclasses too.

As a result, because classes are both types and instances in their own right, all instances are skipped for built-in operation method lookup. This is supposedly applied to normal instances for uniformity and consistency, but both non-built-in names and direct and explicit calls to built-in names still check the instance anyhow. Though perhaps a consequence of the new-style class model, to some this may seem a solution arrived at for the sake of a usage pattern that was more artificial and obscure than the widely used one it broke. Its role as optimization path seems more defensible, but also not without repercussions.

In particular, this has potentially broad implications for the *delegation*-based classes, often known as *proxy* classes, when embedded objects implement operator overloading. In new-style classes, such a proxy object's class must generally *redefine* any such names to catch and delegate, either manually or with tools. The net effect is to either significantly complicate or wholly obviate an *entire category of programs*. We explored delegation in Chapter 28 and Chapter 31; it's a common pattern used to augment or adapt another class's interface—to add validation, tracing, timing, and many other sorts of logic. Though proxies may be more the exception than the rule in typical Python code, many Python programs depend upon them.

Implications for attribute interception

In simple terms, and run in *Python 2.X* to show how new-style classes differ, indexing and prints are routed to __getattr__ in traditional classes, but not for new-style classes, where printing uses a default:[2]

```
>>> class C:
        data = 'spam'
        def __getattr__(self, name):            # Classic in 2.X: catches built-ins
            print(name)
            return getattr(self.data, name)

>>> X = C()
>>> X[0]
__getitem__
```

---

2. As of this chapter's interaction listings, I've started omitting some blank lines and shortening some hex addresses to 32 bits in object displays, to reduce size and clutter. I'm going to assume that by this point in the book, you'll find such small details irrelevant.

```
's'
>>> print(X)                                        # Classic doesn't inherit default
__str__
spam

>>> class C(object):                                # New-style in 2.X and 3.X
        ...rest of class unchanged...

>>> X = C()                                         # Built-ins not routed to getattr
>>> X[0]
TypeError: 'C' object does not support indexing
>>> print(X)
<__main__.C object at 0x02205780>
```

Though apparently rationalized in the name of class metaclass methods and optimizing built-in operations, this divergence is not addressed by special-casing normal instances having a __getattr__, and applies only to built-in operations—not to normally named methods, or explicit calls to built-in methods by name:

```
>>> class C: pass                                   # 2.X classic class
>>> X = C()
>>> X.normal = lambda: 99
>>> X.normal()
99
>>> X.__add__ = lambda(y): 88 + y
>>> X.__add__(1)
89
>>> X + 1
89

>>> class C(object): pass                           # 2.X/3.X new-style class
>>> X = C()
>>> X.normal = lambda: 99
>>> X.normal()                                      # Normals still from instance
99
>>> X.__add__ = lambda(y): 88 + y
>>> X.__add__(1)                                    # Ditto for explicit built-in names
89
>>> X + 1
TypeError: unsupported operand type(s) for +: 'C' and 'int'
```

This behavior winds up being inherited by the __getattr__ attribute interception method:

```
>>> class C(object):
        def __getattr__(self, name): print(name)

>>> X = C()
>>> X.normal                    # Normal names are still routed to getattr
normal
>>> X.__add__                   # Direct calls by name are too, but expressions are not!
__add__
>>> X + 1
TypeError: unsupported operand type(s) for +: 'C' and 'int'
```

Proxy coding requirements

In a more realistic delegation scenario, this means that built-in operations like expressions no longer work the same as their traditional direct-call equivalent. Asymmetrically, direct calls to built-in method names still work, but equivalent expressions do not because through-type calls fail for names not at the class level and above. In other words, this distinction arises in *built-in operations only*; explicit fetches run correctly:

```
>>> class C(object):
        data = 'spam'
        def __getattr__(self, name):
            print('getattr: ' + name)
            return getattr(self.data, name)

>>> X = C()
>>> X.__getitem__(1)          # Traditional mapping works but new-style's does not
getattr: __getitem__
'p'

>>> X[1]
TypeError: 'C' object does not support indexing
>>> type(X).__getitem__(X, 1)
AttributeError: type object 'C' has no attribute '__getitem__'

>>> X.__add__('eggs')          # Ditto for +: instance skipped for expression only
getattr: __add__
'spameggs'

>>> X + 'eggs'
TypeError: unsupported operand type(s) for +: 'C' and 'str'
>>> type(X).__add__(X, 'eggs')
AttributeError: type object 'C' has no attribute '__add__'
```

The net effect: to code a proxy of an object whose interface may in part be invoked by built-in operations, new-style classes require both __getattr__ for normal names, as well as method *redefinitions* for all names accessed by built-in operations—whether coded manually, obtained from superclasses, or generated by tools. When redefinitions are so incorporated, calls through *both* instances and types are equivalent to built-in operations, though redefined names are no longer routed to the generic __getattr__ undefined name handler, even for explicit name calls:

```
>>> class C(object):                                  # New-style: 3.X and 2.X
        data = 'spam'
        def __getattr__(self, name):                  # Catch normal names
            print('getattr: ' + name)
            return getattr(self.data, name)
        def __getitem__(self, i):                     # Redefine built-ins
            print('getitem: ' + str(i))
            return self.data[i]                       # Run expr or getattr
        def __add__(self, other):
            print('add: ' + other)
            return getattr(self.data, '__add__')(other)

>>> X = C()
```

```
>>> X.upper
getattr: upper
<built-in method upper of str object at 0x0233D670>
>>> X.upper()
getattr: upper
'SPAM'

>>> X[1]                          # Built-in operation (implicit)
getitem: 1
'p'
>>> X.__getitem__(1)              # Traditional equivalence (explicit)
getitem: 1
'p'
>>> type(X).__getitem__(X, 1)     # New-style equivalence
getitem: 1
'p'

>>> X + 'eggs'                    # Ditto for + and others
add: eggs
'spameggs'
>>> X.__add__('eggs')
add: eggs
'spameggs'
>>> type(X).__add__(X, 'eggs')
add: eggs
'spameggs'
```

For more details

We will revisit this change in Chapter 40 on metaclasses, and by example in the contexts of attribute management in Chapter 38 and privacy decorators in Chapter 39. In the latter of these, we'll also explore coding structures for providing proxies with the required operator methods generically—it's not an impossible task, and may need to be coded just once if done well. For more of the sort of code influenced by this issue, see those later chapters, as well as the earlier examples in Chapter 28 and Chapter 31.

Because we'll expand on this issue later in the book, we'll cut the coverage short here. For external links and pointers on this issue, though, see the following (along with your local search engine):

- *Python Issue 643841*: this issue has been discussed widely, but its most official history seems to be documented at *http://bugs.python.org/issue643841*. There, it was raised as a concern for real programs and escalated to be addressed, but a proposed library remedy or broader change in Python was struck down in favor of a simple documentation change to describe the new mandated behavior.

- *Tool recipes*: also see *http://code.activestate.com/recipes/252151*, an Active State Python recipe that describes a tool that automatically fills in special method names as generic call dispatchers in a proxy class created with metaclass techniques introduced later in this chapter. This tool still must ask you to pass in the operator method names that a wrapped object may implement, though (it must, as interface components of a wrapped object may be inherited from arbitrary sources).

- *Other approaches:* a web search today will uncover numerous additional tools that similarly populate proxy classes with overloading methods; it's a widespread concern! Again, in Chapter 39, we'll also see how to code straightforward and general superclasses once that provide the required methods or attributes as *mix-ins*, without metaclasses, redundant code generation, or similarly complex techniques.

This story may evolve over time, of course, but has been an issue for many years. As this stands today, classic class proxies for objects that do any operator overloading are effectively broken as new-style classes. Such classes in both 2.X and 3.X require coding or generating wrappers for all the implicitly invoked operator methods a wrapped object may support. This is not ideal for such programs—some proxies may require dozens of wrapper methods (potentially over 50!)—but reflects, or is at least an artifact of, the design goals of new-style class developers.

 Be sure to see Chapter 40's *metaclass* coverage for an additional illustration of this issue and its rationale. We'll also see there that this behavior of built-ins qualifies as a special case in new-style *inheritance*. Understanding this well requires more background on metaclasses than the current chapter can provide, a regrettable byproduct of metaclasses in general—they've become prerequisite to more usage than their originators may have foreseen.

Type Model Changes

On to our next new-style change: depending on your assessment, in new-style classes the distinction between *type* and *class* has either been greatly muted or has vanished entirely. Specifically:

Classes are types

The **type** object generates classes as its instances, and classes generate instances of themselves. Both are considered types, because they generate instances. In fact, there is no real difference between built-in types like lists and strings and user-defined types coded as classes. This is why we can subclass built-in types, as shown earlier in this chapter—a subclass of a built-in type such as **list** qualifies as a new-style class and becomes a new user-defined type.

Types are classes

New class-generating types may be coded in Python as the *metaclasses* we'll meet later in this chapter—user-defined **type** subclasses that are coded with normal **class** statements, and control creation of the classes that are their instances. As we'll see, metaclasses are both class and type, though they are distinct enough to support a reasonable argument that the prior type/class dichotomy has become one of metaclass/class, perhaps at the cost of added complexity in normal classes.

Besides allowing us to subclass built-in types and code metaclasses, one of the most practical contexts where this type/class merging becomes most obvious is when we do explicit type testing. With Python 2.X's classic classes, the type of a class instance is a generic "instance," but the types of built-in objects are more specific:

```
C:\code> c:\python27\python
>>> class C: pass                    # Classic classes in 2.X

>>> I = C()                          # Instances are made from classes
>>> type(I), I.__class__
(<type 'instance'>, <class __main__.C at 0x02399768>)

>>> type(C)                          # But classes are not the same as types
<type 'classobj'>
>>> C.__class__
AttributeError: class C has no attribute '__class__'

>>> type([1, 2, 3]), [1, 2, 3].__class__
(<type 'list'>, <type 'list'>)

>>> type(list), list.__class__
(<type 'type'>, <type 'type'>)
```

But with new-style classes in 2.X, the type of a class instance is the class it's created from, since classes are simply user-defined types—the type of an instance is its class, and the type of a user-defined class is the same as the type of a built-in object type. Classes have a __class__ attribute now, too, because they are instances of type:

```
C:\code> c:\python27\python
>>> class C(object): pass            # New-style classes in 2.X

>>> I = C()                          # Type of instance is class it's made from
>>> type(I), I.__class__
(<class '__main__.C'>, <class '__main__.C'>)

>>> type(C), C.__class__             # Classes are user-defined types
(<type 'type'>, <type 'type'>)
```

The same is true for all classes in Python 3.X, since all classes are automatically new-style, even if they have no explicit superclasses. In fact, the distinction between built-in types and user-defined class types seems to melt away altogether in 3.X:

```
C:\code> c:\python33\python
>>> class C: pass

>>> I = C()                          # All classes are new-style in 3.X
>>> type(I), I.__class__             # Type of instance is class it's made from
(<class '__main__.C'>, <class '__main__.C'>)

>>> type(C), C.__class__             # Class is a type, and type is a class
(<class 'type'>, <class 'type'>)

>>> type([1, 2, 3]), [1, 2, 3].__class__
(<class 'list'>, <class 'list'>)
```

```
>>> type(list), list.__class__          # Classes and built-in types work the same
(<class 'type'>, <class 'type'>)
```

As you can see, in 3.X classes are types, but types are also classes. Technically, each
class is generated by a *metaclass*—a class that is normally either **type** itself, or a subclass
of it customized to augment or manage generated classes. Besides impacting code that
does type testing, this turns out to be an important hook for tool developers. We'll talk
more about metaclasses later in this chapter, and again in more detail in Chapter 40.

Implications for type testing

Besides providing for built-in type customization and metaclass hooks, the merging of
classes and types in the new-style class model can impact code that does type testing.
In Python 3.X, for example, the types of class instances compare directly and meaningfully, and in the same way as built-in type objects. This follows from the fact that
classes are now types, and an instance's type is the instance's class:

```
C:\code> c:\python33\python
>>> class C: pass
>>> class D: pass

>>> c, d = C(), D()
>>> type(c) == type(d)                  # 3.X: compares the instances' classes
False

>>> type(c), type(d)
(<class '__main__.C'>, <class '__main__.D'>)
>>> c.__class__, d.__class__
(<class '__main__.C'>, <class '__main__.D'>)

>>> c1, c2 = C(), C()
>>> type(c1) == type(c2)
True
```

With classic classes in 2.X, though, comparing instance types is almost useless, because
all instances have the same "instance" type. To truly compare types, the instance
__class__ attributes must be compared (if you care about portability, this works in 3.X,
too, but it's not required there):

```
C:\code> c:\python27\python
>>> class C: pass
>>> class D: pass

>>> c, d = C(), D()
>>> type(c) == type(d)                  # 2.X: all instances are same type!
True
>>> c.__class__ == d.__class__          # Compare classes explicitly if needed
False

>>> type(c), type(d)
(<type 'instance'>, <type 'instance'>)
>>> c.__class__, d.__class__
(<class __main__.C at 0x024585A0>, <class __main__.D at 0x024588D0>)
```

And as you should expect by now, new-style classes in 2.X work the same as all classes in 3.X in this regard—comparing instance types compares the instances' classes automatically:

```
C:\code> c:\python27\python
>>> class C(object): pass
>>> class D(object): pass

>>> c, d = C(), D()
>>> type(c) == type(d)                    # 2.X new-style: same as all in 3.X
False

>>> type(c), type(d)
(<class '__main__.C'>, <class '__main__.D'>)
>>> c.__class__, d.__class__
(<class '__main__.C'>, <class '__main__.D'>)
```

Of course, as I've pointed out numerous times in this book, type checking is usually the wrong thing to do in Python programs (we code to object interfaces, not object types), and the more general `isinstance` built-in is more likely what you'll want to use in the rare cases where instance class types must be queried. However, knowledge of Python's type model can help clarify the class model in general.

All Classes Derive from "object"

Another ramification of the type change in the new-style class model is that because all classes derive (inherit) from the class `object` either implicitly or explicitly, and because all types are now classes, every object derives from the `object` built-in class, whether directly or through a superclass. Consider the following interaction in Python 3.X:

```
>>> class C: pass                         # For new-style classes
>>> X = C()
>>> type(X), type(C)                       # Type is class instance was created from
(<class '__main__.C'>, <class 'type'>)
```

As before, the type of a class *instance* is the class it was made from, and the type of a *class* is the `type` class because classes and types have merged. It is also true, though, that the instance and class are both derived from the built-in `object` class and type, an implicit or explicit superclass of every class:

```
>>> isinstance(X, object)
True
>>> isinstance(C, object)                  # Classes always inherit from object
True
```

The preceding returns the same results for both new-style and classic classes in 2.X today, though 2.X `type` results differ. More importantly, as we'll see ahead, `object` is not added to or present in a 2.X classic class's __bases__ tuple, and so is not a true superclass.

The same relationship holds true for built-in types like lists and strings, because types are classes in the new-style model—built-in types are now classes, and their instances derive from object, too:

```
>>> type('spam'), type(str)
(<class 'str'>, <class 'type'>)

>>> isinstance('spam', object)        # Same for built-in types (classes)
True
>>> isinstance(str, object)
True
```

In fact, type itself derives from object, and object derives from type, even though the two are different objects—a circular relationship that caps the object model and stems from the fact that types are classes that generate classes:

```
>>> type(type)                        # All classes are types, and vice versa
<class 'type'>
>>> type(object)
<class 'type'>

>>> isinstance(type, object)          # All classes derive from object, even type
True
>>> isinstance(object, type)          # Types make classes, and type is a class
True
>>> type is object
False
```

Implications for defaults

The preceding may seem obscure, but this model has a number of practical implications. For one thing, it means that we sometimes must be aware of the method defaults that come with the explicit or implicit object root class in new-style classes only:

```
c:\code> py -2
>>> dir(object)
['__class__', '__delattr__', '__doc__', '__format__', '__getattribute__', '__hash__'
, '__init__', '__new__', '__reduce__', '__reduce_ex__', '__repr__', '__setattr__', '
__sizeof__', '__str__', '__subclasshook__']

>>> class C: pass
>>> C.__bases__                       # Classic classes do not inherit from object
()
>>> X = C()
>>> X.__repr__
AttributeError: C instance has no attribute '__repr__'

>>> class C(object): pass             # New-style classes inherit object defaults
>>> C.__bases__
(<type 'object'>,)
>>> X = C()
>>> X.__repr__
<method-wrapper '__repr__' of C object at 0x00000000020B5978>

c:\code> py -3
```

```
>>> class C: pass                    # This means all classes get defaults in 3.X
>>> C.__bases__
(<class 'object'>,)
>>> C().__repr__
<method-wrapper '__repr__' of C object at 0x0000000002955630>
```

This model also makes for fewer special cases than the prior type/class distinction of classic classes, and it allows us to write code that can safely assume and use an `object` superclass (e.g., by assuming it as an "anchor" in some `super` built-in roles described ahead, and by passing it method calls to invoke default behavior). We'll see examples of the latter later in the book; for now, let's move on to explore the last major new-style change.

Diamond Inheritance Change

Our final new-style class model change is also one of its most visible: its slightly different inheritance search order for so-called *diamond* pattern multiple inheritance trees—a tree pattern in which more than one superclass leads to the same higher superclass further above (and whose name comes from the diamond shape of the tree if you sketch out—a square resting on one of its corners).

The diamond pattern is a fairly advanced design concept, only occurs in multiple inheritance trees, and tends to be coded rarely in Python practice, so we won't cover this topic in full depth. In short, though, the differing search orders were introduced briefly in the prior chapter's multiple inheritance coverage:

For classic classes (the default in 2.X): DFLR
    The inheritance search path is strictly depth first, and then left to right—Python climbs all the way to the top, hugging the left side of the tree, before it backs up and begins to look further to the right. This search order is known as *DFLR* for the first letters in its path's directions.

For new-style classes (optional in 2.X and automatic in 3.X): MRO
    The inheritance search path is more breadth-first in diamond cases—Python first looks in any superclasses to the right of the one just searched before ascending to the common superclass at the top. In other words, this search proceeds across by levels before moving up. This search order is called the new-style *MRO* for "method resolution order" (and often just MRO for short when used in contrast with the DFLR order). Despite the name, this is used for all attributes in Python, not just methods.

The new-style MRO algorithm is a bit more complex than just described—and we'll expand on it a bit more formally later—but this is as much as many programmers need to know. Still, it has both important benefits for new-style class code, as well as program-breaking potential for existing classic class code.

For example, the new-style MRO allows lower superclasses to overload attributes of higher superclasses, regardless of the sort of multiple inheritance trees they are mixed into. Moreover, the new-style search rule avoids visiting the same superclass more than once when it is accessible from multiple subclasses. It's arguably better than DFLR, but applies to a small subset of Python user code; as we'll see, though, the new-style class model *itself* makes diamonds much more common, and the MRO more important.

At the same time, the new MRO will locate attributes differently, creating a potential incompatibility for 2.X classic classes. Let's move on to some code to see how its differences pan out in practice.

Implications for diamond inheritance trees

To illustrate how the new-style MRO search differs, consider this simplistic incarnation of the diamond multiple inheritance pattern for *classic classes*. Here, D's superclasses B and C both lead to the same common ancestor, A:

```
>>> class A:        attr = 1     # Classic (Python 2.X)
>>> class B(A):     pass         # B and C both lead to A
>>> class C(A):     attr = 2
>>> class D(B, C):  pass         # Tries A before C

>>> x = D()
>>> x.attr                       # Searches x, D, B, A
1
```

The attribute `x.attr` here is found in superclass A, because with classic classes, the inheritance search climbs as high as it can before backing up and moving right. The full DFLR search order would visit x, D, B, A, C, and then A. For this attribute, the search stops as soon as `attr` is found in A, above B.

However, with *new-style classes* derived from a built-in like `object` (and all classes in 3.X), the search order is different: Python looks in C to the right of B, before trying A above B. The full MRO search order would visit x, D, B, C, and then A. For this attribute, the search stops as soon as `attr` is found in C:

```
>>> class A(object): attr = 1    # New-style ("object" not required in 3.X)
>>> class B(A):      pass
>>> class C(A):      attr = 2
>>> class D(B, C):   pass         # Tries C before A

>>> x = D()
>>> x.attr                        # Searches x, D, B, C
2
```

This change in the inheritance search procedure is based upon the assumption that if you mix in C lower in the tree, you probably intend to grab its attributes in preference to A's. It also assumes that C is always intended to override A's attributes in all contexts, which is probably true when it's used standalone but may not be when it's mixed into a diamond with classic classes—you might not even know that C may be mixed in like this when you code it.

Since it is most likely that the programmer meant that C should override A in this case, though, new-style classes visit C first. Otherwise, C could be essentially pointless in a diamond context for any names in A too—it could not customize A and would be used only for names unique to C.

Explicit conflict resolution

Of course, the problem with assumptions is that they assume things! If this search order deviation seems too subtle to remember, or if you want more control over the search process, you can always force the selection of an attribute from anywhere in the tree by assigning or otherwise naming the one you want at the place where the classes are mixed together. The following, for example, chooses new-style order in a classic class by resolving the choice explicitly:

```
>>> class A:       attr = 1          # Classic
>>> class B(A):    pass
>>> class C(A):    attr = 2
>>> class D(B, C): attr = C.attr     # <== Choose C, to the right

>>> x = D()
>>> x.attr                           # Works like new-style (all 3.X)
2
```

Here, a tree of classic classes is emulating the search order of new-style classes for a specific attribute: the assignment to the attribute in D picks the version in C, thereby subverting the normal inheritance search path (D.attr will be lowest in the tree). New-style classes can similarly emulate classic classes by choosing the higher version of the target attribute at the place where the classes are mixed together:

```
>>> class A(object): attr = 1        # New-style
>>> class B(A):      pass
>>> class C(A):      attr = 2
>>> class D(B, C):   attr = B.attr   # <== Choose A.attr, above

>>> x = D()
>>> x.attr                           # Works like classic (default 2.X)
1
```

If you are willing to always resolve conflicts like this, you may be able to largely ignore the search order difference and not rely on assumptions about what you meant when you coded your classes.

Naturally, attributes picked this way can also be method functions—methods are normal, assignable attributes that happen to reference callable function objects:

```
>>> class A:
        def meth(s): print('A.meth')

>>> class C(A):
        def meth(s): print('C.meth')

>>> class B(A):
```

```
        pass

>>> class D(B, C): pass              # Use default search order
>>> x = D()                          # Will vary per class type
>>> x.meth()                         # Defaults to classic order in 2.X
A.meth

>>> class D(B, C): meth = C.meth     # <== Pick C's method: new-style (and 3.X)
>>> x = D()
>>> x.meth()
C.meth

>>> class D(B, C): meth = B.meth     # <== Pick B's method: classic
>>> x = D()
>>> x.meth()
A.meth
```

Here, we select methods by explicitly assigning to names lower in the tree. We might also simply call the desired class explicitly; in practice, this pattern might be more common, especially for things like constructors:

```
class D(B, C):
    def meth(self):                  # Redefine lower
        ...
        C.meth(self)                 # <== Pick C's method by calling
```

Such selections by assignment or call at mix-in points can effectively insulate your code from this difference in class flavors. This applies only to the attributes you handle this way, of course, but explicitly resolving the conflicts ensures that your code won't vary per Python version, at least in terms of attribute conflict selection. In other words, this can serve as a *portability* technique for classes that may need to be run under both the new-style and classic class models.

Explicit is better than implicit—for method resolution too: Even without the classic/new-style class divergence, the explicit method resolution technique shown here may come in handy in multiple inheritance scenarios in general. For instance, if you want part of a superclass on the left and part of a superclass on the right, you might need to tell Python which same-named attributes to choose by using explicit assignments or calls in subclasses. We'll revisit this notion in a "gotcha" at the end of this chapter.

Also note that diamond inheritance patterns might be more problematic in some cases than I've implied here (e.g., what if B and C both have required constructors that call to the constructor in A?). Since such contexts are rare in real-world Python, we'll defer this topic until we explore the super built-in function near the end of this chapter; besides providing generic access to superclasses in single inheritance trees, super supports a cooperative mode for resolving conflicts in multiple inheritance trees by ordering method calls per the MRO—assuming this order makes sense in this context too!

Scope of search order change

In sum, by default, the diamond pattern is searched differently for classic and new-style classes, and this is a non-backward-compatible change. Keep in mind, though, that this change primarily affects diamond pattern cases of multiple inheritance; new-style class inheritance works the same for most other inheritance tree structures. Further, it's not impossible that this entire issue may be of more theoretical than practical importance —because the new-style search wasn't significant enough to address until Python 2.2 and didn't become standard until 3.0, it seems unlikely to impact most Python code.

Having said that, I should also note that even though you might not code diamond patterns in classes you write yourself, because the implied object superclass is above every root class in 3.X as we saw earlier, *every* case of multiple inheritance exhibits the diamond pattern today. That is, in new-style classes, object automatically plays the role that the class A does in the example we just considered. Hence the new-style MRO search rule not only modifies logical semantics, but is also an important *performance optimization*—it avoids visiting and searching the same class more than once, even the automatic object.

Just as important, we've also seen that the implied object superclass in the new-style model provides *default methods* for a variety of built-in operations, including the __str__ and __repr__ display format methods. Run a dir(object) to see which methods are provided. Without the new-style MRO search order, in multiple inheritance cases the defaults in object would always override redefinitions in user-coded classes, unless they were always made in the leftmost superclass. In other words, the new-style class model itself makes using the new-style search order more critical!

For a more visual example of the implied object superclass in 3.X, and other examples of diamond patterns created by it, see the ListTree class's output in the *lister.py* example in the preceding chapter, as well as the *classtree.py* tree walker example in Chapter 29— and the next section.

More on the MRO: Method Resolution Order

To trace how new-style inheritance works by default, we can also use the new *class.*__mro__ attribute mentioned in the preceding chapter's class lister examples— technically a new-style extension, but useful here to explore a change. This attribute returns a class's *MRO*—the order in which inheritance searches classes in a new-style class tree. This MRO is based on the C3 superclass linearization algorithm initially developed in the Dylan programming language, but later adopted by other languages including Python 2.3 and Perl 6.

The MRO algorithm

This book avoids a full description of the MRO algorithm deliberately, because many Python programmers don't need to care (this only impacts diamonds, which are relatively rare in real-world code); because it differs between 2.X and 3.X; and because the details of the MRO are a bit too arcane and academic for this text. As a rule, this book avoids formal algorithms and prefers to teach informally by example.

On the other hand, some readers may still have an interest in the formal theory behind new-style MRO. If this set includes you, it's described in full detail online; search Python's manuals and the Web for current MRO links. In short, though, the MRO essentially works like this:

1. List all the classes that an instance inherits from using the classic class's *DFLR* lookup rule, and include a class multiple times if it's visited more than once.

2. Scan the resulting list for duplicate classes, removing all but the *last* occurrence of duplicates in the list.

The resulting MRO list for a given class includes the class, its superclasses, and all higher superclasses up to the `object` root class at the top of the tree. It's ordered such that each class appears before its parents, and multiple parents retain the order in which they appear in the `__bases__` superclass tuple.

Crucially, though, because common parents in *diamonds* appear only at the position of their *last* visitation, lower classes are searched first when the MRO list is later used by attribute inheritance. Moreover, each class is included and thus visited just once, no matter how many classes lead to it.

We'll see applications of this algorithm later in this chapter, including that in `super`— a built-in that elevates the MRO to required reading if you wish to fully understand how methods are dispatched by this call, should you choose to use it. As we'll see, despite its name, this call invokes the next class on the MRO, which might not be a superclass at all.

Tracing the MRO

If you just want to see how Python's new-style inheritance orders superclasses in general, though, new-style classes (and hence all classes in 3.X) have a *class*.`__mro__` attribute, which is a tuple giving the linear search order Python uses to look up attributes in superclasses. Really, this attribute *is* the inheritance order in new-style classes, and is often as much MRO detail as many Python users need.

Here are some illustrative examples, run in 3.X; for *diamond* inheritance patterns only, the search is the new order we've been studying—*across* before up, per the MRO for new-style classes always used in 3.X, and available as an option in 2.X:

```
>>> class A: pass
>>> class B(A): pass          # Diamonds: order differs for newstyle
>>> class C(A): pass          # Breadth-first across lower levels
>>> class D(B, C): pass
>>> D.__mro__
(<class '__main__.D'>, <class '__main__.B'>, <class '__main__.C'>,
<class '__main__.A'>, <class 'object'>)
```

For *nondiamonds*, though, the search is still as it has always been (albeit with an extra `object` root)—to the top, and then to the right (a.k.a. *DFLR*, depth first and left to right, the model used for all classic classes in 2.X):

```
>>> class A: pass
>>> class B(A): pass          # Nondiamonds: order same as classic
>>> class C: pass             # Depth first, then left to right
>>> class D(B, C): pass
>>> D.__mro__
(<class '__main__.D'>, <class '__main__.B'>, <class '__main__.A'>,
<class '__main__.C'>, <class 'object'>)
```

The MRO of the following tree, for example, is the same as the earlier diamond, per DFLR:

```
>>> class A: pass
>>> class B: pass             # Another nondiamond: DFLR
>>> class C(A): pass
>>> class D(B, C): pass
>>> D.__mro__
(<class '__main__.D'>, <class '__main__.B'>, <class '__main__.C'>,
<class '__main__.A'>, <class 'object'>)
```

Notice how the implied object superclass always shows up at the *end* of the MRO; as we've seen, it's added automatically above root (*topmost*) classes in new-style class trees in 3.X (and optionally in 2.X):

```
>>> A.__bases__               # Superclass links: object at two roots
(<class 'object'>,)
>>> B.__bases__
(<class 'object'>,)
>>> C.__bases__
(<class '__main__.A'>,)
>>> D.__bases__
(<class '__main__.B'>, <class '__main__.C'>)
```

Technically, the implied `object` superclass always creates a diamond in multiple inheritance even if your classes do not—your classes are searched as before, but the new-style MRO ensures that `object` is visited last, so your classes can override its defaults:

```
>>> class X: pass
>>> class Y: pass
>>> class A(X): pass          # Nondiamond: depth first then left to right
>>> class B(Y): pass          # Though implied "object" always forms a diamond
>>> class D(A, B): pass
>>> D.mro()
[<class '__main__.D'>, <class '__main__.A'>, <class '__main__.X'>,
<class '__main__.B'>, <class '__main__.Y'>, <class 'object'>]

>>> X.__bases__, Y.__bases__
((<class 'object'>,), (<class 'object'>,))
>>> A.__bases__, B.__bases__
((<class '__main__.X'>,), (<class '__main__.Y'>,))
```

The *class.__mro__* attribute is available only on new-style classes; it's not present in 2.X unless classes derive from `object`. Strictly speaking, new-style classes also have a *class*.mro() method used in the prior example for variety; it's called at class instantiation time and its return value is a list used to initialize the __mro__ attribute when the class is created (the method is available for customization in metaclasses, described later). You can also select MRO names if classes' object displays are too detailed, though this book usually shows the *objects* to remind you of their true form:

```
>>> D.mro() == list(D.__mro__)
True
>>> [cls.__name__ for cls in D.__mro__]
['D', 'A', 'X', 'B', 'Y', 'object']
```

However you access or display them, class MRO paths might be useful to resolve confusion, and in tools that must imitate Python's inheritance search order. The next section shows the latter role in action.

Example: Mapping Attributes to Inheritance Sources

As a prime MRO use case, we noted at the end of the prior chapter that class tree climbers—such as the class tree lister mix-in we wrote there—might benefit from the MRO. As coded, the tree lister gave the *physical* locations of attributes in a class tree. However, by mapping the list of inherited attributes in a `dir` result to the linear MRO sequence (or DFLR order for classic classes), such tools can more directly associate attributes with the classes from which they are *inherited*—also a useful relationship for programmers.

We won't recode our tree lister here, but as a first major step, the following file, *mapattrs.py*, implements tools that can be used to associate attributes with their inheritance source; as an added bonus, its `mapattrs` function demonstrates how inheritance actually searches for attributes in class tree objects, though the new-style MRO is largely automated for us:

```
"""
File mapattrs.py (3.X + 2.X)

Main tool: mapattrs() maps all attributes on or inherited by an
instance to the instance or class from which they are inherited.

Assumes dir() gives all attributes of an instance.  To simulate
inheritance, uses either the class's MRO tuple, which gives the
search order for new-style classes (and all in 3.X), or a recursive
traversal to infer the DFLR order of classic classes in 2.X.

Also here: inheritance() gives version-neutral class ordering;
assorted dictionary tools using 3.X/2.7 comprehensions.
"""

import pprint
def trace(X, label='', end='\n'):
```

```
        print(label + pprint.pformat(X) + end)   # Print nicely

def filterdictvals(D, V):
    """
    dict D with entries for value V removed.
    filterdictvals(dict(a=1, b=2, c=1), 1) => {'b': 2}
    """
    return {K: V2 for (K, V2) in D.items() if V2 != V}

def invertdict(D):
    """
    dict D with values changed to keys (grouped by values).
    Values must all be hashable to work as dict/set keys.
    invertdict(dict(a=1, b=2, c=1)) => {1: ['a', 'c'], 2: ['b']}
    """
    def keysof(V):
        return sorted(K for K in D.keys() if D[K] == V)
    return {V: keysof(V) for V in set(D.values())}

def dflr(cls):
    """
    Classic depth-first left-to-right order of class tree at cls.
    Cycles not possible: Python disallows on __bases__ changes.
    """
    here = [cls]
    for sup in cls.__bases__:
        here += dflr(sup)
    return here

def inheritance(instance):
    """
    Inheritance order sequence: new-style (MRO) or classic (DFLR)
    """
    if hasattr(instance.__class__, '__mro__'):
        return (instance,) + instance.__class__.__mro__
    else:
        return [instance] + dflr(instance.__class__)

def mapattrs(instance, withobject=False, bysource=False):
    """
    dict with keys giving all inherited attributes of instance,
    with values giving the object that each is inherited from.
    withobject: False=remove object built-in class attributes.
    bysource:   True=group result by objects instead of attributes.
    Supports classes with slots that preclude __dict__ in instances.
    """
    attr2obj = {}
    inherits = inheritance(instance)
    for attr in dir(instance):
        for obj in inherits:
            if hasattr(obj, '__dict__') and attr in obj.__dict__:     # See slots
                attr2obj[attr] = obj
                break

    if not withobject:
```

```
            attr2obj = filterdictvals(attr2obj, object)
        return attr2obj if not bysource else invertdict(attr2obj)

if __name__ == '__main__':
    print('Classic classes in 2.X, new-style in 3.X')
    class A:         attr1 = 1
    class B(A):      attr2 = 2
    class C(A):      attr1 = 3
    class D(B, C):   pass
    I = D()
    print('Py=>%s' % I.attr1)                          # Python's search == ours?
    trace(inheritance(I),              'INH\n')        # [Inheritance order]
    trace(mapattrs(I),                 'ATTRS\n')      # Attrs => Source
    trace(mapattrs(I, bysource=True),  'OBJS\n')       # Source => [Attrs]


    print('New-style classes in 2.X and 3.X')
    class A(object): attr1 = 1                          # "(object)" optional in 3.X
    class B(A):      attr2 = 2
    class C(A):      attr1 = 3
    class D(B, C):   pass
    I = D()
    print('Py=>%s' % I.attr1)
    trace(inheritance(I),              'INH\n')
    trace(mapattrs(I),                 'ATTRS\n')
    trace(mapattrs(I, bysource=True),  'OBJS\n')
```

This file assumes dir gives all an instance's attributes. It maps each attribute in a dir result to its source by scanning either the MRO order for new-style classes, or the DFLR order for classic classes, searching each object's namespace __dict__ along the way. For classic classes, the DFLR order is computed with a simple recursive scan. The net effect is to simulate Python's inheritance search in both class models.

This file's self-test code applies its tools to the diamond multiple-inheritance trees we saw earlier. It uses Python's pprint library module to display lists and dictionaries nicely —pprint.pprint is its basic call, and its pformat returns a print string. Run this on Python 2.7 to see both classic DFLR and new-style MRO search orders; on Python 3.3, the object derivation is unnecessary, and both tests give the same, new-style results. Importantly, attr1, whose value is labeled with "Py=>" and whose name appears in the results lists, is inherited from class A in classic search, but from class C in new-style search:

```
c:\code> py -2 mapattrs.py
Classic classes in 2.X, new-style in 3.X
Py=>1
INH
[<__main__.D instance at 0x000000000225A688>,
 <class __main__.D at 0x0000000002248828>,
 <class __main__.B at 0x0000000002248768>,
 <class __main__.A at 0x0000000002248708>,
 <class __main__.C at 0x00000000022487C8>,
 <class __main__.A at 0x0000000002248708>]

ATTRS
```

```
{'__doc__': <class __main__.D at 0x0000000002248828>,
 '__module__': <class __main__.D at 0x0000000002248828>,
 'attr1': <class __main__.A at 0x0000000002248708>,
 'attr2': <class __main__.B at 0x0000000002248768>}

OBJS
{<class __main__.A at 0x0000000002248708>: ['attr1'],
 <class __main__.B at 0x0000000002248768>: ['attr2'],
 <class __main__.D at 0x0000000002248828>: ['__doc__', '__module__']}

New-style classes in 2.X and 3.X
Py=>3
INH
(<__main__.D object at 0x0000000002257B38>,
 <class '__main__.D'>,
 <class '__main__.B'>,
 <class '__main__.C'>,
 <class '__main__.A'>,
 <type 'object'>)

ATTRS
{'__dict__': <class '__main__.A'>,
 '__doc__': <class '__main__.D'>,
 '__module__': <class '__main__.D'>,
 '__weakref__': <class '__main__.A'>,
 'attr1': <class '__main__.C'>,
 'attr2': <class '__main__.B'>}

OBJS
{<class '__main__.A'>: ['__dict__', '__weakref__'],
 <class '__main__.B'>: ['attr2'],
 <class '__main__.C'>: ['attr1'],
 <class '__main__.D'>: ['__doc__', '__module__']}
```

As a larger application of these tools, the following is our inheritance simulator at work in 3.3 on the preceding chapter's *testmixin0.py* file's test classes (I've deleted some built-in names here for space; as usual, run live for the whole list). Notice how __X pseudo-private names are mapped to their defining classes, and how ListInstance appears in the MRO *before* object, which has a __str__ that would otherwise be chosen first—as you'll recall, mixing this method in was the whole point of the lister classes!

```
c:\code> py -3
>>> from mapattrs import trace, dflr, inheritance, mapattrs
>>> from testmixin0 import Sub
>>> I = Sub()                          # Sub inherits from Super and ListInstance roots
>>> trace(dflr(I.__class__))           # 2.X search order: implied object before lister!
[<class 'testmixin0.Sub'>,
 <class 'testmixin0.Super'>,
 <class 'object'>,
 <class 'listinstance.ListInstance'>,
 <class 'object'>]

>>> trace(inheritance(I))              # 3.X (+ 2.X newstyle) search order: lister first
(<testmixin0.Sub object at 0x0000000002974630>,
 <class 'testmixin0.Sub'>,
```

```
  <class 'testmixin0.Super'>,
  <class 'listinstance.ListInstance'>,
  <class 'object'>)

>>> trace(mapattrs(I))
{'_ListInstance__attrnames': <class 'listinstance.ListInstance'>,
 '__init__': <class 'testmixin0.Sub'>,
 '__str__': <class 'listinstance.ListInstance'>,
 ...etc...
 'data1': <testmixin0.Sub object at 0x0000000002974630>,
 'data2': <testmixin0.Sub object at 0x0000000002974630>,
 'data3': <testmixin0.Sub object at 0x0000000002974630>,
 'ham': <class 'testmixin0.Super'>,
 'spam': <class 'testmixin0.Sub'>}

>>> trace(mapattrs(I, bysource=True))
{<testmixin0.Sub object at 0x0000000002974630>: ['data1', 'data2', 'data3'],
 <class 'listinstance.ListInstance'>: ['_ListInstance__attrnames', '__str__'],
 <class 'testmixin0.Super'>: ['__dict__', '__weakref__', 'ham'],
 <class 'testmixin0.Sub'>: ['__doc__',
                            '__init__',
                            '__module__',
                            '__qualname__',
                            'spam']}

>>> trace(mapattrs(I, withobject=True))
{'_ListInstance__attrnames': <class 'listinstance.ListInstance'>,
 '__class__': <class 'object'>,
 '__delattr__': <class 'object'>,
 ...etc...
```

Here's the bit you might run if you want to label class objects with names inherited by an instance, though you may want to filter out some built-in double-underscore names for the sake of users' eyesight!

```
>>> amap = mapattrs(I, withobject=True, bysource=True)
>>> trace(amap)
{<testmixin0.Sub object at 0x0000000002974630>: ['data1', 'data2', 'data3'],
 <class 'listinstance.ListInstance'>: ['_ListInstance__attrnames', '__str__'],
 <class 'testmixin0.Super'>: ['__dict__', '__weakref__', 'ham'],
 <class 'testmixin0.Sub'>: ['__doc__',
                            '__init__',
                            '__module__',
                            '__qualname__',
                            'spam'],
 <class 'object'>: ['__class__',
                    '__delattr__',
                    ...etc...
                    '__sizeof__',
                    '__subclasshook__']}
```

Finally, and as both a follow-up to the prior chapter's ruminations and segue to the next section here, the following shows how this scheme works for class-based *slots* attributes too. Because a class's __dict__ includes both normal class attributes and individual entries for the instance attributes defined by its __slots__ list, the slots at-

---

tributes inherited by an instance will be correctly associated with the implementing class from which they are acquired, even though they are not physically stored in the instance's __dict__ itself:

```
# mapattrs-slots.py: test __slots__ attribute inheritance
from mapattrs import mapattrs, trace

class A(object): __slots__ = ['a', 'b']; x = 1; y = 2
class B(A):      __slots__ = ['b', 'c']
class C(A):      x = 2
class D(B, C):
    z = 3
    def __init__(self): self.name = 'Bob';

I = D()
trace(mapattrs(I, bysource=True))     # Also: trace(mapattrs(I))
```

For explicitly new-style classes like those in this file, the results are the same under both 2.7 and 3.3, though 3.3 adds an extra built-in name to the set. The attribute names here reflect all those inherited by the instance from user-defined classes, even those implemented by slots defined at classes and stored in space allocated in the instance:

```
c:\code> py -3 mapattrs-slots.py
{<__main__.D object at 0x00000000028988E0>: ['name'],
 <class '__main__.C'>: ['x'],
 <class '__main__.D'>: ['__dict__',
                        '__doc__',
                        '__init__',
                        '__module__',
                        '__qualname__',
                        '__weakref__',
                        'z'],
 <class '__main__.A'>: ['a', 'y'],
 <class '__main__.B'>: ['__slots__', 'b', 'c']}
```

But we need to move ahead to understand the role of slots better—and understand why mapattrs must be careful to check to see if a __dict__ is present before fetching it!

Study this code for more insight. For the prior chapter's tree lister, your next step might be to index the mapattrs function's bysource=True dictionary result to obtain an object's attributes during the tree sketch traversal, instead of (or perhaps in addition to?) its current physical __dict__ scan. You'll probably need to use getattr on the instance to fetch attribute values, because some may be implemented as slots or other "virtual" attributes at their source classes, and fetching these at the class directly won't return the instance's value. If I code anymore here, though, I'll deprive readers of the remaining fun, and the next section of its subject matter.

Python's `pprint` module used in this example works as shown in Pythons 3.3 and 2.7, but appears to have an issue in Pythons 3.2 and 3.1 where it raises a wrong-number-arguments exception internally for the objects displayed here. Since I've already devoted too much space to covering transitory Python defects, and since this has been repaired in the versions of Python used in this edition, we'll leave working around this in the suggested exercises column for readers running this on the infected Pythons; change `trace` to simple prints as needed, and mind the note on *battery dependence* in Chapter 1!

New-Style Class Extensions

Beyond the changes described in the prior section (some of which, frankly, may seem too academic and obscure to matter to many readers of this book), new-style classes provide a handful of more advanced class tools that have more direct and practical application—*slots*, *properties*, *descriptors*, and more. The following sections provide an overview of each of these additional features, available for new-style class in Python 2.X and all classes in Python 3.X. Also in this extensions category are the `__mro__` attribute and the `super` call, both covered elsewhere—the former in the previous section to explore a change, and the latter postponed until chapter end to serve as a larger case study.

Slots: Attribute Declarations

By assigning a sequence of string attribute names to a special `__slots__` class attribute, we can enable a new-style class to both limit the set of legal attributes that instances of the class will have, and optimize memory usage and possibly program speed. As we'll find, though, slots should be used only in applications that clearly warrant the added complexity. They will complicate your code, may complicate or break code you may use, and require universal deployment to be effective.

Slot basics

To use slots, assign a sequence of string names to the special `__slots__` variable and attribute at the top level of a `class` statement: only those names in the `__slots__` list can be assigned as instance attributes. However, like all names in Python, instance attribute names must still be assigned before they can be referenced, even if they're listed in `__slots__`:

```
>>> class limiter(object):
        __slots__ = ['age', 'name', 'job']

>>> x = limiter()
>>> x.age                              # Must assign before use
AttributeError: age
```

```
>>> x.age = 40                              # Looks like instance data
>>> x.age
40
>>> x.ape = 1000                            # Illegal: not in __slots__
AttributeError: 'limiter' object has no attribute 'ape'
```

This feature is envisioned as both a way to catch typo errors like this (assignments to illegal attribute names not in __slots__ are detected) as well as an optimization mechanism.

Allocating a namespace dictionary for every instance object can be expensive in terms of memory if many instances are created and only a few attributes are required. To save space, instead of allocating a dictionary for each instance, Python reserves just enough space in each *instance* to hold a value for each slot attribute, along with inherited attributes in the common *class* to manage slot access. This might additionally speed execution, though this benefit is less clear and might vary per program, platform, and Python.

Slots are also something of a major break with Python's core dynamic nature, which dictates that any name may be created by assignment. In fact, they imitate C++ for efficiency at the expense of flexibility, and even have the potential to *break* some programs. As we'll see, slots also come with a plethora of special-case usage rules. Per Python's own manual, they should *not* be used except in clearly warranted cases—they are difficult to use correctly, and are, to quote the manual:

> best reserved for rare cases where there are large numbers of instances in a memory-critical application.

In other words, this is yet another feature that should be used only if clearly warranted. Unfortunately, slots seem to be showing up in Python code much more often than they should; their obscurity seems to be a draw in itself. As usual, knowledge is your best ally in such things, so let's take a quick look here.

 In Python 3.3, *non-slots* attribute space requirements have been reduced with a *key-sharing dictionary* model, where the __dict__ dictionaries used for objects' attributes may share part of their internal storage, including that of their keys. This may lessen some of the value of __slots__ as an optimization tool; per benchmark reports, this change reduces memory use by 10% to 20% for object-oriented programs, gives a small improvement in speed for programs that create many similar objects, and may be optimized further in the future. On the other hand, this won't negate the presence of __slots__ in existing code you may need to understand!

Slots and namespace dictionaries

Potential benefits aside, slots can complicate the class model—and code that relies on it—substantially. In fact, some instances with slots may not have a __dict__ attribute namespace dictionary at all, and others will have data attributes that this dictionary does not include. To be clear: this is a *major incompatibility* with the traditional class model—one that can complicate any code that accesses attributes generically, and may even cause some programs to fail altogether.

For instance, programs that list or access instance attributes by name string may need to use more storage-neutral interfaces than __dict__ if slots may be used. Because an instance's data may include class-level names such as slots—either in addition to or instead of namespace dictionary storage—both attribute sources may need to be queried for completeness.

Let's see what this means in terms of code, and explore more about slots along the way. First off, when slots are used, instances do not normally have an attribute dictionary —instead, Python uses the class *descriptors* feature introduced ahead to allocate and manage space reserved for slot attributes in the instance. In Python 3.X, and in 2.X for new-style classes derived from object:

```
>>> class C:                          # Requires "(object)" in 2.X only
        __slots__ = ['a', 'b']        # __slots__ means no __dict__ by default

>>> X = C()
>>> X.a = 1
>>> X.a
1
>>> X.__dict__
AttributeError: 'C' object has no attribute '__dict__'
```

However, we can still fetch and set slot-based attributes by name string using storage-neutral tools such as getattr and setattr (which look beyond the instance __dict__ and thus include class-level names like slots) and dir (which collects all inherited names throughout a class tree):

```
>>> getattr(X, 'a')
1
>>> setattr(X, 'b', 2)                # But getattr() and setattr() still work
>>> X.b
2
>>> 'a' in dir(X)                      # And dir() finds slot attributes too
True
>>> 'b' in dir(X)
True
```

Also keep in mind that without an attribute namespace dictionary, it's not possible to assign new names to instances that are not names in the slots list:

```
>>> class D:                          # Use D(object) for same result in 2.X
        __slots__ = ['a', 'b']
        def __init__(self):
            self.d = 4                # Cannot add new names if no __dict__

>>> X = D()
AttributeError: 'D' object has no attribute 'd'
```

We can still accommodate extra attributes, though, by including _dict_ explicitly in _slots_, in order to create an attribute namespace dictionary too:

```
>>> class D:
        __slots__ = ['a', 'b', '__dict__']   # Name __dict__ to include one too
        c = 3                                 # Class attrs work normally
        def __init__(self):
            self.d = 4                        # d stored in __dict__, a is a slot

>>> X = D()
>>> X.d
4
>>> X.c
3
>>> X.a                            # All instance attrs undefined until assigned
AttributeError: a
>>> X.a = 1
>>> X.b = 2
```

In this case, *both* storage mechanisms are used. This renders _dict_ too limited for code that wishes to treat slots as instance data, but generic tools such as getattr still allow us to process both storage forms as a single set of attributes:

```
>>> X.__dict__                  # Some objects have both __dict__ and slot names
{'d': 4}                        # getattr() can fetch either type of attr
>>> X.__slots__
['a', 'b', '__dict__']
>>> getattr(X, 'a'), getattr(X, 'c'), getattr(X, 'd')    # Fetches all 3 forms
(1, 3, 4)
```

Because dir also returns all *inherited* attributes, though, it might be too broad in some contexts; it also includes class-level methods, and even all object defaults. Code that wishes to list *just* instance attributes may in principle still need to allow for both storage forms explicitly. We might at first naively code this as follows:

```
>>> for attr in list(X.__dict__) + X.__slots__:      # Wrong...
        print(attr, '=>', getattr(X, attr))
```

Since either can be omitted, we may more correctly code this as follows, using get attr to allow for defaults—a noble but nonetheless inaccurate approach, as the next section will explain:

```
>>> for attr in list(getattr(X, '__dict__', [])) + getattr(X, '__slots__', []):
        print(attr, '=>', getattr(X, attr))

d => 4
a => 1                                              # Less wrong...
b => 2
__dict__  => {'d': 4}
```

Multiple __slot__ lists in superclasses

The preceding code works in this specific case, but in general it's *not entirely accurate*. Specifically, this code addresses only slot names in the *lowest* _slots_ attribute inherited by an instance, but slot lists may appear more than once in a class tree. That is, a name's absence in the lowest __slots__ list does not preclude its existence in a higher __slots__. Because slot names become class-level attributes, instances acquire the union of all slot names anywhere in the tree, by the normal inheritance rule:

```
>>> class E:
        __slots__ = ['c', 'd']          # Superclass has slots
>>> class D(E):
        __slots__ = ['a', '__dict__']   # But so does its subclass

>>> X = D()
>>> X.a = 1; X.b = 2; X.c = 3           # The instance is the union (slots: a, c)
>>> X.a, X.c
(1, 3)
```

Inspecting just the inherited slots list won't pick up slots defined higher in a class tree:

```
>>> E.__slots__                         # But slots are not concatenated
['c', 'd']
>>> D.__slots__
['a', '__dict__']
>>> X.__slots__                         # Instance inherits "lowest" __slots__
['a', '__dict__']
>>> X.__dict__                          # And has its own an attr dict
{'b': 2}

>>> for attr in list(getattr(X, '__dict__', [])) + getattr(X, '__slots__', []):
        print(attr, '=>', getattr(X, attr))

b => 2                                  # Other superclass slots missed!
a => 1
__dict__ => {'b': 2}

>>> dir(X)                              # But dir() includes all slot names
[...many names omitted... 'a', 'b', 'c', 'd']
```

In other words, in terms of listing instance attributes generically, one __slots__ isn't always enough—they are potentially subject to the full inheritance search procedure. See the earlier *mapattrs-slots.py* for another example of slots appearing in multiple superclasses. If multiple classes in a class tree have their own __slots__ attributes, generic programs must develop other policies for listing attributes—as the next section explains.

Handling slots and other "virtual" attributes generically

At this point, you may wish to review the discussion of slots policy options at the coverage of the *lister.py* display mix-in classes near the end of the preceding chapter— a prime example of why generic programs may need to care about slots. Such tools that attempt to list instance data attributes generically must account for slots, and perhaps other such "virtual" instance attributes like *properties* and *descriptors* discussed ahead —names that similarly reside in classes but may provide attribute values for instances on request. Slots are the most data-centric of these, but are representative of a larger category.

Such attributes require inclusive approaches, special handling, or general avoidance—the latter of which becomes unsatisfactory as soon as any programmer uses slots in subject code. Really, class-level instance attributes like slots probably necessitate a re-definition of the term *instance data*—as locally stored attributes, the union of all inherited attributes, or some subset thereof.

For example, some programs might classify slot names as attributes of *classes* instead of instances; these attributes do not exist in instance namespace dictionaries, after all. Alternatively, as shown earlier, programs can be more inclusive by relying on `dir` to fetch all inherited attribute names and `getattr` to fetch their corresponding values for the instance—without regard to their physical location or implementation. If you must support slots as instance data, this is likely the most robust way to proceed:

```
>>> class Slotful:
        __slots__ = ['a', 'b', '__dict__']
        def __init__(self, data):
            self.c = data

>>> I = Slotful(3)
>>> I.a, I.b = 1, 2
>>> I.a, I.b, I.c                              # Normal attribute fetch
(1, 2, 3)

>>> I.__dict__                                 # Both __dict__ and slots storage
{'c': 3}
>>> [x for x in dir(I) if not x.startswith('__')]
['a', 'b', 'c']

>>> I.__dict__['c']                            # __dict__ is only one attr source
3
>>> getattr(I, 'c'), getattr(I, 'a')           # dir+getattr is broader than __dict__
(3, 1)                                         # applies to slots, properties, descrip

>>> for a in (x for x in dir(I) if not x.startswith('__')):
        print(a, getattr(I, a))

a 1
b 2
c 3
```

Under this `dir`/`getattr` model, you can still map attributes to their inheritance sources, and filter them more selectively by source or type if needed, by scanning the *MRO*—as we did earlier in both *mapattrs.py* and its application to slots in *mapattrs-slots.py*. As an added bonus, such tools and policies for handling slots will potentially apply automatically to *properties* and *descriptors* too, though these attributes are more explicitly computed values, and less obviously instance-related data than slots.

Also keep in mind that this is not just a tools issue. Class-based instance attributes like slots also impact the traditional coding of the `__setattr__` operator overloading method we met in Chapter 30. Because slots and some other attributes are not stored in the instance `__dict__`, and may even imply its *absence*, new-style classes must instead generally run attribute assignments by routing them to the `object` superclass. In practice, this may make this method fundamentally different in some classic and new-style classes.

Slot usage rules

Slot declarations can appear in multiple classes in a class tree, but when they do they are subject to a number of constraints that are somewhat difficult to rationalize unless you understand the implementation of slots as class-level *descriptors* for each slot name that are inherited by the instances where the managed space is reserved (descriptors are an advanced tool we'll study in detail in the last part of this book):

- *Slots in subs are pointless when absent in supers*: If a subclass inherits from a superclass without a `__slots__`, the instance `__dict__` attribute created for the superclass will always be accessible, making a `__slots__` in the subclass largely pointless. The subclass still manages its slots, but doesn't compute their values in any way, and doesn't avoid a dictionary—the main reason to use slots.

- *Slots in supers are pointless when absent in subs*: Similarly, because the meaning of a `__slots__` declaration is limited to the class in which it appears, subclasses will produce an instance `__dict__` if they do not define a `__slots__`, rendering a `__slots__` in a superclass largely pointless.

- *Redefinition renders super slots pointless*: If a class defines the same slot name as a superclass, its redefinition hides the slot in the superclass per normal inheritance. You can access the version of the name defined by the superclass slot only by fetching its descriptor directly from the superclass.

- *Slots prevent class-level defaults*: Because slots are implemented as class-level descriptors (along with per-instance space), you cannot use class attributes of the same name to provide defaults as you can for normal instance attributes: assigning the same name in the class overwrites the slot descriptor.

- *Slots and `__dict__`*: As shown earlier, `__slots__` preclude both an instance `__dict__` and assigning names not listed, unless `__dict__` is listed explicitly too.

We've already seen the last of these in action, and the earlier *mapattrs-slots.py* illustrates the third. It's easy to demonstrate how the new rules here translate to actual code—most crucially, a namespace dictionary is created when any class in a tree omits slots, thereby negating the memory optimization benefit:

```
>>> class C: pass                          # Bullet 1: slots in sub but not super
>>> class D(C): __slots__ = ['a']          # Makes instance dict for nonslots
>>> X = D()                                 # But slot name still managed in class
>>> X.a = 1; X.b = 2
>>> X.__dict__
{'b': 2}
>>> D.__dict__.keys()
```

```
dict_keys([... 'a', '__slots__', ...])

>>> class C: __slots__ = ['a']          # Bullet 2: slots in super but not sub
>>> class D(C): pass                     # Makes instance dict for nonslots
>>> X = D()                              # But slot name still managed in class
>>> X.a = 1; X.b = 2
>>> X.__dict__
{'b': 2}
>>> C.__dict__.keys()
dict_keys([... 'a', '__slots__', ...])

>>> class C: __slots__ = ['a']          # Bullet 3: only lowest slot accessible
>>> class D(C): __slots__ = ['a']

>>> class C: __slots__ = ['a']; a = 99  # Bullet 4: no class-level defaults
ValueError: 'a' in __slots__ conflicts with class variable
```

In other words, besides their program-breaking potential, slots essentially require *both universal and careful deployment* to be effective—because slots do not compute values dynamically like properties (coming up in the next section), they are largely pointless unless each class in a tree uses them and is cautious to define only new slot names not defined by other classes. It's an *all-or-nothing* feature—an unfortunate property shared by the super call discussed ahead:

```
>>> class C: __slots__ = ['a']          # Assumes universal use, differing names
>>> class D(C): __slots__ = ['b']
>>> X = D()
>>> X.a = 1; X.b = 2
>>> X.__dict__
AttributeError: 'D' object has no attribute '__dict__'
>>> C.__dict__.keys(), D.__dict__.keys()
(dict_keys([... 'a', '__slots__', ...]), dict_keys([... 'b', '__slots__', ...]))
```

Such rules—among others regarding *weak references* omitted here for space—are part of the reason slots are not generally recommended, except in pathological cases where their space reduction is significant. Even then, their potential to complicate or break code should be ample cause to carefully consider the tradeoffs. Not only must they be spread almost *neurotically* throughout a framework, they may also break tools you rely on.

Example impacts of slots: ListTree and mapattrs

As a more realistic example of slots' effects, due to the first bullet in the prior section, Chapter 31's ListTree class does *not fail* when mixed in to a class that defines __slots__, even though it scans instance namespace dictionaries. The lister class's own lack of slots is enough to ensure that the instance will still have a __dict__, and hence not trigger an exception when fetched or indexed. For example, both of the following display without error—the second also allows names not in the slots list to be assigned as instances attributes, including any required by the superclass:

```
class C(ListTree): pass
X = C()                                  # OK: no __slots__ used
```

```
    print(X)

    class C(ListTree): __slots__ = ['a', 'b']       # OK: superclass produces __dict__
    X = C()
    X.c = 3
    print(X)                                         # Displays c at X, a and b at C
```

The following classes display correctly as well—*any* nonslot class like `ListTree` generates an instance `__dict__`, and can thus safely assume its presence:

```
    class A: __slots__ = ['a']                       # Both OK by bullet 1 above
    class B(A, ListTree): pass

    class A: __slots__ = ['a']
    class B(A, ListTree): __slots__ = ['b']          # Displays b at B, a at A
```

Although it renders subclass slots pointless, this is a positive side effect for tools classes
like `ListTree` (and its Chapter 28 predecessor). In general, though, some tools might
need to catch exceptions when `__dict__` is absent or use a `hasattr` or `getattr` to test or
provide defaults if slot usage may preclude a namespace dictionary in instance objects
inspected.

For example, you should now be able to understand why the *mapattrs.py* program
earlier in this chapter must check for the presence of a `__dict__` before fetching it—
instance objects created from classes with `__slots__` won't have one. In fact, if we use
the highlighted alternative line in the following, the `mapattrs` function fails with an
exception when attempting to look for an attribute name in the instance at the front of
the inheritance path sequence:

```
    def mapattrs(instance, withobject=False, bysource=False):
        for attr in dir(instance):
            for obj in inherits:
                if attr in obj.__dict__:             # May fail if __slots__ used

    >>> class C: __slots__ = ['a']
    >>> X = C()
    >>> mapattrs(X)
    AttributeError: 'C' object has no attribute '__dict__'
```

Either of the following works around the issue, and allows the tool to support slots—
the first provides a default, and the second is more verbose but seems marginally more
explicit in its intent:

```
                    if attr in getattr(obj, '__dict__', {}):

                    if hasattr(obj, '__dict__') and attr in obj.__dict__:
```

As mentioned earlier, some tools may benefit from mapping `dir` results to objects in
the MRO this way, instead of scanning an instance `__dict__` in general—without this
more inclusive approach, attributes implemented by class-level tools like slots won't
be reported as instance data. Even so, this doesn't necessarily excuse such tools from
allowing for a missing `__dict__` in the instance too!

What about slots speed?

Finally, while slots primarily optimize memory use, their speed impact is less clear-cut. Here's a simple test script using the `timeit` techniques we studied in Chapter 21. For both the slots and nonslots (instance dictionary) storage models, it makes 1,000 instances, assigns and fetches 4 attributes on each, and repeats 1,000 times—for both models taking the best of 3 runs that each exercise a total of 8M attribute operations:

```python
# File slots-test.py
from __future__ import print_function
import timeit
base = """
Is = []
for i in range(1000):
    X = C()
    X.a = 1; X.b = 2; X.c = 3; X.d = 4
    t = X.a + X.b + X.c + X.d
    Is.append(X)
"""

stmt = """
class C:
    __slots__ = ['a', 'b', 'c', 'd']
""" + base
print('Slots    =>', end=' ')
print(min(timeit.repeat(stmt, number=1000, repeat=3)))

stmt = """
class C:
    pass
""" + base
print('Nonslots=>', end=' ')
print(min(timeit.repeat(stmt, number=1000, repeat=3)))
```

At least on this code, on my laptop, and in my installed versions (Python 3.3 and 2.7), the best times imply that slots are slightly quicker in 3.X and a wash in 2.X, though this says little about memory space, and is prone to change arbitrarily in the future:

```
c:\code> py -3 slots-test.py
Slots    => 0.7780903942045899
Nonslots=> 0.9888108080898417

c:\code> py -2 slots-test.py
Slots    => 0.80868754371
Nonslots=> 0.802224740747
```

For more on slots in general, see the Python standard manual set. Also watch for the `Private` decorator case study of Chapter 39—an example that naturally allows for attributes based on both `__slots__` and `__dict__` storage, by using delegation and storage-neutral accessor tools like `getattr`.

Properties: Attribute Accessors

Our next new-style extension is *properties*—a mechanism that provides another way for new-style classes to define methods called automatically for access or assignment to instance attributes. This feature is similar to properties (a.k.a. "getters" and "setters") in languages like Java and C#, but in Python is generally best used sparingly, as a way to add accessors to attributes *after the fact* as needs evolve and warrant. Where needed, though, properties allow attribute values to be computed dynamically without requiring method calls at the point of access.

Though properties cannot support generic attribute routing goals, at least for specific attributes they are an alternative to some traditional uses of the __getattr__ and __setattr__ overloading methods we first studied in Chapter 30. Properties have a similar effect to these two methods, but by contrast incur an extra method call only for accesses to names that require dynamic computation—other nonproperty names are accessed normally with no extra calls. Although __getattr__ is invoked only for *undefined* names, the __setattr__ method is instead called for assignment to *every* attribute.

Properties and slots are related too, but serve different goals. Both implement instance attributes that are not physically stored in instance namespace dictionaries—a sort of "virtual" attribute—and both are based on the notion of class-level attribute *descriptors*. In contrast, slots manage instance storage, while properties intercept access and compute values arbitrarily. Because their underlying descriptor implementation tool is too advanced for us to cover here, properties and descriptors both get full treatment in Chapter 38.

Property basics

As a brief introduction, though, a property is a type of object assigned to a class attribute name. You generate a property by calling the property built-in function, passing in up to three accessor methods—handlers for get, set, and delete operations—as well as an optional docstring for the property. If any argument is passed as None or omitted, that operation is not supported.

The resulting property object is typically assigned to a name at the top level of a class statement (e.g., *name*=property()), and a special @ syntax we'll meet later is available to automate this step. When thus assigned, later accesses to the class property name itself as an object attribute (e.g., obj.*name*) are automatically routed to one of the accessor methods passed into the property call.

For example, we've seen how the __getattr__ operator overloading method allows classes to intercept undefined attribute references in both classic and new-style classes:

```
>>> class operators:
        def __getattr__(self, name):
            if name == 'age':
                return 40
            else:
```

```
                raise AttributeError(name)
>>> x = operators()
>>> x.age                                            # Runs __getattr__
40
>>> x.name                                           # Runs __getattr__
AttributeError: name
```

Here is the same example, coded with properties instead; note that properties are available for all classes but require the new-style `object` derivation in 2.X to work properly for intercepting attribute *assignments* (and won't complain if you forget this—but will silently overwrite your property with the new data!):

```
>>> class properties(object):                        # Need object in 2.X for setters
        def getage(self):
            return 40
        age = property(getage, None, None, None)     # (get, set, del, docs), or use @

>>> x = properties()
>>> x.age                                            # Runs getage
40
>>> x.name                                           # Normal fetch
AttributeError: 'properties' object has no attribute 'name'
```

For some coding tasks, properties can be less complex and quicker to run than the traditional techniques. For example, when we add attribute *assignment* support, properties become more attractive—there's less code to type, and no extra method calls are incurred for assignments to attributes we don't wish to compute dynamically:

```
>>> class properties(object):                        # Need object in 2.X for setters
        def getage(self):
            return 40
        def setage(self, value):
            print('set age: %s' % value)
            self._age = value
        age = property(getage, setage, None, None)

>>> x = properties()
>>> x.age                                            # Runs getage
40
>>> x.age = 42                                       # Runs setage
set age: 42
>>> x._age                                           # Normal fetch: no getage call
42
>>> x.age                                            # Runs getage
40
>>> x.job = 'trainer'                                # Normal assign: no setage call
>>> x.job                                            # Normal fetch: no getage call
'trainer'
```

The equivalent class based on operator overloading incurs extra method calls for assignments to attributes not being managed and needs to route attribute assignments through the attribute dictionary to avoid loops (or, for new-style classes, to the object superclass's __setattr__ to better support "virtual" attributes such as slots and properties coded in other classes):

```
>>> class operators:
        def __getattr__(self, name):              # On undefined reference
            if name == 'age':
                return 40
            else:
                raise AttributeError(name)
        def __setattr__(self, name, value):        # On all assignments
            print('set: %s %s' % (name, value))
            if name == 'age':
                self.__dict__['_age'] = value       # Or object.__setattr__()
            else:
                self.__dict__[name] = value

>>> x = operators()
>>> x.age                                          # Runs __getattr__
40
>>> x.age = 41                                     # Runs __setattr__
set: age 41
>>> x._age                                         # Defined: no __getattr__ call
41
>>> x.age                                          # Runs __getattr__
40
>>> x.job = 'trainer'                              # Runs __setattr__ again
set: job trainer
>>> x.job                                          # Defined: no __getattr__ call
'trainer'
```

Properties seem like a win for this simple example. However, some applications of __getattr__ and __setattr__ still require more dynamic or generic interfaces than properties directly provide.

For example, in many cases the set of attributes to be supported cannot be determined when the class is coded, and may not even exist in any tangible form (e.g., when *delegating* arbitrary attribute references to a wrapped/embedded object generically). In such contexts, a generic __getattr__ or a __setattr__ attribute handler with a passed-in attribute name is usually preferable. Because such generic handlers can also support simpler cases, properties are often an optional and redundant extension—albeit one that may avoid extra calls on assignments, and one that some programmers may prefer when applicable.

For more details on both options, stay tuned for Chapter 38 in the final part of this book. As we'll see there, it's also possible to code properties using the @ symbol *function decorator syntax*—a topic introduced later in this chapter, and an equivalent and automatic alternative to manual assignment in the class scope:

```
class properties(object):
    @property                                       # Coding properties with decorators: ahead
    def age(self):
        ...
    @age.setter
```

```
    def age(self, value):
        ...
```

To make sense of this decorator syntax, though, we must move ahead.

__getattribute__ and Descriptors: Attribute Tools

Also in the class extensions department, the __getattribute__ operator overloading method, available for new-style classes only, allows a class to intercept *all* attribute references, not just undefined references. This makes it more potent than its __get attr__ cousin we used in the prior section, but also trickier to use—it's prone to loops much like __setattr__, but in different ways.

For more specialized attribute interception goals, in addition to properties and operator overloading methods, Python supports the notion of attribute *descriptors*—classes with __get__ and __set__ methods, assigned to class attributes and inherited by instances, that intercept read and write accesses to specific attributes. As a preview, here's one of the simplest descriptors you're likely to encounter:

```
>>> class AgeDesc(object):
        def __get__(self, instance, owner): return 40
        def __set__(self, instance, value): instance._age = value

>>> class descriptors(object):
        age = AgeDesc()

>>> x = descriptors()
>>> x.age                            # Runs AgeDesc.__get__
40
>>> x.age = 42                       # Runs AgeDesc.__set__
>>> x._age                           # Normal fetch: no AgeDesc call
42
```

Descriptors have access to state in instances of themselves as well as their client class, and are in a sense a more general form of properties; in fact, properties are a simplified way to define a specific type of descriptor—one that runs functions on access. Descriptors are also used to implement the slots feature we met earlier, and other Python tools.

Because __getattribute__ and descriptors are too substantial to cover well here, we'll defer the rest of their coverage, as well as much more on properties, to Chapter 38 in the final part of this book. We'll also employ them in examples in Chapter 39 and study how they factor into inheritance in Chapter 40.

Other Class Changes and Extensions

As mentioned, we're also postponing coverage of the super built-in—an additional major new-style class extension that relies on its MRO—until the end of this chapter. Before we get there, though, we're going to explore additional class-related changes and extensions that are not necessarily bound to new-style classes, but were introduced at roughly the same time: static and class methods, decorators, and more.

Many of the changes and feature additions of new-style classes integrate with the notion of subclassable types mentioned earlier in this chapter, because subclassable types and new-style classes were introduced in conjunction with a merging of the type/class dichotomy in Python 2.2 and beyond. As we've seen, in 3.X, this merging is complete: classes are now types, and types are classes, and Python classes today still reflect both that conceptual merging and its implementation.

Along with these changes, Python also grew a more coherent and generalized protocol for coding *metaclasses*—classes that subclass the **type** object, intercept class creation calls, and may provide behavior acquired by classes. Accordingly, they provide a well-defined hook for management and augmentation of class objects. They are also an advanced topic that is optional for most Python programmers, so we'll postpone further details here. We'll glimpse metaclasses again later in this chapter in conjunction with class decorators—a feature whose roles often overlap—but we'll postpone their full coverage until Chapter 40, in the final part of this book. For our purpose here, let's move on to a handful of additional class-related extensions.

Static and Class Methods

As of Python 2.2, it is possible to define two kinds of methods within a class that can be called without an instance: *static* methods work roughly like simple instance-less functions inside a class, and *class* methods are passed a class instead of an instance. Both are similar to tools in other languages (e.g., C++ static methods). Although this feature was added in conjunction with the new-style classes discussed in the prior sections, static and class methods work for classic classes too.

To enable these method modes, you must call special built-in functions named `staticmethod` and `classmethod` within the class, or invoke them with the special @*name* decoration syntax we'll meet later in this chapter. These functions are required to enable these special method modes in Python 2.X, and are generally needed in 3.X. In Python 3.X, a `staticmethod` declaration is not required for instance-less methods called only through a class name, but is still required if such methods are called through instances.

Why the Special Methods?

As we've learned, a class's method is normally passed an instance object in its first argument, to serve as the implied subject of the method call—that's the "object" in "object-oriented programming." Today, though, there are two ways to modify this model. Before I explain what they are, I should explain why this might matter to you.

Sometimes, programs need to process data associated with classes instead of instances. Consider keeping track of the number of instances created from a class, or maintaining a list of all of a class's instances that are currently in memory. This type of information and its processing are associated with the class rather than its instances. That is, the information is usually stored on the class itself and processed apart from any instance.

For such tasks, simple functions coded outside a class can often suffice—because they can access class attributes through the class name, they have access to class data and never require access to an instance. However, to better associate such code with a class, and to allow such processing to be customized with inheritance as usual, it would be better to code these types of functions *inside* the class itself. To make this work, we need methods in a class that are not passed, and do not expect, a self instance argument.

Python supports such goals with the notion of *static methods*—simple functions with no self argument that are nested in a class and are designed to work on class attributes instead of instance attributes. Static methods never receive an automatic self argument, whether called through a class or an instance. They usually keep track of information that spans all instances, rather than providing behavior for instances.

Although less commonly used, Python also supports the notion of *class methods*—methods of a class that are passed a class object in their first argument instead of an instance, regardless of whether they are called through an instance or a class. Such methods can access class data through their class argument—what we've called self thus far—even if called through an instance. Normal methods, now known in formal circles as *instance methods*, still receive a subject instance when called; static and class methods do not.

Static Methods in 2.X and 3.X

The concept of static methods is the same in both Python 2.X and 3.X, but its implementation requirements have evolved somewhat in Python 3.X. Since this book covers both versions, I need to explain the differences in the two underlying models before we get to the code.

Really, we already began this story in the preceding chapter, when we explored the notion of unbound methods. Recall that both Python 2.X and 3.X always pass an instance to a method that is called through an instance. However, Python 3.X treats methods fetched directly from a class differently than 2.X—a difference in Python lines that has nothing to do with new-style classes:

- Both Python 2.X and 3.X produce a *bound method* when a method is fetched through an instance.
- In Python 2.X, fetching a method from a class produces an *unbound method*, which cannot be called without manually passing an instance.
- In Python 3.X, fetching a method from a class produces a *simple function*, which can be called normally with no instance present.

In other words, Python 2.X class methods always require an instance to be passed in, whether they are called through an instance or a class. By contrast, in Python 3.X we are required to pass an instance to a method only if the method expects one—methods that do not include an instance argument can be called through the class without passing an instance. That is, 3.X allows simple functions in a class, as long as they do not expect and are not passed an instance argument. The net effect is that:

- In Python 2.X, we must always declare a method as static in order to call it without an instance, whether it is called through a class or an instance.
- In Python 3.X, we need not declare such methods as static if they will be called through a class only, but we must do so in order to call them through an instance.

To illustrate, suppose we want to use class attributes to count how many instances are generated from a class. The following file, *spam.py*, makes a first attempt—its class has a counter stored as a class attribute, a constructor that bumps up the counter by one each time a new instance is created, and a method that displays the counter's value. Remember, class attributes are shared by all instances. Therefore, storing the counter in the class object itself ensures that it effectively spans all instances:

```
class Spam:
    numInstances = 0
    def __init__(self):
        Spam.numInstances = Spam.numInstances + 1
    def printNumInstances():
        print("Number of instances created: %s" % Spam.numInstances)
```

The `printNumInstances` method is designed to process class data, not instance data—it's about *all* the instances, not any one in particular. Because of that, we want to be able to call it without having to pass an instance. Indeed, we don't want to make an instance to fetch the number of instances, because this would change the number of instances we're trying to fetch! In other words, we want a `self`-less "static" method.

Whether this code's `printNumInstances` works or not, though, depends on which Python you use, and which way you call the method—through the class or through an instance. In 2.X, calls to a `self`-less method function through both the class and instances fail (as usual, I've omitted some error text here for space):

```
C:\code> c:\python27\python
>>> from spam import Spam
>>> a = Spam()                    # Cannot call unbound class methods in 2.X
>>> b = Spam()                    # Methods expect a self object by default
>>> c = Spam()

>>> Spam.printNumInstances()
TypeError: unbound method printNumInstances() must be called with Spam instance
as first argument (got nothing instead)
>>> a.printNumInstances()
TypeError: printNumInstances() takes no arguments (1 given)
```

The problem here is that unbound instance methods aren't exactly the same as simple functions in 2.X. Even though there are no arguments in the `def` header, the method still expects an instance to be passed in when it's called, because the function is associated with a class. In Python 3.X, calls to self-less methods made through classes work, but calls from instances fail:

```
C:\code> c:\python33\python
>>> from spam import Spam
>>> a = Spam()                          # Can call functions in class in 3.X
>>> b = Spam()                          # Calls through instances still pass a self
>>> c = Spam()

>>> Spam.printNumInstances()            # Differs in 3.X
Number of instances created: 3
>>> a.printNumInstances()
TypeError: printNumInstances() takes 0 positional arguments but 1 was given
```

That is, calls to instance-less methods like printNumInstances made through the *class* fail in Python 2.X but work in Python 3.X. On the other hand, calls made through an *instance* fail in both Pythons, because an instance is automatically passed to a method that does not have an argument to receive it:

```
Spam.printNumInstances()                # Fails in 2.X, works in 3.X
instance.printNumInstances()            # Fails in both 2.X and 3.X (unless static)
```

If you're able to use 3.X and stick with calling self-less methods through classes only, you already have a static method feature. However, to allow self-less methods to be called through classes in 2.X and through instances in both 2.X and 3.X, you need to either adopt other designs or be able to somehow mark such methods as special. Let's look at both options in turn.

Static Method Alternatives

Short of marking a self-less method as special, you can sometimes achieve similar results with different coding structures. For example, if you just want to call functions that access class members without an instance, perhaps the simplest idea is to use normal functions outside the class, not class methods. This way, an instance isn't expected in the call. The following mutation of *spam.py* illustrates, and works the same in Python 3.X and 2.X:

```
def printNumInstances():
    print("Number of instances created: %s" % Spam.numInstances)

class Spam:
    numInstances = 0
    def __init__(self):
        Spam.numInstances = Spam.numInstances + 1

C:\code> c:\python33\python
>>> import spam
>>> a = spam.Spam()
>>> b = spam.Spam()
>>> c = spam.Spam()
>>> spam.printNumInstances()            # But function may be too far removed
```

```
Number of instances created: 3          # And cannot be changed via inheritance
>>> spam.Spam.numInstances
3
```

Because the class name is accessible to the simple function as a global variable, this works fine. Also, note that the name of the function becomes global, but only to this single module; it will not clash with names in other files of the program.

Prior to static methods in Python, this structure was the general prescription. Because Python already provides modules as a namespace-partitioning tool, one could argue that there's not typically any need to package functions in classes unless they implement object behavior. Simple functions within modules like the one here do much of what instance-less class methods could, and are already associated with the class because they live in the same module.

Unfortunately, this approach is still less than ideal. For one thing, it adds to this file's scope an extra name that is used only for processing a single class. For another, the function is much less directly associated with the class by structure; in fact, its definition could be hundreds of lines away. Perhaps worse, simple functions like this cannot be customized by inheritance, since they live outside a class's namespace: subclasses cannot directly replace or extend such a function by redefining it.

We might try to make this example work in a version-neutral way by using a normal method and always calling it through (or with) an instance, as usual:

```
class Spam:
    numInstances = 0
    def __init__(self):
        Spam.numInstances = Spam.numInstances + 1
    def printNumInstances(self):
        print("Number of instances created: %s" % Spam.numInstances)

C:\code> c:\python33\python
>>> from spam import Spam
>>> a, b, c = Spam(), Spam(), Spam()
>>> a.printNumInstances()
Number of instances created: 3
>>> Spam.printNumInstances(a)
Number of instances created: 3
>>> Spam().printNumInstances()          # But fetching counter changes counter!
Number of instances created: 4
```

Unfortunately, as mentioned earlier, such an approach is completely unworkable if we don't have an instance available, and making an instance changes the class data, as illustrated in the last line here. A better solution would be to somehow mark a method inside a class as never requiring an instance. The next section shows how.

Using Static and Class Methods

Today, there is another option for coding simple functions associated with a class that may be called through either the class or its instances. As of Python 2.2, we can code classes with static and class methods, neither of which requires an instance argument to be passed in when invoked. To designate such methods, classes call the built-in functions `staticmethod` and `classmethod`, as hinted in the earlier discussion of new-style classes. Both mark a function object as special—that is, as requiring no instance if static and requiring a class argument if a class method. For example, in the file *bothmethods.py* (which unifies 2.X and 3.X printing with lists, though displays still vary slightly for 2.X classic classes):

```
# File bothmethods.py

class Methods:
    def imeth(self, x):          # Normal instance method: passed a self
        print([self, x])

    def smeth(x):                # Static: no instance passed
        print([x])

    def cmeth(cls, x):           # Class: gets class, not instance
        print([cls, x])

    smeth = staticmethod(smeth)  # Make smeth a static method (or @: ahead)
    cmeth = classmethod(cmeth)   # Make cmeth a class method (or @: ahead)
```

Notice how the last two assignments in this code simply *reassign* (a.k.a. rebind) the method names `smeth` and `cmeth`. Attributes are created and changed by any assignment in a `class` statement, so these final assignments simply overwrite the assignments made earlier by the `def`s. As we'll see in a few moments, the special @ syntax works here as an alternative to this just as it does for properties—but makes little sense unless you first understand the assignment form here that it automates.

Technically, Python now supports three kinds of class-related methods, with differing argument protocols:

- *Instance methods*, passed a `self` instance object (the default)
- *Static methods*, passed no extra object (via `staticmethod`)
- *Class methods*, passed a class object (via `classmethod`, and inherent in metaclasses)

Moreover, Python 3.X extends this model by also allowing simple functions in a class to serve the role of static methods without extra protocol, when called through a class object only. Despite its name, the *bothmethods.py* module illustrates all three method types, so let's expand on these in turn.

Instance methods are the normal and default case that we've seen in this book. An instance method must always be called with an instance object. When you call it through an *instance*, Python passes the instance to the first (leftmost) argument automatically; when you call it through a *class*, you must pass along the instance manually:

```
>>> from bothmethods import Methods    # Normal instance methods
>>> obj = Methods()                     # Callable through instance or class
>>> obj.imeth(1)
[<bothmethods.Methods object at 0x0000000002A15710>, 1]
```

```
>>> Methods.imeth(obj, 2)
[<bothmethods.Methods object at 0x0000000002A15710>, 2]
```

Static methods, by contrast, are called without an instance argument. Unlike simple functions outside a class, their names are local to the scopes of the classes in which they are defined, and they may be looked up by inheritance. Instance-less functions can be called through a class normally in Python 3.X, but never by default in 2.X. Using the `staticmethod` built-in allows such methods to also be called through an instance in 3.X and through both a class and an instance in Python 2.X (that is, the first of the following works in 3.X without `staticmethod`, but the second does not):

```
>>> Methods.smeth(3)          # Static method: call through class
[3]                           # No instance passed or expected
>>> obj.smeth(4)              # Static method: call through instance
[4]                           # Instance not passed
```

Class methods are similar, but Python automatically passes the class (not an instance) in to a class method's first (leftmost) argument, whether it is called through a class or an instance:

```
>>> Methods.cmeth(5)                          # Class method: call through class
[<class 'bothmethods.Methods'>, 5]            # Becomes cmeth(Methods, 5)
>>> obj.cmeth(6)                              # Class method: call through instance
[<class 'bothmethods.Methods'>, 6]            # Becomes cmeth(Methods, 6)
```

In Chapter 40, we'll also find that *metaclass methods*—a unique, advanced, and technically distinct method type—behave similarly to the explicitly-declared class methods we're exploring here.

Counting Instances with Static Methods

Now, given these built-ins, here is the static method equivalent of this section's instance-counting example—it marks the method as special, so it will never be passed an instance automatically:

```
class Spam:
    numInstances = 0                         # Use static method for class data
    def __init__(self):
        Spam.numInstances += 1
    def printNumInstances():
        print("Number of instances: %s" % Spam.numInstances)
    printNumInstances = staticmethod(printNumInstances)
```

Using the static method built-in, our code now allows the `self`-less method to be called through the class or any instance of it, in both Python 2.X and 3.X:

```
>>> from spam_static import Spam
>>> a = Spam()
>>> b = Spam()
>>> c = Spam()
>>> Spam.printNumInstances()                 # Call as simple function
Number of instances: 3
```

```
>>> a.printNumInstances()                    # Instance argument not passed
Number of instances: 3
```

Compared to simply moving `printNumInstances` outside the class, as prescribed earlier, this version requires an extra `staticmethod` call (or an @ line we'll see ahead). However, it also localizes the function name in the class scope (so it won't clash with other names in the module); moves the function code closer to where it is used (inside the `class` statement); and allows subclasses to *customize* the static method with inheritance—a more convenient and powerful approach than importing functions from the files in which superclasses are coded. The following subclass and new testing session illustrate (be sure to start a new session after changing files, so that your `from` imports load the latest version of the file):

```
class Sub(Spam):
    def printNumInstances():              # Override a static method
        print("Extra stuff...")           # But call back to original
        Spam.printNumInstances()
    printNumInstances = staticmethod(printNumInstances)
```

```
>>> from spam_static import Spam, Sub
>>> a = Sub()
>>> b = Sub()
>>> a.printNumInstances()                 # Call from subclass instance
Extra stuff...
Number of instances: 2
>>> Sub.printNumInstances()               # Call from subclass itself
Extra stuff...
Number of instances: 2
>>> Spam.printNumInstances()              # Call original version
Number of instances: 2
```

Moreover, classes can inherit the static method without redefining it—it is run without an instance, regardless of where it is defined in a class tree:

```
>>> class Other(Spam): pass               # Inherit static method verbatim

>>> c = Other()
>>> c.printNumInstances()
Number of instances: 3
```

Notice how this also bumps up the *superclass's* instance counter, because its constructor is inherited and run—a behavior that begins to encroach on the next section's subject.

Counting Instances with Class Methods

Interestingly, a *class method* can do similar work here—the following has the same behavior as the static method version listed earlier, but it uses a class method that receives the instance's class in its first argument. Rather than hardcoding the class name, the class method uses the automatically passed class object generically:

```
class Spam:
    numInstances = 0                                    # Use class method instead of static
    def __init__(self):
        Spam.numInstances += 1
    def printNumInstances(cls):
        print("Number of instances: %s" % cls.numInstances)
    printNumInstances = classmethod(printNumInstances)
```

This class is used in the same way as the prior versions, but its `printNumInstances` method receives the `Spam` class, not the instance, when called from both the class and an instance:

```
>>> from spam_class import Spam
>>> a, b = Spam(), Spam()
>>> a.printNumInstances()                               # Passes class to first argument
Number of instances: 2
>>> Spam.printNumInstances()                            # Also passes class to first argument
Number of instances: 2
```

When using class methods, though, keep in mind that they receive the most specific (i.e., *lowest*) class of the call's subject. This has some subtle implications when trying to update class data through the passed-in class. For example, if in module *spam_class.py* we subclass to customize as before, augment `Spam.printNumInstances` to also display its `cls` argument, and start a new testing session:

```
class Spam:
    numInstances = 0                                    # Trace class passed in
    def __init__(self):
        Spam.numInstances += 1
    def printNumInstances(cls):
        print("Number of instances: %s %s" % (cls.numInstances, cls))
    printNumInstances = classmethod(printNumInstances)

class Sub(Spam):
    def printNumInstances(cls):                         # Override a class method
        print("Extra stuff...", cls)                    # But call back to original
        Spam.printNumInstances()
    printNumInstances = classmethod(printNumInstances)

class Other(Spam): pass                                 # Inherit class method verbatim
```

The lowest class is passed in whenever a class method is run, even for subclasses that have no class methods of their own:

```
>>> from spam_class import Spam, Sub, Other
>>> x = Sub()
>>> y = Spam()
>>> x.printNumInstances()                               # Call from subclass instance
Extra stuff... <class 'spam_class.Sub'>
Number of instances: 2 <class 'spam_class.Spam'>
>>> Sub.printNumInstances()                             # Call from subclass itself
Extra stuff... <class 'spam_class.Sub'>
Number of instances: 2 <class 'spam_class.Spam'>
>>> y.printNumInstances()                               # Call from superclass instance
Number of instances: 2 <class 'spam_class.Spam'>
```

In the first call here, a class method call is made through an instance of the Sub subclass, and Python passes the lowest class, Sub, to the class method. All is well in this case—since Sub's redefinition of the method calls the Spam superclass's version explicitly, the superclass method in Spam receives its own class in its first argument. But watch what happens for an object that inherits the class method verbatim:

```
>>> z = Other()                              # Call from lower sub's instance
>>> z.printNumInstances()
Number of instances: 3 <class 'spam_class.Other'>
```

This last call here passes Other to Spam's class method. This works in this example because *fetching* the counter finds it in Spam by inheritance. If this method tried to *assign* to the passed class's data, though, it would update Other, not Spam! In this specific case, Spam is probably better off hardcoding its own class name to update its data if it means to count instances of all its subclasses too, rather than relying on the passed-in class argument.

Counting instances per class with class methods

In fact, because class methods always receive the *lowest* class in an instance's tree:

- *Static* methods and explicit class names may be a better solution for processing data local to a class.

- *Class* methods may be better suited to processing data that may differ for each class in a hierarchy.

Code that needs to manage *per-class* instance counters, for example, might be best off leveraging class methods. In the following, the top-level superclass uses a class method to manage state information that varies for and is stored on each class in the tree—similar in spirit to the way instance methods manage state information that varies per class instance:

```
class Spam:
    numInstances = 0
    def count(cls):                    # Per-class instance counters
        cls.numInstances += 1          # cls is lowest class above instance
    def __init__(self):
        self.count()                   # Passes self.__class__ to count
    count = classmethod(count)

class Sub(Spam):
    numInstances = 0
    def __init__(self):                # Redefines __init__
        Spam.__init__(self)

class Other(Spam):                     # Inherits __init__
    numInstances = 0

>>> from spam_class2 import Spam, Sub, Other
>>> x = Spam()
>>> y1, y2 = Sub(), Sub()
```

```
>>> z1, z2, z3 = Other(), Other(), Other()
>>> x.numInstances, y1.numInstances, z1.numInstances        # Per-class data!
(1, 2, 3)
>>> Spam.numInstances, Sub.numInstances, Other.numInstances
(1, 2, 3)
```

Static and class methods have additional advanced roles, which we will finesse here; see other resources for more use cases. In recent Python versions, though, the static and class method designations have become even simpler with the advent of *function decoration* syntax—a way to apply one function to another that has roles well beyond the static method use case that was its initial motivation. This syntax also allows us to augment *classes* in Python 2.X and 3.X—to initialize data like the numInstances counter in the last example, for instance. The next section explains how.

 For a postscript on Python's method types, be sure to watch for coverage of *metaclass methods* in Chapter 40—because these are designed to process a *class* that is an instance of a metaclass, they turn out to be very similar to the class methods defined here, but require no classmethod declaration, and apply only to the shadowy metaclass realm.

Decorators and Metaclasses: Part 1

Because the staticmethod and classmethod call technique described in the prior section initially seemed obscure to some observers, a device was eventually added to make the operation simpler. Python *decorators*—similar to the notion and syntax of annotations in Java—both addressed this specific need and provided a general tool for adding logic that manages both functions and classes, or later calls to them.

This is called a "decoration," but in more concrete terms is really just a way to run extra processing steps at function and class definition time with explicit syntax. It comes in two flavors:

- *Function decorators*—the initial entry in this set, added in Python 2.4—augment function definitions. They specify special operation modes for both simple functions and classes' methods by wrapping them in an extra layer of logic implemented as another function, usually called a *metafunction*.

- *Class decorators*—a later extension, added in Python 2.6 and 3.0—augment class definitions. They do the same for classes, adding support for management of whole objects and their interfaces. Though perhaps simpler, they often overlap in roles with *metaclasses*.

Function decorators turn out to be very general tools: they are useful for adding many types of logic to functions besides the static and class method use cases. For instance, they may be used to augment functions with code that logs calls made to them, checks the types of passed arguments during debugging, and so on. Function decorators can be used to manage either functions themselves or later calls to them. In the latter mode, function decorators are similar to the *delegation* design pattern we explored in Chapter 31, but they are designed to augment a specific function or method call, not an entire object interface.

Python provides a few built-in function decorators for operations such as marking static and class methods and defining properties (as sketched earlier, the `property` built-in works as a decorator automatically), but programmers can also code arbitrary decorators of their own. Although they are not strictly tied to classes, user-defined function decorators often are coded as classes to save the original functions for later dispatch, along with other data as state information.

This proved such a useful hook that it was extended in Python 2.6, 2.7, and 3.X—*class decorators* bring augmentation to classes too, and are more directly tied to the class model. Like their function cohorts, class decorators may manage classes themselves or later instance creation calls, and often employ *delegation* in the latter mode. As we'll find, their roles also often overlap with *metaclasses*; when they do, the newer class decorators may offer a more lightweight way to achieve the same goals.

Function Decorator Basics

Syntactically, a function decorator is a sort of runtime declaration about the function that follows. A function decorator is coded on a line by itself just before the `def` statement that defines a function or method. It consists of the @ symbol, followed by what we call a *metafunction*—a function (or other callable object) that manages another function. Static methods since Python 2.4, for example, may be coded with decorator syntax like this:

```
class C:
    @staticmethod              # Function decoration syntax
    def meth():
        ...
```

Internally, this syntax has the same effect as the following—passing the function through the decorator and assigning the result back to the original name:

```
class C:
    def meth():
        ...
    meth = staticmethod(meth)     # Name rebinding equivalent
```

Decoration *rebinds* the method name to the decorator's result. The net effect is that calling the method function's name later actually triggers the result of its `staticme thod` decorator first. Because a decorator can return any sort of object, this allows the decorator to insert a layer of logic to be run on every call. The decorator function is free to return either the original function itself, or a new *proxy* object that saves the original function passed to the decorator to be invoked indirectly after the extra logic layer runs.

With this addition, here's a better way to code our static method example from the prior section in either Python 2.X or 3.X:

```
class Spam:
    numInstances = 0
    def __init__(self):
        Spam.numInstances = Spam.numInstances + 1

    @staticmethod
    def printNumInstances():
        print("Number of instances created: %s" % Spam.numInstances)

>>> from spam_static_deco import Spam
>>> a = Spam()
>>> b = Spam()
>>> c = Spam()
>>> Spam.printNumInstances()            # Calls from classes and instances work
Number of instances created: 3
>>> a.printNumInstances()
Number of instances created: 3
```

Because they also accept and return functions, the `classmethod` and `property` built-in functions may be used as decorators in the same way—as in the following mutation of the prior *bothmethods.py*:

```
# File bothmethods_decorators.py

class Methods(object):              # object needed in 2.X for property setters
    def imeth(self, x):             # Normal instance method: passed a self
        print([self, x])

    @staticmethod
    def smeth(x):                   # Static: no instance passed
        print([x])

    @classmethod
    def cmeth(cls, x):              # Class: gets class, not instance
        print([cls, x])

    @property                       # Property: computed on fetch
    def name(self):
        return 'Bob ' + self.__class__.__name__

>>> from bothmethods_decorators import Methods
>>> obj = Methods()
>>> obj.imeth(1)
[<bothmethods_decorators.Methods object at 0x0000000002A256A0>, 1]
>>> obj.smeth(2)
[2]
>>> obj.cmeth(3)
[<class 'bothmethods_decorators.Methods'>, 3]
>>> obj.name
'Bob Methods'
```

Keep in mind that `staticmethod` and its kin here are still built-in functions; they may be used in decoration syntax, just because they take a function as an argument and return a callable to which the original function name can be rebound. In fact, any such function can be used in this way—even user-defined functions we code ourselves, as the next section explains.

A First Look at User-Defined Function Decorators

Although Python provides a handful of built-in functions that can be used as decorators, we can also write custom decorators of our own. Because of their wide utility, we're going to devote an entire chapter to coding decorators in the final part of this book. As a quick example, though, let's look at a simple user-defined decorator at work.

Recall from Chapter 30 that the __call__ operator overloading method implements a function-call interface for class instances. The following code uses this to define a call *proxy* class that saves the decorated function in the instance and catches calls to the original name. Because this is a class, it also has state information—a counter of calls made:

```python
class tracer:
    def __init__(self, func):              # Remember original, init counter
        self.calls = 0
        self.func  = func
    def __call__(self, *args):             # On later calls: add logic, run original
        self.calls += 1
        print('call %s to %s' % (self.calls, self.func.__name__))
        return self.func(*args)

@tracer                                    # Same as spam = tracer(spam)
def spam(a, b, c):                         # Wrap spam in a decorator object
    return a + b + c

print(spam(1, 2, 3))                       # Really calls the tracer wrapper object
print(spam('a', 'b', 'c'))                 # Invokes __call__ in class
```

Because the spam function is run through the tracer decorator, when the original spam name is called it actually triggers the __call__ method in the class. This method counts and logs the call, and then dispatches it to the original wrapped function. Note how the *name argument syntax is used to pack and unpack the passed-in arguments; because of this, this decorator can be used to wrap any function with any number of positional arguments.

The net effect, again, is to add a layer of logic to the original spam function. Here is the script's 3.X and 2.X output—the first line comes from the tracer class, and the second gives the return value of the spam function itself:

```
c:\code> python tracer1.py
call 1 to spam
6
call 2 to spam
abc
```

Trace through this example's code for more insight. As it is, this decorator works for any function that takes positional arguments, but it does not handle *keyword* argu-

ments, and cannot decorate class-level *method* functions (in short, for methods its
__call__ would be passed a tracer instance only). As we'll see in Part VIII, there are a
variety of ways to code function decorators, including nested def statements; some of
the alternatives are better suited to methods than the version shown here.

For example, by using nested functions with enclosing scopes for state, instead of callable class instances with attributes, function decorators often become more broadly applicable to class-level methods too. We'll postpone the full details on this, but here's a brief look at this *closure* based coding model; it uses function attributes for counter state for portability, but could leverage variables and nonlocal instead in 3.X only:

```python
def tracer(func):                      # Remember original
    def oncall(*args):                 # On later calls
        oncall.calls += 1
        print('call %s to %s' % (oncall.calls, func.__name__))
        return func(*args)
    oncall.calls = 0
    return oncall

class C:
    @tracer
    def spam(self,a, b, c): return a + b + c

x = C()
print(x.spam(1, 2, 3))
print(x.spam('a', 'b', 'c'))           # Same output as tracer1 (in tracer2.py)
```

A First Look at Class Decorators and Metaclasses

Function decorators turned out to be so useful that Python 2.6 and 3.0 expanded the model, allowing decorators to be applied to classes as well as functions. In short, *class decorators* are similar to function decorators, but they are run at the end of a class statement to rebind a class name to a callable. As such, they can be used to either manage classes just after they are created, or insert a layer of wrapper logic to manage instances when they are later created. Symbolically, the code structure:

```python
def decorator(aClass): ...

@decorator                             # Class decoration syntax
class C: ...
```

is mapped to the following equivalent:

```python
def decorator(aClass): ...

class C: ...                           # Name rebinding equivalent
C = decorator(C)
```

The class decorator is free to augment the class itself, or return a *proxy* object that intercepts later instance construction calls. For example, in the code of the section "Counting instances per class with class methods" on page 1033, we could use this hook to automatically augment the classes with instance counters and any other data required:

```
def count(aClass):
    aClass.numInstances = 0
    return aClass                       # Return class itself, instead of a wrapper

@count
class Spam: ...                         # Same as Spam = count(Spam)

@count
class Sub(Spam): ...                    # numInstances = 0 not needed here

@count
class Other(Spam): ...
```

In fact, as coded, this decorator can be applied to class *or* functions—it happily returns the object being defined in either context after initializing the object's attribute:

```
@count
def spam(): pass        # Like spam = count(spam)

@count
class Other: pass       # Like Other = count(Other)

spam.numInstances       # Both are set to zero
Other.numInstances
```

Though this decorator manages a function or class itself, as we'll see later in this book, class decorators can also manage an object's entire *interface* by intercepting construction calls, and wrapping the new instance object in a *proxy* that deploys attribute accessor tools to intercept later requests—a multilevel coding technique we'll use to implement class attribute privacy in Chapter 39. Here's a preview of the model:

```
def decorator(cls):                     # On @ decoration
    class Proxy:
        def __init__(self, *args):      # On instance creation: make a cls
            self.wrapped = cls(*args)
        def __getattr__(self, name):    # On attribute fetch: extra ops here
            return getattr(self.wrapped, name)
    return Proxy

@decorator
class C: ...            # Like C = decorator(C)
X = C()                # Makes a Proxy that wraps a C, and catches later X.attr
```

Metaclasses, mentioned briefly earlier, are a similarly advanced class-based tool whose roles often intersect with those of class decorators. They provide an alternate model, which routes the creation of a class object to a subclass of the top-level **type** class, at the conclusion of a **class** statement:

```
class Meta(type):
    def __new__(meta, classname, supers, classdict):
        ...extra logic + class creation via type call...
```

```
class C(metaclass=Meta):
    ...my creation routed to Meta...            # Like C = Meta('C', (), {...})
```

In Python 2.X, the effect is the same, but the coding differs—use a class attribute instead of a keyword argument in the **class** header:

```
class C:
    __metaclass__ = Meta
    ... my creation routed to Meta...
```

In either line, Python calls a class's metaclass to create the new class object, passing in the data defined during the **class** statement's run; in 2.X, the metaclass simply defaults to the classic class creator:

```
classname = Meta(classname, superclasses, attributedict)
```

To assume control of the creation or initialization of a new class object, a metaclass generally redefines the __new__ or __init__ method of the **type** class that normally intercepts this call. The net effect, as with class decorators, is to define code to be run automatically at class creation time. Here, this step binds the class name to the result of a call to a user-defined metaclass. In fact, a metaclass need not be a class at all—a possibility we'll explore later that blurs some of the distinction between this tool and decorators, and may even qualify the two as functionally equivalent in many roles.

Both schemes, class decorators and metaclasses, are free to augment a class or return an arbitrary object to replace it—a protocol with almost limitless class-based customization possibilities. As we'll see later, metaclasses may also define *methods* that process their instance classes, rather than normal instances of them—a technique that's similar to class methods, and might be emulated in spirit by methods and data in class decorator proxies, or even a class decorator that returns a metaclass instance. Such mind-bending concepts will require Chapter 40's conceptual groundwork (and quite possibly sedation!).

For More Details

Naturally, there's much more to the decorator and metaclass stories than I've shown here. Although they are a general mechanism whose usage may be required by some packages, coding *new* user-defined decorators and metaclasses is an advanced topic of interest primarily to tool writers, not application programmers. Because of this, we'll defer additional coverage until the final and optional part of this book:

- Chapter 38 shows how to code properties using function decorator syntax in more depth.
- Chapter 39 has much more on decorators, including more comprehensive examples.
- Chapter 40 covers metaclasses, and more on the class and instance management story.

Although these chapters cover advanced topics, they'll also provide us with a chance to see Python at work in more substantial examples than much of the rest of the book was able to provide. For now, let's move on to our final class-related topic.

The super Built-in Function: For Better or Worse?

So far, I've mentioned Python's super built-in function only briefly in passing because it is relatively uncommon and may even be controversial to use. Given this call's increased visibility in recent years, though, it merits some further elaboration in this edition. Besides introducing super, this section also serves as a language design case study to close out a chapter on so many tools whose presence may to some seem curious in a scripting language like Python.

Some of this section calls this proliferation of tools into question, and I encourage you to judge any subjective content here for yourself (and we'll return to such things at the end of this book after we've expanded on other advanced tools such as metaclasses and descriptors). Still, Python's rapid growth rate in recent years represents a strategic decision point for its community going forward, and super seems as good a representative example as any.

The Great super Debate

As noted in Chapter 28 and Chapter 29, Python has a super built-in function that can be used to invoke superclass methods generically, but was deferred until this point of the book. This was deliberate—because super has substantial downsides in typical code, and a sole use case that seems obscure and complex to many observers, most beginners are better served by the traditional explicit-name call scheme used so far. See the sidebar "What About super?" on page 831 in Chapter 28 for a brief summary of the rationale for this policy.

The Python community itself seems split on this subject, with online articles about it running the gamut from "Python's Super Considered Harmful" to "Python's super() considered super!"[3] Frankly, in my live classes this call seems to be most often of interest to Java programmers starting to use Python anew, because of its conceptual similarity to a tool in that language (many a new Python feature ultimately owes its existence to programmers of other languages bringing their old habits to a new model). Python's super is not Java's—it translates differently to Python's multiple inheritance, and has

---

3. Both are opinion pieces in part, but are suggested reading. The first was eventually retitled "Python's Super is nifty, but you can't use it," and is today at *https://fuhm.net/super-harmful*. Oddly—and despite its subjective tone—the second article ("Python's super() considered super!") alone somehow found its way into Python's official library manual; see its link in the manual's super section...and consider demanding that differing opinions be represented more evenly in your tools' documentation, or omitted altogether. Python's manuals are not the place for personal opinion and one-sided propaganda!

a use case beyond Java's—but it has managed to generate both controversy and misunderstanding since its conception.

This book postponed the super call until now (and omitted it almost entirely in prior editions) because it has significant issues—it's prohibitively cumbersome to use in 2.X, differs in form between 2.X and 3.X, is based upon unusual semantics in 3.X, and mixes poorly with Python's multiple inheritance and operator overloading in typical Python code. In fact, as we'll see, in some code super can actually mask problems, and discourage a more explicit coding style that offers better control.

In its defense, this call does have a valid use case too—cooperative same-named method dispatch in diamond multiple inheritance trees—but it seems to ask a lot of newcomers. It requires that super be used universally and consistently (if not neurotically), much like __slots__ discussed earlier; relies on the arguably obscure MRO algorithm to order calls; and addresses a use case that seems far more the exception than the norm in Python programs. In this role, super seems an advanced tool based upon esoteric principles, which may be beyond much of Python's audience, and seems artificial to real program goals. That aside, its expectation of universal use seems unrealistic for the vast amount of existing Python code.

Because of all these factors, this introductory-level book has preferred the traditional explicit-name call scheme thus far and recommends the same for newcomers. You're better off learning the traditional scheme first, and might be better off sticking with that in general, rather than using an extra special-case tool that may not work in some contexts, and relies on arcane magic in the valid but atypical use case it addresses. This is not just your author's opinion; despite its advocate's best intentions, super is not widely recognized as "best practice" in Python today, for completely valid reasons.

On the other hand, just as for other tools the increasing use of this call in Python code in recent years makes it no longer optional for many Python programmers—the first time you see it, it's officially mandatory! For readers who may wish to experiment with super, and for other readers who may have it imposed upon them, this section provides a brief look at this tool and its rationale—beginning with alternatives to it.

Traditional Superclass Call Form: Portable, General

In general, this book's examples prefer to call back to superclass methods when needed by naming the superclass explicitly, because this technique is traditional in Python, because it works the same in both Python 2.X and 3.X, and because it sidesteps limitations and complexities related to this call in both 2.X and 3.X. As shown earlier, the traditional superclass method call scheme to augment a superclass method works as follows:

```
>>> class C:                    # In Python 2.X and 3.X
        def act(self):
            print('spam')
```

```
>>> class D(C):
        def act(self):
            C.act(self)              # Name superclass explicitly, pass self
            print('eggs')

>>> X = D()
>>> X.act()
spam
eggs
```

This form works the same in 2.X and 3.X, follows Python's normal method call mapping model, applies to all inheritance tree forms, and does not lead to confusing behavior when operator overloading is used. To see why these distinctions matter, let's see how super compares.

Basic super Usage and Its Tradeoffs

In this section, we'll both introduce super in basic, *single-inheritance mode*, and look at its perceived downsides in this role. As we'll find, in this context super does work as advertised, but is not much different from traditional calls, relies on unusual semantics, and is cumbersome to deploy in 2.X. More critically, as soon as your classes grow to use multiple inheritance, this super usage mode can both mask problems in your code and route calls in ways you may not expect.

Odd semantics: A magic proxy in Python 3.X

The super built-in actually has two intended roles. The more esoteric of these—cooperative multiple inheritance dispatch protocols in diamond multiple-inheritance trees (yes, a mouthful!)—relies on the 3.X MRO, was borrowed from the Dylan language, and will be covered later in this section.

The role we're interested in here is more commonly used, and more frequently requested by people with Java backgrounds—to allow superclasses to be named *generically* in inheritance trees. This is intended to promote simpler code maintenance, and to avoid having to type long superclass reference paths in calls. In Python 3.X, this call seems at least at first glance to achieve this purpose well:

```
>>> class C:                          # In Python 3.X (only: see 2.X super form ahead)
        def act(self):
            print('spam')

>>> class D(C):
        def act(self):
            super().act()             # Reference superclass generically, omit self
            print('eggs')

>>> X = D()
>>> X.act()
spam
eggs
```

This works, and minimizes code changes—you don't need to update the call if D's superclass changes in the future. One of the biggest downsides of this call in 3.X, though, is its *reliance on deep magic*: though prone to change, it operates today by inspecting the call stack in order to automatically locate the self argument and find the superclass, and pairs the two in a special *proxy object* that routes the later call to the superclass version of the method. If that sounds complicated and strange, it's because it is. In fact, this call form doesn't work at all outside the context of a class's method:

```
>>> super                      # A "magic" proxy object that routes later calls
<class 'super'>
>>> super()
SystemError: super(): no arguments

>>> class E(C):
        def method(self):      # self is implicit in super...only!
            proxy = super()    # This form has no meaning outside a method
            print(proxy)       # Show the normally hidden proxy object
            proxy.act()        # No arguments: implicitly calls superclass method!

>>> E().method()
<super: <class 'E'>, <E object>>
spam
```

Really, this call's semantics resembles nothing else in Python—it's neither a bound nor unbound method, and somehow finds a self even though you omit one in the call. In single inheritance trees, a superclass is available from self via the path self.__class__.__bases__[0], but the heavily implicit nature of this call makes this difficult to see, and even flies in the face of Python's explicit self policy that holds true *everywhere else*. That is, this call violates a fundamental Python idiom for a single use case. It also soundly contradicts Python's longstanding EIBTI design rule (run an "import this" for more on this rule).

Pitfall: Adding multiple inheritance naively

Besides its unusual semantics, even in 3.X this super role applies most directly to single inheritance trees, and can become problematic as soon as classes employ multiple inheritance with traditionally coded classes. This seems a major limitation of scope; due to the utility of *mix-in* classes in Python, multiple inheritance from disjoint and independent superclasses is probably more the norm than the exception in realistic code. The super call seems a recipe for disaster in classes coded to naively use its basic mode, without allowing for its much more subtle implications in multiple inheritance trees.

The following illustrates the trap. This code begins its life happily deploying super in single-inheritance mode to invoke a method one level up from C:

```
>>> class A:                   # In Python 3.X
        def act(self): print('A')
>>> class B:
        def act(self): print('B')
```

```
>>> class C(A):
        def act(self):
            super().act()          # super applied to a single-inheritance tree
>>> X = C()
>>> X.act()
A
```

If such classes later grow to use more than one superclass, though, super can become error-prone, and even unusable—it does not raise an exception for multiple inheritance trees, but will naively pick just the *leftmost* superclass having the method being run (technically, the first per the MRO), which may or may not be the one that you want:

```
>>> class C(A, B):                 # Add a B mix-in class with the same method
        def act(self):
            super().act()          # Doesn't fail on multi-inher, but picks just one!
>>> X = C()
>>> X.act()
A
```

```
>>> class C(B, A):
        def act(self):
            super().act()          # If B is listed first, A.act() is no longer run!
>>> X = C()
>>> X.act()
B
```

Perhaps worse, this *silently masks* the fact that you should probably be selecting superclasses *explicitly* in this case, as we learned earlier in both this chapter and its predecessor. In other words, super usage may obscure a common source of errors in Python —one so common that it shows up again in this part's "Gotchas." If you may need to use direct calls later, why not use them earlier too?

```
>>> class C(A, B):                 # Traditional form
        def act(self):             # You probably need to be more explicit here
            A.act(self)            # This form handles both single and multiple inher
            B.act(self)            # And works the same in both Python 3.X and 2.X
>>> X = C()                        # So why use the super() special case at all?
>>> X.act()
A
B
```

As we'll see in a few moments, you might also be able to address such cases by deploying super calls in *every* class of the tree. But that's also one of the biggest downsides of super—why code it in every class, when it's usually not needed, and when using the preceding simpler traditional form in a single class will usually suffice? Especially in existing code—and new code that uses existing code—this super requirement seems harsh, if not unrealistic.

Much more subtly, as we'll also see ahead, once you step up to multiple inheritance calls this way, the super calls in your code might not invoke the class you expect them to. They'll be routed per the MRO order, which, depending on where else super might be used, may invoke a method in a class that is *not the caller's superclass at all*—an implicit ordering that might make for interesting debugging sessions! Unless you completely understand what **super** means once multiple inheritance is introduced, you may be better off not deploying it in single-inheritance mode either.

This coding situation isn't nearly as abstract as it may seem. Here's a real-world example of such a case, taken from the *PyMailGUI* case study in *Programming Python*—the following very typical Python classes use multiple inheritance to mix in both application logic and window tools from independent, standalone classes, and hence must invoke *both* superclass constructors explicitly with direct calls by name. As coded, a super().__init__() here would run only one constructor, and adding **super** throughout this example's disjoint class trees would be more work, would be no simpler, and wouldn't make sense in tools meant for arbitrary deployment in clients that may use **super** or not:

```
class PyMailServerWindow(PyMailServer, windows.MainWindow):
    "a Tk, with extra protocol and mixed-in methods"
    def __init__(self):
        windows.MainWindow.__init__(self, appname, srvrname)
        PyMailServer.__init__(self)

class PyMailFileWindow(PyMailFile, windows.PopupWindow):
    "a Toplevel, with extra protocol and mixed-in methods"
    def __init__(self, filename):
        windows.PopupWindow.__init__(self, appname, filename)
        PyMailFile.__init__(self, filename)
```

The crucial point here is that using **super** for just the single inheritance cases where it applies most clearly is a potential source of error and confusion, and means that programmers must remember two ways to accomplish the same goal, when just one—explicit direct calls—could suffice for all cases.

In other words, unless you can be sure that you will never add a second superclass to a class in a tree over your software's entire lifespan, you cannot use **super** in single-inheritance mode without understanding and allowing for its much more sophisticated role in multiple-inheritance trees. We'll discuss the latter ahead, but it's not optional if you deploy **super** at all.

From a more practical view, it's also not clear that the trivial amount of *code maintenance* that this **super** role is envisioned to avoid fully justifies its presence. In Python practice, superclass names in headers are rarely changed; when they are, there are usually at most a very small number of superclass calls to update within the class. And consider this: if you add a new superclass in the future that doesn't use **super** (as in the preceding example), you'll have to either wrap it in an adaptor proxy or augment all the **super** calls in your class to use the traditional explicit-name call scheme anyhow—a maintenance task that seems just as likely, but perhaps more error-prone if you've grown to rely on **super** magic.

Limitation: Operator overloading

As briefly noted in Python's library manual, super also doesn't fully work in the presence of __X__ operator overloading methods. If you study the following code, you'll see that direct named calls to overload methods in the superclass operate normally, but using the super result in an expression fails to dispatch to the superclass's overload method:

```
>>> class C:                              # In Python 3.X
        def __getitem__(self, ix):        # Indexing overload method
            print('C index')

>>> class D(C):
        def __getitem__(self, ix):        # Redefine to extend here
            print('D index')
            C.__getitem__(self, ix)       # Traditional call form works
            super().__getitem__(ix)       # Direct name calls work too
            super()[ix]                   # But operators do not! (__getattribute__)

>>> X = C()
>>> X[99]
C index
>>> X = D()
>>> X[99]
D index
C index
C index
Traceback (most recent call last):
  File "", line 1, in
  File "", line 6, in __getitem__
TypeError: 'super' object is not subscriptable
```

This behavior is due to the very same new-style (and 3.X) class change described earlier in this chapter (see "Attribute Fetch for Built-ins Skips Instances" on page 987)—because the proxy object returned by super uses __getattribute__ to catch and dispatch later method calls, it fails to intercept the automatic __X__ method invocations run by built-in operations including expressions, as these begin their search in the class instead of the instance. This may seem less severe than the multiple-inheritance limitation, but operators should generally work the same as the equivalent method call, especially for a built-in like this. Not supporting this adds another exception for super users to confront and remember.

Other languages' mileage may vary, but in Python, self is explicit, multiple-inheritance mix-ins and operator overloading are common, and superclass name updates are rare. Because super adds an odd special case to the language—one with strange semantics, limited scope, rigid requirements, and questionable reward—most Python programmers may be better served by the more broadly applicable traditional call scheme. While super has some advanced applications too that we'll study ahead, they may be too obscure to warrant making it a mandatory part of every Python programmer's toolbox.

Use differs in Python 2.X: Verbose calls

If you are a Python 2.X user reading this dual-version book, you should also know that the **super** technique is not portable between Python lines. Its form differs between 2.X and 3.X—and not just between classic and new-style classes. It's really a different tool in 2.X, which cannot run 3.X's simpler form.

To make this call work in Python 2.X, you must first use *new-style classes*. Even then, you must also explicitly pass in the immediate class name and self to super, making this call so complex and verbose that in most cases it's probably easier to avoid it completely, and simply name the superclass explicitly per the previous traditional code pattern (for brevity, I'll leave it to readers to consider what changing a class's own name means for code maintenance when using the 2.X super form!):

```python
>>> class C(object):            # In Python 2.X: for new-style classes only
        def act(self):
            print('spam')

>>> class D(C):
        def act(self):
            super(D, self).act()    # 2.X: different call format - seems too complex
            print('eggs')           # "D" may be just as much to type/change as "C"!

>>> X = D()
>>> X.act()
spam
eggs
```

Although you can use the 2.X call form in 3.X for backward compatibility, it's too cumbersome to deploy in 3.X-only code, and the more reasonable 3.X form is not usable in 2.X:

```python
>>> class D(C):
        def act(self):
            super().act()       # Simpler 3.X call format fails in 2.X
            print('eggs')

>>> X = D()
>>> X.act()
TypeError: super() takes at least 1 argument (0 given)
```

On the other hand, the traditional call form with explicit class names works in 2.X in both classic and new-style classes, and exactly as it does in 3.X:

```python
>>> class D(C):
        def act(self):
            C.act(self)         # But traditional pattern works portably
            print('eggs')       # And may often be simpler in 2.X code

>>> X = D()
>>> X.act()
spam
eggs
```

So why use a technique that works in only limited contexts instead of one that works in many more? Though its basis is complex, the next sections attempt to rally support for the super cause.

The super Upsides: Tree Changes and Dispatch

Having just shown you the downsides of super, I should also confess that I've been tempted to use this call in code that would only ever run on 3.X, and which used a very long superclass reference path through a module package (that is, mostly for laziness, but coding brevity can matter too). To be fair, super may still be useful in some use cases, the chief among which merit a brief introduction here:

- *Changing class trees at runtime*: When a superclass may be changed at runtime, it's not possible to hardcode its name in a call expression, but it is possible to dispatch calls via super.

  On the other hand, this case is extremely rare in Python programming, and other techniques can often be used in this context as well.

- *Cooperative multiple inheritance method dispatch*: When multiple inheritance trees must dispatch to the same-named method in multiple classes, super can provide a protocol for orderly call routing.

  On the other hand, the class tree must rely upon the ordering of classes by the MRO—a complex tool in its own right that is artificial to the problem a program is meant to address—and must be coded or augmented to use super in each version of the method in the tree to be effective. Such dispatch can also often be implemented in other ways (e.g., via instance state).

As discussed earlier, super can also be used to select a superclass generically as long as the MRO's default makes sense, though in traditional code naming a superclass explicitly is often preferable, and may even be required. Moreover, even valid super use cases tend to be uncommon in many Python programs—to the point of seeming academic curiosity to some. The two cases just listed, however, are most often cited as super rationales, so let's take a quick look at each.

Runtime Class Changes and super

Superclass that might be changed at runtime dynamically preclude hardcoding their names in a subclass's methods, while super will happily look up the current superclass dynamically. Still, this case may be too rare in practice to warrant the super model by itself, and can often be implemented in other ways in the exceptional cases where it is needed. To illustrate, the following changes the superclass of C dynamically by changing the subclass's __bases__ tuple in 3.X:

```
>>> class X:
        def m(self): print('X.m')
>>> class Y:
```

```
            def m(self): print('Y.m')
>>> class C(X):                            # Start out inheriting from X
        def m(self): super().m()           # Can't hardcode class name here

>>> i = C()
>>> i.m()
X.m
>>> C.__bases__ = (Y,)                     # Change superclass at runtime!
>>> i.m()
Y.m
```

This works (and shares behavior-morphing goals with other deep magic, such as changing an instance's __class__), but seems rare in the extreme. Moreover, there may be other ways to achieve the same effect—perhaps most simply, calling through the current superclass tuple's value indirectly: special code to be sure, but only for a very special case (and perhaps not any more special than implicit routing by MROs):

```
>>> class C(X):
        def m(self): C.__bases__[0].m(self)    # Special code for a special case

>>> i = C()
>>> i.m()
X.m
>>> C.__bases__ = (Y,)                          # Same effect, without super()
>>> i.m()
Y.m
```

Given the preexisting alternatives, this case alone doesn't seem to justify super, though in more complex trees, the next rationale—based on the tree's MRO order instead of physical superclass links—may apply here as well.

Cooperative Multiple Inheritance Method Dispatch

The second of the use cases listed earlier is the main rationale commonly given for super, and also borrows from other programming languages (most notably, Dylan), where its use case may be more common than it is in typical Python code. It generally applies to diamond pattern multiple inheritance trees, discussed earlier in this chapter, and allows for cooperative and conformant classes to route calls to a *same-named method* coherently among multiple class implementations. Especially for constructors, which have multiple implementations normally, this can simplify call routing protocol when used consistently.

In this mode, each super call selects the method from a *next class* following it in the MRO ordering of the class of the self subject of a method call. The MRO was introduced earlier; it's the path Python follows for inheritance in new-style classes. Because the MRO's linear ordering depends on which class self was made from, the order of method dispatch orchestrated by super can vary per class tree, and visits each class just once as long as all classes use super to dispatch.

Since every class participates in a diamond under `object` in 3.X (and 2.X new-style classes), the applications are broader than you might expect. In fact, some of the earlier examples that demonstrated `super` shortcomings in multiple inheritance trees could use this call to achieve their dispatch goals. To do so, however, `super` must be used *universally* in the class tree to ensure that method call chains are passed on—a fairly major requirement that may be difficult to enforce in much existing and new code.

The basics: Cooperative super call in action

Let's take a look at what this role means in code. In this and the following sections, we'll both learn how `super` works, and explore the tradeoffs it implies along the way. To get started, consider the following *traditionally* coded Python classes (condensed somewhat here as usual for space):

```
>>> class B:
        def __init__(self): print('B.__init__')        # Disjoint class tree branches
>>> class C:
        def __init__(self): print('C.__init__')
>>> class D(B, C): pass

>>> x = D()                                            # Runs leftmost only by default
B.__init__
```

In this case, superclass tree branches are *disjoint* (they don't share a common explicit ancestor), so subclasses that combine them must call through each superclass by name —a common situation in much existing Python code that `super` cannot address directly without code changes:

```
>>> class D(B, C):
        def __init__(self):                            # Traditional form
            B.__init__(self)                           # Invoke supers by name
            C.__init__(self)

>>> x = D()
B.__init__
C.__init__
```

In *diamond* class tree patterns, though, *explicit-name* calls may by default trigger the top-level class's method more than once, though this might be subverted with additional protocols (e.g., status markers in the instance):

```
>>> class A:
        def __init__(self): print('A.__init__')
>>> class B(A):
        def __init__(self): print('B.__init__'); A.__init__(self)
>>> class C(A):
        def __init__(self): print('C.__init__'); A.__init__(self)

>>> x = B()
B.__init__
A.__init__
>>> x = C()                                            # Each super works by itself
C.__init__
```

```
        A.__init__

>>> class D(B, C): pass              # Still runs leftmost only
>>> x = D()
B.__init__
A.__init__

>>> class D(B, C):
        def __init__(self):         # Traditional form
            B.__init__(self)        # Invoke both supers by name
            C.__init__(self)

>>> x = D()                          # But this now invokes A twice!
B.__init__
A.__init__
C.__init__
A.__init__
```

By contrast, if all classes use super, or are appropriately coerced by proxies to behave as if they do, the method calls are dispatched according to class order in the MRO, such that the top-level class's method is run just once:

```
>>> class A:
        def __init__(self): print('A.__init__')
>>> class B(A):
        def __init__(self): print('B.__init__'); super().__init__()
>>> class C(A):
        def __init__(self): print('C.__init__'); super().__init__()

>>> x = B()                 # Runs B.__init__, A is next super in self's B MRO
B.__init__
A.__init__
>>> x = C()
C.__init__
A.__init__

>>> class D(B, C): pass
>>> x = D()                 # Runs B.__init__, C is next super in self's D MRO!
B.__init__
C.__init__
A.__init__
```

The real magic behind this is the linear MRO list constructed for the class of self— because each class appears just once on this list, and because super dispatches to the *next* class on this list, it ensures an orderly invocation chain that visits each class just once. Crucially, the *next* class following B in the MRO differs depending on the class of self—it's A for a B instance, but C for a D instance, accounting for the order of constructors run:

```
>>> B.__mro__
(<class '__main__.B'>, <class '__main__.A'>, <class 'object'>)

>>> D.__mro__
(<class '__main__.D'>, <class '__main__.B'>, <class '__main__.C'>,
<class '__main__.A'>, <class 'object'>)
```

The MRO and its algorithm were presented earlier in this chapter. By selecting a next class in the MRO sequence, a super call in a class's method *propagates* the call through the tree, so long as all classes do the same. In this mode super does not necessarily choose a superclass at all; it picks the next in the linearized MRO, which might be a *sibling*—or even a *lower* relative—in the class tree of a given instance. See "Tracing the MRO" on page 1002 for other examples of the path super dispatch would follow, especially for nondiamonds.

The preceding works—and may even seem clever at first glance—but its scope may also appear limited to some. Most Python programs do not rely on the nuances of diamond pattern multiple inheritance trees (in fact, many Python programmers I've met do not know what the term means!). Moreover, super applies most directly to single inheritance and cooperative diamond cases, and may seem superfluous for disjoint nondiamond cases, where we might want to invoke superclass methods selectively or independently. Even cooperative diamonds can be managed in other ways that may afford programmers more control than an automatic MRO ordering can. To evaluate this tool objectively, though, we need to look deeper.

Constraint: Call chain anchor requirement

The super call comes with complexities that may not be apparent on first encounter, and may even seem initially like features. For example, because *all* classes inherit from object in 3.X automatically (and explicitly in 2.X new-style classes), the MRO ordering can be used even in cases where the diamond is only implicit—in the following, triggering constructors in independent classes automatically:

```
>>> class B:
        def __init__(self): print('B.__init__'); super().__init__()
>>> class C:
        def __init__(self): print('C.__init__'); super().__init__()

>>> x = B()                      # object is an implied super at the end of MRO
B.__init__
>>> x = C()
C.__init__

>>> class D(B, C): pass          # Inherits B.__init__ but B's MRO differs for D
>>> x = D()                      # Runs B.__init__, C is next super in self's D MRO!
B.__init__
C.__init__
```

Technically, this dispatch model generally requires that the method being called by super must exist, and must have the same argument signature across the class tree, and every appearance of the method but the last must use super itself. This prior example works only because the implied object superclass at the end of the MRO of all three classes happens to have a compatible __init__ that satisfies these rules:

```
>>> B.__mro__
(<class '__main__.B'>, <class 'object'>)
```

```
>>> D.__mro__
(<class '__main__.D'>, <class '__main__.B'>, <class '__main__.C'>, <class 'object'>)
```

Here, for a D instance, the next class in the MRO after B is C, which is followed by object whose __init__ silently accepts the call from C and ends the chain. Thus, B's method calls C's, which ends in object's version, even though C is not a superclass to B.

Really, though, this example is atypical—and perhaps even *lucky*. In most cases, no such suitable default will exist in object, and it may be less trivial to satisfy this model's expectations. Most trees will require an explicit—*and possibly extra*—superclass to serve the anchoring role that object does here, to accept but not forward the call. Other trees may require careful design to adhere to this requirement. Moreover, unless Python optimizes it away, the call to object (or other anchor) defaults at the end of the chain may also add extra *performance costs*.

By contrast, in such cases direct calls incur neither extra coding requirements nor added performance cost, and make dispatch more explicit and direct:

```
>>> class B:
        def __init__(self): print('B.__init__')
>>> class C:
        def __init__(self): print('C.__init__')
>>> class D(B, C):
        def __init__(self): B.__init__(self); C.__init__(self)

>>> x = D()
B.__init__
C.__init__
```

Scope: An all-or-nothing model

Also keep in mind that traditional classes that were not written to use super in this role cannot be directly used in such cooperative dispatch trees, as they will not forward calls along the MRO chain. It's possible to incorporate such classes with *proxies* that wrap the original object and add the requisite super calls, but this imposes both additional coding requirements and performance costs on the model. Given that there are many millions of lines of existing Python code that *do not* use super, this seems a major detriment.

Watch what happens, for example, if any one class fails to pass along the call chain by omitting a super, ending the call chain prematurely—like __slots__, super is generally an *all-or-nothing* feature:

```
>>> class B:
        def __init__(self): print('B.__init__'); super().__init__()
>>> class C:
        def __init__(self): print('C.__init__'); super().__init__()
>>> class D(B, C):
        def __init__(self): print('D.__init__'); super().__init__()
>>> X = D()
D.__init__
B.__init__
```

```
         C.__init__
         >>> D.__mro__
         (<class '__main__.D'>, <class '__main__.B'>, <class '__main__.C'>, <class 'object'>)

         # What if you must use a class that doesn't call super?

         >>> class B:
                 def __init__(self): print('B.__init__')
         >>> class D(B, C):
                 def __init__(self): print('D.__init__'); super().__init__()
         >>> X = D()
         D.__init__
         B.__init__                    # It's an all-or-nothing tool...
```

Satisfying this mandatory propagation requirement may be no simpler than direct by-name calls—which you might still forget, but which you won't need to require of all the code your classes employ. As mentioned, it's possible to adapt a class like B by inheriting from a *proxy* class that embeds B instances, but that seems artificial to program goals, adds an extra call to each wrapped method, is subject to the new-style class problems we met earlier regarding interface proxies and built-ins, and seems an extraordinary and even stunning *added coding requirement* inherent in a model intended to simplify code.

Flexibility: Call ordering assumptions

Routing with super also assumes that you really mean to pass method calls throughout all your classes per the MRO, which may or may not match your *call ordering* requirements. For example, imagine that—irrespective of other inheritance ordering needs—the following requires that the class C's version of a given method be run before B's in some contexts. If the MRO says otherwise, you're back to traditional calls, which may conflict with super usage—in the following, invoking C's method twice:

```
         # What if method call ordering needs differ from the MRO?

         >>> class B:
                 def __init__(self): print('B.__init__'); super().__init__()
         >>> class C:
                 def __init__(self): print('C.__init__'); super().__init__()
         >>> class D(B, C):
                 def __init__(self): print('D.__init__'); C.__init__(self); B.__init__(self)
         >>> X = D()
         D.__init__
         C.__init__
         B.__init__
         C.__init__                    # It's the MRO xor explicit calls...
```

Similarly, if you want some methods to *not run at all*, the super automatic path won't apply as directly as explicit calls may, and will make it difficult to take more explicit control of the dispatch process. In realistic programs with many methods, resources, and state variables, these seem entirely plausible scenarios. While you could reorder superclasses in D for this method, that may break other expectations.

Customization: Method replacement

On a related note, the universal deployment expectations of **super** may make it difficult for a single class to *replace* (override) an inherited method altogether. Not passing the call higher with **super**—intentionally in this case—works fine for the class itself, but may break the call chain of trees it's mixed into, thereby preventing methods elsewhere in the tree from running. Consider the following tree:

```
>>> class A:
        def method(self): print('A.method'); super().method()
>>> class B(A):
        def method(self): print('B.method'); super().method()
>>> class C:
        def method(self): print('C.method')       # No super: must anchor the chain!
>>> class D(B, C):
        def method(self): print('D.method'); super().method()
>>> X = D()
>>> X.method()
D.method
B.method
A.method               # Dispatch to all per the MRO automatically
C.method
```

Method replacement here breaks the **super** model, and probably leads us back to the traditional form:

```
# What if a class needs to replace a super's default entirely?

>>> class B(A):
        def method(self): print('B.method')       # Drop super to replace A's method
>>> class D(B, C):
        def method(self): print('D.method'); super().method()
>>> X = D()
>>> X.method()
D.method
B.method               # But replacement also breaks the call chain...

>>> class D(B, C):
        def method(self): print('D.method'); B.method(self); C.method(self)
>>> D().method()
D.method
B.method
C.method               # It's back to explicit calls...
```

Once again, the problem with assumptions is that they assume things! Although the assumption of universal routing might be reasonable for constructors, it would also seem to conflict with one of the core tenets of OOP—unrestricted *subclass customization*. This might suggest restricting **super** usage to constructors, but even these might sometimes warrant replacement, and this adds an odd special-case requirement for one specific context. A tool that can be used only for certain categories of methods might be seen by some as redundant—and even spurious, given the extra complexity it implies.

Coupling: Application to mix-in classes

Subtly, when we say super selects the *next class* in the MRO, we really mean the next class in the MRO *that implements the requested method*—it technically skips ahead until it finds a class with the requested name. This matters for independent mix-in classes, which might be added to arbitrary client trees. Without this skipping-ahead behavior, such mix-ins wouldn't work at all—they would otherwise drop the call chain of their clients' arbitrary methods, and couldn't rely on their own super calls to work as expected.

In the following independent branches, for example, C's call to method is passed on, even though Mixin, the next class in the C instance's MRO, doesn't define that method's name. As long as method name sets are disjoint, this just works—the call chains of each branch can exist independently:

```
# Mix-ins work for disjoint method sets
>>> class A:
        def other(self): print('A.other')
>>> class Mixin(A):
        def other(self): print('Mixin.other'); super().other()

>>> class B:
        def method(self): print('B.method')
>>> class C(Mixin, B):
        def method(self): print('C.method'); super().other(); super().method()

>>> C().method()
C.method
Mixin.other
A.other
B.method

>>> C.__mro__
(<class '__main__.C'>, <class '__main__.Mixin'>, <class '__main__.A'>,
<class '__main__.B'>, <class 'object'>)
```

Similarly, mixing the other way doesn't break call chains of the mix-in either. For instance, in the following, even though B doesn't define other when called in C, classes do later in the MRO. In fact, the call chains work even if one of the branches doesn't use super at all—as long as a method is defined somewhere ahead on the MRO, its call works:

```
>>> class C(B, Mixin):
        def method(self): print('C.method'); super().other(); super().method()

>>> C().method()
C.method
Mixin.other
A.other
B.method

>>> C.__mro__
```

```
(<class '__main__.C'>, <class '__main__.B'>, <class '__main__.Mixin'>,
<class '__main__.A'>, <class 'object'>)
```

This is also true in the presence of *diamonds*—disjoint method sets are dispatched as expected, even if not implemented by each disjoint branch, because we select the next on the MRO with the method. Really, because the MRO contains the same classes in these cases, and because a subclass always appears before its superclass in the MRO, they are equivalent contexts. For example, the call in `Mixin` to `other` in the following still finds it in `A`, even though the next class after `Mixin` on the MRO is `B` (the call to `method` in `C` works again for similar reasons):

```
# Explicit diamonds work too

>>> class A:
        def other(self): print('A.other')
>>> class Mixin(A):
        def other(self): print('Mixin.other'); super().other()

>>> class B(A):
        def method(self): print('B.method')
>>> class C(Mixin, B):
        def method(self): print('C.method'); super().other(); super().method()

>>> C().method()
C.method
Mixin.other
A.other
B.method

>>> C.__mro__
(<class '__main__.C'>, <class '__main__.Mixin'>, <class '__main__.B'>,
<class '__main__.A'>, <class 'object'>)

# Other mix-in orderings work too

>>> class C(B, Mixin):
        def method(self): print('C.method'); super().other(); super().method()

>>> C().method()
C.method
Mixin.other
A.other
B.method

>>> C.__mro__
(<class '__main__.C'>, <class '__main__.B'>, <class '__main__.Mixin'>,
<class '__main__.A'>, <class 'object'>)
```

Still, this has an effect that is no different—but may seem *wildly more implicit*—than direct by-name calls, which also work the same in this case regardless of superclass ordering, and whether there is a diamond or not. In this case, the motivation for relying on MRO ordering seems on shaky ground, if the traditional form is both simpler and more explicit, and offers more control and flexibility:

```
# But direct calls work here too: explicit is better than implicit

>>> class C(Mixin, B):
        def method(self): print('C.method'); Mixin.other(self); B.method(self)

>>> X = C()
>>> X.method()
C.method
Mixin.other
A.other
B.method
```

More crucially, this example so far assumes that method names are disjoint in its branches; the dispatch order for *same-named methods* in diamonds like this may be much less fortuitous. In a diamond like the preceding, for example, it's not impossible that a client class could invalidate a super call's intent—the call to method in Mixin in the following works to run A's version as expected, *unless* it's mixed into a tree that drops the call chain:

```
# But for nondisjoint methods: super creates overly strong coupling

>>> class A:
        def method(self): print('A.method')
>>> class Mixin(A):
        def method(self): print('Mixin.method'); super().method()
>>> Mixin().method()
Mixin.method
A.method

>>> class B(A):
        def method(self): print('B.method')           # super here would invoke A after B
>>> class C(Mixin, B):
        def method(self): print('C.method'); super().method()
>>> C().method()
C.method
Mixin.method
B.method                                               # We miss A in this context only!
```

It may be that B shouldn't redefine this method anyhow (and frankly, we may be encroaching on problems inherent in multiple inheritance in general), but this need not *also* break the mix-in—*direct calls* give you more control in such cases, and allow mix-in classes to be much more independent of usage contexts:

```
# And direct calls do not: they are immune to context of use

>>> class A:
        def method(self): print('A.method')
>>> class Mixin(A):
        def method(self): print('Mixin.method'); A.method(self)          # C irrelevant

>>> class C(Mixin, B):
        def method(self): print('C.method'); Mixin.method(self)
>>> C().method()
C.method
```

```
Mixin.method
A.method
```

More to the point, by making mix-ins more *self-contained*, direct calls minimize *component coupling* that always skews program complexity higher—a fundamental software principle that seems neglected by **super**'s variable and context-specific dispatch model.

Customization: Same-argument constraints

As a final note, you should also consider the consequences of using **super** when method *arguments differ* per class—because a class coder can't be sure which version of a method **super** might invoke (indeed, this may vary per tree!), every version of the method must generally accept the same arguments list, or choose its inputs with analysis of generic argument lists—either of which imposes additional requirements on your code. In realistic programs, this constraint may in fact be a true *showstopper* for many potential **super** applications, precluding its use entirely.

To illustrate why this can matter, recall the pizza shop employee classes we wrote in Chapter 31. As coded there, both subclasses use direct *by-name* calls to invoke the superclass constructor, filling in an expected **salary** argument automatically—the logic being that the subclass implies the pay grade:

```
>>> class Employee:
        def __init__(self, name, salary):            # Common superclass
            self.name = name
            self.salary = salary

>>> class Chef1(Employee):
        def __init__(self, name):                    # Differing arguments
            Employee.__init__(self, name, 50000)     # Dispatch by direct call

>>> class Server1(Employee):
        def __init__(self, name):
            Employee.__init__(self, name, 40000)

>>> bob = Chef1('Bob')
>>> sue = Server1('Sue')
>>> bob.salary, sue.salary
(50000, 40000)
```

This works, but since this is a single-inheritance tree, we might be tempted to deploy **super** here to route the constructor calls generically. Doing so works for either subclass in isolation, since its MRO includes just itself and its actual superclass:

```
>>> class Chef2(Employee):
        def __init__(self, name):
            super().__init__(name, 50000)            # Dispatch by super()

>>> class Server2(Employee):
        def __init__(self, name):
            super().__init__(name, 40000)
```

```
>>> bob = Chef2('Bob')
>>> sue = Server2('Sue')
>>> bob.salary, sue.salary
(50000, 40000)
```

Watch what happens, though, when an employee is a member of *both* categories. Because the constructors in the tree have differing argument lists, we're in trouble:

```
>>> class TwoJobs(Chef2, Server2): pass

>>> tom = TwoJobs('Tom')
TypeError: __init__() takes 2 positional arguments but 3 were given
```

The problem here is that the super call in Chef2 no longer invokes its Employee superclass, but instead invokes its *sibling* class and follower on the MRO, Server2. Since this sibling has a differing argument list than the true superclass—expecting just self and name—the code breaks. This is inherent in super use: because the MRO can differ per tree, it might call different versions of a method in different trees—even some you may not be able to anticipate when coding a class by itself:

```
>>> TwoJobs.__mro__
(<class '__main__.TwoJobs'>, <class '__main__.Chef2'>, <class '__main__.Server2'>
<class '__main__.Employee'>, <class 'object'>)

>>> Chef2.__mro__
(<class '__main__.Chef2'>, <class '__main__.Employee'>, <class 'object'>)
```

By contrast, the direct by-name call scheme still works when the classes are mixed, though the results are a bit dubious—the combined category gets the pay of the leftmost superclass:

```
>>> class TwoJobs(Chef1, Server1): pass

>>> tom = TwoJobs('Tom')
>>> tom.salary
50000
```

Really, we probably want to route the call to the top-level class in this event with a new salary—a model that is possible with direct calls but not with super alone. Moreover, calling Employee directly in this one class means our code uses *two* dispatch techniques when just one—direct calls—would suffice:

```
>>> class TwoJobs(Chef1, Server1):
        def __init__(self, name): Employee.__init__(self, name, 70000)

>>> tom = TwoJobs('Tom')
>>> tom.salary
70000

>>> class TwoJobs(Chef2, Server2):
        def __init__(self, name): super().__init__(name, 70000)

>>> tom = TwoJobs('Tom')
TypeError: __init__() takes 2 positional arguments but 3 were given
```

This example may warrant redesign in general—splitting off shareable parts of `Chef` and `Server` to mix-in classes without a constructor, for example. It's also true that polymorphism in general assumes that the methods in an object's *external* interface have the same argument signature, though this doesn't quite apply to customization of superclass methods—an *internal* implementation technique that should by nature support variation, especially in constructors.

But the crucial point here is that because direct calls do not make code dependent on a magic ordering that can vary per tree, they more directly support argument list flexibility. More broadly, the questionable (or weak) performances `super` turns in on method replacement, mix-in coupling, call ordering, and argument constraints should make you evaluate its deployment carefully. Even in single-inheritance mode, its potential for *later* impacts as trees grow is considerable.

In sum, the three requirements of `super` in this role are also the source of most of its usability issues:

- The method called by `super` must exist—which requires extra code if no anchor is present.
- The method called by `super` must have the same argument signature across the class tree—which impairs flexibility, especially for implementation-level methods like constructors.
- Every appearance of the method called by `super` but the last must use `super` itself —which makes it difficult to use existing code, change call ordering, override methods, and code self-contained classes.

Taken together, these seem to make for a tool with both substantial complexity and significant tradeoffs—downsides that will assert themselves the moment the code grows to incorporate multiple inheritance.

Naturally, there may be creative workarounds for the `super` dilemmas just posed, but additional coding steps would further dilute the call's benefits—and we've run out of space here in any event. There are also alternative *non*-`super` solutions to some diamond method dispatch problems, but these will have to be left as a user exercise for space reasons too. In general, when superclass methods are called by explicit name, root classes of diamonds might check state in instances to avoid firing twice—a similarly complex coding pattern, but required rarely in most code, and which to some may seem no more difficult than using `super` itself.

The super Summary

So there it is—the bad and the good. As with all Python extensions, you should be the judge on this one too. I've tried to give both sides of the debate a fair shake here to help you decide. But because the `super` call:

- Differs in form between 2.X and 3.X

- In 3.X, relies on arguably non-Pythonic magic, and does not fully apply to operator overloading or traditionally coded multiple-inheritance trees
- In 2.X, seems so verbose in this intended role that it may make code more complex instead of less
- Claims code maintenance benefits that may be more hypothetical than real in Python practice

even ex–Java programmers should also consider this book's preferred traditional technique of explicit-name superclass calls to be at least as valid a solution as Python's super —a call that on some levels seems an unusual and limited answer to a question that was not being asked by most Python programmers, and was not deemed important for much of Python's history.

At the same time, the super call offers one solution to the difficult problem of same-named method dispatch in multiple inheritance trees, for programs that choose to use it *universally* and consistently. But therein lies one of its largest obstacles: it requires universal deployment to address a problem most programmers probably do not have. Moreover, at this point in Python's history, asking programmers to change their existing code to use this call widely enough to make it reliable seems highly *unrealistic*.

Perhaps the chief problem of this role, though, is the *role itself*—same-named method dispatch in multiple inheritance trees is relatively rare in real Python programs, and obscure enough to have generated both much controversy and much misunderstanding surrounding this role. People don't use Python the same way they use C++, Java, or Dylan, and lessons from other such languages do not necessarily apply.

Also keep in mind that using super makes your program's behavior dependent on the MRO algorithm—a procedure that we've covered only informally here due to its complexity, that is *artificial* to your program's purpose, and that seems tersely documented and understood in the Python world. As we've seen, even if you understand the MRO, its implications on *customization*, *coupling*, and *flexibility* are remarkably subtle. If you don't completely understand this algorithm—or have goals that its application does not address—you may be better served not relying on it to implicitly trigger actions in your code.

Or, to quote a Python motto from its `import this` creed:

> If the implementation is hard to explain, it's a bad idea.

The super call seems firmly in this category. Most programmers won't use an arcane tool aimed at a rare use case, no matter how clever it may be. This is especially true in a scripting language that bills itself as friendly to nonspecialists. Regrettably, use by any programmer can impose such a tool on others anyhow—the real reason I've covered it here, and a theme we'll revisit at the end of this book.

As usual, time and user base will tell if this call's tradeoffs or momentum lead to broader adoption or not. At the least, it behooves you to also know about the traditional explicit-name superclass call technique, as it is still commonly used and often either simpler or required in today's real-world Python programming. If you do choose to use this tool, my own advice to readers is to remember that using super:

- In *single-inheritance* mode can mask later problems and lead to unexpected behavior as trees grow
- In *multiple-inheritance* mode brings with it substantial complexity for an atypical Python use case

For other opinions on Python's super that go into further details both good and bad, search the Web for related articles. You can find plenty of additional positions, though in the end, Python's future relies as much on yours as any other.

 Also watch for Chapter 40's formal description of full inheritance—a procedure which super objects eschew for a custom scan of a context-specific MRO tail, looking for the first appearance of an attribute (descriptor or value) along the way. Full inheritance is used on the super object itself only if this scan fails. The net effect is a special case for basic name resolution, imposed on both the language and your code for the sake of a relatively rare use case.

Class Gotchas

We've reached the end of the primary OOP coverage in this book. After exceptions, we'll explore additional class-related examples and topics in the last part of the book, but that part mostly just gives expanded coverage to concepts introduced here. As usual, let's wrap up this part with the standard warnings about pitfalls to avoid.

Most class issues can be boiled down to namespace issues—which makes sense, given that classes are just namespaces with a handful of extra tricks. Some of the items in this section are more like class usage pointers than problems, but even experienced class coders have been known to stumble on a few.

Changing Class Attributes Can Have Side Effects

Theoretically speaking, classes (and class instances) are *mutable* objects. As with built-in lists and dictionaries, you can change them in place by assigning to their attributes —and as with lists and dictionaries, this means that changing a class or instance object may impact multiple references to it.

That's usually what we want, and is how objects change their state in general, but awareness of this issue becomes especially critical when changing class attributes. Because all instances generated from a class share the class's namespace, any changes at the class level are reflected in all instances, unless they have their own versions of the changed class attributes.

Because classes, modules, and instances are all just objects with attribute namespaces, you can normally change their attributes at runtime by assignments. Consider the following class. Inside the class body, the assignment to the name a generates an attribute X.a, which lives in the class object at runtime and will be inherited by all of X's instances:

```
>>> class X:
        a = 1          # Class attribute

>>> I = X()
>>> I.a                # Inherited by instance
1
>>> X.a
1
```

So far, so good—this is the normal case. But notice what happens when we change the class attribute dynamically outside the **class** statement: it also changes the attribute in every object that inherits from the class. Moreover, new instances created from the class during this session or program run also get the dynamically set value, regardless of what the class's source code says:

```
>>> X.a = 2            # May change more than X
>>> I.a                # I changes too
2
>>> J = X()            # J inherits from X's runtime values
>>> J.a                # (but assigning to J.a changes a in J, not X or I)
2
```

Is this a useful feature or a dangerous trap? You be the judge. As we learned in Chapter 27, you can actually get work done by changing class attributes without ever making a single instance—a technique that can simulate the use of "records" or "structs" in other languages. As a refresher, consider the following unusual but legal Python program:

```
class X: pass                       # Make a few attribute namespaces
class Y: pass

X.a = 1                             # Use class attributes as variables
X.b = 2                             # No instances anywhere to be found
X.c = 3
Y.a = X.a + X.b + X.c

for X.i in range(Y.a): print(X.i)   # Prints 0..5
```

Here, the classes X and Y work like "fileless" modules—namespaces for storing variables we don't want to clash. This is a perfectly legal Python programming trick, but it's less appropriate when applied to classes written by others; you can't always be sure that class attributes you change aren't critical to the class's internal behavior. If you're out to simulate a C struct, you may be better off changing instances than classes, as that way only one object is affected:

```
class Record: pass
X = Record()
```

```
X.name = 'bob'
X.job  = 'Pizza maker'
```

Changing Mutable Class Attributes Can Have Side Effects, Too

This gotcha is really an extension of the prior. Because class attributes are shared by all instances, if a class attribute references a mutable object, changing that object in place from any instance impacts all instances at once:

```
>>> class C:
        shared = []              # Class attribute
        def __init__(self):
            self.perobj = []     # Instance attribute

>>> x = C()                      # Two instances
>>> y = C()                      # Implicitly share class attrs
>>> y.shared, y.perobj
([], [])

>>> x.shared.append('spam')      # Impacts y's view too!
>>> x.perobj.append('spam')      # Impacts x's data only
>>> x.shared, x.perobj
(['spam'], ['spam'])

>>> y.shared, y.perobj           # y sees change made through x
(['spam'], [])
>>> C.shared                     # Stored on class and shared
['spam']
```

This effect is no different than many we've seen in this book already: mutable objects are shared by simple variables, globals are shared by functions, module-level objects are shared by multiple importers, and mutable function arguments are shared by the caller and the callee. All of these are cases of general behavior—multiple references to a mutable object—and all are impacted if the shared object is changed in place from any reference. Here, this occurs in class attributes shared by all instances via inheritance, but it's the same phenomenon at work. It may be made more subtle by the different behavior of assignments to instance attributes themselves:

```
x.shared.append('spam')     # Changes shared object attached to class in place
x.shared = 'spam'           # Changed or creates instance attribute attached to x
```

But again, this is not a problem, it's just something to be aware of; shared mutable class attributes can have many valid uses in Python programs.

Multiple Inheritance: Order Matters

This may be obvious by now, but it's worth underscoring: if you use multiple inheritance, the order in which superclasses are listed in the class statement header can be critical. Python always searches superclasses from left to right, according to their order in the header line.

For instance, in the multiple inheritance example we studied in Chapter 31, suppose that the Super class implemented a __str__ method, too:

```
class ListTree:
    def __str__(self): ...

class Super:
    def __str__(self): ...

class Sub(ListTree, Super):     # Get ListTree's __str__ by listing it first

x = Sub()                       # Inheritance searches ListTree before Super
```

Which class would we inherit it from—ListTree or Super? As inheritance searches proceed from left to right, we would get the method from whichever class is listed first (leftmost) in Sub's class header. Presumably, we would list ListTree first because its whole purpose is its custom __str__ (indeed, we had to do this in Chapter 31 when mixing this class with a tkinter.Button that had a __str__ of its own).

But now suppose Super and ListTree have their own versions of other same-named attributes, too. If we want one name from Super and another from ListTree, the order in which we list them in the class header won't help—we will have to override inheritance by manually assigning to the attribute name in the Sub class:

```
class ListTree:
    def __str__(self): ...
    def other(self): ...

class Super:
    def __str__(self): ...
    def other(self): ...

class Sub(ListTree, Super):     # Get ListTree's __str__ by listing it first
    other = Super.other         # But explicitly pick Super's version of other
    def __init__(self):
        ...

x = Sub()                       # Inheritance searches Sub before ListTree/Super
```

Here, the assignment to other within the Sub class creates Sub.other—a reference back to the Super.other object. Because it is lower in the tree, Sub.other effectively hides ListTree.other, the attribute that the inheritance search would normally find. Similarly, if we listed Super first in the class header to pick up its other, we would need to select ListTree's method explicitly:

```
class Sub(Super, ListTree):     # Get Super's other by order
    __str__ = Lister.__str__    # Explicitly pick Lister.__str__
```

Multiple inheritance is an advanced tool. Even if you understood the last paragraph, it's still a good idea to use it sparingly and carefully. Otherwise, the meaning of a name may come to depend on the order in which classes are mixed in an arbitrarily far-removed subclass. (For another example of the technique shown here in action, see the discussion of explicit conflict resolution in "The 'New-Style' Class Model", as well as the earlier super coverage.)

As a rule of thumb, multiple inheritance works best when your mix-in classes are as self-contained as possible—because they may be used in a variety of contexts, they should not make assumptions about names related to other classes in a tree. The pseudoprivate _X attributes feature we studied in Chapter 31 can help by localizing names that a class relies on owning and limiting the names that your mix-in classes add to the mix. In this example, for instance, if ListTree only means to export its custom __str__, it can name its other method __other to avoid clashing with like-named classes in the tree.

Scopes in Methods and Classes

When working out the meaning of names in class-based code, it helps to remember that classes introduce local scopes, just as functions do, and methods are simply further nested functions. In the following example, the generate function returns an instance of the nested Spam class. Within its code, the class name Spam is assigned in the gener ate function's local scope, and hence is visible to any further nested functions, including code inside method; it's the E in the "LEGB" scope lookup rule:

```
def generate():
    class Spam:                       # Spam is a name in generate's local scope
        count = 1
        def method(self):
            print(Spam.count)         # Visible in generate's scope, per LEGB rule (E)
    return Spam()

generate().method()
```

This example works in Python since version 2.2 because the local scopes of all enclosing function defs are automatically visible to nested defs (including nested method defs, as in this example).

Even so, keep in mind that method defs cannot see the local scope of the enclosing *class*; they can see only the local scopes of enclosing defs. That's why methods must go through the self instance or the class name to reference methods and other attributes defined in the enclosing class statement. For example, code in the method must use self.count or Spam.count, not just count.

To avoid nesting, we could restructure this code such that the class Spam is defined at the top level of the module: the nested method function and the top-level generate will then both find Spam in their global scopes; it's not localized to a function's scope, but is still local to a single module:

```
def generate():
    return Spam()

class Spam:                           # Define at top level of module
    count = 1
```

```
    def method(self):
        print(Spam.count)         # Works: in global (enclosing module)

generate().method()
```

In fact, this approach is recommended for all Python releases—code tends to be simpler in general if you avoid nesting classes and functions. On the other hand, class nesting is useful in *closure* contexts, where the enclosing function's scope retains *state* used by the class or its methods. In the following, the nested method has access to its own scope, the enclosing function's scope (for label), the enclosing module's global scope, anything saved in the self instance by the class, and the class itself via its nonlocal name:

```
>>> def generate(label):       # Returns a class instead of an instance
        class Spam:
            count = 1
            def method(self):
                print("%s=%s" % (label, Spam.count))
        return Spam

>>> aclass = generate('Gotchas')
>>> I = aclass()
>>> I.method()
Gotchas=1
```

Miscellaneous Class Gotchas

Here's a handful of additional class-related warnings, mostly as review.

Choose per-instance or class storage wisely

On a similar note, be careful when you decide whether an attribute should be stored on a class or its instances: the former is shared by all instances, and the latter will differ per instance. This can be a crucial design issue in practice. In a GUI program, for instance, if you want information to be shared by all of the window class objects your application will create (e.g., the last directory used for a Save operation, or an already entered password), it must be stored as class-level data; if stored in the instance as self attributes, it will vary per window or be missing entirely when looked up by inheritance.

You usually want to call superclass constructors

Remember that Python runs only one __init__ constructor method when an instance is made—the lowest in the class inheritance tree. It does not automatically run the constructors of all superclasses higher up. Because constructors normally perform required startup work, you'll usually need to run a superclass constructor from a subclass constructor—using a manual call through the superclass's name (or super), passing along whatever arguments are required—unless you mean to replace the super's constructor altogether, or the superclass doesn't have or inherit a constructor at all.

Delegation-based classes in 3.X: __getattr__ and built-ins

Another reminder: as described earlier in this chapter and elsewhere, classes that use the __getattr__ operator overloading method to delegate attribute fetches to wrapped objects may fail in Python 3.X (and 2.X when new-style classes are used) unless operator overloading methods are redefined in the wrapper class. The names of operator overloading methods implicitly fetched by built-in operations are not routed through generic attribute-interception methods. To work around this, you must redefine such methods in wrapper classes, either manually, with tools, or by definition in superclasses; we'll see how in Chapter 40.

KISS Revisited: "Overwrapping-itis"

When used well, the code reuse features of OOP make it excel at cutting development time. Sometimes, though, OOP's abstraction potential can be abused to the point of making code difficult to understand. If classes are layered too deeply, code can become obscure; you may have to search through many classes to discover what an operation does.

For example, I once worked in a C++ shop with thousands of classes (some machine-generated), and up to 15 levels of inheritance. Deciphering method calls in such a complex system was often a monumental task: multiple classes had to be consulted for even the most basic of operations. In fact, the logic of the system was so deeply wrapped that understanding a piece of code in some cases required days of wading through related files. This obviously isn't ideal for programmer productivity!

The most general rule of thumb of Python programming applies here, too: *don't make things complicated unless they truly must be*. Wrapping your code in multiple layers of classes to the point of incomprehensibility is always a bad idea. Abstraction is the basis of polymorphism and encapsulation, and it can be a very effective tool when used well. However, you'll simplify debugging and aid maintainability if you make your class interfaces intuitive, avoid making your code overly abstract, and keep your class hierarchies short and flat unless there is a good reason to do otherwise. Remember: code you write is generally code that others must read. See Chapter 20 for more on KISS.

Chapter Summary

This chapter presented an assortment of advanced class-related topics, including subclassing built-in types, new-style classes, static methods, and decorators. Most of these are optional extensions to the OOP model in Python, but they may become more useful as you start writing larger object-oriented programs, and are fair game if they appear in code you must understand. As mentioned earlier, our discussion of some of the more advanced class tools continues in the final part of this book; be sure to look ahead if you need more details on properties, descriptors, decorators, and metaclasses.

This is the end of the class part of this book, so you'll find the usual lab exercises at the end of the chapter: be sure to work through them to get some practice coding real classes. In the next chapter, we'll begin our look at our last core language topic, *exceptions*—Python's mechanism for communicating errors and other conditions to your code. This is a relatively lightweight topic, but I've saved it for last because new exceptions are supposed to be coded as classes today. Before we tackle that final core subject, though, take a look at this chapter's quiz and the lab exercises.

Test Your Knowledge: Quiz

1. Name two ways to extend a built-in object type.
2. What are function and class decorators used for?
3. How do you code a new-style class?
4. How are new-style and classic classes different?
5. How are normal and static methods different?
6. Are tools like __slots__ and super valid to use in your code?
7. How long should you wait before lobbing a "Holy Hand Grenade"?

Test Your Knowledge: Answers

1. You can embed a built-in object in a wrapper class, or subclass the built-in type directly. The latter approach tends to be simpler, as most original behavior is automatically inherited.

2. Function decorators are generally used to manage a function or method, or add to it a layer of logic that is run each time the function or method is called. They can be used to log or count calls to a function, check its argument types, and so on. They are also used to "declare" static methods (simple functions in a class that are not passed an instance when called), as well as class methods and properties. Class decorators are similar, but manage whole objects and their interfaces instead of a function call.

3. New-style classes are coded by inheriting from the object built-in class (or any other built-in type). In Python 3.X, all classes are new-style automatically, so this derivation is not required (but doesn't hurt); in 2.X, classes with this explicit derivation are new-style and those without it are "classic."

4. New-style classes search the diamond pattern of multiple inheritance trees differently—they essentially search breadth-first (across), instead of depth-first (up) in diamond trees. New-style classes also change the result of the type built-in for instances and classes, do not run generic attribute fetch methods such as __getattr__ for built-in operation methods, and support a set of advanced extra tools including properties, descriptors, super, and __slots__ instance attribute lists.

5. Normal (instance) methods receive a `self` argument (the implied instance), but static methods do not. Static methods are simple functions nested in class objects. To make a method static, it must either be run through a special built-in function or be decorated with decorator syntax. Python 3.X allows simple functions in a class to be called through the class without this step, but calls through instances still require static method declaration.

6. Of course, but you shouldn't use advanced tools automatically without carefully considering their implications. Slots, for example, can break code; `super` can mask later problems when used for single inheritance, and in multiple inheritance brings with it substantial complexity for an isolated use case; and both require universal deployment to be most useful. Evaluating new or advanced tools is a primary task of any engineer, and is why we explored tradeoffs so carefully in this chapter. This book's goal is not to tell you which tools to use, but to underscore the importance of objectively analyzing them—a task often given too low a priority in the software field.

7. Three seconds. (Or, more accurately: "And the Lord spake, saying, 'First shalt thou take out the Holy Pin. Then, shalt thou count to three, no more, no less. Three shalt be the number thou shalt count, and the number of the counting shall be three. Four shalt thou not count, nor either count thou two, excepting that thou then proceed to three. Five is right out. Once the number three, being the third number, be reached, then lobbest thou thy Holy Hand Grenade of Antioch towards thy foe, who, being naughty in my sight, shall snuff it.'")[4]

Test Your Knowledge: Part VI Exercises

These exercises ask you to write a few classes and experiment with some existing code. Of course, the problem with existing code is that it must be existing. To work with the set class in exercise 5, either pull the class source code off this book's website (see the preface for a pointer) or type it up by hand (it's fairly brief). These programs are starting to get more sophisticated, so be sure to check the solutions at the end of the book for pointers. You'll find them in Appendix D, under "Part VI, Classes and OOP" on page 1489.

1. *Inheritance*. Write a class called `Adder` that exports a method `add(self, x, y)` that prints a "Not Implemented" message. Then, define two subclasses of `Adder` that implement the `add` method:

   `ListAdder`

   With an `add` method that returns the concatenation of its two list arguments

---

4. This quote is from *Monty Python and the Holy Grail* (and if you didn't know that, it may be time to find a copy!).

`DictAdder`
>
> With an `add` method that returns a new dictionary containing the items in both its two dictionary arguments (any definition of dictionary addition will do)

Experiment by making instances of all three of your classes interactively and calling their `add` methods.

Now, extend your `Adder` superclass to save an object in the instance with a constructor (e.g., assign `self.data` a list or a dictionary), and overload the + operator with an `__add__` method to automatically dispatch to your `add` methods (e.g., X + Y triggers X.add(X.data,Y)). Where is the best place to put the constructors and operator overloading methods (i.e., in which classes)? What sorts of objects can you add to your class instances?

In practice, you might find it easier to code your `add` methods to accept just one real argument (e.g., `add(self,y)`), and add that one argument to the instance's current data (e.g., `self.data + y`). Does this make more sense than passing two arguments to `add`? Would you say this makes your classes more "object-oriented"?

2. *Operator overloading*. Write a class called `MyList` that shadows ("wraps") a Python list: it should overload most list operators and operations, including +, indexing, iteration, slicing, and list methods such as `append` and `sort`. See the Python reference manual or other documentation for a list of all possible methods to support. Also, provide a constructor for your class that takes an existing list (or a `MyList` instance) and copies its components into an instance attribute. Experiment with your class interactively. Things to explore:

   a. Why is copying the initial value important here?

   b. Can you use an empty slice (e.g., `start[:]`) to copy the initial value if it's a `MyList` instance?

   c. Is there a general way to route list method calls to the wrapped list?

   d. Can you add a `MyList` and a regular list? How about a list and a `MyList` instance?

   e. What type of object should operations like + and slicing return? What about indexing operations?

   f. If you are working with a reasonably recent Python release (version 2.2 or later), you may implement this sort of wrapper class by embedding a real list in a standalone class, or by extending the built-in list type with a subclass. Which is easier, and why?

3. *Subclassing*. Make a subclass of `MyList` from exercise 2 called `MyListSub`, which extends `MyList` to print a message to `stdout` before each call to the + overloaded operation and counts the number of such calls. `MyListSub` should inherit basic method behavior from `MyList`. Adding a sequence to a `MyListSub` should print a message, increment the counter for + calls, and perform the superclass's method. Also, introduce a new method that prints the operation counters to `stdout`, and experiment with your class interactively. Do your counters count calls per instance, or per class (for all instances of the class)? How would you program the other

option? (Hint: it depends on which object the count members are assigned to: class members are shared by instances, but `self` members are per-instance data.)

4. *Attribute methods*. Write a class called `Attrs` with methods that intercept every attribute qualification (both fetches and assignments), and print messages listing their arguments to `stdout`. Create an `Attrs` instance, and experiment with qualifying it interactively. What happens when you try to use the instance in expressions? Try adding, indexing, and slicing the instance of your class. (Note: a fully generic approach based upon __getattr__ will work in 2.X's classic classes but not in 3.X's new-style classes—which are optional in 2.X—for reasons noted in Chapter 28, Chapter 31, and Chapter 32, and summarized in the solution to this exercise.)

5. *Set objects*. Experiment with the set class described in "Extending Types by Embedding". Run commands to do the following sorts of operations:

   a. Create two sets of integers, and compute their intersection and union by using `&` and `|` operator expressions.

   b. Create a set from a string, and experiment with indexing your set. Which methods in the class are called?

   c. Try iterating through the items in your string set using a `for` loop. Which methods run this time?

   d. Try computing the intersection and union of your string set and a simple Python string. Does it work?

   e. Now, extend your set by subclassing to handle arbitrarily many operands using the `*args` argument form. (Hint: see the function versions of these algorithms in Chapter 18.) Compute intersections and unions of multiple operands with your set subclass. How can you intersect three or more sets, given that `&` has only two sides?

   f. How would you go about emulating other list operations in the set class? (Hint: __add__ can catch concatenation, and __getattr__ can pass most named list method calls like **append** to the wrapped list.)

6. *Class tree links*. In "Namespaces: The Whole Story" in Chapter 29 and in "Multiple Inheritance: 'Mix-in' Classes" in Chapter 31, we learned that classes have a __bases__ attribute that returns a tuple of their superclass objects (the ones listed in parentheses in the class header). Use __bases__ to extend the *lister.py* mix-in classes we wrote in Chapter 31 so that they print the names of the immediate superclasses of the instance's class. When you're done, the first line of the string representation should look like this (your address will almost certainly vary):

   ```
   <Instance of Sub(Super, Lister), address 7841200:
   ```

7. *Composition*. Simulate a fast-food ordering scenario by defining four classes:

   Lunch
      A container and controller class

Customer

    The actor who buys food

Employee

    The actor from whom a customer orders

Food

    What the customer buys

To get you started, here are the classes and methods you'll be defining:

```
class Lunch:
    def __init__(self)              # Make/embed Customer and Employee
    def order(self, foodName)       # Start a Customer order simulation
    def result(self)                # Ask the Customer what Food it has

class Customer:
    def __init__(self)                      # Initialize my food to None
    def placeOrder(self, foodName, employee)  # Place order with an Employee
    def printFood(self)                     # Print the name of my food

class Employee:
    def takeOrder(self, foodName)       # Return a Food, with requested name

class Food:
    def __init__(self, name)        # Store food name
```

The order simulation should work as follows:

a. The Lunch class's constructor should make and embed an instance of Customer and an instance of Employee, and it should export a method called order. When called, this order method should ask the Customer to place an order by calling its placeOrder method. The Customer's placeOrder method should in turn ask the Employee object for a new Food object by calling Employee's takeOrder method.

b. Food objects should store a food name string (e.g., "burritos"), passed down from Lunch.order, to Customer.placeOrder, to Employee.takeOrder, and finally to Food's constructor. The top-level Lunch class should also export a method called result, which asks the customer to print the name of the food it received from the Employee via the order (this can be used to test your simulation).

Note that Lunch needs to pass either the Employee or itself to the Customer to allow the Customer to call Employee methods.

Experiment with your classes interactively by importing the Lunch class, calling its order method to run an interaction, and then calling its result method to verify that the Customer got what he or she ordered. If you prefer, you can also simply code test cases as self-test code in the file where your classes are defined, using the module __name__ trick of Chapter 25. In this simulation, the Customer is the active agent; how would your classes change if Employee were the object that initiated customer/employee interaction instead?

8. *Zoo animal hierarchy.* Consider the class tree shown in Figure 32-1.

Code a set of six `class` statements to model this taxonomy with Python *inheritance*. Then, add a `speak` method to each of your classes that prints a unique message, and a `reply` method in your top-level `Animal` superclass that simply calls `self.speak` to invoke the category-specific message printer in a subclass below (this will kick off an independent inheritance search from `self`). Finally, remove the `speak` method from your `Hacker` class so that it picks up the default above it. When you're finished, your classes should work this way:

```
% python
>>> from zoo import Cat, Hacker
>>> spot = Cat()
>>> spot.reply()                    # Animal.reply: calls Cat.speak
meow
>>> data = Hacker()                 # Animal.reply: calls Primate.speak
>>> data.reply()
Hello world!
```

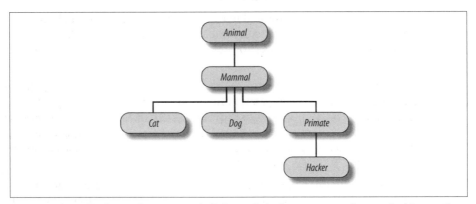

Figure 32-1. A zoo hierarchy composed of classes linked into a tree to be searched by attribute inheritance. Animal has a common "reply" method, but each class may have its own custom "speak" method called by "reply".

9. *The Dead Parrot Sketch.* Consider the object embedding structure captured in Figure 32-2.

Code a set of Python classes to implement this structure with *composition*. Code your `Scene` object to define an `action` method, and embed instances of the `Customer`, `Clerk`, and `Parrot` classes (each of which should define a `line` method that prints a unique message). The embedded objects may either inherit from a common superclass that defines `line` and simply provide message text, or define `line` themselves. In the end, your classes should operate like this:

```
% python
>>> import parrot
>>> parrot.Scene().action()         # Activate nested objects
customer: "that's one ex-bird!"
```

```
clerk: "no it isn't..."
parrot: None
```

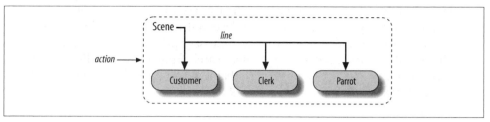

Figure 32-2. A scene composite with a controller class (Scene) that embeds and directs instances of three other classes (Customer, Clerk, Parrot). The embedded instance's classes may also participate in an inheritance hierarchy; composition and inheritance are often equally useful ways to structure classes for code reuse.

Why You Will Care: OOP by the Masters

When I teach Python classes, I invariably find that about halfway through the class, people who have used OOP in the past are following along intensely, while people who have not are beginning to glaze over (or nod off completely). The point behind the technology just isn't apparent.

In a book like this, I have the luxury of including material like the new Big Picture overview in Chapter 26, and the gradual tutorial of Chapter 28—in fact, you should probably review that section if you're starting to feel like OOP is just some computer science mumbo-jumbo. Though it adds much more structure than the generators we met earlier, OOP similarly relies on some magic (inheritance search and a special first argument) that beginners can find difficult to rationalize.

In real classes, however, to help get the newcomers on board (and keep them awake), I have been known to stop and ask the experts in the audience why they use OOP. The answers they've given might help shed some light on the purpose of OOP, if you're new to the subject.

Here, then, with only a few embellishments, are the most common reasons to use OOP, as cited by my students over the years:

Code reuse
> This one's easy (and is the main reason for using OOP). By supporting inheritance, classes allow you to program by customization instead of starting each project from scratch.

Encapsulation
> Wrapping up implementation details behind object interfaces insulates users of a class from code changes.

Structure
> Classes provide new local scopes, which minimizes name clashes. They also provide a natural place to write and look for implementation code, and to manage object state.

Maintenance

Classes naturally promote code factoring, which allows us to minimize redundancy. Thanks both to the structure and code reuse support of classes, usually only one copy of the code needs to be changed.

Consistency

Classes and inheritance allow you to implement common interfaces, and hence create a common look and feel in your code; this eases debugging, comprehension, and maintenance.

Polymorphism

This is more a property of OOP than a reason for using it, but by supporting code generality, polymorphism makes code more flexible and widely applicable, and hence more reusable.

Other

And, of course, the number one reason students gave for using OOP: it looks good on a résumé! (OK, I threw this one in as a joke, but it is important to be familiar with OOP if you plan to work in the software field today.)

Finally, keep in mind what I said at the beginning of this part of the book: you won't fully appreciate OOP until you've used it for a while. Pick a project, study larger examples, work through the exercises—do whatever it takes to get your feet wet with OO code; it's worth the effort.

Exceptions and Tools

Exception Basics

This part of the book deals with *exceptions*, which are events that can modify the flow of control through a program. In Python, exceptions are triggered automatically on errors, and they can be triggered and intercepted by your code. They are processed by four statements we'll study in this part, the first of which has two variations (listed separately here) and the last of which was an optional extension until Python 2.6 and 3.0:

try/except
: Catch and recover from exceptions raised by Python, or by you.

try/finally
: Perform cleanup actions, whether exceptions occur or not.

raise
: Trigger an exception manually in your code.

assert
: Conditionally trigger an exception in your code.

with/as
: Implement context managers in Python 2.6, 3.0, and later (optional in 2.5).

This topic was saved until nearly the end of the book because you need to know about classes to code exceptions of your own. With a few exceptions (pun intended), though, you'll find that exception handling is simple in Python because it's integrated into the language itself as another high-level tool.

Why Use Exceptions?

In a nutshell, exceptions let us jump out of arbitrarily large chunks of a program. Consider the hypothetical pizza-making robot we discussed earlier in the book. Suppose we took the idea seriously and actually built such a machine. To make a pizza, our culinary automaton would need to execute a plan, which we would implement as a

Python program: it would take an order, prepare the dough, add toppings, bake the pie, and so on.

Now, suppose that something goes very wrong during the "bake the pie" step. Perhaps the oven is broken, or perhaps our robot miscalculates its reach and spontaneously combusts. Clearly, we want to be able to jump to code that handles such states quickly. As we have no hope of finishing the pizza task in such unusual cases, we might as well abandon the entire plan.

That's exactly what exceptions let you do: you can jump to an exception handler in a single step, abandoning all function calls begun since the exception handler was entered. Code in the exception handler can then respond to the raised exception as appropriate (by calling the fire department, for instance!).

One way to think of an exception is as a sort of structured "super go to." An *exception handler* (`try` statement) leaves a marker and executes some code. Somewhere further ahead in the program, an exception is raised that makes Python jump back to that marker, abandoning any active functions that were called after the marker was left. This protocol provides a coherent way to respond to unusual events. Moreover, because Python jumps to the handler statement immediately, your code is simpler—there is usually no need to check status codes after every call to a function that could possibly fail.

Exception Roles

In Python programs, exceptions are typically used for a variety of purposes. Here are some of their most common roles:

Error handling
>   Python raises exceptions whenever it detects errors in programs at runtime. You can catch and respond to the errors in your code, or ignore the exceptions that are raised. If an error is ignored, Python's default exception-handling behavior kicks in: it stops the program and prints an error message. If you don't want this default behavior, code a `try` statement to catch and recover from the exception—Python will jump to your `try` handler when the error is detected, and your program will resume execution after the `try`.

Event notification
>   Exceptions can also be used to signal valid conditions without you having to pass result flags around a program or test them explicitly. For instance, a search routine might raise an exception on failure, rather than returning an integer result code—and hoping that the code will never be a valid result!

Special-case handling
>   Sometimes a condition may occur so rarely that it's hard to justify convoluting your code to handle it in multiple places. You can often eliminate special-case code by handling unusual cases in exception handlers in higher levels of your program. An

`assert` can similarly be used to check that conditions are as expected during development.

Termination actions

As you'll see, the `try`/`finally` statement allows you to guarantee that required closing-time operations will be performed, regardless of the presence or absence of exceptions in your programs. The newer `with` statement offers an alternative in this department for objects that support it.

Unusual control flows

Finally, because exceptions are a sort of high-level and structured "go to," you can use them as the basis for implementing exotic control flows. For instance, although the language does not explicitly support backtracking, you can implement it in Python by using exceptions and a bit of support logic to unwind assignments.[1] There is no "go to" statement in Python (thankfully!), but exceptions can sometimes serve similar roles; a `raise`, for instance, can be used to jump out of multiple loops.

We saw some of these roles briefly earlier, and will study typical exception use cases in action later in this part of the book. For now, let's get started with a look at Python's exception-processing tools.

Exceptions: The Short Story

Compared to some other core language topics we've met in this book, exceptions are a fairly lightweight tool in Python. Because they are so simple, let's jump right into some code.

Default Exception Handler

Suppose we write the following function:

```
>>> def fetcher(obj, index):
        return obj[index]
```

There's not much to this function—it simply indexes an object on a passed-in index. In normal operation, it returns the result of a legal index:

```
>>> x = 'spam'
>>> fetcher(x, 3)                          # Like x[3]
'm'
```

---

1. But true backtracking is not part of the Python language. Backtracking undoes all computations before it jumps, but Python exceptions do not: variables assigned between the time a `try` statement is entered and the time an exception is raised are not reset to their prior values. Even the generator functions and expressions we met in Chapter 20 don't do full backtracking—they simply respond to `next(G)` requests by restoring state and resuming. For more on backtracking, see books on artificial intelligence or the Prolog or Icon programming languages.

However, if we ask this function to index off the end of the string, an exception will be triggered when the function tries to run `obj[index]`. Python detects out-of-bounds indexing for sequences and reports it by *raising* (triggering) the built-in `IndexError` exception:

```
>>> fetcher(x, 4)                       # Default handler - shell interface
Traceback (most recent call last):
  File "<stdin>", line 1, in <module>
  File "<stdin>", line 2, in fetcher
IndexError: string index out of range
```

Because our code does not explicitly catch this exception, it filters back up to the top level of the program and invokes the *default exception handler*, which simply prints the standard error message. By this point in the book, you've probably seen your share of standard error messages. They include the exception that was raised, along with a *stack trace*—a list of all the lines and functions that were active when the exception occurred.

The error message text here was printed by Python 3.3; it can vary slightly per release, and even per interactive shell, so you shouldn't rely upon its exact form—in either this book or your code. When you're coding interactively in the basic shell interface, the filename is just "<stdin>," meaning the standard input stream.

When working in the IDLE GUI's interactive shell, the filename is "<pyshell>," and source lines are displayed, too. Either way, file line numbers are not very meaningful when there is no file (we'll see more interesting error messages later in this part of the book):

```
>>> fetcher(x, 4)                       # Default handler - IDLE GUI interface
Traceback (most recent call last):
  File "<pyshell#6>", line 1, in <module>
    fetcher(x, 4)
  File "<pyshell#3>", line 2, in fetcher
    return obj[index]
IndexError: string index out of range
```

In a more realistic program launched outside the interactive prompt, after printing an error message the default handler at the top also *terminates* the program immediately. That course of action makes sense for simple scripts; errors often should be fatal, and the best you can do when they occur is inspect the standard error message.

Catching Exceptions

Sometimes, this isn't what you want, though. Server programs, for instance, typically need to remain active even after internal errors. If you don't want the default exception behavior, wrap the call in a `try` statement to catch exceptions yourself:

```
>>> try:
...     fetcher(x, 4)
... except IndexError:                  # Catch and recover
...     print('got exception')
...
```

```
got exception
>>>
```

Now, Python jumps to your *handler*—the block under the except clause that names the exception raised—automatically when an exception is triggered while the try block is running. The net effect is to wrap a nested block of code in an error handler that intercepts the block's exceptions.

When working interactively like this, after the except clause runs, we wind up back at the Python prompt. In a more realistic program, try statements not only catch exceptions, but also *recover* from them:

```
>>> def catcher():
        try:
            fetcher(x, 4)
        except IndexError:
            print('got exception')
        print('continuing')

>>> catcher()
got exception
continuing
>>>
```

This time, after the exception is caught and handled, the program resumes execution after the entire try statement that caught it—which is why we get the "continuing" message here. We don't see the standard error message, and the program continues on its way normally.

Notice that there's no way in Python to *go back* to the code that triggered the exception (short of rerunning the code that reached that point all over again, of course). Once you've caught the exception, control continues after the entire try that caught the exception, not after the statement that kicked it off. In fact, Python clears the memory of any functions that were exited as a result of the exception, like fetcher in our example; they're not resumable. The try both catches exceptions, and is where the program resumes.

 Presentation note: The interactive prompt's "..." reappears in this part for some top-level try statements, because their code won't work if cut and pasted unless nested in a function or class (the except and other lines must align with the try, and not have extra preceding spaces that are needed to illustrate their indentation structure). To run, simply type or paste statements with "..." prompts one line at a time.

Raising Exceptions

So far, we've been letting Python raise exceptions for us by making mistakes (on purpose this time!), but our scripts can raise exceptions too—that is, exceptions can be raised by Python or by your program, and can be caught or not. To trigger an exception manually, simply run a `raise` statement. User-triggered exceptions are caught the same way as those Python raises. The following may not be the most useful Python code ever penned, but it makes the point—raising the built-in `IndexError` exception:

```
>>> try:
...     raise IndexError                    # Trigger exception manually
... except IndexError:
...     print('got exception')
...
got exception
```

As usual, if they're not caught, user-triggered exceptions are propagated up to the top-level default exception handler and terminate the program with a standard error message:

```
>>> raise IndexError
Traceback (most recent call last):
  File "<stdin>", line 1, in <module>
IndexError
```

As we'll see in the next chapter, the `assert` statement can be used to trigger exceptions, too—it's a conditional `raise`, used mostly for debugging purposes during development:

```
>>> assert False, 'Nobody expects the Spanish Inquisition!'
Traceback (most recent call last):
  File "<stdin>", line 1, in <module>
AssertionError: Nobody expects the Spanish Inquisition!
```

User-Defined Exceptions

The `raise` statement introduced in the prior section raises a *built-in* exception defined in Python's built-in scope. As you'll learn later in this part of the book, you can also define new exceptions of your own that are specific to your programs. User-defined exceptions are coded with *classes*, which inherit from a built-in exception class: usually the class named `Exception`:

```
>>> class AlreadyGotOne(Exception): pass     # User-defined exception

>>> def grail():
...     raise AlreadyGotOne()                # Raise an instance

>>> try:
...     grail()
... except AlreadyGotOne:                    # Catch class name
...     print('got exception')
...
got exception
>>>
```

As we'll see in the next chapter, an `as` clause on an `except` can gain access to the exception object itself. Class-based exceptions allow scripts to build exception categories, which can inherit behavior, and have attached state information and methods. They can also customize their error message text displayed if they're not caught:

```
>>> class Career(Exception):
        def __str__(self): return 'So I became a waiter...'

>>> raise Career()
Traceback (most recent call last):
  File "<stdin>", line 1, in <module>
__main__.Career: So I became a waiter...
>>>
```

Termination Actions

Finally, **try** statements can say "finally"—that is, they may include **finally** blocks. These look like **except** handlers for exceptions, but the **try**/**finally** combination specifies termination actions that always execute "on the way out," regardless of whether an exception occurs in the **try** block or not;

```
>>> try:
...     fetcher(x, 3)
... finally:                          # Termination actions
...     print('after fetch')
...
'm'
after fetch
>>>
```

Here, if the **try** block finishes without an exception, the **finally** block will run, and the program will resume after the entire **try**. In this case, this statement seems a bit silly —we might as well have simply typed the **print** right after a call to the function, and skipped the **try** altogether:

```
fetcher(x, 3)
print('after fetch')
```

There is a problem with coding this way, though: if the function call raises an exception, the **print** will never be reached. The **try**/**finally** combination avoids this pitfall—when an exception does occur in a **try** block, **finally** blocks are executed while the program is being unwound:

```
>>> def after():
        try:
            fetcher(x, 4)
        finally:
            print('after fetch')
        print('after try?')

>>> after()
after fetch
Traceback (most recent call last):
  File "<stdin>", line 1, in <module>
  File "<stdin>", line 3, in after
  File "<stdin>", line 2, in fetcher
IndexError: string index out of range
>>>
```

Here, we don't get the "after try?" message because control does not resume after the try/finally block when an exception occurs. Instead, Python jumps back to run the finally action, and then *propagates* the exception up to a prior handler (in this case, to the default handler at the top). If we change the call inside this function so as not to trigger an exception, the finally code still runs, but the program continues after the try:

```
>>> def after():
        try:
            fetcher(x, 3)
        finally:
            print('after fetch')
        print('after try?')

>>> after()
after fetch
after try?
>>>
```

In practice, try/except combinations are useful for catching and recovering from exceptions, and try/finally combinations come in handy to guarantee that termination actions will fire regardless of any exceptions that may occur in the try block's code. For instance, you might use try/except to catch errors raised by code that you import from a third-party library, and try/finally to ensure that calls to close files or terminate server connections are always run. We'll see some such practical examples later in this part of the book.

Although they serve conceptually distinct purposes, as of Python 2.5, we can mix except and finally clauses in the same try statement—the finally is run on the way out regardless of whether an exception was raised, and regardless of whether the exception was caught by an except clause.

As we'll learn in the next chapter, Python 2.X and 3.X both provide an alternative to try/finally when using some types of objects. The with/as statement runs an object's *context management* logic to guarantee that termination actions occur, irrespective of any exceptions in its nested block:

```
>>> with open('lumberjack.txt', 'w') as file:     # Always close file on exit
        file.write('The larch!\n')
```

Although this option requires fewer lines of code, it's applicable only when processing certain object types, so try/finally is a more general termination structure, and is often simpler than coding a class in cases where with is not already supported. On the other hand, with/as may also run startup actions too, and supports user-defined context management code with access to Python's full OOP toolset.

Why You Will Care: Error Checks

One way to see how exceptions are useful is to compare coding styles in Python and languages without exceptions. For instance, if you want to write robust programs in the C language, you generally have to test return values or status codes after every

---

operation that could possibly go astray, and propagate the results of the tests as your programs run:

```
doStuff()
{                               # C program
    if (doFirstThing() == ERROR)  # Detect errors everywhere
        return ERROR;             # even if not handled here
    if (doNextThing() == ERROR)
        return ERROR;
    ...
    return doLastThing();
}

main()
{
    if (doStuff() == ERROR)
        badEnding();
    else
        goodEnding();
}
```

In fact, realistic C programs often have as much code devoted to error detection as to doing actual work. But in Python, you don't have to be so methodical (and neurotic!). You can instead wrap arbitrarily vast pieces of a program in exception handlers and simply write the parts that do the actual work, assuming all is normally well:

```
def doStuff():        # Python code
    doFirstThing()    # We don't care about exceptions here,
    doNextThing()     # so we don't need to detect them
    ...
    doLastThing()

if __name__ == '__main__':
    try:
        doStuff()     # This is where we care about results,
    except:           # so it's the only place we must check
        badEnding()
    else:
        goodEnding()
```

Because control jumps immediately to a handler when an exception occurs, there's no need to instrument all your code to guard for errors, and there's no extra performance overhead to run all the tests. Moreover, because Python detects errors automatically, your code often doesn't need to check for errors in the first place. The upshot is that exceptions let you largely ignore the unusual cases and avoid error-checking code that can distract from your program's goals.

Chapter Summary

And that is the majority of the exception story; exceptions really are a simple tool.

To summarize, Python exceptions are a high-level control flow device. They may be raised by Python, or by your own programs. In both cases, they may be ignored (to trigger the default error message), or caught by **try** statements (to be processed by your code). The `try` statement comes in two logical formats that, as of Python 2.5, can be combined—one that handles exceptions, and one that executes finalization code regardless of whether exceptions occur or not. Python's `raise` and `assert` statements trigger exceptions on demand—both built-ins and new exceptions we define with classes—and the `with`/`as` statement is an alternative way to ensure that termination actions are carried out for objects that support it.

In the rest of this part of the book, we'll fill in some of the details about the statements involved, examine the other sorts of clauses that can appear under a `try`, and discuss class-based exception objects. The next chapter begins our tour by taking a closer look at the statements we introduced here. Before you turn the page, though, here are a few quiz questions to review.

Test Your Knowledge: Quiz

1. Name three things that exception processing is good for.
2. What happens to an exception if you don't do anything special to handle it?
3. How can your script recover from an exception?
4. Name two ways to trigger exceptions in your script.
5. Name two ways to specify actions to be run at termination time, whether an exception occurs or not.

Test Your Knowledge: Answers

1. Exception processing is useful for error handling, termination actions, and event notification. It can also simplify the handling of special cases and can be used to implement alternative control flows as a sort of structured "go to" operation. In general, exception processing also cuts down on the amount of error-checking code your program may require—because all errors filter up to handlers, you may not need to test the outcome of every operation.

2. Any uncaught exception eventually filters up to the default exception handler Python provides at the top of your program. This handler prints the familiar error message and shuts down your program.

3. If you don't want the default message and shutdown, you can code `try`/`except` statements to catch and recover from exceptions that are raised within its nested code block. Once an exception is caught, the exception is terminated and your program continues after the `try`.

4. The `raise` and `assert` statements can be used to trigger an exception, exactly as if it had been raised by Python itself. In principle, you can also raise an exception by making a programming mistake, but that's not usually an explicit goal!

5. The `try/finally` statement can be used to ensure actions are run after a block of code exits, regardless of whether the block raises an exception or not. The `with/as` statement can also be used to ensure termination actions are run, but only when processing object types that support it.

Exception Coding Details

In the prior chapter we took a quick look at exception-related statements in action. Here, we're going to dig a bit deeper—this chapter provides a more formal introduction to exception processing syntax in Python. Specifically, we'll explore the details behind the `try`, `raise`, `assert`, and `with` statements. As we'll see, although these statements are mostly straightforward, they offer powerful tools for dealing with exceptional conditions in Python code.

> One procedural note up front: The exception story has changed in major ways in recent years. As of Python 2.5, the `finally` clause can appear in the same `try` statement as `except` and `else` clauses (previously, they could not be combined). Also, as of Python 3.0 and 2.6, the new `with` context manager statement has become official, and user-defined exceptions must now be coded as class instances, which should inherit from a built-in exception superclass. Moreover, 3.X sports slightly modified syntax for the `raise` statement and `except` clauses, some of which is available in 2.6 and 2.7.
>
> I will focus on the state of exceptions in recent Python 2.X and 3.X releases in this edition, but because you are still very likely to see the original techniques in code for some time to come, along the way I'll point out how things have evolved in this domain.

The try/except/else Statement

Now that we've seen the basics, it's time for the details. In the following discussion, I'll first present `try/except/else` and `try/finally` as separate statements, because in versions of Python prior to 2.5 they serve distinct roles and cannot be combined, and still are at least logically distinct today. Per the preceding note, in Python 2.5 and later `except` and `finally` can be mixed in a single `try` statement; we'll see the implications of that merging after we've explored the two original forms in isolation.

Syntactically, the **try** is a compound, multipart statement. It starts with a **try** header line, followed by a block of (usually) indented statements; then one or more **except** clauses that identify exceptions to be caught and blocks to process them; and an optional **else** clause and block at the end. You associate the words **try**, **except**, and **else** by indenting them to the same level (i.e., lining them up vertically). For reference, here's the general and most complete format in Python 3.X:

```
try:
    statements              # Run this main action first
except name1:
    statements              # Run if name1 is raised during try block
except (name2, name3):
    statements              # Run if any of these exceptions occur
except name4 as var:
    statements              # Run if name4 is raised, assign instance raised to var
except:
    statements              # Run for all other exceptions raised
else:
    statements              # Run if no exception was raised during try block
```

Semantically, the block under the **try** header in this statement represents the *main action* of the statement—the code you're trying to run and wrap in error processing logic. The **except** clauses define *handlers* for exceptions raised during the **try** block, and the **else** clause (if coded) provides a handler to be run if *no* exceptions occur. The *var* entry here has to do with a feature of **raise** statements and exception classes, which we will discuss in full later in this chapter.

How try Statements Work

Operationally, here's how **try** statements are run. When a **try** statement is entered, Python marks the current program context so it can return to it if an exception occurs. The statements nested under the **try** header are run first. What happens next depends on whether exceptions are raised while the **try** block's statements are running, and whether they match those that the **try** is watching for:

- If an exception *occurs* while the **try** block's statements are running, and the exception *matches* one that the statement names, Python jumps back to the **try** and runs the statements under the first **except** clause that matches the raised exception, after assigning the raised exception object to the variable named after the **as** keyword in the clause (if present). After the **except** block runs, control then resumes below the entire **try** statement (unless the **except** block itself raises another exception, in which case the process is started anew from this point in the code).

- If an exception *occurs* while the **try** block's statements are running, but the exception *does not* match one that the statement names, the exception is propagated up to the next most recently entered **try** statement that matches the exception; if no such matching **try** statement can be found and the search reaches the top level of the process, Python kills the program and prints a default error message.

- If an exception *does not* occur while the `try` block's statements are running, Python runs the statements under the `else` line (if present), and control then resumes below the entire `try` statement.

In other words, `except` clauses catch any matching exceptions that happen while the `try` block is running, and the `else` clause runs only if no exceptions happen while the `try` block runs. Exceptions raised are *matched* to exceptions named in `except` clauses by superclass relationships we'll explore in the next chapter, and the `empty` except clause (with no exception name) matches all (or all other) exceptions.

The `except` clauses are *focused* exception handlers—they catch exceptions that occur only within the statements in the associated `try` block. However, as the `try` block's statements can call functions coded elsewhere in a program, the source of an exception may be outside the `try` statement itself.

In fact, a `try` block might invoke arbitrarily large amounts of program code—including code that may have `try` statements of its own, which will be searched first when exceptions occur. That is, `try` statements can *nest at runtime*, a topic I'll have more to say about in Chapter 36.

try Statement Clauses

When you write a `try` statement, a variety of clauses can appear after the `try` header. Table 34-1 summarizes all the possible forms—you must use at least one. We've already met some of these: as you know, `except` clauses catch exceptions, `finally` clauses run on the way out, and `else` clauses run if no exceptions are encountered.

Formally, there may be any number of `except` clauses, but you can code `else` only if there is at least one `except`, and there can be only one `else` and one `finally`. Through Python 2.4, the `finally` clause must appear alone (without `else` or `except`); the `try/finally` is really a different statement. As of Python 2.5, however, a `finally` can appear in the same statement as `except` and `else` (more on the ordering rules later in this chapter when we meet the unified `try` statement).

Table 34-1. try statement clause forms

Clause form	Interpretation
`except:`	Catch all (or all other) exception types.
`except name:`	Catch a specific exception only.
`except name as value:`	Catch the listed exception and assign its instance.
`except (name1, name2):`	Catch any of the listed exceptions.
`except (name1, name2) as value:`	Catch any listed exception and assign its instance.
`else:`	Run if no exceptions are raised in the `try` block.
`finally:`	Always perform this block on exit.

We'll explore the entries with the extra as *value* part in more detail when we meet the `raise` statement later in this chapter. They provide access to the objects that are raised as exceptions.

Catching any and all exceptions

The first and fourth entries in Table 34-1 are new here:

- `except` clauses that list no exception name (`except:`) catch *all* exceptions not previously listed in the `try` statement.
- `except` clauses that list a set of exceptions in parentheses (`except (e1, e2, e3):`) catch *any* of the listed exceptions.

Because Python looks for a match within a given `try` by inspecting the `except` clauses from *top to bottom*, the parenthesized version has the same effect as listing each exception in its own `except` clause, but you have to code the statement body associated with each only once. Here's an example of multiple `except` clauses at work, which demonstrates just how specific your handlers can be:

```
try:
    action()
except NameError:
    ...
except IndexError:
    ...
except KeyError:
    ...
except (AttributeError, TypeError, SyntaxError):
    ...
else:
    ...
```

In this example, if an exception is raised while the call to the `action` function is running, Python returns to the `try` and searches for the first `except` that names the exception raised. It inspects the `except` clauses from top to bottom and left to right, and runs the statements under the first one that matches. If none match, the exception is propagated past this `try`. Note that the `else` runs only when *no* exception occurs in `action`—it does not run when an exception without a matching `except` is raised.

Catching all: The empty except and Exception

If you really want a general "catchall" clause, an empty `except` does the trick:

```
try:
    action()
except NameError:
    ...                         # Handle NameError
except IndexError:
    ...                         # Handle IndexError
except:
    ...                         # Handle all other exceptions
```

```
    else:
        ...                          # Handle the no-exception case
```

The empty except clause is a sort of *wildcard* feature—because it catches everything, it allows your handlers to be as general or specific as you like. In some scenarios, this form may be more convenient than listing all possible exceptions in a try. For example, the following catches everything without listing anything:

```
    try:
        action()
    except:
        ...                          # Catch all possible exceptions
```

Empty excepts also raise some design issues, though. Although convenient, they may catch unexpected system exceptions unrelated to your code, and they may inadvertently intercept exceptions meant for another handler. For example, even system exit calls and Ctrl-C key combinations in Python trigger exceptions, and you usually want these to pass. Even worse, the empty except may also catch genuine programming mistakes for which you probably want to see an error message. We'll revisit this as a gotcha at the end of this part of the book. For now, I'll just say, "use with care."

Python 3.X more strongly supports an alternative that solves one of these problems—catching an exception named Exception has almost the same effect as an empty except, but ignores exceptions related to system exits:

```
    try:
        action()
    except Exception:
        ...                          # Catch all possible exceptions, except exits
```

We'll explore how this form works its voodoo formally in the next chapter when we study exception classes. In short, it works because exceptions match if they are a subclass of one named in an except clause, and Exception is a superclass of all the exceptions you should generally catch this way. This form has most of the same convenience of the empty except, without the risk of catching exit events. Though better, it also has some of the same dangers—especially with regard to masking programming errors.

 Version skew note: See also the raise statement ahead for more on the as portion of except clauses in try. Syntactically, Python 3.X requires the except E as V: handler clause form listed in Table 34-1 and used in this book, rather than the older except E, V: form. The latter form is still available (but not recommended) in Python 2.6 and 2.7: if used, it's converted to the former.

The change was made to eliminate confusion regarding the dual role of commas in the older form. In this form, two alternate exceptions are properly coded as except (E1, E2):. Because 3.X supports the as form only, commas in a handler clause are always taken to mean a tuple, regardless of whether parentheses are used or not, and the values are interpreted as alternative exceptions to be caught.

As we'll see ahead, though, this option does not modify the scoping rules in 2.X: even with the new **as** syntax, the variable V is still available after the except block in 2.X. In 3.X, V is not available later, and is in fact forcibly deleted.

The try else Clause

The purpose of the `else` clause is not always immediately obvious to Python newcomers. Without it, though, there is no direct way to tell (without setting and checking Boolean flags) whether the flow of control has proceeded past a **try** statement because no exception was raised, or because an exception occurred and was handled. Either way, we wind up after the **try**:

```
try:
    ...run code...
except IndexError:
    ...handle exception...
# Did we get here because the try failed or not?
```

Much like the way `else` clauses in loops make the exit cause more apparent, the `else` clause provides syntax in a **try** that makes what has happened obvious and unambiguous:

```
try:
    ...run code...
except IndexError:
    ...handle exception...
else:
    ...no exception occurred...
```

You can *almost* emulate an `else` clause by moving its code into the **try** block:

```
try:
    ...run code...
    ...no exception occurred...
except IndexError:
    ...handle exception...
```

This can lead to incorrect exception classifications, though. If the "no exception occurred" action triggers an IndexError, it will register as a failure of the **try** block and erroneously trigger the exception handler below the **try** (subtle, but true!). By using an explicit `else` clause instead, you make the logic more obvious and guarantee that except handlers will run only for real failures in the code you're wrapping in a **try**, not for failures in the `else` no-exception case's action.

Example: Default Behavior

Because the control flow through a program is easier to capture in Python than in English, let's run some examples that further illustrate exception basics in the context of larger code samples in files.

I've mentioned that exceptions not caught by **try** statements percolate up to the top level of the Python process and run Python's default exception-handling logic (i.e., Python terminates the running program and prints a standard error message). To illustrate, running the following module file, *bad.py*, generates a divide-by-zero exception:

```
def gobad(x, y):
    return x / y

def gosouth(x):
    print(gobad(x, 0))

gosouth(1)
```

Because the program ignores the exception it triggers, Python kills the program and prints a message:

```
% python bad.py
Traceback (most recent call last):
  File "bad.py", line 7, in <module>
    gosouth(1)
  File "bad.py", line 5, in gosouth
    print(gobad(x, 0))
  File "bad.py", line 2, in gobad
    return x / y
ZeroDivisionError: division by zero
```

I ran this in a shell window with Python 3.X. The message consists of a stack trace ("Traceback") and the name of and details about the exception that was raised. The stack trace lists all lines active when the exception occurred, from oldest to newest. Note that because we're not working at the interactive prompt, in this case the file and line number information is more useful. For example, here we can see that the bad divide happens at the last entry in the trace—line 2 of the file *bad.py*, a **return** statement.[1]

Because Python detects and reports all errors at runtime by raising exceptions, exceptions are intimately bound up with the ideas of error handling and debugging in general. If you've worked through this book's examples, you've undoubtedly seen an exception or two along the way—even typos usually generate a **SyntaxError** or other exception when a file is imported or executed (that's when the compiler is run). By default, you get a useful error display like the one just shown, which helps you track down the problem.

Often, this standard error message is all you need to resolve problems in your code. For more heavy-duty debugging jobs, you can catch exceptions with **try** statements,

---

1. As mentioned in the prior chapter, the text of error messages and stack traces tends to vary slightly over time and shells. Don't be alarmed if your error messages don't exactly match mine. When I ran this example in Python 3.3's IDLE GUI, for instance, its error message text showed filenames with full absolute directory paths.

or use one of the debugging tools that I introduced in Chapter 3 and will summarize again in Chapter 36, such as the `pdb` standard library module.

Example: Catching Built-in Exceptions

Python's default exception handling is often exactly what you want—especially for code in a top-level script file, an error often should terminate your program immediately. For many programs, there is no need to be more specific about errors in your code.

Sometimes, though, you'll want to catch errors and recover from them instead. If you don't want your program terminated when Python raises an exception, simply catch it by wrapping the program logic in a `try`. This is an important capability for programs such as network servers, which must keep running persistently. For example, the following code, in the file *kaboom.py*, catches and recovers from the `TypeError` Python raises immediately when you try to concatenate a list and a string (remember, the `+` operator expects the same sequence type on both sides):

```
def kaboom(x, y):
    print(x + y)                # Trigger TypeError

try:
    kaboom([0, 1, 2], 'spam')
except TypeError:               # Catch and recover here
    print('Hello world!')
print('resuming here')         # Continue here if exception or not
```

When the exception occurs in the function `kaboom`, control jumps to the `try` statement's `except` clause, which prints a message. Since an exception is "dead" after it's been caught like this, the program continues executing below the `try` rather than being terminated by Python. In effect, the code processes and clears the error, and your script recovers:

```
% python kaboom.py
Hello world!
resuming here
```

Keep in mind that once you've caught an error, control resumes at the place where you caught it (i.e., after the `try`); there is no direct way to go back to the place where the exception occurred (here, in the function `kaboom`). In a sense, this makes exceptions more like simple jumps than function calls—there is no way to return to the code that triggered the error.

The try/finally Statement

The other flavor of the `try` statement is a specialization that has to do with finalization (a.k.a. termination) actions. If a `finally` clause is included in a `try`, Python will always run its block of statements "on the way out" of the `try` statement, whether an exception occurred while the `try` block was running or not. Its general form is:

```
try:
    statements                      # Run this action first
finally:
    statements                      # Always run this code on the way out
```

With this variant, Python begins by running the statement block associated with the try header line as usual. What happens next depends on whether an exception occurs during the try block:

- If an exception *does not* occur while the try block is running, Python continues on to run the finally block, and then continues execution past the try statement.

- If an exception *does* occur during the try block's run, Python still comes back and runs the finally block, but it then propagates the exception up to a previously entered try or the top-level default handler; the program does not resume execution below the finally clause's try statement. That is, the finally block is run even if an exception is raised, but unlike an except, the finally does not terminate the exception—it continues being raised after the finally block runs.

The try/finally form is useful when you want to be completely sure that an action will happen after some code runs, regardless of the exception behavior of the program. In practice, it allows you to specify cleanup actions that always must occur, such as file closes and server disconnects where required.

Note that the finally clause cannot be used in the same try statement as except and else in Python 2.4 and earlier, so the try/finally is best thought of as a distinct statement form if you are using an older release. In Python 2.5, and later, however, finally can appear in the same statement as except and else, so today there is really a single try statement with many optional clauses (more about this shortly). Whichever version you use, though, the finally clause still serves the same purpose—to specify "cleanup" actions that must always be run, regardless of any exceptions.

 As we'll also see later in this chapter, as of Python 2.6 and 3.0, the new with statement and its context managers provide an object-based way to do similar work for exit actions. Unlike finally, this new statement also supports entry actions, but it is limited in scope to objects that implement the context manager protocol it leverages.

Example: Coding Termination Actions with try/finally

We saw some simple try/finally examples in the prior chapter. Here's a more realistic example that illustrates a typical role for this statement:

```
class MyError(Exception): pass

def stuff(file):
    raise MyError()

file = open('data', 'w')        # Open an output file (this can fail too)
```

```
try:
    stuff(file)                    # Raises exception
finally:
    file.close()                   # Always close file to flush output buffers
print('not reached')               # Continue here only if no exception
```

When the function in this code raises its exception, the control flow jumps back and runs the `finally` block to close the file. The exception is then propagated on to either another `try` or the default top-level handler, which prints the standard error message and shuts down the program. Hence, the statement after this `try` is never reached. If the function here did *not* raise an exception, the program would still execute the `finally` block to close the file, but it would then continue below the entire `try` statement.

In this specific case, we've wrapped a call to a file-processing function in a `try` with a `finally` clause to make sure that the file is always closed, and thus finalized, whether the function triggers an exception or not. This way, later code can be sure that the file's output buffer's content has been flushed from memory to disk. A similar code structure can guarantee that server connections are closed, and so on.

As we learned in Chapter 9, file objects are automatically closed on garbage collection in standard Python (CPython); this is especially useful for temporary files that we don't assign to variables. However, it's not always easy to predict when garbage collection will occur, especially in larger programs or alternative Python implementations with differing garbage collection policies (e.g., Jython, PyPy). The `try` statement makes file closes more explicit and predictable and pertains to a specific block of code. It ensures that the file will be closed on block exit, regardless of whether an exception occurs or not.

This particular example's function isn't all that useful (it just raises an exception), but wrapping calls in `try`/`finally` statements is a good way to ensure that your closing-time termination activities always run. Again, Python always runs the code in your `finally` blocks, regardless of whether an exception happens in the `try` block.[2]

Notice how the user-defined exception here is again defined with a *class*—as we'll see more formally in the next chapter, exceptions today must all be class instances in 2.6, 3.0, and later releases in both lines.

Unified try/except/finally

In all versions of Python prior to release 2.5 (for its first 15 years of life, more or less), the `try` statement came in two flavors and was really two separate statements—we could either use a `finally` to ensure that cleanup code was always run, or write

---

2. Unless Python crashes completely, of course. It does a good job of avoiding this, though, by checking all possible errors as a program runs. When a program does crash hard, it is usually due to a bug in linked-in C extension code, outside of Python's scope.

except blocks to catch and recover from specific exceptions and optionally specify an else clause to be run if no exceptions occurred.

That is, the finally clause could not be mixed with except and else. This was partly because of implementation issues, and partly because the meaning of mixing the two seemed obscure—catching and recovering from exceptions seemed a disjoint concept from performing cleanup actions.

In Python 2.5 and later, though, the two statements have merged. Today, we can mix finally, except, and else clauses in the same statement—in part because of similar utility in the Java language. That is, we can now write a statement of this form:

```
try:                            # Merged form
    main-action
except Exception1:
    handler1
except Exception2:              # Catch exceptions
    handler2
...
else:                           # No-exception handler
    else-block
finally:                        # The finally encloses all else
    finally-block
```

The code in this statement's *main-action* block is executed first, as usual. If that code raises an exception, all the except blocks are tested, one after another, looking for a match to the exception raised. If the exception raised is Exception1, the *handler1* block is executed; if it's Exception2, *handler2* is run, and so on. If no exception is raised, the *else-block* is executed.

No matter what's happened previously, the *finally-block* is executed once the main action block is complete and any raised exceptions have been handled. In fact, the code in the *finally-block* will be run even if there is an error in an exception handler or the *else-block* and a new exception is raised.

As always, the finally clause does not end the exception—if an exception is active when the *finally-block* is executed, it continues to be propagated after the *finally-block* runs, and control jumps somewhere else in the program (to another try, or to the default top-level handler). If no exception is active when the finally is run, control resumes after the entire try statement.

The net effect is that the finally is always run, regardless of whether:

- An exception occurred in the main action and was handled.
- An exception occurred in the main action and was not handled.
- No exceptions occurred in the main action.
- A new exception was triggered in one of the handlers.

Again, the finally serves to specify cleanup actions that must always occur on the way out of the try, regardless of what exceptions have been raised or handled.

Unified try Statement Syntax

When combined like this, the `try` statement must have either an `except` or a `finally`, and the order of its parts must be like this:

```
try -> except -> else -> finally
```

where the `else` and `finally` are optional, and there may be zero or more `except`s, but there must be at least one `except` if an `else` appears. Really, the `try` statement consists of two parts: `except`s with an optional `else`, and/or the `finally`.

In fact, it's more accurate to describe the merged statement's syntactic form this way (square brackets mean optional and star means zero-or-more here):

```
try:                              # Format 1
    statements
except [type [as value]]:         # [type [, value]] in Python 2.X
    statements
[except [type [as value]]:
    statements]*
[else:
    statements]
[finally:
    statements]


try:                              # Format 2
    statements
finally:
    statements
```

Because of these rules, the `else` can appear only if there is at least one `except`, and it's always possible to mix `except` and `finally`, regardless of whether an `else` appears or not. It's also possible to mix `finally` and `else`, but only if an `except` appears too (though the `except` can omit an exception name to catch everything and run a `raise` statement, described later, to reraise the current exception). If you violate any of these ordering rules, Python will raise a syntax error exception before your code runs.

Combining finally and except by Nesting

Prior to Python 2.5, it is actually possible to combine `finally` and `except` clauses in a `try` by syntactically nesting a `try/except` in the `try` block of a `try/finally` statement. We'll explore this technique more fully in Chapter 36, but the basics may help clarify the meaning of a combined `try`—the following has the same effect as the new merged form shown at the start of this section:

```
try:                              # Nested equivalent to merged form
    try:
        main-action
    except Exception1:
        handler1
    except Exception2:
        handler2
```

```
    ...
    else:
        no-error
finally:
    cleanup
```

Again, the `finally` block is always run on the way out, regardless of what happened in the main action and regardless of any exception handlers run in the nested `try` (trace through the four cases listed previously to see how this works the same). Since an `else` always requires an `except`, this nested form even sports the same mixing constraints of the unified statement form outlined in the preceding section.

However, this nested equivalent seems more obscure to some, and requires more code than the new merged form—though just one four-character line plus extra indentation. Mixing `finally` into the same statement makes your code arguably easier to write and read, and is a generally preferred technique today.

Unified try Example

Here's a demonstration of the merged `try` statement form at work. The following file, *mergedexc.py*, codes four common scenarios, with `print` statements that describe the meaning of each:

```python
# File mergedexc.py (Python 3.X + 2.X)
sep = '-' * 45 + '\n'


print(sep + 'EXCEPTION RAISED AND CAUGHT')
try:
    x = 'spam'[99]
except IndexError:
    print('except run')
finally:
    print('finally run')
print('after run')


print(sep + 'NO EXCEPTION RAISED')
try:
    x = 'spam'[3]
except IndexError:
    print('except run')
finally:
    print('finally run')
print('after run')


print(sep + 'NO EXCEPTION RAISED, WITH ELSE')
try:
    x = 'spam'[3]
except IndexError:
    print('except run')
else:
```

```
    print('else run')
finally:
    print('finally run')
print('after run')


print(sep + 'EXCEPTION RAISED BUT NOT CAUGHT')
try:
    x = 1 / 0
except IndexError:
    print('except run')
finally:
    print('finally run')
print('after run')
```

When this code is run, the following output is produced in Python 3.3; in 2.X, its behavior and output are the same because the **print** calls each print a single item, though the error message text varies slightly. Trace through the code to see how exception handling produces the output of each of the four tests here:

```
c:\code> py -3 mergedexc.py
-----------------------------------------------
EXCEPTION RAISED AND CAUGHT
except run
finally run
after run
-----------------------------------------------
NO EXCEPTION RAISED
finally run
after run
-----------------------------------------------
NO EXCEPTION RAISED, WITH ELSE
else run
finally run
after run
-----------------------------------------------
EXCEPTION RAISED BUT NOT CAUGHT
finally run
Traceback (most recent call last):
  File "mergedexc.py", line 39, in <module>
    x = 1 / 0
ZeroDivisionError: division by zero
```

This example uses built-in operations in the main action to trigger exceptions (or not), and it relies on the fact that Python always checks for errors as code is running. The next section shows how to raise exceptions manually instead.

The raise Statement

To trigger exceptions explicitly, you can code **raise** statements. Their general form is simple—a **raise** statement consists of the word **raise**, optionally followed by the class to be raised or an instance of it:

```
raise instance          # Raise instance of class
raise class             # Make and raise instance of class: makes an instance
raise                   # Reraise the most recent exception
```

As mentioned earlier, exceptions are always instances of classes in Python 2.6, 3.0, and later. Hence, the first **raise** form here is the most common—we provide an *instance* directly, either created before the **raise** or within the **raise** statement itself. If we pass a *class* instead, Python calls the class with no constructor arguments, to create an instance to be raised; this form is equivalent to adding parentheses after the class reference. The last form reraises the most recently raised exception; it's commonly used in exception handlers to propagate exceptions that have been caught.

Version skew note: Python 3.X no longer supports the **raise** *Exc, Args* form that is still available in Python 2.X. In 3.X, use the **raise** *Exc(Args)* instance-creation call form described in this book instead. The equivalent comma form in 2.X is legacy syntax provided for compatibility with the now-defunct string-based exceptions model, and it's deprecated in 2.X. If used, it is converted to the 3.X call form.

As in earlier releases, a **raise** *Exc* form is also allowed to name a class—it is converted to **raise** *Exc()* in both versions, calling the class constructor with no arguments. Besides its defunct comma syntax, Python 2.X's **raise** also allowed for either string or class exceptions, but the former is removed in 2.6, deprecated in 2.5, and not covered here except for a brief mention in the next chapter. Use classes for new exceptions today.

Raising Exceptions

To make this clearer, let's look at some examples. With built-in exceptions, the following two forms are equivalent—both raise an instance of the exception class named, but the first creates the instance implicitly:

```
raise IndexError        # Class (instance created)
raise IndexError()      # Instance (created in statement)
```

We can also create the instance ahead of time—because the **raise** statement accepts any kind of object reference, the following two examples raise IndexError just like the prior two:

```
exc = IndexError()      # Create instance ahead of time
raise exc

excs = [IndexError, TypeError]
raise excs[0]
```

When an exception is raised, Python sends the raised instance along with the exception. If a **try** includes an **except** *name* **as** *X*: clause, the variable *X* will be assigned the instance provided in the **raise**:

```
try:
    ...
except IndexError as X:          # X assigned the raised instance object
    ...
```

The **as** is optional in a **try** handler (if it's omitted, the instance is simply not assigned to a name), but including it allows the handler to access both data in the instance and methods in the exception class.

This model works the same for user-defined exceptions we code with classes—the following, for example, passes to the exception class constructor arguments that become available in the handler through the assigned instance:

```
class MyExc(Exception): pass
...
raise MyExc('spam')              # Exception class with constructor args
...
try:
    ...
except MyExc as X:               # Instance attributes available in handler
    print(X.args)
```

Because this encroaches on the next chapter's topic, though, I'll defer further details until then.

Regardless of how you name them, exceptions are always identified by class *instance objects*, and at most one is active at any given time. Once caught by an **except** clause anywhere in the program, an exception dies (i.e., won't propagate to another **try**), unless it's reraised by another **raise** statement or error.

Scopes and try except Variables

We'll study exception objects in more detail in the next chapter. Now that we've seen the **as** variable in action, though, we can finally clarify the related version-specific scope issue summarized in Chapter 17. In *Python 2.X*, the exception reference variable name in an **except** clause is *not* localized to the clause itself, and is available after the associated block runs:

```
c:\code> py -2
>>> try:
...     1 / 0
... except Exception as X:                # 2.X does not localize X either way
...     print X
...
integer division or modulo by zero
>>> X
ZeroDivisionError('integer division or modulo by zero',)
```

This is true in 2.X whether we use the 3.X-style **as** or the earlier comma syntax:

```
>>> try:
...     1 / 0
... except Exception, X:
```

```
...          print X
...
integer division or modulo by zero
>>> X
ZeroDivisionError('integer division or modulo by zero',)
```

By contrast, *Python 3.X* localizes the exception reference name to the **except** block—
the variable is not available after the block exits, much like a temporary loop variable
in 3.X comprehension expressions (3.X also doesn't accept 2.X's **except** comma syntax,
as noted earlier):

```
c:\code> py -3
>>> try:
...          1 / 0
... except Exception, X:
SyntaxError: invalid syntax

>>> try:
...          1 / 0
... except Exception as X:              # 3.X localizes 'as' names to except block
...          print(X)
...
division by zero
>>> X
NameError: name 'X' is not defined
```

Unlike comprehension loop variables, though, this variable is *removed* after the
except block exits in 3.X. It does so because it would otherwise retain a reference to
the runtime call stack, which would defer garbage collection and thus retain excess
memory space. This removal occurs, though, even if you're using the name elsewhere,
and is more extreme policy than that used for comprehensions:

```
>>> X = 99
>>> try:
...          1 / 0
... except Exception as X:              # 3.X localizes _and_ removes on exit!
...          print(X)
...
division by zero
>>> X
NameError: name 'X' is not defined

>>> X = 99
>>> {X for X in 'spam'}                 # 2.X/3.X localizes only: not removed
{'s', 'a', 'p', 'm'}
>>> X
99
```

Because of this, you should generally use unique variable names in your **try** statement's
except clauses, even if they are localized by scope. If you do need to reference the
exception instance after the **try** statement, simply assign it to another name that won't
be automatically removed:

```
>>> try:
...     1 / 0
... except Exception as X:                  # Python removes this reference
...     print(X)
...     Saveit = X                           # Assign exc to retain exc if needed
...
division by zero
>>> X
NameError: name 'X' is not defined
>>> Saveit
ZeroDivisionError('division by zero',)
```

Propagating Exceptions with raise

The raise statement is a bit more feature-rich than we've seen thus far. For example,
a raise that does not include an exception name or extra data value simply reraises the
current exception. This form is typically used if you need to catch and handle an exception but don't want the exception to die in your code:

```
>>> try:
...     raise IndexError('spam')            # Exceptions remember arguments
... except IndexError:
...     print('propagating')
...     raise                                # Reraise most recent exception
...
propagating
Traceback (most recent call last):
  File "<stdin>", line 2, in <module>
IndexError: spam
```

Running a raise this way reraises the exception and propagates it to a higher handler
(or the default handler at the top, which stops the program with a standard error message). Notice how the argument we passed to the exception class shows up in the error
messages; you'll learn why this happens in the next chapter.

Python 3.X Exception Chaining: raise from

Exceptions can sometimes be triggered in response to other exceptions—both deliberately and by new program errors. To support full disclosure in such cases, Python
3.X (but not 2.X) also allows raise statements to have an optional from clause:

```
raise newexception from otherexception
```

When the from is used in an explicit raise request, the expression following from specifies another exception class or instance to attach to the __cause__ attribute of the new
exception being raised. If the raised exception is not caught, Python prints both exceptions as part of the standard error message:

```
>>> try:
...     1 / 0
... except Exception as E:
...     raise TypeError('Bad') from E        # Explicitly chained exceptions
```

```
   ...
Traceback (most recent call last):
  File "<stdin>", line 2, in <module>
ZeroDivisionError: division by zero

The above exception was the direct cause of the following exception:

Traceback (most recent call last):
  File "<stdin>", line 4, in <module>
TypeError: Bad
```

When an exception is raised implicitly by a program error inside an exception handler, a similar procedure is followed automatically: the previous exception is attached to the new exception's __context__ attribute and is again displayed in the standard error message if the exception goes uncaught:

```
>>> try:
...     1 / 0
... except:
...     badname                              # Implicitly chained exceptions
...
Traceback (most recent call last):
  File "<stdin>", line 2, in <module>
ZeroDivisionError: division by zero

During handling of the above exception, another exception occurred:

Traceback (most recent call last):
  File "<stdin>", line 4, in <module>
NameError: name 'badname' is not defined
```

In both cases, because the original exception objects thus attached to new exception objects may *themselves* have attached causes, the causality chain can be *arbitrary long*, and is displayed in full in error messages. That is, error messages might give more than two exceptions. The net effect in both explicit and implicit contexts is to allow programmers to know all exceptions involved, when one exception triggers another:

```
>>> try:
...     try:
...         raise IndexError()
...     except Exception as E:
...         raise TypeError() from E
... except Exception as E:
...     raise SyntaxError() from E
...
Traceback (most recent call last):
  File "<stdin>", line 3, in <module>
IndexError

The above exception was the direct cause of the following exception:

Traceback (most recent call last):
  File "<stdin>", line 5, in <module>
TypeError
```

```
The above exception was the direct cause of the following exception:

Traceback (most recent call last):
  File "<stdin>", line 7, in <module>
SyntaxError: None
```

Code like the following would similarly display three exceptions, though implicitly triggered here:

```
try:
    try:
        1 / 0
    except:
        badname
except:
    open('nonesuch')
```

Like the unified try, chained exceptions are similar to utility in other languages (including Java and C#) though it's not clear which languages were borrowers. In Python, it's a still somewhat obscure extension, so we'll defer to Python's manuals for more details. In fact, Python 3.3 adds a way to *stop* exceptions from chaining, per the following note.

> *Python 3.3 chained exception suppression:* raise from None. Python 3.3 introduces a new syntax form—using None as the exception name in the raise from statement:
>
> ```
> raise newexception from None
> ```
>
> This allows the display of the chained exception context described in the preceding section to be disabled. This makes for less cluttered error messages in applications that convert between exception types while processing exception chains.

The assert Statement

As a somewhat special case for debugging purposes, Python includes the assert statement. It is mostly just syntactic shorthand for a common raise usage pattern, and an assert can be thought of as a *conditional* raise statement. A statement of the form:

```
assert test, data            # The data part is optional
```

works like the following code:

```
if __debug__:
    if not test:
        raise AssertionError(data)
```

In other words, if the *test* evaluates to false, Python raises an exception: the *data* item (if it's provided) is used as the exception's constructor argument. Like all exceptions, the AssertionError exception will kill your program if it's not caught with a try, in which case the *data* item shows up as part of the standard error message.

As an added feature, assert statements may be removed from a compiled program's byte code if the -O Python command-line flag is used, thereby optimizing the program. AssertionError is a built-in exception, and the __debug__ flag is a built-in name that is automatically set to True unless the -O flag is used. Use a command line like `python -O main.py` to run in optimized mode and disable (and hence skip) asserts.

Example: Trapping Constraints (but Not Errors!)

Assertions are typically used to verify program conditions during development. When displayed, their error message text automatically includes source code line information and the value listed in the assert statement. Consider the file *asserter.py*:

```
def f(x):
    assert x < 0, 'x must be negative'
    return x ** 2

% python
>>> import asserter
>>> asserter.f(1)
Traceback (most recent call last):
  File "<stdin>", line 1, in <module>
  File ".\asserter.py", line 2, in f
    assert x < 0, 'x must be negative'
AssertionError: x must be negative
```

It's important to keep in mind that assert is mostly intended for trapping user-defined constraints, not for catching genuine programming errors. Because Python traps programming errors itself, there is usually no need to code assert to catch things like out-of-bounds indexes, type mismatches, and zero divides:

```
def reciprocal(x):
    assert x != 0            # A generally useless assert!
    return 1 / x             # Python checks for zero automatically
```

Such assert use cases are usually superfluous—because Python raises exceptions on errors automatically, you might as well let it do the job for you. As a rule, you don't need to do error checking explicitly in your own code.

Of course, there are exceptions for most rules—as suggested earlier in the book, if a function has to perform long-running or unrecoverable actions before it reaches the place where an exception will be triggered, you still might want to test for errors. Even in this case, though, be careful not to make your tests overly specific or restrictive, or you will limit your code's utility.

For another example of common assert usage, see the abstract superclass example in Chapter 29; there, we used assert to make calls to undefined methods fail with a message. It's a rare but useful tool.

with/as Context Managers

Python 2.6 and 3.0 introduced a new exception-related statement—the `with`, and its optional `as` clause. This statement is designed to work with *context manager* objects, which support a new method-based protocol, similar in spirit to the way that iteration tools work with methods of the iteration protocol. This feature is also available as an option in 2.5, but must be enabled there with an `import` of this form:

```
from __future__ import with_statement
```

The `with` statement is also similar to a "using" statement in the C# language. Although a somewhat optional and advanced tools-oriented topic (and once a candidate for the next part of the book), context managers are lightweight and useful enough to group with the rest of the exception toolset here.

In short, the `with`/`as` statement is designed to be an alternative to a common `try`/`finally` usage idiom; like that statement, `with` is in large part intended for specifying termination-time or "cleanup" activities that must run regardless of whether an exception occurs during a processing step.

Unlike `try`/`finally`, the `with` statement is based upon an object protocol for specifying actions to be run around a block of code. This makes `with` less general, qualifies it as redundant in termination roles, and requires coding classes for objects that do not support its protocol. On the other hand, `with` also handles entry actions, can reduce code size, and allows code contexts to be managed with full OOP.

Python enhances some built-in tools with context managers, such as files that automatically close themselves and thread locks that automatically lock and unlock, but programmers can code context managers of their own with classes, too. Let's take a brief look at the statement and its implicit protocol.

Basic Usage

The basic format of the `with` statement looks like this, with an optional part in square brackets here:

```
with expression [as variable]:
    with-block
```

The *expression* here is assumed to return an object that supports the context management protocol (more on this protocol in a moment). This object may also return a value that will be assigned to the name *variable* if the optional `as` clause is present.

Note that the *variable* is not necessarily assigned the *result* of the *expression*; the result of the *expression* is the object that supports the context protocol, and the *variable* may be assigned something else intended to be used inside the statement. The object returned by the *expression* may then run startup code before the *with-block* is started, as well as termination code after the block is done, regardless of whether the block raised an exception or not.

Some built-in Python objects have been augmented to support the context management protocol, and so can be used with the `with` statement. For example, file objects (covered in Chapter 9) have a context manager that automatically closes the file after the `with` block regardless of whether an exception is raised, and regardless of if or when the version of Python running the code may close automatically:

```
with open(r'C:\misc\data') as myfile:
    for line in myfile:
        print(line)
        ...more code here...
```

Here, the call to `open` returns a simple file object that is assigned to the name `myfile`. We can use `myfile` with the usual file tools—in this case, the file iterator reads line by line in the `for` loop.

However, this object also supports the context management protocol used by the `with` statement. After this `with` statement has run, the context management machinery guarantees that the file object referenced by `myfile` is automatically closed, even if the `for` loop raised an exception while processing the file.

Although file objects may be automatically closed on garbage collection, it's not always straightforward to know when that will occur, especially when using alternative Python implementations. The `with` statement in this role is an alternative that allows us to be sure that the close will occur after execution of a specific block of code.

As we saw earlier, we can achieve a similar effect with the more general and explicit `try/finally` statement, but it requires three more lines of administrative code in this case (four instead of just one):

```
myfile = open(r'C:\misc\data')
try:
    for line in myfile:
        print(line)
        ...more code here...
finally:
    myfile.close()
```

We won't cover Python's multithreading modules in this book (for more on that topic, see follow-up application-level texts such as *Programming Python*) but the lock and condition synchronization objects they define may also be used with the `with` statement, because they support the context management protocol—in this case adding both entry and exit actions around a block:

```
lock = threading.Lock()                    # After: import threading
with lock:
    # critical section of code
    ...access shared resources...
```

Here, the context management machinery guarantees that the lock is automatically acquired before the block is executed and released once the block is complete, regardless of exception outcomes.

As introduced in Chapter 5, the decimal module also uses context managers to simplify saving and restoring the current decimal context, which specifies the precision and rounding characteristics for calculations:

```
with decimal.localcontext() as ctx:          # After: import decimal
    ctx.prec = 2
    x = decimal.Decimal('1.00') / decimal.Decimal('3.00')
```

After this statement runs, the current thread's context manager state is automatically restored to what it was before the statement began. To do the same with a try/finally, we would need to save the context before and restore it manually after the nested block.

The Context Management Protocol

Although some built-in types come with context managers, we can also write new ones of our own. To implement context managers, classes use special methods that fall into the operator overloading category to tap into the with statement. The interface expected of objects used in with statements is somewhat complex, and most programmers only need to know how to use existing context managers. For tool builders who might want to write new application-specific context managers, though, let's take a quick look at what's involved.

Here's how the with statement actually works:

1. The expression is evaluated, resulting in an object known as a *context manager* that must have __enter__ and __exit__ methods.

2. The context manager's __enter__ method is called. The value it returns is assigned to the variable in the as clause if present, or simply discarded otherwise.

3. The code in the nested with block is executed.

4. If the with block raises an exception, the __exit__(*type, value, traceback*) method is called with the exception details. These are the same three values returned by sys.exc_info, described in the Python manuals and later in this part of the book. If this method returns a false value, the exception is reraised; otherwise, the exception is terminated. The exception should normally be reraised so that it is propagated outside the with statement.

5. If the with block does not raise an exception, the __exit__ method is still called, but its *type*, *value*, and *traceback* arguments are all passed in as None.

Let's look at a quick demo of the protocol in action. The following, file *withas.py*, defines a context manager object that traces the entry and exit of the with block in any with statement it is used for:

```
class TraceBlock:
    def message(self, arg):
        print('running ' + arg)
    def __enter__(self):
```

```
            print('starting with block')
            return self
        def __exit__(self, exc_type, exc_value, exc_tb):
            if exc_type is None:
                print('exited normally\n')
            else:
                print('raise an exception! ' + str(exc_type))
                return False      # Propagate

if __name__ == '__main__':
    with TraceBlock() as action:
        action.message('test 1')
        print('reached')

    with TraceBlock() as action:
        action.message('test 2')
        raise TypeError
        print('not reached')
```

Notice that this class's __exit__ method returns False to propagate the exception; deleting the return statement would have the same effect, as the default None return value of functions is False by definition. Also notice that the __enter__ method returns self as the object to assign to the as variable; in other use cases, this might return a completely different object instead.

When run, the context manager traces the entry and exit of the with statement block with its __enter__ and __exit__ methods. Here's the script in action being run under either Python 3.X or 2.X (as usual, mileage varies slightly in some 2.X displays, and this runs on 2.6, 2.7, and 2.5 if enabled):

```
c:\code> py -3 withas.py
starting with block
running test 1
reached
exited normally

starting with block
running test 2
raise an exception! <class 'TypeError'>
Traceback (most recent call last):
  File "withas.py", line 22, in <module>
    raise TypeError
TypeError
```

Context managers can also utilize OOP state information and inheritance, but are somewhat advanced devices for tool builders, so we'll skip additional details here (see Python's standard manuals for the full story—for example, there's a new contextlib standard module that provides additional tools for coding context managers). For simpler purposes, the try/finally statement provides sufficient support for termination-time activities without coding classes.

Multiple Context Managers in 3.1, 2.7, and Later

Python 3.1 introduced a `with` extension that eventually appeared in Python 2.7 as well. In these and later Pythons, the `with` statement may also specify multiple (sometimes referred to as "nested") context managers with new comma syntax. In the following, for example, both files' exit actions are automatically run when the statement block exits, regardless of exception outcomes:

```
with open('data') as fin, open('res', 'w') as fout:
    for line in fin:
        if 'some key' in line:
            fout.write(line)
```

Any number of context manager items may be listed, and multiple items work the same as nested `with` statements. In Pythons that support this, the following code:

```
with A() as a, B() as b:
    ...statements...
```

is equivalent to the following, which also works in 3.0 and 2.6:

```
with A() as a:
    with B() as b:
        ...statements...
```

Python 3.1's release notes have additional details, but here's a quick look at the extension in action—to implement a parallel lines scan of two files, the following uses `with` to open two files at once and zip together their lines, without having to manually close when finished (assuming manual closes are required):

```
>>> with open('script1.py') as f1, open('script2.py') as f2:
...     for pair in zip(f1, f2):
...         print(pair)
...
('# A first Python script\n', 'import sys\n')
('import sys                 # Load a library module\n', 'print(sys.path)\n')
('print(sys.platform)\n', 'x = 2\n')
('print(2 ** 32)             # Raise 2 to a power\n', 'print(x ** 32)\n')
```

You might use this coding structure to do a line-by-line *comparison* of two text files, for example—replace the `print` with an `if` for a simple file comparison operation, and use `enumerate` for line numbers:

```
with open('script1.py') as f1, open('script2.py') as f2:
    for (linenum, (line1, line2)) in enumerate(zip(f1, f2)):
        if line1 != line2:
            print('%s\n%r\n%r' % (linenum, line1, line2))
```

Still, the preceding technique isn't all that useful in CPython, because input file objects don't require a buffer flush, and file objects are closed automatically when reclaimed if still open. In CPython, the files would be reclaimed immediately if the parallel scan were coded the following simpler way:

```
for pair in zip(open('script1.py'), open('script2.py')):    # Same effect, auto close
    print(pair)
```

On the other hand, alternative implementations such as PyPy and Jython may require more direct closure inside loops to avoid taxing system resources, due to differing garbage collectors. Even more usefully, the following automatically closes the output file on statement exit, to ensure that any buffered text is transferred to disk immediately:

```
>>> with open('script2.py') as fin, open('upper.py', 'w') as fout:
...     for line in fin:
...         fout.write(line.upper())
...
>>> print(open('upper.py').read())
IMPORT SYS
PRINT(SYS.PATH)
X = 2
PRINT(X ** 32)
```

In both cases, we can instead simply open files in individual statements and close after processing if needed, and in some scripts we probably should—there's no point in using statements that catch an exception if it means your program is out of business anyhow!

```
fin  = open('script2.py')
fout = open('upper.py', 'w')
for line in fin:                        # Same effect as preceding code, auto close
    fout.write(line.upper())
```

However, in cases where programs must continue after exceptions, the `with` forms also implicitly catch exceptions, and thereby also avoid a `try`/`finally` in cases where close is required. The equivalent without `with` is more explicit, but requires noticeably more code:

```
fin  = open('script2.py')
fout = open('upper.py', 'w')
try:                                    # Same effect but explicit close on error
    for line in fin:
        fout.write(line.upper())
finally:
    fin.close()
    fout.close()
```

On the other hand, the `try`/`finally` is a single tool that applies to all finalization cases, whereas the `with` adds a second tool that can be more concise, but applies to only certain objects types, and doubles the required knowledge base of programmers. As usual, you'll have to weigh the tradeoffs for yourself.

Chapter Summary

In this chapter, we took a more detailed look at exception processing by exploring the statements related to exceptions in Python: `try` to catch them, `raise` to trigger them, `assert` to raise them conditionally, and `with` to wrap code blocks in context managers that specify entry and exit actions.

Up to this point, exceptions probably seem like a fairly lightweight tool, and in fact, they are; the only substantially complex thing about them is how they are identified. The next chapter continues our exploration by describing how to implement exception objects of your own; as you'll see, classes allow you to code new exceptions specific to your programs. Before we move ahead, though, let's work through the following short quiz on the basics covered here.

Test Your Knowledge: Quiz

1. What is the `try` statement for?
2. What are the two common variations of the `try` statement?
3. What is the `raise` statement for?
4. What is the `assert` statement designed to do, and what other statement is it like?
5. What is the `with/as` statement designed to do, and what other statement is it like?

Test Your Knowledge: Answers

1. The `try` statement catches and recovers from exceptions—it specifies a block of code to run, and one or more handlers for exceptions that may be raised during the block's execution.

2. The two common variations on the `try` statement are `try/except/else` (for catching exceptions) and `try/finally` (for specifying cleanup actions that must occur whether an exception is raised or not). Through Python 2.4, these were separate statements that could be combined by syntactic nesting; in 2.5 and later, `except` and `finally` blocks may be mixed in the same statement, so the two statement forms are merged. In the merged form, the `finally` is still run on the way out of the `try`, regardless of what exceptions may have been raised or handled. In fact, the merged form is equivalent to nesting a `try/except/else` in a `try/finally`, and the two still have logically distinct roles.

3. The `raise` statement raises (triggers) an exception. Python raises built-in exceptions on errors internally, but your scripts can trigger built-in or user-defined exceptions with `raise`, too.

4. The `assert` statement raises an `AssertionError` exception if a condition is false. It works like a conditional `raise` statement wrapped up in an `if` statement, and can be disabled with a -0 switch.

5. The `with/as` statement is designed to automate startup and termination activities that must occur around a block of code. It is roughly like a `try/finally` statement in that its exit actions run whether an exception occurred or not, but it allows a richer object-based protocol for specifying entry *and* exit actions, and may reduce

code size. Still, it's not quite as general, as it applies only to objects that support its protocol; `try` handles many more use cases.

Exception Objects

So far, I've been deliberately vague about what an exception actually *is*. As suggested in the prior chapter, as of Python 2.6 and 3.0 both built-in and user-defined exceptions are identified by *class instance objects*. This is what is raised and propagated along by exception processing, and the source of the class matched against exceptions named in try statements.

Although this means you must use object-oriented programming to define new exceptions in your programs—and introduces a knowledge dependency that deferred full exception coverage to this part of the book—basing exceptions on classes and OOP offers a number of benefits. Among them, class-based exceptions:

- **Can be organized into categories**. Exceptions coded as classes support future changes by providing categories—adding new exceptions in the future won't generally require changes in try statements.

- **Have state information and behavior**. Exception classes provide a natural place for us to store context information and tools for use in the try handler—instances have access to both attached state information and callable methods.

- **Support inheritance**. Class-based exceptions can participate in inheritance hierarchies to obtain and customize common behavior—inherited display methods, for example, can provide a common look and feel for error messages.

Because of these advantages, class-based exceptions support program evolution and larger systems well. As we'll find, all built-in exceptions are identified by classes and are organized into an inheritance tree, for the reasons just listed. You can do the same with user-defined exceptions of your own.

In fact, in Python 3.X the built-in exceptions we'll study here turn out to be integral to new exceptions you define. Because 3.X requires user-defined exceptions to inherit from built-in exception superclasses that provide useful defaults for printing and state retention, the task of coding user-defined exceptions also involves understanding the roles of these built-ins.

Version skew note: Python 2.6, 3.0, and later require exceptions to be defined by classes. In addition, 3.X requires exception classes to be derived from the `BaseException` built-in exception superclass, either directly or indirectly. As we'll see, most programs inherit from this class's `Exception` subclass, to support catchall handlers for normal exception types—naming it in a handler will thus catch everything most programs should. Python 2.X allows standalone classic classes to serve as exceptions, too, but it requires new-style classes to be derived from built-in exception classes, the same as 3.X.

Exceptions: Back to the Future

Once upon a time (well, prior to Python 2.6 and 3.0), it was possible to define exceptions in two different ways. This complicated `try` statements, `raise` statements, and Python in general. Today, there is only one way to do it. This is a good thing: it removes from the language substantial cruft accumulated for the sake of backward compatibility. Because the old way helps explain why exceptions are as they are today, though, and because it's not really possible to completely erase the history of something that has been used by on the order of a million people over the course of nearly two decades, let's begin our exploration of the present with a brief look at the past.

String Exceptions Are Right Out!

Prior to Python 2.6 and 3.0, it was possible to define exceptions with both class instances and string objects. String-based exceptions began issuing deprecation warnings in 2.5 and were removed in 2.6 and 3.0, so today you should use class-based exceptions, as shown in this book. If you work with legacy code, though, you might still come across string exceptions. They might also appear in books, tutorials, and web resources written a few years ago (which qualifies as an eternity in Python years!).

String exceptions were straightforward to use—any string would do, and they matched by object identity, not value (that is, using `is`, not `==`):

```
C:\code> C:\Python25\python
>>> myexc = "My exception string"              # Were we ever this young?...
>>> try:
...     raise myexc
... except myexc:
...     print('caught')
...
caught
```

This form of exception was removed because it was not as good as classes for larger programs and code maintenance. In modern Pythons, string exceptions trigger exceptions instead:

```
C:\code> py -3
>>> raise 'spam'
```

```
TypeError: exceptions must derive from BaseException

C:\code> py -2
>>> raise 'spam'
TypeError: exceptions must be old-style classes or derived from BaseException, ...etc
```

Although you can't use string exceptions today, they actually provide a natural vehicle for introducing the class-based exceptions model.

Class-Based Exceptions

Strings were a simple way to define exceptions. As described earlier, however, classes have some added advantages that merit a quick look. Most prominently, they allow us to identify exception *categories* that are more flexible to use and maintain than simple strings. Moreover, classes naturally allow for attached exception details and support inheritance. Because they are seen by many as the better approach, they are now required.

Coding details aside, the chief difference between string and class exceptions has to do with the way that exceptions raised are matched against except clauses in try statements:

- String exceptions were matched by simple *object identity*: the raised exception was matched to except clauses by Python's is test.
- Class exceptions are matched by *superclass relationships*: the raised exception matches an except clause if that except clause names the exception instance's class or any superclass of it.

That is, when a try statement's except clause lists a superclass, it catches instances of that superclass, as well as instances of all its subclasses lower in the class tree. The net effect is that class exceptions naturally support the construction of exception *hierarchies*: superclasses become category names, and subclasses become specific kinds of exceptions within a category. By naming a general exception superclass, an except clause can catch an entire category of exceptions—any more specific subclass will match.

String exceptions had no such concept: because they were matched by simple object identity, there was no direct way to organize exceptions into more flexible categories or groups. The net result was that exception handlers were coupled with exception sets in a way that made changes difficult.

In addition to this category idea, class-based exceptions better support exception *state information* (attached to instances) and allow exceptions to participate in *inheritance hierarchies* (to obtain common behaviors). Because they offer all the benefits of classes and OOP in general, they provide a more powerful alternative to the now-defunct string-based exceptions model in exchange for a small amount of additional code.

Coding Exceptions Classes

Let's look at an example to see how class exceptions translate to code. In the following file, *classexc.py*, we define a superclass called `General` and two subclasses called `Specific1` and `Specific2`. This example illustrates the notion of exception categories—`General` is a category name, and its two subclasses are specific types of exceptions within the category. Handlers that catch `General` will also catch any subclasses of it, including `Specific1` and `Specific2`:

```
class General(Exception): pass
class Specific1(General): pass
class Specific2(General): pass

def raiser0():
    X = General()          # Raise superclass instance
    raise X

def raiser1():
    X = Specific1()        # Raise subclass instance
    raise X

def raiser2():
    X = Specific2()        # Raise different subclass instance
    raise X

for func in (raiser0, raiser1, raiser2):
    try:
        func()
    except General:        # Match General or any subclass of it
        import sys
        print('caught: %s' % sys.exc_info()[0])

C:\code> python classexc.py
caught: <class '__main__.General'>
caught: <class '__main__.Specific1'>
caught: <class '__main__.Specific2'>
```

This code is mostly straightforward, but here are a few points to notice:

Exception superclass

    Classes used to build exception category trees have very few requirements—in fact, in this example they are mostly empty, with bodies that do nothing but `pass`. Notice, though, how the top-level class here inherits from the built-in `Exception` class. This is required in Python 3.X; Python 2.X allows standalone classic classes to serve as exceptions too, but it requires new-style classes to be derived from built-in exception classes just as in 3.X. Although we don't employ it here, because `Exception` provides some useful behavior we'll meet later, it's a good idea to inherit from it in either Python.

Raising instances

    In this code, we call classes to make *instances* for the `raise` statements. In the class exception model, we always raise and catch a class instance object. If we list a class name without parentheses in a `raise`, Python calls the class with no constructor argument to make an instance for us. Exception instances can be created before the `raise`, as done here, or within the `raise` statement itself.

Catching categories

This code includes functions that raise instances of all three of our classes as exceptions, as well as a top-level `try` that calls the functions and catches `General` exceptions. The same `try` also catches the two specific exceptions, because they are subclasses of `General`—members of its category.

Exception details

The exception handler here uses the `sys.exc_info` call—as we'll see in more detail in the next chapter, it's how we can grab hold of the most recently raised exception in a generic fashion. Briefly, the first item in its result is the class of the exception raised, and the second is the actual instance raised. In a general `except` clause like the one here that catches all classes in a category, `sys.exc_info` is one way to determine exactly what's occurred. In this particular case, it's equivalent to fetching the instance's `__class__` attribute. As we'll see in the next chapter, the `sys.exc_info` scheme is also commonly used with empty `except` clauses that catch everything.

The last point merits further explanation. When an exception is caught, we can be sure that the instance raised is an instance of the class listed in the `except`, or one of its more specific subclasses. Because of this, the `__class__` attribute of the instance also gives the exception type. The following variant in *classexc2.py*, for example, works the same as the prior example—it uses the `as` extension in its `except` clause to assign a variable to the instance actually raised:

```
class General(Exception): pass
class Specific1(General): pass
class Specific2(General): pass

def raiser0(): raise General()
def raiser1(): raise Specific1()
def raiser2(): raise Specific2()

for func in (raiser0, raiser1, raiser2):
    try:
        func()
    except General as X:                    # X is the raised instance
        print('caught: %s' % X.__class__)   # Same as sys.exc_info()[0]
```

Because `__class__` can be used like this to determine the specific type of exception raised, `sys.exc_info` is more useful for empty `except` clauses that do not otherwise have a way to access the instance or its class. Furthermore, more realistic programs usually should *not have to care* about which specific exception was raised at all—by calling methods of the exception class instance generically, we automatically dispatch to behavior tailored for the exception raised.

More on this and `sys.exc_info` in the next chapter; also see Chapter 29 and Part VI at large if you've forgotten what `__class__` means in an instance, and the prior chapter for a review of the `as` used here.

Why Exception Hierarchies?

Because there are only three possible exceptions in the prior section's example, it doesn't really do justice to the utility of class exceptions. In fact, we could achieve the same effects by coding a list of exception names in parentheses within the **except** clause:

```
try:
    func()
except (General, Specific1, Specific2):     # Catch any of these
    ...
```

This approach worked for the defunct string exception model too. For large or high exception hierarchies, however, it may be easier to catch categories using class-based categories than to list every member of a category in a single **except** clause. Perhaps more importantly, you can extend exception hierarchies as software needs evolve by adding new subclasses without breaking existing code.

Suppose, for example, you code a numeric programming library in Python, to be used by a large number of people. While you are writing your library, you identify two things that can go wrong with numbers in your code—division by zero, and numeric overflow. You document these as the two standalone exceptions that your library may raise:

```
# mathlib.py

class Divzero(Exception): pass
class Oflow(Exception): pass

def func():
    ...
    raise Divzero()

...and so on...
```

Now, when people use your library, they typically wrap calls to your functions or classes in **try** statements that catch your two exceptions; after all, if they do not catch your exceptions, exceptions from your library will kill their code:

```
# client.py

import mathlib

try:
    mathlib.func(...)
except (mathlib.Divzero, mathlib.Oflow):
    ...handle and recover...
```

This works fine, and lots of people start using your library. Six months down the road, though, you revise it (as programmers are prone to do!). Along the way, you identify a new thing that can go wrong—underflow, perhaps—and add that as a new exception:

```
# mathlib.py

class Divzero(Exception): pass
class Oflow(Exception): pass
class Uflow(Exception): pass
```

Unfortunately, when you re-release your code, you create a maintenance problem for your users. If they've listed your exceptions explicitly, they now have to go back and change every place they call your library to include the newly added exception name:

```
# client.py

try:
    mathlib.func(...)
except (mathlib.Divzero, mathlib.Oflow, mathlib.Uflow):
    ...handle and recover...
```

This may not be the end of the world. If your library is used only in-house, you can make the changes yourself. You might also ship a Python script that tries to fix such code automatically (it would probably be only a few dozen lines, and it would guess right at least some of the time). If many people have to change all their **try** statements each time you alter your exception set, though, this is not exactly the most polite of upgrade policies.

Your users might try to avoid this pitfall by coding empty **except** clauses to catch *all* possible exceptions:

```
# client.py

try:
    mathlib.func(...)
except:                          # Catch everything here (or catch Exception super)
    ...handle and recover...
```

But this workaround might catch more than they bargained for—things like running out of memory, keyboard interrupts (Ctrl-C), system exits, and even typos in their own **try** block's code will all trigger exceptions, and such things should pass, not be caught and erroneously classified as library errors. Catching the **Exception** super class improves on this, but still intercepts—and thus may mask—program errors.

And really, in this scenario users want to catch and recover from *only* the specific exceptions the library is defined and documented to raise. If any other exception occurs during a library call, it's likely a genuine bug in the library (and probably time to contact the vendor!). As a rule of thumb, it's usually better to be specific than general in exception handlers—an idea we'll revisit as a "gotcha" in the next chapter.[1]

So what to do, then? Class exception hierarchies fix this dilemma completely. Rather than defining your library's exceptions as a set of autonomous classes, arrange them into a class tree with a common superclass to encompass the entire category:

```
# mathlib.py

class NumErr(Exception): pass
class Divzero(NumErr): pass
class Oflow(NumErr): pass

def func():
    ...
    raise DivZero()

...and so on...
```

This way, users of your library simply need to list the common superclass (i.e., category) to catch all of your library's exceptions, both now and in the future:

```
# client.py

import mathlib

try:
    mathlib.func(...)
except mathlib.NumErr:
    ...report and recover...
```

When you go back and hack (update) your code again, you can add new exceptions as new subclasses of the common superclass:

```
# mathlib.py

...
class Uflow(NumErr): pass
```

The end result is that user code that catches your library's exceptions will keep working, *unchanged*. In fact, you are free to add, delete, and change exceptions arbitrarily in the future—as long as clients name the superclass, and that superclass remains intact, they are insulated from changes in your exceptions set. In other words, class exceptions provide a better answer to maintenance issues than strings could.

Class-based exception hierarchies also support state retention and inheritance in ways that make them ideal in larger programs. To understand these roles, though, we first

---

1. As a clever student of mine suggested, the library module could also provide a tuple object that contains all the exceptions the library can possibly raise—the client could then import the tuple and name it in an except clause to catch all the library's exceptions (recall that including a tuple in an except means catch *any* of its exceptions). When new exceptions are added later, the library can just expand the exported tuple. This would work, but you'd still need to keep the tuple up-to-date with raised exceptions inside the library module. Also, class hierarchies offer more benefits than just categories—they also support inherited state and methods and a customization model that individual exceptions do not.

need to see how user-defined exception classes relate to the built-in exceptions from which they inherit.

Built-in Exception Classes

I didn't really pull the prior section's examples out of thin air. All built-in exceptions that Python itself may raise are predefined class objects. Moreover, they are organized into a shallow hierarchy with general superclass categories and specific subclass types, much like the prior section's exceptions class tree.

In Python 3.X, all the familiar exceptions you've seen (e.g., `SyntaxError`) are really just predefined classes, available as built-in names in the module named `builtins`; in Python 2.X, they instead live in `__builtin__` and are also attributes of the standard library module `exceptions`. In addition, Python organizes the built-in exceptions into a hierarchy, to support a variety of catching modes. For example:

`BaseException`: *topmost root, printing and constructor defaults*
> The top-level root superclass of exceptions. This class is not supposed to be directly inherited by user-defined classes (use `Exception` instead). It provides default printing and state retention behavior inherited by subclasses. If the `str` built-in is called on an instance of this class (e.g., by `print`), the class returns the display strings of the constructor arguments passed when the instance was created (or an empty string if there were no arguments). In addition, unless subclasses replace this class's constructor, all of the arguments passed to this class at instance construction time are stored in its `args` attribute as a tuple.

`Exception`: *root of user-defined exceptions*
> The top-level root superclass of application-related exceptions. This is an immediate subclass of `BaseException` and is a superclass to every other built-in exception, except the system exit event classes (`SystemExit`, `KeyboardInterrupt`, and `GeneratorExit`). Nearly all user-defined classes should inherit from this class, not `BaseException`. When this convention is followed, naming `Exception` in a `try` statement's handler ensures that your program will catch everything but system exit events, which should normally be allowed to pass. In effect, `Exception` becomes a catchall in `try` statements and is more accurate than an empty `except`.

`ArithmeticError`: *root of numeric errors*
> A subclass of `Exception`, and the superclass of all numeric errors. Its subclasses identify specific numeric errors: `OverflowError`, `ZeroDivisionError`, and `FloatingPointError`.

`LookupError`: *root of indexing errors*
> A subclass of `Exception`, and the superclass category for indexing errors for both sequences and mappings—`IndexError` and `KeyError`—as well as some Unicode lookup errors.

And so on—because the built-in exception set is prone to frequent changes, this book doesn't document it exhaustively. You can read further about this structure in reference texts such as *Python Pocket Reference* or the Python library manual. In fact, the exceptions class tree differs slightly between Python 3.X and 2.X in ways we'll omit here, because they are not relevant to examples.

You can also see the built-in exceptions class tree in the help text of the `exceptions` module in Python 2.X only (see Chapter 4 and Chapter 15 for help on `help`):

```
>>> import exceptions
>>> help(exceptions)
...lots of text omitted...
```

This module is removed in 3.X, where you'll find up-to-date help in the other resources mentioned.

Built-in Exception Categories

The built-in class tree allows you to choose how specific or general your handlers will be. For example, because the built-in exception `ArithmeticError` is a superclass for more specific exceptions such as `OverflowError` and `ZeroDivisionError`:

- By listing `ArithmeticError` in a `try`, you will catch *any* kind of numeric error raised.
- By listing `ZeroDivisionError`, you will intercept *just* that specific type of error, and no others.

Similarly, because `Exception` is the superclass of all application-level exceptions in Python 3.X, you can generally use it as a *catchall*—the effect is much like an empty `except`, but it allows system exit exceptions to pass and propagate as they usually should:

```
try:
    action()
except Exception:                      # Exits not caught here
    ...handle all application exceptions...
else:
    ...handle no-exception case...
```

This doesn't quite work universally in Python 2.X, however, because standalone user-defined exceptions coded as classic classes are not required to be subclasses of the `Exception` root class. This technique is more reliable in Python 3.X, since it requires all classes to derive from built-in exceptions. Even in Python 3.X, though, this scheme suffers most of the same potential pitfalls as the empty `except`, as described in the prior chapter—it might intercept exceptions intended for elsewhere, and it might mask genuine programming errors. Since this is such a common issue, we'll revisit it as a "gotcha" in the next chapter.

Whether or not you will leverage the categories in the built-in class tree, it serves as a good example; by using similar techniques for class exceptions in your own code, you can provide exception sets that are flexible and easily modified.

 Python 3.3 reworks the built-in IO and OS exception hierarchies. It adds new specific exception classes corresponding to common file and system error numbers, and groups these and others related to operating system calls under the `OSError` category superclass. Former exception names are retained for backward compatibility.

Prior to this, programs inspect the data attached to the exception instance to see what specific error occurred, and possibly reraise others to be propagated (the `errno` module has names preset to the error codes for convenience, and the error number is available in both the generic tuple as `V.args[0]` and attribute `V.errno`):

```
c:\temp> py -3.2
>>> try:
...     f = open('nonesuch.txt')
... except IOError as V:
...     if V.errno == 2:                    # Or errno.N, V.args[0]
...         print('No such file')
...     else:
...         raise                           # Propagate others
...
No such file
```

This code still works in 3.3, but with the new classes, programs in 3.3 and later can be more specific about the exceptions they mean to process, and ignore others:

```
c:\temp> py -3.3
>>> try:
...     f = open('nonesuch.txt')
... except FileNotFoundError:
...     print('No such file')
...
No such file
```

For full details on this extension and its classes, see the other resources listed earlier.

Default Printing and State

Built-in exceptions also provide default print displays and state retention, which is often as much logic as user-defined classes require. Unless you redefine the constructors your classes inherit from them, any constructor arguments you pass to these classes are automatically saved in the instance's `args` tuple attribute, and are automatically displayed when the instance is printed. An empty tuple and display string are used if no constructor arguments are passed, and a single argument displays as itself (not as a tuple).

This explains why arguments passed to *built-in* exception classes show up in error messages—any constructor arguments are attached to the instance and displayed when the instance is printed:

```
>>> raise IndexError                      # Same as IndexError(): no arguments
Traceback (most recent call last):
  File "<stdin>", line 1, in <module>
IndexError

>>> raise IndexError('spam')              # Constructor argument attached, printed
Traceback (most recent call last):
  File "<stdin>", line 1, in <module>
IndexError: spam

>>> I = IndexError('spam')                # Available in object attribute
>>> I.args
('spam',)
>>> print(I)                              # Displays args when printed manually
spam
```

The same holds true for *user-defined* exceptions in Python 3.X (and for new-style classes in 2.X), because they inherit the constructor and display methods present in their built-in superclasses:

```
>>> class E(Exception): pass
...
>>> raise E
Traceback (most recent call last):
  File "<stdin>", line 1, in <module>
__main__.E

>>> raise E('spam')
Traceback (most recent call last):
  File "<stdin>", line 1, in <module>
__main__.E: spam

>>> I = E('spam')
>>> I.args
('spam',)
>>> print(I)
spam
```

When intercepted in a `try` statement, the exception instance object gives access to both the original constructor arguments and the display method:

```
>>> try:
...     raise E('spam')
... except E as X:
...     print(X)                          # Displays and saves constructor arguments
...     print(X.args)
...     print(repr(X))
...
spam
('spam',)
E('spam',)
```

```
>>> try:                                    # Multiple arguments save/display a tuple
...     raise E('spam', 'eggs', 'ham')
... except E as X:
...     print('%s %s' % (X, X.args))
...
('spam', 'eggs', 'ham') ('spam', 'eggs', 'ham')
```

Note that exception instance objects are not strings themselves, but use the __str__ operator overloading protocol we studied in Chapter 30 to provide display strings when printed; to concatenate with real strings, perform manual conversions: str(X) + 'as tr', '%s' % X, and the like.

Although this automatic state and display support is useful by itself, for more specific display and state retention needs you can always redefine inherited methods such as __str__ and __init__ in Exception subclasses—as the next section shows.

Custom Print Displays

As we saw in the preceding section, by default, instances of class-based exceptions display whatever you passed to the class constructor when they are caught and printed:

```
>>> class MyBad(Exception): pass
...
>>> try:
...     raise MyBad('Sorry--my mistake!')
... except MyBad as X:
...     print(X)
...
Sorry--my mistake!
```

This inherited default display model is also used if the exception is displayed as part of an error message when the exception is not caught:

```
>>> raise MyBad('Sorry--my mistake!')
Traceback (most recent call last):
  File "<stdin>", line 1, in <module>
__main__.MyBad: Sorry--my mistake!
```

For many roles, this is sufficient. To provide a more custom display, though, you can define one of two string-representation overloading methods in your class (__repr__ or __str__) to return the string you want to display for your exception. The string the method returns will be displayed if the exception either is caught and printed or reaches the default handler:

```
>>> class MyBad(Exception):
...     def __str__(self):
...         return 'Always look on the bright side of life...'
...
>>> try:
...     raise MyBad()
... except MyBad as X:
...     print(X)
```

```
...
Always look on the bright side of life...

>>> raise MyBad()
Traceback (most recent call last):
  File "<stdin>", line 1, in <module>
__main__.MyBad: Always look on the bright side of life...
```

Whatever your method returns is included in error messages for uncaught exceptions and used when exceptions are printed explicitly. The method returns a hardcoded string here to illustrate, but it can also perform arbitrary text processing, possibly using state information attached to the instance object. The next section looks at state information options.

> A subtle point here: you generally must redefine __str__ for exception display purposes, because the built-in exception superclasses already have a __str__ method, and __str__ is preferred to __repr__ in some contexts—including error message displays. If you define a __repr__, printing will happily call the built-in superclass's __str__ instead!
>
> ```
> >>> class E(Exception):
>         def __repr__(self): return 'Not called!'
> >>> raise E('spam')
> ...
> __main__.E: spam
>
> >>> class E(Exception):
>         def __str__(self): return 'Called!'
> >>> raise E('spam')
> ...
> __main__.E: Called!
> ```
>
> See Chapter 30 for more details on these special operator overloading methods.

Custom Data and Behavior

Besides supporting flexible hierarchies, exception classes also provide storage for extra state information as instance attributes. As we saw earlier, built-in exception superclasses provide a default constructor that automatically saves constructor arguments in an instance tuple attribute named args. Although the default constructor is adequate for many cases, for more custom needs we can provide a constructor of our own. In addition, classes may define methods for use in handlers that provide precoded exception processing logic.

Providing Exception Details

When an exception is raised, it may cross arbitrary file boundaries—the raise statement that triggers an exception and the try statement that catches it may be in completely different module files. It is not generally feasible to store extra details in global variables because the try statement might not know which file the globals reside in. Passing extra state information along in the exception itself allows the try statement to access it more reliably.

With classes, this is nearly automatic. As we've seen, when an exception is raised, Python passes the class instance object along with the exception. Code in try statements can access the raised instance by listing an extra variable after the as keyword in an except handler. This provides a natural hook for supplying data and behavior to the handler.

For example, a program that parses data files might signal a formatting error by raising an exception instance that is filled out with extra details about the error:

```
>>> class FormatError(Exception):
        def __init__(self, line, file):
            self.line = line
            self.file = file

>>> def parser():
        raise FormatError(42, file='spam.txt')      # When error found

>>> try:
...     parser()
... except FormatError as X:
...     print('Error at: %s %s' % (X.file, X.line))
...
Error at: spam.txt 42
```

In the except clause here, the variable X is assigned a reference to the instance that was generated when the exception was raised. This gives access to the attributes attached to the instance by the custom constructor. Although we could rely on the default state retention of built-in superclasses, it's less relevant to our application (and doesn't support the keyword arguments used in the prior example):

```
>>> class FormatError(Exception): pass          # Inherited constructor

>>> def parser():
        raise FormatError(42, 'spam.txt')           # No keywords allowed!

>>> try:
...     parser()
... except FormatError as X:
...     print('Error at:', X.args[0], X.args[1])     # Not specific to this app
...
Error at: 42 spam.txt
```

Providing Exception Methods

Besides enabling application-specific state information, custom constructors also better support extra behavior for exception objects. That is, the exception class can also define *methods* to be called in the handler. The following code in *excparse.py*, for example, adds a method that uses exception state information to log errors to a file automatically:

```
from __future__ import print_function   # 2.X compatibility

class FormatError(Exception):
    logfile = 'formaterror.txt'
    def __init__(self, line, file):
        self.line = line
        self.file = file
    def logerror(self):
        log = open(self.logfile, 'a')
        print('Error at:', self.file, self.line, file=log)

def parser():
    raise FormatError(40, 'spam.txt')

if __name__ == '__main__':
    try:
        parser()
    except FormatError as exc:
        exc.logerror()
```

When run, this script writes its error message to a file in response to method calls in the exception handler:

```
c:\code> del formaterror.txt
c:\code> py -3 excparse.py
c:\code> py -2 excparse.py
c:\code> type formaterror.txt
Error at: spam.txt 40
Error at: spam.txt 40
```

In such a class, methods (like `logerror`) may also be inherited from superclasses, and instance attributes (like `line` and `file`) provide a place to save state information that provides extra context for use in later method calls. Moreover, exception classes are free to customize and extend inherited behavior:

```
class CustomFormatError(FormatError):
    def logerror(self):
        ...something unique here...

raise CustomFormatError(...)
```

In other words, because they are defined with classes, all the benefits of OOP that we studied in Part VI are available for use with exceptions in Python.

Two final notes here: first, the raised instance object assigned to `exc` in this code is also available generically as the second item in the result tuple of the `sys.exc_info()` call—a tool that returns information about the most recently raised exception. This interface must be used if you do not list an exception name in an `except` clause but still need access to the exception that occurred, or to any of its attached state information or methods. Second, although our class's `logerror` method appends a custom message to a logfile, it could also generate Python's standard error message with stack trace using tools in the `traceback` standard library module, which uses traceback objects.

To learn more about `sys.exc_info` and tracebacks, though, we need to move ahead to the next chapter.

Chapter Summary

In this chapter, we explored coding user-defined exceptions. As we learned, exceptions are implemented as class instance objects as of Python 2.6 and 3.0 (an earlier string-based exception model alternative was available in earlier releases but has now been deprecated). Exception classes support the concept of exception hierarchies that ease maintenance, allow data and behavior to be attached to exceptions as instance attributes and methods, and allow exceptions to inherit data and behavior from super-classes.

We saw that in a `try` statement, catching a superclass catches that class as well as all subclasses below it in the class tree—superclasses become exception category names, and subclasses become more specific exception types within those categories. We also saw that the built-in exception superclasses we must inherit from provide usable defaults for printing and state retention, which we can override if desired.

The next chapter wraps up this part of the book by exploring some common use cases for exceptions and surveying tools commonly used by Python programmers. Before we get there, though, here's this chapter's quiz.

Test Your Knowledge: Quiz

1. What are the two new constraints on user-defined exceptions in Python 3.X?
2. How are raised class-based exceptions matched to handlers?
3. Name two ways that you can attach context information to exception objects.
4. Name two ways that you can specify the error message text for exception objects.
5. Why should you not use string-based exceptions anymore today?

Test Your Knowledge: Answers

1. In 3.X, exceptions must be defined by classes (that is, a class instance object is raised and caught). In addition, exception classes must be derived from the built-in class `BaseException`; most programs inherit from its `Exception` subclass, to support catchall handlers for normal kinds of exceptions.
2. Class-based exceptions match by superclass relationships: naming a superclass in an exception handler will catch instances of that class, as well as instances of any of its subclasses lower in the class tree. Because of this, you can think of superclasses as general exception categories and subclasses as more specific types of exceptions within those categories.

3. You can attach context information to class-based exceptions by filling out instance attributes in the instance object raised, usually in a custom class constructor. For simpler needs, built-in exception superclasses provide a constructor that stores its arguments on the instance automatically (as a tuple in the attribute `args`). In exception handlers, you list a variable to be assigned to the raised instance, then go through this name to access attached state information and call any methods defined in the class.

4. The error message text in class-based exceptions can be specified with a custom `__str__` operator overloading method. For simpler needs, built-in exception superclasses automatically display anything you pass to the class constructor. Operations like `print` and `str` automatically fetch the display string of an exception object when it is printed either explicitly or as part of an error message.

5. Because Guido said so—they have been removed as of both Python 2.6 and 3.0. There are arguably good reasons for this: string-based exceptions did not support categories, state information, or behavior inheritance in the way class-based exceptions do. In practice, this made string-based exceptions easier to use at first when programs were small, but more complex to use as programs grew larger.

   The downsides of requiring exceptions to be classes are to *break* existing code, and create a forward *knowledge dependency*—beginners must first learn classes and OOP before they can code new exceptions, or even truly understand exceptions at all. In fact, this is why this relatively straightforward topic was largely postponed until this point in the book. For better or worse, such dependencies are not uncommon in Python today (see the preface and conclusion for more on such things).

CHAPTER 36

Designing with Exceptions

This chapter rounds out this part of the book with a collection of exception design topics and common use case examples, followed by this part's gotchas and exercises. Because this chapter also closes out the fundamentals portion of the book at large, it includes a brief overview of development tools as well to help you as you make the migration from Python beginner to Python application developer.

Nesting Exception Handlers

Most of our examples so far have used only a single **try** to catch exceptions, but what happens if one **try** is physically nested inside another? For that matter, what does it mean if a **try** calls a function that runs another **try**? Technically, **try** statements can nest, in terms of both syntax and the runtime control flow through your code. I've mentioned this briefly, but let's clarify the idea here.

Both of these cases can be understood if you realize that Python *stacks* **try** statements at runtime. When an exception is raised, Python returns to the most recently entered **try** statement with a matching **except** clause. Because each **try** statement leaves a marker, Python can jump back to earlier **trys** by inspecting the stacked markers. This nesting of active handlers is what we mean when we talk about propagating exceptions up to "higher" handlers—such handlers are simply **try** statements entered *earlier* in the program's execution flow.

Figure 36-1 illustrates what occurs when **try** statements with **except** clauses nest at runtime. The amount of code that goes into a **try** block can be substantial, and it may contain function calls that invoke other code watching for the same exceptions. When an exception is eventually raised, Python jumps back to the most recently entered **try** statement that names that exception, runs that statement's **except** clause, and then resumes execution after that **try**.

Once the exception is caught, its life is over—control does not jump back to *all* matching **trys** that name the exception; only the first (i.e., most recent) one is given the opportunity to handle it. In Figure 36-1, for instance, the **raise** statement in the func-

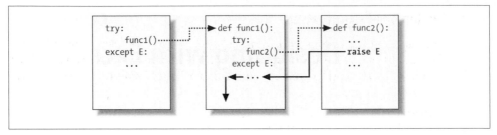

Figure 36-1. Nested try/except statements: when an exception is raised (by you or by Python), control jumps back to the most recently entered try statement with a matching except clause, and the program resumes after that try statement. except clauses intercept and stop the exception—they are where you process and recover from exceptions.

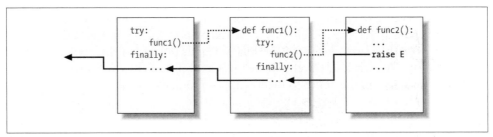

Figure 36-2. Nested try/finally statements: when an exception is raised here, control returns to the most recently entered try to run its finally statement, but then the exception keeps propagating to all finallys in all active try statements and eventually reaches the default top-level handler, where an error message is printed. finally clauses intercept (but do not stop) an exception—they are for actions to be performed "on the way out."

tion `func2` sends control back to the handler in `func1`, and then the program continues within `func1`.

By contrast, when `try` statements that contain only `finally` clauses are nested, *each* `finally` block is run in turn when an exception occurs—Python continues propagating the exception up to other `trys`, and eventually perhaps to the top-level default handler (the standard error message printer). As Figure 36-2 illustrates, the `finally` clauses do not kill the exception—they just specify code to be run on the way out of each `try` during the exception propagation process. If there are many `try`/`finally` clauses active when an exception occurs, they will *all* be run, unless a `try`/`except` catches the exception somewhere along the way.

In other words, where the program goes when an exception is raised depends entirely upon *where it has been*—it's a function of the runtime flow of control through the script, not just its syntax. The propagation of an exception essentially proceeds backward through time to `try` statements that have been entered but not yet exited. This propagation stops as soon as control is unwound to a matching `except` clause, but not as it passes through `finally` clauses on the way.

Example: Control-Flow Nesting

Let's turn to an example to make this nesting concept more concrete. The following module file, *nestexc.py*, defines two functions. `action2` is coded to trigger an exception (you can't add numbers and sequences), and `action1` wraps a call to `action2` in a `try` handler, to catch the exception:

```
def action2():
    print(1 + [])              # Generate TypeError

def action1():
    try:
        action2()
    except TypeError:          # Most recent matching try
        print('inner try')

try:
    action1()
except TypeError:              # Here, only if action1 re-raises
    print('outer try')
```

```
% python nestexc.py
inner try
```

Notice, though, that the top-level module code at the bottom of the file wraps a call to `action1` in a `try` handler, too. When `action2` triggers the `TypeError` exception, there will be two active `try` statements—the one in `action1`, and the one at the top level of the module file. Python picks and runs just the most recent `try` with a matching `except`—which in this case is the `try` inside `action1`.

Again, the place where an exception winds up jumping to depends on the control flow through the program at runtime. Because of this, to know where you will go, you need to know where you've been. In this case, where exceptions are handled is more a function of control flow than of statement syntax. However, we can also nest exception handlers syntactically—an equivalent case we turn to next.

Example: Syntactic Nesting

As I mentioned when we looked at the new unified `try/except/finally` statement in Chapter 34, it is possible to nest `try` statements syntactically by their position in your source code:

```
try:
    try:
        action2()
    except TypeError:          # Most recent matching try
        print('inner try')
except TypeError:              # Here, only if nested handler re-raises
    print('outer try')
```

Really, though, this code just sets up the same handler-nesting structure as (and behaves identically to) the prior example. In fact, syntactic nesting works just like the cases sketched in Figure 36-1 and Figure 36-2. The only difference is that the nested handlers are physically embedded in a **try** block, not coded elsewhere in functions that are called from the **try** block. For example, nested **finally** handlers all fire on an exception, whether they are nested syntactically or by means of the runtime flow through physically separated parts of your code:

```
>>> try:
...     try:
...         raise IndexError
...     finally:
...         print('spam')
... finally:
...     print('SPAM')
...
spam
SPAM
Traceback (most recent call last):
  File "<stdin>", line 3, in <module>
IndexError
```

See Figure 36-2 for a graphic illustration of this code's operation; the effect is the same, but the function logic has been inlined as nested statements here. For a more useful example of syntactic nesting at work, consider the following file, *except-finally.py*:

```
def raise1():  raise IndexError
def noraise():  return
def raise2():  raise SyntaxError

for func in (raise1, noraise, raise2):
    print('<%s>' % func.__name__)
    try:
        try:
            func()
        except IndexError:
            print('caught IndexError')
    finally:
        print('finally run')
    print('...')
```

This code catches an exception if one is raised and performs a **finally** termination-time action regardless of whether an exception occurs. This may take a few moments to digest, but the effect is the same as combining an **except** and a **finally** clause in a single **try** statement in Python 2.5 and later:

```
% python except-finally.py
<raise1>
caught IndexError
finally run
...
<noraise>
finally run
...
```

```
<raise2>
finally run
Traceback (most recent call last):
  File "except-finally.py", line 9, in <module>
    func()
  File "except-finally.py", line 3, in raise2
    def raise2():  raise SyntaxError
SyntaxError: None
```

As we saw in Chapter 34, as of Python 2.5, except and finally clauses can be mixed in the same try statement. This, along with multiple except clause support, makes some of the syntactic nesting described in this section unnecessary, though the equivalent runtime nesting is common in larger Python programs. Moreover, syntactic nesting still works today, may still appear in code written prior to Python 2.5 that you may encounter, can make the disjoint roles of except and finally more explicit, and can be used as a technique for implementing alternative exception-handling behaviors in general.

Exception Idioms

We've seen the mechanics behind exceptions. Now let's take a look at some of the other ways they are typically used.

Breaking Out of Multiple Nested Loops: "go to"

As mentioned at the start of this part of the book, exceptions can often be used to serve the same roles as other languages' "go to" statements to implement more arbitrary control transfers. Exceptions, however, provide a more structured option that localizes the jump to a specific block of nested code.

In this role, raise is like "go to," and except clauses and exception names take the place of program labels. You can jump only out of code wrapped in a try this way, but that's a crucial feature—truly arbitrary "go to" statements can make code extraordinarily difficult to understand and maintain.

For example, Python's break statement exits just the single closest enclosing loop, but we can always use exceptions to break out of more than one loop level if needed:

```
>>> class Exitloop(Exception): pass
...
>>> try:
...     while True:
...         while True:
...             for i in range(10):
...                 if i > 3: raise Exitloop          # break exits just one level
...                 print('loop3: %s' % i)
...             print('loop2')
...         print('loop1')
... except Exitloop:
...     print('continuing')                           # Or just pass, to move on
```

```
...
loop3: 0
loop3: 1
loop3: 2
loop3: 3
continuing
>>> i
4
```

If you change the `raise` in this to `break`, you'll get an infinite loop, because you'll break only out of the most deeply nested `for` loop, and wind up in the second-level loop nesting. The code would then print "loop2" and start the `for` again.

Also notice that variable `i` is still what it was after the `try` statement exits. Variable assignments made in a `try` are not undone in general, though as we've seen, exception instance variables listed in `except` clause headers are localized to that clause, and the local variables of any functions that are exited as a result of a `raise` are discarded. Technically, active functions' local variables are popped off the call stack and the objects they reference may be garbage-collected as a result, but this is an automatic step.

Exceptions Aren't Always Errors

In Python, all errors are exceptions, but not all exceptions are errors. For instance, we saw in Chapter 9 that file object read methods return an empty string at the end of a file. In contrast, the built-in `input` function—which we first met in Chapter 3, deployed in an interactive loop in Chapter 10, and learned is named `raw_input` in 2.X—reads a line of text from the standard input stream, `sys.stdin`, at each call and raises the built-in `EOFError` at end-of-file.

Unlike file methods, this function does not return an empty string—an empty string from `input` means an empty line. Despite its name, though, the `EOFError` exception is just a signal in this context, not an error. Because of this behavior, unless the end-of-file should terminate a script, `input` often appears wrapped in a `try` handler and nested in a loop, as in the following code:

```
while True:
    try:
        line = input()              # Read line from stdin (raw_input in 2.X)
    except EOFError:
        break                       # Exit loop at end-of-file
    else:
        ...process next line here...
```

Several other built-in exceptions are similarly signals, not errors—for example, calling `sys.exit()` and pressing Ctrl-C on your keyboard raise `SystemExit` and `KeyboardInterrupt`, respectively.

Python also has a set of built-in exceptions that represent *warnings* rather than errors; some of these are used to signal use of deprecated (phased out) language features. See the standard library manual's description of built-in exceptions for more information, and consult the `warnings` module's documentation for more on exceptions raised as warnings.

Functions Can Signal Conditions with raise

User-defined exceptions can also signal nonerror conditions. For instance, a search routine can be coded to raise an exception when a match is found instead of returning a status flag for the caller to interpret. In the following, the `try`/`except`/`else` exception handler does the work of an `if`/`else` return-value tester:

```
class Found(Exception): pass

def searcher():
    if ...success...:
        raise Found()          # Raise exceptions instead of returning flags
    else:
        return

try:
    searcher()
except Found:                  # Exception if item was found
    ...success...
else:                          # else returned: not found
    ...failure...
```

More generally, such a coding structure may also be useful for any function that cannot return a *sentinel value* to designate success or failure. In a widely applicable function, for instance, if all objects are potentially valid return values, it's impossible for any return value to signal a failure condition. Exceptions provide a way to signal results without a return value:

```
class Failure(Exception): pass

def searcher():
    if ...success...:
        return ...founditem...
    else:
        raise Failure()

try:
    item = searcher()
except Failure:
    ...not found...
else:
    ...use item here...
```

Because Python is dynamically typed and polymorphic to the core, exceptions, rather than sentinel return values, are the generally preferred way to signal such conditions.

Closing Files and Server Connections

We encountered examples in this category in Chapter 34. As a summary, though, exception processing tools are also commonly used to ensure that system resources are finalized, regardless of whether an error occurs during processing or not.

For example, some servers require connections to be closed in order to terminate a session. Similarly, output files may require close calls to flush their buffers to disk for waiting consumers, and input files may consume file descriptors if not closed; although file objects are automatically closed when garbage-collected if still open, in some Pythons it may be difficult to be sure when that will occur.

As we saw in Chapter 34, the most general and explicit way to guarantee termination actions for a specific block of code is the try/finally statement:

```
myfile = open(r'C:\code\textdata', 'w')
try:
    ...process myfile...
finally:
    myfile.close()
```

As we also saw, some objects make this potentially easier in Python 2.6, 3.0, and later by providing *context managers* that terminate or close the objects for us automatically when run by the with/as statement:

```
with open(r'C:\code\textdata', 'w') as myfile:
    ...process myfile...
```

So which option is better here? As usual, it depends on your programs. Compared to the traditional try/finally, context managers are *more implicit*, which runs contrary to Python's general design philosophy. Context managers are also arguably *less general* —they are available only for select objects, and writing user-defined context managers to handle general termination requirements is more complex than coding a try/finally.

On the other hand, using existing context managers requires *less code* than using try/finally, as shown by the preceding examples. Moreover, the context manager protocol supports *entry* actions in addition to exit actions. In fact, it can save a line of code when no exceptions are expected at all (albeit at the expense of further nesting and indenting file processing logic):

```
myfile = open(filename, 'w')        # Traditional form
...process myfile...
myfile.close()

with open(filename) as myfile:      # Context manager form
    ...process myfile...
```

Still, the implicit exception processing of with makes it more directly comparable to the explicit exception handling of try/finally. Although try/finally is the more widely applicable technique, context managers may be preferable where they are already available, or where their extra complexity is warranted.

Debugging with Outer try Statements

You can also make use of exception handlers to replace Python's default top-level exception-handling behavior. By wrapping an entire program (or a call to it) in an outer try in your top-level code, you can catch any exception that may occur while your program runs, thereby subverting the default program termination.

In the following, the empty except clause catches any uncaught exception raised while the program runs. To get hold of the actual exception that occurred in this mode, fetch the sys.exc_info function call result from the built-in sys module; it returns a tuple whose first two items contain the current exception's class and the instance object raised (more on sys.exc_info in a moment):

```
try:
    ...run program...
except:                              # All uncaught exceptions come here
    import sys
    print('uncaught!', sys.exc_info()[0], sys.exc_info()[1])
```

This structure is commonly used during development, to keep programs active even after errors occur—within a loop, it allows you to run additional tests without having to restart. It's also used when testing other program code, as described in the next section.

 On a related note, for more about handling program shutdowns *without* recovery from them, see also Python's atexit standard library module. It's also possible to customize what the top-level exception handler does with sys.excepthook. These and other related tools are described in Python's library manual.

Running In-Process Tests

Some of the coding patterns we've just looked at can be combined in a test-driver application that tests other code within the same process. The following partial code sketches the general model:

```
import sys
log = open('testlog', 'a')
from testapi import moreTests, runNextTest, testName
def testdriver():
    while moreTests():
        try:
            runNextTest()
        except:
            print('FAILED', testName(), sys.exc_info()[:2], file=log)
        else:
            print('PASSED', testName(), file=log)
testdriver()
```

The `testdriver` function here cycles through a series of test calls (the module `testapi` is left abstract in this example). Because an uncaught exception in a test case would normally kill this test driver, you need to wrap test case calls in a `try` if you want to continue the testing process after a test fails. The empty `except` catches any uncaught exception generated by a test case as usual, and it uses `sys.exc_info` to log the exception to a file. The `else` clause is run when no exception occurs—the test success case.

Such boilerplate code is typical of systems that test functions, modules, and classes by running them in the *same process* as the test driver. In practice, however, testing can be much more sophisticated than this. For instance, to test *external programs*, you could instead check status codes or outputs generated by program-launching tools such as `os.system` and `os.popen`, used earlier in this book and covered in the standard library manual. Such tools do not generally raise exceptions for errors in the external programs —in fact, the test cases may run in parallel with the test driver.

At the end of this chapter, we'll also briefly meet more complete testing frameworks provided by Python, such as `doctest` and PyUnit, which provide tools for comparing expected outputs with actual results.

More on sys.exc_info

The `sys.exc_info` result used in the last two sections allows an exception handler to gain access to the most recently raised exception generically. This is especially useful when using the empty `except` clause to catch everything blindly, to determine what was raised:

```
try:
    ...
except:
    # sys.exc_info()[0:2] are the exception class and instance
```

If no exception is being handled, this call returns a tuple containing three `None` values. Otherwise, the values returned are (*type, value, traceback*), where:

- *type* is the exception class of the exception being handled.
- *value* is the exception class instance that was raised.
- *traceback* is a traceback object that represents the call stack at the point where the exception originally occurred, and used by the `traceback` module to generate error messages.

As we saw in the prior chapter, `sys.exc_info` can also sometimes be useful to determine the specific exception type when catching exception category superclasses. As we've also learned, though, because in this case you can also get the exception type by fetching the `__class__` attribute of the instance obtained with the `as` clause, `sys.exc_info` is often redundant apart from the empty `except`:

```
try:
    ...
```

```
except General as instance:
    # instance.__class__ is the exception class
```

As we've seen, using `Exception` for the *General* exception name here would catch all nonexit exceptions, similar to an empty `except` but less extreme, and still giving access to the exception instance and its class. Even so, using the instance object's interfaces and *polymorphism* is often a better approach than testing exception types—exception methods can be defined per class and run generically:

```
try:
    ...
except General as instance:
    # instance.method() does the right thing for this instance
```

As usual, being too specific in Python can limit your code's flexibility. A polymorphic approach like the last example here generally supports future evolution better than explicitly type-specific tests or actions.

Displaying Errors and Tracebacks

Finally, the exception traceback object available in the prior section's `sys.exc_info` result is also used by the standard library's `traceback` module to generate the standard error message and stack display manually. This file has a handful of interfaces that support wide customization, which we don't have space to cover usefully here, but the basics are simple. Consider the following aptly named file, *badly.py*:

```python
import traceback

def inverse(x):
    return 1 / x

try:
    inverse(0)
except Exception:
    traceback.print_exc(file=open('badly.exc', 'w'))
print('Bye')
```

This code uses the `print_exc` convenience function in the `traceback` module, which uses `sys.exc_info` data by default; when run, the script prints the error message to a file—handy in testing programs that need to catch errors but still record them in full:

```
c:\code> python badly.py
Bye

c:\code> type badly.exc
Traceback (most recent call last):
  File "badly.py", line 7, in <module>
    inverse(0)
  File "badly.py", line 4, in inverse
    return 1 / x
ZeroDivisionError: division by zero
```

For much more on traceback objects, the traceback module that uses them, and related topics, consult other reference resources and manuals.

 Version skew note: In Python 2.X, the older tools sys.exc_type and sys.exc_value still work to fetch the most recent exception type and value, but they can manage only a single, global exception for the entire process. These two names have been removed in Python 3.X. The newer and preferred sys.exc_info() call available in both 2.X and 3.X instead keeps track of each thread's exception information, and so is thread-specific. Of course, this distinction matters only when using multiple threads in Python programs (a subject beyond this book's scope), but 3.X forces the issue. See other resources for more details.

Exception Design Tips and Gotchas

I'm lumping design tips and gotchas together in this chapter, because it turns out that the most common gotchas largely stem from design issues. By and large, exceptions are easy to use in Python. The real art behind them is in deciding how specific or general your except clauses should be and how much code to wrap up in try statements. Let's address the second of these concerns first.

What Should Be Wrapped

In principle, you could wrap every statement in your script in its own try, but that would just be silly (the try statements would then need to be wrapped in try statements!). What to wrap is really a design issue that goes beyond the language itself, and it will become more apparent with use. But for now, here are a few rules of thumb:

- Operations that commonly fail should generally be wrapped in try statements. For example, operations that interface with system state (file opens, socket calls, and the like) are prime candidates for try.

- However, there are exceptions to the prior rule—in a simple script, you may *want* failures of such operations to kill your program instead of being caught and ignored. This is especially true if the failure is a showstopper. Failures in Python typically result in useful error messages (not hard crashes), and this is the best outcome some programs could hope for.

- You should implement termination actions in try/finally statements to guarantee their execution, unless a context manager is available as a with/as option. The try/finally statement form allows you to run code whether exceptions occur or not in arbitrary scenarios.

- It is sometimes more convenient to wrap the call to a large function in a single try statement, rather than littering the function itself with many try statements.

That way, all exceptions in the function percolate up to the try around the call, and you reduce the amount of code within the function.

The types of programs you write will probably influence the amount of exception handling you code as well. *Servers*, for instance, must generally keep running persistently and so will likely require try statements to catch and recover from exceptions. In-process *testing* programs of the kind we saw in this chapter will probably handle exceptions as well. Simpler one-shot scripts, though, will often ignore exception handling completely because failure at any step requires script shutdown.

Catching Too Much: Avoid Empty except and Exception

As mentioned, exception handler generality is a key design choice. Python lets you pick and choose which exceptions to catch, but you sometimes have to be careful to not be too inclusive. For example, you've seen that an empty except clause catches *every* exception that might be raised while the code in the try block runs.

That's easy to code, and sometimes desirable, but you may also wind up intercepting an error that's expected by a try handler higher up in the exception nesting structure. For example, an exception handler such as the following catches and stops *every* exception that reaches it, regardless of whether another handler is waiting for it:

```
def func():
    try:
        ...                      # IndexError is raised in here
    except:
        ...                      # But everything comes here and dies!
try:
    func()
except IndexError:               # Exception should be processed here
    ...
```

Perhaps worse, such code might also catch unrelated system exceptions. Even things like memory errors, genuine programming mistakes, iteration stops, keyboard interrupts, and system exits raise exceptions in Python. Unless you're writing a debugger or similar tool, such exceptions should not usually be intercepted in your code.

For example, scripts normally exit when control falls off the end of the top-level file. However, Python also provides a built-in sys.exit(*statuscode*) call to allow early terminations. This actually works by raising a built-in SystemExit exception to end the program, so that try/finally handlers run on the way out and special types of programs can intercept the event.[1] Because of this, a try with an empty except might unknowingly prevent a crucial exit, as in the following file (*exiter.py*):

---

1. A related call, os._exit, also ends a program, but via an immediate termination — it skips cleanup actions, including any registered with the atexit module noted earlier, and cannot be intercepted with try/except or try/finally blocks. It is usually used only in spawned child processes, a topic beyond this book's scope. See the library manual or follow-up texts for details.

```
import sys
def bye():
    sys.exit(40)                    # Crucial error: abort now!
try:
    bye()
except:
    print('got it')                 # Oops--we ignored the exit
print('continuing...')

% python exiter.py
got it
continuing...
```

You simply might not expect all the kinds of exceptions that could occur during an operation. Using the built-in exception classes of the prior chapter can help in this particular case, because the Exception superclass is not a superclass of SystemExit:

```
try:
    bye()
except Exception:                   # Won't catch exits, but _will_ catch many others
    ...
```

In other cases, though, this scheme is no better than an empty except clause—because Exception is a superclass above all built-in exceptions except system-exit events, it still has the potential to catch exceptions meant for elsewhere in the program.

Probably worst of all, *both* using an empty except and catching the Exception superclass will also catch genuine programming errors, which should be allowed to pass most of the time. In fact, these two techniques can effectively *turn off* Python's error-reporting machinery, making it difficult to notice mistakes in your code. Consider this code, for example:

```
mydictionary = {...}
...
try:
    x = myditctionary['spam']       # Oops: misspelled
except:
    x = None                        # Assume we got KeyError
...continue here with x...
```

The coder here assumes that the only sort of error that can happen when indexing a dictionary is a missing key error. But because the name myditctionary is misspelled (it should say mydictionary), Python raises a NameError instead for the undefined name reference, which the handler will silently catch and ignore. The event handler will incorrectly fill in a None default for the dictionary access, masking the program error.

Moreover, catching Exception here will not help—it would have the exact same effect as an empty except, happily and silently filling in a default and masking a genuine program error you will probably want to know about. If this happens in code that is far removed from the place where the fetched values are used, it might make for a very interesting debugging task!

As a rule of thumb, be as *specific* in your handlers as you can be—empty `except` clauses and `Exception` catchers are handy, but potentially error-prone. In the last example, for instance, you would be better off saying `except KeyError:` to make your intentions explicit and avoid intercepting unrelated events. In simpler scripts, the potential for problems might not be significant enough to outweigh the convenience of a catchall, but in general, general handlers are generally trouble.

Catching Too Little: Use Class-Based Categories

On the other hand, neither should handlers be too specific. When you list specific exceptions in a `try`, you catch only what you actually list. This isn't necessarily a bad thing, but if a system evolves to raise other exceptions in the future, you may need to go back and add them to exception lists elsewhere in your code.

We saw this phenomenon at work in the prior chapter. For instance, the following handler is written to treat `MyExcept1` and `MyExcept2` as normal cases and everything else as an error. If you add a `MyExcept3` in the future, though, it will be processed as an error unless you update the exception list:

```
try:
    ...
except (MyExcept1, MyExcept2):      # Breaks if you add a MyExcept3 later
    ...                             # Nonerrors
else:
    ...                             # Assumed to be an error
```

Luckily, careful use of the class-based exceptions we discussed in Chapter 34 can make this code maintenance trap go away completely. As we saw, if you catch a general superclass, you can add and raise more specific subclasses in the future without having to extend `except` clause lists manually—the superclass becomes an extendible exceptions category:

```
try:
    ...
except SuccessCategoryName:         # OK if you add a MyExcept3 subclass later
    ...                             # Nonerrors
else:
    ...                             # Assumed to be an error
```

In other words, a little design goes a long way. The moral of the story is to be careful to be neither too general nor too specific in exception handlers, and to pick the granularity of your `try` statement wrappings wisely. Especially in larger systems, exception policies should be a part of the overall design.

Core Language Summary

Congratulations! This concludes your look at the fundamentals of the Python programming language. If you've gotten this far, you've become a fully operational Python programmer. There's more optional reading in the advanced topics part ahead that I'll describe in a moment. In terms of the essentials, though, the Python story—and this book's main journey—is now complete.

Along the way, you've seen just about everything there is to see in the language itself, and in enough depth to apply to most of the code you are likely to encounter in the open source "wild." You've studied built-in types, statements, and exceptions, as well as tools used to build up the larger program units of functions, modules, and classes. You've also explored important software design issues, the complete OOP paradigm, functional programming tools, program architecture concepts, alternative tool trade-offs, and more—compiling a skill set now qualified to be turned loose on the task of developing real applications.

The Python Toolset

From this point forward, your future Python career will largely consist of becoming proficient with the toolset available for application-level Python programming. You'll find this to be an ongoing task. The standard library, for example, contains hundreds of modules, and the public domain offers still more tools. It's possible to spend decades seeking proficiency with all these tools, especially as new ones are constantly appearing to address new technologies (trust me on this—I'm at 20 years and counting!).

Speaking generally, Python provides a hierarchy of toolsets:

Built-ins
> Built-in types like strings, lists, and dictionaries make it easy to write simple programs fast.

Python extensions
> For more demanding tasks, you can extend Python by writing your own functions, modules, and classes.

Compiled extensions
> Although we don't cover this topic in this book, Python can also be extended with modules written in an external language like C or C++.

Because Python layers its toolsets, you can decide how deeply your programs need to delve into this hierarchy for any given task—you can use built-ins for simple scripts, add Python-coded extensions for larger systems, and code compiled extensions for advanced work. We've only covered the first two of these categories in this book, and that's plenty to get you started doing substantial programming in Python.

Beyond this, there are tools, resources, or precedents for using Python in nearly any computer domain you can imagine. For pointers on where to go next, see Chapter 1's overview of Python applications and users. You'll likely find that with a powerful open source language like Python, common tasks are often much easier, and even enjoyable, than you might expect.

Development Tools for Larger Projects

Most of the examples in this book have been fairly small and self-contained. They were written that way on purpose, to help you master the basics. But now that you know all about the core language, it's time to start learning how to use Python's built-in and third-party interfaces to do real work.

In practice, Python programs can become substantially larger than the examples you've experimented with so far in this book. Even in Python, *thousands* of lines of code are not uncommon for nontrivial and useful programs, once you add up all the individual modules in the system. Though Python basic program structuring tools such as modules and classes help much to manage this complexity, other tools can sometimes offer additional support.

For developing larger systems, you'll find such support available in both Python and the public domain. You've seen some of these in action, and I've mentioned a few others. To help you on your next steps, here is a quick tour and summary of some of the most commonly used tools in this domain:

PyDoc and docstrings
> PyDoc's `help` function and HTML interfaces were introduced in Chapter 15. PyDoc provides a documentation system for your modules and objects, integrates with Python's docstrings syntax, and is a standard part of the Python system. See Chapter 15 and Chapter 4 for more documentation source hints.

PyChecker and PyLint
> Because Python is such a dynamic language, some programming errors are not reported until your program runs (even syntax errors are not caught until a file is run or imported). This isn't a big drawback—as with most languages, it just means that you have to test your Python code before shipping it. At worst, with Python you essentially trade a compile phase for an initial testing phase. Furthermore, Python's dynamic nature, automatic error messages, and exception model make it easier and quicker to find and fix errors than it is in some other languages. Unlike C, for example, Python does not crash completely on errors.

> Still, tools can help here too. The PyChecker and PyLint systems provide support for catching common errors ahead of time, before your script runs. They serve similar roles to the *lint* program in C development. Some Python developers run their code through PyChecker prior to testing or delivery, to catch any lurking potential problems. In fact, it's not a bad idea to try this when you're first starting out—some of these tools' warnings may help you learn to spot and avoid common Python mistakes. PyChecker and PyLint are third-party open source packages, available at the PyPI website or your friendly neighborhood web search engine. They may appear in IDE GUIs as well.

PyUnit (a.k.a. `unittest`)
> In Chapter 25, we learned how to add self-test code to a Python file by using the `__name__ == '__main__'` trick at the bottom of the file—a simple unit-testing pro-

tocol. For more advanced testing purposes, Python comes with two testing support tools. The first, PyUnit (called `unittest` in the library manual), provides an object-oriented class framework for specifying and customizing test cases and expected results. It mimics the JUnit framework for Java. This is a sophisticated class-based unit testing system; see the Python library manual for details.

doctest

> The `doctest` standard library module provides a second and simpler approach to regression testing, based upon Python's docstrings feature. Roughly, to use `doctest`, you cut and paste a log of an interactive testing session into the docstrings of your source files. `doctest` then extracts your docstrings, parses out the test cases and results, and reruns the tests to verify the expected results. `doctest`'s operation can be tailored in a variety of ways; see the library manual for more details.

IDEs

> We discussed IDEs for Python in Chapter 3. IDEs such as IDLE provide a graphical environment for editing, running, debugging, and browsing your Python programs. Some advanced IDEs—such as Eclipse, Komodo, NetBeans, and others listed in Chapter 3—may support additional development tasks, including source control integration, code refactoring, project management tools, and more. See Chapter 3, the text editors page at *http://www.python.org*, and your favorite web search engine for more on available IDEs and GUI builders for Python.

Profilers

> Because Python is so high-level and dynamic, intuitions about performance gleaned from experience with other languages usually don't apply to Python code. To truly isolate performance bottlenecks in your code, you need to add timing logic with clock tools in the `time` or `timeit` modules, or run your code under the `profile` module. We saw an example of the timing modules at work when comparing the speed of iteration tools and Pythons in Chapter 21.

> Profiling is usually your first optimization step—code for clarity, then profile to isolate bottlenecks, and then time alternative codings of the slow parts of your program. For the second of these steps, `profile` is a standard library module that implements a source code profiler for Python. It runs a string of code you provide (e.g., a script file import, or a call to a function) and then, by default, prints a report to the standard output stream that gives performance statistics—number of calls to each function, time spent in each function, and more.

> The `profile` module can be run as a script or imported, and it may be customized in various ways; for example, it can save run statistics to a file to be analyzed later with the `pstats` module. To profile interactively, import the `profile` module and call `profile.run('code')`, passing in the code you wish to profile as a string (e.g., a call to a function, an import of a file, or code read from a file). To profile from a system shell command line, use a command of the form `python -m profile main.py` *args* (see Appendix A for more on this format). Also see Python's standard library manuals for other profiling options; the `cProfile` module, for example, has

identical interfaces to `profile` but runs with less overhead, so it may be better suited to profiling long-running programs.

Debuggers

We also discussed debugging options in Chapter 3 (see its sidebar "Debugging Python Code" on page 83). As a review, most development IDEs for Python support GUI-based debugging, and the Python standard library also includes a source code debugger module called `pdb`. This module provides a command-line interface and works much like common C language debuggers (e.g., *dbx*, *gdb*).

Much like the profiler, the *pdb* debugger can be run either interactively or from a command line and can be imported and called from a Python program. To use it interactively, import the module, start running code by calling a `pdb` function (e.g., `pdb.run('main()')`), and then type debugging commands from *pdb*'s interactive prompt. To launch *pdb* from a system shell command line, use a command of the form `python -m pdb main.py` *args*. *pdb* also includes a useful postmortem analysis call, `pdb.pm()`, which starts the debugger after an exception has been encountered, possibly in conjunction with Python's `-i` flag. See Appendix A for more on these tools.

Because IDEs such as IDLE also include point-and-click debugging interfaces, *pdb* isn't as critical a tool today, except when a GUI isn't available or when more control is desired. See Chapter 3 for tips on using IDLE's debugging GUI interfaces. Really, neither *pdb* nor IDEs seem to be used much in practice—as noted in Chapter 3, most programmers either insert `print` statements or simply read Python's error messages: perhaps not the most high-tech of approaches, but the practical tends to win the day in the Python world!

Shipping options

In Chapter 2, we introduced common tools for packaging Python programs. *py2exe*, *PyInstaller*, and others listed in that chapter can package byte code and the Python Virtual Machine into "frozen binary" standalone executables, which don't require that Python be installed on the target machine and hide your system's code. In addition, we learned in Chapter 2 that Python programs may be shipped in their source (.*py*) or byte code (.*pyc*) forms, and that import hooks support special packaging techniques such as automatic extraction of .*zip* files and byte code encryption.

We also briefly met the standard library's `distutils` modules, which provide packaging options for Python modules and packages, and C-coded extensions; see the Python manuals for more details. The emerging Python "eggs" third-party packaging system provides another alternative that also accounts for dependencies; search the Web for more details.

Optimization options

When speed counts, there are a handful of options for optimizing your programs. The PyPy system described in Chapter 2 provides a just-in-time compiler for translating Python byte code to binary machine code, and Shed Skin offers a Python-to-

C++ translator. You may also occasionally see *.pyo* optimized byte code files, generated and run with the `-O` Python command-line flag discussed in Chapter 22 and Chapter 34, and to be deployed in Chapter 39; because this provides a very modest performance boost, however, it is not commonly used except to remove debugging code.

As a last resort, you can also move parts of your program to a compiled language such as C to boost performance. See the book *Programming Python* and the Python standard manuals for more on C extensions. In general, Python's speed tends to also improve over time, so upgrading to later releases may improve speed too— once you verify that they are faster for your code, that is (though largely repaired since, Python 3.0's initial release was up to 1000X slower than 2.X on some IO operations!).

Other hints for larger projects

We've met a variety of core language features in this text that will also tend to become more useful once you start coding larger projects. These include module packages (Chapter 24), class-based exceptions (Chapter 34), class pseudoprivate attributes (Chapter 31), documentation strings (Chapter 15), module path configuration files (Chapter 22), hiding names from `from *` with `__all__` lists and `_X`-style names (Chapter 25), adding self-test code with the `__name__ == '__main__'` trick (Chapter 25), using common design rules for functions and modules (Chapter 17, Chapter 19, and Chapter 25), using object-oriented design patterns (Chapter 31 and others), and so on.

To learn about other large-scale Python development tools available in the public domain, be sure to browse the pages at the PyPI website at *http://www.python.org*, and the Web at large. Applying Python is actually a larger topic than learning Python, and one we'll have to delegate to follow-up resources here.

Chapter Summary

This chapter wrapped up the exceptions part of the book with a survey of design concepts, a look at common exception use cases, and a brief summary of commonly used development tools.

This chapter also wrapped up the core material of this book. At this point, you've been exposed to the full subset of Python that most programmers use—and probably more. In fact, if you have read this far, you should feel free to consider yourself an *official Python programmer*. Be sure to pick up a t-shirt or laptop sticker the next time you're online (and don't forget to add Python to your résumé the next time you dig it out).

The next and final part of this book is a collection of chapters dealing with topics that are advanced, but still in the core language category. These chapters are all *optional reading*, or at least *deferrable reading*, because not every Python programmer must delve into their subjects, and others can postpone these chapters' topics until they are needed.

Indeed, many of you can stop here and begin exploring Python's roles in your application domains. Frankly, application libraries tend to be more important in practice than advanced—and to some, esoteric—language features.

On the other hand, if you do need to care about things like Unicode or binary data, have to deal with API-building tools such as descriptors, decorators, and metaclasses, or just want to dig a bit further in general, the next part of the book will help you get started. The larger examples in the final part will also give you a chance to see the concepts you've already learned being applied in more realistic ways.

As this is the end of the core material of this book, though, you get a break on the chapter quiz—just one question this time. As always, be sure to work through this part's closing exercises to cement what you've learned in the past few chapters; because the next part is optional reading, this is the final end-of-part exercises session. If you want to see some examples of how what you've learned comes together in real scripts drawn from common applications, be sure to check out the "solution" to exercise 4 in Appendix D.

And if this is the end of your journey in this book, be sure to also see the "Encore" section at the end of Chapter 41, the very last chapter in this book (for the sake of readers continuing on to the Advanced Topics part, I won't spill the beans here).

Test Your Knowledge: Quiz

1. (This question is a repeat from the first quiz in Chapter 1—see, I told you it would be easy! :-) Why does "spam" show up in so many Python examples in books and on the Web?

Test Your Knowledge: Answers

1. Because Python is named after the British comedy group Monty Python (based on surveys I've conducted in classes, this is a much-too-well-kept secret in the Python world!). The spam reference comes from a Monty Python skit, set in a cafeteria whose menu items all seem to come with Spam. A couple trying to order food there keeps getting drowned out by a chorus of Vikings singing a song about Spam. No, really. And if I could insert an audio clip of that song here, I would...

Test Your Knowledge: Part VII Exercises

As we've reached the end of this part of the book, it's time for a few exception exercises to give you a chance to practice the basics. Exceptions really are simple tools; if you get these, you've probably mastered the exceptions domain. See "Part VII, Exceptions and Tools" on page 1497 in Appendix D for the solutions.

1. **try/except**. Write a function called oops that explicitly raises an IndexError exception when called. Then write another function that calls oops inside a try/except statement to catch the error. What happens if you change oops to raise a KeyError instead of an IndexError? Where do the names KeyError and IndexError come from? (Hint: recall that all unqualified names generally come from one of four scopes.)

2. *Exception objects and lists*. Change the oops function you just wrote to raise an exception you define yourself, called MyError. Identify your exception with a class (unless you're using Python 2.5 or earlier, you must). Then, extend the try statement in the catcher function to catch this exception and its instance in addition to IndexError, and print the instance you catch.

3. *Error handling*. Write a function called safe(func, *pargs, **kargs) that runs any function with any number of positional and/or keyword arguments by using the * arbitrary arguments header and call syntax, catches any exception raised while the function runs, and prints the exception using the exc_info call in the sys module. Then use your safe function to run your oops function from exercise 1 or 2. Put safe in a module file called *exctools.py*, and pass it the oops function interactively. What kind of error messages do you get? Finally, expand safe to also print a Python stack trace when an error occurs by calling the built-in print_exc function in the standard traceback module; see earlier in this chapter, and consult the Python library reference manual for usage details. We could probably code safe as a *function decorator* using Chapter 32 techniques, but we'll have to move on to the next part of the book to learn fully how (see the solutions for a preview).

4. *Self-study examples*. At the end of Appendix D, I've included a handful of example scripts developed as group exercises in live Python classes for you to study and run on your own in conjunction with Python's standard manual set. These are not described, and they use tools in the Python standard library that you'll have to research on your own. Still, for many readers, it helps to see how the concepts we've discussed in this book come together in real programs. If these whet your appetite for more, you can find a wealth of larger and more realistic application-level Python program examples in follow-up books like *Programming Python* and on the Web.

Advanced Topics

Unicode and Byte Strings

So far, our exploration of strings in this book has been deliberately incomplete. Chapter 4's types preview briefly introduced Python's Unicode strings and files without giving many details, and the *strings* chapter in the core types part of this book (Chapter 7) deliberately limited its scope to the subset of string topics that most Python programmers need to know about.

This was by design: because many programmers, including most beginners, deal with simple forms of text like ASCII, they can happily work with Python's basic `str` string type and its associated operations and don't need to come to grips with more advanced string concepts. In fact, such programmers can often ignore the string changes in Python 3.X and continue to use strings as they may have in the past.

On the other hand, many other programmers deal with more specialized types of data: non-ASCII character sets, image file contents, and so on. For those programmers, and others who may someday join them, in this chapter we're going to fill in the rest of the Python string story and look at some more advanced concepts in Python's string model.

Specifically, we'll explore the basics of Python's support for *Unicode text*—rich character strings used in internationalized applications—as well as *binary data*—strings that represent absolute byte values. As we'll see, the advanced string representation story has diverged in recent versions of Python:

- *Python 3.X* provides an alternative string type for binary data, and supports Unicode text (including ASCII) in its normal string type.

- *Python 2.X* provides an alternative string type for non-ASCII Unicode text, and supports both simple text and binary data in its normal string type.

In addition, because Python's string model has a direct impact on how you process non-ASCII *files*, we'll explore the fundamentals of that related topic here as well. Finally, we'll take a brief look at some advanced string and binary *tools*, such as pattern matching, object pickling, binary data packing, and XML parsing, and the ways in which they are impacted by 3.X's string changes.

This is officially an advanced topics chapter, because not all programmers will need to delve into the worlds of Unicode encodings or binary data. For some readers, Chapter 4's preview may suffice, and others may wish to file this chapter away for future reference. If you ever need to care about processing either of these, though, you'll find that Python's string models provide the support you need.

String Changes in 3.X

One of the most noticeable changes in the Python 3.X line is the mutation of string object types. In a nutshell, 2.X's `str` and `unicode` types have morphed into 3.X's `bytes` and `str` types, and a new mutable `bytearray` type has been added. The `bytear ray` type is technically available in Python 2.6 and 2.7 too (though not earlier), but it's a back-port from 3.X and does not as clearly distinguish between text and binary content in 2.X.

Especially if you process data that is either Unicode or binary in nature, these changes can have substantial impacts on your code. As a general rule of thumb, how much you need to care about this topic depends in large part upon which of the following categories you fall into:

- If you deal with non-ASCII *Unicode text*—for instance, in the context of internationalized domains like the Web, or the results of some XML and JSON parsers and databases—you will find support for text encodings to be different in 3.X, but also probably more direct, accessible, and seamless than in 2.X.

- If you deal with *binary data*—for example, in the form of image or audio files or packed data processed with the `struct` module—you will need to understand 3.X's new `bytes` object and 3.X's different and sharper distinction between text and binary data and files.

- If you fall into *neither* of the prior two categories, you can generally use strings in 3.X much as you would in 2.X, with the general `str` string type, text files, and all the familiar string operations we studied earlier. Your strings will be encoded and decoded by 3.X using your platform's default encoding (e.g., ASCII, or UTF-8 on Windows in the U.S.—`sys.getdefaultencoding` gives your default if you care to check), but you probably won't notice.

In other words, if your text is always ASCII, you can get by with normal string objects and text files and can avoid most of the following story for now. As we'll see in a moment, ASCII is a simple kind of Unicode and a subset of other encodings, so string operations and files generally "just work" if your programs process only ASCII text.

Even if you fall into the last of the three categories just mentioned, though, a basic understanding of Unicode and 3.X's string model can help both to demystify some of the underlying behavior now, and to make mastering Unicode or binary data issues easier if they impact you later.

To put that more strongly: like it or not, Unicode will be part of most software development in the interconnected future we've sown, and will probably impact you eventually. Though applications are beyond our scope here, if you work with the Internet, files, directories, network interfaces, databases, pipes, JSON, XML, and even GUIs, Unicode may no longer be an optional topic for you in Python 3.X.

Python 3.X's support for Unicode and binary data is also available in 2.X, albeit in different forms. Although our main focus in this chapter is on string types in 3.X, we'll also explore how 2.X's equivalent support differs along the way for readers using 2.X. Regardless of which version you use, the tools we'll explore here can become important in many types of programs.

String Basics

Before we look at any code, let's begin with a general overview of Python's string model. To understand why 3.X changed the way it did on this front, we have to start with a brief look at how characters are actually represented in computers—both when encoded in files and when stored in memory.

Character Encoding Schemes

Most programmers think of strings as series of characters used to represent textual data. While that's accurate, the way characters are stored can vary, depending on what sort of character set must be recorded. When text is stored on files, for example, its character set determines its format.

Character sets are standards that assign integer codes to individual characters so they can be represented in computer memory. The *ASCII* standard, for example, was created in the U.S., and it defines many U.S. programmers' notion of text strings. ASCII defines character codes from 0 through 127 and allows each character to be stored in one 8-bit byte, only 7 bits of which are actually used.

For example, the ASCII standard maps the character 'a' to the integer value 97 (0x61 in hex), which can be stored in a single byte in memory and files. If you wish to see how this works, Python's ord built-in function gives the binary identifying value for a character, and chr returns the character for a given integer code value:

```
>>> ord('a')        # 'a' is a byte with binary value 97 in ASCII (and others)
97
>>> hex(97)
'0x61'
>>> chr(97)         # Binary value 97 stands for character 'a'
'a'
```

Sometimes one byte per character isn't enough, though. Various symbols and accented characters, for instance, do not fit into the range of possible characters defined by ASCII. To accommodate special characters, some standards use all the possible values in an 8-bit byte, 0 through 255, to represent characters, and assign the values 128 through 255 (outside ASCII's range) to special characters.

One such standard, known as the *Latin-1* character set, is widely used in Western Europe. In Latin-1, character codes above 127 are assigned to accented and otherwise special characters. The character assigned to byte value 196, for example, is a specially marked non-ASCII character:

```
>>> 0xC4
196
>>> chr(196)        # Python 3.X result form shown
'Ä'
```

This standard allows for a wide array of extra special characters, but still supports ASCII as a 7-bit subset of its 8-bit representation.

Still, some alphabets define so many characters that it is impossible to represent each of them as one byte. *Unicode* allows more flexibility. Unicode text is sometimes referred to as "wide-character" strings, because characters may be represented with multiple bytes if needed. Unicode is typically used in *internationalized* programs, to represent European, Asian, and other non-English character sets that have more characters than 8-bit bytes can represent.

To store such rich text in computer memory, we say that characters are translated to and from raw bytes using an *encoding*—the rules for translating a string of Unicode characters to a sequence of bytes, and extracting a string from a sequence of bytes. More procedurally, this translation back and forth between bytes and strings is defined by two terms:

- *Encoding* is the process of translating a string of characters into its raw bytes form, according to a desired encoding name.

- *Decoding* is the process of translating a raw string of bytes into its character string form, according to its encoding name.

That is, we *encode* from string to raw bytes, and *decode* from raw bytes to string. To scripts, decoded strings are just characters in memory, but may be encoded into a variety of byte string representations when stored on files, transferred over networks, embedded in documents and databases, and so on.

For some encodings, the translation process is trivial—ASCII and Latin-1, for instance, map each character to a *fixed-size* single byte, so no translation work is required. For other encodings, the mapping can be more complex and yield multiple bytes per character, even for simple 8-bit forms of text.

The widely used *UTF-8* encoding, for example, allows a wide range of characters to be represented by employing a *variable-sized* number of bytes scheme. Character codes less than 128 are represented as a single byte; codes between 128 and 0x7ff (2047) are turned into 2 bytes, where each byte has a value between 128 and 255; and codes above 0x7ff are turned into 3- or 4-byte sequences having values between 128 and 255. This keeps simple ASCII strings compact, sidesteps byte ordering issues, and avoids null (zero value) bytes that can cause problems for C libraries and networking.

Because their encodings' character maps assign characters to the same codes for compatibility, ASCII is a *subset* of both Latin-1 and UTF-8. That is, a valid ASCII character string is also a valid Latin-1- and UTF-8-encoded string. For example, every ASCII file is a valid UTF-8 file, because the ASCII character set is a 7-bit subset of UTF-8.

Conversely, the UTF-8 encoding is binary compatible with ASCII, but only for character codes less than 128. Latin-1 and UTF-8 simply allow for additional characters: Latin-1 for characters mapped to values 128 through 255 within a byte, and UTF-8 for characters that may be represented with multiple bytes.

Other encodings allow for richer character sets in different ways. *UTF-16* and *UTF-32*, for example, format text with a fixed-size 2 and 4 bytes per each character scheme, respectively, even for characters that could otherwise fit in a single byte. Some encodings may also insert prefixes that identify byte ordering.

To see this for yourself, run a string's `encode` method, which gives its encoded byte-string format under a named scheme—a two-character ASCII string is 2 bytes in ASCII, Latin-1, and UTF-8, but it's much wider in UTF-16 and UTF-32, and includes header bytes:

```
>>> S = 'ni'
>>> S.encode('ascii'), S.encode('latin1'), S.encode('utf8')
(b'ni', b'ni', b'ni')

>>> S.encode('utf16'), len(S.encode('utf16'))
(b'\xff\xfen\x00i\x00', 6)

>>> S.encode('utf32'), len(S.encode('utf32'))
(b'\xff\xfe\x00\x00n\x00\x00\x00i\x00\x00\x00', 12)
```

These results differ slightly in Python 2.X (you won't get the leading b for byte strings). But all of these encoding schemes—ASCII, Latin-1, UTF-8, and many others—are considered to be Unicode.

To Python programmers, encodings are specified as strings containing the encoding's name. Python comes with roughly 100 different encodings; see the Python library reference for a complete list. Importing the module `encodings` and running `help(encodings)` shows you many encoding names as well; some are implemented in Python, and some in C. Some encodings have multiple names, too; for example, *latin-1*, *iso_8859_1*, and *8859* are all synonyms for the same encoding, Latin-1. We'll revisit encodings later in this chapter, when we study techniques for writing Unicode strings in a script.

For more on the underlying Unicode story, see the Python standard manual set. It includes a "Unicode HOWTO" in its "Python HOWTOs" section, which provides additional background that we will skip here in the interest of space.

How Python Stores Strings in Memory

The prior section's encodings really only apply when text is stored or transferred externally, in files and other mediums. In memory, Python always stores decoded text strings in an *encoding-neutral* format, which may or may not use multiple bytes for each character. All text processing occurs in this uniform internal format. Text is translated to and from an encoding-specific format only when it is transferred to or from external text files, byte strings, or APIs with specific encoding requirements. Once in memory, though, strings have no encoding. They are just the string object presented in this book.

Though irrelevant to your code, it may help some readers to make this more tangible. The way Python actually stores text in memory is prone to change over time, and in fact mutated substantially as of 3.3:

Python 3.2 and earlier
> Through Python 3.2, strings are stored internally in *fixed-length* UTF-16 (roughly, UCS-2) format with 2 bytes per character, unless Python is configured to use 4 bytes per character (UCS-4).

Python 3.3 and later
> Python 3.3 and later instead use a *variable-length* scheme with 1, 2, or 4 bytes per character, depending on a string's content. The size is chosen based upon the character with the largest Unicode ordinal value in the represented string. This scheme allows a space-efficient representation in common cases, but also allows for full UCS-4 on all platforms.

Python 3.3's new scheme is an optimization, especially compared to former wide Unicode builds. Per Python documentation: memory footprint is divided by 2 to 4 depending on the text; encoding an ASCII string to UTF-8 doesn't need to encode characters anymore, because its ASCII and UTF-8 representations are the same; repeating a single ASCII letter and getting a substring of an ASCII strings is 4 times faster; UTF-8 is 2 to 4 times faster; and UTF-16 encoding is up to 10 times faster. On some benchmarks, Python 3.3's overall memory usage is 2 to 3 times smaller than 3.2, and similar to the less Unicode-centric 2.7.

Regardless of the storage scheme used, as noted in Chapter 6 Unicode clearly requires us to think of strings in terms of *characters*, instead of *bytes*. This may be a bigger hurdle for programmers accustomed to the simpler ASCII-only world where each character mapped to a single byte, but that idea no longer applies, in terms of both the results of text string tools and physical character size:

Text tools
> Today, both string content and length really correspond to Unicode *code points*— identifying ordinal numbers for characters. For instance, the built-in `ord` function now returns a character's Unicode code point ordinal, which is not necessarily an ASCII code, and which may or may not fit in a single 8-bit byte's value. Similarly,

`len` returns the number of characters, not bytes; the string is probably larger in memory, and its characters may not fit in bytes anyhow.

Text size

As we saw by example in Chapter 4, under Unicode a single character does not necessarily map directly to a single byte, either when encoded in a file or when stored in memory. Even characters in simple 7-bit ASCII text may not map to bytes —UTF-16 uses multiple bytes per character in files, and Python may allocate 1, 2, or 4 bytes per character in memory. Thinking in terms of characters allows us to abstract away the details of external and internal storage.

The key point here, though, is that *encoding* pertains mostly to files and transfers. Once loaded into a Python string, text in memory has no notion of an "encoding," and is simply a sequence of Unicode characters (a.k.a. code points) stored generically. In your script, that string is accessed as a Python string object—the next section's topic.

Python's String Types

At a more concrete level, the Python language provides string data types to represent character text in your scripts. The string types you will use in your scripts depend upon the version of Python you're using. *Python 2.X* has a general string type for representing binary data and simple 8-bit text like ASCII, along with a specific type for representing richer Unicode text:

- `str` for representing 8-bit text and binary data
- `unicode` for representing decoded Unicode text

Python 2.X's two string types are different (`unicode` allows for the extra size of some Unicode characters and has extra support for encoding and decoding), but their operation sets largely overlap. The `str` string type in 2.X is used for text that can be represented with 8-bit bytes (including ASCII and Latin-1), as well as binary data that represents absolute byte values.

By contrast, *Python 3.X* comes with three string object types—one for textual data and two for binary data:

- `str` for representing decoded Unicode text (including ASCII)
- `bytes` for representing binary data (including encoded text)
- `bytearray`, a mutable flavor of the `bytes` type

As mentioned earlier, `bytearray` is also available in Python 2.6 and 2.7, but it's simply a back-port from 3.X with less content-specific behavior and is generally considered a 3.X type.

Why the different string types?

All three string types in 3.X support similar operation sets, but they have different roles. The main goal behind this change in 3.X was to *merge* the normal and Unicode string types of 2.X into a single string type that supports both simple and Unicode text: developers wanted to remove the 2.X string dichotomy and make Unicode processing more natural. Given that ASCII and other 8-bit text is really a simple kind of Unicode, this convergence seems logically sound.

To achieve this, 3.X stores text in a redefined `str` type—*an immutable sequence of characters* (not necessarily bytes), which may contain either simple text such as ASCII whose character values fit in single bytes, or richer character set text such as UTF-8 whose character values may require multiple bytes. Strings processed by your script with this type are stored generically in memory, and are encoded to and decoded from byte strings per either the platform Unicode default or an explicit encoding name. This allows scripts to translate text to different encoding schemes, both in memory and when transferring to and from files.

While 3.X's new `str` type does achieve the desired string/`unicode` merging, many programs still need to process raw binary data that is not encoded per any text format. Image and audio files, as well as packed data used to interface with devices or C programs you might process with Python's `struct` module, fall into this category. Because Unicode strings are decoded *from* bytes, they cannot be used to represent bytes.

To support processing of such truly binary data, a new string type, `bytes`, also was introduced—*an immutable sequence of 8-bit integers* representing absolute byte values, which prints as ASCII characters when possible. Though a distinct object type, `bytes` supports almost all the same operations that the `str` type does; this includes string methods, sequence operations, and even `re` module pattern matching, but not string formatting. In 2.X, the general `str` type fills this binary data role, because its strings are just sequences of bytes; the separate `unicode` type handles richer text strings.

In more detail, a 3.X `bytes` object really is a sequence of small integers, each of which is in the range 0 through 255; indexing a `bytes` returns an `int`, slicing one returns another `bytes`, and running the `list` built-in on one returns a list of integers, not characters. When processed with operations that assume characters, though, the contents of `bytes` objects are assumed to be ASCII-encoded bytes (e.g., the `isalpha` method assumes each byte is an ASCII character code). Further, `bytes` objects are printed as character strings instead of integers for convenience.

While they were at it, Python developers also added a `bytearray` type in 3.X. `bytearray` is a variant of `bytes` that is *mutable* and so supports in-place changes. It supports the usual string operations that `str` and `bytes` do, as well as many of the same in-place change operations as lists (e.g., the `append` and `extend` methods, and assignment to indexes). This can be useful both for truly binary data and simple types of text. Assuming your text strings can be treated as raw 8-bit bytes (e.g., ASCII or Latin-1 text), `bytearray` finally adds direct in-place mutability for text data—something not possible without conversion to a mutable type in Python 2.X, and not supported by Python 3.X's str or bytes.

Although Python 2.X and 3.X offer much the same functionality, they package it differently. In fact, the mapping from 2.X to 3.X string types is not completely direct—2.X's str equates to both str and bytes in 3.X, and 3.X's str equates to both str and unicode in 2.X. Moreover, the mutability of 3.X's bytearray is unique.

In practice, though, this asymmetry is not as daunting as it might sound. It boils down to the following: in 2.X, you will use str for simple text and binary data and unicode for advanced forms of text whose character sets don't map to 8-bit bytes; in 3.X, you'll use str for any kind of text (ASCII, Latin-1, and all other kinds of Unicode) and bytes or bytearray for binary data. In practice, the choice is often made for you by the tools you use—especially in the case of file processing tools, the topic of the next section.

Text and Binary Files

File I/O (input and output) was also revamped in 3.X to reflect the str/bytes distinction and automatically support encoding Unicode text on transfers. Python now makes a sharp platform-independent distinction between text files and binary files; in 3.X:

Text files
> When a file is opened in *text mode*, reading its data automatically decodes its content and returns it as a str; writing takes a str and automatically encodes it before transferring it to the file. Both reads and writes translate per a platform default or a provided encoding name. Text-mode files also support universal end-of-line translation and additional encoding specification arguments. Depending on the encoding name, text files may also automatically process the byte order mark sequence at the start of a file (more on this momentarily).

Binary files
> When a file is opened in *binary mode* by adding a b (lowercase only) to the mode-string argument in the built-in open call, reading its data does not decode it in any way but simply returns its content raw and unchanged, as a bytes object; writing similarly takes a bytes object and transfers it to the file unchanged. Binary-mode files also accept a bytearray object for the content to be written to the file.

Because the language sharply differentiates between str and bytes, you must decide whether your data is text or binary in nature and use either str or bytes objects to represent its content in your script, as appropriate. Ultimately, the mode in which you open a file will dictate which type of object your script will use to represent its content:

- If you are processing image files, data transferred over networks, packed binary data whose content you must extract, or some device data streams, chances are good that you will want to deal with it using bytes and *binary-mode* files. You might also opt for bytearray if you wish to update the data without making copies of it in memory.

- If instead you are processing something that is textual in nature, such as program output, HTML, email content, or CSV or XML files, you'll probably want to use str and *text-mode* files.

Notice that the *mode string* argument to built-in function open (its second argument) becomes fairly crucial in Python 3.X—its content not only specifies a file *processing mode*, but also implies a Python *object type*. By adding a b to the mode string, you specify binary mode and will receive, or must provide, a bytes object to represent the file's content when reading or writing. Without the b, your file is processed in text mode, and you'll use str objects to represent its content in your script. For example, the modes rb, wb, and rb+ imply bytes; r, w+, and rt (the default) imply str.

Text-mode files also handle the *byte order marker* (BOM) sequence that may appear at the start of files under some encoding schemes. In the UTF-16 and UTF-32 encodings, for example, the BOM specifies big- or little-endian format (essentially, which end of a bit-string is most significant)—see the leading bytes in the results of the UTF-16 and UTF-32 encoding calls we ran earlier for examples. A UTF-8 text file might also include a BOM to declare that it is UTF-8 in general. When reading and writing data using these encoding schemes, Python skips or writes the BOM according to rules we'll study later in this chapter.

In Python 2.X, the same behavior is supported, but normal files created by open are used to access bytes-based data, and Unicode files opened with the codecs.open call are used to process Unicode text data. The latter of these also encode and decode on transfer, as we'll see later in this chapter. First, let's explore Python's Unicode string model live.

Coding Basic Strings

Let's step through a few examples that demonstrate how the 3.X string types are used. One note up front: the code in this section was run with and applies to 3.X only. Still, basic string operations are generally portable across Python versions. Simple ASCII strings represented with the str type work the same in 2.X and 3.X (and exactly as we saw in Chapter 7 of this book).

Moreover, although there is no bytes type in Python 2.X (it has just the general str), it can usually run code that thinks there is—in 2.6 and 2.7, the call bytes(X) is present as a synonym for str(X), and the new literal form b'...' is taken to be the same as the normal string literal '...'. You may still run into version skew in some isolated cases, though; the 2.6/2.7 bytes call, for instance, does not require or allow the second argument (encoding name) that is required by 3.X's bytes.

Python 3.X String Literals

Python 3.X string objects originate when you call a built-in function such as str or bytes, read a file created by calling open (described in the next section), or code literal syntax in your script. For the latter, a new literal form, b'xxx' (and equivalently, B'xxx') is used to create bytes objects in 3.X, and you may create bytearray objects by calling the bytearray function, with a variety of possible arguments.

More formally, in 3.X all the current string literal forms—'xxx', "xxx", and triple-quoted blocks—generate a str; adding a b or B just before any of them creates a bytes instead. This new b'...' bytes literal is similar in form to the r'...' raw string used to suppress backslash escapes. Consider the following, run in 3.X:

```
C:\code> C:\python33\python
>>> B = b'spam'            # 3.X bytes literal make a bytes object (8-bit bytes)
>>> S = 'eggs'             # 3.X str literal makes a Unicode text string

>>> type(B), type(S)
(<class 'bytes'>, <class 'str'>)

>>> B                      # bytes: sequence of int, prints as character string
b'spam'
>>> S
'eggs'
```

The 3.X bytes object is actually a sequence of short integers, though it prints its content as characters whenever possible:

```
>>> B[0], S[0]             # Indexing returns an int for bytes, str for str
(115, 'e')
>>> B[1:], S[1:]           # Slicing makes another bytes or str object
(b'pam', 'ggs')
>>> list(B), list(S)
([115, 112, 97, 109], ['e', 'g', 'g', 's'])       # bytes is really 8-bit small ints
```

The bytes object is also immutable, just like str (though bytearray, described later, is not); you cannot assign a str, bytes, or integer to an offset of a bytes object.

```
>>> B[0] = 'x'                              # Both are immutable
TypeError: 'bytes' object does not support item assignment
>>> S[0] = 'x'
TypeError: 'str' object does not support item assignment
```

Finally, note that the bytes literal's b or B prefix also works for any string literal form, including triple-quoted blocks, though you get back a string of raw bytes that may or may not map to characters:

```
>>> # bytes prefix works on single, double, triple quotes, raw
>>> B = B"""
... xxxx
... yyyy
... """
>>> B
b'\nxxxx\nyyyy\n'
```

Python 2.X Unicode literals in Python 3.3

Python 2.X's u'xxx' and U'xxx' Unicode string literal forms were removed in Python 3.0 because they were deemed redundant—normal strings are Unicode in 3.X. To aid both forward and backward compatibility, though, they are available again as of 3.3, where they are treated as normal str strings:

```
C:\code> C:\python33\python
>>> U = u'spam'                  # 2.X Unicode literal accepted in 3.3+
>>> type(U)                      # It is just str, but is backward compatible
<class 'str'>
>>> U
'spam'
>>> U[0]
's'
>>> list(U)
['s', 'p', 'a', 'm']
```

These literals are gone in 3.0 through 3.2, where you must use 'xxx' instead. You should generally use 3.X 'xxx' text literals in new 3.X-only code, because the 2.X form is superfluous. However, in 3.3 and later, using the 2.X literal form can ease the task of porting 2.X code, and boost 2.X code compatibility (for a case in point, see Chapter 25's *currency* example, described in an upcoming note). Regardless of how text strings are coded in 3.X, though, they are all Unicode, even if they contain only ASCII characters (more on writing non-ASCII Unicode text in the section "Coding Non-ASCII Text" on page 1179).

Python 2.X String Literals

All three of the 3.X string forms of the prior section can be coded in 2.X, but their meaning differs. As mentioned earlier, in Python 2.6 and 2.7 the b'xxx' bytes literal is present for forward compatibility with 3.X, but is the same as 'xxx' and makes a str (the b is ignored), and bytes is just a synonym for str; as you've seen, in 3.X both of these address the distinct bytes type:

```
C:\code> C:\python27\python
>>> B = b'spam'                  # 3.X bytes literal is just str in 2.6/2.7
>>> S = 'eggs'                   # str is a bytes/character sequence

>>> type(B), type(S)
(<type 'str'>, <type 'str'>)
>>> B, S
('spam', 'eggs')
>>> B[0], S[0]
('s', 'e')
>>> list(B), list(S)
(['s', 'p', 'a', 'm'], ['e', 'g', 'g', 's'])
```

In 2.X the special Unicode literal and type accommodates richer forms of text:

```
>>> U = u'spam'                  # 2.X Unicode literal makes a distinct type
>>> type(U)                      # Works in 3.3 too, but is just a str there
```

```
<type 'unicode'>
>>> U
u'spam'
>>> U[0]
u's'
>>> list(U)
[u's', u'p', u'a', u'm']
```

As we saw, for compatibility this form works in 3.3 and later too, but it simply makes a normal `str` there (the `u` is ignored).

String Type Conversions

Although Python 2.X allowed `str` and `unicode` type objects to be mixed in expressions (when the `str` contained only 7-bit ASCII text), 3.X draws a much sharper distinction —`str` and `bytes` type objects *never* mix automatically in expressions and *never* are converted to one another automatically when passed to functions. A function that expects an argument to be a `str` object won't generally accept a `bytes`, and vice versa.

Because of this, Python 3.X basically requires that you commit to one type or the other, or perform manual, explicit conversions when needed:

- `str.encode()` and `bytes(S, encoding)` translate a string to its raw bytes form and create an encoded `bytes` from a decoded `str` in the process.
- `bytes.decode()` and `str(B, encoding)` translate raw bytes into its string form and create a decoded `str` from an encoded `bytes` in the process.

These `encode` and `decode` methods (as well as file objects, described in the next section) use either a default encoding for your platform or an explicitly passed-in encoding name. For example, in *Python 3.X*:

```
>>> S = 'eggs'
>>> S.encode()                          # str->bytes: encode text into raw bytes
b'eggs'
>>> bytes(S, encoding='ascii')          # str->bytes, alternative
b'eggs'

>>> B = b'spam'
>>> B.decode()                          # bytes->str: decode raw bytes into text
'spam'
>>> str(B, encoding='ascii')            # bytes->str, alternative
'spam'
```

Two cautions here. First of all, your platform's default encoding is available in the `sys` module, but the encoding argument to `bytes` is not optional, even though it is in `str.encode` (and `bytes.decode`).

Second, although calls to `str` do not require the encoding argument like `bytes` does, leaving it off in `str` calls does not mean that it defaults—instead, a `str` call without an encoding returns the `bytes` object's *print string*, not its `str` converted form (this is usually not what you'll want!). Assuming B and S are still as in the prior listing:

```
>>> import sys
>>> sys.platform                        # Underlying platform
'win32'
>>> sys.getdefaultencoding()            # Default encoding for str here
'utf-8'

>>> bytes(S)
TypeError: string argument without an encoding

>>> str(B)                              # str without encoding
"b'spam'"                               # A print string, not conversion!
>>> len(str(B))
7
>>> len(str(B, encoding='ascii'))       # Use encoding to convert to str
4
```

When in doubt, pass in an encoding name argument in 3.X, even if it may have a default. Conversions are similar in *Python 2.X*, though 2.X's support for mixing string types in expressions makes conversions optional for ASCII text, and the tool names differ for the different string type model—conversions in 2.X occur between encoded `str` and decoded `unicode`, rather than 3.X's encoded `bytes` and decoded `str`:

```
>>> S = 'spam'                          # 2.X type string conversion tools
>>> U = u'eggs'
>>> S, U
('spam', u'eggs')
>>> unicode(S), str(U)                  # 2.X converts str->uni, uni->str
(u'spam', 'eggs')
>>> S.decode(), U.encode()              # versus 3.X byte->str, str->bytes
(u'spam', 'eggs')
```

Coding Unicode Strings

Encoding and decoding become more meaningful when you start dealing with non-ASCII Unicode text. To code arbitrary Unicode characters in your strings, some of which you might not even be able to type on your keyboard, Python string literals support both "\xNN" hex byte value escapes and "\uNNNN" and "\UNNNNNNNN" Unicode escapes in string literals. In Unicode escapes, the first form gives four hex digits to encode a 2-byte (16-bit) character code point, and the second gives eight hex digits for a 4-byte (32-bit) code point. Byte strings support only hex escapes for encoded text and other forms of byte-based data.

Coding ASCII Text

Let's step through some examples that demonstrate text coding basics. As we've seen, ASCII text is a simple type of Unicode, stored as a sequence of byte values that represent characters:

```
C:\code> C:\python33\python
>>> ord('X')              # 'X' is binary code point value 88 in the default encoding
```

```
88
>>> chr(88)                  # 88 stands for character 'X'
'X'

>>> S = 'XYZ'                # A Unicode string of ASCII text
>>> S
'XYZ'
>>> len(S)                   # Three characters long
3
>>> [ord(c) for c in S]      # Three characters with integer ordinal values
[88, 89, 90]
```

Normal 7-bit ASCII text like this is represented with one character per byte under each of the Unicode encoding schemes described earlier in this chapter:

```
>>> S.encode('ascii')        # Values 0..127 in 1 byte (7 bits) each
b'XYZ'
>>> S.encode('latin-1')      # Values 0..255 in 1 byte (8 bits) each
b'XYZ'
>>> S.encode('utf-8')        # Values 0..127 in 1 byte, 128..2047 in 2, others 3 or 4
b'XYZ'
```

In fact, the bytes objects returned by encoding ASCII text this way are really a sequence of short integers, which just happen to print as ASCII characters when possible:

```
>>> S.encode('latin-1')
b'XYZ'
>>> S.encode('latin-1')[0]
88
>>> list(S.encode('latin-1'))
[88, 89, 90]
```

Coding Non-ASCII Text

Formally, to code non-ASCII characters, we can use:

- *Hex* or *Unicode* escapes to embed Unicode code point ordinal values in *text strings* —normal string literals in 3.X, and Unicode string literals in 2.X (and in 3.3 for compatibility).

- *Hex* escapes to embed the encoded representation of characters in *byte strings*— normal string literals in 2.X, and bytes string literals in 3.X (and in 2.X for compatibility).

Note that text strings embed actual code point values, while byte strings embed their encoded form. The value of a character's encoded representation in a byte string is the same as its decoded Unicode code point value in a text string for only certain characters and encodings. In any event, hex escapes are limited to coding a single byte's value, but Unicode escapes can name characters with values 2 and 4 bytes wide. The chr function can also be used to create a single non-ASCII character from its code point value, and as we'll see later, source code declarations apply to such characters embedded in your script.

For instance, the hex values 0xCD and 0xE8 are codes for two special accented characters outside the 7-bit range of ASCII, but we can embed them in 3.X str objects because str supports Unicode:

```
>>> chr(0xc4)              # 0xC4, 0xE8: characters outside ASCII's range
'Ä'
>>> chr(0xe8)
'è'

>>> S = '\xc4\xe8'         # Single 8-bit value hex escapes: two digits
>>> S
'Äè'

>>> S = '\u00c4\u00e8'     # 16-bit Unicode escapes: four digits each
>>> S
'Äè'
>>> len(S)                 # Two characters long (not number of bytes!)
2
```

Note that in Unicode text string literals like these, hex and Unicode escapes denote a Unicode code point value, not byte values. The x hex escapes require exactly two digits (for 8-bit code point values), and u and U Unicode escapes require exactly four and eight hexadecimal digits, respectively, for denoting code point values that can be as big as 16 and 32 bits will allow:

```
>>> S = '\U000000c4\U000000e8'     # 32-bit Unicode escapes: eight digits each
>>> S
'Äè'
```

As shown later, Python 2.X works similarly in this regard, but Unicode escapes are allowed only in its Unicode literal form. They work in normal string literals in 3.X here simply because its normal strings are always Unicode.

Encoding and Decoding Non-ASCII text

Now, if we try to *encode* the prior section's non-ASCII text string into raw bytes using as *ASCII*, we'll get an error, because its characters are outside ASCII's 7-bit code point value range:

```
>>> S = '\u00c4\u00e8'             # Non-ASCII text string, two characters long
>>> S
'Äè'
>>> len(S)
2

>>> S.encode('ascii')
UnicodeEncodeError: 'ascii' codec can't encode characters in position 0-1:
ordinal not in range(128)
```

Encoding this as *Latin-1* works, though, because each character falls into that encoding's 8-bit range, and we get 1 byte per character allocated in the encoded byte string. Encoding as *UTF-8* also works: this encoding supports a wide range of Unicode code points, but allocates 2 bytes per non-ASCII character instead. If these encoded strings are written to a file, the raw **bytes** shown here for encoding results are what is actually stored on the file for the encoding types given:

```
>>> S.encode('latin-1')          # 1 byte per character when encoded
b'\xc4\xe8'

>>> S.encode('utf-8')            # 2 bytes per character when encoded
b'\xc3\x84\xc3\xa8'

>>> len(S.encode('latin-1'))     # 2 bytes in latin-1, 4 in utf-8
2
>>> len(S.encode('utf-8'))
4
```

Note that you can also go the other way, reading raw bytes from a file and *decoding* them back to a Unicode string. However, as we'll see later, the encoding mode you give to the **open** call causes this decoding to be done for you automatically on input (and avoids issues that may arise from reading partial character sequences when reading by blocks of bytes):

```
>>> B = b'\xc4\xe8'              # Text encoded per Latin-1
>>> B
b'\xc4\xe8'
>>> len(B)                      # 2 raw bytes, two encoded characters
2
>>> B.decode('latin-1')         # Decode to text per Latin-1
'Äè'

>>> B = b'\xc3\x84\xc3\xa8'     # Text encoded per UTF-8
>>> len(B)                      # 4 raw bytes, two encoded characters
4
>>> B.decode('utf-8')           # Decode to text per UTF-8
'Äè'
>>> len(B.decode('utf-8'))      # Two Unicode characters in memory
2
```

Other Encoding Schemes

Some encodings use even larger byte sequences to represent characters. When needed, you can specify both 16- and 32-bit Unicode code point values for characters in your strings—as shown earlier, we can use "\u..." with four hex digits for the former, and "\U..." with eight hex digits for the latter, and can mix these in literals with simpler ASCII characters freely:

```
>>> S = 'A\u00c4B\U000000e8C'
>>> S                           # A, B, C, and 2 non-ASCII characters
'AÄBèC'
>>> len(S)                      # Five characters long
5

>>> S.encode('latin-1')
b'A\xc4B\xe8C'
```

```
>>> len(S.encode('latin-1'))              # 5 bytes when encoded per latin-1
5

>>> S.encode('utf-8')
b'A\xc3\x84B\xc3\xa8C'
>>> len(S.encode('utf-8'))                # 7 bytes when encoded per utf-8
7
```

Technically speaking, you can also build Unicode strings piecemeal using chr instead of Unicode or hex escapes, but this might become tedious for large strings:

```
>>> S = 'A' + chr(0xC4) + 'B' + chr(0xE8) + 'C'
>>> S
'AÄBèC'
```

Some other encodings may use very different byte formats, though. The cp500 EBCDIC encoding, for example, doesn't even encode ASCII the same way as the encodings we've been using so far; since Python encodes and decodes for us, we only generally need to care about this when providing encoding names for data sources:

```
>>> S
'AÄBèC'
>>> S.encode('cp500')                     # Two other Western European encodings
b'\xc1c\xc2T\xc3'
>>> S.encode('cp850')                     # 5 bytes each, different encoded values
b'A\x8eB\x8aC'

>>> S = 'spam'                            # ASCII text is the same in most
>>> S.encode('latin-1')
b'spam'
>>> S.encode('utf-8')
b'spam'
>>> S.encode('cp500')                     # But not in cp500: IBM EBCDIC!
b'\xa2\x97\x81\x94'
>>> S.encode('cp850')
b'spam'
```

The same holds true for the UTF-16 and UTF-32 encodings, which use fixed 2- and 4-byte-per-character schemes with same-sized headers—non-ASCII encodes differently, and ASCII is not 1 byte per character:

```
>>> S = 'A\u00c4B\U000000e8C'
>>> S.encode('utf-16')
b'\xff\xfeA\x00\xc4\x00B\x00\xe8\x00C\x00'

>>> S = 'spam'
>>> S.encode('utf-16')
b'\xff\xfes\x00p\x00a\x00m\x00'
>>> S.encode('utf-32')
b'\xff\xfe\x00\x00s\x00\x00\x00p\x00\x00\x00a\x00\x00\x00m\x00\x00\x00'
```

Byte String Literals: Encoded Text

Two cautions here too. First, Python 3.X allows special characters to be coded with both hex and Unicode escapes in `str` strings, but only with hex escapes in `bytes` strings —Unicode escape sequences are silently taken *verbatim* in `bytes` literals, not as escapes. In fact, `bytes` must be decoded to `str` strings to print their non-ASCII characters properly:

```
>>> S = 'A\xC4B\xE8C'                    # 3.X: str recognizes hex and Unicode escapes
>>> S
'AÄBèC'
>>> S = 'A\u00C4B\U000000E8C'
>>> S
'AÄBèC'

>>> B = b'A\xC4B\xE8C'                    # bytes recognizes hex but not Unicode
>>> B
b'A\xc4B\xe8C'
>>> B = b'A\u00C4B\U000000E8C'           # Escape sequences taken literally!
>>> B
b'A\\u00C4B\\U000000E8C'

>>> B = b'A\xC4B\xE8C'                    # Use hex escapes for bytes
>>> B                                     # Prints non-ASCII as hex
b'A\xc4B\xe8C'
>>> print(B)
b'A\xc4B\xe8C'
>>> B.decode('latin-1')                   # Decode as latin-1 to interpret as text
'AÄBèC'
```

Second, `bytes` literals require characters either to be ASCII characters or, if their values are greater than 127, to be escaped; `str` stings, on the other hand, allow literals containing any character in the source character set—which, as discussed later, defaults to UTF-8 unless an encoding declaration is given in the source file:

```
>>> S = 'AÄBèC'                           # Chars from UTF-8 if no encoding declaration
>>> S
'AÄBèC'

>>> B = b'AÄBèC'
SyntaxError: bytes can only contain ASCII literal characters.

>>> B = b'A\xC4B\xE8C'                    # Chars must be ASCII, or escapes
>>> B
b'A\xc4B\xe8C'
>>> B.decode('latin-1')
'AÄBèC'

>>> S.encode()                            # Source code encoded per UTF-8 by default
b'A\xc3\x84B\xc3\xa8C'                     # Uses system default to encode, unless passed
>>> S.encode('utf-8')
b'A\xc3\x84B\xc3\xa8C'
```

```
>>> B.decode()                          # Raw bytes do not correspond to utf-8
UnicodeDecodeError: 'utf8' codec can't decode bytes in position 1-2: ...
```

Both these constraints make sense if you remember that byte strings hold bytes-based data, not decoded Unicode code point ordinals; while they may contain the encoded form of text, decoded code point values don't quite apply to byte strings unless the characters are first encoded.

Converting Encodings

So far, we've been encoding and decoding strings to inspect their structure. It's also possible to *convert* a string to a different encoding than its original, but we must provide an explicit encoding name to encode to and decode from. This is true whether the original text string originated in a file or a literal.

The term *conversion* may be a misnomer here—it really just means encoding a text string to raw bytes per a different encoding scheme than the one it was decoded from. As stressed earlier, decoded text in memory has no encoding type, and is simply a string of Unicode code points (a.k.a. characters); there is no concept of changing its encoding in this form. Still, this scheme allows scripts to read data in one encoding and store it in another, to support multiple clients of the same data:

```
>>> B = b'A\xc3\x84B\xc3\xa8C'        # Text encoded in UTF-8 format originally
>>> S = B.decode('utf-8')             # Decode to Unicode text per UTF-8
>>> S
'AÄBèC'

>>> T = S.encode('cp500')             # Convert to encoded bytes per EBCDIC
>>> T
b'\xc1c\xc2T\xc3'

>>> U = T.decode('cp500')             # Convert back to Unicode per EBCDIC
>>> U
'AÄBèC'

>>> U.encode()                        # Per default utf-8 encoding again
b'A\xc3\x84B\xc3\xa8C'
```

Keep in mind that the special Unicode and hex character escapes are only necessary when you code non-ASCII Unicode strings manually. In practice, you'll often load such text from files instead. As we'll see later in this chapter, 3.X's file object (created with the open built-in function) automatically decodes text strings as they are read and encodes them when they are written; because of this, your script can often deal with strings generically, without having to code special characters directly.

Later in this chapter we'll also see that it's possible to convert between encodings when transferring strings to and from files, using a technique very similar to that in the last example; although you'll still need to provide explicit encoding names when opening a file, the file interface does most of the conversion work for you automatically.

Coding Unicode Strings in Python 2.X

I stress Python 3.X Unicode support in this chapter because it's new. But now that I've shown you the basics of Unicode strings in 3.X, I need to explain more fully how you can do much the same in 2.X, though the tools differ. `unicode` is available in Python 2.X, but is a distinct type from `str`, supports most of the same operations, and allows mixing of normal and Unicode strings when the `str` is all ASCII.

In fact, you can essentially pretend 2.X's `str` is 3.X's `bytes` when it comes to decoding raw bytes into a Unicode string, as long as it's in the proper form. Here is 2.X in action; Unicode characters display in hex in 2.X unless you explicitly print, and non-ASCII displays can vary per shell (most of this section ran outside IDLE, which sometimes detects and prints Latin-1 characters in encoded byte strings—see ahead for more on `PYTHONIOENCODING` and Windows Command Prompt display issues):

```
C:\code> C:\python27\python
>>> S = 'A\xC4B\xE8C'              # String of 8-bit bytes
>>> S                             # Text encoded per Latin-1, some non-ASCII
'A\xc4B\xe8C'
>>> print S                       # Nonprintable characters (IDLE may differ)
A—BΦC


>>> U = S.decode('latin1')        # Decode bytes to Unicode text per latin-1
>>> U
u'A\xc4B\xe8C'
>>> print U
AÄBèC

>>> S.decode('utf-8')             # Encoded form not compatible with utf-8
UnicodeDecodeError: 'utf8' codec can't decode byte 0xc4 in position 1: invalid c
ontinuation byte

>>> S.decode('ascii')             # Encoded bytes are also outside ASCII range
UnicodeDecodeError: 'ascii' codec can't decode byte 0xc4 in position 1: ordinal
not in range(128)
```

To code Unicode text, make a `unicode` object with the `u'xxx'` literal form (as mentioned, this literal is available again in 3.3, but superfluous in 3.X in general, since its normal strings support Unicode):

```
>>> U = u'A\xC4B\xE8C'            # Make Unicode string, hex escapes
>>> U
u'A\xc4B\xe8C'
>>> print U
AÄBèC
```

Once you've created it, you can convert Unicode text to different raw byte encodings, similar to encoding `str` objects into `bytes` objects in 3.X:

```
>>> U.encode('latin-1')           # Encode per latin-1: 8-bit bytes
'A\xc4B\xe8C'
```

```
>>> U.encode('utf-8')                    # Encode per utf-8: multibyte
'A\xc3\x84B\xc3\xa8C'
```

Non-ASCII characters can be coded with hex or Unicode escapes in string literals in 2.X, just as in 3.X. However, as with bytes in 3.X, the "\u..." and "\U..." escapes are recognized only for unicode strings in 2.X, not 8-bit str strings—again, these are used to give the values of decoded Unicode ordinal integers, which don't make sense in a raw byte string:

```
C:\code> C:\python27\python
>>> U = u'A\xC4B\xE8C'                    # Hex escapes for non-ASCII
>>> U
u'A\xc4B\xe8C'
>>> print U
AÄBèC

>>> U = u'A\u00C4B\U000000E8C'            # Unicode escapes for non-ASCII
>>> U                                      # u'' = 16 bits, U'' = 32 bits
u'A\xc4B\xe8C'
>>> print U
AÄBèC

>>> S = 'A\xC4B\xE8C'                      # Hex escapes work
>>> S
'A\xc4B\xe8C'
>>> print S                                # But some may print oddly, unless decoded
A—BØC
>>> print S.decode('latin-1')
AÄBèC

>>> S = 'A\u00C4B\U000000E8C'              # Not Unicode escapes: taken literally!
>>> S
'A\\u00C4B\\U000000E8C'
>>> print S
A\u00C4B\U000000E8C
>>> len(S)
19
```

Mixing string types in 2.X

Like 3.X's str and bytes, 2.X's unicode and str share nearly identical operation sets, so unless you need to convert to other encodings you can often treat unicode as though it were str. One of the primary differences between 2.X and 3.X, though, is that uni code and non-Unicode str objects can be freely *mixed* in 2.X expressions—as long as the str is compatible with the unicode object, Python will automatically convert it up to unicode:

```
>>> u'ab' + 'cd'                          # Can mix if compatible in 2.X
u'abcd'                                    # But 'ab' + b'cd' not allowed in 3.X
```

However, this liberal approach to mixing string types in 2.X works *only* if the 8-bit string happens to contain only 7-bit (ASCII) bytes:

```
>>> S =  'A\xC4B\xE8C'                # Can't mix in 2.X if str is non-ASCII!
>>> U = u'A\xC4B\xE8C'
>>> S + U
UnicodeDecodeError: 'ascii' codec can't decode byte 0xc4 in position 1: ordinal
not in range(128)

>>> 'abc' + U                         # Can mix only if str is all 7-bit ASCII
u'abcA\xc4B\xe8C'
>>> print 'abc' + U                   # Use print to display characters
abcAÄBèC

>>> S.decode('latin-1') + U           # Manual conversion may be required in 2.X too
u'A\xc4B\xe8CA\xc4B\xe8C'
>>> print S.decode('latin-1') + U
AÄBèCAÄBèC

>>> print u'\xA3' + '999.99'          # Also see Chapter 25's currency example
£999.99
```

By contrast, in 3.X, str and bytes *never* mix automatically and require manual conversions—the preceding code actually runs in 3.3, but only because 2.X's Unicode literal is taken to be the same as a normal string by 3.X (the u is ignored); the 3.X equivalent would be a str added to a bytes (i.e., 'ab' + b'cd') which fails in 3.X, unless objects are converted to a common type.

In 2.X, though, the difference in types is often trivial to your code. Like normal strings, Unicode strings may be concatenated, indexed, sliced, matched with the re module, and so on, and they cannot be changed in place. If you ever need to convert between the two types explicitly, you can use the built-in str and unicode functions as shown earlier:

```
>>> str(u'spam')                      # Unicode to normal
'spam'
>>> unicode('spam')                   # Normal to Unicode
u'spam'
```

If you are using Python 2.X, also watch for an example of your different file interface later in this chapter. Your open call supports only files of 8-bit bytes, returning their contents as str strings, and it's up to you to interpret the contents as text or binary data and decode if needed. To read and write Unicode files and encode or decode their content automatically, use 2.X's codecs.open call we'll see in action later in this chapter. This call provides much the same functionality as 3.X's open and uses 2.X unicode objects to represent file content—reading a file translates encoded bytes into decoded Unicode characters, and writing translates strings to the desired encoding specified when the file is opened.

Source File Character Set Encoding Declarations

Finally, Unicode escape codes are fine for the occasional Unicode character in string literals, but they can become tedious if you need to embed non-ASCII text in your strings frequently. To interpret the content of strings you code and hence embed within the text of your script files, Python uses the UTF-8 encoding by default, but it allows you to change this to support arbitrary character sets by including a comment that names your desired encoding. The comment must be of this form and must appear as either the first or second line in your script in either Python 2.X or 3.X:

```
# -*- coding: latin-1 -*-
```

When a comment of this form is present, Python will recognize strings represented natively in the given encoding. This means you can edit your script file in a text editor that accepts and displays accented and other non-ASCII characters correctly, and Python will decode them correctly in your string literals. For example, notice how the comment at the top of the following file, *text.py*, allows Latin-1 characters to be embedded in strings, which are themselves embedded in the script file's text:

```
# -*- coding: latin-1 -*-
# Any of the following string literal forms work in latin-1.
# Changing the encoding above to either ascii or utf-8 fails,
# because the 0xc4 and 0xe8 in myStr1 are not valid in either.

myStr1 = 'aÄBèC'

myStr2 = 'A\u00c4B\U000000e8C'

myStr3 = 'A' + chr(0xC4) + 'B' + chr(0xE8) + 'C'

import sys
print('Default encoding:', sys.getdefaultencoding())

for aStr in myStr1, myStr2, myStr3:
    print('{0}, strlen={1}, '.format(aStr, len(aStr)), end='')

    bytes1 = aStr.encode()            # Per default utf-8: 2 bytes for non-ASCII
    bytes2 = aStr.encode('latin-1')   # One byte per char
    #bytes3 = aStr.encode('ascii')    # ASCII fails: outside 0..127 range

    print('byteslen1={0}, byteslen2={1}'.format(len(bytes1), len(bytes2)))
```

When run, this script produces the following output, giving, for each of three coding techniques, the string, its length, and the lengths of its UTF-8 and Latin-1 encoded byte string forms.

```
C:\code> C:\python33\python text.py
Default encoding: utf-8
aÄBèC, strlen=5, byteslen1=7, byteslen2=5
AÄBèC, strlen=5, byteslen1=7, byteslen2=5
AÄBèC, strlen=5, byteslen1=7, byteslen2=5
```

Since many programmers are likely to fall back on the standard UTF-8 encoding, I'll defer to Python's standard manual set for more details on this option and other advanced Unicode support topics, such as properties and character name escapes in strings I'm omitting here. For this chapter, let's take a quick look at the new byte string object types in Python 3.X, before moving on to its file and tool changes.

For an additional example of non-ASCII character coding and source file declarations, see the currency symbols used in the money formatting example of Chapter 25, as well as its associated file in this book's examples package, *formats_currency2.py*. The latter requires a source-file declaration to be usable by Python, because it embeds non-ASCII currency symbol characters. This example also illustrates the portability gains possible when using 2.X's Unicode literal in 3.X code in 3.3 and later.

Using 3.X bytes Objects

We studied a wide variety of operations available for Python 3.X's general `str` string type in Chapter 7; the basic string type works identically in 2.X and 3.X, so we won't rehash this topic. Instead, let's dig a bit deeper into the operation sets provided by the new `bytes` type in 3.X.

As mentioned previously, the 3.X `bytes` object is a sequence of small integers, each of which is in the range 0 through 255, that happens to print as ASCII characters when displayed. It supports sequence operations and most of the same methods available on `str` objects (and present in 2.X's `str` type). However, `bytes` does *not* support the `for mat` method or the `%` formatting expression, and you cannot mix and match `bytes` and `str` type objects without explicit conversions—you generally will use all `str` type objects and text files for *text data*, and all `bytes` type objects and binary files for *binary data*.

Method Calls

If you really want to see what attributes `str` has that `bytes` doesn't, you can always check their `dir` built-in function results. The output can also tell you something about the expression operators they support (e.g., `__mod__` and `__rmod__` implement the `%` operator):

```
C:\code> C:\python33\python

# Attributes in str but not bytes
>>> set(dir('abc')) - set(dir(b'abc'))
{'isdecimal', '__mod__', '__rmod__', 'format_map', 'isprintable',
'casefold', 'format', 'isnumeric', 'isidentifier', 'encode'}

# Attributes in bytes but not str
>>> set(dir(b'abc')) - set(dir('abc'))
{'decode', 'fromhex'}
```

As you can see, `str` and `bytes` have almost identical functionality. Their unique attributes are generally methods that don't apply to the other; for instance, `decode` translates a raw `bytes` into its `str` representation, and `encode` translates a string into its raw `bytes` representation. Most of the methods are the same, though `bytes` methods require `bytes` arguments (again, 3.X string types don't mix). Also recall that `bytes` objects are immutable, just like `str` objects in both 2.X and 3.X (error messages here have been shortened for brevity):

```
>>> B = b'spam'                    # b'...' bytes literal
>>> B.find(b'pa')
1

>>> B.replace(b'pa', b'XY')        # bytes methods expect bytes arguments
b'sXYm'

>>> B.split(b'pa')                 # bytes methods return bytes results
[b's', b'm']

>>> B
b'spam'
>>> B[0] = 'x'
TypeError: 'bytes' object does not support item assignment
```

One notable difference is that *string formatting* works only on `str` objects in 3.X, not on `bytes` objects (see Chapter 7 for more on string formatting expressions and methods):

```
>>> '%s' % 99
'99'
>>> b'%s' % 99
TypeError: unsupported operand type(s) for %: 'bytes' and 'int'

>>> '{0}'.format(99)
'99'
>>> b'{0}'.format(99)
AttributeError: 'bytes' object has no attribute 'format'
```

Sequence Operations

Besides method calls, all the usual generic sequence operations you know (and possibly love) from Python 2.X strings and lists work as expected on both `str` and `bytes` in 3.X; this includes indexing, slicing, concatenation, and so on. Notice in the following that indexing a `bytes` object returns an integer giving the byte's binary value; `bytes` really is a *sequence of 8-bit integers*, but for convenience prints as a string of ASCII-coded characters where possible when displayed as a whole. To check a given byte's value, use the `chr` built-in to convert it back to its character, as in the following:

```
>>> B = b'spam'                    # A sequence of small ints
>>> B                              # Prints as ASCII characters (and/or hex escapes)
b'spam'

>>> B[0]                           # Indexing yields an int
115
>>> B[-1]
109

>>> chr(B[0])                      # Show character for int
's'
```

```
>>> list(B)                        # Show all the byte's int values
[115, 112, 97, 109]

>>> B[1:], B[:-1]
(b'pam', b'spa')
>>> len(B)
4
>>> B + b'lmn'
b'spamlmn'
>>> B * 4
b'spamspamspamspam'
```

Other Ways to Make bytes Objects

So far, we've been mostly making `bytes` objects with the `b'...'` literal syntax. We can also create them by calling the `bytes` constructor with a `str` and an encoding name, calling the `bytes` constructor with an iterable of integers representing byte values, or encoding a `str` object per the default (or passed-in) encoding. As we've seen, encoding takes a text `str` and returns the raw encoded byte values of the string per the encoding specified; conversely, decoding takes a raw `bytes` sequence and translates it to its `str` text string representation—a series of Unicode characters. Both operations create new string objects:

```
>>> B = b'abc'                     # Literal
>>> B
b'abc'

>>> B = bytes('abc', 'ascii')      # Constructor with encoding name
>>> B
b'abc'

>>> ord('a')
97
>>> B = bytes([97, 98, 99])        # Integer iterable
>>> B
b'abc'

>>> B = 'spam'.encode()            # str.encode() (or bytes())
>>> B
b'spam'
>>>
>>> S = B.decode()                 # bytes.decode() (or str())
>>> S
'spam'
```

From a functional perspective, the last two of these operations are really tools for *converting* between `str` and `bytes`, a topic introduced earlier and expanded upon in the next section.

Mixing String Types

In the `replace` call of the section "Method Calls" on page 1189, we had to pass in two `bytes` objects—`str` types won't work there. Although Python 2.X automatically converts `str` to and from `unicode` when possible (i.e., when the `str` is 7-bit ASCII text), Python 3.X requires specific string types in some contexts and expects manual conversions if needed:

```
# Must pass expected types to function and method calls

>>> B = b'spam'

>>> B.replace('pa', 'XY')
TypeError: expected an object with the buffer interface

>>> B.replace(b'pa', b'XY')
b'sXYm'

>>> B = B'spam'
>>> B.replace(bytes('pa'), bytes('xy'))
TypeError: string argument without an encoding

>>> B.replace(bytes('pa', 'ascii'), bytes('xy', 'utf-8'))
b'sxym'

# Must convert manually in 3.X mixed-type expressions

>>> b'ab' + 'cd'
TypeError: can't concat bytes to str

>>> b'ab'.decode() + 'cd'          # bytes to str
'abcd'
>>> b'ab' + 'cd'.encode()          # str to bytes
b'abcd'
>>> b'ab' + bytes('cd', 'ascii')   # str to bytes
b'abcd'
```

Although you can create `bytes` objects yourself to represent packed binary data, they can also be made automatically by reading files opened in binary mode, as we'll see in more detail later in this chapter. First, though, let's introduce `bytes`'s very close, and mutable, cousin.

Using 3.X/2.6+ bytearray Objects

So far we've focused on `str` and `bytes`, because they subsume Python 2's `unicode` and `str`. Python 3.X grew a third string type, though—`bytearray`, a mutable sequence of integers in the range 0 through 255, which is a mutable variant of `bytes`. As such, it supports the same string methods and sequence operations as `bytes`, as well as many of the mutable in-place-change operations supported by *lists*.

Bytearrays support in-place changes to both truly binary data as well as simple forms of text such as ASCII, which can be represented with 1 byte per character (richer Unicode text generally requires Unicode strings, which are still immutable). The `bytearray` type is also available in Python 2.6 and 2.7 as a back-port from 3.X, but it does not enforce the strict text/binary distinction there that it does in 3.X.

bytearrays in Action

Let's take a quick tour. We can create `bytearray` objects by calling the `bytearray` built-in. In Python 2.X, any string may be used to initialize:

```
# Creation in 2.6/2.7: a mutable sequence of small (0..255) ints

>>> S = 'spam'
>>> C = bytearray(S)                    # A back-port from 3.X in 2.6+
>>> C                                   # b'..' == '..' in 2.6+ (str)
bytearray(b'spam')
```

In Python 3.X, an encoding name or byte string is required, because text and binary strings do not mix (though byte strings may reflect encoded Unicode text):

```
# Creation in 3.X: text/binary do not mix

>>> S = 'spam'
>>> C = bytearray(S)
TypeError: string argument without an encoding

>>> C = bytearray(S, 'latin1')          # A content-specific type in 3.X
>>> C
bytearray(b'spam')

>>> B = b'spam'                         # b'..' != '..' in 3.X (bytes/str)
>>> C = bytearray(B)
>>> C
bytearray(b'spam')
```

Once created, `bytearray` objects are sequences of small integers like `bytes` and are mutable like lists, though they require an integer for index assignments, not a string (all of the following is a continuation of this session and is run under Python 3.X unless otherwise noted—see comments for 2.X usage notes):

```
# Mutable, but must assign ints, not strings

>>> C[0]
115

>>> C[0] = 'x'                          # This and the next work in 2.6/2.7
TypeError: an integer is required
>>> C[0] = b'x'
TypeError: an integer is required

>>> C[0] = ord('x')                     # Use ord() to get a character's ordinal
>>> C
```

```
bytearray(b'xpam')

>>> C[1] = b'Y'[0]                          # Or index a byte string
>>> C
bytearray(b'xYam')
```

Processing bytearray objects borrows from both strings and lists, since they are mutable
byte strings. While the byterrray's methods overlap with both str and bytes, it also
has many of the list's mutable methods. Besides named methods, the __iadd__ and
__setitem__ methods in bytearray implement += in-place concatenation and index assignment, respectively:

```
# in bytes but not bytearray
>>> set(dir(b'abc')) - set(dir(bytearray(b'abc')))
{'__getnewargs__'}

# in bytearray but not bytes
>>> set(dir(bytearray(b'abc'))) - set(dir(b'abc'))
{'__iadd__', 'reverse', '__setitem__', 'extend', 'copy', '__alloc__',
'__delitem__', '__imul__', 'remove', 'clear', 'insert', 'append', 'pop'}
```

You can change a bytearray in place with both index assignment, as you've just seen,
and list-like methods like those shown here (to change text in place prior to 2.6, you
would need to convert to and then from a list, with list(str) and ''.join(list)—see
Chapter 4 and Chapter 6 for examples):

```
# Mutable method calls

>>> C
bytearray(b'xYam')

>>> C.append(b'LMN')                        # 2.X requires string of size 1
TypeError: an integer is required

>>> C.append(ord('L'))
>>> C
bytearray(b'xYamL')

>>> C.extend(b'MNO')
>>> C
bytearray(b'xYamLMNO')
```

All the usual sequence operations and string methods work on bytearrays, as you would
expect (notice that like bytes objects, their expressions and methods expect bytes arguments, not str arguments):

```
# Sequence operations and string methods

>>> C
bytearray(b'xYamLMNO')

>>> C + b'!#'
bytearray(b'xYamLMNO!#')
>>> C[0]
120
```

```
>>> C[1:]
bytearray(b'YamLMNO')
>>> len(C)
8

>>> C.replace('xY', 'sp')                    # This works in 2.X
TypeError: Type str doesn't support the buffer API
>>> C.replace(b'xY', b'sp')
bytearray(b'spamLMNO')

>>> C
bytearray(b'xYamLMNO')
>>> C * 4
bytearray(b'xYamLMNOxYamLMNOxYamLMNOxYamLMNO')
```

Python 3.X String Types Summary

Finally, by way of summary, the following examples demonstrate how **bytes** and **byte array** objects are sequences of **ints**, and **str** objects are sequences of characters:

```
# Binary versus text

>>> B                               # B is same as S in 2.6/2.7
b'spam'
>>> list(B)
[115, 112, 97, 109]

>>> C
bytearray(b'xYamLMNO')
>>> list(C)
[120, 89, 97, 109, 76, 77, 78, 79]

>>> S
'spam'
>>> list(S)
['s', 'p', 'a', 'm']
```

Although all three Python 3.X string types can contain character values and support many of the same operations, again, you should always:

- Use **str** for textual data.
- Use **bytes** for binary data.
- Use **bytearray** for binary data you wish to change in place.

Related tools such as files, the next section's topic, often make the choice for you.

Using Text and Binary Files

This section expands on the impact of Python 3.X's string model on the file processing basics introduced earlier in the book. As mentioned earlier, the mode in which you open a file is crucial—it determines which object type you will use to represent the file's content in your script. Text mode implies str objects, and binary mode implies bytes objects:

- *Text-mode files* interpret file contents according to a Unicode *encoding*—either the default for your platform, or one whose name you pass in. By passing in an encoding name to open, you can force conversions for various types of Unicode files. Text-mode files also perform universal *line-end translations*: by default, all line-end forms map to the single '\n' character in your script, regardless of the platform on which you run it. As described earlier, text files also handle reading and writing the *byte order mark* (BOM) stored at the start-of-file in some Unicode encoding schemes.

- *Binary-mode files* instead return file content to you *raw*, as a sequence of integers representing byte values, with no encoding or decoding and no line-end translations.

The second argument to open determines whether you want text or binary processing, just as it does in 2.X Python—adding a b to this string implies binary mode (e.g., "rb" to read binary data files). The default mode is "rt"; this is the same as "r", which means text input (just as in 2.X).

In 3.X, though, this mode argument to open also implies an *object type* for file content representation, regardless of the underlying platform—text files return a str for reads and expect one for writes, but binary files return a bytes for reads and expect one (or a bytearray) for writes.

Text File Basics

To demonstrate, let's begin with basic file I/O. As long as you're processing basic text files (e.g., ASCII) and don't care about circumventing the platform-default encoding of strings, files in 3.X look and feel much as they do in 2.X (for that matter, so do strings in general). The following, for instance, writes one line of text to a file and reads it back in 3.X, exactly as it would in 2.X (note that file is no longer a built-in name in 3.X, so it's perfectly OK to use it as a variable here):

```
C:\code> C:\python33\python
# Basic text files (and strings) work the same as in 2.X

>>> file = open('temp', 'w')
>>> size = file.write('abc\n')      # Returns number of characters written
>>> file.close()                    # Manual close to flush output buffer

>>> file = open('temp')             # Default mode is "r" (== "rt"): text input
>>> text = file.read()
>>> text
'abc\n'
>>> print(text)
abc
```

Text and Binary Modes in 2.X and 3.X

In Python 2.X, there is no major distinction between text and binary files—both accept and return content as str strings. The only major difference is that text files automatically map \n end-of-line characters to and from \r\n on Windows, while binary files do not (I'm stringing operations together into one-liners here just for brevity):

```
C:\code> C:\python27\python
>>> open('temp', 'w').write('abd\n')          # Write in text mode: adds \r
>>> open('temp', 'r').read()                   # Read in text mode: drops \r
'abd\n'
>>> open('temp', 'rb').read()                  # Read in binary mode: verbatim
'abd\r\n'

>>> open('temp', 'wb').write('abc\n')          # Write in binary mode
>>> open('temp', 'r').read()                   # \n not expanded to \r\n
'abc\n'
>>> open('temp', 'rb').read()
'abc\n'
```

In Python 3.X, things are a bit more complex because of the distinction between str for text data and bytes for binary data. To demonstrate, let's write a *text file* and read it back in both modes in 3.X. Notice that we are required to provide a str for writing, but reading gives us a str or a bytes, depending on the open mode:

```
C:\code> C:\python33\python
# Write and read a text file
>>> open('temp', 'w').write('abc\n')           # Text mode output, provide a str
4
>>> open('temp', 'r').read()                   # Text mode input, returns a str
'abc\n'
>>> open('temp', 'rb').read()                  # Binary mode input, returns a bytes
b'abc\r\n'
```

Notice how on Windows text-mode files translate the \n *end-of-line* character to \r\n on output; on input, text mode translates the \r\n back to \n, but binary-mode files do not. This is the same in 2.X, and it's normally what we want—text files should for portability map end-of-line markers to and from \n (which is what is actually present in files in Linux, where no mapping occurs), and such translations should never occur for binary data (where end-of-line bytes are irrelevant). Although you can control this behavior with extra open arguments in 3.X if desired, the default usually works well.

Now let's do the same again, but with a *binary file*. We provide a bytes to write in this case, and we still get back a str or a bytes, depending on the input mode:

```
# Write and read a binary file
>>> open('temp', 'wb').write(b'abc\n')         # Binary mode output, provide a bytes
4
>>> open('temp', 'r').read()                   # Text mode input, returns a str
'abc\n'
>>> open('temp', 'rb').read()                  # Binary mode input, returns a bytes
b'abc\n'
```

Note that the \n end-of-line character is not expanded to \r\n in binary-mode output —again, a desired result for binary data. Type requirements and file behavior are the same even if the data we're writing to the binary file is truly binary in nature. In the following, for example, the "\x00" is a binary zero byte and not a printable character:

```
# Write and read truly binary data
>>> open('temp', 'wb').write(b'a\x00c')        # Provide a bytes
3
>>> open('temp', 'r').read()                   # Receive a str
'a\x00c'
>>> open('temp', 'rb').read()                  # Receive a bytes
b'a\x00c'
```

Binary-mode files always return contents as a **bytes** object, but accept either a **bytes** or **bytearray** object for writing; this naturally follows, given that **bytearray** is basically just a mutable variant of **bytes**. In fact, most APIs in Python 3.X that accept a **bytes** also allow a **bytearray**:

```
# bytearrays work too
>>> BA = bytearray(b'\x01\x02\x03')

>>> open('temp', 'wb').write(BA)
3
>>> open('temp', 'r').read()
'\x01\x02\x03'
>>> open('temp', 'rb').read()
b'\x01\x02\x03'
```

Type and Content Mismatches in 3.X

Notice that you cannot get away with violating Python's **str/bytes** type distinction when it comes to files. As the following examples illustrate, we get errors (shortened here) if we try to write a **bytes** to a text file or a **str** to a binary file (the exact text of the error messages here is prone to change):

```
# Types are not flexible for file content
>>> open('temp', 'w').write('abc\n')           # Text mode makes and requires str
4
>>> open('temp', 'w').write(b'abc\n')
TypeError: must be str, not bytes

>>> open('temp', 'wb').write(b'abc\n')          # Binary mode makes and requires bytes
4
>>> open('temp', 'wb').write('abc\n')
TypeError: 'str' does not support the buffer interface
```

This makes sense: text has no meaning in binary terms, before it is encoded. Although it is often possible to convert between the types by encoding **str** and decoding **bytes**, as described earlier in this chapter, you will usually want to stick to *either* **str** for text data or **bytes** for binary data. Because the **str** and **bytes** operation sets largely intersect, the choice won't be much of a dilemma for most programs (see the string tools coverage in the final section of this chapter for some prime examples of this).

In addition to type constraints, *file content* can matter in 3.X. Text-mode output files require a `str` instead of a `bytes` for content, so there is no way in 3.X to write truly binary data to a text-mode file. Depending on the encoding rules, bytes outside the default character set can sometimes be embedded in a normal string, and they can always be written in binary mode (some of the following raise errors when displaying their string results in Pythons prior to 3.3, but the file operations work successfully):

```
# Can't read truly binary data in text mode
>>> chr(0xFF)                                  # FF is a valid char, FE is not
'ÿ'
>>> chr(0xFE)                                  # An error in some Pythons
'\xfe'

>>> open('temp', 'w').write(b'\xFF\xFE\xFD')   # Can't use arbitrary bytes!
TypeError: must be str, not bytes

>>> open('temp', 'w').write('\xFF\xFE\xFD')    # Can write if embeddable in str
3
>>> open('temp', 'wb').write(b'\xFF\xFE\xFD')  # Can also write in binary mode
3

>>> open('temp', 'rb').read()                  # Can always read as binary bytes
b'\xff\xfe\xfd'

>>> open('temp', 'r').read()                   # Can't read text unless decodable!
'ÿ\xfe\xfd'                                     # An error in some Pythons
```

In general, however, because text-mode input files in 3.X must be able to decode content per a Unicode encoding, there is no way to read truly binary data in text mode, as the next section explains.

Using Unicode Files

So far, we've been reading and writing basic text and binary files. It turns out to be easy to read and write Unicode text stored in files too, because the 3.X `open` call accepts an encoding for text files, and arranges to run the required encoding and decoding for us automatically as data is transferred. This allows us to process a variety of Unicode text created with different encodings than the default for the platform, and store the same text in different encodings for different purposes.

Reading and Writing Unicode in 3.X

In fact, we can effectively *convert* a string to different encoded forms both manually with method calls as we did earlier, and automatically on file input and output. We'll use the following Unicode string in this section to demonstrate:

```
C:\code> C:\python33\python
>>> S = 'A\xc4B\xe8C'          # Five-character decoded string, non-ASCII
>>> S
'AÄBèC'
```

```
>>> len(S)
5
```

Manual encoding

As we've already learned, we can always encode such a string to raw bytes according to the target encoding name:

```
# Encode manually with methods
>>> L = S.encode('latin-1')        # 5 bytes when encoded as latin-1
>>> L
b'A\xc4B\xe8C'
>>> len(L)
5

>>> U = S.encode('utf-8')          # 7 bytes when encoded as utf-8
>>> U
b'A\xc3\x84B\xc3\xa8C'
>>> len(U)
7
```

File output encoding

Now, to write our string to a text file in a particular encoding, we can simply pass the desired encoding name to open—although we could manually encode first and write in binary mode, there's no need to:

```
# Encoding automatically when written
>>> open('latindata', 'w', encoding='latin-1').write(S)       # Write as latin-1
5
>>> open('utf8data', 'w', encoding='utf-8').write(S)          # Write as utf-8
5

>>> open('latindata', 'rb').read()                            # Read raw bytes
b'A\xc4B\xe8C'

>>> open('utf8data', 'rb').read()                             # Different in files
b'A\xc3\x84B\xc3\xa8C'
```

File input decoding

Similarly, to read arbitrary Unicode data, we simply pass in the file's encoding type name to open, and it decodes from raw bytes to strings automatically; we could read raw bytes and decode manually too, but that can be tricky when reading in blocks (we might read an incomplete character), and it isn't necessary:

```
# Decoding automatically when read
>>> open('latindata', 'r', encoding='latin-1').read()         # Decoded on input
'AÄBèC'
>>> open('utf8data', 'r', encoding='utf-8').read()            # Per encoding type
'AÄBèC'

>>> X = open('latindata', 'rb').read()                        # Manual decoding:
>>> X.decode('latin-1')                                       # Not necessary
```

```
'AÄBèC'
>>> X = open('utf8data', 'rb').read()
>>> X.decode()                                   # UTF-8 is default
'AÄBèC'
```

Decoding mismatches

Finally, keep in mind that this behavior of files in 3.X limits the kind of content you can load as text. As suggested in the prior section, Python 3.X really must be able to decode the data in text files into a str string, according to either the default or a passed-in Unicode encoding name. Trying to open a truly binary data file in text mode, for example, is unlikely to work in 3.X even if you use the correct object types:

```
>>> file = open(r'C:\Python33\python.exe', 'r')
>>> text = file.read()
UnicodeDecodeError: 'charmap' codec can't decode byte 0x90 in position 2: ...

>>> file = open(r'C:\Python33\python.exe', 'rb')
>>> data = file.read()
>>> data[:20]
b'MZ\x90\x00\x03\x00\x00\x00\x04\x00\x00\x00\xff\xff\x00\x00\xb8\x00\x00\x00'
```

The first of these examples might not fail in Python 2.X (normal files do not decode text), even though it probably should: reading the file may return corrupted data in the string, due to automatic end-of-line translations in text mode (any embedded \r\n bytes will be translated to \n on Windows when read). To treat file content as Unicode text in 2.X, we need to use special tools instead of the general open built-in function, as we'll see in a moment. First, though, let's turn to a more explosive topic.

Handling the BOM in 3.X

As described earlier in this chapter, some encoding schemes store a special *byte order marker* (BOM) sequence at the start of files, to specify data *endianness* (which end of a string of bits is most significant to its value) or declare the encoding type. Python both skips this marker on input and writes it on output if the encoding name implies it, but we sometimes must use a specific encoding name to force BOM processing explicitly.

For example, in the UTF-16 and UTF-32 encodings, the BOM specifies big- or little-endian format. A UTF-8 text file may also include a BOM, but this isn't guaranteed, and serves only to declare that it is UTF-8 in general. When reading and writing data using these encoding schemes, Python automatically skips or writes the BOM if it is either implied by a general encoding name, or if you provide a more specific encoding name to force the issue. For instance:

- In UTF-16, the BOM is always processed for "utf-16," and the more specific encoding name "utf-16-le" denotes little-endian format.
- In UTF-8, the more specific encoding "utf-8-sig" forces Python to both skip and write a BOM on input and output, respectively, but the general "utf-8" does not.

Dropping the BOM in Notepad

Let's make some files with BOMs to see how this works in practice. When you save a text file in Windows Notepad, you can specify its encoding type in a drop-down list—simple ASCII text, UTF-8, or little- or big-endian UTF-16. If a two-line text file named *spam.txt* is saved in Notepad as the encoding type *ANSI*, for instance, it's written as simple ASCII text without a BOM. When this file is read in binary mode in Python, we can see the actual bytes stored in the file. When it's read as text, Python performs end-of-line translation by default; we can also decode it as explicit UTF-8 text since ASCII is a subset of this scheme (and UTF-8 is Python 3.X's default encoding):

```
C:\code> C:\python33\python            # File saved in Notepad
>>> import sys
>>> sys.getdefaultencoding()
'utf-8'
>>> open('spam.txt', 'rb').read()      # ASCII (UTF-8) text file
b'spam\r\nSPAM\r\n'
>>> open('spam.txt', 'r').read()       # Text mode translates line end
'spam\nSPAM\n'
>>> open('spam.txt', 'r', encoding='utf-8').read()
'spam\nSPAM\n'
```

If this file is instead saved as *UTF-8* in Notepad, it is prepended with a 3-byte UTF-8 BOM sequence, and we need to give a more specific encoding name ("utf-8-sig") to force Python to skip the marker:

```
>>> open('spam.txt', 'rb').read()      # UTF-8 with 3-byte BOM
b'\xef\xbb\xbfspam\r\nSPAM\r\n'
>>> open('spam.txt', 'r').read()
'ï»¿spam\nSPAM\n'
>>> open('spam.txt', 'r', encoding='utf-8').read()
'\ufeffspam\nSPAM\n'
>>> open('spam.txt', 'r', encoding='utf-8-sig').read()
'spam\nSPAM\n'
```

If the file is stored as *Unicode big endian* in Notepad, we get UTF-16-format data in the file, with 2-byte (16-bit) characters prepended with a 2-byte BOM sequence—the encoding name "utf-16" in Python skips the BOM because it is implied (since all UTF-16 files have a BOM), and "utf-16-be" handles the big-endian format but does not skip the BOM (the second of the following fails to print on older Pythons):

```
>>> open('spam.txt', 'rb').read()
b'\xfe\xff\x00s\x00p\x00a\x00m\x00\r\x00\n\x00S\x00P\x00A\x00M\x00\r\x00\n'
>>> open('spam.txt', 'r').read()
'\xfeÿ\x00s\x00p\x00a\x00m\x00\n\x00\n\x00S\x00P\x00A\x00M\x00\n\x00\n'
>>> open('spam.txt', 'r', encoding='utf-16').read()
'spam\nSPAM\n'
>>> open('spam.txt', 'r', encoding='utf-16-be').read()
'\ufeffspam\nSPAM\n'
```

Notepad's "Unicode," by the way, is UTF-16 little endian (which, of course, is one of very many kinds of Unicode encoding!).

Dropping the BOM in Python

The same patterns generally hold true for *output*. When writing a Unicode file in Python code, we need a more explicit encoding name to force the BOM in UTF-8—"utf-8" does not write (or skip) the BOM, but "utf-8-sig" does:

```
>>> open('temp.txt', 'w', encoding='utf-8').write('spam\nSPAM\n')
10
>>> open('temp.txt', 'rb').read()                    # No BOM
b'spam\r\nSPAM\r\n'

>>> open('temp.txt', 'w', encoding='utf-8-sig').write('spam\nSPAM\n')
10
>>> open('temp.txt', 'rb').read()                    # Wrote BOM
b'\xef\xbb\xbfspam\r\nSPAM\r\n'

>>> open('temp.txt', 'r').read()
'ï»¿spam\nSPAM\n'
>>> open('temp.txt', 'r', encoding='utf-8').read()   # Keeps BOM
'\ufeffspam\nSPAM\n'
>>> open('temp.txt', 'r', encoding='utf-8-sig').read()   # Skips BOM
'spam\nSPAM\n'
```

Notice that although "utf-8" does not drop the BOM, data *without* a BOM can be read with both "utf-8" and "utf-8-sig"—use the latter for input if you're not sure whether a BOM is present in a file (and don't read this paragraph out loud in an airport security line!):

```
>>> open('temp.txt', 'w').write('spam\nSPAM\n')
10
>>> open('temp.txt', 'rb').read()                    # Data without BOM
b'spam\r\nSPAM\r\n'

>>> open('temp.txt', 'r').read()                     # Either utf-8 works
'spam\nSPAM\n'
>>> open('temp.txt', 'r', encoding='utf-8').read()
'spam\nSPAM\n'
>>> open('temp.txt', 'r', encoding='utf-8-sig').read()
'spam\nSPAM\n'
```

Finally, for the encoding name "utf-16," the BOM is handled automatically: on *output*, data is written in the platform's native endianness, and the BOM is always written; on *input*, data is decoded per the BOM, and the BOM is always stripped because it's standard in this scheme:

```
>>> sys.byteorder
'little'
>>> open('temp.txt', 'w', encoding='utf-16').write('spam\nSPAM\n')
10
>>> open('temp.txt', 'rb').read()
b'\xff\xfes\x00p\x00a\x00m\x00\r\x00\n\x00S\x00P\x00A\x00M\x00\r\x00\n\x00'
>>> open('temp.txt', 'r', encoding='utf-16').read()
'spam\nSPAM\n'
```

More specific UTF-16 encoding names can specify different endianness, though you may have to manually write and skip the BOM yourself in some scenarios if it is required or present—study the following examples for more BOM-making instructions:

```
>>> open('temp.txt', 'w', encoding='utf-16-be').write('\ufeffspam\nSPAM\n')
11
>>> open('spam.txt', 'rb').read()
b'\xfe\xff\x00s\x00p\x00a\x00m\x00\r\x00\n\x00S\x00P\x00A\x00M\x00\r\x00\n'
>>> open('temp.txt', 'r', encoding='utf-16').read()
'spam\nSPAM\n'
>>> open('temp.txt', 'r', encoding='utf-16-be').read()
'\ufeffspam\nSPAM\n'
```

The more specific UTF-16 encoding names work fine with BOM-less files, though "utf-16" requires one on input in order to determine byte order:

```
>>> open('temp.txt', 'w', encoding='utf-16-le').write('SPAM')
4
>>> open('temp.txt', 'rb').read()                 # OK if BOM not present or expected
b'S\x00P\x00A\x00M\x00'
>>> open('temp.txt', 'r', encoding='utf-16-le').read()
'SPAM'
>>> open('temp.txt', 'r', encoding='utf-16').read()
UnicodeError: UTF-16 stream does not start with BOM
```

Experiment with these encodings yourself or see Python's library manuals for more details on the BOM.

Unicode Files in 2.X

The preceding discussion applies to Python 3.X's string types and files. You can achieve similar effects for Unicode files in 2.X, but the interface is different. However, if you replace str with unicode and open with codecs.open, the result is essentially the same in 3.X:

```
C:\code> C:\python27\python
>>> S = u'A\xc4B\xe8C'                              # 2.X type
>>> print S
AÄBèC
>>> len(S)
5
>>> S.encode('latin-1')                            # Manual calls
'A\xc4B\xe8C'
>>> S.encode('utf-8')
'A\xc3\x84B\xc3\xa8C'

>>> import codecs                                  # 2.X files
>>> codecs.open('latindata', 'w', encoding='latin-1').write(S)   # Writes encode
>>> codecs.open('utfdata', 'w', encoding='utf-8').write(S)

>>> open('latindata', 'rb').read()
'A\xc4B\xe8C'
>>> open('utfdata', 'rb').read()
'A\xc3\x84B\xc3\xa8C'
```

```
>>> codecs.open('latindata', 'r', encoding='latin-1').read()          # Reads decode
u'A\xc4B\xe8C'
>>> codecs.open('utfdata', 'r', encoding='utf-8').read()
u'A\xc4B\xe8C'
>>> print codecs.open('utfdata', 'r', encoding='utf-8').read()         # Print to view
AÄBèC
```

For more 2.X Unicode details, see earlier sections of this chapter and Python 2.X manuals.

Unicode Filenames and Streams

In closing, this section has focused on the encoding and decoding of Unicode text file *content*, but Python also supports the notion of non-ASCII file *names*. In fact, they are independent settings in sys, which can vary per Python version and platform (2.X returns ASCII for the first of the following on Windows):

```
>>> import sys
>>> sys.getdefaultencoding(), sys.getfilesystemencoding()      # File content, names
('utf-8', 'mbcs')
```

Filenames: Text versus bytes

Filename encoding is often a nonissue. In short, for filenames given as Unicode text strings, the open call encodes automatically to and from the underlying platform's filename conventions. Passing arbitrarily pre-encoded filenames as byte strings to file tools (including open and directory walkers and listers) overrides automatic encodings, and forces filename results to be returned in encoded byte string form too—useful if filenames are undecodable per the underlying platform's conventions (I'm using Windows, but some of the following may fail on other platforms):

```
>>> f = open('xxx\u00A5', 'w')               # Non-ASCII filename
>>> f.write('\xA5999\n')                      # Writes five characters
>>> f.close()
>>> print(open('xxx\u00A5').read())           # Text: auto-encoded
¥999
>>> print(open(b'xxx\xA5').read())            # Bytes: pre-encoded
¥999

>>> import glob                               # Filename expansion tool
>>> glob.glob('*\u00A5*')                     # Get decoded text for decoded text
['xxx¥']
>>> glob.glob(b'*\xA5*')                       # Get encoded bytes for encoded bytes
[b'xxx\xa5']
```

Stream content: PYTHONIOENCODING

In addition, the environment variable PYTHONIOENCODING can be used to set the encoding used for text in the standard *streams*   input, output, and error. This setting overrides Python's default encoding for printed text, which on Windows currently uses a Windows format on 3.X and ASCII on 2.X. Setting this to a general Unicode format like UTF-8 may sometimes be required to print non-ASCII text, and to display such text in shell windows (possibly in conjunction with code page changes on some Windows machines). A script that prints non-ASCII filenames, for example, may fail unless this setting is made.

For more background on this subject, see also "Currency Symbols: Unicode in Action" in Chapter 25. There, we work through an example that demonstrates the essentials of portable Unicode coding, as well as the roles and requirements of PYTHONIOENCODING settings, which we won't rehash here.

For more on these topics in general, see Python manuals or books such as *Programming Python, 4th Edition* (or later, if later may be). The latter of these digs deeper into streams and files from an applications-level perspective.

Other String Tool Changes in 3.X

Many of the other popular string-processing tools in Python's standard library have also been revamped for the new str/bytes type dichotomy. We won't cover any of these application-focused tools in much detail in this core language book, but to wrap up this chapter, here's a quick look at four of the major tools impacted: the re pattern-matching module, the struct binary data module, the pickle object serialization module, and the xml package for parsing XML text. As noted ahead, other Python tools, such as its json module, differ in ways similar to those presented here.

The re Pattern-Matching Module

Python's re pattern-matching module supports text processing that is more general than that afforded by simple string method calls such as find, split, and replace. With re, strings that designate searching and splitting targets can be described by general patterns, instead of absolute text. This module has been generalized to work on objects of any string type in 3.X—str, bytes, and bytearray—and returns result substrings of the same type as the subject string. In 2.X it supports both unicode and str.

Here it is at work in 3.X, extracting substrings from a line of text—borrowed, of course, from Monty Python's *The Meaning of Life*. Within pattern strings, (.*) means any character (the .), zero or more times (the *), saved away as a matched substring (the ()). Parts of the string matched by the parts of a pattern enclosed in parentheses are available after a successful match, via the group or groups method:

```
C:\code> C:\python33\python
>>> import re
>>> S = 'Bugger all down here on earth!'      # Line of text
>>> B = b'Bugger all down here on earth!'     # Usually from a file

>>> re.match('(.*) down (.*) on (.*)', S).groups()   # Match line to pattern
('Bugger all', 'here', 'earth!')                     # Matched substrings
```

```
>>> re.match(b'(.*) down (.*) on (.*)', B).groups()          # bytes substrings
(b'Bugger all', b'here', b'earth!')
```

In Python 2.X results are similar, but the unicode type is used for non-ASCII text, and str handles both 8-bit and binary text:

```
C:\code> C:\python27\python
>>> import re
>>> S = 'Bugger all down here on earth!'          # Simple text and binary
>>> U = u'Bugger all down here on earth!'          # Unicode text

>>> re.match('(.*) down (.*) on (.*)', S).groups()
('Bugger all', 'here', 'earth!')

>>> re.match('(.*) down (.*) on (.*)', U).groups()
(u'Bugger all', u'here', u'earth!')
```

Since bytes and str support essentially the same operation sets, this type distinction is largely transparent. But note that, like in other APIs, you can't mix str and bytes types in its calls' arguments in 3.X (although if you don't plan to do pattern matching on binary data, you probably don't need to care):

```
C:\code> C:\python33\python
>>> import re
>>> S = 'Bugger all down here on earth!'
>>> B = b'Bugger all down here on earth!'

>>> re.match('(.*) down (.*) on (.*)', B).groups()
TypeError: can't use a string pattern on a bytes-like object

>>> re.match(b'(.*) down (.*) on (.*)', S).groups()
TypeError: can't use a bytes pattern on a string-like object

>>> re.match(b'(.*) down (.*) on (.*)', bytearray(B)).groups()
(bytearray(b'Bugger all'), bytearray(b'here'), bytearray(b'earth!'))

>>> re.match('(.*) down (.*) on (.*)', bytearray(B)).groups()
TypeError: can't use a string pattern on a bytes-like object
```

The struct Binary Data Module

The Python struct module, used to create and extract packed binary data from strings, also works the same in 3.X as it does in 2.X, but in 3.X packed data is represented as bytes and bytearray objects only, not str objects (which makes sense, given that it's intended for processing binary data, not decoded text); and "s" data code values must be bytes as of 3.2 (the former str UTF-8 auto-encode is dropped).

Here are both Pythons in action, packing three objects into a string according to a binary type specification (they create a 4-byte integer, a 4-byte string, and a 2-byte integer):

```
C:\code> C:\python33\python
>>> from struct import pack
>>> pack('>i4sh', 7, b'spam', 8)          # bytes in 3.X (8-bit strings)
```

```
b'\x00\x00\x00\x07spam\x00\x08'

C:\code> C:\python27\python
>>> from struct import pack
>>> pack('>i4sh', 7, 'spam', 8)          # str in 2.X (8-bit strings)
'\x00\x00\x00\x07spam\x00\x08'
```

Since `bytes` has an almost identical interface to that of `str` in 3.X and 2.X, though, most programmers probably won't need to care—the change is irrelevant to most existing code, especially since reading from a binary file creates a `bytes` automatically. Although the last test in the following example fails on a type mismatch, most scripts will read binary data from a file, not create it as a string as we do here:

```
C:\code> C:\python33\python
>>> import struct
>>> B = struct.pack('>i4sh', 7, b'spam', 8)
>>> B
b'\x00\x00\x00\x07spam\x00\x08'

>>> vals = struct.unpack('>i4sh', B)
>>> vals
(7, b'spam', 8)

>>> vals = struct.unpack('>i4sh', B.decode())
TypeError: 'str' does not support the buffer interface
```

Apart from the new syntax for bytes, creating and reading binary files works almost the same in 3.X as it does in 2.X. Still, code like this is one of the main places where programmers will notice the `bytes` object type:

```
C:\code> C:\python33\python
# Write values to a packed binary file
>>> F = open('data.bin', 'wb')                    # Open binary output file
>>> import struct
>>> data = struct.pack('>i4sh', 7, b'spam', 8)    # Create packed binary data
>>> data                                          # bytes in 3.X, not str
b'\x00\x00\x00\x07spam\x00\x08'
>>> F.write(data)                                 # Write to the file
10
>>> F.close()

# Read values from a packed binary file
>>> F = open('data.bin', 'rb')                    # Open binary input file
>>> data = F.read()                               # Read bytes
>>> data
b'\x00\x00\x00\x07spam\x00\x08'
>>> values = struct.unpack('>i4sh', data)         # Extract packed binary data
>>> values                                        # Back to Python objects
(7, b'spam', 8)
```

Once you've extracted packed binary data into Python objects like this, you can dig even further into the binary world if you have to—strings can be indexed and sliced to get individual bytes' values, individual bits can be extracted from integers with bitwise operators, and so on (see earlier in this book for more on the operations applied here):

```
>>> values                                       # Result of struct.unpack
(7, b'spam', 8)

# Accessing bits of parsed integers
>>> bin(values[0])                               # Can get to bits in ints
'0b111'
>>> values[0] & 0x01                             # Test first (lowest) bit in int
1
>>> values[0] | 0b1010                           # Bitwise or: turn bits on
15
>>> bin(values[0] | 0b1010)                      # 15 decimal is 1111 binary
'0b1111'
>>> bin(values[0] ^ 0b1010)                      # Bitwise xor: off if both true
'0b1101'
>>> bool(values[0] & 0b100)                      # Test if bit 3 is on
True
>>> bool(values[0] & 0b1000)                     # Test if bit 4 is set
False
```

Since parsed `bytes` strings are sequences of small integers, we can do similar processing with their individual bytes:

```
# Accessing bytes of parsed strings and bits within them
>>> values[1]
b'spam'
>>> values[1][0]                                 # bytes string: sequence of ints
115
>>> values[1][1:]                                # Prints as ASCII characters
b'pam'
>>> bin(values[1][0])                            # Can get to bits of bytes in strings
'0b1110011'
>>> bin(values[1][0] | 0b1100)                   # Turn bits on
'0b1111111'
>>> values[1][0] | 0b1100
127
```

Of course, most Python programmers don't deal with binary bits; Python has higher-level object types, like lists and dictionaries that are generally a better choice for representing information in Python scripts. However, if you must use or produce lower-level data used by C programs, networking libraries, or other interfaces, Python has tools to assist.

The pickle Object Serialization Module

We met the `pickle` module briefly in Chapter 9, Chapter 28, and Chapter 31. In Chapter 28, we also used the `shelve` module, which uses `pickle` internally. For completeness here, keep in mind that the Python 3.X version of the `pickle` module always creates a `bytes` object, regardless of the default or passed-in "protocol" (data format level). You can see this by using the module's `dumps` call to return an object's pickle string:

```
C:\code> C:\python33\python
>>> import pickle                                # dumps() returns pickle string
```

```
>>> pickle.dumps([1, 2, 3])                    # Python 3.X default protocol=3=binary
b'\x80\x03]q\x00(K\x01K\x02K\x03e.'

>>> pickle.dumps([1, 2, 3], protocol=0)        # ASCII protocol 0, but still bytes!
b'(lp0\nL1L\naL2L\naL3L\na.'
```

This implies that files used to store pickled objects must always be opened in *binary mode* in Python 3.X, since text files use `str` strings to represent data, not `bytes`—the `dump` call simply attempts to write the pickle string to an open output file:

```
>>> pickle.dump([1, 2, 3], open('temp', 'w'))   # Text files fail on bytes!
TypeError: must be str, not bytes                # Despite protocol value

>>> pickle.dump([1, 2, 3], open('temp', 'w'), protocol=0)
TypeError: must be str, not bytes

>>> pickle.dump([1, 2, 3], open('temp', 'wb'))   # Always use binary in 3.X

>>> open('temp', 'r').read()                     # This works, but just by luck
'\u20ac\x03]q\x00(K\x01K\x02K\x03e.'
```

Notice the last result here didn't issue an error in text mode only because the stored binary data was compatible with the Windows platform's UTF-8 default decoder; this was really just luck (and in fact, this command failed when printing in older Pythons, and may fail on other platforms). Because pickle data is not generally decodable Unicode text, the same rule holds on input—correct usage in 3.X requires always both writing and reading pickle data in binary modes, whether unpickling or not:

```
>>> pickle.dump([1, 2, 3], open('temp', 'wb'))
>>> pickle.load(open('temp', 'rb'))
[1, 2, 3]
>>> open('temp', 'rb').read()
b'\x80\x03]q\x00(K\x01K\x02K\x03e.'
```

In Python 2.X, we can get by with text-mode files for pickled data, as long as the protocol is level 0 (the default in 2.X) and we use text mode consistently to convert line ends:

```
C:\code> C:\python27\python
>>> import pickle
>>> pickle.dumps([1, 2, 3])                    # Python 2.X default=0=ASCII
'(lp0\nI1\naI2\naI3\na.'

>>> pickle.dumps([1, 2, 3], protocol=1)
']q\x00(K\x01K\x02K\x03e.'

>>> pickle.dump([1, 2, 3], open('temp', 'w'))   # Text mode works in 2.X
>>> pickle.load(open('temp'))
[1, 2, 3]
>>> open('temp').read()
'(lp0\nI1\naI2\naI3\na.'
```

If you care about version neutrality, though, or don't want to care about protocols or their version-specific defaults, always use binary-mode files for pickled data—the following works the same in Python 3.X and 2.X:

```
>>> import pickle
>>> pickle.dump([1, 2, 3], open('temp', 'wb'))     # Version neutral
>>> pickle.load(open('temp', 'rb'))                 # And required in 3.X
[1, 2, 3]
```

Because almost all programs let Python pickle and unpickle objects automatically and do not deal with the content of pickled data itself, the requirement to always use binary file modes is the only significant incompatibility in Python 3.X's newer pickling model. See reference books or Python's manuals for more details on object pickling.

XML Parsing Tools

XML is a tag-based language for defining structured information, commonly used to define documents and data shipped over the Web. Although some information can be extracted from XML text with basic string methods or the re pattern module, XML's nesting of constructs and arbitrary attribute text tend to make full parsing more accurate.

Because XML is such a pervasive format, Python itself comes with an entire package of XML parsing tools that support the SAX and DOM parsing models, as well as a package known as *ElementTree*—a Python-specific API for parsing and constructing XML. Beyond basic parsing, the open source domain provides support for additional XML tools, such as XPath, Xquery, XSLT, and more.

XML by definition represents text in Unicode form, to support internationalization. Although most of Python's XML parsing tools have always returned Unicode strings, in Python 3.X their results have mutated from the 2.X unicode type to the 3.X general str string type—which makes sense, given that 3.X's str string *is* Unicode, whether the encoding is ASCII or other.

We can't go into many details here, but to sample the flavor of this domain, suppose we have a simple XML text file, *mybooks.xml*:

```
<books>
    <date>1995~2013</date>
    <title>Learning Python</title>
    <title>Programming Python</title>
    <title>Python Pocket Reference</title>
    <publisher>O'Reilly Media</publisher>
</books>
```

and we want to run a script to extract and display the content of all the nested title tags, as follows:

```
Learning Python
Programming Python
Python Pocket Reference
```

There are at least four basic ways to accomplish this (not counting more advanced tools like XPath). First, we could run basic *pattern matching* on the file's text, though this tends to be inaccurate if the text is unpredictable. Where applicable, the `re` module we met earlier does the job—its `match` method looks for a match at the start of a string, `search` scans ahead for a match, and the `findall` method used here locates all places where the pattern matches in the string (the result comes back as a list of matched substrings corresponding to parenthesized pattern groups, or tuples of such for multiple groups):

```python
# File patternparse.py

import re
text = open('mybooks.xml').read()
found = re.findall('<title>(.*)</title>', text)
for title in found: print(title)
```

Second, to be more robust, we could perform complete XML parsing with the standard library's *DOM parsing* support. DOM parses XML text into a tree of objects and provides an interface for navigating the tree to extract tag attributes and values; the interface is a formal specification, independent of Python:

```python
# File domparse.py

from xml.dom.minidom import parse, Node
xmltree = parse('mybooks.xml')
for node1 in xmltree.getElementsByTagName('title'):
    for node2 in node1.childNodes:
        if node2.nodeType == Node.TEXT_NODE:
            print(node2.data)
```

As a third option, Python's standard library supports *SAX parsing* for XML. Under the SAX model, a class's methods receive callbacks as a parse progresses and use state information to keep track of where they are in the document and collect its data:

```python
# File saxparse.py

import xml.sax.handler
class BookHandler(xml.sax.handler.ContentHandler):
    def __init__(self):
        self.inTitle = False
    def startElement(self, name, attributes):
        if name == 'title':
            self.inTitle = True
    def characters(self, data):
        if self.inTitle:
            print(data)
    def endElement(self, name):
        if name == 'title':
            self.inTitle = False

import xml.sax
parser = xml.sax.make_parser()
handler = BookHandler()
```

```
parser.setContentHandler(handler)
parser.parse('mybooks.xml')
```

Finally, the *ElementTree* system available in the **etree** package of the standard library can often achieve the same effects as XML DOM parsers, but with remarkably less code. It's a Python-specific way to both parse and generate XML text; after a parse, its API gives access to components of the document:

```
# File etreeparse.py

from xml.etree.ElementTree import parse
tree = parse('mybooks.xml')
for E in tree.findall('title'):
    print(E.text)
```

When run in either 2.X or 3.X, all four of these scripts display the same printed result:

```
C:\code> C:\python27\python domparse.py
Learning Python
Programming Python
Python Pocket Reference

C:\code> C:\python33\python domparse.py
Learning Python
Programming Python
Python Pocket Reference
```

Technically, though, in 2.X some of these scripts produce **unicode** string objects, while in 3.X all produce **str** strings, since that type includes Unicode text (whether ASCII or other):

```
C:\code> C:\python33\python
>>> from xml.dom.minidom import parse, Node
>>> xmltree = parse('mybooks.xml')
>>> for node in xmltree.getElementsByTagName('title'):
        for node2 in node.childNodes:
            if node2.nodeType == Node.TEXT_NODE:
                node2.data

'Learning Python'
'Programming Python'
'Python Pocket Reference'

C:\code> C:\python27\python
>>> ...same code...

u'Learning Python'
u'Programming Python'
u'Python Pocket Reference'
```

Programs that must deal with XML parsing results in nontrivial ways will need to account for the different object type in 3.X. Again, though, because all strings have nearly identical interfaces in both 2.X and 3.X, most scripts won't be affected by the change; tools available on **unicode** in 2.X are generally available on **str** in 3.X. The major feat, if there is one, is likely in getting the encoding names right when transferring the parsed-out data to and from files, network connections, GUIs, and so on.

Regrettably, going into further XML parsing details is beyond this book's scope. If you are interested in text or XML parsing, it is covered in more detail in the applications-focused follow-up book *Programming Python*. For more details on `re`, `struct`, `pickle`, and XML, as well as the additional impacts of Unicode on other library tools such as filename expansion and directory walkers, consult the Web, the aforementioned book and others, and Python's standard library manual.

For a related topic, see also the *JSON* example in Chapter 9—a language-neutral data exchange format, whose structure is very similar to Python dictionaries and lists, and whose strings are all Unicode that differs in type between Pythons 2.X and 3.X much the same as shown for XML here.

Why You Will Care: Inspecting Files, and Much More

As I was updating this chapter, I stumbled onto a use case for some of its tools. After saving a formerly ASCII HTML file in Notepad as "UTF8," I found that it had grown a mystery non-ASCII character along the way due to an apparent keyboard operator error, and would no longer work as ASCII in text tools. To find the bad character, I simply started Python, decoded the file's content from its UTF-8 format via a *text mode* file, and scanned character by character looking for the first byte that was not a valid ASCII character too:

```
>>> f = open('py33-windows-launcher.html', encoding='utf8')
>>> t = f.read()
>>> for (i, c) in enumerate(t):
        try:
            x = c.encode(encoding='ascii')
        except:
            print(i, sys.exc_info()[0])
    9886 <class 'UnicodeEncodeError'>
```

With the bad character's index in hand, it's easy to slice the Unicode string for more details:

```
>>> len(t)
31021
>>> t[9880:9890]
'ugh.  \u206cThi'
>>> t[9870:9890]
'trace through.  \u206cThi'
```

After fixing, I could also open in *binary mode* to verify and explore actual undecoded file content further:

```
>>> f = open('py33-windows-launcher.html', 'rb')
>>> b = f.read()
>>> b[0]
60
>>> b[:10]
b'<HTML>\r\n<T'
```

Not rocket science, perhaps, and there are other approaches, but Python makes for a convenient tactical tool in such cases, and its file objects give you a tangible window on your data when needed, both in scripts and interactive mode.

For more realistically scaled examples of Unicode at work, I suggest my other book *Programming Python, 4th Edition* (or later). That book develops much larger programs than we can here, and has numerous up close and personal encounters with Unicode along the way, in the context of files, directory walkers, network sockets, GUIs, email content and headers, web page content, databases, and more. Though clearly an important topic in today's global software world, Unicode is more mandatory than you might expect, especially in a language like Python 3.X, which elevates it to its core string and file types, thus bringing all its users into the Unicode fold—ready or not!

Chapter Summary

This chapter explored in-depth the advanced string types available in Python 3.X and 2.X for processing Unicode text and binary data. As we saw, many programmers use ASCII text and can get by with the basic string type and its operations. For more advanced applications, Python's string models fully support both richer Unicode text (via the normal string type in 3.X and a special type in 2.X) and byte-oriented data (represented with a **bytes** type in 3.X and normal strings in 2.X).

In addition, we learned how Python's file object has mutated in 3.X to automatically encode and decode Unicode text and deal with byte strings for binary-mode files, and saw similar utility for 2.X. Finally, we briefly met some text and binary data tools in Python's library, and sampled their behavior in 3.X and 2.X.

In the next chapter, we'll shift our focus to tool-builder topics, with a look at ways to manage access to object attributes by inserting automatically run code. Before we move on, though, here's a set of questions to review what we've learned here. This has been a substantial chapter, so be sure to read the quiz answers eventually for a more in-depth summary.

Test Your Knowledge: Quiz

1. What are the names and roles of string object types in Python 3.X?
2. What are the names and roles of string object types in Python 2.X?
3. What is the mapping between 2.X and 3.X string types?
4. How do Python 3.X's string types differ in terms of operations?
5. How can you code non-ASCII Unicode characters in a string in 3.X?
6. What are the main differences between text- and binary-mode files in Python 3.X?
7. How would you read a Unicode text file that contains text in a different encoding than the default for your platform?

8. How can you create a Unicode text file in a specific encoding format?

9. Why is ASCII text considered to be a kind of Unicode text?

10. How large an impact does Python 3.X's string types change have on your code?

Test Your Knowledge: Answers

1. Python 3.X has three string types: `str` (for Unicode text, including ASCII), `bytes` (for binary data with absolute byte values), and `bytearray` (a mutable flavor of `bytes`). The `str` type usually represents content stored on a text file, and the other two types generally represent content stored on binary files.

2. Python 2.X has two main string types: `str` (for 8-bit text and binary data) and `unicode` (for possibly wider character Unicode text). The `str` type is used for both text and binary file content; `unicode` is used for text file content that is generally more complex than 8-bit characters. Python 2.6 (but not earlier) also has 3.X's `bytearray` type, but it's mostly a back-port and doesn't exhibit the sharp text/binary distinction that it does in 3.X.

3. The mapping from 2.X to 3.X string types is not direct, because 2.X's `str` equates to both `str` and `bytes` in 3.X, and 3.X's `str` equates to both `str` and `unicode` in 2.X. The mutability of `bytearray` in 3.X is also unique. In general, though: Unicode text is handled by 3.X `str` and 2.X `unicode`, byte-based data is handled by 3.X `bytes` and 2.X `str`, and 3.X `bytes` and 2.X `str` can both handle some simpler types of text.

4. Python 3.X's string types share almost all the same operations: method calls, sequence operations, and even larger tools like pattern matching work the same way. On the other hand, only `str` supports string formatting operations, and `bytearray` has an additional set of operations that perform in-place changes. The `str` and `bytes` types also have methods for encoding and decoding text, respectively.

5. Non-ASCII Unicode characters can be coded in a string with both hex (`\xNN`) and Unicode (`\uNNNN`, `\UNNNNNNNN`) escapes. On some machines, some non-ASCII characters—certain Latin-1 characters, for example—can also be typed or pasted directly into code, and are interpreted per the UTF-8 default or a source code encoding directive comment.

6. In 3.X, text-mode files assume their file content is Unicode text (even if it's all ASCII) and automatically decode when reading and encode when writing. With binary-mode files, bytes are transferred to and from the file unchanged. The contents of text-mode files are usually represented as `str` objects in your script, and the contents of binary files are represented as `bytes` (or `bytearray`) objects. Text-mode files also handle the BOM for certain encoding types and automatically translate end-of-line sequences to and from the single `\n` character on input and output unless this is explicitly disabled; binary-mode files do not perform either of these steps. Python 2.X uses `codecs.open` for Unicode files, which encodes and decodes similarly; 2.X's `open` only translates line ends in text mode.

---

7. To read files encoded in a different encoding than the default for your platform, simply pass the name of the file's encoding to the `open` built-in in 3.X (`codecs.open()` in 2.X); data will be decoded per the specified encoding when it is read from the file. You can also read in binary mode and manually decode the bytes to a string by giving an encoding name, but this involves extra work and is somewhat error-prone for multibyte characters (you may accidentally read a partial character sequence).

8. To create a Unicode text file in a specific encoding format, pass the desired encoding name to `open` in 3.X (`codecs.open()` in 2.X); strings will be encoded per the desired encoding when they are written to the file. You can also manually encode a string to bytes and write it in binary mode, but this is usually extra work.

9. ASCII text is considered to be a kind of Unicode text, because its 7-bit range of values is a subset of most Unicode encodings. For example, valid ASCII text is also valid Latin-1 text (Latin-1 simply assigns the remaining possible values in an 8-bit byte to additional characters) and valid UTF-8 text (UTF-8 defines a variable-byte scheme for representing more characters, but ASCII characters are still represented with the same codes, in a single byte). This makes Unicode backward-compatible with the mass of ASCII text data in the world (though it also may have limited its options—self-identifying text, for instance, may have been difficult (though BOMs serve much the same role).

10. The impact of Python 3.X's string types change depends upon the types of strings you use. For scripts that use simple ASCII text on platforms with ASCII-compatible default encodings, the impact is probably minor: the `str` string type works the same in 2.X and 3.X in this case. Moreover, although string-related tools in the standard library such as `re`, `struct`, `pickle`, and `xml` may technically use different types in 3.X than in 2.X, the changes are largely irrelevant to most programs because 3.X's `str` and `bytes` and 2.X's `str` support almost identical interfaces. If you process Unicode data, the toolset you need has simply moved from 2.X's `unicode` and `codecs.open()` to 3.X's `str` and `open`. If you deal with binary data files, you'll need to deal with content as `bytes` objects; since they have a similar interface to 2.X strings, though, the impact should again be minimal. That said, the update of the book *Programming Python* for 3.X ran across numerous cases where Unicode's mandatory status in 3.X implied changes in standard library APIs—from networking and GUIs, to databases and email. In general, Unicode will probably impact most 3.X users eventually.

Managed Attributes

This chapter expands on the *attribute interception* techniques introduced earlier, introduces another, and employs them in a handful of larger examples. Like everything in this part of the book, this chapter is classified as an advanced topic and optional reading, because most applications programmers don't need to care about the material discussed here—they can fetch and set attributes on objects without concern for attribute implementations.

Especially for tools builders, though, managing attribute access can be an important part of flexible APIs. Moreover, an understanding of the descriptor model covered here can make related tools such as slots and properties more tangible, and may even be required reading if it appears in code you must use.

Why Manage Attributes?

Object attributes are central to most Python programs—they are where we often store information about the entities our scripts process. Normally, attributes are simply names for objects; a person's `name` attribute, for example, might be a simple string, fetched and set with basic attribute syntax:

```
person.name              # Fetch attribute value
person.name = value      # Change attribute value
```

In most cases, the attribute lives in the object itself, or is inherited from a class from which it derives. That basic model suffices for most programs you will write in your Python career.

Sometimes, though, more flexibility is required. Suppose you've written a program to use a `name` attribute directly, but then your requirements change—for example, you decide that names should be validated with logic when set or mutated in some way when fetched. It's straightforward to code methods to manage access to the attribute's value (`valid` and `transform` are abstract here):

```
class Person:
    def getName(self):
```

```
            if not valid():
                raise TypeError('cannot fetch name')
            else:
                return self.name.transform()

        def setName(self, value):
            if not valid(value):
                raise TypeError('cannot change name')
            else:
                self.name = transform(value)

    person = Person()
    person.getName()
    person.setName('value')
```

However, this also requires changing all the places where names are used in the entire program—a possibly nontrivial task. Moreover, this approach requires the program to be aware of how values are exported: as simple names or called methods. If you begin with a method-based interface to data, clients are immune to changes; if you do not, they can become problematic.

This issue can crop up more often than you might expect. The value of a cell in a spreadsheet-like program, for instance, might begin its life as a simple discrete value, but later mutate into an arbitrary calculation. Since an object's interface should be flexible enough to support such future changes without breaking existing code, switching to methods later is less than ideal.

Inserting Code to Run on Attribute Access

A better solution would allow you to run code automatically on attribute access, if needed. That's one of the main roles of managed attributes—they provide ways to add *attribute accessor* logic after the fact. More generally, they support arbitrary attribute usage modes that go beyond simple data storage.

At various points in this book, we've met Python tools that allow our scripts to dynamically compute attribute values when fetching them and validate or change attribute values when storing them. In this chapter, we're going to expand on the tools already introduced, explore other available tools, and study some larger use-case examples in this domain. Specifically, this chapter presents *four* accessor techniques:

- The __getattr__ and __setattr__ methods, for routing undefined attribute fetches and all attribute assignments to generic handler methods.
- The __getattribute__ method, for routing all attribute fetches to a generic handler method.
- The property built-in, for routing specific attribute access to get and set handler functions.

- The *descriptor protocol*, for routing specific attribute accesses to instances of classes with arbitrary get and set handler methods, and the basis for other tools such as properties and slots.

The tools in the first of these bullets are available in all Pythons. The last three bullets' tools are available in Python 3.X and new-style classes in 2.X—they first appeared in Python 2.2, along with many of the other advanced tools of Chapter 32 such as slots and super. We briefly met the first and third of these in Chapter 30 and Chapter 32, respectively; the second and fourth are largely new topics we'll explore in full here.

As we'll see, all four techniques share goals to some degree, and it's usually possible to code a given problem using any one of them. They do differ in some important ways, though. For example, the last two techniques listed here apply to *specific* attributes, whereas the first two are generic enough to be used by delegation-based proxy classes that must route *arbitrary* attributes to wrapped objects. As we'll see, all four schemes also differ in both complexity and aesthetics, in ways you must see in action to judge for yourself.

Besides studying the specifics behind the four attribute interception techniques listed in this section, this chapter also presents an opportunity to explore larger programs than we've seen elsewhere in this book. The `CardHolder` case study at the end, for example, should serve as a self-study example of larger classes in action. We'll also be using some of the techniques outlined here in the next chapter to code decorators, so be sure you have at least a general understanding of these topics before you move on.

Properties

The property protocol allows us to route a specific attribute's get, set, and delete operations to functions or methods we provide, enabling us to insert code to be run automatically on attribute access, intercept attribute deletions, and provide documentation for the attributes if desired.

Properties are created with the `property` built-in and are assigned to class attributes, just like method functions. Accordingly, they are inherited by subclasses and instances, like any other class attributes. Their access-interception functions are provided with the `self` instance argument, which grants access to state information and class attributes available on the subject instance.

A property manages a single, specific attribute; although it can't catch all attribute accesses generically, it allows us to control both fetch and assignment accesses and enables us to change an attribute from simple data to a computation freely, without breaking existing code. As we'll see, properties are strongly related to descriptors; in fact, they are essentially a restricted form of them.

The Basics

A property is created by assigning the result of a built-in function to a class attribute:

```
attribute = property(fget, fset, fdel, doc)
```

None of this built-in's arguments are required, and all default to None if not passed. For the first three, this None means that the corresponding operation is not supported, and attempting it will raise an AttributeError exception automatically.

When these arguments are used, we pass fget a function for intercepting attribute fetches, fset a function for assignments, and fdel a function for attribute deletions. Technically, all three of these arguments accept any callable, including a class's method, having a first argument to receive the instance being qualified. When later invoked, the fget function returns the computed attribute value, fset and fdel return nothing (really, None), and all three may raise exceptions to reject access requests.

The doc argument receives a documentation string for the attribute, if desired; otherwise, the property copies the docstring of the fget function, which as usual defaults to None.

This built-in property call returns a property object, which we assign to the name of the attribute to be managed in the class scope, where it will be inherited by every instance.

A First Example

To demonstrate how this translates to working code, the following class uses a property to trace access to an attribute named name; the actual stored data is named _name so it does not clash with the property (if you're working along with the book examples package, some filenames in this chapter are implied by the command-lines that run them following their listings):

```
class Person:                          # Add (object) in 2.X
    def __init__(self, name):
        self._name = name
    def getName(self):
        print('fetch...')
        return self._name
    def setName(self, value):
        print('change...')
        self._name = value
    def delName(self):
        print('remove...')
        del self._name
    name = property(getName, setName, delName, "name property docs")

bob = Person('Bob Smith')              # bob has a managed attribute
print(bob.name)                        # Runs getName
bob.name = 'Robert Smith'              # Runs setName
print(bob.name)
```

```
del bob.name                        # Runs delName

print('-'*20)
sue = Person('Sue Jones')           # sue inherits property too
print(sue.name)
print(Person.name.__doc__)          # Or help(Person.name)
```

Properties are available in both 2.X and 3.X, but they require new-style `object` derivation in 2.X to work correctly for *assignments*—add `object` as a superclass here to run this in 2.X. You can list the superclass in 3.X too, but it's implied and not required, and is sometimes omitted in this book to reduce clutter.

This particular property doesn't do much—it simply intercepts and traces an attribute —but it serves to demonstrate the protocol. When this code is run, two instances inherit the property, just as they would any other attribute attached to their class. However, their attribute accesses are caught:

```
c:\code> py -3 prop-person.py
fetch...
Bob Smith
change...
fetch...
Robert Smith
remove...
--------------------
fetch...
Sue Jones
name property docs
```

Like all class attributes, properties are *inherited* by both instances and lower subclasses. If we change our example as follows, for instance:

```
class Super:
    ...the original Person class code...
    name = property(getName, setName, delName, 'name property docs')

class Person(Super):
    pass                            # Properties are inherited (class attrs)

bob = Person('Bob Smith')
...rest unchanged...
```

the output is the same—the `Person` subclass inherits the `name` property from `Super`, and the `bob` instance gets it from `Person`. In terms of inheritance, properties work the same as normal methods; because they have access to the `self` instance argument, they can access instance state information and methods irrespective of subclass depth, as the next section further demonstrates.

Computed Attributes

The example in the prior section simply traces attribute accesses. Usually, though, properties do much more—computing the value of an attribute dynamically when fetched, for example. The following example illustrates:

```
class PropSquare:
    def __init__(self, start):
        self.value = start
    def getX(self):                       # On attr fetch
        return self.value ** 2
    def setX(self, value):                # On attr assign
        self.value = value
    X = property(getX, setX)              # No delete or docs

P = PropSquare(3)       # Two instances of class with property
Q = PropSquare(32)      # Each has different state information

print(P.X)              # 3 ** 2
P.X = 4
print(P.X)              # 4 ** 2
print(Q.X)              # 32 ** 2 (1024)
```

This class defines an attribute X that is accessed as though it were static data, but really runs code to compute its value when fetched. The effect is much like an implicit method call. When the code is run, the value is stored in the instance as state information, but each time we fetch it via the managed attribute, its value is automatically squared:

```
c:\code> py -3 prop-computed.py
9
16
1024
```

Notice that we've made two different instances—because property methods automatically receive a `self` argument, they have access to the state information stored in instances. In our case, this means the fetch computes the square of the subject instance's own data.

Coding Properties with Decorators

Although we're saving additional details until the next chapter, we introduced *function decorator* basics earlier, in Chapter 32. Recall that the function decorator syntax:

```
@decorator
def func(args): ...
```

is automatically translated to this equivalent by Python, to rebind the function name to the result of the `decorator` callable:

```
def func(args): ...
func = decorator(func)
```

Because of this mapping, it turns out that the **property** built-in can serve as a decorator, to define a function that will run automatically when an attribute is fetched:

```
class Person:
    @property
    def name(self): ...          # Rebinds: name = property(name)
```

When run, the decorated method is automatically passed to the first argument of the **property** built-in. This is really just alternative syntax for creating a property and rebinding the attribute name manually, but may be seen as more explicit in this role:

```
class Person:
    def name(self): ...
    name = property(name)
```

Setter and deleter decorators

As of Python 2.6 and 3.0, property objects also have **getter**, **setter**, and **deleter** methods that assign the corresponding property accessor methods and return a copy of the property itself. We can use these to specify components of properties by decorating normal methods too, though the **getter** component is usually filled in automatically by the act of creating the property itself:

```
class Person:
    def __init__(self, name):
        self._name = name

    @property
    def name(self):              # name = property(name)
        "name property docs"
        print('fetch...')
        return self._name

    @name.setter
    def name(self, value):       # name = name.setter(name)
        print('change...')
        self._name = value

    @name.deleter
    def name(self):              # name = name.deleter(name)
        print('remove...')
        del self._name

bob = Person('Bob Smith')        # bob has a managed attribute
print(bob.name)                  # Runs name getter (name 1)
bob.name = 'Robert Smith'        # Runs name setter (name 2)
print(bob.name)
del bob.name                     # Runs name deleter (name 3)

print('-'*20)
sue = Person('Sue Jones')        # sue inherits property too
print(sue.name)
print(Person.name.__doc__)       # Or help(Person.name)
```

In fact, this code is equivalent to the first example in this section—decoration is just an alternative way to code properties in this case. When it's run, the results are the same:

```
c:\code> py -3 prop-person-deco.py
fetch...
Bob Smith
change...
fetch...
Robert Smith
remove...
--------------------
fetch...
Sue Jones
name property docs
```

Compared to manual assignment of `property` results, in this case using decorators to code properties requires just three extra lines of code—a seemingly negligible difference. As is so often the case with alternative tools, though, the choice between the two techniques is largely subjective.

Descriptors

Descriptors provide an alternative way to intercept attribute access; they are strongly related to the properties discussed in the prior section. Really, a property *is* a kind of descriptor—technically speaking, the `property` built-in is just a simplified way to create a specific type of descriptor that runs method functions on attribute accesses. In fact, descriptors are the underlying implementation mechanism for a variety of class tools, including both properties and slots.

Functionally speaking, the descriptor protocol allows us to route a specific attribute's get, set, and delete operations to methods of a separate class's instance object that we provide. This allows us to insert code to be run automatically on attribute fetches and assignments, intercept attribute deletions, and provide documentation for the attributes if desired.

Descriptors are created as independent *classes*, and they are assigned to class attributes just like method functions. Like any other class attribute, they are inherited by subclasses and instances. Their access-interception methods are provided with both a `self` for the descriptor instance itself, as well as the instance of the client class whose attribute references the descriptor object. Because of this, they can retain and use state information of their own, as well as state information of the subject instance. For example, a descriptor may call methods available in the client class, as well as descriptor-specific methods it defines.

Like a property, a descriptor manages a single, specific attribute; although it can't catch all attribute accesses generically, it provides control over both fetch and assignment accesses and allows us to change an attribute name freely from simple data to a computation without breaking existing code. Properties really are just a convenient way to create a specific kind of descriptor, and as we shall see, they can be coded as descriptors directly.

Unlike properties, descriptors are broader in scope, and provide a more general tool. For instance, because they are coded as normal classes, descriptors have their own state, may participate in descriptor inheritance hierarchies, can use composition to aggregate objects, and provide a natural structure for coding internal methods and attribute documentation strings.

The Basics

As mentioned previously, descriptors are coded as separate classes and provide specially named accessor methods for the attribute access operations they wish to intercept —get, set, and deletion methods in the descriptor class are automatically run when the attribute assigned to the descriptor class instance is accessed in the corresponding way:

```
class Descriptor:
    "docstring goes here"
    def __get__(self, instance, owner): ...      # Return attr value
    def __set__(self, instance, value): ...      # Return nothing (None)
    def __delete__(self, instance): ...          # Return nothing (None)
```

Classes with any of these methods are considered descriptors, and their methods are special when one of their instances is assigned to another class's attribute—when the attribute is accessed, they are automatically invoked. If any of these methods are absent, it generally means that the corresponding type of access is not supported. Unlike properties, however, omitting a __set__ allows the descriptor attribute's name to be assigned and thus redefined in an instance, thereby *hiding* the descriptor—to make an attribute *read-only*, you must define __set__ to catch assignments and raise an exception.

Descriptors with __set__ methods also have some special-case implications for inheritance that we'll largely defer until Chapter 40's coverage of metaclasses and the complete inheritance specification. In short, a descriptor with a __set__ is known formally as *data descriptor*, and is given precedence over other names located by normal inheritance rules. The inherited descriptor for name __class__, for example, overrides the same name in an instance's namespace dictionary. This also works to ensure that data descriptors you code in your own classes take precedence over others.

Descriptor method arguments

Before we code anything realistic, let's take a brief look at some fundamentals. All three descriptor methods outlined in the prior section are passed both the descriptor class instance (self), and the instance of the client class to which the descriptor instance is attached (instance).

The __get__ access method additionally receives an owner argument, specifying the class to which the descriptor instance is attached. Its instance argument is either the instance through which the attribute was accessed (for *instance*.attr), or None when the attribute is accessed through the owner class directly (for *class*.attr). The former of these generally computes a value for instance access, and the latter usually returns self if descriptor object access is supported.

For example, in the following 3.X session, when X.attr is fetched, Python automatically runs the __get__ method of the Descriptor class instance to which the Subject.attr class attribute is assigned. In 2.X, use the print statement equivalent, and derive *both* classes here from object, as descriptors are a new-style class tool; in 3.X this derivation is implied and can be omitted, but doesn't hurt:

```
>>> class Descriptor:                    # Add "(object)" in 2.X
        def __get__(self, instance, owner):
            print(self, instance, owner, sep='\n')

>>> class Subject:                       # Add "(object)" in 2.X
        attr = Descriptor()              # Descriptor instance is class attr

>>> X = Subject()
>>> X.attr
<__main__.Descriptor object at 0x0281E690>
<__main__.Subject object at 0x028289B0>
<class '__main__.Subject'>

>>> Subject.attr
<__main__.Descriptor object at 0x0281E690>
None
<class '__main__.Subject'>
```

Notice the arguments automatically passed in to the __get__ method in the first attribute fetch—when X.attr is fetched, it's as though the following translation occurs (though the Subject.attr here doesn't invoke __get__ again):

```
X.attr  ->  Descriptor.__get__(Subject.attr, X, Subject)
```

The descriptor knows it is being accessed directly when its instance argument is None.

Read-only descriptors

As mentioned earlier, unlike properties, simply omitting the __set__ method in a descriptor isn't enough to make an attribute read-only, because the descriptor name can be assigned to an instance. In the following, the attribute assignment to X.a stores a in the instance object X, thereby hiding the descriptor stored in class C:

```
>>> class D:
        def __get__(*args): print('get')

>>> class C:
        a = D()                          # Attribute a is a descriptor instance

>>> X = C()
>>> X.a                                  # Runs inherited descriptor __get__
get
>>> C.a
```

```
get
>>> X.a = 99                              # Stored on X, hiding C.a!
>>> X.a
99
>>> list(X.__dict__.keys())
['a']
>>> Y = C()
>>> Y.a                                   # Y still inherits descriptor
get
>>> C.a
get
```

This is the way all instance attribute assignments work in Python, and it allows classes to selectively override class-level defaults in their instances. To make a descriptor-based attribute read-only, catch the assignment in the descriptor class and raise an exception to prevent attribute assignment—when assigning an attribute that is a descriptor, Python effectively bypasses the normal instance-level assignment behavior and routes the operation to the descriptor object:

```
>>> class D:
        def __get__(*args): print('get')
        def __set__(*args): raise AttributeError('cannot set')

>>> class C:
        a = D()

>>> X = C()
>>> X.a                                   # Routed to C.a.__get__
get
>>> X.a = 99                              # Routed to C.a.__set__
AttributeError: cannot set
```

 Also be careful not to confuse the descriptor __delete__ method with the general __del__ method. The former is called on attempts to delete the managed attribute name on an instance of the owner class; the latter is the general instance destructor method, run when an instance of any kind of class is about to be garbage-collected. __delete__ is more closely related to the __delattr__ generic attribute deletion method we'll meet later in this chapter. See Chapter 30 for more on operator overloading methods.

A First Example

To see how this all comes together in more realistic code, let's get started with the same first example we wrote for properties. The following defines a descriptor that intercepts access to an attribute named name in its clients. Its methods use their instance argument to access state information in the subject instance, where the name string is actually stored. Like properties, descriptors work properly only for new-style classes, so be sure to derive *both* classes in the following from object if you're using 2.X—it's not enough to derive just the descriptor, or just its client:

```
class Name:                              # Use (object) in 2.X
    "name descriptor docs"
    def __get__(self, instance, owner):
        print('fetch...')
        return instance._name
    def __set__(self, instance, value):
        print('change...')
        instance._name = value
    def __delete__(self, instance):
        print('remove...')
        del instance._name

class Person:                            # Use (object) in 2.X
    def __init__(self, name):
        self._name = name
    name = Name()                        # Assign descriptor to attr

bob = Person('Bob Smith')                # bob has a managed attribute
print(bob.name)                          # Runs Name.__get__
bob.name = 'Robert Smith'                # Runs Name.__set__
print(bob.name)
del bob.name                             # Runs Name.__delete__

print('-'*20)
sue = Person('Sue Jones')                # sue inherits descriptor too
print(sue.name)
print(Name.__doc__)                      # Or help(Name)
```

Notice in this code how we assign an instance of our descriptor class to a *class attribute* in the client class; because of this, it is inherited by all instances of the class, just like a class's methods. Really, we *must* assign the descriptor to a class attribute like this —it won't work if assigned to a self instance attribute instead. When the descriptor's __get__ method is run, it is passed three objects to define its context:

- self is the Name class instance.
- instance is the Person class instance.
- owner is the Person class.

When this code is run the descriptor's methods intercept accesses to the attribute, much like the property version. In fact, the output is the same again:

```
c:\code> py -3 desc-person.py
fetch...
Bob Smith
change...
fetch...
Robert Smith
remove...
--------------------
fetch...
Sue Jones
name descriptor docs
```

Also like in the property example, our descriptor class instance is a class attribute and thus is *inherited* by all instances of the client class and any subclasses. If we change the `Person` class in our example to the following, for instance, the output of our script is the same:

```
...
class Super:
    def __init__(self, name):
        self._name = name
    name = Name()

class Person(Super):                     # Descriptors are inherited (class attrs)
    pass
...
```

Also note that when a descriptor class is not useful outside the client class, it's perfectly reasonable to embed the descriptor's definition inside its client syntactically. Here's what our example looks like if we use a *nested class*:

```
class Person:
    def __init__(self, name):
        self._name = name

    class Name:                          # Using a nested class
        "name descriptor docs"
        def __get__(self, instance, owner):
            print('fetch...')
            return instance._name
        def __set__(self, instance, value):
            print('change...')
            instance._name = value
        def __delete__(self, instance):
            print('remove...')
            del instance._name
    name = Name()
```

When coded this way, `Name` becomes a local variable in the scope of the `Person` class statement, such that it won't clash with any names outside the class. This version works the same as the original—we've simply moved the descriptor class definition into the client class's scope—but the last line of the testing code must change to fetch the docstring from its new location (per the example file *desc-person-nested.py*):

```
...
print(Person.Name.__doc__)      # Differs: not Name.__doc__ outside class
```

Computed Attributes

As was the case when using properties, our first descriptor example of the prior section didn't do much—it simply printed trace messages for attribute accesses. In practice, descriptors can also be used to compute attribute values each time they are fetched. The following illustrates—it's a rehash of the same example we coded for properties, which uses a descriptor to automatically square an attribute's value each time it is fetched:

```
class DescSquare:
    def __init__(self, start):              # Each desc has own state
        self.value = start
    def __get__(self, instance, owner):     # On attr fetch
        return self.value ** 2
    def __set__(self, instance, value):     # On attr assign
        self.value = value                  # No delete or docs

class Client1:
    X = DescSquare(3)         # Assign descriptor instance to class attr

class Client2:
    X = DescSquare(32)        # Another instance in another client class
                              # Could also code two instances in same class
c1 = Client1()
c2 = Client2()

print(c1.X)                   # 3 ** 2
c1.X = 4
print(c1.X)                   # 4 ** 2
print(c2.X)                   # 32 ** 2 (1024)
```

When run, the output of this example is the same as that of the original property-based version, but here a descriptor class object is intercepting the attribute accesses:

```
c:\code> py -3 desc-computed.py
9
16
1024
```

Using State Information in Descriptors

If you study the two descriptor examples we've written so far, you might notice that they get their information from different places—the first (the name attribute example) uses data stored on the client *instance*, and the second (the attribute squaring example) uses data attached to the *descriptor* object itself (a.k.a. self). In fact, descriptors can use *both* instance state and descriptor state, or any combination thereof:

- *Descriptor state* is used to manage either data internal to the workings of the descriptor, or data that spans all instances. It can vary per attribute appearance (often, per client class).

- *Instance state* records information related to and possibly created by the client class. It can vary per client class instance (that is, per application object).

In other words, descriptor state is per-descriptor data and instance state is per-client-instance data. As usual in OOP, you must choose state carefully. For instance, you would not normally use *descriptor* state to record employee names, since each client instance requires its own value—if stored in the descriptor, each client class instance will effectively share the same single copy. On the other hand, you would not usually use *instance* state to record data pertaining to descriptor implementation internals—if stored in each instance, there would be multiple varying copies.

Descriptor methods may use either state form, but descriptor state often makes it unnecessary to use special naming conventions to avoid name collisions in the instance for data that is not instance-specific. For example, the following descriptor attaches information to its own instance, so it doesn't clash with that on the client class's instance—but also shares that information between two client instances:

```python
class DescState:                            # Use descriptor state, (object) in 2.X
    def __init__(self, value):
        self.value = value
    def __get__(self, instance, owner):     # On attr fetch
        print('DescState get')
        return self.value * 10
    def __set__(self, instance, value):     # On attr assign
        print('DescState set')
        self.value = value

# Client class
class CalcAttrs:
    X = DescState(2)                        # Descriptor class attr
    Y = 3                                   # Class attr
    def __init__(self):
        self.Z = 4                          # Instance attr

obj = CalcAttrs()
print(obj.X, obj.Y, obj.Z)                  # X is computed, others are not
obj.X = 5                                   # X assignment is intercepted
CalcAttrs.Y = 6                             # Y reassigned in class
obj.Z = 7                                   # Z assigned in instance
print(obj.X, obj.Y, obj.Z)

obj2 = CalcAttrs()                          # But X uses shared data, like Y!
print(obj2.X, obj2.Y, obj2.Z)
```

This code's internal `value` information lives only in the *descriptor*, so there won't be a collision if the same name is used in the client's instance. Notice that only the descriptor attribute is managed here—get and set accesses to X are intercepted, but accesses to Y and Z are not (Y is attached to the client class and Z to the instance). When this code is run, X is computed when fetched, but its value is also the same for all client instances because it uses descriptor-level state:

```
c:\code> py -3 desc-state-desc.py
DescState get
20 3 4
DescState set
DescState get
50 6 7
DescState get
50 6 4
```

It's also feasible for a descriptor to store or use an attribute attached to the client class's *instance*, instead of itself. Crucially, unlike data stored in the descriptor itself, this allows for data that can vary per client class instance. The descriptor in the following example assumes the instance has an attribute _X attached by the client class, and uses it to compute the value of the attribute it represents:

```
class InstState:                                 # Using instance state, (object) in 2.X
    def __get__(self, instance, owner):
        print('InstState get')                   # Assume set by client class
        return instance._X * 10
    def __set__(self, instance, value):
        print('InstState set')
        instance._X = value

# Client class
class CalcAttrs:
    X = InstState()                              # Descriptor class attr
    Y = 3                                        # Class attr
    def __init__(self):
        self._X = 2                              # Instance attr
        self.Z  = 4                              # Instance attr

obj = CalcAttrs()
print(obj.X, obj.Y, obj.Z)                       # X is computed, others are not
obj.X = 5                                        # X assignment is intercepted
CalcAttrs.Y = 6                                  # Y reassigned in class
obj.Z = 7                                        # Z assigned in instance
print(obj.X, obj.Y, obj.Z)

obj2 = CalcAttrs()                               # But X differs now, like Z!
print(obj2.X, obj2.Y, obj2.Z)
```

Here, X is assigned to a descriptor as before that manages accesses. The new descriptor here, though, has no information itself, but it uses an attribute assumed to exist in the instance—that attribute is named _X, to avoid collisions with the name of the descriptor itself. When this version is run the results are similar, but the value of the descriptor attribute can vary per client instance due to the differing state policy:

```
c:\code> py -3 desc-state-inst.py
InstState get
20 3 4
InstState set
InstState get
50 6 7
InstState get
20 6 4
```

Both descriptor and instance state have roles. In fact, this is a general advantage that descriptors have over properties—because they have state of their own, they can easily retain data internally, without adding it to the namespace of the client instance object. As a summary, the following uses *both* state sources—its self.data retains per-attribute information, while its instance.data can vary per client instance:

```
>>> class DescBoth:
        def __init__(self, data):
            self.data = data
        def __get__(self, instance, owner):
            return '%s, %s' % (self.data, instance.data)
        def __set__(self, instance, value):
            instance.data = value

>>> class Client:
        def __init__(self, data):
            self.data = data
        managed = DescBoth('spam')

>>> I = Client('eggs')
>>> I.managed                       # Show both data sources
'spam, eggs'
>>> I.managed = 'SPAM'              # Change instance data
>>> I.managed
'spam, SPAM'
```

We'll revisit the implications of this choice in a larger case study later in this chapter. Before we move on, recall from Chapter 32's coverage of slots that we can access "virtual" attributes like properties and descriptors with tools like dir and getattr, even though they don't exist in the instance's namespace dictionary. Whether you *should* access these this way probably varies per program—properties and descriptors may run arbitrary computation, and may be less obviously instance "data" than slots:

```
>>> I.__dict__
{'data': 'SPAM'}
>>> [x for x in dir(I) if not x.startswith('__')]
['data', 'managed']

>>> getattr(I, 'data')
'SPAM'
>>> getattr(I, 'managed')
'spam, SPAM'

>>> for attr in (x for x in dir(I) if not x.startswith('__')):
        print('%s => %s' % (attr, getattr(I, attr)))

data => SPAM
managed => spam, SPAM
```

The more generic __getattr__ and __getattribute__ tools we'll meet later are not designed to support this functionality—because they have no class-level attributes, their "virtual" attribute names do not appear in dir results.[1] In exchange, they are also not limited to specific attribute names coded as properties or descriptors: tools that share even more than this behavior, as the next section explains.

---

1. As noted in Chapter 31, such dynamic classes can also use a __dir__ method to provide an attribute result list for dir calls, though general tools cannot depend on this optional interface.

How Properties and Descriptors Relate

As mentioned earlier, properties and descriptors are strongly related—the property built-in is just a convenient way to create a descriptor. Now that you know how both work, you should also be able to see that it's possible to simulate the property built-in with a descriptor class like the following:

```
class Property:
    def __init__(self, fget=None, fset=None, fdel=None, doc=None):
        self.fget = fget
        self.fset = fset
        self.fdel = fdel                        # Save unbound methods
        self.__doc__ = doc                      # or other callables

    def __get__(self, instance, instancetype=None):
        if instance is None:
            return self
        if self.fget is None:
            raise AttributeError("can't get attribute")
        return self.fget(instance)              # Pass instance to self
                                                # in property accessors
    def __set__(self, instance, value):
        if self.fset is None:
            raise AttributeError("can't set attribute")
        self.fset(instance, value)

    def __delete__(self, instance):
        if self.fdel is None:
            raise AttributeError("can't delete attribute")
        self.fdel(instance)

class Person:
    def getName(self): print('getName...')
    def setName(self, value): print('setName...')
    name = Property(getName, setName)           # Use like property()

x = Person()
x.name
x.name = 'Bob'
del x.name
```

This `Property` class catches attribute accesses with the descriptor protocol and routes requests to functions or methods passed in and saved in descriptor state when the class is created. Attribute fetches, for example, are routed from the `Person` class, to the `Property` class's `__get__` method, and back to the `Person` class's `getName`. With descriptors, this "just works":

```
c:\code> py -3 prop-desc-equiv.py
getName...
setName...
AttributeError: can't delete attribute
```

Note that this descriptor class equivalent only handles basic property usage, though; to use @ *decorator syntax* to also specify set and delete operations, we'd have to extend our `Property` class with `setter` and `deleter` methods, which would save the decorated accessor function and return the property object (`self` should suffice). Since the `prop erty` built-in already does this, we'll omit a formal coding of this extension here.

Descriptors and slots and more

You can also probably now at least in part imagine how descriptors are used to implement Python's *slots* extension: instance attribute dictionaries are avoided by creating class-level descriptors that intercept slot name access, and map those names to sequential storage space in the instance. Unlike the explicit `property` call, though, much of the magic behind slots is orchestrated at class creation time both automatically and implicitly, when a `__slots__` attribute is present in a class.

See Chapter 32 for more on slots (and why they're not recommended except in pathological use cases). Descriptors are also used for other class tools, but we'll omit further internals details here; see Python's manuals and source code for more details.

 In Chapter 39, we'll also make use of descriptors to implement function *decorators* that apply to both functions and methods. As you'll see there, because descriptors receive both descriptor *and* subject class instances they work well in this role, though nested functions are usually a conceptually much simpler solution. We'll also deploy descriptors as one way to intercept *built-in* operation method fetches in Chapter 39.

Be sure to also see Chapter 40's coverage of *data descriptors'* precedence in the full inheritance model mentioned earlier: with a `__set__`, descriptors override other names, and are thus fairly binding—they cannot be hidden by names in instance dictionaries.

__getattr__ and __getattribute__

So far, we've studied properties and descriptors—tools for managing specific attributes. The `__getattr__` and `__getattribute__` operator overloading methods provide still other ways to intercept attribute fetches for class instances. Like properties and descriptors, they allow us to insert code to be run automatically when attributes are accessed. As we'll see, though, these two methods can also be used in more general ways. Because they intercept arbitrary names, they apply in broader roles such as delegation, but may also incur extra calls in some contexts, and are too dynamic to register in `dir` results.

Attribute fetch interception comes in two flavors, coded with two different methods:

- `__getattr__` is run for *undefined* attributes—because it is run only for attributes not stored on an instance or inherited from one of its classes, its use is straightforward.

- __getattribute__ is run for *every* attribute—because it is all-inclusive, you must be cautious when using this method to avoid recursive loops by passing attribute accesses to a superclass.

We met the former of these in Chapter 30; it's available for all Python versions. The latter of these is available for new-style classes in 2.X, and for all (implicitly new-style) classes in 3.X. These two methods are representatives of a set of attribute interception methods that also includes __setattr__ and __delattr__. Because these methods have similar roles, though, we will generally treat them all as a single topic here.

Unlike properties and descriptors, these methods are part of Python's general *operator overloading* protocol—specially named methods of a class, inherited by subclasses, and run automatically when instances are used in the implied built-in operation. Like all normal methods of a class, they each receive a first `self` argument when called, giving access to any required instance state information as well as other methods of the class in which they appear.

The __getattr__ and __getattribute__ methods are also more *generic* than properties and descriptors—they can be used to intercept access to any (or even all) instance attribute fetches, not just a single specific name. Because of this, these two methods are well suited to general *delegation*-based coding patterns—they can be used to implement wrapper (a.k.a. *proxy*) objects that manage all attribute accesses for an embedded object. By contrast, we must define one property or descriptor for every attribute we wish to intercept. As we'll see ahead, this role is impaired somewhat in new-style classes for built-in operations, but still applies to all named methods in a wrapped object's interface.

Finally, these two methods are more *narrowly focused* than the alternatives we considered earlier: they intercept attribute fetches only, not assignments. To also catch attribute changes by assignment, we must code a __setattr__ method—an operator overloading method run for every attribute assignment, which must take care to avoid recursive loops by routing attribute assignments through the instance namespace dictionary or a superclass method. Although less common, we can also code a __delattr__ overloading method (which must avoid looping in the same way) to intercept attribute deletions. By contrast, properties and descriptors catch get, set, *and* delete operations by design.

Most of these operator overloading methods were introduced earlier in the book; here, we'll expand on their usage and study their roles in larger contexts.

The Basics

__getattr__ and __setattr__ were introduced in Chapter 30 and Chapter 32, and __getattribute__ was mentioned briefly in Chapter 32. In short, if a class defines or inherits the following methods, they will be run automatically when an instance is used in the context described by the comments to the right:

```
def __getattr__(self, name):            # On undefined attribute fetch [obj.name]
def __getattribute__(self, name):       # On all attribute fetch [obj.name]
def __setattr__(self, name, value):     # On all attribute assignment [obj.name=value]
def __delattr__(self, name):            # On all attribute deletion [del obj.name]
```

In all of these, self is the subject instance object as usual, name is the string name of the attribute being accessed, and value is the object being assigned to the attribute. The two get methods normally return an attribute's value, and the other two return nothing (None). All can raise exceptions to signal prohibited access.

For example, to catch every attribute fetch, we can use either of the first two previous methods, and to catch every attribute assignment we can use the third. The following uses __getattr__ and works *portably* on both Python 2.X and 3.X, not requiring new-style object derivation in 2.X:

```
class Catcher:
    def __getattr__(self, name):
        print('Get: %s' % name)
    def __setattr__(self, name, value):
        print('Set: %s %s' % (name, value))

X = Catcher()
X.job                                   # Prints "Get: job"
X.pay                                   # Prints "Get: pay"
X.pay = 99                              # Prints "Set: pay 99"
```

Using __getattribute__ works exactly the same in this specific case, but requires object derivation in 2.X (only), and has subtle looping potential, which we'll take up in the next section:

```
class Catcher(object):                  # Need (object) in 2.X only
    def __getattribute__(self, name):   # Works same as getattr here
        print('Get: %s' % name)         # But prone to loops on general
    ...rest unchanged...
```

Such a coding structure can be used to implement the *delegation* design pattern we met earlier, in Chapter 31. Because all attributes are routed to our interception methods generically, we can validate and pass them along to embedded, managed objects. The following class (borrowed from Chapter 31), for example, traces *every* attribute fetch made to another object passed to the wrapper (proxy) class:

```
class Wrapper:
    def __init__(self, object):
        self.wrapped = object           # Save object
    def __getattr__(self, attrname):
        print('Trace: ' + attrname)     # Trace fetch
        return getattr(self.wrapped, attrname)  # Delegate fetch

X = Wrapper([1, 2, 3])
X.append(4)                             # Prints "Trace: append"
print(X.wrapped)                        # Prints "[1, 2, 3, 4]"
```

There is no such analog for properties and descriptors, short of coding accessors for *every* possible attribute in *every* possibly wrapped object. On the other hand, when such generality is not required, generic accessor methods may incur additional calls for assignments in some contexts—a tradeoff described in Chapter 30 and mentioned in the context of the case study example we'll explore at the end of this chapter.

Avoiding loops in attribute interception methods

These methods are generally straightforward to use; their only substantially complex aspect is the potential for *looping* (a.k.a. recursing). Because __getattr__ is called for undefined attributes only, it can freely fetch other attributes within its own code. However, because __getattribute__ and __setattr__ are run for *all* attributes, their code needs to be careful when accessing other attributes to avoid calling themselves again and triggering a recursive loop.

For example, another attribute fetch run inside a __getattribute__ method's code will trigger __getattribute__ again, and the code will usually loop until memory is exhausted:

```
def __getattribute__(self, name):
    x = self.other                      # LOOPS!
```

Technically, this method is even more loop-prone than this may imply—a self attribute reference run *anywhere* in a class that defines this method will trigger __getattribute__, and also has the potential to loop depending on the class's logic. This is normally desired behavior—intercepting every attribute fetch is this method's purpose, after all—but you should be aware that this method catches all attribute fetches wherever they are coded. When coded within __getattribute__ itself, this almost always causes a loop. To avoid this loop, route the fetch through a higher superclass instead to skip this level's version—because the object class is always a new-style superclass, it serves well in this role:

```
def __getattribute__(self, name):
    x = object.__getattribute__(self, 'other')   # Force higher to avoid me
```

For __setattr__, the situation is similar, as summarized in Chapter 30—assigning *any* attribute inside this method triggers __setattr__ again and may create a similar loop:

```
def __setattr__(self, name, value):
    self.other = value                  # Recurs (and might LOOP!)
```

Here too, self attribute assignments *anywhere* in a class defining this method trigger __setattr__ as well, though the potential for looping is much stronger when they show up in __setattr__ itself. To work around this problem, you can assign the attribute as a key in the instance's __dict__ namespace dictionary instead. This avoids direct attribute assignment:

```
def __setattr__(self, name, value):
    self.__dict__['other'] = value      # Use attr dict to avoid me
```

Although it's a less traditional approach, __setattr__ can also pass its own attribute assignments to a higher superclass to avoid looping, just like __getattribute__ (and per the upcoming note, this scheme is sometimes preferred):

```
def __setattr__(self, name, value):
    object.__setattr__(self, 'other', value)     # Force higher to avoid me
```

By contrast, though, we *cannot* use the __dict__ trick to avoid loops in __getattribute__:

```
def __getattribute__(self, name):
    x = self.__dict__['other']                   # Loops!
```

Fetching the __dict__ attribute itself triggers __getattribute__ again, causing a recursive loop. Strange but true!

The __delattr__ method is less commonly used in practice, but when it is, it is called for every attribute deletion (just as __setattr__ is called for every attribute assignment). When using this method, you must take care to avoid loops when deleting attributes, by using the same techniques: namespace dictionaries operations or superclass method calls.

 As noted in Chapter 30, attributes implemented with new-style class features such as *slots* and *properties* are not physically stored in the instance's __dict__ namespace dictionary (and slots may even preclude its existence entirely). Because of this, code that wishes to support such attributes should code __setattr__ to assign with the object.__setattr__ scheme shown here, not by self.__dict__ indexing. Namespace __dict__ operations suffice for classes known to store data in instances, like this chapter's self-contained examples; general tools, though, should prefer object.

A First Example

Generic attribute management is not nearly as complicated as the prior section may have implied. To see how to put these ideas to work, here is the same first example we used for properties and descriptors in action again, this time implemented with attribute operator overloading methods. Because these methods are so generic, we test attribute names here to know when a managed attribute is being accessed; others are allowed to pass normally:

```
class Person:                          # Portable: 2.X or 3.X
    def __init__(self, name):          # On [Person()]
        self._name = name              # Triggers __setattr__!

    def __getattr__(self, attr):       # On [obj.undefined]
        print('get: ' + attr)
        if attr == 'name':             # Intercept name: not stored
            return self._name          # Does not loop: real attr
        else:                          # Others are errors
```

```
                raise AttributeError(attr)
        def __setattr__(self, attr, value):       # On [obj.any = value]
            print('set: ' + attr)
            if attr == 'name':
                attr = '_name'                     # Set internal name
            self.__dict__[attr] = value            # Avoid looping here

        def __delattr__(self, attr):               # On [del obj.any]
            print('del: ' + attr)
            if attr == 'name':
                attr = '_name'                     # Avoid looping here too
            del self.__dict__[attr]                # but much less common

bob = Person('Bob Smith')               # bob has a managed attribute
print(bob.name)                         # Runs __getattr__
bob.name = 'Robert Smith'               # Runs __setattr__
print(bob.name)
del bob.name                            # Runs __delattr__

print('-'*20)
sue = Person('Sue Jones')               # sue inherits property too
print(sue.name)
#print(Person.name.__doc__)             # No equivalent here
```

Notice that the attribute assignment in the __init__ constructor triggers __setattr__ too—this method catches *every* attribute assignment, even those anywhere within the class itself. When this code is run, the same output is produced, but this time it's the result of Python's normal operator overloading mechanism and our attribute interception methods:

```
c:\code> py -3 getattr-person.py
set: _name
get: name
Bob Smith
set: name
get: name
Robert Smith
del: name
--------------------
set: _name
get: name
Sue Jones
```

Also note that, unlike with properties and descriptors, there's no direct notion of specifying *documentation* for our attribute here; managed attributes exist within the code of our interception methods, not as distinct objects.

Using __getattribute__

To achieve exactly the same results with __getattribute__, replace __getattr__ in the example with the following; because it catches *all* attribute fetches, this version must be careful to avoid looping by passing new fetches to a superclass, and it can't generally assume unknown names are errors:

```
# Replace __getattr__ with this

def __getattribute__(self, attr):          # On [obj.any]
    print('get: ' + attr)
    if attr == 'name':                      # Intercept all names
        attr = '_name'                      # Map to internal name
    return object.__getattribute__(self, attr)   # Avoid looping here
```

When run with this change, the output is similar, but we get an extra __getattribute__ call for the fetch in __setattr__ (the first time originating in __init__):

```
c:\code> py -3 getattribute-person.py
set: _name
get: __dict__
get: name
Bob Smith
set: name
get: __dict__
get: name
Robert Smith
del: name
get: __dict__
--------------------
set: _name
get: __dict__
get: name
Sue Jones
```

This example is equivalent to that coded for properties and descriptors, but it's a bit artificial, and it doesn't really highlight these tools' assets. Because they are generic, __getattr__ and __getattribute__ are probably more commonly used in delegation-base code (as sketched earlier), where attribute access is validated and routed to an embedded object. Where just a *single* attribute must be managed, properties and descriptors might do as well or better.

Computed Attributes

As before, our prior example doesn't really do anything but trace attribute fetches; it's not much more work to compute an attribute's value when fetched. As for properties and descriptors, the following creates a virtual attribute X that runs a calculation when fetched:

```
class AttrSquare:
    def __init__(self, start):
        self.value = start          # Triggers __setattr__!

    def __getattr__(self, attr):     # On undefined attr fetch
        if attr == 'X':
            return self.value ** 2   # value is not undefined
        else:
```

```
                    raise AttributeError(attr)

        def __setattr__(self, attr, value):          # On all attr assignments
            if attr == 'X':
                attr = 'value'
            self.__dict__[attr] = value

A = AttrSquare(3)          # 2 instances of class with overloading
B = AttrSquare(32)         # Each has different state information

print(A.X)                 # 3 ** 2
A.X = 4
print(A.X)                 # 4 ** 2
print(B.X)                 # 32 ** 2 (1024)
```

Running this code results in the same output that we got earlier when using properties and descriptors, but this script's mechanics are based on generic attribute interception methods:

```
c:\code> py -3 getattr-computed.py
9
16
1024
```

Using __getattribute__

As before, we can achieve the same effect with __getattribute__ instead of __getattr__; the following replaces the fetch method with a __getattribute__ and changes the __setattr__ assignment method to avoid looping by using direct superclass method calls instead of __dict__ keys:

```
class AttrSquare:                              # Add (object) for 2.X
    def __init__(self, start):
        self.value = start                     # Triggers __setattr__!

    def __getattribute__(self, attr):          # On all attr fetches
        if attr == 'X':
            return self.value ** 2             # Triggers __getattribute__ again!
        else:
            return object.__getattribute__(self, attr)

    def __setattr__(self, attr, value):        # On all attr assignments
        if attr == 'X':
            attr = 'value'
        object.__setattr__(self, attr, value)
```

When this version, *getattribute-computed.py*, is run, the results are the same again. Notice, though, the implicit routing going on inside this class's methods:

- self.value=start inside the constructor triggers __setattr__
- self.value inside __getattribute__ triggers __getattribute__ again

In fact, __getattribute__ is run *twice* each time we fetch attribute X. This doesn't happen in the __getattr__ version, because the value attribute is not undefined. If you care about speed and want to avoid this, change __getattribute__ to use the superclass to fetch value as well:

```
def __getattribute__(self, attr):
    if attr == 'X':
        return object.__getattribute__(self, 'value') ** 2
```

Of course, this still incurs a call to the superclass method, but not an additional recursive call before we get there. Add print calls to these methods to trace how and when they run.

__getattr__ and __getattribute__ Compared

To summarize the coding differences between __getattr__ and __getattribute__, the following example uses both to implement three attributes—attr1 is a class attribute, attr2 is an instance attribute, and attr3 is a virtual managed attribute computed when fetched:

```
class GetAttr:
    attr1 = 1
    def __init__(self):
        self.attr2 = 2
    def __getattr__(self, attr):          # On undefined attrs only
        print('get: ' + attr)             # Not on attr1: inherited from class
        if attr == 'attr3':               # Not on attr2: stored on instance
            return 3
        else:
            raise AttributeError(attr)

X = GetAttr()
print(X.attr1)
print(X.attr2)
print(X.attr3)
print('-'*20)

class GetAttribute(object):               # (object) needed in 2.X only
    attr1 = 1
    def __init__(self):
        self.attr2 = 2
    def __getattribute__(self, attr):     # On all attr fetches
        print('get: ' + attr)             # Use superclass to avoid looping here
        if attr == 'attr3':
            return 3
        else:
            return object.__getattribute__(self, attr)

X = GetAttribute()
print(X.attr1)
print(X.attr2)
print(X.attr3)
```

When run, the __getattr__ version intercepts only attr3 accesses, because it is undefined. The __getattribute__ version, on the other hand, intercepts all attribute fetches
and must route those it does not manage to the superclass fetcher to avoid loops:

```
c:\code> py -3 getattr-v-getattr.py
1
2
get: attr3
3
--------------------
get: attr1
1
get: attr2
2
get: attr3
3
```

Although __getattribute__ can catch more attribute fetches than __getattr__, in practice they are often just variations on a theme—if attributes are not physically stored,
the two have the same effect.

Management Techniques Compared

To summarize the coding differences in all four attribute management schemes we've
seen in this chapter, let's quickly step through a somewhat more comprehensive com-
puted-attribute example using each technique, coded to run in either Python 3.X or
2.X. The following first version uses *properties* to intercept and calculate attributes
named square and cube. Notice how their base values are stored in names that begin
with an underscore, so they don't clash with the names of the properties themselves:

```
# Two dynamically computed attributes with properties

class Powers(object):                       # Need (object) in 2.X only
    def __init__(self, square, cube):
        self._square = square               # _square is the base value
        self._cube   = cube                 # square is the property name

    def getSquare(self):
        return self._square ** 2
    def setSquare(self, value):
        self._square = value
    square = property(getSquare, setSquare)

    def getCube(self):
        return self._cube ** 3
    cube = property(getCube)

X = Powers(3, 4)
print(X.square)        # 3 ** 2 = 9
print(X.cube)          # 4 ** 3 = 64
X.square = 5
print(X.square)        # 5 ** 2 = 25
```

To do the same with *descriptors*, we define the attributes with complete classes. Note that these descriptors store base values as instance state, so they must use leading underscores again so as not to clash with the names of descriptors; as we'll see in the final example of this chapter, we could avoid this renaming requirement by storing base values as descriptor state instead, but that doesn't as directly address data that must vary per client class instance:

```
# Same, but with descriptors (per-instance state)

class DescSquare(object):
    def __get__(self, instance, owner):
        return instance._square ** 2
    def __set__(self, instance, value):
        instance._square = value

class DescCube(object):
    def __get__(self, instance, owner):
        return instance._cube ** 3

class Powers(object):                          # Need all (object) in 2.X only
    square = DescSquare()
    cube   = DescCube()
    def __init__(self, square, cube):
        self._square = square                  # "self.square = square" works too,
        self._cube   = cube                    # because it triggers desc __set__!

X = Powers(3, 4)
print(X.square)        # 3 ** 2 = 9
print(X.cube)          # 4 ** 3 = 64
X.square = 5
print(X.square)        # 5 ** 2 = 25
```

To achieve the same result with __getattr__ fetch interception, we again store base values with underscore-prefixed names so that accesses to managed names are undefined and thus invoke our method; we also need to code a __setattr__ to intercept assignments, and take care to avoid its potential for looping:

```
# Same, but with generic __getattr__ undefined attribute interception

class Powers:
    def __init__(self, square, cube):
        self._square = square
        self._cube   = cube

    def __getattr__(self, name):
        if name == 'square':
            return self._square ** 2
        elif name == 'cube':
            return self._cube ** 3
        else:
            raise TypeError('unknown attr:' + name)

    def __setattr__(self, name, value):
        if name == 'square':
```

```
        self.__dict__['_square'] = value          # Or use object
    else:
        self.__dict__[name] = value

X = Powers(3, 4)
print(X.square)      # 3 ** 2 = 9
print(X.cube)        # 4 ** 3 = 64
X.square = 5
print(X.square)      # 5 ** 2 = 25
```

The final option, coding this with __getattribute__, is similar to the prior version. Because we catch every attribute now, though, we must also route base value fetches to a superclass to avoid looping or extra calls—fetching self._square directly works too, but runs a second __getattribute__ call:

```
# Same, but with generic __getattribute__ all attribute interception

class Powers(object):                                # Need (object) in 2.X only
    def __init__(self, square, cube):
        self._square = square
        self._cube   = cube

    def __getattribute__(self, name):
        if name == 'square':
            return object.__getattribute__(self, '_square') ** 2
        elif name == 'cube':
            return object.__getattribute__(self, '_cube') ** 3
        else:
            return object.__getattribute__(self, name)

    def __setattr__(self, name, value):
        if name == 'square':
            object.__setattr__(self, '_square', value)    # Or use __dict__
        else:
            object.__setattr__(self, name , value)

X = Powers(3, 4)
print(X.square)      # 3 ** 2 = 9
print(X.cube)        # 4 ** 3 = 64
X.square = 5
print(X.square)      # 5 ** 2 = 25
```

As you can see, each technique takes a different form in code, but all four produce the same result when run:

```
9
64
25
```

For more on how these alternatives compare, and other coding options, stay tuned for a more realistic application of them in the attribute validation example in the section "Example: Attribute Validations" on page 1256. First, though, we need to take a short side trip to study a new-style-class pitfall associated with two of these tools—the generic attribute interceptors presented in this section.

Intercepting Built-in Operation Attributes

If you've been reading this book linearly, some of this section is review and elaboration on material covered earlier, especially in Chapter 32. For others, this topic is presented in this chapter's context here.

When I introduced __getattr__ and __getattribute__, I stated that they intercept undefined and all attribute fetches, respectively, which makes them ideal for delegation-based coding patterns. While this is true for both *normally named* and *explicitly called* attributes, their behavior needs some additional clarification: for method-name attributes implicitly fetched by *built-in* operations, these methods may *not be run at all*. This means that operator overloading method calls cannot be delegated to wrapped objects unless wrapper classes somehow redefine these methods themselves.

For example, attribute fetches for the __str__, __add__, and __getitem__ methods run implicitly by printing, + expressions, and indexing, respectively, are not routed to the generic attribute interception methods in 3.X. Specifically:

- In Python 3.X, *neither* __getattr__ nor __getattribute__ is run for such attributes.
- In Python 2.X classic classes, __getattr__ *is* run for such attributes if they are undefined in the class.
- In Python 2.X, __getattribute__ is available for new-style classes only and works as it does in 3.X.

In other words, in all Python 3.X classes (and 2.X new-style classes), there is no direct way to generically intercept built-in operations like printing and addition. In Python 2.X's default classic classes, the methods such operations invoke are looked up at runtime in *instances*, like all other attributes; in Python 3.X's new-style classes such methods are looked up in *classes* instead. Since 3.X mandates new-style classes and 2.X defaults to classic, this is understandably attributed to 3.X, but it can happen in 2.X new-style code too. In 2.X, though, you at least have a way to avoid this change; in 3.X, you do not.

Per Chapter 32, the official (though tersely documented) rationale for this change appears to revolve around metaclasses and optimization of built-in operations. Regardless, given that all attributes—both normally named and others—still dispatch generically through the instance and these methods when accessed *explicitly* by name, this does not seem meant to preclude delegation in general; it seems more an optimization step for built-in operations' implicit behavior. This does, however, make delegation-based coding patterns more complex in 3.X, because object interface proxies cannot generically intercept operator overloading method calls and route them to an embedded object.

This is an inconvenience, but is not necessarily a showstopper—wrapper classes can work around this constraint by redefining all relevant operator overloading methods in the wrapper itself, in order to delegate calls. These extra methods can be added either manually, with tools, or by definition in and inheritance from common superclasses. This does, however, make object wrappers more work than they used to be when operator overloading methods are a part of a wrapped object's interface.

Keep in mind that this issue applies only to __getattr__ and __getattribute__. Because properties and descriptors are defined for specific attributes only, they don't really apply to delegation-based classes at all—a single property or descriptor cannot be used to intercept arbitrary attributes. Moreover, a class that defines *both* operator overloading methods and attribute interception will work correctly, regardless of the type of attribute interception defined. Our concern here is only with classes that do not have operator overloading methods defined, but try to intercept them generically.

Consider the following example, the file *getattr-bultins.py*, which tests various attribute types and built-in operations on instances of classes containing __getattr__ and __get attribute__ methods:

```
class GetAttr:
    eggs = 88                          # eggs stored on class, spam on instance
    def __init__(self):
        self.spam = 77
    def __len__(self):                 # len here, else __getattr__ called with __len__
        print('__len__: 42')
        return 42
    def __getattr__(self, attr):       # Provide __str__ if asked, else dummy func
        print('getattr: ' + attr)
        if attr == '__str__':
            return lambda *args: '[Getattr str]'
        else:
            return lambda *args: None

class GetAttribute(object):            # object required in 2.X, implied in 3.X
    eggs = 88                          # In 2.X all are isinstance(object) auto
    def __init__(self):                # But must derive to get new-style tools,
        self.spam = 77                 # incl __getattribute__, some __X__ defaults
    def __len__(self):
        print('__len__: 42')
        return 42
    def __getattribute__(self, attr):
        print('getattribute: ' + attr)
        if attr == '__str__':
            return lambda *args: '[GetAttribute str]'
        else:
            return lambda *args: None

for Class in GetAttr, GetAttribute:
    print('\n' + Class.__name__.ljust(50, '='))

    X = Class()
    X.eggs                             # Class attr
    X.spam                             # Instance attr
    X.other                            # Missing attr
    len(X)                             # __len__ defined explicitly
```

```
# New-styles must support [], +, call directly: redefine

    try:    X[0]                 # __getitem__?
    except: print('fail []')

    try:    X + 99               # __add__?
    except: print('fail +')

    try:    X()                  # __call__? (implicit via built-in)
    except: print('fail ()')

    X.__call__()                 # __call__? (explicit, not inherited)
    print(X.__str__())           # __str__? (explicit, inherited from type)
    print(X)                     # __str__? (implicit via built-in)
```

When run under Python 2.X as coded, __getattr__ *does* receive a variety of implicit attribute fetches for built-in operations, because Python looks up such attributes in instances normally. Conversely, __getattribute__ is *not* run for any of the operator overloading names invoked by built-in operations, because such names are looked up in classes only in the new-style class model:

```
c:\code> py -2 getattr-builtins.py
```

```
GetAttr==========================================
getattr: other
__len__: 42
getattr: __getitem__
getattr: __coerce__
getattr: __add__
getattr: __call__
getattr: __call__
getattr: __str__
[Getattr str]
getattr: __str__
[Getattr str]

GetAttribute=====================================
getattribute: eggs
getattribute: spam
getattribute: other
__len__: 42
fail []
fail +
fail ()
getattribute: __call__
getattribute: __str__
[GetAttribute str]
<__main__.GetAttribute object at 0x02287898>
```

Note how __getattr__ intercepts both implicit and explicit fetches of __call__ and __str__ in 2.X here. By contrast, __getattribute__ fails to catch implicit fetches of either attribute name for built-in operations.

Really, the __getattribute__ case is the same in 2.X as it is in 3.X, because in 2.X classes must be made new-style by deriving from object to use this method. This code's object derivation is optional in 3.X because all classes are new-style.

When run under Python 3.X, though, results for __getattr__ differ—*none* of the implicitly run operator overloading methods trigger *either* attribute interception method when their attributes are fetched by built-in operations. Python 3.X (and new-style classes in general) skips the normal instance lookup mechanism when resolving such names, though normally named methods are still intercepted as before:

```
c:\code> py -3 getattr-builtins.py
```

```
GetAttr===========================================
getattr: other
__len__: 42
fail []
fail +
fail ()
getattr: __call__
<__main__.GetAttr object at 0x02987CC0>
<__main__.GetAttr object at 0x02987CC0>

GetAttribute======================================
getattribute: eggs
getattribute: spam
getattribute: other
__len__: 42
fail []
fail +
fail ()
getattribute: __call__
getattribute: __str__
[GetAttribute str]
<__main__.GetAttribute object at 0x02987CF8>
```

Trace these outputs back to prints in the script to see how this works. Some highlights:

- __str__ access fails to be caught twice by __getattr__ in 3.X: once for the built-in print, and once for explicit fetches because a default is inherited from the class (really, from the built-in object, which is an automatic superclass to every class in 3.X).

- __str__ fails to be caught only once by the __getattribute__ catchall, during the built-in print operation; explicit fetches bypass the inherited version.

- __call__ fails to be caught in both schemes in 3.X for built-in call expressions, but it is intercepted by both when fetched explicitly; unlike __str__, there is no inherited __call__ default for object instances to defeat __getattr__.

- __len__ is caught by both classes, simply because it is an explicitly defined method in the classes themselves—though its name it is not routed to either __getattr__ or __getattribute__ in 3.X if we delete the class's __len__ methods.

- All other built-in operations fail to be intercepted by both schemes in 3.X.

Again, the net effect is that operator overloading methods implicitly run by built-in operations are never routed through either attribute interception method in 3.X: Python 3.X's new-style classes search for such attributes in *classes* and skip instance lookup entirely. Normally named attributes do not.

This makes delegation-based wrapper classes more difficult to code in 3.X's new-style classes—if wrapped classes may contain operator overloading methods, those methods must be redefined redundantly in the wrapper class in order to delegate to the wrapped object. In general delegation tools, this can add dozens of extra methods.

Of course, the addition of such methods can be partly automated by tools that augment classes with new methods (the class decorators and metaclasses of the next two chapters might help here). Moreover, a superclass might be able to define all these extra methods once, for inheritance in delegation-based classes. Still, delegation coding patterns require extra work in 3.X's classes.

For a more realistic illustration of this phenomenon as well as its workaround, see the Private decorator example in the following chapter. There, we'll explore alternatives for coding the operator methods required of proxies in 3.X's classes—including reusable *mix-in superclass* models. We'll also see there that it's possible to insert a __getattribute__ in the client class to retain its original type, although this method still won't be called for operator overloading methods; printing still runs a __str__ defined in such a class directly, for example, instead of routing the request through __getattribute__.

As a more realistic example of this, the next section resurrects our class tutorial example. Now that you understand how attribute interception works, I'll be able to explain one of its stranger bits.

Delegation-based managers revisited

The object-oriented tutorial of Chapter 28 presented a Manager class that used object embedding and method delegation to customize its superclass, rather than inheritance. Here is the code again for reference, with some irrelevant testing removed:

```python
class Person:
    def __init__(self, name, job=None, pay=0):
        self.name = name
        self.job  = job
        self.pay  = pay
    def lastName(self):
        return self.name.split()[-1]
    def giveRaise(self, percent):
        self.pay = int(self.pay * (1 + percent))
    def __repr__(self):
        return '[Person: %s, %s]' % (self.name, self.pay)

class Manager:
    def __init__(self, name, pay):
        self.person = Person(name, 'mgr', pay)    # Embed a Person object
    def giveRaise(self, percent, bonus=.10):
```

```
            self.person.giveRaise(percent + bonus)        # Intercept and delegate
        def __getattr__(self, attr):
            return getattr(self.person, attr)              # Delegate all other attrs
        def __repr__(self):
            return str(self.person)                        # Must overload again (in 3.X)

if __name__ == '__main__':
    sue = Person('Sue Jones', job='dev', pay=100000)
    print(sue.lastName())
    sue.giveRaise(.10)
    print(sue)
    tom = Manager('Tom Jones', 50000)        # Manager.__init__
    print(tom.lastName())                    # Manager.__getattr__ -> Person.lastName
    tom.giveRaise(.10)                       # Manager.giveRaise -> Person.giveRaise
    print(tom)                               # Manager.__repr__ -> Person.__repr__
```

Comments at the end of this file show which methods are invoked for a line's operation. In particular, notice how `lastName` calls are undefined in `Manager`, and thus are routed into the generic `__getattr__` and from there on to the embedded `Person` object. Here is the script's output—Sue receives a 10% raise from `Person`, but Tom gets 20% because `giveRaise` is customized in `Manager`:

```
c:\code> py -3 getattr-delegate.py
Jones
[Person: Sue Jones, 110000]
Jones
[Person: Tom Jones, 60000]
```

By contrast, though, notice what occurs when we *print* a `Manager` at the end of the script: the wrapper class's `__repr__` is invoked, and it delegates to the embedded `Person` object's `__repr__`. With that in mind, watch what happens if we *delete* the `Manager.__repr__` method in this code:

```
# Delete the Manager __str__ method

class Manager:
    def __init__(self, name, pay):
        self.person = Person(name, 'mgr', pay)         # Embed a Person object
    def giveRaise(self, percent, bonus=.10):
        self.person.giveRaise(percent + bonus)         # Intercept and delegate
    def __getattr__(self, attr):
        return getattr(self.person, attr)              # Delegate all other attrs
```

Now printing does *not* route its attribute fetch through the generic `__getattr__` interceptor under Python 3.X's new-style classes for `Manager` objects. Instead, a default `__repr__` display method inherited from the class's implicit `object` superclass is looked up and run (`sue` still prints correctly, because `Person` has an explicit `__repr__`):

```
c:\code> py -3 getattr-delegate.py
Jones
[Person: Sue Jones, 110000]
Jones
<__main__.Manager object at 0x029E7B70>
```

As coded, running without a __repr__ like this *does* trigger __getattr__ in Python 2.X's default classic classes, because operator overloading attributes are routed through this method, and such classes do not inherit a default for __repr__:

```
c:\code> py -2 getattr-delegate.py
Jones
[Person: Sue Jones, 110000]
Jones
[Person: Tom Jones, 60000]
```

Switching to __getattribute__ won't help 3.X here either—like __getattr__, it is *not* run for operator overloading attributes implied by built-in operations in either Python 2.X or 3.X:

```
# Replace __getattr__ with __getattribute__

class Manager(object):                                    # Use "(object)" in 2.X
    def __init__(self, name, pay):
        self.person = Person(name, 'mgr', pay)            # Embed a Person object
    def giveRaise(self, percent, bonus=.10):
        self.person.giveRaise(percent + bonus)            # Intercept and delegate
    def __getattribute__(self, attr):
        print('**', attr)
        if attr in ['person', 'giveRaise']:
            return object.__getattribute__(self, attr)    # Fetch my attrs
        else:
            return getattr(self.person, attr)             # Delegate all others
```

Regardless of which attribute interception method is used in 3.X, we still must include a redefined __repr__ in Manager (as shown previously) in order to intercept printing operations and route them to the embedded Person object:

```
C:\code> py -3 getattr-delegate.py
Jones
[Person: Sue Jones, 110000]
** lastName
** person
Jones
** giveRaise
** person
<__main__.Manager object at 0x028E0590>
```

Notice that __getattribute__ gets called *twice* here for methods—once for the method name, and again for the self.person embedded object fetch. We could avoid that with a different coding, but we would still have to redefine __repr__ to catch printing, albeit differently here (self.person would cause this __getattribute__ to fail):

```
# Code __getattribute__ differently to minimize extra calls

class Manager:
    def __init__(self, name, pay):
        self.person = Person(name, 'mgr', pay)
    def __getattribute__(self, attr):
        print('**', attr)
        person = object.__getattribute__(self, 'person')
```

```
            if attr == 'giveRaise':
                return lambda percent: person.giveRaise(percent+.10)
            else:
                return getattr(person, attr)
    def __repr__(self):
        person = object.__getattribute__(self, 'person')
        return str(person)
```

When this alternative runs, our object prints properly, but only because we've added an explicit __repr__ in the wrapper—this attribute is still not routed to our generic attribute interception method:

```
Jones
[Person: Sue Jones, 110000]
** lastName
Jones
** giveRaise
[Person: Tom Jones, 60000]
```

The short story here is that delegation-based classes like Manager must redefine some operator overloading methods (like __repr__ and __str__) to route them to embedded objects in Python 3.X, but not in Python 2.X unless new-style classes are used. Our only direct options seem to be using __getattr__ and Python 2.X, or redefining operator overloading methods in wrapper classes redundantly in 3.X.

Again, this isn't an impossible task; many wrappers can predict the set of operator overloading methods required, and tools and superclasses can automate part of this task—in fact, we'll study coding patterns that can fill this need in the next chapter. Moreover, not all classes use operator overloading methods (indeed, most application classes usually should not). It is, however, something to keep in mind for delegation coding models used in Python 3.X; when operator overloading methods are part of an object's interface, wrappers must accommodate them portably by redefining them locally.

Example: Attribute Validations

To close out this chapter, let's turn to a more realistic example, coded in all four of our attribute management schemes. The example we will use defines a CardHolder object with four attributes, three of which are managed. The managed attributes validate or transform values when fetched or stored. All four versions produce the same results for the same test code, but they implement their attributes in very different ways. The examples are included largely for self-study; although I won't go through their code in detail, they all use concepts we've already explored in this chapter.

Using Properties to Validate

Our first coding in the file that follows uses properties to manage three attributes. As usual, we could use simple methods instead of managed attributes, but properties help if we have been using attributes in existing code already. Properties run code automatically on attribute access, but are focused on a specific set of attributes; they cannot be used to intercept all attributes generically.

To understand this code, it's crucial to notice that the attribute assignments inside the __init__ constructor method trigger property setter methods too. When this method assigns to self.name, for example, it automatically invokes the setName method, which transforms the value and assigns it to an instance attribute called __name so it won't clash with the property's name.

This renaming (sometimes called *name mangling*) is necessary because properties use common instance state and have none of their own. Data is stored in an attribute called __name, and the attribute called name is always a property, not data. As we saw in Chapter 31, names like __name are known as *pseudoprivate* attributes, and are changed by Python to include the enclosing class's name when stored in the instance's namespace; here, this helps keep the implementation-specific attributes distinct from others, including that of the property that manages them.

In the end, this class manages attributes called name, age, and acct; allows the attribute addr to be accessed directly; and provides a read-only attribute called remain that is entirely virtual and computed on demand. For comparison purposes, this property-based coding weighs in at 39 lines of code, not counting its two initial lines, and includes the object derivation required in 2.X but optional in 3.X:

```
# File validate_properties.py

class CardHolder(object):                              # Need "(object)" for setter in 2.X
    acctlen = 8                                        # Class data
    retireage = 59.5

    def __init__(self, acct, name, age, addr):
        self.acct = acct                               # Instance data
        self.name = name                               # These trigger prop setters too!
        self.age  = age                                # __X mangled to have class name
        self.addr = addr                               # addr is not managed
                                                       # remain has no data
    def getName(self):
        return self.__name
    def setName(self, value):
        value = value.lower().replace(' ', '_')
        self.__name = value
    name = property(getName, setName)

    def getAge(self):
        return self.__age
    def setAge(self, value):
        if value < 0 or value > 150:
            raise ValueError('invalid age')
        else:
            self.__age = value
    age = property(getAge, setAge)
```

```
    def getAcct(self):
        return self.__acct[:-3] + '***'
    def setAcct(self, value):
        value = value.replace('-', '')
        if len(value) != self.acctlen:
            raise TypeError('invald acct number')
        else:
            self.__acct = value
    acct = property(getAcct, setAcct)

    def remainGet(self):                     # Could be a method, not attr
        return self.retireage - self.age     # Unless already using as attr
    remain = property(remainGet)
```

Testing code

The following code, *validate_tester.py*, tests our class; run this script with the name of the class's module (sans ".py") as a single command-line argument (you could also add most of its test code to the bottom of each file, or interactively import it from a module after importing the class). We'll use this same testing code for all four versions of this example. When it runs, it makes two instances of our managed-attribute class and fetches and changes their various attributes. Operations expected to fail are wrapped in try statements, and identical behavior on 2.X is supported by enabling the 3.X print function:

```
# File validate_tester.py
from __future__ import print_function # 2.X

def loadclass():
    import sys, importlib
    modulename = sys.argv[1]                              # Module name in command line
    module = importlib.import_module(modulename)          # Import module by name string
    print('[Using: %s]' % module.CardHolder)             # No need for getattr() here
    return module.CardHolder

def printholder(who):
    print(who.acct, who.name, who.age, who.remain, who.addr, sep=' / ')

if __name__ == '__main__':
    CardHolder = loadclass()
    bob = CardHolder('1234-5678', 'Bob Smith', 40, '123 main st')
    printholder(bob)
    bob.name = 'Bob Q. Smith'
    bob.age  = 50
    bob.acct = '23-45-67-89'
    printholder(bob)

    sue = CardHolder('5678-12-34', 'Sue Jones', 35, '124 main st')
    printholder(sue)
    try:
        sue.age = 200
    except:
        print('Bad age for Sue')
```

```
    try:
        sue.remain = 5
    except:
        print("Can't set sue.remain")

    try:
        sue.acct = '1234567'
    except:
        print('Bad acct for Sue')
```

Here is the output of our self-test code on both Python 3.X and 2.X; again, this is the same for all versions of this example, except for the tested class's name. Trace through this code to see how the class's methods are invoked; accounts are displayed with some digits hidden, names are converted to a standard format, and time remaining until retirement is computed when fetched using a class attribute cutoff:

```
c:\code> py -3 validate_tester.py validate_properties
[Using: <class 'validate_properties.CardHolder'>]
12345*** / bob_smith / 40 / 19.5 / 123 main st
23456*** / bob_q._smith / 50 / 9.5 / 123 main st
56781*** / sue_jones / 35 / 24.5 / 124 main st
Bad age for Sue
Can't set sue.remain
Bad acct for Sue
```

Using Descriptors to Validate

Now, let's recode our example using *descriptors* instead of properties. As we've seen, descriptors are very similar to properties in terms of functionality and roles; in fact, properties are basically a restricted form of descriptor. Like properties, descriptors are designed to handle specific attributes, not generic attribute access. Unlike properties, descriptors can also have their own state, and are a more general scheme.

Option 1: Validating with shared descriptor instance state

To understand the following code, it's again important to notice that the attribute assignments inside the __init__ constructor method trigger descriptor __set__ methods. When the constructor method assigns to self.name, for example, it automatically invokes the Name.__set__() method, which transforms the value and assigns it to a descriptor attribute called name.

In the end, this class implements the same attributes as the prior version: it manages attributes called name, age, and acct; allows the attribute addr to be accessed directly; and provides a read-only attribute called remain that is entirely virtual and computed on demand. Notice how we must catch assignments to the remain name in its descriptor and raise an exception; as we learned earlier, if we did not do this, assigning to this attribute of an instance would silently create an instance attribute that hides the class attribute descriptor.

For comparison purposes, this descriptor-based coding takes 45 lines of code; I've added the required `object` derivation to the main descriptor classes for 2.X compatibility (they can be omitted for code to be run in 3.X only, but don't hurt in 3.X, and aid portability if present):

```python
# File validate_descriptors1.py: using shared descriptor state

class CardHolder(object):                      # Need all "(object)" in 2.X only
    acctlen = 8                                # Class data
    retireage = 59.5

    def __init__(self, acct, name, age, addr):
        self.acct = acct                       # Instance data
        self.name = name                       # These trigger __set__ calls too!
        self.age  = age                        # __X not needed: in descriptor
        self.addr = addr                       # addr is not managed
                                               # remain has no data
    class Name(object):
        def __get__(self, instance, owner):    # Class names: CardHolder locals
            return self.name
        def __set__(self, instance, value):
            value = value.lower().replace(' ', '_')
            self.name = value
    name = Name()

    class Age(object):
        def __get__(self, instance, owner):
            return self.age                    # Use descriptor data
        def __set__(self, instance, value):
            if value < 0 or value > 150:
                raise ValueError('invalid age')
            else:
                self.age = value
    age = Age()

    class Acct(object):
        def __get__(self, instance, owner):
            return self.acct[:-3] + '***'
        def __set__(self, instance, value):
            value = value.replace('-', '')
            if len(value) != instance.acctlen:  # Use instance class data
                raise TypeError('invald acct number')
            else:
                self.acct = value
    acct = Acct()

    class Remain(object):
        def __get__(self, instance, owner):
            return instance.retireage - instance.age   # Triggers Age.__get__
        def __set__(self, instance, value):
            raise TypeError('cannot set remain')       # Else set allowed here
    remain = Remain()
```

When run with the prior testing script, all examples in this section produce the same output as shown for properties earlier, except that the name of the class in the first line varies:

```
C:\code> python validate_tester.py validate_descriptors1
...same output as properties, except class name...
```

Option 2: Validating with per-client-instance state

Unlike in the prior property-based variant, though, in this case the actual name value is attached to the *descriptor* object, not the client class instance. Although we could store this value in either instance or descriptor state, the latter avoids the need to mangle names with underscores to avoid collisions. In the CardHolder client class, the attribute called name is always a descriptor object, not data.

Importantly, the downside of this scheme is that state stored inside a descriptor itself is class-level data that is effectively *shared* by all client class instances, and so cannot vary between them. That is, storing state in the *descriptor* instance instead of the *owner* (client) class instance means that the state will be the same in all owner class instances. Descriptor state can vary only per attribute appearance.

To see this at work, in the preceding descriptor-based CardHolder example, try printing attributes of the bob instance after creating the second instance, sue. The values of sue's managed attributes (name, age, and acct) *overwrite* those of the earlier object bob, because both share the same, single descriptor instance attached to their class:

```
# File validate_tester2.py
from __future__ import print_function # 2.X

from validate_tester import loadclass
CardHolder = loadclass()

bob = CardHolder('1234-5678', 'Bob Smith', 40, '123 main st')
print('bob:', bob.name, bob.acct, bob.age, bob.addr)

sue = CardHolder('5678-12-34', 'Sue Jones', 35, '124 main st')
print('sue:', sue.name, sue.acct, sue.age, sue.addr)    # addr differs: client data
print('bob:', bob.name, bob.acct, bob.age, bob.addr)    # name,acct,age overwritten?
```

The results confirm the suspicion—in terms of managed attributes, bob has morphed into sue!

```
c:\code> py -3 validate_tester2.py validate_descriptors1
[Using: <class 'validate_descriptors1.CardHolder'>]
bob: bob_smith 12345*** 40 123 main st
sue: sue_jones 56781*** 35 124 main st
bob: sue_jones 56781*** 35 123 main st
```

There are valid uses for descriptor state, of course—to manage descriptor implementation and data that spans all instance—and this code was implemented to illustrate the technique. Moreover, the state scope implications of class versus instance attributes should be more or less a given at this point in the book.

However, in this particular use case, attributes of `CardHolder` objects are probably better stored as *per-instance* data instead of descriptor instance data, perhaps using the same __X naming convention as the property-based equivalent to avoid name clashes in the instance—a more important factor this time, as the client is a different class with its own state attributes. Here are the required coding changes; it doesn't change line counts (we're still at 45):

```python
# File validate_descriptors2.py: using per-client-instance state

class CardHolder(object):                       # Need all "(object)" in 2.X only
    acctlen = 8                                 # Class data
    retireage = 59.5

    def __init__(self, acct, name, age, addr):
        self.acct = acct                        # Client instance data
        self.name = name                        # These trigger __set__ calls too!
        self.age  = age                         #  __X needed: in client instance
        self.addr = addr                        # addr is not managed
                                                # remain managed but has no data
    class Name(object):
        def __get__(self, instance, owner):     # Class names: CardHolder locals
            return instance.__name
        def __set__(self, instance, value):
            value = value.lower().replace(' ', '_')
            instance.__name = value
    name = Name()                               # class.name vs mangled attr

    class Age(object):
        def __get__(self, instance, owner):
            return instance.__age               # Use descriptor data
        def __set__(self, instance, value):
            if value < 0 or value > 150:
                raise ValueError('invalid age')
            else:
                instance.__age = value
    age = Age()                                 # class.age vs mangled attr

    class Acct(object):
        def __get__(self, instance, owner):
            return instance.__acct[:-3] + '***'
        def __set__(self, instance, value):
            value = value.replace('-', '')
            if len(value) != instance.acctlen:  # Use instance class data
                raise TypeError('invald acct number')
            else:
                instance.__acct = value
    acct = Acct()                               # class.acct vs mangled name

    class Remain(object):
        def __get__(self, instance, owner):
            return instance.retireage - instance.age    # Triggers Age.__get__
        def __set__(self, instance, value):
            raise TypeError('cannot set remain')        # Else set allowed here
    remain = Remain()
```

This supports per-instance data for the name, age, and acct managed fields as expected (bob remains bob), and other tests work as before:

```
c:\code> py -3 validate_tester2.py validate_descriptors2
[Using: <class 'validate_descriptors2.CardHolder'>]
bob: bob_smith 12345*** 40 123 main st
sue: sue_jones 56781*** 35 124 main st
bob: bob_smith 12345*** 40 123 main st

c:\code> py -3 validate_tester.py validate_descriptors2
...same output as properties, except class name...
```

One small caveat here: as coded, this version doesn't support *through-class* descriptor access, because such access passes a None to the instance argument (also notice the attribute __*X* name mangling to _Name__name in the error message when the fetch attempt is made):

```
>>> from validate_descriptors1 import CardHolder
>>> bob = CardHolder('1234-5678', 'Bob Smith', 40, '123 main st')
>>> bob.name
'bob_smith'
>>> CardHolder.name
'bob_smith'

>>> from validate_descriptors2 import CardHolder
>>> bob = CardHolder('1234-5678', 'Bob Smith', 40, '123 main st')
>>> bob.name
'bob_smith'
>>> CardHolder.name
AttributeError: 'NoneType' object has no attribute '_Name__name'
```

We could detect this with a minor amount of additional code to trigger the error more explicitly, but there's probably no point—because this version stores data in the *client instance*, there's no meaning to its descriptors unless they're accompanied by a client instance (much like a normal unbound instance method). In fact, that's really the entire point of this version's change!

Because they are classes, descriptors are a useful and powerful tool, but they present choices that can deeply impact a program's behavior. As always in OOP, choose your state retention policies carefully.

Using __getattr__ to Validate

As we've seen, the __getattr__ method intercepts all undefined attributes, so it can be more generic than using properties or descriptors. For our example, we simply test the attribute name to know when a managed attribute is being fetched; others are stored physically on the instance and so never reach __getattr__. Although this approach is more general than using properties or descriptors, extra work may be required to imitate the specific-attribute focus of other tools. We need to check names at runtime, and we must code a __setattr__ in order to intercept and validate attribute assignments.

As for the property and descriptor versions of this example, it's critical to notice that the attribute assignments inside the __init__ constructor method trigger the class's __setattr__ method too. When this method assigns to self.name, for example, it automatically invokes the __setattr__ method, which transforms the value and assigns it to an instance attribute called name. By storing name on the instance, it ensures that future accesses will not trigger __getattr__. In contrast, acct is stored as _acct, so that later accesses to acct do invoke __getattr__.

In the end, this class, like the prior two, manages attributes called name, age, and acct; allows the attribute addr to be accessed directly; and provides a read-only attribute called remain that is entirely virtual and is computed on demand.

For comparison purposes, this alternative comes in at 32 lines of code—7 fewer than the property-based version, and 13 fewer than the version using descriptors. Clarity matters more than code size, of course, but extra code can sometimes imply extra development and maintenance work. Probably more important here are *roles*: generic tools like __getattr__ may be better suited to generic delegation, while properties and descriptors are more directly designed to manage specific attributes.

Also note that the code here incurs *extra calls* when setting unmanaged attributes (e.g., addr), although no extra calls are incurred for fetching unmanaged attributes, since they are defined. Though this will likely result in negligible overhead for most programs, the more narrowly focused *properties* and *descriptors* incur an extra call only when managed attributes are accessed, and also appear in dir results when needed by generic tools.

Here's the __getattr__ version of our validations code:

```
# File validate_getattr.py

class CardHolder:
    acctlen = 8                                      # Class data
    retireage = 59.5

    def __init__(self, acct, name, age, addr):
        self.acct = acct                             # Instance data
        self.name = name                             # These trigger __setattr__ too
        self.age  = age                              # _acct not mangled: name tested
        self.addr = addr                             # addr is not managed
                                                     # remain has no data
    def __getattr__(self, name):
        if name == 'acct':                           # On undefined attr fetches
            return self._acct[:-3] + '***'           # name, age, addr are defined
        elif name == 'remain':
            return self.retireage - self.age         # Doesn't trigger __getattr__
        else:
            raise AttributeError(name)

    def __setattr__(self, name, value):
        if name == 'name':                           # On all attr assignments
            value = value.lower().replace(' ', '_')  # addr stored directly
```

```
        elif name == 'age':                          # acct mangled to _acct
            if value < 0 or value > 150:
                raise ValueError('invalid age')
        elif name == 'acct':
            name  = '_acct'
            value = value.replace('-', '')
            if len(value) != self.acctlen:
                raise TypeError('invald acct number')
        elif name == 'remain':
            raise TypeError('cannot set remain')
        self.__dict__[name] = value                  # Avoid looping (or via object)
```

When this code is run with either test script, it produces the same output (with a different class name):

```
c:\code> py -3 validate_tester.py validate_getattr
...same output as properties, except class name...

c:\code> py -3 validate_tester2.py validate_getattr
...same output as instance-state descriptors, except class name...
```

Using __getattribute__ to Validate

Our final variant uses the __getattribute__ catchall to intercept attribute fetches and manage them as needed. Every attribute fetch is caught here, so we test the attribute names to detect managed attributes and route all others to the superclass for normal fetch processing. This version uses the same __setattr__ to catch assignments as the prior version.

The code works very much like the __getattr__ version, so I won't repeat the full description here. Note, though, that because *every* attribute fetch is routed to __getattribute__, we don't need to mangle names to intercept them here (acct is stored as acct). On the other hand, this code must take care to route nonmanaged attribute fetches to a superclass to avoid looping or extra calls.

Also notice that this version incurs extra calls for both setting and fetching unmanaged attributes (e.g., addr); if speed is paramount, this alternative may be the slowest of the bunch. For comparison purposes, this version amounts to 32 lines of code, just like the prior version, and includes the requisite object derivation for 2.X compatibility; like properties and descriptors, __getattribute__ is a new-style class tool:

```
# File validate_getattribute.py

class CardHolder(object):                       # Need "(object)" in 2.X only
    acctlen = 8                                 # Class data
    retireage = 59.5

    def __init__(self, acct, name, age, addr):
        self.acct = acct                        # Instance data
        self.name = name                        # These trigger __setattr__ too
        self.age  = age                         # acct not mangled: name tested
        self.addr = addr                        # addr is not managed
```

```
                                                           # remain has no data
    def __getattribute__(self, name):
        superget = object.__getattribute__          # Don't loop: one level up
        if name == 'acct':                          # On all attr fetches
            return superget(self, 'acct')[:-3] + '***'
        elif name == 'remain':
            return superget(self, 'retireage') - superget(self, 'age')
        else:
            return superget(self, name)             # name, age, addr: stored

    def __setattr__(self, name, value):
        if name == 'name':                          # On all attr assignments
            value = value.lower().replace(' ', '_')  # addr stored directly
        elif name == 'age':
            if value < 0 or value > 150:
                raise ValueError('invalid age')
        elif name == 'acct':
            value = value.replace('-', '')
            if len(value) != self.acctlen:
                raise TypeError('invald acct number')
        elif name == 'remain':
            raise TypeError('cannot set remain')
        self.__dict__[name] = value                 # Avoid loops, orig names
```

Both the getattr and getattribute scripts work the same as the property and per-client-instance descriptor versions, when run by both tester scripts on either 2.X or 3.X.—*four ways to achieve the same goal in Python*, though they vary in structure, and are perhaps less redundant in some other roles. Be sure to study and run this section's code on your own for more pointers on managed attribute coding techniques.

Chapter Summary

This chapter covered the various techniques for managing access to attributes in Python, including the __getattr__ and __getattribute__ operator overloading methods, class properties, and class attribute descriptors. Along the way, it compared and contrasted these tools and presented a handful of use cases to demonstrate their behavior.

Chapter 39 continues our tool-building survey with a look at *decorators*—code run automatically at function and class creation time, rather than on attribute access. Before we continue, though, let's work through a set of questions to review what we've covered here.

Test Your Knowledge: Quiz

1. How do __getattr__ and __getattribute__ differ?
2. How do properties and descriptors differ?
3. How are properties and decorators related?

4. What are the main functional differences between __getattr__ and __getattri
   bute__ and properties and descriptors?

5. Isn't all this feature comparison just a kind of argument?

Test Your Knowledge: Answers

1. The __getattr__ method is run for fetches of *undefined* attributes only (i.e., those
   not present on an instance and not inherited from any of its classes). By contrast,
   the __getattribute__ method is called for *every* attribute fetch, whether the attribute is defined or not. Because of this, code inside a __getattr__ can freely fetch
   other attributes if they are defined, whereas __getattribute__ must use special code
   for all such attribute fetches to avoid looping or extra calls (it must route fetches
   to a superclass to skip itself).

2. Properties serve a specific role, while descriptors are more general. Properties define
   get, set, and delete functions for a specific attribute; descriptors provide a class
   with methods for these actions, too, but they provide extra flexibility to support
   more arbitrary actions. In fact, properties are really a simple way to create a specific
   kind of descriptor—one that runs functions on attribute accesses. Coding differs
   too: a property is created with a built-in function, and a descriptor is coded with
   a class; thus, descriptors can leverage all the usual OOP features of classes, such
   as inheritance. Moreover, in addition to the instance's state information, descriptors have local state of their own, so they can sometimes avoid name collisions in
   the instance.

3. Properties can be coded with decorator syntax. Because the `property` built-in accepts a single function argument, it can be used directly as a function decorator to
   define a fetch access property. Due to the name rebinding behavior of decorators,
   the name of the decorated function is assigned to a property whose get accessor is
   set to the original function decorated (`name = property(name)`). Property `setter`
   and `deleter` attributes allow us to further add set and delete accessors with decoration syntax—they set the accessor to the decorated function and return the augmented property.

4. The __getattr__ and __getattribute__ methods are more generic: they can be used
   to catch arbitrarily many attributes. In contrast, each property or descriptor provides access interception for only one *specific* attribute—we can't catch every attribute fetch with a single property or descriptor. On the other hand, properties
   and descriptors handle both attribute fetch and *assignment* by design: __get
   attr__ and __getattribute__ handle fetches only; to intercept assignments as well,
   __setattr__ must also be coded. The implementation is also different: __get
   attr__ and __getattribute__ are operator overloading methods, whereas properties and descriptors are objects manually assigned to class attributes. Unlike the
   others, properties and descriptors can also sometimes avoid extra calls on assignment to unmanaged names, and show up in `dir` results automatically, but are also

narrower in scope—they can't address generic dispatch goals. In Python evolution, new features tend to offer alternatives, but do not fully subsume what came before.

5. No it isn't. To quote from Python namesake *Monty Python's Flying Circus*:

An argument is a connected series of statements intended to establish a proposition.
No it isn't.
Yes it is! It's not just contradiction.
Look, if I argue with you, I must take up a contrary position.
Yes, but that's not just saying "No it isn't."
Yes it is!
No it isn't!
Yes it is!
No it isn't. Argument is an intellectual process. Contradiction is just the automatic gainsaying of any statement the other person makes.
(short pause) No it isn't.
It is.
Not at all.
Now look...

Decorators

In the advanced class topics chapter of this book (Chapter 32), we met static and class methods, took a quick look at the @ decorator syntax Python offers for declaring them, and previewed decorator coding techniques. We also met function decorators briefly in Chapter 38, while exploring the `property` built-in's ability to serve as one, and in Chapter 29 while studying the notion of abstract superclasses.

This chapter picks up where this previous decorator coverage left off. Here, we'll dig deeper into the inner workings of decorators and study more advanced ways to code new decorators ourselves. As we'll see, many of the concepts we studied earlier—especially state retention—show up regularly in decorators.

This is a somewhat advanced topic, and decorator construction tends to be of more interest to tool builders than to application programmers. Still, given that decorators are becoming increasingly common in popular Python frameworks, a basic understanding can help demystify their role, even if you're just a decorator user.

Besides covering decorator construction details, this chapter serves as a more realistic *case study* of Python in action. Because its examples grow somewhat larger than most of the others we've seen in this book, they better illustrate how code comes together into more complete systems and tools. As an extra perk, some of the code we'll write here may be used as general-purpose tools in your day-to-day programs.

What's a Decorator?

Decoration is a way to specify management or augmentation code for functions and classes. Decorators themselves take the form of callable objects (e.g., functions) that process other callable objects. As we saw earlier in this book, Python decorators come in two related flavors, neither of which requires 3.X or new-style classes:

- *Function decorators*, added in Python 2.4, do name rebinding at function definition time, providing a layer of logic that can manage functions and methods, or later calls to them.

- *Class decorators*, added in Python 2.6 and 3.0, do name rebinding at class definition time, providing a layer of logic that can manage classes, or the instances created by later calls to them.

In short, decorators provide a way to insert *automatically run code* at the end of function and class definition statements—at the end of a `def` for function decorators, and at the end of a `class` for class decorators. Such code can play a variety of roles, as described in the following sections.

Managing Calls and Instances

In typical use, this automatically run code may be used to augment calls to functions and classes. It arranges this by installing *wrapper* (a.k.a. *proxy*) objects to be invoked later:

Call proxies
> Function decorators install wrapper objects to intercept later *function calls* and process them as needed, usually passing the call on to the original function to run the managed action.

Interface proxies
> Class decorators install wrapper objects to intercept later *instance creation calls* and process them as required, usually passing the call on to the original class to create a managed instance.

Decorators achieve these effects by automatically rebinding function and class names to other callables, at the end of `def` and `class` statements. When later invoked, these callables can perform tasks such as tracing and timing function calls, managing access to class instance attributes, and so on.

Managing Functions and Classes

Although most examples in this chapter deal with using wrappers to intercept later calls to functions and classes, this is not the only way decorators can be used:

Function managers
> Function decorators can also be used to manage *function objects*, instead of or in addition to later calls to them—to register a function to an API, for instance. Our primary focus here, though, will be on their more commonly used call wrapper application.

Class managers
> Class decorators can also be used to manage *class objects* directly, instead of or in addition to instance creation calls—to augment a class with new methods, for example. Because this role intersects strongly with that of *metaclasses*, we'll see additional use cases in the next chapter. As we'll find, both tools run at the end of the class creation process, but class decorators often offer a lighter-weight solution.

In other words, function decorators can be used to manage both function calls and function objects, and class decorators can be used to manage both class instances and classes themselves. By returning the decorated object itself instead of a wrapper, decorators become a simple post-creation step for functions and classes.

Regardless of the role they play, decorators provide a convenient and explicit way to code tools useful both during program development and in live production systems.

Using and Defining Decorators

Depending on your job description, you might encounter decorators as a user or a provider (you might also be a maintainer, but that just means you straddle the fence). As we've seen, Python itself comes with built-in decorators that have specialized roles —static and class method declaration, property creation, and more. In addition, many popular Python toolkits include decorators to perform tasks such as managing database or user-interface logic. In such cases, we can get by without knowing how the decorators are coded.

For more general tasks, programmers can code arbitrary decorators of their own. For example, function decorators may be used to augment functions with code that adds call tracing or logging, performs argument validity testing during debugging, automatically acquires and releases thread locks, times calls made to functions for optimization, and so on. Any behavior you can imagine adding to—really, wrapping around—a function call is a candidate for custom function decorators.

On the other hand, function decorators are designed to augment only a specific function or method *call*, not an entire *object interface*. Class decorators fill the latter role better —because they can intercept instance creation calls, they can be used to implement arbitrary object interface augmentation or management tasks. For example, custom class decorators can trace, validate, or otherwise augment every attribute reference made for an object. They can also be used to implement proxy objects, singleton classes, and other common coding patterns. In fact, we'll find that many class decorators bear a strong resemblance to—and in fact are a prime application of—the *delegation* coding pattern we met in Chapter 31.

Why Decorators?

Like many advanced Python tools, decorators are never strictly required from a purely technical perspective: we can often implement their functionality instead using simple helper function calls or other techniques. And at a base level, we can always manually code the name rebinding that decorators perform automatically.

That said, decorators provide an explicit syntax for such tasks, which makes intent clearer, can minimize augmentation code redundancy, and may help ensure correct API usage.

- Decorators have a very *explicit* syntax, which makes them easier to spot than helper function calls that may be arbitrarily far-removed from the subject functions or classes.

- Decorators are applied *once*, when the subject function or class is defined; it's not necessary to add extra code at every call to the class or function, which may have to be changed in the future.

- Because of both of the prior points, decorators make it less likely that a user of an API will *forget* to augment a function or class according to API requirements.

In other words, beyond their technical model, decorators offer some advantages in terms of both code maintenance and consistency. Moreover, as structuring tools, decorators naturally foster *encapsulation* of code, which reduces redundancy and makes future changes easier.

Decorators do have some potential *drawbacks*, too—when they insert wrapper logic, they can alter the types of the decorated objects, and they may incur extra calls when used as call or interface proxies. On the other hand, the same considerations apply to any technique that adds wrapping logic to objects.

We'll explore these tradeoffs in the context of real code later in this chapter. Although the choice to use decorators is still somewhat subjective, their advantages are compelling enough that they are quickly becoming best practice in the Python world. To help you decide for yourself, let's turn to the details.

> *Decorators versus macros*: Python's decorators bear similarities to what some call *aspect-oriented programming* in other languages—code inserted to run automatically before or after a function call runs. Their syntax also very closely resembles (and is likely borrowed from) Java's *annotations*, though Python's model is usually considered more flexible and general.
>
> Some liken decorators to *macros* too, but this isn't entirely apt, and might even be misleading. Macros (e.g., C's `#define` preprocessor directive) are typically associated with textual replacement and expansion, and designed for generating code. By contrast, Python's decorators are a *runtime* operation, based upon name rebinding, callable objects, and often, proxies. While the two may have use cases that sometimes overlap, decorators and macros are fundamentally different in scope, implementation, and coding patterns. Comparing the two seems akin to comparing Python's `import` with a C `#include`, which similarly confuses a runtime object-based operation with text insertion.
>
> Of course, the term *macro* has been a bit diluted over time—to some, it now can also refer to any canned series of steps or procedure—and users of other languages might find the analogy to descriptors useful anyhow. But they should probably also keep in mind that decorators are about callable *objects* managing callable *objects*, not text expansion. Python tends to be best understood and used in terms of Python idioms.

The Basics

Let's get started with a first-pass look at decoration behavior from a symbolic perspective. We'll write real and more substantial code soon, but since most of the magic of decorators boils down to an automatic rebinding operation, it's important to understand this mapping first.

Function Decorators

Function decorators have been available in Python since version 2.4. As we saw earlier in this book, they are largely just syntactic sugar that runs one function through another at the end of a def statement, and rebinds the original function name to the result.

Usage

A function decorator is a kind of *runtime declaration* about the function whose definition follows. The decorator is coded on a line just before the def statement that defines a function or method, and it consists of the @ symbol followed by a reference to a *metafunction*—a function (or other callable object) that manages another function.

In terms of code, function decorators automatically map the following syntax:

```
@decorator              # Decorate function
def F(arg):
    ...

F(99)                   # Call function
```

into this equivalent form, where `decorator` is a one-argument callable object that returns a callable object with the same number of arguments as F (if not F itself):

```
def F(arg):
    ...
F = decorator(F)        # Rebind function name to decorator result

F(99)                   # Essentially calls decorator(F)(99)
```

This automatic name rebinding works on any def statement, whether it's for a simple function or a method within a class. When the function F is later called, it's actually calling the object *returned* by the decorator, which may be either another object that implements required wrapping logic, or the original function itself.

In other words, decoration essentially maps the first of the following into the second —though the decorator is really run only once, at decoration time:

```
func(6, 7)
decorator(func)(6, 7)
```

This automatic name rebinding accounts for the static method and property decoration syntax we met earlier in the book.

```
class C:
    @staticmethod
    def meth(...): ...              # meth = staticmethod(meth)

class C:
    @property
    def name(self): ...            # name = property(name)
```

In both cases, the method name is rebound to the result of a built-in function decorator, at the end of the def statement. Calling the original name later invokes whatever object the decorator returns. In these specific cases, the original names are rebound to a static method router and property descriptor, but the process is much more general than this —as the next section explains.

Implementation

A decorator itself is a *callable that returns a callable*. That is, it returns the object to be called later when the decorated function is invoked through its original name—either a wrapper object to intercept later calls, or the original function augmented in some way. In fact, decorators can *be* any type of callable and *return* any type of callable: any combination of functions and classes may be used, though some are better suited to certain contexts.

For example, to tap into the decoration protocol in order to manage a function just after it is created, we might code a decorator of this form:

```
def decorator(F):
    # Process function F
    return F

@decorator
def func(): ...                    # func = decorator(func)
```

Because the original decorated function is assigned back to its name, this simply adds a post-creation step to function definition. Such a structure might be used to register a function to an API, assign function attributes, and so on.

In more typical use, to insert logic that intercepts later calls to a function, we might code a decorator to return a different object than the original function—a proxy for later calls:

```
def decorator(F):
    # Save or use function F
    # Return a different callable: nested def, class with __call__, etc.

@decorator
def func(): ...                    # func = decorator(func)
```

This decorator is invoked at decoration time, and the callable it returns is invoked when the original function name is later called. The decorator itself receives the decorated function; the callable returned receives whatever arguments are later passed to the decorated function's name. When coded properly, this works the same for class-level

---

methods: the implied instance object simply shows up in the first argument of the returned callable.

In skeleton terms, here's one common coding pattern that captures this idea—the decorator returns a wrapper that retains the original function in an enclosing scope:

```
def decorator(F):                    # On @ decoration
    def wrapper(*args):              # On wrapped function call
        # Use F and args
        # F(*args) calls original function
    return wrapper

@decorator                           # func = decorator(func)
def func(x, y):                      # func is passed to decorator's F
    ...

func(6, 7)                           # 6, 7 are passed to wrapper's *args
```

When the name `func` is later called, it really invokes the `wrapper` function returned by `decorator`; the `wrapper` function can then run the original `func` because it is still available in an *enclosing scope*. When coded this way, each decorated function produces a new scope to retain state.

To do the same with *classes*, we can overload the call operation and use instance attributes instead of enclosing scopes:

```
class decorator:
    def __init__(self, func):        # On @ decoration
        self.func = func
    def __call__(self, *args):       # On wrapped function call
        # Use self.func and args
        # self.func(*args) calls original function

@decorator                           # func = decorator(func)
def func(x, y):                      # func is passed to __init__
    ...

func(6, 7)                           # 6, 7 are passed to __call__'s *args
```

When the name `func` is later called now, it really invokes the `__call__` operator overloading method of the instance created by `decorator`; the `__call__` method can then run the original `func` because it is still available in an *instance attribute*. When coded this way, each decorated function produces a new instance to retain state.

Supporting method decoration

One subtle point about the prior class-based coding is that while it works to intercept simple *function* calls, it does not quite work when applied to class-level *method* functions:

```
class decorator:
    def __init__(self, func):        # func is method without instance
        self.func = func
    def __call__(self, *args):       # self is decorator instance
```

```
                      # self.func(*args) fails!      # C instance not in args!
          class C:
              @decorator
              def method(self, x, y):                # method = decorator(method)
                  ...                                # Rebound to decorator instance
```

When coded this way, the decorated method is rebound to an instance of the decorator class, instead of a simple function.

The problem with this is that the `self` in the decorator's __call__ receives the **decora tor** class instance when the method is later run, and the instance of class C is never included in `*args`. This makes it impossible to dispatch the call to the original method —the decorator object retains the original method function, but it has no instance to pass to it.

To support *both* functions and methods, the nested function alternative works better:

```
          def decorator(F):                         # F is func or method without instance
              def wrapper(*args):                    # class instance in args[0] for method
                                                     # F(*args) runs func or method
              return wrapper

          @decorator
          def func(x, y):                            # func = decorator(func)
              ...
          func(6, 7)                                 # Really calls wrapper(6, 7)

          class C:
              @decorator
              def method(self, x, y):                # method = decorator(method)
                  ...                                # Rebound to simple function

          X = C()
          X.method(6, 7)                             # Really calls wrapper(X, 6, 7)
```

When coded this way `wrapper` receives the C class instance in its first argument, so it can dispatch to the original method and access state information.

Technically, this nested-function version works because Python creates a bound method object and thus passes the subject class instance to the `self` argument only when a method attribute references a simple function; when it references an instance of a callable class instead, the callable class's instance is passed to `self` to give the callable class access to its own state information. We'll see how this subtle difference can matter in more realistic examples later in this chapter.

Also note that nested functions are perhaps the most straightforward way to support decoration of both functions and methods, but not necessarily the only way. The prior chapter's *descriptors*, for example, receive both the descriptor and subject class instance when called. Though more complex, later in this chapter we'll see how this tool can be leveraged in this context as well.

Class Decorators

Function decorators proved so useful that the model was extended to allow class decoration as of Python 2.6 and 3.0. They were initially resisted because of role overlap with *metaclasses*; in the end, though, they were adopted because they provide a simpler way to achieve many of the same goals.

Class decorators are strongly related to function decorators; in fact, they use the same syntax and very similar coding patterns. Rather than wrapping individual functions or methods, though, class decorators are a way to manage classes, or wrap up instance construction calls with extra logic that manages or augments instances created from a class. In the latter role, they may manage full object interfaces.

Usage

Syntactically, class decorators appear just before `class` statements, in the same way that function decorators appear just before `def` statements. In symbolic terms, for a `decorator` that must be a one-argument callable that returns a callable, the class decorator syntax:

```
@decorator                  # Decorate class
class C:
    ...

x = C(99)                   # Make an instance
```

is equivalent to the following—the class is automatically passed to the decorator function, and the decorator's result is assigned back to the class name:

```
class C:
    ...
C = decorator(C)            # Rebind class name to decorator result

x = C(99)                   # Essentially calls decorator(C)(99)
```

The net effect is that calling the class name later to create an instance winds up triggering the callable returned by the decorator, which may or may not call the original class itself.

Implementation

New class decorators are coded with many of the same techniques used for function decorators, though some may involve *two levels* of augmentation—to manage both instance construction calls, as well as instance interface access. Because a class decorator is also a *callable that returns a callable*, most combinations of functions and classes suffice.

However it's coded, the decorator's result is what runs when an instance is later created. For example, to simply manage a class just after it is created, return the original class itself:

```
def decorator(C):
    # Process class C
    return C

@decorator
class C: ...                                    # C = decorator(C)
```

To instead insert a wrapper layer that intercepts later instance creation calls, return a different callable object:

```
def decorator(C):
    # Save or use class C
    # Return a different callable: nested def, class with __call__, etc.

@decorator
class C: ...                                    # C = decorator(C)
```

The callable returned by such a class decorator typically creates and returns a new instance of the original class, augmented in some way to manage its interface. For example, the following inserts an object that intercepts undefined attributes of a class instance:

```
def decorator(cls):                             # On @ decoration
    class Wrapper:
        def __init__(self, *args):              # On instance creation
            self.wrapped = cls(*args)
        def __getattr__(self, name):            # On attribute fetch
            return getattr(self.wrapped, name)
    return Wrapper

@decorator
class C:                                         # C = decorator(C)
    def __init__(self, x, y):                    # Run by Wrapper.__init__
        self.attr = 'spam'

x = C(6, 7)                                      # Really calls Wrapper(6, 7)
print(x.attr)                                    # Runs Wrapper.__getattr__, prints "spam"
```

In this example, the decorator rebinds the class name to another class, which retains the original class in an enclosing scope and creates and embeds an instance of the original class when it's called. When an attribute is later fetched from the instance, it is intercepted by the wrapper's __getattr__ and delegated to the embedded instance of the original class. Moreover, each decorated class creates a new scope, which remembers the original class. We'll flesh out this example into some more useful code later in this chapter.

Like function decorators, class decorators are commonly coded as either "factory" functions that create and return callables, classes that use __init__ or __call__ methods to intercept call operations, or some combination thereof. Factory functions typically retain state in enclosing scope references, and classes in attributes.

Supporting multiple instances

As for function decorators, some callable type combinations work better for class decorators than others. Consider the following invalid alternative to the class decorator of the prior example:

```
class Decorator:
    def __init__(self, C):           # On @ decoration
        self.C = C
    def __call__(self, *args):       # On instance creation
        self.wrapped = self.C(*args)
        return self
    def __getattr__(self, attrname): # On attribute fetch
        return getattr(self.wrapped, attrname)

@Decorator
class C: ...                         # C = Decorator(C)

x = C()
y = C()                              # Overwrites x!
```

This code handles multiple decorated classes (each makes a new `Decorator` instance) and will intercept instance creation calls (each runs `__call__`). Unlike the prior version, however, this version fails to handle *multiple instances* of a given class—each instance creation call overwrites the prior saved instance. The original version does support multiple instances, because each instance creation call makes a new independent wrapper object. More generally, either of the following patterns supports multiple wrapped instances:

```
def decorator(C):                    # On @ decoration
    class Wrapper:
        def __init__(self, *args):   # On instance creation: new Wrapper
            self.wrapped = C(*args)  # Embed instance in instance
    return Wrapper

class Wrapper: ...
def decorator(C):                    # On @ decoration
    def onCall(*args):               # On instance creation: new Wrapper
        return Wrapper(C(*args))     # Embed instance in instance
    return onCall
```

We'll study this phenomenon in a more realistic context later in the chapter too; in practice, though, we must be careful to combine callable types properly to support our intent, and choose state policies wisely.

Decorator Nesting

Sometimes one decorator isn't enough. For instance, suppose you've coded *two* function decorators to be used during development—one to test argument types before function calls, and another to test return value types after function calls. You can use either independently, but what to do if you want to employ *both* on a single function? What you really need is a way to *nest* the two, such that the result of one decorator is the function decorated by the other. It's irrelevant which is nested, as long as both steps run on later calls.

To support multiple nested steps of augmentation this way, decorator syntax allows you to add multiple layers of wrapper logic to a decorated function or method. When this feature is used, each decorator must appear on a line of its own. Decorator syntax of this form:

```
@A
@B
@C
def f(...):
    ...
```

runs the same as the following:

```
def f(...):
    ...
f = A(B(C(f)))
```

Here, the original function is passed through three different decorators, and the resulting callable object is assigned back to the original name. Each decorator processes the result of the prior, which may be the original function or an inserted wrapper.

If all the decorators insert wrappers, the net effect is that when the original function name is called, three different layers of wrapping object logic will be invoked, to augment the original function in three different ways. The last decorator listed is the first applied, and is the most deeply nested when the original function name is later called (insert joke about Python "interior decorators" here).

Just as for functions, multiple class decorators result in multiple nested function calls, and possibly multiple levels and steps of wrapper logic around instance creation calls. For example, the following code:

```
@spam
@eggs
class C:
    ...

X = C()
```

is equivalent to the following:

```
class C:
    ...
C = spam(eggs(C))

X = C()
```

Again, each decorator is free to return either the original class or an inserted wrapper object. With wrappers, when an instance of the original C class is finally requested, the call is redirected to the wrapping layer objects provided by both the spam and eggs decorators, which may have arbitrarily different roles—they might trace and validate attribute access, for example, and both steps would be run on later requests.

For instance, the following do-nothing decorators simply return the decorated function:

```
def d1(F): return F
def d2(F): return F
def d3(F): return F

@d1
@d2
@d3
def func():                # func = d1(d2(d3(func)))
    print('spam')

func()                     # Prints "spam"
```

The same syntax works on classes, as do these same do-nothing decorators.

When decorators insert wrapper function objects, though, they may augment the original function when called—the following concatenates to its result in the decorator layers, as it runs the layers from inner to outer:

```
def d1(F): return lambda: 'X' + F()
def d2(F): return lambda: 'Y' + F()
def d3(F): return lambda: 'Z' + F()

@d1
@d2
@d3
def func():                # func = d1(d2(d3(func)))
    return 'spam'

print(func())              # Prints "XYZspam"
```

We use `lambda` functions to implement wrapper layers here (each retains the wrapped function in an enclosing scope); in practice, wrappers can take the form of functions, callable classes, and more. When designed well, decorator nesting allows us to combine augmentation steps in a wide variety of ways.

Decorator Arguments

Both function and class decorators can also seem to take *arguments*, although really these arguments are passed to a callable that in effect *returns* the decorator, which in turn returns a callable. By nature, this usually sets up multiple levels of state retention. The following, for instance:

```
@decorator(A, B)
def F(arg):
    ...

F(99)
```

is automatically mapped into this equivalent form, where `decorator` is a callable that *returns* the actual decorator. The returned decorator in turn returns the callable run later for calls to the original function name:

```
def F(arg):
    ...
F = decorator(A, B)(F)       # Rebind F to result of decorator's return value

F(99)                        # Essentially calls decorator(A, B)(F)(99)
```

Decorator arguments are resolved before decoration ever occurs, and they are usually used to retain state information for use in later calls. The decorator function in this example, for instance, might take a form like the following:

```
def decorator(A, B):
    # Save or use A, B
    def actualDecorator(F):
        # Save or use function F
        # Return a callable: nested def, class with __call__, etc.
        return callable
    return actualDecorator
```

The outer function in this structure generally saves the decorator arguments away as state information, for use in the actual decorator, the callable it returns, or both. This code snippet retains the state information argument in enclosing function scope references, but class attributes are commonly used as well.

In other words, decorator arguments often imply *three levels of callables*: a callable to accept decorator arguments, which returns a callable to serve as decorator, which returns a callable to handle calls to the original function or class. Each of the three levels may be a function or class and may retain state in the form of scopes or class attributes.

Decorator arguments can be used to provide attribute initialization values, call trace message labels, attribute names to be validated, and much more—any sort of configuration parameter for objects or their proxies is a candidate. We'll see concrete examples of decorator arguments employed later in this chapter.

Decorators Manage Functions and Classes, Too

Although much of the rest of this chapter focuses on wrapping later calls to functions and classes, it's important to remember that the decorator mechanism is more general than this—it is a protocol for passing functions and classes through any callable immediately after they are created. As such, it can also be used to invoke arbitrary post-creation processing:

```
def decorator(O):
    # Save or augment function or class O
    return O

@decorator
def F(): ...                 # F = decorator(F)
```

```
@decorator
class C: ...                    # C = decorator(C)
```

As long as we return the original decorated object this way instead of a proxy, we can manage functions and classes themselves, not just later calls to them. We'll see more realistic examples later in this chapter that use this idea to register callable objects to an API with decoration and assign attributes to functions when they are created.

Coding Function Decorators

On to the code—in the rest of this chapter, we are going to study working examples that demonstrate the decorator concepts we just explored. This section presents a handful of function decorators at work, and the next shows class decorators in action. Following that, we'll close out with some larger case studies of class and function decorator usage—complete implementations of class privacy and argument range tests.

Tracing Calls

To get started, let's revive the call tracer example we met in Chapter 32. The following defines and applies a function decorator that counts the number of calls made to the decorated function and prints a trace message for each call:

```
# File decorator1.py

class tracer:
    def __init__(self, func):          # On @ decoration: save original func
        self.calls = 0
        self.func = func
    def __call__(self, *args):         # On later calls: run original func
        self.calls += 1
        print('call %s to %s' % (self.calls, self.func.__name__))
        self.func(*args)

@tracer
def spam(a, b, c):                     # spam = tracer(spam)
    print(a + b + c)                   # Wraps spam in a decorator object
```

Notice how each function decorated with this class will create a new instance, with its own saved function object and calls counter. Also observe how the *args argument syntax is used to pack and unpack arbitrarily many passed-in arguments. This generality enables this decorator to be used to wrap any function with any number of positional arguments; this version doesn't yet work on keyword arguments or class-level methods, and doesn't return results, but we'll fix these shortcomings later in this section.

Now, if we import this module's function and test it interactively, we get the following sort of behavior—each call generates a trace message initially, because the decorator class intercepts it. This code runs as is under both Python 2.X and 3.X, as does all code in this chapter unless otherwise noted (I've made prints version-neutral, and decorators do not require new-style classes; some hex addresses have also been shortened to protect the sighted):

```
>>> from decorator1 import spam

>>> spam(1, 2, 3)              # Really calls the tracer wrapper object
call 1 to spam
6

>>> spam('a', 'b', 'c')       # Invokes __call__ in class
call 2 to spam
abc

>>> spam.calls                # Number calls in wrapper state information
2
>>> spam
<decorator1.tracer object at 0x02D9A730>
```

When run, the `tracer` class saves away the decorated function, and intercepts later calls to it, in order to add a layer of logic that counts and prints each call. Notice how the total number of calls shows up as an attribute of the decorated function—`spam` is really an instance of the `tracer` class when decorated, a finding that may have ramifications for programs that do type checking, but is generally benign (decorators might copy the original function's `__name__`, but such forgery is limited, and could lead to confusion).

For function calls, the @ decoration syntax can be more convenient than modifying each call to account for the extra logic level, and it avoids accidentally calling the original function directly. Consider a nondecorator equivalent such as the following:

```
calls = 0
def tracer(func, *args):
    global calls
    calls += 1
    print('call %s to %s' % (calls, func.__name__))
    func(*args)

def spam(a, b, c):
    print(a, b, c)

>>> spam(1, 2, 3)             # Normal nontraced call: accidental?
1 2 3

>>> tracer(spam, 1, 2, 3)    # Special traced call without decorators
call 1 to spam
1 2 3
```

This alternative can be used on any function without the special @ syntax, but unlike the decorator version, it requires extra syntax at every place where the function is called in your code. Furthermore, its intent may not be as obvious, and it does not ensure that the extra layer will be invoked for normal calls. Although decorators are never *required* (we can always rebind names manually), they are often the most convenient and uniform option.

Decorator State Retention Options

The last example of the prior section raises an important issue. Function decorators have a variety of options for retaining state information provided at decoration time, for use during the actual function call. They generally need to support multiple decorated objects and multiple calls, but there are a number of ways to implement these goals: instance attributes, global variables, nonlocal closure variables, and function attributes can all be used for retaining state.

Class instance attributes

For example, here is an augmented version of the prior example, which adds support for *keyword* arguments with ** syntax, and *returns* the wrapped function's result to support more use cases (for nonlinear readers, we first studied keyword arguments in Chapter 18, and for readers working with the book examples package, some filenames in this chapter are again implied by the command-lines that follow their listings):

```
class tracer:                              # State via instance attributes
    def __init__(self, func):              # On @ decorator
        self.calls = 0                     # Save func for later call
        self.func  = func
    def __call__(self, *args, **kwargs):   # On call to original function
        self.calls += 1
        print('call %s to %s' % (self.calls, self.func.__name__))
        return self.func(*args, **kwargs)

@tracer
def spam(a, b, c):          # Same as: spam = tracer(spam)
    print(a + b + c)        # Triggers tracer.__init__

@tracer
def eggs(x, y):             # Same as: eggs = tracer(eggs)
    print(x ** y)           # Wraps eggs in a tracer object

spam(1, 2, 3)               # Really calls tracer instance: runs tracer.__call__
spam(a=4, b=5, c=6)         # spam is an instance attribute

eggs(2, 16)                 # Really calls tracer instance, self.func is eggs
eggs(4, y=4)                # self.calls is per-decoration here
```

Like the original, this uses *class instance attributes* to save state explicitly. Both the wrapped function and the calls counter are *per-instance* information—each decoration gets its own copy. When run as a script under either 2.X or 3.X, the output of this version is as follows; notice how the spam and eggs functions each have their own calls counter, because each decoration creates a new class instance:

```
c:\code> python decorator2.py
call 1 to spam
6
call 2 to spam
15
call 1 to eggs
```

```
65536
call 2 to eggs
256
```

While useful for decorating functions, this coding scheme still has issues when applied to methods—a shortcoming we'll address in a later revision.

Enclosing scopes and globals

Closure functions—with enclosing `def` scope references and nested `defs`—can often achieve the same effect, especially for static data like the decorated original function. In this example, though, we would also need a counter in the enclosing scope that *changes* on each call, and that's not possible in Python 2.X (recall from Chapter 17 that the `nonlocal` statement is 3.X-only).

In 2.X, we can still use either classes and attributes per the prior section, or other options. Moving state variables out to the *global scope* with declarations is one candidate, and works in both 2.X and 3.X:

```
calls = 0
def tracer(func):                    # State via enclosing scope and global
    def wrapper(*args, **kwargs):    # Instead of class attributes
        global calls                 # calls is global, not per-function
        calls += 1
        print('call %s to %s' % (calls, func.__name__))
        return func(*args, **kwargs)
    return wrapper

@tracer
def spam(a, b, c):          # Same as: spam = tracer(spam)
    print(a + b + c)

@tracer
def eggs(x, y):             # Same as: eggs = tracer(eggs)
    print(x ** y)

spam(1, 2, 3)              # Really calls wrapper, assigned to spam
spam(a=4, b=5, c=6)        # wrapper calls spam

eggs(2, 16)                # Really calls wrapper, assigned to eggs
eggs(4, y=4)               # Global calls is not per-decoration here!
```

Unfortunately, moving the counter out to the common global scope to allow it to be changed like this also means that it will be *shared* by every wrapped function. Unlike class instance attributes, global counters are cross-program, not per-function—the counter is incremented for *any* traced function call. You can tell the difference if you compare this version's output with the prior version's—the single, shared global call counter is incorrectly updated by calls to every decorated function:

```
c:\code> python decorator3.py
call 1 to spam
6
call 2 to spam
```

```
15
call 3 to eggs
65536
call 4 to eggs
256
```

Enclosing scopes and nonlocals

Shared global state may be what we want in some cases. If we really want a *per-function* counter, though, we can either use classes as before, or make use of *closure* (a.k.a. *factory*) functions and the `nonlocal` statement in Python 3.X, described in Chapter 17. Because this new statement allows enclosing function scope variables to be changed, they can serve as per-decoration and changeable data. In 3.X only:

```
def tracer(func):                           # State via enclosing scope and nonlocal
    calls = 0                               # Instead of class attrs or global
    def wrapper(*args, **kwargs):           # calls is per-function, not global
        nonlocal calls
        calls += 1
        print('call %s to %s' % (calls, func.__name__))
        return func(*args, **kwargs)
    return wrapper

@tracer
def spam(a, b, c):          # Same as: spam = tracer(spam)
    print(a + b + c)

@tracer
def eggs(x, y):             # Same as: eggs = tracer(eggs)
    print(x ** y)

spam(1, 2, 3)              # Really calls wrapper, bound to func
spam(a=4, b=5, c=6)        # wrapper calls spam

eggs(2, 16)                # Really calls wrapper, bound to eggs
eggs(4, y=4)               # Nonlocal calls _is_ per-decoration here
```

Now, because enclosing scope variables are not cross-program globals, each wrapped function gets its own counter again, just as for classes and attributes. Here's the new output when run under 3.X:

```
c:\code> py -3 decorator4.py
call 1 to spam
6
call 2 to spam
15
call 1 to eggs
65536
call 2 to eggs
256
```

Function attributes

Finally, if you are not using Python 3.X and don't have a `nonlocal` statement—or you want your code to work portably on *both* 3.X and 2.X—you may still be able to avoid globals and classes by making use of *function attributes* for some changeable state instead. In all Pythons since 2.1, we can assign arbitrary attributes to functions to attach them, with `func.attr=value`. Because a factory function makes a new function on each call, its attributes become per-call state. Moreover, you need to use this technique only for state variables that must *change*; enclosing scope references are still retained and work normally.

In our example, we can simply use `wrapper.calls` for state. The following works the same as the preceding `nonlocal` version because the counter is again per-decorated-function, but it also runs in Python 2.X:

```python
def tracer(func):                          # State via enclosing scope and func attr
    def wrapper(*args, **kwargs):          # calls is per-function, not global
        wrapper.calls += 1
        print('call %s to %s' % (wrapper.calls, func.__name__))
        return func(*args, **kwargs)
    wrapper.calls = 0
    return wrapper

@tracer
def spam(a, b, c):          # Same as: spam = tracer(spam)
    print(a + b + c)

@tracer
def eggs(x, y):             # Same as: eggs = tracer(eggs)
    print(x ** y)

spam(1, 2, 3)               # Really calls wrapper, assigned to spam
spam(a=4, b=5, c=6)         # wrapper calls spam

eggs(2, 16)                 # Really calls wrapper, assigned to eggs
eggs(4, y=4)                # wrapper.calls _is_ per-decoration here
```

As we learned in Chapter 17, this works only because the name `wrapper` is retained in the enclosing `tracer` function's scope. When we later increment `wrapper.calls`, we are not changing the name `wrapper` itself, so no `nonlocal` declaration is required. This version runs in either Python line:

```
c:\code> py -2 decorator5.py
...same output as prior version, but works on 2.X too...
```

This scheme was almost relegated to a footnote, because it may be more obscure than `nonlocal` in 3.X and might be better saved for cases where other schemes don't help. However, function attributes also have substantial advantages. For one, they allow access to the saved state from *outside* the decorator's code; nonlocals can only be seen inside the nested function itself, but function attributes have wider visibility. For another, they are far more *portable*; this scheme also works in 2.X, making it version-neutral.

We will employ function attributes again in an answer to one of the end-of-chapter questions, where their visibility outside callables becomes an asset. As changeable state associated with a context of use, they are equivalent to enclosing scope nonlocals. As usual, choosing from multiple tools is an inherent part of the programming task.

Because decorators often imply multiple levels of callables, you can combine functions with enclosing scopes, classes with attributes, and function attributes to achieve a variety of coding structures. As we'll see later, though, this sometimes may be subtler than you expect—each decorated function should have its own state, and each decorated class may require state both for itself and for each generated instance.

In fact, as the next section will explain in more detail, if we want to apply function decorators to class-level methods, too, we also have to be careful about the distinction Python makes between decorators coded as callable class instance objects and decorators coded as functions.

Class Blunders I: Decorating Methods

When I wrote the first class-based `tracer` function decorator in *decorator1.py* earlier, I naively assumed that it could also be applied to any *method*—decorated methods should work the same, I reasoned, but the automatic `self` instance argument would simply be included at the front of `*args`. The only real downside to this assumption is that it is *completely wrong*! When applied to a class's method, the first version of the `tracer` fails, because `self` is the instance of the decorator class and the instance of the decorated subject class is not included in `*args` at all. This is true in both Python 3.X and 2.X.

I introduced this phenomenon earlier in this chapter, but now we can see it in the context of realistic working code. Given the class-based tracing decorator:

```
class tracer:
    def __init__(self, func):           # On @ decorator
        self.calls = 0                  # Save func for later call
        self.func  = func
    def __call__(self, *args, **kwargs):  # On call to original function
        self.calls += 1
        print('call %s to %s' % (self.calls, self.func.__name__))
        return self.func(*args, **kwargs)
```

decoration of simple functions works as advertised earlier:

```
@tracer
def spam(a, b, c):                      # spam = tracer(spam)
    print(a + b + c)                    # Triggers tracer.__init__

>>> spam(1, 2, 3)                       # Runs tracer.__call__
call 1 to spam
6
>>> spam(a=4, b=5, c=6)                 # spam saved in an instance attribute
call 2 to spam
15
```

However, decoration of class-level methods fails (more lucid sequential readers might recognize this as an adaptation of our `Person` class resurrected from the object-oriented tutorial in Chapter 28):

```
class Person:
    def __init__(self, name, pay):
        self.name = name
        self.pay  = pay

    @tracer
    def giveRaise(self, percent):           # giveRaise = tracer(giveRaise)
        self.pay *= (1.0 + percent)

    @tracer
    def lastName(self):                      # lastName = tracer(lastName)
        return self.name.split()[-1]

>>> bob = Person('Bob Smith', 50000)         # tracer remembers method funcs
>>> bob.giveRaise(.25)                        # Runs tracer.__call__(???, .25)
call 1 to giveRaise
TypeError: giveRaise() missing 1 required positional argument: 'percent'

>>> print(bob.lastName())                     # Runs tracer.__call__(???)
call 1 to lastName
TypeError: lastName() missing 1 required positional argument: 'self'
```

The root of the problem here is in the `self` argument of the tracer class's `__call__` method—is it a `tracer` instance or a `Person` instance? We really need *both* as it's coded: the `tracer` for decorator state, and the `Person` for routing on to the original method. Really, `self` *must* be the `tracer` object, to provide access to `tracer`'s state information (its `calls` and `func`); this is true whether decorating a simple function or a method.

Unfortunately, when our decorated method name is rebound to a class instance object with a `__call__`, Python passes only the `tracer` *instance* to `self`; it doesn't pass along the `Person` subject in the arguments list at all. Moreover, because the `tracer` knows nothing about the `Person` instance we are trying to process with method calls, there's no way to create a bound method with an instance, and thus no way to correctly dispatch the call. This isn't a bug, but it's wildly subtle.

In the end, the prior listing winds up passing too few arguments to the decorated method, and results in an error. Add a line to the decorator's `__call__` to print all its arguments to verify this—as you can see, `self` is the `tracer` instance, and the `Person` instance is entirely absent:

```
>>> bob.giveRaise(.25)
<__main__.tracer object at 0x02A486D8> (0.25,) {}
call 1 to giveRaise
Traceback (most recent call last):
  File "<stdin>", line 1, in <module>
  File "<stdin>", line 9, in __call__
TypeError: giveRaise() missing 1 required positional argument: 'percent'
```

As mentioned earlier, this happens because Python passes the implied subject instance to `self` when a method name is bound to a simple function only; when it is an instance of a callable class, that class's instance is passed instead. Technically, Python makes a bound method object containing the subject instance only when the method is a simple function, not when it is a callable instance of another class.

Using nested functions to decorate methods

If you want your function decorators to work on *both* simple functions and class-level methods, the most straightforward solution lies in using one of the other state retention solutions described earlier—code your function decorator as nested `def`s, so that you don't depend on a single `self` instance argument to be both the wrapper class instance and the subject class instance.

The following alternative applies this fix using Python 3.X nonlocals; recode this to use function attributes for the changeable `calls` to use in 2.X. Because decorated methods are rebound to simple functions instead of instance objects, Python correctly passes the `Person` object as the first argument, and the decorator propagates it on in the first item of `*args` to the `self` argument of the real, decorated methods:

```
# A call tracer decorator for both functions and methods

def tracer(func):                              # Use function, not class with __call__
    calls = 0                                  # Else "self" is decorator instance only!
    def onCall(*args, **kwargs):               # Or in 2.X+3.X: use [onCall.calls += 1]
        nonlocal calls
        calls += 1
        print('call %s to %s' % (calls, func.__name__))
        return func(*args, **kwargs)
    return onCall


if __name__ == '__main__':

    # Applies to simple functions
    @tracer
    def spam(a, b, c):                         # spam = tracer(spam)
        print(a + b + c)                       # onCall remembers spam

    @tracer
    def eggs(N):
        return 2 ** N

    spam(1, 2, 3)                              # Runs onCall(1, 2, 3)
    spam(a=4, b=5, c=6)
    print(eggs(32))

    # Applies to class-level method functions too!
    class Person:
        def __init__(self, name, pay):
            self.name = name
            self.pay  = pay
```

```
        @tracer
        def giveRaise(self, percent):          # giveRaise = tracer(giveRaise)
            self.pay *= (1.0 + percent)         # onCall remembers giveRaise

        @tracer
        def lastName(self):                     # lastName = tracer(lastName)
            return self.name.split()[-1]

    print('methods...')
    bob = Person('Bob Smith', 50000)
    sue = Person('Sue Jones', 100000)
    print(bob.name, sue.name)
    sue.giveRaise(.10)                          # Runs onCall(sue, .10)
    print(int(sue.pay))
    print(bob.lastName(), sue.lastName())       # Runs onCall(bob), lastName in scopes
```

We've also indented the file's self-test code under a __name__ test so the decorator can be imported and used elsewhere. This version works the same on both functions and methods, but runs in 3.X only due to its `nonlocal`:

```
c:\code> py -3 calltracer.py
call 1 to spam
6
call 2 to spam
15
call 1 to eggs
4294967296
methods...
Bob Smith Sue Jones
call 1 to giveRaise
110000
call 1 to lastName
call 2 to lastName
Smith Jones
```

Trace through these results to make sure you have a handle on this model; the next section provides an alternative to it that supports classes, but is also substantially more complex.

Using descriptors to decorate methods

Although the nested function solution illustrated in the prior section is the most straightforward way to support decorators that apply to both functions and class-level methods, other schemes are possible. The *descriptor* feature we explored in the prior chapter, for example, can help here as well.

Recall from our discussion in that chapter that a descriptor is normally a class attribute assigned to an object with a __get__ method run automatically whenever that attribute is referenced and fetched; new-style class `object` derivation is required for descriptors in Python 2.X, but not 3.X:

```
class Descriptor(object):
    def __get__(self, instance, owner): ...
```

```
class Subject:
    attr = Descriptor()

X = Subject()
X.attr              # Roughly runs Descriptor.__get__(Subject.attr, X, Subject)
```

Descriptors may also have __set__ and __del__ access methods, but we don't need them here. More relevant to this chapter's topic, because the descriptor's __get__ method receives *both* the descriptor class instance and subject class instance when invoked, it's well suited to decorating methods when we need both the decorator's state and the original class instance for dispatching calls. Consider the following alternative tracing decorator, which *also* happens to be a descriptor when used for a class-level method:

```
class tracer(object):                               # A decorator+descriptor
    def __init__(self, func):                       # On @ decorator
        self.calls = 0                              # Save func for later call
        self.func  = func
    def __call__(self, *args, **kwargs):            # On call to original func
        self.calls += 1
        print('call %s to %s' % (self.calls, self.func.__name__))
        return self.func(*args, **kwargs)
    def __get__(self, instance, owner):             # On method attribute fetch
        return wrapper(self, instance)

class wrapper:
    def __init__(self, desc, subj):                 # Save both instances
        self.desc = desc                            # Route calls back to deco/desc
        self.subj = subj
    def __call__(self, *args, **kwargs):
        return self.desc(self.subj, *args, **kwargs)   # Runs tracer.__call__

@tracer
def spam(a, b, c):                                  # spam = tracer(spam)
    ...same as prior...                             # Uses __call__ only

class Person:
    @tracer
    def giveRaise(self, percent):                   # giveRaise = tracer(giveRaise)
        ...same as prior...                         # Makes giveRaise a descriptor
```

This works the same as the preceding nested function coding. Its operation varies by usage context:

- Decorated *functions* invoke only its __call__, and never invoke its __get__.
- Decorated *methods* invoke its __get__ first to resolve the method name fetch (on *I.method*); the object returned by __get__ retains the subject class instance and is then invoked to complete the call expression, thereby triggering the decorator's __call__ (on ()).

For example, the test code's call to:

```
    sue.giveRaise(.10)                          # Runs __get__ then __call__
```

runs `tracer.__get__` first, because the `giveRaise` attribute in the `Person` class has been
rebound to a descriptor by the method function decorator. The call expression then
triggers the `__call__` method of the returned `wrapper` object, which in turn invokes
`tracer.__call__`. In other words, decorated method calls trigger a four-step process:
`tracer.__get__`, followed by three call operations— `wrapper.__call__`,
`tracer.__call__`, and finally the original wrapped method.

The `wrapper` object retains both descriptor and subject instances, so it can route control
back to the original decorator/descriptor class instance. In effect, the `wrapper` object
saves the subject class instance available during method attribute fetch and adds it to
the later call's arguments list, which is passed to the decorator `__call__`. Routing the
call back to the descriptor class instance this way is required in this application so that
all calls to a wrapped method use the same `calls` counter state information in the
descriptor instance object.

Alternatively, we could use a nested function and enclosing scope references to achieve
the same effect—the following version works the same as the preceding one, by swapping a class and object attributes for a nested function and scope references. It requires
noticeably less code, but follows the same four-step process on each decorated method
call:

```
    class tracer(object):
        def __init__(self, func):              # On @ decorator
            self.calls = 0                     # Save func for later call
            self.func  = func
        def __call__(self, *args, **kwargs):   # On call to original func
            self.calls += 1
            print('call %s to %s' % (self.calls, self.func.__name__))
            return self.func(*args, **kwargs)
        def __get__(self, instance, owner):        # On method fetch
            def wrapper(*args, **kwargs):          # Retain both inst
                return self(instance, *args, **kwargs)   # Runs __call__
            return wrapper
```

Add `print` statements to these alternatives' methods to trace the multistep get/call process on your own, and run them with the same test code as in the nested function
alternative shown earlier (see file *calltracer-descr.py* for their source). In either coding,
this descriptor-based scheme is also substantially subtler than the nested function option, and so is probably a second choice here. To be more blunt, if its complexity doesn't
send you screaming into the night, its performance costs probably should! Still, this
may be a useful coding pattern in other contexts.

It's also worth noting that we might code this descriptor-based decorator more simply
as follows, but it would then apply only to methods, not to simple functions—an intrinsic limitation of attribute descriptors (and just the inverse of the problem we're
trying to solve: application to both functions and methods):

```
    class tracer(object):                       # For methods, but not functions!
        def __init__(self, meth):               # On @ decorator
```

```
            self.calls = 0
            self.meth  = meth
    def __get__(self, instance, owner):          # On method fetch
        def wrapper(*args, **kwargs):            # On method call: proxy with self+inst
            self.calls += 1
            print('call %s to %s' % (self.calls, self.meth.__name__))
            return self.meth(instance, *args, **kwargs)
        return wrapper

class Person:
    @tracer                              # Applies to class methods
    def giveRaise(self, percent):        # giveRaise = tracer(giveRaise)
        ...                              # Makes giveRaise a descriptor

@tracer                                  # But fails for simple functions
def spam(a, b, c):                       # spam = tracer(spam)
    ...                                  # No attribute fetch occurs here
```

In the rest of this chapter we're going to be fairly casual about using classes or functions to code our function decorators, as long as they are applied only to functions. Some decorators may not require the instance of the original class, and will still work on both functions and methods if coded as a class—something like Python's own staticmethod decorator, for example, wouldn't require an instance of the subject class (indeed, its whole point is to remove the instance from the call).

The moral of this story, though, is that if you want your decorators to work on both simple functions and methods, you're probably better off using the nested-function-based coding pattern outlined here instead of a class with call interception.

Timing Calls

To sample the fuller flavor of what function decorators are capable of, let's turn to a different use case. Our next decorator times calls made to a decorated function—both the time for one call, and the total time among all calls. The decorator is applied to two functions, in order to compare the relative speed of list comprehensions and the map built-in call:

```
# File timerdeco1.py
# Caveat: range still differs - a list in 2.X, an iterable in 3.X
# Caveat: timer won't work on methods as coded (see quiz solution)

import time, sys
force = list if sys.version_info[0] == 3 else (lambda X: X)

class timer:
    def __init__(self, func):
        self.func    = func
        self.alltime = 0
    def __call__(self, *args, **kargs):
        start  = time.clock()
        result = self.func(*args, **kargs)
```

```
        elapsed = time.clock() - start
        self.alltime += elapsed
        print('%s: %.5f, %.5f' % (self.func.__name__, elapsed, self.alltime))
        return result

@timer
def listcomp(N):
    return [x * 2 for x in range(N)]

@timer
def mapcall(N):
    return force(map((lambda x: x * 2), range(N)))

result = listcomp(5)                    # Time for this call, all calls, return value
listcomp(50000)
listcomp(500000)
listcomp(1000000)
print(result)
print('allTime = %s' % listcomp.alltime)        # Total time for all listcomp calls

print('')
result = mapcall(5)
mapcall(50000)
mapcall(500000)
mapcall(1000000)
print(result)
print('allTime = %s' % mapcall.alltime)          # Total time for all mapcall calls

print('\n**map/comp = %s' % round(mapcall.alltime / listcomp.alltime, 3))
```

When run in either Python 3.X or 2.X, the output of this file's self-test code is as follows —giving for each function call the function name, time for this call, and time for all calls so far, along with the first call's return value, cumulative time for each function, and the map-to-comprehension time ratio at the end:

```
c:\code> py -3 timerdeco1.py
listcomp: 0.00001, 0.00001
listcomp: 0.00499, 0.00499
listcomp: 0.05716, 0.06215
listcomp: 0.11565, 0.17781
[0, 2, 4, 6, 8]
allTime = 0.17780527629411225

mapcall: 0.00002, 0.00002
mapcall: 0.00988, 0.00990
mapcall: 0.10601, 0.11591
mapcall: 0.21690, 0.33281
[0, 2, 4, 6, 8]
allTime = 0.3328064956447921

**map/comp = 1.872
```

Times vary per Python line and test machine, of course, and cumulative time is available as a class instance attribute here. As usual, map calls are almost twice as slow as list comprehensions when the latter can avoid a function call (or equivalently, its require-ment of function calls can make map slower).

Decorators versus per-call timing

For comparison, see Chapter 21 for a *nondecorator* approach to timing iteration alternatives like these. As a review, we saw two per-call timing techniques there, homegrown and library—here deployed to time the 1M list comprehension case of the decorator's test code, though incurring extra costs for management code including an outer loop and function calls:

```
>>> def listcomp(N): [x * 2 for x in range(N)]

>>> import timer                                        # Chapter 21 techniques
>>> timer.total(1, listcomp, 1000000)
(0.1461295268088542, None)

>>> import timeit
>>> timeit.timeit(number=1, stmt=lambda: listcomp(1000000))
0.14964829430189397
```

In this specific case, a nondecorator approach would allow the subject functions to be used with or without timing, but it would also complicate the call signature when timing is desired—we'd need to add code at every call instead of once at the def. Moreover, in the nondecorator scheme there would be no direct way to guarantee that all list builder calls in a program are routed through timer logic, short of finding and potentially changing them all. This may make it difficult to collect cumulative data for all calls.

In general, *decorators* may be preferred when functions are already deployed as part of a larger system, and may not be easily passed to analysis functions at calls. On the other hand, because decorators charge each call to a function with augmentation logic, a *nondecorator* approach may be better if you wish to augment calls more selectively. As usual, different tools serve different roles.

 Timer call portability and new options in 3.3: Also see Chapter 21's more complete handling and selection of time module functions, as well as its sidebar concerning the new and improved timer functions in this module available as of Python 3.3 (e.g., perf_counter). We're taking a simplistic approach here for both brevity and version neutrality, but time.clock may not be best on some platforms even prior to 3.3, and platform or version tests may be required outside Windows.

Testing subtleties

Notice how this script uses its force setting to make it portable between 2.X and 3.X. As described in Chapter 14, the map built-in returns an *iterable* that generates results on demand in 3.X, but an actual list in 2.X. Hence, 3.X's map by itself doesn't compare directly to a list comprehension's work. In fact, without wrapping it in a list call to force results production, the map test takes virtually no time at all in 3.X—it returns an iterable without iterating!

At the same time, adding this list call in 2.X too charges map with an unfair penalty—the map test's results would include the time required to build *two* lists, not one. To work around this, the script selects a map enclosing function per the Python version number in sys: in 3.X, picking list, and in 2.X using a no-op function that simply returns its input argument unchanged. This adds a very minor constant time in 2.X, which is probably fully overshadowed by the cost of the inner loop iterations in the timed function.

While this makes the comparison between list comprehensions and map more fair in either 2.X or 3.X, because range is also an iterator in 3.X, the results for 2.X and 3.X won't compare directly unless you also hoist this call out of the timed code. They'll be relatively comparable—and will reflect best practice code in each line anyhow—but a range iteration adds extra time in 3.X only. For more on all such things, see Chapter 21's benchmark recreations; producing comparable numbers is often a nontrivial task.

Finally, as we did for the tracer decorator earlier, we could make this timing decorator reusable in other modules by indenting the self-test code at the bottom of the file under a __name__ test so it runs only when the file is run, not when it's imported. We won't do this here, though, because we're about to add another feature to our code.

Adding Decorator Arguments

The timer decorator of the prior section works, but it would be nice if it were more configurable—providing an output label and turning trace messages on and off, for instance, might be useful in a general-purpose tool like this. Decorator arguments come in handy here: when they're coded properly, we can use them to specify configuration options that can vary for each decorated function. A label, for instance, might be added as follows:

```
def timer(label=''):
    def decorator(func):
        def onCall(*args):          # Multilevel state retention:
            ...                     # args passed to function
            func(*args)             # func retained in enclosing scope
            print(label, ...)       # label retained in enclosing scope
        return onCall
    return decorator                # Returns the actual decorator

@timer('==>')                       # Like listcomp = timer('==>')(listcomp)
def listcomp(N): ...                # listcomp is rebound to new onCall

listcomp(...)                       # Really calls onCall
```

This code adds an enclosing scope to retain a decorator argument for use on a later actual call. When the listcomp function is defined, Python really invokes decorator—

the result of `timer`, run before decoration actually occurs—with the `label` value available in its enclosing scope. That is, `timer` *returns* the decorator, which remembers both the decorator argument and the original function, and returns the callable `onCall`, which ultimately invokes the original function on later calls. Because this structure creates new `decorator` and `onCall` functions, their enclosing scopes are per-decoration state retention.

We can put this structure to use in our timer to allow a label and a trace control flag to be passed in at decoration time. Here's an example that does just that, coded in a module file named *timerdeco2.py* so it can be imported as a general tool; it uses a class for the second state retention level instead of a nested function, but the net result is similar:

```python
import time

def timer(label='', trace=True):            # On decorator args: retain args
    class Timer:
        def __init__(self, func):           # On @: retain decorated func
            self.func    = func
            self.alltime = 0
        def __call__(self, *args, **kargs):  # On calls: call original
            start   = time.clock()
            result  = self.func(*args, **kargs)
            elapsed = time.clock() - start
            self.alltime += elapsed
            if trace:
                format = '%s %s: %.5f, %.5f'
                values = (label, self.func.__name__, elapsed, self.alltime)
                print(format % values)
            return result
    return Timer
```

Mostly all we've done here is embed the original `Timer` class in an enclosing function, in order to create a scope that retains the decorator arguments per deployment. The outer `timer` function is called before decoration occurs, and it simply returns the `Timer` class to serve as the actual decorator. On decoration, an instance of `Timer` is made that remembers the decorated function itself, but also has access to the decorator arguments in the enclosing function scope.

Timing with decorator arguments

This time, rather than embedding self-test code in this file, we'll run the decorator in a different file. Here's a client of our timer decorator, the module file *testseqs.py*, applying it to sequence iteration alternatives again:

```python
import sys
from timerdeco2 import timer
force = list if sys.version_info[0] == 3 else (lambda X: X)

@timer(label='[CCC]==>')
def listcomp(N):                        # Like listcomp = timer(...)(listcomp)
    return [x * 2 for x in range(N)]    # listcomp(...) triggers Timer.__call__
```

```
@timer(trace=True, label='[MMM]==>')
def mapcall(N):
    return force(map((lambda x: x * 2), range(N)))

for func in (listcomp, mapcall):
    result = func(5)            # Time for this call, all calls, return value
    func(50000)
    func(500000)
    func(1000000)
    print(result)
    print('allTime = %s\n' % func.alltime)    # Total time for all calls

print('**map/comp = %s' % round(mapcall.alltime / listcomp.alltime, 3))
```

Again, to make this fair, `map` is wrapped in a `list` call in 3.X only. When run as is in 3.X or 2.X, this file prints the following—each decorated function now has a label of its own defined by decorator arguments, which will be more useful when we need to find trace displays mixed in with a larger program's output:

```
c:\code> py -3 testseqs.py
[CCC]==> listcomp: 0.00001, 0.00001
[CCC]==> listcomp: 0.00504, 0.00505
[CCC]==> listcomp: 0.05839, 0.06344
[CCC]==> listcomp: 0.12001, 0.18344
[0, 2, 4, 6, 8]
allTime = 0.1834406801777564

[MMM]==> mapcall: 0.00003, 0.00003
[MMM]==> mapcall: 0.00961, 0.00964
[MMM]==> mapcall: 0.10929, 0.11892
[MMM]==> mapcall: 0.22143, 0.34035
[0, 2, 4, 6, 8]
allTime = 0.3403542519173618

**map/comp = 1.855
```

As usual, we can also test interactively to see how the decorator's configuration arguments come into play:

```
>>> from timerdeco2 import timer
>>> @timer(trace=False)                      # No tracing, collect total time
... def listcomp(N):
...     return [x * 2 for x in range(N)]
...
>>> x = listcomp(5000)
>>> x = listcomp(5000)
>>> x = listcomp(5000)
>>> listcomp.alltime
0.0037191417530599152
>>> listcomp
<timerdeco2.timer.<locals>.Timer object at 0x02957518>

>>> @timer(trace=True, label='\t=>')         # Turn on tracing, custom label
... def listcomp(N):
```

```
...        return [x * 2 for x in range(N)]
...
>>> x = listcomp(5000)
        => listcomp: 0.00106, 0.00106
>>> x = listcomp(5000)
        => listcomp: 0.00108, 0.00214
>>> x = listcomp(5000)
        => listcomp: 0.00107, 0.00321
>>> listcomp.alltime
0.0032089204665562404
```

As is, this timing function decorator can be used for any function, both in modules and interactively. In other words, it automatically qualifies as a *general-purpose tool* for timing code in our scripts. Watch for another example of decorator arguments in the section "Implementing Private Attributes" on page 1314, and again in "A Basic Range-Testing Decorator for Positional Arguments".

 Supporting methods: This section's timer decorator works on any *function*, but a minor rewrite is required to be able to apply it to class-level *methods* too. In short, as our earlier section "Class Blunders I: Decorating Methods" on page 1289 illustrated, it must avoid using a nested class. Because this mutation was deliberately reserved to be a subject of one of our end-of-chapter quiz questions, though, I'll avoid giving away the answer completely here.

Coding Class Decorators

So far we've been coding function decorators to manage function calls, but as we've seen, decorators have been extended to work on classes too as of Python 2.6 and 3.0. As described earlier, while similar in concept to function decorators, class decorators are applied to classes instead—they may be used either to manage *classes* themselves, or to intercept instance creation calls in order to manage *instances*. Also like function decorators, class decorators are really just optional syntactic sugar, though many believe that they make a programmer's intent more obvious and minimize erroneous or missed calls.

Singleton Classes

Because class decorators may intercept instance creation calls, they can be used to either manage all the instances of a class, or augment the interfaces of those instances. To demonstrate, here's a first class decorator example that does the former—managing all instances of a class. This code implements the classic *singleton* coding pattern, where at most one instance of a class ever exists. Its `singleton` function defines and returns a function for managing instances, and the @ syntax automatically wraps up a subject class in this function:

```
# 3.X and 2.X: global table

instances = {}

def singleton(aClass):                          # On @ decoration
    def onCall(*args, **kwargs):                # On instance creation
        if aClass not in instances:             # One dict entry per class
            instances[aClass] = aClass(*args, **kwargs)
        return instances[aClass]
    return onCall
```

To use this, decorate the classes for which you want to enforce a single-instance model (for reference, all the code in this section is in the file *singletons.py*):

```
@singleton                                      # Person = singleton(Person)
class Person:                                   # Rebinds Person to onCall
    def __init__(self, name, hours, rate):      # onCall remembers Person
        self.name = name
        self.hours = hours
        self.rate = rate
    def pay(self):
        return self.hours * self.rate

@singleton                                      # Spam = singleton(Spam)
class Spam:                                      # Rebinds Spam to onCall
    def __init__(self, val):                     # onCall remembers Spam
        self.attr = val

bob = Person('Bob', 40, 10)                     # Really calls onCall
print(bob.name, bob.pay())

sue = Person('Sue', 50, 20)                     # Same, single object
print(sue.name, sue.pay())

X = Spam(val=42)                                # One Person, one Spam
Y = Spam(99)
print(X.attr, Y.attr)
```

Now, when the Person or Spam class is later used to create an instance, the wrapping logic layer provided by the decorator routes instance construction calls to onCall, which in turn ensures a single instance per class, regardless of how many construction calls are made. Here's this code's output (2.X prints extra tuple parentheses):

```
c:\code> python singletons.py
Bob 400
Bob 400
42 42
```

Coding alternatives

Interestingly, you can code a more self-contained solution here if you're able to use the nonlocal statement (available in Python 3.X only) to change enclosing scope names, as described earlier—the following alternative achieves an identical effect, by using one *enclosing scope* per class, instead of one global table entry per class. It works the same, but it does not depend on names in the global scope outside the decorator (note that the None check could use is instead of == here, but it's a trivial test either way):

```
# 3.X only: nonlocal

def singleton(aClass):                              # On @ decoration
    instance = None
    def onCall(*args, **kwargs):                    # On instance creation
        nonlocal instance                           # 3.X and later nonlocal
        if instance == None:
            instance = aClass(*args, **kwargs)      # One scope per class
        return instance
    return onCall
```

In either Python 3.X or 2.X (2.6 and later), you can also code a self-contained solution with either function attributes or a class instead. The first of the following codes the former, leveraging the fact that there will be one onCall *function* per decoration—the object namespace serves the same role as an enclosing scope. The second uses one *instance* per decoration, rather than an enclosing scope, function object, or global table. In fact, the second relies on the same coding pattern that we will later see is a common decorator class blunder—here we *want* just one instance, but that's not usually the case:

```
# 3.X and 2.X: func attrs, classes (alternative codings)

def singleton(aClass):                              # On @ decoration
    def onCall(*args, **kwargs):                    # On instance creation
        if onCall.instance == None:
            onCall.instance = aClass(*args, **kwargs)  # One function per class
        return onCall.instance
    onCall.instance = None
    return onCall


class singleton:
    def __init__(self, aClass):                     # On @ decoration
        self.aClass = aClass
        self.instance = None
    def __call__(self, *args, **kwargs):            # On instance creation
        if self.instance == None:
            self.instance = self.aClass(*args, **kwargs)  # One instance per class
        return self.instance
```

To make this decorator a fully general-purpose tool, choose one, store it in an importable module file, and indent the self-test code under a __name__ check—steps we'll leave as suggested exercise. The final class-based version offers a portability and explicit option, with extra structure that may better support later evolution, but OOP might not be warranted in all contexts.

Tracing Object Interfaces

The singleton example of the prior section illustrated using class decorators to manage *all* the instances of a class. Another common use case for class decorators augments the interface of *each* generated instance. Class decorators can essentially install on instances a wrapper or "proxy" logic layer that manages access to their interfaces in some way.

For example, in Chapter 31, the __getattr__ operator overloading method is shown as a way to wrap up entire object interfaces of embedded instances, in order to implement the *delegation* coding pattern. We saw similar examples in the managed attribute coverage of the prior chapter. Recall that __getattr__ is run when an undefined attribute name is fetched; we can use this hook to intercept method calls in a controller class and propagate them to an embedded object.

For reference, here's the original nondecorator delegation example, working on two built-in type objects:

```python
class Wrapper:
    def __init__(self, object):
        self.wrapped = object                    # Save object
    def __getattr__(self, attrname):
        print('Trace:', attrname)                # Trace fetch
        return getattr(self.wrapped, attrname)   # Delegate fetch

>>> x = Wrapper([1,2,3])                          # Wrap a list
>>> x.append(4)                                   # Delegate to list method
Trace: append
>>> x.wrapped                                     # Print my member
[1, 2, 3, 4]

>>> x = Wrapper({"a": 1, "b": 2})                 # Wrap a dictionary
>>> list(x.keys())                                # Delegate to dictionary method
Trace: keys                                       # Use list() in 3.X
['a', 'b']
```

In this code, the Wrapper class intercepts access to any of the wrapped object's named attributes, prints a trace message, and uses the getattr built-in to pass off the request to the wrapped object. Specifically, it traces attribute accesses made *outside* the wrapped object's class; accesses inside the wrapped object's methods are not caught and run normally by design. This *whole-interface* model differs from the behavior of function decorators, which wrap up just one specific method.

Tracing interfaces with class decorators

Class decorators provide an alternative and convenient way to code this __getattr__ technique to wrap an entire interface. As of both 2.6 and 3.0, for example, the prior class example can be coded as a class decorator that triggers wrapped instance creation, instead of passing a premade instance into the wrapper's constructor (also augmented here to support keyword arguments with **kargs and to count the number of accesses made to illustrate changeable state):

```python
def Tracer(aClass):                               # On @ decorator
    class Wrapper:
        def __init__(self, *args, **kargs):       # On instance creation
            self.fetches = 0
```

```
                    self.wrapped = aClass(*args, **kargs)      # Use enclosing scope name
            def __getattr__(self, attrname):
                print('Trace: ' + attrname)                    # Catches all but own attrs
                self.fetches += 1
                return getattr(self.wrapped, attrname)         # Delegate to wrapped obj
        return Wrapper


    if __name__ == '__main__':

        @Tracer
        class Spam:                                            # Spam = Tracer(Spam)
            def display(self):                                 # Spam is rebound to Wrapper
                print('Spam!' * 8)

        @Tracer
        class Person:                                          # Person = Tracer(Person)
            def __init__(self, name, hours, rate):             # Wrapper remembers Person
                self.name = name
                self.hours = hours
                self.rate = rate
            def pay(self):                                     # Accesses outside class traced
                return self.hours * self.rate                  # In-method accesses not traced

        food = Spam()                                          # Triggers Wrapper()
        food.display()                                         # Triggers __getattr__
        print([food.fetches])

        bob = Person('Bob', 40, 50)                            # bob is really a Wrapper
        print(bob.name)                                        # Wrapper embeds a Person
        print(bob.pay())

        print('')
        sue = Person('Sue', rate=100, hours=60)                # sue is a different Wrapper
        print(sue.name)                                        # with a different Person
        print(sue.pay())

        print(bob.name)                                        # bob has different state
        print(bob.pay())
        print([bob.fetches, sue.fetches])                      # Wrapper attrs not traced
```

It's important to note that this is very different from the tracer decorator we met earlier (despite the name!). In "Coding Function Decorators", we looked at decorators that enabled us to trace and time calls to a given function or method. In contrast, by intercepting instance creation calls, the class decorator here allows us to trace an entire object interface—that is, accesses to any of the instance's attributes.

The following is the output produced by this code under both 3.X and 2.X (2.6 and later): attribute fetches on instances of both the Spam and Person classes invoke the __getattr__ logic in the Wrapper class, because food and bob are really instances of Wrapper, thanks to the decorator's redirection of instance creation calls:

```
c:\code> python interfacetracer.py
Trace: display
```

```
Spam!Spam!Spam!Spam!Spam!Spam!Spam!Spam!
[1]
Trace: name
Bob
Trace: pay
2000

Trace: name
Sue
Trace: pay
6000
Trace: name
Bob
Trace: pay
2000
[4, 2]
```

Notice how there is one `Wrapper` class with state retention per decoration, generated by the nested `class` statement in the `Tracer` function, and how each instance gets its own fetches counter by virtue of generating a new `Wrapper` instance. As we'll see ahead, orchestrating this is trickier than you may expect.

Applying class decorators to built-in types

Also notice that the preceding decorates a user-defined class. Just like in the original example in Chapter 31, we can also use the decorator to wrap up a built-in type such as a list, as long as we either subclass to allow decoration syntax or perform the decoration manually—decorator syntax requires a `class` statement for the @ line. In the following, x is really a `Wrapper` again due to the indirection of decoration:

```
>>> from interfacetracer import Tracer

>>> @Tracer
... class MyList(list): pass        # MyList = Tracer(MyList)

>>> x = MyList([1, 2, 3])           # Triggers Wrapper()
>>> x.append(4)                     # Triggers __getattr__, append
Trace: append
>>> x.wrapped
[1, 2, 3, 4]

>>> WrapList = Tracer(list)         # Or perform decoration manually
>>> x = WrapList([4, 5, 6])         # Else subclass statement required
>>> x.append(7)
Trace: append
>>> x.wrapped
[4, 5, 6, 7]
```

The decorator approach allows us to move instance creation into the decorator itself, instead of requiring a premade object to be passed in. Although this seems like a minor difference, it lets us retain normal instance creation syntax and realize all the benefits of decorators in general. Rather than requiring all instance creation calls to route objects through a wrapper manually, we need only augment class definitions with decorator syntax:

```
@Tracer                                        # Decorator approach
class Person: ...
bob = Person('Bob', 40, 50)
sue = Person('Sue', rate=100, hours=60)

class Person: ...                              # Nondecorator approach
bob = Wrapper(Person('Bob', 40, 50))
sue = Wrapper(Person('Sue', rate=100, hours=60))
```

Assuming you will make more than one instance of a class, and want to apply the augmentation to every instance of a class, decorators will generally be a net win in terms of both code size and code maintenance.

 Attribute version skew note: The preceding tracer decorator works for explicitly accessed attribute names on all Pythons. As we learned in Chapter 38, Chapter 32, and elsewhere, though, __getattr__ intercepts built-ins' implicit accesses to operator overloading methods like __str__ and __repr__ in Python 2.X's default classic classes, but not in 3.X's new-style classes.

In Python 3.X's classes, instances inherit defaults for some, but not all of these names from the class (really, from the object superclass). Moreover, in 3.X, implicitly invoked attributes for built-in operations like printing and + are *not* routed through __getattr__, or its cousin, __get attribute__. In new-style classes, built-ins start such searches at *classes* and skip the normal instance lookup entirely.

Here, this means that the __getattr__ based tracing wrapper will automatically trace and propagate operator overloading calls for built-ins in 2.X as coded, but not in 3.X. To see this, display "x" directly at the end of the preceding interactive session—in 2.X the attribute __repr__ is traced and the list prints as expected, but in 3.X no trace occurs and the list prints using a default display for the Wrapper class:

```
>>> x                              # 2.X
Trace: __repr__
[4, 5, 6, 7]
>>> x                              # 3.X
<interfacetracer.Tracer.<locals>.Wrapper object at 0x02946358>
```

To work the same in 3.X, operator overloading methods generally must be redefined redundantly in the wrapper class, either by hand, by tools, or by definition in superclasses. We'll see this at work again in a Pri vate decorator later in this chapter—where we'll also study ways to add the methods required of such code in 3.X.

Class Blunders II: Retaining Multiple Instances

Curiously, the decorator function in this example can *almost* be coded as a class instead of a function, with the proper operator overloading protocol. The following slightly simplified alternative works similarly because its __init__ is triggered when the @ decorator is applied to the class, and its __call__ is triggered when a subject class instance is created. Our objects are really instances of Tracer this time, and we essentially just trade an enclosing scope reference for an instance attribute here:

```
class Tracer:
    def __init__(self, aClass):        # On @decorator
        self.aClass = aClass           # Use instance attribute
    def __call__(self, *args):         # On instance creation
        self.wrapped = self.aClass(*args)  # ONE (LAST) INSTANCE PER CLASS!
        return self
    def __getattr__(self, attrname):
        print('Trace: ' + attrname)
        return getattr(self.wrapped, attrname)

@Tracer                                # Triggers __init__
class Spam:                            # Like: Spam = Tracer(Spam)
    def display(self):
        print('Spam!' * 8)


...
food = Spam()                          # Triggers __call__
food.display()                         # Triggers __getattr__
```

As we saw in the abstract earlier, though, this class-only alternative handles multiple *classes* as before, but it won't quite work for *multiple instances* of a given class: each instance construction call triggers __call__, which overwrites the prior instance. The net effect is that Tracer saves just one instance—the last one created. Experiment with this yourself to see how, but here's an example of the problem:

```
@Tracer
class Person:                          # Person = Tracer(Person)
    def __init__(self, name):          # Wrapper bound to Person
        self.name = name

bob = Person('Bob')                    # bob is really a Wrapper
print(bob.name)                        # Wrapper embeds a Person
Sue = Person('Sue')
print(sue.name)                        # sue overwrites bob
print(bob.name)                        # OOPS: now bob's name is 'Sue'!
```

This code's output follows—because this tracer only has a single shared instance, the second overwrites the first:

```
Trace: name
Bob
Trace: name
Sue
Trace: name
Sue
```

The problem here is bad *state retention*—we make one decorator instance per class, but not per class instance, such that only the last instance is retained. The solution, as in our prior class blunder for decorating methods, lies in abandoning class-based decorators.

The earlier function-based `Tracer` version *does* work for multiple instances, because each instance construction call makes a new `Wrapper` instance, instead of overwriting the state of a single shared `Tracer` instance; the original nondecorator version handles multiple instances correctly for the same reason. The moral here: decorators are not only arguably magical, they can also be incredibly subtle!

Decorators Versus Manager Functions

Regardless of such subtleties, the `Tracer` class decorator example ultimately still relies on `__getattr__` to intercept fetches on a wrapped and embedded instance object. As we saw earlier, all we've really accomplished is moving the instance creation call inside a class, instead of passing the instance into a manager function. With the original nondecorator tracing example, we would simply code instance creation differently:

```
class Spam:                              # Nondecorator version
    ...                                  # Any class will do
food = Wrapper(Spam())                   # Special creation syntax

@Tracer
class Spam:                              # Decorator version
    ...                                  # Requires @ syntax at class
food = Spam()                            # Normal creation syntax
```

Essentially, *class decorators* shift special syntax requirements from the instance creation call to the class statement itself. This is also true for the singleton example earlier in this section—rather than decorating a class and using normal instance creation calls, we could simply pass the class and its construction arguments into a manager function:

```
instances = {}
def getInstance(aClass, *args, **kwargs):
    if aClass not in instances:
        instances[aClass] = aClass(*args, **kwargs)
    return instances[aClass]

bob = getInstance(Person, 'Bob', 40, 10)     # Versus: bob = Person('Bob', 40, 10)
```

Alternatively, we could use Python's introspection facilities to fetch the class from an already created instance (assuming creating an initial instance is acceptable):

```
instances = {}
def getInstance(object):
    aClass = object.__class__
    if aClass not in instances:
        instances[aClass] = object
    return instances[aClass]

bob = getInstance(Person('Bob', 40, 10))      # Versus: bob = Person('Bob', 40, 10)
```

The same holds true for *function decorators* like the tracer we wrote earlier: rather than decorating a function with logic that intercepts later calls, we could simply pass the function and its arguments into a manager that dispatches the call:

```
def func(x, y):                    # Nondecorator version
    ...                            # def tracer(func, args): ... func(*args)
result = tracer(func, (1, 2))      # Special call syntax

@tracer
def func(x, y):                    # Decorator version
    ...                            # Rebinds name: func = tracer(func)
result = func(1, 2)                # Normal call syntax
```

Manager function approaches like this place the burden of using special syntax on *calls*, instead of expecting decoration syntax at function and class definitions, but also allow you to selectively apply augmentation on a call-by-call basis.

Why Decorators? (Revisited)

So why did I just show you ways to *not* use decorators to implement singletons? As I mentioned at the start of this chapter, decorators present us with tradeoffs. Although syntax matters, we all too often forget to ask the "why" questions when confronted with new tools. Now that we've seen how decorators actually work, let's step back for a minute to glimpse the big picture here before moving on to more code.

Like most language features, decorators have both pros and cons. For example, in the negatives column, decorators may suffer from three potential drawbacks, which can vary per decorator type:

Type changes

As we've seen, when wrappers are inserted, a decorated function or class does not retain its *original type*—it is rebound to a wrapper (proxy) object, which might matter in programs that use object names or test object types. In the singleton example, both the decorator and manager function approaches retain the original class type for instances; in the tracer code, neither approach does, because wrappers are required. Of course, you should avoid type checks in a polymorphic language like Python anyhow, but there are exceptions to most rules.

Extra calls

A wrapping layer added by decoration incurs the additional performance cost of an *extra call* each time the decorated object is invoked—calls are relatively time-expensive operations, so decoration wrappers can make a program slower. In the tracer code, both approaches require each attribute to be routed through a wrapper layer; the singleton example avoids extra calls by retaining the original class type.

All or nothing

Because decorators augment a function or class, they generally apply to *every* later call to the decorated object. That ensures uniform deployment, but can also be a negative if you'd rather apply an augmentation more selectively on a call-by-call basis.

That said, none of these is a very serious issue. For most programs, decorations' uniformity is an asset, the type difference is unlikely to matter, and the speed hit of the extra calls will be insignificant. Furthermore, the latter of these occurs only when wrappers are used, can often be negated if we simply remove the decorator when optimal performance is required, and is also incurred by nondecorator solutions that add wrapping logic (including *metaclasses*, as we'll see in Chapter 40).

Conversely, as we saw at the start of this chapter, decorators have three main advantages. Compared to the manager (a.k.a. "helper") function solutions of the prior section, decorators offer:

Explicit syntax
Decorators make augmentation explicit and obvious. Their @ syntax is easier to recognize than special code in calls that may appear anywhere in a source file—in our singleton and tracer examples, for instance, the decorator lines seem more likely to be noticed than extra code at calls would be. Moreover, decorators allow function and instance creation calls to use normal syntax familiar to all Python programmers.

Code maintenance
Decorators avoid repeated augmentation code at each function or class call. Because they appear just once, at the definition of the class or function itself, they obviate redundancy and simplify future code maintenance. For our singleton and tracer cases, we need to use special code at each call to use a manager function approach—extra work is required both initially and for any modifications that must be made in the future.

Consistency
Decorators make it less likely that a programmer will forget to use required wrapping logic. This derives mostly from the two prior advantages—because decoration is explicit and appears only once, at the decorated objects themselves, decorators promote more consistent and uniform API usage than special code that must be included at each call. In the singleton example, for instance, it would be easy to forget to route all class creation calls through special code, which would subvert the singleton management altogether.

Decorators also promote code *encapsulation* to reduce redundancy and minimize future maintenance effort; augmentation code appears just once in the decorator callable, instead of being copied for each deployment. Although manager functions can achieve this too, decorators also offer an explicit syntax and seamless call model that makes them natural for augmentation tasks.

None of these benefits completely requires decorator syntax to be achieved, though, and decorator usage is ultimately a stylistic choice. That said, most programmers find them to be a net win, especially as a tool for using libraries and APIs correctly.

Historic anecdote: I can recall similar arguments being made both for and against *constructor* functions in classes—prior to the introduction of _init_ methods, programmers achieved the same effect by running an instance through a method manually when creating it (e.g., X=Class().init()). Over time, though, despite being fundamentally a stylistic choice, the _init_ syntax came to be universally preferred because it was more explicit, consistent, and maintainable. Although you should be the judge, decorators seem to bring many of the same assets to the table.

Managing Functions and Classes Directly

Most of our examples in this chapter have been designed to intercept function and instance creation calls. Although this is typical for decorators, they are not limited to this role. Because decorators work by running new functions and classes through decorator code, they can also be used to manage function and class objects themselves, not just later calls made to them.

Imagine, for example, that you require methods or classes used by an application to be registered to an API for later processing (perhaps that API will call the objects later, in response to events). Although you could provide a registration function to be called manually after the objects are defined, decorators make your intent more explicit.

The following simple implementation of this idea defines a decorator that can be applied to *both* functions and classes, to add the object to a dictionary-based registry. Because it returns the object itself instead of a wrapper, it does not intercept later calls:

```python
# Registering decorated objects to an API
from __future__ import print_function      # 2.X

registry = {}
def register(obj):                          # Both class and func decorator
    registry[obj.__name__] = obj            # Add to registry
    return obj                              # Return obj itself, not a wrapper

@register
def spam(x):
    return(x ** 2)                          # spam = register(spam)

@register
def ham(x):
    return(x ** 3)

@register
class Eggs:                                 # Eggs = register(Eggs)
    def __init__(self, x):
        self.data = x ** 4
    def __str__(self):
        return str(self.data)
```

```
print('Registry:')
for name in registry:
    print(name, '=>', registry[name], type(registry[name]))

print('\nManual calls:')
print(spam(2))                                # Invoke objects manually
print(ham(2))                                 # Later calls not intercepted
X = Eggs(2)
print(X)

print('\nRegistry calls:')
for name in registry:
    print(name, '=>', registry[name](2))      # Invoke from registry
```

When this code is run the decorated objects are added to the registry by name, but they still work as originally coded when they're called later, without being routed through a wrapper layer. In fact, our objects can be run both manually and from inside the registry table:

```
c:\code> py -3 registry-deco.py
Registry:
spam => <function spam at 0x02969158> <class 'function'>
ham => <function ham at 0x02969400> <class 'function'>
Eggs => <class '__main__.Eggs'> <class 'type'>

Manual calls:
4
8
16

Registry calls:
spam => 4
ham => 8
Eggs => 16
```

A user interface might use this technique, for example, to register callback handlers for user actions. Handlers might be registered by function or class name, as done here, or decorator arguments could be used to specify the subject event; an extra **def** statement enclosing our decorator could be used to retain such arguments for use on decoration.

This example is artificial, but its technique is very general. For example, function decorators might also be used to process function attributes, and class decorators might insert new class attributes, or even new methods, dynamically. Consider the following function decorators—they assign function attributes to record information for later use by an API, but they do not insert a wrapper layer to intercept later calls:

```
# Augmenting decorated objects directly

>>> def decorate(func):
        func.marked = True          # Assign function attribute for later use
        return func

>>> @decorate
    def spam(a, b):
```

```
        return a + b

>>> spam.marked
True

>>> def annotate(text):              # Same, but value is decorator argument
        def decorate(func):
            func.label = text
            return func
        return decorate

>>> @annotate('spam data')
    def spam(a, b):                   # spam = annotate(...)(spam)
        return a + b

>>> spam(1, 2), spam.label
(3, 'spam data')
```

Such decorators augment functions and classes directly, without catching later calls to them. We'll see more examples of class decorations managing classes directly in the next chapter, because this turns out to encroach on the domain of *metaclasses*; for the remainder of this chapter, let's turn to two larger case studies of decorators at work.

Example: "Private" and "Public" Attributes

The final two sections of this chapter present larger examples of decorator use. Both are presented with minimal description, partly because this chapter has hit its size limits, but mostly because you should already understand decorator basics well enough to study these on your own. Being general-purpose tools, these examples give us a chance to see how decorator concepts come together in more useful code.

Implementing Private Attributes

The following *class decorator* implements a `Private` declaration for class instance attributes—that is, attributes stored on an instance, or inherited from one of its classes. It disallows fetch and change access to such attributes from *outside* the decorated class, but still allows the class itself to access those names freely within its own methods. It's not exactly C++ or Java, but it provides similar access control as an option in Python.

We saw an incomplete first-cut implementation of instance attribute privacy for *changes* only in Chapter 30. The version here extends this concept to validate attribute *fetches* too, and it uses delegation instead of inheritance to implement the model. In fact, in a sense this is just an extension to the attribute tracer class decorator we met earlier.

Although this example utilizes the new syntactic sugar of class decorators to code attribute privacy, its attribute interception is ultimately still based upon the __get attr__ and __setattr__ operator overloading methods we met in prior chapters. When a private attribute access is detected, this version uses the **raise** statement to raise an exception, along with an error message; the exception may be caught in a **try** or allowed to terminate the script.

Here is the code, along with a self test at the bottom of the file. It will work under both Python 3.X and 2.X (2.6 and later) because it employs version-neutral **print** and **raise** syntax, though as coded it catches built-ins' dispatch to operator overloading method attributes in 2.X only (more on this in a moment):

```
"""
File access1.py (3.X + 2.X)

Privacy for attributes fetched from class instances.
See self-test code at end of file for a usage example.

Decorator same as: Doubler = Private('data', 'size')(Doubler).
Private returns onDecorator, onDecorator returns onInstance,
and each onInstance instance embeds a Doubler instance.
"""

traceMe = False
def trace(*args):
    if traceMe: print('[' + ' '.join(map(str, args)) + ']')

def Private(*privates):                              # privates in enclosing scope
    def onDecorator(aClass):                         # aClass in enclosing scope
        class onInstance:                            # wrapped in instance attribute
            def __init__(self, *args, **kargs):
                self.wrapped = aClass(*args, **kargs)

            def __getattr__(self, attr):             # My attrs don't call getattr
                trace('get:', attr)                  # Others assumed in wrapped
                if attr in privates:
                    raise TypeError('private attribute fetch: ' + attr)
                else:
                    return getattr(self.wrapped, attr)

            def __setattr__(self, attr, value):      # Outside accesses
                trace('set:', attr, value)           # Others run normally
                if attr == 'wrapped':                # Allow my attrs
                    self.__dict__[attr] = value      # Avoid looping
                elif attr in privates:
                    raise TypeError('private attribute change: ' + attr)
                else:
                    setattr(self.wrapped, attr, value)   # Wrapped obj attrs
        return onInstance                                # Or use __dict__
    return onDecorator


if __name__ == '__main__':
    traceMe = True

    @Private('data', 'size')                         # Doubler = Private(...)(Doubler)
    class Doubler:
```

```
        def __init__(self, label, start):
            self.label = label              # Accesses inside the subject class
            self.data  = start              # Not intercepted: run normally
        def size(self):
            return len(self.data)           # Methods run with no checking
        def double(self):                   # Because privacy not inherited
            for i in range(self.size()):
                self.data[i] = self.data[i] * 2
        def display(self):
            print('%s => %s' % (self.label, self.data))

X = Doubler('X is', [1, 2, 3])
Y = Doubler('Y is', [-10, -20, -30])

# The following all succeed
print(X.label)                              # Accesses outside subject class
X.display(); X.double(); X.display()        # Intercepted: validated, delegated
print(Y.label)
Y.display(); Y.double()
Y.label = 'Spam'
Y.display()

# The following all fail properly
"""
print(X.size())         # prints "TypeError: private attribute fetch: size"
print(X.data)
X.data = [1, 1, 1]
X.size = lambda S: 0
print(Y.data)
print(Y.size())
"""
```

When traceMe is True, the module file's self-test code produces the following output. Notice how the decorator catches and validates both attribute fetches and assignments run *outside* of the wrapped class, but does not catch attribute accesses *inside* the class itself:

```
c:\code> py -3 access1.py
[set: wrapped <__main__.Doubler object at 0x00000000029769B0>]
[set: wrapped <__main__.Doubler object at 0x00000000029769E8>]
[get: label]
X is
[get: display]
X is => [1, 2, 3]
[get: double]
[get: display]
X is => [2, 4, 6]
[get: label]
Y is
[get: display]
Y is => [-10, -20, -30]
[get: double]
[set: label Spam]
[get: display]
Spam => [-20, -40, -60]
```

Implementation Details I

This code is a bit complex, and you're probably best off tracing through it on your own to see how it works. To help you study, though, here are a few highlights worth mentioning.

Inheritance versus delegation

The first-cut privacy example shown in Chapter 30 used *inheritance* to mix in a __setattr__ to catch accesses. Inheritance makes this difficult, however, because differentiating between accesses from inside or outside the class is not straightforward (inside access should be allowed to run normally, and outside access should be restricted). To work around this, the Chapter 30 example requires inheriting classes to use __dict__ assignments to set attributes—an incomplete solution at best.

The version here uses *delegation* (embedding one object inside another) instead of inheritance; this pattern is better suited to our task, as it makes it much easier to distinguish between accesses inside and outside of the subject class. Attribute accesses from outside the subject class are intercepted by the wrapper layer's overloading methods and delegated to the class if valid. Accesses inside the class itself (i.e., through self within its methods' code) are not intercepted and are allowed to run normally without checks, because privacy is not inherited in this version.

Decorator arguments

The class decorator used here accepts any number of arguments, to name private attributes. What really happens, though, is that the arguments are passed to the Private function, and Private returns the decorator function to be applied to the subject class. That is, the arguments are used before decoration ever occurs; Private returns the decorator, which in turn "remembers" the privates list as an enclosing scope reference.

State retention and enclosing scopes

Speaking of enclosing scopes, there are actually *three levels* of state retention at work in this code:

- The arguments to Private are used before decoration occurs and are retained as an enclosing scope reference for use in both onDecorator and onInstance.
- The class argument to onDecorator is used at decoration time and is retained as an enclosing scope reference for use at instance construction time.
- The wrapped instance object is retained as an instance attribute in the onInstance proxy object, for use when attributes are later accessed from outside the class.

This all works fairly naturally, given Python's scope and namespace rules.

Using __dict__ and __slots__ (and other virtual names)

The __setattr__ method in this code relies on an instance object's __dict__ attribute namespace dictionary in order to set onInstance's own wrapped attribute. As we learned in the prior chapter, this method cannot assign an attribute directly without looping. However, it uses the setattr built-in instead of __dict__ to set attributes in the *wrapped* object itself. Moreover, getattr is used to fetch attributes in the wrapped object, since they may be stored in the object itself or inherited by it.

Because of that, this code will work for most classes—including those with "virtual" class-level attributes based on *slots*, *properties*, *descriptors*, and even __getattr__ and its ilk. By assuming a namespace dictionary for itself only and using storage-neutral tools for the wrapped object, the wrapper class avoids limitations inherent in other tools.

For example, you may recall from Chapter 32 that new-style classes with __slots__ may not store attributes in a __dict__ (and in fact may not even have one of these at all). However, because we rely on a __dict__ only at the onInstance level here, and not in the wrapped instance, this concern does not apply. In addition, because setattr and getattr apply to attributes based on both __dict__ and __slots__, our decorator applies to classes using either storage scheme. By the same reasoning, the decorator also applies to new-style properties and similar tools: delegated names will be looked up anew in the wrapped instance, irrespective of attributes of the decorator proxy object itself.

Generalizing for Public Declarations, Too

Now that we have a Private implementation, it's straightforward to generalize the code to allow for Public declarations too—they are essentially the inverse of Private declarations, so we need only negate the inner test. The example listed in this section allows a class to use decorators to define a set of either Private or Public instance attributes —attributes of any kind stored on an instance or inherited from its classes—with the following semantics:

- Private declares attributes of a class's instances that *cannot* be fetched or assigned, except from within the code of the class's methods. That is, any name declared Private cannot be accessed from outside the class, while any name not declared Private can be freely fetched or assigned from outside the class.

- Public declares attributes of a class's instances that *can* be fetched or assigned from both outside the class and within the class's methods. That is, any name declared Public can be freely accessed anywhere, while any name not declared Public cannot be accessed from outside the class.

Private and Public declarations are intended to be mutually exclusive: when using Private, all undeclared names are considered Public, and when using Public, all undeclared names are considered Private. They are essentially inverses, though undeclared names not created by a class's methods behave slightly differently—new names can be assigned and thus created outside the class under `Private` (all undeclared names are accessible), but not under `Public` (all undeclared names are inaccessible).

Again, study this code on your own to get a feel for how this works. Notice that this scheme adds an additional *fourth level of state retention* at the top, beyond that described in the preceding section: the test functions used by the `lambda`s are saved in an extra enclosing scope. This example is coded to run under either Python 3.X or 2.X (2.6 or later), though it comes with a caveat when run under 3.X (explained briefly in the file's docstring and expanded on after the code):

```
"""
File access2.py (3.X + 2.X)
Class decorator with Private and Public attribute declarations.

Controls external access to attributes stored on an instance, or
Inherited by it from its classes. Private declares attribute names
that cannot be fetched or assigned outside the decorated class,
and Public declares all the names that can.

Caveat: this works in 3.X for explicitly named attributes only: __X__
operator overloading methods implicitly run for built-in operations
do not trigger either __getattr__ or __getattribute__ in new-style
classes.  Add __X__ methods here to intercept and delegate built-ins.
"""

traceMe = False
def trace(*args):
    if traceMe: print('[' + ' '.join(map(str, args)) + ']')

def accessControl(failIf):
    def onDecorator(aClass):
        class onInstance:
            def __init__(self, *args, **kargs):
                self.__wrapped = aClass(*args, **kargs)

            def __getattr__(self, attr):
                trace('get:', attr)
                if failIf(attr):
                    raise TypeError('private attribute fetch: ' + attr)
                else:
                    return getattr(self.__wrapped, attr)

            def __setattr__(self, attr, value):
                trace('set:', attr, value)
                if attr == '_onInstance__wrapped':
                    self.__dict__[attr] = value
                elif failIf(attr):
                    raise TypeError('private attribute change: ' + attr)
                else:
                    setattr(self.__wrapped, attr, value)
        return onInstance
    return onDecorator

def Private(*attributes):
```

```
        return accessControl(failIf=(lambda attr: attr in attributes))

    def Public(*attributes):
        return accessControl(failIf=(lambda attr: attr not in attributes))
```

See the prior example's self-test code for a usage example. Here's a quick look at these class decorators in action at the interactive prompt; they work the same in 2.X and 3.X for attributes referenced by explicit name like those tested here. As advertised, non-Private or Public names can be fetched and changed from outside the subject class, but Private or non-Public names cannot:

```
>>> from access2 import Private, Public

>>> @Private('age')                             # Person = Private('age')(Person)
    class Person:                               # Person = onInstance with state
        def __init__(self, name, age):
            self.name = name
            self.age  = age                      # Inside accesses run normally

>>> X = Person('Bob', 40)
>>> X.name                                       # Outside accesses validated
'Bob'
>>> X.name = 'Sue'
>>> X.name
'Sue'
>>> X.age
TypeError: private attribute fetch: age
>>> X.age = 'Tom'
TypeError: private attribute change: age

>>> @Public('name')
    class Person:
        def __init__(self, name, age):
            self.name = name
            self.age  = age

>>> X = Person('bob', 40)                        # X is an onInstance
>>> X.name                                       # onInstance embeds Person
'bob'
>>> X.name = 'Sue'
>>> X.name
'Sue'
>>> X.age
TypeError: private attribute fetch: age
>>> X.age = 'Tom'
TypeError: private attribute change: age
```

Implementation Details II

To help you analyze the code, here are a few final notes on this version. Since this is just a generalization of the preceding section's version, the implementation notes there apply here as well.

Using __X pseudoprivate names

Besides generalizing, this version also makes use of Python's _X pseudoprivate name mangling feature (which we met in Chapter 31) to localize the wrapped attribute to the proxy control class, by automatically prefixing it with this class's name. This avoids the prior version's risk for collisions with a wrapped attribute that may be used by the real, wrapped class, and it's useful in a general tool like this. It's not quite "privacy," though, because the mangled version of the name can be used freely outside the class. Notice that we also have to use the fully expanded name string—'_onInstance__wrapped'— as a test value in __setattr__, because that's what Python changes it to.

Breaking privacy

Although this example does implement access controls for attributes of an instance and its classes, it is possible to subvert these controls in various ways—for instance, by going through the expanded version of the wrapped attribute explicitly (bob.pay might not work, but the fully mangled bob._onInstance__wrapped.pay could!). If you have to explicitly try to do so, though, these controls are probably sufficient for normal intended use. Of course, privacy controls can generally be subverted in other languages if you try hard enough (#define private public may work in some C++ implementations, too). Although access controls can reduce accidental changes, much of this is up to programmers in any language; whenever source code may be changed, airtight access control will always be a bit of a pipe dream.

Decorator tradeoffs

We could again achieve the same results without decorators, by using manager functions or coding the name rebinding of decorators manually; the decorator syntax, however, makes this consistent and a bit more obvious in the code. The chief potential downsides of this and any other wrapper-based approach are that attribute access incurs an extra call, and instances of decorated classes are not really instances of the original decorated class—if you test their type with X.__class__ or isinstance(X, C), for example, you'll find that they are instances of the *wrapper* class. Unless you plan to do introspection on objects' types, though, the type issue is probably irrelevant, and the extra call may apply mostly to development time; as we'll see later, there are ways to remove decorations automatically if desired.

Open Issues

As is, this example works as planned under both Python 2.X and 3.X for methods called explicitly by name. As with most software, though, there is always room for improvement. Most notably, this tool turns in mixed performance on operator overloading methods if they are used by client classes.

As coded, the proxy class is a classic class when run under 2.X, but a new-style class when run by 3.X. As such, the code supports any client class in 2.X, but in 3.X fails to validate or delegate operator overloading methods dispatched implicitly by built-in operations, unless they are redefined in the proxy. Clients that do not use operator overloading are fully supported, but others may require additional code in 3.X.

Importantly, this is not a new-style class issue here, it's a Python *version* issue—the same code runs differently and fails in 3.X only. Because the nature of the wrapped object's class is irrelevant to the proxy, we are concerned only with the proxy's own code, which works under 2.X but not 3.X.

We've met this issue a few times already in this book, but let's take a quick look at its impact on the very realistic code we've written here, and explore a workaround to it.

Caveat: Implicitly run operator overloading methods fail to delegate under 3.X

Like all delegation-based classes that use `__getattr__`, this decorator works cross-version for normally named or explicitly called attributes only. When run implicitly by built-in operations, operator overloading methods like `__str__` and `__add__` work differently for new-style classes. Because this code is interpreted as a new-style class in 3.X only, such operations fail to reach an embedded object that defines them when run under this Python line as currently coded.

As we learned in the prior chapter, built-in operations look for operator overloading names in *instances* for classic classes, but not for new-style classes—for the latter, they skip the instance entirely and begin the search for such methods in *classes* (technically, in the namespace dictionaries of all classes in the instance's tree). Hence, the `__X__` operator overloading methods implicitly run for built-in operations do *not* trigger either `__getattr__` or `__getattribute__` in new-style classes; because such attribute fetches skip our `onInstance` class's `__getattr__` altogether, they cannot be validated or delegated.

Our decorator's class is not coded as explicitly new-style (by deriving from `object`), so it will catch operator overloading methods if run under 2.X as a default classic class. In 3.X, though, because all classes are new-style automatically (and by mandate), such methods will *fail* if they are implemented by the embedded object—because they are not caught by the proxy, they won't be passed on.

The most direct workaround in 3.X is to redefine redundantly in `onInstance` all the operator overloading methods that can possibly be used in wrapped objects. Such extra methods can be added by hand, by tools that partly automate the task (e.g., with class decorators or the metaclasses discussed in the next chapter), or by definition in reusable superclasses. Though tedious—and code-intensive enough to largely omit here—we'll explore approaches to satisfying this 3.X-only requirement in a moment.

First, though, to see the difference for yourself, try applying the decorator to a class that uses operator overloading methods under 2.X; validations work as before, and both the `__str__` method used by printing and the `__add__` method run for + invoke the decorator's __getattr__ and hence wind up being validated and delegated to the subject Person object correctly:

```
C:\code> c:\python27\python
>>> from access2 import Private
>>> @Private('age')
    class Person:
        def __init__(self):
            self.age = 42
        def __str__(self):
            return 'Person: ' + str(self.age)
        def __add__(self, yrs):
            self.age += yrs

>>> X = Person()
>>> X.age                               # Name validations fail correctly
TypeError: private attribute fetch: age
>>> print(X)                            # __getattr__ => runs Person.__str__
Person: 42
>>> X + 10                              # __getattr__ => runs Person.__add__
>>> print(X)                            # __getattr__ => runs Person.__str__
Person: 52
```

When the same code is run under Python 3.X, though, the implicitly invoked __str__ and __add__ skip the decorator's __getattr__ and look for definitions in or above the decorator class itself; print winds up finding the default display inherited from the class type (technically, from the implied object superclass in 3.X), and + generates an error because no default is inherited:

```
C:\code> c:\python33\python
>>> from access2 import Private
>>> @Private('age')
    class Person:
        def __init__(self):
            self.age = 42
        def __str__(self):
            return 'Person: ' + str(self.age)
        def __add__(self, yrs):
            self.age += yrs

>>> X = Person()                        # Name validations still work
>>> X.age                               # But 3.X fails to delegate built-ins!
TypeError: private attribute fetch: age
>>> print(X)
<access2.accessControl.<locals>.onDecorator.<locals>.onInstance object at ...etc>
>>> X + 10
TypeError: unsupported operand type(s) for +: 'onInstance' and 'int'
>>> print(X)
<access2.accessControl.<locals>.onDecorator.<locals>.onInstance object at ...etc>
```

Strangely, this occurs only for dispatch from built-in operations; explicit direct calls to overload methods are routed to __getattr__, though clients using operator overloading can't be expected to do the same:

```
>>> X.__add__(10)                   # Though calls by name work normally
>>> X._onInstance__wrapped.age      # Break privacy to view result...
52
```

In other words, this is a matter of *built-in operations versus explicit calls*; it has little to do with the actual names of the methods involved. Just for built-in operations, Python skips a step for 3.X's new-style classes.

Using the alternative `__getattribute__` method won't help here—although it is defined to catch every attribute reference (not just undefined names), it is also not run by built-in operations. Python's `property` feature, which we met in Chapter 38, won't help directly here either; recall that properties are automatically run code associated with *specific* attributes defined when a class is written, and are not designed to handle arbitrary attributes in wrapped objects.

Approaches to redefining operator overloading methods for 3.X

As mentioned earlier, the most straightforward solution under 3.X is to redundantly redefine operator overloading names that may appear in embedded objects in delegation-based classes like our decorator. This isn't ideal because it creates some code redundancy, especially compared to 2.X solutions. However, it isn't an impossibly major coding effort; can be automated to some extent with tools or superclasses; suffices to make our decorator work in 3.X; and may allow operator overloading names to be declared `Private` or `Public` too, assuming overloading methods trigger the `failIf` test internally.

Inline definition. For instance, the following is an *inline* redefinition approach—add method redefinitions to the proxy for every operator overloading method a wrapped object may define itself, to catch and delegate. We're adding just four operation interceptors to illustrate, but others are similar (new code is in bold font here):

```
def accessControl(failIf):
    def onDecorator(aClass):
        class onInstance:
            def __init__(self, *args, **kargs):
                self.__wrapped = aClass(*args, **kargs)

            # Intercept and delegate built-in operations specifically
            def __str__(self):
                return str(self.__wrapped)
            def __add__(self, other):
                return self.__wrapped + other          # Or getattr(x, '__add__')(y)
            def __getitem__(self, index):
                return self.__wrapped[index]           # If needed
            def __call__(self, *args, **kargs):
                return self.__wrapped(*args, **kargs)  # If needed
            # plus any others needed

            # Intercept and delegate by-name attribute access generically
            def __getattr__(self, attr): ...
            def __setattr__(self, attr, value): ...
```

```
        return onInstance
    return onDecorator
```

Mix-in superclasses. Alternatively, these methods can be inserted by a common *superclass* —given that there are dozens of such methods, an external class may be better suited to the task, especially if it is general enough to be used in any such interface proxy class. Either of the following mix-in class schemes (among likely others) suffice to catch and delegate built-ins operations:

- The *first* catches built-ins and forcibly reroutes down to the subclass __get attr__. It requires that operator overloading names be public per the decorator's specifications, but built-in operation calls will work the same as both explicit name calls and 2.X's classic classes.

- The *second* catches built-ins and reroutes to the wrapped object directly. It requires access to and assumes a proxy attribute named _wrapped giving access to the embedded object—which is less than ideal because it precludes wrapped objects from using the same name and creates a subclass dependency, but better than using the mangled and class-specific _onInstance__wrapped, and no worse than a similarly named method.

Like the inline approach, both of these mix-ins also require one method per built-in operation in general tools that proxy arbitrary objects' interfaces. Notice how these classes catch operation *calls* rather than operation attribute *fetches*, and thus must perform the actual operation by delegating a call or expression:

```
    class BuiltinsMixin:
        def __add__(self, other):
            return self.__class__.__getattr__(self, '__add__')(other)
        def __str__(self):
            return self.__class__.__getattr__(self, '__str__')()
        def __getitem__(self, index):
            return self.__class__.__getattr__(self, '__getitem__')(index)
        def __call__(self, *args, **kargs):
            return self.__class__.__getattr__(self, '__call__')(*args, **kargs)
        # plus any others needed

def accessControl(failIf):
    def onDecorator(aClass):
        class onInstance(BuiltinsMixin):
            ...rest unchanged...
            def __getattr__(self, attr): ...
            def __setattr__(self, attr, value): ...


    class BuiltinsMixin:
        def __add__(self, other):
            return self._wrapped + other          # Assume a _wrapped
        def __str__(self):                         # Bypass __getattr__
            return str(self._wrapped)
        def __getitem__(self, index):
            return self._wrapped[index]
```

```
        def __call__(self, *args, **kargs):
            return self._wrapped(*args, **kargs)
        # plus any others needed

    def accessControl(failIf):
        def onDecorator(aClass):
            class onInstance(BuiltinsMixin):
                ...and use self._wrapped instead of self.__wrapped...
                def __getattr__(self, attr): ...
                def __setattr__(self, attr, value): ...
```

Either one of these superclass mix-ins will be extraneous code, but must be implemented only once, and seem much more straightforward than the various *metaclass*- or *decorator*-based tool approaches you'll find online that populate each proxy class with the requisite methods redundantly (see the class augmentation examples in Chapter 40 for the principles behind such tools).

Coding variations: Routers, descriptors, automation. Naturally, both of the prior section's mix-in superclasses might be improved with additional code changes we'll largely pass on here, except for two variations worth noting briefly. First, compare the following mutation of the *first* mix-in—which uses a simpler coding structure but will incur an extra call per built-in operation, making it slower (though perhaps not significantly so in a proxy context):

```
    class BuiltinsMixin:
        def reroute(self, attr, *args, **kargs):
            return self.__class__.__getattr__(self, attr)(*args, **kargs)

        def __add__(self, other):
            return self.reroute('__add__', other)
        def __str__(self):
            return self.reroute('__str__')
        def __getitem__(self, index):
            return self.reroute('__getitem__', index)
        def __call__(self, *args, **kargs):
            return self.reroute('__call__', *args, **kargs)
        # plus any others needed
```

Second, all the preceding built-in mix-in classes code each operator overloading method *explicitly*, and intercept the *call* issued for the operation. With an alternative coding, we could instead *generate* methods from a list of names mechanically, and intercept only the attribute *fetch* preceding the call by creating class-level *descriptors* of the prior chapter—as in the following, which, like the second mix-in alternative, assumes the proxied object is named _wrapped in the proxy instance itself:

```
    class BuiltinsMixin:
        class ProxyDesc(object):                                    # object for 2.X
            def __init__(self, attrname):
                self.attrname = attrname
            def __get__(self, instance, owner):
                return getattr(instance._wrapped, self.attrname)    # Assume a _wrapped

        builtins = ['add', 'str', 'getitem', 'call']                # Plus any others
```

```
    for attr in builtins:
        exec('__%s__ = ProxyDesc("__%s__")' % (attr, attr))
```

This coding may be the most concise, but also the most implicit and complex, and is fairly tightly coupled with its subclasses by the shared name. The loop at the end of this class is equivalent to the following, run in the mix-in class's local scope—it creates descriptors that respond to initial name lookups by fetching from the wrapped object in __get__, rather than catching the later operation call itself:

```
__add__ = ProxyDesc("__add__")
__str__ = ProxyDesc("__str__")
...etc...
```

With such operator overloading methods added—either inline or by mix-in inheritance —the prior `Private` example client that overloaded + and `print` with __str__ and __add__ works correctly under 2.X and 3.X, as do subclasses that overload indexing and calls. If you care to experiment further, see files *access2_builtins*.py* in the book examples package for complete codings of these options; we'll also employ the third of the mix-in options in a solution to an end-of-chapter quiz.

Should operator methods be validated?

Adding support for operator overloading methods is required of interface proxies in general, to delegate calls correctly. In our specific privacy application, though, it also raises some additional design choices. In particular, privacy of operator overloading methods differs per implementation:

- Because they invoke __getattr__, the rerouter mix-ins require either that all __X__ names accessed be listed in `Public` decorations, or that `Private` be used instead when operator overloading is present in clients. In classes that use overloading heavily, `Public` may be impractical.

- Because they bypass __getattr__ entirely, as coded here both the inline scheme and `self._wrapped` mix-ins do not have these constraints, but they preclude built-in operations from being made private, and cause built-in operation dispatch to work asymmetrically from both explicit __X__ calls by-name and 2.X's default classic classes.

- Python 2.X classic classes have the first bullet's constraints, simply because all __X__ names are routed through __getattr__ automatically.

- Operator overloading names and protocols differ between 2.X and 3.X, making truly cross-version decoration less than trivial (e.g., `Public` decorators may need to list names from both lines).

We'll leave final policy here a TBD, but some interface proxies might prefer to allow __X__ operator names to always pass unchecked when delegated.

In the general case, though, a substantial amount of extra code is required to accommodate 3.X's new-style classes as delegation proxies—in principle, *every* operator

---

overloading method that is no longer dispatched as a normal instance attribute auto-matically will need to be defined redundantly in a general tool class like this privacy decorator. This is why this extension is omitted in our code: there are potentially more than 50 such methods! Because all its classes are new-style, delegation-based code is more difficult—though not necessarily impossible—in Python 3.X.

Implementation alternatives: __getattribute__ inserts, call stack inspection

Although redundantly defining operator overloading methods in wrappers is probably the most straightforward workaround to Python 3.X dilemma outlined in the prior section, it's not necessarily the only one. We don't have space to explore this issue much further here, so deeper investigation will have to be relegated to suggested exer-cise. Because one dead-end alternative illustrates class concepts well, though, it merits a brief mention.

One downside of the privacy example is that instance objects are not truly instances of the original class—they are instances of the *wrapper* instead. In some programs that rely on type testing, this might matter. To support such cases, we might try to achieve similar effects by *inserting* a __getattribute__ and a __setattr__ method into the orig-inal class, to catch *every* attribute reference and assignment made on its instances. These inserted methods would pass valid requests up to their superclass to avoid loops, using the techniques we studied in the prior chapter. Here is the potential change to our class decorator's code:

```
# Method insertion: rest of access2.py code as before

def accessControl(failIf):
    def onDecorator(aClass):
        def getattributes(self, attr):
            trace('get:', attr)
            if failIf(attr):
                raise TypeError('private attribute fetch: ' + attr)
            else:
                return object.__getattribute__(self, attr)

        def setattributes(self, attr, value):
            trace('set:', attr)
            if failIf(attr):
                raise TypeError('private attribute change: ' + attr)
            else:
                return object.__setattr__(self, attr, value)

        aClass.__getattribute__ = getattributes
        aClass.__setattr__ = setattributes        # Insert accessors
        return aClass                             # Return original class
    return onDecorator
```

This alternative addresses the type-testing issue but suffers from others. For one thing, this decorator can be used by *new-style class* clients only: because __getattribute__ is a new-style-only tool (as is this __setattr__ coding), decorated classes in 2.X must use new-style derivation, which may or may not be appropriate for their goals. In fact, the set of classes supported is even further limited: inserting methods will break clients that are *already using* a __setattr__ or __getattribute__ of their own.

Worse, this scheme does not address the *built-in* operation attributes issue described in the prior section, because __getattribute__ is also not run in these contexts. In our case, if Person had a __str__ it would be run by print operations, but only because it was actually present in that class. As before, the __str__ attribute would *not* be routed to the inserted __getattribute__ method generically—printing would bypass this method altogether and call the class's __str__ directly.

Although this is probably better than not supporting operator overloading methods in a wrapped object at all (barring redefinition, at least), this scheme still cannot intercept and validate __*X*__ methods, making it impossible for any of them to be private. Whether operator overloading methods should be private is another matter, but this structure precludes the possibility.

Much worse, because this nonwrapper approach works by adding a __getattribute__ and __setattr__ to the decorated class, it also intercepts attribute accesses made *by the class itself* and validates them the same as accesses made from outside. In other words, the class's own method won't be able to use its private names either! This is a show-stopper for the insertion approach.

In fact, inserting these methods this way is functionally equivalent to *inheriting* them, and implies the same constraints as our original Chapter 30 privacy code. To know whether an attribute access originated inside or outside the class, our methods might need to inspect frame objects on the Python *call stack*. This might ultimately yield a solution—implementing private attributes as properties or descriptors that check the stack and validate for outside accesses only, for example—but it would slow access further, and is far too dark a magic for us to explore here. (Descriptors seem to make all things possible, even when they shouldn't!)

While interesting, and possibly relevant for some other use cases, this method insertion technique doesn't meet our goals. We won't explore this option's coding pattern further here because we will study class augmentation techniques in the next chapter, in conjunction with metaclasses. As we'll see there, metaclasses are not strictly required for changing classes this way, because class decorators can often serve the same role.

Python Isn't About Control

Now that I've gone to such great lengths to implement Private and Public attribute declarations for Python code, I must again remind you that it is not entirely *Pythonic* to add access controls to your classes like this. In fact, most Python programmers will probably find this example to be largely or totally irrelevant, apart from serving as a demonstration of decorators in action. Most large Python programs get by successfully without any such controls at all.

That said, you might find this tool useful in limited scopes during development. If you do wish to regulate attribute access in order to eliminate coding mistakes, or happen to be a soon-to-be-ex-C++-or-Java programmer, most things are possible with Python's operator overloading and introspection tools.

Example: Validating Function Arguments

As a final example of the utility of decorators, this section develops a *function decorator* that automatically tests whether arguments passed to a function or method are within a valid numeric range. It's designed to be used during either development or production, and it can be used as a template for similar tasks (e.g., argument type testing, if you must). Because this chapter's size limits have been broached, this example's code is largely self-study material, with limited narrative; as usual, browse the code for more details.

The Goal

In the object-oriented tutorial of Chapter 28, we wrote a class that gave a pay raise to objects representing people based upon a passed-in percentage:

```
class Person:
    ...
    def giveRaise(self, percent):
        self.pay = int(self.pay * (1 + percent))
```

There, we noted that if we wanted the code to be robust it would be a good idea to check the percentage to make sure it's not too large or too small. We could implement such a check with either **if** or **assert** statements in the method itself, using *inline tests*:

```
class Person:
    def giveRaise(self, percent):                    # Validate with inline code
        if percent < 0.0 or percent > 1.0:
            raise TypeError, 'percent invalid'
        self.pay = int(self.pay * (1 + percent))
```

```
class Person:                                        # Validate with asserts
    def giveRaise(self, percent):
        assert percent >= 0.0 and percent <= 1.0, 'percent invalid'
        self.pay = int(self.pay * (1 + percent))
```

However, this approach clutters up the method with inline tests that will probably be useful only during development. For more complex cases, this can become tedious (imagine trying to inline the code needed to implement the attribute privacy provided by the last section's decorator). Perhaps worse, if the validation logic ever needs to change, there may be arbitrarily many inline copies to find and update.

A more useful and interesting alternative would be to develop a general tool that can perform range tests for us automatically, for the arguments of any function or method we might code now or in the future. A *decorator* approach makes this explicit and convenient:

```
class Person:
    @rangetest(percent=(0.0, 1.0))          # Use decorator to validate
    def giveRaise(self, percent):
        self.pay = int(self.pay * (1 + percent))
```

Isolating validation logic in a decorator simplifies both clients and future maintenance.

Notice that our goal here is different than the attribute validations coded in the prior chapter's final example. Here, we mean to validate the values of *function arguments* when passed, rather than *attribute values* when set. Python's decorator and introspection tools allow us to code this new task just as easily.

A Basic Range-Testing Decorator for Positional Arguments

Let's start with a basic range test implementation. To keep things simple, we'll begin by coding a decorator that works only for positional arguments and assumes they always appear at the same position in every call; they cannot be passed by keyword name, and we don't support additional **args keywords in calls because this can invalidate the positions declared in the decorator. Code the following in a file called *rangetest1.py*:

```
def rangetest(*argchecks):                  # Validate positional arg ranges
    def onDecorator(func):
        if not __debug__:                   # True if "python -O main.py args..."
            return func                     # No-op: call original directly
        else:                               # Else wrapper while debugging
            def onCall(*args):
                for (ix, low, high) in argchecks:
                    if args[ix] < low or args[ix] > high:
                        errmsg = 'Argument %s not in %s..%s' % (ix, low, high)
                        raise TypeError(errmsg)
                return func(*args)
            return onCall
    return onDecorator
```

As is, this code is mostly a rehash of the coding patterns we explored earlier: we use decorator arguments, nested scopes for state retention, and so on.

We also use nested def statements to ensure that this works for both simple functions and *methods*, as we learned earlier. When used for a class's method, onCall receives the subject class's instance in the first item in *args and passes this along to self in the original method function; argument numbers in range tests start at 1 in this case, not 0.

New here, notice this code's use of the __debug__ built-in variable—Python sets this to True, unless it's being run with the -O optimize command-line flag (e.g., python -O main.py). When __debug__ is False, the decorator returns the origin function unchanged, to avoid extra later calls and their associated performance penalty. In other words, the decorator automatically *removes* its augmentation logic when -O is used, without requiring you to physically remove the decoration lines in your code.

This first iteration solution is used as follows:

```
# File rangetest1_test.py
from __future__ import print_function   # 2.X
from rangetest1 import rangetest
print(__debug__)                                    # False if "python -O main.py"

@rangetest((1, 0, 120))                             # persinfo = rangetest(...)(persinfo)
def persinfo(name, age):                            # age must be in 0..120
    print('%s is %s years old' % (name, age))

@rangetest([0, 1, 12], [1, 1, 31], [2, 0, 2009])
def birthday(M, D, Y):
    print('birthday = {0}/{1}/{2}'.format(M, D, Y))

class Person:
    def __init__(self, name, job, pay):
        self.job = job
        self.pay = pay

    @rangetest([1, 0.0, 1.0])                       # giveRaise = rangetest(...)(giveRaise)
    def giveRaise(self, percent):                   # Arg 0 is the self instance here
        self.pay = int(self.pay * (1 + percent))

# Comment lines raise TypeError unless "python -O" used on shell command line

persinfo('Bob Smith', 45)                           # Really runs onCall(...) with state
#persinfo('Bob Smith', 200)                         # Or person if -O cmd line argument

birthday(5, 31, 1963)
#birthday(5, 32, 1963)

sue = Person('Sue Jones', 'dev', 100000)
sue.giveRaise(.10)                                  # Really runs onCall(self, .10)
print(sue.pay)                                      # Or giveRaise(self, .10) if -O
#sue.giveRaise(1.10)
#print(sue.pay)
```

When run, valid calls in this code produce the following output (all the code in this section works the same under Python 2.X and 3.X, because function decorators are supported in both, we're not using attribute delegation, and we use version-neutral exception construction and printing techniques):

```
C:\code> python rangetest1_test.py
True
Bob Smith is 45 years old
birthday = 5/31/1963
110000
```

Uncommenting any of the invalid calls causes a TypeError to be raised by the decorator. Here's the result when the last two lines are allowed to run (as usual, I've omitted some of the error message text here to save space):

```
C:\code> python rangetest1_test.py
True
```

```
Bob Smith is 45 years old
birthday = 5/31/1963
110000
TypeError: Argument 1 not in 0.0..1.0
```

Running Python with its -O flag at a system command line will disable range testing, but also avoid the performance overhead of the wrapping layer—we wind up calling the original undecorated function directly. Assuming this is a debugging tool only, you can use this flag to optimize your program for production use:

```
C:\code> python -O rangetest1_test.py
False
Bob Smith is 45 years old
birthday = 5/31/1963
110000
231000
```

Generalizing for Keywords and Defaults, Too

The prior version illustrates the basics we need to employ, but it's fairly limited—it supports validating arguments passed by position only, and it does not validate keyword arguments (in fact, it assumes that no keywords are passed in a way that makes argument position numbers incorrect). Additionally, it does nothing about arguments with defaults that may be omitted in a given call. That's fine if all your arguments are passed by position and never defaulted, but less than ideal in a general tool. Python supports much more flexible argument-passing modes, which we're not yet addressing.

The mutation of our example shown next does better. By matching the wrapped function's expected arguments against the actual arguments passed in a call, it supports range validations for arguments passed by either position or keyword name, and it skips testing for default arguments omitted in the call. In short, arguments to be validated are specified by keyword arguments to the decorator, which later steps through both the *pargs positionals tuple and the **kargs keywords dictionary to validate.

```
    """
    File rangetest.py: function decorator that performs range-test
    validation for arguments passed to any function or method.

    Arguments are specified by keyword to the decorator. In the actual
    call, arguments may be passed by position or keyword, and defaults
    may be omitted.  See rangetest_test.py for example use cases.
    """
    trace = True

    def rangetest(**argchecks):                  # Validate ranges for both+defaults
        def onDecorator(func):                   # onCall remembers func and argchecks
            if not __debug__:                    # True if "python -O main.py args..."
                return func                      # Wrap if debugging; else use original
            else:
                code     = func.__code__
                allargs  = code.co_varnames[:code.co_argcount]
                funcname = func.__name__
```

```
def onCall(*pargs, **kargs):
    # All pargs match first N expected args by position
    # The rest must be in kargs or be omitted defaults
    expected    = list(allargs)
    positionals = expected[:len(pargs)]

    for (argname, (low, high)) in argchecks.items():
        # For all args to be checked
        if argname in kargs:
            # Was passed by name
            if kargs[argname] < low or kargs[argname] > high:
                errmsg = '{0} argument "{1}" not in {2}..{3}'
                errmsg = errmsg.format(funcname, argname, low, high)
                raise TypeError(errmsg)

        elif argname in positionals:
            # Was passed by position
            position = positionals.index(argname)
            if pargs[position] < low or pargs[position] > high:
                errmsg = '{0} argument "{1}" not in {2}..{3}'
                errmsg = errmsg.format(funcname, argname, low, high)
                raise TypeError(errmsg)
        else:
            # Assume not passed: default
            if trace:
                print('Argument "{0}" defaulted'.format(argname))

    return func(*pargs, **kargs)     # OK: run original call
    return onCall
return onDecorator
```

The following test script shows how the decorator is used—arguments to be validated are given by keyword decorator arguments, and at actual calls we can pass by name or position and omit arguments with defaults even if they are to be validated otherwise:

```
"""
File rangetest_test.py (3.X + 2.X)
Comment lines raise TypeError unless "python -O" used on shell command line
"""

from __future__ import print_function # 2.X
from rangetest import rangetest

# Test functions, positional and keyword

@rangetest(age=(0, 120))                     # persinfo = rangetest(...)(persinfo)
def persinfo(name, age):
    print('%s is %s years old' % (name, age))

@rangetest(M=(1, 12), D=(1, 31), Y=(0, 2013))
def birthday(M, D, Y):
    print('birthday = {0}/{1}/{2}'.format(M, D, Y))

persinfo('Bob', 40)
persinfo(age=40, name='Bob')
```

```
birthday(5, D=1, Y=1963)
#persinfo('Bob', 150)
#persinfo(age=150, name='Bob')
#birthday(5, D=40, Y=1963)

# Test methods, positional and keyword

class Person:
    def __init__(self, name, job, pay):
        self.job  = job
        self.pay  = pay

                                          # giveRaise = rangetest(...)(giveRaise)
    @rangetest(percent=(0.0, 1.0))        # percent passed by name or position
    def giveRaise(self, percent):
        self.pay = int(self.pay * (1 + percent))

bob = Person('Bob Smith', 'dev', 100000)
sue = Person('Sue Jones', 'dev', 100000)
bob.giveRaise(.10)
sue.giveRaise(percent=.20)
print(bob.pay, sue.pay)
#bob.giveRaise(1.10)
#bob.giveRaise(percent=1.20)

# Test omitted defaults: skipped

@rangetest(a=(1, 10), b=(1, 10), c=(1, 10), d=(1, 10))
def omitargs(a, b=7, c=8, d=9):
    print(a, b, c, d)

omitargs(1, 2, 3, 4)
omitargs(1, 2, 3)
omitargs(1, 2, 3, d=4)
omitargs(1, d=4)
omitargs(d=4, a=1)
omitargs(1, b=2, d=4)
omitargs(d=8, c=7, a=1)

#omitargs(1, 2, 3, 11)        # Bad d
#omitargs(1, 2, 11)           # Bad c
#omitargs(1, 2, 3, d=11)      # Bad d
#omitargs(11, d=4)            # Bad a
#omitargs(d=4, a=11)          # Bad a
#omitargs(1, b=11, d=4)       # Bad b
#omitargs(d=8, c=7, a=11)     # Bad a
```

When this script is run, out-of-range arguments raise an exception as before, but arguments may be passed by either name or position, and omitted defaults are not validated. This code runs on both 2.X and 3.X. Trace its output and test this further on your own to experiment; it works as before, but its scope has been broadened:

```
C:\code> python rangetest_test.py
Bob is 40 years old
Bob is 40 years old
birthday = 5/1/1963
```

```
110000 120000
1 2 3 4
Argument "d" defaulted
1 2 3 9
1 2 3 4
Argument "c" defaulted
Argument "b" defaulted
1 7 8 4
Argument "c" defaulted
Argument "b" defaulted
1 7 8 4
Argument "c" defaulted
1 2 8 4
Argument "b" defaulted
1 7 7 8
```

On validation errors, we get an exception as before when one of the method test lines is uncommented, unless the -O command-line argument is passed to Python to disable the decorator's logic:

```
TypeError: giveRaise argument "percent" not in 0.0..1.0
```

Implementation Details

This decorator's code relies on both introspection APIs and subtle constraints of argument passing. To be fully general we could in principle try to mimic Python's argument matching logic in its entirety to see which names have been passed in which modes, but that's far too much complexity for our tool. It would be better if we could somehow match arguments passed by name against the set of all expected arguments' names, in order to determine which position arguments actually appear in during a given call.

Function introspection

It turns out that the introspection API available on function objects and their associated code objects has exactly the tool we need. This API was briefly introduced in Chapter 19, but we'll actually put it to use here. The set of expected argument names is simply the first *N* variable names attached to a function's code object:

```
# In Python 3.X (and 2.6+ for compatibility)
>>> def func(a, b, c, e=True, f=None):     # Args: three required, two defaults
        x = 1                               # Plus two more local variables
        y = 2

>>> code = func.__code__                    # Code object of function object
>>> code.co_nlocals
7
>>> code.co_varnames                        # All local variable names
('a', 'b', 'c', 'e', 'f', 'x', 'y')
>>> code.co_varnames[:code.co_argcount]     # <== First N locals are expected args
('a', 'b', 'c', 'e', 'f')
```

And as usual, *starred-argument* names in the call proxy allow it to collect arbitrarily many arguments to be matched against the expected arguments so obtained from the function's introspection API:

```
>>> def catcher(*pargs, **kargs): print('%s, %s' % (pargs, kargs))

>>> catcher(1, 2, 3, 4, 5)
(1, 2, 3, 4, 5), {}
>>> catcher(1, 2, c=3, d=4, e=5)            # Arguments at calls
(1, 2), {'d': 4, 'e': 5, 'c': 3}
```

The function object's API is available in older Pythons, but the `func.__code__` attribute is named `func.func_code` in 2.5 and earlier; the newer `__code__` attribute is also redundantly available in 2.6 and later for portability. Run a `dir` call on function and code objects for more details. Code like the following would support 2.5 and earlier, though the `sys.version_info` result itself is similarly nonportable—it's a named tuple in recent Pythons, but we can use offsets on newer and older Pythons alike:

```
>>> import sys                               # For backward compatibility
>>> tuple(sys.version_info)                  # [0] is major release number
(3, 3, 0, 'final', 0)
>>> code = func.__code__ if sys.version_info[0] == 3 else func.func_code
```

Argument assumptions

Given the decorated function's set of expected argument names, the solution relies upon two constraints on argument passing *order* imposed by Python (these still hold true in both 2.X and 3.X current releases):

- At the call, all positional arguments appear before all keyword arguments.
- In the `def`, all nondefault arguments appear before all default arguments.

That is, a nonkeyword argument cannot generally follow a keyword argument at a *call*, and a nondefault argument cannot follow a default argument at a *definition*. All "name=value" syntax must appear after any simple "name" in both places. As we've also learned, Python matches argument values passed by position to argument names in function headers from left to right, such that these values always match the *leftmost* names in headers. Keywords match by name instead, and a given argument can receive only one value.

To simplify our work, we can also make the assumption that a call is *valid* in general —that is, that all arguments either will receive values (by name or position), or will be omitted intentionally to pick up defaults. This assumption won't necessarily hold, because the function has not yet actually been called when the wrapper logic tests validity —the call may still fail later when invoked by the wrapper layer, due to incorrect argument passing. As long as that doesn't cause the wrapper to fail any more badly, though, we can finesse the validity of the call. This helps, because validating calls before they are actually made would require us to emulate Python's argument-matching algorithm in full—again, too complex a procedure for our tool.

Matching algorithm

Now, given these constraints and assumptions, we can allow for both keywords and omitted default arguments in the call with this algorithm. When a call is intercepted, we can make the following assumptions and deductions:

1. Let *N* be the number of passed positional arguments, obtained from the length of the *pargs tuple.

2. All *N* positional arguments in *pargs must match the first *N* expected arguments obtained from the function's code object. This is true per Python's call ordering rules, outlined earlier, since all positionals precede all keywords in a call.

3. To obtain the names of arguments actually passed by position, we can slice the list of all expected arguments up to the length *N* of the *pargs passed positionals tuple.

4. Any arguments after the first *N* expected arguments either were passed by keyword or were defaulted by omission at the call.

5. For each argument name to be validated by the decorator:

    a. If the name is in **kargs, it was passed by name—indexing **kargs gives its passed value.

    b. If the name is in the first *N* expected arguments, it was passed by position— its relative position in the expected list gives its relative position in *pargs.

    c. Otherwise, we can assume it was omitted in the call and defaulted, and need not be checked.

In other words, we can skip tests for arguments that were omitted in a call by assuming that the first *N* actually passed positional arguments in *pargs must match the first *N* argument names in the list of all expected arguments, and that any others must either have been passed by keyword and thus be in **kargs, or have been defaulted. Under this scheme, the decorator will simply skip any argument to be checked that was omitted between the rightmost positional argument and the leftmost keyword argument; between keyword arguments; or after the rightmost positional in general. Trace through the decorator and its test script to see how this is realized in code.

Open Issues

Although our range-testing tool works as planned, three caveats remain—it doesn't detect invalid calls, doesn't handle some arbitrary-argument signatures, and doesn't fully support nesting. Improvements may require extension or altogether different approaches. Here's a quick rundown of the issues.

Invalid calls

First, as mentioned earlier, calls to the original function that are *not valid* still fail in our final decorator. The following both trigger exceptions, for example:

```
omitargs()
omitargs(d=8, c=7, b=6)
```

These only fail, though, where we try to invoke the original function, at the end of the wrapper. While we could try to imitate Python's argument matching to avoid this, there's not much reason to do so—since the call would fail at this point anyhow, we might as well let Python's own argument-matching logic detect the problem for us.

Arbitrary arguments

Second, although our final version handles positional arguments, keyword arguments, and omitted defaults, it still doesn't do anything explicit about *pargs* and **kargs* starred-argument names that may be used in a decorated function that accepts *arbitrarily many* arguments itself. We probably don't need to care for our purposes, though:

- If an extra *keyword* argument is passed, its name will show up in **kargs* and can be tested normally if mentioned to the decorator.

- If an extra keyword argument is *not* passed, its name won't be in either **kargs* or the sliced expected positionals list, and it will thus not be checked—it is treated as though it were defaulted, even though it is really an optional extra argument.

- If an extra *positional* argument is passed, there's no way to reference it in the decorator anyhow—its name won't be in either **kargs* or the sliced expected arguments list, so it will simply be skipped. Because such arguments are not listed in the function's definition, there's no way to map a name given to the decorator back to an expected relative position.

In other words, as it is the code supports testing arbitrary keyword arguments by name, but not arbitrary positionals that are unnamed and hence have no set position in the function's argument signature. In terms of the function object's API, here's the effect of these tools in decorated functions:

```
>>> def func(*kargs, **pargs): pass
>>> code = func.__code__
>>> code.co_nlocals, code.co_varnames
(2, ('kargs', 'pargs'))
>>> code.co_argcount, code.co_varnames[:code.co_argcount]
(0, ())

>>> def func(a, b, *kargs, **pargs): pass
>>> code = func.__code__
>>> code.co_argcount, code.co_varnames[:code.co_argcount]
(2, ('a', 'b'))
```

Because starred-argument names show up as locals but *not* as expected arguments, they won't be a factor in our matching algorithm—names preceding them in function headers can be validated as usual, but not any extra positional arguments passed. In principle, we could extend the decorator's interface to support *pargs* in the decorated function, too, for the rare cases where this might be useful (e.g., a special argument name with a test to apply to all arguments in the wrapper's *pargs* beyond the length of the expected arguments list), but we'll pass on such an extension here.

Decorator nesting

Finally, and perhaps most subtly, this code's approach does not fully support use of *decorator nesting* to combine steps. Because it analyzes arguments using names in function definitions, and the names of the call proxy function returned by a nested decoration won't correspond to argument names in either the original function or decorator arguments, it does not fully support use in nested mode.

Technically, when nested, only the most deeply nested appearance's validations are run in full; all other nesting levels run tests on arguments passed by keyword only. Trace the code to see why; because the `onCall` proxy's call signature expects no named positional arguments, any to-be-validated arguments passed to it by position are treated as if they were omitted and hence defaulted, and are thus skipped.

This may be inherent in this tool's approach—proxies change the argument name signatures at their levels, making it impossible to directly map names in decorator arguments to positions in passed argument sequences. When proxies are present, argument *names* ultimately apply to keywords only; by contrast, the first-cut solution's argument *positions* may support proxies better, but do not fully support keywords.

In lieu of this nesting capability, we'll generalize this decorator to support multiple types of validations in a single decoration in an end-of-chapter quiz solution, which also gives examples of the nesting limitation in action. Since we've already neared the space allocation for this example, though, if you care about these or any other further improvements, you've officially crossed over into the realm of suggested exercises.

Decorator Arguments Versus Function Annotations

Interestingly, the function annotation feature introduced in Python 3.X (3.0 and later) could provide an alternative to the decorator arguments used by our example to specify range tests. As we learned in Chapter 19, annotations allow us to associate expressions with arguments and return values, by coding them in the `def` header line itself; Python collects annotations in a dictionary and attaches it to the annotated function.

We could use this in our example to code range limits in the header line, instead of in decorator arguments. We would still need a function decorator to wrap the function in order to intercept later calls, but we would essentially trade decorator argument syntax:

```
@rangetest(a=(1, 5), c=(0.0, 1.0))
def func(a, b, c):                      # func = rangetest(...)(func)
    print(a + b + c)
```

for annotation syntax like this:

```
@rangetest
def func(a:(1, 5), b, c:(0.0, 1.0)):
    print(a + b + c)
```

That is, the range constraints would be moved into the function itself, instead of being coded externally. The following script illustrates the structure of the resulting decorators under both schemes, in incomplete skeleton code for brevity. The decorator arguments code pattern is that of our complete solution shown earlier; the annotation alternative requires one less level of nesting, because it doesn't need to retain decorator arguments as state:

```
# Using decorator arguments (3.X + 2.X)

def rangetest(**argchecks):
    def onDecorator(func):
        def onCall(*pargs, **kargs):
            print(argchecks)
            for check in argchecks:
                pass                           # Add validation code here
            return func(*pargs, **kargs)
        return onCall
    return onDecorator

@rangetest(a=(1, 5), c=(0.0, 1.0))
def func(a, b, c):                             # func = rangetest(...)(func)
    print(a + b + c)

func(1, 2, c=3)                                # Runs onCall, argchecks in scope


# Using function annotations (3.X only)

def rangetest(func):
    def onCall(*pargs, **kargs):
        argchecks = func.__annotations__
        print(argchecks)
        for check in argchecks:
            pass                               # Add validation code here
        return func(*pargs, **kargs)
    return onCall

@rangetest
def func(a:(1, 5), b, c:(0.0, 1.0)):           # func = rangetest(func)
    print(a + b + c)

func(1, 2, c=3)                                # Runs onCall, annotations on func
```

When run, both schemes have access to the same validation test information, but in different forms—the decorator argument version's information is retained in an argument in an enclosing scope, and the annotation version's information is retained in an attribute of the function itself. In 3.X only, due to the use of function annotations:

```
C:\code> py -3 decoargs-vs-annotation.py
{'a': (1, 5), 'c': (0.0, 1.0)}
6
```

```
{'a': (1, 5), 'c': (0.0, 1.0)}
6
```

I'll leave fleshing out the rest of the annotation-based version as a suggested exercise; its code would be identical to that of our complete solution shown earlier, because range-test information is simply on the function instead of in an enclosing scope. Really, all this buys us is a different user interface for our tool—it will still need to match argument names against expected argument names to obtain relative positions as before.

In fact, using annotation instead of decorator arguments in this example actually *limits its utility*. For one thing, annotation only works under Python 3.X, so 2.X is no longer supported; function decorators with arguments, on the other hand, work in both versions.

More importantly, by moving the validation specifications into the `def` header, we essentially commit the function to a *single role*—since annotation allows us to code only one expression per argument, it can have only one purpose. For instance, we cannot use range-test annotations for any other role.

By contrast, because decorator arguments are coded outside the function itself, they are both easier to remove and *more general*—the code of the function itself does not imply a single decoration purpose. Crucially, by *nesting* decorators with arguments, we can apply multiple augmentation steps to the same function; annotation directly supports only one. With decorator arguments, the function itself also retains a simpler, normal appearance.

Still, if you have a single purpose in mind, and you can commit to supporting 3.X only, the choice between annotation and decorator arguments is largely stylistic and subjective. As is so often true in life, one person's decoration or annotation may well be another's syntactic clutter!

Other Applications: Type Testing (If You Insist!)

The coding pattern we've arrived at for processing arguments in decorators could be applied in other contexts. Checking argument data types at development time, for example, is a straightforward extension:

```python
def typetest(**argchecks):
    def onDecorator(func):
        ...
        def onCall(*pargs, **kargs):
            positionals = list(allargs)[:len(pargs)]
            for (argname, type) in argchecks.items():
                if argname in kargs:
                    if not isinstance(kargs[argname], type):
                        ...
                        raise TypeError(errmsg)
                elif argname in positionals:
                    position = positionals.index(argname)
```

```
                if not isinstance(pargs[position], type):
                    ...
                    raise TypeError(errmsg)
            else:
                # Assume not passed: default
        return func(*pargs, **kargs)
    return onCall
return onDecorator

@typetest(a=int, c=float)
def func(a, b, c, d):              # func = typetest(...)(func)
    ...

func(1, 2, 3.0, 4)                 # OK
func('spam', 2, 99, 4)             # Triggers exception correctly
```

Using function annotations instead of decorator arguments for such a decorator, as described in the prior section, would make this look even more like type declarations in other languages:

```
@typetest
def func(a: int, b, c: float, d):     # func = typetest(func)
    ...                               # Gasp!...
```

But we're getting dangerously close to triggering a "flag on the play" here. As you should have learned in this book, this particular role is generally a bad idea in working code, and, much like private declarations, is not at all *Pythonic* (and is often a symptom of an ex-C++ programmer's first attempts to use Python).

Type testing restricts your function to work on specific types only, instead of allowing it to operate on any types with compatible *interfaces*. In effect, it limits your code and breaks its *flexibility*. On the other hand, every rule has exceptions; type checking may come in handy in isolated cases while debugging and when interfacing with code written in more restrictive languages, such as C++.

Still, this general pattern of argument processing might also be applicable in a variety of less controversial roles. We might even generalize further by passing in a *test function*, much as we did to add `Public` decorations earlier; a single copy of this sort of code would then suffice for both range and type testing, and perhaps other similar goals. In fact, we *will* generalize this way in the end-of-chapter quiz coming up, so we'll leave this extension as a cliffhanger here.

Chapter Summary

In this chapter, we explored decorators—both the function and class varieties. As we learned, decorators are a way to insert code to be run automatically when a function or class is defined. When a decorator is used, Python rebinds a function or class name to the callable object it returns. This hook allows us to manage functions and classes themselves, or later calls to them—by adding a layer of wrapper logic to catch later calls, we can augment both function calls and instance interfaces. As we also saw, manager functions and manual name rebinding can achieve the same effect, but decorators provide a more explicit and uniform solution.

As we also learned, class decorators can be used to manage classes themselves, rather than just their instances. Because this functionality overlaps with *metaclasses*—the topic of the next and final technical chapter— you'll have to read ahead for the conclusion to this story, and that of this book at large. First, though, let's work through the following quiz. Because this chapter was mostly focused on its examples, its quiz will ask you to modify some of its code in order to review. You can find the original versions' code in the book's examples package (see the preface for access pointers). If you're pressed for time, study the modifications listed in the answers instead—programming is as much about reading code as writing it.

Test Your Knowledge: Quiz

1. *Method decorators*: As mentioned in one of this chapter's notes, the *timerdeco2.py* module's timer function decorator with decorator arguments that we wrote in the section "Adding Decorator Arguments" on page 1298 can be applied only to simple *functions*, because it uses a nested class with a `__call__` operator overloading method to catch calls. This structure does not work for a class's *methods* because the decorator instance is passed to `self`, not the subject class instance.

   Rewrite this decorator so that it can be applied to both simple functions and methods in classes, and test it on both functions and methods. (Hint: see the section "Class Blunders I: Decorating Methods" on page 1289 for pointers.) Note that you will probably need to use function object *attributes* to keep track of total time, since you won't have a nested class for state retention and can't access nonlocals from outside the decorator code. As an added bonus, this makes your decorator usable on both Python 3.X and 2.X.

2. *Class decorators*: The `Public`/`Private` class decorators we wrote in module *access2.py* in this chapter's first case study example will add *performance costs* to every attribute fetch in a decorated class. Although we could simply delete the `@` decoration line to gain speed, we could also augment the decorator itself to check the `__debug__` switch and perform no wrapping at all when the `-O` Python flag is passed on the command line—just as we did for the argument range-test decorators. That way, we can speed our program without changing its source, via command-line arguments (`python -O main.py...`). While we're at it, we could also use one of the mix-in superclass techniques we studied to catch a few *built-in operations* in Python 3.X too. Code and test these two extensions.

3. *Generalized argument validations*: The function and method decorator we wrote in *rangetest.py* checks that passed arguments are in a valid range, but we also saw that the same pattern could apply to similar goals such as argument type testing, and possibly more. Generalize the range tester so that its single code base can be used for multiple argument validations. Passed-in functions may be the simplest

solution given the coding structure here, though in more OOP-based contexts, subclasses that provide expected methods can often provide similar generalization routes as well.

Test Your Knowledge: Answers

1. Here's one way to code the first question's solution, and its output (though some methods may run too fast to register reported time). The trick lies in replacing nested classes with *nested functions*, so the self argument is not the decorator's instance, and assigning the total time to the decorator function itself so it can be fetched later through the original rebound name (see the section "State Information Retention Options" of this chapter for details—functions support arbitrary attribute attachment, and the function name is an enclosing scope reference in this context). If you wish to expand this further, it might be useful to also record the *best* (minimum) call time in addition to the total time, as we did in Chapter 21's timer examples.

```
"""
File timerdeco.py (3.X + 2.X)
Call timer decorator for both functions and methods.
"""

import time

def timer(label='', trace=True):              # On decorator args: retain args
    def onDecorator(func):                     # On @: retain decorated func
        def onCall(*args, **kargs):            # On calls: call original
            start   = time.clock()             # State is scopes + func attr
            result  = func(*args, **kargs)
            elapsed = time.clock() - start
            onCall.alltime += elapsed
            if trace:
                format = '%s%s: %.5f, %.5f'
                values = (label, func.__name__, elapsed, onCall.alltime)
                print(format % values)
            return result
        onCall.alltime = 0
        return onCall
    return onDecorator
```

I've coded tests in a separate file here to allow the decorator to be easily reused:

```
"""
File timerdeco-test.py
"""

from __future__ import print_function # 2.X
from timerdeco import timer
import sys
force = list if sys.version_info[0] == 3 else (lambda X: X)

print('-----------------------------------------------------')
# Test on functions
```

```
@timer(trace=True, label='[CCC]==>')
def listcomp(N):                              # Like listcomp = timer(...)(listcomp)
    return [x * 2 for x in range(N)]          # listcomp(...) triggers onCall

@timer('[MMM]==>')
def mapcall(N):
    return force(map((lambda x: x * 2), range(N)))    # list() for 3.X views

for func in (listcomp, mapcall):
    result = func(5)                          # Time for this call, all calls, return value
    func(5000000)
    print(result)
    print('allTime = %s\n' % func.alltime)    # Total time for all calls

print('------------------------------------------------------')
# Test on methods

class Person:
    def __init__(self, name, pay):
        self.name = name
        self.pay  = pay

    @timer()
    def giveRaise(self, percent):             # giveRaise = timer()(giveRaise)
        self.pay *= (1.0 + percent)           # tracer remembers giveRaise

    @timer(label='**')
    def lastName(self):                       # lastName = timer(...)(lastName)
        return self.name.split()[-1]          # alltime per class, not instance

bob = Person('Bob Smith', 50000)
sue = Person('Sue Jones', 100000)
bob.giveRaise(.10)
sue.giveRaise(.20)                            # runs onCall(sue, .10)
print(int(bob.pay), int(sue.pay))
print(bob.lastName(), sue.lastName())         # runs onCall(bob), remembers lastName
print('%.5f %.5f' % (Person.giveRaise.alltime, Person.lastName.alltime))
```

If all goes according to plan, you'll see the following output in both Python 3.X and 2.X, albeit with timing results that will vary per Python and machine:

```
c:\code> py -3 timerdeco-test.py
------------------------------------------------------
[CCC]==>listcomp: 0.00001, 0.00001
[CCC]==>listcomp: 0.57930, 0.57930
[0, 2, 4, 6, 8]
allTime = 0.5793010457092784

[MMM]==>mapcall: 0.00002, 0.00002
[MMM]==>mapcall: 1.08609, 1.08611
[0, 2, 4, 6, 8]
allTime = 1.0861149923442373

------------------------------------------------------
giveRaise: 0.00001, 0.00001
```

```
giveRaise: 0.00000, 0.00001
55000 120000
**lastName: 0.00001, 0.00001
**lastName: 0.00000, 0.00001
Smith Jones
0.00001 0.00001
```

2. The following three files satisfy the second question. The first gives the *decorator* —it's been augmented to return the original class in optimized mode (-0), so attribute accesses don't incur a speed hit. Mostly, it just adds the debug mode test statements and indents the class further to the right:

```
"""
File access.py (3.X + 2.X)
Class decorator with Private and Public attribute declarations.
Controls external access to attributes stored on an instance, or
inherited by it from its classes in any fashion.

Private declares attribute names that cannot be fetched or assigned
outside the decorated class, and Public declares all the names that can.

Caveats: in 3.X catches built-ins coded in BuiltinMixins only (expand me);
as coded, Public may be less useful than Private for operator overloading.
"""
from access_builtins import BuiltinsMixin     # A partial set!

traceMe = False
def trace(*args):
    if traceMe: print('[' + ' '.join(map(str, args)) + ']')

def accessControl(failIf):
    def onDecorator(aClass):
        if not __debug__:
            return aClass
        else:
            class onInstance(BuiltinsMixin):
                def __init__(self, *args, **kargs):
                    self.__wrapped = aClass(*args, **kargs)

                def __getattr__(self, attr):
                    trace('get:', attr)
                    if failIf(attr):
                        raise TypeError('private attribute fetch: ' + attr)
                    else:
                        return getattr(self.__wrapped, attr)

                def __setattr__(self, attr, value):
                    trace('set:', attr, value)
                    if attr == '_onInstance__wrapped':
                        self.__dict__[attr] = value
                    elif failIf(attr):
                        raise TypeError('private attribute change: ' + attr)
                    else:
                        setattr(self.__wrapped, attr, value)
            return onInstance
```

```
        return onDecorator

    def Private(*attributes):
        return accessControl(failIf=(lambda attr: attr in attributes))

    def Public(*attributes):
        return accessControl(failIf=(lambda attr: attr not in attributes))
```

I've also used one of our mix-in techniques to add some operator overloading method redefinitions to the wrapper class, so that in 3.X it correctly delegates built-in operations to subject classes that use these methods. As coded, the proxy is a default classic class in 2.X that routes these through __getattr__ already, but in 3.X is a new-style class that does not. The mix-in used here requires listing such methods in Public decorators; see earlier for alternatives that do not (but that also do not allow built-ins to be made private), and expand this class as needed:

```
"""
File access_builtins.py (from access2_builtins2b.py)
Route some built-in operations back to proxy class __getattr__, so they
work the same in 3.X as direct by-name calls and 2.X's default classic classes.
Expand me as needed to include other __X__ names used by proxied objects.
"""

class BuiltinsMixin:
    def reroute(self, attr, *args, **kargs):
        return self.__class__.__getattr__(self, attr)(*args, **kargs)

    def __add__(self, other):
        return self.reroute('__add__', other)
    def __str__(self):
        return self.reroute('__str__')
    def __getitem__(self, index):
        return self.reroute('__getitem__', index)
    def __call__(self, *args, **kargs):
        return self.reroute('__call__', *args, **kargs)

        # Plus any others used by wrapped objects in 3.X only
```

Here too I split the self-test code off to a separate file, so the decorator could be imported elsewhere without triggering the tests, and without requiring a __name__ test and indenting:

```
"""
File: access-test.py
Test code: separate file to allow decorator reuse.
"""

import sys
from access import Private, Public

print('-----------------------------------------------------------')
# Test 1: names are public if not private

@Private('age')                          # Person = Private('age')(Person)
class Person:                            # Person = onInstance with state
```

```
        def __init__(self, name, age):
            self.name = name
            self.age  = age                    # Inside accesses run normally
        def __add__(self, N):
            self.age += N                      # Built-ins caught by mix-in in 3.X
        def __str__(self):
            return '%s: %s' % (self.name, self.age)

X = Person('Bob', 40)
print(X.name)                                  # Outside accesses validated
X.name = 'Sue'
print(X.name)
X + 10
print(X)

try:    t = X.age                              # FAILS unless "python -O"
except: print(sys.exc_info()[1])
try:    X.age = 999                            # ditto
except: print(sys.exc_info()[1])

print('----------------------------------------------------------')
# Test 2: names are private if not public
# Operators must be non-Private or Public in BuiltinMixin used

@Public('name', '__add__', '__str__', '__coerce__')
class Person:
    def __init__(self, name, age):
        self.name = name
        self.age  = age
    def __add__(self, N):
        self.age += N                          # Built-ins caught by mix-in in 3.X
    def __str__(self):
        return '%s: %s' % (self.name, self.age)

X = Person('bob', 40)                          # X is an onInstance
print(X.name)                                  # onInstance embeds Person
X.name = 'sue'
print(X.name)
X + 10
print(X)

try:    t = X.age                              # FAILS unless "python -O"
except: print(sys.exc_info()[1])
try:    X.age = 999                            # ditto
except: print(sys.exc_info()[1])
```

Finally, if all works as expected, this test's output is as follows in both Python 3.X
and 2.X—the same code applied to the same class decorated with Private and then
with Public:

```
c:\code> py -3 access-test.py
-------------------------------------------------------
Bob
Sue
Sue: 50
```

```
private attribute fetch: age
private attribute change: age
----------------------------------------------------------
bob
sue
sue: 50
private attribute fetch: age
private attribute change: age
```

c:\code> **py -3 -O access-test.py**   *# Suppresses the four access error messages*

3. Here's a generalized argument validator for you to study on your own. It uses a passed-in validation function, to which it passes the test's criteria value coded for the argument in the decorator. This handles ranges, type tests, value testers, and almost anything else you can dream up in an expressive language like Python. I've also refactored the code a bit to remove some redundancy, and automated test failure processing. See this module's self-test for usage examples and expected output. Per this example's caveats described earlier, this decorator doesn't fully work in nested mode as is—only the most deeply nested validation is run for positional arguments—but its arbitrary **valuetest** can be used to combine differing types of tests in a single decoration (though the amount of code needed in this mode may negate much of its benefits over a simple **assert**!).

```
"""
File argtest.py: (3.X + 2.X) function decorator that performs
arbitrary passed-in validations for arguments passed to any
function method. Range and type tests are two example uses;
valuetest handles more arbitrary tests on an argument's value.

Arguments are specified by keyword to the decorator. In the actual
call, arguments may be passed by position or keyword, and defaults
may be omitted.  See self-test code below for example use cases.

Caveats: doesn't fully support nesting because call proxy args
differ; doesn't validate extra args passed to a decoratee's *args;
and may be no easier than an assert except for canned use cases.
"""
trace = False


def rangetest(**argchecks):
    return argtest(argchecks, lambda arg, vals: arg < vals[0] or arg > vals[1])

def typetest(**argchecks):
    return argtest(argchecks, lambda arg, type: not isinstance(arg, type))

def valuetest(**argchecks):
    return argtest(argchecks, lambda arg, tester: not tester(arg))


def argtest(argchecks, failif):          # Validate args per failif + criteria
    def onDecorator(func):               # onCall retains func, argchecks, failif
        if not __debug__:                # No-op if "python -O main.py args..."
```

```
                return func
        else:
            code = func.__code__
            expected = list(code.co_varnames[:code.co_argcount])
            def onError(argname, criteria):
                errfmt = '%s argument "%s" not %s'
                raise TypeError(errfmt % (func.__name__, argname, criteria))

            def onCall(*pargs, **kargs):
                positionals = expected[:len(pargs)]
                for (argname, criteria) in argchecks.items():      # For all to test
                    if argname in kargs:                           # Passed by name
                        if failif(kargs[argname], criteria):
                            onError(argname, criteria)

                    elif argname in positionals:                   # Passed by posit
                        position = positionals.index(argname)
                        if failif(pargs[position], criteria):
                            onError(argname, criteria)
                    else:                                          # Not passed-dflt
                        if trace:
                            print('Argument "%s" defaulted' % argname)
                return func(*pargs, **kargs)   # OK: run original call
            return onCall
    return onDecorator


if __name__ == '__main__':
    import sys
    def fails(test):
        try:    result = test()
        except: print('[%s]' % sys.exc_info()[1])
        else:   print('?%s?' % result)

    print('------------------------------------------------------------------')
    # Canned use cases: ranges, types

    @rangetest(m=(1, 12), d=(1, 31), y=(1900, 2013))
    def date(m, d, y):
        print('date = %s/%s/%s' % (m, d, y))

    date(1, 2, 1960)
    fails(lambda: date(1, 2, 3))

    @typetest(a=int, c=float)
    def sum(a, b, c, d):
        print(a + b + c + d)

    sum(1, 2, 3.0, 4)
    sum(1, d=4, b=2, c=3.0)
    fails(lambda: sum('spam', 2, 99, 4))
    fails(lambda: sum(1, d=4, b=2, c=99))

    print('------------------------------------------------------------------')
    # Arbitrary/mixed tests
```

```
@valuetest(word1=str.islower, word2=(lambda x: x[0].isupper()))
def msg(word1='mighty', word2='Larch', label='The'):
    print('%s %s %s' % (label, word1, word2))

msg()   # word1 and word2 defaulted
msg('majestic', 'Moose')
fails(lambda: msg('Giant', 'Redwood'))
fails(lambda: msg('great', word2='elm'))

print('----------------------------------------------------------------')
# Manual type and range tests

@valuetest(A=lambda x: isinstance(x, int), B=lambda x: x > 0 and x < 10)
def manual(A, B):
    print(A + B)

manual(100, 2)
fails(lambda: manual(1.99, 2))
fails(lambda: manual(100, 20))

print('----------------------------------------------------------------')
# Nesting: runs both, by nesting proxies on original.
# Open issue: outer levels do not validate positionals due
# to call proxy function's differing argument signature;
# when trace=True, in all but the last of these "X" is
# classified as defaulted due to the proxy's signature.

@rangetest(X=(1, 10))
@typetest(Z=str)                              # Only innermost validates positional args
def nester(X, Y, Z):
    return('%s-%s-%s' % (X, Y, Z))

print(nester(1, 2, 'spam'))                   # Original function runs properly
fails(lambda: nester(1, 2, 3))                # Nested typetest is run: positional
fails(lambda: nester(1, 2, Z=3))              # Nested typetest is run: keyword
fails(lambda: nester(0, 2, 'spam'))           # <==Outer rangetest not run: posit.
fails(lambda: nester(X=0, Y=2, Z='spam'))     # Outer rangetest is run: keyword
```

This module's self-test output in both 3.X and 2.X follows (some 2.X object displays vary slightly): as usual, correlate with the source for more insights.

```
c:\code> py -3 argtest.py
----------------------------------------------------------------
date = 1/2/1960
[date argument "y" not (1900, 2013)]
10.0
10.0
[sum argument "a" not <class 'int'>]
[sum argument "c" not <class 'float'>]
----------------------------------------------------------------
The mighty Larch
The majestic Moose
[msg argument "word1" not <method 'islower' of 'str' objects>]
[msg argument "word2" not <function <lambda> at 0x0000000002A096A8>]
----------------------------------------------------------------
```

```
102
[manual argument "A" not <function <lambda> at 0x0000000002A09950>]
[manual argument "B" not <function <lambda> at 0x0000000002A09B70>]
-----------------------------------------------------------------
1-2-spam
[nester argument "Z" not <class 'str'>]
[nester argument "Z" not <class 'str'>]
?0-2-spam?
[onCall argument "X" not (1, 10)]
```

Finally, as we've learned, this decorator's coding structure works for both functions and methods:

```
# File argtest_testmeth.py
from argtest import rangetest, typetest

class C:
    @rangetest(a=(1, 10))
    def meth1(self, a):
        return a * 1000

    @typetest(a=int)
    def meth2(self, a):
        return a * 1000

>>> from argtest_testmeth import C
>>> X = C()
>>> X.meth1(5)
5000
>>> X.meth1(20)
TypeError: meth1 argument "a" not (1, 10)
>>> X.meth2(20)
20000
>>> X.meth2(20.9)
TypeError: meth2 argument "a" not <class 'int'>
```

Metaclasses

In the prior chapter, we explored decorators and studied various examples of their use. In this final technical chapter of the book, we're going to continue our tool-builders focus and investigate another advanced topic: *metaclasses*.

In a sense, metaclasses simply extend the code-insertion model of decorators. As we learned in the prior chapter, function and class decorators allow us to intercept and augment function calls and class instance creation calls. In a similar spirit, metaclasses allow us to intercept and augment *class creation*—they provide an API for inserting extra logic to be run at the conclusion of a `class` statement, albeit in different ways than decorators. Accordingly, they provide a general protocol for managing class objects in a program.

Like all the subjects dealt with in this part of the book, this is an *advanced topic* that can be investigated on an as-needed basis. In practice, metaclasses allow us to gain a high level of control over how a set of classes works. This is a powerful concept, and metaclasses are not intended for most application programmers. Nor, frankly, is this a topic for the faint of heart—some parts of this chapter may warrant extra focus (and others might even owe attribution to Dr. Seuss!).

On the other hand, metaclasses open the door to a variety of coding patterns that may be difficult or impossible to achieve otherwise, and they are especially of interest to programmers seeking to write flexible *APIs* or programming tools for others to use. Even if you don't fall into that category, though, metaclasses can teach you much about Python's class model in general (as we'll see, they even impact *inheritance*), and are prerequisite to understanding code that employs them. Like other advanced tools, metaclasses have begun appearing in Python programs more often than their creators may have intended.

As in the prior chapter, part of our goal here is also to show more realistic code examples than we did earlier in this book. Although metaclasses are a core language topic and not themselves an application domain, part of this chapter's agenda is to spark your interest in exploring larger application-programming examples after you finish this book.

Because this is the final technical chapter in this book, it also begins to wrap up some threads concerning Python itself that we've met often along the way and will finalize in the conclusion that follows. Where you go after this book is up to you, of course, but in an open source project it's important to keep the big picture in mind while hacking the small details.

To Metaclass or Not to Metaclass

Metaclasses are perhaps the most advanced topic in this book, if not the Python language as a whole. To borrow a quote from the *comp.lang.python* newsgroup by veteran Python core developer Tim Peters (who is also the author of the famous "import this" Python motto):

> [Metaclasses] are deeper magic than 99% of users should ever worry about. If you wonder whether you need them, you don't (the people who actually need them know with certainty that they need them, and don't need an explanation about why).

In other words, metaclasses are primarily intended for a subset of programmers building APIs and tools for others to use. In many (if not most) cases, they are probably not the best choice in applications work. This is especially true if you're developing code that other people will use in the future. Coding something "because it seems cool" is not generally a reasonable justification, unless you are experimenting or learning.

Still, metaclasses have a wide variety of potential roles, and it's important to know when they can be useful. For example, they can be used to enhance classes with features like tracing, object persistence, exception logging, and more. They can also be used to construct portions of a class at runtime based upon configuration files, apply function decorators to every method of a class generically, verify conformance to expected interfaces, and so on.

In their more grandiose incarnations, metaclasses can even be used to implement alternative coding patterns such as aspect-oriented programming, object/relational mappers (ORMs) for databases, and more. Although there are often alternative ways to achieve such results—as we'll see, the roles of *class decorators* and metaclasses often intersect—metaclasses provide a formal model tailored to those tasks. We don't have space to explore all such applications first-hand in this chapter, of course, but you should feel free to search the Web for additional use cases after studying the basics here.

Probably the reason for studying metaclasses most relevant to this book is that this topic can help demystify Python's class mechanics in general. For instance, we'll see that they are an intrinsic part of the language's new-style inheritance model finally formalized in full here. Although you may or may not code or reuse them in your work, a cursory understanding of metaclasses can impart a deeper understanding of Python at large.[1]

Increasing Levels of "Magic"

Most of this book has focused on straightforward application-coding techniques—the modules, functions, and classes that most programmers spend their time writing to achieve real-world goals. The majority of Python's users may use classes and make instances, and might even do a bit of operator overloading, but they probably won't get too deep into the details of how their classes actually work.

However, in this book we've also seen a variety of tools that allow us to control Python's behavior in generic ways, and that often have more to do with Python internals or tool building than with application-programming domains. As a review, and to help us place metaclasses in the tools spectrum:

Introspection attributes and tools
> Special attributes like `__class__` and `__dict__` allow us to inspect internal implementation aspects of Python objects, in order to process them generically—to list all attributes of an object, display a class's name, and so on. As we've also seen, tools such as `dir` and `getattr` can serve similar roles when "virtual" attributes such as slots must be supported.

Operator overloading methods
> Specially named methods such as `__str__` and `__add__` coded in classes intercept and provide behavior for built-in operations applied to class instances, such as printing, expression operators, and so on. They are run automatically in response to built-in operations and allow classes to conform to expected interfaces.

Attribute interception methods
> A special category of operator overloading methods provides a way to intercept attribute accesses on instances generically: `__getattr__`, `__setattr__`, `__delattr__`, and `__getattribute__` allow wrapper (a.k.a. proxy) classes to insert automatically run code that may validate attribute requests and delegate them to embedded objects. They allow any number of attributes of an object to be computed when accessed—either selected attributes, or all of them.

Class properties
> The `property` built-in allows us to associate code with a specific class attribute that is automatically run when the attribute is fetched, assigned, or deleted. Though not as generic as the prior paragraph's tools, properties allow for automatic code invocation on access to specific attributes.

Class attribute descriptors
> Really, `property` is a succinct way to define an attribute descriptor that runs functions on access automatically. Descriptors allow us to code in a separate class

---

1. And to quote a Python 3.3 error message I just came across: "TypeError: metaclass conflict: the metaclass of a derived class must be a (non-strict) subclass of the metaclasses of all its bases" (!). This reflects an erroneous use of a module as a superclass, but metaclasses may not be as optional as developers imply —a theme we'll revisit in the next chapter's conclusion to this book.

__get__, __set__, and __delete__ handler methods that are run automatically when an attribute assigned to an instance of that class is accessed. They provide a general way to insert arbitrary code that is run implicitly when a specific attribute is accessed as part of the normal attribute lookup procedure.

Function and class decorators

As we saw in Chapter 39, the special `@callable` syntax for decorators allows us to add logic to be automatically run when a function is called or a class instance is created. This wrapper logic can trace or time calls, validate arguments, manage all instances of a class, augment instances with extra behavior such as attribute fetch validation, and more. Decorator syntax inserts name-rebinding logic to be run at the end of function and class definition statements—decorated function and class names may be rebound to either augmented original objects, or to object proxies that intercept later calls.

Metaclasses

The last topic of magic introduced in Chapter 32, which we take up here.

As mentioned in this chapter's introduction, *metaclasses* are a continuation of this story —they allow us to insert logic to be run automatically at the end of a `class` statement, when a class object is being created. Though strongly reminiscent of class decorators, the metaclass mechanism doesn't rebind the class name to a decorator callable's result, but rather routes *creation of the class itself* to specialized logic.

A Language of Hooks

In other words, metaclasses are ultimately just another way to define *automatically run code*. With the tools listed in the prior section, Python provides ways for us to interject logic in a variety of contexts—at operator evaluation, attribute access, function calls, class instance creation, and now class object creation. It's a language with *hooks galore* —a feature open to abuse like any other, but one that also offers the flexibility that some programmers desire, and that some programs may require.

As we've also seen, many of these advanced Python tools have *intersecting roles*. For example, attributes can often be managed with properties, descriptors, or attribute interception methods. As we'll see in this chapter, class decorators and metaclasses can often be used interchangeably as well. By way of preview:

- Although *class decorators* are often used to manage instances, they can also be used to manage classes instead, much like metaclasses.

- Similarly, while *metaclasses* are designed to augment class construction, they can also insert proxies to manage instances instead, much like class decorators.

In fact, the main functional difference between these two tools is simply their place in the *timing* of class creation. As we saw in the prior chapter, class decorators run *after* the decorated class has already been created. Thus, they are often used to add logic to be run at *instance* creation time. When they do provide behavior for a class, it is typically through changes or proxies, instead of a more direct relationship.

As we'll see here, metaclasses, by contrast, run *during* class creation to make and return the new client class. Therefore, they are often used for managing or augmenting *classes* themselves, and can even provide methods to process the classes that are created from them, via a direct instance relationship.

For example, metaclasses can be used to add decoration to all methods of classes automatically, register all classes in use to an API, add user-interface logic to classes automatically, create or extend classes from simplified specifications in text files, and so on. Because they can control how classes are made—and by proxy the behavior their instances acquire—metaclass applicability is potentially very wide.

As we'll also see here, though, these two tools are more similar than different in many common roles. Since tool choices are sometimes partly subjective, knowledge of the alternatives can help you pick the right tool for a given task. To understand the options better, let's see how metaclasses stack up.

The Downside of "Helper" Functions

Also like the decorators of the prior chapter, metaclasses are often optional from a theoretical perspective. We can usually achieve the same effect by passing class objects through *manager functions*—sometimes known as *helper* functions—much as we can achieve the goals of decorators by passing functions and instances through manager code. Just like decorators, though, metaclasses:

- Provide a more formal and explicit structure
- Help ensure that application programmers won't forget to augment their classes according to an API's requirements
- Avoid code redundancy and its associated maintenance costs by factoring class customization logic into a single location, the metaclass

To illustrate, suppose we want to automatically insert a method into a set of classes. Of course, we could do this with simple *inheritance*, if the subject method is known when we code the classes. In that case, we can simply code the method in a superclass and have all the classes in question inherit from it:

```
class Extras:
    def extra(self, args):          # Normal inheritance: too static
        ...

class Client1(Extras): ...          # Clients inherit extra methods
class Client2(Extras): ...
class Client3(Extras): ...

X = Client1()                       # Make an instance
X.extra()                           # Run the extra methods
```

Sometimes, though, it's impossible to predict such augmentation when classes are co-ded. Consider the case where classes are augmented in response to choices made in a user interface at runtime, or to specifications typed in a configuration file. Although we could code every class in our imaginary set to *manually* check these, too, it's a lot to ask of clients (`required` is abstract here—it's something to be filled in):

```
def extra(self, arg): ...

class Client1: ...                      # Client augments: too distributed
if required():
    Client1.extra = extra

class Client2: ...
if required():
    Client2.extra = extra

class Client3: ...
if required():
    Client3.extra = extra

X = Client1()
X.extra()
```

We can add methods to a class after the `class` statement like this because a class-level method is just a function that is associated with a class and has a first argument to receive the `self` instance. Although this works, it might become untenable for larger method sets, and puts all the burden of augmentation on client classes (and assumes they'll remember to do this at all!).

It would be better from a maintenance perspective to isolate the choice logic in a single place. We might encapsulate some of this extra work by routing classes through a *manager function*—such a manager function would extend the class as required and handle all the work of runtime testing and configuration:

```
def extra(self, arg): ...

def extras(Class):                      # Manager function: too manual
    if required():
        Class.extra = extra

class Client1: ...
extras(Client1)

class Client2: ...
extras(Client2)

class Client3: ...
extras(Client3)

X = Client1()
X.extra()
```

This code runs the class through a manager function immediately after it is created. Although manager functions like this one can achieve our goal here, they still put a fairly heavy burden on class coders, who must understand the requirements and adhere to them in their code. It would be better if there was a simple way to enforce the augmentation in the subject classes, so that they don't need to deal with the augmentation so explicitly, and would be less likely to forget to use it altogether. In other words, we'd like to be able to insert some code to run *automatically* at the end of a `class` statement, to augment the class.

This is exactly what *metaclasses* do—by declaring a metaclass, we tell Python to route the creation of the class object to another class we provide:

```
def extra(self, arg): ...

class Extras(type):
    def __init__(Class, classname, superclasses, attributedict):
        if required():
            Class.extra = extra

class Client1(metaclass=Extras): ...        # Metaclass declaration only (3.X form)
class Client2(metaclass=Extras): ...        # Client class is instance of meta
class Client3(metaclass=Extras): ...

X = Client1()                               # X is instance of Client1
X.extra()
```

Because Python invokes the metaclass automatically at the end of the `class` statement when the new class is created, it can augment, register, or otherwise manage the class as needed. Moreover, the only requirement for the client classes is that they declare the metaclass; every class that does so will automatically acquire whatever augmentation the metaclass provides, both now and in the future if the metaclass changes.

Of course, this is the standard rationale, which you'll need to judge for yourself—in truth, clients might forget to list a metaclass just as easily as they could forget to call a manager function! Still, the explicit nature of metaclasses may make this less likely. Moreover, metaclasses have additional potentials we haven't yet seen. Although it may be difficult to glean from this small example, metaclasses generally handle such tasks better than more manual approaches.

Metaclasses Versus Class Decorators: Round 1

Having said that, it's also important to note that the *class decorators* described in the preceding chapter sometimes overlap with metaclasses—in terms of both utility and benefit. Although they are often used for managing instances, class decorators can also augment classes, independent of any created instances. Their syntax makes their usage similarly explicit, and arguably more obvious than manager function calls.

For example, suppose we coded our manager function to return the augmented class, instead of simply modifying it in place. This would allow a greater degree of flexibility, because the manager would be free to return any type of object that implements the class's expected interface:

```
def extra(self, arg): ...

def extras(Class):
    if required():
        Class.extra = extra
    return Class

class Client1: ...
Client1 = extras(Client1)

class Client2: ...
Client2 = extras(Client2)

class Client3: ...
Client3 = extras(Client3)

X = Client1()
X.extra()
```

If you think this is starting to look reminiscent of class decorators, you're right. In the prior chapter we emphasized class decorators' role in augmenting *instance* creation calls. Because they work by automatically rebinding a class name to the result of a function, though, there's no reason that we can't use them to augment the class by changing it before any instances are ever created. That is, class decorators can apply extra logic to *classes*, not just *instances*, at class creation time:

```
def extra(self, arg): ...

def extras(Class):
    if required():
        Class.extra = extra
    return Class

@extras
class Client1: ...            # Client1 = extras(Client1)

@extras
class Client2: ...            # Rebinds class independent of instances

@extras
class Client3: ...

X = Client1()                 # Makes instance of augmented class
X.extra()                     # X is instance of original Client1
```

Decorators essentially automate the prior example's manual name rebinding here. Just as for metaclasses, because this decorator returns the original class, instances are made from it, not from a wrapper object. In fact, instance creation is not intercepted at all in this example.

In this specific case—adding methods to a class when it's created—the choice between metaclasses and decorators is somewhat arbitrary. Decorators can be used to manage both instances and classes, and intersect most strongly with metaclasses in the second of these roles, but this discrimination is not absolute. In fact, the roles of each are determined in part by their mechanics.

As we'll see ahead, decorators technically correspond to metaclass `__init__` methods, used to initialize newly created classes. Metaclasses have additional customization hooks beyond class initialization, though, and may perform arbitrary class construction tasks that might be more difficult with decorators. This can make them more complex, but also better suited for augmenting classes as they are being formed.

For example, metaclasses also have a `__new__` method used to create a class, which has no analogy in decorators; making a new class in a decorator would incur an extra step. Moreover, metaclasses may also provide behavior acquired by classes in the form of *methods*, which have no direct counterpart in decorators either; decorators must provide class behavior in less direct ways.

Conversely, because metaclasses are designed to manage classes, applying them to managing *instances* alone is less optimal. Because they are also responsible for making the class itself, metaclasses incur this as an *extra* step in instance management roles.

We'll explore these differences in code later in this chapter, and will flesh out this section's partial code into a real working example later in this chapter. To understand how metaclasses do their work, though, we first need to get a clearer picture of their underlying model.

There's Magic, and Then There's Magic

This chapter's "Increasing Levels of Magic" list deals with types of magic beyond those widely seen as beneficial by programmers. Some might add Python's *functional* tools like closures and generators, and even its basic *OOP* support, to this list—the former relying on scope retention and automatic generator object creation, and the latter on inheritance attribute search and a special first function argument. Though based on magic too, these represent paradigms that ease the task of programming by providing abstractions above and beyond the underlying hardware architecture.

For example, *OOP*—Python's earlier paradigm—is broadly accepted in the software world. It provides a model for writing programs that is more complete, explicit, and richly structured than functional tools. That is, some levels of magic are considered more warranted than others; after all, if it were not for some magic, programs would still consist of machine code (or physical switches).

It's usually the *accumulation* of new magic that puts systems at risk of breaching a complexity threshold—such as adding a functional paradigm to what was always an OO language, or adding redundant or advanced ways to achieve goals that are rarely pursued in the common practice of most users. Such magic can set the entry bar far too high for a large part of your tool's audience.

Moreover, some magic is imposed on its users more than others. The translation step of a compiler, for instance, does not generally require its users to be compiler developers. By contrast, Python's **super** assumes full mastery and deployment of the arguably obscure and artificial MRO algorithm. The new-style *inheritance* algorithm presented in this chapter similarly assumes descriptors, metaclasses, and the MRO as its prerequisites—all advanced tools in their own right. Even implicit "hooks" like descriptors remain implicit only until their first failure or maintenance cycle. Such *magic exposed* escalates a tool's prerequisites and downgrades its usability.

In open source systems, only time and downloads can determine where such thresholds may lie. Finding the proper *balance* of power and complexity depends as much on shifting opinion as on technology. Subjective factors aside, though, new magic that imposes itself on users inevitably skews a system's learning curve higher—a topic we'll return to in the next chapter's final words.

The Metaclass Model

To understand metaclasses, you first need to understand a bit more about Python's type model and what happens at the end of a **class** statement. As we'll see here, the two are intimately related.

Classes Are Instances of type

So far in this book, we've done most of our work by making instances of built-in types like lists and strings, as well as instances of classes we code ourselves. As we've seen, instances of *classes* have some state information attributes of their own, but they also inherit behavioral attributes from the classes from which they are made. The same holds true for *built-in* types; list instances, for example, have values of their own, but they inherit methods from the list type.

While we can get a lot done with such instance objects, Python's type model turns out to be a bit richer than I've formally described. Really, there's a hole in the model we've seen thus far: if instances are created from classes, what is it that creates our *classes*? It turns out that classes are instances of something, too:

- In *Python 3.X*, user-defined class objects are instances of the object named **type**, which is itself a class.
- In *Python 2.X*, new-style classes inherit from **object**, which is a subclass of **type**; classic classes are instances of **type** and are not created from a class.

We explored the notion of types in Chapter 9 and the relationship of classes to types in Chapter 32, but let's review the basics here so we can see how they apply to metaclasses.

Recall that the **type** built-in returns the type of any object (which is itself an object) when called with a single argument. For built-in types like lists, the type of the instance is the built-in list type, but the type of the list type is the type **type** itself—the **type** object at the top of the hierarchy creates specific types, and specific types create instances. You can see this for yourself at the interactive prompt. In Python 3.X, for example, the type of a list instance is the list class, and the type of the list class is the type class:

```
C:\code> py -3                              # In 3.X:
>>> type([]), type(type([]))               # List instance is created from list class
(<class 'list'>, <class 'type'>)           # List class is created from type class
>>> type(list), type(type)                 # Same, but with type names
(<class 'type'>, <class 'type'>)           # Type of type is type: top of hierarchy
```

As we learned when studying new-style class changes in Chapter 32, the same is generally true in Python 2.X, but types are not quite the same as classes—**type** is a unique kind of built-in object that caps the type hierarchy and is used to construct types:

```
C:\code> py -2
>>> type([]), type(type([]))               # In 2.X, type is a bit different
(<type 'list'>, <type 'type'>)
>>> type(list), type(type)
(<type 'type'>, <type 'type'>)
```

As it happens, the type/instance relationship holds true for user-defined classes as well: instances are created from classes, and classes are created from **type**. In Python 3.X, though, the notion of a "type" is merged with the notion of a "class." In fact, the two are essentially synonyms—*classes are types, and types are classes*. That is:

- Types are defined by classes that derive from **type**.
- User-defined classes are instances of type classes.
- User-defined classes are types that generate instances of their own.

As we saw earlier, this equivalence affects code that tests the type of instances: the type of an instance is the class from which it was generated. It also has implications for the way that classes are created that turn out to be the key to this chapter's subject. Because classes are normally created from a root type class by default, most programmers don't need to think about this type/class equivalence. However, it opens up new possibilities for customizing both classes and their instances.

For example, all user-defined classes in 3.X (and new-style classes in 2.X) are instances of the **type** class, and instance objects are instances of their classes; in fact, classes now have a __class__ that links to **type**, just as an instance has a __class__ that links to the class from which it was made:

```
C:\code> py -3
>>> class C: pass                          # 3.X class object (new-style)
>>> X = C()                                # Class instance object

>>> type(X)                                # Instance is instance of class
<class '__main__.C'>
>>> X.__class__                            # Instance's class
<class '__main__.C'>

>>> type(C)                                # Class is instance of type
```

```
<class 'type'>
>>> C.__class__                          # Class's class is type
<class 'type'>
```

Notice especially the last two lines here—classes are instances of the **type** class, just as normal instances are instances of a user-defined class. This works the same for both built-ins and user-defined class types in 3.X. In fact, classes are not really a separate concept at all: they are simply user-defined types, and **type** itself is defined by a class.

In Python 2.X, things work similarly for new-style classes derived from **object**, because this enables 3.X class behavior (as we've seen, 3.X adds **object** to the **__bases__** super-class tuple of top-level root classes automatically to qualify them as new-style):

```
C:\code> py -2
>>> class C(object): pass                # In 2.X new-style classes,
>>> X = C()                              # classes have a class too

>>> type(X)
<class '__main__.C'>
>>> X.__class__
<class '__main__.C'>

>>> type(C)
<type 'type'>
>>> C.__class__
<type 'type'>
```

Classic classes in 2.X are a bit different, though—because they reflect the original class model in older Pythons, they do not have a **__class__** link, and like built-in types in 2.X they are instances of **type**, not a type class (I've shortened some of the hex addresses in object displays in this chapter for clarity):

```
C:\code> py -2
>>> class C: pass                        # In 2.X classic classes,
>>> X = C()                              # classes have no class themselves

>>> type(X)
<type 'instance'>
>>> X.__class__
<class __main__.C at 0x005F85A0>

>>> type(C)
<type 'classobj'>
>>> C.__class__
AttributeError: class C has no attribute '__class__'
```

Metaclasses Are Subclasses of Type

Why would we care that classes are instances of a **type** class in 3.X? It turns out that this is the hook that allows us to code metaclasses. Because the notion of *type* is the same as *class* today, we can subclass **type** with normal object-oriented techniques and class syntax to customize it. And because classes are really instances of the **type** class, creating classes from customized subclasses of type allows us to implement custom kinds of classes. In full detail, this all works out quite naturally—in 3.X, and in 2.X new-style classes:

- type is a class that generates user-defined classes.
- Metaclasses are subclasses of the type class.
- Class objects are instances of the type class, or a subclass thereof.
- Instance objects are generated from a class.

In other words, to control the way classes are created and augment their behavior, all we need to do is specify that a user-defined class be created from a user-defined metaclass instead of the normal type class.

Notice that this *type instance* relationship is not quite the same as normal *inheritance*. User-defined classes may also have superclasses from which they and their instances inherit attributes as usual. As we've seen, inheritance superclasses are listed in parentheses in the class statement and show up in a class's __bases__ tuple. The type from which a class is created, though, and of which it is an instance, is a different relationship. Inheritance searches instance and class namespace dictionaries, but classes may also acquire behavior from their type that is not exposed to the normal inheritance search.

To lay the groundwork for understanding this distinction, the next section describes the procedure Python follows to implement this instance-of type relationship.

Class Statement Protocol

Subclassing the type class to customize it is really only half of the magic behind metaclasses. We still need to somehow route a class's creation to the metaclass, instead of the default type. To fully understand how this is arranged, we also need to know how class statements do their business.

We've already learned that when Python reaches a class statement, it runs its nested block of code to create its attributes—all the names assigned at the top level of the nested code block generate attributes in the resulting class object. These names are usually method functions created by nested defs, but they can also be arbitrary attributes assigned to create class data shared by all instances.

Technically speaking, Python follows a standard protocol to make this happen: at the *end of a class statement*, and after running all its nested code in a namespace dictionary corresponding to the class's local scope, Python calls the type object to create the class object like this:

```
class = type(classname, superclasses, attributedict)
```

The type object in turn defines a __call__ operator overloading method that runs two other methods when the type object is called:

```
type.__new__(typeclass, classname, superclasses, attributedict)
type.__init__(class, classname, superclasses, attributedict)
```

The __new__ method creates and returns the new **class** object, and then the __init__ method initializes the newly created object. As we'll see in a moment, these are the hooks that metaclass subclasses of **type** generally use to customize classes.

For example, given a class definition like the following for **Spam**:

```
class Eggs: ...                      # Inherited names here

class Spam(Eggs):                    # Inherits from Eggs
    data = 1                         # Class data attribute
    def meth(self, arg):             # Class method attribute
        return self.data + arg
```

Python will internally run the nested code block to create two attributes of the class (**data** and **meth**), and then call the **type** object to generate the **class** object at the end of the **class** statement:

```
Spam = type('Spam', (Eggs,), {'data': 1, 'meth': meth, '__module__': '__main__'})
```

In fact, you can call **type** this way yourself to create a class dynamically—albeit here with a fabricated method function and empty superclasses tuple (Python adds **object** automatically in both 3.X and 2.X):

```
>>> x = type('Spam', (), {'data': 1, 'meth': (lambda x, y: x.data + y)})
>>> i = x()
>>> x, i
(<class '__main__.Spam'>, <__main__.Spam object at 0x029E7780>)
>>> i.data, i.meth(2)
(1, 3)
```

The class produced is exactly like that you'd get from running a **class** statement:

```
>>> x.__bases__
(<class 'object'>,)
>>> [(a, v) for (a, v) in x.__dict__.items() if not a.startswith('__')]
[('data', 1), ('meth', <function <lambda> at 0x0297A158>)]
```

Because this **type** call is made automatically at the end of the **class** statement, though, it's an ideal hook for augmenting or otherwise processing a class. The trick lies in replacing the default **type** with a custom subclass that will intercept this call. The next section shows how.

Declaring Metaclasses

As we've just seen, classes are created by the **type** class by default. To tell Python to create a class with a custom metaclass instead, you simply need to declare a metaclass to intercept the normal instance creation call in a user-defined class. How you do so depends on which Python version you are using.

Declaration in 3.X

In Python 3.X, list the desired metaclass as a *keyword* argument in the `class` header:

```
class Spam(metaclass=Meta):                    # 3.X version (only)
```

Inheritance superclasses can be listed in the header as well. In the following, for example, the new class `Spam` inherits from superclass `Eggs`, but is also an instance of and is created by metaclass `Meta`:

```
class Spam(Eggs, metaclass=Meta):              # Normal supers OK: must list first
```

In this form, superclasses must be listed before the metaclass; in effect, the ordering rules used for keyword arguments in function calls apply here.

Declaration in 2.X

We can get the same effect in Python 2.X, but we must specify the metaclass differently —using a *class attribute* instead of a keyword argument:

```
class Spam(object):                            # 2.X version (only), object optional?
    __metaclass__ = Meta

class Spam(Eggs, object):                      # Normal supers OK: object suggested
    __metaclass__ = Meta
```

Technically, some classes in 2.X do *not* have to derive from `object` explicitly to make use of metaclasses. The generalized metaclass dispatch mechanism was added at the same time as new-style classes, but is not itself bound to them. It does, however, *produce* them—in the presence of a `__metaclass__` declaration, 2.X makes the resulting class new-style automatically, adding `object` to its `__bases__` sequence. In the absence of this declaration, 2.X simply uses the classic class creator as the metaclass default. Because of this, some classes in 2.X require only the `__metaclass__` attribute.

On the other hand, notice that metaclasses *imply* that your class will be new-style in 2.X even without an explicit `object`. They'll behave somewhat differently as outlined in Chapter 32, and as we'll see ahead 2.X may require that they or their superclasses derive from `object` explicitly, because a new-style class cannot have only classic superclasses in this context. Given this, deriving from `object` doesn't hurt as a sort of warning about the class's nature, and may be required to avoid potential problems.

Also in 2.X, a *module* level `__metaclass__` global variable is available to link all classes in the module to a metaclass. This is no longer supported in 3.X, as it was intended as a temporary measure to make it easier to default to new-style classes without deriving every class from `object`. Python 3.X also ignores the 2.X class attribute, and the 3.X keyword form is a syntax error in 2.X, so there is no simple portability route. Apart from differing syntax, though, metaclass declaration in 2.X and 3.X has the same effect, which we turn to next.

Metaclass Dispatch in Both 3.X and 2.X

When a specific metaclass is declared per the prior sections' syntax, the call to create the `class` object run at the end of the `class` statement is modified to invoke the *metaclass* instead of the `type` default:

```
class = Meta(classname, superclasses, attributedict)
```

And because the metaclass is a subclass of `type`, the `type` class's __call__ delegates the calls to create and initialize the new `class` object to the metaclass, if it defines custom versions of these methods:

```
Meta.__new__(Meta, classname, superclasses, attributedict)
Meta.__init__(class, classname, superclasses, attributedict)
```

To demonstrate, here's the prior section's example again, augmented with a 3.X metaclass specification:

```
class Spam(Eggs, metaclass=Meta):     # Inherits from Eggs, instance of Meta
    data = 1                          # Class data attribute
    def meth(self, arg):              # Class method attribute
        return self.data + arg
```

At the end of this `class` statement, Python internally runs the following to create the `class` object—again, a call you could make manually too, but automatically run by Python's `class` machinery:

```
Spam = Meta('Spam', (Eggs,), {'data': 1, 'meth': meth, '__module__': '__main__'})
```

If the metaclass defines its own versions of __new__ or __init__, they will be invoked in turn during this call by the inherited `type` class's __call__ method, to create and initialize the new class. The net effect is to automatically run methods the metaclass provides, as part of the class construction process. The next section shows how we might go about coding this final piece of the metaclass puzzle.

 This chapter uses Python 3.X metaclass keyword argument syntax, not the 2.X class attribute. 2.X readers will need to translate, but version neutrality is not straightforward here—3.X doesn't recognize the attribute and 2.X doesn't allow keyword syntax—and listing examples twice doesn't address portability (or chapter size!).

Coding Metaclasses

So far, we've seen how Python routes class creation calls to a metaclass, if one is specified and provided. How, though, do we actually code a metaclass that customizes `type`?

It turns out that you already know most of the story—metaclasses are coded with normal Python `class` statements and semantics. By definition, they are simply classes that inherit from `type`. Their only substantial distinctions are that Python calls them *automatically* at the end of a `class` statement, and that they must adhere to the *interface* expected by the `type` superclass.

A Basic Metaclass

Perhaps the simplest metaclass you can code is simply a subclass of `type` with a `__new__` method that creates the class object by running the default version in `type`. A metaclass `__new__` like this is run by the `__call__` method inherited from `type`; it typically performs whatever customization is required and calls the `type` superclass's `__new__` method to create and return the new class object:

```
class Meta(type):
    def __new__(meta, classname, supers, classdict):
        # Run by inherited type.__call__
        return type.__new__(meta, classname, supers, classdict)
```

This metaclass doesn't really do anything (we might as well let the default `type` class create the class), but it demonstrates the way a metaclass taps into the metaclass hook to customize—because the metaclass is called at the end of a `class` statement, and because the `type` object's `__call__` dispatches to the `__new__` and `__init__` methods, code we provide in these methods can manage all the classes created from the metaclass.

Here's our example in action again, with prints added to the metaclass and the file at large to trace (again, some filenames are implied by later command-lines in this chapter):

```
class MetaOne(type):
    def __new__(meta, classname, supers, classdict):
        print('In MetaOne.new:', meta, classname, supers, classdict, sep='\n...')
        return type.__new__(meta, classname, supers, classdict)

class Eggs:
    pass

print('making class')
class Spam(Eggs, metaclass=MetaOne):       # Inherits from Eggs, instance of MetaOne
    data = 1                               # Class data attribute
    def meth(self, arg):                   # Class method attribute
        return self.data + arg

print('making instance')
X = Spam()
print('data:', X.data, X.meth(2))
```

Here, `Spam` inherits from `Eggs` and is an instance of `MetaOne`, but `X` is an instance of and inherits from `Spam`. When this code is run with Python 3.X, notice how the metaclass is invoked at the *end* of the `class` statement, before we ever make an instance—metaclasses are for processing *classes*, and classes are for processing normal *instances*:

```
c:\code> py −3 metaclass1.py
making class
In MetaOne.new:
```

```
...<class '__main__.MetaOne'>
...Spam
...(<class '__main__.Eggs'>,)
...{'data': 1, 'meth': <function Spam.meth at 0x02A191E0>, '__module__': '__main__'}
making instance
data: 1 3
```

Presentation note: I'm truncating addresses and omitting some irrelevant built-in __X__ names in namespace dictionaries in this chapter for brevity, and as noted earlier am forgoing 2.X portability due to differing declaration syntax. To run in 2.X, use the class attribute form, and change print operations as desired. This example works in 2.X with the following modifications, in the file *metaclass1-2x.py*; notice that either Eggs *or* Spam must be derived from object explicitly, or else 2.X issues a warning because new-style class can't have only classic bases here—when in doubt, use object in 2.X metaclasses clients:

```
from __future__ import print_function      # To run the same in 2.X (only)
class Eggs(object):                          # One of the "object" optional
class Spam(Eggs, object):
    __metaclass__ = MetaOne
```

Customizing Construction and Initialization

Metaclasses can also tap into the __init__ protocol invoked by the type object's __call__. In general, __new__ creates and returns the class object, and __init__ initializes the already created class passed in as an argument. Metaclasses can use either or both hooks to manage the class at creation time:

```
class MetaTwo(type):
    def __new__(meta, classname, supers, classdict):
        print('In MetaTwo.new: ', classname, supers, classdict, sep='\n...')
        return type.__new__(meta, classname, supers, classdict)

    def __init__(Class, classname, supers, classdict):
        print('In MetaTwo.init:', classname, supers, classdict, sep='\n...')
        print('...init class object:', list(Class.__dict__.keys()))

class Eggs:
    pass

print('making class')
class Spam(Eggs, metaclass=MetaTwo):         # Inherits from Eggs, instance of MetaTwo
    data = 1                                  # Class data attribute
    def meth(self, arg):                      # Class method attribute
        return self.data + arg

print('making instance')
X = Spam()
print('data:', X.data, X.meth(2))
```

In this case, the class initialization method is run after the class construction method, but both run at the end of the class statement before any instances are made. Con-

---

versely, an __init__ in Spam would run at *instance* creation time, and is not affected or run by the metaclass's __init__:

```
c:\code> py -3 metaclass2.py
making class
In MetaTwo.new:
...Spam
...(<class '__main__.Eggs'>,)
...{'data': 1, 'meth': <function Spam.meth at 0x02967268>, '__module__': '__main__'}
In MetaTwo.init:
...Spam
...(<class '__main__.Eggs'>,)
...{'data': 1, 'meth': <function Spam.meth at 0x02967268>, '__module__': '__main__'}
...init class object: ['__qualname__', 'data', '__module__', 'meth', '__doc__']
making instance
data: 1 3
```

Other Metaclass Coding Techniques

Although redefining the type superclass's __new__ and __init__ methods is the most common way to insert logic into the class object creation process with the metaclass hook, other schemes are possible.

Using simple factory functions

For example, metaclasses need not really be classes at all. As we've learned, the class statement issues a simple call to create a class at the conclusion of its processing. Because of this, *any callable object* can in principle be used as a metaclass, provided it accepts the arguments passed and returns an object compatible with the intended class. In fact, a simple object factory function may serve just as well as a type subclass:

```
# A simple function can serve as a metaclass too

def MetaFunc(classname, supers, classdict):
    print('In MetaFunc: ', classname, supers, classdict, sep='\n...')
    return type(classname, supers, classdict)

class Eggs:
    pass

print('making class')
class Spam(Eggs, metaclass=MetaFunc):      # Run simple function at end
    data = 1                               # Function returns class
    def meth(self, arg):
        return self.data + arg

print('making instance')
X = Spam()
print('data:', X.data, X.meth(2))
```

When run, the function is called at the end of the declaring **class** statement, and it returns the expected new class object. The function is simply catching the call that the type object's __call__ normally intercepts by default:

```
c:\code> py -3 metaclass3.py
making class
In MetaFunc:
...Spam
...(<class '__main__.Eggs'>,)
...{'data': 1, 'meth': <function Spam.meth at 0x029471E0>, '__module__': '__main__'}
making instance
data: 1 3
```

Overloading class creation calls with normal classes

Because normal class instances can respond to call operations with operator overloading, they can serve in some metaclass roles too, much like the preceding function. The output of the following is similar to the prior class-based versions, but it's based on a simple class—one that doesn't inherit from **type** at all, and provides a __call__ for its instances that catches the metaclass call using normal operator overloading. Note that __new__ and __init__ must have different names here, or else they will run when the Meta instance is *created*, not when it is later called in the role of metaclass:

```
# A normal class instance can serve as a metaclass too

class MetaObj:
    def __call__(self, classname, supers, classdict):
        print('In MetaObj.call: ', classname, supers, classdict, sep='\n...')
        Class = self.__New__(classname, supers, classdict)
        self.__Init__(Class, classname, supers, classdict)
        return Class

    def __New__(self, classname, supers, classdict):
        print('In MetaObj.new: ', classname, supers, classdict, sep='\n...')
        return type(classname, supers, classdict)

    def __Init__(self, Class, classname, supers, classdict):
        print('In MetaObj.init:', classname, supers, classdict, sep='\n...')
        print('...init class object:', list(Class.__dict__.keys()))

class Eggs:
    pass

print('making class')
class Spam(Eggs, metaclass=MetaObj()):      # MetaObj is normal class instance
    data = 1                                # Called at end of statement
    def meth(self, arg):
        return self.data + arg

print('making instance')
X = Spam()
print('data:', X.data, X.meth(2))
```

When run, the three methods are dispatched via the normal instance's __call__ inherited from its normal class, but without any dependence on **type** dispatch mechanics or semantics:

```
c:\code> py -3 metaclass4.py
making class
In MetaObj.call:
...Spam
...(<class '__main__.Eggs'>,)
...{'data': 1, 'meth': <function Spam.meth at 0x029492F0>, '__module__': '__main__'}
In MetaObj.new:
...Spam
...(<class '__main__.Eggs'>,)
...{'data': 1, 'meth': <function Spam.meth at 0x029492F0>, '__module__': '__main__'}
In MetaObj.init:
...Spam
...(<class '__main__.Eggs'>,)
...{'data': 1, 'meth': <function Spam.meth at 0x029492F0>, '__module__': '__main__'}
...init class object: ['__module__', '__doc__', 'data', '__qualname__', 'meth']
making instance
data: 1 3
```

In fact, we can use normal superclass inheritance to acquire the call interceptor in this coding model—the superclass here is serving essentially the same role as **type**, at least in terms of metaclass dispatch:

```
# Instances inherit from classes and their supers normally

class SuperMetaObj:
    def __call__(self, classname, supers, classdict):
        print('In SuperMetaObj.call: ', classname, supers, classdict, sep='\n...')
        Class = self.__New__(classname, supers, classdict)
        self.__Init__(Class, classname, supers, classdict)
        return Class

class SubMetaObj(SuperMetaObj):
    def __New__(self, classname, supers, classdict):
        print('In SubMetaObj.new: ', classname, supers, classdict, sep='\n...')
        return type(classname, supers, classdict)

    def __Init__(self, Class, classname, supers, classdict):
        print('In SubMetaObj.init:', classname, supers, classdict, sep='\n...')
        print('...init class object:', list(Class.__dict__.keys()))

class Spam(Eggs, metaclass=SubMetaObj()):    # Invoke Sub instance via Super.__call__
    ...rest of file unchanged...

c:\code> py -3 metaclass4-super.py
making class
In SuperMetaObj.call:
...as before...
In SubMetaObj.new:
...as before...
In SubMetaObj.init:
...as before...
```

```
making instance
data: 1 3
```

Although such alternative forms work, most metaclasses get their work done by redefining the `type` superclass's `__new__` and `__init__`; in practice, this is usually as much
control as is required, and it's often simpler than other schemes. Moreover, metaclasses
have access to additional tools, such as class *methods* we'll explore ahead, which can
influence class behavior more directly than some other schemes.

Still, we'll see later that a simple callable-based metaclass can often work much like a
class decorator, which allows the metaclasses to manage instances as well as classes.
First, though, the next section presents an example drawn from the Python "Twilight
Zone" to introduce metaclass name resolution concepts.

Overloading class creation calls with metaclasses

Since they participate in normal OOP mechanics, it's also possible for metaclasses to
catch the creation call at the end of a `class` statement directly, by redefining the `type`
object's `__call__`. The redefinitions of both `__new__` and `__call__` must be careful to
call back to their defaults in `type` if they mean to make a class in the end, and
`__call__` must invoke `type` to kick off the other two here:

```python
# Classes can catch calls too (but built-ins look in metas, not supers!)

class SuperMeta(type):
    def __call__(meta, classname, supers, classdict):
        print('In SuperMeta.call: ', classname, supers, classdict, sep='\n...')
        return type.__call__(meta, classname, supers, classdict)

    def __init__(Class, classname, supers, classdict):
        print('In SuperMeta init:', classname, supers, classdict, sep='\n...')
        print('...init class object:', list(Class.__dict__.keys()))

print('making metaclass')
class SubMeta(type, metaclass=SuperMeta):
    def __new__(meta, classname, supers, classdict):
        print('In SubMeta.new: ', classname, supers, classdict, sep='\n...')
        return type.__new__(meta, classname, supers, classdict)

    def __init__(Class, classname, supers, classdict):
        print('In SubMeta init:', classname, supers, classdict, sep='\n...')
        print('...init class object:', list(Class.__dict__.keys()))

class Eggs:
    pass

print('making class')
class Spam(Eggs, metaclass=SubMeta):           # Invoke SubMeta, via SuperMeta.__call__
    data = 1
    def meth(self, arg):
        return self.data + arg

print('making instance')
```

```
X = Spam()
print('data:', X.data, X.meth(2))
```

This code has some oddities I'll explain in a moment. When run, though, all three redefined methods run in turn for Spam as in the prior section. This is again essentially what the type object does by default, but there's an additional metaclass call for the metaclass subclass (*metasubclass?*):

```
c:\code> py -3 metaclass5.py
making metaclass
In SuperMeta init:
...SubMeta
...(<class 'type'>,)
...{'__init__': <function SubMeta.__init__ at 0x028F92F0>, ...}
...init class object: ['__doc__', '__module__', '__new__', '__init__', ...]
making class
In SuperMeta.call:
...Spam
...(<class '__main__.Eggs'>,)
...{'data': 1, 'meth': <function Spam.meth at 0x028F9378>, '__module__': '__main__'}
In SubMeta.new:
...Spam
...(<class '__main__.Eggs'>,)
...{'data': 1, 'meth': <function Spam.meth at 0x028F9378>, '__module__': '__main__'}
In SubMeta init:
...Spam
...(<class '__main__.Eggs'>,)
...{'data': 1, 'meth': <function Spam.meth at 0x028F9378>, '__module__': '__main__'}
...init class object: ['__qualname__', '__module__', '__doc__', 'data', 'meth']
making instance
data: 1 3
```

This example is complicated by the fact that it overrides a method invoked by a *built-in* operation—in this case, the call run automatically to create a class. Metaclasses are used to create class objects, but only generate instances of themselves when called in a metaclass role. Because of this, name lookup with metaclasses may be somewhat different than what we are accustomed to. The __call__ method, for example, is looked up by built-ins in the class (a.k.a. type) of an object; for metaclasses, this means the metaclass of a metaclass!

As we'll see ahead, metaclasses also *inherit* names from other metaclasses normally, but as for normal classes, this seems to apply to *explicit* name fetches only, not to the *implicit* lookup of names for built-in operations such as calls. The latter appears to look in the metaclass's *class*, available in its __class__ link—which is either the default type or a metaclass. This is the same built-ins routing issue we've seen so often in this book for normal class instances. The metaclass in SubMeta is required to set this link, though this also kicks off a metaclass construction step for the metaclass itself.

Trace the invocations in the output. SuperMeta's __call__ method is *not* run for the call to SuperMeta when making SubMeta (this goes to type instead), but *is* run for the Sub Meta call when making Spam. Inheriting normally from SuperMeta does not suffice to catch SubMeta calls, and for reasons we'll see later is actually the wrong thing to do for operator overloading methods: SuperMeta's __call__ is then acquired by Spam, causing Spam instance creation calls to fail before any instance is ever created. Subtle but true!

Here's an illustration of the issue in simpler terms—a normal superclass is skipped for *built-ins*, but not for *explicit* fetches and calls, the latter relying on normal attribute name inheritance:

```
class SuperMeta(type):
    def __call__(meta, classname, supers, classdict):    # By name, not built-in
        print('In SuperMeta.call:', classname)
        return type.__call__(meta, classname, supers, classdict)

class SubMeta(SuperMeta):                                  # Created by type default
    def __init__(Class, classname, supers, classdict):     # Overrides type.__init__
        print('In SubMeta init:', classname)

print(SubMeta.__class__)
print([n.__name__ for n in SubMeta.__mro__])
print()
print(SubMeta.__call__)                          # Not a data descriptor if found by name
print()
SubMeta.__call__(SubMeta, 'xxx', (), {})         # Explicit calls work: class inheritance
print()
SubMeta('yyy', (), {})                           # But implicit built-in calls do not: type

c:\code> py -3 metaclass5b.py
<class 'type'>
['SubMeta', 'SuperMeta', 'type', 'object']

<function SuperMeta.__call__ at 0x029B9158>

In SuperMeta.call: xxx
In SubMeta init: xxx

In SubMeta init: yyy
```

Of course, this specific example is a special case: catching a built-in run on a metaclass, a likely rare usage related to __call__ here. But it underscores a core asymmetry and apparent inconsistency: *normal attribute inheritance is not fully used for built-in dispatch* —for both instances and classes.

To truly understand this example's subtleties, though, we need to get more formal about what metaclasses mean for Python name resolution in general.

Inheritance and Instance

Because metaclasses are specified in similar ways to inheritance superclasses, they can be a bit confusing at first glance. A few key points should help summarize and clarify the model:

Metaclasses inherit from the type *class (usually)*

Although they have a special role, metaclasses are coded with class statements and follow the usual OOP model in Python. For example, as subclasses of type, they can redefine the type object's methods, overriding and customizing them as needed. Metaclasses typically redefine the type class's __new__ and __init__ to customize class creation and initialization. Although it's less common, they can also redefine __call__ if they wish to catch the end-of-class creation call directly (albeit with the complexities we saw in the prior section), and can even be simple functions or other callables that return arbitrary objects, instead of type subclasses.

Metaclass declarations are inherited by subclasses

The metaclass=M declaration in a user-defined class is *inherited* by the class's normal subclasses, too, so the metaclass will run for the construction of each class that inherits this specification in a superclass inheritance chain.

Metaclass attributes are not inherited by class instances

Metaclass declarations specify an *instance* relationship, which is not the same as what we've called inheritance thus far. Because classes are instances of metaclasses, the behavior defined in a metaclass applies to the class, but not the class's later instances. Instances obtain behavior from their classes and superclasses, but not from any metaclasses. Technically, attribute inheritance for normal instances usually searches only the __dict__ dictionaries of the instance, its class, and all its superclasses; metaclasses are *not* included in inheritance lookup for normal instances.

Metaclass attributes are acquired by classes

By contrast, classes *do* acquire methods of their metaclasses by virtue of the instance relationship. This is a source of class behavior that processes classes themselves. Technically, classes acquire metaclass attributes through the class's __class__ link just as normal instances acquire names from their class, but inheritance via __dict__ search is attempted first: when the same name is available to a class in *both* a metaclass and a superclass, the superclass (inheritance) version is used instead of that on a metaclass (instance). The class's __class__, however, is not followed for its own instances: metaclass attributes are made available to their instance classes, but not to instances of those instance classes (and see the earlier reference to Dr. Seuss...).

This may be easier to understand in code than in prose. To illustrate all these points, consider the following example:

```
# File metainstance.py

class MetaOne(type):
    def __new__(meta, classname, supers, classdict):      # Redefine type method
        print('In MetaOne.new:', classname)
        return type.__new__(meta, classname, supers, classdict)
    def toast(self):
      return 'toast'
```

```
class Super(metaclass=MetaOne):          # Metaclass inherited by subs too
    def spam(self):                      # MetaOne run twice for two classes
        return 'spam'

class Sub(Super):                        # Superclass: inheritance versus instance
    def eggs(self):                      # Classes inherit from superclasses
        return 'eggs'                    # But not from metaclasses
```

When this code is run (as a script or module), the metaclass handles construction of *both* client classes, and *instances* inherit class attributes but *not* metaclass attributes:

```
>>> from metainstance import *          # Runs class statements: metaclass run twice
In MetaOne.new: Super
In MetaOne.new: Sub

>>> X = Sub()                # Normal instance of user-defined class
>>> X.eggs()                 # Inherited from Sub
'eggs'
>>> X.spam()                 # Inherited from Super
'spam'
>>> X.toast()                # Not inherited from metaclass
AttributeError: 'Sub' object has no attribute 'toast'
```

By contrast, *classes* both inherit names from their superclasses, and acquire names from their metaclass (which in this example is *itself* inherited from a superclass):

```
>>> Sub.eggs(X)             # Own method
'eggs'
>>> Sub.spam(X)             # Inherited from Super
'spam'
>>> Sub.toast()            # Acquired from metaclass
'toast'
>>> Sub.toast(X)           # Not a normal class method
TypeError: toast() takes 1 positional argument but 2 were given
```

Notice how the last of the preceding calls fails when we pass in an instance, because the name resolves to a metaclass method, not a normal class method. In fact, both the object you fetch a name from and its source become crucial here. Methods acquired from metaclasses are bound to the subject *class*, while methods from normal classes are *unbound* if fetched through the class but *bound* when fetched through the instance:

```
>>> Sub.toast
<bound method MetaOne.toast of <class 'metainstance.Sub'>>
>>> Sub.spam
<function Super.spam at 0x0298A2F0>
>>> X.spam
<bound method Sub.spam of <metainstance.Sub object at 0x02987438>>
```

We've studied the last two of these rules before in Chapter 31's bound method coverage; the first is new, but reminiscent of class methods. To understand why this works the way it does, we need to explore the metaclass instance relationship further.

Metaclass Versus Superclass

In even simpler terms, watch what happens in the following: as an *instance* of the A metaclass type, class B acquires A's attribute, but this attribute is not made available for inheritance by B's own instances—the acquisition of names by metaclass instances is *distinct* from the normal inheritance used for class instances:

```
>>> class A(type): attr = 1
>>> class B(metaclass=A): pass      # B is meta instance and acquires meta attr
>>> I = B()                         # I inherits from class but not meta!
>>> B.attr
1
>>> I.attr
AttributeError: 'B' object has no attribute 'attr'
>>> 'attr' in B.__dict__, 'attr' in A.__dict__
(False, True)
```

By contrast, if A morphs from metaclass to superclass, then names *inherited* from an A superclass become available to later instances of B, and are located by searching namespace dictionaries in classes in the tree—that is, by checking the __dict__ of objects in the method resolution order (MRO), much like the mapattrs example we coded back in Chapter 32:

```
>>> class A: attr = 1
>>> class B(A): pass                # I inherits from class and supers
>>> I = B()
>>> B.attr
1
>>> I.attr
1
>>> 'attr' in B.__dict__, 'attr' in A.__dict__
(False, True)
```

This is why metaclasses often do their work by manipulating a new class's namespace dictionary, if they wish to influence the behavior of later instance objects—instances will see names in a class, but not its metaclass. Watch what happens, though, if the same name is available in *both* attribute sources—the *inheritance* name is used instead of instance acquisition:

```
>>> class M(type): attr = 1
>>> class A: attr = 2
>>> class B(A, metaclass=M): pass       # Supers have precedence over metas
>>> I = B()
>>> B.attr, I.attr
(2, 2)
>>> 'attr' in B.__dict__, 'attr' in A.__dict__, 'attr' in M.__dict__
(False, True, True)
```

This is true regardless of the relative height of the inheritance and instance sources—Python checks the __dict__ of each class on the MRO (*inheritance*), before falling back on metaclass acquisition (*instance*):

```
>>> class M(type): attr = 1
>>> class A: attr = 2
```

```
>>> class B(A): pass
>>> class C(B, metaclass=M): pass        # Super two levels above meta: still wins
>>> I = C()
>>> I.attr, C.attr
(2, 2)
>>> [x.__name__ for x in C.__mro__]      # See Chapter 32 for all things MRO
['C', 'B', 'A', 'object']
```

In fact, classes acquire metaclass attributes through their __class__ link, in the same way that normal instances inherit from classes through their __class__, which makes sense, given that classes are also instances of metaclasses. The chief distinction is that instance inheritance does not follow a class's __class__, but instead restricts its scope to the __dict__ of each class in a tree per the MRO—following __bases__ at each class only, and using only the instance's __class__ link once:

```
>>> I.__class__                # Followed by inheritance: instance's class
<class '__main__.C'>
>>> C.__bases__                # Followed by inheritance: class's supers
(<class '__main__.B'>,)
>>> C.__class__                # Followed by instance acquisition: metaclass
<class '__main__.M'>
>>> C.__class__.attr           # Another way to get to metaclass attributes
1
```

If you study this, you'll probably notice a nearly glaring symmetry here, which leads us to the next section.

Inheritance: The Full Story

As it turns out, instance inheritance works in similar ways, whether the "instance" is created from a normal class, or is a class created from a metaclass subclass of type—a single attribute search rule, which fosters the grander and parallel notion of metaclass inheritance hierarchies. To illustrate the basics of this conceptual merger, in the following, the instance inherits from all its classes; the class inherits from both classes and metaclasses; and metaclasses inherit from higher metaclasses (*supermetaclasses?*):

```
>>> class M1(type): attr1 = 1             # Metaclass inheritance tree
>>> class M2(M1):    attr2 = 2            # Gets __bases__, __class__, __mro__

>>> class C1: attr3 = 3                    # Superclass inheritance tree
>>> class C2(C1,metaclass=M2): attr4 = 4   # Gets __bases__, __class__, __mro__

>>> I = C2()                               # I gets __class__ but not others
>>> I.attr3, I.attr4                       # Instance inherits from super tree
(3, 4)
>>> C2.attr1, C2.attr2, C2.attr3, C2.attr4 # Class gets names from both trees!
(1, 2, 3, 4)
>>> M2.attr1, M2.attr2                      # Metaclass inherits names too!
(1, 2)
```

Both inheritance paths—class and metaclass—employ the same links, though not recursively: instances do not inherit their class's metaclass names, but may request them explicitly:

```
>>> I.__class__                    # Links followed at instance with no __bases__
<class '__main__.C2'>
>>> C2.__bases__
(<class '__main__.C1'>,)

>>> C2.__class__                   # Links followed at class after __bases__
<class '__main__.M2'>
>>> M2.__bases__
(<class '__main__.M1'>,)

>>> I.__class__.attr1              # Route inheritance to the class's meta tree
1
>>> I.attr1                        # Though class's __class__ not followed normally
AttributeError: 'C2' object has no attribute 'attr1'

>>> M2.__class__                   # Both trees have MROs and instance links
<class 'type'>
>>> [x.__name__ for x in C2.__mro__]    # __bases__ tree from I.__class__
['C2', 'C1', 'object']
>>> [x.__name__ for x in M2.__mro__]    # __bases__ tree from C2.__class__
['M2', 'M1', 'type', 'object']
```

If you care about metaclasses, or must use code that does, study these examples, and then study them again. In effect, inheritance follows __bases__ before following a single __class__; normal instances have no __bases__; and classes have both—whether normal or metaclass. In fact, understanding this example is important to Python name resolution in general, as the next section explains.

Python's inheritance algorithm: The simple version

Now that we know about metaclass acquisition, we're finally able to formalize the inheritance rules that they augment. Technically, inheritance deploys two distinct but similar lookup routines, and is based on MROs. Because __bases__ are used to construct the __mro__ ordering at class creation time, and because a class's __mro__ includes itself, the prior section's generalization is the same as the following—a first-cut definition of Python's new-style inheritance algorithm:

To look up an explicit attribute name:

1. From an *instance* I, search the instance, then its class, and then all its superclasses, using:

    a. The __dict__ of the instance I

    b. The __dict__ of all classes on the __mro__ found at I's __class__, from left to right

2. From a *class* C, search the class, then all its superclasses, and then its metaclasses tree, using:

a. The __dict__ of all classes on the __mro__ found at C itself, from left to right

b. The __dict__ of all metaclasses on the __mro__ found at C's __class__, from left to right

3. In both rule 1 and 2, give precedence to *data descriptors* located in step *b* sources (see ahead).

4. In both rule 1 and 2, skip step *a* and begin the search at step *b* for *built-in* operations (see ahead).

The first two steps are followed for normal, explicit attribute fetch only. There are exceptions for both *built-ins* and *descriptors*, both of which we'll clarify in a moment. In addition, a __getattr__ or __getattribute__ may also be used for missing or all names, respectively, per Chapter 38.

Most programmers need only be aware of the first of these rules, and perhaps the first step of the second—which taken together correspond to 2.X *classic class* inheritance. There's an extra acquisition step added for metaclasses (*2b*), but it's essentially the same as others—a fairly subtle equivalence to be sure, but metaclass acquisition is not as novel as it may seem. In fact, it's just one component of the larger model.

The descriptors special case

At least that's the normal—and *simplistic*—case. I listed step 3 in the prior section specially, because it doesn't apply to most code, and complicates the algorithm substantially. It turns out, though, that inheritance also has a special case interaction with Chapter 38's attribute descriptors. In short, some descriptors known as *data descriptors*—those that define __set__ methods to intercept assignments—are given precedence, such that their names override other inheritance sources.

This exception serves some practical roles. For example, it is used to ensure that the special __class__ and __dict__ attributes cannot be redefined by the same names in an instance's own __dict__:

```
>>> class C: pass                          # Inheritance special case #1...
>>> I = C()                                # Class data descriptors have precedence
>>> I.__class__, I.__dict__
(<class '__main__.C'>, {})

>>> I.__dict__['name'] = 'bob'             # Dynamic data in the instance
>>> I.__dict__['__class__'] = 'spam'       # Assign keys, not attributes
>>> I.__dict__['__dict__'] = {}

>>> I.name                                 # I.name comes from I.__dict__ as usual
'bob'                                      # But I.__class__ and I.__dict__ do not!
>>> I.__class__, I.__dict__
(<class '__main__.C'>, {'__class__': 'spam', '__dict__': {}, 'name': 'bob'})
```

This data descriptor exception is tested before the preceding two inheritance rules as a preliminary step, may be more important to Python implementers than Python programmers, and can be reasonably ignored by most application code in any event—that is, unless *you* code data descriptors of your own, which follow the same inheritance special case precedence rule:

```
>>> class D:
        def __get__(self, instance, owner): print('__get__')
        def __set__(self, instance, value): print('__set__')

>>> class C: d = D()              # Data descriptor attribute
>>> I = C()
>>> I.d                           # Inherited data descriptor access
__get__
>>> I.d = 1
__set__
>>> I.__dict__['d'] = 'spam'      # Define same name in instance namespace dict
>>> I.d                           # But doesn't hide data descriptor in class!
__get__
```

Conversely, if this descriptor did *not* define a __set__, the name in the instance's dictionary would hide the name in its class instead, per normal inheritance:

```
>>> class D:
        def __get__(self, instance, owner): print('__get__')

>>> class C: d = D()
>>> I = C()
>>> I.d                           # Inherited nondata descriptor access
__get__
>>> I.__dict__['d'] = 'spam'      # Hides class names per normal inheritance rules
>>> I.d
'spam'
```

In both cases, Python automatically runs the descriptor's __get__ when it's found by inheritance, rather than returning the descriptor object itself—part of the attribute magic we met earlier in the book. The special status afforded to data descriptors, however, also modifies the meaning of attribute *inheritance*, and thus the meaning of names in your code.

Python's inheritance algorithm: The somewhat-more-complete version

With both the data descriptor special case and general descriptor invocation factored in with class and metaclass trees, Python's full new-style inheritance algorithm can be stated as follows—a complex procedure, which assumes knowledge of descriptors, metaclasses, and MROs, but is the final arbiter of attribute names nonetheless (in the following, items are attempted in sequence either as numbered, or per their left-to-right order in "or" conjunctions):

To look up an explicit attribute name:

1. From an *instance* I, search the instance, its class, and its superclasses, as follows:
    a. Search the __dict__ of all classes on the __mro__ found at I's __class__
    b. If a data descriptor was found in step *a*, call its __get__ and exit

c. Else, return a value in the `__dict__` of the instance I

d. Else, call a nondata descriptor or return a value found in step *a*

2. From a *class* C, search the class, its superclasses, and its metaclasses tree, as follows:

   a. Search the `__dict__` of all metaclasses on the `__mro__` found at C's `__class__`

   b. If a data descriptor was found in step *a*, call its `__get__` and exit

   c. Else, call a descriptor or return a value in the `__dict__` of a class on C's own `__mro__`

   d. Else, call a nondata descriptor or return a value found in step *a*

3. In both rule 1 and 2, *built-in* operations essentially use just step *a* sources (see ahead)

Note here again that this applies to normal, *explicit* attribute fetch only. The *implicit* lookup of method names for *built-ins* doesn't follow these rules, and essentially uses just step *a* sources in both cases, as the next section will demonstrate.

As always, the implied `object` superclass provides some defaults at the top of every class and metaclass tree (that is, at the end of every MRO). And beyond all this, method `__getattr__` may be run if defined when an attribute is not found, and method `__getattribute__` may be run for every attribute fetch, though they are special-case extensions to the name lookup model. See Chapter 38 for more on these tools and descriptors, and Chapter 32 for the `super` special-case MRO scan.

Assignment inheritance

Also note that the prior section defines inheritance in terms of attribute *reference* (lookup), but parts of it apply to attribute *assignment* as well. As we've learned, assignment normally changes attributes in the subject object itself, but inheritance is also invoked on assignment to test first for some of Chapter 38's attribute management tools, including descriptors and properties. When present, such tools intercept attribute assignment, and may route it arbitrarily.

For example, when an attribute assignment is run for new-style classes, a data descriptor with a `__set__` method is acquired from a class by inheritance using the MRO, and has precedence over the normal storage model. In terms of the prior section's rules:

- When applied to an *instance*, such assignments essentially follow steps *a* through *c* of rule 1, searching the instance's class tree, though step *b* calls `__set__` instead of `__get__`, and step *c* stops and stores in the instance instead of attempting a fetch.

- When applied to a *class*, such assignments run the same procedure on the class's metaclass tree: roughly the same as rule 2, but step *c* stops and stores in the class.

Because descriptors are also the basis for other advanced attribute tools such as properties and slots, this inheritance pre-check on assignment is utilized in multiple contexts. The net effect is that descriptors are treated as an inheritance special case in new-style classes, for *both* reference and assignment.

The built-ins special case

At least that's *almost* the full story. As we've seen, built-ins don't follow these rules. Instances and classes may both be skipped for built-in operations only, as a special case that differs from normal or explicit name inheritance. Because this is a *context-specific* divergence, it's easier to demonstrate in code than to weave into a single algorithm. In the following, str is the built-in, __str__ is its explicit name equivalent, and the instance is skipped for the built-in only:

```
>>> class C:                                  # Inheritance special case #2...
        attr = 1                              # Built-ins skip a step
        def __str__(self): return('class')

>>> I = C()
>>> I.__str__(), str(I)                        # Both from class if not in instance
('class', 'class')

>>> I.__str__ = lambda: 'instance'
>>> I.__str__(), str(I)                        # Explicit=>instance, built-in=>class!
('instance', 'class')

>>> I.attr                                     # Asymmetric with normal or explicit names
1
>>> I.attr = 2; I.attr
2
```

As we saw in *metaclass5.py* earlier, the same holds true for *classes*: explicit names start at the class, but built-ins start at the class's class, which is its metaclass, and defaults to type:

```
>>> class D(type):
        def __str__(self): return('D class')

>>> class C(D):
        pass
>>> C.__str__(C), str(C)                        # Explicit=>super, built-in=>metaclass!
('D class', "<class '__main__.C'>")

>>> class C(D):
        def __str__(self): return('C class')
>>> C.__str__(C), str(C)                        # Explicit=>class, built-in=>metaclass!
('C class', "<class '__main__.C'>")

>>> class C(metaclass=D):
        def __str__(self): return('C class')
>>> C.__str__(C), str(C)                        # Built-in=>user-defined metaclass
('C class', 'D class')
```

In fact, it can sometimes be nontrivial to know *where* a name comes from in this model, since all classes also inherit from object—including the default type metaclass. In the following's explicit call, C appears to get a default __str__ from object instead of the metaclass, per the first source of class inheritance (the class's own MRO); by contrast, the built-in skips ahead to the metaclass as before:

```
>>> class C(metaclass=D):
        pass
>>> C.__str__(C), str(C)                      # Explicit=>object, built-in=>metaclass
("<class '__main__.C'>", 'D class')

>>> C.__str__
<slot wrapper '__str__' of 'object' objects>

>>> for k in (C, C.__class__, type): print([x.__name__ for x in k.__mro__])
['C', 'object']
['D', 'type', 'object']
['type', 'object']
```

All of which leads us to this book's final `import this` quote—a tenet that seems to conflict with the status given to descriptors and built-ins in the attribute inheritance mechanism of new-style classes:

> Special cases aren't special enough to break the rules.

Some practical needs warrant exceptions, of course. We'll forgo rationales here, but you should carefully consider the implications of an object-oriented language that applies inheritance—*its foundational operation*—in such an uneven and inconsistent fashion. At a minimum, this should underscore the importance of keeping your code *simple*, to avoid making it dependent on such convoluted rules. As always, your code's users and maintainers will be glad you did.

For more fidelity on this story, see Python's internal implementation of inheritance—a complete saga chronicled today in its *object.c* and *typeobject.c*, the former for normal instances, and the latter for classes. Delving into internals shouldn't be required to use Python, of course, but it's the ultimate source of truth in a complex and evolving system, and sometimes the best you'll find. This is especially true in boundary cases born of accrued exceptions. For our purposes here, let's move on to the last bit of metaclass magic.

Metaclass Methods

Just as important as the inheritance of names, *methods* in metaclasses process their instance *classes*—not the normal instance objects we've known as "self," but classes themselves. This makes them similar in spirit and form to the *class methods* we studied in Chapter 32, though they again are available in the metaclasses instance realm only, not to normal instance inheritance. The failure at the end of the following, for example, stems from the explicit name inheritance rules of the prior section:

```
>>> class A(type):
        def x(cls): print('ax', cls)          # A metaclass (instances=classes)
        def y(cls): print('ay', cls)          # y is overridden by instance B

>>> class B(metaclass=A):
        def y(self): print('by', self)        # A normal class (normal instances)
        def z(self): print('bz', self)        # Namespace dict holds y and z
```

```
>>> B.x                                          # x acquired from metaclass
<bound method A.x of <class '__main__.B'>>
>>> B.y                                          # y and z defined in class itself
<function B.y at 0x0295F1E0>
>>> B.z
<function B.z at 0x0295F378>
>>> B.x()                                        # Metaclass method call: gets cls
ax <class '__main__.B'>

>>> I = B()                                      # Instance method calls: get inst
>>> I.y()
by <__main__.B object at 0x02963BE0>
>>> I.z()
bz <__main__.B object at 0x02963BE0>
>>> I.x()                                        # Instance doesn't see meta names
AttributeError: 'B' object has no attribute 'x'
```

Metaclass Methods Versus Class Methods

Though they differ in inheritance visibility, much like class methods, metaclass methods are designed to manage *class-level data*. In fact, their roles can overlap—much as metaclasses do in general with class decorators—but metaclass methods are not accessible except through the class, and do not require an explicit classmethod class-level data declaration in order to be bound with the class. In other words, metaclass methods can be thought of as implicit class methods, with limited visibility:

```
>>> class A(type):
        def a(cls):                   # Metaclass method: gets class
            cls.x = cls.y + cls.z

>>> class B(metaclass=A):
        y, z = 11, 22
        @classmethod                  # Class method: gets class
        def b(cls):
            return cls.x

>>> B.a()           # Call metaclass method; visible to class only
>>> B.x             # Creates class data on B, accessible to normal instances
33

>>> I = B()
>>> I.x, I.y, I.z
(33, 11, 22)

>>> I.b()           # Class method: sends class, not instance; visible to instance
33
>>> I.a()           # Metaclass methods: accessible through class only
AttributeError: 'B' object has no attribute 'a'
```

Operator Overloading in Metaclass Methods

Just like normal classes, metaclasses may also employ operator overloading to make built-in operations applicable to their instance classes. The __getitem__ indexing method in the following metaclass, for example, is a metaclass method designed to process *classes* themselves—the classes that are instances of the metaclass, not those classes' own later instances. In fact, per the inheritance algorithms sketched earlier, normal class instances don't inherit names acquired via the metaclass instance relationship at all, though they can access names present on their own classes:

```
>>> class A(type):
        def __getitem__(cls, i):        # Meta method for processing classes:
            return cls.data[i]          # Built-ins skip class, use meta
                                        # Explicit names search class + meta
>>> class B(metaclass=A):               # Data descriptors in meta used first
        data = 'spam'

>>> B[0]                        # Metaclass instance names: visible to class only
's'
>>> B.__getitem__
<bound method A.__getitem__ of <class '__main__.B'>>

>>> I = B()
>>> I.data, B.data              # Normal inheritance names: visible to instance and class
('spam', 'spam')
>>> I[0]
TypeError: 'B' object does not support indexing
```

It's possible to define a __getattr__ on a metaclass too, but it can be used to process its instance *classes* only, not their normal instances—as usual, it's not even acquired by a class's instances:

```
>>> class A(type):
        def __getattr__(cls, name):         # Acquired by class B getitem
            return getattr(cls.data, name)  # But not run same by built-ins

>>> class B(metaclass=A):
        data = 'spam'

>>> B.upper()
'SPAM'
>>> B.upper
<built-in method upper of str object at 0x029E7420>
>>> B.__getattr__
<bound method A.__getattr__ of <class '__main__.B'>>

>>> I = B()
>>> I.upper
AttributeError: 'B' object has no attribute 'upper'
>>> I.__getattr__
AttributeError: 'B' object has no attribute '__getattr__'
```

Moving the __getattr__ to a metaclass doesn't help with its built-in interception shortcomings, though. In the following continuation, explicit attributes are routed to the metaclass's __getattr__, but built-ins are not, despite that fact the indexing *is* routed to a metaclass's __getitem__ in the first example of the section—strongly suggesting that new-style __getattr__ is a *special case of a special case*, and further recommending code simplicity that avoids dependence on such boundary cases:

```
>>> B.data = [1, 2, 3]
>>> B.append(4)         # Explicit normal names routed to meta's getattr
>>> B.data
[1, 2, 3, 4]
>>> B.__getitem__(0)    # Explicit special names routed to meta's gettarr
1
>>> B[0]                # But built-ins skip meta's gettatr too?!
TypeError: 'A' object does not support indexing
```

As you can probably tell, metaclasses are interesting to explore, but it's easy to lose track of their big picture. In the interest of space, we'll omit additional fine points here. For the purposes of this chapter, it's more important to show why you'd care to use such a tool in the first place. Let's move on to some larger examples to sample the roles of metaclasses in action. As we'll find, like so many tools in Python, metaclasses are first and foremost about easing maintenance work by eliminating redundancy.

Example: Adding Methods to Classes

In this and the following section, we're going to study examples of two common use cases for metaclasses: adding methods to a class, and decorating all methods automatically. These are just two of the many metaclass roles, which unfortunately will consume the space we have left for this chapter; again, you should consult the Web for more advanced applications. These examples are representative of metaclasses in action, though, and they suffice to illustrate their application.

Moreover, both give us an opportunity to contrast class decorators and metaclasses— our first example compares metaclass- and decorator-based implementations of class augmentation and instance wrapping, and the second applies a decorator with a metaclass first and then with another decorator. As you'll see, the two tools are often interchangeable, and even complementary.

Manual Augmentation

Earlier in this chapter, we looked at skeleton code that augmented classes by adding methods to them in various ways. As we saw, simple class-based inheritance suffices if the extra methods are statically known when the class is coded. Composition via object embedding can often achieve the same effect too. For more dynamic scenarios, though, other techniques are sometimes required—helper functions can usually suffice, but metaclasses provide an explicit structure and minimize the maintenance costs of changes in the future.

Let's put these ideas in action here with working code. Consider the following example of manual class augmentation—it adds two methods to two classes, after they have been created:

```
# Extend manually - adding new methods to classes

class Client1:
    def __init__(self, value):
        self.value = value
    def spam(self):
        return self.value * 2

class Client2:
    value = 'ni?'

def eggsfunc(obj):
    return obj.value * 4

def hamfunc(obj, value):
    return value + 'ham'

Client1.eggs = eggsfunc
Client1.ham  = hamfunc

Client2.eggs = eggsfunc
Client2.ham  = hamfunc

X = Client1('Ni!')
print(X.spam())
print(X.eggs())
print(X.ham('bacon'))

Y = Client2()
print(Y.eggs())
print(Y.ham('bacon'))
```

This works because methods can always be assigned to a class after it's been created, as long as the methods assigned are functions with an extra first argument to receive the subject `self` instance—this argument can be used to access state information accessible from the class instance, even though the function is defined independently of the class.

When this code runs, we receive the output of a method coded inside the first class, as well as the two methods added to the classes after the fact:

```
c:\code> py -3 extend-manual.py
Ni!Ni!
Ni!Ni!Ni!Ni!
baconham
ni?ni?ni?ni?
baconham
```

This scheme works well in isolated cases and can be used to fill out a class arbitrarily at runtime. It suffers from a potentially major downside, though: we have to repeat the augmentation code for every class that needs these methods. In our case, it wasn't too onerous to add the two methods to both classes, but in more complex scenarios this approach can be time-consuming and error-prone. If we ever forget to do this consistently, or we ever need to change the augmentation, we can run into problems.

Metaclass-Based Augmentation

Although manual augmentation works, in larger programs it would be better if we could apply such changes to an entire set of classes automatically. That way, we'd avoid the chance of the augmentation being botched for any given class. Moreover, coding the augmentation in a single location better supports future changes—all classes in the set will pick up changes automatically.

One way to meet this goal is to use metaclasses. If we code the augmentation in a metaclass, every class that declares that metaclass will be augmented uniformly and correctly and will automatically pick up any changes made in the future. The following code demonstrates:

```
# Extend with a metaclass - supports future changes better

def eggsfunc(obj):
    return obj.value * 4

def hamfunc(obj, value):
    return value + 'ham'

class Extender(type):
    def __new__(meta, classname, supers, classdict):
        classdict['eggs'] = eggsfunc
        classdict['ham']  = hamfunc
        return type.__new__(meta, classname, supers, classdict)

class Client1(metaclass=Extender):
    def __init__(self, value):
        self.value = value
    def spam(self):
        return self.value * 2

class Client2(metaclass=Extender):
    value = 'ni?'

X = Client1('Ni!')
print(X.spam())
print(X.eggs())
print(X.ham('bacon'))

Y = Client2()
print(Y.eggs())
print(Y.ham('bacon'))
```

This time, both of the client classes are extended with the new methods because they are instances of a metaclass that performs the augmentation. When run, this version's output is the same as before—we haven't changed what the code does, we've just re-factored it to encapsulate the augmentation more cleanly:

```
c:\code> py -3 extend-meta.py
Ni!Ni!
Ni!Ni!Ni!Ni!
baconham
ni?ni?ni?ni?
baconham
```

Notice that the metaclass in this example still performs a fairly static task: adding two known methods to every class that declares it. In fact, if all we need to do is always add the same two methods to a set of classes, we might as well code them in a normal superclass and inherit in subclasses. In practice, though, the metaclass structure supports much more dynamic behavior. For instance, the subject class might also be configured based upon arbitrary logic at runtime:

```
# Can also configure class based on runtime tests

class MetaExtend(type):
    def __new__(meta, classname, supers, classdict):
        if sometest():
            classdict['eggs'] = eggsfunc1
        else:
            classdict['eggs'] = eggsfunc2
        if someothertest():
            classdict['ham']  = hamfunc
        else:
            classdict['ham']  = lambda *args: 'Not supported'
        return type.__new__(meta, classname, supers, classdict)
```

Metaclasses Versus Class Decorators: Round 2

Keep in mind again that the prior chapter's class decorators often overlap with this chapter's metaclasses in terms of functionality. This derives from the fact that:

- *Class decorators* rebind class names to the result of a function at the end of a class statement, after the new class has been created.

- *Metaclasses* work by routing class object creation through an object at the end of a class statement, in order to create the new class.

Although these are slightly different models, in practice they can often achieve the same goals, albeit in different ways. As you've now seen, class decorators correspond directly to metaclass __init__ methods called to initialize newly created classes. Decorators have no direct analog to the metaclass __new__ (called to make classes in the first place) or to metaclass methods (used to process instance classes), but many or most use cases for these tools do not require these extra steps.

Because of this, both tools in principle can be used to manage both instances of a class and the class itself. In practice, though, metaclasses incur extra steps to manage instances, and decorators incur extra steps to create new classes. Hence, while their roles often overlap, metaclasses are probably best used for class object management. Let's translate these ideas to code.

Decorator-based augmentation

In pure augmentation cases, decorators can often stand in for metaclasses. For example, the prior section's metaclass example, which adds methods to a class on creation, can also be coded as a class decorator; in this mode, decorators roughly correspond to the __init__ method of metaclasses, since the class object has already been created by the time the decorator is invoked. Also as for metaclasses, the original class type is retained, since no wrapper object layer is inserted. The output of the following, file *extend-deco.py*, is the same as that of the prior metaclass code:

```
# Extend with a decorator: same as providing __init__ in a metaclass

def eggsfunc(obj):
    return obj.value * 4

def hamfunc(obj, value):
    return value + 'ham'

def Extender(aClass):
    aClass.eggs = eggsfunc        # Manages class, not instance
    aClass.ham  = hamfunc         # Equiv to metaclass __init__
    return aClass

@Extender
class Client1:                    # Client1 = Extender(Client1)
    def __init__(self, value):    # Rebound at end of class stmt
        self.value = value
    def spam(self):
        return self.value * 2

@Extender
class Client2:
    value = 'ni?'

X = Client1('Ni!')                # X is a Client1 instance
print(X.spam())
print(X.eggs())
print(X.ham('bacon'))

Y = Client2()
print(Y.eggs())
print(Y.ham('bacon'))
```

In other words, at least in certain cases, decorators can manage classes as easily as metaclasses. The converse isn't quite so straightforward, though; metaclasses can be used to manage instances, but only with a certain amount of extra magic. The next section demonstrates.

Managing instances instead of classes

As we've just seen, class decorators can often serve the same *class-management* role as metaclasses. Metaclasses can often serve the same *instance-management* role as decorators, too, but this requires extra code and may seem less natural. That is:

- *Class decorators* can manage both classes and instances, but don't create classes normally.

- *Metaclasses* can manage both classes and instances, but instances require extra work.

That said, certain applications may be better coded in one or the other. For example, consider the following class decorator example from the prior chapter; it's used to print a trace message whenever any normally named attribute of a class instance is fetched:

```
# Class decorator to trace external instance attribute fetches

def Tracer(aClass):                                    # On @ decorator
    class Wrapper:
        def __init__(self, *args, **kargs):            # On instance creation
            self.wrapped = aClass(*args, **kargs)      # Use enclosing scope name
        def __getattr__(self, attrname):
            print('Trace:', attrname)                  # Catches all but .wrapped
            return getattr(self.wrapped, attrname)     # Delegate to wrapped object
    return Wrapper

@Tracer
class Person:                                          # Person = Tracer(Person)
    def __init__(self, name, hours, rate):             # Wrapper remembers Person
        self.name = name
        self.hours = hours
        self.rate = rate                               # In-method fetch not traced
    def pay(self):
        return self.hours * self.rate

bob = Person('Bob', 40, 50)                            # bob is really a Wrapper
print(bob.name)                                        # Wrapper embeds a Person
print(bob.pay())                                       # Triggers __getattr__
```

When this code is run, the decorator uses class name rebinding to wrap instance objects in an object that produces the trace lines in the following output:

```
c:\code> py -3 manage-inst-deco.py
Trace: name
Bob
Trace: pay
2000
```

Although it's possible for a metaclass to achieve the same effect, it seems less straightforward conceptually. Metaclasses are designed explicitly to manage class object creation, and they have an interface tailored for this purpose. To use a metaclass just to manage instances, we have to also take on responsibility for creating the class too—an extra step if normal class creation would otherwise suffice. The following metaclass, in file *manage-inst-meta.py*, has the same effect as the prior decorator:

```
# Manage instances like the prior example, but with a metaclass

def Tracer(classname, supers, classdict):          # On class creation call
    aClass = type(classname, supers, classdict)    # Make client class
    class Wrapper:
        def __init__(self, *args, **kargs):        # On instance creation
            self.wrapped = aClass(*args, **kargs)
        def __getattr__(self, attrname):
            print('Trace:', attrname)              # Catches all but .wrapped
            return getattr(self.wrapped, attrname) # Delegate to wrapped object
    return Wrapper

class Person(metaclass=Tracer):                    # Make Person with Tracer
    def __init__(self, name, hours, rate):         # Wrapper remembers Person
        self.name = name
        self.hours = hours
        self.rate = rate                           # In-method fetch not traced
    def pay(self):
        return self.hours * self.rate

bob = Person('Bob', 40, 50)                        # bob is really a Wrapper
print(bob.name)                                    # Wrapper embeds a Person
print(bob.pay())                                   # Triggers __getattr__
```

This works, but it relies on two tricks. First, it must use a simple function instead of a class, because **type** subclasses must adhere to object creation protocols. Second, it must manually create the subject class by calling **type** manually; it needs to return an instance wrapper, but metaclasses are also responsible for creating and returning the subject class. Really, we're using the metaclass protocol to imitate decorators in this example, rather than vice versa; because both run at the conclusion of a **class** statement, in many roles they are just variations on a theme. This metaclass version produces the same output as the decorator when run live:

```
c:\code> py -3 manage-inst-meta.py
Trace: name
Bob
Trace: pay
2000
```

You should study both versions of these examples for yourself to weigh their tradeoffs. In general, though, metaclasses are probably best suited to class management, due to their design; class decorators can manage either instances or classes, though they may not be the best option for more advanced metaclass roles that we don't have space to cover in this book. See the Web for more metaclass examples, but keep in mind that some are more appropriate than others (and some of their authors may know less of Python than you do!).

Metaclass and class decorator equivalence?

The preceding section illustrated that metaclasses incur an extra step to create the class when used in instance management roles, and hence can't quite subsume decorators in all use cases. But what about the inverse—are decorators a replacement for metaclasses?

Just in case this chapter has not yet managed to make your head explode, consider the following metaclass coding alternative too—a class decorator that returns a metaclass instance:

```
# A decorator can call a metaclass, though not vice versa without type()

>>> class Metaclass(type):
        def __new__(meta, clsname, supers, attrdict):
            print('In M.__new__:')
            print([clsname, supers, list(attrdict.keys())])
            return type.__new__(meta, clsname, supers, attrdict)

>>> def decorator(cls):
        return Metaclass(cls.__name__, cls.__bases__, dict(cls.__dict__))

>>> class A:
        x = 1

>>> @decorator
    class B(A):
        y = 2
        def m(self): return self.x  + self.y

In M.__new__:
['B', (<class '__main__.A'>,), ['__qualname__', '__doc__', 'm', 'y', '__module__']]
>>> B.x, B.y
(1, 2)
>>> I = B()
>>> I.x, I.y, I.m()
(1, 2, 3)
```

This nearly proves the equivalence of the two tools, but really just in terms of *dispatch* at class construction time. Again, decorators essentially serve the same role as metaclass __init__ methods. Because this decorator returns a metaclass instance, metaclasses—or at least their type superclass—are still assumed here. Moreover, this winds up triggering an *additional* metaclass call after the class is created, and isn't an ideal scheme in real code—you might as well move this metaclass to the first creation step:

```
>>> class B(A, metaclass=Metaclass): ...        # Same effect, but makes just one class
```

Still, there is some tool redundancy here, and decorator and metaclass roles often overlap in practice. And although decorators don't directly support the notion of class-level methods in metaclasses discussed earlier, methods and state in *proxy* objects created by decorators can achieve similar effects, though for space we'll leave this last observation in the suggested explorations column.

The *inverse* may not seem applicable—a metaclass can't generally defer to a nonmetaclass decorator, because the class doesn't yet exist until the metaclass call completes —although a metaclass *can* take the form of a simple callable that invokes **type** to create the class directly and passes it on to the decorator. In other words, the crucial hook in the model is the **type** call issued for class construction. Given that, metaclasses and class decorators are often functionally equivalent, with varying *dispatch protocol* models:

```
>>> def Metaclass(clsname, supers, attrdict):
        return decorator(type(clsname, supers, attrdict))

>>> def decorator(cls): ...
>>> class B(A, metaclass=Metaclass): ...        # Metas can call decos and vice versa
```

In fact, metaclasses need not necessarily return a **type** instance either—*any* object compatible with the class coder's expectations will do—and this further blurs the decorator/metaclass distinction:

```
>>> def func(name, supers, attrs):
        return 'spam'

>>> class C(metaclass=func):               # A class whose metaclass makes it a string!
        attr = 'huh?'

>>> C, C.upper()
('spam', 'SPAM')

>>> def func(cls):
        return 'spam'

>>> @func
    class C:                               # A class whose decorator makes it a string!
        attr = 'huh?'

>>> C, C.upper()
('spam', 'SPAM')
```

Odd metaclass and decorator tricks like these aside, timing often determines roles in practice, as stated earlier:

- Because *decorators* run after a class is created, they incur an extra *runtime* step in class creation roles.

- Because *metaclasses* must create classes, they incur an extra *coding* step in instance management roles.

In other words, neither completely subsumes the other. Strictly speaking, metaclasses might be a functional superset, as they can call decorators during class creation; but metaclasses can also be substantially heavier to understand and code, and many roles intersect completely. In practice, the need to take over class creation entirely is probably much less important than tapping into the process in general.

Rather than follow this rabbit hole further, though, let's move on to explore metaclass roles that may be a bit more typical and practical. The next section concludes this chapter with one more common use case—applying operations to a class's methods automatically at class creation time.

Example: Applying Decorators to Methods

As we saw in the prior section, because they are both run at the end of a `class` statement, metaclasses and decorators can often be used *interchangeably*, albeit with different syntax. The choice between the two is arbitrary in many contexts. It's also possible to use them in *combination*, as complementary tools. In this section, we'll explore an example of just such a combination—applying a function decorator to all the methods of a class.

Tracing with Decoration Manually

In the prior chapter we coded two function decorators, one that traced and counted all calls made to a decorated function and another that timed such calls. They took various forms there, some of which were applicable to both functions and methods and some of which were not. The following collects both decorators' final forms into a module file for reuse and reference here:

```
# File decotools.py: assorted decorator tools
import time

def tracer(func):                              # Use function, not class with __call__
    calls = 0                                  # Else self is decorator instance only
    def onCall(*args, **kwargs):
        nonlocal calls
        calls += 1
        print('call %s to %s' % (calls, func.__name__))
        return func(*args, **kwargs)
    return onCall

def timer(label='', trace=True):               # On decorator args: retain args
    def onDecorator(func):                      # On @: retain decorated func
        def onCall(*args, **kargs):             # On calls: call original
            start   = time.clock()              # State is scopes + func attr
            result  = func(*args, **kargs)
            elapsed = time.clock() - start
            onCall.alltime += elapsed
            if trace:
                format = '%s%s: %.5f, %.5f'
                values = (label, func.__name__, elapsed, onCall.alltime)
                print(format % values)
            return result
        onCall.alltime = 0
        return onCall
    return onDecorator
```

As we learned in the prior chapter, to use these decorators manually, we simply import them from the module and code the decoration @ syntax before each method we wish to trace or time:

```
from decotools import tracer

class Person:
    @tracer
    def __init__(self, name, pay):
        self.name = name
        self.pay  = pay

    @tracer
    def giveRaise(self, percent):          # giveRaise = tracer(giverRaise)
        self.pay *= (1.0 + percent)        # onCall remembers giveRaise

    @tracer
    def lastName(self):                     # lastName = tracer(lastName)
        return self.name.split()[-1]

bob = Person('Bob Smith', 50000)
sue = Person('Sue Jones', 100000)
print(bob.name, sue.name)
sue.giveRaise(.10)                          # Runs onCall(sue, .10)
print('%.2f' % sue.pay)
print(bob.lastName(), sue.lastName())       # Runs onCall(bob), remembers lastName
```

When this code is run, we get the following output—calls to decorated methods are routed to logic that intercepts and then delegates the call, because the original method names have been bound to the decorator:

```
c:\code> py -3 decoall-manual.py
call 1 to __init__
call 2 to __init__
Bob Smith Sue Jones
call 1 to giveRaise
110000.00
call 1 to lastName
call 2 to lastName
Smith Jones
```

Tracing with Metaclasses and Decorators

The manual decoration scheme of the prior section works, but it requires us to add decoration syntax before *each* method we wish to trace and to later remove that syntax when we no longer desire tracing. If we want to trace every method of a class, this can become tedious in larger programs. In more dynamic contexts where augmentations depend upon runtime parameters, it may not be possible at all. It would be better if we could somehow apply the tracer decorator to all of a class's methods automatically.

With metaclasses, we can do exactly that—because they are run when a class is constructed, they are a natural place to add decoration wrappers to a class's methods. By scanning the class's attribute dictionary and testing for function objects there, we can automatically run methods through the decorator and rebind the original names to the results. The effect is the same as the automatic method name rebinding of decorators, but we can apply it more globally:

```
# Metaclass that adds tracing decorator to every method of a client class

from types import FunctionType
from decotools import tracer

class MetaTrace(type):
    def __new__(meta, classname, supers, classdict):
        for attr, attrval in classdict.items():
            if type(attrval) is FunctionType:           # Method?
                classdict[attr] = tracer(attrval)       # Decorate it
        return type.__new__(meta, classname, supers, classdict)   # Make class

class Person(metaclass=MetaTrace):
    def __init__(self, name, pay):
        self.name = name
        self.pay  = pay
    def giveRaise(self, percent):
        self.pay *= (1.0 + percent)
    def lastName(self):
        return self.name.split()[-1]

bob = Person('Bob Smith', 50000)
sue = Person('Sue Jones', 100000)
print(bob.name, sue.name)
sue.giveRaise(.10)
print('%.2f' % sue.pay)
print(bob.lastName(), sue.lastName())
```

When this code is run, the results are the same as before—calls to methods are routed to the tracing decorator first for tracing, and then propagated on to the original method:

```
c:\code> py -3 decoall-meta.py
call 1 to __init__
call 2 to __init__
Bob Smith Sue Jones
call 1 to giveRaise
110000.00
call 1 to lastName
call 2 to lastName
Smith Jones
```

The result you see here is a *combination* of decorator and metaclass work—the metaclass automatically applies the function decorator to every method at class creation time, and the function decorator automatically intercepts method calls in order to print the trace messages in this output. The combination "just works," thanks to the generality of both tools.

Applying Any Decorator to Methods

The prior metaclass example works for just one specific function decorator—tracing. However, it's trivial to generalize this to apply *any* decorator to all the methods of a class. All we have to do is add an outer scope layer to retain the desired decorator, much like we did for decorators in the prior chapter. The following, for example, codes such a generalization and then uses it to apply the tracer decorator again:

```python
# Metaclass factory: apply any decorator to all methods of a class

from types import FunctionType
from decotools import tracer, timer

def decorateAll(decorator):
    class MetaDecorate(type):
        def __new__(meta, classname, supers, classdict):
            for attr, attrval in classdict.items():
                if type(attrval) is FunctionType:
                    classdict[attr] = decorator(attrval)
            return type.__new__(meta, classname, supers, classdict)
    return MetaDecorate

class Person(metaclass=decorateAll(tracer)):        # Apply a decorator to all
    def __init__(self, name, pay):
        self.name = name
        self.pay  = pay
    def giveRaise(self, percent):
        self.pay *= (1.0 + percent)
    def lastName(self):
        return self.name.split()[-1]

bob = Person('Bob Smith', 50000)
sue = Person('Sue Jones', 100000)
print(bob.name, sue.name)
sue.giveRaise(.10)
print('%.2f' % sue.pay)
print(bob.lastName(), sue.lastName())
```

When this code is run as it is, the output is again the same as that of the previous examples—we're still ultimately decorating every method in a client class with the tracer function decorator, but we're doing so in a more generic fashion:

```
c:\code> py -3 decoall-meta-any.py
call 1 to __init__
call 2 to __init__
Bob Smith Sue Jones
call 1 to giveRaise
110000.00
call 1 to lastName
call 2 to lastName
Smith Jones
```

Now, to apply a *different* decorator to the methods, we can simply replace the decorator name in the **class** header line. To use the timer function decorator shown earlier, for example, we could use either of the last two header lines in the following when defining our class—the first accepts the timer's default arguments, and the second specifies label text:

```
class Person(metaclass=decorateAll(tracer)):          # Apply tracer

class Person(metaclass=decorateAll(timer())):         # Apply timer, defaults
class Person(metaclass=decorateAll(timer(label='**'))):   # Decorator arguments
```

Notice that this scheme cannot support nondefault decorator arguments differing per method in the client class, but it can pass in decorator arguments that apply to all such methods, as done here. To test, use the last of these metaclass declarations to apply the timer, and add the following lines at the end of the script to see the timer's extra informational attributes:

```
# If using timer: total time per method

print('-'*40)
print('%.5f' % Person.__init__.alltime)
print('%.5f' % Person.giveRaise.alltime)
print('%.5f' % Person.lastName.alltime)
```

The new output is as follows—the metaclass wraps methods in timer decorators now, so we can tell how long each and every call takes, for every method of the class:

```
c:\code> py -3 decoall-meta-any2.py
**__init__: 0.00001, 0.00001
**__init__: 0.00001, 0.00001
Bob Smith Sue Jones
**giveRaise: 0.00002, 0.00002
110000.00
**lastName: 0.00002, 0.00002
**lastName: 0.00002, 0.00004
Smith Jones
----------------------------------------
0.00001
0.00002
0.00004
```

Metaclasses Versus Class Decorators: Round 3 (and Last)

As you might expect, class decorators intersect with metaclasses here, too. The following version replaces the preceding example's metaclass with a class decorator. That is, it defines and uses a *class decorator that applies a function decorator* to all methods of a class. Although the prior sentence may sound more like a Zen statement than a technical description, this all works quite naturally—Python's decorators support arbitrary nesting and combinations:

```
# Class decorator factory: apply any decorator to all methods of a class

from types import FunctionType
from decotools import tracer, timer
```

```
def decorateAll(decorator):
    def DecoDecorate(aClass):
        for attr, attrval in aClass.__dict__.items():
            if type(attrval) is FunctionType:
                setattr(aClass, attr, decorator(attrval))        # Not __dict__
        return aClass
    return DecoDecorate

@decorateAll(tracer)                    # Use a class decorator
class Person:                           # Applies func decorator to methods
    def __init__(self, name, pay):      # Person = decorateAll(..)(Person)
        self.name = name                # Person = DecoDecorate(Person)
        self.pay  = pay
    def giveRaise(self, percent):
        self.pay *= (1.0 + percent)
    def lastName(self):
        return self.name.split()[-1]

bob = Person('Bob Smith', 50000)
sue = Person('Sue Jones', 100000)
print(bob.name, sue.name)
sue.giveRaise(.10)
print('%.2f' % sue.pay)
print(bob.lastName(), sue.lastName())
```

When this code is run as it is, the class decorator applies the tracer function decorator to every method and produces a trace message on calls (the output is the same as that of the preceding metaclass version of this example):

```
c:\code> py -3 decoall-deco-any.py
call 1 to __init__
call 2 to __init__
Bob Smith Sue Jones
call 1 to giveRaise
110000.00
call 1 to lastName
call 2 to lastName
Smith Jones
```

Notice that the class decorator returns the original, augmented class, not a wrapper layer for it (as is common when wrapping instance objects instead). As for the metaclass version, we retain the type of the original class—an instance of Person is an instance of Person, not of some wrapper class. In fact, this class decorator deals with class creation only; instance creation calls are not intercepted at all.

This distinction can matter in programs that require type testing for instances to yield the original class, not a wrapper. When augmenting a class instead of an instance, class decorators can retain the original class type. The class's methods are not their original functions because they are rebound to decorators, but this is likely less important in practice, and it's true in the metaclass alternative as well.

Also note that, like the metaclass version, this structure cannot support function decorator arguments that differ per method in the decorated class, but it can handle such arguments if they apply to all such methods. To use this scheme to apply the timer decorator, for example, either of the last two decoration lines in the following will suffice if coded just before our class definition—the first uses decorator argument defaults, and the second provides one explicitly:

```
@decorateAll(tracer)                  # Decorate all with tracer

@decorateAll(timer())                 # Decorate all with timer, defaults
@decorateAll(timer(label='@@'))       # Same but pass a decorator argument
```

As before, let's use the last of these decorator lines and add the following at the end of the script to test our example with a different decorator (better schemes are possible on both the testing and timing fronts here, of course, but we're at chapter end; improve as desired):

```
# If using timer: total time per method

print('-'*40)
print('%.5f' % Person.__init__.alltime)
print('%.5f' % Person.giveRaise.alltime)
print('%.5f' % Person.lastName.alltime)
```

The same sort of output appears—for every method we get timing data for each and all calls, but we've passed a different label argument to the timer decorator:

```
c:\code> py -3 decoall-deco-any2.py
@@__init__: 0.00001, 0.00001
@@__init__: 0.00001, 0.00001
Bob Smith Sue Jones
@@giveRaise: 0.00002, 0.00002
110000.00
@@lastName: 0.00002, 0.00002
@@lastName: 0.00002, 0.00004
Smith Jones
----------------------------------------
0.00001
0.00002
0.00004
```

Finally, it's possible to *combine* decorators such that each runs per method call, but it will likely require changes to those we've coded here. As is, nesting calls to them directly winds up tracing or timing the other's creation-time application, listing the two on separate lines results in tracing or timing the other's wrapper before running the original method, and metaclasses seem to fare no better on this front:

```
@decorateAll(tracer(timer(label='@@')))    # Traces applying the timer
class Person:

@decorateAll(tracer)                        # Traces onCall wrapper, times methods
@decorateAll(timer(label='@@'))
class Person:

@decorateAll(timer(label='@@'))
```

```
@decorateAll(tracer)                  # Times onCall wrapper, traces methods
class Person:
```

Pondering this further will have to remain suggested study—both because we're out of space and time, and because this may quite possibly be illegal in some states!

As you can see, metaclasses and class decorators are not only often interchangeable, but also commonly complementary. Both provide advanced but powerful ways to customize and manage both class and instance objects, because both ultimately allow you to insert code into the class creation process. Although some more advanced applications may be better coded with one or the other, the way you choose or combine these two tools in many cases is largely up to you.

Chapter Summary

In this chapter, we studied metaclasses and explored examples of them in action. Metaclasses allow us to tap into the class creation protocol of Python, in order to manage or augment user-defined classes. Because they automate this process, they may provide better solutions for API writers than manual code or helper functions; because they encapsulate such code, they may minimize maintenance costs better than some other approaches.

Along the way, we also saw how the roles of class decorators and metaclasses often intersect: because both run at the conclusion of a `class` statement, they can sometimes be used interchangeably. Class decorators and metaclasses can both be used to manage both class and instance objects, though each tool may present tradeoffs in some use cases.

Since this chapter covered an advanced topic, we'll work through just a few quiz questions to review the basics (candidly, if you've made it this far in a chapter on metaclasses, you probably already deserve extra credit!). Because this is the last part of the book, we'll forgo the end-of-part exercises. Be sure to see the appendixes that follow for Python changes, the solutions to the prior parts' exercises, and more; the last of these includes a sampling of typical application-level programs for self-study.

Once you finish the quiz, you've officially reached the end of this book's technical material. The next and final chapter offers some brief closing thoughts to wrap up the book at large. I'll see you there in the Python benediction after you work through this final quiz.

Test Your Knowledge: Quiz

1. What is a metaclass?
2. How do you declare the metaclass of a class?
3. How do class decorators overlap with metaclasses for managing classes?

4. How do class decorators overlap with metaclasses for managing instances?

5. Would you rather count decorators or metaclasses amongst your weaponry? (And please phrase your answer in terms of a popular Monty Python skit.)

Test Your Knowledge: Answers

1. A metaclass is a class used to create a class. Normal new-style classes are instances of the `type` class by default. Metaclasses are usually subclasses of the `type` class, which redefines class creation protocol methods in order to customize the class creation call issued at the end of a `class` statement; they typically redefine the methods `__new__` and `__init__` to tap into the class creation protocol. Metaclasses can also be coded other ways—as simple functions, for example—but they are always responsible for making and returning an object for the new class. Metaclasses may have methods and data to provide behavior for their classes too—and constitute a secondary pathway for inheritance search—but their attributes are accessible only to their class instances, not to their instance's instances.

2. In Python 3.X, use a keyword argument in the `class` header line: `class C(metaclass=M)`. In Python 2.X, use a class attribute instead: `__metaclass__` = `M`. In 3.X, the `class` header line can also name normal superclasses before the `metaclass` keyword argument; in 2.X you generally should derive from `object` too, though this is sometimes optional.

3. Because both are automatically triggered at the end of a `class` statement, class decorators and metaclasses can both be used to manage classes. Decorators rebind a class name to a callable's result and metaclasses route class creation through a callable, but both hooks can be used for similar purposes. To manage classes, decorators simply augment and return the original class objects. Metaclasses augment a class after they create it. Decorators may have a slight disadvantage in this role if a new class must be defined, because the original class has already been created.

4. Because both are automatically triggered at the end of a `class` statement, we can use both class decorators and metaclasses to manage class instances, by inserting a wrapper (proxy) object to catch instance creation calls. Decorators may rebind the class name to a callable run on instance creation that retains the original class object. Metaclasses can do the same, but may have a slight disadvantage in this role, because they must also create the class object.

5. Our chief weapon is decorators...decorators and metaclasses...metaclasses and decorators... Our two weapons are metaclasses and decorators...and ruthless efficiency... Our *three* weapons are metaclasses, decorators, and ruthless efficiency...and an almost fanatical devotion to Python... Our *four*...no... *Amongst* our weapons... Amongst our weaponry...are such elements as metaclasses, decorators... I'll come in again...

All Good Things

Welcome to the end of the book! Now that you've made it this far, I want to say a few words in closing about Python's evolution before turning you loose on the software field. This topic is subjective by nature, of course, but vital to all Python users nonetheless.

You've now had a chance to see the entire language yourself—including some advanced features that may seem at odds with its scripting paradigm. Though many will understandably accept this as status quo, in an open source project it's crucial that some ask the "why" questions too. Ultimately, the trajectory of the Python story—and its true conclusion—is at least in part up to you.

The Python Paradox

If you've read this book, or reasonable subsets of it, you should now be able to weigh Python's tradeoffs fairly. As you've seen, Python is a powerful, expressive, and even fun programming language, which will serve as an enabling technology for wherever you choose to go next. At the same time, you've also seen that today's Python is something of a paradox: it has expanded to incorporate tools that many consider both needlessly redundant and curiously advanced—and at a rate that appears to be only accelerating.

For my part, as one of Python's earliest advocates, I've watched it morph over the years from simple to sophisticated tool, with a steadily shifting scope. By most measures, it seems to have grown at least as complex as other languages that drove many of us to Python in the first place. And just as in those other languages, this has inevitably fostered a growing culture in which obscurity is a badge of honor.

That's as contrary to Python's original goals as it could be. Run an `import this` in any Python interactive session to see what I mean—the creed I've quoted from repeatedly in this book in contexts where it was clearly violated. On many levels, its core ideals of explicitness, simplicity, and lack of redundancy have been either naively forgotten or carelessly abandoned.

The end result is a language and community that could in part be described today in some of the same terms I used in the Perl sidebar of Chapter 1. While Python still has much to offer, this trend threatens to negate much of its perceived advantage, as the next section explains.

On "Optional" Language Features

I included a quote near the start of the prior chapter about metaclasses not being of interest to 99% of Python programmers, to underscore their perceived obscurity. That statement is not quite accurate, though, and not just numerically so. The quote's author is a noted Python contributor and friend from the early days of Python, and I don't mean to pick on anyone unfairly. Moreover, I've often made such statements about language feature obscurity myself—in the various editions of this very book, in fact.

The problem, though, is that such statements really apply only to people who work alone and only ever use code that they've written themselves. As soon as an "optional" advanced language feature is used by *anyone* in an organization, it is no longer optional —it is effectively imposed on *everyone* in the organization. The same holds true for externally developed software you use in your systems—if the software's author uses an advanced or extraneous language feature, it's no longer entirely optional for you, because you have to understand the feature to reuse or change the code.

This observation applies to all the *advanced* topics covered in this book, including those listed as "magic" hooks near the beginning of the prior chapter, and many others:

> Generators, decorators, slots, properties, descriptors, metaclasses, context managers, closures, super, namespace packages, Unicode, function annotations, relative imports, keyword-only arguments, class and static methods, and even obscure applications of comprehensions and operator overloading

If any person or program you need to work with uses such tools, they automatically become part of your *required knowledge base* too.

To see just how daunting this can be, one need only consider Chapter 40's *new-style inheritance* procedure—a horrifically convoluted model that can make descriptors and metaclasses prerequisite to understanding even basic name resolution. Chapter 32's super similarly ups the intellectual ante—imposing an obscenely implicit and artificial MRO algorithm on readers of any code that uses this tool.

The net effect of such over-engineering is to either escalate learning requirements radically, or foster a user base that only partially understands the tools they employ. This is obviously less than ideal for those hoping to use Python in simpler ways, and contradictory to the scripting motif.

Against Disquieting Improvements

This observation also applies to the many *redundant* features we've seen, such as Chapter 7's `str.format` method and Chapter 34's `with` statement—tools borrowed from other languages, and overlapping with others long present in Python. When programmers use multiple ways to achieve the same goal, all become required knowledge.

Let's be honest: Python has grown rife with redundancy in recent years. As I suggested in the preface—and as you've now seen first-hand—today's Python world comes replete with all the functional duplications and expansions chronicled in Table 41-1, among others we've seen in this book.

Table 41-1. A sampling of redundancy and feature explosion in Python

Category	Specifics
3 major paradigms	Procedural, functional, object-oriented
2 incompatible lines	2.X and 3.X, with new-style classes in both
3 string formatting tools	% expression, str.format, string.Template
4 attribute accessor tools	__getattr__, __getattribute__, properties, descriptors
2 finalization statements	try/finally, with
4 varieties of comprehension	List, generator, set, dictionary
3 class augmentation tools	Function calls, decorators, metaclasses
4 kinds of methods	Instance, static, class, metaclass
2 attribute storage systems	Dictionaries, slots
4 flavors of imports	Module, package, package relative, namespace package
2 superclass dispatch protocols	Direct calls, super + MRO
5 assignment statement forms	Basic, multiname, augmented, sequence, starred
2 types of functions	Normal, generator
5 function argument forms	Basic, name=value, *pargs, **kargs, keyword-only
2 class behavior sources	Superclasses, metaclasses
4 state retention options	Classes, closures, function attributes, mutables
2 class models	Classic + new-style in 2.X, mandated new-style in 3.X
2 Unicode models	Optional in 2.X, mandated in 3.X
2 PyDoc modes	GUI client, required all-browser in recent 3.X
2 byte code storage schemes	Original, __pycache__ only in recent 3.X

If you care about Python, you should take a moment to browse this table. It reflects a virtual explosion in functionality and toolbox size—59 concepts that are all fair game for newcomers. Most of its categories began with *just one original member* in Python; many were expanded in part to imitate other languages; and only the last few can be simplified by pretending that the latest Python is the only Python that matters to its programmers.

I've stressed avoiding unwarranted complexity in this book, but in practice, both advanced and new tools tend to encourage their own adoption—often for no better reason than a programmer's personal desire to demonstrate prowess. The net result is that much Python code today is littered with these complex and extraneous tools. That is, *nothing is truly "optional" if nothing is truly optional.*

Complexity Versus Power

This is why some Python old-timers (myself included) sometimes worry that Python seems to have grown larger and more complex over time. New features added by veterans, converts, and even amateurs may have raised the intellectual bar for newcomers. Although Python's core ideas, like dynamic typing and built-in types, have remained essentially the same, its advanced additions can become required reading for any Python programmer. I chose to cover these topics here for this reason, despite their omission in early editions. It's not possible to skip the advanced stuff if it's in code you have to understand.

On the other hand, as mentioned in Chapter 1, to most observers Python is still *noticeably simpler* than most of its contemporaries, and perhaps only as complex as its many roles require. Though it's acquired many of the same tools as Java, C#, and C++, they tend to be lighter weight in the context of a dynamically typed scripting language. For all its growth over the years, Python is still relatively easy to learn and use when compared to the alternatives, and new learners can often pick up advanced topics as needed.

And frankly, application programmers tend to spend most of their time dealing with *libraries and extensions*, not advanced and sometimes-arcane language features. For instance, the book *Programming Python*—a follow-up to this one—deals mostly with the marriage of Python to application libraries for tasks such as GUIs, databases, and the Web, not with esoteric language tools (though Unicode still forces itself onto many stages, and the odd generator expression and `yield` crop up along the way).

Moreover, the flipside of this growth is that Python has become more *powerful*. When used well, tools like decorators and metaclasses are not only arguably "cool," but allow creative programmers to build more flexible and useful APIs for other programmers to use. As we've seen, they can also provide good solutions to problems of encapsulation and maintenance.

Simplicity Versus Elitism

Whether this justifies the potential expansion of required Python knowledge is up to you to decide. For better or worse, a person's skill level often decides this issue by default—more advanced programmers like more advanced tools and tend to forget about their impact on other camps. Fortunately, though, this isn't an absolute; good programmers also understand that *simplicity is good engineering*, and advanced tools should be used only when warranted. This is true in any programming language, but especially in one like Python that is frequently exposed to new or novice programmers as an extension tool.

And if you're still not buying this, keep in mind that many people using Python are not comfortable with even *basic OOP*. Trust me on this; I've met thousands of them. Although Python was never a trivial subject, the reports from the software trenches are very clear on this point: unwarranted added complexity is never a welcome feature, especially when it is driven by the personal preferences of an unrepresentative few. Whether intended or not, this is often understandably perceived as *elitism*—a mindset that is both unproductive and rude, and has no place in a tool as widely used as Python.

This is also a social issue, of course, and pertains as much to individual programmers as to language designers. In the "real world" where open source software is measured, though, Python-based systems that require their users to master the nuances of metaclasses, descriptors, and the like should probably scale their market expectations accordingly. Hopefully, if this book has done its job, you'll find the importance of simplicity in programming to be one of its most important and lasting takeaways.

Closing Thoughts

So there you have it—some observations from someone who has been using, teaching, and advocating Python for two decades, and still wishes nothing but the best for its future. None of these concerns are entirely new, of course. Indeed, the growth of this very book over the years seems testament to the effect of Python's own growth—if not an *ironic eulogy* to its original conception as a tool that would simplify programming and be accessible to both experts and nonspecialists alike. Judging by language heft alone, that dream seems to have been either neglected or abandoned entirely.

That said, Python's present rise in *popularity* seems to show no signs of abating—a powerful counterargument to complexity concerns. Today's Python world may be understandably less concerned with its original and perhaps idealistic goals than with applying its present form in their work. Python gets many a job done in the practical world of complex programming requirements, and this is still ample cause to recommend it for many tasks. Original goals aside, mass appeal does qualify as one form of success, though one whose significance will have to await the verdict of time.

If you're interested in musing further over Python's evolution and learning curve, I wrote a more in-depth article in 2012 on such things: *Answer Me These Questions Three...*, available online at *http://learning-python.com/pyquestions3.html*. These are important pragmatic questions that are crucial to Python's future, and deserve more attention than I've given here. But these are highly subjective issues; this is not a philosophy text; and this book has already exceeded its page-count targets.

More importantly, in an open source project like Python the answers to such questions must be formed anew by each wave of newcomers. I hope the wave you ride in will have as much common sense as fun while plotting Python's future.

Where to Go From Here

And that's a wrap, folks. You've officially reached the end of this book. Now that you know Python inside and out, your next step, should you choose to take it, is to explore the libraries, techniques, and tools available in the application domains in which you work.

Because Python is so widely used, you'll find ample resources for using it in almost any application you can think of—from GUIs, the Web, and databases to numeric programming, robotics, and system administration. See Chapter 1 and your favorite web browser for pointers to popular tools and topics.

This is where Python starts to become truly fun, but this is also where this book's story ends, and others' begin. For pointers on where to turn after this book, see the recommended follow-up texts mentioned in the preface. I hope to see you in an applications programming domain soon.

Good luck with your journey. And of course, "Always look on the bright side of Life!"

Encore: Print Your Own Completion Certificate!

And one last thing: in lieu of exercises for this part of the book, I'm going to post a bonus script here for you to study and run on your own. I can't provide completion certificates for readers of this book (and the certificates would be worthless if I could), but I can include an arguably cheesy Python script that does—the following file, *certificate.py*, is a Python 2.X and 3.X script that creates a simple book completion certificate in both text and HTML file forms, and pops them up in a web browser on your machine by default.

```
#!/usr/bin/python
"""
File certificate.py: a Python 2.X and 3.X script.
Generate a bare-bones class completion certificate: printed,
and saved in text and html files displayed in a web browser.
"""

from __future__ import print_function            # 2.X compatibility
import time, sys, webbrowser

if sys.version_info[0] == 2:                      # 2.X compatibility
    input = raw_input
    import cgi
    htmlescape = cgi.escape
else:
    import html
```

```
    htmlescape = html.escape

maxline  = 60                    # For seperator lines
browser  = True                  # Display in a browser
saveto   = 'Certificate.txt'     # Output filenames
template = """
%s

 ===> Official Certificate <===

Date: %s

This certifies that:

\t%s

has survived the massive tome:

\t%s

and is now entitled to all privileges thereof, including
the right to proceed on to learning how to develop Web
sites, desktop GUIs, scientific models, and assorted apps,
with the possible assistance of follow-up applications
books such as Programming Python (shameless plug intended).

--Mark Lutz, Instructor

(Note: certificate void where obtained by skipping ahead.)

%s
"""

# Interact, setup
for c in 'Congratulations!'.upper():
    print(c, end=' ')
    sys.stdout.flush()           # Else some shells wait for \n
    time.sleep(0.25)
print()

date = time.asctime()
name = input('Enter your name: ').strip() or 'An unknown reader'
sept = '*' * maxline
book = 'Learning Python 5th Edition'

# Make text file version
file = open(saveto, 'w')
text = template % (sept, date, name, book, sept)
print(text, file=file)
file.close()

# Make html file version
htmlto = saveto.replace('.txt', '.html')
file = open(htmlto, 'w')
```

```
    tags = text.replace(sept,    '<hr>')                          # Insert a few tags
    tags = tags.replace('===>', '<h1 align=center>')
    tags = tags.replace('<===', '</h1>')

    tags = tags.split('\n')                                        # Line-by-line mods
    tags = ['<p>' if line == ''
                 else line for line in tags]
    tags = ['<i>%s</i>' % htmlescape(line) if line[:1] == '\t'
                 else line for line in tags]
    tags = '\n'.join(tags)

    link = '<i><a href="http://www.rmi.net/~lutz">Book support site</a></i>\n'
    foot = '<table>\n<td><img src="ora-lp.jpg" hspace=5>\n<td>%s</table>\n' % link
    tags = '<html><body bgcolor=beige>' + tags + foot + '</body></html>'

    print(tags, file=file)
    file.close()

    # Display results
    print('[File: %s]' % saveto, end='')
    print('\n' * 2, open(saveto).read())

    if browser:
        webbrowser.open(saveto, new=True)
        webbrowser.open(htmlto, new=False)

    if sys.platform.startswith('win'):
        input('[Press Enter]')   # Keep window open if clicked on Windows
```

Run this script on your own, and study its code for a summary of some of the ideas we've covered in this book. Fetch it from this book's website described in the preface if you wish. You won't find any descriptors, decorators, metaclasses, or **super** calls in this code, but it's typical Python nonetheless.

When run, it generates the web page captured in the fully gratuitous Figure 41-1. This could be much more grandiose, of course; see the Web for pointers to Python support for PDFs and other document tools such as Sphinx surveyed in Chapter 15. But hey: if you've made it to the end of this book, you deserve another joke or two...

Figure 41-1. Web page created and opened by certificate.py.

Appendixes

Installation and Configuration

This appendix provides additional installation and configuration details as a resource for people new to these topics. It's located here because not all readers will need to deal with these subjects up front. Because it covers some peripheral topics such as environment variables and command-line arguments, though, this material probably merits at least a quick scan for most readers.

Installing the Python Interpreter

Because you need the Python interpreter to run Python scripts, the first step in using Python is usually installing Python. Unless one is already available on your machine, you'll need to fetch, install, and possibly configure a recent version of Python on your computer. You'll only need to do this once per machine, and if you will be running a frozen binary (described in Chapter 2) or self-installing system, your setup tasks may be trivial or null.

Is Python Already Present?

Before you do anything else, check whether you already have a recent Python on your machine. If you are working on Linux, Mac OS X, or some Unix systems, Python is probably already installed on your computer, though it may be one or two releases behind the cutting edge. Here's how to check:

- On *Windows* 7 and earlier, check whether there is a Python entry in the Start button's All Programs menu (at the bottom left of the screen). On *Windows 8*, look for Python in a Start screen tile, your Search tool, the "All apps" display on your Start screen, or a File Explorer in desktop mode (more on Windows 8 in an upcoming sidebar).
- On *Mac OS X*, open a Terminal window (Applications→Utilities→Terminal) and type **python** at the prompt. Python, IDLE, and its tkinter GUI toolkit are standard components of this system.

- On *Linux* and *Unix*, type **python** at a shell prompt (a.k.a. terminal window), and see what happens. Alternatively, try searching for "python" in the usual places —*/usr/bin*, */usr/local/bin*, etc. As on Macs, Python is a standard part of Linux systems.

If you find a Python, make sure it's a recent version. Although any recent Python will do for most of this text, this edition focuses on Python 3.3 and 2.7 specifically, so you may want to install one of these to run some of the examples in this book.

Speaking of *versions*, per the preface, I recommend starting out with Python 3.3 or later if you're learning Python anew and don't need to deal with existing 2.X code; otherwise, you should generally use Python 2.7. Some popular Python-based systems still use older releases, though (2.6 and even 2.5 are still widespread), so if you're working with existing systems be sure to use a version relevant to your needs; the next section describes locations where you can fetch a variety of Python versions.

Where to Get Python

If there is no Python on your machine, you will need to install one yourself. The good news is that Python is an open source system that is freely available on the Web and very easy to install on most platforms.

You can always fetch the latest and greatest *standard Python* release from *http://www .python.org*, Python's official website. Look for the Downloads link on that page, and choose a release for the platform on which you will be working. You'll find prebuilt self-installer files for *Windows* (run to install), Installer Disk Images for *Mac OS X* (installed per Mac conventions), the full source code distribution (typically compiled on Linux, Unix, or OS X machines to generate an interpreter), and more.

Although Python is standard on *Linux* these days, you can also find RPMs for Linux on the Web (unpack them with *rpm*). Python's website also has links to pages where versions for other platforms are maintained, either at Python.org (*http://www.python .org*) itself or offsite. For example, you can find third-party Python installers for Google's *Android*, as well as apps to install Python on Apple's *iOS*.

A Google web search is another great way to find Python installation packages. Among other platforms, you can find Python prebuilt for iPods, Palm handhelds, Nokia cell phones, PlayStation and PSP, Solaris, AS/400, and Windows Mobile, though some of these are typically a few releases behind the curve.

If you find yourself pining for a Unix environment on a Windows machine, you might also be interested in installing *Cygwin* and its version of Python (see *http://www.cygwin .com*). Cygwin is a GPL-licensed library and toolset that provides full Unix functionality on Windows machines, and it includes a prebuilt Python that makes use of all the Unix tools provided.

You can also find Python on CD-ROMs supplied with Linux distributions, included with some products and computer systems, and enclosed with some other Python books. These tend to lag behind the current release somewhat, but usually not seriously so.

In addition, you can find Python in some free and commercial development bundles. At this writing, this *alternative distributions* category includes:

ActiveState ActivePython
A package that combines Python with extensions for scientific, Windows, and other development needs, including PyWin32 and the PythonWin IDE

Enthought Python Distribution
A combination of Python and a host of additional libraries and tools oriented toward scientific computing needs

Portable Python
A blend of Python and add-on packages configured to run directly from a portable device

Pythonxy
A scientific-oriented Python distribution based on Qt and Spyder

Conceptive Python SDK
A bundle targeted at business, desktop, and database applications

PyIMSL Studio
A commercial distribution for numerical analysis

Anaconda Python
A distribution for analysis and visualization of large data sets

This set is prone to change, so search the Web for details on all of the above, and others. Some of these are free, some are not, and some have both free and nonfree versions. All combine the standard Python freely available at *http://www.python.org* with additional tools, but can simplify install tasks for many.

Finally, if you are interested in alternative Python implementations, run a web search to check out *Jython* (the Python port to the Java environment) and *IronPython* (Python for the C#/.NET world), both of which are described in Chapter 2. Installation of these systems is beyond the scope of this book.

Installation Steps

Once you've downloaded Python, you need to install it. Installation steps are very platform-specific, but here are a few pointers for the major Python platforms (biased in volume toward Windows, only because that is the platform where most Python newcomers are likely to encounter the language first):

Windows

For Windows (including XP, Vista, 7, and 8), Python comes as a *self-installer* MSI program file—simply double-click on its file icon, and answer Yes or Next at every prompt to perform a default install. The default install includes Python's documentation set and support for `tkinter` (Tkinter in Python 2.X) GUIs, shelve databases, and the IDLE development GUI. Python 3.3 and 2.7 are normally installed in the directories *C:\Python33* and *C:\Python27* though this can be changed at install time.

For convenience, on Windows 7 and earlier Python shows up after the install in the *Start button*'s All Programs menu (see ahead for Windows 8 notes). Python's menu there has five entries that give quick access to common tasks: starting the IDLE user interface, reading module documentation, starting an interactive session, reading Python's standard manuals, and uninstalling. Most of these options involve concepts explored in detail elsewhere in this text.

When installed on Windows, Python also automatically uses *filename associations* to register itself to be the program that opens Python files when their icons are clicked (a program launch technique described in Chapter 3). It is also possible to build Python from its source code on Windows, but this is not commonly done so we'll skip the details here (see python.org).

Three additional install-related notes for Windows users: first, be sure to see the next appendix for an introduction to the new *Windows launcher* shipped with 3.3; it changes some of the rules for installation, file associations, and command lines, but can be an asset if you have multiple Python versions on your computer (e.g., both 2.X and 3.X). Per Appendix B, Python 3.3's MSI installer also has an option to set your PATH variable to include Python's directory.

Second, *Windows 8* users should see the sidebar in this appendix "Using Python on Windows 8" on page 1425. Standard Python installs and works the same on Windows 8, where it runs in desktop mode, but you won't get the Start button menu described earlier, and the tablet interface on top is not yet directly supported.

Finally, some *Windows Vista* users may run into install issues related to security features. This seems to have been resolved over time (and Vista is relatively rare these days), but if running the MSI installer file directly doesn't work as expected, it's probably because MSI files are not true executables and do not correctly inherit administrator permissions (they run per the registry). To fix, run the installer from a command line with appropriate permissions: Select Command Prompt, choose "Run as administrator," cd to the directory where your Python MSI file resides, and run the MSI installer with a command line of the form: `msiexec /i python-2.5.1.msi`.

Linux

For Linux, if Python or your desired flavor of it is not already present, you can probably obtain it as one or more RPM files, which you unpack in the usual way (consult the RPM manpage for details). Depending on which RPMs you download, there may be one for Python itself, and another that adds support for `tkinter` GUIs and the IDLE environment. Because Linux is a Unix-like system, the next paragraph applies as well.

Unix

For Unix systems, Python is usually compiled from its full C source code distribution. This usually only requires you to unpack the file and run simple `config` and `make` commands; Python configures its own build procedure automatically, according to the system on which it is being compiled. However, be sure to see the package's *README* file for more details on this process. Because Python is open source, its source code may be used and distributed free of charge.

On other platforms the installation details can differ widely, but they generally follow the platform's normal conventions. For example, installing the "Pippy" port of Python for PalmOS required a hotsync operation with your PDA, and Python for the Sharp Zaurus Linux-based PDA was one or more *.ipk* files, which you simply ran to install (these likely still work, though finding the devices today may be a logistical challenge!).

More recently, Python can be installed and used on *Android* and *iOS* platforms too, but installation and usage techniques are too platform-specific to cover here. For additional install procedures and the latest on available ports, try both Python's website and a web search.

Using Python on Windows 8

Windows 8 was released as this edition was being written. As mentioned in the preface, this book was developed on both Windows 7 and 8, but mostly under Windows 7 because the choice is irrelevant to almost everything in this book—both Python 2.X and 3.X presently work only in *desktop mode* on Windows 8, but install and run there the same as in Windows 7, Vista, XP, and others. Once you navigate past the tablet-like layer at the top, usage is almost entirely as before.

The only notable exception to this is Windows 8's lack of a *Start button menu* in desktop mode. You don't get the nice menu of Python options automatically, though you can simulate it manually. Although this story is prone to change (and you should take this sidebar as an early report), here are a few Windows 8 usage notes.

At this writing, the standard Python Windows MSI installer program installs Python on Windows 8 correctly, and exactly as in the past: you get the same filename associations for icon clicks, access from command lines, and so on. The installer also creates a Start screen button on Windows 8, but Python itself runs in Windows 8's desktop mode, which is essentially the same as Windows 7 without a Start button menu. For example, the Windows 8 Start screen button created by the Python install simply switches control to desktop mode to open a Python interactive shell.

The upside to this is that all existing Python software works on Windows 8's desktop just as before. One downside is that you'll need to create shortcuts for the user-friendly Start button menu items created automatically on former Windows versions. This in-

---

cludes the former menu's links to the IDLE GUI, PyDoc, Python's command-line interface, and Python's manuals set.

This isn't a showstopper—you can emulate the former Start button menu's items with either tiles on the Start screen or shortcuts on the desktop taskbar. To do so, you might look up these tools in a variety of ways:

- By navigating to their corresponding filename in a File Explorer, opened by right-clicking the screen's lower-left corner.
- By searching for their name in the Search "charm," opened by pulling down the screen's top-right corner.
- By finding their entry after right-clicking on the Start screen to open the *All apps* display, which is reminiscent of the former Start button menus.
- By locating their tiles on your Start screen, if they have any.

For example, you can locate *IDLE* by navigating to the file *idle.py* in *C:\Python33\Lib*, by searching on "idle," by finding IDLE in "All apps," or by clicking a Start screen tile if one exists. You can find Python itself in the same ways (and probably others). This isn't quite as nice as the original Start button menus out of the box, but it suffices.

Probably the bigger potential *downside* on Windows 8 is that while Python runs fine in desktop mode, it doesn't yet have an official port to run as a Start screen style "app." That is, standard Python does not yet run programs in the *WinRT* (formerly known as *Metro*) environment—the tile-based media consumption layer that appears first when you start Windows 8, and before you can click your way to the desktop. This may be a temporary state, though, as a number of options either already exist or are being actively explored.

On one front, it's not impossible that Python's *installer* may be enhanced for Windows 8's nondesktop mode. There has already been work on porting Python to run as a Start screen "app," though this may appear as a separate installer package due to differences in the underlying libraries (in short, WinRT runs programs in a classic "sandbox" model, with a restricted subset of the libraries available normally).

On other fronts, the C#/.NET-based *IronPython* system may offer additional Windows 8 "app" development options, and some of Python's major *GUI toolkits* such as tkinter, wxPython, and PyQt could eventually provide portability to the Windows 8 "apps" environment as well. The Qt library underlying the latter of these seems to have already showed some progress in this department.

For now, existing Python software runs fine in Windows 8's desktop mode unchanged. Developing or running Python code in the Start screen "apps" environment will likely require special handling and platform-specific APIs not unlike those required to run Python on other tablet- and phone-oriented platforms based on Google's *Android* and Apple's *iOS* (iPhone and iPad) operating systems.

Also note that much of this sidebar applies to Window 8, but not *Windows RT*. The latter does not run third-party desktop mode applications directly, and may need to await a sanctioned Python installer that supports the WinRT "app" API in general.

Then again, the Windows 8 story remains to be told. Be sure to watch for developments in both Windows and Python's installer for it. For now, a simple tile click or Windows-key press to hop into desktop mode will allow most Python programmers on Windows to safely ignore the tablet-like interface on top—at least until "apps" trounce "programs" altogether.[1]

Configuring Python

After you've installed Python, you may want to configure some system settings that impact the way Python runs your code. (If you are just getting started with the language, you can probably skip this section completely; there is usually no need to specify any system settings for basic programs.)

Generally speaking, parts of the Python interpreter's behavior can be configured with environment variable settings and command-line options. In this section, we'll take a brief look at both, but be sure to see other documentation sources for more details on the topics we introduce here.

Python Environment Variables

Environment variables—known to some as shell variables, or DOS variables—are system-wide settings that live outside Python and thus can be used to customize the interpreter's behavior each time it is run on a given computer. Python recognizes a handful of environment variable settings, but only a few are used often enough to warrant explanation here. Table A-1 summarizes the main Python-related environment variable settings (you'll find information on others in Python reference resources).

Table A-1. Important environment variables

Variable	Role
PATH (or path)	System shell search path (for finding "python")
PYTHONPATH	Python module search path (for imports)
PYTHONSTARTUP	Path to Python interactive startup file
TCL_LIBRARY, TK_LIBRARY	GUI extension variables (tkinter)
PY_PYTHON, PY_PYTHON3, PY_PYTHON2	Windows launcher defaults (see Appendix B)

These variables are straightforward to use, but here are a few pointers:

---

1. Lest that seem too sarcastic, I should note that Windows 8.1 may address some launch screen and Start button (if not menu) concerns per late-breaking rumors, and this edition's new Windows 8 sidebar replaces one in prior editions that discussed a Windows Vista issue. Any similarities you might deduce from that are officially coincidental.

PATH

The PATH setting lists a set of directories that the operating system searches for executable programs, when they are invoked without a full directory path. It should normally include the directory where your Python interpreter lives (the *python* program on Unix, or the *python.exe* file on Windows).

You don't need to set this variable at all if you are willing to work in the directory where Python resides, or type the full path to Python in command lines. On Windows, for instance, the PATH is irrelevant if you run a **cd C:\Python33** before running any code (to change to the directory where Python lives—though you shouldn't generally store your own code in this directory per Chapter 3), or always type **C:\Python33\python** instead of just **python** (giving a full path).

Also note that PATH settings are mostly for launching programs from command lines; they are usually irrelevant when launching via icon clicks and IDEs—the former uses filename associations, and the latter uses built-in mechanisms, and doesn't generally require this configuration step. See also Appendix B for details on 3.3's automatic PATH setting option at install time.

PYTHONPATH

The PYTHONPATH setting serves a role similar to PATH: the Python interpreter consults the PYTHONPATH variable to locate module files when you *import* them in a program. If used, this variable is set to a platform-dependent list of directory names, separated by colons on Unix and semicolons on Windows. This list normally includes just your own source code directories. Its content is merged into the sys.path module import search path, along with the script's container directory, any *.pth* path file settings, and standard library directories.

You don't need to set this variable unless you will be performing *cross-directory imports*—because Python always searches the home directory of the program's top-level file automatically, this setting is required only if a module needs to import another module that lives in a different directory. See also the discussion of *.pth* path files later in this appendix for an alternative to PYTHONPATH. For more on the module search path, refer to Chapter 22.

PYTHONSTARTUP

If PYTHONSTARTUP is set to the pathname of a file of Python code, Python executes the file's code automatically whenever you start the interactive interpreter, as though you had typed it at the interactive command line. This is a rarely used but handy way to make sure you always load certain utilities when working interactively; it saves an import each time you start a Python session.

tkinter *settings*

If you wish to use the tkinter GUI toolkit (named Tkinter in 2.X), you might have to set the two GUI variables in the last line of Table A-1 to the names of the source library directories of the Tcl and Tk systems (much like PYTHONPATH). However, these settings are not required on Windows systems (where tkinter support is installed alongside Python), and are usually not required on Mac OS X and Linux systems, unless the underlying Tcl and Tk libraries are either invalid or reside in nonstandard directories (see python.org's Download page for more details).

PY_PYTHON, PY_PYTHON3, PY_PYTHON2

These settings are used to specify default Pythons when you are using the new (at this writing) Windows launcher that ships with Python 3.3 and is available separately for other versions. Since we'll be exploring the launcher in Appendix B, I'll postpone further details here.

Note that because these environment settings are external to Python itself, *when* you set them is usually irrelevant: this can be done before or after Python is installed, as long as they are set the way you require before Python is actually *run*—be sure to restart your Python IDEs and interactive sessions after making such changes if you want them to apply.

---

tkinter and IDLE GUIs on Linux and Macs

The IDLE interface described in Chapter 3 is a Python `tkinter` GUI program. The `tkinter` module (named `Tkinter` in 2.X) is a GUI toolkit that is automatically installed with standard Python on Windows, and is an inherent part of Mac OS X and most Linux installations.

On some *Linux* systems, though, the underlying GUI library may not be a standard installed component. To add GUI support to your Python on Linux if needed, try running a command line of the form **yum tkinter** to automatically install `tkinter`'s underlying libraries. This should work on Linux distributions (and some other systems) on which the *yum* installation program is available; for others, see your platform's installation documentation.

As also discussed in Chapter 3, on *Mac OS X* IDLE probably lives in the *MacPython* (or *Python N.M*) folder of your *Applications* folder (along with PythonLauncher, used for starting programs with clicks in Finder), but be sure to see the Download page at python.org if IDLE has problems; you may need to install an update on some OS X versions (see Chapter 3).

How to Set Configuration Options

The way to set Python-related environment variables, and what to set them to, depends on the type of computer you're working on. And again, remember that you won't necessarily have to set these at all right away; especially if you're working in IDLE (described in Chapter 3) and save all your files in the same directory, configuration is probably not required up front.

But suppose, for illustration, that you have generally useful module files in directories called *utilities* and *package1* somewhere on your machine, and you want to be able to import these modules from files located in other directories. That is, to load a file called *spam.py* in either the *utilities* or *package1* directories, you want to be able to say this in another file in another directory:

```
import spam
```

To make this work, you'll have to configure your module search path one way or another to include the directory containing *spam.py*. Here are a few tips on this process using PYTHONPATH as an example; do the same for other settings like PATH as needed (though 3.3 can set PATH automatically: see Appendix B).

Unix/Linux shell variables

On Unix systems, the way to set environment variables depends on the shell you use. Under the *csh* shell, you might add a line like the following in your *.cshrc* or *.login* file to set the Python module search path:

```
setenv PYTHONPATH /usr/home/pycode/utilities:/usr/lib/pycode/package1
```

This tells Python to look for imported modules in two user-defined directories. Alternatively, if you're using the *ksh* shell, the setting might instead appear in your *.kshrc* file and look like this:

```
export PYTHONPATH="/usr/home/pycode/utilities:/usr/lib/pycode/package1"
```

Other shells may use different (but analogous) syntax.

DOS variables (and older Windows)

If you are using MS-DOS or some now fairly old flavors of Windows, you may need to add an environment variable configuration command to your *C:\autoexec.bat* file, and reboot your machine for the changes to take effect. The configuration command on such machines has a syntax unique to DOS:

```
set PYTHONPATH=c:\pycode\utilities;d:\pycode\package1
```

You can type such a command in a DOS console window, too, but the setting will then be active only for that one console window. Changing your *.bat* file makes the change permanent and global to all programs, though this technique has been superseded in recent years by that described in the next section.

Windows environment variable GUI

On all recent versions of Windows (including XP, Vista, 7, and 8), you can instead set PYTHONPATH and other variables via the system environment variable GUI without having to edit files, type command lines, or reboot. Select the Control Panel (in your Start button in Windows 7 and earlier, and in the desktop mode's Settings "charm" on Windows 8), choose the System icon, pick the Advanced settings tab or link, and click the Environment Variables button at the bottom to edit or add new variables (PYTHON PATH is usually a new user variable). Use the same variable name and values syntax shown in the DOS `set` command in the preceding section. On Vista you may have to verify operations along the way.

You do not need to reboot your machine after this, but be sure to restart Python if it's open so that it picks up your changes—it configures its import search path at startup time only. If you're working in a Windows Command Prompt window, you'll probably need to restart that to pick up your changes as well.

Windows registry

If you are an experienced Windows user, you may also be able to configure the module search path by using the Windows Registry Editor. To open this tool, type **regedit** in the Start→Run... interface on some Windows, in the search field at the bottom of the Start button display on Windows 7, and in a Command Prompt window on Windows 8 and others (among other routes). Assuming the typical registry tool is available on your machine, you can then navigate to Python's entries and make your changes. This is a delicate and error-prone procedure, though, so unless you're familiar with the registry, I suggest using other options (indeed, this is akin to performing brain surgery on your computer, so be careful!).

Path files

Finally, if you choose to extend the module search path with a *.pth* path file instead of the `PYTHONPATH` variable, you might instead code a text file that looks like the following on Windows (e.g., file *C:\Python33\mypath.pth*):

```
c:\pycode\utilities
d:\pycode\package1
```

Its contents will differ per platform, and its container directory may differ per both platform and Python release. Python locates this file automatically when it starts up.

Directory names in path files may be absolute, or relative to the directory containing the path file; multiple *.pth* files can be used (all their directories are added), and *.pth* files may appear in various automatically checked directories that are platform- and version-specific. In general, a Python release numbered Python *N.M* typically looks for path files in *C:\PythonNM* and *C:\PythonNM\Lib\site-packages* on Windows, and in */usr/local/lib/pythonN.M/site-packages* and */usr/local/lib/site-python* on Unix and Linux. See Chapter 22 for more on using path files to configure the `sys.path` import search path.

Because environment settings are often optional, and because this isn't a book on operating system shells, I'll defer to other sources for further details. Consult your system shell's manpages or other documentation for more information, and if you have trouble figuring out what your settings should be, ask your system administrator or another local expert for help.

Python Command-Line Arguments

When you start Python from a system command line (a.k.a. a shell prompt, or Command Prompt window), you can pass in a variety of option flags to control how Python runs your code. Unlike the system-wide environment variables of the prior section, command-line arguments can be different each time you run a script. The complete form of a Python command-line invocation in 3.3 looks like this (2.7 is roughly the same, with a few differences described ahead):

```
python [-bBdEhiOqsSuvVWxX] [-c command | -m module-name | script | - ] [args]
```

The rest of this section briefly demonstrates some of Python's most commonly used arguments. For more details on available command-line options not covered here, see the Python manuals or reference texts. Or better yet, ask Python itself—run a command line form like this:

```
C:\code> python -h
```

to request Python's help display, which documents all available command-line options. If you deal with complex command lines, be sure to also check out the standard library modules in this domain: the original `getop`, the newer `argparse`, and the now-deprecated (since 3.2) `optparse`, which support more sophisticated command-line processing. Also see Python's library manuals and other references for more on the `pdb` and `profile` modules the following tour deploys.

Running script files with arguments

Most command lines make use of only the *script* and *args* parts of the last section's Python command-line format, to run a program's source file with arguments to be used by the program itself. To illustrate, consider the following script—a text file named *showargs.py*, created in directory *C:\code* or another of your choosing—which prints the command-line arguments made available to the script as `sys.argv`, a Python list of Python strings (if you don't yet know how to create or run Python script files, see the full coverage in Chapter 2 and Chapter 3; we're interested only in command-line arguments here):

```
# File showargs.py
import sys
print(sys.argv)
```

In the following command line, both `python` and `showargs.py` can also be complete directory paths—the former is assumed to be on your `PATH` here, and the latter is assumed to be in the current directory. The three arguments (`a b -c`) meant for the script show up in the `sys.argv` list and can be inspected by your script's code there; the first item in `sys.argv` is always the script file's name, when it is known:

```
C:\code> python showargs.py a b -c        # Most common: run a script file
['showargs.py', 'a', 'b', '-c']
```

As covered elsewhere in this book, Python *lists* print in square brackets and *strings* display in quotes.

Running code given in arguments and standard input

Other code format specification options allow you to give Python code to be run on the command line itself (-c), and accept code to run from the standard input stream (a - means read from a pipe or redirected input stream file, terms also defined in full elsewhere in this text):

```
C:\code> python -c "print(2 ** 100)"        # Read code from command argument
1267650600228229401496703205376

C:\code> python -c "import showargs"        # Import a file to run its code
['-c']

C:\code> python - < showargs.py a b -c      # Read code from standard input
['-', 'a', 'b', '-c']

C:\code> python - a b -c < showargs.py       # Same effect as prior line
['-', 'a', 'b', '-c']
```

Running modules on the search path

The –m code specification locates a module on Python's module search path and then runs it as a top-level script (as module __main__). That is, it looks up a script the same way import operations do, using the directory list normally known as sys.path, which includes the current directory, PYTHONPATH settings, and standard libraries. Leave off the ".py" suffix here, as the filename is treated as a module.

```
C:\code> python -m showargs a b -c          # Locate/run module as script
['c:\\code\\showargs.py', 'a', 'b', '-c']
```

The –m option also supports running tools, modules in packages with and without relative import syntax, and modules located in *.zip* archives. For instance, this switch is commonly used to run the pdb debugger and profile profiler modules from a command line for a script invocation, rather than interactively:

```
C:\code> python                             # Interactve debugger session
>>> import pdb
>>> pdb.run('import showargs')
...more omitted: see pdb docs

C:\code> python -m pdb showargs.py a b -c    # Debugging a script (c=continue)
> C:\code\showargs.py(2)<module>()
-> import sys
(Pdb) c
['showargs.py', 'a', 'b', '-c']
...more omitted: q to exit
```

The profiler runs and times your code; its output can vary per Python, operating system, and computer:

```
C:\code> python -m profile showargs.py a b -c          # Profiling a script
['showargs.py', 'a', 'b', '-c']
         9 function calls in 0.016 seconds

   Ordered by: standard name

   ncalls  tottime  percall  cumtime  percall filename:lineno(function)
        2    0.000    0.000    0.000    0.000 :0(charmap_encode)
        1    0.000    0.000    0.000    0.000 :0(exec)
...more omitted: see profile docs
```

You might also use the -m switch to spawn Chapter 3's IDLE GUI program located in the standard library from any other directory, and to start the `pydoc` and `timeit` tools modules with command lines as we do in this book in Chapter 15 and Chapter 21 (see those chapters for more details on the tools launched here):

```
c:\code> python -m idlelib.idle -n          # Run IDLE in package, no subprocess

c:\code> python -m pydoc -b          # Run pydoc and timeit tools modules

c:\code> python -m timeit -n 1000 -r 3 -s "L = [1,2,3,4,5]" "M = [x + 1 for x in L]"
```

Optimized and unbuffered modes

Immediately after the "python" and before the designation of code to be run, Python accepts additional arguments that control its own behavior. These arguments are consumed by Python itself and are not meant for the script being run. For example, -O runs Python in optimized mode and -u forces standard streams to be unbuffered—with the latter, any printed text will be finalized immediately, and won't be delayed in a buffer:

```
C:\code> python -O showargs.py a b -c          # Optimized: make/run ".pyo" byte code

C:\code> python -u showargs.py a b -c          # Unbuffered standard output stream
```

Post-run interactive mode

Finally, the –i flag enters interactive mode after running a script—especially useful as a debugging tool, because you can print variables' final values after a successful run to get more details:

```
C:\code> python -i showargs.py a b -c          # Go to interactive mode on script exit
['showargs.py', 'a', 'b', '-c']
>>> sys                                         # Final value of sys: imported module
<module 'sys' (built-in)>
>>> ^Z
```

You can also print variables this way after an exception shuts down your script to see what they looked like when the exception occurred, even if not running in debug mode —though you can start the debugger's postmortem tool here as well (`type` is the Windows file display command; try a `cat` or other elsewhere):

```
C:\code> type divbad.py
X = 0
```

```
    print(1 / X)

C:\code> python divbad.py                        # Run the buggy script
...error text omitted
ZeroDivisionError: division by zero

C:\code> python -i divbad.py                     # Print variable values at error
...error text omitted
ZeroDivisionError: division by zero
>>> X
0
>>> import pdb                                    # Start full debugger session now
>>> pdb.pm()
> C:\code\divbad.py(2)<module>()
-> print(1 / X)
(Pdb) quit
```

Python 2.X command-line arguments

Besides those just mentioned, Python 2.7 supports additional options that promote 3.X compatibility (-3 to warn about incompatibilities, and -Q to control division operator models) and detecting inconsistent tab indentation usage, which is always detected and reported in 3.X (-t; see Chapter 12). Again, you can always ask Python 2.X itself for more on the subject as needed:

```
C:\code> c:\python27\python -h
```

Python 3.3 Windows Launcher Command Lines

Technically, the preceding section described the arguments you can pass to the Python interpreter itself—the program usually named python.exe on Windows, and python on Linux (the .exe is normally omitted on Windows). As we'll see in the next appendix, the Windows launcher shipped with Python 3.3 augments this story for users of 3.3 and later or the standalone launcher package. It adds new executables that accept Python version numbers as arguments in command lines used to start Python and your scripts (file *what.py* is listed and described in the next appendix, and simply prints the Python version number):

```
C:\code> py what.py                 # Windows launcher command lines
3.3.0

C:\code> py -2 what.py              # Version number switch
2.7.3

C:\code> py -3.3 -i what.py -a -b -c   # Arguments for all 3: py, python, script
3.3.0
>>> ^Z
```

In fact, as the last run of the preceding example shows, command lines using the launcher can give arguments for the launcher itself (-3.3), Python itself (-i), and your script (-a, -b, and -c). The launcher can also parse version numbers out of #! Unix lines at the top of script files instead. Because the next appendix is devoted to this launcher entirely, though, you'll have to read on for the rest of this story.

For More Help

Python's standard manual set today includes valuable pointers for usage on various platforms. The standard manual set is available in your Start button on Windows 7 and earlier after Python is installed (option "Python Manuals"), and online at *http://www .python.org*. Look for the manual set's top-level section titled "Using Python" for more platform-specific pointers and hints, as well as up-to-date cross-platform environment and command-line details.

As always, the Web is your ally, too, especially in a field that often evolves faster than books like this can be updated. Given Python's widespread adoption, chances are good that answers to any high-level usage questions you may have can be found with a web search.

The Python 3.3 Windows Launcher

This appendix describes the new Windows launcher for Python, installed with Python 3.3 automatically, and available separately on the Web for use with older versions. Though the new launcher comes with some pitfalls, it provides some much-needed coherence for program execution when multiple Pythons coexist on the same computer.

I've written this page for programmers using Python on Windows. Though it is platform-specific by nature, it's targeted at both Python beginners (most of whom get started on this platform), as well as Python developers who write code to work portably between Windows and Unix. As we will see, the new launcher changes the rules on Windows radically enough to impact *everyone* who uses Python on Windows, or may in the future.

The Unix Legacy

To fully understand the launcher's protocols, we have to begin with a short history lesson. Unix developers long ago devised a protocol for designating a program to run a script's code. On Unix systems (including Linux and Mac OS X), the first line in a script's text file is special if it begins with a two-character sequence: #!, sometimes called a *shebang* (an arguably silly phrase I promise not to repeat from here on).

Chapter 3 gives a brief overview of this topic, but here's another look. In Unix scripts, such lines designate a program to run the rest of the script's contents, by coding it after the #!—using either the directory path to the desired program itself, or an invocation of the env Unix utility that looks up the target per your PATH setting, the customizable system environment variable that lists directories to be searched for executables:

```
#!/usr/local/bin/python
...script's code                 # Run under this specific program

#!/usr/bin/env python
...script's code                 # Run under "python" found on PATH
```

By making such a script executable (e.g., via `chmod +x script.py`), you can run it by giving just its filename in a command line; the #! line at the top then directs the Unix shell to a program that will run the rest of the file's code. Depending on the platform's install structure, the `python` that these #! lines name might be a real executable, or a symbolic link to a version-specific executable located elsewhere. These lines might also name a more specific executable explicitly, such as `python3`. Either way, by changing #! lines, symbolic links, or `PATH` settings, Unix developers can route a script to the appropriate installed Python.

None of this applies to Windows itself, of course, where #! lines have no inherent meaning. Python itself has historically ignored such lines as comments if present on Windows ("#" starts a comment in the language). Still, the idea of selecting Python executables on a per-file basis is a compelling feature in a world where Python 2.X and 3.X often coexist on the same machine. Given that many programmers coded #! lines for portability to Unix anyhow, the idea seemed ripe for emulating.

The Windows Legacy

The install model has been very different on the other side of the fence. In the past (well, in every Python until 3.3), the Windows installer updated the global Windows registry such that the latest Python version installed on your computer was the version that opened Python files when they were clicked or run by direct filename in command lines.

Some Windows users may know this registry as filename *associations*, configurable in Control Panel's Default Programs dialog. You do not need to give files executable privileges for this to work, as you do for Unix scripts. In fact, there's no such concept on Windows—filename associations and commands suffice to launch files as programs.

Under this install model, if you wished to open a file with a different version than the latest install, you had to run a command line giving the full path to the Python you wanted, or update your filename associations manually to use the desired version. You could also point generic `python` command lines to a specific Python by setting or changing your `PATH` setting, but Python didn't set this for you, and this wouldn't apply to scripts launched by icon clicks and other contexts.

This reflects the natural order on Windows (when you click on a *.doc* file, Windows usually opens it in the latest Word installed), and has been the state of things ever since there was a Python on Windows. It's less ideal if you have Python scripts that require different versions on the same machine, though—a situation that has become increasingly common, and perhaps even normal in the dual Python 2.X/3.X era. Running multiple Pythons on Windows prior to 3.3 can be tedious for developers, and discouraging for newcomers.

Introducing the New Windows Launcher

The new Windows launcher, shipped and installed automatically with Python 3.3 (and presumably later), and available as a standalone package for use with other versions, addresses these deficits in the former install model by providing two new executables:

- `py.exe` for console programs
- `pyw.exe` for nonconsole (typically GUI) programs

These two programs are registered to open *.py* and *.pyw* files, respectively, via Windows filename associations. Like Python's original `python.exe` main program (which they do not deprecate but can largely subsume), these new executables are also registered to open byte code files launched directly. Amongst their weapons, these two new executables:

- Automatically open Python source and byte-code files launched by icon clicks or filename commands, via Windows associations
- Are normally installed on your system search path and do not require a directory path or `PATH` settings when used as command lines
- Allow Python version numbers to be passed in easily as command-line arguments, when starting both scripts and interactive sessions
- Attempt to parse Unix-style `#!` comment lines at the top of scripts to determine which Python version should be used to run a file's code

The net effect is that under the new launcher, when multiple Pythons are installed on Windows, you are no longer limited to either the latest version installed or explicit/full command lines. Instead, you can now select versions explicitly on both a per-file and per-command basis, and specify versions in either partial or full form in both contexts. Here's how this works:

1. To select versions *per file*, use Unix-style top-of-script comments like these:

   ```
   #!python2
   #!/usr/bin/python2.7
   #!/usr/bin/env python3
   ```

2. To select versions *per command*, use command lines of the following forms:

   ```
   py -2 m.py
   py -2.7 m.py
   py -3 m.py
   ```

For example, the *first* of these techniques can serve as a sort of directive to declare which Python version the script depends upon, and will be applied by the launcher whenever the script is run by command line or icon click (these are variants of a file named *script.py*):

```
#!python3
...
...a 3.X script                    # Runs under latest 3.X installed
...

#!python2
...
...a 2.X script                    # Runs under latest 2.X installed
...

#!python2.6
...
...a 2.6 script                    # Runs under 2.6 (only)
...
```

On Windows, command lines are typed in a Command Prompt window, designated by its `C:\code>` prompt in this appendix. The first of the following is the same as both the second and an icon click, because of filename associations:

```
C:\code> script.py          # Run per file's #! line if present, else per default
C:\code> py script.py       # Ditto, but py.exe is run explicitly
```

Alternatively, the *second* technique just listed can select versions with argument switches in command lines instead:

```
C:\code> py -3 script.py      # Runs under latest 3.X
C:\code> py -2 script.py      # Runs under latest 2.X
C:\code> py -2.6 script.py    # Runs under 2.6 (only)
```

This works both when launching scripts and starting the interactive interpreter (when no script is named):

```
C:\code> py -3       # Starts latest 3.X, interactive
C:\code> py -2       # Starts latest 2.X, interactive
C:\code> py -3.1     # Starts 3.1 (only), interactive
C:\code> py          # Starts default Python (initially 2.X: see ahead)
```

If there are *both* `#!` lines in the file and a version number switch in the command line used to start it, the command line's version overrides that in the file's directive:

```
#! python3.2
...
...a 3.X script
...

C\code> py script.py          # Runs under 3.2, per file directive
C\code> py -3.1 script.py     # Runs under 3.1, even if 3.2 present
```

The launcher also applies *heuristics* to select a specific Python version when it is missing or only partly described. For instance, the latest 2.X is run when only a `2` is specified, and a 2.X is preferred for files that do not name a version in a `#!` line when launched by icon click or generic command lines (e.g., `py m.py`, `m.py`), unless you configure the default to use 3.X instead by setting `PY_PYTHON` or a configuration file entry (more on this ahead).

Especially in the current dual 2.X/3.X Python world, explicit version selection seems a useful addition for Windows, where many (and probably most) newcomers get their first exposure to the language. Although it is not without potential pitfalls—including failures on unrecognized Unix #! lines and a puzzling 2.X default—it does allow for a more graceful coexistence of 2.X and 3.X files on the same machine, and provides a rational approach to version control in command lines.

For the complete story on the Windows launcher, including more advanced features and use cases I'll either condense or largely omit here, see Python's release notes and try a web search to find the PEP (the proposal document). Among other things, the launcher also allows selecting between 32- and 64-bit installs, specifying defaults in configuration files, and defining custom #! command string expansion.

A Windows Launcher Tutorial

Some readers familiar with Unix scripting may find the prior section enough to get started. For others, this section provides additional context in the form of a tutorial, which gives concrete examples of the launcher in action for you to trace through. This section also discloses additional launcher details along the way, though, so even well-seasoned Unix veterans may benefit from a quick scan here before FTPing all their Python scripts to the local Windows box.

To get started, we'll be using the following simple script, *what.py*, which can be run under both 2.X and 3.X to echo the version number of the Python that runs its code. It uses sys.version—a string whose first component after splitting on whitespace is Python's version number:

```
#!python3
import sys
print(sys.version.split()[0])      # First part of string
```

If you want to work along, type this script's code in your favorite text file editor, open a Command Prompt window for typing the command lines we'll be running, and cd to the directory where you've save the script (C:\code is where I'm working, but feel free to save this wherever you wish, and see Chapter 3 for more Windows usage pointers).

This script's first-line comment serves to designate the required Python version; it must begin with #! per Unix convention, and allows for a space before the python3 or not. On my machine I currently have Pythons 2.7, 3,1, 3.2, and 3.3 all installed; let's watch which version is invoked as the script's first line is modified in the following sections, exploring file directives, command lines, and defaults along the way.

Step 1: Using Version Directives in Files

As this script is coded, when run by icon click or command line, the first line directs the registered py.exe launcher to run using the latest 3.X installed:

```
#! python3
import sys
print(sys.version.split()[0])
```

```
C:\code> what.py                    # Run per file directive
3.3.0
```

```
C:\code> py what.py                 # Ditto: latest 3.X
3.3.0
```

Again, the space after #! is optional; I added a space to demonstrate the point here. Note that the first `what.py` command here is equivalent to both an icon click and a full `py what.py`, because the `py.exe` program is registered to open *.py* files automatically in the Windows filename associations registry when the launcher is installed.

Also note that when launcher documentation (including this appendix) talks about the *latest* version, it means the *highest-numbered* version. That is, it refers to the latest released, not the latest installed on your computer (e.g., if you install 3.1 after 3.3, #! python3 selects the latter). The launcher cycles through the Pythons on your computer to find the highest-numbered version that matches your specification or defaults; this differs from the former last-installed-wins model.

Now, changing the first line name to `python2` triggers the latest (really, highest-numbered) 2.X installed instead. Here's this change at work; I'll omit the last two lines of our script from this point on because they won't be altered:

```
#! python2
...rest of script unchanged
```

```
C:\code> what.py                    # Run with latest 2.X per #!
2.7.3
```

And you can request a more specific version if needed—for example, if you don't want the latest in a Python line:

```
#! python3.1
...
```

```
C:\code> what.py                    # Run with 3.1 per #!
3.1.4
```

This is true even if the requested version is *not installed*—which is treated as an error case by the launcher:

```
#! python2.6
...
```

```
C:\code> what.py
Requested Python version (2.6) is not installed
```

Unrecognized Unix #! lines are also treated as errors, unless you give a version number as a command-line switch to compensate, as the next section describes in more detail (and as the section on launcher issues will revisit as a pitfall):

```
#!/bin/python
...
```

```
C:\code> what.py
Unable to create process using '/bin/python "C:\code\what.py" '
```

```
C:\code> py what.py
Unable to create process using '/bin/python what.py'
```

```
C:\code> py -3 what.py
3.3.0
```

Technically, the launcher recognizes Unix-style #! lines at the top of script files that follow one of the following four patterns:

```
#!/usr/bin/env python*
#!/usr/bin/python*
#!/usr/local/bin/python*
#!python*
```

Any #! line that does not take one of these recognized and parseable forms is assumed to be a fully specified command line to start a process to run the file, which is passed to Windows as is, and generates the error message we saw previously if it is not a valid Windows command. (The launcher also supports "customized" command expansions via its configuration files, which are attempted before passing unrecognized commands on to Windows, but we'll gloss over these here.)

In recognizable #! lines, directory paths are coded per Unix convention, for portability to that platform. The * part at the end of the four preceding recognized patterns denotes an optional Python version number, in one of three forms:

Partial (e.g., python3*)*
> To run the version installed with the highest minor release number among those with the major release number given

Full (e.g., python3.1*)*
> To run that specific version only, optionally suffixed by -32 to prefer a 32-bit version (e.g., python3.1-32)

Omitted (e.g., python*)*
> To run the launcher's default version, which is 2 unless changed (e.g., by setting the PY_PYTHON environment variable to 3), another pitfall described ahead

Files with *no* #! line at all behave the same as those that name just a generic python— the aforementioned omitted case—and are influenced by PY_PYTHON default settings. The first case, partials, may also be affected by version-specific environment settings (e.g., set PY_PYTHON3 to 3.1 to select 3.1 for python3, and set PY_PYTHON2 to 2.6 to pick 2.6 for python2). We'll revisit defaults later in this tutorial.

First, though, note that anything after the * part in a #! line's format is assumed to be command-line arguments to Python itself (i e , program python.exe), unless you also give arguments in a `py` command line that are deemed to supersede #! line arguments by the launcher:

```
#!python3 [any python.exe arguments go here]
...
```

These include all the Python command-line arguments we met in Appendix A. But this leads us to launcher command lines in general, and will suffice as a natural segue to the next section.

Step 2: Using Command-Line Version Switches

As mentioned, version switches on command lines can be used to select a Python version if one isn't present in the file. You run a `py` or `pyw` command line to pass them a switch this way, instead of relying on filename associations in the registry, and instead of (or in addition to) giving versions in #! lines in files. In the following, we modify our script so that it has no #! directive:

```
# not a launcher directive
...

C:\code> py -3 what.py          # Run per command-line switch
3.3.0

C:\code> py -2 what.py          # Ditto: latest 2.X installed
2.7.3

C:\code> py -3.2 what.py        # Ditto: 3.2 specifically (and only)
3.2.3

C:\code> py what.py             # Run per launcher's default (ahead)
2.7.3
```

But command-line switches also take precedence over a version designation in a file's directive:

```
#! python3.1
...

C:\code> what.py                # Run per file directive
3.1.4

C:\code> py what.py             # Ditto
3.1.4

C:\code> py -3.2 what.py        # Switches override directives
3.2.3

C:\code> py -2 what.py          # Ditto
2.7.3
```

Formally, the launcher accepts the following command-line argument types (which exactly mirror the * part at the end of a file's #! line described in the prior section):

And the launcher's command lines take the following general form:

```
py [py.exe arg] [python.exe args] script.py [script.py args]
```

Anything following the launcher's own argument (if present) is treated as though it were passed to the `python.exe` program—typically, this includes any arguments for Python itself, followed by the script filename, followed by any arguments meant for the script.

The usual `-m mod`, `-c cmd`, and `-` program specification forms work in a `py` command line too, as do all the other Python command-line arguments covered in Appendix A. As mentioned earlier, arguments to `python.exe` can also appear at the end of the `#!` directive line in a file, if used, though arguments in `py` command lines override them.

To see how this works, let's write a new script that extends the prior to display command-line arguments; `sys.argv` is the script's own arguments, and I'm using the Python (`python.exe`) `-i` switch, which directs it to the interactive prompt (`>>>`) after a script runs:

```
# args.py, show my arguments too
import sys
print(sys.version.split()[0])
print(sys.argv)

C:\code> py -3 -i args.py -a 1 -b -c        # -3: py, -i: python, rest: script
3.3.0
['args.py', '-a', '1', '-b', '-c']
>>> ^Z

C:\code> py -i args.py -a 1 -b -c           # Args to python, script
2.7.3
['args.py', '-a', '1', '-b', '-c']
>>> ^Z

C:\code> py -3 -c print(99)                 # -3 to py, rest to python: "-c cmd"
99

C:\code> py -2 -c "print 99"
99
```

Notice how the first two launches run the default Python unless a version is given in the command line, because no `#!` line appears in the script itself. Somewhat coincidentally, that leads us to the last topic of this tutorial.

Step 3: Using and Changing Defaults

As also mentioned, the launcher defaults to 2.X for a generic python in a #! directive with no specific version number. This is true whether this generic form appears in a full Unix path (e.g., `#!/usr/bin/python`) or not (`#!python`). Here's the latter case in action, coded in our original *what.py* script:

```
#!python
...                                    # Same as #!/usr/bin/python

C:\code> what.py                       # Run per launcher default
2.7.3
```

The default is also applied when no directive is present at all—perhaps the most common case for code written to be used on Windows primarily or exclusively:

```
# not a launcher directive
...

C:\code> what.py                       # Also run per default
2.7.3

C:\code> py what.py                    # Ditto
2.7.3
```

But you can set the launcher's default to 3.X with initialization file or environment variable settings, which will apply to both files run from command lines and by icon clicks via their name's association with `py.exe` or `pyw.exe` in the Windows registry:

```
# not a launcher directive
...

C:\code> what.py                       # Run per default
2.7.3

C:\code> set PY_PYTHON=3               # Or via Control Panel/System
C:\code> what.py                       # Run per changed default
3.3.0
```

As suggested earlier, for more fine-grained control you can also set version-specific environment variables to direct *partial* selections to a specific release, instead of falling back on the installed release with the highest minor number:

```
#!python3
...

C:\code> py what.py                    # Runs "latest" 3.X
3.3.0

C:\code> set PY_PYTHON3=3.1            # Use PY_PYTHON2 for 2.X
C:\code> py what.py                    # Override highest-minor choice
3.1.4
```

The `set` used in these interactions applies to its Command Prompt window only; making such settings in the Control Panel's System window will make them apply globally across your machine (see Appendix A for help with these settings). You may or may not want to set defaults this way depending on the majority of the Python code you'll be running. Many Python 2.X users can probably rely on defaults unchanged, and override them in #! lines or py command lines as needed.

However, the setting used for directive-less files, PY_PYTHON, seems fairly crucial. Most programmers who have used Python on Windows in the past will probably expect 3.X to be the default after installing 3.3, especially given that the launcher is installed by 3.3 in the first place—a seeming paradox, which leads us to the next section.

Pitfalls of the New Windows Launcher

Though the new Windows launcher in 3.3 is a nice addition, like much in 3.X it may have been nicer had it appeared years ago. Unfortunately, it comes with some backward incompatibilities, which may be an inevitable byproduct of today's multiversion Python world, but which may also break some existing programs. This includes examples in books I've written, and probably many others. While porting code to 3.3, I've come across three launcher issues worth noting:

- Unrecognized Unix #! lines now make scripts fail on Windows.
- The launcher defaults to using 2.X unless told otherwise.
- The new PATH extension is off by default and seems contradictory.

The rest of this section gives a rundown of each of these three issues in turn. In the following, I use the programs in my book *Programming Python, 4th Edition*, as an example to illustrate the impacts of launcher incompatibilities, because porting these 3.1/3.2 examples to 3.3 was my first exposure to the new launcher. In my specific case, installing 3.3 broke numerous book examples that worked formerly under 3.2 and 3.1. The causes for these failures outlined here may break your code too.

Pitfall 1: Unrecognized Unix #! Lines Fail

The new Windows launcher recognizes Unix #! lines that begin with #!/usr/bin/env python but *not* the other common Unix form #!/bin/env python (which is actually mandated on some Unixes). Scripts that use the latter of these, including some of my book examples, worked on Windows in the past because their #! lines coded for Unix compatibility have been ignored as comments by all Windows Pythons to date. These scripts now fail to run in 3.3 because the new launcher doesn't recognize their directive's format and posts an error message.

More generally, scripts with *any* #! Unix line not recognized will now fail to run on Windows. This includes scripts having any first line that begins with a #! that is not followed by one of the four recognized patterns described earlier: /usr/bin/env python*, /usr/bin/python*, /usr/local/bin/python*, or python*. Anything else won't work, and requires code changes. For instance, a somewhat common #!/bin/python line also causes a script to now fail on Windows, unless a version number is given in command-line switches.

Unix-style #! lines probably aren't present in Windows-only programs, but can be common in programs meant to be run on Unix too. Treating unrecognized Unix directives as errors on Windows seems a bit extreme, especially given that this is new behavior in 3.3, and will likely be unexpected. Why not just ignore unrecognized #! lines and run the file with the default Python—like every Windows Python to date has? It's possible that this might be improved in a future 3.X release (there may be some pushback on this), but today you must change any files using a #!/bin/env or other unrecognized pattern, if you want them to run under the launcher installed with Python 3.3 on Windows.

Book examples impact and fix

With respect to the book examples I ported to 3.3, this broke roughly a dozen scripts that started with #!/bin/env python. Regrettably, this includes some of the book's user-friendly and top-level demo launcher scripts (*PyGadgets* and *PyDemos*). To fix, I changed these to use the accepted #!/usr/bin/env python form instead. Altering your Windows file associations to omit the launcher altogether may be another option (e.g., associating *.py* files with python.exe instead of py.exe), but this negates the launcher's benefits, and seems a bit much to ask of users, especially newcomers.

One open issue here: strangely, passing *any* command-line switch to the launcher, even a python.exe argument, seems to negate this effect and fall back on the default Python —m.py and py m.py both issue errors on unrecognized #! lines, but py -i m.py runs such a file with the default Python. This seems a possible launcher bug, but also relies on the default, the subject of the next issue.

Pitfall 2: The Launcher Defaults to 2.X

Oddly, the Windows 3.3 launcher defaults to using an installed Python 2.X when running scripts that don't select 3.X explicitly. That is, scripts that either have no #! directive or use one that names python generically will be run by a 2.X Python by default when launched by icon clicks, direct filename command lines (m.py), or launcher command lines that give no version switch (py m.py). This is true even if 3.3 is installed after a 2.X on your machine, and has the potential to make many 3.X scripts fail initially.

The implications of this are potentially broad. As one example, clicking the icon of a directive-less 3.X file just after installing 3.3 may now fail, because the associated launcher assumes you mean to use 2.X by default. This probably won't be a pleasant first encounter for some Python newcomers! This assumes the 3.X file has no #! directive that provides an explicit python3 version number, but most scripts meant to run on Windows won't have a #! line at all, and many files coded before the launcher came online won't accommodate its version number expectations. Most 3.X users will be basically compelled to set PY_PYTHON after installing 3.3—hardly a usability win.

Program launches that don't give an explicit version number might be arguably ambiguous on Unix too, and often rely on symbolic links from python to a specific version (which is most likely 2.X today—a state the new Windows launcher seems to emulate). But as for the prior issue, this probably shouldn't trigger a *new* error on Windows in 3.3 for scripts that worked there formerly. Most programmers wouldn't expect Unix comment lines to matter on Windows, and wouldn't expect 2.X to be used by default just after installing 3.X.

Book examples impact and fix

In terms of my book examples port, this 2.X default caused multiple 3.X script failures after installing 3.3, for both scripts with no #! line, as well as scripts with a Unix-compatible `#!/usr/bin/python` line. To fix just the latter, change all scripts in this category to name `python3` explicitly instead of just `python`. To fix both the former and the latter in a single step, set the Windows launcher's default to be 3.X globally with either a *py.ini* configuration file (see the launcher's documentation for details) or a `PY_PYTHON` environment variable setting as shown in the earlier examples (e.g., `set PY_PYTHON=3`). As mentioned in the prior point, manually changing your file associations is another solution, but none of these options seem simpler than those imposed by prior install schemes.

Pitfall 3: The New PATH Extension Option

Besides installing the new launcher, the Windows Python 3.3 installer can automatically add the directory containing 3.3's `python.exe` executable to your system `PATH` setting. The reasoning behind this is that it might make life easier for some Windows beginners—they can type just `python` instead of the full directory path to it. This isn't a feature of the launcher per se, and shouldn't cause scripts to fail in general. It had no impact on the book examples. But it seems to clash with the launcher's operation and goals, and may be best avoided. This is a bit subtle, but I'll explain why.

As described, the new launcher's `py` and `pyw` executables are by default installed on your system search path, and running them requires neither directory paths nor `PATH` settings. If you start scripts with `py` instead of `python` command lines, the new `PATH` feature is irrelevant. In fact, `py` completely *subsumes* `python` in most contexts. Given that file associations will launch `py` or `pyw` instead of `python` anyhow, you probably should too —using `python` instead of `py` may prove redundant and inconsistent, and might even launch a version different than that used in launcher contexts should the two schemes' settings grow out of sync. In short, adding `python` to `PATH` seems *contradictory* to the new launcher's worldview, and potentially error-prone.

Also note that updating your `PATH` assumes you *want* a `python` command to run 3.3 normally, and this feature is *disabled* by default; be sure to select this in the install screen if you want this to work (but not if you don't!). Due to the second pitfall mentioned earlier, many users may still need to set `PY_PYTHON` to 3 for programs run by icon clicks that invoke the new launcher, which seems no simpler than setting `PATH`, a step that the launcher was meant to remove. You may be better served by using just the launcher's executables, and changing just PY_PYTHON as needed.

Conclusions: A Net Win for Windows

To be fair, some of the prior section's pitfalls may be an inevitable consequence of trying to simultaneously support a Unix feature on Windows and multiple installed versions. In exchange, it provides a coherent way to manage mixed-version scripts and installations. You'll probably find the Windows launcher shipped with 3.3 and later to be a major asset once you start using it, and get past any initial incompatibilities you may encounter.

In fact, you may also want to start getting into the habit of coding compatible Unix-style #! lines in your Windows scripts, with explicit version numbers (e.g., #!/usr/bin/python3). Not only does this declare your code's requirements and arrange for its proper execution on Windows, it will also subvert the launcher's defaults, and may also make your script usable as a Unix executable in the future.

But you should be aware that the launcher may break some formerly valid scripts having #! lines, may choose a default version that you don't expect and your scripts can't use, and may require configuration and code changes on the order of those it was intended to obviate. The new boss is better than the old boss, but seems to have gone to the same school.

For more on Windows usage, see Appendix A for installation and configuration, Chapter 3 for general concepts, and platform-specific documents in Python's manuals set.

Python Changes and This Book

This appendix briefly summarizes changes made in recent releases of Python organized by the book editions where they first appeared, and gives links to their coverage in this book. It is intended as a reference for both readers of prior editions, as well as developers migrating from prior Python releases.

Here's how changes in Python relate to this book's recent editions:

- This *fifth* edition of 2013 covers Python 3.3 and 2.7.
- The *fourth* edition of 2009 covered Python 2.6 and 3.0 (with some 3.1 features).
- The *third* edition of 2007 covered Python 2.5.
- The *first* and *second* editions of 1999 and 2003 covered Pythons 2.0 and 2.2.
- The predecessor of this book, 1996's *Programming Python*, covered Python 1.3.

Hence, to see changes made in just this *fifth* edition, see the Python 2.7, 3.2, and 3.3 changes listed ahead. For changes incorporated into both the *fourth and fifth* editions (that is, since the *third*), also see Python 2.6, 3.0, and 3.1 changes here. Third edition language changes are listed very briefly too, though this seems of only historical value today.

Also note that this appendix focuses on major changes and book impacts, and is not intended as a complete guide to Python's evolution. For the fuller story on changes applied in each new Python release, consult the "What's New" documents that are part of its standard documentation set, and available at the Documentation page of python.org (*http://python.org*). Chapter 15 covers Python documentation and its manuals set.

Major 2.X/3.X Differences

Much of this appendix relates Python changes to book coverage. If you're instead looking for a quick summary of the most prominent 2.X/3.X distinctions, the following may suffice. Note that this section primarily compares the latest 3.X and 2.X releases

—3.3 and 2.7. Many 3.X features are not listed here because they were either also added to 2.6 (e.g., the `with` statement and class decorators), or back-ported later to 2.7 (e.g., set and dictionary comprehensions), but are not available in earlier 2.X releases. See later sections for more fine-grained information about changes in earlier versions, and see Python's "What's New" documents for changes that may appear in future releases.

3.X Differences

The following summarizes tools that differ across Python lines.

- *Unicode string model*: In 3.X, normal `str` strings support all Unicode text including ASCII, and the separate `bytes` type represents raw 8-bit byte sequences. In 2.X, normal `str` strings support both 8-bit text including ASCII, and a separate `uni code` type represents richer Unicode text as an option.

- *File model*: In 3.X, files created by `open` are specialized by content—text files implement Unicode encodings and represent content as `str` strings, and binary files represent content as `bytes` strings. In 2.X, files use distinct interfaces—files created by `open` represent content as `str` strings for content that is either 8-bit text or bytes-based data, and `codecs.open` implements Unicode text encodings.

- *Class model*: In 3.X, all classes derive from `object` automatically and acquire the numerous changes and extensions of *new-style* classes, including their differing inheritance algorithm, built-ins dispatch, and MRO search order for diamond-pattern trees. In 2.X, normal classes follow the *classic* model, and explicit inheritance from `object` or other built-in types enables the new-style model as an option.

- *Built-in iterables*: In 3.X, `map`, `zip`, `range`, `filter`, and dictionary `keys`, `values`, and `items` are all iterable objects that generate values on request. In 2.X, these calls create physical lists.

- *Printing*: 3.X provides a built-in function with keyword arguments for configuration, while 2.X provides a statement with special syntax for configuration.

- *Relative imports*: Both 2.X and 3.X support `from .` relative import statements, but 3.X changes the search rule to skip a package's own directory for normal imports.

- *True division*: Both 2.X and 3.X support the `//` floor division operator, but the `/` is true division in 3.X and retains fractional remainders, while `/` is type-specific in 2.X.

- *Integer types*: 3.X has a single integer type that supports extended precision. 2.X has both normal `int` and extended `long`, and automatic conversion to `long`.

- *Comprehension scopes*: In 3.X, all comprehension forms—list, set, dictionary, generator—localize variables to the expression. In 2.X, list comprehensions do not.

- *PyDoc*: An all-browser `pydoc -b` interface is supported as of 3.2 and required as of 3.3. In 2.X, the original `pydoc -g` GUI client interface may be used instead.

- *Byte code storage*: As of 3.2, 3.X stores byte code files in a __pycache__ subdirectory of the source directory, with version-identifying names. In 2.X, byte code is stored in the source file directory with generic names.

- *Built-in system exceptions*: As of 3.3, 3.X has a reworked exception hierarchy for OS and IO classes that includes additional categories and granularity. In 2.X, exception attributes must sometimes be inspected on system errors.

- *Comparisons and sorts*: In 3.X, relative magnitude comparisons of both mixed-types and dictionaries are errors, and sorts do not support mixed types or general comparison functions (use `key` mappers instead). In 2.X all these forms work.

- *String exceptions and module functions*: String-based exceptions are fully removed in 3.X, though they are also gone in 2.X as of 2.6 (use classes instead). `string` module functions redundant with string object methods are also removed in 3.X.

- *Language removals*: Per Table C-2, 3.X removes, renames, or relocates many 2.X language items: `reload`, `apply`, `` `x` ``, `<>`, `0177`, `999L`, `dict.has_key`, `raw_input`, `xrange`, `file`, `reduce`, and `file.xreadlines`.

3.X-Only Extensions

The following summarizes tools available in 3.X only.

- *Extended sequence assignment*: 3.X allows a * in sequence assignment targets to collect remaining unmatched iterable items in a list. 2.X can achieve similar effects with slicing.

- *Nonlocal*: 3.X provides a `nonlocal` statement, which allows names in enclosing function scopes to be changed from within nested functions. 2.X can achieve similar effects with function attributes, mutable objects, and class state.

- *Function annotations*: 3.X allows function arguments and return types to be annotated with objects that are retained in the function but not otherwise used. 2.X may often achieve similar effects with extra objects or decorator arguments.

- *Keyword-only arguments*: 3.X allows specification of function arguments that must be passed as keywords, typically used for extra configuration options. 2.X may often achieve similar effects with argument analysis and dictionary pops.

- *Chained exceptions*: 3.X allows exceptions to be chained and thus appear in error messages, with a `raise from` extension; 3.3 allows a `None` to cancel the chain.

- *Yield from*: As of 3.3, the `yield` statement may delegate to a nested generator with `from`. 2.X can often achieve similar results with a `for` loop in simpler use cases.

- *Namespace packages*: As of 3.3, the package model is extended to allow packages that span multiple directories with no initialization file, as a fallback option. 2.X might achieve similar effects with import extensions.

- *Windows launcher*: As of 3.3, a launcher is shipped with Python for Windows, though this is also available separately for use on other Pythons, including 2.X.

- *Internals*: As of 3.2, threading is implemented with time slices instead of virtual machine instruction counts, and 3.3 stores Unicode text in a variable-length scheme instead of fixed-size bytes. 2.X's string model minimizes Unicode use in general.

General Remarks: 3.X Changes

Although the Python 3.X line covered in the two most recent editions of this book is largely the same language as its 2.X predecessor, it differs in some crucial ways. As discussed in the preface and summarized in the preceding section, 3.X's nonoptional Unicode model, mandatory new-style classes, and broader emphasis on generators and other functional tools alone can make it a materially different experience.

On the whole, Python 3.X may be a *cleaner* language, but it is also in many ways a more *sophisticated* language, relying upon concepts that are substantially more advanced. In fact, some of its changes seem to assume you must already know Python in order to learn Python. The preface mentioned some of the more prominent circular knowledge dependencies in 3.X that imply forward topic dependencies.

As a random example, the rationale for wrapping dictionary views in a `list` call in 3.X is incredibly subtle and requires substantial foreknowledge—of views, generators, and the iteration protocol, at the least. Keyword arguments are similarly required in simple tools (e.g., printing, string formatting, dictionary creation, and sorting) that crop up long before a newcomer learns enough about functions to understand them fully. One of this book's goals is to help bridge this knowledge gap in today's 2.X/3.X dual-version world.

Changes in Libraries and Tools

There are additional changes in Python 3.X not listed in this appendix, simply because they don't affect this book. For example, some standard libraries and development tools are outside this book's core language scope, though some are mentioned along the way (e.g., `timeit`), and others have always been covered here (e.g., *PyDoc*).

For completeness, the following sections note 3.X developments in these categories. Some of the changes in these categories are also listed later in this appendix, in conjunction with the book edition and Python version in which they were introduced.

Standard library changes

Formally speaking, the Python standard library is not a part of this book's core language subject, even though it's always available with Python, and permeates realistic Python programs. In fact, the libraries were not subject to the temporary 3.X language changes moratorium enacted during 3.2's development.

Because of this, changes in the standard library have a larger impact on applications-focused books like *Programming Python* than they do here. Although most standard library functionality is still present, Python 3.X takes further liberties with renaming modules, grouping them into packages, and changing API call patterns.

Some library changes are much broader, though. Python 3.X's *Unicode* model, for example, creates widespread differences in 3.X's standard library—it potentially impacts any program that processes file content, filenames, directory walkers, pipes, descriptor files, sockets, text in GUIs, Internet protocols such as FTP and email, CGI scripts, web content of many kinds, and even some persistence tools such as DBM files, shelves, and pickles.

For a more comprehensive list of changes in 3.X's standard libraries, see the "What's New" documents for 3.X releases (especially 3.0) in Python's standard manual set. Because it uses Python 3.X throughout, the aforementioned *Programming Python* can also serve as a guide to 3.X library changes.

Tools changes

Though most development tools are the same between 2.X and 3.X (e.g., for debugging, profiling, timing, and testing), a few have undergone changes in 3.X along with the language and library. Among these, the *PyDoc* module documentation system has moved away from its former GUI client model in 3.2 and earlier, replacing it with an all web browser interface.

Other noteworthy changes in this category: the *distutils* package, used to distribute and install third-party software, is to be subsumed by a new *packaging* system in 3.X; the new _pycache_ byte code storage scheme described in this book, though an improvement, potentially impacts many Python tools and programs; and the internal implementation of *threading* changed as of 3.2 to reduce contention by modifying the global interpreter lock (GIL) to use absolute time slices instead of a virtual machine instruction counter.

Migrating to 3.X

If you are migrating from Python 2.X to Python 3.X, be sure to also see the *2to3* automatic code conversion script that is shipped with Python 3.X. It's currently available in Python's `Tools\Scripts` install folder, or via a web search. This script cannot translate everything, and attempts to translate core language code primarily—3.X standard library APIs may differ further. Still, it does a reasonable job of converting much 2.X code to run under 3.X.

Conversely, the *3to2* back-conversion program, currently available in the third-party domain, can also translate much Python 3.X code to run in 2.X environments. Depending on your goals and constraints, either *2to3* or *3to2* may prove useful if you must maintain code for both Python lines; see the Web for details, and additional tools and techniques.

It's also possible to write code that runs *portably* on both 2.X and 3.X using techniques presented in this book—importing 3.X features from __future__, avoiding version-specific tools, and so on. Many of the examples in this book are platform-neutral. For examples, see the benchmarking tools in Chapter 21, the module reloaders and comma formatter in Chapter 25, the class tree listers in Chapter 31, most of the larger decorator examples in Chapter 38 and Chapter 39, the joke script at the end of Chapter 41, and more. As long as you understand 2.X/3.X core language differences, coding around them is often straightforward.

If you're interested in writing code for both 2.X and 3.X, see also *six*—a library of cross-version mapping and renaming tools, which currently lives at *http://packages.python .org/six*. Naturally, this package can't offset every difference in language semantics and library APIs, and in many cases you must use its library tools instead of straight Python to realize its portability gains. In exchange, though, your programs become much more version-neutral when using this library's tools.

Fifth Edition Python Changes: 2.7, 3.2, 3.3

The following specific changes were made in the Python 2.X and 3.X lines after the fourth edition was published, and have been incorporated into this edition. Specifically, this section documents Python book-related changes in Pythons 2.7, 3.2, and 3.3.

Changes in Python 2.7

On the technical front, Python 2.7 mostly incorporates as back-ports a handful of 3.X features that were covered in the prior edition of this book, but formerly as 3.X-only features. This new fifth edition presents these as 2.7 tools as well. Among these:

- Set literals:

      {1, 4, 2, 3, 4}

- Set and dictionary comprehensions:

      {c * 4 for c in 'spam'}, {c: c * 4 for c in 'spam'}

- Dictionary views, incorporated as optional methods:

      dict.viewkeys(), dict.viewvalues(), dict.viewitems()

- Comma separators and field autonumbering in str.format (from 3.1):

      '{:,.2f} {}'.format(1234567.891, 'spam')

- Nested with statement context managers (from 3.1):

      with X() as x, Y() as y: ...

- Float object repr display improvements (back-ported from 3.1: see ahead)

To see where these topics are covered in the book, look for their entries in the 3.0 changes list of Table C-1, or the Python 3.1 changes section, both ahead. They were already present for 3.X, but have been updated to reflect their availability in 2.7 as well.

On the logistical front, per current plans 2.7 will be the last major 2.X series release, but will have a long maintenance period in which it will continue to be used in production work. After 2.7, new development is to shift to the Python 3.X line.

That said, it's impossible to foresee how this official posture will stand the test of time, given 2.X's still very wide user base. See the preface for more on this; the optimized PyPy implementation, for example, is still Python 2.X only. Or, to borrow a Monty Python line, "*I'm not dead yet...*"—stay tuned for developments on the Python 2.X story.

Changes in Python 3.3

Python 3.3 includes a surprisingly large number of changes for a point release. Some of these are not entirely compatible with code written for prior releases in the 3.X line. Among these, the new Windows launcher, installed as a mandatory part of 3.3, has broad potential to break existing 3.X scripts run on Windows.

Here's a brief rundown of noteworthy 3.3 changes, along with their location in this book where applicable. Python 3.3 comes with:

- A reduced *memory footprint* that is more in line with 2.X, thanks mainly to its new variable-length string storage scheme, and also to its attribute name-sharing dictionaries system (see Chapter 37 and Chapter 32)
- A new *namespace package model*, where new-style packages may span multiple directories and require no *__init__.py* file (see Chapter 24)
- New syntax for delegating to subgenerators: `yield from ...` (see Chapter 20)
- New syntax for suppressing exception context: `raise ... from None` (see Chapter 34)
- New syntax for accepting 2.X's Unicode literal form to ease migration: 3.3 now treats 2.X's Unicode literal `u'xxxx'` the same as its normal string `'xxxx'`, similar to the way 2.X treats 3.X's bytes literal `b'xxxx'` the same as its normal string `'xxxx'` (see Chapter 4, Chapter 7, and Chapter 37)
- Reworked OS and IO *exception hierarchies*, which provide more inclusive general superclasses, as well as new subclasses for common errors that can obviate the need to inspect exception object attributes (see Chapter 35)
- An all-web-browser-based interface to *PyDoc documentation* started via `pydoc -b`, replacing its former standalone GUI client search interface, which was in the Windows 7 and earlier Start button and invoked by `pydoc -g` (see Chapter 15)

- Changes to some longstanding *standard library* modules, including `ftplib`, `time`, and `email`, and potentially `distutils`; impacts in this book: `time` has new portable calls in 3.X (see Chapter 21 and Chapter 39)
- An implementation of the `__import__` function in `importlib.__import__`, in part to unify and more clearly expose its implementation (see Chapter 22 and Chapter 25)
- A new capability in the Windows 3.3 installer that extends the system `PATH` setting to include 3.3's directory as an install-time option to simplify some command lines (see Appendixes A and B)
- A new *Windows launcher*, which attempts to interpret Unix-style #! lines for dispatching Python scripts on Windows, and allows both #! lines and new `py` command lines to select between Python 2.X and 3.X versions explicitly on both a per-file and per-command basis (see the new Appendix B)

Changes in Python 3.2

Python 3.2 continued the 3.X line's evolution. It was developed during a moratorium on 3.X core language changes, so its relevant changes were minor. Here's a quick review of major 3.2 changes, and their location in this fifth edition where relevant:

- Byte-code files storage model change: `__pycache__` (see Chapter 2 and Chapter 22)
- The `struct` module's autoencoding for strings is gone (see Chapter 9 and Chapter 37)
- 3.X `str`/`bytes` split supported better by Python itself (not relevant to this book)
- The `cgi.escape` call was to be moved in 3.2+ (not relevant to this book)
- Threading implementation change: time slices (not relevant to this book)

Fourth Edition Python Changes: 2.6, 3.0, 3.1

The fourth edition was updated to cover Python *3.0* and *2.6*, and incorporated a small number of major changes made in *3.1*. Its 3.0 and 3.1 changes apply to all future releases in the 3.X line including this fifth edition's Python 3.3, and its 2.6 changes are also part of this edition's 2.7. As noted earlier, some of the changes described here as 3.X changes also later found their way into Python 2.7 as back-ports (e.g., set literals, and set and dictionary comprehensions).

Changes in Python 3.1

In addition to the 3.0 and 2.6 changes listed in upcoming sections, shortly before going to press the fourth edition was also augmented with notes about prominent extensions in the then upcoming Python 3.1 release, including:

- Comma separators and automatic field numbering in string `format` method calls (Chapter 7)
- Multiple context manager syntax in `with` statements (Chapter 34)
- New methods for number objects (Chapter 5)
- (Not added until this fifth edition) Floating-point display changes (Chapter 4 and Chapter 5)

This fifth edition covers these topics in the chapters just noted. Because Python 3.1 was targeted primarily at optimization and was released relatively soon after 3.0, the fourth edition also applied directly to 3.1. In fact, because Python 3.1 superseded 3.0 entirely, and because the latest Python is usually the best Python to fetch and use anyhow, whenever that edition used the term "Python 3.0" it generally referred to the language variations introduced by Python 3.0 but that are present in the entire 3.X line, including this edition's Python 3.3.

One notable exception: the fourth edition did *not* incorporate 3.1's new `repr` display scheme for *floating-point* numbers. The new display algorithm attempts to display floating-point numbers more intelligently when possible, usually with fewer (but occasionally with more) decimal digits—a change that is reflected in this fifth edition.

Changes in Python 3.0 and 2.6

The fourth edition's language changes stem from Python 3.0 and 2.6. All of its 2.6 and many of its 3.0 changes are shared by Python 2.7 and 3.3 today. Python 2.7 was extended with some 3.0 features not present in 2.6 (see earlier in this appendix), and Python 3.3 inherits all the features introduced by 3.0.

Because there were so many changes in the initial 3.X release, they are noted only briefly in tables here, with links to more details in this book. Table C-1 provides the first set of 3.X changes, listing the most prominent new language features covered in the fourth edition, along with the primary chapters in the current fifth edition in which they appear.

Table C-1. Extensions in Python 2.6 and 3.0

Extension	Covered in chapter(s)
The `print` function in 3.0	11
The `nonlocal x,y` statement in 3.0	17
The `str.format` method in 2.6 and 3.0	7
String types in 3.0: `str` for Unicode text, `bytes` for binary data	7, 37
Text and binary file distinctions in 3.0	9, 37
Class decorators in 2.6 and 3.0: `@private('age')`	32, 39
New iterators in 3.0: `range`, `map`, `zip`	14, 20
Dictionary views in 3.0: `D.keys`, `D.values`, `D.items`	8, 14

Extension	Covered in chapter(s)
Division operators in 3.0: remainders, / and //	5
Set literals in 3.0: {a, b, c}	5
Set comprehensions in 3.0: {x**2 for x in seq}	4, 5, 14, 20
Dictionary comprehensions in 3.0: {x: x**2 for x in seq}	4, 8, 14, 20
Binary digit-string support in 2.6 and 3.0: 0b0101, bin(I)	5
The fraction number type in 2.6 and 3.0: Fraction(1, 3)	5
Function annotations in 3.0: def f(a:99, b:str)->int	19
Keyword-only arguments in 3.0: def f(a, *b, c, **d)	18, 20
Extended sequence unpacking in 3.0: a, *b = seq	11, 13
Relative import syntax for packages enabled in 3.0: from .	24
Context managers enabled in 2.6 and 3.0: with/as	34, 36
Exception syntax changes in 3.0: raise, except/as, superclass	34, 35
Exception chaining in 3.0: raise e2 from e1	34
Reserved word changes in 2.6 and 3.0	11
New-style class cutover in 3.0	32
Property decorators in 2.6 and 3.0: @property	38
Descriptor use in 2.6 and 3.0	32, 38
Metaclass use in 2.6 and 3.0	32, 40
Abstract base classes support in 2.6 and 3.0	29

Specific Language Removals in 3.0

In addition to extensions, a number of 2.X language tools have been removed in 3.X in an effort to clean up its design. Table C-2 summarizes the 3.X removals that impact this book, covered in various chapters of this edition as noted. As also shown in this table, many of the 3.X removals have direct replacements, some of which are also available in 2.6 and 2.7 to support future migration to 3.X.

Table C-2. Removals in Python 3.0 that impact this book

Removed	Replacement	Covered in chapter(s)
reload(M)	imp.reload(M) (or exec)	3, 23
apply(f, ps, ks)	f(*ps, **ks)	18
`X`	repr(X)	5
X <> Y	X != Y	5
long	int	5
9999L	9999	5
D.has_key(K)	K in D (or D.get(key) != None)	8

Removed	Replacement	Covered in chapter(s)
`raw_input`	`input`	3, 10
`old input`	`eval(input())`	3
`xrange`	`range`	13, 14
`file`	`open` (and `io` module classes)	9
`X.next`	`X.__next__`, called by `next(X)`	14, 20, 30
`X.__getslice__`	`X.__getitem__` passed a slice object	7, 30
`X.__setslice__`	`X.__setitem__` passed a slice object	7, 30
`reduce`	`functools.reduce` (or loop code)	14, 19
`execfile(filename)`	`exec(open(file name).read())`	3
`exec open(filename)`	`exec(open(file name).read())`	3
`0777`	`0o777`	5
`print x, y`	`print(x, y)`	11
`print >> F, x, y`	`print(x, y, file=F)`	11
`print x, y,`	`print(x, y, end=' ')`	11
`u'ccc'` (back in 3.3)	`'ccc'`	4, 7, 37
`'bbb'` for byte strings	`b'bbb'`	4, 7, 9, 37
`raise E, V`	`raise E(V)`	33, 34, 35
`except E, X:`	`except E as X:`	33, 34, 35
`def f((a, b)):`	`def f(x): (a, b) = x`	11, 18, 20
`file.xreadlines`	`for line in file:` (or `X=iter(file)`)	13, 14
`D.keys()`, etc. as lists	`list(D.keys())` (dictionary views)	8, 14
`map()`, `range()`, etc. as lists	`list(map())`, `list(range())` (built-ins)	14
`map(None, ...)`	`zip` (or manual code to pad results)	13, 20
`X=D.keys(); X.sort()`	`sorted(D)` (or `list(D.keys())`)	4, 8, 14
`cmp(x, y)`	`(x > y) - (x < y)`	30
`X.__cmp__(y)`	`__lt__`, `__gt__`, `__eq__`, etc.	30
`X.__nonzero__`	`X.__bool__`	30
`X.__hex__`, `X.__oct__`	`X.__index__`	30
Sort comparison functions	Use `key=transform` or `reverse=True`	8

Removed	Replacement	Covered in chapter(s)
Dictionary `<, >, <=, >=`	Compare `sorted(D.items())` (or loop code)	8, 9
`types.ListType`	`list` (types is for non-built-in names only)	9
`__metaclass__ = M`	`class C(metaclass=M):`	29, 32, 40
`__builtin__`	`builtins` (renamed)	17
`Tkinter`	`tkinter` (renamed)	18, 19, 25, 30, 31
`sys.exc_type, exc_value`	`sys.exc_info()[0], [1]`	35, 36
`function.func_code`	`function.__code__`	19, 39
`__getattr__` run by built-ins	Redefine `__X__` methods in wrapper classes	31, 38, 39
`-t, -tt` command-line switches	Inconsistent tabs/spaces use is always an error	10, 12
`from ... *`, within a function	May only appear at the top level of a file	23
`import mod`, in same package	`from . import mod`, package-relative form	24
`class MyException:`	`class MyException(Exception):`	35
exceptions module	Built-in scope, library manual	35
thread, Queue modules	`_thread, queue` (both renamed)	17
anydbm module	dbm (renamed)	28
`cPickle` module	`_pickle` (renamed, used automatically)	9
`os.popen2/3/4`	`subprocess.Popen` (`os.popen` retained)	14
String-based exceptions	Class-based exceptions (also required in 2.6)	33, 34, 35
String module functions	String object methods	7
Unbound methods	Functions (`staticmethod` to call via instance)	31, 32
Mixed type comparisons, sorts	Nonnumeric mixed type magnitude comparisons (and sorts) are errors	5, 9

Third Edition Python Changes: 2.3, 2.4, 2.5

The third edition of this book was thoroughly updated to reflect *Python 2.5* and all changes to the language made after the publication of the second edition in late 2003. (The second edition was based largely on *Python 2.2*, with some 2.3 features grafted on at the end of the project.) In addition, brief discussions of anticipated changes in the upcoming Python 3.0 release were incorporated where appropriate. Here are some of the major language topics for which new or expanded coverage was provided (chapter numbers here have been updated to reflect this fifth edition):

- The new `B if A else C` conditional expression (Chapter 12, Chapter 19)
- `with`/`as` context managers (Chapter 34)
- `try`/`except`/`finally` unification (Chapter 34)
- Relative import syntax (Chapter 24)
- Generator expressions (Chapter 20)
- New generator function features (Chapter 20)
- Function decorators (Chapter 32, Chapter 39)
- The set object type (Chapter 5)
- New built-in functions: `sorted`, `sum`, `any`, `all`, `enumerate` (Chapter 13 and Chapter 14)
- The decimal fixed-precision object type (Chapter 5)
- Files, list comprehensions, and iterators (Chapter 14 and Chapter 20)
- New development tools: Eclipse, `distutils`, `unittest` and `doctest`, IDLE enhancements, Shed Skin, and so on (Chapter 2 and Chapter 36)

Smaller language changes (for instance, the widespread use of `True` and `False`; the new `sys.exc_info` for fetching exception details; and the demise of string-based exceptions, string methods, and the `apply` and `reduce` built-ins) were incorporated throughout the book. The third edition also expanded coverage of some of the features that were new in the second edition, including three-limit slices and the arbitrary arguments call syntax that subsumed `apply`.

Earlier and Later Python Changes

Each edition before the third also incorporated Python changes too—the first two editions from 1999 and 2003 covered Pythons 2.0 and 2.2, and their 1996 *Programming Python 1st Edition* predecessor, from which my three later books were all derived, began the process with Python 1.3—but I've omitted these here because they are now ancient history (well, in computer field terms, at least).

See the first and second editions for more details, if you can manage to scare one up. While it's impossible to predict the future, given how much has stood the test of time, it's likely that the core ideas stressed in this book will likely apply to future Pythons as well.

Solutions to End-of-Part Exercises

Part I, Getting Started

See "Test Your Knowledge: Part I Exercises" on page 87 in Chapter 3 for the exercises.

1. *Interaction.* Assuming Python is configured properly, the interaction should look something like the following (you can run this any way you like (in IDLE, from a shell prompt, and so on):

   ```
   % python
   ...copyright information lines...
   >>> "Hello World!"
   'Hello World!'
   >>>                       # Use Ctrl-D or Ctrl-Z to exit, or close window
   ```

2. *Programs.* Your code (i.e., module) file *module1.py* and the operating system shell interactions should look like this:

   ```
   print('Hello module world!')
   ```

   ```
   % python module1.py
   Hello module world!
   ```

   Again, feel free to run this other ways—by clicking the file's icon, by using IDLE's Run→Run Module menu option, and so on.

3. *Modules.* The following interaction listing illustrates running a module file by importing it:

   ```
   % python
   >>> import module1
   Hello module world!
   >>>
   ```

   Remember that you will need to reload the module to run it again without stopping and restarting the interpreter. The question about moving the file to a different directory and importing it again is a trick question: if Python generates a *module1.pyc* file in the original directory, it uses that when you import the module, even if the source code (*.py*) file has been moved to a directory not in Python's search path. The *.pyc* file is written automatically if Python has access to the source file's directory; it contains the compiled byte code version of a module. See Chapter 3 for more on modules.

4. *Scripts.* Assuming your platform supports the #! trick, your solution will look like the following (although your #! line may need to list another path on your machine). Note that these lines are significant under the Windows launcher shipped and installed with Python 3.3, where they are parsed to select a version of Python to run the script, along with a default setting; see Appendix B for details and examples.

```
#!/usr/local/bin/python            (or #!/usr/bin/env python)
print('Hello module world!')
% chmod +x module1.py

% module1.py
Hello module world!
```

5. *Errors.* The following interaction (run in Python 3.X) demonstrates the sorts of error messages you'll get when you complete this exercise. Really, you're triggering Python exceptions; the default exception-handling behavior terminates the running Python program and prints an error message and stack trace on the screen. The stack trace shows where you were in a program when the exception occurred (if function calls are active when the error happens, the "Traceback" section displays all active call levels). In Chapter 10 and Part VII, you will learn that you can catch exceptions using **try** statements and process them arbitrarily; you'll also see there that Python includes a full-blown source code debugger for special error-detection requirements. For now, notice that Python gives meaningful messages when programming errors occur, instead of crashing silently:

```
% python
>>> 2 ** 500
327339060789614187001318969682759915221664204604306478948329136809613379640467455488327009232590415715088668412756007100921725654588539305332852758937 6
>>>
>>> 1 / 0
Traceback (most recent call last):
  File "<stdin>", line 1, in <module>
ZeroDivisionError: int division or modulo by zero
>>>
>>> spam
Traceback (most recent call last):
  File "<stdin>", line 1, in <module>
NameError: name 'spam' is not defined
```

6. *Breaks and cycles.* When you type this code:

```
L = [1, 2]
L.append(L)
```

you create a cyclic data structure in Python. In Python releases before 1.5.1, the Python printer wasn't smart enough to detect cycles in objects, and it would print

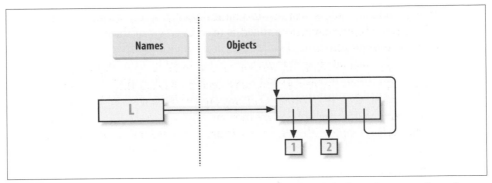

Figure D-1. A cyclic object, created by appending a list to itself. By default, Python appends a reference to the original list, not a copy of the list.

an unending stream of [1, 2, [1, 2, [1, 2, [1, 2, and so on, until you hit the break-key combination on your machine (which, technically, raises a keyboard-interrupt exception that prints a default message). Beginning with Python 1.5.1, the printer is clever enough to detect cycles and prints [[...]] instead to let you know that it has detected a loop in the object's structure and avoided getting stuck printing forever.

The reason for the cycle is subtle and requires information you will glean in Part II, so this is something of a preview. But in short, assignments in Python always generate *references* to objects, not copies of them. You can think of objects as chunks of memory and of references as implicitly followed pointers. When you run the first assignment above, the name L becomes a named reference to a two-item list object—a pointer to a piece of memory. Python lists are really arrays of object references, with an append method that changes the array in place by tacking on another object reference at the end. Here, the append call adds a reference to the front of L at the end of L, which leads to the cycle illustrated in Figure D-1: a pointer at the end of the list that points back to the front of the list.

Besides being printed specially, as you'll learn in Chapter 6 cyclic objects must also be handled specially by Python's garbage collector, or their space will remain un-reclaimed even when they are no longer in use. Though rare in practice, in some programs that traverse arbitrary objects or structures you might have to detect such cycles yourself by keeping track of where you've been to avoid looping. Believe it or not, cyclic data structures can sometimes be useful, despite their special-case printing.

Part II, Types and Operations

See "Test Your Knowledge: Part II Exercises" on page 313 in Chapter 9 for the exercises.

1. *The basics.* Here are the sorts of results you should get, along with a few comments about their meaning. Again, note that ; is used in a few of these to squeeze more than one statement onto a single line (the ; is a statement separator), and commas build up tuples displayed in parentheses. Also keep in mind that the / division result near the top differs in Python 2.X and 3.X (see Chapter 5 for details), and the list wrapper around dictionary method calls is needed to display results in 3.X, but not 2.X (see Chapter 8):

```
# Numbers

>>> 2 ** 16                          # 2 raised to the power 16
65536
>>> 2 / 5, 2 / 5.0                   # Integer / truncates in 2.X, but not 3.X
(0.40000000000000002, 0.40000000000000002)

# Strings

>>> "spam" + "eggs"                  # Concatenation
'spameggs'
>>> S = "ham"
>>> "eggs " + S
'eggs ham'
>>> S * 5                            # Repetition
'hamhamhamhamham'
>>> S[:0]                            # An empty slice at the front -- [0:0]
''                                   # Empty of same type as object sliced

>>> "green %s and %s" % ("eggs", S)  # Formatting
'green eggs and ham'
>>> 'green {0} and {1}'.format('eggs', S)
'green eggs and ham'

# Tuples

>>> ('x',)[0]                        # Indexing a single-item tuple
'x'
>>> ('x', 'y')[1]                    # Indexing a two-item tuple
'y'

# Lists

>>> L = [1,2,3] + [4,5,6]            # List operations
>>> L, L[:], L[:0], L[-2], L[-2:]
([1, 2, 3, 4, 5, 6], [1, 2, 3, 4, 5, 6], [], 5, [5, 6])
>>> ([1,2,3]+[4,5,6])[2:4]
[3, 4]
>>> [L[2], L[3]]                     # Fetch from offsets; store in a list
[3, 4]
>>> L.reverse(); L                   # Method: reverse list in place
[6, 5, 4, 3, 2, 1]
>>> L.sort(); L                      # Method: sort list in place
[1, 2, 3, 4, 5, 6]
>>> L.index(4)                       # Method: offset of first four (search)
3
```

```
# Dictionaries
>>> {'a':1, 'b':2}['b']                        # Index a dictionary by key
2
>>> D = {'x':1, 'y':2, 'z':3}
>>> D['w'] = 0                                 # Create a new entry
>>> D['x'] + D['w']
1
>>> D[(1,2,3)] = 4                             # A tuple used as a key (immutable)

>>> D
{'w': 0, 'z': 3, 'y': 2, (1, 2, 3): 4, 'x': 1}

>>> list(D.keys()), list(D.values()), (1,2,3) in D         # Methods, key test
(['w', 'z', 'y', (1, 2, 3), 'x'], [0, 3, 2, 4, 1], True)

# Empties
>>> [[]], ["",[],(),{},None]                   # Lots of nothings: empty objects
([[]], ['', [], (), {}, None])
```

2. *Indexing and slicing.* Indexing out of bounds (e.g., L[4]) raises an error; Python always checks to make sure that all offsets are within the bounds of a sequence.

On the other hand, slicing out of bounds (e.g., L[-1000:100]) works because Python scales out-of-bounds slices so that they always fit (the limits are set to zero and the sequence length, if required).

Extracting a sequence in reverse, with the lower bound greater than the higher bound (e.g., L[3:1]), doesn't really work. You get back an empty slice ([ ]) because Python scales the slice limits to make sure that the lower bound is always less than or equal to the upper bound (e.g., L[3:1] is scaled to L[3:3], the empty insertion point at offset 3). Python slices are always extracted from left to right, even if you use negative indexes (they are first converted to positive indexes by adding the sequence length). Note that Python 2.3's three-limit slices modify this behavior somewhat. For instance, L[3:1:-1] does extract from right to left:

```
>>> L = [1, 2, 3, 4]
>>> L[4]
Traceback (innermost last):
  File "<stdin>", line 1, in ?
IndexError: list index out of range
>>> L[-1000:100]
[1, 2, 3, 4]
>>> L[3:1]
[]
>>> L
[1, 2, 3, 4]
>>> L[3:1] = ['?']
>>> L
[1, 2, 3, '?', 4]
```

3. *Indexing, slicing, and del.* Your interaction with the interpreter should look something like the following code. Note that assigning an empty list to an offset stores an empty list object there, but assigning an empty list to a slice deletes the slice. Slice assignment expects another sequence, or you'll get a type error; it inserts items *inside* the sequence assigned, not the sequence itself:

```
>>> L = [1,2,3,4]
>>> L[2] = []
>>> L
[1, 2, [], 4]
>>> L[2:3] = []
>>> L
[1, 2, 4]
>>> del L[0]
>>> L
[2, 4]
>>> del L[1:]
>>> L
[2]
>>> L[1:2] = 1
Traceback (innermost last):
  File "<stdin>", line 1, in ?
TypeError: illegal argument type for built-in operation
```

4. *Tuple assignment.* The values of X and Y are swapped. When tuples appear on the left and right of an assignment symbol (=), Python assigns objects on the right to targets on the left according to their positions. This is probably easiest to understand by noting that the targets on the left aren't a real tuple, even though they look like one; they are simply a set of independent assignment targets. The items on the right are a tuple, which gets unpacked during the assignment (the tuple provides the temporary assignment needed to achieve the swap effect):

```
>>> X = 'spam'
>>> Y = 'eggs'
>>> X, Y = Y, X
>>> X
'eggs'
>>> Y
'spam'
```

5. *Dictionary keys.* Any immutable object can be used as a dictionary key, including integers, tuples, strings, and so on. This really is a dictionary, even though some of its keys look like integer offsets. Mixed-type keys work fine, too:

```
>>> D = {}
>>> D[1] = 'a'
>>> D[2] = 'b'
>>> D[(1, 2, 3)] = 'c'
>>> D
{1: 'a', 2: 'b', (1, 2, 3): 'c'}
```

6. *Dictionary indexing.* Indexing a nonexistent key (D['d']) raises an error; assigning to a nonexistent key (D['d']='spam') creates a new dictionary entry. On the other hand, out-of-bounds indexing for lists raises an error too, but so do out-of-bounds

assignments. Variable names work like dictionary keys; they must have already been assigned when referenced, but they are created when first assigned. In fact, variable names can be processed as dictionary keys if you wish (they're made visible in module namespace or stack-frame dictionaries):

```
>>> D = {'a':1, 'b':2, 'c':3}
>>> D['a']
1
>>> D['d']
Traceback (innermost last):
  File "<stdin>", line 1, in ?
KeyError: d
>>> D['d'] = 4
>>> D
{'b': 2, 'd': 4, 'a': 1, 'c': 3}
>>>
>>> L = [0, 1]
>>> L[2]
Traceback (innermost last):
  File "<stdin>", line 1, in ?
IndexError: list index out of range
>>> L[2] = 3
Traceback (innermost last):
  File "<stdin>", line 1, in ?
IndexError: list assignment index out of range
```

7. *Generic operations.* Question answers:

   - The + operator doesn't work on different/mixed types (e.g., string + list, list + tuple).

   - + doesn't work for dictionaries, as they aren't sequences.

   - The append method works only for lists, not strings, and keys works only on dictionaries. append assumes its target is mutable, since it's an in-place extension; strings are immutable.

   - Slicing and concatenation always return a new object of the same type as the objects processed:

```
>>> "x" + 1
Traceback (innermost last):
  File "<stdin>", line 1, in ?
TypeError: illegal argument type for built-in operation
>>>
>>> {} + {}
Traceback (innermost last):
  File "<stdin>", line 1, in ?
TypeError: bad operand type(s) for +
>>>
>>> [].append(9)
>>> "".append('s')
Traceback (innermost last):
  File "<stdin>", line 1, in ?
AttributeError: attribute-less object
>>>
```

```
>>> list({}.keys())                          # list() needed in 3.X, not 2.X
[]
>>> [].keys()
Traceback (innermost last):
  File "<stdin>", line 1, in ?
AttributeError: keys
>>>
>>> [][:]
[]
>>> ""[:]
''
```

8. *String indexing.* This is a bit of a trick question—because strings are collections of one-character strings, every time you index a string, you get back a string that can be indexed again. S[0][0][0][0][0] just keeps indexing the first character over and over. This generally doesn't work for lists (lists can hold arbitrary objects) unless the list contains strings:

```
>>> S = "spam"
>>> S[0][0][0][0][0]
's'
>>> L = ['s', 'p']
>>> L[0][0][0]
's'
```

9. *Immutable types.* Either of the following solutions works. Index assignment doesn't, because strings are immutable:

```
>>> S = "spam"
>>> S = S[0] + 'l' + S[2:]
>>> S
'slam'
>>> S = S[0] + 'l' + S[2] + S[3]
>>> S
'slam'
```

(See also the Python 3.X and 2.6+ `bytearray` string type in Chapter 37—it's a mutable sequence of small integers that is essentially processed the same as a string.)

10. *Nesting.* Here is a sample:

```
>>> me = {'name':('John', 'Q', 'Doe'), 'age':'?', 'job':'engineer'}
>>> me['job']
'engineer'
>>> me['name'][2]
'Doe'
```

11. *Files.* Here's one way to create and read back a text file in Python (`ls` is a Unix command; use `dir` on Windows):

```
# File: maker.py
file = open('myfile.txt', 'w')
file.write('Hello file world!\n')        # Or: open().write()
file.close()                             # close not always needed

# File: reader.py
file = open('myfile.txt')                # 'r' is default open mode
```

```
        print(file.read())                           # Or print(open().read())

        % python maker.py
        % python reader.py
        Hello file world!

        % ls -l myfile.txt
        -rwxrwxrwa   1 0          0         19 Apr 13 16:33 myfile.txt
```

Part III, Statements and Syntax

See "Test Your Knowledge: Part III Exercises" on page 467 in Chapter 15 for the exercises.

1. *Coding basic loops.* As you work through this exercise, you'll wind up with code that looks like the following:

```
        >>> S = 'spam'
        >>> for c in S:
        ...     print(ord(c))
        ...
        115
        112
        97
        109

        >>> x = 0
        >>> for c in S: x += ord(c)           # Or: x = x + ord(c)
        ...
        >>> x
        433

        >>> x = []
        >>> for c in S: x.append(ord(c))
        ...
        >>> x
        [115, 112, 97, 109]

        >>> list(map(ord, S))                 # list() required in 3.X, not 2.X
        [115, 112, 97, 109]
        >>> [ord(c) for c in S]               # map and listcomps automate list builders
        [115, 112, 97, 109]
```

2. *Backslash characters.* The example prints the bell character (\a) 50 times; assuming your machine can handle it, and when it's run outside of IDLE, you may get a series of beeps (or one sustained tone, if your machine is fast enough). Hey—I warned you.

3. *Sorting dictionaries.* Here's one way to work through this exercise (see Chapter 8 or Chapter 14 if this doesn't make sense). Remember, you really do have to split up the keys and sort calls like this because sort returns None. In Python 2.2 and later, you can iterate through dictionary keys directly without calling keys (e.g.,

for key in D:), but the keys list will not be sorted like it is by this code. In more recent Pythons, you can achieve the same effect with the sorted built-in, too:

```
>>> D = {'a':1, 'b':2, 'c':3, 'd':4, 'e':5, 'f':6, 'g':7}
>>> D
{'f': 6, 'c': 3, 'a': 1, 'g': 7, 'e': 5, 'd': 4, 'b': 2}
>>>
>>> keys = list(D.keys())            # list() required in 3.X, not in 2.X
>>> keys.sort()
>>> for key in keys:
...     print(key, '=>', D[key])
...
a => 1
b => 2
c => 3
d => 4
e => 5
f => 6
g => 7

>>> for key in sorted(D):            # Better, in more recent Pythons
...     print(key, '=>', D[key])
```

4. *Program logic alternatives.* Here's some sample code for the solutions. For step e, assign the result of 2 ** X to a variable outside the loops of steps a and b, and use it inside the loop. Your results may vary a bit; this exercise is mostly designed to get you playing with code alternatives, so anything reasonable gets full credit:

```
# a

L = [1, 2, 4, 8, 16, 32, 64]
X = 5

i = 0
while i < len(L):
    if 2 ** X == L[i]:
        print('at index', i)
        break
    i += 1
else:
    print(X, 'not found')

# b

L = [1, 2, 4, 8, 16, 32, 64]
X = 5

for p in L:
    if (2 ** X) == p:
        print((2 ** X), 'was found at', L.index(p))
        break
else:
    print(X, 'not found')

# c
```

```
L = [1, 2, 4, 8, 16, 32, 64]
X = 5

if (2 ** X) in L:
    print((2 ** X), 'was found at', L.index(2 ** X))
else:
    print(X, 'not found')
```

d

```
X = 5
L = []
for i in range(7): L.append(2 ** i)
print(L)

if (2 ** X) in L:
    print((2 ** X), 'was found at', L.index(2 ** X))
else:
    print(X, 'not found')
```

f

```
X = 5
L = list(map(lambda x: 2**x, range(7)))     # Or [2**x for x in range(7)]
print(L)                                     # list() to print all in 3.X, not 2.X

if (2 ** X) in L:
    print((2 ** X), 'was found at', L.index(2 ** X))
else:
    print(X, 'not found')
```

5. *Code maintenance.* There is no fixed solution to show here; see *mypydoc.py* in the book's examples package for my edits on this code as one example.

Part IV, Functions and Generators

See "Test Your Knowledge: Part IV Exercises" on page 663 in Chapter 21 for the exercises.

1. *The basics.* There's not much to this one, but notice that using `print` (and hence your function) is technically a *polymorphic* operation, which does the right thing for each type of object:

```
% python
>>> def func(x): print(x)
...
>>> func("spam")
spam
>>> func(42)
42
>>> func([1, 2, 3])
[1, 2, 3]
```

```
>>> func({'food': 'spam'})
{'food': 'spam'}
```

2. *Arguments.* Here's a sample solution. Remember that you have to use `print` to see results in the test calls because a file isn't the same as code typed interactively; Python doesn't normally echo the results of expression statements in files:

```
def adder(x, y):
    return x + y

print(adder(2, 3))
print(adder('spam', 'eggs'))
print(adder(['a', 'b'], ['c', 'd']))

% python mod.py
5
spameggs
['a', 'b', 'c', 'd']
```

3. *varargs.* Two alternative `adder` functions are shown in the following file, *adders.py*. The hard part here is figuring out how to initialize an accumulator to an empty value of whatever type is passed in. The first solution uses manual type testing to look for an integer, and an empty slice of the first argument (assumed to be a sequence) if the argument is determined not to be an integer. The second solution uses the first argument to initialize and scan items 2 and beyond, much like one of the `min` function variants shown in Chapter 18.

The second solution is better. Both of these assume all arguments are of the same type, and neither works on dictionaries (as we saw in Part II, + doesn't work on mixed types or dictionaries). You could add a type test and special code to allow dictionaries, too, but that's extra credit.

```
def adder1(*args):
    print('adder1', end=' ')
    if type(args[0]) == type(0):      # Integer?
        sum = 0                       # Init to zero
    else:                             # else sequence:
        sum = args[0][:0]             # Use empty slice of arg1
    for arg in args:
        sum = sum + arg
    return sum

def adder2(*args):
    print('adder2', end=' ')
    sum = args[0]                     # Init to arg1
    for next in args[1:]:
        sum += next                   # Add items 2..N
    return sum

for func in (adder1, adder2):
    print(func(2, 3, 4))
    print(func('spam', 'eggs', 'toast'))
    print(func(['a', 'b'], ['c', 'd'], ['e', 'f']))
```

```
% python adders.py
adder1 9
adder1 spameggstoast
adder1 ['a', 'b', 'c', 'd', 'e', 'f']
adder2 9
adder2 spameggstoast
adder2 ['a', 'b', 'c', 'd', 'e', 'f']
```

4. *Keywords.* Here is my solution to the first and second parts of this exercise (coded in the file *mod.py*). To iterate over keyword arguments, use the **args form in the function header and use a loop (e.g., for x in args.keys(): use args[x]), or use args.values() to make this the same as summing *args positionals:

```
def adder(good=1, bad=2, ugly=3):
    return good + bad + ugly

print(adder())
print(adder(5))
print(adder(5, 6))
print(adder(5, 6, 7))
print(adder(ugly=7, good=6, bad=5))
```

```
% python mod.py
6
10
14
18
18
```

```
# Second part solutions

def adder1(*args):                      # Sum any number of positional args
    tot = args[0]
    for arg in args[1:]:
        tot += arg
    return tot

def adder2(**args):                     # Sum any number of keyword args
    argskeys = list(args.keys())        # list needed in 3.X!
    tot = args[argskeys[0]]
    for key in argskeys[1:]:
        tot += args[key]
    return tot

def adder3(**args):                     # Same, but convert to list of values
    args = list(args.values())          # list needed to index in 3.X!
    tot = args[0]
    for arg in args[1:]:
        tot += arg
    return tot

def adder4(**args):                     # Same, but reuse positional version
    return adder1(*args.values())

print(adder1(1, 2, 3),        adder1('aa', 'bb', 'cc'))
```

```
print(adder2(a=1, b=2, c=3), adder2(a='aa', b='bb', c='cc'))
print(adder3(a=1, b=2, c=3), adder3(a='aa', b='bb', c='cc'))
print(adder4(a=1, b=2, c=3), adder4(a='aa', b='bb', c='cc'))
```

5. (and 6.) *Dictionary tools.* Here are my solutions to exercises 5 and 6 (file *dicts.py*). These are just coding exercises, though, because Python 1.5 added the dictionary methods D.copy() and D1.update(D2) to handle things like copying and adding (merging) dictionaries. See Chapter 8 for dict.update examples, and Python's library manual or O'Reilly's *Python Pocket Reference* for more details. X[:] doesn't work for dictionaries, as they're not sequences (see Chapter 8 for details). Also, remember that if you assign (e = d) rather than copying, you generate a reference to a *shared* dictionary object; changing d changes e, too:

```
def copyDict(old):
    new = {}
    for key in old.keys():
        new[key] = old[key]
    return new

def addDict(d1, d2):
    new = {}
    for key in d1.keys():
        new[key] = d1[key]
    for key in d2.keys():
        new[key] = d2[key]
    return new
```

```
% python
>>> from dicts import *
>>> d = {1: 1, 2: 2}
>>> e = copyDict(d)
>>> d[2] = '?'
>>> d
{1: 1, 2: '?'}
>>> e
{1: 1, 2: 2}

>>> x = {1: 1}
>>> y = {2: 2}
>>> z = addDict(x, y)
>>> z
{1: 1, 2: 2}
```

6. See #5.

7. *More argument-matching examples.* Here is the sort of interaction you should get, along with comments that explain the matching that goes on:

```
def f1(a, b): print(a, b)              # Normal args

def f2(a, *b): print(a, b)             # Positional varargs

def f3(a, **b): print(a, b)            # Keyword varargs

def f4(a, *b, **c): print(a, b, c)     # Mixed modes
```

```
def f5(a, b=2, c=3): print(a, b, c)        # Defaults

def f6(a, b=2, *c): print(a, b, c)         # Defaults and positional varargs


% python
>>> f1(1, 2)                               # Matched by position (order matters)
1 2
>>> f1(b=2, a=1)                           # Matched by name (order doesn't matter)
1 2

>>> f2(1, 2, 3)                            # Extra positionals collected in a tuple
1 (2, 3)

>>> f3(1, x=2, y=3)                        # Extra keywords collected in a dictionary
1 {'x': 2, 'y': 3}

>>> f4(1, 2, 3, x=2, y=3)                  # Extra of both kinds
1 (2, 3) {'x': 2, 'y': 3}

>>> f5(1)                                  # Both defaults kick in
1 2 3
>>> f5(1, 4)                               # Only one default used
1 4 3

>>> f6(1)                                  # One argument: matches "a"
1 2 ()
>>> f6(1, 3, 4)                            # Extra positional collected
1 3 (4,)
```

8. *Primes revisited.* Here is the primes example, wrapped up in a function and a module (file *primes.py*) so it can be run multiple times. I added an `if` test to trap negatives, 0, and 1. I also changed / to // in this edition to make this solution immune to the Python 3.X / true division changes we studied in Chapter 5, and to enable it to support floating-point numbers (uncomment the `from` statement and change // to / to see the differences in 2.X):

```
#from __future__ import division

def prime(y):
    if y <= 1:                             # For some y > 1
        print(y, 'not prime')
    else:
        x = y // 2                         # 3.X / fails
        while x > 1:
            if y % x == 0:                 # No remainder?
                print(y, 'has factor', x)
                break                      # Skip else
            x -= 1
        else:
            print(y, 'is prime')

prime(13); prime(13.0)
prime(15); prime(15.0)
```

```
prime(3);  prime(2)
prime(1);  prime(-3)
```

Here is the module in action; the `//` operator allows it to work for floating-point numbers too, even though it perhaps should not:

```
% python primes.py
13 is prime
13.0 is prime
15 has factor 5
15.0 has factor 5.0
3 is prime
2 is prime
1 not prime
-3 not prime
```

This function still isn't very reusable—it could return values, instead of printing —but it's enough to run experiments. It's also not a strict mathematical prime (floating points work), and it's still inefficient. Improvements are left as exercises for more mathematically minded readers. (Hint: a `for` loop over `range(y, 1, -1)` may be a bit quicker than the `while`, but the algorithm is the real bottleneck here.) To time alternatives, use the homegrown `timer` or standard library `timeit` modules and coding patterns like those used in Chapter 21's timing sections (and see Solution 10).

9. *Iterations and comprehensions.* Here is the sort of code you should write; I may have a preference, but yours may vary:

```
>>> values = [2, 4, 9, 16, 25]
>>> import math

>>> res = []
>>> for x in values: res.append(math.sqrt(x))
...
>>> res
[1.4142135623730951, 2.0, 3.0, 4.0, 5.0]

>>> list(map(math.sqrt, values))
[1.4142135623730951, 2.0, 3.0, 4.0, 5.0]

>>> [math.sqrt(x) for x in values]
[1.4142135623730951, 2.0, 3.0, 4.0, 5.0]

>>> list(math.sqrt(x) for x in values)
[1.4142135623730951, 2.0, 3.0, 4.0, 5.0]
```

10. *Timing tools.* Here is some code I wrote to time the three square root options, along with the results in CPythons 3.3 and 2.7 and PyPy 1.9 (which implements Python 2.7). Each test takes the best of three runs; each run takes the total time required to call the test function 1,000 times; and each test function iterates 1,000 times. The last result of each function is printed to verify that all three do the same work:

```
# File timer2.py (2.X and 3.X)
...same as listed in Chapter 21...
```

```
# File timesqrt.py
import sys, timer2
reps = 10000
repslist = range(reps)                        # Pull out range list time for 2.X

from math import sqrt                          # Not math.sqrt: adds attr fetch time
def mathMod():
    for i in repslist:
        res = sqrt(i)
    return res

def powCall():
    for i in repslist:
        res = pow(i, .5)
    return res

def powExpr():
    for i in repslist:
        res = i ** .5
    return res

print(sys.version)
for test in (mathMod, powCall, powExpr):
    elapsed, result = timer2.bestoftotal(test, _reps1=3, _reps=1000)
    print ('%s: %.5f => %s' % (test.__name__, elapsed, result))
```

Following are the test results for the three Pythons. The 3.3 and 2.7 results are roughly twice as fast as 3.0 and 2.6 in the prior edition, due largely to a faster test machine. For each Python tested, it looks like the `math` module is quicker than the `**` expression, which is quicker than the `pow` call; however, you should try this with your code and on your own machine and version of Python. Also, note that Python 3.3 is essentially twice as slow as 2.7 on this test, and PyPy is a rough order of magnitude (10X) faster than both CPythons, despite the fact that this is running floating-point math and iterations. Later versions of any of these Pythons might differ, so time this in the future to see for yourself:

```
c:\code> py -3 timesqrt.py
3.3.0 (v3.3.0:bd8afb90ebf2, Sep 29 2012, 10:57:17) [MSC v.1600 64 bit (AMD64)]
mathMod: 2.04481 => 99.99499987499375
powCall: 3.40973 => 99.99499987499375
powExpr: 2.56458 => 99.99499987499375

c:\code> py -2 timesqrt.py
2.7.3 (default, Apr 10 2012, 23:24:47) [MSC v.1500 64 bit (AMD64)]
mathMod: 1.04337 => 99.994999875
powCall: 2.57516 => 99.994999875
powExpr: 1.89560 => 99.994999875

c:\code> c:\pypy\pypy-1.9\pypy timesqrt.py
2.7.2 (341e1e3821ff, Jun 07 2012, 15:43:00)
[PyPy 1.9.0 with MSC v.1500 32 bit]
mathMod: 0.07491 => 99.994999875
```

```
powCall: 0.85678 => 99.994999875
powExpr: 0.85453 => 99.994999875
```

To time the relative speeds of Python 3.X and 2.7 *dictionary comprehensions* and equivalent for loops interactively, you can run a session like the following. It appears that the two are roughly the same in this regard under Python 3.3; unlike list comprehensions, though, manual loops are slightly faster than dictionary comprehensions today (though the difference isn't exactly earth-shattering—at the end we save half a second when making 50 dictionaries of 1,000,000 items each). Again, rather than taking these results as gospel you should investigate further on your own, on your computer and with your Python:

```
C:\code> c:\python33\python
>>>
>>> def dictcomp(I):
        return {i: i for i in range(I)}

>>> def dictloop(I):
        new = {}
        for i in range(I): new[i] = i
        return new

>>> dictcomp(10)
{0: 0, 1: 1, 2: 2, 3: 3, 4: 4, 5: 5, 6: 6, 7: 7, 8: 8, 9: 9}
>>> dictloop(10)
{0: 0, 1: 1, 2: 2, 3: 3, 4: 4, 5: 5, 6: 6, 7: 7, 8: 8, 9: 9}
>>>
>>> from timer2 import total, bestof
>>> bestof(dictcomp, 10000)[0]             # 10,000-item dict
0.0017095345403959072
>>> bestof(dictloop, 10000)[0]
0.002097576400046819
>>>
>>> bestof(dictcomp, 100000)[0]            # 100,000-items: 10X slower
0.012716923463358398
>>> bestof(dictloop, 100000)[0]
0.014129806355413166
>>>
>>> bestof(dictcomp, 1000000)[0]           # 1 of 1M-items: 10X time
0.11614425187337929
>>> bestof(dictloop, 1000000)[0]
0.1331144855439561
>>>
>>> total(dictcomp, 1000000, _reps=50)[0]  # Total to make 50 1M-item dicts
5.8162020671780965
>>> total(dictloop, 1000000, _reps=50)[0]
6.626680761285343
```

11. *Recursive functions.* I coded this function as follows; a simple range, comprehension, or map will do the job here as well, but recursion is useful enough to experiment with here (print is a function in 3.X only, unless you import it from __future__ or code your own equivalent):

```
def countdown(N):
    if N == 0:
        print('stop')                    # 2.X: print 'stop'
    else:
        print(N, end=' ')                 # 2.X: print N,
        countdown(N-1)

>>> countdown(5)
5 4 3 2 1 stop
>>> countdown(20)
20 19 18 17 16 15 14 13 12 11 10 9 8 7 6 5 4 3 2 1 stop

# Nonrecursive options:
>>> list(range(5, 0, -1))
[5, 4, 3, 2, 1]

# On 3.X only:
>>> t = [print(i, end=' ') for i in range(5, 0, -1)]
5 4 3 2 1
>>> t = list(map(lambda x: print(x, end=' '), range(5, 0, -1)))
5 4 3 2 1
```

I didn't include a *generator*-based solution in this exercise on the grounds of merit (and humanity!), but one is listed below; all the other techniques seem much simpler in this case—a good example of cases where generators should probably be avoided. Remember that generators produce no results until iterated, so we need a `for` or `yield from` here (`yield from` works in 3.3 and later only):

```
def countdown2(N):                        # Generator function, recursive
    if N == 0:
        yield 'stop'
    else:
        yield N
        for x in countdown2(N-1): yield x    # 3.3+: yield from countdown2(N-1)

>>> list(countdown2(5))
[5, 4, 3, 2, 1, 'stop']

# Nonrecursive options:
>>> def countdown3():                     # Generator function, simpler
        yield from range(5, 0, -1)        # Pre 3.3: for x in range(): yield x

>>> list(countdown3())
[5, 4, 3, 2, 1]

>>> list(x for x in range(5, 0, -1))      # Equivalent generator expression
[5, 4, 3, 2, 1]

>>> list(range(5, 0, -1))                 # Equivalent nongenerator form
[5, 4, 3, 2, 1]
```

12. *Computing factorials.* The following file shows how I coded this exercise; it runs on Python 3.X and 2.X, and its output on 3.3 is given in a string literal at the end of the file. Naturally, there are many possible variations on its code; its ranges, for

instance, could run from `2..N+1` to skip an iteration, and `fact2` could use `reduce(operator.mul, range(N, 1, -1))` to avoid a lambda.

```python
#!python
from __future__ import print_function              # File factorials.py
from functools import reduce
from timeit import repeat
import math

def fact0(N):                                       # Recursive
    if N == 1:                                       # Fails at 999 by default
        return N
    else:
        return N * fact0(N-1)

def fact1(N):
    return N if N == 1 else N * fact1(N-1)           # Recursive, one-liner

def fact2(N):                                        # Functional
    return reduce(lambda x, y: x * y, range(1, N+1))

def fact3(N):
    res = 1
    for i in range(1, N+1): res *= i                 # Iterative
    return res

def fact4(N):
    return math.factorial(N)                         # Stdlib "batteries"

# Tests
print(fact0(6), fact1(6), fact2(6), fact3(6), fact4(6))      # 6*5*4*3*2*1: all 720
print(fact0(500) == fact1(500) == fact2(500) == fact3(500) == fact4(500))   # True

for test in (fact0, fact1, fact2, fact3, fact4):
    print(test.__name__, min(repeat(stmt=lambda: test(500), number=20, repeat=3)))

r"""
C:\code> py -3 factorials.py
720 720 720 720 720
True
fact0 0.003990868798355564
fact1 0.003901433457907475
fact2 0.002732909419593966
fact3 0.002052614370939676
fact4 0.0003401475243271501
"""
```

Conclusions: recursion is slowest on my Python and machine, and fails once `N` reaches 999 due to the default stack size setting in `sys`; per Chapter 19, this limit can be increased, but simple loops or the standard library tool seem the best route here in any event.

This general finding holds true often. For instance, `''.join(reversed(S))` may be the preferred way to reverse a string, even though recursive solutions are possible.

Time the following to see how: as for factorials in 3.X, recursion is today an order of magnitude slower in CPython, though these results vary in PyPy:

```
def rev1(S):
    if len(S) == 1:
        return S
    else:
        return S[-1] + rev1(S[:-1])        # Recursive: 10x slower in CPython today

def rev2(S):
    return ''.join(reversed(S))            # Nonrecursive iterable: simpler, faster

def rev3(S):
    return S[::-1]                         # Even better?: sequence reversal by slice
```

Part V, Modules and Packages

See "Test Your Knowledge: Part V Exercises" on page 778 in Chapter 25 for the exercises.

1. *Import basics.* When you're done, your file (*mymod.py*) and interaction should look similar to the following; remember that Python can read a whole file into a list of line strings, and the len built-in returns the lengths of strings and lists:

```
def countLines(name):
    file = open(name)
    return len(file.readlines())

def countChars(name):
    return len(open(name).read())

def test(name):                                # Or pass file object
    return countLines(name), countChars(name)  # Or return a dictionary

% python
>>> import mymod
>>> mymod.test('mymod.py')
(10, 291)
```

Your counts may vary, as mine may or may not include comments and an extra line at the end. Note that these functions load the entire file in memory all at once, so they won't work for pathologically large files too big for your machine's memory. To be more robust, you could read line by line with iterators instead and count as you go:

```
def countLines(name):
    tot = 0
    for line in open(name): tot += 1
    return tot

def countChars(name):
    tot = 0
```

```
    for line in open(name): tot += len(line)
    return tot
```

A generator expression can have the same effect (though the instructor might take off points for excessive magic!):

```
def countlines(name): return sum(+1 for line in open(name))
def countchars(name): return sum(len(line) for line in open(name))
```

On Unix, you can verify your output with a wc command; on Windows, right-click on your file to view its properties. Note that your script may report fewer characters than Windows does—for portability, Python converts Windows \r\n line-end markers to \n, thereby dropping 1 byte (character) per line. To match byte counts with Windows exactly, you must open in binary mode ('rb'), or add the number of bytes corresponding to the number of lines. See Chapter 9 and Chapter 37 for more on end-of-line translations in text files.

The "ambitious" part of this exercise (passing in a file object so you only open the file once), will require you to use the seek method of the built-in file object. It works like C's fseek call (and may call it behind the scenes): seek resets the current position in the file to a passed-in offset. After a seek, future input/output operations are relative to the new position. To rewind to the start of a file without closing and reopening it, call file.seek(0); the file read methods all pick up at the current position in the file, so you need to rewind to reread. Here's what this tweak would look like:

```
def countLines(file):
    file.seek(0)                                # Rewind to start of file
    return len(file.readlines())

def countChars(file):
    file.seek(0)                                # Ditto (rewind if needed)
    return len(file.read())

def test(name):
    file = open(name)                           # Pass file object
    return countLines(file), countChars(file)   # Open file only once

>>> import mymod2
>>> mymod2.test("mymod2.py")
(11, 392)
```

2. from/from *. Here's the from * part; replace * with countChars to do the rest:

```
% python
>>> from mymod import *
>>> countChars("mymod.py")
291
```

3. __main__. If you code it properly, this file works in either mode—program run or module import:

```
def countLines(name):
    file = open(name)
```

```
        return len(file.readlines())

    def countChars(name):
        return len(open(name).read())

    def test(name):                                     # Or pass file object
        return countLines(name), countChars(name)       # Or return a dictionary

    if __name__ == '__main__':
        print(test('mymod.py'))

    % python mymod.py
    (13, 346)
```

This is where I would probably begin to consider using command-line arguments or user input to provide the filename to be counted, instead of hardcoding it in the script (see Chapter 25 for more on `sys.argv`, and Chapter 10 for more on `input`— and use `raw_input` instead in 2.X):

```
    if __name__ == '__main__':
        print(test(input('Enter file name:')))          # Console (raw_input in 2.X)

    if __name__ == '__main__':
        import sys
        print(test(sys.argv[1]))                         # Command line
```

4. *Nested imports.* Here is my solution (file *myclient.py*):

```
    from mymod import countLines, countChars
    print(countLines('mymod.py'), countChars('mymod.py'))

    % python myclient.py
    13 346
```

As for the rest of this one, `mymod`'s functions are accessible (that is, importable) from the top level of `myclient`, since `from` simply assigns to names in the importer (it works as if `mymod`'s `def`s appeared in `myclient`). For example, another file can say:

```
    import myclient
    myclient.countLines(...)

    from myclient import countChars
    countChars(...)
```

If `myclient` used `import` instead of `from`, you'd need to use a path to get to the functions in `mymod` through `myclient`:

```
    import myclient
    myclient.mymod.countLines(...)

    from myclient import mymod
    mymod.countChars(...)
```

In general, you can define *collector* modules that import all the names from other modules so they're available in a single convenience module. The following partial

code, for example, creates three different copies of the name somename—mod1.some
name, collector.somename, and __main__.somename; all three share the same integer
object initially, and only the name somename exists at the interactive prompt as is:

```
# File mod1.py
somename = 42

# File collector.py
from mod1 import *                          # Collect lots of names here
from mod2 import *                          # from assigns to my names
from mod3 import *
```

```
>>> from collector import somename
```

5. *Package imports.* For this, I put the *mymod.py* solution file listed for exercise 3 into
   a directory package. The following is what I did in a Windows console interface to
   set up the directory and the *__init__.py* file that it's required to have until Python
   3.3; you'll need to interpolate for other platforms (e.g., use cp and vi instead of
   copy and notepad). This works in any directory (I'm using my own code directory
   here), and you can do some of this from a file explorer GUI, too.

   When I was done, I had a *mypkg* subdirectory that contained the files
   __init__.py and *mymod.py*. Until Python 3.3's namespace package extension, you
   need an *__init__.py* in the *mypkg* directory, but not in its parent; technically,
   mypkg is located in the home directory component of the module search path.
   Notice how a print statement coded in the directory's initialization file fires only
   the first time it is imported, not the second; raw strings are also used here to avoid
   escape issues in the file paths:

   ```
   C:\code> mkdir mypkg
   C:\code> copy mymod.py mypkg\mymod.py
   C:\code> notepad mypkg\__init__.py
   ...coded a print statement...

   C:\code> python
   >>> import mypkg.mymod
   initializing mypkg
   >>> mypkg.mymod.countLines(r'mypkg\mymod.py')
   13
   >>> from mypkg.mymod import countChars
   >>> countChars(r'mypkg\mymod.py')
   346
   ```

6. *Reloads.* This exercise just asks you to experiment with changing the *changer.py*
   example in the book, so there's nothing to show here.

7. *Circular imports.* The short story is that importing recur2 first works because the
   recursive import then happens at the import in recur1, not at a from in recur2.

   The long story goes like this: importing recur2 first works because the recursive
   import from recur1 to recur2 fetches recur2 as a whole, instead of getting specific
   names. recur2 is incomplete when it's imported from recur1, but because it uses
   import instead of from, you're safe: Python finds and returns the already created

recur2 module object and continues to run the rest of `recur1` without a glitch. When the `recur2` import resumes, the second from finds the name Y in `recur1` (it's been run completely), so no error is reported.

Running a file as a *script* is not the same as importing it as a module; these cases are the same as running the first import or from in the script interactively. For instance, running `recur1` as a script works, because it is the same as importing `recur2` interactively, as `recur2` is the first module imported in `recur1`. Running `recur2` as a script fails for the same reason—it's the same as running its first import interactively.

Part VI, Classes and OOP

See "Test Your Knowledge: Part VI Exercises" on page 1072 in Chapter 32 for the exercises.

1. *Inheritance*. Here's the solution code for this exercise (file *adder.py*), along with some interactive tests. The __add__ overload has to appear only once, in the superclass, as it invokes type-specific add methods in subclasses:

```
class Adder:
    def add(self, x, y):
        print('not implemented!')
    def __init__(self, start=[]):
        self.data = start
    def __add__(self, other):            # Or in subclasses?
        return self.add(self.data, other)  # Or return type?

class ListAdder(Adder):
    def add(self, x, y):
        return x + y

class DictAdder(Adder):
    def add(self, x, y):
        new = {}
        for k in x.keys(): new[k] = x[k]
        for k in y.keys(): new[k] = y[k]
        return new
```

```
% python
>>> from adder import *
>>> x = Adder()
>>> x.add(1, 2)
not implemented!
>>> x = ListAdder()
>>> x.add([1], [2])
[1, 2]
>>> x = DictAdder()
>>> x.add({1:1}, {2:2})
{1: 1, 2: 2}

>>> x = Adder([1])
```

```
>>> x + [2]
not implemented!
>>>
>>> x = ListAdder([1])
>>> x + [2]
[1, 2]
>>> [2] + x
In 3.3:  TypeError: can only concatenate list (not "ListAdder") to list
Earlier: TypeError: __add__ nor __radd__ defined for these operands
```

Notice in the last test that you get an error for expressions where a class instance appears on the right of a +; if you want to fix this, use __radd__ methods, as described in "Operator Overloading" in Chapter 30.

If you are saving a value in the instance anyhow, you might as well rewrite the add method to take just one argument, in the spirit of other examples in this part of the book (this is *adder2.py*):

```
class Adder:
    def __init__(self, start=[]):
        self.data = start
    def __add__(self, other):          # Pass a single argument
        return self.add(other)         # The left side is in self
    def add(self, y):
        print('not implemented!')

class ListAdder(Adder):
    def add(self, y):
        return self.data + y

class DictAdder(Adder):
    def add(self, y):
        d = self.data.copy()           # Change to use self.data instead of x
        d.update(y)                    # Or "cheat" by using quicker built-ins
        return d

x = ListAdder([1, 2, 3])
y = x + [4, 5, 6]
print(y)                               # Prints [1, 2, 3, 4, 5, 6]

z = DictAdder(dict(name='Bob')) + {'a':1}
print(z)                               # Prints {'name': 'Bob', 'a': 1}
```

Because values are attached to objects rather than passed around, this version is arguably more object-oriented. And, once you've gotten to this point, you'll probably find that you can get rid of add altogether and simply define type-specific __add__ methods in the two subclasses.

2. *Operator overloading.* The solution code (file *mylist.py*) uses a handful of operator overloading methods we explored in Chapter 30. Copying the initial value in the constructor is important because it may be mutable; you don't want to change or have a reference to an object that's possibly shared somewhere outside the class. The __getattr__ method routes calls to the wrapped list. For hints on an easier

way to code this in Python 2.2 and later, see "Extending Types by Subclassing" on page 981 in Chapter 32:

```
class MyList:
    def __init__(self, start):
        #self.wrapped = start[:]           # Copy start: no side effects
        self.wrapped = list(start)         # Make sure it's a list here
    def __add__(self, other):
        return MyList(self.wrapped + other)
    def __mul__(self, time):
        return MyList(self.wrapped * time)
    def __getitem__(self, offset):         # Also passed a slice in 3.X
        return self.wrapped[offset]        # For iteration if no __iter__
    def __len__(self):
        return len(self.wrapped)
    def __getslice__(self, low, high):     # Ignored in 3.X: uses __getitem__
        return MyList(self.wrapped[low:high])
    def append(self, node):
        self.wrapped.append(node)
    def __getattr__(self, name):           # Other methods: sort/reverse/etc
        return getattr(self.wrapped, name)
    def __repr__(self):                    # Catchall display method
        return repr(self.wrapped)

if __name__ == '__main__':
    x = MyList('spam')
    print(x)
    print(x[2])
    print(x[1:])
    print(x + ['eggs'])
    print(x * 3)
    x.append('a')
    x.sort()
    print(' '.join(c for c in x))
```

```
c:\code> python mylist.py
['s', 'p', 'a', 'm']
a
['p', 'a', 'm']
['s', 'p', 'a', 'm', 'eggs']
['s', 'p', 'a', 'm', 's', 'p', 'a', 'm', 's', 'p', 'a', 'm']
a a m p s
```

Note that it's important to copy the start value by calling `list` instead of slicing here, because otherwise the result may not be a true list and so will not respond to expected list methods, such as `append` (e.g., slicing a string returns another string, not a list). You would be able to copy a `MyList` start value by slicing because its class overloads the slicing operation and provides the expected list interface; however, you need to avoid slice-based copying for objects such as strings.

3. *Subclassing.* My solution (*mysub.py*) appears as follows. Your solution should be similar:

```
from mylist import MyList

class MyListSub(MyList):
    calls = 0                                   # Shared by instances
    def __init__(self, start):
        self.adds = 0                           # Varies in each instance
        MyList.__init__(self, start)

    def __add__(self, other):
        print('add: ' + str(other))
        MyListSub.calls += 1                    # Class-wide counter
        self.adds += 1                          # Per-instance counts
        return MyList.__add__(self, other)

    def stats(self):
        return self.calls, self.adds            # All adds, my adds

if __name__ == '__main__':
    x = MyListSub('spam')
    y = MyListSub('foo')
    print(x[2])
    print(x[1:])
    print(x + ['eggs'])
    print(x + ['toast'])
    print(y + ['bar'])
    print(x.stats())
```

```
c:\code> python mysub.py
a
['p', 'a', 'm']
add: ['eggs']
['s', 'p', 'a', 'm', 'eggs']
add: ['toast']
['s', 'p', 'a', 'm', 'toast']
add: ['bar']
['f', 'o', 'o', 'bar']
(3, 2)
```

4. *Attribute methods.* I worked through this exercise as follows. Notice that in Python
   2.X's classic classes, operators try to fetch attributes through __getattr__, too; you
   need to return a value to make them work. As noted in Chapter 32 and elsewhere,
   __getattr__ is *not* called for built-in operations in Python 3.X (and in 2.X if new-
   style classes are used), so the expressions aren't intercepted at all here; in new-style
   classes, a class like this must redefine __X__ operator overloading methods explicitly. More on this in Chapter 28, Chapter 31, Chapter 32, Chapter 38, and Chapter 39: it can impact much code!

```
c:\code> py -2
>>> class Attrs:
        def __getattr__(self, name):
            print('get %s' % name)
        def __setattr__(self, name, value):
            print('set %s %s' % (name, value))
```

```
>>> x = Attrs()
>>> x.append
get append
>>> x.spam = 'pork'
set spam pork
>>> x + 2
get __coerce__
TypeError: 'NoneType' object is not callable
>>> x[1]
get __getitem__
TypeError: 'NoneType' object is not callable
>>> x[1:5]
get __getslice__
TypeError: 'NoneType' object is not callable

c:\code> py -3
>>> ...same startup code...
>>> x + 2
TypeError: unsupported operand type(s) for +: 'Attrs' and 'int'
>>> x[1]
TypeError: 'Attrs' object does not support indexing
>>> x[1:5]
TypeError: 'Attrs' object is not subscriptable
```

5. *Set objects*. Here's the sort of interaction you should get. Comments explain which methods are called. Also, note that sets are a built-in type in Python today, so this is largely just a coding exercise (see Chapter 5 for more on sets).

```
% python
>>> from setwrapper import Set
>>> x = Set([1, 2, 3, 4])               # Runs __init__
>>> y = Set([3, 4, 5])

>>> x & y                               # __and__, intersect, then __repr__
Set:[3, 4]
>>> x | y                               # __or__, union, then __repr__
Set:[1, 2, 3, 4, 5]

>>> z = Set("hello")                    # __init__ removes duplicates
>>> z[0], z[-1], z[2:]                  # __getitem__
('h', 'o', ['l', 'o'])

>>> for c in z: print(c, end=' ')       # __iter__ (else __getitem__)  [3.X print]
...
h e l o
>>> ''.join(c.upper() for c in z)       # __iter__ (else __getitem__)
'HELO'
>>> len(z), z                           # __len__, __repr__
(4, Set:['h', 'e', 'l', 'o'])

>>> z & "mello", z | "mello"
(Set:['e', 'l', 'o'], Set:['h', 'e', 'l', 'o', 'm'])
```

My solution to the multiple-operand extension subclass looks like the following class (file *multiset.py*). It needs to replace only two methods in the original set. The class's documentation string explains how it works:

```
from setwrapper import Set

class MultiSet(Set):
    """
    Inherits all Set names, but extends intersect and union to support
    multiple operands; note that "self" is still the first argument
    (stored in the *args argument now); also note that the inherited
    & and | operators call the new methods here with 2 arguments, but
    processing more than 2 requires a method call, not an expression;
    intersect doesn't remove duplicates here: the Set constructor does;
    """
    def intersect(self, *others):
        res = []
        for x in self:                          # Scan first sequence
            for other in others:                # For all other args
                if x not in other: break        # Item in each one?
            else:                               # No: break out of loop
                res.append(x)                   # Yes: add item to end
        return Set(res)

    def union(*args):                           # self is args[0]
        res = []
        for seq in args:                        # For all args
            for x in seq:                       # For all nodes
                if not x in res:
                    res.append(x)               # Add new items to result
        return Set(res)
```

Your interaction with the extension will look something like the following. Note that you can intersect by using & or calling `intersect`, but you must call `intersect` for three or more operands; & is a binary (two-sided) operator. Also, note that we could have called `MultiSet` simply `Set` to make this change more transparent if we used `setwrapper.Set` to refer to the original within `multiset` (the `as` clause in an import could rename the class too if desired):

```
>>> from multiset import *
>>> x = MultiSet([1, 2, 3, 4])
>>> y = MultiSet([3, 4, 5])
>>> z = MultiSet([0, 1, 2])

>>> x & y, x | y                                # Two operands
(Set:[3, 4], Set:[1, 2, 3, 4, 5])

>>> x.intersect(y, z)                           # Three operands
Set:[]
>>> x.union(y, z)
Set:[1, 2, 3, 4, 5, 0]
>>> x.intersect([1,2,3], [2,3,4], [1,2,3])      # Four operands
Set:[2, 3]
>>> x.union(range(10))                          # Non-MultiSets work, too
```

```
Set:[1, 2, 3, 4, 0, 5, 6, 7, 8, 9]

>>> w = MultiSet('spam')                              # String sets
>>> w
Set:['s', 'p', 'a', 'm']
>>> ''.join(w | 'super')
'spamuer'
>>> (w | 'super') & MultiSet('slots')
Set:['s']
```

6. *Class tree links.* Here is the way I changed the lister classes, and a rerun of the test to show its format. Do the same for the dir-based version, and also do this when formatting class objects in the tree climber variant:

```
class ListInstance:
    def __attrnames(self):
        ...unchanged...

    def __str__(self):
        return '<Instance of %s(%s), address %s:\n%s>' % (
                           self.__class__.__name__,          # My class's name
                           self.__supers(),                  # My class's own supers
                           id(self),                         # My address
                           self.__attrnames())               # name=value list

    def __supers(self):
        names = []
        for super in self.__class__.__bases__:               # One level up from class
            names.append(super.__name__)                     # name, not str(super)
        return ', '.join(names)

    # Or: ', '.join(super.__name__ for super in self.__class__.__bases__)

c:\code> py listinstance-exercise.py
<Instance of Sub(Super, ListInstance), address 43671000:
        data1=spam
        data2=eggs
        data3=42
>
```

7. *Composition.* My solution is as follows (file *lunch.py*), with comments from the description mixed in with the code. This is one case where it's probably easier to express a problem in Python than it is in English:

```
class Lunch:
    def __init__(self):                          # Make/embed Customer, Employee
        self.cust = Customer()
        self.empl = Employee()
    def order(self, foodName):                   # Start Customer order simulation
        self.cust.placeOrder(foodName, self.empl)
    def result(self):                            # Ask the Customer about its Food
        self.cust.printFood()

class Customer:
    def __init__(self):                          # Initialize my food to None
        self.food = None
```

```
        def placeOrder(self, foodName, employee):    # Place order with Employee
            self.food = employee.takeOrder(foodName)
        def printFood(self):                          # Print the name of my food
            print(self.food.name)

    class Employee:
        def takeOrder(self, foodName):                # Return Food, with desired name
            return Food(foodName)

    class Food:
        def __init__(self, name):                     # Store food name
            self.name = name

    if __name__ == '__main__':
        x = Lunch()                                   # Self-test code
        x.order('burritos')                           # If run, not imported
        x.result()
        x.order('pizza')
        x.result()

    % python lunch.py
    burritos
    pizza
```

8. *Zoo animal hierarchy.* Here is the way I coded the taxonomy in Python (file *zoo.py*); it's artificial, but the general coding pattern applies to many real structures, from GUIs to employee databases to spacecraft. Notice that the self.speak reference in Animal triggers an independent inheritance search, which finds speak in a subclass. Test this interactively per the exercise description. Try extending this hierarchy with new classes, and making instances of various classes in the tree:

```
    class Animal:
        def reply(self):    self.speak()          # Back to subclass
        def speak(self):    print('spam')         # Custom message

    class Mammal(Animal):
        def speak(self):    print('huh?')

    class Cat(Mammal):
        def speak(self):    print('meow')

    class Dog(Mammal):
        def speak(self):    print('bark')

    class Primate(Mammal):
        def speak(self):    print('Hello world!')

    class Hacker(Primate): pass                   # Inherit from Primate
```

9. *The Dead Parrot Sketch.* Here's how I implemented this one (file *parrot.py*). Notice how the line method in the Actor superclass works: by accessing self attributes twice, it sends Python back to the instance twice, and hence invokes *two* inheritance searches—self.name and self.says() find information in the specific subclasses:

```
class Actor:
    def line(self): print(self.name + ':', repr(self.says()))

class Customer(Actor):
    name = 'customer'
    def says(self): return "that's one ex-bird!"

class Clerk(Actor):
    name = 'clerk'
    def says(self): return "no it isn't..."

class Parrot(Actor):
    name = 'parrot'
    def says(self): return None

class Scene:
    def __init__(self):
        self.clerk    = Clerk()          # Embed some instances
        self.customer = Customer()       # Scene is a composite
        self.subject  = Parrot()

    def action(self):
        self.customer.line()             # Delegate to embedded
        self.clerk.line()
        self.subject.line()
```

Part VII, Exceptions and Tools

See "Test Your Knowledge: Part VII Exercises" on page 1161 in Chapter 36 for the exercises.

1. **try/except.** My version of the oops function (file *oops.py*) follows. As for the non-coding questions, changing oops to raise a KeyError instead of an IndexError means that the **try** handler won't catch the exception—it "percolates" to the top level and triggers Python's default error message. The names KeyError and IndexError come from the outermost built-in names scope (the *B* in "LEGB"). Import builtins in 3.X (and __builtin__ in Python 2.X) and pass it as an argument to the dir function to see this for yourself.

```
def oops():
    raise IndexError()

def doomed():
    try:
        oops()
    except IndexError:
        print('caught an index error!')
    else:
        print('no error caught...')

if __name__ == '__main__': doomed()
```

```
% python oops.py
caught an index error!
```

2. *Exception objects and lists.* Here's the way I extended this module for an exception of my own, file *oops2.py*:

```
from __future__ import print_function    # 2.X

class MyError(Exception): pass

def oops():
    raise MyError('Spam!')

def doomed():
    try:
        oops()
    except IndexError:
        print('caught an index error!')
    except MyError as data:
        print('caught error:', MyError, data)
    else:
        print('no error caught...')

if __name__ == '__main__':
    doomed()
```

```
% python oops2.py
caught error: <class '__main__.MyError'> Spam!
```

Like all class exceptions, the instance is accessible via the **as** variable **data**; the error message shows both the class (**<...>**) and its instance (**Spam!**). The instance must be inheriting both an __init__ and a __repr__ or __str__ from Python's **Excep tion** class, or it would print much like the class does. See Chapter 35 for details on how this works in built-in exception classes.

3. *Error handling.* Here's one way to solve this one (file *exctools.py*). I did my tests in a file, rather than interactively, but the results are similar enough for full credit. Notice that the empty **except** and **sys.exc_info** approach used here will catch exit-related exceptions that listing **Exception** with an **as** variable won't; that's probably not ideal in most applications code, but might be useful in a tool like this designed to work as a sort of exceptions firewall.

```
import sys, traceback

def safe(callee, *pargs, **kargs):
    try:
        callee(*pargs, **kargs)            # Catch everything else
    except:                                # Or "except Exception as E:"
        traceback.print_exc()
        print('Got %s %s' % (sys.exc_info()[0], sys.exc_info()[1]))

if __name__ == '__main__':
    import oops2
    safe(oops2.oops)
```

```
c:\code> py -3 exctools.py
Traceback (most recent call last):
  File "C:\code\exctools.py", line 5, in safe
    callee(*pargs, **kargs)              # Catch everything else
  File "C:\code\oops2.py", line 6, in oops
    raise MyError('Spam!')
oops2.MyError: Spam!
Got <class 'oops2.MyError'> Spam!
```

The following sort of code could turn this into a *function decorator* that could wrap and catch exceptions raised by any function, using techniques introduced in Chapter 32, but covered more fully in Chapter 39 in the next part of the book—it augments a function, rather than expecting it to be passed in explicitly:

```
import sys, traceback

def safe(callee):
    def callproxy(*pargs, **kargs):
        try:
            return callee(*pargs, **kargs)
        except:
            traceback.print_exc()
            print('Got %s %s' % (sys.exc_info()[0], sys.exc_info()[1]))
            raise
    return callproxy

if __name__ == '__main__':
    import oops2

    @safe
    def test():
        oops2.oops()

    test()
```

4. *Self-study examples.* Here are a few examples for you to study as time allows; for more, see follow-up books—such as *Programming Python*, from which these examples were borrowed or derived—and the Web:

```
# Find the largest Python source file in a single directory

import os, glob
dirname = r'C:\Python33\Lib'

allsizes = []
allpy = glob.glob(dirname + os.sep + '*.py')
for filename in allpy:
    filesize = os.path.getsize(filename)
    allsizes.append((filesize, filename))

allsizes.sort()
print(allsizes[:2])
print(allsizes[-2:])
```

```
# Find the largest Python source file in an entire directory tree

import sys, os, pprint
if sys.platform[:3] == 'win':
    dirname = r'C:\Python33\Lib'
else:
    dirname = '/usr/lib/python'

allsizes = []
for (thisDir, subsHere, filesHere) in os.walk(dirname):
    for filename in filesHere:
        if filename.endswith('.py'):
            fullname = os.path.join(thisDir, filename)
            fullsize = os.path.getsize(fullname)
            allsizes.append((fullsize, fullname))

allsizes.sort()
pprint.pprint(allsizes[:2])
pprint.pprint(allsizes[-2:])


# Find the largest Python source file on the module import search path

import sys, os, pprint
visited  = {}
allsizes = []
for srcdir in sys.path:
    for (thisDir, subsHere, filesHere) in os.walk(srcdir):
        thisDir = os.path.normpath(thisDir)
        if thisDir.upper() in visited:
            continue
        else:
            visited[thisDir.upper()] = True
        for filename in filesHere:
            if filename.endswith('.py'):
                pypath  = os.path.join(thisDir, filename)
                try:
                    pysize = os.path.getsize(pypath)
                except:
                    print('skipping', pypath)
                allsizes.append((pysize, pypath))

allsizes.sort()
pprint.pprint(allsizes[:3])
pprint.pprint(allsizes[-3:])


# Sum columns in a text file separated by commas

filename = 'data.txt'
sums = {}

for line in open(filename):
    cols = line.split(',')
```

```
        nums = [int(col) for col in cols]
        for (ix, num) in enumerate(nums):
            sums[ix] = sums.get(ix, 0) + num

for key in sorted(sums):
    print(key, '=', sums[key])
```

Similar to prior, but using lists instead of dictionaries for sums

```
import sys
filename = sys.argv[1]
numcols  = int(sys.argv[2])
totals   = [0] * numcols

for line in open(filename):
    cols = line.split(',')
    nums = [int(x) for x in cols]
    totals = [(x + y) for (x, y) in zip(totals, nums)]

print(totals)
```

Test for regressions in the output of a set of scripts

```
import os
testscripts = [dict(script='test1.py', args=''),        # Or glob script/args dir
               dict(script='test2.py', args='spam')]

for testcase in testscripts:
    commandline = '%(script)s %(args)s' % testcase
    output = os.popen(commandline).read()
    result = testcase['script'] + '.result'
    if not os.path.exists(result):
        open(result, 'w').write(output)
        print('Created:', result)
    else:
        priorresult = open(result).read()
        if output != priorresult:
            print('FAILED:', testcase['script'])
            print(output)
        else:
            print('Passed:', testcase['script'])
```

Build GUI with tkinter (Tkinter in 2.X) with buttons that change color and grow

```
from tkinter import *                          # Use Tkinter in 2.X
import random
fontsize = 25
colors = ['red', 'green', 'blue', 'yellow', 'orange', 'white', 'cyan', 'purple']

def reply(text):
    print(text)
    popup = Toplevel()
```

```
        color = random.choice(colors)
        Label(popup, text='Popup', bg='black', fg=color).pack()
        L.config(fg=color)

    def timer():
        L.config(fg=random.choice(colors))
        win.after(250, timer)

    def grow():
        global fontsize
        fontsize += 5
        L.config(font=('arial', fontsize, 'italic'))
        win.after(100, grow)

win = Tk()
L = Label(win, text='Spam',
          font=('arial', fontsize, 'italic'), fg='yellow', bg='navy',
          relief=RAISED)
L.pack(side=TOP, expand=YES, fill=BOTH)
Button(win, text='press', command=(lambda: reply('red'))).pack(side=BOTTOM, fill=X)
Button(win, text='timer', command=timer).pack(side=BOTTOM, fill=X)
Button(win, text='grow', command=grow).pack(side=BOTTOM, fill=X)
win.mainloop()


# Similar to prior, but use classes so each window has own state information

from tkinter import *
import random

class MyGui:
    """
    A GUI with buttons that change color and make the label grow
    """
    colors = ['blue', 'green', 'orange', 'red', 'brown', 'yellow']

    def __init__(self, parent, title='popup'):
        parent.title(title)
        self.growing = False
        self.fontsize = 10
        self.lab = Label(parent, text='Gui1', fg='white', bg='navy')
        self.lab.pack(expand=YES, fill=BOTH)
        Button(parent, text='Spam', command=self.reply).pack(side=LEFT)
        Button(parent, text='Grow', command=self.grow).pack(side=LEFT)
        Button(parent, text='Stop', command=self.stop).pack(side=LEFT)

    def reply(self):
        "change the button's color at random on Spam presses"
        self.fontsize += 5
        color = random.choice(self.colors)
        self.lab.config(bg=color,
                font=('courier', self.fontsize, 'bold italic'))

    def grow(self):
        "start making the label grow on Grow presses"
```

```
            self.growing = True
            self.grower()

    def grower(self):
        if self.growing:
            self.fontsize += 5
            self.lab.config(font=('courier', self.fontsize, 'bold'))
            self.lab.after(500, self.grower)

    def stop(self):
        "stop the button growing on Stop presses"
        self.growing = False

class MySubGui(MyGui):
    colors = ['black', 'purple']          # Customize to change color choices

MyGui(Tk(), 'main')
MyGui(Toplevel())
MySubGui(Toplevel())
mainloop()
```

Email inbox scanning and maintenance utility

```
"""
scan pop email box, fetching just headers, allowing
deletions without downloading the complete message
"""

import poplib, getpass, sys

mailserver = 'your pop email server name here'          # pop.server.net
mailuser   = 'your pop email user name here'
mailpasswd = getpass.getpass('Password for %s?' % mailserver)

print('Connecting...')
server = poplib.POP3(mailserver)
server.user(mailuser)
server.pass_(mailpasswd)

try:
    print(server.getwelcome())
    msgCount, mboxSize = server.stat()
    print('There are', msgCount, 'mail messages, size ', mboxSize)
    msginfo = server.list()
    print(msginfo)
    for i in range(msgCount):
        msgnum  = i+1
        msgsize = msginfo[1][i].split()[1]
        resp, hdrlines, octets = server.top(msgnum, 0)         # Get hdrs only
        print('-'*80)
        print('[%d: octets=%d, size=%s]' % (msgnum, octets, msgsize))
        for line in hdrlines: print(line)

        if input('Print?') in ['y', 'Y']:
```

```
                for line in server.retr(msgnum)[1]: print(line)    # Get whole msg
            if input('Delete?') in ['y', 'Y']:
                print('deleting')
                server.dele(msgnum)                                  # Delete on srvr
            else:
                print('skipping')
finally:
    server.quit()                                    # Make sure we unlock mbox
input('Bye.')                                        # Keep window up on Windows
```

 # CGI server-side script to interact with a web browser

```
#!/usr/bin/python
import cgi
form = cgi.FieldStorage()                            # Parse form data
print("Content-type: text/html\n")                   # hdr plus blank line
print("<HTML>")
print("<title>Reply Page</title>")                   # HTML reply page
print("<BODY>")
if not 'user' in form:
    print("<h1>Who are you?</h1>")
else:
    print("<h1>Hello <i>%s</i>!</h1>" % cgi.escape(form['user'].value))
print("</BODY></HTML>")
```

 # Database script to populate a shelve with Python objects

 # see also Chapter 28 shelve and Chapter 31 pickle examples

```
rec1 = {'name': {'first': 'Bob', 'last': 'Smith'},
        'job':  ['dev', 'mgr'],
        'age':  40.5}

rec2 = {'name': {'first': 'Sue', 'last': 'Jones'},
        'job':  ['mgr'],
        'age':  35.0}

import shelve
db = shelve.open('dbfile')
db['bob'] = rec1
db['sue'] = rec2
db.close()
```

 # Database script to print and update shelve created in prior script

```
import shelve
db = shelve.open('dbfile')
for key in db:
    print(key, '=>', db[key])

bob = db['bob']
bob['age'] += 1
```

```
db['bob'] = bob
db.close()
```

Database script to populate and query a MySql database

```
from MySQLdb import Connect
conn = Connect(host='localhost', user='root', passwd='XXXXXXX')
curs = conn.cursor()
try:
    curs.execute('drop database testpeopledb')
except:
    pass                                            # Did not exist

curs.execute('create database testpeopledb')
curs.execute('use testpeopledb')
curs.execute('create table people (name char(30), job char(10), pay int(4))')

curs.execute('insert people values (%s, %s, %s)', ('Bob', 'dev', 50000))
curs.execute('insert people values (%s, %s, %s)', ('Sue', 'dev', 60000))
curs.execute('insert people values (%s, %s, %s)', ('Ann', 'mgr', 40000))

curs.execute('select * from people')
for row in curs.fetchall():
    print(row)

curs.execute('select * from people where name = %s', ('Bob',))
print(curs.description)
colnames = [desc[0] for desc in curs.description]
while True:
    print('-' * 30)
    row = curs.fetchone()
    if not row: break
    for (name, value) in zip(colnames, row):
        print('%s => %s' % (name, value))

conn.commit()                                       # Save inserted records
```

Fetch and open/play a file by FTP

```
import webbrowser, sys
from ftplib import FTP                              # Socket-based FTP tools
from getpass import getpass                         # Hidden password input
if sys.version[0] == '2': input = raw_input         # 2.X compatibility

nonpassive = False                                  # Force active mode FTP for server?
filename   = input('File?')                         # File to be downloaded
dirname    = input('Dir? ') or '.'                  # Remote directory to fetch from
sitename   = input('Site?')                         # FTP site to contact
user       = input('User?')                         # Use () for anonymous
if not user:
    userinfo = ()
else:
    from getpass import getpass                      # Hidden password input
```

```
            userinfo = (user, getpass('Pswd?'))

    print('Connecting...')
    connection = FTP(sitename)                          # Connect to FTP site
    connection.login(*userinfo)                         # Default is anonymous login
    connection.cwd(dirname)                             # Xfer 1k at a time to localfile
    if nonpassive:                                      # Force active FTP if server requires
        connection.set_pasv(False)

    print('Downloading...')
    localfile = open(filename, 'wb')                    # Local file to store download
    connection.retrbinary('RETR ' + filename, localfile.write, 1024)
    connection.quit()
    localfile.close()

    print('Playing...')
    webbrowser.open(filename)
```

Index

Symbols

\# character
   comments, 48, 55, 141, 444
   directives, 48
\#! characters, 59, 60–62, 1441–1444
% (percent sign)
   formatting expression operator, 217, 227–229, 1189
   system shell prompt, 44, 48, 56
( ) (parentheses)
   comprehensions and, 112
   expression operators and, 139
   statements and, 323, 328
   superclasses and, 801
   tuples and, 277
* (multiplication) operator
   multiplying numbers, 97
   repeating lists, 242
   repeating strings, 100, 200
\+ (plus) operator
   adding numbers, 97
   concatenating lists, 242, 1100
   concatenating strings, 100, 200, 1100
+= in-place addition, 920, 1194
, (comma), 277
/ / operator, 146–150
/ operator, 146–150
: (colon), 322
; (semicolon), 323, 327
<< (left-shift) operator, 207
== (equivalence) operator, 301
>>> prompt
   about, 45, 49
   common usage mistakes, 52

@ symbol
   about, 1029, 1035
   function decorators and, 1022, 1035, 1273
[ ] (square brackets), 96, 224, 328
\ (backslash)
   escape sequences and, 105, 193–197
   multiline statements and, 328, 378
_ (underscore)
   class names, 845
   module names, 70, 747
   name mangling and, 945
   operator overloading, 104, 805
   showing name values, 971
{ } (curly braces), 114, 328

A

abs built-in function, 155
absolute imports, 718, 722, 726, 731
abstract superclasses, 869–871, 939
access-by-key databases and filesystems
   dictionary interfaces, 848
   exploring interactively, 849–851
   iterations and, 423
   object persistence and, 116, 847
   pickle module, 290
   storing objects on, 271, 848
   updating objects, 851
accessor functions, 498, 554
__add__ method, 104, 808, 889, 918
addition operation, 97
all built-in function, 432
__all__ variable, 711, 747
Android platform, 1425
annotations, 565–567, 1340–1342
__annotations__ attribute, 565

We'd like to hear your suggestions for improving our indexes. Send email to *index@oreilly.com*.

B

backslash (\)
    escape sequences and, 105, 193–197
    multiline statements and, 328, 378
backtracking, exception handlers and, 1083
base classes, 787
BaseException class, 1123, 1131
__bases__ attribute
    about, 811, 878
    inheritance and, 843, 967, 1383
BDFL (Benevolent Dictator for Life), 17
benchmarking
    pystone.py program, 656
    quiz questions and answers, 662
    timeit module, 647–655
    timing iteration, 629–655
    usage examples, 651
Benevolent Dictator for Life (BDFL), 17
big-endian format, 1201–1204
bin built-in function, 135, 207
binary files
    about, 107, 123, 1173–1174, 1196
    escape sequences and, 196
    frozen executables, 39, 82
    storing data, 293
    struct module and, 1207–1209
    text files and, 123
    version considerations, 287, 1197
binary formatting, 231
binary notation, 135, 151–153
binary operator methods, 917–921
bitwise operations, 137, 153–155
blank lines
    common usage mistakes, 53
    statements and, 53, 375
block strings, 198–199
blocks of code
    delimiting, 376–378
    indenting, 376–378
    loop coding techniques, 402–411
    nesting, 335, 376–378
    special case rules, 329
BOM (byte order marker), 1174, 1201–1204
__bool__ method, 889, 927–929
Booleans (bool type)
    about, 127, 384
    operator overloading and, 927–929
    truth test and, 171, 305, 380–382
    version considerations, 928

bound methods, 573, 948–953, 1025
bounds checking for lists, 110
branching in if statements, 372–374
break statement
    about, 320, 389
    nested loops and, 391, 1145
bsddb extension module, 850
built-in attributes, 839, 1249–1256
built-in exception classes
    about, 1131
    built-in categories, 1132
    default printing and state, 1133–1135
built-in exceptions, 1086, 1100
built-in object types
    about, 19, 94, 295
    attribute fetches for, 985, 987–992
    class decorators and, 1306
    common usage mistakes, 308–311
    comparison operations, 300–303
    core data types, 95, 295
    dictionaries (see dictionaries)
    equality and, 300–303
    extending, 980–983
    files (see files)
    general type categories, 235–236
    generation in, 606–609
    iteration and, 422–424
    lists (see lists)
    metaclasses and, 1387–1388
    numbers (see numbers)
    object flexibility, 297
    references versus copies, 297–300, 308
    strings (see strings)
    tuples (see tuples)
    type hierarchies, 306–308
built-in scope
    about, 487, 491–493
    LEGB rule and, 488
__builtin__ module, 156, 493
builtins module, 156, 491–493
byte code
    about, 30–31
    modules and, 676–678
    optimizing, 684
    PVM and, 31
    Python versions and, 31
    source changes and, 31
byte order marker (BOM), 1174, 1201–1204
bytearray string type

termination actions, 1083, 1088, 1152
version considerations, 1118–1119
working directory, 47
wrappers (proxy classes)
about, 942–943
decorators installing, 1270
delegation and, 988
writing scripts, 55
wxPython GUI API, 11

X

_x naming convention, 747, 1321
XML parsing tools, 1211–1214
xrange built-in function, 403, 435

Y

yield operator, 137
yield statement
about, 320
coding example, 902–906
coding functions, 475
extended syntax, 605
function gotchas, 660
generator functions and, 591
iteration and, 423, 440
return statement versus, 592–597

Z

ZeroDivisionError exception, 1131, 1132
zip built-in function
dictionary keys and, 262, 265
iteration and, 430, 433, 434, 437, 617–621
loop coding techniques and, 402, 407–410
parallel traversals, 407–410
.zip file extension, 684
ZODB object-oriented database system, 854

About the Author

Mark Lutz is a leading Python trainer, the author of Python's earliest and best-selling texts, and a pioneering figure in the Python world.

Mark is the author of the three O'Reilly books *Learning Python*, *Programming Python*, and *Python Pocket Reference*, all currently in fourth or fifth editions. He has been using and promoting Python since 1992, started writing Python *books* in 1995, and began teaching *Python classes* in 1997. As of Spring 2013, Mark has instructed 260 Python training sessions, taught roughly 4,000 students in live classes, and written Python books that have sold 400,000 units and been translated to at least a dozen languages.

Together, his two decades of *Python* efforts have helped to establish it as one of the most widely used programming languages in the world today. In addition, Mark has been in the software field for 30 years. He holds BS and MS degrees in computer science from the University of Wisconsin where he explored implementations of the Prolog language, and over his career has worked as a professional software developer on compilers, programming tools, scripting applications, and assorted client/server systems.

Mark maintains a training website (*http://learning-python.com/*) and an additional book support site on the Web (*http://www.rmi.net/~lutz*).

Colophon

The animal on the cover of *Learning Python*, Fifth Edition, is a wood rat (*Neotoma Muridae*). The wood rat lives in a wide range of conditions (mostly rocky, scrub, and desert areas) over much of North and Central America, generally at some distance from humans. Wood rats are good climbers, nesting in trees or bushes up to six meters off the ground; some species burrow underground or in rock crevices or inhabit other species' abandoned holes.

These grayish-beige, medium-size rodents are the original pack rats: they carry anything and everything into their homes, whether or not it's needed, and are especially attracted to shiny objects such as tin cans, glass, and silverware.

The cover image is a 19th-century engraving from *Cuvier's Animals*. The cover font is Adobe ITC Garamond. The text font is Linotype Birka; the heading font is Adobe Myriad Condensed; and the code font is LucasFont's TheSansMonoCondensed.

Get even more for your money.

Join the O'Reilly Community, and register the O'Reilly books you own. It's free, and you'll get:

- $4.99 ebook upgrade offer
- 40% upgrade offer on O'Reilly print books
- Membership discounts on books and events
- Free lifetime updates to ebooks and videos
- Multiple ebook formats, DRM FREE
- Participation in the O'Reilly community
- Newsletters
- Account management
- 100% Satisfaction Guarantee

Signing up is easy:

1. Go to: oreilly.com/go/register
2. Create an O'Reilly login.
3. Provide your address.
4. Register your books.

Note: English-language books only

To order books online:
oreilly.com/store

For questions about products or an order:
orders@oreilly.com

To sign up to get topic-specific email announcements and/or news about upcoming books, conferences, special offers, and new technologies:
elists@oreilly.com

For technical questions about book content:
booktech@oreilly.com

To submit new book proposals to our editors:
proposals@oreilly.com

O'Reilly books are available in multiple DRM-free ebook formats. For more information:
oreilly.com/ebooks

O'REILLY®

Have it your way.